PIPE FITTINGS

NIPPLES

PIPE LENGTHS UP TO 22 FT.

STRAIGHT COUPLING

REDUCING COUPLING

COUPLING

NUT

CAP

STRAIGHT TEE

REDUCING TEE

STREET TEE

STRAIGHT CROSS

REDUCING CROSS

90° ELBOW

90° ELBOW

90° ELBOW

45° ELBOW

REDUCING ELBOW

90° STREET ELBOW

45° STREET ELBOW

45° Y-BEND

REDUCING TEE

REDUCER

UNION (3 PARTS)

PLUG

BUSHING

CAP

RETURN BEND

90°

45°

UNION ELBOWS

STREET

UNION TEES

PLUG

45° ELBOW

TEE

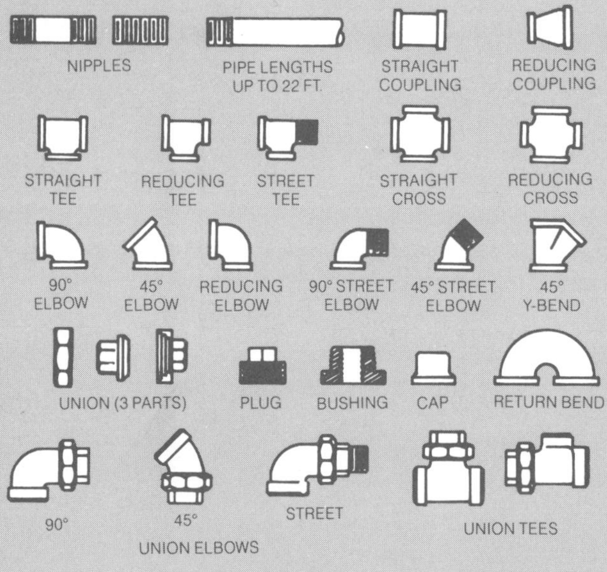

MEASURES OF CAPACITY

1 cup   = 8 fl oz
2 cups   = 1 pint
2 pints   = 1 quart
4 quarts   = 1 gallon
2 gallons = 1 peck
4 pecks   = 1 bushel

STANDARD STEEL PIPE ((All Dimensions in inches)					
Nominal Size	Outside Diameter	Inside Diameter	Nominal Size	Outside Diameter	Inside Diameter
⅛	0.405	0.269	1	1.315	1.049
¼	0.540	0.364	1¼	1.660	1.380
⅜	0.675	0.493	1½	1.900	1.610
½	0.840	0.622	2	2.375	2.067
¾	1.050	0.824	2½	2.875	2.469

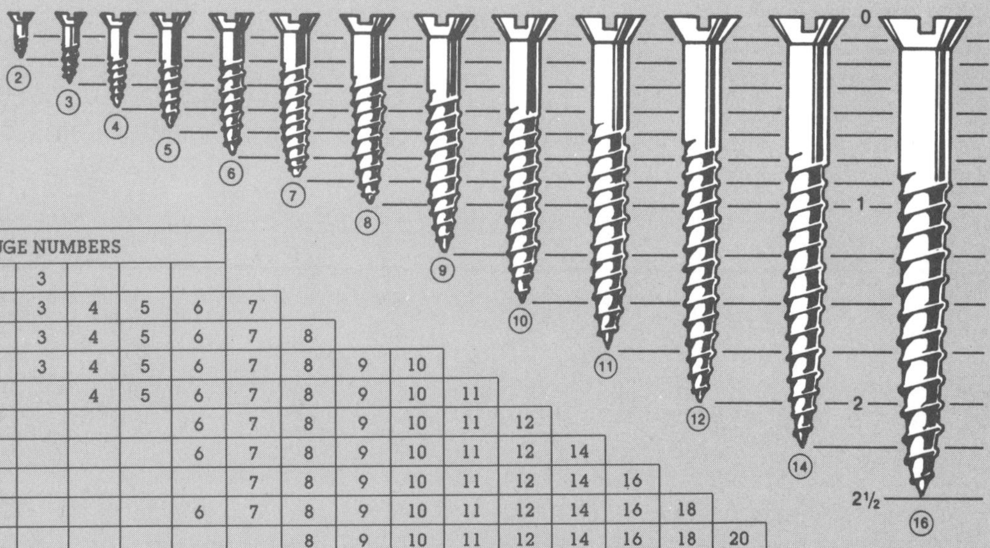

WOOD SCREWS

LENGTH	GAUGE NUMBERS														
¼ INCH	0	1	2	3											
⅜ INCH			2	3	4	5	6	7							
½ INCH			2	3	4	5	6	7	8						
⅝ INCH				3	4	5	6	7	8	9	10				
¾ INCH					4	5	6	7	8	9	10	11			
⅞ INCH							6	7	8	9	10	11	12		
1 INCH							6	7	8	9	10	11	12	14	
1¼ INCH								7	8	9	10	11	12	14	16
1½ INCH							6	7	8	9	10	11	12	14	16	18
1¾ INCH									8	9	10	11	12	14	16	18	20
2 INCH									8	9	10	11	12	14	16	18	20
2¼ INCH										9	10	11	12	14	16	18	20
2½ INCH													12	14	16	18	20
2¾ INCH														14	16	18	20
3 INCH															16	18	20
3½ INCH																18	20	24
4 INCH																18	20	24

WHEN YOU BUY SCREWS, SPECIFY (1) LENGTH, (2) GAUGE NUMBER, (3) TYPE OF HEAD—FLAT, ROUND, OR OVAL, (4) MATERIAL—STEEL, BRASS, BRONZE, ETC., (5) FINISH—BRIGHT, STEEL BLUED, CADMIUM, NICKEL, OR CHROMIUM PLATED.

POPULAR MECHANICS

HOME HOW-TO

POPULAR MECHANICS

HOME HOW-TO

ALBERT JACKSON AND DAVID DAY

HEARST BOOKS

POPULAR MECHANICS HOME HOW-TO

Previously published in the U. K. as Collins Complete Do-It -Yourself Manual.
Copyright © 1986 by William Collins Sons & Co. Ltd.

This book was conceived and designed by Jackson Day Jennings Ltd
trading as Inklink.

Library of Congress Cataloging-in-Publication Data

Jackson, Albert. 1943--
  Popular mechanics home how-to/Albert Jackson and David Day.
    p. cm.
  Rev. ed. of: Collins complete do-it-yourself manual, c 1986.
  ISBN 0-688-08512-1
  1. Dwellings -- Maintenance and repair -- Amateurs' manuals, I, Day.
  David, 1944-- II. Jackson, Albert. 1943-- . Collins complete do-
  it-yourself manual. III. Title.
  TH4817.3.J33 1989
  643'.7--dc19

                                              88-17760
                                                CIP

Phototypeset in Great Britain by Rowland Phototypesetting Ltd

Printed in the United States of America

12345678910

Popular Mechanics
Joe Oldham, *Editor-in-Chief*
William Collins Sons & Co. Ltd
Robin Wood, *Executive Editor*
Inklink
Editorial
Albert Jackson & David Day
Art direction
Simon Jennings
Design
Alan Marshall
Illustrations
David Day, Robin Harris
Additional illustrations
Brian Craker, Michael Parr, Brian Sayers
Photographs
Paul Chave, Peter Higgins,
Simon Jennings, Albert Jackson

Please note
Great care has been taken to ensure the accuracy of the information
in this book. However, in view of the complex and changing nature of
building regulations, codes and by-laws, the authors and publishers
advise consultation with specialists in appropriate instances and
cannot assume responsibility for any loss or damage resulting from
reliance solely upon the information herein

HOW TO USE THIS BOOK

This book has been written and designed to make the location of specific information as easy as possible by dividing the subject matter into clearly defined, color-coded chapters. Each chapter has its own contents list, and each page is divided into easy-to-follow sections. In addition to a detailed index at the back of the book, every page has a list of cross-references to other information related to the task at hand.

Running heads
identify the subjects covered on each page.

Tinted boxes
are used to separate certain information from the main text. Red-tinted boxes indicate special safety precautions.

Numbers in bold type
in the text refer to illustrations that will help to clarify the instructions at that point.

Headings
divide the main text into sections so that you can locate specific information or a single stage in the work. They are especially useful when you want to refresh your memory without having to reread the whole page.

Color coding
of bands and margin tabs let you know immediately what chapter you're in.

Cross-references
When additional information about a subject is discussed in more than one section of the book, the subject is marked in the text with the symbol (▷), and the cross-references to it are listed in the margin of the page. Those printed in bold type are directly related to the task at hand. Other references that will broaden your understanding of the subject are printed in lighter type.

APPLICATION
TILING

CUTTING CERAMIC TILES

Having finished the main field of tiles you will have to cut the ceramic tiles to fill the border and to fit around obstructions such as window frames, electrical fixtures, pipes and the basin. Making straight cuts is easy using a tile cutter, but shaping tiles to fit curves takes practice. There are a number of ways to do it.

SEE ALSO
Details for: ◁	
Slipstone	46
Preparing plaster	14
Ceramic tiles	45

Cutting thin strips
A tile cutter is the most accurate way to cut a thin strip cleanly from the edge of a tile. If you do not want to use the strip itself, nibble away the waste a little at a time with pliers or special tile nibblers.

Tile cutter
A worthwhile investment if you're cutting a lot of tiles, a tile cutter incorporates a device for measuring and scoring tiles. The cutter is drawn down the channel of the adjustable guide. The tile is snapped with a special pincer-action tool.

Tiling around a window
Tile up to the edges of a window, then stick bullnose tiles to the reveal to lap the edges of surrounding tiles. Fill in behind the edging tiles with cut tiles.

Cutting a curve
To fit a tile against a curved shape, cut a template from thin cardboard to the exact size of a tile. Cut "fingers" along one edge; press them against the curve to reproduce the shape. Transfer the curve onto the face of the tile and score the line freehand. Nibble away the waste a little at a time using pliers or a tile nibbler and smooth the edge with a silicone carbide abrasive.

Making straight cuts
Mark a border tile by placing it face down over its neighbor with one edge against the adjacent wall (1). Make an allowance for normal spacing between the tiles. Transfer the marks to the edge of the tiles using a felt-tip pen.

Use a proprietary tile scorer held against a straightedge to score across the face with one firm stroke to cut through the glaze (2). You may have to score the edge of thick tiles.

Stretch a length of thin wire across a panel of chipboard, place the scored line directly over the wire and press down on both sides to snap the tile (3).

Alternatively, use a tile cutter, which has a wheel to score the tile and jaws to snap it along the line. If you're doing a lot of tiling, invest in a tile cutter. The jig will hold the tile square with a cutting edge; pressing down on the guide snaps the tile cleanly. Some cutters include a device for measuring border tiles, too.

Smooth the cut edges of the tile with a tile sander or small slipstone (◁).

Fitting around a pipe
Mark the center of the pipe on the top and side edges of a tile and draw lines across the tile from these points. Where they cross, draw around a coin or something slightly larger than the diameter of the pipe.

Make one straight cut through the center of the circle and either nibble out the waste, having scored the curve, or clamp it in a vise, protected with wood blocks, and cut it out with a saw file—a thin rod coated with hard, abrasive particles which will cut in any direction. Saw one half of the tile on each side of the pipe.

Fitting around a socket or switch
In order to fit around a socket or switch you may have to cut the corner out of a tile. Mark it from the socket then clamp the tile in a vise, protected with wood blocks. Score both lines then use a saw file to make one diagonal cut from the corner of the tile to where the lines meet. Snap out both triangles.

If you have to cut a notch out of a large tile, cut down both sides with a hacksaw then score between them and snap the piece out of the middle.

Mark two edges

Cut and fit tile

CUTTING BORDER TILES
It's necessary to cut border tiles one at a time to fit the gap between the field tiles and the adjacent wall. Walls are rarely true square and the margin is bound to be uneven.

1 Mark the edge tile

2 Score the marked line

3 Snap the tile over a wire

104

APPLICATION
TILING

HANGING OTHER WALL TILES

Mosaic tiles
Ceramic mosaic tiles are applied to a wall in a similar way to large square tiles. Set out the wall (▷) and use the same adhesive and grout.

The mesh backing on some sheets is pressed into the adhesive. The facing paper on other sheets is left intact on the surface until the adhesive sets.

Fill the main area of the wall, spacing the sheets to equal the gaps between individual tiles. Place a carpet-covered board over the sheets and tap it with a mallet to set the tiles into the adhesive.

For borders by cutting strips from the sheet. Cut individual tiles to fit into awkward shapes and around fixtures. If necessary, soak off the facing paper with a damp sponge and grout the tiles (▷).

Mirror tiles
Set out the wall with guide sticks (▷) but avoid using mirror tiles in an area which would entail complicated fittings, as it is difficult to cut glass except in straight lines. Mirror tiles are fixed, close-butted, with self-adhesive pads. No grout is necessary.

Peel the protective paper from the pads and lightly position each tile. Check its alignment with a level then press it firmly into place with a soft cloth.

Use a wooden straightedge and a wheel glass cutter to score a line across a tile. Make one firm stroke. Lay the tile over a stretched wire and press down on both sides. Finish the cut edge with silicone carbide abrasive.

Add spare adhesive pads and set the tile in place. Finally, polish the tiles to remove any unsightly fingerprints.

Metal tiles
Set out metallic tiles as for ceramic ones. No adhesive or grout is required. Don't fit metal tiles behind electrical fixtures—there's a risk that they could conduct the current.

Remove the protective paper from the adhesive pads on the back and press each tile onto the wall. Check the alignment of the tiles regularly; they are not always perfectly made.

Cut border tiles with scissors or tinsnips, but nick the edges before cutting across the face or the surface is likely to distort.

To round over a cut edge, cut a wooden block to fit inside the tile, and align it with the edge. Tap and rub along the edge with another block.

To fit into a corner, file a V-shape into the opposite edges, then bend the tile over the edge of the table.

When the wall is complete, peel off any protective film which may be covering the tiles.

Cork tiles
Set up a horizontal guide stick (▷) to make sure you lay the tiles accurately. It isn't necessary to use a guide, however; the large tiles are easy to align without one. Simply mark a vertical line centrally on the wall and hang the tiles in both directions from it.

Use a rubber-based contact adhesive to fix cork tiles, if possible the type that allows a degree of movement when positioning them. If any adhesive gets onto the surface of a tile, clean it off immediately with a suitable solvent (▷) on a cloth.

Spread adhesive thinly and evenly onto the wall and backs of the tiles and leave it to dry. Lay each tile by placing one edge only against the guide or a neighboring tile, then gradually press the rest of the tile onto the wall. Smooth it down with your palms.

Cut cork tiles with a sharp trimming knife. Because the edges are butted tightly, you'll need to be very accurate when marking out border tiles. Use the same method as for laying cork and vinyl floor tiles (▷). Cut and fit curved shapes using a template.

Unless the tiles are precoated, apply two coats of varnish after 24 hours.

Tiling around curves
In many older houses some walls might be rounded at the outside corners. Flexible tiles such as vinyl, rubber and carpet types are easy to bend into quite tight radii, but cork will snap if bent too far.

Cut a series of shallow slits vertically across the back within its central section, using a back saw, then bend it gently to the curve required.

SEE ALSO
Details for: ▷	
Setting out	42
Grouting	40
Vinyl/cork tiles	106-109
Adhesive solvents	
Preparing plaster	40

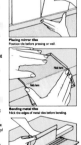

Setting mosaics
Set tiles by tapping a carpet-covered board.

Placing mirror tiles
Position tile before pressing on wall.

Bending metal tiles
Nick the edges of metal tiles before bending.

Bending a cork tile
Cut a series of shallow slits vertically down the back of a tile using a back saw within the central section, then bend it gently. The slits should enable the tile to assume even a fairly tight curve without snapping, but experiment first.

105

● **Illustrations**
On every page you'll find easy-to-understand color diagrams and photos illustrating the techniques, tools and materials discussed in the text.

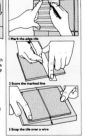

PLANNING AHEAD

DECORATING

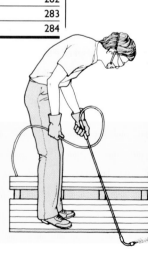

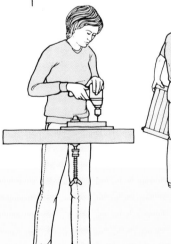

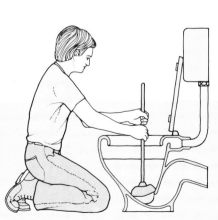

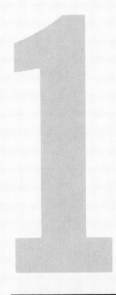

PLANNING AHEAD

PLANNING AHEAD: ASSESSING A PROPERTY

Embarking on a substantial scheme of home improvement can be an enjoyable and rewarding experience or a nightmare. Much depends on getting off on the right foot. If you plan each step in advance you are more likely to spend your money on real improvements that will benefit you and your family while adding to the value of your property.

On the other hand, if you buy a property that proves to be unsuitable for your present or future needs, or launch into an ambitious project without thinking through the consequences, you could be disillusioned and waste time and money.

SEE ALSO

◁ Details for:

What is involved?   13

Checklists
Buying a house or an apartment is an exciting event, and when you find just what you have been searching for, it can be such a heady moment that it becomes all too easy to get carried away without checking the essential requirements. Your first impressions can be totally misleading so that the disadvantages and shortcomings of a particular dwelling begin to emerge only after you have moved in. If you carry with you a checklist of salient points when you visit a prospective house you are less likely to be

disappointed later when it can cost a great deal to bring the building up to the required standard.

In some ways, assessing the potential of your present home can be even more difficult. Everything fits like an old glove and it is hard to be objective about possible improvements. Try to step back from the familiarity by using the same sort of checklist as if you were considering it as a new house.

No single property is ever absolutely ideal, but planning ahead will provide you with the means to make the best of what any house has to offer.

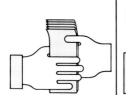

Before you buy
Buying a home will probably be your biggest single investment: don't be misled by first impressions. Check your list of essential points carefully so that you can fully consider the property before investing in a professional inspection.

STRUCTURAL CONDITION

Before you make up your mind to buy a house or apartment the building should be inspected by a professional inspector to make sure it is structurally sound. But make some spot checks yourself before spending money on an inspection. A pair of binoculars will help you inspect the building from ground level.

Look for cracks in the walls, both inside and out. Cracked plaster may simply be the result of shrinkage, but if the fault is visible on the outside, it may indicate deformation of the foundation.

Inspect chimney stacks for faults. A loose stack could cause considerable damage if it were to collapse.

Check the condition of the roof. A few loose shingles can be repaired easily, but if a whole section appears to be deteriorated it could mean a new roof.

Ask if the house has been inspected or treated for rot or insect infestation. If so, is there a guarantee available? Don't rely entirely upon your own inspection, but if the baseboards look distorted, or a floor feels unduly springy, expect trouble.

Look for moisture problems. In hot weather the worst effects may have disappeared, but stained wallpapers and peeling paint should make you leery.

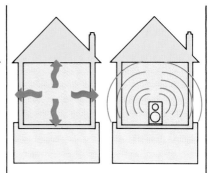

INSULATION

In locales where homes are heated in winter, roof or ceiling insulation on the uppermost floor is essential. Wall and foundation insulation also help to conserve energy both in heated and air conditioned spaces. The type of material used and its thickness can help you judge its adequacy. Water damage to walls and ceilings may be an indication that insulation is wet and, therefore, ineffective.

If urea formaldehyde foam insulation is present, it's a good idea to have the air inside the home tested to determine the concentration of potentially harmful gases. While UF foam is not likely to present a problem if it is properly installed, some people are sensitive to the gases and may experience headaches and nausea when exposed to them.

HOME SECURITY

Look to see whether all doors and windows are secured with good-quality locks and catches. You will probably want to change the front-door lock anyway. A burglar alarm is an advantage only if it is reliable and intelligently installed. If you are buying an apartment, make sure there is adequate provision for escape during a fire.

SERVICES

A real estate agent's written details of the property will describe recent rewiring, but in the absence of such assurance, try to determine the likely condition of the installation. The presence of old-fashioned switches and sockets may indicate out-of-date wiring, but new equipment is no guarantee at all that the cables themselves have been replaced. If light fixtures hang from old, fabric-covered flex, be very suspicious. The age of the wiring around the main service panel will be your best indication. Check that there are enough sockets in every room for your needs. Is the lighting well planned? Pay particular attention to safe lighting over stairs.

Is the plumbing of an age and type that can be extended easily to take new fittings? Extensive lead pipework will need to be replaced. Take note of the size of the hot water heater to make sure it can supply enough hot water, and check that it is insulated.

If the house is centrally heated, check the system's age, overall adequacy and efficiency. Check whether exposed heat pipes and ducts are insulated. Is the heating system fitted with proper thermostatic controls to keep down running costs? Ask whether fireplaces and flues are in working order.

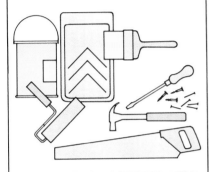

● Apartments
When buying an apartment, make additional checks on the building management and maintenance. Ask about shared facilities like laundry and waste disposal, and joint responsibilities such as maintenance of public areas and drainage problems.

DECOR/IMPROVEMENT

Decorative condition
Is the house decorated to a high standard both inside and out to protect the structure and enhance the appearance of the building? The decorative condition of the house is reflected in the price, and the chances are that you will be expected to pay the same whether the work is up to a good professional standard or shoddily applied. It is up to you to point out the difference to the vendor.

Improvements
Make up your own mind whether "improvements" have been carried out tastefully. Ask yourself if you can live in a house where the original doors and windows have been replaced with alternatives that do not suit the style of the architecture. A neighboring house may give you some idea of its intended appearance.

There is considerable doubt about the advantages claimed for certain types of stone cladding, and painted brickwork is costly to strip back to the original. There is an understandable desire for personalizing one's home, but a small terraced house masquerading as a Tudor cottage may be a doubtful investment.

WHAT IS INVOLVED?

Having checked the condition of the building, refer to other sections of this book to ascertain how much work is involved to correct any faults you have noticed. It will help you to decide whether to do the work yourself, hire a professional or look elsewhere.

Structural condition

Repointing	47
Spalled masonry	48
Cracked walls	48
Damaged concrete	49, 182
Damaged plaster	53–54, 153–157
Foundations	121–122, 409
Replacing floors	178–181
Rotted doors	188, 190–191
Broken windows	200–203
Rotted windows	205–206
Repairing staircases	214–220
Major roof problems	222
Roof repairs	225–233
New gutters	236
Treating woodwork	246–249
Wet and dry rot	251–252
Treating dampness	253–258

Insulation

Roof insulation	265–268
Wall insulation	268–269
Floor insulation	270

Home security

Fitting locks and catches	240–243
Burglar alarms	243
Fire precautions	244

Services

Electrical installations	286–335
Plumbing	338–380
Fireplaces and flues	383–389
Furnaces	392–393, 397
Heating controls	396
Replacing radiators	401

Decoration

Preparation	43–62
Application	63–118

Improvements

Replacing doors	186
Replacing windows	209–210
Double glazing	271–274

PLANNING FOR PEOPLE

Function, comfort and appearance should take equal priority when you plan your home, but the best designers build their concepts around the human frame using statistics gleaned from research into the way people use their home and working environments.

Ergonomics
Although human stature varies a great deal, the study of ergonomics, as it is called, has determined the optimum dimensions of furniture and the spaces that surround it to accommodate people of average build. These conclusions have been adopted by manufacturers and designers so that most shop-bought items for kitchens, bathrooms and living and dining areas are built to standardized dimensions.

This is especially true of kitchen units that are designed for compatibility with appliances such as ranges and refrigerators to make a scheme that fits together as an integrated, functional whole. The standard worktop height allows a dishwasher or washing machine to fit neatly beneath it, while a range is designed to fit flush with countertops and base units. Designers adopt the same criteria for other items of furniture. Standard-size chairs, tables and desks are matched to allow most people to work and eat comfortably.

An appreciation of ergonomics avoids accidents as well. Correctly positioned shelves and worktops avoid unnecessary stretching or climbing onto a chair to reach high surfaces. Low-level easy chairs or soft beds that offer no support are bad for back sufferers, and high stools are not suitable for young children. Understanding ergonomics will help you choose appropriate furniture.

Using available space
As well as the size and function of the furniture itself, its positioning within the room falls within the province of ergonomics. An efficient use of floor area is an essential ingredient of good planning, providing people with a freedom of action and the room to make use of furniture and appliances.

When you are buying furniture or planning the furnishings and fixtures for your own home, it is worthwhile familiarizing yourself with the dimensions shown on the following pages. They will help you buy wisely and make the best use of available space.

ASSESSING A PROPERTY: ROOM BY ROOM

Assuming the structural condition of the house is such that you are quite willing to take on the work involved, begin to check out those points that a structural inspector won't be looking for. Is it the right home for you and your family? It takes a bit of imagination to see how a room might look when it has been divided in two or when a wall has been removed, but it is even more difficult to predict what your life-style might be in five or ten years' time. Unless you intend to live in a home for a couple of years only before moving on, you must try to assess whether the house will be able to evolve with you.

You will need to take measurements before you can make some decisions, so carry a tape measure with you.

MEASURING A ROOM

If you think there is a possibility that you might want to change the shape of a room, or you suspect there may be a problem with fitting certain items of furniture into it, measure the floor area and the ceiling height so that you can make a scale drawing later to clarify your thoughts. Take the main dimensions, including alcoves, the chimney breast and so on. Make a note of which way the doors swing and the positions of windows, radiators and built-in furniture. Transfer the measurements to graph paper with each square representing a set unit of measurement.

When you have drawn your plan of the room, cut out pieces of paper to represent your furniture using the same scale measurements. Rearrange them until you arrive at a satisfactory solution.

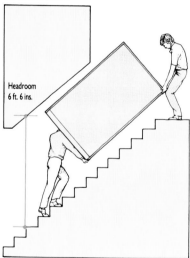

Draw a measured plan on graph paper

The hallway

When you are invited into the house, you will be able to gauge whether the entrance hall is large enough to receive visitors. Is the staircase wide enough to allow you to carry large pieces of furniture to the bedrooms?

Will there be room to store top coats, hats, boots, umbrellas and so on?

It is an advantage if there is some facility for deliveries to be stored outside but under cover when the house is unoccupied.

Check whether it is possible to identify a visitor before opening the door, especially after dark.

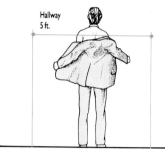

Hallway
5 ft.

Removing a coat
When planning a hallway, allow 5 ft. to remove a top coat or jacket.

Headroom
6 ft. 6 ins.

▲
Staircase headroom
Headroom of 6 ft. 6 in. above a staircase will allow you to carry a wardrobe to the next floor.

◀ **Negotiating a bend**
You can turn a large piece of furniture around a bend in a 3-ft.-wide passageway.

Passageway
3 ft.

Living rooms

How many sitting rooms are there in the house? More than one living room provides an opportunity for members of the family to engage in different pursuits without inconveniencing each other.

If there is one living room only, make sure there are facilities elsewhere for private study, music practice or hobbies.

Is the living room large enough to accommodate the seating arrangement you have in mind, or will you have to remove a wall to incorporate extra space? If you do, it is worth considering folding doors so that you can divide the area again when it suits you.

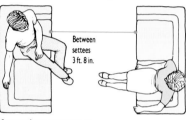

Between settees
3 ft. 8 in.

Arranging two settees
Allow a minimum of 3 ft. 8 in. between two settees facing each other.

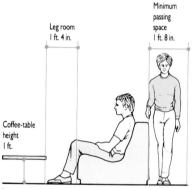

Leg room
1 ft. 4 in.

Minimum passing space
1 ft. 8 in.

Coffee-table height
1 ft.

Low seating
The density of upholstery and the dimensions of the seat and back vary so much that it is impossible to suggest a standard, but make certain your back is supported properly and you can get out of a chair without help. If you place a coffee table in front of a settee, try to position the settee so that people can get into it from each end to avoid treading on the toes of someone seated.

Dining room

Is there a separate formal dining room? Estimate whether there will be space for table and chairs with enough room for people to circulate freely.

A dining room should be positioned conveniently close to the kitchen so that meals are still warm when they get to the table. You may have to install a serving hutch.

Whether or not the dining area is part of the kitchen, efficient ventilation will be necessary to extract the odors of cooking and steam. Some cooks prefer a kitchen screened from visitors. Are the present arrangements suitable?

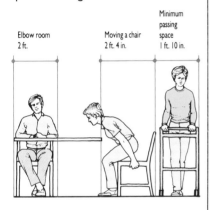

Elbow room
2 ft.

Moving a chair
2 ft. 4 in.

Minimum
passing
space
1 ft. 10 in.

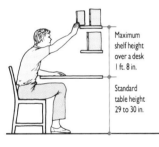

Maximum shelf height over a desk
1 ft. 8 in.

Standard table height
29 to 30 in.

Sitting at a table

Sitting at a dining table, desk or dressing table requires the same area. Arrange the furniture for people to get in and out of a chair while leaving enough room for moving about with a cart.

Breakfast bar

A 36-in.-high breakfast bar aligns with a worktop.

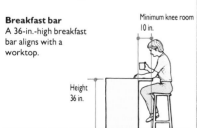

Minimum knee room
10 in.

Height
36 in.

Bedrooms

The number of rooms may be adequate for your present needs but what about the future? There may be additions to the family, and although young children can share a room, individual accommodations will be required eventually. You may want to put up a guest from time to time or even have an elderly relative stay for extended periods, in which case, can they cope with stairs? It might be possible to divide a large room with a simple partition, or perhaps a room on the ground floor can double as a bedroom. As a long-term solution, you could plan for an extension or attic conversion.

Are all the bedrooms of an adequate size? As well as a bed or bunks, a bedroom must accommodate clothes storage and in some cases books, toys and facilities for homework or pastimes. A guest room may have to function as a private sitting room. You could dismantle or move a dividing wall, or possibly incorporate part of a large landing providing it does not interfere with access to other rooms or obstruct an escape route in case of fire. Try not to rely on using a bedroom which can be reached only by passing through another. This arrangement is fine when you want to be close to a young child, but a connected room could be used as a dressing room or bathroom suite.

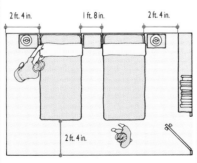

2 ft. 4 in.

1 ft. 8 in.

2 ft. 4 in.

2 ft. 4 in.

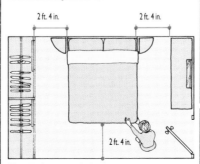

2 ft. 4 in.

2 ft. 4 in.

2 ft. 4 in.

Circulating space in bedrooms

The bathroom

If the bathroom does not provide the amenities you require, estimate whether there is space to incorporate extra appliances, even if it means rearranging the existing layout, or incorporating an adjacent toilet.

Is there a separate toilet for use when the bathroom is occupied?

You should investigate the possibility of installing a second bathroom or shower stall elsewhere if the present bathroom is not accessible to all the bedrooms. Alternatively, consider plumbing a basin in some bedrooms.

Make a note of electrical installations in a bathroom. They must comply with accepted recommendations or be replaced with new units.

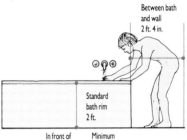

Between bath and wall
2 ft. 4 in.

Standard bath rim
2 ft.

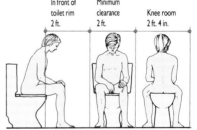

In front of toilet rim
2 ft.

Minimum clearance
2 ft.

Knee room
2 ft. 4 in.

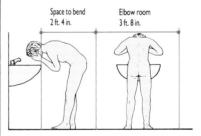

Space to bend
2 ft. 4 in.

Elbow room
3 ft. 8 in.

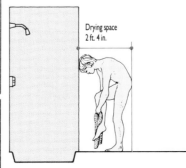

Drying space
2 ft. 4 in.

Between bath and wall

Allow sufficient room between bath and wall to dry yourself with a towel. You can bend in the same amount of space in order to clean the bath.

Toilet and bidet

Allow for the same space in front of a toilet and bidet but provide extra leg room on each side of a bidet. The same spaces provide room to maintain and clean an appliance.

Using a basin

The generous space allows you to bend over a basin even when there is a wall behind you and provides plenty of elbow room for washing hair. You can also wash a child in the same space.

Drying after a shower

This is the minimum space required to dry yourself in front of an open shower stall. If the stall is screened, allow an extra foot.

ASSESSING A PROPERTY: ROOM BY ROOM

The kitchen

The quality of kitchen cabinets and fixtures varies enormously, but every well-designed kitchen should incorporate the following features:

A labor-saving layout

Preparing meals becomes tiresome unless the facilities for cooking, food preparation and washing up are grouped in a layout that avoids unnecessary movement. To use designer's parlance, the kitchen must form an efficient work triangle. In ideal conditions, the sides of the triangle combined should not exceed 20 to 22 feet in length.

Work triangle
A typical work triangle links washing, cooking and preparation areas.

Storage

When you are building storage into a kitchen, workshop, bedroom or living room, make sure every item is within easy reach and that there is room to open drawers and doors without backing into a wall or injuring others.

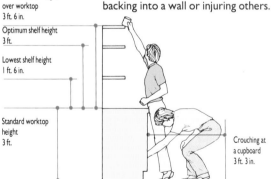

Maximum shelf height over worktop
3 ft. 6 in.

Optimum shelf height
3 ft.

Lowest shelf height
1 ft. 6 in.

Standard worktop height
3 ft.

Crouching at a cupboard
3 ft. 3 in.

Kitchen storage
Plan your kitchen storage for safe and efficient access.

Access to drawers
Crouching at a drawer unit
4 ft. 2 in.

Storage and appliances

If the work triangle is to be effective, a kitchen must incorporate enough storage space in each area. The refrigerator and foodstuffs should be close to where meals are prepared, and adequate work surfaces must be provided. A freezer could be housed elsewhere but should be somewhere close to the kitchen.

The cooktop and oven should be grouped together with heat-proof surfaces nearby to receive hot dishes. Cooking utensils should be stored within easy reach.

Appliances that require plumbing are best grouped together, with the sink on an outside wall. In a small house, this area will contain a washing machine and tumble dryer, although a separate laundry room is an ideal solution.

KITCHEN SAFETY

How safe is the layout of the kitchen? A cramped kitchen can lead to accidents, so ensure that more than one person at a time can circulate in safety.

- **Where possible, avoid an arrangement that encourages people to use the working part of the kitchen as a through passage to other parts of the house or garden.**
- **Make sure children cannot reach the cooktop and construct a barrier that will keep small children out of the work triangle.**
- **Placing the range in a corner or at the end of a run of cupboards is not advisable. Try to plan for a clear worktop on each side. Don't place it under a window, either. Eventually, someone will get burned trying to open the window, and a draft could extinguish a gas pilot light.**

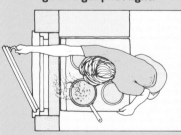

A dangerously placed cooker
Do not position cookers under windows.

OUTBUILDINGS AND GARDENS

Garage and workshop

Is the garage large enough for your car, or one you aspire to, or will you need to garage two cars?

If the garage is too small to use as a workshop, you could possibly fit out a cellar so long as there is storage space for materials and you can deliver them without disruption or damaging the decorations and furniture in the house.

A new shed or outbuilding is another solution, providing there is room in the yard, and a utilitarian building will not spoil the appearance of the property.

Long-term storage is always a problem. Every household accumulates bulky items, like camping or sports equipment, which have to be stored for much of the year. Once again, a garage or outbuilding is ideal, but if necessary, can you use the attic for storage? Check the size of the hatchway, and decide whether you need to install flooring over the joists.

The garden

If you are not a keen gardener, you will want to avoid a large garden requiring a lot of attention. Does it receive enough sunlight for the type of plants you want to grow or simply for sunbathing?

Check the view. When foliage drops, you may be confronted with an eyesore that is screened during the summer months.

Make sure the fences or walls are high enough to provide privacy. If you view a house on a weekend, ask whether there are any factories, workshops or playgrounds nearby that may disturb your peace and quiet during the week.

It is an advantage if the garden has access for building materials and equipment to avoid carrying them through the house.

Can children play safely in the garden without supervision? Make sure that gates are secure and high enough to prevent them wandering out of the garden and out of sight.

Why pay someone to do a job when you can do it perfectly well yourself? There are plenty of skilled amateurs who can tackle just about any job to a high standard, but it usually takes them longer than a professional specialist, and to most of us time is the enemy.

In some circumstances it is worth paying to have a job done quickly and efficiently because it is holding up a whole series of other projects. Or perhaps you do not feel sufficiently confident to handle a certain type of work. You may prefer to ask an electrician to do major wiring or a plumber to install a new bathroom, although you would carry out all the peripheral labor and finishing yourself. Then there are certain skills such as plastering that require time and practice before you become really proficient at them. In the average-size house, you might just about develop the knack as the work is coming to an end, but you probably won't plaster another wall until you buy another house.

Essential professional advice

You must seek professional advice to obtain a building permit, and if you need a mortgage, the bank or credit union will insist on the building being professionally inspected. If the inspector's report highlights a serious defect, the mortgage company will also want the fault rectified by a professional who will guarantee the work.

The Inspector

When you apply for a mortgage, the bank or other lender may appoint an inspector who is trained to evaluate a property in order to protect the mortgage company's investment. His or her job is to check that the building is structurally sound and to pinpoint anything that needs attention. You will have to pay for the service, but the inspector will report directly to the mortgage company. There was a time when the lender as not obliged to show you the report but simply told you what work had to be carried out in order to secure your mortgage. Many mortgage companies are now more lenient, however, and will probably give you a copy of the inspector's report.

Unless you are buying a fairly new property, an inspector's report usually makes depressing reading. If the inspector has done a thorough job, the report will list everything that is in need of attention, from peeling paintwork to dry rot in the basement. No inspector will take the responsibility for guaranteeing the condition of areas of the house that were inaccessible at the time of inspection. For example, if the house is occupied, wall-to-wall carpets will make it very difficult to examine thoroughly the condition of the floors. The report will point out that these areas cannot be guaranteed as sound but that does not necessarily imply that there is likely to be a problem.

Study the report for specific references to serious faults that may be expensive to correct, such as damage to the foundation, dry or wet rot, termite damage, water seepage or a badly deteriorating roof. Also take note of points that could lead to trouble in the future even if there is no evidence of it at the moment. If the survey points out leaking gutters that are soaking a wall, for instance, they will have to be repaired to avoid moisture damage.

If you are not given a copy of the report you should consider having your own private survey before committing yourself to a purchase. Use a qualified inspector. Contact the American Society of Home Inspectors for referrals to professional inspectors in your area.

Construction professionals with varied backgrounds may offer home inspection services. While membership in the American Society of Home Inspectors is not a guarantee of an inspector's professionalism, it does indicate an active interest in the professional community. Another reliable qualifying credential is that the home inspector holds a professional engineering (P.E.) degree. For further information contact:

> **American Society of Home Inspectors**
> 655 15th St., N.W., Suite 320
> Washington, D.C. 20005
> Telephone: (202) 842-3096

The Architect

If you are planning ambitious home improvements, especially involving major structural alterations or extensions, you should consult a qualified architect. He or she is trained to design buildings and interiors that are not only structurally sound but aesthetically pleasing. An architect will prepare scale drawings of the project for submission to the authorities of the local building department. You can even employ the same architect to supervise the construction of the building to ensure that it meets the required specifications. You and your architect must work as a partnership. Brief him or her by discussing the type of project you have in mind, how you plan to use the space, how much you want to spend and so on.

You can contact the American Institute of Architects (AIA) for a list of professionals working in your area, but a personal recommendation from a friend or colleague is far more valuable. Arrange to meet the architect and to see some recent work before you commit yourself to engaging him or her.

> **American Institute of Architects**
> 1735 New York Ave., N.W.
> Washington, D.C. 20006
> Telephone: (202) 626-7300

OFFICIAL PERMISSION

Before starting certain building projects, it is necessary to obtain official permission from local authorities. Depending on the type of project and local regulations, you may need to apply for a building permit, zoning variance or a certificate of appropriateness. In some cases, you may need all three.

Many homeowners, especially do-it-yourselfers, and some contractors as well, fail to apply for the official approvals necessary because they are unaware of the need to do so, because they want to avoid what they fear will be a tedious bureaucratic process, and because they believe they can get away with it. You can't.

If you fail to apply for official permission when it is required, you could become liable for demolition of new work or any remedies necessary to bring the project into conformity with local standards. You could also be fined.

Building codes, zoning ordinances and historic preservation rules vary widely. Consequently, the information provided on the following pages should be seen only as a general guide rather than an authoritative statement of law. When in doubt about permissions needed, consult your local building department or an architect.

BUILDING CODES, PERMITS AND OTHER LEGAL CONSIDERATIONS

Building codes

Building codes are comprehensive guidelines intended to set standards for construction practices and material specifications. Their purpose is to ensure the adequate structural and mechanical performance, fire safety and overall quality of buildings and to address health and environmental concerns related to the way buildings are constructed. By setting minimum standards, building codes also limit unfair competitive practices among contractors.

Building codes address nearly every detail of building construction from the acceptable recipes for concrete used in the foundation to the permissible fire rating of the roof finish material—and many features in between. Partly because codes attempt to be as comprehensive as possible and also because they must address different concerns in varied locales, they are very lengthy, complex and lack uniformity from region to region. A further complication is that many new building products become available each year that are not accounted for in existing codes. Model codes promulgated by four major organizations are widely used for reference throughout the United States.

The Uniform Building Code, published by the International Conference of Building Officials, is perhaps the most widely accepted code. ICBO republishes the entire code every three years and publishes revisions annually. A short form of the Uniform Building Code covering buildings with less than three stories and less than 6,000 square feet of ground floor area is available—easier for home builders, and remodelers' reference.

The BOCA-Basic Building Code, issued by the Building Officials and Code Administrators International, Inc., is also widely used. An abridged form designed for residential construction, which includes plumbing and wiring standards, is available.

A third model code, prepared under the supervision of the American Insurance Association and known as the National Building Code, serves as the basis for codes adopted by many communities. It, too, is available in a short form for matters related to home construction.

The Standard Building Code is published by the Southern Building Code Congress International, Inc. It addresses conditions and problems prevalent in the southern United States.

While it is likely that one of the model codes named above serves as the basis for the building code in your community, municipal governments and states frequently add standards and restrictions. It is your local building department that ultimately decides what is acceptable and what is not. Consult that agency if a code question should arise.

Building codes are primarily designed for the safety of the building occupants and the general welfare of the community at large. It is wise to follow *all* practices outlined by the prevailing code in your area.

Building permits

A building permit is generally required for new construction, remodeling projects that involve structural changes or additions, and major demolition projects. In some locales it may be necessary to obtain a building permit for constructing in-ground pools, and you may need a building permit or rigger's license to erect scaffolding as an adjunct to nonstructural work on a house.

To obtain a building permit, you must file forms prescribed by your local building department that answer questions about the proposed site and project. In addition, it is necessary to file a complete set of drawings of the project along with detailed specifications. A complete set normally includes a plot plan or survey, foundation plan, floor plans, wall sections and electrical, plumbing and mechanical plans. Building permit fees are usually assessed based on the estimated cost of construction and records of the application are usually passed along to the local tax department for reassessment of the property value.

At the time you apply for a building permit, you may be advised of other applications for official permission that are required. For example, you may need to apply to the county health department concerning projects that may affect sewerage facilities and natural water supplies. It is important to arrange inspections in a timely way since finish stages cannot proceed until the structural, electrical, plumbing and mechanical work are approved.

Anyone may apply for a building permit, but it is usually best to have an architect or contractor file in your behalf, even if you plan to do the work yourself.

Zoning restrictions

Even for projects that do not require a building permit, local zoning regulations may limit the scope and nature of the construction permitted. Whereas building codes and permit regulations relate to a building itself, zoning rules address the needs and conditions of the community as a whole by regulating the development and uses of property. Zoning restrictions may apply to such various cases as whether a single-family house can be remodeled into apartments, whether a commercial space can be converted to residential use or the permissible height of a house or outbuilding.

It is advisable to apply to the local zoning board for approval before undertaking any kind of construction or remodeling that involves a house exterior or yard or if the project will substantially change the way a property is used. If the project does not conform with the standing zoning guidelines, you may apply to the zoning board for a variance. It is best to enlist the help of an architect or attorney for this.

Landmark regulations

Homes in historic districts may be subject to restrictions placed to help the neighborhood retain its architectural distinction and character. For the most part in designated landmark areas, changes in house exteriors are closely regulated. While extensive remodeling that would significantly change the architectural style are almost never permitted, even seemingly small modifications of existing structures are scrutinized. For example, metal or vinyl replacement windows may not be permitted for Victorian homes in designated areas, or the exterior paint and roof colors may be subject to approval. Even the color of the mortar used to repoint brickwork may be specified by the local landmarks commission or similar regulating body. Designs for new construction must conform to the prevalent architectural character. If you live in an historic district, it is advised that you apply to the governing body for approval of any plans for exterior renovation.

WILL YOU NEED A PERMIT OR VARIANCE?

Building code requirements and zoning regulations vary from city to city and frequently have county and state restrictions added to them. For this reason, it is impossible to state categorically which home-improvement projects require official permission and which do not. The chart below, which lists some of the most frequently undertaken projects, is meant to serve as a rough guide. Taken as a whole, it suggests a certain logic for anticipating when and what type of approval may be needed. Whether or not official approval is required, all work should be carried out in conformity with local code standards.

SEE ALSO

Details for: ▷

| NEC Regulations | 287 |
| Drainage systems | 338, 378 |

TYPE OF WORK	●	BUILDING PERMIT NEEDED		ZONING APPROVAL NEEDED	
Exterior painting and repairs Interior decoration and repairs	119 39	NO	Permit or rigger's license may be needed to erect exterior scaffolding	NO	Certificate of appropriateness may be needed in historic areas
Replacing windows and doors	184 196	NO		NO	Permissible styles may be restricted in historic districts
Electrical	285	NO	Have work performed or checked by a licensed contractor	NO	Outdoor lighting may be subject to approval
Plumbing	337	NO	Have work performed or checked by a licensed contractor	NO	Work involving new water supply, septic or sewerage systems may require county health department
Heating	390	NO		NO	Installation of new oil storage tanks may require state environmental agency approval
Constructing patios and decks	438	Possibly		Possibly	
Installing a hot tub	369	NO		NO	
Structural alterations	119	YES		NO	Unless alterations change building height above limit or proximity of building to lot line
Attic remodeling	147 266	NO	Ascertain whether joists can safely support the floor load	NO	
Building a fence or garden wall	410 420	NO		YES	In cases where structure is adjacent to public road or easement or extends above a height set by board
Planting a hedge	406	NO		NO	
Path or sidewalk paving	444	NO		Possibly	Public sidewalks must conform to local standards and specifications
Clearing land	406	NO		YES	County and state environmental approval may also be needed
Constructing an in-ground pool	460	YES		YES	County and state environmental approval may also be needed
Constructing outbuildings	119 420	YES	For buildings larger than set limit	Possibly	
Adding a porch	119 420	NO	Unless larger than set limit	Possibly	Regulations often set permissible setback from public road
Adding a sunspace or greenhouse	119 420	YES		Possibly	Yes, if local rules apply to extensions
Constructing a garage	119 420	YES		Possibly	Yes, if used for a commercial vehicle and within set proximity to lot line
Driveway paving	438	NO		Possibly	Yes where access to public road created, also restrictions on proximity to lot lines
Constructing a house extension	119 420	YES		Possibly	Regulations may limit permissible house size and proximity to lot lines
Demolition		YES	If work involves structural elements	NO	Structures in historic districts may be protected by regulations
Converting 1-family house to multiunit dwelling		YES	Fire safety and ventilation codes are frequently more stringent for multiple dwellings	YES	
Converting a residential building to commercial use		YES		YES	

● Refer to these pages for further information

EMPLOYING A BUILDER

• Estimates and quotations
A builder's estimate is an approximate price only. Before you engage him or her, ask for a written contract that is a binding agreement to carry out the work for the price stated.

You must do careful research to find a builder who is proficient and reliable. You will hear many stories of clients being overcharged for shoddy work or being left with a half-completed job for months on end. It's not that good builders don't exist, but there are unscrupulous individuals who masquerade as professional tradesmen and give the whole industry a bad name.

One of the problems in finding a reputable builder is a matter of timing. A good builder will be booked up for months, so allow plenty of time to find someone who will be free when you need him or her. A builder might come so highly recommended that you won't want to look elsewhere, but unless you get two or three firms to estimate for the same job you won't know whether the price is fair. A builder who is in demand might suggest a high price because he really doesn't need the work. An inexperienced builder could submit a tempting price but might cut corners or ask for more money later because he had not anticipated all the problems.

Choosing a builder
Recommendation is the only safe way to find a builder. If someone whose opinion you respect has found a professional who is skillful, reliable and easy to communicate with, then the chances are you will enjoy the same experience. Even so, you should inspect the builder's work yourself before you make up your mind. If a recommendation is hard to come by, choose a builder who is a member of a professional or business association. While association membership is not a guarantee of skill or character, it does indicate an active participation in the professional community.

SUBCONTRACTORS

Unless a builder is a jack-of-all-trades he will have to employ electricians, plumbers, plasterers or whatever. The builder is responsible for the quality of the subcontracted work unless you agree beforehand that you will hire the specialists yourself. Agree to discuss anything concerning subcontracted work with the builder himself. A subcontractor must receive clear instructions from one person only or there is bound to be confusion.

Writing a specification

Many of the disagreements that arise between builder and client are a result of insufficient briefing before the work was started. Do not give a builder vague instructions. He may do his best to provide the kind of work he thinks you want, but it might be wide of the mark, and he can't possibly quote an accurate price unless he knows exactly what you require. You don't have to write a legal document, nor do you have to tell the builder how to do his job. Just write a detailed list of the work you want him to carry out and, as far as possible, the materials you want him to use. If you have not made up your mind about the wallcovering you want to use or the exact make of bathroom fixture, then at least say so in the specification. You can always discuss it with the builder before he submits a quotation. Read the relevant sections in this book to find out what is involved in a particular job or, if the work is complicated, ask an architect to write the specifications for you.

The specifications should include a date for starting the work and an estimate of how long it will take to complete. You will have to obtain that information from the builder when he submits his estimate, but make sure it is added to the specifications before you both agree to the terms and price. There may be legitimate reasons why a job doesn't start and finish on time, but at least the builder will be aware that you expect him to behave in a professional manner.

Getting an estimate

When you ask several builders to bid for the work, you will receive their estimates of costs. They will be based on current prices and the amount of information you have supplied at the time. If you take a long time to make up your mind or alter the specifications in the meantime, prices may have changed. Before you hire a builder, ask him for a firm quotation with a detailed breakdown of his costs. Part of that quotation may still be estimated. If you still haven't decided on certain items, you can both agree on a provisional sum to cover them, but make it clear that you are to be consulted before that money is spent. Also, a builder might have to employ a specialist for some of the work, and that fee might be estimated. Try to get the builder to firm up the price before you employ him and certainly before the work begins.

Agree on a method of payment. Many builders will complete the work before any money changes hands. Some firms will ask for installments to cover the cost of materials. If you agree to paying in installments, payments it must be on the understanding that you will hold the last payment until the work is completed to your satisfaction. Never agree to an advance payment. If you make it clear to the builder before he accepts the contract, you can retain a figure for an agreed period after the work is completed to cover the cost of faulty workmanship. Between 5 and 10 percent of the overall cost is reasonable.

Neither you nor the builder can anticipate all the problems that might arise. If something unexpected occurs which affects the price for the job, ask the builder for an estimate of costs before you decide on a course of action. Similarly, if you change your mind or ask for work extra to the specification you must expect to pay for any resulting increase in costs—but have it agreed at the time, not at the end of the job.

Working with your builder

Most people find they get a better job from a builder if they create a friendly working atmosphere. You must provide access to electricity and water if they are required for the job, and somewhere to store materials and tools. Some mess is inevitable, but a builder should leave the site fairly tidy at the end of a working day, and you should not have to put up with mud in areas of the house that are not part of the building site.

Unless you have an architect to supervise the job, keep your eye on the progress of the work. Disagreements will occur if you constantly interrupt the builder, but inspect the job when the workers have left the site to satisfy yourself on the standard of the workmanship and that it is keeping up to schedule. If you have to go out before the builder arrives, leave a note if you want to discuss something.

GUIDE TO CONTRACTORS' ASSOCIATIONS AND INFORMATION SOURCES

The best source for finding a qualified professional or tradesperson is through personal recommendation. But if you cannot come by a referral that way, you may wish to contact one of the professional associations or organizations listed below for referrals to tradespeople in your area. These groups may also be helpful in answering questions you might have about standards and business practices.

ARCHITECTS

American Institute of Architects
1735 New York Ave., N.W.
Washington, D.C. 20006
(202) 626-7300

ASBESTOS ABATEMENT

Asbestos Information Association/N.A.
1745 Jefferson Davis Hwy., Suite 509
Arlington, Va. 22202
(703) 979-1150

National Association of Asbestos Abatement Contractors
Box 477, Lawrence, Kan. 66044
(913) 749-4032

BUILDING & REMODELING

National Association of Home Builders
15th and M Sts., N.W.
Washington, D.C. 20005
(202) 822-0200

National Association of the Remodeling Industry
1901 N. Moore St., Suite 808
Arlington, Va. 22209
(703) 276-7600

CONCRETE

American Concrete Institute
Box 19150, Detroit, Mich. 48219
(313) 532-2600

ELECTRICAL CONTRACTORS

Independent Electrical Contractors
1101 Connecticut Ave., N.W.,
Suite 700
Washington, D.C. 20036
(202) 857-1141

National Electrical Contractors Association
1715 Wisconsin Ave.
Bethesda, Md. 20814
(301) 657-3110

FLOOR COVERING INSTALLERS

Floor Covering Installation Contractors Association
P.O. Box 2048
Dalton, Ga. 30720
(404) 226-5488

HEATING & AIR CONDITIONING CONTRACTORS

National Association of Plumbing, Heating and Cooling Contractors
P.O. Box 6808
180 S. Washington St.
Falls Church, Va. 22046
(703) 237-8100

HOME INSPECTORS

American Society of Home Inspectors
655 15th St., N.W., Suite 320
Washington, D.C. 20005
(202) 842-3096

INSULATION CONTRACTORS

Insulation Contractors Association of America
15819 Crabbs Branch Way
Rockville, Md. 20855
(301) 926-3083

National Insulation Contractors Association
1025 Vermont Ave., N.W., Suite 410
Washington, D.C. 20005
(202) 783-6277

INTERIOR DESIGNERS

American Society of Interior Designers
1430 Broadway
New York, N.Y. 10018
(212) 944-9220

KITCHEN DESIGNERS

Society of Certified Kitchen Designers
124 Main St.
Hackettstown, N.J. 07840
(201) 852-0033

LANDSCAPE ARCHITECTS

American Society of Landscape Architects
1733 Connecticut Ave., N.W.
Washington, D.C. 20009
(202) 466-7730

LIGHTING DESIGNERS

American Home Lighting Institute
435 N. Michigan Ave., Suite 1717
Chicago, Ill. 60611
(312) 644-0828

International Association of Lighting Designers
30 W. 22nd St., 4th floor
New York, N.Y. 10010
(212) 206-1281

PAINTING & WALLPAPERING CONTRACTORS

Independent Professional Painting Contractors Association
P.O. Box 233
Huntington, N.Y. 11743
(516) 423-3654

National Guild of Professional Paperhangers
P.O. Box 574
Farmingdale, N.Y. 11735
(516) 795-3557

Painting and Decorating Contractors of America
7223 Lee Hwy.
Falls Church, Va. 22056
(703) 534-1201.

ROOFING CONTRACTORS

National Roofing Contractors Association
8600 Bryn Mawr Ave.
Chicago, Ill. 60631
(312) 693-0700

SECURITY DEVICE INSTALLERS & EQUIPMENT

Locksmith Security Association
200 S. Washington
Royal Oak, Mich. 48067
(313) 589-0318

National Burglar and Fire Alarm Association
1120 19th St., N.W., Suite LL-20
Washington, D.C. 20036
(202) 296-9595

Security Equipment Industry Association
2665 30th St.
Santa Monica, Ca. 90405
(213) 450-4141

SOLAR ENERGY INFORMATION

American Solar Energy Society
2030 17th St., Boulder, Colo. 80350
(303) 443-3130

SEE ALSO

Details for: ▷

Crime Prevention Officer	238
Fire Prevention Officer	238

DOING IT YOURSELF

In the majority of cases you will save money by doing most of the work yourself. You will probably have to pay more for materials than a tradesperson who benefits from discounts and can buy in greater quantities, but you will save the labor costs that account for a large part of the professional's bill. You will also gain satisfaction from producing good-quality work yourself, especially since a tradesperson must equate the time he or she spends with the price for the job and may not be able to spend as much time attending to details.

Planning work priorities

Although forward planning might not be so important when you are doing all the work yourself, careful forethought will reduce disruption of the household to a minimum and will avoid spoiling finished decor and carpets with dust generated in other parts of the building. Work out a schedule for yourself, listing the jobs in order of priority. Some work should be carried out urgently to safeguard the structure of the house or because the prospect of bad weather dictates the order of work. However, it is mostly dictated by what appears to be the most logical sequence to ensure that you won't have to backtrack because you forgot to complete an earlier stage.

Planning your time

Another important aspect to consider is the amount of time you can devote to the work, because that can determine how you tackle a long-term project. Unless you can work full time for periods of weeks or even months on end, it will take several years to completely renovate even a small house. Therefore you have to decide whether you and your family are prepared to put up with the inconvenience caused by tackling the entire house in one shot or whether you would be better off to divide up the work so that part of the house is still relatively comfortable. Just how you plan the work will depend on the layout of the building. If you have more than one entrance it may be possible to seal off one section completely while you work on it. If the house is built on several floors, then work out a sequence whereby you are not treading dust and dirt from a work site on an upper level through finished carpeted areas below. Leave linking areas such as stairs, landings and hallways undecorated until the last moment.

WORKING TO A SEQUENCE

PRIORITY WORK

URGENT REPAIRS

Attend to the faults mentioned in a professional survey (these repairs are often insisted upon by a mortgage company). Repair anything in a dangerous condition or which is damaging to the structure of the building and getting rapidly worse. This may include:

● Rot, moisture infiltration.
See pages 251–258.

● Structural faults.
See pages 120–136.

● Pest infestation.
See pages 246–247.

● Faulty plumbing, downspouts and drains.
See pages 338–380, 234–236.

● Faulty electrical wiring.
See pages 286–336.

● Faulty masonry.
See pages 46–50, 64–66, 254–255, 258, 409.

● Roof work.
See next column and pages 222–236.

SECURITY

● Fit locks to all vulnerable doors and windows.
See pages 240–243.

● Change front door lock if you have just moved in to a new house. You cannot know who has a key.
See pages 240–241.

● Install fire extinguisher and smoke alarm.
See page 244.

APPROVAL

● Seek planning permission and Building Regulation approval from your local authority for any work likely to require official permission.
See pages 17–19.

No two homes or family circumstances are identical, but the chart will help you plan your own sequence of events. You should always tackle first those measures which will arrest deterioration, and it is usually best to repair and decorate the exterior before the interior to make sure the house is weatherproof. In practice, you will find that it is very

ROOF WORK

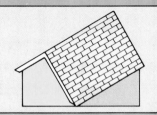

ROOF COVERING

● Repair or replace damaged or missing shingles, slates or tiles.
See pages 223–227, 230–231.

● Repair faulty flashing.
See pages 232–233.

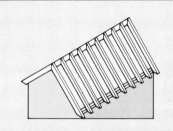

ROOF FRAME

● Treat or replace rotten or damaged frame members. You may have to hire a professional.
See pages 20–21, 222, 246, 251.

ROOF INSULATION

● Insulate and ventilate the roof space.
See pages 265–268, 277–278.

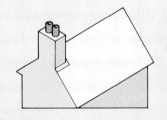

CHIMNEY

● Repoint chimney.
See pages 47, 232, 430.

● Repair damaged flashing.
See pages 232–233.

● Clean and repair flue lining.
See page 388.

difficult to stick rigidly to your schedule. Unexpected problems will dictate a change of plan, and family pressures or financial constraints often demand that a task be given priority or left to a later stage even though logic would suggest another solution.

SEE ALSO

Details for: ▷
Assessing a property   12–16
Using professionals   17–21

INDOOR WORK

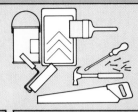

ALTERATIONS

Undertake major interior structural changes such as:

● Building or removing dividing walls. See pages 123, 128–141, 434.

● Lowering ceilings. See pages 142–146.

● Opening up or closing off doors and pass-throughs. See pages 124–127.

● Add, repair, or replace fireplace mantels. See pages 384–387.

SERVICES

PLUMBING

● Undertake new plumbing and heating work. See pages 338–380, 382–404.

ELECTRICAL

● Wire new electrical sockets and appliances. See pages 286–336.

INSULATION

CEILING, WALL AND FLOOR INSULATION

● Install insulation wherever appropriate. See pages 260–270.

DOUBLE GLAZING

● Install double glazing. See pages 271–274.

VENTILATION

● Provide adequate ventilation. See pages 275–284.

REPAIRS AND RENOVATIONS

FLOORS

● Repair or replace floors. See pages 172–183.

PLASTERWORK

● Repair or replace plasterwork. See pages 53–54, 148–167.

WOODWORK

● Fit new baseboards. See page 181.

● Fit new door and window casings. See pages 185, 198.

● Replace or add crown moldings. See pages 88, 156, 167, 468.

FURNITURE

● Build cabinets and shelves. See page 16.

DECORATION

CEILINGS

● Paint or paper ceilings. See pages 67–69, 98.

WALLS

● Paint walls at this stage. See pages 67–73.

FINISH WOODWORK

● Paint or varnish woodwork. See pages 74–84.

WALL-COVERINGS

● Hang wallpapers and wallcoverings. See pages 90–97.

FLOOR-COVERINGS

● Lay carpets and floor coverings. See pages 60, 61, 107–118.

OUTDOOR WORK

OUTSIDE WALLS

REPAIRING WALLS

● Repoint brickwork and repair damaged siding. See pages 47–48, 168–171, 430.

● Patch damaged stucco. See page 49.

● Repair damaged masonry. See page 48.

INSULATING WALLS

● Consider installing external insulation for foundations and blown-in insulation for frame walls at this stage. See pages 268–269.

WEATHER-PROOF WALLS

● Waterproof or paint exterior walls. See pages 48, 50, 64–66.

WINDOWS, DOORS, WOOD AND METAL

● Repair or replace doors and windows. See pages 184–211.

● Refit locks and latches. See pages 240–243.

● Paint or varnish all wood and metalwork. See pages 55, 74–82, 85–86.

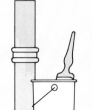

GARDEN WORK

WALLS AND FENCES

● Repair or build garden walls and fences. See pages 410–417, 420–437.

PAVING AND STEPS

● Lay paving. See pages 446–454.

● Build a patio or deck. See pages 438–440, 448–450.

PONDS AND WATERGARDENS

● Construct garden ponds and waterfalls. See pages 455–459.

ROCKERY

● Build a rock garden before planting. See page 459.

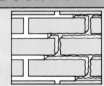
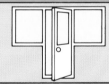

A BASIS FOR SELECTING COLOR

Developing a sense of the "right" color is not the same as learning to paint a door or hang wallpaper. There are no "rules" as such, but there are simple guidelines which will help. In magazine articles on interior design or color selection you will come across terms such as harmony and contrast. Colors are described as being cool or warm, or as tints or shades. These specialized terms form a basis for developing a color scheme. By considering colors as the spokes of a wheel, you will see how one color relates to another and how such relationships create a particular mood or effect.

Primary colors
All colors are derived from three basic "pure" colors—red, blue and yellow. They are known as the primary colors.

Secondary colors
When you mix two primary colors in equal proportions, a secondary color is produced. Red plus blue makes violet, blue with yellow makes green and red plus yellow makes orange. When a secondary color is placed between its constituents on the wheel, it sits opposite its complementary color—the one primary not used in its make-up. Complementary colors are the the most contrasting colors in the spectrum and are used in color schemes for dramatic effects.

Tertiary colors
When a primary is mixed equally with one of its neighboring secondaries, it produces a tertiary color. The complete wheel illustrates a simplified version of all color groupings. Colors on opposite sides of the wheel are used in combination to produce vibrant, contrasting color schemes, while those colors grouped together on one side of the wheel form the basis of a harmonious scheme.

Warm and cool colors
The wheel also groups colors with similar characteristics. On one side are the warm red and yellow combinations, colors we associate with fire and sunlight. A room decorated with warm colors feels cozy or exciting depending on the intensity of the colors used. Cool colors are grouped on the opposite side of the wheel. Blues and greens suggest vegetation, water and sky, and create a relaxed, airy feeling when used together.

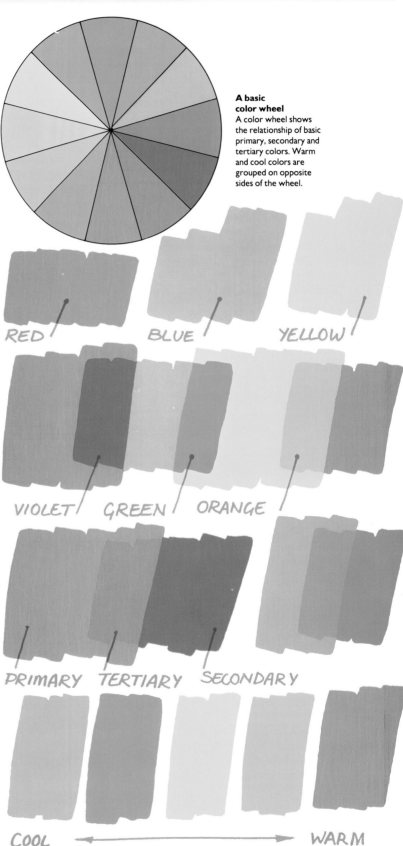

A basic color wheel
A color wheel shows the relationship of basic primary, secondary and tertiary colors. Warm and cool colors are grouped on opposite sides of the wheel.

SELECTING COLOR

1△

3▷

2▽

4▷

5▷

SEE ALSO

Details for: ▷	
Tone	26–27
Texture	28
Pattern	29
Manipulating space	30–31
Decorating	40–118

1 Bold treatment for a living room
A bold red treatment always creates a warm atmosphere. In this interior, obvious brush strokes add the extra element of texture.

2 A child's playroom
Primary colors make a lively, invigorating playroom. The gray floor and expanse of white accentuate the bright colors.

3 Colored fixtures
Basic appliances such as baths, sinks or storage heaters were invariably produced in neutral colors so that they blended into any interior. Now it is possible to order equipment like these wall-mounted radiators which become important elements of a color scheme.

4 Adding color with window blinds
Colored or patterned curtains are fairly commonplace but fewer people choose from the available range of brightly colored venetian blinds. Strong sunlight contributes to the colorful effect.

5 Using color outside
Most buildings do not lend themselves to being painted in bright colors. In areas of the country where color is traditionally acceptable, a bold treatment can be very exciting.

USING TONE FOR SUBTLETY

Pure colors are used to great effect for exterior color schemes and interior decor, but a more subtle combination of colors is called for in the majority of situations. Subtle colors are made by mixing different percentages of pure color, or simply by changing the tone of a color by adding a neutral.

Neutrals

The purest form of neutral is the complete absence of "color"—black or white. By mixing the two together, the range of neutrals is extended almost indefinitely as varying tones of gray. Neutrals are used extensively by decorators because they do not clash with any other color, but in their simplest forms neutrals can be either stark or rather bland. Consequently, a touch of color is normally added to a gray to give it a warm or cool bias so that it can pick up the character of another color in harmony, or provide an almost imperceptible contrast within a range of colors.

Tints

Changing the tone of pure colors by adding white creates pastel colors or tints. Used in combination, tints are safe colors. It is difficult to produce anything but a harmonious scheme whatever colors you use together. The effect can be very different, however, if a pale tint is contrasted with dark tones to produce a dramatic result.

Shades

The shades of a color are produced by adding black to it. Shades are rich, dramatic colors which are used for bold yet sophisticated schemes. It is within this range of colors that browns appear —the interior designer's stock in trade. Brown blends so harmoniously into almost any color scheme that it is tantamount to a neutral.

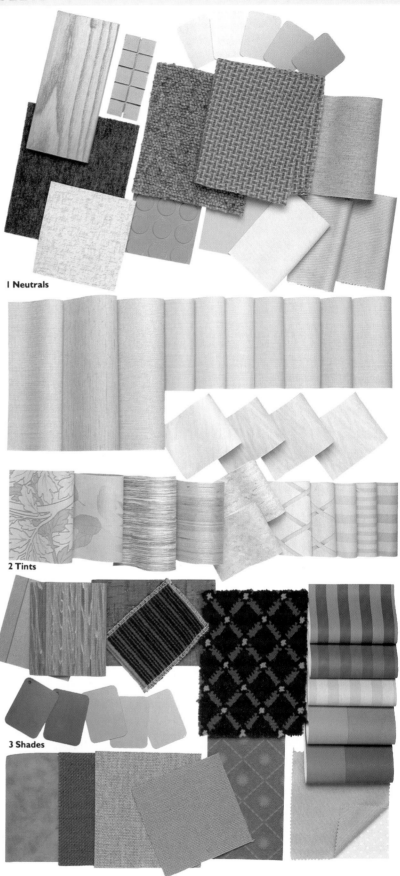

1 Neutrals

1 Neutrals
A range of neutral tones introduces all manner of subtle colors.

2 Tints
A composition of pale tints is always harmonious and attractive.

3 Shades
Use darker tones, or shades, for rich dramatic effects.

2 Tints

3 Shades

USING TONE

1△

◁2

3▷

1 White makes a room spacious
White paint, fabric and carpet take full advantage of available natural light to create a fresh, airy interior. In this bedroom, the crisp black frames accentuate the beautifully proportioned windows.

2 Using tints creatively
Pale colors are often used when a safe harmonious scheme is required, but you can create vibrant effects by juxtaposing cool and warm tints.

3 Dark dramatic tones
The very dark tone used for walls, ceiling and floors in this room is relieved by a carefully painted frieze and white accessories. Gloss paint will reflect some light even when such a dark color is used.

27

TAKING TEXTURE INTO ACCOUNT

Color is an abstraction, merely the way we perceive different wavelengths of light, and yet we are far more aware of the color of a surface than its more tangible texture, which we almost take for granted. Texture is a vital ingredient of any decorative scheme and merits careful thought.

Natural and man-made textures
(Far right)
Many people are not conscious of the actual texture of materials. This selection ranges from the warmth of wood and coarsely woven materials to the smooth coolness of marble, ceramics, plastic and metal.

Textural variety
(Below)
It's relatively simple to achieve interesting textural variety with almost any group of objects. Here, a few stylish kitchen artifacts contrast beautifully with a patterned tile splashback and warm oak cupboards.

The visual effect of texture is also created by light. A smooth surface reflects more light than one that is rough. Coarse textures absorb light, even creating shadows if the light falls at a shallow angle. Consequently, when you paint a coarse texture, the color will look entirely different from the same color applied to a smooth one.

Even without applied color, texture adds interest to a scheme. You can contrast bare brickwork with smooth painted wood, for instance, or use the reflective qualities of glass, metal or glazed ceramics to produce some stunning decorative effects.

Just as color is used to create an atmosphere, texture will produce an almost instinctive impression—it's as if we could feel texture with our eyes. Cork, wood, coarsely woven fabrics or rugs add warmth, even a sense of luxury, to an interior, while smooth, hard materials such as polished stone, stainless steel, vinyl, or even a black lacquered surface give a clean, almost clinical feeling to a room.

Carefully chosen textures *(Right)*
Soft and hard textures have been selected with care for this cool, sophisticated environment.

USING PATTERN FOR EFFECT

Recent, purist approaches to design have made us afraid to use pattern boldly, and yet our less-inhibited forefathers felt free to cover their homes with pattern and applied decoration with spectacular results, creating a sense of gaiety, excitement—"punch," if you like—which is difficult to evoke in any other way.

A well-designed patterned wallpaper, fabric or rug can provide the basis for the entire color scheme, and a professional designer will have chosen the colors to form a pleasing combination. There is no reason why the same colors shouldn't look equally attractive when applied to the other surfaces of a room, but perhaps the safest way to incorporate a pattern is to use it on one surface only to contrast with plain colors elsewhere.

Combining different patterns can be tricky, but a small, regular pattern normally works well with large, bold decoration. Also, different patterns with a similar dominating color can coordinate well even if you experiment with contrasting tones. Another approach is to use the same pattern in different colors, one for the walls, perhaps, and the other for curtains. You should also select patterns according to the atmosphere you want to create. Simple geometric shapes are likely to be more restful than bold, swirling motifs.

Be bold with pattern
There is no reason to be afraid of using pattern when you consider that manufacturers have done most of the thinking for you. Well-designed materials are available to clad just about any surface in your home.

1 Coordinated pattern
The colors used for the striped curtain and furniture fabrics are the basis of this coordinated color scheme.

2 A profusion of pattern
This bedroom combines a wealth of pattern with the rich color of natural mahogany furniture. It shows what can be achieved if one has the courage to opt for the bold approach.

MANIPULATING SPACE

There are nearly always areas of a house that feel uncomfortably small or, conversely, so spacious that one feels isolated, almost vulnerable. Perhaps the first reaction is to consider structural alterations like knocking down a wall or installing a false ceiling. In some cases, such measures will prove to be the most effective solution, but there is no doubt that they will be more expensive and disruptive than the alternative measures of manipulating space—using color, tone and pattern.

Our eyes perceive colors and tones in such a way that it is possible to create optical illusions that apparently change the dimensions of a room. Warm colors appear to advance, so that a room painted overall with brown or red, for instance, will feel smaller than the same room decorated in cool colors such as blue or green, which have a tendency to recede.

Tone can be used to modify or reinforce the desired illusion. Dark tones, even when you are using cool colors, will advance, while pale tones will open up a space visually.

The same qualities of color and tone will change the proportion of a space. Adjusting the height of a ceiling is an obvious example. If you paint a ceiling a darker tone than the walls it will appear lower. If you treated the floor in a similar way, the room would seem squeezed between the two. A long narrow passageway will feel less claustrophobic if you push out the walls by decorating them with pale, cool colors which, incidentally, reflect more light as well.

Using linear pattern is another way to alter our perception of space. A vertically striped wallpaper or woodstrip panelling on the walls counteracts the effect of a low ceiling. Venetian blinds make windows seem wider, and wooden strip floors are stretched in the direction of the boards. Any large-scale pattern draws attention to itself and will advance like warm, dark colors, but small patterns appear as an overall texture from a distance and therefore have less effect.

Practical experiments *(Right)*
A model helps to determine whether an optical illusion will have the desired effect.

Warm colors appear to advance

A cool color or pale tone will recede

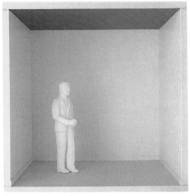

A dark ceiling will appear lower

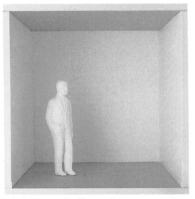

A dark floor and ceiling make a room smaller

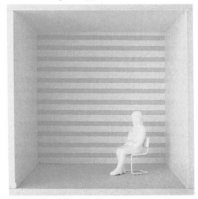

Horizontal stripes make a wall seem wider

Vertical stripes increase the height

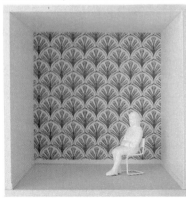

Large-scale patterns advance

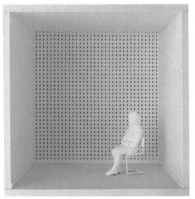

A small regular pattern recedes

1 Using mirrors
Floor-to-ceiling mirrors appear to double the size of a room.

2 Lowering a ceiling
A dark-tone carpet and deep-blue ceiling reduce the height of a room.

3 Incorporating an alcove
Disguise a small kitchen alcove by using colors or pattern which make it feel like part of the living room.

4 Creating space with pattern
A three-dimensional pattern can make a small space seem larger.

1△

2△

◁3

4▷

VERIFYING YOUR SCHEME

Before you spend money on paint, carpet or wallcoverings, collect samples of the materials you propose to use in order to gauge the effect of one color or texture on another.

Collecting samples
Make your first selection from the limited choice of furniture fabrics or carpets. Collect scraps of the other materials you are considering or borrow sample books or display samples from the suppliers to compare them at home. As paint charts are printed, you can never be absolutely confident they will match the actual paint you buy. Consequently, some manufacturers produce small sample pots of paint to try on the wall or woodwork.

Making a sample board
Professional designers make sample boards to check the relative proportions of materials as they will appear in the room. Usually a patch of floor- or wallcovering will be the largest dominating area of color, painted woodwork will be proportionally smaller and accessories might be represented by small spots of color. Make your own board by gluing your assembly of materials to stiff card, butting one piece against another to avoid leaving a white border around each sample, which would change the combined effect.

Incorporating existing features
Most schemes will have to incorporate existing features such as bathroom fixtures or kitchen cabinets. Use these items as starting points, building the color scheme around them. Cut a hole in your sample board as a window for viewing existing materials or borrowed samples against those on the card.

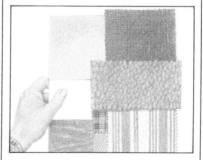

Checking your color selection
View your completed sample board in natural and artificial light to check your color selection.

SCHEMES FOR LIVING ROOMS

In most homes the living room is the largest area in the house. It's where you spend most of your leisure time and entertain your friends. It's the room on which most money is spent on furnishings, curtains and carpets, not to mention expensive audio and video units and so on. For all these reasons, you will want to make sure that the living room decor has lasting appeal. After all, you are unlikely to replace costly furniture and materials frequently.

Unless you are lucky enough to have more than one sitting or living room, it is an area that must feel comfortable during the day, relaxing in the evening and lively enough for the occasional party. Unless the room receives an unusual amount of sunlight, a warm color scheme is often the best to create a cozy atmosphere. Dark, cool tones will produce a similar result under artificial light, but very deep tones can have the opposite effect by creating dark, shadowy areas. Predominantly neutral schemes or a range of browns and beiges lend themselves to change in the future by simply swapping the

accessories without having to spend a lot of money on replacing the essentials. Natural textures are equally versatile.

Patterned carpets or rugs are less likely to be ruined by the inevitable spills than plain colors, but very dark tones are almost as difficult to keep clean as pale colors.

Curtains or blinds provide the perfect solution to a change of mood. During the day, they are pulled aside or lifted and therefore contribute very little to the general appearance of the room, but in the evening they can become a wall of color or pattern which can transform the scheme.

An adaptable scheme
(Right)
A safe yet comfortable scheme lends itself to change by swapping the accessories.

Typically traditional
(Far right)
Pink-washed walls and floral patterns suit a typical country cottage.

Sympathetic style
(Below)
A period living room needs appropriate styling.

Simple styling suits a modern house *(Right)*
A modern home can be treated successfully with restrained colors and natural textures.

SCHEMES FOR BEDROOMS

A bedroom is first and foremost a personal room. Its decor should reflect the character of its occupant and the functions to which the room is put. At night, a bedroom should be relaxing, even romantic. Much depends on the lighting, but pattern and color can create a luxurious and seductive mood.

Strangely, very few people ever use pattern on a ceiling, and yet a bedroom provides the ideal opportunity, especially as you are unlikely to spend much of your waking life there and so can afford to be adventurous with the decor. Bedroom carpet is often of inferior quality because it need not be hardwearing, but you could give the color scheme a real lift by investing in an expensive rug or deep-pile carpet, knowing that it will come to no harm.

If a bedroom faces south, early sunlight will provide the necessary stimulus to wake you up, but a north-facing room will benefit from bright, invigorating colors.

Some bedrooms may serve a dual function. A teenager's bedroom may have to double as a study or a private sitting room and so needs to be stimulating rather than restful. A child's room will almost certainly function as a playroom. The obvious choice would be for strong, even primary colors, but as most children accumulate brightly colored toys, books and pictures, you might select a neutral background to the colorful accessories. The smallest bedrooms are usually reserved for guests, but they can be made to appear larger and more inviting by the judicious manipulation of the proportions with color or tone.

1 An elegant master bedroom
The peaceful character of this elegant bedroom is a result of a basically neutral scheme which is warmed very slightly by a hint of cream and pale yellow.

2 Bright and refreshing
The combination of bright yellow and white makes for a cheerful start to the day.

3 Dual-purpose room
When a bedroom doubles as a sitting room it needs to be stimulating during the day and cozy at night.

4 A guest room
A guest room should make a visitor feel at home immediately. The warmth of stripped pine makes this room very inviting.

DECOR FOR COOKING AND EATING

Kitchens need to be functional areas capable of taking a great deal of wear and tear, so the materials you choose will be dictated largely by practicalities. But that doesn't meant you have to restrict your use of color in any way. Kitchen sinks and appliances are made in bright colors as well as the standard stainless steel and white enamel. Tiled worktops and splashbacks, vinyl floorcoverings and plastic-laminate surfaces offer further opportunity to introduce a range of colors.

Textures are an important consideration with a range of possibilities. Natural wood is still a popular material for kitchen cupboards, and wherever wood is employed, it will provide a warm element which you can choose to contrast with cool colors and textures, or pick up the warm theme with paint, paper or floorcovering. Some people prefer to rely entirely on metallic, ceramic and plastic surfaces that impose a clean, purposeful and practical character.

If the kitchen incorporates a dining area, you may decide to create within the same room a separate space that is more conducive to relaxation and conversation. Softer textures such as carpet tiles, cork flooring and fabric upholstery absorb some of the sound generated by appliances and the clatter of kitchen utensils. You could also decorate the walls in a different way to change the mood, perhaps using darker tones or a patterned wallcovering to define the dining area.

1 A functional kitchen
This simple kitchen, laid out to form a perfect work triangle, looks extremely functional without feeling clinical.

2 A family kitchen
Some people like the kitchen to be part of an informal sitting and dining area where the family can relax.

3 A breakfast room
A sunny alcove linked to the kitchen makes an ideal breakfast room.

4 A kitchen extension
Colorful fabric blinds shade this kitchen extension from direct sunlight.

BATHROOMS

Bathrooms, like kitchens, must fulfill quite definite functions efficiently, but they should never look clinical. Even when a bathroom is centrally heated, a cold uninviting color scheme would not be a wise choice as enameled and tiled surfaces are inevitable. Colored bathroom appliances are commonplace, but choose carefully as they are likely to remain the dominating influence on any future color schemes.

A bathroom is another area where you can afford to be inventive with your use of color or pattern. A bold treatment that might become tiresome with overexposure can be highly successful in a room used at intervals only. Try to introduce some sound-absorbing materials like ceiling tiles, carpet or cork flooring to avoid the hollow acoustics associated with old-fashioned tiled bathrooms. If you want to use delicate materials that might be affected by steam, make sure the bathroom is properly ventilated. Bathrooms are usually small rooms with relatively high ceilings, but painting a ceiling a dark tone, which might improve the proportion of a larger room, can make a bathroom feel like a box. A more successful way to counter the effect of a high ceiling is to divide the walls with a chair rail, using a different color or material above and below the line.

If you live in a hard-water area, avoid dark-colored bathroom fixtures that will emphasize mineral deposits.

1 Warm and luxurious
There is no reason why a bathroom cannot be warm and inviting when there is such a choice of luxurious wallcoverings and ceramic tiles.

2 Changing the proportion
Improve the proportion of a bathroom with a high ceiling by a change of color at chair-rail height.

3 Fashionable styling
A clever combination of color and shape changes a simple bathroom into a room with distinctive character.

4 A period bathroom
Reproduction fixtures and marbled paintwork re-create a period bathroom.

SINGLE ROOMS OR SMALL APARTMENTS

When you live in one room, every activity takes place in the same area, so its decor must be versatile. But much depends on your life-style. If you are out at work during the day you may decide to concentrate on creating a mood for the evening. On the other hand, if you work at home, your priority will be to provide a stimulating daytime environment, but not one that is too distracting.

1 An open-plan apartment
Create an impression of space with a fitted carpet and white walls. Vertical louvered blinds can be used to screen one area from another.

2 One large room
A warm color scheme makes a large room feel cozier. Foldaway furniture is an advantage when you live in one room.

3 Dividing a single room
Custom-built furniture and different floor levels can be used to relieve the monotony of four walls.

Ideally, you should attempt to design an interior that can be changed at will to suit the time of day or your disposition. We have mentioned the fact that curtains or blinds can be used to greater effect after dark, but more positive measures are required to make the room as adaptable as possible.

Some means of screening off a sleeping alcove is always an advantage. Floor-length curtains hung from a ceiling-mounted track can form a soft wall of color or texture. Or use vertical louvered blinds—with the flick of a pull cord, you can let in the sunlight. A concertina-folding wall of panels or louvered shutters give the impression of a permanent screen during the day, and provide the opportunity to introduce natural or stained wood to a scheme. Alternatively, construct a portable screen from flat panels that you can decorate to suit yourself.

Dividing the floor area will define areas of activity: soft rugs for seating, polished boards or tiling for cooking or eating. You can even change the floor level with a simple wooden dais covered in carpet. Areas of wall can be sharply defined to pick up the theme using different finishes.

A small, open-plan apartment suggests other options. Prevailing natural light might persuade you to treat areas differently, either to freshen up a dark corner or to cool down an area that is constantly sunlit. You can create the impression of greater space by running the same flooring throughout the apartment, and white or pastel-painted walls will have a similar effect. Picking out some walls with strong color or pattern will lead the eye into another area. You could play with ceiling levels using color or tone, possibly pulling it down over a cozy sitting area or bedroom while apparently increasing the volume of another space by painting the ceiling with a pale neutral or pastel tint.

1△

2▽

3▽

PLANNING YOUR LIGHTING

Successful lighting must be functional to enable you to work efficiently and read or study without eyestrain. It must define areas of potential danger and provide general background illumination. But the decorative element of lighting is equally important. It can create an atmosphere of warmth and wellbeing, highlight objects of beauty or interest and transform an interior with areas of light and shadow.

Living areas

For the living areas of the house, the accent should be one of versatility, creating areas of light where they are needed most, both for function and dramatic effect. Seating areas are best served by lighting placed at a low level so that naked bulbs are not directed straight into the eyes, and in such a position that the pages of a book or newspaper are illuminated from beside the reader. Choose lighting that is not so harsh that it would cause glare from white paper, and supplement it with additional low-level lighting to reduce the effects of contrast between the page and darker areas beyond.

Working at a desk demands similar conditions, but the light source must be situated in front of you to avoid throwing your own shadow across the work. Choose a properly shaded desk lamp, or conceal lighting under wall storage or bookshelves above the desk.

Similar concealed lighting is ideal for a wall-hung audio system, but you may require extra lighting in the form of ceiling-mounted downlights to illuminate the shelves themselves. Alternatively, use fixtures designed to clip onto the shelves or wall uprights.

Concealed lighting in other areas of the living room can be very attractive. Strip lights placed on top and at the back of high cupboards will bounce light off the ceiling into the room. Hide lighting behind valances or soffits to accentuate curtains, or along a wall to light pictures. Individual artworks can be picked out with track lights placed above them, or use a ceiling spot light that is adjustable to place light exactly where it is required. Take care with pictures protected by glass as reflections may destroy the desired effect. Use lighting in an alcove or recess to give maximum impact to an attractive display of collected items.

SEE ALSO

Details for: ▷	
Light fixtures	298–299, 330
Electrical circuits	306–309

Concealed lighting
Interesting effects are created by concealing the actual source of artificial light and allowing it to bounce off adjacent surfaces to illuminate areas of the room.

Atmospheric lighting
Carefully placed light fixtures produce an atmosphere of warmth and wellbeing.

PLANNING YOUR LIGHTING

Sleeping areas

Lamps at the side of the bed are essential requirements in any bedroom. Or, better still, use concealed lighting above the headboard. Position the fitting low enough to prevent light from falling on your face as you lie in bed. Install two lights behind the baffle over a double bed, each controlled individually so that your partner can sleep undisturbed if you want to read into the early hours. A dressing table needs its own light source placed so that it cannot be seen in the mirror but illuminates the person using it. Wall lights or downlights in the ceiling will provide atmospheric lighting, but install two-way switching (◁) so that you can control them from the bed and the door. Make sure bedside light fixtures in a child's room are completely tamperproof and completely safe(◁). A dimmer switch controlling the main room lighting will provide enough light to comfort a child at night but can be turned to full brightness when he or she is playing in the evening.

Dining areas/kitchens

An adjustable unit is the ideal type to light a dining table because its height can be adjusted exactly. If you eat in the kitchen, have separate controls for the table lighting and work areas so that you can create a cozy dining area without having to illuminate the rest of the room. In addition to a good background light, illuminate kitchen worktops with strip lights placed under the wall cabinets but hidden from view by baffles along the front edges. Place a track light or downlights over the sink to eliminate your own shadow.

Bathrooms

Safety must be your first priority when lighting a bathroom. Fixtures should be designed to protect electrical connections from moisture and steam, and switches must be protected with ground-fault circuit interrupters for safety. It can be difficult to create atmospheric lighting in a bathroom, but concealed light directed onto the ceiling is one solution as long as you provide another source of light over the basin mirror.

Stairways

Light staircases from above so that treads are illuminated clearly, throwing the risers into shadow. This will define the steps clearly for anyone with poor eyesight. Place a light over each landing or turn of the staircase. Three-way switching is essential to be certain that no one has to negotiate the stairs in darkness.

Workshops

Plan workshop lighting with efficiency and safety in mind. Light a workbench like a desk and provide individual, adjustable fixtures for machine tools.

Bedside lamps
(Below)
You can expend a great deal of thought on planning the lighting in your bedroom only to find that two simple bedside lamps are the perfect solution.

Bathroom lighting
(Right)
Light fixtures concealed behind a translucent screen produce an original and safe form of lighting for a bathroom.

Concentrating areas of illumination
(Above)
Spotlights will concentrate pools of light to illuminate the functional area of a kitchen and a dining table.

An improvised lampshade
(Left)
This Oriental sunshade will throw a diffused light on the dining table while bouncing extra light off the ceiling.

2

DECORATING

Ladder accessories
Fit out your ladder with a range of helpful devices to make working easier and safer. This ladder features adjustable feet (**1**) for uneven ground, a foot rest for comfort (**2**), a clamp for a paint can (**3**), a tool tray (**4**), and a stay (**5**), to hold the top away from eaves or gutters.

BEFORE YOU BEGIN

Timing, weather and the condition of the site are important factors to consider before you decorate outside. Indoors, you have the problem of what to do with a room full of furniture and furnishings while you work.

OUTSIDE THE HOUSE

Plan your work so that you can begin the actual decoration of the house exterior in spring and autumn. Working conditions will be comfortable and the paint, adhesives and other materials will have a chance to cure before exposure to climatic extremes.

The best weather for decorating is a warm but overcast day. Avoid painting on rainy days or in direct sunlight, as both can ruin new paintwork. You should follow the sun around the house, however, so that its warmth dries out the night's dew before you get there.

Don't work on windy days either, or dust will be deposited on the fresh paint. Sprinkle water around doorways or spray with a houseplant sprayer before you paint as this settles dust, which you would churn up with your feet.

Clear away any rubbish from around the house, which will slow down your progress and could even cause accidents. Cut back overhanging foliage from trees or shrubs. Protect plants and paving with drop cloths.

INSIDE THE HOUSE

Before you decorate a room inside, carry out all repairs necessary and have the chimney swept if you use an open fire: a soot fall would ruin your decorations. Clear as much furniture from the room as possible, and group what is left under drop cloths.

Lift any rugs or carpets, then spray water on the floor and sweep it to collect loose dust before you begin to paint. Protect finished wood or tiled floors with drop cloths.

Remove all furnishings such as pictures and lampshades and unscrew door handles and other hardware. Keep the knob handy in the room with you, in case you get shut in accidentally.

WHAT TO WEAR

Naturally, you will wear old clothes when decorating, but avoid woolen garments, which tend to leave hairs sticking to paintwork. Jeans with loops and large pockets for tools are ideal for decorating.

MEANS OF ACCESS

Whether you are decorating inside or outside, you must provide adequate means of reaching the area you are working on. Using inefficient equipment and makeshift structures is dangerous; but even if you don't want to buy your own ladders and scaffolding equipment, you can rent them quite cheaply. Safety and comfort while working are other important considerations, and there's a wide range of devices and accessories to make the job that much easier.

Types of ladders and access equipment

Stepladders are essential for interior decoration. Traditional wooden stepladders are still available, but they have been largely superseded by lightweight aluminum alloy types. You should have at least one which stands about 6 feet high to reach a ceiling without having to stand on the top step. Another, shorter ladder might be more convenient for other jobs and you can use them both, with scaffold boards, to build a platform.

Outdoors you'll need ladders to reach up to the roof. Double and triple wooden extension ladders are very heavy, so consider a metal one.

Extension ladders are operated by a rope and pulley so that they can be extended single-handed.

To estimate the length of ladder you need, add together the ceiling heights of your house. Add at least 3 feet to the length to allow for the angle and safe access to the roof.

There are many versions of dual- or even multipurpose ladders, which convert from stepladder to straight ladder. A well-designed, versatile ladder is a good compromise.

Sectional scaffold frames can be built up to form towers at any convenient height for decorating inside and outside. Wide feet prevent the tower from sinking into the ground, and adjustable versions allow you to level it. Some models have locking casters, which enable you to move the tower.

Towers are ideal for painting a large expanse of wall outdoors. Indoors, smaller platforms made from the same scaffold components bring high ceilings within easy reach.

Accessories for ladders

- **Ladder stay** A stay holds the ladder away from the wall. It is an essential piece of equipment when painting overhanging eaves and gutters. You may otherwise be forced to lean back too far and possibly fall.
- **Clip-on platform** A wide flat board, which clamps to the rungs, provides a comfortable platform to stand on while working for long periods.
- **Adjustable legs** Bolt-on accessories, which enable you to level the foot of a ladder on uneven ground.

- **Paint can holder** You should always support yourself with one hand on a ladder, so use a metal S-hook to hang the paint can from a rung. A special clamp, which can be fixed to the rail, enables you to position the can at one side of the ladder.
- **Tool tray** A clip-on tray is ideal for holding a small selection of tools.

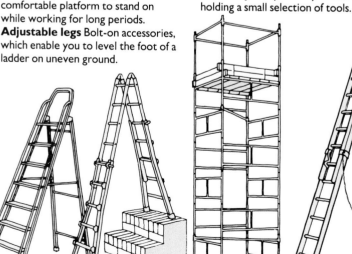

Alloy stepladder   **Dual-purpose ladder**   **Scaffold tower**   **Extension ladder**

WORKING WITH LADDERS

When you buy or rent a ladder, wooden or metal, bear in mind that:
- Wooden ladders should be made from straight-grained, knot-free lumber.
- Good-quality wooden ladders have hardwood rungs tenoned through the upright stiles and secured with wedges.
- Wooden rungs with reinforcing metal rods stretched under them are safer than ones without.
- End caps or foot pads are an advantage to prevent the ladder from slipping on hard ground.
- Adjustability is a prime consideration. Choose a ladder that enables you to gain access to various parts of the building and which converts to a compact unit for storage.
- The rungs of overlapping sections of an extension ladder should align or the gap between the rungs might be too small for toes to catch accidentally.
- Choose an extension ladder with a rope, pulley and automatic latch, which locks the extension to its rung.
- Check that you can buy or rent a range of accessories (see opposite) to fit your make of ladder.
- Choose a stepladder with a platform at the top to take cans and trays.
- Treads should be comfortable to stand on. Stepladders with wide, flat treads are the best choice.
- Stepladders with extended rails give you a handhold at the top of the steps.
- Wooden stepladders often have a rope to stop the two halves sliding apart. A better solution used on most metal stepladders is a folding stay, which locks in the open position.

Is the ladder safe to use?

Check ladders regularly and before you use them after a winter's break. Inspect a rented ladder before use.

Look for splits opening along the rails, check that there are no missing or broken rungs and that the joints are tight. Sight along the rails to make sure they are aligned, or the ladder could rock when leaning against a wall.

Inspect wooden ladders for rot and other defects. Even a few checks or sponginess could signify serious damage below the surface. Test that the wood is sound before using the ladder and treat it regularly with a wood preservative.

Check that fasteners for hinges and pulleys are secure and lubricate them. Inspect the pulley rope for fraying and renew if necessary.

Oil or varnish wooden ladders regularly to keep them from drying out. Apply extra coats to the rungs (which take most wear). Don't paint a ladder, since this may hide serious defects.

How to handle a ladder

Carry a ladder upright, not slung across your shoulder. Hold the ladder vertically, bend your knees slightly then rock the ladder back against your shoulder. Grip one rung lower down while you support the ladder at head height with your other hand, then straighten your knees.

To erect a ladder, lay it on the ground with its feet against the wall. Gradually raise it to vertical as you walk towards the wall. Pull the feet out from the wall so that the ladder is resting at an angle of about 70 degrees. The ladder's feet should be one-quarter of its height from the wall (for a 20-foot ladder, wall-to-ladder distance at the bottom should be 5 feet).

Raise an extension ladder to the required height while holding it upright. If it is a heavy ladder, get someone to hold it while you operate the pulley.

Handling a ladder
Carry the ladder upright, leaning it back against your shoulder; grip one rung low down, another at head height. When erected, the base of the ladder should be one-quarter of its height away from the wall so that it is correctly balanced.

HOW TO USE A LADDER SAFELY

More accidents are caused by using ladders unwisely than as a result of faulty equipment. Erect the ladder safely before you ascend and move it when the work is out of reach—never lean out to the side or you'll tilt over. Follow these simple, common-sense rules:

Securing the ladder

If the ground is soft, spread the load of the ladder by placing a wide board under the feet; screw a batten across the board to wedge the ladder in place.

On hard ground, make sure the ladder has antislip end caps and lay a sandbag (or a tough polyethylene bag filled with earth) at the base.

Secure the stiles near the base with rope tied to wooden stakes driven into the ground at each side and just behind the ladder (**1**). When extending a ladder, the sections should overlap by at least one-quarter of their length—but don't lean the top against unstable gutters, soil pipes, drainpipes, and especially glass, as they may give way.

Anchor the ladder near the top by tying it to a stout length of lumber, held across the inside of the window frame. Make sure the rail extends about 1 foot on each side of the window and pad the ends to protect the wall (**2**).

It's a good idea to fix ring bolts at regular intervals into the masonry just below the fascia board. This is an excellent way to secure the top of a ladder as you have equally good anchor points wherever you position it. Alternatively, fix screw eyes to the wall or a sound fascia board and attach the ladder to them.

Safety aloft

Never climb higher than four rungs from the top of the ladder; handholds will be out of reach. Don't lean sideways from a ladder either. Keep both feet on a rung and your hips centered between the stiles.

Avoid a slippery foothold by placing a sack or old doormat at the foot of the ladder to dry your boots before you ascend.

Unless the manufacturer states otherwise, do not use a ladder to form a horizontal walkway, even with a scaffold board lying on it.

Stepladders are prone to topple sideways. Clamp a strut to the ladder on uneven floors (**3**).

1 Staking a ladder
Secure the base of the ladder by lashing it to stakes in the ground.

2 Securing the top
Anchor the ladder to a bar held inside the window frame.

3 Supporting a stepladder
Clamp a strut to the rail to prevent a stepladder from toppling sideways.

41

ERECTING WORK PLATFORMS INDOORS

A lot of work can be carried out by moving a ladder little by little as the work progresses, but it can become tedious, perhaps leading to an accident as you try to reach just a bit further before having to move along, and then tip over.

It's more convenient to build a work platform that allows you to tackle a large area without moving the structure. You can rent a pair of decorator's trestles and bridge them with a scaffold board, or make a similar structure with two stepladders (1).

Clamp or tie the board to the rungs and use two boards, one on top of the other, if two people need to use the platform at once.

An even better arrangement is to use scaffold tower components to make a mobile platform (2). Choose one with locking casters for the ideal solution for painting or papering ceilings.

SEE ALSO
◁ Details for:
Scaffold tower   40
Ladders   40–41

1 Improvised platform
A simple yet safe platform made from stepladders and a scaffold board.

2 Mobile platform
An efficient structure made from scaffold tower frames.

Gaining access to a stairwell

Stairwells present particular problems when building platforms. The simplest method is to use a dual-purpose staircase ladder, which can be adjusted to stand evenly on a flight (3). Anchor the steps with rope through a couple of screw eyes fixed to the stair treads if the holes will be concealed by carpet later. Rest a scaffold board between the ladder and the landing to form a bridge.

Screw the board to the landing and tie the other end.

Alternatively, construct a tailor-made platform from ladders and boards to suit your staircase (4). Make sure the boards and ladders are clamped or lashed together, and that ladders can't slip on the treads. If necessary, screw wooden stops to the stairs to prevent the foot of the ladder from moving.

Stair scaffold
Erect a platform with scaffold frames to compensate for the slope of a staircase.

3 Dual-purpose ladder
Use a stair ladder to straddle the flight with a scaffold board to give a level work platform.

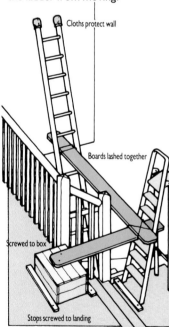

Cloths protect wall

Boards lashed together

Screwed to box

Stops screwed to landing

4 Tailor-made platform
Build a network of scaffold boards, stepladders, ladders and boxes to suit your stairwell layout.

ERECTING PLATFORMS OUTSIDE

Scaffolding is by far the best method of building a work platform to do work on the outside of a house. Towers made from slot-together frames are available for rent. Heights up to about 30 feet are possible; the tallest ones require supporting outriggers.

Build the lower section of the frame first and level it with adjustable feet before erecting a tower on top. As you build, climb and stand on the inside of the tower.

Erect a proper platform at the top with toe boards all round to prevent tools and materials being knocked off the tower, and extend the framework to provide hand rails all around.

Secure the tower to the house by tying it to screw eyes fixed into the structural members, as with ladders.

Some towers incorporate a staircase inside the scaffold frame; floors with a trapdoor enable you to ascend to the top of the tower. If you cannot find such a tower, the safest access is via a ladder. Make sure it extends at least 3 feet above the staging so that you can step on and off safely.

It is difficult to reach windows and walls above an extension with just a ladder. With a scaffold tower, however, you can construct a cantilevered section fixed to the main tower, which rests on the roof of the extension.

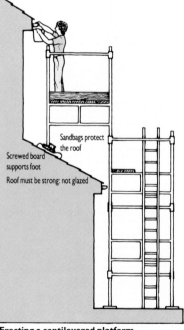

Sandbags protect the roof

Screwed board supports foot

Roof must be strong: not glazed

Erecting a cantilevered platform
Cantilever section rests on a board to spread load.

ROUTINE MAINTENANCE

It sometimes seems that simply taking care of your home involves so much time and energy that it is difficult to even think about making substantial improvements. Indeed, maintenance of even a modest home involves looking after a rather complex system of structural, mechanical and decorative features.

But it is routine, methodical maintenance that prevents small problems from turning into large, expensive ones and that keeps a home running efficiently and economically. Attending to chores both inside and outside the home keeps what's already there intact and so provides the best opportunity for continuing improvement.

To keep maintenance tasks from seeming overwhelming, it's best to approach them on a seasonal basis. In most locales, spring and fall will be the busiest times as it seems best to take advantage of the moderate weather to repair damage from the extremes of the prior season and prepare for those of the upcoming one. The chart below suggests a schedule that would be appropriate for most regions of the country, and throughout the book you will find methods and measures for the various maintenance concerns discussed in greater detail.

SEASONAL MAINTENANCE SCHEDULE

WINTER

Doors and windows: Check for drafts and weatherstrip where necessary.
Heating system: Replace filters in forced-air systems once a month.
Fireplaces, stoves and chimneys: Clean and inspect flues in midseason.
Gutters, leaders and outdoor drains: Keep them clear of ice and debris.
Yard: Prune trees early to midseason.

SPRING

Roofing: Repair damaged shingles and flashing.
Gutters, leaders and outdoor drains: Clear debris and flush with water. Straighten and correct pitch of misaligned gutters. Reset leaders and tighten fasteners.
Siding and trim: Caulk and renail loose pieces. Restore failing paint. Wash all exterior surfaces.
Masonry: Repair cracks; repoint failing brick mortar joints.
Windows: Clean and unstick sash, repair damaged putty. Install insect screens in ventilating windows and shading devices on south-facing windows.
Pests: Check for termite and ant infestation. Check vent louvers, chimneys and other protective areas for bird and insect nests.
Heating system: Shut off unneeded appliances with standing pilots. Drain hydronic systems.
Fireplaces, stoves, and chimneys: Clean and inspect flues when seasonal use-period ends.
Air-conditioning equipment: Vacuum internal parts and clear drainage tubes.
Garden equipment: Clean and lubricate: fill oil reservoirs in gas-powered equipment and change air filters.

Lawn: Clear away accumulated leaves and debris. Test soil pH and amend as necessary. Dethatch, roll, and aerate; reseed as necessary. Apply preemergent weed killers and 25% of annual fertilizer allotment.

SUMMER

Air-conditioning equipment: Clean filters once monthly.
Mildew control: Clean away incipient growth with bleach solution; operate dehumidifiers in damp areas.
Lawn: Feed lawn with 50% of annual fertilizer allotment. Weed on a biweekly basis.

FALL

Gutters, leaders and outdoor drains: Clear debris and flush with water. Inspect joints and tighten brackets as necessary.
Heating system: Have equipment professionally serviced. Blow dust from thermostat contacts.
Air-conditioning equipment: Vacuum internal parts and wrap equipment.
Outdoor water supply: In frost-prone areas, shut off supply, drain lines and leave valves open.
Siding, trim and foundation: Patch and seal open cracks. Seal openings where animals may take refuge. Close vents of unheated crawlspaces.
Windows and doors: Put storm sash in place. Clean and repair screens, spray with protective coating before storing. Inspect and fortify weatherstripping. Clear debris from basement window wells.
Garden equipment: Drain fuel from gas engines. Clean metal surfaces and spray with protective coating.
Lawn: Clear leaves, dethatch and reseed.

KEEPING A CLEAN HOUSE

Regular cleaning of a home's exterior surfaces not only keeps them looking well-kept and attractive, it is an important aspect of preventive maintenance that can help stave off the need to refinish or replace materials on the outside of the home. We're not talking here about weekly scrubbings but only about taking a couple of hours once or twice a year to remove the buildup of grime and pollutants that can eat away at the skin of a home.

Even so-called no-maintenance materials such as vinyl and aluminum siding can benefit from a little care. Just dissolve 1 teaspoon of trisodium phosphate per gallon of water used, wash with a scrub brush and rinse with a garden hose.

TSP is also great for cleaning light soil from wood, painted surfaces and masonry. Household bleach will kill mildew and lift the dark stains. To remove heavy stains including mortar, efflorescence and paint from masonry, mix 1 part muriatic acid with 10 parts water and scrub with a wire brush. Lift grease and oil stains from concrete by sprinkling portland cement or corn starch over the area and wetting it with paint thinner or benzene. Keep the poultice moist for 24 hours, then rinse it away with clear water.

Weathered natural wood can be restored to its original color by scrubbing with oxalic acid solution. Kerosene is effective for removing rust stains and protecting steel screens.

SEE ALSO

Details for: ▷	
Painted woodwork	44–45
Maintaining masonry	46–48, 50
Repairing concrete	49
Maintaining metalwork	51–52
Wall finishes	53
Repairing plaster	54
Interior woodwork	55

Using a power washer
A power washer, which can be rented and attached to a garden hose, can be used to clean siding.

PAINTED WOODWORK

In time, all painted wood surfaces require renewal by repainting. But you can reduce the need to repaint frequently through effective maintenance. The maintenance program for painted wood should include regular washing with nondestructive cleaners to remove the buildup of agents that can attack finishes, diagnosing the cause of any particular type of paint failure and correcting the condition before repainting, and preparing the surface properly before applying a new finish coat.

Liquid sander
You can chemically prepare paintwork in good condition using a liquid sander: wipe it onto the surface and leave it to slightly soften the top layer of paint, leaving a matte finish. It is an ideal surface for applying the new top coat of paint. The chemical cleans and degreases the painted surface, too.

Maintaining paintwork in good condition

Wash painted surfaces from the bottom upwards with a solution of warm water and trisodium phosphate, about one teaspoon per gallon of water. Pay particular attention to the areas around door handles and window catches, where dirt and grease will be heaviest. Rinse with fresh water from top to bottom to prevent runs of dirty liquid on a newly cleaned surface.

If painted surfaces are spotted with mildew but otherwise sound, clean away the growth with direct application of household bleach.

Since paint finishes are susceptible to abrasion, trim back tree branches or any other growth that may rub against the surface.

Fill any open joints or holes with filler and rub down when set. Renew old and crumbling window putty and seal around window and door frames with a good-quality caulk. If you plan to repaint, no further preparation may be necessary except light sanding to roughen glossy surfaces slightly.

Diagnosing paint problems

When a painted finish fails, there's always a reason for it. Causes may range from simple breakdown of the resins because of age to improper preparation of the surface. Or the causes may have their roots in incorrect paint selection or environmental conditions. Most types of paint failure are related to moisture problems.

It is important to analyze the symptoms of any particular type of paint failure, pinpoint the underlying cause and then correct it before going to the trouble and expense of repainting, only to have paint fail again after a brief period. Examples of the most common types of paint failure are illustrated at the left and below. The possible causes and remedies for each are discussed below.

Peeling, flaking paint may result from two causes. If the peeling exposes bare wood, the cause is most likely a moisture problem—moisture originating inside the house or seeping in through improperly caulked joints is literally pushing the paint off the surface as it evaporates into the air. If exterior joints seem satisfactorily caulked, the remedy is to improve ventilation. Consider installing or enlarging roof vents, adding soffit vents under the eaves and installing small circular vents in the siding itself to allow moisture generated inside the home to escape in a less destructive way. If you see paint beneath a peeling top coat, the cause may be inadequate preparation before paint was applied or incompatibility of the top coat with the coat beneath.

In any case, scrape away all loose, peeling paint and sand sharply raised edges to create a reasonably smooth surface. Prime bare and peeled spots before applying the top coat.

Blistering can also be symptomatic of a moisture problem. If water is present when you cut open blisters, then improving ventilation and fortifying the caulking are the measures to take before repainting. If water isn't present and if there's paint instead of bare wood beneath the blister, the probable cause is that the surface was too hot at the time it was painted. Again, remove all loose paint, sand and prime before repainting.

Wrinkled paint may result from two causes. The previous painter may have tried to apply too heavy a coat, which sagged before drying. Or, the surface over which the top coat was applied may have been too glossy. In either case, sand away the wrinkles and prime lightly before applying the top coat.

Alligatoring results from the buildup of too many layers of paint, each expanding and contracting unevenly and cracking the surface. The remedy here is to strip the surface down to the bare wood before priming and repainting.

Peeling/flaking

Blistering

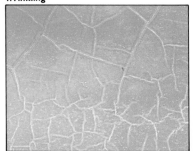

Wrinkling

Alligatoring

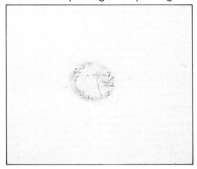

Bleeding
Stains can bleed through top coats when a surface hasn't been properly sealed. Particularly prevalent are knot stains caused by the leaching out of a chemical that is naturally concentrated in knots. Sealing stained areas with shellac, then applying a stain-blocking primer is the best way to assure the integrity of the top coat.

SELECTING AND USING CHEMICAL STRIPPERS

An old finish can be removed using a stripper which reacts chemically with paint or varnish. There are basically two types: those with a liquid or gel consistency based on methylene chloride and strippers in the form of a thick paste, which are caustic based.

All chemical strippers can be dangerous if splashed on your skin or eyes, so take proper precautions:

- Wear vinyl work gloves and safety glasses. Wear a respiratory face mask as well.
- Work in a well-ventilated area and never smoke near the chemicals; some give off fumes which are toxic when inhaled through a cigarette.
- If you get stripper on your skin, wash it off immediately with copious amounts of cold water. If it gets in your eyes, wash it out under running water and seek medical advice.
- Keep pets and children out of the way when using chemical strippers.

GEL OR LIQUID STRIPPERS

Liquid strippers are suitable only when you can lay an object horizontally. For stripping moldings and other woodwork in place, use a gel stripper, which is stiff enough to cling to vertical surfaces.

Lay polyethylene sheet or plenty of newspaper on the floor, then apply a liberal coat of stripper to the paint, working well into any contours.

Leave it for about 10 minutes, then try scraping a patch to see if the paint has softened through to the wood. If not, don't waste time removing the top layers only, but apply more stripper and stipple the softened paint back down with a brush. Leave for 5 minutes.

Once the chemicals have completed their work, use a scraper to remove the paint from flat surfaces and a shavehook to remove it from recesses.

Wipe the paint from deep carvings with fine steel wool; use small pieces of burlap when stripping oak, since particles of metal can stain the wood.

When you have removed the bulk of the paint, clean off residual patches with a wad of steel wool dipped in fresh stripper. Rub with the grain, turning the wad inside out to present a clean face as it becomes clogged with paint.

Neutralize the stripper by washing the wood with turpentine or water (depending on the stripper manufacturer's advice). It is cheaper to use water when washing large areas but water will raise the grain and can cause joints to swell. Let the surfaces dry out thoroughly, then treat as new wood (▷).

PASTE STRIPPERS

Spread a paste stripper onto wood in a thick layer, working it well into crevices and recesses and making sure all air bubbles are expelled.

The paste must be kept moist long enough for the chemicals to work—it may dry out too quickly in direct sunlight or a heated room—so cover it with a thin polyethylene sheet. Some manufacturers supply a blanket which seals the moisture in. Leave the stripper in place for several hours, then lift the leathery substance at the edge with a scraper and peel it off, complete with paint, in one layer. If it has become too hard to peel, soften it by soaking.

Discard the paste wrapped in newspaper, then wash the wood with water and a scrub brush. Let it dry before priming and finishing.

INDUSTRIAL STRIPPING

Any portable woodwork can be taken to a professional stripper, who will immerse the whole thing in a tank of stripping solution. Many companies use a solution of hot caustic chemicals, which must be washed out of the wood by hosing down with water. It is an efficient process (which incidentally kills organic growths at the same time) but there is a risk of splitting the panels, warping and opening up joints. At best, you can expect a reasonable amount of raised grain, which you will have to sand smooth before refinishing.

Some companies use a cold chemical dip, which does little harm to solid timber and raises the grain less. This process is likely to be more expensive than the hot dipping method.

Most stripping companies will collect, many will rehang a door for you, and some offer a finishing service, too.

Never submit veneered items to either treatment: it may peel off.

Using a hot-air stripper

Although stripping paint with a flame is fast and efficient, there is always the risk that you will burn the wood. Scorching can be covered by paint, but if you want to varnish the stripped wood, scorch marks will mar the finish.

Electrically heated guns—like powerful hair dryers—work almost as quickly as a torch with less risk of scorching or fire. They do operate at an extremely high temperature; under no circumstances test the stripper by holding your hand over the nozzle.

Some guns come with variable heat settings and a selection of nozzles for various uses (see below). Hold the gun about 2 inches from the surface of the paint and move it slowly backward and forward until the paint blisters and bubbles. Immediately remove the paint with a shavehook or scraper. Aim to heat the paint just head of the scraper so you develop a continuous work action.

Fit a shaped nozzle onto the gun when stripping window muntins to concentrate the jet of hot air and reduce the risk of cracking the glass.

Old primer can sometimes be difficult to remove with a hot-air scraper. If you are repainting the wood this is no problem; just rub the surface down with abrasive paper. For a clear finish remove residues of paint from the grain with wads of steel wool dipped in chemical stripper (see left).

SEE ALSO

Details for: ▷	
Preparing wood	44, 45
Primers	62
Finishing wood	63, 74–84
Scrapers	470

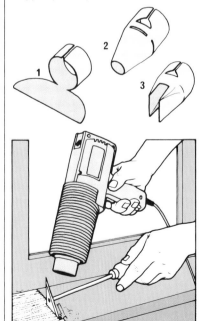

Nozzles for hot-air guns
Hot-air strippers come with a standard wide mouth for general usage, but most offer optional extras, typically a push-on nozzle for stripping window muntins (**1**) and a conical nozzle to concentrate the heat on a small area (**2**). Some offer nozzles for a wide spread of heat (**3**).

With a hot-air gun there's less risk of scorching

CLEANING BRICK AND STONE

At regular intervals and before you decorate the outside of your house, check the condition of the brick and stonework, and carry out any necessary repairs. There's no reason why you can't paint brick or stone walls, but if you consider masonry most attractive in its natural state, you could be faced with a problem: once masonry is painted, it is difficult to restore it to its original condition. There will always be particles of paint left in the texture of brickwork, and even smooth stone, which can be stripped successfully, may be stained by the paint.

Stained brickwork

Organic growth

Efflorescence

Treating new masonry

New brickwork or stonework should be left for about three months until it is completely dry before any further treatment is considered. White, powdery deposits called efflorescence may come to the surface over this period, but you can simply brush it off with a stiff-bristled brush or a piece of burlap (◁). After that, bricks and mortar should be weatherproof and therefore require no further protection or treatment.

Cleaning organic growth from masonry

There are innumerable species of mold growth or lichens, which appear as tiny colored specks or patches on masonry. They gradually merge until the surface is covered with colors ranging from bright orange to yellow or green, gray and black.

Molds and lichen will flourish only in damp conditions, so try to cure the source of the problem before treating the growth (◁). If one side of the house always faces away from the sun, it will have little chance to dry out. Relieve the situation by cutting back overhanging trees or shrubs to increase ventilation to the wall.

Make sure the earth surrounding masonry walls is graded so that surface water flows away from them.

Cracked or corroded downspouts leaking onto the wall are another common cause of organic growth. Feel behind the pipe with your fingers or use a hand mirror to locate the leak.

Removing the growth
Brush the wall vigorously with a stiff-bristled brush. This can be an unpleasant, dusty job, so wear a gauze facemask. Brush away from you to avoid debris being sprayed into your eyes.

Microscopic spores will remain even after brushing. Kill these with a solution of bleach or, if the wall suffers persistently from fungal growth, use a proprietary fungicide, available from most home centers.

Using a bleach solution
Mix one part household bleach with four parts water. Paint the solution onto the wall using an old paintbrush, then 48 hours later wash the surface with clean water, using a scrub brush. Brush on a second application of bleach solution if the original fungal growth was severe.

Using a fungicidal solution
Dilute the fungicide with water according to the manufacturer's instructions and apply it liberally to the wall with an old paintbrush. Leave it for 24 hours, then rinse the wall with clean water. In extreme cases, give the wall two washes of fungicide, allowing 24 hours between applications and a further 24 hours before washing it down with water.

Removing efflorescence from masonry

Soluble salts within building materials such as cement, brick, stone and plaster gradually migrate to the surface along with the water as a wall dries out. The result is a white crystalline deposit called efflorescence.

The same condition can occur on old masonry if it is subjected to more than average moisture. Efflorescence itself is not harmful, but the source of moisture causing it must be identified and cured if the surface is to remain unstained and before painting.

Regularly brush the deposit from the wall with a dry stiff-bristled brush until the crystals cease to form—don't attempt to wash off the crystals; they'll merely dissolve in the water and soak back into the wall. Above all, don't attempt to paint a wall which is still efflorescing, and therefore damp.

When the wall is completely dry, paint the surface with an alkali-resistant primer to neutralize the effect of the crystals before you paint with oil paint; water-thinned paints or clear sealants let the wall breathe, so are not affected by the alkali content of the masonry. Most exterior latex paints can be used without primer (◁).

CLEANING OLD MASONRY

Whether you intend to finish a wall or leave it natural, all loose debris and dirt must be brushed off with a stiff-bristled brush. Don't use a wire brush unless the masonry is badly soiled; the wire brush may leave scratch marks.

Brush along the mortar joints to dislodge loose pointing. Defective mortar can be repaired easily at this stage (see right), but if you fail to disturb it now by being too cautious, it may fall out after you paint, creating far more work in the long run.

Removing unsightly stains

Improve the appearance of stone or brick left in its natural state by washing it with clean water. Play a hose gently onto the masonry while you scrub it with a stiff-bristled brush (1). Scrub heavy deposits with half a cup of ammonia added to a bucketful of water, then rinse again.

Abrade small cement stains or other marks from brickwork with a piece of similar-colored brick, or scrub the area with a household kitchen cleanser.

Remove spilled oil paint from masonry with a proprietary paint stripper (▷). Put on gloves and protective goggles, then paint on the stripper, stippling it into the rough texture (2). After about ten minutes, remove it with a scraper and a soft wire brush. If paint remains in the crevices, dip the brush in stripper and gently scrub it with small circular strokes. When the wall is clean, rinse with water.

1 Remove dirt and dust by washing

2 Stipple paint stripper onto spilled oil paint

REPOINTING MASONRY

The mortar joints between bricks and stones can become porous with age, allowing rainwater to penetrate to the inside, causing damp patches to appear, ruining decorations. Replacing the mortar pointing, which deflects the water, is quite straightforward but time-consuming. Tackle only a small, manageable area at a time, using a ready-mixed mortar or your own mix.

Applying the pointing mortar

Rake out the old mortar pointing with a thin wooden stick to a depth of about ½ inch. Use a cold chisel or a special plugging chisel and sledgehammer to dislodge firmly embedded sections, then brush out the joints with a stiff-bristled brush.

Apply water to the joints using an old paintbrush, making sure the bricks or stones are soaked so they will not absorb too much water from the fresh mortar. Mix up some mortar in a bucket and transfer it to a hawk. If you're mixing your own mortar, use the proportions 1 part cement: 1 part lime: 6 parts builders' sand.

Pick up a little sausage of mortar on the back of a small pointing trowel and push it firmly into the vertical joints. This can be difficult to do without the mortar dropping off, so hold the hawk under each joint to catch it.

Try not to smear the face of the bricks with mortar, as it will stain. Repeat the process for the horizontal joints. The actual shape of the pointing is not vital at this stage.

Once the mortar is firm enough to retain a thumb print, it is ready for shaping. Match the style of pointing used on the rest of the house (see below). When the pointing has almost hardened, brush the wall to remove traces of surplus mortar.

Shaping the mortar joints

The joints shown here are commonly used for brickwork but they are also suitable for stonework. Additionally, stone may have raised mortar joints.

Flush joints
The easiest profile to produce, a flush joint is used where the wall is sheltered or painted. Rub each joint with burlap; start with the verticals.

Rubbed (rounded) joints
Bricklayers make a rubbed or rounded joint with a tool shaped like a sled runner with a handle; the semicircular blade is run along the joints.

Improvise by bending a short length of metal tube or rod. Use the curved section only or you'll gouge the mortar. Alternatively, use a length of ⅜-inch-diameter plastic tube.

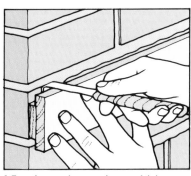

A Frenchman trims weatherstruck joints

Raked joints
A raked joint is used to emphasize the type of bonding pattern of a brick wall. It's not suitable for soft bricks or for a wall that takes a lot of weathering. Scrape out a little of the mortar, then tidy up the joints by running a ⅜-inch stick along them.

Weatherstruck joints
The sloping profile is intended to shed rainwater from the wall. Shape the mortar with the edge of a pointing trowel. Start with the vertical joints, and slope them in either direction but be consistent. During the process, mortar will tend to spill from the bottom of a joint, as surplus is cut off. Bricklayers use a tool called a "frenchman" to neaten the work. It has a narrow blade with the tip bent at right angles. Make your own by bending a thin metal strip, then bind electrical tape around the other end to form a handle. Or bend the tip of an old kitchen knife after heating it with a torch.

You will find it easiest to use a wooden batten to guide the blade of the frenchman along the joints, but nail scraps of plywood at each end of the batten to hold it off the wall.

Align the batten with the bottom of the horizontal joints, then draw the tool along it, cutting off the excess mortar, which drops to the ground.

SEE ALSO

Details for: ▷

Paint stripper	45
Penetrating dampness	253–255
Mixing mortar	425
Pointing tools	478
Plugging chisel	480
Banister brush	482

● **Mortar dyes**
Liquid or powder additives are available for changing the color of mortar to match existing pointing. Color matching is difficult and smears can stain the bricks permanently.

Flush joint

Rubbed joint

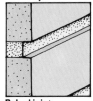

Raked joint

Weatherstruck joint

REPAIRING MASONRY

REPAIRING SPALLED MASONRY

Cracks in external walls can be either the source of penetrating moisture (◁), which ruins your decoration inside, or the result of a much more serious problem: sinking of the foundations. Whatever the cause, it's obvious that you shouldn't just ignore the danger signs, but effect immediate cures.

Filling cracked masonry

If substantial cracks are apparent in a brick or stone wall, consult a builder or engineer to ascertain the cause.

If the crack seems to be stable, it can be filled. Where the crack follows the line of the mortar joints, rake out those affected and repoint in the normal way, as previously described. A crack that splits one or more bricks or stones cannot be repaired, and the damaged area should be removed and replaced, unless you are going to paint the wall afterwards.

Use a ready-mixed mortar with a little PVA bonding agent added to help it to stick. Soak the cracked masonry with a hose to encourage the mortar to flow deeply into the crack.

Crack may follow pointing only

Cracked bricks could signify serious faults

Priming brickwork

Brickwork will need to be primed only in certain circumstances. An alkali-resistant primer will guard against efflorescence (◁) and a stabilizing solution will bind crumbling masonry and help to seal it at the same time.

If you are planning to paint the wall for the first time with an exterior latex, you may find that the first coat is difficult to apply due to the suction of the dry, porous brick. Thin the first coat slightly with water.

To economize when using a thixotropic latex (◁), prime the wall with a cement paint with a little fine sand mixed in thoroughly.

Waterproofing masonry

I Replacing a spalled brick
Having mortared top and one end, slip the new brick into the hole you have cut.

Colorless water-repellent fluids are intended to make masonry impervious to water without coloring it or stopping it from breathing (important to allow moisture within the walls to dry out).

Prepare the surface thoroughly before applying the fluid; repair any cracks in bricks or pointing and remove organic growth (◁) and allow the wall to dry out thoroughly.

Apply the fluid generously with a large paintbrush and stipple it into the joints. Apply a second coat as soon as the first has been absorbed to ensure that there are no bare patches where water could seep in. To be sure that you're covering the wall properly, use a sealant containing a fugitive dye, which will disappear gradually after a few weeks.

Carefully paint up to surrounding woodwork; if you accidentally splash sealant onto it, wash it down immediately with a cloth dampened with solvent.

If the area you need to treat is large, consider spraying on the fluid, using a rented spray gun. You'll need to rig up a sturdy work platform (◁) and mask off all wood- and metalwork that adjoins the wall. The fumes from the fluid can be dangerous if inhaled, so be sure to wear a proper respirator, which you can also rent.

Moisture penetrating soft masonry will expand in icy weather, flaking off the outer face of brickwork and stonework. The process, known as spalling, not only looks unattractive but also allows water to seep into the surface. Repairs to spalled bricks or stones can be made, although the treatment depends on the severity of the problem.

If spalling is localized, it is possible to cut out individual bricks or stones and replace them with matching ones. The sequence below describes how it's tackled with brickwork, but the process is similar for a stone wall.

Where the spalling is extensive, it's likely that the whole wall is porous and your best remedy is to paint on a stabilizing solution to bind the loose material together, then apply a textured wall finish, as used to patch stucco, which will disguise the faults and waterproof the wall at the same time.

Replacing a spalled brick

Use a cold chisel and sledgehammer to rake out the pointing surrounding the brick, then chop out the brick itself. If the brick is difficult to pry out, drill into it many times with a large-diameter masonry bit, then attack the brick with a cold chisel and hammer. It should crumble, enabling you to remove the pieces easily.

To fit the replacement brick, first dampen the opening and spread mortar on the base and one side. Butter the dampened replacement brick on the top and one end and slot it into the hole (I).

Shape the pointing to match the surrounding brickwork then, once it is dry, apply a clear water repellent.

REPAIRING CONCRETE AND STUCCO

Concrete is used in and around the house as a surface for solid floors, drives, paths and walls. In common with other building materials, it suffers from the effects of moisture—spalling and efflorescence—and related defects such as cracking and crumbling. Stucco can also suffer from excessive moisture and may crack as a result of temperature shifts throughout the seasonal cycle. In both cases, if small faults are caught and repaired in time, you may prevent further damage from occurring and stave off costly replacement.

Sealing concrete

New concrete has a high alkali content and efflorescence can develop on the surface as it leaches out. Do not use any finish other than a water-thinned paint until the concrete is completely dry. Treat efflorescence on concrete as for brickwork (▷).

A porous concrete wall should be waterproofed with a clear sealant on the exterior. Some latex paints will cover bitumen satisfactorily, but it will bleed through most paints unless you prime it with a PVA bonding agent diluted 50 percent with water. Alternatively, use an aluminium-based sealer.

Cleaning dirty concrete

Clean dirty concrete as you would brickwork. Where a concrete drive or garage floor, for instance, is stained with patches of oil or grease, soak up fresh spillages immediately to prevent them becoming permanent stains. Sprinkle dry sand onto patches of oil to absorb any liquid deposits, collect it up and wash the area with mineral spirits or degreasing solution.

Binding dusty concrete

Concrete is troweled when it is laid to give a flat finish; if this is overdone, cement is brought to the surface and when the concrete dries out, this thin layer begins to break up within a short time, producing a loose, dusty surface. You must not apply a decorative finish to concrete in this condition.

Treat a concrete wall with stabilizing primer, but paint a dusty floor with one or two coats of PVA bonding agent mixed with five parts of water. Use the same solution to prime a particularly porous surface.

Repairing cracks and holes

Rake out and brush away loose debris from cracks or holes in concrete. If the crack is less than about 1/4 inch wide, open it up a little with a cold chisel so that it will accept a filling. Undercut the edges to form a lip so the filler will grip.

To fill a hole in concrete, add a fine aggregate such as gravel to the sand and cement mix. Make sure the fresh concrete sticks in shallow depressions by priming the damaged surface with 3 parts bonding agent: 1 part water. When the primed surface becomes tacky, trowel in the concrete and smooth it. Don't overwork the surface as that will cause improper curing.

Treating spalled concrete

When concrete breaks up or spalls due to the action of frost, the process is accelerated when steel reinforcement is exposed and begins to corrode. Fill the concrete as described above but prepare and prime the metalwork first (▷). If spalling recurs, particularly in exposed conditions, protect the wall with a bitumen base coat and a compatible latex paint.

Spalling concrete ▷
Rusting metalwork causes concrete to spall.

REPAIRING STUCCO

Stucco is a cementious exterior plaster that may be applied directly over block or brick, or over wire lath that has been fastened to wood sheathing. One or two layers of rough stucco are applied, followed by a finish coat.

Large, long cracks in stucco, especially those that run vertically from the roofline and door or window openings, may indicate structural problems that should be remedied before making repairs to the finish. Consult an engineer or builder if you suspect structural faults. Bulges in stucco may mean that the wire lath has pulled loose from the sheathing, a condition that must be corrected before a proper path can be made.

Fine, hairline cracks need no other repair than painting with exterior latex paint. Elastomeric paints are also excellent finishes for stucco because they can expand and contract as the stucco heats and cools without cracking. Rake out larger cracks using a cold chisel, dampen with water and fill flush with the surface with a mortar mix comprised of 1 part portland cement to 4 parts builder's sand and enough water to create a stiff but workable consistency. Use PVA bonding agent to help the patching mixture stick to masonry substrates.

To reinforce especially large cracks or those that seem to open repeatedly, rake out the crack and clean away loose material. Dampen the substrate and crack edges, then fill with mortar mix as described above. Once the patching material has stiffened, apply a coat of bituminous material such as roof cement and embed a piece of fiberglass flashing fabric in it with bitumen and flashing fabric extending at least 3 inches beyond the edges of the crack (1). Flatten and feather the fabric with a roller (2). Wait a day, then apply a second coat of bitumen, and tool or stipple the wet coating to match the texture of the surrounding stucco (3). After it has dried, seal the tar with aluminum primer, then paint.

Large, deep holes in stucco may need to be repaired with two applications of patching mortar. After removing all unsound material and cleaning the area thoroughly, apply a rough coat to the dampened substrate, leaving it about an inch shy of the finished surface. Wait a day or so, then apply the finish coat, working the surface with a hand float to match the surrounding surface texture and feather the edges.

SEE ALSO

Details for: ▷	
Efflorescence	46
Priming metal	51
Repairing brickwork	48
Primers	62
Masonry paints	65
Mixing concrete	439
Floats and trowels	478

1 Embed the scrim

2 Feather with roller

3 Stipple the texture

PAINTED MASONRY

ASBESTOS MATERIALS

Painted masonry inside the house is usually in fairly good order, and apart from a good wash-down to remove dust and grease and a light sanding to give a key for the new finish, there's little else you need to do. Outside, however, it's a different matter. Subjected to extremes of heat, cold and rain, the surface is likely to be detrimentally affected by stains, flaking and chalkiness.

Chalky surface needs stabilizing

Strip flaky paintwork to a sound surface

Chimney stained by tar deposits from flue

Curing a chalky surface

Rub the palm of your hand lightly over the surface of the wall to see if it is chalky. If the paint rubs off as a powdery deposit, treat the wall before you repaint. Brush the surface with a stiff-bristled brush then liberally paint the whole wall with a stabilizing primer, which binds the chalky surface so that paint will adhere to it. Use a white stabilizing primer, which can act as an undercoat. Clean splashes of the fluid from surrounding woodwork with solvent. If the wall is very dusty, apply a second coat of stabilizer after about 12 hours. Wait another 12 hours before painting over.

Dealing with flaky paint

Flaking is commonly due to poor surface preparation or because the paint and preparatory treatments were incompatible. Damp walls will cause flaking, so remedy this and let the wall dry out before further treatment. Another cause could be too many previous coats of paint, which makes the top layers flake off.

Subsequent coats of paint will not bind to a flaky surface. Loose paint must be removed. Use a paint scraper and stiff-bristled brush to remove all loose material. Coarse aluminum oxide abrasive should finish the job or at least feather the edges of any sturbborn patches. Stabilize the surface as for chalky walls before repainting.

If the flaking is as a result of spalling brickwork (◁), stabilize the affected bricks with a bitumen base coat. Feather the edges with a foam roller, let the bitumen harden for 24 hours, then paint the wall with successive coats of stain-blocking primer and latex paint.

Treating a stained chimney

A painted brick chimney with the outline of courses showing clearly through the paint as brown staining is caused by a breakdown of the internal lining or "pargeting" of the chimney; this allows creosote deposits to migrate through the mortar to the outer paint. To solve the problem, fit a flue liner in the chimney (◁), then treat the stains with an aluminum sealer before applying a new coat of paint.

Asbestos cement has been used to make various items in and around the home, typically ceiling tiles, flooring, siding, roofing and various insulating materials. Nowadays, asbestos is regarded as an unnecessary danger—the dust is a real health hazard if inhaled—and it's consequently not recommended where an alternative is available. But if your home already contains the material, there's a safe way to treat it and keep it looking good.

Whenever you are working with any material containing asbestos, wear a gauze facemask and damp the surface with water whenever rubbing down. If asbestos sheets or boards are in a friable (crumbly) condition, seek professional advice.

Dealing with asbestos
Heavy exposure to asbestos has been associated with lung disease and cancer, yet the mere presence of asbestos in the home does not necessarily pose a serious health threat. Asbestos is potentially harmful only when fibers are airborne. If you find materials that you suspect to contain asbestos in degenerating condition—that is, with broken seals or chalky deposits on or near asbestos-composition surfaces, don't try to clean them up yourself. You will probably only succeed in stirring up the dust and making the condition truly hazardous. Asbestos fibers are generally too fine for household vacuum cleaners and will be discharged into the air with the exhaust.

Specialized training in proper procedures is needed to accomplish removal safely. If you suspect that a health-threatening asbestos condition exists in your home, contact the National Association of Asbestos Abatement Contractors, whose address and phone number are listed on page 21, for a specialist in your area.

Previously painted asbestos
Wash down surfaces that are in good condition with a trisodium phosphate solution, then rinse with clean water. Do not sand and, when scrubbing surfaces with a brush, avoid rubbing through to the surface of the asbestos.

Use a stiff-bristled brush to remove flaky paint, then wash down as previously described. Let the surface dry, then bind it with a stabilizing primer before painting. Build up low patches with successive undercoats.

METALWORK: IRON AND STEEL

Metal is a strong, hardwearing material that's used extensively throughout the home—for window frames, railings, gutters, pipes and radiators, to name but a few items. Oddly, they're areas that are in close proximity to water, and consequently particularly prone to attack by metal's worst enemy: rust. Paint alone won't guard against this corrosive menace, so special treatments are necessary to ensure the long life of metal.

What is rust?

Rust is a form of corrosion that affects only the ferrous metals—notably iron and steel—due to the combination of water, oxygen and carbon dioxide. Although paint slows down the rate at which moisture penetrates, it doesn't stop it; inhibitors and primers are needed to complete the protection, and the type you use depends on the condition of the metal and how you plan to decorate it. Prepare thoroughly or the job will be ruined.

SEE ALSO

Details for: ▷	
Industrial stripping	45
Primers	62
Finishing metal	85–86
Wire brushes	481

Treating bare metal

Remove light deposits of rust by rubbing with steel wool or wet-and-dry abrasive paper dipped in mineral spirits. If the rust is heavy and the surface of the metal pitted, use a wire brush, or, for extensive corrosion, a wire wheel or cup brush in a power drill. Wear goggles while wire brushing to protect your eyes from flying particles.

Paint a proprietary rust inhibitor onto the cleaned metal, following the manufacturer's instructions. Some inhibitors remain on the surface to protect the metal, others must be washed off after a few minutes. Some car accessory shops carry a range of suitable inhibitors.

Wash off deposits of grease with mineral spirits and steel wool. As soon as the metal is clean and dry, apply a primer. For general inside use, choose a zinc phosphate or red oxide primer. For exterior priming, zinc-rich or latex primers specially formulated for metals are recommended. Work the primer into crevices and fasteners, and make sure sharp edges and corners are coated generously.

Cast iron railings deeply pitted with rust

Preparing previously painted metal

If the paint is perfectly sound, wash it with trisodium phosphate solution, rinse and dry. Key gloss paint with fine wet-and-dry abrasive.

If the paint film is blistered or flaking where water has penetrated and corrosion has set in, remove all loose paint and rust with a wire brush or rotary attachment to an electric drll. Apply rust inhibitor to bare patches, working it well into joints, bolt heads and other fasteners. Prime bare metal immediately; rust can reform rapidly.

The insides of metal gutters can be protected with bituminous coatings. Should the asphalt sealant splash over to the outer gutter surface, seal it with aluminum paint before applying the top coat. Two thin top coat applications will last longer than one heavy coat.

Flaking casement window as a result of rust

Stripping painted metal

Delicately molded sections—on fire surrounds, garden furniture and other cast or wrought ironwork—can't easily be rubbed down with a wire brush, and will often benefit from stripping off old paint and rust which is masking fine detail. A hot-air stripper cannot be used here as the metal dissipates the heat before the paint softens. A propane torch can be used to strip wrought ironwork, but cast iron might crack if it becomes distorted by localized heating.

Chemical stripping is the safest method, but before you begin, check that what appears to be a metal fire surround is not in fact made from plaster moldings on a wooden background; the stripping process can play havoc with soft plaster. Tap the surround to see if it is metallic, or scrape an inconspicuous section.

Apply a proprietary rust-killing jelly or liquid, chemicals which will remove and neutralize rust; usually based on phosphoric acid, they combine with the rust to leave it quite inert in the form of iron phosphate. Some rust killers will deal with minute particles invisible to the naked eye, and are self-priming, so no additional primer is required.

Alternatively, if the metalwork is portable, you can take it to a sandblaster or an industrial stripper (▷). None of the disadvantages of industrial stripping apply to metal.

Clean the stripped metal with a wire brush then wash with mineral spirits before finishing it.

Severely corroded cast iron drainpipe

TREATING OTHER METALS

Corrosion in aluminum

Aluminum does not corrode to the same extent as ferrous metals. Indeed, modern aluminum alloy window and door frames, for example, are designed to withstand weathering without a coat of protective paint. Nevertheless, in adverse conditions, aluminum may corrode to a dull gray and even produce white crystals on the surface.

To remove the corrosion, rub the aluminum with fine wet-and-dry abrasive paper using mineral spirits as a lubricant until you get back to bright, but not gleaming, metal. Wipe the metal with a cloth dampened with mineral spirits to remove particles and traces of grease. When dry, prime the surface with a chromate primer. Never use a primer containing lead on aluminum, as there is likely to be an adverse chemical reaction between the metals in the presence of moisture.

Painting galvanized metal

Galvanized iron and steel has a coating of zinc applied by hot dipping; when new, it provides a poor key for most paints. Leaving the galvanizing to weather for six months will remedy this, but in many cases the manufacturer of galvanized metalwork will prepare it chemically for instant priming. If possible, check when you purchase it.

Treating chipped galvanizing
Any small rust spots caused by accidental chipping of the zinc coating should be removed by gentle abrasion with wire wool. But take care not to damage the surrounding coating. Wash the area with mineral spirits, then allow the surface to dry. Prime with calcium plumbate primer.

Protecting corrugated iron
For long-term protection of corrugated iron, first remove rust deposits, then prime with a bitumen base coat before finishing with a compatible reinforced emulsion paint.

Maintaining brass and copper

Ornamental brassware—typically door knobs, fingerplates and other door furniture—should not be painted, especially as there are clear lacquers which protect it from the elements. Strip painted brass with a chemical stripper; deal with corroded brass as described right.

Copper—mainly plumbing pipework and fittings—doesn't require painting for protection, but visible pipe runs are usually painted so they blend in with the room decor (it is possible to make a feature of them by polishing, but it's a chore to keep them looking pristine).

Don't just paint onto the bare pipes; degrease and key the surface with fine wire wool lubricated with mineral spirits. Wipe away metal particles with a cloth dampened with mineral spirits. Apply under coat and top coats direct; no primer is needed.

Painting over lead

In order to decorate old lead pipework, scour the surface with wire wool dipped in mineral spirits; no further preparation is required before you apply paint.

Advanced lead corrosion
The cames (grooved retaining strips) of stained glass windows can become corroded, producing white stains.

Mix some mild white vinegar in a little water and rub the cames thoroughly with the solution until the corrosion disappears. Next, apply a solution of washing soda and water to neutralize the acid content of the vinegar, then rinse several times with clean water and cloths.

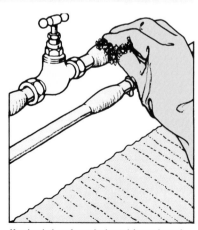
Key lead pipes for painting with steel wool

REMOVING CORROSION FROM BRASS FITTINGS

Brass corrodes to a dull brown color but corrosion is normally easy to remove with a standard metal polish. However, if exterior brass door fixtures have been left unprotected, deposits build up until they are difficult to polish off.

Mix one level tablespoonful of salt plus the same amount of vinegar in a half-pint of hot water. Soften the corrosion by applying liberal washes of the solution to the brass using very fine steel wool.

Wash the metal in hot water containing a little detergent, then rinse and dry it before polishing.

Clean brass with salt and vinegar solution

Removing verdigris
Badly weathered brass can develop green deposits called verdigris. This heavy corrosion may leave the metal pitted, so clean it as soon as possible.

Line a plastic bowl with ordinary aluminum foil. Attach a piece of string to each item of brassware, then place them in the bowl on top of the foil. Dissolve a cup of baking soda in four pints of hot water and pour it into the bowl to cover the metalware.

Leave the solution to fizz and bubble for a couple of minutes, then lift out the brass items with the string. Replace any that are still corroded. If necessary, the process can be repeated using fresh solution and new foil.

Rinse the brass with hot water, dry it with a soft cloth, then polish.

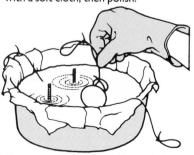
Remove verdigris with a baking soda dip

PATCHING HOLES IN WALLS

A lath-and-plaster wall

If the laths are intact, plaster up the holes as for solid plasterwork. A hole under 3 inches wide can simply be packed out with a ball of wet newspaper dipped in plaster. Fill flush to the surface with wallboard joint compound.

If some laths are broken, reinforce the repair with a piece of fine expanded wire lath. Rake out loose plaster and undercut the edge of the hole with a cold chisel. Use tinsnips to cut the wire lath to the shape of the hole but a little larger (1).

The wire lath is flexible so you can bend it in order to tuck the edge behind the sound plaster all around (2). Flatten it against the wood lath with light taps from a hammer and, if possible, staple the mesh to a wall stud to hold it (3).

Gently apply one thin coat of brown coat (4) and let it dry for about one hour before you continue patching.

1 Cut with tinsnips **2 Tuck mesh into hole** **3 Staple mesh to stud** **4 Trowel on plaster**

A wallboard wall or ceiling

A large hole punched through a wallboard wall or ceiling cannot be patched with wet plaster only. Cut back the damaged board to the nearest studs or joists at each side using a sharp utility knife against a straightedge. Keep the cutout slim to avoid having to fit braces at the long sides (1).

Cut a new panel of wallboard to fit snugly within the hole and nail it to the joists or studs using galvanized wallboard nails. Use a 3-inch wallboard taping knife to spread joint compound over the seams, then embed wallboard tape in the wet compound. Let the compound dry, then apply additional coats of compound with successively wider knives to feather two patch edges.

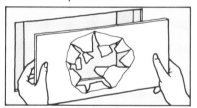
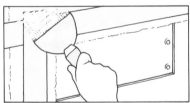

1 Cut damaged panel to nearest supports **2 Finish patch seams with tape compound**

A small hole in wallboard

For very small holes in wallboard use wallboard compound instead of plaster. Use a joint tape for holes up to 3½ inches across. Stick on the self-adhesive strips in a star shape over the hole, then apply filler (1).

Alternatively, use a scrap of wallboard just larger than the hole yet narrow enough to slot through. Bore a hole in the middle and thread a length of string through. Tie a galvanized nail to one end of the string (2). Butter the ends of the scrap with filler, then feed it into the hole (3). Pull on the string to force it against the back of the wall finish, then press more compound into the hole so it's not quite flush with the surface, When the compound is hard, cut off the string then apply a thin coat of filler for a flush finish.

1 Fill and feather the patch **2 Fix the string to scrap** **3 Pull on string**

WORKING WITH JOINT COMPOUND

Joint compound is a cellulose-fiber that is formulated for finishing wallboard seams but can also be used as a patching material and filler in a variety of applications. It is much easier to use and far more forgiving than plaster and can also be used as a fast-drying filler for wood that is to be painted.

Joint compound comes ready-mixed in tubs ranging from 1 pint to 5 gallons. While it takes a certain knack to spread compound smoothly with a joint knife, an imperfectly finished surface of dry compound can easily be sanded and feathered and filled with fresh applications.

To work effectively with joint compound, you should have a hawk, which is similar to a painter's palette and used to hold large dollops of compound as you work, a variety of joint knives with different widths, and a supply of wallboard tape—either plain paper tape or fiber-reinforced tape with an adhesive backing.

To fill a seam or the edges around a patch, first apply a coat of compound about ⅛ inch thick over the seams with a 3- or 4-inch-wide joint knife (1). (This step is not necessary if you will also be using self-adhesive joint tape; then, simply stick the tape over the seams.)

Quickly apply joint tape centered over the seams to the wet compound. Press the tape flat into the wet compound. Press the tape flat into the compound using the joint knife edge (2). Press out any air bubbles and with long, smooth strokes, remove excess compound that may squeeze out. While for efficiency's sake it is important to smooth the compound as well as possible, don't continue to work the surface after the compound has begun to dry. Crumbs will begin to form and the tape will begin to roughen and shred. Scrape the knife edges and hawk frequently.

Let the first application dry thoroughly; it usually takes about 24 hours. Lightly sand any burrs or raised edges. Cut away any sections of tape that have air bubbles under them. Then apply a second thin coat of compound with a wider joint knife (3), say 6 inches, to fill depressions and feather the edges of the first coat. Let the second application dry, polish lightly with sandpaper, then apply a third coat with an 8- to 10-inch knife (4).

Joint compound can be applied to hairline cracks in plaster without tape.

1 Apply compound to joint

2 Apply tape

3 Apply wider second coat

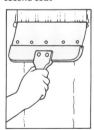

4 Apply third, wider coat

53

REPAIRING PLASTER

Plaster has been used to finish the walls and ceilings of many older houses and is enjoying renewed popularity in many custom homes today. While plaster walls are relatively more expensive to construct, finish and repair than those made with gypsum wallboard, many people prefer them for their superior sound insulating characteristics and their smoothness and quality of solidity. While repairs to plaster finishes can be made by breaking out damaged sections and inserting wallboard patches or by simply applying wallboard over the plaster surface, you may prefer to preserve the original finish by replastering or simply redecorating. Plaster can be applied directly to a masonry substrate, to wood or wire lath, or as a skim-coat over wallboard. Some useful techniques and considerations related to working with plaster are discussed below.

PREPARING TO DECORATE

NEW PLASTER

New plaster must dry out thoroughly before it can be decorated with paint or paper. Allow efflorescence to form on the surface, then wipe off with coarse burlap; repeat periodically until the crystals cease to appear.

Use an alkali-resistant primer if you are applying oil paint. Priming isn't necessary for latex, but apply a thinned coat on absorbent plaster.

Size new, absorbent plaster before wallpapering, or the water will be sucked too quickly from the paste, resulting in poor adhesion. Use a proprietary size or shellac sealer. If you are hanging vinyl wallcovering, make sure the size contains fungicide, since the covering can't breathe like a plain paper can.

For tiling, no further preparation is needed, once the plaster is dry.

OLD PLASTER

Apart from filling minor defects and dusting down, old, dry plaster needs no further preparation. If the wall is patchy, apply a general-purpose primer. If the surface is friable, apply a stabilizing solution before you decorate.

Don't decorate damp plaster; cure, then let the plaster dry out first.

Smooth finish
Smooth the surface of small repairs with a wet brush or knife to reduce the amount of sanding required later.

WALLBOARD

Fill all joints between newly hung wallboard (◁) then, whether you're painting or papering the board, fill all nail heads with joint compound.

Before you paint wallboard with oil paint, prime it with one coat of general-purpose primer. One coat of thinned latex may be needed on an absorbent board before the normal full-strength coats are applied.

Prior to hanging wallcovering on wallboard, seal the surface with a general-purpose primer thinned with solvent. After 48 hours, apply a coat of size. This allows wet-stripping without disturbing the board's paper facing.

PAINTED PLASTER

Wash any painted walls in good condition with TSP or detergent solution to remove dirt and grease. Use water and medium-grade wet-and-dry abrasive paper to key the surface of gloss paint, particularly if covering with latex. Prime and allow to dry.

If the ceiling is severely stained by smoke and nicotine, prime it with an alkali-resistant primer or an aluminum-based sealer.

If you want to hang wallcovering on oil paint, key then size the wall. Add dry plaster or compound to the size to provide an additional key. Cross-line the wall with lining paper (◁) before hanging a heavy embossed paper on oil paint.

Remove flaky materials with a scraper or stiff-bristled brush. Feather off the edges of the bare spots with wet-and-dry abrasive paper. Treat bare plaster patches with a general-purpose primer. Should the edges of old paint continue to show, prime those areas again, rubbing down afterwards. Apply stabilizing primer if the paint is friable.

Apply tiles over sound plaster after you have removed any loose material.

Cracks in solid plaster

Rake loose material from a crack with the blade of a scraper or putty knife (**1**). Undercut the edges of larger cracks to provide a key for the filling. Mix up joint compound to a stiff consistency or use a premixed filler.

Dampen the crack with a paintbrush, then press the filler in with a putty knife. Drag the blade across the crack to force the filler in, then draw it along the crack (**2**) to smooth the filler. Leave the filler standing slightly raised above the surface, ready for rubbing down smooth and flush with abrasive paper.

Fill shallow cracks with one application, but for deep ones, build up the filler in stages, letting each set before adding more.

Cracks sometimes appear in the corner between walls or a wall and ceiling; fill these by running your finger dipped in filler along the crack. When the filler has hardened, rub it down with medium-grade abrasive paper.

Fill and rub down small holes and dents in solid plasterwork in same way as for filling cracks.

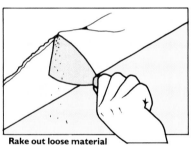

Rake out loose material

2 Press filler into crack

INTERIOR WOODWORK

Wood is used throughout the interiors of homes for trim, cabinetry and furniture. Valued for its workability and natural beauty, wooden trim and furniture brings detail and refinement along with its natural warmth into a home. It must be treated with special care to retain its special character.

A wider variety of woods is used indoors than outdoors, and while interior wood is not as subject to the ravages of weather, it is more likely to become damaged by abuse. While the wood itself may become dented and worn, interior finishes are also more prone to scratching, staining and marring.

Treating new wood

Interior woodwork should be sealed and if it is to be painted, primed before the final finish is applied. Because a higher degree of refinement and, therefore, a higher finish quality is desirable indoors, special care should be taken to build up thin finish coats to ensure that trim and highly figured woods retain their detail and clarity.

For economy, many mills that produce trim moldings, windows and doors make them from finger-jointed stock—short lengths are are laminated end-to-end to create longer pieces. These look best when painted rather than clear-finished. Start by fine-sanding, then applying a stain-blocking sealer or primer, which is especially important

Seal resinous knots with shellac

when knots are present in the wood. It is important to sand lightly between coats applied to woodwork. Gloss or semigloss top coats are usually selected because of their washability, which reduces the frequency of the need to refinish.

Hardwoods may be painted, but because of their natural richness, are often treated with stains, oils, and/or clear varnished to bring out the beauty of their grain patterns. Sander-sealer may be applied as a prime coat for varnish, but more often than not a first coat of diluted varnish will seal

adequately. Open-grained woods should be treated initially with paste filler in order to prepare for a smooth, glossy finish. Woodwork that's to be treated with oil finish or stain should not be sealed until after those substances are applied and completely dry.

Varnishes are the toughest top coat for surfaces that will get a lot of wear. Modern polyurethane varnishes, available gloss, semigloss and satin finishes, are highly durable and nearly impervious to water, alcohol and heat stains. Polyurethane varnishes are suitable for floors and all furniture surfaces including table tops, but are not recommended for surfaces on which food will be prepared. On those, use an oil specially recommended for the application.

Stains and oils protect wood only slightly, but are used as color-enhancing agents. Because various woods differ greatly in the way they react to stains, it is important to test a stain on a sample of the wood to be treated before going ahead with the application. For durability and washability, apply paste wax or varnish over stains and oils to provide a protective coating. Take into consideration that polyurethane varnish will slightly darken surfaces it's applied to and will yellow with age, particularly under strong exposure to sunlight.

Finish maintenance and repair

Finished wood in good condition should be washed routinely with mild soap and water to keep a fresh look. Rinse thoroughly and dry after washing.

Superficial scratches in a finish can usually be rubbed out with a fine buffing compound, or in a pinch, a bit of toothpaste. When scratches have penetrated through the finish to the wood surface, it is necessary to sand off the entire finish, smooth the scratch and then refinish. The same is true of superficial finish stains caused by water, alcohol and heat. If staining has penetrated through the finish to the wood itself, apply wood bleach to the

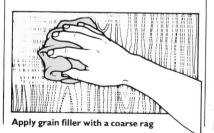
Apply grain filler with a coarse rag

surface after removing the finish. Be careful when working with veneered pieces not to sand through or otherwise damage the thin laminated surface.

Deep dents and scratches must be filled. Joint compound is an excellent substance for repairing wood that is to be repainted, while numerous colored fillers are available for repairing clear-finished wood. Always apply fillers a little higher than the surface and when dry, sand them smooth. As a stopgap to avoid refinishing dented woodwork, repair irregularities with wax-stick filler of a matching color.

Filling the grain

If you plan to clear-finish an open-grained wood, apply a proprietary grain filler after sanding. Use a natural filler for pale woods; for darker wood, buy a filler that matches the tone. Rub the filler across the grain with a coarse rag, leave to harden for several hours, then rub off the excess along the grain with a clean coarse rag.

Preparing for a clear finish

There's no need to apply shellac when you intend to finish the wood with a clear varnish or lacquer. Sand the wood in the direction of the grain using progressively finer grades of abrasive paper, then seal it with a slightly thinned coat of the intended finish.

If the wood is subject to rot, treat it first with a liberal wash of clear wood

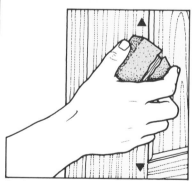
Sand along the grain with abrasive paper

preservative. Badly damaged wood can be restored with two-part wood filler that can be shaped after hardening—but this type of filler can't be stained or treated with a clear finish. Check with the maker's recommendations that the liquid is compatible with the finish. This treatment is equally well suited to a painted finish.

SEE ALSO

Details for: ▷	
Primers	62
Finishing woodwork	74–84
Wood stains	76
Wood preservatives	252

● **Cellulose filler** would show through a clear finish, so use one of many alternative products to fill imperfections. These are thick pastes made in a range of colors to suit the type of wood. You can adjust the color further by mixing it with wood stains. As fillers can be oil- or water-based, make sure you use a similarly-based stain.

ERADICATING ORGANIC GROWTHS

Under damp conditions, organic growths can develop, usually in the form of mold or mildew. The cause of the damp should be remedied before you treat the walls or ceiling.

Kill organic growths before you carry out any other preparatory work to avoid distributing spores into the atmosphere. Apply a liberal wash of a solution made from 1 part household bleach to 16 parts water. Don't make the solution any stronger as it may damage the wall decoration. Leave the solution for at least 4 hours then carefully scrape off the growth, wipe it onto newspaper and burn it outside if local regulations permit.

Wash the wall again with the solution but leave it for three days to sterilize the wall completely. When the wall is dry, paint it with a stabilizing primer. If you plan to hang wallpaper, size the wall using a size containing a fungicide solution.

Where organic growth is affecting wallpaper, soak the area in a warm water and bleach solution, then scrape off the contaminated paper. Wash the wall with a fresh bleach solution to remove paste residue.

Apply a liberal wash of similar solution to sterilize the wall and leave it for at least three days, but preferably one week, to make sure no further growth occurs. When the wall is completely dry, apply a stabilizing primer followed by a coat of size if you plan to repaper the wall.

2 Steam stripper
To remove painted and washable wallpapers, use a steam stripper—little more than a water boiler which exudes steam from a sole plate. To use the machine, hold the plate against the wall until the steam penetrates, soaks and softens the paper, then remove it with a scraper. Wash the wall to remove traces of paste.

Mold growth ▷
Mold, typified by black specks, will grow on damp plaster or paper.

PREPARING WALLCOVERINGS

Faced with a previously papered surface, the best solution is to strip it completely before hanging new wallcoverings. However, if the paper is perfectly sound, you can paint it with latex or oil paints (but be warned: it will be difficult to remove in the future). Don't paint vinyl wallcovering except blown vinyl (◁). If the paper has strong reds, greens or blues, the colors may show through the finished paint; *metallic inks have a similar tendency. You can mask strong colors by applying shellac thinned by 25 percent with denatured alcohol, but over a large area, use an aluminum-based sealer. If you opt for stripping off the old covering, the method you use depends on the material and how it's been treated.*

Stripping wallpaper

Soak the paper with warm water with a little dish soap or proprietary stripping powder or liquid added to soften the adhesive. Apply the liquid with a sponge or houseplant sprayer. Repeat and allow the water to penetrate for 15 to 20 minutes.

Use a wide metal-bladed scraper to lift the softened paper, starting at the seams. Take care not to dig the points of the blade into the wall underneath. Resoak stubborn areas of paper and return to strip them later.

Electricity and water are a lethal combination; where possible, dry-strip around switches and sockets. If the paper cannot be stripped dry, switch off the power at the service panel (◁) when you come to strip around electrical fixtures. Unscrew the faceplates so that you can get at the paper trapped behind. Don't use the sprayer near electrical accessories.

Collect all the stripped paper in plastic sacks, then wash the wall with warm water containing a little detergent. From then on, treat the wall as for plaster (◁).

Scoring washable wallpaper

Washable wallpaper has an impervious plastic surface film, which you must break through to allow the water to penetrate to the adhesive.

Use a wire brush, coarse abrasive paper or a serrated scraper to score the surface, then soak it with warm water and stripper. It may take several applications of the liquid before the paper begins to lift.

Peeling off vinyl wallcovering

Vinyl wallcovering consists of a thin vinyl layer, which is fused with the pattern, on a paper backing. It is possible to peel off the film, leaving the backing paper on the wall; this can then be painted or used as a lining for a new wallcovering.

To remove the top layer, lift both bottom corners, then pull firmly but steadily away from the wall. Either soak and scrape off the backing paper or, if you want to leave it as a lining paper, smooth the seams with medium-grade abrasive paper. But use very light pressure or you'll wear a hole.

Stripping painted wallcoverings

Wallcoverings which have been painted previously can be difficult to remove, especially if a heavy embossed paper was used. If the paper is sound, prepare in the same way as painted plaster (◁) and paint over it.

Use a wire brush or homemade scraper (**1**) to score the surface, then soak with warm water plus a little paper stripper. Painted papers (and washables) can easily be stripped using a rented steam stripper. Hold the stripper plate against the paper until the steam penetrates, then remove the soaked paper with a wide-bladed scraper (**2**).

1 Wallpaper scorer
Drive nails through a block of softwood measuring 1 × 5 × 6 inches, so that the points just protrude.

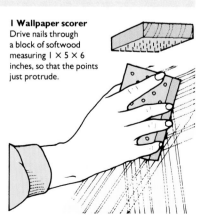

BLEACHING STAINS FROM WOOD

Discolored or stained wood can be bleached in preparation for color-staining and polishing. If possible, try to bleach the entire area rather than an isolated part to avoid a light patch in place of the stain.

Traditionally, oxalic acid in the form of white crystals (available from druggists) is used to bleach the wood. Make a solution with warm water; add water until no more crystals will dissolve. Oxalic acid is poisonous, so handle only when wearing protective gloves, and do not use where it could contaminate food. Keep it out of reach of children and pets.

To use the bleaching solution, apply a liberal wash to the wood, using an old paintbrush (or a wad of cloth). Watch carefully until the stain has disappeared, then rinse the wood thoroughly with clean water and allow to dry.

Two-part bleach

An alternative to the oxalic acid solution is to use a proprietary two-part wood bleach. One part is brushed onto the wood and ten to twenty minutes later the second part is applied over the first. The bleach is then left to work on the stain.

After three to four hours, the bleach should have removed the discoloration from the wood and can be washed off with an acid such as white vinegar (but follow the manufacturer's instructions).

Bleaching wood
Apply a solution of bleach to stained wood using a paintbrush and leave until the discoloration has disappeared, then wash off with water or vinegar.

MAN-MADE BOARDS

Versatile and relatively inexpensive, man-made boards are used extensively in the home, typically for cladding walls, leveling floors, shelving—even for building cabinets for the kitchen or bedroom. Preparation for decoration depends on whether you plan to paint the surface or hang wallcovering.

Preparing man-made boards for decoration

Wallboards such as plywood, chipboard, hardboard and fiberboard (◁) are all wood products, but they must be prepared for decoration in a different way to natural wood. Their surface finish, for instance, varies according to the quality of the board. Some are compact and smooth and may even be presealed ready for painting; others must be filled and sanded before a smooth finish is achieved.

As a rough guide, no primer will be required when using latex other than a sealing coat of the paint itself, slightly thinned with water. However, any nail or screw heads must be driven below the surface and coated with rust-blocking primer so as to prevent stains.

If you are using oil paint, prime the boards first with a general-purpose primer (stabilizing primer for porous fiberboard). Where possible, you should prime both sides of the board. If the boards are presealed, apply undercoat directly to the surface.

1 Hardboard face
2 Hardboard back
3 Lumber-core plywood
4 Chipboard
5 Veneer-core plywood
6 Fiberboard

Wallpapering man-made boards

If you want to wallpaper a panelled wall, careful preparation is required to ensure that the boards will not shrink and split the paper. If the panelling is insufficiently fastened, water absorbed from the paste could make untreated boards buckle and warp. Unless the boards are primed, the same could happen if the wall is wet-stripped later (◁). The surface must be clean and dry prior to priming. Sand it down and dust off. Treat nail and screw heads with metal primer.

Fill joints with compound, using tape as reinforcement (◁). Fill any holes, too. Sand the filler, dust off and treat the boards with a stabilizing primer thinned slightly with solvent. When the paint is dry, size the wall or use a heavy wallpaper paste.

SANDING A WOOD FLOOR

A sanded wood floor sealed with a clear finish that highlights its grain is a most attractive feature for many rooms. Although simple, the job is laborious, dusty *and extremely noisy. Considerable patience is also required in order to achieve an even, scratch-free and long-lasting finish.*

Repairing the floorboards

There's no point in spending time and money sanding floorboards which are in poor condition, so examine them first. Look for signs of decay and excessive wear. Serious defects in the wood strips or boards such as checks (cracks), capping, warping, and insect damage will either be impossible to correct with sanding and refinishing or will require so much sanding that it would be more practical to replace the flooring. Wide gaps caused by shrinkage constitute another serious problem—proprietary fillers won't take stains and varnishes in the same way as the natural wood surface. Methods of repairing gaps are discussed below.

If you find signs of dry or wet rot when you lift a floorboard, correct the moisture problem before you continue with the sanding (▷).

Examine the floor for boards which

have been lifted previously by electricians and plumbers. Replace any that are split, too short or badly jointed (▷). Try to find secondhand boards to match the rest of the floor, but if you have to use new wood, stain it after the floor is sanded to match the color of the old boards. Drive all nail heads below the surface with a nailset and hammer; a raised head will rip the abrasive paper on the sander's drum.

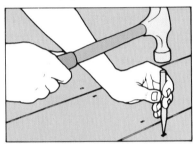

Sink nail heads below the surface

Filling gaps between floorboards

What you do about gaps between boards depends on how much they bother you. Many people simply ignore them, but you will end up with a superior job as well as improved draftproofing if you make the effort to fill them invisibly or close them up.

Closing up
Over a large area, the quickest and most satisfactory solution is to lift the boards a few at a time and reposition them butted side by side, filling in the final gap with a new board (▷).

Filling with papier mâché
If there are a few gaps only, make up a stiff papier mâché paste with white newsprint and wallpaper paste, plus a

little water-based wood dye to color it to match the sanded floor. Scrape out dirt and wax from between the boards and press the paste into the gap with a putty knife. Press it well below the level likely to be reached by the sander, and fill flush with the floor surface. Run the blade along the filler to smooth it.

Inserting a wooden lath
Large gaps can be filled by a thin wood lath planed to fit tightly between the boards. Apply a little PVA adhesive to the gap and tap the lath in with a hammer until it is flush with the surface. Skim it with a plane if necessary. Don't bother to fill several gaps this way. It is easier to close up the boards and fill one gap only with a new floorboard (▷).

Force papier mâché between boards

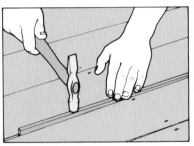

Wedge a wooden lath into a wide gap

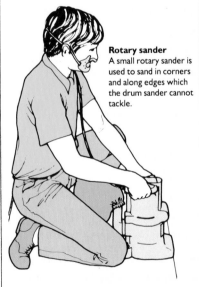

Hook scraper
Use a small hook scraper for removing paint spots from the floor, and for reaching into spaces that are inaccessible to the rotary sander. The tool cuts on the backward stroke; various sizes and blade shapes are available to deal with most situations.

CHOOSING A SANDING MACHINE

The area of a floor is far too large to contemplate sanding with anything but an industrial sanding machine. You can obtain such equipment from the usual tool rental outlets, which also supply the abrasive papers. You will need three grades of paper: coarse, to level the boards initially, medium and fine to achieve a smooth finish.

It's best to rent a large upright drum sander for the main floor area and a smaller rotary sander for tackling the edges. For small rooms such as bathrooms, you can use the rotary sander only.

Some companies also supply a scraper for cleaning out the inaccessible corners, but do make sure it is fitted with a new blade when you rent.

Drum sander
An upright drum sander is used for sanding the main floor area with coarse, medium then fine-grade abrasive papers for a smooth flat finish.

Rotary sander
A small rotary sander is used to sand in corners and along edges which the drum sander cannot tackle.

Fitting the abrasive sheet

Precise instructions for fitting the abrasive paper to the sanding machine should be included with the rental tool, or the store clerk will demonstrate what you need to do. Never attempt to change abrasive papers while the machine is plugged into a socket. With most machines the paper is wrapped round the drum and secured with a screw-down bar (1). Ensure that the paper is wrapped tightly around the drum; if it is slack it may slip from its clamp and be torn to pieces.

Edging sanders take an abrasive disc, usually clamped to the sole plate by a central nut (2).

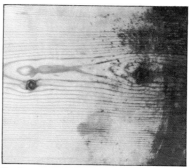

1 Drum sander   2 Rotary sander

Operating a drum sander

Stand at the beginning of a run with the drum raised so that the abrasive itself is clear of the floor. Drape the electric cord over one shoulder to make sure it cannot become caught in the sander.

Switch on the machine and gently lower the drum onto the floor. To hold the machine still for even a short time will sand a deep hollow in the floor. There is no need to push a drum sander; it will move forward under its own power. Hold the machine in check so that it proceeds at a slow but steady walking pace along a straight line.

When you reach the other side of the room, tilt the machine back, switch off and wait for it to stop before lowering it to the floor.

If the paper rips, tilt the machine onto its back casters and switch off. Wait for the drum to stop revolving, disconnect the power, then change the paper. If you let go of the machine it will run across the room on its own almost certainly damaging the floor in the process.

Sanding cleans and rejuvenates floors

Using an edging sander

Hold the handles on top of the machine and drape the cord over your shoulder. Tilt the sander onto its back casters to lift the disc off the floor. Switch on and lower the machine. As soon as you contact the boards, sweep the machine in any direction but keep it moving.

There is no need to press down on the machine. As soon as it comes to rest the disc will score deep, scorched swirl marks in the wood, which are difficult to remove. When you have finished, tilt back the machine and switch off, letting the motor run down.

1 Sand diagonally across the floorboards

Sanding procedure

A great deal of dust is produced by sanding a floor, so before you begin, empty the room of furniture and take down curtains, lampshades and pictures. Seal around the room door with masking tape and stuff folded newspaper under it. Open all windows. Wear old clothes and a gauze facemask.

Sweep the floor to remove grit and other debris. Old floorboards will most likely be curved across their width, or cupped, so the first task is to level the floor across its entire area.

With coarse paper fitted in the drum sander, sand diagonally across the room (1). At the end of the run, tilt the machine, pull it back and make a second run parallel to the first. Allow each pass to slightly overlap the last.

When you have covered the floor once, sand it again in the same way, but this time across the opposite diagonal of the room (2). Sweep the sawdust from the floor after each run is completed.

Once the floor is flat, so that the boards are clean all over, change to a medium-grade paper and sand parallel to the boards (3). Overlap each pass as before. Finally, switch to the fine-grade paper to remove all obvious scratches and give a smooth finish.

Sand the edges of the room with the rotary machine. As soon as you change the grade of paper on the drum sander put the same grade on the edging sander. In this way, the edges of the room are finished to the same standard as the main area (4).

Even the edging sander cannot clean right up to the baseboard or into the corners; finish these small areas with a scraper, or fit a flexible abrasive disc in a power drill.

Vacuum the floor and wipe it over with a tack cloth to leave it ready for finishing.

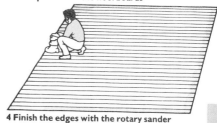

2 Sand across the opposite diagonal

3 Sand parallel to the floorboards

4 Finish the edges with the rotary sander

TILED SURFACES

Tiles are used to clad walls, floors and ceilings, and are made in a vast range of materials—ceramic, cork, vinyl and polystyrene are popular—and in a host of different surface textures and finishes. If they're looking shabby it's possible to either revive their existing finish or decorate them with paint or wallcoverings—with some it's even possible to stick new tiles on top for a completely new look.

CLEANING AN OLD QUARRY-TILED FLOOR

Old quarry tiles are absorbent and dirt and grease become ingrained in the surface. If normal washing with detergent fails to revitalize their color and finish, clean the tiles with a diluted hydrochloric acid or muriatic acid solution.

Add a drop or two of acid to some warm water in a plastic bucket. Stir it gently with a wooden stick and try it on a small patch of floor. Don't make the solution any stronger than is necessary; the solution attacks the grouting, so work quickly in small sections. Wash the floor with the solution, rinsing off the diluted acid with clean, warm water.

Removing ingrained dirt
Wash tiles with hydrochloric acid solution

WHEN USING ACID

- **Wear PVC gloves, old clothes and goggles.**
- **Add acid to water, never the other way around.**
- **Keep acid out of reach of children and animals.**

Removing ceramic or quarry tiles
To remove old tiles, first chop out at least one of them with a cold chisel, then pry the others off the surface by driving a bolster chisel behind them. Chop away any remaining tile adhesive or mortar with the bolster.

Ceramic wall and floor tiles

Ceramic tiles are stuck to the wall or floor with a special adhesive, or, in many cases, mortar. Removing them in their entirety in order to redecorate the wall is messy and time-consuming, but is often the most satisfactory long-term solution.

So long as a ceramic tiled wall is sound, you can paint it with oil-based paint. Wash the surface thoroughly with TSP or detergent solution. The problem with this treatment is that glazed tiles do not provide a good key for paint, and you'd find that the new surface would chip easily. You can lay new tiles directly over old ones but make sure the surface is perfectly flat—check by holding a long level or straight-edged metal molding across the surface. Tap the tiles to locate any loose ones and either glue them firmly in place or chop them out with a cold chisel and sledgehammer and fill the space with mortar. Wash the wall to remove grease and dirt.

It's also possible to tile over old quarry or ceramic floor tiles in the same way. Treat an uneven floor with a self-leveling compound.

It is not possible to paper over old ceramic wall tiles, as the adhesive would not be able to grip on the shiny surface. Instead, you could hang a woven fiberglass wallcovering, which is designed to be painted afterwards (◁). The tiles must be perfectly sound and free from dirt and grease. Otherwise this rather coarse material might peel off.

Polystyrene ceiling tiles

Polystyrene tiles are stuck directly onto the surface with a water- or solvent-based adhesive that can be difficult to remove. The adhesive was commonly applied in five small dabs. This method is now unapproved due to the risk of fire. Manufacturers recommend a complete bed of adhesive, which makes removal even worse.

Remove tiles by prying them off with a wide-bladed scraper, then pry off the adhesive dabs. On stubborn patches, try to soften the adhesive with warm water, wallpaper stripper or even paint stripper (but wear goggles and PVC gloves; it's difficult to avoid splashes). For larger areas of adhesive try a solution of ammonia (see below). One way to give the tiles a facelift is to paint them. These tiles should never be painted with an oil paint, which increases the risk of fire spreading across the tiles. Brush the tiles to remove dust, then apply latex paint.

Vinyl floor tiles

Vinyl floor tiles are not a good foundation, so resurface them or remove them completely. Soften the tiles and their adhesive with a clothes iron, then use a scraper to pry them up. Remove the old adhesive by applying a solution of half a cupful of household ammonia and a drop of liquid detergent in a bucketful of cold water. When the floor is clean, rinse it with water.

If vinyl tiles are firmly glued to the floor, you can clean them, then resurface them with a latex self-leveling screed (◁). Before you apply this method, however, check the recommendations of your floorcovering manufacturer; it may not be suitable for laying after this treatment.

Cork floor and wall tiles

It's possible to decorate over cork tiles, although absorbent tiles will need priming first. The advice given for vinyl floor tiles applies for cork tiles also. Hard, sound wall tiles can be painted so long as they are clean. Prime absorbent cork first with a general-purpose primer before painting over it.

Unless the tiles are textured or pierced, they can be papered over. But size the surface with commercial size or heavy-duty wallpaper paste, then line the tiles horizontally (◁) to prevent joints from showing through.

Fiber ceiling tiles

Acoustic fiber tiles can be painted with water-based paints. Wash them with a mild detergent but do not soak the tiles, as they're quite absorbent.

LEVELING A WOOD FLOOR

Tiles, sheet vinyl or carpet must not be laid directly onto an uneven wood floor surface. The undulations would cause the tiles or covering to lift or even crack. The solution is to panel over the floorboards with ⅛-inch-thick tempered hardboard or, preferably, dense hardwood or plywood. The methods are identical whichever board you use.

Priming and conditioning boards

Before you seal your floor with plywood or hardboard, make sure that the existing flooring is structurally sound and provides a firm nailing base. Bear in mind, too, that once the floor is sealed you will not have ready access to underfloor pipes and electric cables, which could be a problem should you need to make repairs at some time in the future.

Because it is not dimensionally stable,

it is necessary to condition hardboard to prevent buckling after it has been laid by soaking its textured back with warm water, then leaving the sheets stacked back-to-back for 24 hours.

In wintertime when the home is heated for some time, there is no need for such treatment. Just stack the plywood or hardboard sheets on edge in the room for 48 hours so that they can adjust to the atmosphere.

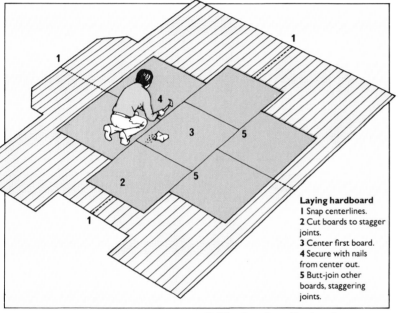

Laying hardboard
1 Snap centerlines.
2 Cut boards to stagger joints.
3 Center first board.
4 Secure with nails from center out.
5 Butt-join other boards, staggering joints.

Nail hardboard over floorboards
Secure from center outwards, then fill margin.

FILL THE BORDER | **FIT TO A DOORWAY**

1 Butt to baseboard | **4 Scribe to baseboard**

2 Scribe to fit | **5 Trace frame shape**

3 Nail to floor | **6 Cut and nail down**

LAYING A BASE FOR CERAMIC TILES

A concrete platform is the most suitable base for ceramic floor tiles, but you can lay them on a suspended wood floor so long as the joists are perfectly rigid so that the floor cannot flex. The space below must be adequately ventilated with air bricks to prevent the formation of rot. Level the floor using ½-inch plywood and screw it down every 1 foot for a firm fixing.

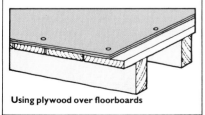

Using plywood over floorboards

Laying the boards

Unless flooring manufacturers suggest otherwise, lay hardboard rough side up, as a key for the adhesive. Cut boards to stagger the joints. Nail loose floorboards and plane off high points, then set the nail heads.

Use a chalkline to snap two center lines across the room, crossing at right angles. Lay the first board on the center; adjust it so that its edges do not align with the gaps between floorboards. Loose-lay the boards in both directions: if you'll be left with narrow borders, reposition the boards.

Nail the first board to the floor with 1-inch ring nails. Start near the center of the board and nail it every 6 inches until you get within 1 inch of the edge, then nail around the edge every 4 inches. Nail other boards butted up to the first (see above). Scribe the narrow edge strips to

fit the border. Lay the board on the floor touching the baseboard but square to the edges of the nailed boards (**1**). Hold the board firmly and scribe along it to fit the baseboard (**2**). Cut the scribed line and butt it up to the baseboard, then mark the position of the nailed boards on both edges. Join the marks then cut along this line. Nail the board to the floor (**3**).

To fit into a doorway, butt a board up to the frame; measure to the door stop. Cut a block of wood to this size and scribe to the baseboard (**4**). Use the same block to transfer the key points of reference for the shape of the door frame (**5**). Cut out the shape with a coping saw. Slide the board into the doorway, mark and cut the other edge to meet the nailed boards, then fasten it to the floor (**6**).

● **Shortening a door**
If you level a floor with hardboard or ply, you may have to plane the bottom of the door for clearance. Take it off its hinges and plane towards the center from each end.

61

PREPARATION AND PRIMING

Thorough preparation of all surfaces is the vital first step in redecorating. If you neglect this stage, subsequent finishes will be affected. Preparation means removing dirt, grease and loose or flaky previous finishes, as well as repairing serious deterioration such as cracks, holes, corrosion and decay. It's not just old surfaces that need attention; new masonry, wood and metals must be sealed against attack and priming is called for to ensure that a surface is in a suitable condition to accept its finish. Consult the charts on this page for details of primers and sealers for all the materials you're likely to encounter in and around the home, then read the following sections, which examine each material in detail.

THE PURPOSE OF PRIMING

Deciding whether or not to prime and then selecting the proper priming material depends largely on the condition and special problems of the particular surface.

Generally speaking, the purpose of priming is to seal absorbent surfaces for economical application of the top coat and to provide a good bonding surface for the finish. In many cases, diluted solution of the top coat material will be the best primer. Since primers for various materials are formulated using a variety of the common paint resins, make sure the paint is formulated for the material and application in which you plan to use it.

In general, all bare wood should be primed before painting. But even wood that isn't to be painted, especially when it is used outdoors, should be treated with preservative and clear moisture repellent. Even pressure-treated wood needs water-repellent treatment if it is to remain free of cracks and other common defects.

There are a variety of materials formulated to seal against moisture and stain-bleeding and others made to stabilize existing coatings before new paint or adhesives are applied. The chart below suggests a range of choices.

PRIMERS AND SEALERS: SUITABILITY, DRYING TIME, COVERAGE

● Black dot denotes that primer and surface are compatible

	Latex primer	Alkyd primer	Stain-blocking primer	Zinc-rich primer	Oil-cement primer	Aluminum paint	Clear sander-sealer	Clear wood preservative	Clear moisture repellent	Bitumen primer	Masonry sealer	Shellac	Wood-filler paste
SUITABLE FOR													
Wood to be painted	●	●	●			●	●	●	●	●		●	●
Wood to be clear or unfinished							●	●	●			●	●
Brick	●				●					●	●		
Stone	●				●					●	●		
Concrete	●				●	●				●	●		
Cinder block	●				●	●				●	●		
Stucco	●				●	●				●	●		
Gypsum wallboard	●	●	●									●	
Plaster	●	●	●								●	●	
Hardboard	●	●	●			●	●		●			●	
Particleboard	●	●	●				●		●			●	●
Iron, steel	●	●		●		●							
Galvanized metals	●	●		●		●							
Aluminum	●	●		●		●							
Copper or bronze		●		●									
Tile, glass	●	●											
PROBLEM SURFACES													
Bleed-prone staining			●			●						●	
Pressure-treated wood	●	●						●					
Bitumen-primed surfaces						●							
Resinous woods		●				●						●	
Open-grained woods							●						●
Below-grade, covered masonry					●					●			
Unidentifiable finish		●				●						●	
DRYING TIME: HOURS													
Touch dry	½	8	8	4	8	8	1	2	2	24	1	½	1
Recoatable	1	24	24	10	24	24	4	24	24	72	4	12	8
COVERAGE (SQ. FT.)													
Smooth surface	450	450	450	450	450	550	600	600	600	300	450	450	—
Rough or absorbent surface	250	250	250	250	250	300	300	300	300	150	250	300	—

APPLYING FINISHES

A finish in coating terms means a liquid or semiliquid substance which sets, dries or cures to protect and sometimes color materials such as wood or masonry. Apart from paint, other finishes for wood include stains, varnishes, oil, wax and French polish, all of which are used specifically where you want to display the grain of wood for its natural beauty.

The makeup of paint

Paint is basically made from solid particles of pigment suspended in a liquid binder or medium. The pigment provides the color and body of the paint, the medium allows the material to be brushed, rolled or sprayed and, once applied, forms a solid film binding the pigment together and adhering to the surface. Binder and pigment vary from paint to paint, but the commonest two families are solvent-based (sometimes known as oil paint) and water-based.

COMMON PAINT FINISHES AND ADDITIVES

The type of paint you choose depends on the finish you want and the material you're decorating. Various additives adapt the paint's qualities.

SOLVENT-BASED (OIL) PAINT

The medium for solvent-based paints (commonly called oil paints) is a mixture of oils and resin. A paint made from a natural resin is slow-drying, but modern paints contain synthetic resins such as alkyd, urea, epoxy, acrylic and vinyl, which all make for fast-drying paints. A white pigment, titanium dioxide, is added, plus other pigments to alter the color.

WATER-BASED PAINT

Latex is the commonest water-based paint. It has a binder made from synthetic resins similar to those used for oil paints, but it is dispersed in a solution of water. Titanium is the white pigment used for good-quality paints. It is also used with additional pigments for a wide range of colors.

ADDITIVES IN PAINT

No paint is made from simply binder and pigment. Certain additives are included during manufacture to give the paint qualities such as faster drying, high gloss, easy flow, longer pot life, or to make the paint nondrip.
- **Thixotropic** paints are the typical nondrip types; they are thick, almost jellylike in the can, enabling you to pick up a brush load without dripping.
- **Extenders** are added as fillers to strengthen the paint film. Cheap paint contains too much filler, reducing its covering power.

PAINT THINNERS

If a paint is too thick it cannot be applied properly and must be thinned before it is used. Some finishes require special thinners provided by the manufacturer, but most oil paints can be thinned with mineral spirits, and latexes with water.

Turpentine will thin oil paint but has no advantages over mineral spirits for household paints, and it is much more expensive.

GLOSS OR MATTE FINISH?

The proportion of pigment to resin affects the way the paint sets. A gloss (shiny) paint contains approximately equal amounts of resin and pigment, whereas a higher proportion of pigment produces a flat (dull) paint. By adjusting the proportions, it is possible to make satin or semigloss paints. Flat paints tend to cover best due to their high pigment content, but the greater proportion of resin in gloss paints is responsible for their strength.

Applying a paint system

No paint will provide protection for long if you apply one coat only. It is necessary to apply successive layers to build up a paint system.
- Paint for walls requires a simple system comprising two or three coats of the same paint.
- Paint intended for woodwork and metalwork needs a more complex system using paints with different qualities. A typical paint system for woodwork is illustrated below.

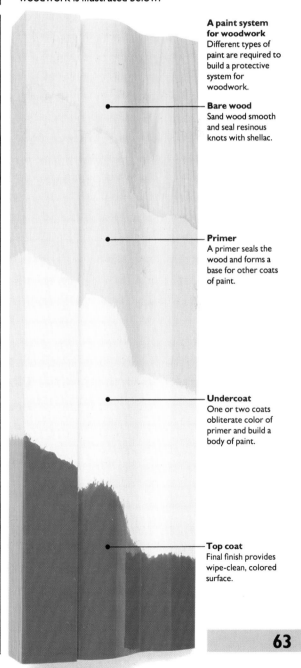

A paint system for woodwork
Different types of paint are required to build a protective system for woodwork.

Bare wood
Sand wood smooth and seal resinous knots with shellac.

Primer
A primer seals the wood and forms a base for other coats of paint.

Undercoat
One or two coats obliterate color of primer and build a body of paint.

Top coat
Final finish provides wipe-clean, colored surface.

Strain old paint
If you're using leftover paint, filter it through a piece of muslin or old hose stretched over the rim of a container.

Resealing the lid
Wipe the rim of the can clean before you replace the lid, then tap it down all around with a hammer over a wood block.

SAFETY WHEN PAINTING

Decorating isn't dangerous so long as you take sensible precautions to protect your health.

- **Ensure good ventilation indoors while applying a finish and when it is drying. Wear a facemask if you have respiratory problems.**
- **Do not smoke while painting or in the vicinity of drying paint.**
- **Contain paint spills outside with sand or earth and don't allow spills to enter a drain.**
- **If you splash paint in your eyes, flush them with copious amounts of water with your lids held open; if you have ill effects, visit a doctor.**
- **Wear barrier cream or gloves on sensitive hands. Use a proprietary skin cleanser to remove paint from the skin or wash it off with warm soapy water. Do not use paint thinners to clean your skin.**
- **Keep any finish and thinners out of reach of children. If a child swallows a substance, do not induce vomiting; seek medical treatment.**

PREPARING THE PAINT

Whether you're using newly purchased paint or leftovers from previous jobs, there are some basic rules to observe before you apply it.

- Wipe dust from the paint can, then pry off the lid with the side of a knife blade. Don't use a screwdriver: it only buckles the edge of the lid, preventing an airtight seal and making subsequent removal difficult.
- Gently stir liquid paints with a wooden stick to blend the pigment and medium. There's no need to stir thixotropic paints unless the medium has separated; if you have to stir it, leave it to gel again before using.
- If a skin has formed on paint, cut around the edge with a knife and lift out in one piece with a stick. Store the can on its lid, so that a skin cannot form on top of the paint.
- Whether the paint is old or new, transfer a small amount into a paint pot or plastic bucket. Filter old paint at the same time by tying a piece of muslin or old nylon hose across the rim of the pot.

PAINTING EXTERIOR MASONRY

The outside walls of your house need painting for two major reasons: to give a clean, bright appearance and to protect the surface from the rigors of the climate. What you use as a finish and how you apply it depend on what the walls are made of, their condition and the degree of protection they need. Bricks are traditionally left bare, but may require a coat of paint if they're in bad condition or previous attempts to decorate have resulted in a poor finish. Stucco walls are often painted to brighten the naturally dull gray color of the cement; sometimes masonry surfaces may need a colorful coat to disguise previous conspicuous patches. On the other hand, you may just want to change the present color of your walls for a fresh appearance.

Working to a plan

Before you start painting the outside walls of your house, plan your time carefully. Depending on the preparation, even a small house will take a few weeks to complete.

You need not tackle the whole job at once, although it is preferable—the weather may change to the detriment of your timetable. You can split the work into separate stages with days (even weeks) in between, so long as you divide the walls into manageable sections. Use window and door frames, bays, pipes and corners of walls to form break lines that will disguise lap marks.

Start at the top of the house, working right to left if you are right-handed (vice versa if you are left-handed).

FINISHES FOR MASONRY

● Black dot denotes compatibility. All surfaces must be clean, sound, dry and free from organic growth.

	Cement paint	Exterior latex paint	Reinforced latex paint	Solvent-thinned masonry paint	Textured coating	Floor paint
SUITABLE TO COVER						
Brick	●	●	●	●	●	●
Stone	●	●	●	●	●	●
Concrete	●	●	●	●	●	●
Stucco	●	●	●	●	●	●
Exposed-aggregate concrete	●	●	●	●	●	●
Asbestos cement	●		●	●	●	●
Latex paint		●	●	●	●	●
Oil-based paint		●	●	●	●	●
Cement paint	●	●	●	●	●	●
DRYING TIME: HOURS						
Touch dry	1–2	1–2	2–3	1–2	6	2–3
Recoatable	24	4	24	24	24–48	12–24
THINNERS: SOLVENTS						
Water-thinned	●	●	●		●	
Solvent-thinned				●		●
NUMBER OF COATS						
Normal conditions	2	2	1–2	2	1	1–2
COVERAGE: DEPENDING ON WALL TEXTURE						
Sq. ft. per quart		150–400	120–250	120–225		180–550
Sq. ft. per pound	30–75				20–40	
METHOD OF APPLICATION						
Brush	●	●	●	●	●	●
Roller	●	●	●	●	●	●
Spray gun	●		●	●		●

64

SUITABLE PAINTS FOR EXTERIOR MASONRY

There are various grades of paint suitable for decorating and protecting exterior masonry, which take into account economy, standard of finish, durability and coverage. Use the chart opposite for quick reference.

CEMENT PAINT

Cement paint is supplied as a dry powder, to which water is added. It is based on portland cement but pigments are added to produce a range of colors. Cement paint is the cheapest of the paints suitable for exterior use, although it is not as weatherproof as some others. Spray new or porous surfaces with water before you apply two coats.

Mixing cement paint
Shake or roll the container to loosen the powder, then add two parts powder to one of water in a clean bucket. Stir it to a smooth paste, then add a little more water until you achieve a full-bodied, creamy consistency. Mix up no more than you can use in one hour, or it will start to dry.

Adding an aggregate
When you're painting a dense wall or one treated with a stabilizing solution so that it its porosity is substantially reduced, it is advisable to add clean sand to the mix. It also provides added protection for an exposed wall and helps to cover dark colors. If the sand changes the color of the paint, add it to the first coat only. Use one part sand to four of powder, but stir it in when the paint is still in its pastelike consistency.

EXTERIOR LATEX

Exterior latex paint resembles the interior type; it is water-thinnable and dries to a similar smooth, flat finish. However, it is formulated to make it weatherproof and includes an additive to prevent organic growth; so apart from reinforced latexes, it is the only water-soluble paint that is recommended for use on outside walls.

The paint is ready for use, but thin the first coat on porous walls with 20 percent water. Follow up with one or two full-strength coats (depending on the color of the paint).

REINFORCED LATEX

Reinforced latex is a water-thinnable, resin-based paint to which has been added powdered mica or a similar fine aggregate. It dries with a textured finish that is extremely weatherproof, even in coastal districts or industrial areas and where darker colors are especially suitable. Although cracks and holes must be filled prior to painting, reinforced latex will cover hairline cracks and crazing. Apply two coats of paint in normal conditions, but you can economize by using sanded cement paint for the first coat.

SOLVENT-BASED MASONRY PAINT

A few masonry paints suitable for exterior walls are thinned with mineral spirits, but they are based on special resins so that, unlike most oil-based paints, they can be used on new walls without priming first with an alkali-resistant primer (▷). Check with manufacturer's recommendations. However, it is advisable to thin the first coat with 15 percent mineral spirits.

TEXTURED COATING

A thick textured coating can be applied to exterior walls. Such coatings are thoroughly weatherproof and often can be overpainted to match other colors. The usual preparation is necessary and brickwork should be pointed flush. Large cracks should be filled, but a textured coating will cover fine cracks. The paste is brushed or rolled onto the wall, then left to harden, forming an even texture. On the other hand, you can produce a texture of your choice using a variety of simple tools (▷). It's an easy process, but practice on a small section first.

Concrete floor paints

Floor paints are specially prepared to withstand hard wear. They are especially suitable for concrete garage or workshop floors, but they are also used for stone paving, steps and other concrete structures. They can be used inside for playroom floors.

The floor must be clean and dry and free from oil or grease. If the concrete is freshly laid, allow it to cure for at least three months before painting. Thin the first coat of paint with 10 percent mineral spirits.

Don't use floor paint over a surface sealed with a proprietary concrete sealer, but you can cover other paints so long as they are keyed first.

The best way to paint a large area is to use a paintbrush around the edges, then fit an extension to a paint roller for the bulk of the floor.

SEE ALSO

Details for: ▷	
Primers	62
Textured coating	73
Preparing masonry	46–50
Paint rollers	483

Apply paint with a roller on an extension

Paint in manageable sections
You can't hope to paint an entire house in one session, so divide each elevation into manageable sections to disguise the joints. The horizontal molding divide the wall neatly into two sections, and the raised door and window surrounds are convenient break lines.

TECHNIQUES FOR PAINTING MASONRY

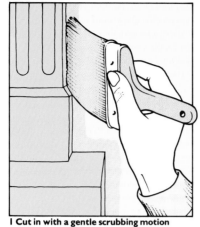

1 Cut in with a gentle scrubbing motion

3 Use a banister brush
Tackle deeply textured wall surfaces with a banister brush, using a scrubbing action.

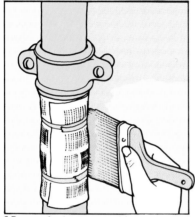

2 Protect the downspouts with newspaper

4 Use a roller
For speed in application, use a paint roller with a deep pile for heavy textures, a medium pile for light textures and smooth wall surfaces.

5 Spray onto the apex of external corners

6 Spray internal corners as separate surfaces

Using paintbrushes

Choose a 4- to 6-inch-wide paintbrush for walls; larger ones are heavy and tiring to use. A good-quality brush with coarse bristles will last longer on rough walls. For a good coverage, apply the paint with vertical strokes, criss-crossed with horizontal ones. You will find it necessary to stipple paint into textured surfaces.

Cutting in

Painting up to a feature such as a door or window frame is known as cutting in. On a smooth surface, you should be able to paint a reasonably straight edge following the line of the feature, but it's difficult to apply the paint to a heavily textured wall with a normal brush stroke. Don't just apply more paint to overcome the problem; instead, touch the tip of the brush only to the wall, using a gentle scrubbing action (1), then brush excess paint away from the feature once the texture is filled.

Wipe splashed paint from window and door frames with a cloth dampened with the appropriate thinner.

Painting behind pipes

To protect rainwater downspouts, tape a roll of newspaper around them. Stipple behind the pipe with a brush, then slide the paper tube down the pipe to mask the next section (2).

Painting with a banister brush

Use a banister brush (3) to paint deeply textured masonry surfaces. Pour some paint into a roller tray and dab the brush in to load it. Scrub the paint onto the wall using circular strokes to work it well into the uneven surface.

Using a paint roller

A roller (4) will apply paint three times faster than a brush. Use a deep-pile roller for heavy textures or a medium-pile for lightly textured or smooth walls. Rollers wear quickly on rough walls, so have a spare sleeve handy. Vary the angle of the stroke when using a roller to ensure even coverage and use a brush to cut into angles and obstructions.

A paint tray is difficult to use at the top of a ladder, unless you fit a tool support or, better still, erect a flat platform to work from (◁).

Using a spray gun

Spraying is the quickest and most efficient way to apply paint to a large expanse of wall. But you will have to mask all the parts you do not want to paint, using newspaper and masking tape. The paint must be thinned by about 10 percent for spraying. Set the spray gun according to the manufacturer's instructions to suit the particular paint. It is advisable to wear a respirator when spraying.

Hold the gun about a foot away from the wall and keep it moving with even, parallel passes. Slightly overlap each pass and try to keep the gun pointing directly at the surface—tricky while standing on a ladder. Trigger the gun just before each pass and release it at the end of the stroke.

When spraying a large, blank wall, paint it into vertical bands, overlapping each band about 4 inches.

Spray external corners by aiming the gun directly at the apex so that paint falls evenly on both surfaces (5). When two walls meet at an internal angle, treat each surface separately (6).

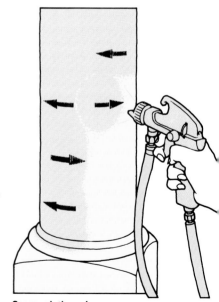

Spray-painting columns
Columns, part of a front door portico, for instance, should be painted in a series of overlapping vertical bands. Apply the bands by running the spray gun from side to side as you work down the column.

Most interior walls and ceilings will be wallboard or plaster and most probably papered or painted, unless the house has been recently built. Apart from their preparation, the methods for painting them are identical, and they can be considered smooth surfaces in terms of paint coverage. Although a flat finish is usually preferred indoors for walls and ceilings, there's no reason why you shouldn't use a gloss or even a textured paint in your scheme.

Finishes for bare masonry

Some interior walls are left unplastered—and some may even have been stripped on purpose—either for their decorative appearance or because it was considered unnecessary to clad the walls of certain rooms such as the basement, workshop or garage. A stripped brick or stone chimney breast makes an attractive focal point in a room, and an entire wall of bare masonry can create a dramatic effect or suggest a country cottage style.

If you want to finish brick, concrete or stone walls, follow the methods described for exterior walls. However, because they will not have to withstand weathering, you can use paint designed for interior use. Newly stripped masonry will require sealing to bind the surface (▷).

SEE ALSO

Details for: ▷
Primers and sealers	62
Cement paint	65
Choosing colors	24–25
Preparing masonry	46–50
Stripping wallcoverings	56

SELECTING PAINTS FOR INTERIOR SURFACES

Although you really have a choice of only two finishes for interior walls and ceilings—latex or oil paint—there are various qualities which offer depth of sheen, texture, one-coat coverage and good hiding power.

LATEX PAINT

The most popular and practical finish for walls and ceilings, latex paints are available in liquid or thixotropic consistencies with flat and semigloss finishes.

A semigloss latex is less likely to show fingerprints or scuffs. A nondrip, thixotropic paint has obvious advantages when painting ceilings, and covers in one coat. But apply a thinned coat on new, porous plaster, then a full-strength coat to achieve the required finish.

Latex is also available in a solid form, which comes in its own roller tray. It paints out well with minimal spatter and no drips.

REINFORCED LATEX

Latex paints, reinforced with fine aggregate, are primarily for use on exterior walls, but their fine textured finish is just as attractive inside and will cover minor imperfections, which would show through standard latex finishes.

OIL PAINT

Oil paints dry to a hard, durable finish. Although these paints are mainly intended for woodwork, they can be used on walls that require an extra degree of protection; they were once popular in bathrooms and kitchens, where you might expect condensation, but this is unnecessary with the development of modern water-thinned latexes, which resist moisture.

High-gloss paints accentuate uneven wall surfaces, so most people prefer a flat finish. Both types are available in liquid or thixotropic form. Most gloss paints should be preceded by one or two undercoats, but flat finishes, which have a very fine texture, form their own undercoats.

UNDERCOAT

Undercoat is a relatively cheap paint used to build up the full system of protective paintwork. It will obliterate underlying colors and fill minor irregularities. If speed is essential, choose a quick-drying primer/undercoat—a three-coat system of two undercoats and a top coat can be built up in one day.

CEMENT PAINT

Cement paint is an inexpensive exterior finish which is ideal for a utilitarian area indoors, such as a cellar, workshop or garage. Sold in dry powder form, it must be made up with water and dries to a matte finish (▷).

Paints for walls and ceilings
Latex paint, in its many forms, is the most practical finish for interior walls and ceilings, but many prefer oil paints on wood trim like baseboards and picture rails. The example above illustrates the advantage of contrasting textures: flat latex for the cornice up to the ceiling; gloss oil paint for the picture rail; semigloss latex for the textured walls.

USING BRUSHES, PADS AND ROLLERS

Applying paint by brush

Choose a good-quality brush for painting walls and ceilings. Cheap brushes tend to shed bristles—infuriating and less economical in the long run. Buy a wide brush 8 inches wide for quickest coverage. If you're not used to handling a brush, your wrist will soon tire and you may find a 4-inch brush, plus a 2-inch brush for the edges and corners, more comfortable to use. Take into account that the job will take longer with narrower brushes.

Loading the brush
Don't overload a brush; it leads to messy work and ruins the bristles if paint is allowed to dry in the roots. Dip no more than the first third of the brush, wiping off excess on the side of the container to prevent drips (1).

When using thixotropic paint, load the brush and apply paint without removing excess.

Using a brush
You can hold the brush whichever way feels comfortable to you, but the "pencil" grip is the most versatile, enabling your wrist to move the brush freely in any direction. Hold the brush handle between your thumb and forefinger, with your fingers on the ferrule (metal band) and your thumb supporting it from the other side (2).

Apply the paint in vertical strokes, then spread it at right angles to even out the coverage. Latex paint will not show brush marks when it dries, but finish oil paints with light upward vertical strokes for the best results.

1 Dip only the first third of bristles in paint

2 Place fingers on ferrule, thumb behind

Applying paint by roller

A paint roller with interchangeable sleeves is an excellent tool for applying paint to large areas. Choose a 9-inch roller for painting walls and ceilings.

There are a number of different sleeves to suit the type of paint and texture of the surface. Long-nap sheepskin and woven wool sleeves are excellent on textured surfaces, especially with latex paint. Choose a short-pile for smooth surfaces and with oil paints.

Disposable plastic foam rollers can be used to apply any paint to a smooth surface, but they soon lose their resilience and have a greater tendency to skid across the wall.

Special rollers
Rollers with long extension handles are designed for painting ceilings without having to erect a work platform (◁).

Some have a built-in paint reservoir for automatic reloading.

Narrow rollers are available for painting behind radiators, if you are unable to remove them (◁).

Loading a roller
You will need a paint tray to load a standard roller. Having dipped the sleeve lightly into the paint reservoir, roll it gently onto the ribbed part of the tray to coat the roller evenly (1).

Using a roller
Use zigzag strokes with a roller (2), covering the surface in all directions. Keep it on the surface at all times. If you let it spin at the end of a stroke it will spray paint onto the floor or adjacent surface. When applying oil paint, finish in one direction, preferably towards prevailing light.

1 Dip roller in paint, roll onto ribbed tray

2 Apply in zigzags, finish in one direction

● **Spraying**
It is possible to spray paint onto interior walls and ceilings, but it is only practical for large rooms. You'll have to mask everything you don't want to paint; and the sprayed paint would be forced through even the narrowest gaps between doors and frames. Adequate ventilation is vital when spraying indoors.

Applying paint by pad

Paint pads for large surfaces have flat rectangular faces covered with a short mohair pile. A plastic foam backing gives the pad flexibility so that the pile will always be in contact with the wall, even on a rough surface.

The exact size of the pad will be determined by the brand you choose, but one about 8 inches long is best for applying paint evenly and smoothly to walls and ceilings. You will also need a small pad or paintbrush for cutting in at corners and ceilings.

Loading a pad
Load a pad from its own special tray, drawing the pad across the captive roller so that you pick up an even amount of paint (1).

Using a pad
To apply the paint consistently, keep the pad flat on the wall and sweep it gently and evenly in any direction (2). Use criss-cross strokes for latex, but finish with vertical strokes with oil paints to prevent streaking.

1 Loading a pad
Load the pad evenly by drawing it across the integral roller on the tray without squeezing.

2 Sweep pad gently in any direction

Even the most experienced painter can't help dripping a little paint, so always paint a ceiling before the wall, especially if they are to be different colors. Erect a work platform so that you can cover as much of the surface as possible without having to change position; you will achieve a better finish and will be able to work in safety. When you start to paint, follow a strict working routine to ensure a faultless finish. Choose your tools wisely so you can work efficiently. Refer to the chart below for professional results.

FINISHES FOR INTERIOR WALLS & CEILINGS

● Black dot denotes compatibility. All surfaces must be clean, sound, dry and free from organic growth.

	Latex paint	Reinforced latex paint	Oil-based paint	Undercoat	Primer/ undercoat	Cement paint	Textured coating
SUITABLE TO COVER							
Plaster	●	●	●	●	●	●	●
Wallpaper	●		●	●	●		
Brick	●	●	●	●		●	●
Stone	●	●	●	●		●	●
Concrete	●	●	●	●		●	●
Previously painted surface	●	●	●	●	●		●
DRYING TIME: HOURS							
Touch dry	1–2	2–3		4	½	1–2	6
Recoatable	4	24	16	16	2	24	24–48
THINNERS: SOLVENTS							
Water	●	●				●	●
Mineral spirits			●	●	●		
NUMBER OF COATS							
Normal conditions	2	1–2	1–2	1–2	1–2	2	1
COVERAGE: APPROXIMATE							
Sq. ft. per gallon	350–400	175–200	400–500	500–600	500		
Sq. ft. per pound						30–75	10–20
METHOD OF APPLICATION							
Brush	●	●	●	●	●	●	●
Roller	●	●	●	●	●	●	●
Paint pad	●	●	●	●		●	
Spray	●	●	●	●	●		

Painting the walls

Use a small brush to paint the edges starting at a top corner of the room. If you are right-handed, work right to left. Paint an area of about 2 square feet at a time. If you are left-handed, paint the wall in the opposite direction. When using latex, paint in horizontal bands (1),

but, with oil paints, use vertical strips (2) as the junctions are more likely to show unless you blend in the wet edges quickly. Always finish a complete wall before you take a break or a change of tone will show between separate painted sections.

1 Paint latex in horizontal bands

2 Apply oil paints in vertical strips

Painting the ceiling

Start in a corner near the window and carefully paint along the edges with a small paintbrush.

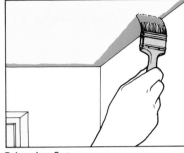

Paint edges first

Working from the wet edges, paint in 2-foot-wide bands, working away from the light. Whether you use a brush, a pad or a roller, apply each fresh load of paint just clear of the previous application, blending in the junctions for even coverage.

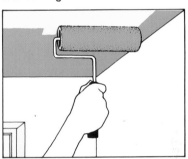

Work from wet edges

Electrical fixtures

Unscrew ceiling fixtures so that you can paint right up to the backplate with a small brush. Loosen the faceplate or mounting box of sockets and switches to paint behind them.

Remember: switch off at the main service panel before exposing electrical connections (▷).

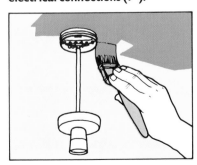

Unscrew fixture cover to keep it clean

SEE ALSO

Details for: ▷	
Service panel	291, 319
Work platforms	40–42
Preparing masonry	46–50
Preparing concrete	49
Preparing paint surfaces	50, 54
Preparing plaster	53–54
Stripping wallcoverings	56
Primers	62
Pressurized roller	483

Paint reservoir
Use a special roller with a pressurized paint reservoir to avoid having to reload a roller constantly. It's an excellent tool for painting ceilings and high walls, when frequent returns to the tray would be tiresome.

DECORATIVE EFFECTS: SPATTERING AND STIPPLING

Decorative effects with paint, once common practice, can be applied to walls, ceilings, furniture and trim to give an individual look to a scheme. Some of the more complex effects—traditionally the domain of the skilled craftsman—are made easier to achieve using easily workable modern materials and improvised equipment.

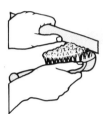

1 Spatter paint
Produce a speckled effect by drawing a ruler across a banister brush.

The speckled effect of spattering

2 Sponge stipple
Apply delicate stipple textures by patting a paint-dampened natural sponge on the wall.

Subtle textures with sponge stippling

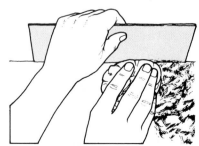

3 Rag stipple
Create vivid stipple textures using a crumpled cotton rag.

More vivid effects of rag stippling

The importance of practice

Although some of the techniques are easy, it is worth practicing them on a piece of flat board before you tackle a whole room. The texture of the actual wall might influence the finished effect, but at least you will be familiar with the basic techniques. If the result is not to your satisfaction, don't worry—you can always paint or paper over it.

Spattering

Achieve a speckled effect by spattering two or three contrasting colors onto a solid background. When planning your color scheme, consider the background as your dominant color. Cover the floor with drop cloths and mask door and window frames (plus the panes) unless you want to cover them with the same effect. Use masking tape to cover electrical fixtures.

Use oil paint for the spatter colors, reduced to the required consistency with a little mineral spirits; this is best achieved by trial and error on your practice board. Avoid making the paint too liquid or your speckled effect will become a mass of runs. If an accident

Sponge stippling

Stipple simple textures onto a latex background with a natural sponge. Use a dark-toned latex paint to stipple over a lighter base color for a two-tone effect. When choosing, remember that the base color will be the dominant color in the room.

Dampen a natural sponge with water until it swells to its full size. Squeeze out excess water to leave it moist. Pour a tablespoonful of paint into a shallow tray and dip the sponge into it. Blot off

Rag stippling

Using a ball of cotton rag instead of a sponge produces a more vivid stippled effect, although the technique is similar. Crumple a piece of cotton rag about the size of a large handkerchief into a ball and dip it into the paint until it is saturated. Squeeze it out and try stippling onto scrap paper. Use a wrinkled part of the ball rather than a smooth section to achieve the most interesting patterns. When you achieve the effect you like on the paper, apply the rag lightly to the wall (**3**).

Use different parts of the ball as you work across the wall and refold it to

Applying a base coat

Although decorative effects can be applied successfully to woodwork, nevertheless they are best when applied to a flat plaster surface, and thorough preparation is essential as with any decoration. Any of the following finishes require a flat base coat in your choice of color. This initial coat can be applied by brush, roller or paint pad. Leave to dry.

occurs, blot the paint immediately with an absorbent rag or paper tissue and allow it to dry. Obliterate the mistake by dabbing with a sponge dipped in the base color.

Choose any stiff-bristled brush, such as a banister brush. Dip the tips of the bristles only into the paint, then, holding the brush about 4 inches from the wall, drag an old ruler towards you, across the bristles. This flicks tiny drops of paint onto the wall (**1**). Produce an even or random coverage as you prefer, but avoid concentrating the effect in one place. When the first spatter coat is dry, apply other colors in turn, if required, in the same way.

excess paint onto a piece of plain scrap paper until it leaves a mottled effect, then apply it lightly to the wall (**2**).

Do not press hard or the sponge will leave a patch of almost solid paint. Group the impressions closely to form an even texture across the wall. If any area appears too dark when dry, stipple base color over it to tone it down.

When the first stipple coat has dried, sponge another tone or color over it.

vary the pattern. Stipple out mistakes using a clean rag dipped in base color once the first stipple coat is dry.

Mask adjoining areas with cardboard

GRAINING AND MARBLING

Bag graining

Bag graining involves a stippling action, but it is used to remove paint from the wall instead of to apply it. Use a darker graining paint over a pale latex background. The graining color is likely to be the more dominant of the two. It is more convenient if two people work together, one to apply the paint while the other patterns it.

Dilute latex paint with about 50 percent water and stir it to an even consistency. Make up enough paint to cover at least one complete wall at a time in case a fresh batch differs slightly in tone. Before you start, mask off areas you don't want to treat with newspaper and masking tape.

Use a wide brush to paint the graining color over the base with vertical strokes (1). Take care to avoid runs. After you have applied a band of paint about 2 feet wide, take a plastic bag half-filled with rags and use it to stipple the wet paint (2). Overlap each impression to produce an overall crinkled effect. When paint builds up on the bag, wipe it off onto a piece of absorbent rag.

Your helper should work just ahead of you, applying fresh paint so that you can texture it before it dries.

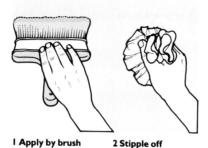

1 Apply by brush   2 Stipple off

SEE ALSO	
Details for: ▷	
Paints	67
Varnish	75
Brushes	482

Two-tone patterns with bag graining

Marbling

Producing a marblelike effect with paint is not an easy technique to master, so be prepared to experiment on a practice board until you achieve a convincing result. Study some examples of marble, taking note of the basic colors and tones involved. Choose a limited color range, which you can mix to produce a variety of hues.

Artist's student oil paints are the best materials to use for veining and mottling—characteristic patterns in marble—as they take longer to dry (it's necessary to work the whole effect with wet paint), and they blend extremely well. They are relatively expensive, however, so you may prefer to use ordinary oil paints in semigloss finish instead.

Starting with an oil glaze
A transparent oil glaze, obtainable from a professional paint supplier, is the best material to use as a base coat and as a medium for the mottling and veining paints. Dip a lint-free rag into the glaze and rub it evenly over the wall surface. A light coating is usually quite sufficient to achieve the best surface.

Applying a mottled pattern
Mix up one or two color washes using oil paints and glaze. Use a 1-inch paintbrush to paint uneven patches onto the wet glazed surface. Space them randomly and you can then overlap color and tones.

Take the rag used to apply the glaze and stipple the patches to blend them and lose the distinct edges. Complete the effect using a clean, soft-bristled paintbrush; sweep it very gently back and forth across the wet paint to produce a delicately softened effect.

Adjust the tone of any dark areas by applying small patches of lighter paint on top, then soften them in again.

Mottled effects typical of marbling

Forming the veining
Use an artist's paintbrush to draw on the veins using color washes, mixed as for mottling. Veins are best freely painted with varying thicknesses of line. note carefully the branching lines typical of marble veining. Blot any thick paint carefully with a tissue, then blur the veins by brushing back and forth with a soft paintbrush until they appear as subtle, soft-edged lines.

Sealing with varnish
Allow the paintwork to dry thoroughly, then paint on a coat of semigloss polyurethane varnish. When the varnish is hard, burnish the wall with a soft cloth to give a delicate sheen. Apply a little wax paste if necessary.

Veining characteristic of marbling

RAG ROLLING, LINEAR AND STENCILED EFFECTS

1 Rag rolling
Roll off a dark finish to reveal a paler base coat.

2 Paint a clean edge
Use masking tape to define a line; brush paint away from the tape to avoid a thick edge forming.

3 Striping tape
Paint bands of color with striping tape.

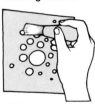

4 Cutting a stencil

5 Stipple on color

Define areas with linear effects

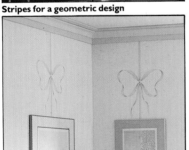

Stripes for a geometric design

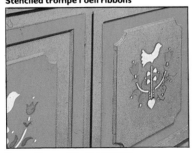

Stenciled trompe l'oeil ribbons

Decorative motif using stencils

Rag rolling

Also known as scumbling, rag rolling is a technique similar to bag graining. You will need a helper to paint vertical bands of diluted color ahead of you. The best results are achieved with a flat base coat of pale semigloss finish oil paint overlaid with a darker semigloss finish oil paint mixed with 50 percent mineral spirits. The top coat will be the dominant color.

Take a piece of rag about the size of a dish towel, fold it into quarters then twist it into a roll. Start at the bottom of the wall and roll the rag upwards to remove wet paint, producing a texture resembling watered silk **(1)**.

As you reach the ceiling, use the roll to stipple the margin. If you touch the ceiling accidentally, wipe off the paint immediately with a clean rag dampened with mineral spirits.

Start the next band of texturing at the bottom again, but don't attempt to produce straight strips of pattern. Change direction constantly to overlap and blend with previous impressions. Remake the rolled rag each time it becomes impregnated with paint, or use a clean rag.

Masking straight edges

Use low-tack masking tape when you want to paint two areas of color, or even a colored band, perhaps, to finish off a painted dado. This tape can be peeled off without removing the painted surface below. Don't use transparent ordinary tape for this reason.

Marking the line
Draw straight horizontal lines with a level and straightedge. Vertical lines can be marked by snapping a chalked plumbline on the wall.

Painting the edge
Run masking tape along one side of the marked line, taking care not to stretch or curve the tape. Using a small brush, paint away from the tape so that you do not build a thick edge of paint against it, which could peel off with the tape **(2)**. Paint the rest of the wall with a roller or brush. When the paint is touch-dry, peel off the tape. Pull back and away from the edge to leave a clean line. If you happen to pull away specks of paint, touch up with an artist's paintbrush.

Painting a band of color
To paint a band of color, complete the background, then mask the top and bottom of the band. Apply the paint and when touch-dry, remove both tapes.

Alternatively, use striping tape designed to paint lines on car bodies. Once the tape is applied to the wall, the center section is peeled away, leaving a gap between two masked edges, which you fill in with paint **(3)**.

Stenciling

Ready-made paper stencils for painting patterns or motifs onto a wall are available from artists' shops. If you cannot find a stencil which suits your purpose, buy blank sheets of stencil paper from the same outlets and cut your own design with a razor knife **(4)**. Design your stencil with thin strips to hold the shapes together.

Ordinary latex paint is ideal for stenciling. You will need a stencil brush. It has short stiff bristles and is used with a stippling action **(5)**.

Mark out the wall lightly to position the stencil horizontally and vertically. At the same time, make small marks to indicate the position of repeat patterns. Use small pieces of masking tape to hold the stencil on the wall. Spoon a little paint onto a flat board. Take a stencil brush and touch the tips of the bristles into the paint. Stipple excess paint onto waste paper until it deposits paint evenly, then transfer it to the wall.

Hold the stencil flat against the wall. Stipple the edges of the motif first, then fill in the center. If necessary, apply a second coat immediately to build up the required depth of color.

When the motif is complete, hold the stencil perfectly still while you slowly peel it away from the wall. Make sure paint has not crept under the stencil before repositioning it to repeat the motif next to the painted area.

If paint has crept under the stencil, try to dab it off with a piece of absorbent paper rolled into a thin taper. Alternatively, allow the paint to become touch-dry, then scrape it carefully away with a razor blade. Touch up the scraped area with background paint.

APPLYING TEXTURED COATING

You can apply the coating with either a roller or a broad wall brush: finer textures are possible using the latter. Buy a special roller if recommended by the coating manufacturer.

With a well-loaded roller, apply a generous coat in a 2-foot-wide band across the ceiling or down a wall. Do not press too hard and vary the angle of the stroke.

If you decide to brush on the coating, do not spread it out like paint. Lay it on with one stroke and spread it back again with one or two strokes only.

Clean up any splashes, then apply a second band and texture it, blending both bands together. Continue in this way until the wall or ceiling is complete. Keep the room ventilated until the coating has hardened.

Painting around fixtures
Use a small paintbrush to fill in around electrical fixtures and along edges, trying to copy the texture used on the surrounding wall or ceiling. Some people prefer to form a distinct margin around fixtures by drawing a small paintbrush along the perimeter to give a smooth finish.

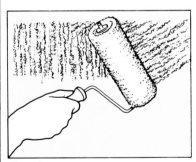

Creating a texture
You can experiment with a variety of tools to make any number of textures. You can use a standard roller, or use ones made with special surfaces to produce diagonal or diamond patterns, or you can apply a swirling, ripple or stipple finish with improvised equipment, as shown at right.

TEXTURED COATINGS

Textured coatings can be obtained as a dry powder for mixing with warm water, or in a ready-mixed form for direct application from the tub. Joint compound can be used. Most manufacturers supply a fine or a thick mix; if you want a heavy texture, choose the thicker mix. Where you're likely to rub against the wall—such as in a narrow hall or small bathroom—a fine texture is preferable. The rough coating dries very hard and it could graze your skin.

Some coatings are suitable for exterior walls as well as indoors. They are also available in a range of colors—you can cover the texture with latex paint if a standard color does not fit your decorative scheme.

Preparing for textured coatings

New surfaces will need virtually no preparation, but joints between plasterboard must be reinforced with tape (▷). Strip any wallcoverings and key gloss paint with fine sandpaper. Old walls and ceilings must be clean, dry, sound and free from organic growth. Treat friable surfaces with stabilizing primer (▷).

Although large cracks and holes must be filled, a textured coating will conceal minor defects in walls and ceilings by filling small cracks and bridging shallow bumps and hollows.

Masking joinery and fittings
Use 2-inch-wide masking tape to cover door and window frames, electrical outlets, switches and ceiling roses, plumbing pipework, picture rails and baseboards. Lay dust sheets over the floor.

1 Diamond pattern

3 Swirl design

5 Tree bark simulation

2 Stipple effect

4 Combed arcs

6 Stucco finish

1 Geometric patterns
Use a roller with diamond or diagonal grooves. Load the roller and draw lightly across the textured surface.

2 Stippled finish
Pat the coating with a damp sponge to create a pitted profile. Rinse out frequently. Alter your wrist angle and overlap sections.

3 Random swirls
Twist a damp sponge on the textured surface, then pull away to make a swirling design. Overlap swirls for a layered effect.

4 Combed arcs
A toothed spatula sold with the finish is used to create combed patterns: arcs, criss-cross patterns or wavy scrolls.

5 Imitation tree bark
Produce a bark texture by applying parallel strokes with a roller, then lightly drawing the straight edge of a spatula over it.

6 Stucco finish
Apply parallel roller strokes, then run the rounded corner of a spatula over it in short, straight strokes.

FINISHING WOODWORK

Paint is the usual finish for woodwork in and around the house—it gives a protective, decorative coating and there's a vast choice of colors and surface finishes. But stains, varnishes or polishes can also be used not just for furniture but as an attractive, durable finish for wood trim. They enable you to add color to woodwork without obliterating the natural beauty of its grain; transparent finishes are also a good alternative where you don't want to alter the natural wood color. Bear in mind the location of the woodwork and the amount of wear it is likely to get when choosing a finish. Each has somewhat different characteristics and tolerances.

Left to right
1 Wax polish
2 Colored preserver
3 Satin oil paint
4 Cold-cure lacquer
5 Gloss oil paint
6 Oil finish
7 Unsealed wood stain
8 Opaque microporous wood stain
9 Clear microporous wood stain
10 Polyurethane varnish

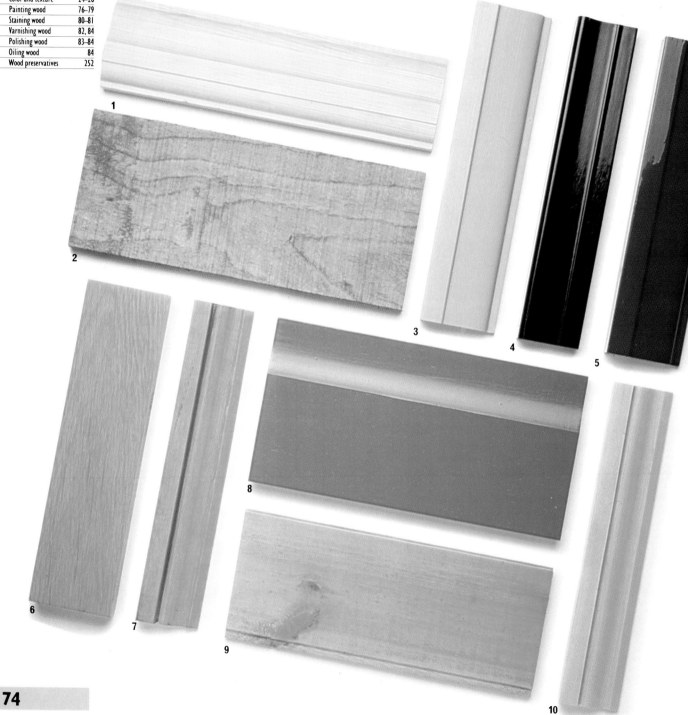

THE CHOICE OF FINISHES FOR WOOD

The list below comprises a comprehensive range of finishes available for decorating and protecting woodwork in and around the house. Each finish has qualities particular to its intended usage, although many can be used simply for their attractive appearance rather than for any practical considerations—this, however, depends on the location of woodwork, as some finishes are much more durable than others.

OIL PAINT

Oil (solvent-based) paints are still preferred by many, primarily for the range of colors offered by all paint manufacturers, secondarily because they last for many years with only the occasional wash-down to remove finger marks. Outside, their durability is reduced considerably due to the combined action of sun and rain: consider redecoration every two or three years. They are available as a gloss or semigloss finish with both liquid and thixotropic consistencies.

One or two undercoats are essential, especially for outside.

GLOSS LATEX PAINT

Latex-based gloss paint was introduced by several manufacturers but is still quite rare. Beneficially, it dries much faster than oil paint and without the strong smell associated with such paint. It is suitable for both interior and exterior use. It allows moisture to escape from the wood while protecting it from rainwater—which oil paint does not—so reduces the risk of flaking and blistering. Gloss latex requires its own compatible primer/undercoat. The usual system of two undercoats and one top coat can be applied in one day.

WOOD STAIN

Unlike paint, which after the initial priming coat rests on the surface of woodwork, stain penetrates the wood. Its main advantage is to enhance the natural color of the woodwork or to unify the slight variation in color found in even the same species.

Water- or oil-based stains are available ready for use but powdered pigments are available for mixing with denatured alcohol. None of these stains will actually protect the wood, and you will have to seal them with a clear varnish or polish.

There are protective wood stains (often sold as *microporous paints* or *breathing paints*) specially made for use on exterior applications. The microporous nature of the coating allows water to escape from the wood, yet provides a weather-resistant flat finish. Being a stain, it does not crack, peel or flake. Choose a semitransparent stain when you want the grain to show, or an opaque one for less attractive woods.

COLORED PRESERVERS

Rough-sawn lumber frequently used for rustic effects looks particularly unattractive when painted, yet it needs protection. Use a wood preserver, which penetrates deeply into the lumber to prevent rot and insect attack (▷). There are clear preservers, plus a range of browns and greens, and ones for redwood.

Traditional preservers such as creosote have a strong, unpleasant smell and are harmful, but there are several organic solvent preservers, which are perfectly safe—even for greenhouses and wood decks.

VARNISH

Varnish is a clear protective coating for wood. Most modern varnishes are made with polyurethane resins to provide a waterproof scratch- and heat-resistant finish. The majority are ready to apply, although some are supplied with a catalyst, which must be added before the varnish is used. These two-component varnishes are even tougher than standard polyurethanes and are especially suitable for treating wood floors (▷). You can choose from high gloss, satin or matte.

An exterior grade of varnish is more weather-resistant. Marine varnish, which is formulated to withstand even salt water, would therefore be an ideal finish for exterior woodwork in a coastal climate.

Colored varnishes are designed to provide a stain and clear finish at the same time. They are available in the normal wood shades and some strong primary colors. Unlike a true stain, a colored varnish does not sink into the wood, so there is a possibility of a local loss of color in areas of heavy wear or abrasion unless you apply additional coats of clear varnish.

COLD-CURE LACQUER

Cold-cure lacquer is a plastic coating which is mixed with a hardener just before it is used. It is extremely durable, even on floors, and is heat- and alcohol-resistant. The standard type dries to a high gloss, which can be burnished to a lacquerlike finish if required. There is also a matte finish grade, but a smoother matte surface can be obtained by rubbing down the gloss coating with fine steel wool and wax. It is available in clear, black or white.

OIL

Oil is a subtle finish which soaks into the wood, leaving a mellow sheen on the surface. Traditional linseed oils remain sticky for hours, but a modern oil will dry in about one hour and provides a tougher, more durable finish. Oil can be used on softwoods as well as open-grained oily hardwoods, such as teak or walnut (▷). It's suitable for interior and exterior woodwork.

WAX POLISH

Wax can be used as a dressing to preserve and maintain another finish, or it can be used as a finish itself. A good wax should be a blend of beeswax and a hard polishing wax such as carnauba. Some contain silicones to make it easier to achieve a high gloss.

Polishes are white or tinted to various shades of brown to darken the wood. Although it is attractive, wax polish is not a durable finish and should be used indoors only.

FRENCH POLISH

French polish is made by dissolving shellac in alcohol and, if properly applied, can be burnished to a mirrorlike finish. It is easily scratched and alcohol, or even water, will etch the surface, leaving white stains. Consequently, it can be used only on furniture unlikely to receive normal wear and tear.

There are several varieties of shellac polish. Button polish is the best quality standard polish and is reddish brown in color. It is bleached to make white polish for light-colored woods and if the natural wax is removed from the shellac, a clear, transparent polish is produced. For mahogany, choose a darker red garnet polish.

SEE ALSO

Details for: ▷	
Wood flooring	58–59, 113
Oiling wood	84
Wood preservatives	252
Primers	62
Hardwood	494

PAINTING WOODWORK

When you're painting wood, take into account that it's a fibrous material, which has a definite grain pattern, different rates of absorbency, knots that may ooze resin—all qualities that influence the type of paint you use and the techniques and tools you'll need to apply it. Different species have different characteristics.

Basic application

Prepare and prime all new woodwork thoroughly (◁) before applying the final finish. If you are using gloss paint, apply one or two undercoats, depending on the covering power of the paint. As each coat hardens, rub down with fine wet-and-dry paper to remove blemishes and wipe the surface with a cloth dampened with mineral spirits to remove the dust residue.

Best quality paintbrushes are the most efficient tools for painting woodwork. You will need 1-inch and 2-inch brushes for general work and perhaps angled sash brushes for painting window muntins. Apply the paint with vertical strokes, then spread sideways to even out the coverage. Finish with light strokes—called laying off—in the direction of the grain. Blend the edges of the next application while the paint is still wet, or a hard edge will show. Don't go back over a painted surface that has started to dry, or it will leave a blemish in the surface.

It is not necessary to spread thixotropic paint in the same way. Simply lay on the paint in almost parallel strokes leaving the brush strokes to settle out naturally.

● **Removing a blemish**
If you find specks of fluff or a brush bristle embedded in fresh paint, don't attempt to remove them once a skin has begun to form on the paint. Let it harden, then rub down with wet-and-dry paper. The same applies if you discover runs.

Painting a panel
When painting up to the edge of a panel, brush from the center out. If you flex the bristles against the edge, the paint will run.

Similarly, molding flexes the bristles unevenly and too much paint flows; spread it well, taking care at corners of molded panels.

Making a straight edge
To finish an area with a straight edge, use one of the smaller brushes and place it a fraction of an inch from the edge. As you flex the bristles, they'll spread to the required width, laying on an even coat of paint.

THE ORDER OF WORK

Follow the sequences recommended below for painting interior and exterior woodwork successfully:

INSIDE

Start painting windows early in the day, so you can close them at night without the new film sticking. Paint doors, then picture rails; finish with baseboards so specks of dust picked up on the brush won't be transferred to other areas.

OUTSIDE

Choose the order of painting according to the position of the sun. Avoid painting in direct sunlight as this will cause glare with light colors and result in runs or blistering. Never paint on wet or windy days; rain specks will pit the finish and airborne dust will ruin the surface. Paint windows and exterior doors early so that they are touch-dry by the evening.

FINISHES FOR WOODWORK

● Black dot denotes compatibility. All surfaces must be clean, sound, dry and free from organic growth.

	Oil paint	Gloss latex	Wood stain	Protective wood stain	Colored preservative	Varnish	Colored varnish	Cold-cure lacquer	Oil	Wax polish	French polish
SUITABLE FOR											
Softwoods	●	●	●	●	●	●	●	●	●	●	
Hardwoods	●	●	●	●	●	●	●	●	●	●	●
Oily hardwoods	●	●	●	●	●	●	●	●	●	●	●
Surfaced boards	●	●	●	●	●	●	●	●	●	●	
Rough-sawn boards				●	●						
Interior use	●	●	●	●			●	●	●	●	●
Exterior use	●	●		●	●	●	●	●	●		
DRYING TIME: HOURS											
Touch-dry	4	1	½	4	1–2	4	4	1	1		½
Recoatable	14	3	6	6–8	2–4	14	14	2	6	1	24
THINNERS: SOLVENTS											
Water		●	●		●						
Mineral spirits	●		●	●	●	●	●		●	●	
Denatured alcohol											●
Special thinner								●			
NUMBER OF COATS											
Interior use	1–2	1–2	2–3	2		2–3	2–3	2–3	3	2	10–15
Exterior use	2–3	1–2		2	2	3–4	3–4		3		
COVERAGE											
Sq. ft. per gallon	450–600	375–550	600–1000	375–900	150–450	550–600	550–600	600–650	375–550	VARIABLE	VARIABLE
METHOD OF APPLICATION											
Brush	●	●	●	●	●	●	●	●	●	●	●
Paint pad	●	●	●	●		●	●				
Cloth pad			●						●	●	●
Spray gun	●	●	●			●	●	●			●

Doors have a variety of faces and conflicting grain patterns that need to be painted separately—yet the end result must look even in color without ugly brush marks or heavily painted edges. There's a strict system for painting panel, flush or glazed doors.

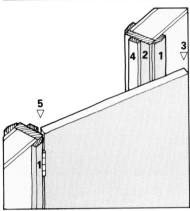

Painting each side a different color
Make sure all the surfaces that face you when the door is open are painted the same color.

Opening side: Paint the casing (1) and door frame up to and including the edge of the door stop (2) one color. Paint the face of the door and its opening edge (3) the same color.

Opposite side: Paint the casing and frame up to and over the door stop (4) the second color. Paint the opposite face of the door and its hinged edge (5) with the second color.

Preparation and technique

Remove all the door handles and wedge the door open so that it cannot be closed accidentally, locking you in the room. Keep the handle in the room with you, just in case.

Aim to paint the door and its frame separately so that there is less chance of touching wet paint when passing through a freshly painted doorway. Paint the door first and when it is dry finish the trim.

If you want to use a different color for each side of the door, paint the hinged edge the color of the closing face (the one that comes to rest against the stop molding). Paint the outer edge of the door the same color as the opening face. This means that there won't be any difference in color when viewed from either side.

Each side of the frame should match the corresponding face of the door. When painting in the room into which the door swings, paint that side of the frame, including the edge of the stop molding against which the door closes, to match the opening face and the rest of the frame the color of the closing face.

System for a flush door

To paint a flush door, start at the top and work down in sections, blending each one into the other. Lay on the paint, then finish each section with light vertical brush strokes. Finally, paint the edges. Brush from edges, never onto them, or the paint will build up, run and a ridge will form.

System for a panel door

The different parts of a paneled door must be painted in logical order. Finish each part with parallel strokes in the direction of the grain.

Whatever the style of paneled door you are painting, start with the moldings (1) followed by the panels (2). Paint the center verticals—muntins (3)—next, then the cross rails (4). Finish the face by painting the outer verticals—stiles (5). Paint the edge of the door (6).

To achieve a superior finish, paint the muntins, rails and stiles together, picking up the wet edges of paint before they begin to dry, show brush strokes and pull out bristles. To get the best results it is important to work quickly.

SEE ALSO

Details for:	▷
Muntins	78
Preparing paintwork	44
Preparing wood	55
Primers	62
Staining a door	81
Doors	184–185

Glazed doors
To paint a glazed door, begin with the muntins (▷), then follow the sequence as described for panel doors.

Flush door
Apply square sections of paint, working down from the top, and pick up the wet edges for a good blend. Lay off with light vertical brush strokes.

Panel door: basic painting method
Follow the numbered sequence for painting the various parts of the door, each finished with strokes along the grain to prevent streaking.

Panel door: advanced painting method
Working rapidly, follow the alternative sequence to produce a finish free from lap marks between sections.

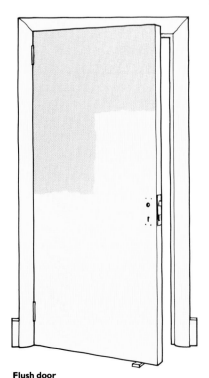

Flush door

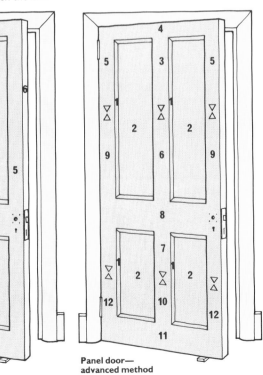

Panel door— basic method

Panel door— advanced method

● **Clean windows first**
Clean the glass in your windows before decorating to avoid picking up particles of dust in the paint.

Cutting-in brush
Paint muntins with a cutting-in brush, which has its bristles cut at an angle to enable you to work right up to the glass with a thin line of paint.

● **Painting French windows**
Although French windows are really glazed doors, treat them like large casement windows.

PROTECTING THE GLASS

When painting the edges of muntins, overlap the glass by about 1/16 inch to prevent rain or condensation from seeping between glass and woodwork.

If you find it difficult to achieve a satisfactory straight edge, use a proprietary plastic or metal paint shield held against the edge of the frame to protect the glass.

Alternatively, run masking tape around the edges of the window pane, leaving a slight gap so that the paint will seal the joint between glass and frame. When the paint is touch-dry, carefully peel off the tape. Don't wait until the paint is completely dry or the film may peel off with the tape.

Scrape off any paint accidentally dripped onto the glass using a razor blade, once it has set. Plastic handles to hold blades are sold by many home centers for this purpose.

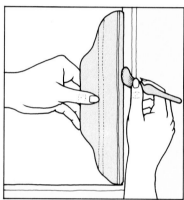

Using a paint shield
A plastic or metal paint shield enables you to paint a straight edge up to glass.

KEEPING THE WINDOW OPEN

With the catch and stay removed there's nothing to stop the sash from closing. Make a stay with a length of stiff wire, hook the other end and slot it into one of the screw holes in the frame.

Temporary stay
Wind wire around a nail driven in the underside of the frame and use as a stay.

PAINTING WINDOW FRAMES

Window frames need to be painted in strict order, like doors, so that the various components will be evenly treated and so that you can close them at night. You also need to take care not to splash panes with paint or apply a crooked line around the glazing bars—the mark of poor workmanship.

Painting a casement window

A casement window hinges like a door, so if you plan to paint each side a different color, follow a procedure similar to that described for painting doors and frames.

Remove the stay and catch before you paint the window. So that you can still operate the window during decorating without touching wet paint, drive a nail into the underside of the bottom rail as a makeshift handle.

Painting sequence
First paint the muntins (**1**), cutting into the glass on both sides. Carry on with the top and bottom horizontal rails (**2**), followed by the vertical stiles (**3**). Finish the casement by painting the edges (**4**), then paint the frame (**5**).

Painting sequence for casement window ▷

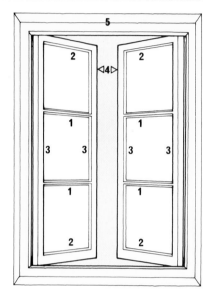

Painting a sash window

Double-hung windows are the most difficult type to paint, as the two panes slide vertically, overlapping each other.

The following sequence describes the painting of a double-hung window from the inside. To paint the outside face, use a similar procedure but start with the lower sash. When using different colors for each side, the demarcation lines are fairly obvious. When the window is closed, all the surfaces visible from one side should be the same.

Painting sequence
Raise the bottom sash and pull down the top one. Paint the bottom meeting rail of the top sash (**1**) and the accessible parts of the vertical members (**2**). Reverse the position of the sashes, leaving a gap top and bottom and complete the painting of the top sash (**3**). Paint the bottom sash (**4**), then the frame (**5**), except for the tracks in which the sashes slide.

Leave the paint to dry, then paint the inner tracks (**6**) plus a short section of the outer tracks (**7**). When painting the tracks, pull the cords aside to avoid splashing paint on them, as this will make them brittle, shortening their working life. Make sure the window slides before the paint dries.

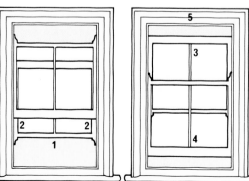

Raise bottom sash and pull down top

Reverse the position of the sashes

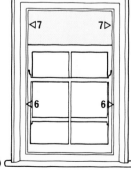

Lower both sashes for access to tracks

PAINTING WOOD TRIM

Staircase

Paint banisters first, making sure that you do not precipitate runs by stroking the brush against the edges or contoured parts. Start at the top of the stairs, painting the treads, risers and stringers ($\triangleright$) together to keep the edges of the paint fresh.

If there is any chance that the paint will not dry before the staircase is used again, paint all risers but alternate treads only. The next day, paint the remainder.

Baseboards

The only problem with painting a baseboard is protecting the floor from paint and at the same time avoid picking up dust on the wet paintbrush.

Slide strips of thin cardboard under the baseboard as a paint shield (don't use newspaper; it will tear and remain stuck to the baseboard).

PAINTING EXTERIOR SIDING

Start at the top of the wall and apply paint to one or two boards at a time. Paint the under-edge first, then the face of the boards; finish parallel with the edge. Make sure you coat exposed end grain well, as it is more absorbent and requires extra protection.

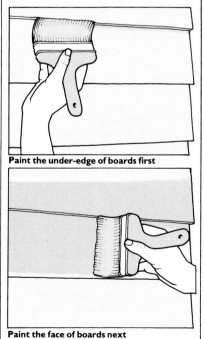

Paint the under-edge of boards first

Paint the face of boards next

GRAINING WOOD

Graining is a technique for simulating natural wood with paint. It was used extensively on cheap softwood joinery to imitate expensive hardwoods. Doors and panels can look attractive treated in this way. The basic method is simple to describe but practice on a flat board is essential before you can achieve convincing results. A skilled grainer can simulate actual species of timber, but just try to suggest ordinary wood grain rather than attempt to produce a perfect copy.

Equipment and preparation for graining

The simplest graining effects can be achieved by removing dark paint to reveal a paler base coat below. The traditional way to carry out this effect is to use a special hog's- or squirrel's-hair brush called a mottler or grainer. To compromise, try any soft-bristled paintbrush or even a dusting brush. You can also buy steel, rubber or leather combs from decorator's suppliers to achieve similar effects.

Applying a base coat (ground)

Prepare the base coat as for normal painting, finishing with a flat oil paint. It should represent the lightest color of the wood you want to reproduce and is normally beige or olive green. The base coat will look more convincing if it is slightly dull rather than being too bright.

Choosing the graining color

Translucent, flat-drying paints are produced especially for graining in a range of appropriate colors. These paints must be thinned with a mixture comprising 2 parts mineral spirits to 1 part raw linseed oil to make a graining glaze. The quantity of thinners controls the color of the graining, so add thinner to the paint sparingly until you achieve the desired result. Try the method on a practice panel before attempting it on an actual piece of woodwork.

Producing the effect

Paint an even coat of glaze onto the ground with a 2-inch paintbrush. After only two or three minutes, lightly drag the tip of the mottler or comb along the line of the rail or panel, leaving faint streaks in the glaze.

When two rails meet at right-angles, mask the joint with a piece of cardboard to prevent the simulated grain being disturbed on one rail while you paint a rail next to it.

The grain does not have to be exactly parallel with the rail. You can vary the pattern by allowing the comb or mottler to streak out the glaze at a slight angle and over the edges of some of the rails.

Let the graining dry overnight, then apply one or two coats of clear varnish to protect and seal the effects.

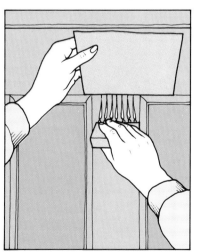

Masking meeting rails
Hold a piece of cardboard over the joint between two meeting rails—on a panel door, for instance, where muntins meet cross rails—to prevent spoiling the graining effect on one while you treat the other.

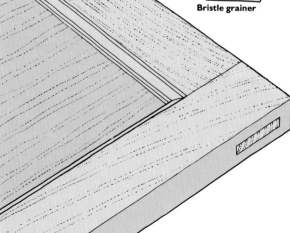

Applying graining patterns
Produce graining patterns that are as authentic as possible. Don't just run the streaks in one direction, or parallel to the timber. Simulate actual wood grain by running the pattern at an angle to the edges of the board.

SEE ALSO

Details for: $\triangleright$	
Staircases	212–214
Preparing wood	55
Painting wood	76
Varnishing wood	82

Steel graining comb

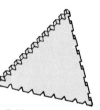

Rubber or leather comb

Bristle grainer

79

STAINING WOODWORK

Unless the wood is perfectly clean and free from grease, the stain will be rejected, producing an uneven, patchy appearance. Strip any previous finish and sand the wood with progressively finer abrasive papers, always in the direction of the grain. Scratches made across the grain will tend to be emphasized by the stain.

Testing the stain
Make a test strip (far right) to assess the depth of color of various stains before starting on the final job. Apply a band of varnish along the bottom half of the strip to see how the colors are affected.

Paint pad

Paintbrush

Making a test strip

The final color is affected by the nature of the wood, the number of coats and the overlying clear finish. You can also mix compatible stains to alter the color or dilute them with the appropriate thinner.

Make a test strip so that you will have an accurate guide from which you can choose the depth of stain to suit your purpose. Use a piece of wood from the same batch you are staining, or one that resembles it closely.

Paint the whole strip with one coat of stain. Allow the stain to be absorbed, then apply a second coat, leaving a strip of the first application showing. It is rarely necessary to apply more than two coats of stain, but for the experiment add a third and even a fourth coat, always leaving a strip of the previous application for comparison.

When the stain has dried completely, paint a band of clear varnish along the strip. Some polyurethane varnishes react unfavorably with oil-based stains, so it is advisable to use products made by the same manufacturer.

USING A RAG FOR STAIN

Wear gloves to protect your skin and pour some stain into a shallow dish. Saturate the rag with stain, then squeeze some out so that it is not dripping but still wet enough to apply a liberal coat of stain to the surface

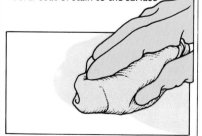

Apply stain with a rag

If you wet a piece of wood, water is absorbed by the wood, raising a mass of tiny fibers across the surface. A water-based stain will produce the same result and the final finish will be ruined. Solve the problem by sanding the wood until it is perfectly smooth, then dampen the whole surface with a wet rag. Let it dry out, then sand the raised grain with very fine abrasive paper before you apply the stain. If you are using an oil-based stain, this preliminary process is unnecessary.

If you want to fill the grain, first apply a seal coat of clear finish over the stain. Choose a grain filler that matches the stain closely, adjusting the color by adding a little stain to it, but make sure that the stain and filler are compatible. An oil-based stain will not mix with a water-based filler and vice versa, so check before you buy either.

How to apply wood stain

Use a 4-inch paintbrush to apply stains over a wide, flat surface. Do not brush out a stain like paint, but apply it liberally and evenly, always in the direction of the grain.

It is essential to blend wet edges of stain, so work fairly quickly and don't take a break until you have completed the job. If you have brushed a water-based stain onto the wood, it is sometimes advantageous to wipe over the wet surface with a soft cloth and remove excess stain.

A paint pad is one of the best applicators for achieving even coverage with wood stain over a flat surface. However, you may find that you will still need a paintbrush to get the stain into awkward corners and for contoured surfaces.

Because stains are so fluid, it's often easier to apply them with a wad of soft, lint-free rag (◁). You'll be able to control runs on a vertical panel, and it's the best way to stain turned wood and rails.

Rag

STAINING PANELS, FLOORS AND DOORS

Staining a flat panel

Whenever possible, set up a panel horizontally for staining, either on sawhorses or raised on wood blocks. Shake the container before use and pour the stain into a flat dish so that you can load your applicator properly.

Apply the stain, working swiftly and evenly along the grain. Stain the edges at the same time as the top surface. The first application may have a slightly patchy appearance as it dries because some parts of the wood will absorb more stain than others. The second coat normally evens out the color without difficulty. If powdery deposits are left on the surface of the dry stain, wipe them off with a coarse, dry cloth before applying the second coat in the same way as the first.

Let the stain dry overnight, then proceed with the clear finish of your choice to seal the colorant.

Staining floors

Because a wooden floor is such a large area, it is more difficult to blend the wet edges of the stain. Work along two or three boards at a time using a paintbrush so that you can finish at the edge of a board each time.

Parquet floors are even trickier, so try to complete one panel at a time, and use a soft cloth to blend in any overlapping areas.

Staining a door

Stain a new or stripped door before it is hung so that it can be laid horizontally. A flush door is stained just like any other panel, but use a rag carefully to color the edges so that stain does not run under to spoil the other side.

When staining a paneled door, it is essential to follow a sequence which will allow you to pick up the edges of stain before they dry. Use a combination of brush and rag to apply the stain.

Follow the numbered sequence below and note that, unlike painting a panel door, the panel moldings are stained last to prevent any overlapping from showing on the finished door. Stain the moldings carefully with a narrow brush and then blend in the color with a rag.

Method for staining a panel door
Follow this practical sequence, using a combination of paintbrush or paint pad and rag to apply the stain evenly to the various sections. Start with the inset panels first (**1**), then continue with half of the center vertical rail (**2**), the bottom cross rail (**3**) and half the stiles (**4**). Pick up the wet edges with the other half of the center vertical (**5**) and the stiles (**6**). Stain the center cross rail (**7**), then repeat the procedure for the second half of the door (**8–12**), finishing with the moldings (**13**) using a narrow brush and rag.

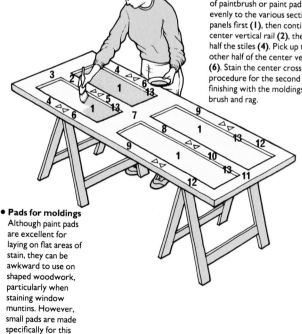

● **Pads for moldings**
Although paint pads are excellent for laying on flat areas of stain, they can be awkward to use on shaped woodwork, particularly when staining window muntins. However, small pads are made specifically for this purpose.

USING WOOD STAINS OUTDOORS

Standard wood stains are not suitable for exterior use. They have no protective properties of their own and they have a tendency to fade in direct sunlight. For surfaced timber and siding, use a microporous protective wood stain (▷). For rough-sawn lumber use a colored wood preserver. Both materials are much thinner than paint, so take care to avoid splashing.

Protective wood stain
Make sure the surface is clean, dry and sanded. All previous paint or varnish must be stripped. For blemished lumber, use an opaque wood stain so that you can fill cracks and holes. For extra protection, treat the wood with a clear wood preserver before staining.

Apply two coats with a paintbrush, making sure that the coating is even, and avoid any overlaps.

Stain lap siding one board at a time (treating the under-edge first).

Wood preserver
Before you apply wood preserver, remove surface dirt with a stiff-bristled brush. Paint or varnish must be stripped completely, but previously preserved or creosoted lumber can be treated, so long as it has weathered.

For additional protection against insect and fungal attack, treat the wood first with a clear wood preserver, either by immersion or by full brush coats (▷).

Paint a full coat of colored preserver onto the wood followed by a second coat as soon as the first has soaked in. Brush out sufficiently to achieve an even color and avoid overlaps by following immediately with the edges of boards, rails and posts.

Replacing putty
Stain will not color putty. In any case, microporous stains allow the wood to breathe, so there's likely to be some movement, which puts greater strain on the glass. For both reasons, remove the old putty (▷) and stain the frame. Seal with fresh putty or caulking (**1**).

Set lengths of stained wooden glass bead into the caulk and secure them with panel nails (**2**). You'll find it easiest to fasten the beading if you tap in the nails beforehand, so they just protrude through the other side. Remove excess caulk squeezed from beneath the beading with a putty knife (**3**).

SEE ALSO	
Details for: ▷	
Protective stains	75
Removing putty	202
Wood preservatives	252
Preparing wood	55
Sanding floors	58–59
Painting a door	77

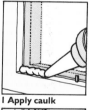
1 Apply caulk

2 Fasten bead

3 Trim excess caulk

VARNISHING WOODWORK

Varnish serves two main purposes: to protect the wood from scratches, stains and other marks, and to give it a sheen that accentuates the beautiful grain pattern. In some cases, it can even be used to change the color of the wood to that of another species—or to give it a fresh, new look with a choice of bright colors.

The effect of varnish
The example below demonstrates how different varnishes affect the same species of wood. From top to bottom: untreated birch plywood; flat clear varnish; gloss clear varnish; wood shade colored varnish; pure colored varnish.

How to apply varnish

Use paintbrushes, foam or lamb's-wool applicators to apply varnish in the same way as paint. You will need a range of sizes for general work: ½-inch, 1-inch and 2-inch are useful widths. For varnishing floors use a lamb's-wool wax applicator brush for quick coverage. With any brush, make sure it's spotlessly clean; any previous traces of paint may mar the finish.

Load a brush with varnish by dipping the first third of the bristles into the liquid, then blot off the excess on the side of the container. Don't scrape the brush across the rim of the container as it causes bubbles in the varnish, which can spoil the finish.

A soft cloth pad or rag (◁) can be used to apply the first thinned coat of varnish into the grain. It is not essential to use a rag—even for the sealing coat—but it is convenient, especially for coating shaped or turned pieces of wood.

Applying the varnish

Thin the first coat of varnish with 10 percent mineral spirits and rub it well into the wood with a cloth pad in the direction of the grain. Brush on the sealer coat where the rag is difficult to use.

Apply the second coat of varnish not less than six hours later. If more than 24 hours have elapsed, key the surface of gloss varnish lightly with fine abrasive paper. Wipe it over with a cloth dampened with mineral spirits to remove dust and grease, then brush on a full coat of varnish as for paint.

Apply a third and fourth coat if the surface is likely to take hard wear.

Using colored varnish

A wood stain can be used only on bare wood, but you can use a colored varnish to darken or alter the color of woodwork that has been varnished previously without having to strip the finish. Clean the surface with steel wool and mineral spirits mixed with a little linseed oil (◁). Dry the surface with a clean cloth, then apply the varnish.

Apply tinted varnish in the same way as the clear type. It might be worth making a test strip to see how many coats you will need to achieve the depth of color you want (◁).

Varnishing floors

Varnishing a floor is no different from finishing any other woodwork, but the greater area can produce an unpleasant concentration of fumes in a confined space. Open all windows for ventilation and wear a Type A respirator.

Start in the corner farthest from the door and work back towards it. Brush the varnish out well to make sure it does not collect in pools.

DEALING WITH DUST PARTICLES

Minor imperfections and particles of dust stuck to the varnished surface can be rubbed down with fine abrasive paper between coats. If your top coat is to be a high-gloss finish, take even more care to ensure that your brush is perfectly clean.

If you are not satisfied with your final finish, dip very fine steel wool in wax polish and rub the varnish with parallel strokes in the direction of the grain. Buff the surface with a soft cloth. This will remove the high gloss, but it leaves a pleasant sheen on the surface with no obvious imperfections.

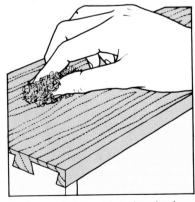

Produce a soft sheen with steel wool and wax

FRENCH POLISHING

The art of French polishing has always been considered the province of the expert, which a wise amateur would leave well alone. It is true that an expert will do a better job of the polishing and can work much faster than an amateur, but there's no reason why anyone cannot produce a satisfactory finish with a little practice.

Woodwork must be prepared immaculately before polishing, as every blemish will be mirrored in the finish. The grain should be filled, either with a proprietary filler (▷) or by layers of polish, which are rubbed down and repeated until the pores of the wood are filled flush with polish.

Work in a warm, dust-free room; dust's effect is obvious, but a low temperature will make the polish cloudy (bloom).

Work in a good light so that you can glance across the surface to gauge the quality of the finish you are applying.

Basic French polishing

Try out French polishing using one of the prepared proprietary kits available from home centers. A kit typically contains a bottle of thin shellac for building up the body of polish and a separate clear burnishing liquid.

Brush coating

Pour some shellac into a shallow dish so that you can use a brush to paint the polish onto the wood. Keep the coating even and work quickly to pick up the moist edges. Don't go over an area more than once.

Half an hour later, brush-coat the work again, then leave it for another hour. Next, lightly sand the polish with a silicone carbide paper (gray with a dry lubricant embedded in its surface) to remove any blemishes.

Building up the polish

With the workpiece set up at a comfortable working height and in good light, distribute the polish along the surface of the wood with continuous, circular strokes of a soft cloth.

There's no need to press too hard at first as a fully charged polishing cloth flows easily. As the applicator gradually dries out, increase the pressure.

Never bring the polishing cloth to rest on the surface of the polish. As you reach the edge of the workpiece, sweep the cloth off the surface and sweep it back on again for the next pass. If you pull the cloth off the workpiece it will leave a blemish in the polish.

Cover the surface, perhaps ten or twelve times. As you feel the cloth drying out, open it up and pour a little more shellac onto the back of the cotton wool filling. Occasionally change the rag for a spare one, leaving the used one to soak in a jar of denatured alcohol to wash out the polish ready for the next exchange.

Seal the polishing cloth in an empty glass jar and let the surface harden for about one hour, then if necessary, lightly flatten the polish with silicone carbide paper using fingertip pressure.

Build up another layer of polish with the cloth. Vary the size and shape of your strokes so that every part of the surface is covered (see below). In between each coat, make straight parallel strokes along the grain.

Repeat the process for a third time, more if you want a deeper color. Make your final coat with slightly less polish; allow it to harden overnight.

Burnishing the polished surface

Take a handful of clean cotton wool and dampen the sole of the pad with burnishing liquid. Use it to burnish a small section at a time, rubbing forcefully along the grain. As the sole of the pad becomes dirty, pull it off to reveal a clean surface. Buff each section with a soft cloth before burnishing the next.

TRADITIONAL FRENCH POLISHING

With traditional polishing, the shellac is thicker; therefore do not soak the rag with alcohol. Charge the rag and dab linseed oil on the sole.

Apply all the shellac with a cotton rag, using a combination of strokes (see below). Recharge the applicator and add a touch of oil to the sole when it starts to drag or catch. Let dry for twenty minutes. Repeat four or five times.

Let finish dry overnight, then build up more layers—ten may be enough, but continue until you're happy with the depth of color. To remove surface marks, rub down the hard polish with silicon carbide paper. The top layer may be streaked; add denatured alcohol to the applicator's cotton wool. Burnish with straight strokes parallel with the grain, sweeping the applicator on and off at each end. As the cloth drags, recharge. Wait a few minutes to see if the streaking disappears. If not, repeat with more solvent. Polish with a clean cloth and let harden.

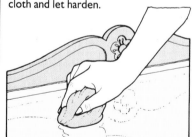

Apply French polish with a soft cotton cloth

SEE ALSO

Details for: ▷	
Grain filler	55
Preparing wood	55
French polish	75
Dust particles	82
Abrasive papers	469

Using the applicator
Apply the polish with a combination of circular and figure-eight strokes so that every part of the surface is covered. When you finish each coat, run the applicator in long straight strokes, parallel to the wood grain. Keep the pad moving constantly and smoothly; if you lift it from the surface a scar will form.

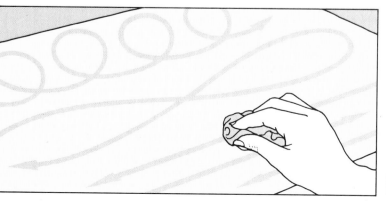

Making an applicator for basic polishing
Saturate a 1-foot square of white cotton rag with denatured alcohol, wring out until damp, dip a handful of cotton wool into the shellac and squeeze out excess. Wrap in rag, twist excess into a handgrip; smooth the sole of the applicator.

COLD CURE LACQUER

Due to its chemical composition, careful preparation is essential or plastic coating will take days to cure instead of only two hours. It must be applied to a clean, grease-free surface, which has been sanded smooth. Strip the old finish but do not use a caustic stripper, as this will react against the coating.

Clean the old wax polish from the wood. You must remove every trace, even from the pores of the wood. Wash it with mineral spirits, using a pad of fine steel wool in the direction of the grain. When the wood is dry, scrub it with water and detergent, then rinse the surface with clean water with a little white vinegar added.

If you use wood stain, make sure it is made by the manufacturer of the lacquer, otherwise it might change color. Use the same manufacturer's filler to repair cracks and holes and never use plaster or plastic fillers.

Mixing cold cure lacquer

In most cases, it's best to use a paintbrush to apply plastic coating, although you can use a plastic foam roller instead, especially for large areas of woodwork.

When you are ready to apply the lacquer, mix the coating and hardener in a glass, polyethylene or enamel container.

Use the proportions recommended by the manufacturer. Mix just enough for your immediate needs, as it will set in two to three days in an open dish. Don't be tempted to economize by pouring mixed lacquer back into its original container; the hardener will ruin any remaining substance.

Applying the lacquer

Plastic coating must be applied in a warm atmosphere. Use a well-loaded applicator and spread the lacquer onto the wood. There is no need to brush out the liquid as it will flow unaided and even a thick coat will cure thoroughly and smoothly. Plastic coating dries quickly and will begin to show brush marks if disturbed after 10 to 15 minutes, so you should work swiftly to pick up the wet edges.

After two hours, apply the second coat. If necessary, rub down the hardened lacquer with fine abrasive paper to remove blemishes, then add a third coat. You will achieve better adhesion between the layers if you can apply all the coats in one day, so long as each has time to dry.

Burnishing lacquer

If you want a mirror finish, wait for 24 hours, then use a proprietary burnishing cream. Rub down the lacquer with very fine abrasive paper or steel wool, then rub the cream onto the surface with a soft cloth. Burnish it vigorously with a clean, soft cloth to achieve the required depth of sheen.

Matting lacquer

To produce a subtle satin coat, rub the hardened lacquer along the grain with fine steel wool dipped in wax polish. The grade of the steel wool will affect the degree of matting. Use very fine 000 grade for a satin finish and a coarse 0 grade for a fully matted surface. Polish with a clean, soft cloth.

● Spontaneous combustion
It is essential to dispose of oily rags immediately as you're finished with them as they have been known to burst into flames.

SAFETY WHEN USING LACQUER

Although cold cure lacquer is safe to use, you should take care when applying it to a large surface such as a floor, due to the concentration of fumes.

Open all windows and doors if possible for ventilation—but remember the necessity for a warm atmosphere, too—and take the extra precaution of wearing a respirator to prevent your breathing in the fumes. You should be sure to get the type that filters organic vapors, and if your finishing will be extensive, get some replacement filters.

OILING AND WAXING WOODWORK

Applying the oil

Clean and prepare wood for oiling by removing previous finishes carefully so that oil can penetrate the grain.

The most efficient way to apply a finishing oil is to rub it into the wood with a soft, lint-free rag similar to a French polish applicator (◁). Don't store oily rags. Keep them in a sealed tin while the job is in progress, then unfold them and leave them outside to dry before throwing them away.

A brush is a convenient way to spread oil liberally over large surfaces and into carvings or deep moldings.

Rub or brush a generous coating of oil into the woodgrain. Leave it to soak in for a few minutes, then rub off excess oil with a clean cloth. After about six hours, coat the wood with oil once more. The next day, apply a third and final coat; raise a faint sheen by burnishing with a soft cloth.

Wax-polishing wood

If you want to wax-polish new timber, seal the wood first with one coat of clear varnish (or French polish on fine furniture). This will stop the wax from being absorbed too deeply into the wood and provides a slightly more durable finish. Before waxing an old clear finish, clean it first to remove deposits of dirt and possibly an old wax dressing.

To remove dirty wax, mix up mineral spirits with 25 percent linseed oil. Use the liquid to rub the surface quite hard with a coarse cloth. If there is no obvious improvement, try dipping very fine steel wool into the cleaner and rub in the direction of the grain. Don't press too hard as you want to remove wax and dirt only without damaging the finish below. Wash the cleaned surface with a cloth dipped in mineral spirits and leave to dry before refinishing.

You can use a soft cloth to apply wax polish, but use a paintbrush to spread liquid wax over a wide area. Pour liquid wax polish onto a cloth pad and rub it into the sealed wood with a circular motion followed by strokes parallel with the grain. Make this first coat a generous one.

Buff up the wax after one hour, then apply a second, thinner coat in the direction of the grain only. Burnish this coat lightly and leave it for several hours to harden. Bring the surface to a high gloss by burnishing vigorously with a soft cloth.

FINISHING METALWORK

Ferrous metals that are rusty will shed any paint film rapidly, so the most important aspect of finishing metalwork is thorough preparation and priming to prevent this corrosion from returning; then applying the finish is virtually the same as painting woodwork.

When you are choosing a finish for metalwork in and around the house (see chart below and table overleaf for suitable types), make sure it fulfills your requirements. Many of the finishes listed are easy to apply to metal, but the ability of some to withstand heavy wear is likely to be poor ($\triangleright$).

Methods of application

Most of the finishes suggested for use on metalwork can be applied with a paintbrush or sprayed on ($\triangleright$). In the main, use the standard techniques for painting woodwork ($\triangleright$), but bitumen-based paints should be laid on only and not brushed out like conventional coatings.

Remove metal door and window hardware for painting, suspending them on wire hooks to dry. Make sure sharp or hard edges are coated properly, as the finish can wear thin quickly.

Some paints can be sprayed but there are few situations where it is advantageous, except perhaps for intricately molded ironwork such as garden furniture, which you can paint outside; otherwise ventilation is a necessity indoors.

A roller is suitable on large flat surfaces and pipework requires its own special V-section roller ($\triangleright$), which is designed to coat curved surfaces.

SEE ALSO

Details for: $\triangleright$	
Painting woodwork	76
Metal finishes	86
Paint brushes	482
Rollers	483
Paint sprayers	484
Primers	62
Removing radiators	399

● Black dot denotes compatibility. Thorough preparation is essential before applying any finish to metals ($\triangleright$).

FINISHES FOR METALWORK

	Oil paint	Latex paint	Metallic paint	Bituminous based paint	Lacquer	Radiator enamel	Zinc-rich finish	Varnish	Epoxy paints	Nonslip paint
DRYING TIME: HOURS										
Touch-dry	4	1–2	4	1–2	½	2–6		0–3	6–10	4–6
Recoatable	14	4	8	6–24	1	7–14		1	16–24	12
THINNERS: SOLVENTS										
Water		●		●						
Mineral spirits	●		●	●	●		●	●	●	●
Special						●				
Cellulose thinners									●	
NUMBER OF COATS										
Normal conditions	1–2	2	1–2	1–3	2	1–2	VARIABLE	1–2	2	2
COVERAGE										
Sq. ft. per gallon	450–600	325–550	375–500	225–550	400	450	VARIABLE	450	450–550	100–180
METHOD OF APPLICATION										
Brush	●	●	●	●	●	●		●	●	●
Roller	●	●	●							
Spray gun	●	●	●						●	
Cloth applicator							●			

PAINTING RADIATORS AND PIPES

Let radiators and hot water pipes cool before you paint them. The only problem with decorating a radiator is how to paint the back: the best solution is to remove it completely or, if possible, swing it away from the wall, paint the back, reposition the radiator, then paint the front.

If this is inconvenient, use a special radiator brush with a long handle (see right). Use the same tool to paint in between the leaves of a double radiator. It is difficult to achieve a perfect finish even with the brush, so aim at covering areas you are likely to see when the radiator is in position rather than a complete application.

Don't paint over radiator valves or fittings or you will not be able to operate them afterwards.

Paint pipes lengthwise rather than across, or runs are likely to form. The first coat on metal piping will be streaky, so be prepared to apply two or three coats. Unless you are using radiator enamel, allow the paint to harden thoroughly before turning on the heat, or it may blister.

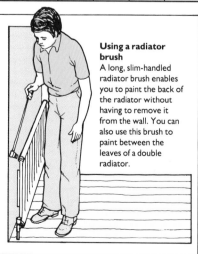

Using a radiator brush
A long, slim-handled radiator brush enables you to paint the back of the radiator without having to remove it from the wall. You can also use this brush to paint between the leaves of a double radiator.

METALWORK

SUITABLE FINISHES FOR METALWORK

Gutters and downspouts

It is best to coat the insides of gutters with a bituminous paint for thorough protection against moisture, but you can finish the outer surfaces with oil paint or latex paint.

To protect the wall behind a downspout, slip a scrap of cardboard in between while painting the back of the pipe (1).

Metal casement windows

Paint metal casement windows using the sequence described for wooden casements (◁), which allows you to close the frame at night without spoiling a freshly painted surface.

Lacquering metalwork

Polish the metal to a high gloss, then use a nail brush to scrub it with warm water containing some liquid detergent. Rinse the metal in clean water, then dry it thoroughly with an absorbent cloth.

Use a large, soft artist's brush to paint on acrylic lacquer (2), working swiftly from the top. Let the lacquer flow naturally, working all around the object to keep the wet edge moving.

If you do leave a brush stroke in partially set lacquer, do not try to overpaint it. Finish the job, then warm the metal (by standing it on a radiator if possible). As soon as the blemish disappears, remove the object from the heat and allow it to cool gradually in a dust-free atmosphere.

Oiling cast iron

Oil dressing produces an attractive finish for cast iron. It is not a permanent or durable finish and will have to be renewed periodically. It may transfer if rubbed hard.

The material is supplied in a toothpaste-like tube. Squeeze some of the oil onto a soft cloth and spread it onto the metal. Use an old toothbrush (3) to scrub it into decorative ironwork for best coverage.

When you have covered the surface, buff the surface to a satin sheen with a clean, dry cloth. Build up a patina with several applications of oil dressing for a moistureproof finish.

1 Protect wall
Use cardboard behind a pipe when painting behind it.

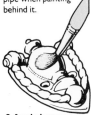

2 Apply lacquer
Use a large, soft artist's paintbrush.

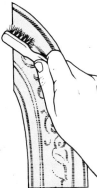

3 Apply oil dressing
Scrub dressing into intricate surfaces using an old toothbrush.

OIL PAINT

Standard oil paints are perfectly suitable for metal. Having primed the surface, interior metalwork will need at least one undercoat plus a top coat. Add an extra undercoat for greater protection of exterior metalwork.

LATEX PAINT

Strictly, latex paint is not suitable for finishing metal. Being water-based, it may promote corrosion on ferrous metals if applied directly; it can be used to paint radiators to match the wall color if the metal has been factory-painted.

METALLIC PAINT

For a metal-like finish, choose a paint containing aluminum, copper, gold or bronze powders. These paints are water-resistant and are able to withstand very high temperatures—up to about 212 degrees F.

BITUMINOUS PAINT

Bitumen-based paints give economical protection for exterior storage tanks and piping. Standard bituminous paint is black, but there is also a limited range of colors, plus modified bituminous paint, which contains aluminum.

Before coating the insides of water tanks, make sure the paint is noncontaminating. Don't apply over other types of paint.

SECURITY PAINT

Nonsetting security paint, primarily for rainwater and waste downpipes, remains slippery to prevent intruders from scaling the wall via the pipe. Restrict it to pipework over about 6 feet above the ground, out of reach.

RADIATOR ENAMEL

A heat-resistant acrylic paint which is applied in two thin coats, it can be used over latex or oil paints so long as these have not been recently applied (don't rub them down first).

Apply a compatible metal primer over new paint or factory priming to prevent strong solvents in the enamel from reacting with the previous coating. A special thinner is required for brush cleaning. A choice of satin and gloss finishes is available.

Finish the radiator in position, then turn the heat on (boiler set to maximum) for a minimum of two hours to bake the enamel onto the metal. Apply a second coat six to eight hours later.

Also use radiator enamel to repaint boiler cabinets, refrigerators, ranges and washing machines.

OIL DRESSING

A cream used to color cast ironwork, it is a mixture of graphite and waxes. After several coats it is moistureproof, but it is not suitable for exterior use.

LACQUERS

Virtually any clear lacquer can be used on polished metalwork without spoiling its appearance. Polyurethanes yellow with age. An acrylic lacquer is clear and will protect chrome plating, brass and copper—even outside.

NONSLIP PAINT

Designed to provide good foot-holding on a wide range of surfaces, including metal, nonslip paint is ideal for painting metal spiral staircase treads and exterior fire escapes. The surface must be primed before application.

INTERIOR PANELING

Walls that are in poor condition—except those that are damp—can be covered with paneling to conceal them and to provide a decorative surface. Paneling can be practical in other ways, too, if used in conjunction with insulation. There are various types of decorative paneling for walls, notably solid wood planking and decorative sheet panels with various patterns.

Tongue-and-groove boards

Solid wooden paneling is made from planks with a tongue along one edge and a matching groove on the other. This provides a way to attach the boards to the wall and allows movement in the wood—due to the atmosphere—to prevent splitting. The meeting edges of some planks—called tongued, grooved and V-jointed (TGV) boards—are machined to produce a decorative V-shaped profile, accentuating the shape of each board. Other types have more decorative profiles. Shiplap has a rabbet on the back face, which holds down the front edge of the next board.

A few hardwoods are available as paneling but the majority of paneling is made from softwood, typically pine, redwood and cedar. Rough-sawn fir is sometimes used for paneling.

Buy boards in one batch
Make sure you buy enough boards to complete the work. If you have to use a few boards from another batch, the machine used to shape the tongues and grooves may not be set to exactly the same tolerances, and the joints won't fit.

Sheet paneling

A wider choice of paneling exists in the form of manufactured sheets. They are made to various standard sizes and in thicknesses ranging from 3/16 to 1/4 inch.

Plywood or hardboard panels are faced with real veneers or paper printed to simulate wood grain, and there are plastic-faced boards in various colors. Typical surfaces include embossed brick, stone, plaster or tiled effects as well as a random V-grooved panel like solid wood boards.

Wall panels made from wood fiber board are 1-inch thick and can sometimes be bought with cork, grass and fabric surfaces, which are sound- and heat-insulating.

CONSTRUCTING A NAILING BASE FOR PANELING

If a wall is flat you can glue thick wallboards directly to the surface, but as most walls are fairly uneven, it is usually better to nail furring strips to an existing wall surface to provide a nailing base. For TGV and thin wallboards, this is the only practical solution. You can nail any type of paneling directly to the studs of a stud partition wall (▷).

Before you start, carefully pry off the baseboards, picture rails and other trim, so that you can reuse these on the paneling, if required. If you are installing paneling on a solid wall, erect the framework using 1 × 2-in. furring strips.

Line an external wall with a polyethylene vapor barrier before attaching the furring strips, to prevent condensation. The simplest way to do this is to tack the polyethylene sheets to the wall using staples, then secure them with the furring.

You can also insulate the wall by sandwiching a layer of fiberglass insulation meterial or polystyrene sheets between it and the paneling. If you do this, fix the polyethylene vapor barrier over the furring strips.

The furring should be nailed 16 inches apart with 2-inch nails, masonry nails or screws and wallplugs. Use a builder's level to align each strip with its neighbor to produce a vertical, flat plane. Shim out hollows with cardboard or wood shingles.

Panels are fixed vertically to the framework, but TGV boards can be arranged in a variety of patterns— vertically, horizontally, diagonally, or even in a zigzag fashion for a really individual effect.

To fix vertical TGV paneling, run the furring strips horizontally. The lowest strip should be level with the top of the baseboard with short vertical strips below it for fixing the new baseboard to. For horizontal boards, run the furring strips from floor to ceiling. Nail scraps of paneling to the bottom of the strips as spacers to support the baseboard at the new level. Stagger the butt joints between boards on alternate rows. Fix diagonal boards to strips running horizontally and stagger the joints also.

To fasten sheet panels, center vertical furring strips on the edges of each sheet. Fill in with horizontal strips spaced 16 inches apart.

Details for: ▷
Stud partition   136–137
Insulation   269

SEE ALSO

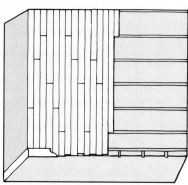

1 Vertical TGV paneling with furring strips running horizontally and short strips for base.

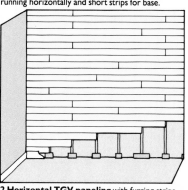

2 Horizontal TGV paneling with furring strips set vertically and panel scraps for baseboard.

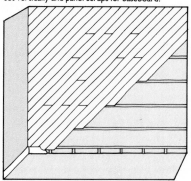

3 Diagonal TGV paneling with furring strips set horizontally. Stagger joints on alternate rows.

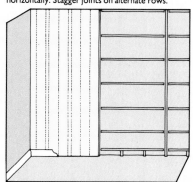

4 Panels need vertical furring strips at the edges and horizontal strips between.

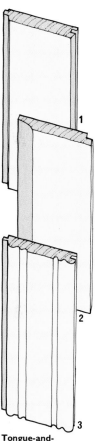

Tongue-and-groove paneling
Solid wood tongue-and-groove planks are sold in various lengths and widths. Prepacked kits of TGV boards are also available. Various profiles are made: tongued, grooved and V-jointed (**1**), shiplap (**2**), molded TGV (**3**).

87

ATTACHING STRIP WOOD PANELING

Nailing vertical paneling

Mark out and cut the boards to length, using a crosscut saw. Sand all the boards before fastening (unless they're in a kit). With the grooved edge against the left-hand wall, plumb the first board with a level. Nail it to the furring through the center of the face, using 1¼-inch panel nails. Use 1½-inch nails when nailing directly to studs.

Slide the next board onto the tongue—protect the edge while you tap it in place with a hammer. Nail the board to the furring using the "blind nailing" technique. Drive nails through the inner corner of the tongue at an angle (**1**). Sink the head below the surface with a nail set. Slide on the next board to hide the nails, and repeat to cover the wall.

Use up short lengths of paneling by butting them end to end over a furring strip, but stagger such joints across the wall to avoid a continuous line.

When you reach the other end of the wall, cut the last board down its length (using a jigsaw or circular saw for accuracy) to fit the gap. Nail it through the face. If it is a tight fit, spring the last two boards in at the same time. Slot them together, slip the last board's groove onto the exposed tongue, then push both into the wall. Nail a small quarter-round molding down the edges, nail the baseboard in place and fit a molding to trim the top edges of the boards.

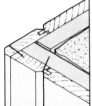

Inside corners
Scribe a butt joint using a block of wood and a pencil, then plane a chamfer on one board. Nail the chamfered board to the furring strips through its face. The detail is identical for either vertical or horizontal boards.

1 Vertical panels

2 Horizontal panels

Outside corners
To join vertical panels, lap one board with another and nail together. Plane a bevel on the outer corner (**1**). For horizontal panels, nail on a beveled molding to cover the end grain (**2**).

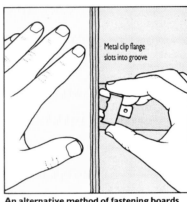

Horizontal furring

Apply boards tongue outwards

1 Blind nailing

Baseboard nailers

Applying vertical TGV boards

An alternative method of fastening boards

Metal clip flange slots into groove

Metal clips

Some prepacked boards are attached to the furring with metal clips which slip into the groove of a board, leaving a tab which takes the nail. With this type of fastener, plane the tongue from the first board and place that edge against the left-hand side walls (or the ceiling). The clips are concealed by the next board.

Fastening horizontal paneling

Follow the same procedure as for vertical paneling but position the first board just below baseboard level, with its groove at the bottom.

Paneling around doors and windows

Remove the casing and sill casing and nail furring strips (**1**) close to the frame. Fasten the paneling (**2**) and cover the edge with a thin wooden strip (**3**) so that it is flush with the inner face of the frame. Refit the moldings (**4**) on top of the paneling.

Adapting the moldings ▷
Follow the numbered sequence to adapt moldings around doors and windows.

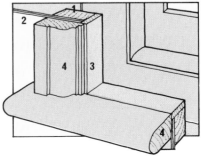

DEALING WITH ELECTRICAL BOXES

Socket outlets and light switches must be brought forward to the new wall surfaces. If they are surface-mounted, simply panel around the box to create a flush mount. If they're flush-mounted already, you'll either have to convert them to surface-mounted types or bring them forward and set them flush with the new wall surface.

Flush-mounted boxes
Turn off the power at the panel (◁), then unscrew the faceplate and draw it away from the wall. Remove the screws that attach the metal mounting box to the wall. There should be enough slack in the cable for you to pull the box flush with the new wall surface (**1**), or mount to the wall finish using metal box mounting flanges intended for use on drywall (◁).

To do this, fur out around the box but allow for a narrow margin of paneling all round. Fit the flanges, then screw on the faceplate; the flanges pull it against the margin.

You can also buy mounting boxes for fastening in this situation; these need no separate flanges (◁).

Surface-mounted fittings
Nail short furring strips on each side of the cable to take the screws holding the box to the wall (**2**). Drill a hole in the paneling, pass the cable through and screw the mounting box over it. Wire and fit the faceplate (◁).

If you don't want to surface-mount the box, frame it with short furring strips nailed to the wall, then cut the paneling to fit around it.

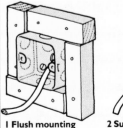

1 Flush mounting   **2 Surface mounting**

Paneling a ceiling

It is relatively straightforward to panel a ceiling with TGV boards, following the methods described for paneling a wall. First locate the joists (◁), then nail or screw the furring strips across them.

ATTACHING SHEET PANELING

Nailing sheet paneling

Scribe the first board to the left-hand side wall and ceiling. Cut the boards with a circular saw, face side up to avoid splitting the grain.

Use a block to hold the panel off the floor (▷) and nail it through the grooves. Tap the nails just below the surface with a fine nail set to make them ready for filling later.

Butt-join subsequent panels. The edges are beveled to make a matching V-groove. Cut the last board to fit against the opposite wall, then fit wood or plastic and moldings.

Gluing on wallboards

Hardboard paneling can be nailed to the furring strips, but nail heads may spoil the appearance. For a better result, use a proprietary panel adhesive to glue the boards to the furring. If the panels are narrower than standard wallboards, reduce the spacing of the furring strips accordingly.

Fit the first sheet to the wall and ceiling. Use a sharp knife to cut the panel. Follow the manufacturer's instructions to apply the glue. Some recommend applying it in patches and some in continuous bands before pressing the panels in place. Strike the edges with the side of your fist to spread the glue.

Contact adhesive can also be used to fix the panels. Apply the adhesive to the strips, then press the board against the furring; peel it off again to leave glue on both surfaces. Wedge a furring strip under the bottom edge to maintain its position relative to the wall. When the glue is touch-dry, press the panel in place again for an immediate bond.

Pin outside corners
Nail softwood blocks to one furring strip to support the edges of the board. Add adhesive to the blocks, then pin the boards along a groove. Bevel the boards at the corner and stain the core.

Pin inside corners
Butt-join the wallboards at an inside corner. For neatness, you can conceal the joint by gluing a matching cover strip into the angle.

Using contact adhesive
Glue strips, press on board, then peel off; refit when touch-dry.

Glue outside corners
Cut a V-shaped groove in the back of the board, leaving the facing intact. Fold it around to make a mitered joint, then glue to the furring strips.

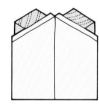

Glue inside corners
Cut through the wallboard as far down as the face material, then fold it—face to face—to fit the corner and glue to the furring strips.

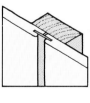

Joining grooved boards
Some boards are grooved along the vertical edges to accept a spline joint strip. Nail or staple along the joint covering the nails with the spline.

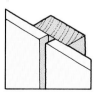

Butt-joining boards
Square-edged boards can be butt-joined or left with a slight reveal between; stain or paint the furring strip behind as a decorative feature of the panels.

Fitting a batten strip
The third method of concealing the joints between panels is to leave a slight gap between butted boards and glue on a rounded batten strip.

REPRODUCTION PANELING

Period solid-timber paneling was an important part of older houses' decorative character and, unless it's in poor condition, is worth preserving (▷). If you don't have any existing paneling but feel that it would enhance your room's decor, reproduction versions are available. There are two basic types. One comprises panels molded from originals in rigid urethane foam; the other consists of veneer-faced panels which you attach to the wall with molded urethane foam channels.

Fitting urethane paneling
Reproduction paneling in rigid form usually comprises standard components:

● **Panels** molded from rigid urethane foam come in various sizes, from about 3¾ × 6½ inches to 11½ × 18 inches, with many intermediate sizes. Face designs are typically linenfold (resembling a fold of fabric) or floral. Panels can be stuck directly to the wall with contact cement. Some have tongue-and-groove edges.

● **Rails and stiles** come in lengths of about 10 feet; they're used to frame doors and windows or to finish the edge of paneling. Some panels require cover strips, which may be grooved to take a tongued panel, to conceal joints.

With some urethane paneling it's necessary to frame the wall with rabbeted edging strips, then stick on the panels within them, covering the joints with cover strips.

Veneered timber paneling
Oak-faced plywood, ¼ inch thick, is available from many lumberyards and gives a more realistic appearance and texture. Cut into panels to suit the size and proportions of your walls, it is fixed with rigid foam rails and stiles that are cut from the same section supplied in 8- and 10-foot lengths, and have a rabbet on each side to hold a panel against the wall.

When a rail is needed to surround a door or window or to finish an edge of paneling, the beaded rabbet is sawn off to leave a square edge.

Ply panels are fastened from one end of the room by nailing stiles, rails and panels in sequence to a bed of panel adhesive. The stiles must be noticed to take the ends of the rails, which must be mitered, and a jig is sold with the battens.

● **Shiplap paneling**
Shiplap boards are normally used outside but there is no reason why you cannot use them to panel an interior. To attach them, start at baseboard level with the rabbet at the bottom (or left-hand side wall). Position the next board and nail it through the face just above the rabbet.

WALLCOVERINGS

Although wallcoverings are often called "wallpaper," only a proportion of the wide range available is made solely from wood pulp. There is a huge range of paper-backed fabrics from exotic silks to coarse hessians; other types include natural textures such as cork or woven grass on a paper backing. Plastics have widened the choice of wallcoverings still further. There are paper- or cotton-backed vinyls, and plain or patterned foamed plastics. Before wallpaper became popular, fabric wall hangings were used to decorate interiors and this is still possible today, using unbacked fabrics glued or stretched across walls.

Ensuring a suitable surface

Although many wallcoverings will cover minor blemishes, walls and ceilings should be clean, sound and smooth. Eradicate moisture and organic growth before hanging any wallcovering. Consider whether you should size the walls to reduce paste absorption (◁).

COVERINGS THAT CAMOUFLAGE

Although a poor surface should be repaired, some coverings hide minor blemishes as well as provide a foundation for other finishes.

Expanded polystyrene sheet
Thin polystyrene sheet is used for lining a wall before papering. It reduces condensation but will also bridge hairline cracks and small holes. Polystyrene dents easily, so don't use it where it will take a lot of punishment. A patterned ceiling version is made.

Lining paper
A cheap, buff-colored wallpaper for lining uneven or impervious walls prior to hanging a heavy or expensive wallcovering. Can also provide an even surface for latex paint.

Woodchip paper
Woodchip or ingrain paper is a relief covering made by sandwiching particles of wood between two layers of paper. It's inexpensive, easy to hang (but a problem to cut), and must be painted.

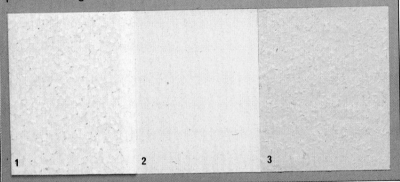

Relief papers ▷
Relief papers, with a deeply embossed pattern, are for hiding minor imperfections and for over-painting.

Anaglypta is made by bonding two sheets of paper together, which then pass between embossing rollers. A stronger version, *Supaglypta*, is made using cotton fibers instead of wood pulp, and withstands deeper embossing.

The raised pattern on *Lincrusta* is a solid film of linseed oil and fillers fused onto a backing paper before the pattern is applied by an engraved steel roller. Deep-relief wallcoverings are made from vinyl—notably *Vinaglypta*—either as solid plastic, or it is heated in an oven, which expands the vinyl, embossing it. Relief vinyls are intended to be painted over.

◁ **Printed wallpapers**
One advantage of ordinary wallpaper is the superb range of printed colors and patterns, which is much wider than for any other covering. Most papers—the cheapest—are machine-printed.

Hand-printed papers are more costly. Inks have a tendency to run if you smear paste on the surface, are prone to tearing when wet, and are not really suitable for walls exposed to wear or condensation. Pattern matching can be awkward, because hand printing isn't as accurate as machine printing.

Washable papers

Ordinary printed papers with a thin, impervious glaze of PVA to make a spongeable surface, washables are suitable for bathrooms and kitchens. The surface must not be scrubbed or the plastic coating will be worn away.

Vinyl wallcoverings

A base paper, or sometimes a cotton backing, is coated with a layer of vinyl upon which the design is printed. Heat is used to fuse the colors and vinyl. The result is a durable, washable wallcovering ideally suited to bathrooms and kitchens. Many vinyls are sold ready-pasted for easy application.

Foamed polyethylene coverings

A lightweight wallcovering made solely of foamed plastic with no backing paper. It is printed with a wide range of patterns, colors and designs. You paste the wall instead of the covering. It is best used on walls that are not exposed to wear.

Flock wallcoverings

Flock papers have the major pattern elements picked out with a fine pile produced by gluing synthetic or natural fibers (such as silk or wool) to the backing paper, so that they stand out in relief, with a velvetlike texture.

Standard flocks are difficult to hang, as paste will ruin the pile. Vinyl flocks are less delicate, can be hung anywhere, and may even be ready-pasted.

You can sponge flock paper to remove stains, but brush to remove dust from the pile. Vinyl flocks can be washed without risk of damage.

Foil wallcoverings

Paper-backed foils are coated with a metallized plastic film to give a shiny finish. They are expensive but come in a range of beautiful contrasting textures (overprinted designs allow the foil to show through). Foils should not be used on uneven walls, as the shine will highlight imperfections.

Glass fiber wallcovering

Woven glass fiber fabric is a durable fire-resistant wallcovering that will bridge minor irregularities. After 24 hours, the fabric can be painted.

Grass cloth

Natural grasses are woven into a mat, which is glued to a paper backing. These wallcoverings are very attractive but fragile and difficult to hang.

Cork-faced paper

A wallpaper surfaced with thin sheets of colored or natural cork, which is not as easily spoiled as other special papers.

Paper-backed fabrics

Finely woven cotton, linen or silk on a paper backing must be applied to a flat surface. They are expensive, not easy to hang, and you must avoid smearing the fabric with adhesive. Most fabrics are delicate but some are plastic-coated to make them scuff-resistant.

Unbacked fabrics

Upholstery-width fabric—typically hessian—can be wrapped around panels and glued to the wall.

Left to right
1 Washable papers
2 Vinyls
3 Foamed polyethylene
4 Flock papers
5 Foil papers
6 Glass fiber
7 Cork-faced papers
8 Paper-backed fabrics
9 Unbacked fabrics
10 Grass cloth mats

WALLCOVERINGS: ESTIMATING QUANTITIES

Calculating the number of rolls of wallcoverings you will need to cover your walls and ceiling depends on the size of the roll—both length and width—the pattern repeat and the obstructions you have to avoid. Because of variations in color between batches, you must take into account all these points—and allow for waste, too. A standard roll of wallcovering will cover approximately 36 square feet of wall surface. Use the two charts on this page to estimate how many rolls you will need for walls and ceilings.

Estimating nonstandard rolls

If the wallcovering is not cut to a standard size, calculate the amount you need in this way:

Walls

Measure the height of the walls from baseboard to ceiling. Divide the length of the roll by this figure to find the number of wall lengths you can cut from a roll.

Measure around the room, excluding windows and doors, to work out how many widths fit into the total length of the walls. Divide this number by the number of wall lengths you can get from one roll to find how many rolls you need. Make an allowance for short lengths above doors and under windows.

Ceilings

Measure the length of the room to determine the length of one strip of paper. Work out how many roll widths fit across the room. Multiply the two figures. Divide the answer by the length of a roll to find out how many rolls you need. Check for waste and allow for it.

Checking for shading

If rolls of wallcovering are printed in one batch, there should be no problem with color-matching one roll to another. When you buy, look for the batch number printed on the wrapping.

Make a visual check before hanging the covering, especially for hand-printed papers or fabrics. Unroll a short length of each roll and lay them side by side. You may get a better color match by changing the rolls around, but if color difference is obvious, ask for a replacement roll.

Some wallcoverings are marked "reverse alternate lengths" in order to even out any color variations. Take this into account when checking.

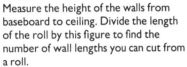

Measuring walls for standard rolls
You can include windows and doors in your estimate.

Measuring walls for nonstandard rolls
Do not include doors and windows when estimating for expensive materials. Allow for short lengths afterwards.

Walls:
Standard rolls
Measure your room, then look down height column and across wall column to assess number of standard rolls required.

MEASUREMENT IN FEET AROUND WALLS INCLUDING DOORS AND WINDOWS	7'-0" to 7'-6"	7'-6" to 8'-0"	8'-0" to 8'-6"	8'-6" to 9'-0"	9'-0" to 9'-6"	9'-6" to 10'-0"	10'-0" to 10'-6"	10'-6" to 11'-0"
WALLS	**NUMBER OF ROLLS REQUIRED FOR WALLS**							
30	7	7	8	8	8	9	9	9
32	7	8	8	8	9	9	10	10
34	8	8	9	9	9	10	10	11
36	8	8	9	9	10	10	11	11
38	8	9	9	10	11	11	11	12
40	9	9	10	10	11	12	12	13
42	9	10	10	11	12	12	13	13
44	10	10	11	11	12	13	13	14
46	10	11	11	12	13	13	14	15
48	10	11	12	12	13	14	14	15
50	11	12	12	13	14	14	15	16
52	11	12	13	13	14	15	16	16
54	12	12	13	14	15	15	16	17
56	12	13	14	14	15	16	17	18
58	13	13	14	15	16	17	17	18
60	13	14	15	15	16	17	18	19
62	13	14	15	16	17	18	19	19
64	14	15	16	16	17	18	19	20
66	14	15	16	17	18	19	20	21
68	15	16	17	17	18	19	20	21
70	15	16	17	18	19	20	21	22
72	15	16	17	18	19	20	21	22
74	16	17	18	19	20	21	22	23
76	16	17	18	19	21	22	23	24
78	17	18	19	20	21	22	23	24
80	17	18	19	20	22	23	24	25
82	18	19	20	21	22	23	24	26
84	18	19	20	21	23	24	25	26
86	18	20	21	22	23	24	26	27
88	19	20	21	22	24	25	26	27
90	19	20	22	23	24	25	27	28
92	20	21	22	23	25	26	27	28
94	20	21	23	24	25	27	28	29
96	20	22	23	24	26	27	28	30
98	21	22	24	25	26	28	29	30
100	21	23	24	25	27	28	30	31
102	22	23	25	26	27	29	30	32
104	22	24	25	26	28	29	31	32
106	23	24	26	27	28	30	31	33
108	23	24	26	27	29	30	32	34
110	23	25	26	28	30	31	33	34

HEIGHT OF ROOM IN FEET FROM BASEBOARD

Ceilings:
Standard rolls
Number of standard rolls required is shown next to overall room dimensions.

CEILINGS: NUMBER OF ROLLS REQUIRED

Measurement around room (ft.)	Number of rolls	Measurement around room (ft.)	Number of rolls	Measurement around room (ft.)	Number of rolls	Measurement around room (ft.)	Number of rolls
34	2	44	4	54	6	64	8
36	3	46	4	56	6	66	8
38	4	48	4	58	6	68	9
40	3	50	5	60	7	70	9
42	4	52	5	62	7	72	9

Dimensions
All dimensions are shown in ft.

TRIMMING AND CUTTING TECHNIQUES

Most wallcoverings are already machine-trimmed to width so that you can butt-join adjacent lengths accurately. Some hand-printed papers and speciality coverings are left untrimmed. These are usually expensive, so don't attempt to trim them yourself; ask the supplier to do this for you—it's worth the slight additional cost.

Cutting plain wallcoverings

To cut a plain paper to length, measure the height of the wall at the point where you will hang the first strip. Add an extra 4 inches for trimming top and bottom. Cut several pieces from your first roll to the same length and mark the top of each one.

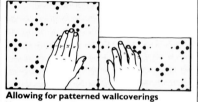

Allowing for patterned wallcoverings
You may have to allow extra on alternate lengths of patterned wallcoverings to match patterns. Check before you cut your second length.

CHOOSING PASTE

Most wallpaper pastes are supplied as powder or flakes for mixing with water. There are several specific types:

Wheat paste

Standard adhesive preferred for untreated, vinyl-coated, cloth-backed and grass cloths.

Cellulose paste

Also for common wallcoverings, natural fabrics such as silk, hemp and burlap.

Fungicidal paste

Most pastes contain a fungicide to prevent mold growth under certain impervious wallcoverings, which slows down the drying rate of the paste. It is essential to use a fungicidal paste when hanging vinyls, washable papers, foils and foamed plastic coverings.

Vinyl adhesive

For vinyls, foils, flocks and leathers. Available in powdered form to be added to water or premixed.

PASTING WALLCOVERINGS

You can use any wipe-clean table for pasting, but a narrow fold-up pasting table is a good investment if you are doing a lot of decorating. Lay several cut lengths of paper on top of each other face-down on the table to keep them clean. Tuck the ends under a length of string tied loosely round the table legs to stop the paper from rolling up while you past it.

Applying the paste

Use a large, soft wall brush or paint roller to apply the paste. Mix the paste in a plastic bucket and tie string across its rim to support the brush, keeping its handle clean while you work.

Align the covering with the far edge of the table (so you don't get paste on the table), then transfer it to the face of the wallcovering. Apply the paste by brushing away from the center. Paste the edges and remove any lumps.

If you prefer, apply the paste with a short-piled paint roller; pour the paste into a roller tray. Roll in one direction only—toward the end of the paper.

Pull the covering to the front edge of the table and paste the other half. Fold the pasted end over—don't press it down—and slide the length along the table to expose an unpasted part.

Paste the other end, then fold it over to almost meet the first cut end. The second fold is invariably deeper than the first, a good way to denote the bottom of patterned wallcoverings. Fold long drops concertina-fashion.

Leave the pasted covering to soak, draped over a broom handle spanning two chair backs. Some heavy or embossed coverings may need to soak for 15 minutes: let one length soak while you hang another. Vinyls and lightweight papers can be hung immediately.

Pasting the wall

Hang exotic wallcoverings by pasting the wall, to reduce the risk of marking their delicate faces. Apply a band of paste just wider than the width of covering so that you will not have to paste right up to its edge for the next length. Use a brush or roller.

Ready-pasted wallcoverings

Many wallcoverings come precoated with adhesive, activated by soaking a cut length in a trough of cold water (▷). Mix ordinary paste to recoat dry edges.

SEE ALSO

Details for: ▷
Ready-pasted
wallcoverings   96
Wallcoverings   90–91

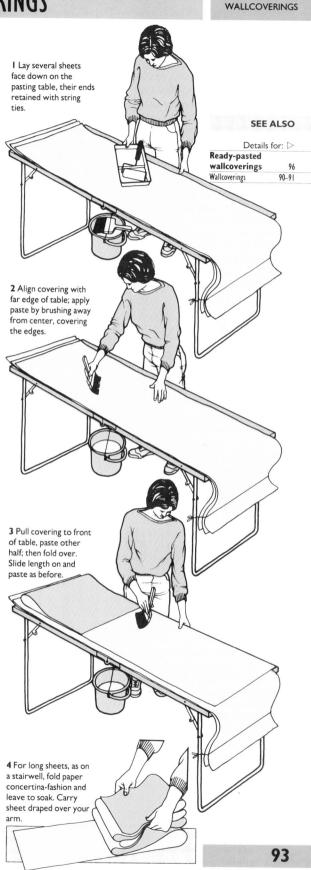

1 Lay several sheets face down on the pasting table, their ends retained with string ties.

2 Align covering with far edge of table; apply paste by brushing away from center, covering the edges.

3 Pull covering to front of table, paste other half; then fold over. Slide length on and paste as before.

4 For long sheets, as on a stairwell, fold paper concertina-fashion and leave to soak. Carry sheet draped over your arm.

93

LINING A WALL

Lining a wall prior to decorating is necessary only if you are hanging embossed or luxury wallcoverings, or if the wall is uneven and imperfections might show through a thin paper. Lining paper is hung horizontally so that the seams cannot align with those in the top layer. Work from right to left if you are right-handed, vice versa if you are left-handed.

Mark a horizontal line near the top of the wall, one roll width from the ceiling. Holding the concertina-folded length in one hand, start at the top right-hand corner of the wall, aligning the bottom edge with the marked line. Smooth the paper onto the wall with a paper-hanger's brush, working from the center towards the edges.

Work along the wall gradually, unfolding the length as you do so. Take care not to stretch or tear the wet paper. Use the brush to gently stipple the edge into the corner at each end.

Use the point of a pair of scissors to lightly mark the corner, peel back the paper and trim to the line. Brush the paper back in place. You may have to perform a similar operation along the ceiling if the paper overlaps slightly. Work down the wall, butting each strip against the last, or leave a tiny gap between the lengths.

Trim the bottom length to the baseboard. Leave the lining paper to dry out for 24 hours before covering.

Lining prior to painting

If you line a wall for latex painting, hang the paper vertically as for other wallcoverings, as the seams will be minimally visible.

● **Hide a mismatch in a corner**
When you are using a wallcovering with a large pattern, try to finish in a corner where you will not notice if the pattern does not match.

Sticking down the edges
Ensure that the edges of the paper adhere firmly by running a seam roller along the butt joint.

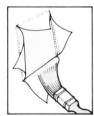

Repairing air bubbles
Slight blistering usually flattens out as wet paper dries and shrinks slightly. If you find that a blister remains, either inject a little paste through it and roll it flat, or cut across it in two directions, peel back the triangular flaps and paste them down.

94

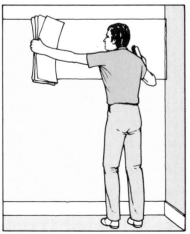

Hanging lining paper horizontally
Hold the concertina-folded paper in one hand and smooth onto the wall from top right, butting strips.

PAPERING A WALL

Where to start

Don't apply wallcovering until all the woodwork has been painted or varnished (◁). Start by painting or papering the ceiling (◁).

The traditional method for papering a room is to hang the first length next to a window close to a corner, then work in both directions away from the light, but you may find it easier to paper the longest uninterrupted wall to get used to the basic techniques before tackling corners or obstructions.

If your wallcovering has a large regular pattern, center the first length over the fireplace for symmetry. You could center this first length between two windows, unless you will be left with narrow strips each side, in which case it's best to butt two lengths on the centerline.

Center a large pattern over fireplace

Or butt two lengths between windows

Hanging on a straight wall

The walls of an average room are rarely truly square, so use a plumb line to mark a vertical guide against which to set the first length of wallcovering. Start at one end of the wall and mark the vertical line one roll width away from the corner, minus ½ inch so the first length will overlap the adjacent wall.

Allowing enough wallcovering for trimming at the ceiling, unfold the top section of the pasted length and hold it against the plumbed line. Using a paperhanger's brush, work gently out from the center in all directions to squeeze out any trapped air.

When you are sure the paper is positioned accurately, mark the ceiling line with back edge of your scissors blade, peel back the top edge and cut along the crease. Smooth the paper back and stipple it down carefully with the brush. Unpeel the lower fold of the paper, smooth it onto the wall with the brush, then stipple it firmly into the corner. Trim the bottom edges against the baseboard, peel away, trim and brush back against the wall.

Hang the next length in the same way. Slide it with your fingertips to align the pattern and produce a perfect butt joint. Wipe excess paste with a damp cloth. Continue to the other side of the wall, allowing the last sheet to overlap the adjoining wall by ½ inch.

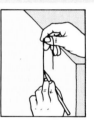

1 Mark first length
Use a roll of paper to mark the wall one width away from the corner—less ½ inch for an overlap onto the return wall—then draw a line from ceiling to baseboard using a plumb line.

2 Hang first sheet
Cut the first sheet of paper, allowing about 2 inches at each end for trimming, paste and allow to soak. Hang the top fold against the plumbed line and brush out from the center, working down.

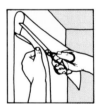

3 Trim at ceiling
When the paper is smoothly brushed on, run the back edge of your scissors along the ceiling angle, peel away the paper, cut off the excess, then brush back onto the wall.

4 Trim at baseboard
Hang the lower fold of paper. At the baseboard, tap your brush gently into the top edge, peel away the paper and cut along the folded line with scissors, then brush back.

PAPERING PROBLEM AREAS

Papering around doors and windows

Hang the length next to a door frame, brushing down the butt joint to align the pattern, but allow the other edge to loosely overlap the door.

Make a diagonal cut in the excess towards the top corner of the frame **(1)**. Crease the waste along the frame with scissors, peel it back, trim it off, then brush it back. Leave a ½-inch strip for turning onto the top of the frame. Fill in over the door.

Butt the next full length over the door and cut the excess diagonally into the frame so that you can paste the rest of the strip down the side of the door. Mark and cut off the waste.

When papering up to flush window frames, treat them like a door. Where a window is set into a reveal, hang the length of wallcovering next to the window and allow it to overhang the opening. Make a horizontal cut just above the edge of the window reveal. Make a similar cut near the bottom, then fold the paper around to cover the side of the reveal. Crease and trim along the window frame and sill.

Cut a strip of paper to match the width and pattern of the overhang above the window reveal. Paste it, slip it under the overhang and fold it around the top of the reveal **(2)**. Cut through the overlap with a smooth, wavy stroke, remove the excess paper and roll down the seam **(3)**.

To continue, hang short lengths on the wall below and above the window, wrapping top lengths into the reveal.

Papering around a fireplace

Paper around a fireplace as for a door. Make a diagonal cut in the waste overlapping the fireplace, up to the edge of the mantel shelf, so that you can tuck the paper in all around for creasing and trimming to the surround.

To cut to an ornate surround, paper the wall above the surround; cut strips to fit under the mantel at each side, turning them around the corners of the chimney breast. Gently press the wallcovering into the molding, peel it away and cut around the impression using nail scissors. Brush the paper back.

Papering inside and outside corners

Turn an inside corner by marking another plumbed line so that the next length of paper covers the overlap from the first wall. If the piece you trimmed off at the corner is wide enough, use it as your first length on the new wall.

To turn an outside corner, trim the last length so that it wraps around it, lapping the next wall by about 1 inch. Plumb and hang the remaining strip with its edge about ½ inch from the corner.

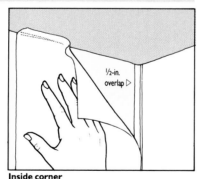

Inside corner

Papering behind radiators

If you can't remove a radiator, turn off the heating and allow it to cool. Use a steel tape to measure the positions of the brackets holding the radiator to the wall. Transfer these measurements to a length of wallcovering; slit it from the bottom up to the top of the bracket. Feed the pasted paper behind the radiator, down both sides of the brackets. Use a radiator roller to press it to the wall (▷). Crease and trim to the baseboard.

Papering around switches and sockets

Turn off the electricity at the panel (▷). Hang the wallcovering over the switch or socket. Make diagonal cuts from the center of the plate to each corner. Trim off the waste, leaving ¼ inch all around.

Loosen the faceplate, tuck the margin behind and retighten it. Don't switch the power back on until the paste is dry. Don't use foil papers for this; the metallic surface can conduct electricity.

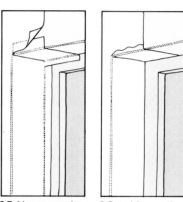

1 Cut the overlap diagonally into the frame

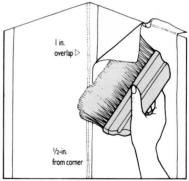

2 Fold onto reveal top   3 Cut with wavy line

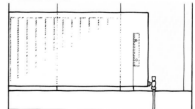

Outside corner

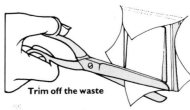

Slit to top of bracket behind radiator

Trim off the waste

SEE ALSO

Details for: ▷	
Service panel	291, 319
Radiator roller	483
Preparing plaster	54
Wallcoverings	90–91

- **Papering archways**
Arrange strips to leave even gaps between arch sides and the next full-length strips. Hang strips over face of arch, cut curve, leaving 1 inch extra. Fold it onto underside, snipping into extra to prevent creasing. Fit a strip on the underside to reach from floor to top of arch. Repeat on opposite side of arch.

- **Trimming foils around electrical fixtures**
Make diagonal cuts (see left), but crease the waste against the fixture and trim off with a sharp knife when the paste has dried.

STAIRWELLS

The only problem with papering a stairwell is the extra long sheets on the side walls. You will need to build a safe work platform over the stairs (◁). Plumb and hang the longest sheet first, lapping the head wall above the stairs by ½ inch.

Carrying the long drops of wallcovering—sometimes as much as 15-feet long—is awkward; paste the covering liberally so it's not likely to dry out while you hang it, then fold it concertina-fashion. Drape it over your arm while you climb the platform. You'll need a helper to support the weight of the pasted length while you apply it. Unfold the flaps as you work down.

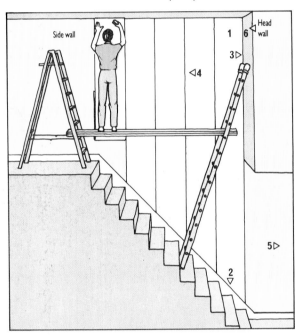

Papering sequence
Follow this sequence for papering a stairwell.
1 Hang the longest sheet.
2 Crease it into the angled baseboard and cut.
3 Lap the paper onto the head wall.
4, 5 Work away from the first sheet in both directions.
6 Paper the head wall.

Crease and cut the bottom of the paper against the angled baseboard. Don't forget—when you first cut the length—to allow for this angle; work to the longest edge measurement. Work away from this first length in both directions, then hang the head wall.

Where the banister rail is let into the stairwell wall, try to arrange the rolls so that the rail falls between the two butted sheets. Hang the sheets to the rail and cut horizontally into the edge of the last strip at the center of the rail, then make radial cuts so the paper can be molded around the rail. Crease the flaps, peel away the wallcovering and cut them off. Smooth the covering back.

Hang the next sheet at the other side of the rail, butting it to the previous piece, and make similar radial cuts.

SPECIAL TECHNIQUES FOR WALLPAPERING

Whatever you are using as a wallcovering, follow the standard wallpapering techniques as explained previously. However, there are some additional considerations and special techniques involved in using certain types of wallcovering, as explained below and opposite.

RELIEF WALLCOVERINGS

When hanging *Anaglypta*, line the wall first and use a heavy-duty paste. Apply the paste liberally and evenly but try not to leave too much paste in the depressions. Allow it to soak for 10 minutes. *Supaglypta* will need 15 minutes soaking time.

Don't use a seam roller on the joints; tap the paper gently with a paperhanger's brush to avoid flattening the embossed pattern.

Don't turn a relief wallcovering around corners. Measure the distance from the last sheet to the corner and cut your next length to fit. Trim and hang the cutoff to meet at the corner. Fill outside corners with cellulose filler once the paper has dried thoroughly.

To use *Lincrusta*, sponge the back with hot water until it is thoroughly soaked. Apply the paste and hang the length, rubbing it down with a felt or rubber roller.

Use a sharp knife and straightedge to trim *Lincrusta*. Treat the corners with filler as for *Anaglypta*.

VINYL WALLCOVERINGS

Paste paper-backed vinyls in the normal way, but cotton-backed vinyl hangs better if you paste the wall and let it become tacky before applying the wallcovering. Use fungicidal paste.

Hang and butt-join lengths of vinyl using a sponge to smooth them onto the wall rather than a brush. Crease a length top and bottom, them trim it to size with a sharp knife.

Vinyl will not stick to itself, so when you turn a corner, use a knife to cut through both pieces of paper where they overlap. Peel away the excess and rub down the vinyl to produce a perfect butt joint.

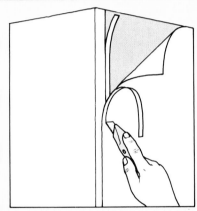
Cut through overlap and remove excess

READY-PASTED WALLCOVERINGS

Place a trough of cold water next to the baseboard at the position of the first sheet. Roll a cut length loosely from the bottom with the pattern on the outside. Immerse the roll in the trough for the prescribed time, according to the manufacturer's instructions.

Take hold of the cut end and lift the paper, allowing it to unroll naturally, draining the surface water back into the trough at the same time.

Hang and butt-join the coverings in the usual way—use a sponge to apply vinyls, but use a paperhanger's brush for other coverings.

Hanging a long, wet length can be difficult if you follow the standard procedure. Instead, roll the length from the top with the pattern outermost. Place it in the trough and immediately reroll it through the water. Take it from the trough in roll form and drain excess water. Hang it by feeding from the roll as you proceed.

Pull paper from trough and hang on the wall

SPECIAL TECHNIQUES FOR WALLPAPERING

METALLIC FOILS

The acid content of old paste may discolor metallic foil papers, so coat either the paper or the wall with fresh fungicidal paste.

FLOCK PAPER

Protect the flocking with a piece of lining paper and remove air bubbles with a paperhanger's brush. Cut through both thicknesses of overlapped joints and remove the surplus; press back the edges to make a neat butt joint.

FOAMED POLYETHYLENE

Foamed polyethylene can be hung straight from the roll onto a pasted wall. Sponge in place and trim it top and bottom with scissors.

FABRICS AND SPECIAL COVERINGS

Try to keep paste off the face of paper-backed fabrics and any other special wallcoverings. There are so many different coverings, so check with the supplier as to which paste to use.

So you don't damage a delicate surface, use a felt or rubber roller to press in place or stipple with a brush.

Most fabric coverings will be machine-trimmed but if the edges are frayed, overlap the joints and cut through both thicknesses; then peel off the waste to make a butt joint. Make a similar joint at a corner.

Many fabrics are sold in wide rolls; even one cut length will be heavy and awkward to handle. Paste the wall, then support the rolled length on a pole between two stepladders. Work from the bottom upwards.

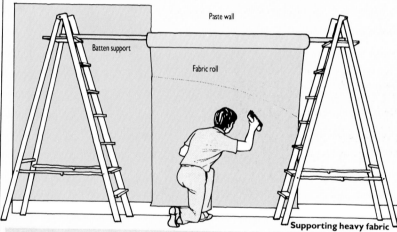
Paste wall
Batten support
Fabric roll
Supporting heavy fabric

FIBERGLASS WALLCOVERINGS

Hang fiberglass coverings by applying the special adhesive to the wall with a roller. Hang and butt the lengths, then use a spatula to smooth the covering from the center outwards (or use a felt or rubber roller).

Crease and trim fiberglass as for ordinary wallcoverings, or use a knife and straightedge. Leave the glue to set for 24 hours, then paint. When the first coat has dried, lightly rub down to remove raised fibers, then recoat.

EXPANDED POLYSTYRENE

Paint or roll special adhesive onto the wall. Hang the covering straight from the roll, smooth gently with the flat of your hand, then roll over it lightly with a dry paint roller.

If the edge is square, butt adjacent sheets. If it is crushed or crumbled, overlap the joint and cut through both thicknesses with a sharp trimming knife, peel away the cutoffs and rub the edges down. Unless the edges are generously glued, they will curl apart. Trim top and bottom with a knife and straightedge. Allow the adhesive to dry for 72 hours, then hang the wallcovering using a thick fungicidal paste.

UNBACKED FABRICS

If you want to apply a plain-colored, medium-weight fabric, you can glue it directly to the wall. However, it is easy to stretch an unbacked fabric so that aligning a pattern is difficult.

For more control, stretch the fabric onto ½-inch thick panels of lightweight insulation board (you'll then have the added advantage of insulation and a pin-board). Stick the boards directly onto the wall.

Using paste

Test a scrap of the fabric first to make sure that the adhesive will not stain it. Use a ready-mixed paste and roll it onto the wall.

Wrap a cut length of fabric around a cardboard tube (from a carpet supplier) and gradually unroll it on the surface, smoothing it down with a dry paint roller. Take care not to distort the weave. Overlap the seams but do not cut through them until the paste has dried, in case the fabric shrinks. Repaste and close the seam.

Press the fabric into the ceiling line and baseboard and trim away the excess with a sharp trimming knife when the paste has set.

Making wall panels

Cut the insulation board to suit the width of the fabric and the height of the wall. Stretch the fabric across the panel, wrap it around the edges, then use latex adhesive to stick it to the back. Hold it temporarily with thumbtacks while the adhesive dries.

Either use wallboard adhesive to glue the panels to the wall or nail them, tapping the nail heads through the weave of the fabric to conceal them.

SEE ALSO

Details for: ▷	
Preparing plaster	54
Preparing tiles	60
Wallcoverings	90–91
Papering tools	484–485

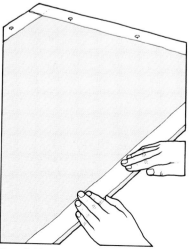
Stretch fabric over insulation board

97

PAPERING A CEILING

Papering a ceiling isn't as difficult as you may think. The techniques are basically the same as for papering a wall, except that the sheets are usually longer and more unwieldy to hold while you brush the paper into place. Set up a sensible work platform—it's virtually impossible to work by moving a single stepladder along— and enlist a helper to support the pasted, folded paper while you position one end, and progress backwards across the room. If you've marked out the ceiling first with guidelines to ensure the strips are applied straight, the result should be faultless.

Setting out the ceiling

Arrange your work platform (▷) before you begin to plan out the papering sequence for the ceiling. The best type of platform to use is a special-purpose decorator's trestle, but you can manage with a scaffold board spanning between two stepladders.

Now mark the ceiling to give a visual guide to positioning the strips of paper. Aim to work parallel with the window wall and away from the light, so you can see what you are doing and so that the light will not highlight the seams between strips. If the distance is shorter the other way, hang the strips in that direction for ease.

Mark a guide line along the ceiling, one roll-width minus ½ inch from the side wall, so that the first strip of paper will lap onto the wall.

Putting up the paper

Paste and fold the paper as for wallcovering, concertina-fashion (◁), drape it over a spare roll and carry it to the work platform. You'll certainly find it easier if you get a helper to hold the folded paper, giving you both hands free for brushing into place.

Hold the strip against the guide line, using a brush to stroke it onto the ceiling. Tap it into the wall angle, then gradually work backwards along the scaffold board, brushing on the paper as your helper unfolds it.

If the ceiling has a crown molding, crease and trim the paper at the ends. Otherwise, leave it to lap the walls by ½ inch so that it will be covered by the wallcovering. Work across the ceiling in the same way, butting the lengths of paper together. Cut the final strip to roughly the width, and trim into the wall angle.

There are usually few obstructions on a ceiling to make papering difficult—unlike walls, which have doors, windows and radiators to contend with. The only problem areas occur where there's a pendant light fixture or decorative plaster.

Cutting around a pendant light

Where the paper passes over a ceiling rose, cut several triangular flaps so that you can pass the light fixture through the hole. Tap the paper all around the rose with a paperhanging brush and continue to the end of the strip. Return to the rose and cut off the flaps with a knife.

Papering around a centerpiece

If you have a decorative plaster centerpiece, work out the position of the strips so that a joint will pass through the middle. Cut long flaps from the side of each piece of paper so that you can tuck it in all around the plaster molding.

Working from a ladder
If you have to work from a stepladder, an assistant can support the paper on a cardboard tube taped to a broom.

Papering a ceiling
The job is so much easier if two people work together.
1 Mark guide line on ceiling.
2 Support folded paper on tube.
3 Brush on paper, from center outwards.
4 Overlap covered by wallpaper.
5 Use two boards to support two people.

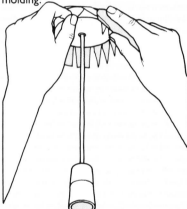

Cut off triangular flaps when paste is dry

Cut long strips to fit around molding

CHOOSING TILES

Tiling is a universally popular method of decorating a surface, with an almost inexhaustible range of colors, textures and patterns to choose from depending on the degree of durability required. Tiling provides the facility of finishing a surface with small, regular units which can be cut and fitted into an awkward shape far easier than sheet materials.

Glazed ceramic tiles

Hard ceramic tiles, usually glazed and fired, are made for walls and floors. Unglazed tiles are available but only to provide a surer grip for flooring. A textured surface reduces the risk of accidents where a floor might become wet. All ceramic tiles are durable and waterproof, but be sure to use special heat- and frost-resistant tiles where appropriate. Do not use wall tiles on the floor, as they cannot take the weight of traffic or furniture.

The majority of tiles are square but dimensions vary according to use and the manufacturer's preference.

Rectangular and more irregular-shaped tiles are available. Typical shapes include hexagons, octagons, diamonds and interlocking units with curved elaborate edges. Other units include slim rectangles with pointed or slanted ends. Use them in combination to produce patterned floors and walls.

Mosaic tiles

Mosaic tiles are small versions of the standard ceramic tiles. To lay them individually would be time-consuming and lead to inaccuracy, so they are usually joined by a paper covering, or a mesh background, into larger panels. Square tiles are common but rectangular, hexagonal and round mosaics are also available. Because they are small, mosaics can be used on curved surfaces and will fit irregular shapes better than large ceramic tiles.

Quarry tiles

Quarry tiles are thick, unglazed ceramic tiles used for floors which need a hard-wearing, waterproof surface. Colors are limited to browns, reds, black and white. Machine-made tiles are regular in size and even in color but handmade tiles are variable, producing a beautiful mottled effect. Quarry tiles are difficult to cut so do not use them where you will have to fit them against a complicated shape. Rounded-edge quarry tiles can be used as treads for steps, and a floor can be finished with bullnose tiles as a baseboard.

Stone and slate flooring

A floor laid with real stone or slate tiles will be exquisite but expensive. Sizes and thicknesses will vary according to the manufacturer—some will even cut to measure. A few materials are so costly that you should consider hiring a professional to lay them; otherwise treat cheaper ones like quarry tiles.

SEE ALSO	
Details for: ▷	
Choosing color/ pattern	24–25, 29
Repairing concrete	49
Preparing plaster	54
Leveling wood floors	61

Standard tile sections
A range of sections is produced for specific functions:

Field tile for general tiling with spacing lugs molded onto them.

Bullnose tile for edging the field.

ACR 4640 with two adjacent rounded edges.

Universal tile with two glazed, square edges for use in any position.

Tile selection
The examples shown left are a typical cross-section of commercially available ceramic tiles.
1 Glazed ceramic
2 Shape and size variation
3 Mosaic tiles
4 Quarry tiles
5 Slate and stone

CHOOSING TILES

Stone and brick tiles

Thin masonry facing tiles can be used to simulate a stone or brick wall as a feature area for a chimney breast, for example, or to clad a whole wall. Stone tiles are typically made from reconstituted stone in molds, and most look unconvincing as an imitation of the real thing. Color choice is intended to reflect local stone types, and is typically white, gray or buff. Some "weathered" versions are also made.

Brick tiles look much more authentic. The best ones are actually brick "slips"—slivers cut from kiln-produced bricks. A very wide range of traditional brick colors is available.

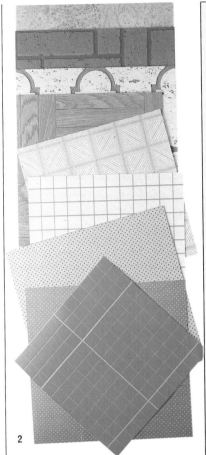

2

Vinyl tiles

Vinyl tiles are among the cheapest and easiest floorcoverings to use. Vinyl can be cut easily, and so long as the tiles are firmly glued, with good joints, the floor will be waterproof. However, it will still be susceptible to scratching. A standard coated tile has a printed pattern between a vinyl backing and a harder, clear vinyl surface. Solid vinyl tiles are made entirely of hard-wearing plastic. Some vinyl tiles have a high proportion of mineral filler. As a result, they are stiff and must be laid on a perfectly flat base. Unlike standard vinyl tiles, they will resist some moisture in a concrete subfloor. Most tiles are square or rectangular but there are interlocking shapes and hexagons. There are many patterns and colors to choose from, including embossed vinyl which represents ceramic, brick or stone tiling.

Left to right
1 Brick tiles
2 Vinyl floor tiles

CARPET TILES

Carpet tiles have advantages over wall-to-wall carpeting. There is less to fear when cutting a single tile to fit and, being loose-laid, worn, burnt or stained tiles can be replaced instantly. However, you can't substitute a brand new tile several years later, as the color will not match. Buy several spares initially and swap them around regularly to even out the wear and color change. Most types of carpet are available as tiles, including cord, loop and twist piles in wool as well as a range of man-made fibers. Tiles are normally plain in color, but some are patterned to give a striking grid effect. Some tiles have an integral rubber underlayment.

A selection of carpet tiles
Tiles are used extensively for commercial carpeting, but they are equally suitable as a hard-wearing floor covering in the home.

1

CHOOSING TILES

Polystyrene tiles
Although expanded polystyrene tiles will not reduce heat loss from a room by any significant amount, they will deter condensation as well as mask a ceiling in poor condition. Polystyrene cuts easily so long as the trimming knife is very sharp. For safety in case of fire, choose a self-extinguishing type and do not overpaint with an oil paint. In many locales, polystyrene is banned altogether for use indoors under prevailing fire code restrictions.

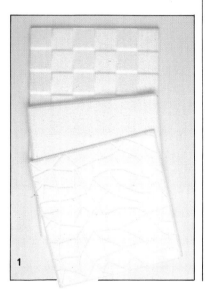

1

Mirror tiles
Square and rectangular mirror tiles can be attached to walls with self-adhesive pads in each corner. There is a choice of silver, bronze or smoke gray finish. Don't expect tiles to produce a perfect reflection unless they are mounted on a really flat surface.

Mineral fiber tiles
Ceiling tiles made from compressed mineral fiber are dense enough to be sound- and heat-insulating. They often have tongue-and-groove edges so that, once stapled to the ceiling, the next interlocking tile covers the fasteners. Fiber tiles can also be glued directly to a flat ceiling. A range of textured surfaces is available.

2

Metal tiles
Lightweight pressed metal tiles are fixed in the same way as mirror tiles. Choose from aluminum, bronze and gold colored tiles with satin or bright finishes. These tiles are not grouted so do not use them where food particles can gather in the crevices.

3

4

Rubber tiles
Soft rubber tiles were originally made for use in shops and offices, but they are equally suitable for the home, being hard-wearing yet soft and quiet to walk on. The surface is usually studded or textured to improve the grip. Choice is limited to a few plain colors.

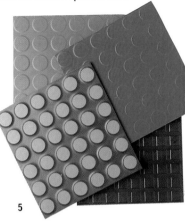

5

SEE ALSO	
Details for: ▷	
Choosing color/	
pattern	24–25, 29
Repairing concrete	49
Repairing plaster	54
Leveling wood	
floors	61
Wall tiling	102–106

Cork tiles
Cork is a popular covering for walls and floors. It is easy to lay with contact adhesive and can be cut to size and shape with a knife. There's a wide range of textures and warm colors to choose from. Presanded but unfinished cork will darken in tone when you varnish it. Alternatively, you can buy ready-finished tiles with various plastic and wax coatings. Soft, granular insulating cork is suitable as a decorative finish for walls only. It crumbles easily, so should not be used where it will be exposed on outside corners.

6

Left to right
1 Polystyrene tiles
2 Mineral fiber tiles
3 Mirror tiles
4 Metal wall tiles
5 Rubber tiles
6 Cork floor tiles

PREPARING FOR WALL TILES

Setting out
The setting out procedure described on this page is applicable to the following tiles: cork, mosaics, ceramic, mirror, metal.

Whatever tiles you plan to use, the walls must be clean, sound and dry. You cannot tile over wallpaper, and flaking or powdery paint must be treated first to give a suitably stable base for the tiles. It's important that you make the surface as flat as possible so the tiles will stick firmly. Setting out the prepared surface accurately is a vital aid to hanging the tiles properly.

MAKING A GAUGE STICK

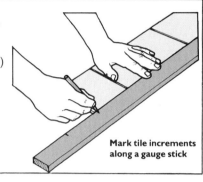

First make a gauge stick (a tool for plotting the position of tiles on the wall) from a length of 1 × 2-inch furring. Lay several tiles along it, butting together those with lugs, or add spacers for square-edged tiles, unless they're intended to be close-butted. Mark the position of each tile on the softwood stick.

Mark tile increments along a gauge stick

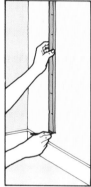

Using a gauge stick
Hold a homemade gauge stick firmly against the wall and mark the positions of the tiles on the surface.

Setting out a plain wall

On a plain uninterrupted wall, use the gauge stick to plan horizontal rows starting at baseboard level. If you are left with a narrow strip at the top, move the rows up half a tile-width to create a wider margin. Mark the bottom of the lowest row of whole tiles. Temporarily nail a thin guide to the wall aligned with the mark (**1**). Make sure it is horizontal by placing a level on top.

Mark the center of the wall (**2**), then use the gauge stick to set out the vertical rows at each side of it. If the border tiles are less than half a width, reposition the rows sideways by half a tile. Use a level to position a guide stick against the last vertical line and nail it (**3**).

Plotting a half-tiled wall

If you are tiling part of a wall only—up to a chair rail, for instance—set out the tiles with a row of whole tiles at the top (**4**). This is even more important if you are using bullnose tiles which are used for the top row of a half-tiled wall.

Setting out for tiling
Plan out the tiling arrangement on the walls as shown right, but first plot the symmetry of the tile field with a gauge stick to ensure a wide margin all around.
1 Temporarily fix a horizontal guide at the base of the field.
2 Mark the center of the wall.
3 Gauge from the mark, then fix a vertical guide to indicate the side of the field.
4 Start under a chair rail with whole tiles.
5 Use a row of whole tiles at sill level.
6 Place cut tiles at back of a reveal.
7 Support tiles over window while they set.

Arranging tiles around a window

Use a window as your starting point so that the tiles surrounding it are equal and not too narrow. If possible, begin a row of whole tiles at sill level (**5**), and position cut tiles at the back of a window reveal (**6**). Fix a guide stick over a window to support the rows of tiles temporarily (**7**).

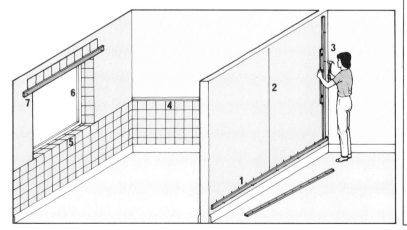

RENOVATING TILES

A properly tiled surface should last for many years, but the appearance is often spoiled by one or two damaged tiles, discolored grouting on ceramic tiles or lifting or curling of cork, vinyl or polystyrene tiles. Most of these problems can be solved fairly easily.

Renewing the grouting
It's necessary to rake out old, cracked grouting. Use a beer can opener to clean all loose or damaged grout from between the joints.

Select among the available grouts—standard type or latex, powdered or premixed, white or colored. Wipe fresh grout over the tiled surface with a sponge. Use an ice cream stick to force new grout into the joints.

After letting the grout set for the prescribed period, clean away the excess with a wet sponge, rinsing it frequently. Allow the grout to dry fully, then wipe off the powdery residue with a soft, dry cloth.

Brush on the liquid colorant (supplied in red, white, blue, green, beige or brown), following the lines of the grout which must be clean and dry. After about an hour, wet the area with a sponge, leave it for three minutes, then wipe excess colorant from the tiles. The liquid bonds with the grout to provide a water-resistant finish which can be polished with a dry cloth.

Replacing a cracked ceramic tile
Scrape the grout from around the damaged tiles, then use a fine cold chisel to carefully chip out the tile, working carefully from the center.

Scrape out the remains of the adhesive and vacuum the recess. Butter the back of the replacement tile with adhesive and press it firmly in place. Wipe off excess adhesive, allow it to set, then renew the grouting.

Lifting a cork or vinyl floor tile
Try to remove a single tile by chopping it out from the center with a wood chisel. If the adhesive is firm, try warming the tile with a clothes iron.

Scrape the floor clean of old adhesive and try the new tile for fit. Trim the edges if necessary. Spread adhesive on the floor, then place one corner of the tile in position. Gradually lower it into the recess. Spread the tile with your fingertips to squeeze out any air bubbles, place a heavy weight on it and leave overnight.

TILING A WALL: CERAMIC TILES

Choosing the correct adhesive

Most ceramic tile adhesives are sold ready-mixed, although a few need to be mixed with water. Tubs or packets will state the coverage.

Standard adhesive is suitable for most applications, but use a waterproof type in areas likely to be subjected to running water or splashing. If the tiles are to be laid on a wallboard, use a flexible adhesive and make sure it is heat resistant for worktops or around a fireplace. Some adhesives can also be used for grouting the finished wall.

A notched plastic spreader is usually supplied with each tub, or you can use a serrated trowel.

Hanging the tiles

Spread enough adhesive on the wall to cover about 3 square feet. Press the teeth of the spreader against the surface and drag it through the adhesive so that it forms horizontal ridges (1).

Press the first tile into the angle formed by the guide sticks (2) until it is firmly stuck, then butt up tiles on each side. Build up three or four rows at a time. If the tiles do not have lugs, place matchsticks, thick cardboard or plastic spacers between them to form the grout lines. Wipe away adhesive from the surface with a damp sponge.

Spread more adhesive and tile along the guide until the first rows of whole tiles are complete. From time to time, check that your tiling is accurate by holding a straightedge and level across the faces and along the top and edge. When you have completed the entire field, scrape adhesive from the border and allow it to set before removing the setting-out guides.

Grouting tiles and sealing joints

Use a ready-mixed paste called grout to fill the gaps between the tiles. Standard grout is white, gray or brown, but there is also a range of colored grouts to match or contrast with the tiles. Alternatively, mix pigments with dry, powdered grout before adding water to match any color.

Waterproof grout is essential for showers and bath surrounds, and you should use an epoxy-based grout for worktops to keep them germ-free.

Leave the adhesive to harden for 24 hours, then use a rubber-bladed squeegee or plastic scraper to press the grout into the joints (3). Spread it in all directions to make sure all joints are well filled.

Wipe grout from the surface of the tiles with a sponge before it sets and smooth the joints with a blunt-ended stick—a dowel will do.

When the grout has dried, polish the tiles with a dry cloth. Do not use a tiled shower for about seven days to let the grout harden thoroughly.

Sealing around bathroom fixtures

Don't use grout or ordinary filler to seal the gap between a tiled wall and shower pan, bath or basin; the fixtures can flex enough to crack a rigid seal, and frequent soakings will allow water to seep in, create stains and damage the floor and wall. Use a silicon rubber caulking compound to fill the gaps; it remains flexible enough to accommodate any movement.

Sealants are sold in a choice of colors to match popular tile and bathroom fixture colors. They come in tubes or cartridges and fill gaps up to ⅛ inch wide; over that, pack gaps with soft rope or twists of soaked newspaper.

If you're using a tube, trim the end off the plastic nozzle and press the tip into the joint at an angle of 45 degrees. Push forward at a steady rate while squeezing the tube to apply a bead of sealant. Smooth any ripples with the back of a wetted teaspoon.

If you're using a cartridge, again, snip the end off the angled nozzle—the amount you cut off dictates the thickness of the bead—and use the container's finger-action dispenser to squirt out the sealant (4).

Alternatively, use ceramic trim tiles to edge a bath or shower unit, or glue on a plastic trim strip.

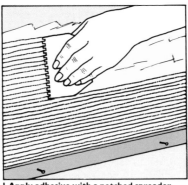

1 Apply adhesive with a notched spreader

2 Stick first tile in angles of guide sticks

3 Press grout into joints with squeegee

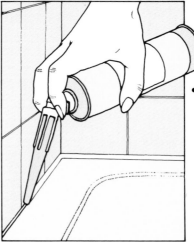

4 Seal between tiles and fixtures with caulk

SEE ALSO

Details for: ▷

Preparing plaster	54
Ceramic tiles	99
Tiling tools	485

Ceramic coving tiles

Bead
Used to fill the joint between bath and wall.

Mitered trim
Use at the end if you want to turn a corner.

Bullnose bead
Use this tile to finish the end of a straight run.

● **Tiling around pipes and fittings**
Check with the gauge stick how the tiles will fit around socket outlets and switches, pipes and other obstructions. Make slight adjustments to the position of the main field to avoid difficult shaping around these features.

CUTTING CERAMIC TILES

Having finished the main field of tiles you will have to cut the ceramic tiles to fill the border and to fit around obstructions such as window frames, electrical fixtures, *pipes and the basin. Making straight cuts is easy using a tile cutter, but shaping tiles to fit curves takes practice. There are a number of ways to do it.*

Cutting thin strips

A tile cutter is the most accurate way to cut a thin strip cleanly from the edge of a tile. If you do not want to use the strip itself, nibble away the waste a little at a time with pliers or special tile nibblers.

Tile cutter
A worthwhile investment if you're cutting a lot of tiles, a tile cutter incorporates a device for measuring and scoring tiles. The cutter is drawn down the channel of the adjustable guide. The tile is snapped with a special pincer-action tool.

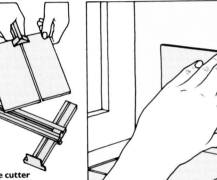

Tiling around a window

Tile up to the edges of a window, then stick bullnose tiles to the reveal to lap the edges of surrounding tiles. Fill in behind the edging tiles with cut tiles.

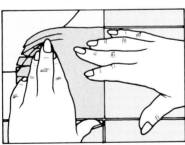

Cutting a curve

To fit a tile against a curved shape, cut a template from thin cardboard to the exact size of a tile. Cut "fingers" along one edge; press them against the curve to reproduce the shape. Transfer the curve onto the face of the tile and score the line freehand. Nibble away the waste a little at a time using pliers or a tile nibbler and smooth the edge with a silicone carbide abrasive.

Mark two edges   **Cut and fit tile**

Fitting around a pipe

Mark the center of the pipe on the top and side edges of a tile and draw lines across the tile from these points. Where they cross, draw around a coin or something slightly larger than the diameter of the pipe.

Make one straight cut through the center of the circle and either nibble out the waste, having scored the curve, or clamp it in a vise, protected with wood blocks, and cut it out with a saw file—a thin rod coated with hard, abrasive particles which will cut in any direction. Stick one half of the tile on each side of the pipe.

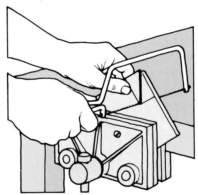

Fitting around a socket or switch

In order to fit around a socket or switch you may have to cut the corner out of a tile. Mark it from the socket then clamp the tile in a vise, protected with wood blocks. Score both lines then use a saw file to make one diagonal cut from the corner of the tile to where the lines meet. Snap out both triangles.

If you have to cut a notch out of a large tile, cut down both sides with a hacksaw then score between them and snap the piece out of the middle.

CUTTING BORDER TILES

It's necessary to cut border tiles one at a time to fit the gap between the field tiles and the adjacent wall. Walls are rarely true square and the margin is bound to be uneven.

Making straight cuts

Mark a border tile by placing it face down over its neighbor with one edge against the adjacent wall (1). Make an allowance for normal spacing between the tiles. Transfer the marks to the edge of the tiles using a felt-tip pen.

Use a proprietary tile scorer held against a straightedge to score across the face with one firm stroke to cut through the glaze (2). You may have to score the edge of thick tiles.

Stretch a length of thin wire across a panel of chipboard, place the scored line directly over the wire and press down on both sides to snap the tile (3).

Alternatively, use a tile cutter, which has a wheel to score the tile and jaws to snap it along the line. If you're doing a lot of tiling, invest in a tile cutter. The jig will hold the tile square with a cutting edge; pressing down on the guide snaps the tile cleanly. Some cutters include a device for measuring border tiles, too.

Smooth the cut edges of the tile with a tile sander or small slipstone (◁).

1 Mark the edge tile

2 Score the marked line

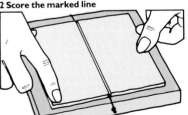

3 Snap the tile over a wire

HANGING OTHER WALL TILES

Mosaic tiles

Ceramic mosaic tiles are applied to a wall in a similar way to large square tiles. Set out the wall (▷) and use the same adhesive and grout.

The mesh backing on some sheets is pressed into the adhesive. The facing paper on other sheets is left intact on the surface until the adhesive sets.

Fill the main area of the wall, spacing the sheets to equal the gaps between individual tiles. Place a carpet-covered board over the sheets and tap it with a mallet to set the tiles into the adhesive.

Fill borders by cutting strips from the sheet. Cut individual tiles to fit into awkward shapes and around fixtures. If necessary, soak off the facing paper with a damp sponge and grout the tiles (▷).

Setting mosaics
Set tiles by tapping a carpet-covered board.

Mirror tiles

Set out the wall with guide sticks (▷) but avoid using mirror tiles in an area which would entail complicated fittings, as it is difficult to cut glass except in straight lines. Mirror tiles are fixed, close-butted, with self-adhesive pads. No grout is necessary.

Peel the protective paper from the pads and lightly position each tile. Check its alignment with a level then press it firmly into place with a soft cloth.

Use a wooden straightedge and a wheel glass cutter to score a line across a tile. Make one firm stroke. Lay the tile over a stretched wire and press down on both sides. Finish the cut edge with silicone carbide abrasive.

Add spare adhesive pads and set the tile in place. Finally, polish the tiles to remove any unsightly fingermarks.

Placing mirror tiles
Position tile before pressing on wall.

Metal tiles

Set out metallic tiles as for ceramic ones. No adhesive or grout is required. Don't fit metal tiles behind electrical fixtures—there's a risk that they could conduct the current.

Remove the protective paper from the adhesive pads on the back and press each tile onto the wall. Check the alignment of the tiles regularly; they are not always perfectly made.

Cut border tiles with scissors or tinsnips, but nick the edges before cutting across the face or the surface is likely to distort.

To round over a cut edge, cut a wooden block to fit inside the tile, and align it with the edge. Tap and rub along the edge with another block.

To fit into a corner, file a V-shape into the opposite edges, then bend the tile over the edge of the table.

When the wall is complete, peel off any protective film which may be covering the tiles.

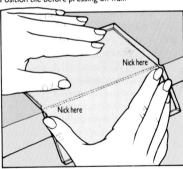

Nick here

Nick here

Bending metal tiles
Nick the edges of metal tiles before bending.

Cork tiles

Set up a horizontal guide stick (▷) to make sure you lay the tiles accurately. It isn't necessary to use a guide, however; the large tiles are easy to align without one. Simply mark a vertical line centrally on the wall and hang the tiles in both directions from it.

Use a rubber-based contact adhesive to fix cork tiles, if possible the type that allows a degree of movement when positioning them. If any adhesive gets onto the surface of a tile, clean it off immediately with a suitable solvent (▷) on a cloth.

Spread adhesive thinly and evenly onto the wall and backs of the tiles and leave it to dry. Lay each tile by placing one edge only against the guide or a neighboring tile, then gradually press the rest of the tile onto the wall. Smooth it down with your palms.

Cut cork tiles with a sharp trimming knife. Because the edges are butted tightly, you'll need to be very accurate when marking out border tiles. Use the same method as for laying cork and vinyl floor tiles (▷). Cut and fit curved shapes using a template.

Unless the tiles are precoated, apply two coats of varnish after 24 hours.

Tiling around curves

In many older houses some walls might be rounded at the outside corners. Flexible tiles such as vinyl, rubber and carpet types are easy to bend into quite tight radii, but cork will snap if bent too far.

Cut a series of shallow slits vertically down the back of a tile within its central section, using a back saw, then bend it gently to the curve required.

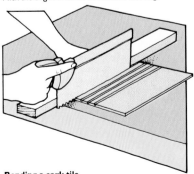

Bending a cork tile
Cut a series of shallow slits vertically down the back of a tile using a back saw within the central section, then bend it gently. The slits should enable the tile to assume even a fairly tight curve without snapping, but experiment first.

105

SETTING BRICK TILES

STONE TILES

Brick tiles can look quite authentic if laid in a standard running bond (◁), although you need not be hampered by structural requirements. You can hang them vertically, horizontally, diagonally or even zigzag to achieve a dramatic effect.

You can either leave the baseboard in place and start the first course of tiles just above it, or remove it and replace it just lapping over the bottom course of tiles. Alternatively, remove the baseboard and set a row of brick tiles on end.

Stone tiles are laid in the same way as brick tiles. Coursed stones should be arranged with a selection of small and large tiles for the most authentic look. Lay the tiles on the floor to plan the setting out, then transfer them to the wall one by one.

Irregularly shaped stones can be laid in any pattern you want, but again, it's best to set them out on the floor to achieve a good balance of large and small sizes for realism.

With some stone tiles you have to coat the wall with a special mortar-colored adhesive, which gives an overall background, then stick the individual tiles on by buttering their backs with adhesive.

Applying adhesive
Butter the tile back using a notched spreader.

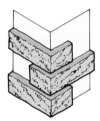

Corner tiles
Start with three corner tiles at each end of a run.

Setting brick tiles
Follow this procedure when setting brick tiles on your wall:
1 Plot the tile courses vertically and horizontally with two gauge sticks. Allow joint spaces between each tile.
2 Use preformed tiles at outside corners.
3 Set a course of tiles on end above a window as a brick lintel.
4 Set the bottom row of tiles on the baseboard on the new wall surface or substitute with a row of brick tiles on end.
5 Leave a gap for ventilating the flue in a blocked off fireplace.
6 Set tiles from the bottom up, staggering the vertical joints.

Setting out the wall

Make two gauge sticks, one for the vertical coursing and another to space the tiles sideways. Allow ⅜ inch spacing between each tile for the mortar joints, but adjust this slightly so there will be a full-width tile top and bottom.

Work out your spacing side to side so that, if possible, you have one course of whole tiles alternating with courses containing a half tile at each end.

If you are using corner tiles at each end, work out your space from them towards the middle of a wall, and place cut tiles centrally.

Fitting around a window
Lay tiles vertically above a window in a "soldier course" to simulate a brick lintel. Use prefabricated corner tiles to take the brickwork into a window reveal for the most realistic effect.

Cutting brick tiles
Most brick tiles can be cut with a hacksaw, but if a cut edge looks too sharp, round it over by rubbing with a scrap piece of tile. You can cut tiles with sledgehammer and cold chisel, or the thinnest type with scissors.

Gluing on the tiles

You can use mortar to stick brick tiles to the wall, but most types are sold with a compatible adhesive. Use a notched spreader to coat the back of each tile (left), then press it on the wall. Some manufacturers recommend spreading the adhesive onto the wall, instead of the tile.

If you are using preformed corner tiles, set them first, three at a time, alternating headers and stretchers (◁). Check that they are level at each side of the wall with a guide and level, then fill in between.

Start filling in by tiling the bottom course, using ⅜-inch wood scraps to space the tiles. Some tiles come with polystyrene packing, which you should cut into pieces to use as spacers. Every third course, use a level to check the alignment of the tiles, and adjust if necessary.

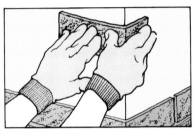

Bending brick tiles
Most brick tiles are made from rigid ceramic, but some plastic tiles can be hand-bent around a corner or even a curved column. Heat the tile gently with a hot air stripper or hair dryer until it is pliable. Wearing thick gloves, grasp the tile and bend it around the angle.

Pointing the joints
After 24 hours, use a ready-mixed mortar to point the wall as for real brickwork (◁). Brush smears of mortar from the face of the tiles with a stiff-bristled brush.

If you don't want to point the joints, simply leave them as they are; the adhesive is colored to resemble mortar and the joints will resemble raked joints (◁).

SETTING OUT FOR DIAGONAL TILING

Arranging the tiles diagonally can create an unusual decorative effect, especially if your choice of tiles enables you to mix colors. Setting out and laying the tiles diagonally isn't complicated—it's virtually the same as setting them at right angles, except that you'll be working into a corner instead of a wall. Mark a centerline, and bisect it at right angles using an improvised compass (right). Draw a line from opposite diagonal corners of the room through the center point. Dry lay a row of tiles to plot the margins (see below). Mark a right angle to the diagonal. Set a straightedge along one diagonal as a guide to laying the first row of tiles.

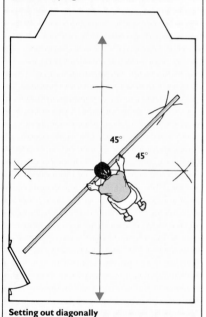

Setting out diagonally
Bisect the quartered room at 45 degrees.

SETTING OUT FOR SOFT FLOOR TILES

Vinyl, rubber, cork and carpet tiles are relatively large, so you can complete the floor fairly quickly. Some vinyl tiles are self-adhesive, and carpet tiles are loose-laid, both of which speed up the process still further. Soft tiles such as these can be cut easily with a sharp trimming knife or even scissors, so fitting to irregular shapes is easier. Use the following techniques to make your layout.

Marking out the floor

You can lay tiles onto a solid concrete or sheathed wooden floor, so long as the surface is level, clean and dry. Most soft tiles can be set out in a similar way. Find the center of two opposite walls, snap a chalkline between them to mark a line across the floor (**1**). Lay loose tiles at right angles to the line up to one wall (see below left). If there is a gap of less than half a tile width, move the line sideways by half a tile to give a wider margin.

To draw a line at right angles to the first, use string and a pencil as an improvised compass to scribe arcs on the marked line, at equal distances each side of the center (**2**).

From each point, scribe arcs on both sides of the line (**3**), which bisect each other. Join the points to form a line across the room (**4**). As before, lay tiles at right angles to the new line to make sure border tiles are at least half width. Nail a straightedge guide against one line in order to align the first row of tiles.

If the room is noticeably irregular in shape, center the first line over the fireplace or the door opening (see below right).

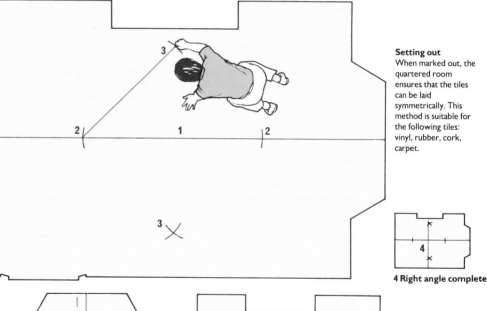

Setting out
When marked out, the quartered room ensures that the tiles can be laid symmetrically. This method is suitable for the following tiles: vinyl, rubber, cork, carpet.

4 Right angle complete

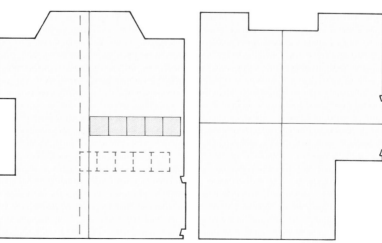

Plotting margin width *(near right)*
Lay loose tiles to make sure there is a reasonable gap at the margins. If not, move the line half a tile width in any direction.

Plotting an odd-shaped room *(far right)*
When a room is not a single rectangle, set out the lines using the fireplace or door as focal points.

LAYING VINYL FLOOR TILES

Tiles precoated with adhesive can be laid quickly and simply with no risk of squeezing glue onto the surface. If you're not using self-adhesive tiles, however, *follow the tile manufacturer's instructions concerning the type of adhesive to use. The surface over which they'll be applied must be clean, flat and stable.*

Fixing self-adhesive tiles

Stack the tiles in the room for 24 hours before you lay them so they become properly acclimatized.

If the tiles have a directional pattern—some have arrows printed on the back to indicate this—make sure you lay them the correct way.

Remove the protective paper backing from the first tile prior to laying (**1**), then press the edge against the straightedge guide. Align one corner with the centerline (**2**). Gradually lower the tile onto the floor and press it down.

Lay the next tile on the other side of the line, butting against the first one (**3**). Form a square with two more tiles. Lay tiles around the square to form a pyramid (**4**). Continue in this way to fill one half of the room, remove the guide and tile the other half.

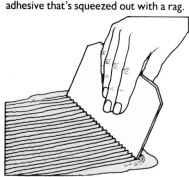

1 Peel off paper backing from adhesive tiles

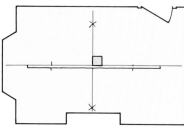

2 Place first tile in angle of intersecting lines

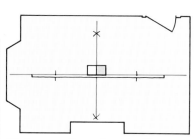

3 Butt up next tile on other side of line

GLUING VINYL TILES

Spread adhesive thinly but evenly across the floor, using a notched spreader, to stick about two or three tiles only. Lay the tiles carefully and wipe off surplus adhesive that's squeezed out with a rag.

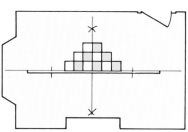

4 Lay tiles in a pyramid, then fill in half room

Apply bed of adhesive with notched spreader

Finishing off the floor

As soon as you have laid all the floor tiles, wash the surface with a damp cloth to remove any finger marks. It is not often necessary to polish vinyl tiles, but you can apply an acrylic floor polish if you wish.

Fit a straight metal strip (available from carpet suppliers) over the edge of the tiles when you finish at a doorway. When the tiles butt up to an area of carpet, fit a single threshold bar onto the edge of the carpeting. (▷)

CUTTING TILES TO FIT

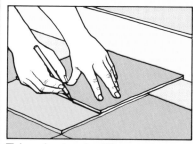

Trimming border tiles
Rooms are rarely square, so cut border tiles to the baseboard profile. To make a border tile, lay a loose one exactly on top of the last full tile. Place another tile on top but with its edge touching the wall. Draw along the edge of this tile with a pencil to mark the tile below. Remove the marked tile and cut along the line, then fit the cut-off portion of the tile into the border.

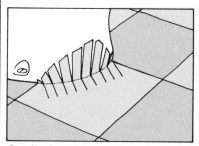

Cutting irregular shapes
To fit curves and moldings, make a template for each tile out of thin cardboard. Cut fingers and press against the object to reproduce its shape. Transfer the template to a tile and cut it out. You can also use a profile gauge to mark tiles for cutting complex curves.

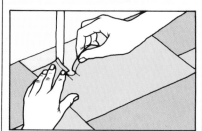

Fitting around pipes
Mark the position of the pipe on the tile using a compass. Draw parallel lines to the edge of the tile, taken from the perimeter of the circle. Measure halfway between the lines and cut a straight slit to the edge of the tile. Fold back the slit and slide the tile in place.

LAYING OTHER TYPES OF SOFT FLOOR TILES

Carpet tiles

Carpet tiles are laid as for vinyl tiles, except that they are not usually glued down. Set out centerlines on the floor (▷), but don't nail down a straightedge; simply aligning the row of tiles with the marked lines is sufficient.

Carpet tiles have a pile which must be laid in the correct direction, sometimes indicated by arrows on the back face. One problem with loose-laid carpet tiles is preventing them from slipping—particularly noticeable in a large room.

Some tiles have ridges of rubber on the back which mean they will slip easily in one direction but not in another. The nonslip direction is typically denoted by an arrow on the back of the tile. It's usual to lay the tiles in pairs so that one prevents the other from moving.

Stick down every third row of tiles using double-sided carpet tape to make sure the tiles don't slide.

Cut and fit carpet tiles as described for vinyl tiles.

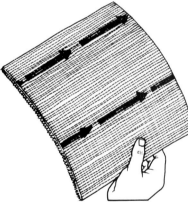

Checking direction of pile
Some carpet tiles have arrows on the back to indicate laying direction.

Using pile for decoration
Two typical arrangements of tiles using the pile to make decorative textures.

Cork tiles

Use the methods described for laying vinyl tiles to cut and fit cork tiles, but use a contact adhesive. Thixotropic types allow a degree of movement as you position the tiles.

Make sure the tiles are level by tapping down the edges with a block of wood. Unfinished tiles can be sanded lightly to remove minor irregularities.

Vacuum then seal unfinished tiles with three or four coats of clear polyurethane varnish.

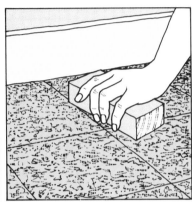

Setting cork tiles
Set the edges of cork tiles with a wood block.

Rubber tiles

Use the same methods to lay rubber tiles as for vinyl types. Use a latex flooring adhesive.

Laying rubber tiles
Lay large rubber tiles by placing one edge and corner against neighboring tiles before lowering it onto a bed of adhesive.

NEAT DETAILING FOR SOFT FLOOR TILES

Covering a recessed base
Create the impression of a floating bath panel or kitchen base units by running floor tiles up the face of the kick space. Fold carpet tiles into a tight bend with a tackless strip (1) or glue other tiles in place for a similar detail. Glue a plastic molding, normally used to seal around the edge of a bath, behind the floor covering to produce a curved detail which makes cleaning the floor a lot easier (2).

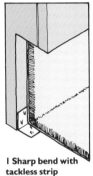 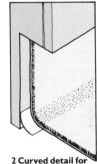

1 Sharp bend with tackless strip   **2 Curved detail for easy cleaning**

Cutting holes for pipes
With most soft floor tiles you can cut neat holes for central heating pipes using a homemade punch. Cut a 6-inch length of the same diameter pipe and sharpen the rim on the inside at one end with a metalworking file. Plot the position for the hole on the tile, then place the punching tool on top. Hit the other end of the punch with a hammer to cut through the tile cleanly. With some carpet tiles you may have to cut around the backing to release the cutout and prevent fraying with tape.

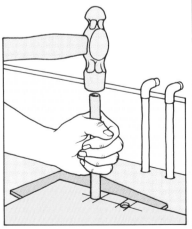

Punch holes for pipes with sharpened cutoff

● **Access to plumbing**
If you are covering completely a bath panel with tiles, remember to make a lift-off section in the panel to gain access to pipes and valves around the bath.

LAYING CERAMIC FLOOR TILES

Ceramic floor tiles make a durable, hard surface that can also be extremely decorative. Laying the tiles on a floor is similar to hanging them on a wall, *although since they are somewhat thicker than wall tiles, you have to be especially careful when cutting them to fit for neat and accurate results.*

● **Wood guides on concrete**
Use masonry nails to hold guides onto a concrete floor.

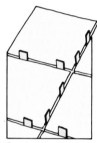

Spacing the tiles
Use scraps of thick cardboard to set floor tiles apart consistently to allow for grouting.

● **Grouting the joints**
Grout the tiles as for walls, but fill the joints flush rather than indenting them, so that dirt will not clog them. A dark grout is less likely to show dirt.

Setting out for tiling
Mark out the floor as for soft floor tiles, then set out the field with battens.
1 Fix temporary guides at the edge of the field on two adjacent walls farthest from the door.
2 Ensure that the guides are at true right angles by measuring the diagonal.
3 Dry-lay a square of 16 tiles in the angle as a final check.

Setting out

You cannot lay ceramic tiles on a wooden strip floor without constructing a solid, level surface that will not flex (◁). A flat, dry concrete floor is an ideal base (◁).

Mark out the floor as for soft floor tiles (◁) and work out the spacing to achieve even, fairly wide border tiles. Nail two straightedge guides to the floor, aligned with the last row of whole tiles on two adjacent walls farthest from the door. Set the guides at a right angle—even a small error will become obvious by the time you reach the other end of the room. Check the angle by measuring three units from one corner along one guide and four units along the other. Measure the diagonal between the marks; it should measure five units if the guides form an angle of 90 degrees. Make a final check by dry-laying a square of tiles in the angle.

Laying the tiles

Use a proprietary floor tile adhesive that is waterproof and slightly flexible when set. Spread it on using a plain or notched trowel, according to the manufacturer's recommendations. The normal procedure is to apply adhesive to the floor for the main area of tiling but to butter the backs of individual cut tiles as well.

Spread enough adhesive on the floor for about sixteen tiles. Press the tiles into the adhesive, starting in the corner. Work along both guides, then fill in between to form the square. Few floor tiles have spacing lugs, so use plastic spacers or cardboard.

Check the alignment of the tiles with a straightedge and make sure they're lying flat by spanning them with a level. Work along one guide, laying squares of sixteen tiles each time. Tile the rest of the floor in the same way, working back towards the door. Leave the floor for 24 hours before you walk on it to remove the guides and fit the border tiles.

Cutting ceramic floor tiles

Measure and cut the tiles to fit the border as described for wall tiles (◁). Because they are thicker, floor tiles will not snap quite so easily, so if you have a large area to fill, buy or rent a tile cutter.

Alternatively, make your own device by nailing two scraps of ½-inch plywood to 1 × 2-inch pine strips, leaving a parallel gap between plywood scraps just wide enough to take a tile. Hold the device on edge, insert a scored tile into the gap, up to the scored line—which should be facing upward—and press down on the free end (see below right). Snap thin strips from the edge in this way. Saw or nibble curved shapes (◁).

LAYING MOSAIC FLOOR TILES

Set out mosaic tiles on a floor as for ceramic floor tiles. Spread on the adhesive, then lay the tiles, paper facing up, with spacers that match the gaps between individual pieces. Press the sheets into the adhesive, using a block of wood to tamp them level. Remove the spacers and soak the tiles with warm water; peel off the facing 24 hours later. Grout as normal.

If you have to fit a sheet of mosaic tiles around an obstruction, remove individual mosaic pieces as close to the profile as possible. Fit the sheet (**1**), then cut and replace the pieces to fit around the shapes.

If you're using mosaics in areas of heavy traffic—a step on the patio, for example—protect vulnerable edges with a nosing of ordinary ceramic floor tiles to match or contrast (**2**).

1 Remove mosaic pieces to fit around pipe

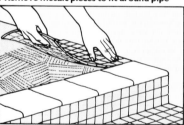

2 Lay a nosing of ceramic tiles on step treads

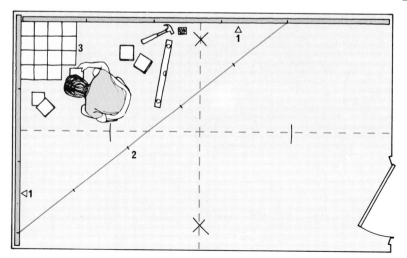

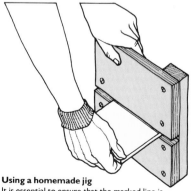

Using a homemade jig
It is essential to ensure that the marked line is positioned parallel to the edge of the plywood or the tile will not snap accurately.

LAYING QUARRY TILES IN MORTAR

Quarry tiles are the best choice for a tough, hard-wearing flooring that will bear a lot of heavy foot traffic. But beware. They're fairly thick and making even a straight cut is not easy. Reserve them for areas that don't require a lot of complex shaping.

Don't lay quarry tiles on a wood-strip floor; replace the floorboards with ⅝ or ¾-inch exterior-grade plywood to provide a sufficiently flat and rigid base (▷). A concrete floor presents no problems, providing it is free from moisture. So long as the floor is reasonably flat, the mortar bed on which the tiles are laid will take care of the fine leveling.

Setting out for tiling

Set out two straightedge guides in a corner of the room at right angles to each other, as described for ceramic floor tiles, opposite. The depth of the guides should measure about twice the thickness of the tiles to allow for the mortar bed. Fasten them temporarily to a concrete floor with masonry nails. The level of the guides is essential, so check with a level; shim up under the guides with scraps of hardboard or shingles where necessary. Mark tile widths along each batten, leaving ⅛-inch gaps between for grouting, as a guide to positioning.

Dry-lay a square of sixteen tiles in the angle, then nail a third guide to the floor, butting the tiles and parallel with one of the other battens. Level and mark it as before.

Laying the tiles

Quarry tiles are laid on a bed of mortar mixed from 1 part cement: 3 parts builder's sand. When water is added, the mortar should be stiff enough to hold an impression when squeezed in your hand.

Soak quarry tiles in water prior to laying to prevent them from sucking water from the mortar too rapidly, when a poor bond could result. Cut a stout board to span the parallel guides; this will be used to level the mortar bed and tiles. Cut a notch in each end to fit between the guides, to the thickness of a tile less ⅛ inch.

Spread the mortar to a depth of about ½ inch to cover the area of sixteen tiles. Level it by dragging the notched side of the board across.

Dust dry cement on the mortar to provide a good key for the tiles, then lay the tiles along three sides of the square against the guides. Fill in the square, spacing the tiles equally by adjusting them with a trowel.

Tamp down the tiles gently with the unnotched side of the board until they are level with the guides. If the mortar is too stiff, brush water into the joints. Wipe mortar from the faces of the tiles before it hardens, or it will stain.

Fill in between the guides, then move one guide back to form another bay of the same dimension. Level it with the first section of tiles. Tile section-by-section until the main floor is complete. When the floor is hard enough to walk on, lift the guides and fill in the border tiles.

CUTTING QUARRY TILES

Because quarry tiles are difficult to cut, you may think it worthwhile having them cut by a tile supplier. Measure border tiles as described for wall tiles; then, having scored in the line, number each one on the bottom and mark the waste with a felt-tip pen.

If you want to cut the tiles yourself, scribe them with a tile cutter, then make a shallow cut down each edge with a saw file (▷). With the face side of the tile held in a gloved hand, strike behind the scored line with the cross pein of a hammer.

Score tile face; tap the back with a hammer

Notching the leveling board
Cut the same notch at each end of the board for leveling the mortar.

Leveling the mortar
With a notch located over each guide, drag the leveling board towards you.

Leveling border tiles
Use a notched piece of plywood to level the mortar in the margin and tamp down the tiles with a block.

● **Finishing off the quarry tiling**
Grout quarry tiles as for ceramic floor tiles, using cement or proprietary waterproof grout. Clean it off the surface by sprinkling sawdust onto it and wiping off with a cloth. Wash the finished floor with a soapless detergent.

The setup for a quarry tiled floor
The arrangement for quarry tiles is similar to that for glazed tiles.
1 Fix two straightedge guides—about twice the tile thickness—at right angles to each other.
2 Fix a third guide parallel with one of the others.
3 Dry-lay sixteen tiles between the guides to check their accuracy, then proceed with tiling.

FITTING CEILING TILES

There are basically two types of tiles which you can use on a ceiling. Lesser-priced polystyrene tiles are easy to cut and—because they're so lightweight—they can be stuck to the ceiling without any difficulty. For a more luxurious finish, consider using mineral fiber ceiling tiles. They, too, can be glued directly to a ceiling, although some have tongue-and-groove edges which are best stapled to a furring framework nailed to the ceiling.

Installing stapled tiles

Mineral fiber tiles are stapled to a furring framework nailed to the ceiling joists. The first job is to locate the joists and arrange the furring to suit the tile size.

Locating the joists

Start by marking out two bisecting lines across the ceiling (◁), so that you can work out the spacing of the tiles with even borders. Mark the edges of the last whole tile on the ceiling.

Check the direction of the joists by examining the floor above if you're in a downstairs room, or by looking in the attic if you're upstairs.

To locate the joists on the ceiling, poke an awl through the ceiling at each side of a few joists (if you can gain access via the attic). Don't go to the trouble of lifting floorboards in a room above. Floorboards run at right angles to joists, so to locate joists, try tapping the ceiling with your knuckles. Listen for the dull thud when you're under a joist. Use the awl—or a small-diameter drill bit—to locate the approximate center of the joists.

Measure from these points to the next joists—they'll usually be 16 or 24 inches apart—and mark their centers. Nail parallel strips of 1 × 2-in. furring to

the joists, at right angles to them. Space them so the distance between the center of each strip is a tile width. Fitting the strips is easier with a spacer—two pine strips nailed together (1) to set the spacing. Finish by nailing the last strip against the far wall. Transfer the line marking the edge of the border tiles to the furring along both sides of the ceiling.

Fitting stapled tiles

Unlike any other form of tiling, you must start by setting stapled tiles at the borders. Mark and cut off the tongued edges of two adjacent rows of border tiles, starting with the one in the corner. Staple them through the grooved edge to the furring strips, but secure the cut edges with panel nails driven through their faces.

Proceed diagonally across the ceiling by setting whole tiles into the angle formed by the border tiles. Slide the tongues of the loose tiles into the grooves of their neighbors, then staple them through their own grooved edge (2).

To fit the remaining border tiles, cut off the tongues and nail them through their face. Use crown or quarter-round molding to finish uneven seams.

1 Make a spacing gauge
Set out the furring strips at the correct spacing using a gauge made from wood strips nailed together.

2 Securing the tiles
Set the tiles groove outwards and staple through the grooved edge. Slot the tongues by butting tiles into them.

How ceiling tiles are fastened
Mineral fiber tiles require a setup of furring strips attached to the ceiling surface.
1 Nail furring to the joists at right angles, a tile width apart. Arrange substantial borders by altering the starting point.
2 Staple the border tiles first on two adjacent rows, starting with the corner tile.
3 Staple the remaining tiles to the furring through their grooves, working diagonally across the ceiling.

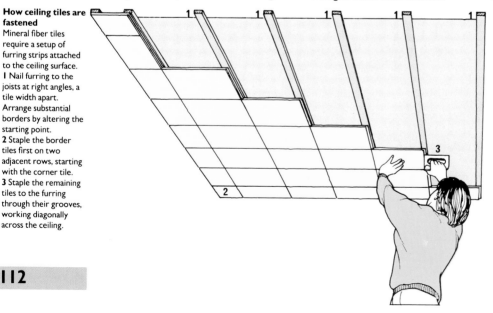

FIXING POLYSTYRENE CEILING TILES

Where to use the tiles
Polystyrene tiles can be used in virtually any room in the house except in the kitchen, where they would be directly over a source of heat—or where they are banned by local building codes.

Preparing the ceiling
Remove any fabric material and make sure the ceiling is clean and free from grease (◁). Snap two chalk lines which cross each other at right angles in the center of the ceiling (◁). Hang the tiles to the chalk lines, checking their alignment frequently (◁).

Sticking up the tiles
Use a proprietary polystyrene adhesive or a heavy-duty wallpaper paste. Spread the adhesive across the back of the tile to cover all but the very edge.

Press the first tile into one of the angles formed by the marked lines. Use the flat of your hand; fingertip pressure can crush polystyrene. Proceed with subsequent tiles to complete one half of the ceiling, then the other.

Cutting the tiles
Mark the border tiles (◁), then use a sharp utility knife with a blade long enough to cut through a tile with one stroke. Cut the tiles on a flat piece of scrap board. Clean up the edges but don't rub too hard or the polystyrene granules will crumble.

Mark out curves with a template (◁), then follow the marked line freehand with a utility knife.

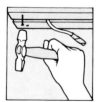

1 Fix furring to joists   **2 Replace ceiling rose**

Dealing with electrical fixtures
Turn off the power at the panel (◁), unscrew the ceiling rose cover and disconnect the wires.

Nail furring to the ceiling joists to correspond with the screw holes of the rose (**1**). Cut a hole through the covering tile for the cable and replace the rose (**2**), screwing it through the tile to the furring. Reconnect the wires (◁), replace the rose cover and restore the power.

ESTIMATING SHEET VINYL AND CARPET

Measure the floor area carefully and draw a freehand plan, including the position of doors, window bay, alcoves and so on, plus the full width of the door frame. Make a note of the dimensions on the plan and take it to the supplier, who will advise you on the most economical way to cover the floor.

The ideal solution is to achieve a seamless wall-to-wall covering, but this is often impossible, either because a particular width is unobtainable or because the room is such an irregular shape that there would be an unacceptable amount of waste if it was cut from one piece. Carpet or sheet vinyl widths have to be butted together in these circumstances, but try to avoid seams in heavy traffic areas. You will also have to consider matching the pattern and the direction of carpet pile. Pile must run in the same direction or each piece of carpet will look different. Remember to order about 3 inches extra all around for fitting.

Standard widths

Most manufacturers produce carpet or vinyl to standard widths. Some can be cut to fit any shape of room but the average waste factor is reflected in the price. Not all carpets are available in the full range of widths and you may have some difficulty in matching a color exactly from one width to another, so ask the supplier to check. Carpet and vinyl are made in a variety of sizes, but not all designs are available in all widths.

Available Widths	
Carpet	**Vinyl**
2 ft. 6 in.*	6 ft.
3 ft.	9 ft.
9 ft.	12 ft.
12 ft.	15 ft.
13 ft.*	
15 ft.*	

*rare

Carpet widths of 9 feet and over are called "broadlooms;" narrower widths are called "strip" or "body" carpets.

Carpet squares

Carpet squares, not to be confused with tiles (▷), are large rectangular loose-laid rugs. Simply order whichever size suits the proportion of your room. Carpet squares should be turned from time to time to even out wear.

SHEET VINYL AND CARPET

Sheet flooring fits wall-to-wall. The coverings most often used today are sheet vinyl (the modern equivalent of linoleum) and carpet in all its forms. Included in the cost of an expensive floorcovering should be an allowance for having it professionally laid—and even if there's an additional charge, you'd be well advised to spend that little extra to avoid the risk of spoiling costly carpet or vinyl. On the other hand, there's no reason why you shouldn't lay the less-expensive ranges, where cost-saving makes more sense. It's not really difficult.

Types of sheet floorcovering

There are many types of carpet and vinyl flooring. Choose according to durability, color and pattern.

Unbacked vinyl

Sheet vinyl is made by sandwiching the printed pattern between a base of PVC and a clear protective PVC covering. All vinyl is relatively hard-wearing, but some have a thicker, reinforced protective layer to increase their durability. Discuss with the supplier the quality to suit your needs and choose from the range of colors, patterns and embossed textures available.

Backed vinyl

Backed vinyl has similar properties to the unbacked type, with the addition of a resilient underlayment to make them softer and warmer to walk on. The backing may be felt or, more often, a cushion of foamed PVC.

Vinyl carpet

Vinyl carpet is a cross between carpet and sheet vinyl originally developed for contract use but now available for domestic installation. It has a velvetlike pile of fine nylon fibers embedded in a waterproof, expanded PVC base. It's popular for kitchens as spills are washed off easily with water and a mild detergent. Rolls are 5 feet wide.

Carpet

Originally, pile carpets were made by knotting strands of wool or other natural fibers into a woven foundation but gradually, with the introduction of machine-made carpets and synthetic fibers, a very wide variety of different types has been developed. There is a good choice available for virtually every situation—whether the need is for something luxurious or practical and hard-wearing.

SEE ALSO

Details for: ▷

Leveling wood floors	61
Carpet tiles	100
Leveling concrete	173
Choosing color/pattern/ texture	24–29
Laying sheet vinyl	118

Vinyl flooring
Being hard-wearing and waterproof, sheet vinyl is one of the most popular floorcoverings for bathrooms and kitchens. Vinyl carpet (6th from right) has a pile but is equally suitable in those areas.

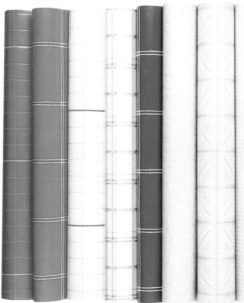

Preparing the floor for floorcovering

Before you lay a sheet covering, make sure the floor is flat and dry. Take out any unevenness by screeding or sheathing the floor (▷). A concrete floor must have a vapor barrier of 15-pound asphalt felt. Don't lay vinyl over wood recently treated with preservative.

CHOOSING CARPET

HOW CARPETS ARE MADE

There are various factors to consider when you're shopping for carpeting, such as fiber content, type of pile and durability. Although wool is luxurious, don't be put off by the synthetic version and other man-made fibers widely available. It has a lot to offer in terms of comfort underfoot, finish and texture.

How fiber content affects the carpet

The best carpets are made from wool or a mixture of wool plus a percentage of man-made fiber. Wool carpets are expensive, so manufacturers have experimented with a variety of fibers to produce cheaper but still durable and attractive carpets. Materials such as nylon, polypropylene, acrylic, rayon and polyester are all used for carpet-making—singly or combined.

Synthetic-fiber carpets were once inferior substitutes, often with an unattractive shiny pile and a reputation for building up a charge of static electricity that produced mild shocks when anyone touched a metal doorknob. Nowadays, manufacturers have largely solved the problem of static, but you can seek the advice of the supplier before you buy.

So far as appearance is concerned, a modern carpet made from good-quality blended fibers is hard to distinguish from one made from wool. Certain combinations produce carpets that are so stain-resistant that they virtually shrug off spilled liquids. To their disadvantage, synthetic fibers tend to react badly to burns, shriveling rapidly from the heat, whereas wool tends only to smolder.

Rush, sisal, coir and jute are natural vegetable fibers used to make coarsely woven rugs or strips.

Which type of pile?

The nature of the pile is even more important to the feel and appearance of a carpet than the fiber content. Pile carpets are woven or tufted. Axminster and Wilton are names used to describe two traditional methods of weaving the pile simultaneously with the foundation so that the strands are wrapped around and through the warp and weft threads.

With tufted carpets, continuous strands are pushed between the threads of a prewoven foundation. Although it is secured with an adhesive backing, tufted pile is not as permanent as woven pile. Consult the box, right, for the various ways tufted and woven piles are created. Where durability is important, see below.

The importance of underlay

It is false economy to try to save on the cost of padding. Without it, carpet wears faster and is not as comfortable underfoot. Eventually, the lines of floorboards will begin to show as dirty lines on a pale carpet as dust from the gaps begins to emerge.

An underlay can be a thick felt or foam rubber and plastic. Rubber or foam-backed carpets need no padding.

As an extra precaution, it is worth laying rolls of brown paper over the floor to stop dust and grit from working their way into the underlay and to prevent rubber-backed carpet from sticking to the floor, and tearing when lifted.

Tufted and woven carpet pile is treated in a number of ways to give some different qualities of finish. With some types the strands are left long and uncut; with others the looped pile is twisted together to give a coarser texture; very hard-wearing types have their looped pile pulled tight against the foundation; cut, velvety and shaggy types have the tops of their loop removed to leave single fiber strands.

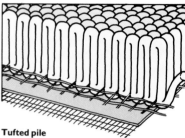

Tufted pile
Continuous strands pushed into a woven foundation secured on an adhesive backing.

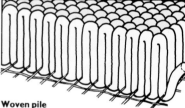

Woven pile
Continuous strands woven onto the warp and weft threads of the foundation.

1 Looped pile
Ordinary looped pile gives a smooth feel.

2 Twisted pile
Looped pile twisted for a coarser texture.

3 Cord pile
Loops are pulled tight against the foundation.

4 Cut pile
Loops are cut, giving a velvety textured pile.

5 Velvet pile
Loops are cut short for a close-stranded pile.

6 Shag pile
A long cut pile up to 4 inches long.

Fiberbonded pile
The most modern method of carpet production, fiberbonded pile consists of synthetic fibers packed tightly together and bonded to an impregnated backing. It produces a texture like coarse felt.

CHOOSING A DURABLE CARPET

Whether it is woven, tufted or bonded, a hard-wearing carpet must have a dense pile. When you fold the carpet and part the pile you should not be able to see the backing it is attached to.

Fortunately, many manufacturers categorize their floorcoverings according to their ability to withstand wear. If the classification is not stated on the carpet, ask the supplier how it is categorized.

● **Light domestic**	Bedrooms
● **Medium domestic**	Light traffic only, dining room, well-used bedroom
● **General domestic**	Living rooms
● **Heavy domestic**	Hallways and stairs

LAYING CARPET

Some people prefer to loose-lay carpet, relying on the weight of furniture to stop its moving around. However, a properly stretched and fixed carpet looks much better, and isn't difficult to accomplish. There are three main methods of fastening, as detailed right.

Laying a standard width

The only special tool required for laying carpet is a knee kicker for stretching the covering. It has a toothed head, which is pressed into the carpet while you nudge the padded end with your knee. You can rent a knee kicker from a dealer.

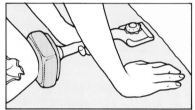

A knee kicker, used to stretch carpet to fit

Join the padding with short strips of carpet tape or secure it with a few tacks to stop its moving. Roll out the carpet, butting one machine-cut edge against a wall and fasten that edge. (If the carpet is patterned, it should run parallel to the main axis of the room.)

Stretch the carpet to the wall directly opposite and temporarily fasten it with tacks, or slip it onto tackless strips, but do not cure it yet. Work from the center towards each corner, stretching and fastening. Do the same along the other sides of the room.

Cut the corners like sheet vinyl (▷) to allow the carpet to lie flat. Adjust it until it is stretched evenly, then fasten it permanently. When you are using tape or strips, press the carpet into the angle between baseboard and floor with a bolster chisel; trim with a knife held at 45 degrees to the baseboard. Tuck the edge behind the strip with the chisel.

Cutting to fit

Cut and fit carpet into doorways and around obstacles like sheet vinyl (▷). Join carpets at a doorway with a single- or double-sided threshold bar.

Joining carpet

Don't join expensive woven carpets; they should be sewn by a professional. Glue straight seams with latex adhesive or use adhesive tape for rubber-backed carpet. Use as described for vinyl (▷).

Methods of fixing

Tacks

A 2-inch strip of carpet is folded under and nailed to a wood floor with carpet tacks about every 8 inches. Lose the head in the pile by rubbing the pile with your fingertips. Padding should be laid short of the baseboard to allow the carpet to lie flat along the edge.

Double-sided tape

For rubber-backed carpets only—stick 2-inch tape around the perimeter of the room. When you are ready to fasten the carpet, peel off the protective paper layer from the adhesive tape to expose the sticky surface.

Tackless strip

Wood or metal strips with fine metal teeth are nailed to the floor and grip the woven foundation of the carpet. Nail strips to the floor, $\frac{1}{4}$ inch from the baseboard with the teeth angled towards the wall. Cut short strips to fit doorways and alcoves and glue to a concrete floor. Cut padding to the edge.

Carpeting a staircase

If possible use one of the narrow standard widths of carpet for a staircase. Order an extra foot and a half over the required length so that the carpet can be moved at a later date to even out the wear. This allowance is turned under onto the bottom step.

You can fit stair carpeting across the entire width of the treads or stop short to reveal a border of polished or painted staircase; you can use the traditional metal or wood stair rods to hold the carpet against the risers. Fastening is simply a matter of screwing brackets on each side.

Alternatively, you can tack the carpet to the stairs every 3 inches across the treads. Push the carpet firmly into the angle between riser and tread with a bolster chisel while you tack the center, then work outwards to each side.

So long as the carpet is not rubber-backed, you can use tackless strip to fix the run in place.

Fitting the padding

Cut padding into separate pads for each tread. Secure each pad next to the riser with tacks or tackless strip, and tack the front edge under the nosing.

Laying a straight run

The pile of a carpet should face down the stairs. Rub the palm of your hand along the carpet in both directions. It will feel smoother in the direction of the pile.

Start at the bottom of the staircase with the carpet laid face down on the first tread. Fasten the back edge with tacks or nail a strip over it. Stretch the carpet over the nosing and fasten it to the bottom of the riser by nailing through a straight strip. Run the carpet up the staircase, pushing it firmly into each tackless strip with a chisel. Nail the end of the carpet against the riser on the last tread. Bring the landing carpet over the top step to meet it.

Carpeting winding stairs

To carpet the winding section of a staircase, keep the carpet in a continuous length but fold the excess under and secure it to the riser with a stair rod or straight tackless strip.

Alternatively, fold the slack against the riser and tack through the three thicknesses of carpet.

To install fitted carpet on winding stairs, cut a pattern for each step and carpet it individually.

SEE ALSO

Details for: ▷	
Laying sheet vinyl	118
Leveling wood floors	61
Leveling concrete	173
Staircases	212–214

Fastening carpet
Use one of three ways:

Fold tacked to floor

Double-sided tape

Tackless strip

Joining at a doorway
Use one of the bars below:

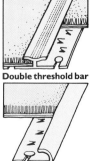

Double threshold bar

Single threshold bar

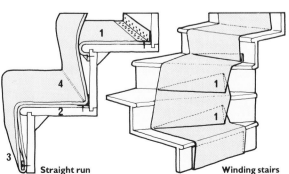

Carpeting stairs
1 Tack pads.
2 Tack carpet face-down on first tread.
3 Pull over nosing and tack to base of riser.
4 Run carpet up stairs, fastening to tackless.

Carpeting winding stairs
1 Don't cut the carpet but fold the excess under and fasten to riser with stair rod or straight strip.

Straight run   **Winding stairs**

117

LAYING SHEET VINYL

Vinyl floorcovering makes a durable, wall-to-wall surface for floors subject to likely water spills, such as the kitchen, utility room and bathroom. There are numerous colors, patterns and embossed effects available, and you will find most types easy to lay if you follow a systematic routine.

SEE ALSO

◁ Details for:

Leveling wood floors	61
Sheet flooring	115
Leveling concrete	173

Leave the vinyl in a room for 24 to 48 hours before laying, preferably opened flat or at least stood on end, loosely rolled. Assuming there are no seams, start by fitting the longest wall first. Drive a nail through a wooden strip 2 inches from one end.

Pull the vinyl away from the wall by approximately 1½ inches. Make sure it is parallel with the wall or the main axis of the room. Use the nailed strip to scribe a line following the baseboard (1). Cut along the vinyl with a sharp knife or scissors and slide the sheet up against the wall.

To get the rest of the sheet to lie as flat as possible, cut a triangular notch out of each corner. Make a straight cut down to the floor at outside corners. Remove as much waste as possible, leaving 2 to 3 inches turned up all around.

Press the vinyl into the angle between baseboard and floor with a chisel. Align a metal straightedge with the crease and run along it with a sharp knife held at a slight angle to the baseboard (2). If your trimming is less than perfect, nail a cover strip of shoe base to the baseboard.

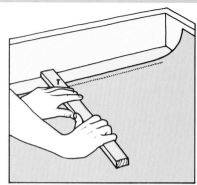

1 Fit to first wall by scribing with a nailed strip

Trimming and gluing sheet vinyl

Trimming to fit a doorway
Work around the door frame molding making straight cuts and removing triangular notches at each change of angle as if they were miniature corners. Crease the vinyl against the floor and trim the waste. Make a straight cut across the opening and fit a threshold bar over the edge of the sheet.

Cutting around an obstruction
To fit a toilet or sink pedestal, fold back the sheet and pierce it with a knife just above floor level. Draw the blade up towards the edge. Make triangular cuts around the base, gradually working around the curve until the sheet can lie flat on the floor (3). Crease and cut off the waste.

Gluing the sheet
Modern vinyls can be loose-laid, but you may prefer to glue the edges and especially along a door opening. Peel back the edge and spread a band of the recommended flooring adhesive with a toothed spreader (4) or use a 2-inch wide double-sided tape.

Making a seam
If you have to join widths of vinyl, scribe one edge as described above, then overlap the free edge with the second sheet until the pattern matches exactly. Cut through both pieces with a knife, then remove the waste strips.

Without moving the sheets, fold back both cut edges, apply tape or adhesive and press the seam together.

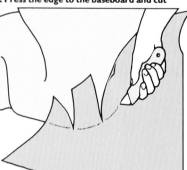

2 Press the edge to the baseboard and cut

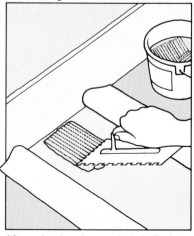

3 Make triangular cuts around a curve

Positioning the vinyl
Aligning the vinyl sheet squarely on the floor is essential.
1 Fit the longest, uninterrupted wall.
2 Cut triangular notches at each external inside and outside corner so the sheet will lie flat.
3 Allow folds of about 3 inches all round for scribing to fit accurately.
4 Make a straight cut against the door opening so a threshold bar can be fastened.

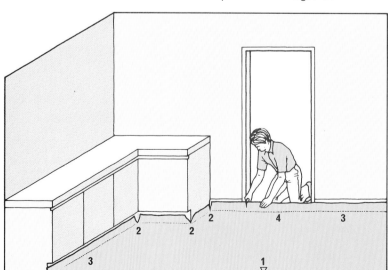

4 Secure butting edges on a bed of adhesive

3

REPAIRS & IMPROVEMENTS

FRAME HOUSE CONSTRUCTION

Wood is the predominant material used in residential construction for both structural and finish applications. While there are several approaches to framing a structure with wood, the platform framing system, illustrated at the right, is most widely used.

Foundations

The foundations for frame houses are generally poured concrete or concrete block. Footings should be present under all perimeter walls and beneath any loadbearing walls or columns.

Floor construction

In platform framing, the first-floor structure is fastened to sill plates that rest on top of the foundation walls (◁). The basic floor structure is made from 2-inch-thick joists. The ends of joists are joined to joist headers, and cross-braces are nailed between joists to prevent twisting. Where openings occur in the joist pattern for stairways or other passages through the floor plane, doubled headers and doubled joists along the sides of the opening are added. Subflooring and finish flooring are applied over the floor frame.

Wall construction

The walls of frame houses are ordinarily built by fastening studs to horizontal members called top and toe plates (◁). The wall frames are fastened to the floor frames. Loadbearing walls have a doubled top plate. Where the ordinary stud spacing pattern is interrupted for window and door openings in bearing walls, special headers are fashioned to support the weight above each opening.

In another framing approach called "balloon framing," wall studs rise from the first floor to the top floor ceiling structure, and intermediate floor frames are attached to the wall studs.

The exterior wall frames are covered with sheathing, and then building paper is applied before the wall finish is added.

Roof structure

In simple pitched roofs, rafters rest on top of house walls and join to a ridge board at the peak. The roof deck is formed by fastening sheathing over the structural members, and is then covered with asphalt felt, which is in turn finished with asphalt or wood shingles. Slate and clay tile finishes are also common (◁).

Foundations

The foundation carries the whole weight of the house. The type, size and depth are determined largely by the loadbearing properties of the subsoil.

Strip foundation
A continuous strip of concrete set well below ground.

Slab on footings
Houses without basements or crawlspaces may have this type of foundation. In cold climates footing must be set deep enough to fall below the frostline.

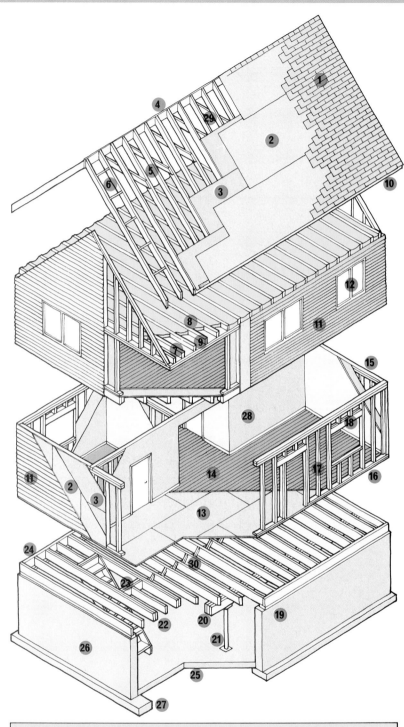

TYPICAL COMPONENTS OF A FRAME HOUSE			
1 Asphalt shingles	9 Vapor barrier	17 Stud	24 Joist header
2 Asphalt felt	10 Fascia	18 Header	25 Concrete slab
3 Sheathing	11 Siding	19 Sill plate	26 Foundation wall
4 Ridge board	12 Window unit	20 Girder	27 Footing
5 Rafters	13 Subflooring	21 Column	28 Loadbearing
6 Lookouts	14 Finish flooring	22 Doubled joist	partition
7 Joists	15 Doubled top plate	23 Doubled joist	29 Collar beam
8 Insulation	16 Toe plate	header	30 Cross-bracing

BRICK HOUSE CONSTRUCTION

While a brick veneer may confer a degree of nobility to a frame house, a true brick house is, to many, the essence of solidity and permanence. Typical construction details for brick houses are illustrated at the left.

Foundation

Brick houses generally have a deep, strip-type foundation of block or concrete. In older houses, stone or brick may have been used to build foundation walls.

Wall structure

Cavity wall construction is used to build the perimeter walls of most brick houses—each wall consists of an inner and outer leaf separated by an airspace (▷). The two leaves are braced with metal or brick ties. A flashing just above ground level keeps dampness from the ground from migrating up the walls. Rigid insulation is often placed in the airspace.

For economy, especially in more recently built homes, concrete blocks are frequently used for the inner wall, and the interior surface is generally finished with plaster. Interior partitions are generally framed with wood studs over which wood or wire lath is placed to hold the plaster finish. In large apartment buildings built prior to World War II, you may find gypsum block partitions finished with plaster.

For structural purposes, the tops of door and window openings in brick walls are treated with lintels of stone, steel or precast concrete. Brick arches are a decorative alternative to lintels.

Floor structure

The ends of floor joists generally rest on recesses in the brick walls (▷). Cross-bracing is used between them and they may be supported between perimeter walls with columns or girders. As in frame houses, subflooring is applied over joists, and the finish flooring is installed over the subfloor.

Roof structure

In many brick houses, the roof structure is similar to that used in frame houses, but if the roof finish is slate or tile (▷), the structure must be reinforced with purlins or trusses to support the additional weight.

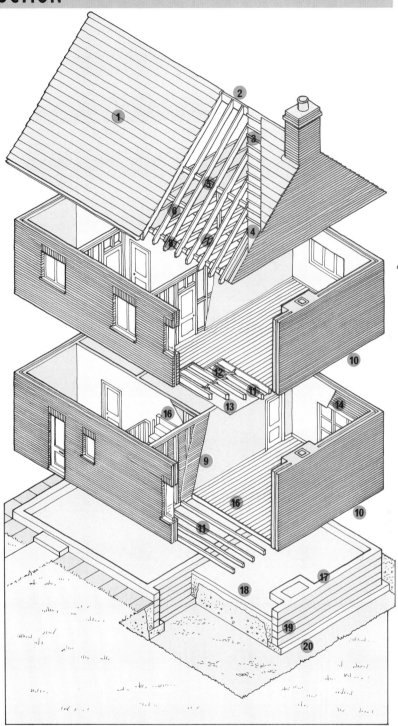

• **Foundation problems**
Consult a professional engineer or architect when dealing with problems or new work involving foundations.

Settlement
Settlement cracks in walls are not uncommon. If they are not too wide and have stabilized, they are not a serious problem.

Subsidence
Subsidence caused by weak or shallow foundations or excessive moisture-loss from the ground—can be more serious. Widening cracks from window or door openings indicate this.

Heave
Weak foundations can also be damaged by ground swell, or "heave."

Light foundations
The walls of extensions or bays with lighter or shallower foundations than the house may show cracks where the two meet due to differential movement.

TYPICAL COMPONENTS OF A BRICK HOUSE

1 Tile or slate	9 Lath-and-plaster stud partition	16 Finish flooring
2 Ridge board	10 Brick cavity wall	17 Flashing
3 Nailers	11 Floor joists	18 Concrete slab
4 Asphalt felt	12 Cross-bracing	19 Foundation wall
5 Purlin	13 Plaster ceiling	20 Footing
6 Rafter	14 Lintel	
7 Ceiling joist	15 Staircase	
8 Wall plate		

WALLS: EXTERIOR WALLS

Exterior walls are built to bear the structural loads of the house, to keep out weather and unwanted noises, to trap heat and to serve as a decorative element in the *home's design. There are numerous structural approaches for exterior walls; the most common ones are illustrated and described below.*

Wall ties
Wall ties are laid in the mortar joints and bridge the airspace between the inner and outer leaves. In brick veneer walls, the ties are fastened to the sheathing.

Wire butterfly tie

Sheet metal tie

Frame wall construction

In wood frame houses, exterior walls are usually built with 2-by-4 studs nailed 16 inches on center to top and toe plates, and since exterior walls carry much of the structural load, wall top plates are doubled.

Sheathing is nailed to the outer surface of the wall frame to add rigidity, and is then covered with a weather-resistant membrane. Wood, plywood, hardboard, vinyl and aluminum sidings are nailed directly to the membrane-covered sheathing. When the exterior finish is made of brick or stucco veneer, there is generally a 1-inch airspace between the sheathing and veneer (◁).

Fiberglass batt or mineral fiber insulation is frequently used in the stud cavities. A vapor barrier is applied to the interior edges of the wall frame before attaching the interior wall finish, which may be gypsum wallboard, plaster or paneling.

Masonry construction

Very old stone houses may be built with solid walls, but in most masonry construction, cavity walls, consisting of an inner and outer leaf separated by an airspace, are the norm. The two leaves are braced with wall ties running between them, which are then set in the mortar joints. In modern masonry construction, rigid insulation may be set in the airspace, and cement block instead of brick may be used for the inner leaf for economy.

Exterior wall construction
1 Frame wall with wood siding
2 Frame wall with brick veneer
3 Brick cavity wall
4 Frame wall with stucco veneer
5 Brick cavity wall with block inner leaf
6 Solid stone wall

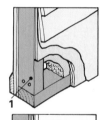

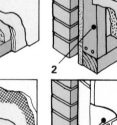

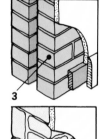

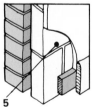

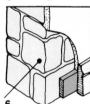

Superinsulated frame walls

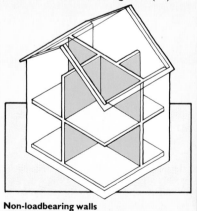

Superinsulated frame wall

In recent years, new approaches to wall framing and insulation have been developed in the interest of conserving energy. Typical of various super-insulation approaches has been the use of 2-by-6 studs and plates to create deeper stud cavities that permit the installation of thicker insulation. The added insulation significantly improves the R-value of house walls, a standard that measures structural resistance to the passage of thermal energy.

In addition to improving R-values with thicker insulation and insulated sheathing materials, superinsulating techniques also protect insulation from moisture damage and reduce air infiltration through seams and joints by special attention to the application of the vapor barrier. The vapor barrier is carefully wrapped around corners and at floor and ceiling joints, and the wall finish is often spaced away from the barrier with furring to prevent its being torn by fasteners. The vapor barrier is also carefully sealed around electrical boxes and other mechanical fixtures. Semi-permeable housewraps have been developed for the membrane between the sheathing and siding; these permit moisture to escape from the wall cavity but screen out drafts.

IDENTIFYING LOADBEARING WALLS

When appraising the condition of a house or planning a remodeling project, distinguishing between loadbearing and non-loadbearing walls is critical (◁). In general, the exterior walls of a house are loadbearing, that is, they transmit the weight of the roof and floor loads of upper stories to the foundation. If you took the finish off exterior walls, you would find that they utilize special structural elements—frame walls have doubled top plates and broad doubled headers over window and door openings where the normal stud-spacing pattern is interrupted to bear the weight above. If, when you inspect a house, exterior walls appear to buckle, show unusual cracks or vertical or horizontal misalignment, it is evidence of a severe structural problem. And if you altered the structural scheme of an existing exterior wall to build an addition to a home, you would have to design an alternative means of supporting the loads formerly borne by the altered wall.

Interior walls may be loadbearing or non-loadbearing. If a wall runs parallel to floor joists, chances are it has no structural purpose other than to divide the interior space. But if a wall runs perpendicular to joists and you find a similar wall or lollicolumns aligned directly below the wall on a lower story, the wall is loadbearing. A loadbearing wall may also rest on a girder, that is, a heavy horizontal member of steel or wood. Like exterior loadbearing walls, interior bearing walls cannot be removed or structurally altered without providing support for related elements of the building. Obtain advice from a professional architect or engineer before proceeding with alterations to loadbearing walls (◁).

Non-loadbearing walls
These walls divide internal space into rooms and could be removed without damaging the structure.

INTERIOR WALLS

The type of interior wall construction and finish will depend to a certain extent on the age of the building and on the function of the wall within the structure. The most common types are illustrated and discussed on this page.

Wood frame walls

Wood framing is by far the most common structural system used for both interior loadbearing and non-loadbearing partitions (▷). Specific structural differences between the two may consist only of a doubled top plate and more extensive cross-bracing in loadbearing walls. In general, wall studs are set 16 inches on center apart and nailed to top and toe plates. In some non-structural walls, wall studs are set 24 inches on center.

In older houses, thin, closely-spaced wood lath strips are nailed to the wall frame to serve as a structural basis for plaster. Plaster is frequently applied in two coats—an undercoat of brown plaster followed by a finish coat of white finish plaster (▷). In newer buildings, metal wire lath is used as the structural ground for plaster instead of wood lath. Metal lath over wood studs is also frequently found where the wall finish is ceramic tile set over concrete plaster.

In the vast majority of homes built after World War II, interior walls are wood frame finished with gypsum wallboard. The wallboard is nailed to the wall frame in sheets, and seams are finished with a cellulose-base wallboard compound. In some cases, a gypsum product similar to wallboard is nailed to the wall frame and finished with a skim-coat of plaster. Where ceramic tile is applied over a wallboard finish, a mastic adhesive is used as the bonding agent.

Metal stud walls

In recent years, metal stud systems have increasingly been used to construct interior partitions for economy and because of their fire resistance (▷). It is likely that those living in apartment buildings constructed after 1970 will find partitions framed with metal studs and finished with gypsum wallboard, which is fastened to the framing with special screws.

Metal studs and the track that is used for top and toe plates are nominally U-shaped. These materials are easily cut with tin snips or aviation shears. Studs are crimped into place in the tracks, which are used for top and toe plates, and are ordinarily easy to remove with a firm twist.

Non-frame walls

In some masonry buildings, especially large apartment buildings constructed between 1890 and 1945, interior partions may be constructed with lightweight gypsum block or hollow clay block. In most cases with this type of interior wall construction, the wall finish is plaster applied directly to the block. While it is advisable to check with a professional before removing any wall or cutting an opening in it, hollow-block partitions are, in most cases, non-loadbearing. After ascertaining that such a wall serves no critical structural purpose, you can easily break down or open hollow block walls with a sledge hammer and cold chisel. The top of openings in block walls will require a lintel for support (▷).

In modern construction, concrete block walls are frequently used as party walls to separate attached housing units. The wall finish may be plaster or gypsum wallboard. Concrete-block walls are designed to contain the spread of fires and also provide good sound insulation. Generally speaking, party walls are structural and should not be altered without obtaining professional advice and legal permission.

In the most advanced building technology that's being increasingly applied in factory-built, modular homes, walls consist of "stressed-skin panels." While many of the systems are proprietary and the terminology is not entirely uniform, the term usually refers to a wall system that is made with an inner core of rigid foam to which plywood, particleboard or gypsum wallboard has been laminated. The panels have interlocking joints. Never alter a stressed-skin panel structure without consulting the manufacturer for the correct procedure and specifications.

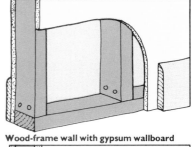

Wood-frame wall with gypsum wallboard

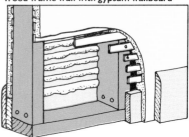

Wood-frame wall with plaster over wood lath

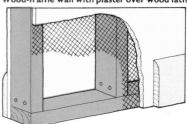

Wood-frame wall with plaster over metal lath

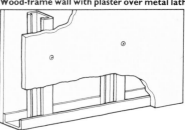

Metal stud wall with gypsum wallboard

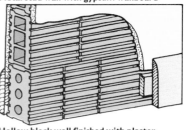

Hollow block wall finished with plaster

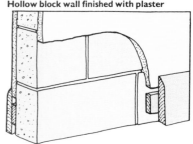

Concrete block wall finished with plaster

Glass blocks
Hollow glass blocks can be used for non-loadbearing walls. Made in square and rectangular shapes and a range of colors they can be laid in mortar or dry-set with plastic jointing strips in a frame.

SEE ALSO

◁ Details for:
**Opening masonry
walls** 130–131

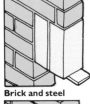
Stone and timber

Brick and steel

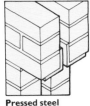
Reinforced concrete

Pressed steel

Rolled steel

TYPES OF LINTELS

A lintel is used in brick, block and stone construction to bridge a gap above a window, door or other wall opening.

WOOD AND STEEL

In frame buildings with a brick veneer, a rolled-steel angle is frequently used to support the brick above a door or window opening. The lintel, however, does little to support the overall roof and wall structure. Instead, a wood header whose dimensions are based on the load and span of the opening is installed behind the steel lintel.

FLAT ROLLED STEEL

A flat rolled-steel lintel is sometimes used to support a soldier course of brick to form a lintel. This lintel construction method is not especially strong and is generally limited to brick veneer structures.

REINFORCED CONCRETE

Precast concrete lintels are among the most widely used in modern masonry construction. While concrete bears compression loads well, it does not resist tension well. Because lintels are subject to both types of forces, precast concrete lintels have steel reinforcing bars embedded in them to improve their tensile strength.

Prestressed concrete lintels, reinforced with wire strands set in the concrete under tension, are lighter than other concrete lintels. Precast concrete lintels are available in a variety of standard sizes to match wall thicknesses and course heights, but may be rather awkward to handle in large sizes. Some concrete lintels are cast with a hollow that is reinforced with steel and filled with grout after being set in place.

ROLLED-STEEL ANGLES

Rolled-steel angles are commonly used for lintels in masonry construction; the size of the angle is based on the load. Inserting an angle at the top of the opening in each leaf of a cavity wall is on standard method, but sometimes angles are bolted together or welded to other steel members of the building's structural frame.

SPANNING OPENINGS IN BRICK WALLS

Creating an opening in a brick or block wall for a door or window requires installation of a lintel to support the *structural load above it. Some structural principles relating to brick walls are discussed below.*

Where supports are needed

Door or window frames aren't designed to carry superimposed loads, so the load from floors above—even the brick-work above the opening—must be supported by a rigid beam called a lintel, which transmits the weight to the sides where the bearings are firm. Wider openings call for stronger beams, such as rolled-steel lintels. There are numerous beams, but all work in the same way.

The forces on a beam

When a load is placed at the center of a beam supported at each end, the beam will bend. The lower portion is being stretched and is in "tension;" the top portion is being squeezed and is in "compression." The beam is also subjected to "shear" forces where the vertical load is trying to sever the beam at the points of support. A beam must be able to resist these forces. This is achieved by the correct choice of material and the depth of the beam in relation to the imposed load and the span of the opening.

Calculating lintel size

The purpose of a lintel is to form a straight bridge across an opening, which can carry the load of the structure above it. The load may be relatively light, being no more than a number of brick or block courses. It is more likely that other loads from upper floors and the roof will also bear on the lintel.

The size of the lintel must be suitable for the job it has to do. The size should be derived from calculations based on the weight of the materials used in the construction of the building. Calculation for specifying a beam is a job for an architect or structural engineer. Tables relating to the weight of the materials are used on which to base the figures.

In practice, for typical situations, a builder can help you decide on the required size of lintel based on his experience. A building inspector usually will be happy to accept this type of specification, but he can insist that proper calculations are also submitted along with your application for a building permit.

When to support a wall

If you are creating a door, window or finished opening which is no wider than 3 feet across in a non-loadbearing wall, you can cut the hole without having to support the wall above providing the wall is properly bonded and sound. The only area of brickwork that is likely to collapse is roughly in the shape of a 45-degree triangle directly above the opening leaving a self-supporting stepped arch of brickwork. This effect is known as "self-corbelling". Do not rely on the self-corbelling effect to support the wall if you plan to make an opening which is more than three feet wide. In that case, temporarily support the wall as if it were loadbearing.

Before you make any opening in a loadbearing wall you will need to erect adjustable props (◁) as temporary supports, not only for the weight of the masonry but also for the loads that bear on it from floors, walls and roof above.

Self-corbelling
The shaded bricks are the only ones at risk of falling out before the lintel is installed because of the self-corbelling effect of the bricks above. Theoretically the lintel supports the weight of the materials within the 60° triangle plus any superimposed floor or roof loading, but when the side walls (piers) are narrow, the load on the lintel is increased to encompass the area of the rectangle.

RIGGING UP ADJUSTABLE PROPS

To remove part of a loadbearing wall it's necessary to temporarily support the wall above the opening. Rent adjustable steel jacks (▷) and scaffold boards to spread the load across the floor. Where part of a bearing wall will remain below the ceiling level, you will also need "needles" to spread the load. Needles can generally be made with 4-by-6 lumber about 6 feet long.

For a window or door opening, probably only one needle and two props will suffice: place the needle centrally over the opening about 6 inches above the lintel or header position. For wider openings, or where a load is great, two needles and four props will be needed, spaced no more than 3 feet apart across the width of the opening.

Cut a hole in the wall for each needle and insert them. Support each end with a prop, which works like a car jack. Stand the props on scaffold boards no more than 2 feet from each side of the wall.

Loadbearing wall
Construct adequate header and support with jack studs.

HEADER

SUPPORTING STUDS

Stud partition
Fit framing at top and bottom of opening.

MAKING A WALL OPENING

A pass-through is a convenient opening in a wall, usually between a kitchen and dining area, through which you can pass food, drinks and equipment. If you are blocking off a doorway, or making a stud wall, it may be advantageous to allow for a pass-through. You may want to make a pass-through in an existing wall.

Planning the size and shape

Ideally the bottom of the opening should be an extension of the kitchen worktop or at least flush with a work surface: 3 feet is a comfortable working height (▷) and the standard height for kitchen worktops. For practicality—passing through a tray and serving dishes, for instance—it should not be narrower than 2 feet 6 inches.

Hatches should be fitted with some means of closing the opening for privacy, preventing cooking odors from drifting and, in some cases, as a fire-check (See right).

Creating the opening in a masonry wall

You can make an opening in either a loadbearing or a solid non-loadbearing wall in much the same way: the main requirement with the former is temporarily supporting the structure above and the load imposed on the wall (▷). Mark the position for the opening on one side of the wall. Align the hole with the vertical and horizontal mortar courses between bricks or blocks to save having to cut too many bricks—break away a square of plaster at the center to locate the joints.

Mark out the shape and position of the opening on the other side of the wall using adjacent walls, the ceiling and floor as references, or drill through at the corners. Make the hole about 1 inch oversize to allow for a jamb. Mark the lintel position.

Set up adjustable props and needles if you're working on a loadbearing wall (see left), then chop a slot for the lintel with a sledgehammer and bolster chisel—on a brick wall this will probably be a single course of bricks deep; on a block wall, remove a whole course of blocks and fill the gap with bricks. Trowel mortar onto the bearings and set the lintel in place. Use a level to check that the lintel is perfectly horizontal—pack under it with pieces of slate if necessary. Replace any bricks above the lintel that have dropped. Leave 24 hours to set, then remove props, needles and the masonry below.

Making an opening in a stud wall

Cutting an opening in a non-loadbearing stud partition wall is simpler than making one in a solid wall, but if the wall bears some weight you'll need to support the floor or ceiling above with props using planks to spread the load.

Mark out, then cut away the wallboard or lath-and-plaster covering from each side to expose the studs. For an opening the width between studs (16 inches), just toenail 2-by-4s between them at the top and bottom of the opening. If it will be wider, make the opening span three studs. Cut away part of the middle stud at the height you want the jamb, allowing for the thickness of a horizontal frame member above and below the opening. Make the framing from 2-by-4 lumber and cut them to fit between the two studs on each side of the cut one. Fit and check for level.

Fitting a finished jamb

Line the four sides of the opening with ¾-inch-thick pine of a width equal to the wall thickness joined at the corners with butt joints or 45-degree miter joints for a neater result. The frame can finish flush with the wall surface and be covered with a casing, or project beyond the wall finish to form a lip.

The sides of the opening in a masonry wall may be rough—it's not easy to cut a clean line. Make and fit the frame, then shim out the gap between masonry and lining with wood shingles—the frame must be square within the opening; check with a level. Screw the frame to masonry with lead anchors, fitted when the frame is positioned. Fill gaps with mortar. Rake back the surface of the mortar. When set finish flush with plaster.

SEE ALSO

Details for: ▷	
Planning spaces	12–16
Propping	130
Opening masonry walls	130–131

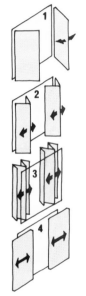

Pass-through doors
1 Double-hinged
2 Twin bi-fold
3 Concertina
4 Horizontal-sliding

Finishing the frame
Use a casing to cover the joint between the jamb and wall or let the frame project to mask it.

Fit a casing

Let jamb project

125

CUTTING AN INTERIOR DOORWAY

In an interior remodeling project, you may wish to create a doorway in an existing solid wall. First determine whether the wall is loadbearing or non-loadbearing, *then depending on which is appropriate for your situation, follow one of the procedures explained and illustrated below.*

Framing a door opening in a loadbearing wall

You can generally tell whether a wall is loadbearing or nonstructural by removing the wall finish in the area where you wish to situate the door up to the ceiling. Gypsum wallboard can easily be stripped away by cutting with a utility knife or wallboard saw; plaster must be chipped off with a bolster chisel and then the lath must be cut away.

If you find a doubled top plate, you can assume that the wall is loadbearing. A little further checking will probably show floor joists resting on top of the wall frame. This is a clear indication that you will have to set up temporary supports to bear the structural load before removing any wall studs and that you will need to construct a structural header when framing the rough opening for the doorway. Seek professional advice from an engineer or building inspector on specifications for the header. If the opening is 3 feet wide or less, chances are that a wood header of 2-by-12s will be sufficient, but wider openings may require a steel beam.

Place temporary props in place as shown at the right; props must be set on both sides of interior bearing walls. Once adequate support is in place, remove any studs that fall within the area of the desired opening. Cut away the toe plate of the wall from the bottom of the opening.

If it is not convenient to use existing studs as sides for the doorway's rough opening, new studs may be nailed in position as desired. Remember that when setting the width of the rough opening, an allowance must be made for the thickness of the jack studs that will support the structural header and for the materials that will be used to finish its inside edges—either a jamb of ¾-inch thick lumber, plaster or wallboard.

Once the full-length studs at the sides of the rough opening are nailed in place with 10d common nails, nail the jack studs in place. They should be cut to a length equal to the rough opening height. Then nail up the header using 2-inch-thick lumber of the necessary width using scraps of ½-inch-thick plywood as spacers between the two lengths used to make up the header. Set the header in place on top of the jack studs and nail. Insert cripple studs to run from the top of the header to the underside of the doubled top plate—these transmit the structural load to the header.

Once the framing is complete, the temporary props can be removed. The wall finish can be restored, and the door opening can be finished, either with a wood jamb and casing, or with ordinary wall finish materials (◁).

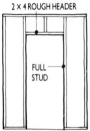

Framing for door opening in a non-loadbearing partition

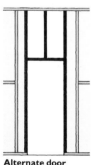

Alternate door framing methods for non-loadbearing partitions

Framing a door opening in a non-loadbearing partition

A door opening in a nonstructural frame partition is fairly straightforward. The task will be simplest if you can situate the doorway between two existing studs in the wall frame. Start at one end of the wall where you want the opening, and measure off increments of 16 inches to locate the wall studs. Probe the area where you think the studs to be used for sides of the rough jamb are. If you don't find them immediately, measure off 16-inch increments from the opposite end of the wall. If you can't put the opening between two existing studs, you will have to insert new studs to serve as vertical rough jambs.

Draw layout lines on the wall for the sides and top of the opening. The opening will look best if the top aligns with other doors and windows in the room. Remove the baseboard molding, and cut away the wall finish inside the layout lines. At the top of the opening you will have to cut away the wall finish about 2½ inches higher than the layout line. Cut any existing studs that fall within the opening at a point 2½ inches higher than the desired height for the finished opening. (Cut the studs 1½ inches plus the thickness of the wall-finish material higher than the layout mark if you do not plan to install a finished door jamb.) Cut a rough header for the opening from one of the studs you removed and nail it across the top with its wide side down, making sure it is level. Then, install the door jamb or finish the opening as desired.

Before you begin to alter the framing of a loadbearing wall to create a doorway or for any reason, it is necessary to set up temporary support. You can rent or purchase adjustable jack posts such as those shown below for this purpose. First, determine the direction of the floor joists and set a length of 2-by-10 lumber on the floor about 2 feet from the wall, perpendicular to the joist direction. Adjust the jack posts to the approximate height needed by setting the pins in the correct holes in the telescoping body. Wedge a second 2-by-10 between the top of the jack posts and the ceiling, setting the jacks plumb. Screw the threaded rod at the top of each jack post upward until the jacks and plates are snug. Make similar setups on both sides of interior walls.

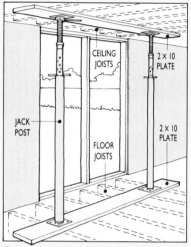

Temporary supports for cutting a door opening

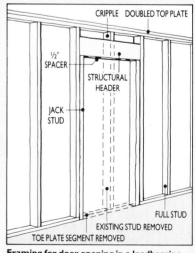

Framing for door opening in a loadbearing wall

FILLING AN OPENING IN A STUD PARTITION

Strip the door jambs as described (see right). Trim the lath-and-plaster or plasterboard back to the center line of the door jamb studs and header, with a sharp utility knife. Remove the old nails with a claw hammer. Nail the new cut edge all around.

Nail a matching toe plate to the floor between the studs. Cut and nail a new stud centrally between header and toe plate. Cut and nail braces between the studs across the opening. Fasten wallboard to each face of the opening. Cut the board 1/8 inch less all around. Fill and tape the joints (▷), then finish as desired with paint or with wallcovering.

Nail the toe plate, stud and braces

BLOCKING OFF A DOORWAY

If you are making a new opening in a wall, it's possible that you will also have to block off the original one. Obviously, you'll want the patch to be invisible, which takes careful plastering or joint filling of wallboard.

Choosing the right materials

It is better to fill in the opening with the same materials used in the construction of the wall—although you can consider bricks and blocks as the same—to prevent cracks forming from movement in the structure. You could use a wooden stud frame with gypsum lath board and a skimcoat of plaster finish to fill an opening in a brick wall, but it would not have the same acoustic properties as block or brick and cracks are difficult to prevent or disguise.

Removing the woodwork

Saw through the door jambs close to the top and pry them away from the structural framework with a wrecking bar. Start levering at the bottom. If the jambs were fitted before the flooring, the ends could be trapped: cut them flush with the floor. Next, pry the jamb header away from the top.

Bricking up the opening

Cut back the plaster about 6 inches all around the opening. It need not be an even line; unevenness helps to disguise the outline of the doorway.

To bond the new brickwork into the old, cut out a half-brick on each side of the opening at every fourth course, using a sledgehammer and bolster chisel. For a block wall, remove a quarter of a block from alternate courses.

It's not vital to tooth-in the infill if you're using blocks (which are easy and quick to lay) as it will require more cutting to fit. Instead, 4-inch steel cut nails driven dovetail fashion into the bed joints of the side brickwork (**1**) can be used to tie the masonry together.

Galvanized angle brackets can also be used to save cutting into the bricks (**2**)—screw them to the wall, resting on every fourth brick.

Lay the bricks or blocks in mortar, following the original courses. If a wooden suspended floor runs through the opening, lay the bricks on a wood toe plate nailed across the opening. When the mortar has set, spread on a base coat of plaster, followed by a finishing coat (▷). Fit two complete lengths of new matching baseboard, or add to the original. When making up the baseboard from odd pieces, make sure the joints do not occur in the same place as the original opening.

SEE ALSO

Details for: ▷
Plastering a wall 157
Finishing
wallboard 164–165

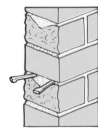

1 Nail ties

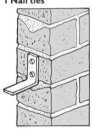

2 Angle bracket tie

Cut out half-bricks

Lay bricks into the courses

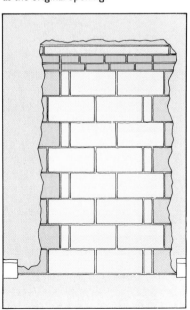

Cut blocks to match bonding

CONVERTING TWO ROOMS TO ONE

Removing a wall may be the best way to improve access between areas frequently used—the dining and living rooms, for instance—and of course it can expand your living space considerably. The job uses similar principles to making a pass-through or a new doorway, although on a much larger scale. Removing a dividing wall—whether it's structural or simply a non-loadbearing partition—is a major undertaking, but it need not be overwhelming. If you follow some basic safety and structural rules, much of the job is straightforward, if messy and disruptive. Before you start, plan out your requirements and consult the flow chart, right, for a breakdown of just what's involved.

SEE ALSO

◁ Details for:
Planning   12–16

WHY DO YOU WANT TO REMOVE A WALL?

Before you go ahead and demolish the wall between two rooms, consider just how the new space might function, its appearance, the time it will take you to carry out the work, and the cost (◁).

Ask yourself the following questions:
● Will the shape and size of the new room suit your needs? Remember, if you have a young family, your needs are likely to change as they grow up.
● Will most of the family activities be carried out in the same room (eating, watching TV, playing music, reading, conversation, playing with toys, hobbies, homework)?
● Will removing the wall deprive you of privacy within the family, or from passersby in the street?
● Will the new room feel like one unit and not a conversion? For example, do the baseboards and moldings match?
● Are the fireplaces acceptable when seen together, or should one be removed? Should one of the doorways, if close together, be blocked off?
● Will the loss of a wall make the furniture arrangements difficult—particularly if central-heating radiators are in use and take up valuable wall space elsewhere?
● Will the heating and lighting need to be modified?
● Will the proposed shape of the opening be in character with the room and the right proportion?

● **Hiring professionals**
If you're in doubt, hire a professional builder: to save costs, you may be able to work as a laborer or do preparation and clearing work.

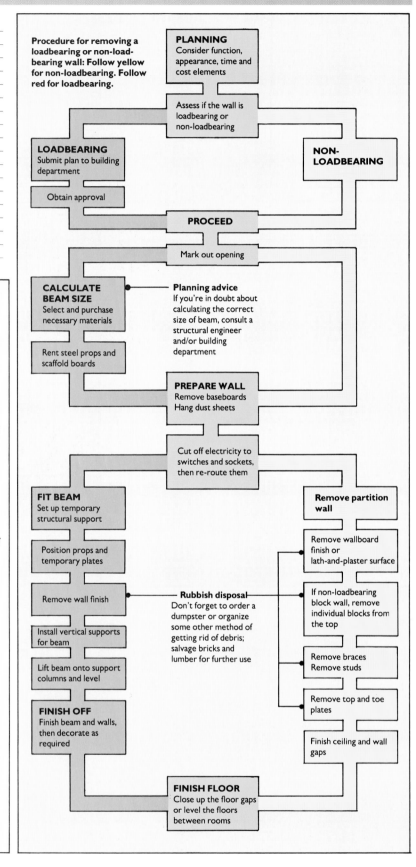

Procedure for removing a loadbearing or non-load-bearing wall: Follow yellow for non-loadbearing. Follow red for loadbearing.

PLANNING
Consider function, appearance, time and cost elements

Assess if the wall is loadbearing or non-loadbearing

LOADBEARING
Submit plan to building department

Obtain approval

NON-LOADBEARING

PROCEED

Mark out opening

CALCULATE BEAM SIZE
Select and purchase necessary materials

Rent steel props and scaffold boards

Planning advice
If you're in doubt about calculating the correct size of beam, consult a structural engineer and/or building department

PREPARE WALL
Remove baseboards
Hang dust sheets

Cut off electricity to switches and sockets, then re-route them

FIT BEAM
Set up temporary structural support

Position props and temporary plates

Remove wall finish

Install vertical supports for beam

Lift beam onto support columns and level

FINISH OFF
Finish beam and walls, then decorate as required

Rubbish disposal
Don't forget to order a dumpster or organize some other method of getting rid of debris; salvage bricks and lumber for further use

Remove partition wall

Remove wallboard finish or lath-and-plaster surface

If non-loadbearing block wall, remove individual blocks from the top

Remove braces
Remove studs

Remove top and toe plates

Finish ceiling and wall gaps

FINISH FLOOR
Close up the floor gaps or level the floors between rooms

If a loadbearing wall is to be removed to create a more open plan, a beam must be installed to maintain the home's structural integrity. *The basic concerns of and options for removing a loadbearing wall are discussed below.*

Structural concerns

An interior loadbearing wall generally supports the weight of an upper floor and sometimes, depending on the design, part of the weight of the roof. When a loadbearing wall is removed, provisions must be made to support the loads on that wall. Typically, a horizontal beam is installed in the area where joists of the upper floor rested on the top plate of the wall that is being removed. The beam is supported by vertical columns that transmit the load to the foundation and other structural elements of the house frame.

The size of the beam is determined by several factors: the load it must bear, the span between the vertical columns that support it, the distance from the beam to other structural elements that run parallel to it, the material from which the beam is made and local standards for minimum floor load capacities. While determining the necessary size required for a beam in any given situation is a matter for a professional engineer, architect or building official, in general, the greater the load, span between vertical supports, and distance from parallel structural elements, the larger the beam must be. The required thickness and depth of a beam can vary based on variations of the number and spacing of support columns and with the introduction of other structural elements running parallel to the beam.

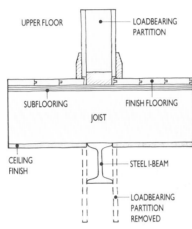

UPPER FLOOR — LOADBEARING PARTITION

SUBFLOORING — FINISH FLOORING

JOIST

CEILING FINISH — STEEL I-BEAM

— LOADBEARING PARTITION REMOVED

Steel I-beam bears load where structural wall is removed

Choosing a beam

Beams of several different materials can be used to provide structural support where a loadbearing wall is removed. In many cases, rolled steel I-beams are used. Because of steel's great strength, the depth of the beam can be relatively shallow compared with the other options, and this may be an important concern where maximum headroom for an opening is critical. But steel beams can present some difficulties for typical do-it-yourselfers. Most codes require that steel beams be supported by steel columns, and that connections be either welded or bolted—both options require special equipment and skills.

Finishing a steel beam can also be problematic (▷).

Laminated wood-beams are a desirable option preferred by do-it-yourselfers and increasingly specified by architects. The beams are made by laminating several thicknesses of dimension lumber, and several appearance grades are available which may either finished with wallboard or left exposed for decorative effect. Laminated beams can be cut and drilled with ordinary woodworking tools, and can be joined to columns with structural joints, lag screws or approved metal fastening plates.

Planning and approval

It is necessary to obtain a building permit before removing a loadbearing wall. In order to obtain a permit, it is necessary to provide the inspector with drawings that include key details of the existing structure and specifications for the installation of the new supporting structure. While a knowledgeable do-it-yourselfer may be able to prepare such drawings, it is highly recommended that you consult with an architect or structural engineer when tackling a project that involves altering structural elements of a home.

HOW A BEAM IS SUPPORTED

Beams are supported by vertical columns that transmit the load to other structural elements within the building. The required number and spacing of columns is contingent on the load and the size of the beam.

The drawing below illustrates a typical configuration. The structural beam supporting the second floor joists is supported by a column that transmits the weight to the end of a girder notched into the foundation wall. As you move to the left you see another column supporting the beam. That column bears directly on the girder and aligns with a column supporting it. The key point is that columns must align either exactly or very nearly to maintain the structural integrity of the beam. Note that a concrete footing appears below the basement floor slab beneath the columns to bear and spread the weight of the imposed load.

SEE ALSO

Details for: ▷
House
construction   120-121
Finishing beams   131

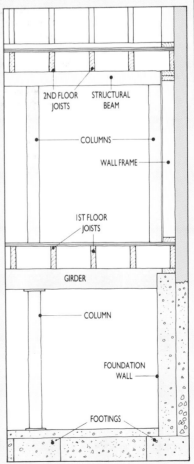

2ND FLOOR JOISTS   STRUCTURAL BEAM

COLUMNS

WALL FRAME

IST FLOOR JOISTS

GIRDER

COLUMN

FOUNDATION WALL

FOOTINGS

SEE ALSO

◁ Details for:
Baseboards   181

I Layout for removing wall flush with ceiling

Supporting the wall
I When removing a
wall up to ceiling level,
support the upper floor
with scaffold boards
and props alone when
the joists pass through
the brickwork to
support the wall.
Otherwise, in addition,
use needles on jacks
placed directly above
the props.
2 Normally brickwork
projects below the
ceiling level and is
supported on needles
passing through holes in
the wall.

2 Layout for removing wall below ceiling

SAFE PROPPING PROCEDURE

To reduce the risk of structural collapse
when opening up walls, it is critical to
set up props in a safe manner. Use a
level to make sure that props are
exactly vertical and always use heavy
boards running perpendicular to the
floor joists at the bearing points of the
jacks to spread the load. If the floor
structure on which props are bearing
seems springy, set jack posts directly
beneath them on the floor below.

OPENING MASONRY WALLS

To remove part of a masonry wall you
must temporarily support the wall
above the opening. You will need to
rent adjustable steel props and scaffold
boards on which to support them.
Where the beam is to be placed at
ceiling level, rent extra boards to
support the ceiling (**I**). Generally you
will have to fit needles through the wall
to transfer the load to the props (**2**).
The needles must be at least 4 by 6
inches in section.

Rent sufficient props to be spaced not
more than 3 feet apart across the width
of the opening. If possible, buy the beam
after the initial inspection by the building
department officer's inspection. It can
then be cut to your exact requirements.

Preparation and marking out
Remove the baseboards from both sides
of the wall (◁). Working from one side,
mark out the position of the beam on
the wall in pencil. Use a steel tape
measure, level and straightedge for
accuracy.

Hang dust sheets around the work
area on the opposite face of the wall to
help contain much of the inevitable
airborne dust; attach them with furring
nailed over them at the top. Seal gaps
around all doors with masking tape to
prevent the dust from traveling
throughout the house. Open windows
in the rooms you're working in.

Inserting the needles
Mark the positions for the needles on
the wall, then cut away the plaster
locally and chisel a hole through the
brickwork at each point. Finish level
with the bottom of one course of
bricks. Make the holes slightly oversize
so you can easily pass the needles
through. Position a pair of adjustable
props under each needle not more than
2 feet from each side of the wall. Stand
the props on scaffold boards to spread
the load over the floor.

Adjust the props to take the weight
of the structure and nail their base
plates to the supporting boards to
prevent them being dislodged.

Supporting the ceiling
If the ceiling needs supporting, stand the
props on scaffold boards at each side of
the wall and adjust so they're virtually to
ceiling height—they should be placed 2
feet from the wall. Place another plank
on top of the pairs of props and adjust
simultaneously until the ceiling joists are
supported.

Removing the wall
Chip off plaster with a sledgehammer
and bolster chisel, then cut out the
brickwork, working from the top. Once
you've removed four or five courses,
cut the bricks on the side of the
opening. Chisel downwards, pointing
towards the wall to cut the bricks
cleanly. Remove all brickwork down to
one course below the floorboards.
Clear the rubble as you work into
garbage bags—it may be worth renting
a dumpster. The job is slow and
laborious, but a circular saw with a
masonry blade can make it easier and
quicker.

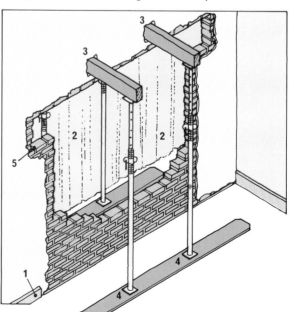

Cutting the opening
I Remove or cut back
the baseboard and mark
the beam's position.
2 Hang dust sheets
around the work area.
3 Cut openings and
insert needles.
4 Stand props on
scaffold boards and
adjust them to support
the needles.
5 Cut away the plaster,
then chisel out the
bricks starting from the
top of the opening.

PLACING THE BEAM

Masonry supports for a beam

A rolled steel I-beam may be used for a lintel to support masonry above a large opening. In loadbearing cavity walls, the ends of a beam can usually be supported in notches cut into the wall itself that are fitted with a solid concrete masonry unit (CMU) to serve as the bearing surface. A structural engineer or building inspector should decide whether the wall structure and foundation can support the concentrated load transmitted by the beam ends. When the foundation structure is inadequate, or where there is no foundation at all as in a non-loadbearing hollow block partition, masonry piers and footings must be constructed. Design of masonry piers should be left to a professional.

Installing the beam

Make two wooden forms or boxes from thick plywood or utility-grade lumber and cast concrete padstones (on which to bed the beam) to the size required by the building code. Mix the concrete to the proportions 1 part cement: 2 parts sand: 4 parts aggregate. When they are set, bed the padstones in mortar at the top of each pier. When a large padstone is required, it may be better to cast it in place: set up formwork at the required height on each side and check the level between the two sides.

Build a work platform by placing doubled-up scaffold boards between steady stepladders, or rent scaffold tower sections. You'll need assistance to lift the beam into position.

Apply mortar to the padstones, then lift and set the beam in place. Pack pieces of slate between the beam and the brickwork above to fill the gap. An alternate method is to pack the gap with a mortar mix of 1 part cement: 3 parts sand, which is just wet enough to bind it together. Work it well into the gap with a bricklaying trowel and compact it with a wooden block and a hammer. Where the gap can take a whole brick or more, apply a bed of mortar and rebuild the brickwork on top of the beam. Work the course between the needles so that when they are removed the holes can be filled in to continue the bonding. Allow two days for the mortar to set, then remove the props and needles and fill in the holes.

When the beam is fitted against ceiling joists you can use a different method. Support the ceiling with props and a board to spread the load (see left), on each side of the wall. Cut away the wall, lift the beam into position and fit a pair of adjustable props under it. Apply mortar to the top of the beam and adjust the props to push it against the joists and brickwork above. Bed the padstones in mortar or build formwork at each end and cast them.

FINISHING THE BEAM

A steel beam should be enclosed to provide protection from fire (which would cause it to distort) and to give a flat surface that can be decorated. Wet plaster, gypsum wallboard or a specially made fireproof board can be used.

Cladding with plaster
Box in a beam with galvanized wire lath to provide a key for the plaster. Fold the mesh around the beam, then lap it onto the brickwork above and secure with galvanized nails.

Alternatively, wedge-shaped wooden blocks (soldiers) into the recessed sides of the beam and nail the metal lath to these. It's a good idea to prime the cut edges of the lath to prevent corrosion, which can stain the plaster.

Boxing in with wallboard
To box in the beam with wallboard, you will need to fit shaped wooden blocks, wedged into the sides. To these fix wooden furring nailed together to make nailers for the wallboard panels (if you plan to install a folding door system in the opening, you can nail the door jamb directly to these same nailers (▷). Set the wallboard about 1/8-inch below plaster level to allow for a skim coat to finish flush with the surrounding wall. Fill and seal the joints with tape compound (▷).

Plaster the piers, then finish the beam and pier together.

Disguising the beam
You can conceal a steel I-beam by fitting a simulated oak beam, molded from rigid urethane foam plastic, which can be simply glued or nailed over the beam, to give a country cottage effect to the room.

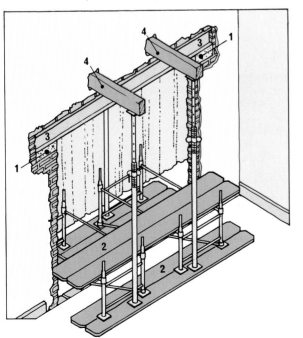

Installing the beam
1 Cast concrete padstones and set them on the brickwork piers.
2 Set up a secure platform to enable two people to work safely.
3 Place the beam on the mortared padstones and check level. Fill the gaps between the beam and the brickwork.
4 When set, remove the props and needles and fill the holes.

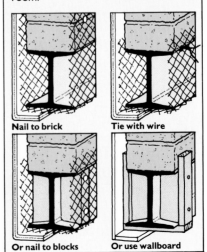

Nail to brick   Tie with wire

Or nail to blocks   Or use wallboard

131

CREATING INTERIOR ARCHES

When opening a partition wall to create one room from two or when creating a passage from one room to another, it may be desirable to create a finished opening in the form of an arch. Methods of constructing and finishing arches with gypsum wallboard and plaster are discussed below.

Wire lath-plaster arches

To create a plaster arch, first construct a frame as if you were going to finish the walls with wallboard, except you don't need to create the scored plywood arch. Apply wire lath to the framing with galvanized or blued fasteners and form the curve of the arch with a strip of wire lath. Fasten the strip to the inside of the rough jamb and to the supporting members overhead. Where the edges of the lath lining the inside of the arch meet with those of the lath on the wall surface, tie the corners together with wire. Apply plaster to the lath in two or more coats, with the first being brown coat or rough plaster followed by smooth coats (◁).

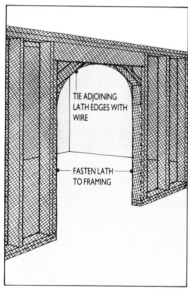

Preparation for plaster arch

TIE ADJOINING LATH EDGES WITH WIRE

FASTEN LATH TO FRAMING

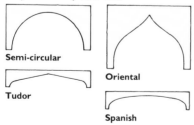

Semi-circular

Tudor

Oriental

Spanish

When designing an arch, proportion and style are key elements. A variety of arch profiles is illustrated above

Plywood-wallboard arch construction

Begin by framing a rectangular opening using 2-by-4 lumber to establish the overall height and width of the arch. Then, based on a scale drawing, determine the best locations for framing members that will run tangent to the arc and provide fastening points for a plywood strip that will be bent to form the curve. These framing members may either be lengths of 2-by-4 set at an angle between the header and rough sidejambs as shown in the drawing at the right, or vertical cripple studs cut to suitable lengths and angles to match the curve of the arch. Using the method of framing with cripples over the arch is the more difficult of the two methods.

Once the framing members are in place, rip a piece of ½-inch plywood to a width equal to that of the framing—if 2-by-4 is being used, then the correct width for the plywood would be 3½-inches. Then, set a portable circular saw to a depth of about ⅜-inch and cut saw kerfs spaced about ½-inch apart across the back of the plywood strip in the areas that must be bent to create the curve. The series of kerfs makes the plywood flexible.

Begin attaching the plywood strip at lower corner formed by the vertical rough jamb and floor. The saw kerfs should be oriented toward the framing, not facing into the opening. Drywall screws 1¼-inches long may be used as fasteners. Continue along working upward and toward the opposite side of the arch until the plywood is in place and the structural frame achieves rigidity. In some cases, it may be desirable to apply two layers of plywood to form the arch for extra stability.

Apply a strip of gypsum wallboard directly to the plywood. If the curve is relatively sharp, it may be necessary to moisten the back of the wallboard with a damp sponge to keep it from cracking as it is bent and fastened. After applying wallboard to the inside of the arch, apply it to the wall surfaces. Then apply corner beads where raw wallboard edges meet and finish with tape and wallboard compound (◁). It will be necessary to make parallel cuts along one of the flanges of the corner bead to make it flexible enough to conform to the arch. The cut flange is positioned against the vertical wall for installation, and each tab should be fastened.

HEADER   2 × 4 BRACES
TANGENT TO ARCH

½" PLYWOOD WITH SCORED BACK

FASTENERS

Framing preparation for wallboard arch

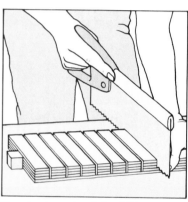

To make plywood easily bendable, cut saw kerfs across the back just deep enough to leave one of the veneer faces intact

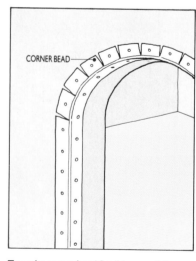

CORNER BEAD

To make corner bead flexible enough to conform to the shape of a wallboard arch, cut a series of notches in one of the flanges

REMOVING A NON-LOADBEARING WALL

Lightweight partition walls which are not loadbearing can be removed safely without consulting the authorities for approval and without the need to add temporary

supports. You must, however, be certain that the wall is not structural before doing so, as some partitions do offer partial structural support.

Dismantling a stud partition

Remove the baseboards from both sides of the wall and any other moldings. It's a good idea to save these for re-use or repairs in the future. If any electrical switches or socket outlets are attached to the wall, they must be disconnected and re-routed before work begins (▷).

Removing the plasterwork
Use a claw hammer or wrecking bar to remove the plaster and laths or wallboard cladding covering the wall frame. Once stripped to the framework, remove the vertical studs. Gather the debris which collects during stripping and remove it for disposal.

Removing the framework
First knock away any nailed bracing

Dismantling a blockwork wall

Partition walls are sometimes made using lightweight concrete blocks (▷). To remove the wall, start to cut away the individual units with a bolster chisel and sledgehammer from the top. Work

from between the studs. If the studs are nailed to the head and sill, they can be knocked apart. If they are difficult to remove, saw through them (at an angle to prevent the saw binding). If you make the cut close to the joint, you will be left with a useful length of re-usable lumber for future work.

Pry off the top and toe plates from the ceiling joists and floor. If the end studs are nailed to the walls, pry them away from the wall with a wrecking bar.

Finishing off
Fill the gap in the ceiling and walls, fitting a narrow strip of wallboard if necessary (▷). Fit floorboards together to close the gap if the boards are not continuous.

from the middle out to the sides.
Cut away an area of plaster first, so that you can locate the joints between blocks, then drive your chisel into these to lever them out.

METHODS OF CLOSING A FLOOR GAP

When you remove a wall to create one room from two or part of a wall to create a passage, a gap may be left in the finish flooring where the toe plate of the wall had been fastened to the subflooring.

If a gap runs parallel to the direction of the boards in wood strip flooring, you can fill it with little disturbance to the pattern. Since floor boards are generally milled with a tongue on one edge and a groove on the other so that they interlock when they are installed, fitting new boards into a confined space can present a problem. If the protuding tongue of an existing floorboard will not allow you to set the filler board in place, chisel away the lower edge of the wood that forms the groove to compensate for the obstruction. If the filler board must be ripped to a narrower width to fit into the space, cut a rabbet to fit over the tongue.

If the gap runs perpendicular to the existing flooring, it will look better to fill it with strips running in the same direction rather than with short strips to match the existing pattern. In this case, match the groove side of a filler board against the ends of existing flooring at one side of the gap and fasten with finish nails driven through the tongue. This technique is called "blind-nailing." Fit the grooves of subsequent rows over the tongues of installed strips and fasten in the same way. To fit the final strip in place, remove the tongue with a chisel or rip the board to the correct width from the tongue edge. The last strip will need to be face-nailed in place.

SEE ALSO

Details for: ▷	
Interior walls	123
Gypsum wallboard	158–167
Switches	310
Receptacles	314
Mismatched floors	134

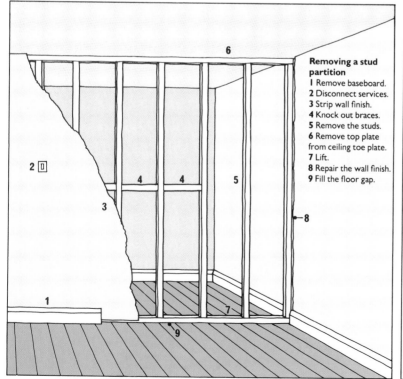

Removing a stud partition
1 Remove baseboard.
2 Disconnect services.
3 Strip wall finish.
4 Knock out braces.
5 Remove the studs.
6 Remove top plate from ceiling toe plate.
7 Lift.
8 Repair the wall finish.
9 Fill the floor gap.

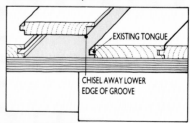

EXISTING TONGUE

CHISEL AWAY LOWER EDGE OF GROOVE

Gap parallel to floor boards

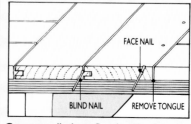

FACE NAIL

BLIND NAIL   REMOVE TONGUE

Gap perpendicular to floor boards

133

ALIGNING MISMATCHED FLOORS

When a partition wall separating two rooms is removed or when an opening is made to create a passageway, it is sometimes the case that the levels of the finished flooring on the two sides of the wall are at different heights. This occurs most frequently when the finished flooring of one room is different from the other, or when a floor has been refinished during a previous remodeling project.

For the sake of both appearance and safety, it is desirable either to create a uniform level or to provide an appropriate transition between the two levels. Several possible solutions to the problem are discussed below.

SEE ALSO

◁ Details for:

Floors   175–181

Treating slight mismatches

The slightest mismatches in floor levels can create tricky steps that cause people to trip, perhaps because of the unconscious habit of lifting one's feet only a certain amount while walking. When a slight mismatch exists, it is desirable to create a distinct visual transition between the two floor surfaces.

For example, a slight mismatch could exist when one part of a floor surface is finished with ceramic tile and the remainder with wood strip flooring. Ordinarily, the tile floor could be anywhere from 1/4- to 7/8-inches higher than the wood floor, attributable to the thickness of the subflooring beneath the tile plus the tile thickness. Three simple treatments would be possible for addressing this problem.

The first would be to install a saddle to cover the gap left by the wall that has been removed. The best way to do this would be to fill the gap with wood blocks or strips level with the wood floor. The saddle, a stock molding available in several widths at any lumber yard, would then be nailed in place over the filler blocks. The top of the saddle should be level with or slightly higher than the higher of the two surfaces.

A second alternative here would be to nail a quarter-round molding to the tile subflooring's edge. This would provide the appropriate visual transition and also would protect the tile edge from cracking.

A third solution that would unify the room and address a slight mismatch in floor levels would be to fill the gap left where the wall was removed with a proprietary cementitious floor-filling compound finished with a slope to make the transition from one level to the other. The entire floor surface could then be covered with carpeting.

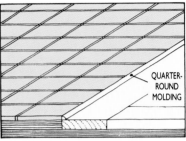

Creating a uniform floor level
Install nailing blocks in gap and nail saddle to blocks.

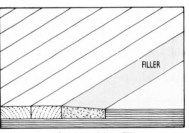

Filling gap with wood flooring strips
Install a quarter-round molding to finish and protect tile edge.

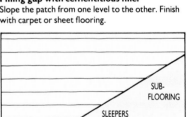

Filling gap with cementitious filler
Slope the patch from one level to the other. Finish with carpet or sheet flooring.

Building up floor levels

Where you want to create a uniform floor level in two rooms that have been made into one by removal of a partition, it may be necessary to build up the existing floor to create a flat, uniform plane. The method and materials you choose for the job should be based on the actual differential between the existing floors. Essentially, building-up methods involve compensating for the height differential between two levels with new subflooring and/or sleepers, which are strips of material installed below the subflooring where they act as spacers.

Before you make a decision on one of the specific approaches illustrated on this page, it is important to consider what type and thicknesses of materials constitute adequate subflooring for various floor finishes. Plywood, particleboard, tempered hardboard, and fiberboard are generally used for subflooring. Pine, plywood, and hardboard strips may be used for sleepers. Ceramic and resilient tile and laminated wood flooring units require a fairly rigid subfloor to prevent them from flexing underfoot, which will ultimately loosen the adhesive and may result in cracking. For these applications, minimum thicknesses of 1/2-inch plywood or 5/8-inch particleboard are recommended. If these materials are to be supported by sleepers, the spacing between them should be no greater than 16 inches. Tempered hardboard should be used as subflooring for tile units only if it is laid directly over an existing floor without sleepers. Solid wood strip flooring, which is generally 1 inch thick, can be nailed directly to an existing strip floor, to any existing sturdy subfloor or perpendicular to sleepers spaced 16 inches apart. Sleepers and subflooring should be fastened either with screws or ring nails that resist popping. Fasteners should be approximately three times longer than the thickness of the material being fastened. Adhesive can be used along with fasteners.

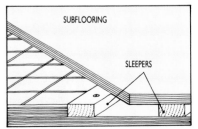

Building up lower floor surface
Match the higher surface with sleepers and subflooring. Treat subflooring or both surfaces.

Setting sleepers
Use sleepers equal in thickness to the differential between floor levels on the lower surface and nail subflooring over both surfaces.

MAKING ONE ROOM INTO TWO

Constructing partitions to divide larger spaces into smaller ones or to alter an existing floor plan is, for the most part, a relatively simple matter of constructing one or more stud walls and finishing with gypsum wallboard or any other appropriate material. Considerations relating to codes, design goals and methods of construction are discussed on the following pages.

Code considerations

Code regulations concerning the construction of partition walls vary widely from locale to locale, but in general, they relate to the amount and type of ventilation that must be provided within an enclosed space, minimum dimensions for hallways, and fire-safety provisions. For example, most rooms that can be categorized as living space (living rooms, dining areas, bedrooms, and the like) must have windows of a certain size in relation to the square footage of the room in order to provide minimally adequate light and ventilation. Bathrooms and kitchens, while not necessarily required to have windows, frequently are required to have mechanical ventilation ($\triangleright$).

With respect to fire regulations, the type and thickness of materials used to construct partitions are frequently specified to ensure that walls can withstand or contain fire for a minimum of one hour. In multiple dwellings in some urban areas, metal studs are frequently required and wood studs are not permitted.

Many local codes specify that hallways may be no less than 3 feet wide to provide sufficient room for passage. While it is a good idea to consult with a professional who can advise you on local code standards relating to your particular project, it is also important to think through the space requirements for activities and room furnishings so that you will arrive at a workable, comfortable design.

Positioning a partition

The frame for a partition wall is generally made from 2-by-3 or 2-by-4 lumber and consists of a top plate, which is attached to the ceiling, a toe plate, which is attached to the floor, and studs, which run vertically between the top and toe plates ($\triangleright$). While it is not usually necessary to remove the existing ceiling, floor or wall finish to fasten new wall frame components to existing structural elements in the house, it is nevertheless important to make sure fasteners used for the top and toe plates and those used to attach end studs to existing walls are driven into existing structural members. As a rule of thumb, use fasteners that are two to three times as long as the plate is thick.

Determine first whether the new partition will run perpendicular or parallel to existing floor and ceiling joists. If it will run perpendicular, then be sure to establish the exact locations of the joists (floor joists are usually spaced on 16-inch centers, ceiling joists on 16- or 24-inch centers), and drive fasteners through the plates and into the joists. If the partition is to run parallel with joists, center the plates on a joist or add blocking between existing joists to provide structural anchoring for fasteners. An end stud that is used to fasten a new partition to an existing wall should be nailed or screwed to a stud in the existing wall. Use expansion bolts to anchor to masonry walls.

FRAMING TO REDUCE SOUND TRANSMISSION

While constructing stud walls finished with gypsum wallboard is a simple, convenient way to attain visual privacy, the conventional system of framing and finishing affords relatively low resistance to sound transmission. The typical wall, framed with 2-by-4s and finished with ½-inch wallboard, has an STC rating of only 30 to 34—STC is the standard by which resistance to sound transmission is measured.

Filling stud cavities with batt insulation and using thicker wallboard, even doubling the layers of wallboard, will improve the resistance to sound transmission. One of the most effective approaches to the problem, however, is to modify the wall framing method by using lumber for the top and toe plates that is wider than that used for the studs. Studs are then fastened in place on 8-inch centers, with edges alternately aligned with opposite edges of the plates. This reduces the amount of sound-induced vibration that is transmitted from one side of the wall to the other. The STC rating of the model illustrated below, which uses 2-by-4 studs set on 2-by-6 plates and is finished with double layers of ⅝-inch wallboard, would have an STC rating of 50 to 54—nearly equal to that of a 7-inch-thick brick cavity wall.

Parts of a stud partition
1 Top plate
2 Toe plate
3 Wall-fastening stud
4 Stud
5 Cross-bracing

Perpendicular to joists
Drive fasteners through plates at 16- or 24-in. intervals anchoring them in joists.

Parallel to joists
Center plates on joists and drive fasteners through them and into joists.

Parallel, between joists
Install perpendicular blocking between joists to serve as anchoring points for plates.

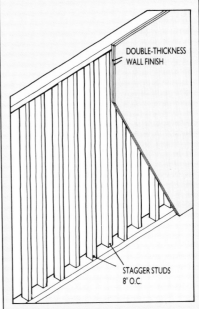

DOUBLE-THICKNESS WALL FINISH

STAGGER STUDS 8" O.C.

Wall framing and finishing design to reduce sound transmission

BUILDING A STUD PARTITION

Making a stud partition wall is the easiest way to divide a room in two: you can construct a plain wall, or add a doorway, pass-through or glazed area to "borrow" light from an existing window. You can build the partition directly onto the floorboards or the joists below. The ends of the partition can be set against the existing wall finish provided there is a stud or other solid material directly beneath it, or the existing wall can be opened to add the necessary structural member.

Marking out and spacing the studs

Mark the position of one edge of the toe plate for the new wall on the floor in chalk. Use a length of 2-by-4 as a guide to draw the line. Continue the guidelines up the walls at each side, using a level and straight-edged plank or a plumb line and bob. Continue the guidelines onto the ceiling, by snapping a chalk line onto the surface with a taut string (1).

Spacing the studs
Lay the top and toe plates together with their face sides facing upward. Mark the position of the studs at 16-inch centers working from one edge. Square the lines across both members against a square (2). Center a 2-by-4 scrap over the layout marks and use the edges as a guide for marking the stud positions.

Attaching the framework

Secure the toe plate to the floor on each side of the door opening using 16d common nails or 4-inch lag screws. Use the top plate as a guide to keep a toe plate interrupted by a door opening in line.

Prop the top plate against the ceiling on its line and check that the stud marks are true with the toe plate using a plumb line. Nail or screw it to the joists (4).

Measure the distance between the top and toe plate at each end and cut the outer wall studs to length: they should be a tight fit between the sill and head plate. Fasten the end studs to the walls with nails or screws.

Attaching door studs
Cut the door studs to fit between the

If you are fixing ⅝-inch wallboard or tongued-and-grooved (T&G) paneling, the 2-foot spacing can be used.

Marking out a doorway
If you are including a doorway in the wall, make an allowance for the width of the opening (◁). The studs that form the sides of the opening must be spaced apart by the width of the door plus a ¼-inch tolerance gap and the thickness of both door jambs. Mark the width of the opening on the top plate at the required positions, then mark the positions for the studs working from the opening. Take the dimensions for the sill from the head and cut both plates to length (3). The door studs overlap the ends of the sills, which must be cut back to allow for them.

top plate and floor. Wedge them in place but do not fasten them yet. Add together the door height and the thickness of the finished header plus ⅜-inch for tolerance, then mark the position of the underside of the header on the edge of one stud. Hold a level on this mark and transfer it accurately to the other door stud.

Attaching the rough header
Nail the door studs to the toe plate and fasten them into the ends of the toe plates (◁). Hold the rough header in position and drive 16d nails through the studs and into the header ends. Fit cripple studs as needed between the rough header and the top plate.

Alternative fastening for door studs

An alternative method for attaching the door studs is to cut the door studs to the required door height and double-up with a stud between the top and toe plates on each side of the rough jamb. Support the door header and nail it to the top of the door studs. Cut a short length of 2-by-4 to fit vertically between the center of the top plate and header. That short stud is called a

"cripple." Secure in place by toe-nailing. Make sure when nailing all the parts together that their faces are flush and that the studs are plumb. The header must be level. The overall size of the rough opening must be large enough to accommodate the new door with necessary clearances, the finished jamb and some shim space for squaring it up.

Double door studs
1 Rough jamb studs
2 Full studs
3 Rough header

1 Snap a chalk line onto the ceiling

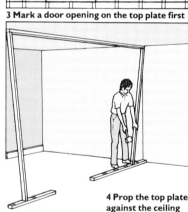

2 Mark the top and toe plate together

3 Mark a door opening on the top plate first

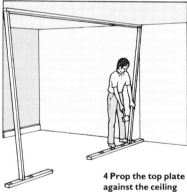

4 Prop the top plate against the ceiling

5 Nail the studs to the rough header

STUD PARTITIONS

Fastening studs and braces

Measure and cut each full-length stud and fasten in turn (see below). Cut the braces to fit between the studs, and working from the wall, toe-nail the first end to the wall stud then nail through the next stud into the end of the brace. One or two rows of braces may be required: if you are going to fit wallboard horizontally, place the center of the braces at 4 feet, working from the ceiling. When the boards are to be fitted vertically, space the line of braces evenly, staggering them to make the fastening easier.

Space studs equally and nail top and bottom

Nail braces between studs to stiffen them

Fastening to an existing stud wall

Stud partitions are used for interior walls of rooms. If your new partition meets a wood-framed wall, align it with the existing solid frame members.

Fasten the wall stud of the new partition to a stud in the existing wall, where possible. Locate the stud by tapping, then drill closely spaced holes through the finish to find its center.

When the new partition wall falls between the studs of the original one, fasten its studs to the braces, top and toe plates of the original wall. Construct the new wall as above but, in this instance, cut the wall stud to fit between the floor and the ceiling and fix it before the top and toe plate are nailed into place.

Fastening wallboard vertically

Start at the doorway with the edge of the first board flush with the stud face. Before fastening, cut a 1-inch-wide strip, from the edge down to the bottom edge of the door header.

Fasten the board with 1¼- or 1½- inch wallboard nails not more than 12 inches apart. Fit the boards on both sides of the doorway then cut and fit a section over the opening. Allow a ⅛-inch gap at the cut joint. Fit the remaining boards.

Fastening wallboard horizontally

Wallboard can be fitted horizontally where it is more economical or convenient to do so. First nail the top line of boards in place so that, should it be necessary to cut the bottom run of boards, the cut edge will fall behind the baseboard. Cut a strip from the edge of the boards on each side of the doorway to allow for the sheets over the door to be fastened to the studs.

Temporarily nail a horizontal support strip to the studs ⅛-inch below the center line of the braces. Sit a board on the strip and nail it to the studs. Fit the remainder of the top boards in this way; then fit the bottom row. Stagger the vertical joints.

A second person should assist you by holding the wallboard steady. If you have to work alone, use a length of lumber to prop the board while you work. Nail from the center of the board.

NAILING TECHNIQUES

Use two 10d common nails to toe-nail each butt joint, one through each side. Temporarily nail a block behind the stud to prevent it moving sideways when driving in the first nail. Blocks cut to fit between each stud can be permanently nailed in place to form housings for extra support.

Alternative stud-nailing method
For a more rigid frame, set the studs into ½-inch-deep housings notched into the top and toe plates before nailing.

Toe-nailing
Toe-nail the butt joints with two nails.

Nailing techniques
Support the stud with a block while driving the first nail.

Supporting joint
Blocks fastened to each side brace the joint.

Housing joints
Housing joints ensure a true and rigid frame.

SEE ALSO

Details for: ▷	
Staggered partitions	138
Fitting pipes and wires	139
Gypsum wallboard	158
Applying wallboard	159
Scribing wallboard	160
Finishing wallboard	164–165

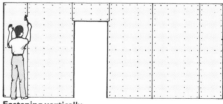

Fastening vertically
Work away from a doorway or start at one end.

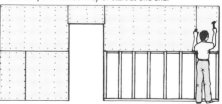

Fastening horizontally
Fix the top row first, stagger the joints on the next.

BUILDING A STAGGERED PARTITION

A stud wall can be built to divide one room into two and provide alcoves for storage at the same time. The method of construction is the same as described for the straight partition (◁) but also includes right-angle junctions. Constructing a staggered partition with a door at one end and a spacious alcove, as shown below, makes sensible use of available space.

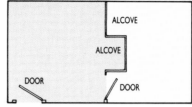

A staggered partition will form storage alcoves on each side, one for each room.

Building the wall
1 Mark toeplate positions.
2 Transfer the marks to the ceiling.
3 Cut and fasten the toeplates to the floor.
4 Fix the top plates to the the ceiling.
5 Make corners from three studs.
6 Fasten the other studs at required spacing.
7 Fit braces, then fasten the wall finish.
8 Fit door frame and complete the wall finish.
9 Fit door jamb, door and moldings.

Positioning the wall

Mark out the toeplate position of the main partition across the floor. Mark the position of the "recessed" partition parallel with it. For clothes storage the recess should be at least 2 feet deep.

Calculate the length of the wall segments by setting them out on the floor. Starting from the wall adjacent to the doorway measure off the thickness of a stud, the door jamb, the width of

the door and the finished jamb. Also add ¼-inch for clearance around the door. This takes you to the face of the first short partition that runs parallel to the wall. Measure from this point to the other wall and divide the dimension in two. This gives you the line for the other short partition. Set out their thicknesses at right angles to the main partitions.

Fastening the top and toeplates

Mark the positions for the top plates on the ceiling. Use a straightedge and level or a plumb line to ensure that the marks exactly correspond with those marked on the floor.

Cut and fasten the toe and top plates to the floor and ceiling respectively, as for erecting a straight partition. Cut and fit the studs at the required spacing to suit the thickness of the wall finish.

CONSTRUCTING THE CORNERS

The right-angled corners and the end of the short partition, which supports the door frame, need extra studs to provide a nailing surface for the wallboard.

Make up a corner from three studs arranged and nailed in place. Fit short cutoffs of studs as spacer blocks. Fasten the cutoffs level with the cross-braces. Fit the boards with one edge overlapping the end of the adjoining panel. For the end of the short partition, fit two studs spaced 1½-inches apart with spacer blocks in between. Nail the board to the two faces of the partition. Leave the end exposed until the door frame is fitted.

Measure and cut the door studs, top plate and door header to length. Nail the top plate in place and fasten one stud to the room wall and one to the stud wall. Make sure they are square and flush with the end of the partition. Fit the door header and cripple stud above it. Apply wall finish over the doorway and to the side faces of the studs, including the end of the wall.

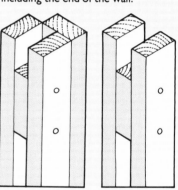

Carpenter's corner
Use three studs at the partition corners.

End post
Use two studs at the end of the partition.

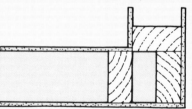

Overlap the wallboard at corners

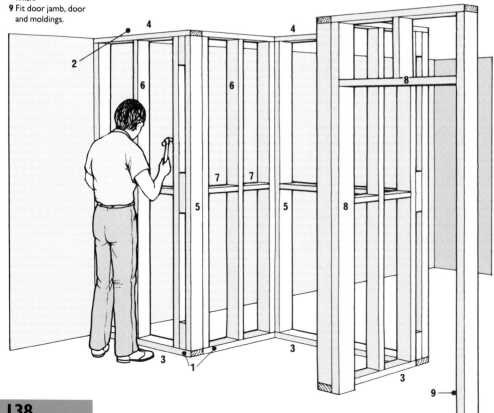

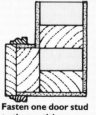

Fasten one door stud to the partition

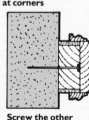

Screw the other stud to wall

Unlike solid walls of brick or block, stud walls are mainly hollow, presenting problems when wall fixtures are to be hung. Wherever possible fixtures should be fastened directly to the structural stud members for maximum support, but if the positions of fixtures are pre-planned, extra studs, braces or mounting boards can be incorporated before the wall finish is applied.

Mounting a hand basin

A wall-mounted hand basin will need a sound enough fastening system to carry its own weight and that of someone leaning on it when it is in use.

Buy the basin before building the wall—or work from the manufacturer's literature, which usually specifies the distance between centers for fixing the brackets—and position two studs to take the mounting screws. Mark the center lines of the studs on the floor before applying the wallboard, then draw plumbed lines from the marks up the face of the sheets. Measure the height from the floor for the brackets and fasten them securely with wood screws.

Another approach would be to mount a plywood mounting board to fit between a pair of standard spaced studs

to carry both the basin and the faucets. Use exterior-grade plywood at least ¾-inch-thick. Plywood is tougher and more stable than ¾-pine and chipboard doesn't hold screws well.

Screw 2-by-2 nailing strips to the inside faces of the studs, set back from their front edges by the thickness of the board. Cut the board to size with enough height to support the basin, then screw it to the nailers to lie flush with the two studs.

Apply the wall finish to the side of the wall that will carry the basin, leaving the other side open for water-supply pipes and vent lines. Drill holes in the studs for pipes. Fasten the basin support brackets, preferably with bolts.

To hide the plumbing within the wall pass the waste pipe through a hole drilled in the wall toe plate and run it under the floor. If the waste pipe must run sideways in the wall, notch the studs (see below).

Fitting a wall cupboard

It is not always possible to arrange studs as needed for wall mounting because walls tend to be put up well before fixtures are considered. If there are no studs where you want them you will have to use hollow-wall fasteners

instead. Choose a type that will adequately support the cabinet (▷).

Hanging shelving

Wall-mounted bookshelves have to carry a considerable weight and must be mounted securely, especially to stud partitions. Use shelving that has strong metal uprights into which adjustable brackets may be locked. Screw into studs if you can; otherwise use suitable hollow-wall fasteners (see below right).

Hanging small fixtures

Load-carrying fixtures with a small contact area can crush the wall finish and strain the fasteners. Mount coat hooks on a board to spread the load, and screw the boards to studs. Hang small pictures on picture hooks secured with steel pins, large ones on a double-pin type, preferably fastened to a stud. Put mirror plates on the frame of a heavy mirror or picture for screw mounting. Use stranded wire for mirrors hung on a hook fastened to a stud.

SEE ALSO

Details for: ▷	
Running new cables	318
Lavatories and sinks	354–355
Hollow-wall fasteners	499
Outlet and fixture boxes	309
Drilling plates	320

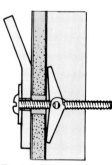

Mounting a basin ▶
Fasten a wall-mounted basin to an exterior-grade plywood board.

FITTING PIPES AND WIRES IN STUD PARTITIONS

It is easy to plan and fit pipes and wires in a stud partition wall before finishing it. To guard against future occupants drilling into them set horizontal cables or pipes no more than 12 inches above floor level.

Plumbing
Plan the runs of supply or waste pipes by marking the faces of the vertical studs or the cross-braces. Remember that a waste pipe must have a slight fall (▷). When you are satisfied with the layout, cut notches in the studs for the pipes (see right).

Transfer the marked lines to the sides of the studs or braces and drill holes for the pipes close to their front edges. Cut in to the holes to make notches. If cut at a slight angle they will hold the pipes while they are being fitted.

Notches cut for waste pipes must be reinforced to prevent them from weakening the studs. Drill the holes in the centers of the studs, following the

pipe run. Before cutting into the holes, cut housings for 1-by-2 furring strips to bridge the notches. Make the notches, set the waste pipe in place, then screw the bridging pieces into their housings flush with the fronts of the studs.

Cross-braces need not be reinforced, but fit one under a pipe bend as a support.

Running electric cable
Drill ½- to ¾-inch holes at the centers of the studs for level runs of cable, and in cross-braces for vertical runs (▷). When possible, it is most convenient to mount electrical boxes for switches and outlets directly to studs. Boxes are available with a number of different types of brackets for this purpose (▷). Boxes with gripping arms are also available for mounting boxes directly to cutouts in wallboard. Surface-mounted boxes may also be used.

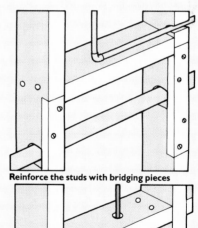

Reinforce the studs with bridging pieces

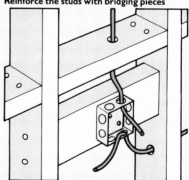

Fit metal boxes to a mounting board

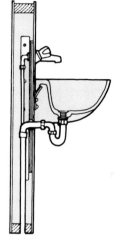

Toggle bolt

Hollow wall fasteners
Various fasteners may be used for insertion into holes and securing with screws or bolts. Some expand to grip the lining as a screw is tightened; some are held in place by a toggle that springs out behind the wall finish.

METAL STUD PARTITIONS

Metal stud and track systems are increasingly being used for wall and ceiling framing in residential construction. Somewhat more economical than wood, metal wall framing components can prove, with a little experience, to be faster and easier to work with than conventional framing. What follows is a discussion of the basic system components, the tools necessary for working with them and some basic approaches to interior, nonstructural framing tasks.

Metal framing components

The basic parts of metal framing systems are studs, which are C-shaped in section view, and track, which is U-shaped. Metal studs have holes punched along their broad surface to permit the passage of wiring or piping and also to serve as mounts for metal cross-bracing, which may be used to stiffen wall frames. Metal track, which is essentially used for top, toe and ledger plates, does not have holes.

Stud and track are available in widths that correspond to the actual dimensions of ordinary framing lumber: 2-by-2s, 2-by-3s, 2-by-4s and 2-by-6s. Available lengths for studs also correspond to those of dimension lumber, starting at 8 feet and increasing in increments of 2 feet up to 20 feet. Track generally comes in 10-foot lengths.

In addition to stud and track, of interest to do-it-yourselfers is metal furring strip. It may be used for ordinary furring-out applications such as preparing a masonry wall for a panel finish and is also sometimes used as support for suspended ceilings.

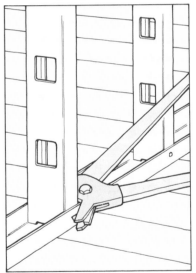

STUD

TRACK

FURRING

Metal framing components

Specialized tools and fasteners

Metal framing components can be cut with ordinary sheetmetal shears—aviation snips, which have a spring-action are most convenient for extensive work.

The majority of joints formed between metal framing components are fastened by crimping. A special crimping tool used for metal framing punches through the flanges of the pieces being joined and bends back the metal to create a sort of negative staple. Where greater strength is needed, joints can be fastened with ¼-inch panhead tapping screws, known as "metal-to-metal screws" in trade jargon.

Gypsum wallboard is fastened to the metal framework with "drywall screws," which are essentially Phillips-type tapping screws with a bugle head. Drywall screws are available in lengths from 1 to 3 inches and may also be used for fastening wood to metal frames. Phillips-type tapping screws with "trim heads," similar to those of finishing nails, are useful for applying wood moldings and door jambs.

It is essential to have a screwgun when working with metal studs. Similar in appearance to electric drills, screw guns have high-speed motors and magnetized chucks that hold Phillips tips needed for driving the various screws. Screwguns are also equipped with clutches and depth-finders. Once a screw is fitted to the tip and the machine is switched on, you press the screw point against the work to engage the clutch, causing the tip to rotate. The depth-finder, once coming in contact with work surface, relieves pressure on the clutch and stops the tip from spinning once the screw has been driven to the desired depth. No. 1 Phillips tips are used to drive pan- and trim-head screws; No. 2 tips are used to drive drywall screws.

Metal-to-metal screw

Drywall screw

Trim-head screw

Tapping screw with high-low threads

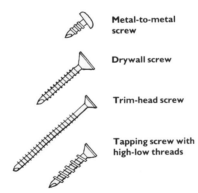

Metal stud crimper

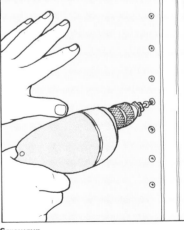

Screwgun

METAL STUD PARTITIONS

Assembling metal wall frames

After snapping layout lines on the ceiling and floor, fasten lengths of track in place to serve as top and toe plates. Use 1½-inch panhead tapping screws no greater than 24 inches apart to fasten the track to wood flooring or to ceilings where wood structural members are beneath the finish. To fasten track or furring to masonry, use either plastic anchors set in predrilled holes and panhead screws, or panhead screws with high-low threads, which will hold in masonry without plugs. Butt tracks at right angles to form corners; do not miter cut.

Cut studs to about ¼-inch shorter than the measurement from floor to ceiling and slip the studs into the tracks, spacing them 16 inches on-center. Crimp the studs in place. Studs and headers forming rough door openings should be screwed together with metal-to-metal screws. Where heavy, solid doors will be used, it is advisable to reinforce door openings with wood framing, which can easily be slipped into and fastened to the track.

A unique feature of metal stud systems is that the flanges of the track may be snipped and bent to create tabs that may be fastened to intersecting or adjacent members. V-shaped cutouts may be made in a track flange and then the broad surface of the track snipped to facilitate forming curved top and toe plates. Customized, two-sided tracks and box beams may also be created by screwing various members together lengthwise.

Apply ½- or ⅝-wallboard to the wall frame with 1¼-inch drywall screws spaced approximately 16 inches apart. Screw heads should be driven slightly below the wallboard surface, but take care not to tear the wallboard's paper binder.

SEE ALSO

Details for: ▷

Stud partitions	137
Staggered partitions	138
Gypsum wallboard	158
Applying wallboard	159
Scribing wallboard	160
Finishing wallboard	164–165

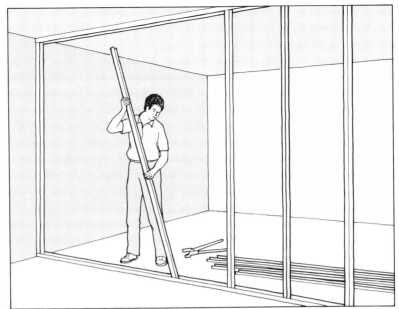

Metal studs are fitted into track that serves as top and toe plates

Box beam formed with two studs

SCREW

CARRY WALLBOARD OVER TRACK

WALLBOARD

METAL STUD

TRACK

Corner detail for wallboard-metal stud assembly

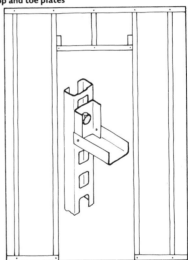

Door header assembly detail

Box beam formed with two studs and pieces of track

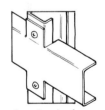

Cross-bracing for stud made by cutting track flanges and bending into tabs

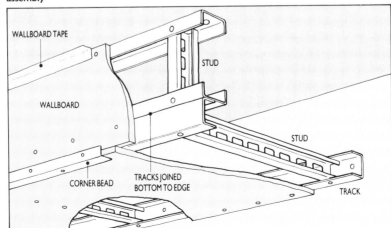

WALLBOARD TAPE

STUD

WALLBOARD

STUD

CORNER BEAD

TRACKS JOINED BOTTOM TO EDGE

TRACK

Soffit construction with metal studs and track

Track notched to form curved plate

CEILINGS: LOWERING A CEILING

When the ceiling of a room presents a problem, either because of the condition of its finish or because its height makes the room seem cavernous, remodeling by lowering the ceiling may be the simplest solution. Several approaches to remodeling a ceiling are discussed on this and the following pages.

High ceilings are generally found in older houses. Some are decorative molded ceilings, while many others have simple but attractive cornice moldings, and these should be preserved to maintain the character of the house. But where a room is plain and the ceiling needs attention, or where the proportions of the room would benefit from alteration, a lowered ceiling can be an improvement. It can be used to hide ducting, improve sound and heat insulation and provide a space for flush or concealed lights.

Changing the character of a room

A room's character is largely determined by the relation of its area to its ceiling height. Low ceilings are considered charming and cozy, while tall rooms are felt to be very imposing, though they are usually larger. Other high-ceilinged rooms feel somewhat uncomfortable.

The sense of coziness or emptiness may be based on practical experience. For example, the volume of a low-ceilinged room is less than that of a high-ceilinged room of the same floor area, so it would be easier to heat evenly, and a room with an even temperature feels more comfortable than one where the temperature varies due to rising air currents. The acoustics in a small room may also be better, inducing a relaxed feeling. Yet the qualities of light and space in a room may be due to its high ceiling, and if it were lowered, changing the room's proportions, the tall windows might look awkward and the sense of space be lost.

Making a model

Making a simple cardboard model of a room's interior is a good way to check that a planned project will suit the room before spending time and money on the real thing.

Measure the length, width and height of the room and the height, width and positions of the windows and doors. Mark out and cut pieces of cardboard for the floor and walls to any convenient

scale—perhaps simplest is to allow 1 inch to equal 1 foot.

Mark the positions of the doors and windows on the cardboard walls and cut out the openings with a craft knife. The openings will allow light into the finished model. You can hinge the doors in place with self-adhesive tape. Draw lines on the walls to represent the baseboards and casings around the doors and windows. You can color these details to make them more realistic. Also mark in the fireplace to the same scale. A projecting chimney breast can be formed in cardboard and glued on.

Punch a small peep-hole in each wall at a height scaled to your eye level and assemble the floor and walls using adhesive tape.

Cut a cardboard panel representing the ceiling to fit closely between the walls. If the real ceiling is to be the suspended type, with lighting around its edges, cut the panel smaller to provide the gap at the sides.

Cut two strips of cardboard about 2 inches wide and as long as the width of the ceiling piece and glue them on edge across the back of the ceiling. Cut two more strips, the same width but a little longer, and use clips to attach them to the shorter ones. The longer strips will rest across the walls and the clips are adjusted to set the ceiling at various heights. Check the effect of this on the room by viewing the interior space through the peepholes and the door and window openings.

To simulate a grid-system illuminated ceiling make a framework with strips of balsa wood to the same scale as the room and covered with tracing paper.

The height of a new ceiling should be no less than 7 feet 6 inches. In some cases 6 feet 6 inches is acceptable under beams or bay windows.

You can construct a slightly lower ceiling in a kitchen, provided at least half of it is at 7 feet 6 inches.

In a roof space the ceiling height should be a minimum of 7 feet 6 inches for at least half the area of the room. However, this area might not represent the whole floor. Mark all the sloping ceilings to the desirable minimum height above the floor, then use a plumb line to mark the floor directly below. The area of the floor within the marked lines represents the actual area used to calculate the ceiling height.

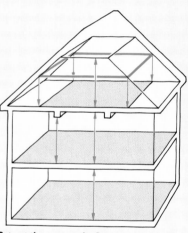

Set out the area on the floor

Cardboard model parts
1 Walls
2 Chimney breast

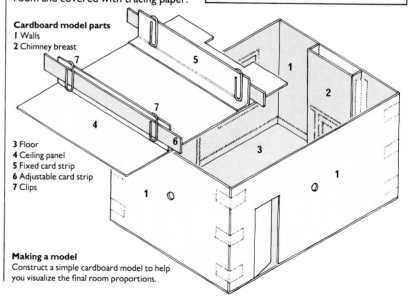

3 Floor
4 Ceiling panel
5 Fixed card strip
6 Adjustable card strip
7 Clips

Making a model
Construct a simple cardboard model to help you visualize the final room proportions.

You might decide to lower a ceiling for practical reasons or simply to change the style of the interior, but whatever the reason, you should consider your options carefully because a ceiling is a large area which can be costly to cover.

Wood framed ceilings are heavy but they can be custom-made to suit the style and shape of a room using basic woodworking skills.

Manufactured suspended-ceiling systems are relatively lightweight, easy to install and offer a wide choice of materials for the paneling, but a strong grid pattern is unavoidable.

Use the chart to help you consider the project in advance and to compare one system with another.

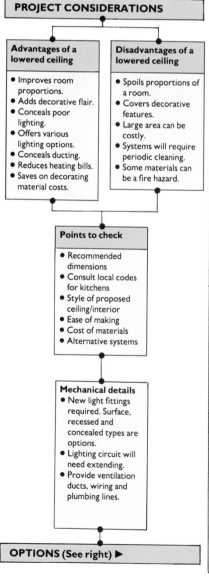

PROJECT CONSIDERATIONS

Advantages of a lowered ceiling
- Improves room proportions.
- Adds decorative flair.
- Conceals poor lighting.
- Offers various lighting options.
- Conceals ducting.
- Reduces heating bills.
- Saves on decorating material costs.

Disadvantages of a lowered ceiling
- Spoils proportions of a room.
- Covers decorative features.
- Large area can be costly.
- Systems will require periodic cleaning.
- Some materials can be a fire hazard.

Points to check
- Recommended dimensions
- Consult local codes for kitchens
- Style of proposed ceiling/interior
- Ease of making
- Cost of materials
- Alternative systems

Mechanical details
- New light fittings required. Surface, recessed and concealed types are options.
- Lighting circuit will need extending.
- Provide ventilation ducts, wiring and plumbing lines.

OPTIONS (See right) ▶

LOWERED CEILING

Design features	Planning the scheme	Type of construction	Covering/finishes
Will change the room proportions. Will hide old ceiling or mechanicals. Least likely to appear a conversion. Can be fitted with cornice moldings. Without a hatch, prevents access to the void above.	Make initial sketches of the proposed interior, then draw scale plans on graph paper to detail and cost the scheme. Make a scale model to visualize the effect of the ceiling.	This type of construction uses new ceiling joists to span room in shortest direction. The joists are supported by headers fastened to the walls. Ties and hangers may be used.	Materials: Gypsum wallboard. Fire-resistant compositions. Plywood. Tongue-and-groove paneling. Mineral-fiber tiles. Finishes: papered, painted, varnished or ready-finished.

PART-LOWERED CEILING

Design features	Planning the scheme	Type of construction	Covering/finishes
Similar to the full lowered ceiling above but has added interest of the split-level. The end transition between levels can be vertical or sloped, sloped being preferable when parallel with a window.	As for lowered ceiling (see above). Consider the line of the "drop" in relation to the window. It should not cut across the window when viewed from the opposite side of the room.	Wood-frame constructions as for lowered ceiling (see above). The end framework is formed from ties and hangers. The hangers are set at an angle for a sloped end.	As for lowered ceiling (see above).

OPEN-BOARD CEILING

Design features	Planning the scheme	Type of construction	Covering/finishes
Not a true ceiling but a framework which appears to be continuous. Most effective in hallways or passage. It does not seal off the old ceiling. Can be dismantled for access to services.	As for lowered ceiling (see above). The spacing and depth of the slats can be varied: you should not be able to see between the slats when looking straight ahead.	Edge-on plank construction using no sub-structure. Perimeter planks are housed and fastened to the wall; the slats are fastened to them.	No covering is used. The ceiling and walls above the slats are painted a dark color. Finish for woodwork: light-colored stain, clear varnish or paint.

SUSPENDED CEILING

Design features	Planning the scheme	Type of construction	Covering/finishes
Appears to be suspended away from the walls and appears to float: concealed lighting enhances this illusion. Has modern character. Will mask old ceiling or mechanicals. Not demountable.	As for lowered ceiling (see above). Locate original ceiling joists and set out their position on your plan drawing: design the structure around them.	Wood-frame construction using ties fastened across ceiling joists and carrying hangers from which the new frame is suspended. The main components are assembled with bolts.	As for lowered ceiling (see above).

SUSPENDED CEILING SYSTEMS

Design features	Planning the scheme	Type of construction	Covering/finishes
A grid system manufactured from lightweight materials for self-assembly. Individual translucent or opaque panels sit in the grid framework. The system is demountable.	As for lowered ceiling (see above). Draw a plan of the room on graph paper and set out a symmetrical grid.	Lightweight alumium T-sectioned extrusions suspended from angle sections screwed to the walls. Tees are loose-fitted.	Metal: anodized. Panel materials: plain, textured and colored translucent plastic; opaque plastic; mineral fiber.

Vapor checks
Provide a vapor check to prevent condensation problems in an unventilated space above a lowered ceiling. Use a waterproof wallboard, an impervious sealer or polyethylene plastic sheeting. The gaps between the boards or the plastic must be sealed effectively.

Wallboard
Bed joints in mastic.

Polyethylene sheeting
Fold and staple edges.

CONSTRUCTING A LOWERED CEILING

You can build the new ceiling at any height provided it complies with the regulations. However, the height of window openings may limit your choice. About 8 feet is a useful height for a lowered ceiling. It is a common room height for modern houses and relates to standard wallboard sheet sizes. Most manufacturers of built-in furniture adopt it as a standard height for ceilings.

Planning the layout

Making a lowered ceiling requires a considerable amount of lumber for the framework and wallboard to cover it. It is critical to select the correct width for the joists and their spacing based on their span and the weight of the ceiling finish material. Arrange the panels with the paper-covered edges set at right angles to the timber supports. Stagger the end joints between each row of boards and arrange them so as to fall on a joist.

If you plan to use tongue-and-groove paneling, buy it in lengths that can be economically cut to suit your joist arrangement, since excessive cut-offs are wasteful. Avoid butt joints coinciding on adjacent boards.

Materials for the framework

Make a cutting list of the materials you will need to make up the structure. In most cases 2-by-3 or 2-by-4 lumber can be used for the ceiling joists. These should span the room in the shortest direction. Calculate the number of joists you will need. These should be spaced at 16 or 24 inches on center according to the thickness of the wallboard (◁). These dimensions will also suit other types of paneling.

You will need extra joist lumber for the braces fitted between the joists. One-by-two strips may be fastened to walls and used as ledgers to support the ceiling frame.

Spans of over 8 feet should be supported by hangers and ties, made from lumber not less than 2-by-2 which are fastened to the ceiling above. Place the hangers about the middle of the joists' span.

It is possible to use more hangers and reduce the section of the joists from 2-by-3 to 2-by-2. In this case place the hangers about 3 feet apart.

Cutting list
A cutting list is your shopping guide. It will enable you to establish your requirements and help your supplier in making up your order. List the individual parts of the structure, and, under separate columns, fill in the quantity, length, width, thickness and material, required.

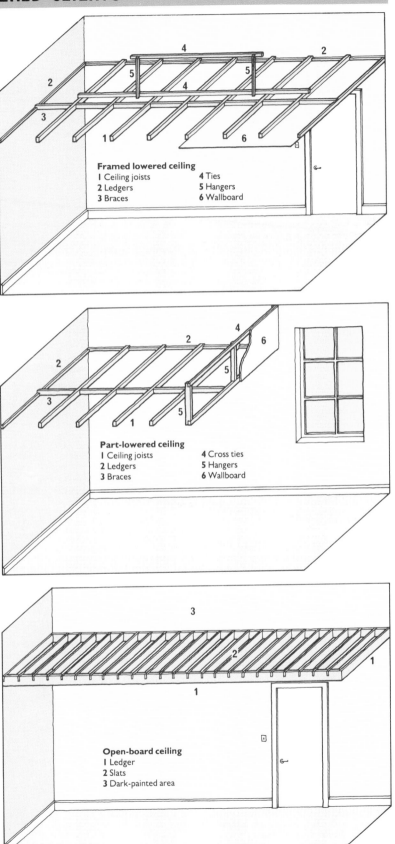

Framed lowered ceiling
1 Ceiling joists　　4 Ties
2 Ledgers　　　　5 Hangers
3 Braces　　　　6 Wallboard

Part-lowered ceiling
1 Ceiling joists　　4 Cross ties
2 Ledgers　　　　5 Hangers
3 Braces　　　　6 Wallboard

Open-board ceiling
1 Ledger
2 Slats
3 Dark-painted area

Constructing the ceiling

Mark the height of the new ceiling, including the thickness of the finish on one wall. At this level draw a horizontal line across the wall using a straightedge and level for accuracy. Continue the line around the room at this height. Cut ledger boards to length. Nail or screw them to the walls at 16-inch intervals with the bottom edge level with the line.

Cut the ceiling joists to length. Notch the ends to sit over the wall ledgers to bring the bottom edges flush. Toenail the joists to the wall ledgers. Cut and fit hangers and ties to prevent long joists from sagging (see left). These supports also stiffen the structure.

Cut and nail braces between the joists to support the edges of the wallboard. Nail tapered-edged wallboard to the joists, braces and wall battening. Fill and tape the joints between boards and walls (▷).

Lowering part of a ceiling

You can lower part of a ceiling to overcome problems around tall window openings or to create a split-level effect. Follow the method for constructing a ceiling (as described above) but enclose the end-drop with wallboard nailed to hangers fixed in a line to a cross-tie member set above the last joist.

Making an open-board ceiling

One-by-six pine boards set on edge and spaced apart can be used to create a simple yet effective open-board ceiling. Smaller sections can be used where the span is short, as with a narrow hallway.

Cut four lengths of ledger strips to line the walls all around. Before nailing or screwing them at the required height, mark and cut housings in two of the planks opposite one another. Space the housings about 9 inches apart. For boards less than 6 inches wide, space them about 4 to 6 inches apart. Cut notches in the ends of the "slat" boards to sit in the housings so that the bottom edges finish flush.

Before fitting the slats, paint walls and ceilings above the lining boards with a dark flat latex paint. Also paint ducts or plumbing to disguise it. Finish the slats with varnish, stain or paint.

A suspended ceiling with reveals around the perimeter appears to float way from the walls. Fluorescent lights can be placed around the edge of the ceiling to enhance the floating effect and provide wall-washing illumination (▷). The fiber can be covered with plasterboard, decorative veneered ply or mineral-fiber ceiling ties.

Locate the position of the ceiling joists by noting the direction of the floorboards of the room above; the joists will run at right angles to them (▷). Pinpoint the joists from below by boring pilot holes through the ceiling (▷). Mark the center of each joist.

Setting out the grid

Measure the lengths of the walls and draw a scaled plan of the room on graph paper. Set out the shape of the ceiling panel on the drawing with its edges approximately 8 inches from each wall. Then set out the position of the 2-by-2 ceiling ties. The ties should run at right angles to the joists of the ceiling above. The ends of the ties and sides of the two outer ones should be about 1 foot from the walls. The number of ties you'll need will depend on the size of the ceiling, but three should be a minimum. They should be spaced not more than 3 feet apart for adequate support.

Constructing the ceiling

Counterbore and securely screw the ties in position to each of the joists they cross. Cut 2-by-2 hangers to the required length and fasten them to the

ties with carriage bolts not more than 3 feet apart.

Cut additional ties to the same length as the planned ceiling panel. Bolt them across the ends of the hangers with an equal space at each end.

Cut the required number of 2-by-2 furring strips to suit the spacings necessary to support the wallboard or tiles used as a ceiling finish. The length of the furring strips should be equal to the width of the ceiling panel minus two 1-by-2 inch capping strips. Equally space and screw the furring strips to the tie members. Countersink the screw heads.

Mark off the positions of the furring strips along the sides of each capping strip. Drive 3-inch nails into, but not quite through, the cappings at these points. Apply woodworking adhesive and nail the cappings to the ends of the furring strips.

Finishing the assembly

Run electrical wiring in preparation for the fluorescent lights to be fitted (▷). Cover the underside of the frame with wallboard, decorative veneered panels or ceiling tiles (▷). Fill and finish the surface and edges of a gypsum wallboard ceiling. Finish the exposed edges of the frame to match other materials as required.

Wire up and fit slim fluorescent light fixtures to loose boards, which sit on top of the projecting frame. The fixtures can then be easily removed for servicing. Leave enough spare cable to allow the lights to be lifted clear.

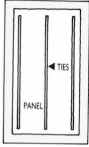

Setting out
Set out the panel on graph paper with an 8-in. gap all round. Insert the ties about 1 ft.

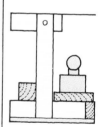

Light fixture
Attach a fluorescent light to a removable board for servicing.

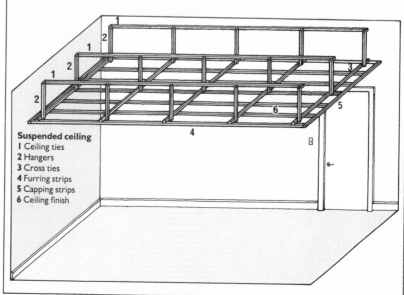

Suspended ceiling
1 Ceiling ties
2 Hangers
3 Cross ties
4 Furring strips
5 Capping strips
6 Ceiling finish

Manufactured suspended-ceilings are made from slim metal sections, which provide a fairly lightweight structure for acoustic or translucent panels. They're quick and easy to fit using no special tools.

Panel layouts

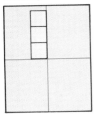

1 Main tee on center

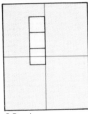

2 Panel on center

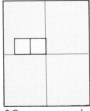

3 Cross-tee centered

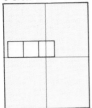

4 Panel on center

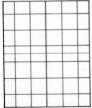

5 Best grid arrangement

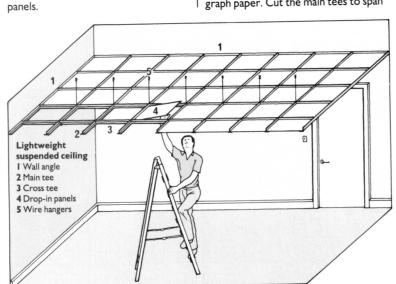

Manufactured systems
Manufacturers offer a choice of colored framing as well as colored-translucent and opaque panels.

The lightweight alloy framework is made from three basic elements: wall angles, which are fastened to walls; main tees, which are similar in function to joists and are usually installed across a room's shorter span; and cross-tees, which are set between and perpendicular to main tees.

The loose panels sit on the flanges of the tees. They can be easily lifted out for access to ducts or to service light fixtures, which can be concealed behind them. You need at least 4 inches of space above the framework to fit the panels.

Setting out the grid

Normally, 2-by-2 or 2-by-4 panels are used for suspended ceiling systems. Before installing the framework, draw a plan of the ceiling on graph paper to ensure that the borders are symmetrical. Draw a plan of the room with two lines taken from the hallway point on each wall to bisect at the center. Lay out the grid on your plan.

Fitting the framework

Before installing a suspended ceiling with translucent panels, remove any flaking materials and repair any cracks in the plaster ceiling above. Paint the ceiling with white latex to improve reflectivity if concealed fluorescent lighting is to be used.

Install fluorescent light fixtures as needed across the ceiling: 16 watts per square yard is recommended for a suitable level of light in most rooms.

Mark the height of the suspended ceiling on the walls with a continuous leveled line. Hacksaw two lengths of wall-angle section to fit the longest walls. Remove burrs from the ends with a file. Drill screw holes at 2-foot intervals. Drill and plug the walls using the angle as a guide and screw the components in place (**1**).

Next cut lengths of wall angle to fit the shorter walls. Their ends should fit on the angles already fitted. Attach them in the same way as the other wall-angle sections.

Mark the positions of the tees along two adjacent walls, as set out on the graph paper. Cut the main tees to span

with a main tee centered on the short bisecting line (**1**), then lay it out again with a line of panels centered on the same line (**2**). Use the grid that provides the widest border panels.

Plot the position of the cross tees in the same way, using the other line (**3**, **4**). Try to get the border panels even on opposite sides of the room (**5**).

the room. Sit them on the wall angles (**2**). Use a ceiling panel to check that they are parallel and at right angles to the wall and each other.

Cut the border of cross-tees to fit between the end of the main tees and wall angles. Set them in line with the points marked on the wall. Position the remainder of the cross-tees following the same line.

Working from the center drop in the full-sized panels. Measure and cut the border panels to fit the grid and then drop them into place.

Spanning wide rooms
If the size of the room exceeds the maximum length of the main tee, join two or more pieces together. A joint bridging piece is provided if the ends of the tees are not made to lock together.

For spans exceeding 10 feet, support the main tees with wire hangers. Fasten each wire, spaced not more than 5 feet apart, through a hole in the tee and hang it from a screw eye in a furring strip or joist in the ceiling.

Lightweight suspended ceiling
1 Wall angle
2 Main tee
3 Cross tee
4 Drop-in panels
5 Wire hangers

1 Screw the angle to the wall

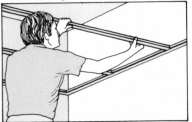

2 Position the main tees

INSTALLING A FOLDING LADDER

Access to the attic space is more convenient and safer if you install a folding ladder. Some are complete with built-in hatch cover, frame and fittings ready to install in a new opening. Normally, the length of the ladders suits standard ceiling heights, 7 feet 6 inches and 8 feet. Some can extend up to 10 feet.

Concertina ladder

To fit a concertina ladder, securely screw the brackets of the aluminum ladder to the framework of the opening. Fit the retaining hooks to the framework to support the ladder in the stowed position. Operate the ladder with a pole, which hooks over the bottom rail. Fit the hatch door to the frame with a continuous hinge, followed by a push-to-release latch installed at the edge of the hatch door.

Ready-to-install folding ladder

Cut the opening and trim the joists to the size specified by the manufacturer. Insert the casing with built-in frame in the opening and screw it to the joists.

A concertina ladder is simple to install

Folding ladders are easy to deploy

MAKING AN ATTIC-ACCESS HATCH

Many houses are provided with a hatch in the ceiling to give access to the attic space for convenient storage and maintaining the roof structure. If your house has a large attic space without access from the house, installing a hatch could be a valuable addition. Pre-fab units are available at many home centers. Although the job is basically straightforward, it does entail cutting into the top-floor ceiling structure.

When cutting into the structure of a ceiling to create an attic entrance, it is important to consider the effect of the alteration on the ability of the framing to support the existing structure. Some roof frames may incorporate purlins, these bearing part of the load on rafters. The purlins may be supported by vertical members that transfer part of the load to ceiling joists. If you have any doubts about the effect of cutting joists to install a hatchway, consult a knowledgeable professional.

If you have a choice, site the hatchway over a landing, but not close to a stair, rather than in a room. In this way a ladder used for access will not interfere with the occupants or function of the room. Allow for the pitch of the roof, as you will need headroom above the hatch.

Making the opening

If you are planning to install a special folding ladder, the size of the new opening will be specified by the manufacturer. Generally aim to cut away no more than one of the ceiling joists: these are usually spaced 16 inches apart.

Locate three of the joists by drilling pilot holes in the ceiling. Mark out a square for the opening between the two outer joists. Cut an inspection hole inside the marked area to check that no obstacles are in the way of the cutting line. Saw through the ceiling finish and strip it away.

Pass a light into the roof space and climb up into it between the joists. Lay a board across the joists to support yourself. Saw through the middle joist, cutting it back 2 inches from each edge of the opening. Cut two new lengths of joist lumber—called headers—to fit between the joists. Nail the joints between the joists and headers. Use two 16d common nails to secure each joist.

Nail the ceiling laths or plasterboard to the underside of the header joists. Cut jambs from nominal 1-inch boards to cover the joists and the edges of the ceiling finish. Repair the damaged edges of the existing finish with filler. When the filler has set, nail a casing around the opening. Make a drop-in or hinged panel of ¾-inch plywood or particleboard. If you plan to use the attic space mainly for storage, fix chipboard panels over the joists. Cut them to fit through the opening.

SEE ALSO

Details for: ▷

| House construction | 120–121 |

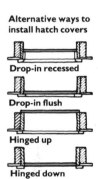

Alternative ways to install hatch covers

Drop-in recessed

Drop-in flush

Hinged up

Hinged down

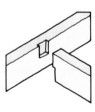

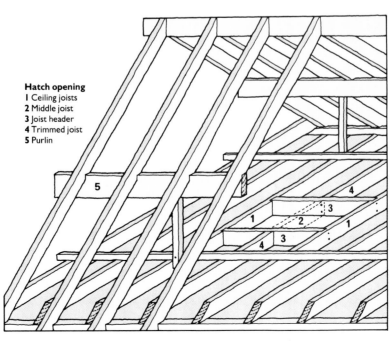

Hatch opening
1 Ceiling joists
2 Middle joist
3 Joist header
4 Trimmed joist
5 Purlin

INTERIOR WALL FINISH

As popular interest in authentic restoration of older houses grows, there is a renewed appreciation for the qualities of a plaster wall finish. While wallboard is generally faster and easier to apply, plaster walls have a look and feel that is unmistakable to the discerning eye, and sound insulation properties that are superior to wallboard. In the following pages you will find both traditional and modern approaches to plastering as well as methods for applying and finishing wallboard.

Storing plaster
Keep an open bag of plaster in a plastic sack sealed with adhesive tape.

Traditional plastering techniques

Traditional plastering uses a mix of plastering materials and water, which is spread over the rough background in one, two or three layers. Each layer is applied with a trowel and leveled accordingly; when set, the plaster forms an integral part of the wall or ceiling. Traditionally, plaster has been applied over masonry walls or wood lath, thin wood strips slightly spaced that make it possible for plaster to key-in and adhere. More recently, metal and gypsum laths have been developed. Plastering well requires practice to achieve a smooth, flat surface over a large area. With care, an amateur can produce satisfactory results, provided the right tools and plaster are employed and the work is divided into manageable sections. All-purpose one-coat plasters are now available to make plastering easier for amateurs.

Gypsum wallboard

Manufactured boards of paper-bound gypsum are widely used to finish the walls and ceilings in modern homes and during renovations. Its use overcomes the drying-out period required for wet plasters and requires less skill to apply.

The large flat boards are nailed or bonded to walls and ceilings to provide a separate finishing layer. The surface may be decorated directly once the boards are sealed, or covered with a thin coat of finish plaster.

BUYING AND STORING PLASTER

Plaster powder is normally sold in 50- and 100-pound paper sacks. Smaller sizes, including 5-pound sacks, are available from DIY stores for repair work. It's generally more economical to buy the larger sacks, but this depends on the scale of the work. Try to buy only as much plaster as you need. It's better to overestimate, however, to allow for waste and prevent running short (◁).

Store plaster in dry conditions: if it is to be kept in an outbuilding for some time, cover it with plastic sheeting to protect it from moisture. Keep the paper bags off a concrete floor by placing them on boards or plastic sheeting. Open bags are more likely to absorb moisture, which can shorten the setting time and weaken the plaster. Keep an opened bag in a sealed plastic sack. Use self-adhesive tape to seal it. Discard plaster which contains lumps.

Ready-to-use joint compound, which can be used for some plaster repairs, is also available in plastic tubs. It can be more expensive to buy it this way but it is easier for amateurs to use and it will keep for a long time, provided the airtight lid is well sealed.

Traditional plastering

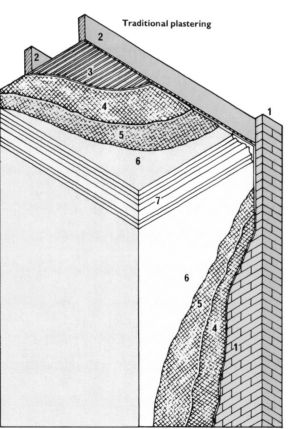

Traditional plastering
(Right)
The construction of a lath-and-plaster ceiling and plastered masonry wall.
1 Brick ground
2 Ceiling joists
3 Lath
4 Base coat
5 Brown coat
6 Finishing coat
7 Cornice molding

Drywall

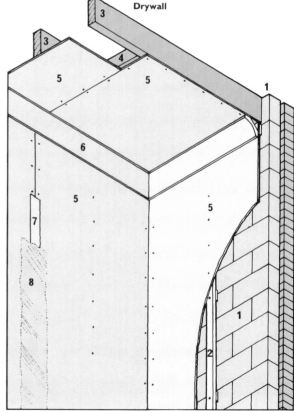

Drywall
(Far right)
The construction of a modern wallboard wall and ceiling.
1 Block wall
2 Furring
3 Ceiling joists
4 Cross-braces
5 Gypsum wallboard
7 Crown molding
8 Joint compound

TYPES OF PLASTER

Plastering is carried out using modern gypsum plasters or mixes based on cement, lime and sand. By varying the process and introducing additives, a range of plasters can be produced within a given type to suit different grounds, or substrate materials.

Plasters are basically produced in two grades—one as a base or floating coat, the other for finishing coats. Base coat gypsum plasters are pre-mixed types, which contain lightweight aggregates. Base-coat sanded plasters, which are based on cement or cement/lime, have to be mixed on site with a suitable grade of clean, sharp sand (although finish plasters are ready to use with the addition of water).

The following information deals only with those materials suitable for domestic work.

PLASTER TYPES AND RELATED MATERIALS

GYPSUM PLASTERS

Most plasters in common use are produced from ground gypsum rock by a process which removes most of the moisture from the rock to produce a powder that sets hard when mixed with water. Setting times are controlled by the use of retarding additives, which give each of the several types of plaster a setting time suitable to its use.

Gypsum plasters are intended for interior work only; they should not be used on permanently damp walls. They must not be remixed with water once they start to set.

PLASTER OF PARIS

This quick-setting non-retarded gypsum plaster gives off heat as it sets. It is white or pinkish, and is mixed to a creamy consistency with clean water. It is unsuitable for general plastering but good for casting, and can be used for repairs to decorative moldings.

BASE-COAT PLASTERS

In traditional plastering, the finish is built up in two or three successive coats. Base-coat plasters are used for all but the last coat.

Several types of base-coat plasters are available, some needing only to be mixed with water before application and others, which may need to be mixed with sand or other aggregate before they can be used effectively. Which type you choose may depend on the substrate, the specific job at hand, the desire for economy and the desired performance and working characteristics. It is crucial to read the package label to determine whether a particular formulation is suitable for the substrate or lath to which the plaster will be applied and to learn the best way to prepare the mixture.

Ordinary gypsum base-coat plaster, which must have sand or other aggregate added, is economical and suitable for most purposes. Wood-fiber base-coat plaster can be used with the addition of water only over wood, metal or gypsum lath, but must be mixed with sand for application over masonry. Wood-fiber plasters are about 25 percent lighter than sanded gypsum base coats and have greater fire resistance.

Special lightweight gypsum-based plasters, some pre-mixed with the aggregate (these are commonly known by the United States Gypsum Co. tradenames "Structo-base" and "Structo-lite") are higher in strength than conventional plasters. Portland cement-lime plaster is suitable for interior applications where a high-moisture condition prevails and for exterior stucco.

GAUGING PLASTER

Gauging plasters are designed to be mixed with lime putty and applied as a finish coat. Some grades are harder and more abrasion-resistant than others; which type is best-suited for a particular application may be determined by consulting with your supplier. In addition to blending gauging plaster with lime putty to improve workability, it may have aggregate added to roughen the finished texture.

FINISH-COAT PLASTER

Finish-coat plasters do not need to be mixed with lime putty. They are mixed with water and may be applied over compatible basecoats, gypsum lath and moisture-resistant-type gypsum wallboard. Some types are formulated for use over portland-cement-lime base coats for walls with moisture problems.

MOLDING PLASTER

With extremely fine grains and controlled set, molding plasters are preferred for casting and running ornamental trim and cornices. When used for running cornices with a template, the addition of lime putty may be necessary.

PATCHING PLASTER

Available in comparatively small packages, patching plasters are formulated for high bonding strength and are fast setting. Patching plasters are best suited to repairs of small areas.

FINISH LIME

Finish lime is added to plaster to provide bulk, plasticity and ease of spreading. It also helps to control the setting time. Conventional finish limes must be slaked, that is saturated with water for 16 to 24 hours to develop the desirable putty consistency and proper working characteristics. Specially processed types develop the necessary qualities immediately on being mixed with water.

OTHER ADDITIVES

Plaster retarders may be added to conventional plasters to slow drying and allow adequate working time. Accelerators may be added to speed hardening where conditions require it.

● **Avoiding old plaster**
Plaster may deteriorate if stored for more than two months, so suppliers try to make sure it is sold in rotation. The paper sacks in which plaster is supplied are usually date-stamped by the manufacturer. If you are buying from a self-service supplier, choose a sack with the latest date.

TYPES OF SURFACE

● **Providing a "key"**
Rake out mortar
joints to help plaster
and stucco grip.

A well-prepared ground is the first step to successful plastering. New surfaces of block or brickwork may need only dampening or priming with a bonding agent, depending on their absorbency. Old plastered surfaces needing repairs should be thoroughly checked. If the plaster is unsound, remove it to leave only stable material, then treat the surface and replaster the area.

Background preparation and absorbency

Brush down the surface of a masonry ground to remove loose particles, dust and efflorescent salts (◁). Test the absorption of the masonry by splashing on water; if it stays wet, consider the surface normal—this means that it will only require light dampening with clean water prior to applying the plaster.

A dry background that absorbs the water immediately takes too much water from the plaster, making it difficult to work, and prevents it from setting properly, which can result in cracking. Soak the masonry with clean water applied with a brush.

High-absorbency surfaces

For very absorbent surfaces, such as aerated concrete blocks, prime the background with 1 part PVA bonding agent: 3 to 5 parts clean water. When dry, apply a bonding coat of 3 parts bonding agent: 1 part water. Apply the plaster when the bonding coat is tacky.

Low-absorbency surfaces

Prime low-absorption smooth brickwork or concrete with a solution of 1 part bonding agent: 3 to 5 parts water. Allow to dry. Apply a second coat of 3 to 5 parts bonding agent: 1 part water, and apply the plaster when tacky or allow it to dry for no more than 24 hours before plastering.

Non-absorbent surfaces

Glazed tiles and painted walls are considered non-absorbent and will require a coating of neat bonding agent to enable the plaster to stick. The plaster is applied while the agent is still wet. An alternative for glazed tiles is to apply a slurry of 2 parts sharp sand: 1 part cement mixed with a solution of 1 part bonding agent: 1 part water. Apply the slurry with a stiff-bristled brush to form a stippled coating. Allow to dry for 24 hours then apply the plaster.

The best option is to chip off the old tiles. Always remove loose tiles.

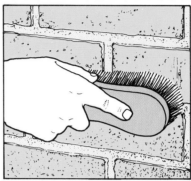
Remove loose particles with a stiff brush

Prime porous surfaces to control the suction

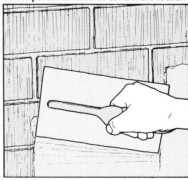
A bonding agent improves adhesion

Smooth tiles can be "keyed" with a slurry

MAKING FILLER AND MORTAR BOARDS

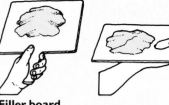

Filler board

You can make a useful board for mixing and working with plaster and compound from marine plywood. Cut out a 1-foot square with a projecting handle on one side, or make a thumb hole like an artist's palette. Seal the surface with a polyurethane varnish or apply a plastic laminate for a smooth finish.

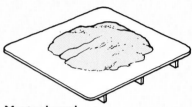

Mortar board

Cut a piece of ½- or ¾-inch marine plywood approximately 3 feet square. Round off the corners and bevel the edges all round. Screw three lengths of 1-by-2 furring across the underside, spread equally apart. A smaller board, known as a spotboard, 2 feet square, can be made in a similar way.

Using a stand ▶
You will find it easier
to handle plaster with
the mix at table height.

Using a stand

A stand is used to support the mortar board at table height, about 30 inches from the ground. This enables the plaster to be picked up on a hawk by placing it under the edge of the board and drawing the plaster onto it.

Make a folding stand using 2-by-3 studs for the legs and 1-by-3 furring for the rails. Make one leg frame fit inside the other and bolt them securely together at the center.

A proprietary folding bench can be used to support the board instead of making a stand: grip the center support in the vise jaws (◁).

MIXING PLASTER

With the ground prepared, the next step for the amateur plasterer is to make a good mix. It is best to mix your plaster close to the working place, since it can be messy. Also cover the floor with old newspapers and remember to wipe your feet when leaving the room.

A plaster that is well-mixed to the right consistency will be easier to apply. Use a plastic bucket to measure the cement, lime and sand, or plaster accurately. For large quantities of plaster, multiply the number of bucket measures. For small quantities, just use half-bucket measures or less.

Old, hard plaster stuck to your equipment can shorten the setting time and reduce the strength of the newly mixed plaster. Do not try to re-work plaster that has begun to set by adding more water: discard it and make a fresh batch. Mix only as much plaster as you will need. For larger areas, mix as much as you can apply in about twenty minutes—judge this by practice.

BONDING AGENTS

Bonding agents modify the suction of the ground or improve the adhesion of the plastering. When used, the base-coat plaster should not exceed 3/8 inches in thickness. If you need to build up the thickness, scratch the surface to provide an extra key, and allow at least 24 hours between coats.

Bonding agents can be mixed with plaster or sand and cement to fill cracks. First brush away any loose particles and then apply a solution of 1 part agent: 3 to 5 parts water with a brush.

Mix the plaster or sand and cement with 1 part bonding agent: 3 parts water to a stiff mix. Apply the filler with a trowel, pressing it well into the crack.

Wash tools and brushes thoroughly in clean water when you are finished. It may be necessary to rinse out the brushes as the work progresses on a large job.

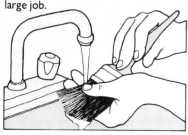

Wash agent from brushes before it sets

Base-coat plasters

Mix base-coat plasters on a mortar board (see opposite). For sanded plasters, measure out each of the materials and thoroughly dry-mix them with a shovel or trowel for small quantities (▷). Make a well in the heaped plaster and pour in some clean water. Turn in the plaster, adding water to produce a thick, creamy consistency.

Just add water to pre-mixed gypsum plaster (which already contains an aggregate). Mix them on the board in the same way. Always wash down the board after use.

You can mix small quantities of pre-mixed plaster in a bucket. Pour the plaster into the water and stir to a creamy consistency; 2½ pounds of plaster will need about 1½ pints of water.

Finish plaster

Mix finish plaster in a clean plastic bucket. Add the powder to the water. Pour no more than 4 pints of water into the bucket. Sprinkle the plaster into the water and stir it with a broad length of wood to a thick, creamy consistency. Tip the plaster out onto a clean, damp mortar board ready for use. Wash the bucket out with clean water before the plaster sets in it.

SEE ALSO

Details for: ▷
Builder's tools 478
Applying plaster 152
Repairing plasterwork 153

COVERAGE OF GAUGED-LIME FINISH PLASTERS*

Plaster product	Ratio of mix			Approximate coverage in sq. yds. per 100 lbs. of plaster
	Lime	Gauging	Sand	
Standard gauging plasters	2	1	–	19.5
	2	1	8	14
Structo-Gauge†	1	1	–	19
	2	1	–	21.5
Keenes cement	2	1	8	13.5
	1	2	–	18.5
	1	2	8	13.5

Mix ratios and approximate coverages are based on information contained in Gypsum Construction Handbook, 2nd edition, published by the United States Gypsum Co. † Structo-Gauge is a USG trademark.

COVERAGE OF BASE-COAT PLASTERS*

Plaster product	Mix	Ratio: aggregate by vol./plaster by weight	Approximate coverage in sq. yds. per 100 lbs. of plaster		
			Gypsum lath	Metal lath	Unit masonry
Standard gypsum base-coat plasters	Sand	2.0–3.0	10.5	5.75	9.25
	Perlite	2.0–3.0	9.25	4.5	7.5
	Vermiculite	2.0–3.0	9	—	8.25
Wood fiber	Neat	—	6.75	2.5	5.25
	Sand	1.0	6.75	3.5	5.25
Structo-Lite†	Regular	—	7	3.75	6.75
Structo-Base†	Sand	2.0–3.0	8.25	5	7.6

Mix ratios and approximate coverages are based on information contained in Gypsum Construction Handbook, 2nd edition, published by the United States Gypsum Co. † Structo-Life and Structo-Base are USG trademarks.

Plaster fillers

Pour out a small heap of the powder on to a small board, make a hollow in its center and pour in water. Stir the mix to a creamy thickness; if it seems too runny add more powder. Use a rather drier mix for filling deeper holes.

APPLYING PLASTER

To the beginner, plastering can seem an overwhelming job, yet it has only two basic requirements: that the plaster should stick well to its ground and that it should be brought to a smooth, flat finish. Good preparation, the careful choice of plaster and working with the right tools should guarantee good adhesion of the material, but the ability to achieve the smooth, flat surface will come only after some practice. Most of the plasterer's tools (◁) are rather specialized and unlikely to be found in the ordinary tool kit, but their cost may prove economical in the long term if you are planning several jobs.

Problems to avoid

Uneven surfaces

Many amateurs tackle plastering jobs, large or small, planning to rub the surface down level when it has set. This approach is very dusty and laborious, and invariably produces a poor result. If a power sander is used, the dust is unpleasant to work in and permeates other parts of the house, making more work. It is better to try for a good surface as you put the plaster on, using wide-bladed tools to spread the material evenly. Ridges left by the corners of the trowel or knife can be carefully shaved down afterwards with the knife—not with abrasive paper.

When covering a large area with finishing plaster, it is not always easy to see if the surface is flat as well as smooth. Look obliquely across the wall or shine a light across it from one side to detect any irregularities.

Crazing

Fine cracks in finished plaster may be due to a sand-and-cement undercoat still drying out, and therefore shrinking. Such an undercoat must be fully dry before the plaster goes on, though if the plaster surface is sound, the fine cracks can be wallpapered over.

Top-coat and undercoat plaster can also crack if made to dry out too fast. Never heat plaster to dry it out.

Loss of strength

Gypsum and cement set chemically when mixed with water. If they dry out before the chemical set takes place, they do not develop their full strength and they become fragile. If this happens it may be necessary to strip the wall and replaster it.

PLASTERING TECHNIQUES

Picking up

Hold the edge of the hawk below the mortar board and scrape a manageable amount of plaster onto the hawk, using the trowel (**1**). Take no more than a trowelful to start with.

Tip the hawk towards you and in one movement cut away about half of the plaster with the trowel, scraping and lifting it off the hawk and onto the face of the trowel (**2**).

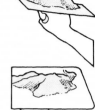

1 Load the hawk   **2 Lift off the plaster**

Application

Hold the loaded trowel horizontally but tilted at an angle to the face of the wall (**1**). Apply the plaster with a vertical upward stroke, pressing firmly so that plaster is fed to the wall. Flatten the angle of the trowel as you go (**2**) but never let its whole face come into contact with the plaster since suction can pull it off the wall again.

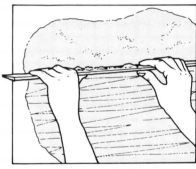

1 Tilt the trowel   **2 Apply the plaster**

Leveling up

Build a slight extra thickness of plaster with the trowel, applying it as evenly as possible. Use the rule (◁) to level the surface, starting at the bottom of the wall, the rule held against original plaster or wooden screeds nailed on at either side. Work the rule upwards while moving it from side to side, then lift it carefully away and the surplus plaster with it. Fill in any hollows with more plaster from the trowel, then level again. Let the plaster stiffen before a final smoothing with the trowel.

Work the rule up the wall to level the surface

Finishing

You can apply the finishing coat to a gypsum-plaster undercoat as soon as it sets. Cement-based sanded plaster must dry thoroughly, but dampen its surface for suction before finish-plastering. The gray face of gypsum lath is finished immediately and is not wetted.

Apply the finish with a plasterer's trowel as described above, spreading it evenly, no more than $1/16$- to $1/8$-inch, judging by eye, as screeds are not used. To gypsum board apply two coats to build a $3/16$-inch thickness.

As the plaster stiffens, brush or lightly spray it with water, then trowel the surface to consolidate it and produce a smooth matte finish. Do not press hard or overwork the surface. Remove surplus water with a sponge.

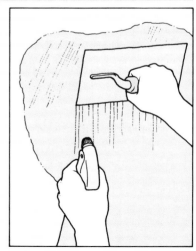

Spray plaster occasionally as you smooth it

REINFORCING A CORNER

When damage to a corner extends along most of the edge, you can reinforce the repair plasterwork with a metal corner bead (1). As well as strengthening and protecting the new corner, it will speed up the repair work because it cuts out the need to use a board as a guide. You can obtain the corner bead from a good builders' supply or DIY store.

Cut the beading to the required length with scissors or a hacksaw. It has a galvanized protective coating, and the cut ends must be sealed with a metal primer or bituminous paint.

Cut back the old plaster from the damaged edge, wet the brickwork and apply patches of undercoat plaster at each side of the corner. Press the expanded metal wings of the bead into the plaster patches (2), using your straightedge to align its outer nose with both original plaster surfaces or checking the bead for evenness with a builder's level. Allow the plaster to set.

Build up the undercoat as before (3), but this time scrape it back to 1/16-inch below the old finished level.

Apply the finishing coat, using the bead as a level to achieve flush surfaces. Take care not to damage the beading's galvanized coating with your trowel; rust can come through later and stain wallcoverings. To be on the safe side, you can brush metal primer over the new corner before decorating.

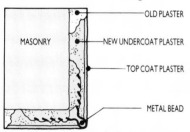

OLD PLASTER

MASONRY — NEW UNDERCOAT PLASTER

TOP COAT PLASTER

METAL BEAD

1 Section through a repaired corner

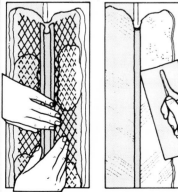

2 Set in plaster   **3 Trim undercoat back**

REPAIRING PLASTERWORK

Every decorator at some time will have to fill small holes and cracks with plaster or filler as part of normal patching preparations (▷), and these should present few problems. But once you start tackling more ambitious jobs, such as removing fireplaces and taking down walls, you will need to develop some of the professional plasterer's skills in order to handle jobs of this magnitude.

Plastering over a fireplace

A bricked-in fireplace provides an area large enough to give the amateur good practice without being overwhelmed. Jobs like this can be done with a one-coat plaster, or with an undercoat plaster followed by a top coat of finishing plaster.

Using a one-coat plaster
Prepare the background by cutting away any loose plaster above and around the brickwork. Remove dust and loose particles with a stiff brush.

Mix the plaster in a tub according to the maker's instructions.

Dampen the background with clean water and place a strip of hardboard below the work area to help you to pick up dropped plaster cleanly.

Tip the mixed plaster onto a dampened mortar board, then scoop some onto a hawk, and with a trowel (or the spreader provided) apply the plaster to the brickwork.

Work in the sequence shown (1), starting at the bottom of each section and spreading the plaster vertically. Work each area in turn, blending the edge of one into the next to build up a slight extra thickness, then level with a rule (▷). Fill any hollows and level again.

Leave the plaster to stiffen for about 45 minutes, when firm finger pressure leaves no impression, then lightly dampen the surface with a close-textured plastic sponge.

Wet the trowel or spreader and give the plaster a smooth finish, using firm pressure vertically and horizontally and keeping the tool wet.

Let the plaster dry thoroughly, for about six weeks, before decorating.

Two-coat plastering
Apply undercoat and finishing coat plasters as described above, scraping the undercoat back to allow for the thickness of the finishing coat.

Repairing a chipped corner

When part of the outside corner of a plastered wall has broken away to show the brickwork behind, you can rebuild it with either one- or two-coat plaster. Use a 4-inch-wide board as a guide to get the corner straight.

With a bolster (▷), cut the plaster back from the damaged edge to reveal about 4 inches of the brickwork.

For two-coat plaster, place the guide board against the old plasterwork, set back about 1/8-inch from the surface of the plaster on the other side of the corner (1). Fasten the board to the brickwork temporarily with masonry nails through the mortar joints, placing them well away from the corner.

Mix up the undercoat plaster, wet the brickwork and edge of the old plaster, then fill the one side of the corner flush with the edge of the board but not the wall (2). Scratch-key the new plaster with the trowel.

When the plaster is stiff, remove the board, pulling it straight from the wall to prevent the new plaster breaking away. The exposed edge represents the finished surface, so scrape it back about 1/8-inch with the trowel and straight-edge (3) to allow for the top coat.

For such a job, a professional would simply hold the board over the new repair and fill the second side of the corner immediately. But this leaves only one hand to lift and apply the plaster, a difficult trick for the amateur. An easier, though slower, method is to let the new plaster harden, then nail the board through it before applying and keying fresh plaster as before (4). Or, if the new plaster is set hard, you can use the scraped edge as a guide.

Let the undercoat set, then nail the board to the wall as before, but this time set it flush with the corner and level off with finishing plaster. Dampen the undercoat if necessary, to help the top coat to stick.

When both sides are firm, polish the new plaster with a wet trowel, rounding over the sharp edge slightly, then leave it to dry out.

If you choose to carry out the repair with a one-coat plaster you must set the board flush with the corner before applying the material.

SEE ALSO

Details for: ▷
Repairing plaster 53–54
Builder's tools 478–479
Background preparation 150

1 Plastering sequence
Divide the area into manageable portions and apply the plaster in the sequence shown.

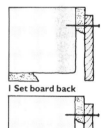

1 Set board back

2 Fill flush with board

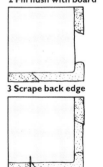

3 Scrape back edge

4 Fill second side

153

PATCHING A WALLBOARD CEILING

A misplaced foot in the attic, a roof leak not attended to, a leaking water pipe—any of these can cause damage to a ceiling. Fortunately the damage is usually of a localized kind that can be simply patch-repaired.

Before starting work, turn off the electricity at the service panel (◁). The next job is to check the direction in which the ceiling joists run and determine whether there is any electrical wiring close by the damaged area. If the damaged ceiling is below a floor, such an inspection can usually be carried out from above, by raising a floorboard. An alternative is to knock an inspection hole through the center of the damage with a hammer. You will find that it is possible to look along the void with the help of a flashlight and a mirror (**1**).

I Use a mirror and flashlight to inspect a void

Close the damaged area, mark out a square or rectangle on the ceiling. Cut away an area of the wallboard slightly larger than the damage, working up to the sides of the nearest joists (**2**). Use a wallboard saw or, if there is wiring nearby, a utility knife, which will just penetrate the thickness of the wallboard.

Cut and toenail 2-by-4 cross-braces between the joists at the ends of the cutout, with half of their thickness projecting beyond the cut edges of the wallboard (**3**).

Nail 1-by-2 furring to the sides of the joists flush with their bottom edges (**4**).

Cut your wallboard patch to fit the opening with a ⅛-inch gap all around, and nail it to the 2-by-4 and furring. Fill and tape over the joints to give a flush surface (◁).

Minor damage
Repair minor damage to wallboard as when preparing to decorate.

2 Cut an opening

3 Nail in cross-braces

4 Nail in furring

REPAIRING LATH AND PLASTER

When the plaster of a lath and plaster wall deteriorates with age it can lose its grip on the laths because its key has gone. This may show itself as a swelling, perhaps with some cracking. It will make a hollow sound if tapped and will yield when it is pressed. The loose plaster should be replaced.

Repairing a wall

Cut out the plaster with a cold chisel and hammer (**1**). If the laths are sound you can replaster over them. Dampen the wooden laths and plaster edges (**2**) around the hole and apply a one-coat plaster with a plasterer's trowel, pressing it firmly between the laths as you coat them (**3**). Build up the coating flush with the surrounding plaster and level it with a rule. Let the plaster stiffen and smooth it with a damp sponge and a trowel. Another option is to apply it in two coats. Scratch-key the first coat and let it set (**4**), then apply the second and finish as before.

For large repairs use two coats of pre-mixed lightweight bonding undercoat, or metal-lathing plaster, followed by a finishing plaster. For a small patch repair use joint compound, pressing it on and between laths (◁).

If laths are damaged, cut them out and replace them, or cover the studs with wallboard and finish with plaster. When using wallboard, nail it in the opening with the grey side towards you.

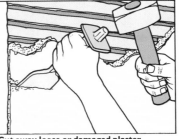

I Cut away loose or damaged plaster

2 Dampen edges of old sound plaster

3 Apply plaster pressing it between laths

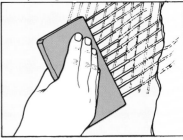

4 Scratch key the undercoat

Repairing a ceiling

A water leak above a lath and plaster ceiling will cause localized damage to the plaster. Repair the ceiling with metal-lathing plaster, finishing with a top-coat gypsum plaster (◁).

Carefully cut back the plaster to sound material. Dampen the background and apply the undercoat (**1**). Don't build up a full thickness. Key the surface and let it set. Give the ceiling a second coat, scrape it back ⅛-inch below the surface and lightly key it. When set, finish-coat the ceiling using a plasterer's trowel (**2**).

I Apply a thin first coat with firm pressure

2 Level top coat over keyed undercoat

CEILING CENTERPIECES

Many older houses have molded cornices and ceiling centerpieces in at least some of their rooms. Though many of these disappeared in the modernism of recent decades, appreciation of them has now revived, and where they cannot be restored they are often replaced with reproductions.

Restoring originals

A ceiling centerpiece, or "rose," is a decorative plaster molding placed at the center of a ceiling and usually has a pendant-light fitting hung from it. Old moldings of this kind are often caked in accretions of ancient paint that mask their fine detail. Restore them whenever possible by cleaning away the old paint buildup and repairing any cracks and chipped details with filler.

Fitting a reproduction molding

To replace original ceiling moldings that are past repair or have been removed, there are now some excellent reproduction moldings which are made from fibrous plaster and are available in a range of styles and sizes to fit most needs.

Prepare to fit such a reproduction by first carefully chipping away the old molding, if present, with a hammer and chisel back to the ceiling plaster. Repair the surface with plaster.

If there is already a light fixture in place on the ceiling, turn off the power supply at the panel ($\triangleright$) and remove the whole fixture. If the ceiling is bare, find its center, using strings stretched across between diagonally opposite corners. The point where the strings cross is the center. Mark the point and drill a hole there for installing the lighting cable.

If the new molding fixture itself lacks a hole for the lighting cable, drill one through its center.

Apply a commercial plaster adhesive to the back of the molding and press it firmly into place after you pass the cable through both holes. On a flat ceiling the suction of the adhesive should be enough, but if you are in any doubt use floor jacks.

The larger types of molding should have the additional support of brass screws driven into the joists, with the screw heads then being covered with filler.

Wipe away surplus adhesive from around the edges of the molding with a damp brush or sponge. Dried adhesive will be hard to remove.

When the adhesive is set, attach the light fixture. Longer screws will now be needed to secure it.

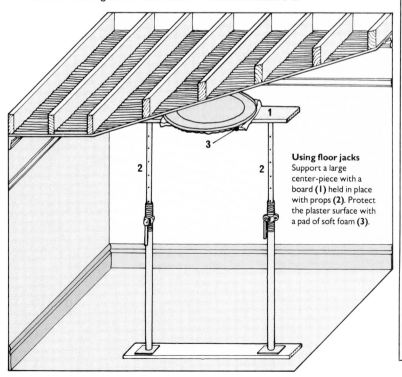

Using floor jacks
Support a large center-piece with a board (1) held in place with props (2). Protect the plaster surface with a pad of soft foam (3).

REPAIRING MOLDED CEILINGS

Sagging plaster on a traditional molded ceiling, if it is left unchecked, can develop into an expensive repair job requiring the services of a professional. But if part of the plaster has broken away from its lath background, yet is otherwise intact, it can be repaired and prevented from collapsing.

Screw repair

Lift and support the sagging portion of the ceiling with wide boards propped in place with lengths of lumber of floor jacks.

Drive countersunk plated screws fitted with galvanized or plated washers through the plaster and into the ceiling joists. The washers should be about 1-inch in diameter and the fasteners should be spaced about 12 inches apart. They will bed themselves down into the plaster and can then be concealed with filler.

Plaster repair

A laborious but more substantial repair to a sagging ceiling can be made by using plaster of paris to bond the plaster back to the laths.

Prop up the ceiling as for the screw repair, then lift the floorboard in the room above—this is not usually necessary in an attic—so that you can get at the back of the ceiling.

Thoroughly brush and vacuum all loose material, dust and dirt away. If the groundwork is not clean, the plaster of paris will not hold.

Liberally soak the back of the ceiling with clean water, then mix the plaster of paris to a creamy consistency and spread it quickly over the whole of the damaged area, covering both the laths and the plaster (1).

Plaster of paris dries very quickly, but leave the props in place until it has set quite hard.

1 Spread plaster over laths and old plaster

REPAIRING CORNICE MOLDINGS

MAKING A NEW LENGTH OF MOLDING

Cornice moldings are decorative plaster features running around the perimeter of a room in the angles between the walls and the ceiling, and they can often be damaged by the settling of a house over a long period of time. Cracks can easily be repaired with filler, while missing sections of moldings have to be re-created.

Small pieces of straight moldings can be formed in place, but longer sections should be made on a bench and then set in place with plaster adhesive. In either case, clean all the old paint off the remaining molding before starting, so as to regain the sharp modeling of the shape and make a better repair.

In-place repair

To start, temporarily nail a straight guide strip to the wall, tucked up against the lower edge of the molding (**1**) and spanning the width of the missing section.

Next, make a template of the molding profile, including the guide strip (**2**). Use a needle template tool (◁) to copy the profile shape, then transfer it to a piece of stiff aluminum or plastic laminate. Cut the shape out of the material with a saw-file blade fitted to a hacksaw and finish off the profile with shaped files, regularly checking the fit against an undamaged section of the molding.

Locate cement, screw the template to a backing board and cut the board to the same shape, but with the contoured edge also cut back to an angle of about 45 degrees from the template (**3**).

Screw a straight-edged base board to

the template so that it just touches the wall when the template is in position. Be sure that the template is at 90 degrees to the edge of the base board. Screw a triangular brace to the back edge of the template and to the base board to make the whole assembly rigid. Finally, fix a "fence" strip to the base board on each side of the template and level with the shaped edge. When the template is in use the fence runs along the face of the wall guide (**4**).

Clear away any loose material and dampen the area to be restored. Mix plaster of paris to a creamy consistency and spread it over the damage. Build the thickness up gradually with progressive layers of plaster, running the template along the guide strip to form the shape as the plaster stiffens. Include pieces of jute scrim in the thick sections to reinforce the plaster.

Long sections of cornice molding can be made up on the bench in a former, constructed by screwing two lengths of board together to represent the angle between the wall and the ceiling, then gluing a triangular strip into the angle between them. Measure the height of the existing cornice and fasten a guide strip to the board representing the wall at that distance from the "ceiling" board. Next paint and wax all of the interior surfaces of the former.

Take the profile of the cornice and make up template assembly (see left). Mix up the plaster and spread it onto the faces of the former while working the template carefully along the guide strip to form the shape as layers of plaster are added and the cornice is built up in stages. Reinforce the thick parts of the molding with pieces of jute scrim. When the molding is hard and dry remove it from the former. Cut back the old damaged cornice to sound material, making square cuts with a fine-toothed saw and cleaning out any broken pieces from the angle with a hammer and chisel. Cut the new section of molding to fit into the cut-out stretch, apply a proprietary plaster adhesive to its back and top, and press it into place. A very large section should have the extra support of brass screws driven into the ceiling joists.

Scrape away any surplus adhesive and fill the joints where the sections butt together, then wipe down with a damp brush or sponge.

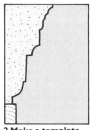

1 Fix a guide to wall

2 Make a template

3 Bevel backing board

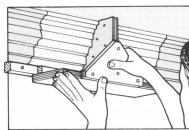

4 Run the fence along the wall guide

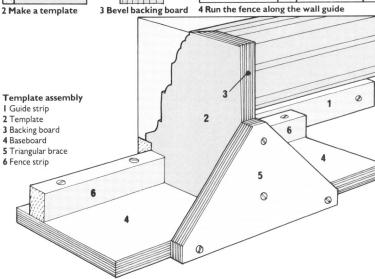

Template assembly
1 Guide strip
2 Template
3 Backing board
4 Baseboard
5 Triangular brace
6 Fence strip

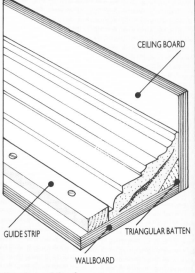

CEILING BOARD

GUIDE STRIP

TRIANGULAR BATTEN

WALLBOARD

Cornice molding former
Run the template assembly along the guide strip.

PLASTERING A WALL

The plastering of a complete wall is usually not necessary in many households. Any new work is much easier to carry out with wallboard (▷), but there are times when repairs are needed due to moisture problems or alterations such as moving doorways, leaving large areas to be plastered. This repair can be done by the non-professional. The key to success is to divide the wall into manageable areas (see below). Some previous practice, for example when patching up decayed plaster, is helpful to do the job without errors.

Applying the plaster

Using the face of the plasterer's trowel, scrape several trowel-loads of plaster onto the hawk and start undercoat plastering at the top of the wall, holding the trowel at an angle to the face of the wall and applying the plaster with vertical strokes. Work from right to left if you are right-handed and from left to right if you are left-handed (see below).

Using firm pressure to guarantee good adhesion, apply first a thin layer and then follow this with more plaster, building up the required thickness. If the final thickness of the plaster needs to be more than ⅜-inch, key the surface with a scratcher and let it set, then apply a second coat to finish the surface.

Fill in the area between two screed strips. It is not necessary to work tight up against them. Level the surface by running the rule upwards, laid across the screeds, and working it from side to side as you go. Fill in any hollows and then level the plaster again. Scratch the surface lightly to provide a key for the finishing coat and let the plaster set. Work along the wall in this way, then remove the screeds and fill the gaps they have left between the plastered areas, again leveling with the rule.

With gypsum plasters, the finishing coat can be applied as soon as the undercoat is set. Cement undercoats must be left to dry for at least 24 hours because of shrinkage (▷), then wetted when the top coat is applied.

PREPARING TO PLASTER

In addition to the plastering tools you need a level and some lengths of ⅜-inch wood strip. The wood strips—known as screeds—are for nailing to the wall, to act as guides when it comes to leveling the plaster. Professional plasterers form plaster screeds by applying bands of undercoat plaster to the required thickness. These may be vertical or horizontal.

Prepare the ground (▷) and fasten the wooden screeds vertically to the wall with masonry nails. Driving the nails home will make it easier for you to work the trowel, but it can also make it more difficult to remove the screeds afterwards. The screeds should be spaced no more than 2 feet apart. Use the level to get them truly even, shimming them out with strips of hardboard or wood as necessary.

Mix the undercoat plaster to a thick, creamy consistency and measure out two bucketfuls to begin with, although you can increase this to larger amounts when you become a little more proficient at working with the material.

Finishing

Cover the undercoat with a thin layer of finishing plaster, working from top to bottom and from left to right (see left) using even, vertical strokes. Work with the trowel held at a slight angle so that only its one edge is touching.

Make sweeping horizontal strokes to level the surface further. You can try using the rule in getting the initial surface even, but you may risk dragging the finish coat off. Use the trowel to smooth out any slight ripples.

Wet the trowel and work over the surface with firm pressure to consolidate the plaster, and as it sets, trowel it to produce a smooth matt finish. Don't overwork it, and wipe away any plaster slurry that appears with a damp sponge.

The walls should be left to dry out for several weeks before decorating.

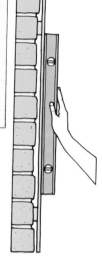

Level the screeds
Shim out the screed strips at the fastening points as required.

The order for applying plaster

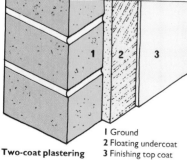

Two-coat plastering

1 Ground
2 Floating undercoat
3 Finishing top coat

Three-coat plastering

1 Ground
2 Roughcoat
3 Floating undercoat
4 Finishing top coat

◀ **Plaster layers**
Plaster is applied in layers to build up a smooth level surface. Two or three coats may be used.

157

GYPSUM WALLBOARD

Wallboard provides a relatively quick and simple method of finishing the rough structural materials of walls and ceilings. It is easy to cut and apply, with adhesives or mechanical fasteners.

A range of gypsum wallboard products is available from builders' supplies. The boards are all based on a core of gypsum plaster covered on both sides with a strong paper liner. They may have a grey paper facing or green, indicating they are moisture-resistant. As well as coming in a range of thicknesses and sheet sizes, the boards can also have tapered or beveled edges. Wallboard joints are usually finished with tape and compound and then decorated. In some cases, a skim coat of plaster is applied to the wallboard before decoration.

SEE ALSO

◁ Details for:
Tools   464, 465, 485

STORING AND CUTTING GYPSUM WALLBOARD

Wallboard is fragile, having very little structural strength, and the sheets are quite heavy, so always get someone to help you carry a sheet, and hold it on its edge. To carry it flat is to run a serious risk of breaking it.

Manufacturers and suppliers of the material store it flat in stacks, but this is usually inconvenient at home and is anyway not necessary for a small number of sheets. Instead store them on edge, leaning them slightly against a wall, their outer faces together to protect them. Place the sheets down carefully to avoid damaging their edges.

Cutting wallboard

Wallboard can be cut with a saw or with a stiff-bladed craft knife.

The sheet must be supported, face side up, on lengths of wood laid across saw horses and with the cutting line marked on it with the aid of a straightedge. When sawing, the saw should be held at a shallow angle to the surface of the wallboard, and if the cutoff is a large one, a helper should support it to prevent it breaking away towards the end of the cut.

When cutting wallboard with a knife, cut well into the material following a straightedge, snap the board along the cutting line over a length of wood and cut through the paper liner on the other side to separate the pieces.

To make openings in wallboard for electrical and other fittings, you can use a keyhole saw, a power jigsaw or a craft knife (◁).

Remove any ragged paper after cutting by rubbing down the cut edges with an abrasive paper.

Tapered edge

Square edge

Beveled edge

Types of edges
Ordinary wallboard used as the primary wall finish have tapered edges to facilitate the building up of compound to create a flush surface. Gypsum bases and lath typically have square edges. Pre-decorated wallboards, which are not finished with compound, have beveled edges to create a pleasing V-joint pattern when installed.

GYPSUM PANEL PRODUCTS

GYPSUM PANEL TYPES AND USES	THICKNESSES (inches)	WIDTHS (inches)	LENGTHS (feet)	EDGE FINISHES
Standard wallboard				
This material is generally used to finish walls and ceilings. The long edges of the panels are tapered to accommodate the built-up layers of tape and compound used to finish joints. Available in a variety of thicknesses, 5⁄8- and 1⁄2-in. panels are typically used for single-layer applications direct to studs, while 3⁄8-in. is normally used over existing wall finishes; 1⁄4-in. wallboard is generally used in multi-layer applications for sound control and for curved surfaces with short radii.	1⁄4 3⁄8, 1⁄2, 5⁄8	48 48	8 8, 9, 10, 12, 14	Tapered
Water-resistant gypsum panels				
With a specially formulated gypsum-asphalt core and chemically-treated face and back papers, this material is recommended for direct application to studs in bathrooms, powder rooms and utility rooms to combat moisture penetration. Suitable as base for ceramic tile and plastic-faced wall panels.	1⁄2, 5⁄8	48	8, 10, 12	Tapered
Predecorated gypsum panels				
These are standard wallboard panels that have a wide range of factory-applied vinyl and fabric facings. Long edges of panels are beveled to form a shallow V-groove at joints.	1⁄2	48	8, 9, 10	Beveled
Gypsum-base panels				
Gypsum bases are used in conjunction with proprietary veneer finishes to create the beauty of a plaster finish with less labor, weight and residual moisture.	1⁄2, 5⁄8	48	8, 10, 12, 14	Square
Gypsum lath				
This product category includes a variety of panel products specially designed as a ground for standard plaster base coats and finishes.	3⁄8, 1⁄2	16, 24	4, 8	Square

APPLYING WALLBOARD

Wallboard can be nailed directly to the framework of a stud partition or to furring strips that are fastened to a solid masonry wall. It can also be bonded straight onto solid walls with an adhesive.

The boards may be fitted horizontally if it is more economical to do so, but generally they are placed vertically. All of the edges should be supported.

When finishing a ceiling and walls, cover the ceiling before you finish the wall.

Methods of fastening wallboard

Nailing to a stud partition

Partition walls may simply be plain room-dividers or they may include doorways. When you are finishing a plain wall, you should work from one corner when you start hanging the board, but where there is a doorway, you may want to work away from it towards the corners.

Starting from a corner

Hold the first board in position. Mark and scribe the edge that meets the adjacent wall if this is necessary ($\triangleright$), then nail or screw the board into position, securing it to all the frame members (see right).

Fasten the rest of the boards in place, working across the partition. Butt the edges of tapered-edged boards, but leave a gap of about ⅛-inch between boards that are going to be coated with tape and compound.

If necessary, scribe the edge of the last board to fit the end corner before nailing it into place.

Cut a baseboard, mitering the joints at the corners or scribing the ends of the new board to the original ($\triangleright$). Fit the baseboard.

Starting from a doorway

Position the first board flush with the door stud and mark the position of the underside of the door's head member on the edge of the board. Between the mark on the board's edge and its top edge, cut out a strip 1-inch wide. Reposition the board and fasten it in place, nailing it to all frame members (see right).

Fasten the rest of the boards in place, working towards the corner. Butt the edges of tapered-edge boards but leave a ⅛-inch gap all around boards which are to be coated afterwards with tape and compound.

If necessary, scribe the last board to fit any irregularities in the corner ($\triangleright$) before fastening it in place.

Cover the rest of the wall on the other side of the doorway in the same way, starting by cutting a 1-inch strip from the first board between its top edge and a mark indicating the lower side of the door's head member.

Cut a wallboard panel to go above the doorway, butting into the cutouts in the boards on each side of the door. Sandpaper away the ragged edges of paper before fitting the panel.

When all of the wallboard is in place, fill and finish the joints ($\triangleright$). Cut and fit door jambs ($\triangleright$) and cover the edges with a casing.

Cut and fit baseboards ($\triangleright$), nailing through the wallboard into studs underneath.

SEE ALSO

Details for: $\triangleright$
Scribing wallboard 160
Finishing
wallboard 164–165
Baseboards 181
Stud partitions 136–137

WALLBOARD NAILS

Use special galvanized drywall nails of lengths appropriate to the thickness of the wallboard, as shown in the table below.

Space the nails about 12 inches apart and place them not less than ⅜-inch from the paper-covered edge and ½-inch from the cut ends. Drive the nails in straight so that they sink just below the surface without tearing through the paper lining.

Board thickness	Nail length
⅜"	1¼"
½"	1⅝"
⅝"	1⅝"

Note that 1¼-inch drywall screws are adequate for most single-layer applications. Use longer screws when applying wallboard in two layers or over existing wall finish.

Drywall nails
1 Galvanized nails
2 Double-headed nail
3 Nailable plug
4 Ring nail

Types of nail used with wallboard

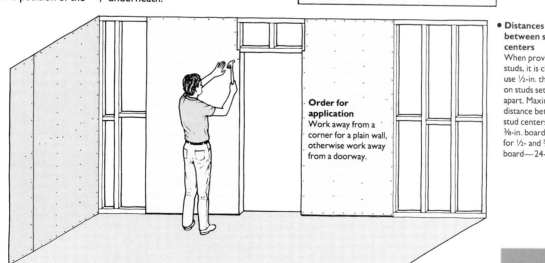

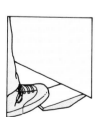

Using a footlifter
Cut the board about ⅝-in. below room height to clear the rootlifter, a simple tool that holds the board against the ceiling leaving both hands free for nailing. You can make one from a 3-in.-wide wood block.

Order for application
Work away from a corner for a plain wall, otherwise work away from a doorway.

• **Distances between stud centers**
When providing new studs, it is cheaper to use ½-in. thick board on studs set 24 in. apart. Maximum distance between stud centers: for ⅜-in. board— 16 in., for ½- and ⅝-in. board—24-in.

SCRIBING WALLBOARD

If the inner edge of the first sheet of wallboard butts against an uneven wall, or its other edge does not fall on the center of the stud, the board must be scribed to fit.

Scribing the first board

Try the first board in position (**1**). The case shown is of an uneven wall pushing the wallboard beyond the studs at the other edge of the wallboard, and of the problem encountered when the end stud in a partition is not set at the normal spacing.

Move and reposition the board (**2**) so that its inner edge lies on the center of the stud and tack it into place with drywall nails driven partway into the intermediate studs. Before temporarily tacking the board, make sure it is set at the right height by using the footlifter. With a pencil and a guide (cut the width of the board), trace a line down the face of the board, copying the contour of the wall. It is essential to keep the guide level while doing this.

Trim the waste away from the scribed edge, following the line, replace the board in the corner and fasten it with nails or screws (**3**).

Scribing the last board

Temporarily nail the board to be scribed over the last fixed board (**4**), making sure that their edges lie flush.

Using a guide and a pencil as above, trace a pencil line down the face of the board, carefully keeping the guide level.

Remove the marked board, cut away the scribed area to cut it to size and nail it into place (**5**).

1 Try the first board in the corner

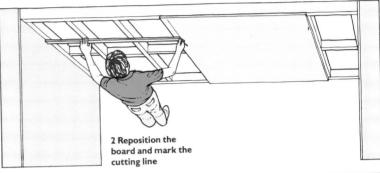

2 Reposition the board and mark the cutting line

3 Cut the board to size and nail in place

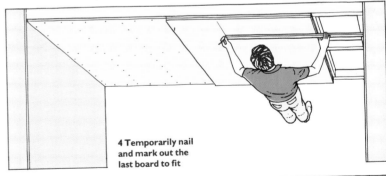

4 Temporarily nail and mark out the last board to fit

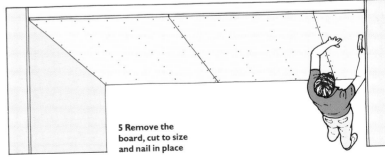

5 Remove the board, cut to size and nail in place

SOLID WALL FURRING

Wallboard cannot be nailed directly to solid masonry walls. One-by-two lengths of wood known as furring strips are used to provide a good basis for the nails and to counter any unevenness of the wall surface. These should be treated with a wood preservative.

You can cover sound old plaster but if it is in poor condition, strip it back to the brickwork. If the failure of the original plaster was caused by moisture, it must be treated (▷) and if possible allowed to dry out before refinishing.

Fit any plumbing pipe runs, electrical conduit or cable to the wall before the furring is applied to conceal them.

Marking out

Use a straightedge to mark the position of the furring strips on the wall with vertical chalk lines. The lines should be placed at 16-inch or 24-inch centers according to the width and thickness of the wallboard being used, bearing in mind that sheets of wallboard must meet on the center lines of the furring strips. Work away from any door or window opening and allow for the thickness of the furring and wallboard at the moldings (▷).

Fastening the furring

Cut the required number of furring strips from 1-by-2 or 1-by-3 lumber. The vertical strips should be cut slightly shorter than the height of the wall. The horizontal strips should be cut to run along the tops and bottoms of the vertical ones and any short vertical lengths above and below openings (see below).

Nail the vertical furring strips on first, setting their bottom ends about 4 inches above the floor. Fasten them with masonry nails or cut nails, with the face of each strip level with the guide line (see right), and check with the straightedge and level that they are also flat and plumb, shimming them out if necessary.

Now nail the horizontal strips across the tops and bottoms of the vertical members, shimming them to the same level if necessary.

Fastening the wallboard

To fasten wallboard to furring strips, follow the same procedure as described for nailing to a stud partition (▷), except that in this case the boards at the sides of doors and windows do not need to be notched to receive panels above or below the openings.

The procedure for filling and finishing the joints between the sheets of wallboard is also identical.

Cut the baseboard to length and nail it through the wallboard to the bottom horizontal furring strip, although if it is a high baseboard of the type used in old, high-ceilinged houses, it can be nailed to the vertical strips.

LEVELING THE FURRING STRIPS

Masonry walls are often uneven and this must be taken into account when fastening the furring if the lining is to finish straight and flat.

To check if the wall is flat hold a long straightedge horizontally against it at different levels. If it proves to be uneven, mark the vertical chalk line already drawn on the wall that is the closest to the highest point (1).

Hold a straight furring strip vertically on the marked chalk line, keeping it plumb with a straightedge and strip level, then mark the floor (2) where the face of the strip falls. Draw a straight guide line across the floor (3), passing through this mark and meeting the walls on each end at right angles.

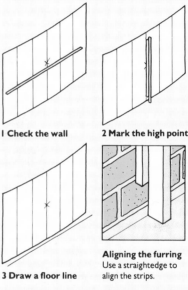

1 Check the wall

2 Mark the high point

3 Draw a floor line

Aligning the furring
Use a straightedge to align the strips.

SEE ALSO

Details for: ▷
Applying wallboard 159
Angles and openings 163
Treating moisture problems 253–257

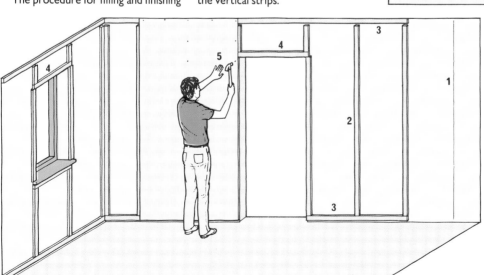

**Using furring strips:
Order of working**
1 Mark furring positions.
2 Fasten vertical strips.
3 Fasten horizontal strips.
4 Fasten short pieces over doors and windows and offset the short vertical ones.
5 Nail boards in place working away from a door or window.

BONDING TO A SOLID WALL

As an alternative to using furring strips on a solid wall as a basis for wallboard, tapered-edged wallboard can be bonded directly to the wall with dabs of plaster or an adhesive. Special pads are produced for leveling up the wall, but squares cut from remnants of the wallboard itself can be used.

The pads are first bonded to the wall in lines that substitute for furring, then dabs of plaster are applied between the lines of pads and the wallboard is temporarily nailed to the pads while the plaster sets. The special double-headed nails are then removed.

Ordinary wallboard may be used with this technique. The wall must first be prepared in the usual way (◁).

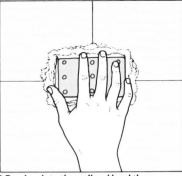

1 Bond pads to the wall and level them

Bonding the pads

Set out vertical chalk lines on the wall 16 inches apart, working from one corner or from a doorway or window opening (see below).

Draw a horizontal line 9 inches from the ceiling, one 4 inches from the floor and another centred between them. If the wall is more than 8 feet high, divide the space between the top and bottom equally with two lines. Place the pads where horizontal and vertical lines intersect.

Using a level and a straightedge almost at the height of the wall, check the wall at each vertical line, noting high spots at the intersections of the lines.

Bond a pad on the most prominent intersection point, using a bonding-coat plaster or a proprietary plaster adhesive, and press it in place to leave not less than $1/8$-inch of adhesive behind it (**1**). The rest of the pads are leveled up to the first one with plaster or adhesive.

Bond and plumb the other pads on the same vertical line, then complete a second vertical row two lines from the first. Check these pads for level vertically, then diagonally with the first row. Work across the wall in this way, then bond remaining pads on the other intersections. Allow two hours to set.

2 Apply thick dabs of plaster between pads

Bonding the wallboard

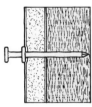

Double-headed nails
Use these special nails to temporarily hold the board while the plaster adhesive sets.

Apply thick dabs of adhesive or bonding plaster to the wall with a trowel (**2**) over an area for one board at a time. Space them 3 inches apart vertically and do not overlap the area of the next board. Press the board firmly against the pads so that the plaster spreads out behind it. Use the straightedge to press it evenly and the footlifter to position it.

Check the alignment, then fasten the board with double-headed nails driven through it into the pads round the edge. Bond the next board in the same way, butting it to the first, and work on across the wall, scribing the last board into the corner (◁). When the plaster has set, remove the nails with pliers or a claw hammer, protecting the wallboard surface (**3**).

Work around angles and openings (see opposite) and when all surfaces are covered, fill and finish the joints (◁).

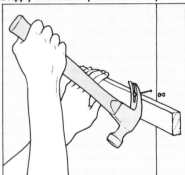

3 Pull out the nails when plaster is set

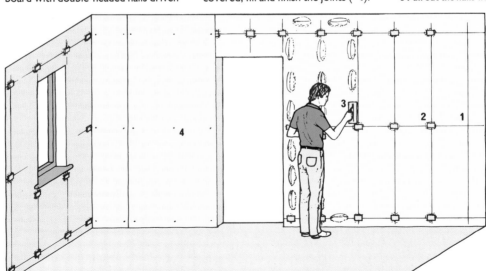

The bonding method order of working
1 Mark pad positions.
2 Stick the pads to the wall.
3 Apply dabs of plaster.
4 Place wallboard and temporarily nail. Remove nails when plaster is set.

WINDOW OPENINGS

Cut the wallboard linings for the window reveals and soffit to length and width. These are put into place before the wall finish. Their front edges should line up with the faces of the wall pads or furring strips.

Apply evenly spaced dabs of plaster adhesive to the back of the soffit lining, press it into place (**1**) and prop it there while the plaster adhesive sets. If the lining covers a wide span also use a wooden board to support it. Fit the reveal linings in the same way (**2**).

Working away from the window, bond the wall linings so that the paper-covered edge of the board laps the cut edge of the reveal lining.

The panels for above and below the window are cut and fitted last. Sandpaper off any rough edges of paper and leave a 1/8-inch gap for filling.

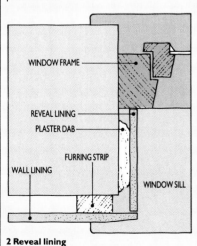

1 Soffit lining
Bond a soffit lining with dabs of plaster and prop in place until set.

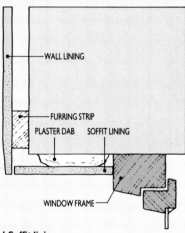

2 Reveal lining
Like the soffit lining, cut and bond the reveal so the wall lining overlaps its cut edge.

Inside corner

Fasten wooden furring strips or bonded gypsum board pads close to the corner. Whenever possible always place the cut edges of the wallboard into an inside corner.

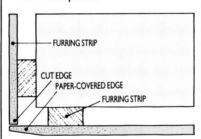

Inside corner
Set cut edges into the angle.

Outside corner

Attach furring strips of gypsum board pads and close to the corner as possible. Use screws and wall plugs to attach the furring so as to prevent the corner breaking away. Apply metal corner bead over the joint and finish with three coats of compound.

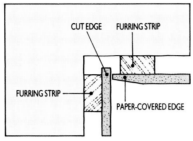

Outside corner
A paper-covered edge should lap the other edge.

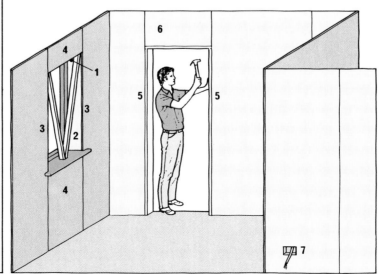

Door openings

The reveals of doorways in exterior walls should be treated in the same way as described for window openings (see left).

In the case of interior door openings, screw wooden furring strips or bond gypsum board pads level with the edge of the blockwork, then nail or bond the wallboard into place.

Fit a new door jamb or modify the old one if necessary and cover the joint with a casing.

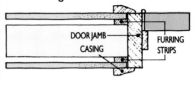

Electrical outlets

Depending on the type of fitting, build a chase or shim out the mounting box for an electrical switch or socket outlet so that it finishes flush with the face of the wallboard lining. Screw short lengths of furring strip at each side of the box, or apply dabs of adhesive or plaster for pads if using the bonding method (see opposite).

Cut the opening for the box before mounting the board. If you find it difficult to mark the opening accurately by transferring measurements to the board, remove the fixture from the box and take an impression of it by placing the board in position and pressing it against the box.

Mount the wallboard panel in place and replace the electrical fixture.

Interior door opening
Fit a new jamb or widen the old one and cover the joint between the jamb and wallboard with a casing.

Electrical outlets
Build a chase or shim out the mounting box to set it flush with the wallboard.

Angle treatments: Order of working
1 Fit soffit lining.
2 Fit reveal lining.
3 Fit boards working away from window.
4 Fit panels over and under window.
5 Fit boards working away from doorway.
6 Cut and fit panel over doorway.
7 Cut openings for electrical fixtures as they occur.

FINISHING WALLBOARD

All of the joints between boards and the indentations left by nailing must be filled and smoothed before the surface of the wallboard is ready for direct decoration.

To finish wallboard for applying decoration, you will need filler, joint tape and a variety of taping knives. The technique is not difficult.

SEE ALSO

◁ Details for:
Applying wallboard   159

Tools and materials

To finish wallboard joints, you will need joint compound—a premixed plaster-like substance that is available in 5-gallon pails, joint tape and a variety of joint knives ranging in width from 3 to 10 inches. In addition to these items, you will need a hawk, which is used to hold the compound and from which you load the knife and apply material to the wall, medium-grade sandpaper and a sanding block. The work area should be neat and dust-free.

Filling tapered-edge board joints

Start by applying a 1/8-inch-thick bed of compound to the recess around a wallboard joint with a 3-inch knife. The bed should be uniform and fairly smooth, with no voids—to accomplish this, work with firm but fluid strokes. After the bed has been prepared, lightly press wallboard tape into it with the 3-inch knife (**1**). It sometimes helps the tape to adhere if it is moistened before application. Once the tape is in position, go over it with the knife, pressing firmly and using the knife edge to smooth the tape and squeeze out excess compound from beneath it. Work in only one direction and after each stroke, scrape the knife blade against the edge of the hawk to remove excess compound. It is critical that no air bubbles are left beneath the tape, but it is equally crucial that the surface is not overworked.

Stop working the surface if the compound begins to dry.

Allow the initial coat of compound and tape to dry for about a day. Inspect the first coat for ridges, burrs and air bubbles beneath the tape. Sand lightly with a block to remove ridges; dried burrs can usually be scraped off with a clean taping knife. Cut away tape over air bubbles with a utility knife.

Apply a thinner second coat of compound over the tape using a 4- or 6-inch taping knife (**2**). Fill all voids and feather the edges of the bead. Allow the second coat to dry thoroughly and remove any surface roughness as after the first application.

The third and final coat should be applied with an 8- or 10-inch knife (**3**). When dry, the final coat may be lightly polished with medium-grade sandpaper.

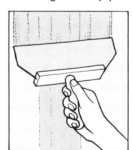

1 Press tape into filler   **2 Apply finish in a wide band**   **3 Finish with wide knife**

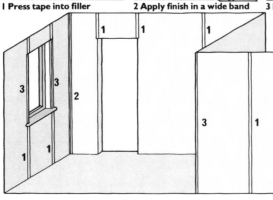

Filling the joints
1 Use the tape flat for flush joints.
2 Fold the tape for inside corners.
3 Use metal-reinforced tape or metal corner bead on outside corners.

CUT EDGES

Treat a butt joint between a tapered edge and a cut edge of wallboard in a way similar to that described for joints between two tapered edges (see left), but build up the tapered edge with compound, level with the cut edge, before applying the tape.

When two cut edges meet press the compound into the 1/8-inch gap to finish flush. When the compound is set, apply a thin band of finish to it and press the paper tape tight against the board. Cover this with a wide but thin coat of compound and feather the edges, then finish off as before.

```
                        ▽ COMPOUND
┌─────────────────────────────────────┐
│ TAPERED EDGE    //    CUT EDGE       │
├─────────────────────────────────────┤
│              TAPE                    │
└─────────────────────────────────────┘
               ▽ COMPOUND
┌─────────────────────────────────────┐
│ CUT EDGE     //     CUT EDGE         │
├─────────────────────────────────────┤
│              TAPE                    │
└─────────────────────────────────────┘
```

FIBERGLASS TAPES

A self-adhesive fiberglass mesh tape can be used instead of traditional paper tape for finishing new wallboard or for making patch repairs. The tape is a strong binder and does not need prior application of compound to bond it in place. The tape is put on first, then the compound is pressed through the mesh afterwards.

Applying the tape
Make sure that the joint edges of the wallboard are dust-free. If the edges of boards have been cut, burnish them with the handle of your taping knife to remove all traces of rough paper.

Starting at the top, center the tape over the joint, unroll and press it into place as your work down the wall. Cut it off to length at the bottom. Do not overlap ends if you have to make a join in the tape; butt them.

Press the compound through the tape into the joint with the knife, then level off the surface so that the mesh of the tape is visible and let the compound set.

Finish the joint with subsequent coats of compound, as with paper tape.

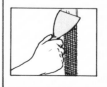

Applying the compound
Press the compound through the tape with a taping knife.

FINISHING WALLBOARD

Inside corners

The inside corners of drywall are finished in a way similar to the method used for flat joints. A bed of joint compound is first applied to the contiguous surfaces where two walls meet to form a corner or where a wall meets the ceiling.

Cut the paper tape to length and fold it down its center. Use a 3-inch joint knife or a specially designed corner knife

to press the paper into the wet compound (1).

Squeeze out excess compound from beneath the tape and remove it. You may wish to apply the second coat of compound over the tape immediately (2). Feather the edges with a wide knife.

When the first coat is completely dry, apply a second, wider coat and feather the edges again.

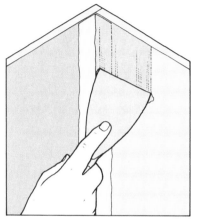

1 Finishing inside corner
Apply bands of compound to adjacent walls, creasing tape, and then pressing tape into wet compound.

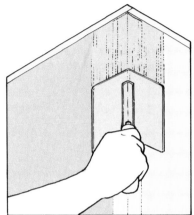

2 Applying coat of compound coat and tape
This can be done with a special corner knife. Feathering coats are applied with wider flat knives.

Outside corners

Wallboard edges that meet to form an outside corner must first have a corner bead applied over them. There are two basic designs for corner beads—one has a thin, metal rod attached to paper flanges, the other is all-metal. The paper type must be embedded in compound, and the all-metal type is fastened to the corner with drywall nails, screws or a

special crimping tool. If nails or screws are used, it is essential that the fastener heads be driven below the protruding surface of the bead, but care must be taken not to distort the metal flanges into which the fasteners are driven.

Once the corner bead has been fastened to the surface, the flanges are covered with successive applications of wallboard compound. The first coat should be applied with one edge of the knife blade resting against the bead extension and the other against the wallboard surface. The slight hollow is filled with a relatively thick coat of compound. Once the first coat is dry, scrape off the burrs with a clean joint knife and apply two more coats with successively wider knives to fill the hollow and feather out the edges of the compound.

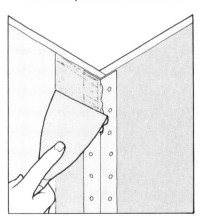

Method for finishing outside corner with corner bead and compound

---

PREPARING FOR DECORATION

Finishing with plaster
The alternative to direct decoration of the gypsum wallboard is to precede decoration by applying a thin finishing-coat of actual plaster to the board. The plastering is not easy for the inexperienced but with some practice, you could tackle your walls. Ceilings should be left to professionals, but you can prepare the wallboard and have it ready for the tradesman to plaster.

Preparing the ground
First fill the gaps between the board joints and at the angles, bringing them flush with the boards. Use board-finish plaster for one-coat plastering, and an undercoat first for two-coat plastering.

Reinforce all of the joints and angles with jute scrim pressed into a thin band of the plaster. Let the plaster set, but don't let it dry out before applying the finishing plaster.

Rolls of jute scrim $3\frac{1}{2}$-inches-wide are available from builders' suppliers.

If you intend to plaster the walls yourself, first study the section on plastering thoroughly (▷).

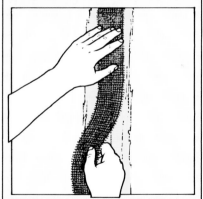

Reinforce joints with scrim before plastering

Decorating direct
Before the wallboard can be directly decorated, it must be given a uniform surface by the application of a sealer.

Brush on or sponge-apply a thin coating of finish mixed to a thin consistency. If applying it by brush, follow it up with the sponge worked in a light circular motion over the entire surface. Alternatively, use a proprietary ready-mixed top coat, which can be applied with a brush or roller and is suitable for all decorative treatments. Two coats of shellac will also provide a vapor barrier.

SEE ALSO

Details for: ▷
Plaster   148–152

165

APPLYING GYPSUM BOARD TO A CEILING

A new ceiling may be made with wallboard, which can also be used to replace an old lath-and-plaster ceiling that is beyond repair.

Fastening wallboard in place and finishing its surface to make it ready for direct decoration can be tackled by the non-professional, but wet plastering of a ceiling should be left to the skilled professional as it is hard work and difficult to do well.

Preparing an old ceiling

Start by stripping away all the old damaged plaster and lath, and pull out all the nails.

This is a messy job, so wear protective clothing, a pair of goggles and a face mask while working. It's also a good idea to seal the gaps around doors in the room to prevent dust escaping through the rest of the house.

If necessary, trim back the top edge of the wall plaster so that the edge of the ceiling wallboard can be tucked in.

Inspect and treat exposed joists for any signs of decay (◁).

FITTING NEW WALLBOARD

Measure the area of the ceiling and select the most economical size of boards to cover it.

The boards should be fitted with their long paper-covered edges running at right angles to the joists. The butting joints between the ends of boards should be staggered on each row and supported by a joist in every case.

Fit perimeter nailers between the joists against the walls and other intermediate ones in lines across the ceilings to support the long edges of the boards. It is not always necessary to fit intermediate supports if the boards are finally to be plastered, but they will guarantee a sound ceiling. The intermediate nailers should be 2-by-4 and should be fitted so that the edges of the boards will fall along their center lines.

If necessary, trim the length of the boards to guarantee that their ends fall on the center lines of the joists.

Start applying the boards working from one corner of the room. It takes two people to support a large sheet of wallboard while it is being fastened. Smaller sizes may be applied single-handed, but even then a temporary wooden prop to hold them in place during nailing will be useful.

Using galvanized wallboard nails, install the first board, working from the joist nearest its center and nailing at 6-inch centers. This is to prevent the boards sagging in the middle, which can happen if their edges are nailed first.

Fasten all the remaining boards in the same way.

If the boards are to be plastered, leave ⅛-inch gaps between the cut ends and the paper-covered edges. For direct decoration, butt the paper-covered edges but leave ⅛-inch gaps at the ends of the boards.

Finish the joints by the method described for gypsum wallboard (◁).

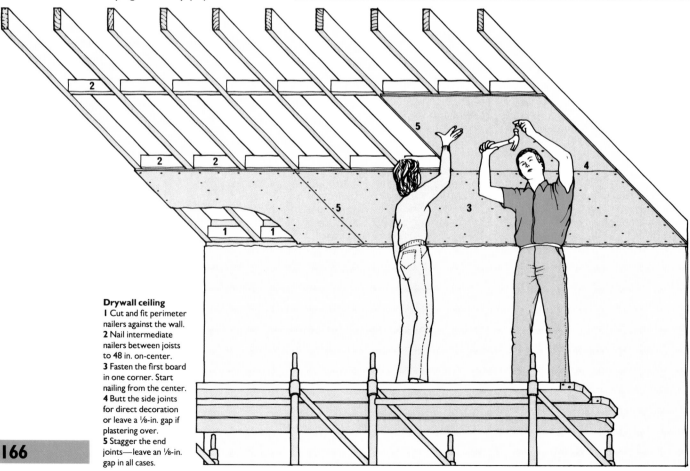

Drywall ceiling
1 Cut and fit perimeter nailers against the wall.
2 Nail intermediate nailers between joists to 48 in. on-center.
3 Fasten the first board in one corner. Start nailing from the center.
4 Butt the side joints for direct decoration or leave a ⅛-in. gap if plastering over.
5 Stagger the end joints—leave an ⅛-in. gap in all cases.

Taping the joint

Where new gypsum wallboard panels meet a ceiling, the joint must be taped and successive coats of compound applied as for any inside corner in gypsum wallboard construction. This is the case whether the ceiling has been also finished with wallboard or it is an existing plaster ceiling.

As you would with an inside corner formed by two walls, apply a thick coat of compound to the adjacent surfaces with a 3-in. joint knife or corner taping knife. Fold the tape lengthwise and press it into the wet compound. Then use the flat or corner knife to smooth the tape and remove excess compound and air bubbles. Let the freshly applied compound dry for about 24 hours, polish and smooth the dry compound as necessary, then apply a second coat of compound to both the wall and ceiling surfaces with a 6-inch knife, feathering the edges flush with the wall and ceiling surfaces. After the second coat dries, prepare the surface and then apply the final coat of compound with an 8- to 10-inch knife. Once the final coat is dry and after it has had minor imperfections either filled or polished out with sandpaper, the walls and ceiling will be ready for decorating.

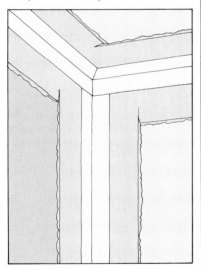

Finishing joints between wallboard and ceiling
Use compound and a folded length of tape, then feather out as ordinary joints.

Crown moldings

Millwork designed to finish the corner formed by a ceiling and the top of a wall is called "crown molding." There are many sizes, patterns and profiles of crown molding, and at least several choices are likely to be available at your local lumberyard or home center. A great number of patterns are also available in molded polystyrene plastic and are available through lumberyards, decorator outlets and by mail order.

Whether you choose a wide, highly detailed style or a simple design, treating walls with crown moldings can provide an extremely nice decorative touch. Of course, the crown molding you select should be in keeping with other trim moldings used in the room and its overall style.

As with other moldings whose ends must be miter-cut to form corners, it is necessary to use a miter box when cutting crown molding. But, because crown moldings are applied between the wall and ceiling at a cant, the ends must take a compound, rather than simple, miter-cut. It is easy to cut compound miters accurately if the crown molding is supported in the miter box at the same angle at which it will be applied to the wall. One method of supporting the molding would be to construct a jig from two pieces of wood joined along their edges to form a right angle, as shown at the right. The widths of the pieces used to make the jig must

be such that the crown molding can be nestled into them to form the hypotenuse of a right triangle. It is also helpful to cut the ends of the top part of the jig to parallel 45-degree angles.

After determining the length needed for a particular run of crown molding, mark the point at which it must be cut along the top of the molding. Nestle the molding into the jig and align the cutting mark with the 45-degree miter box guides. Hold the molding and jig tightly against the back of the miter box and cut on the waste side of the mark with a sharp backsaw. It is important to establish the correct direction of the cut—if the miter is being cut for an inside corner, the back of the cut piece will, in effect, be longer than the patterned face. The opposite will be the case for crown moldings cut to form an outside corner.

SEE ALSO	
Details for: ▷	
Backsaw	463
Miter box	464

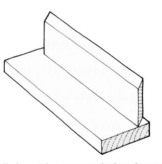

Jig for cutting compound miters for crown molding with a miter box and backsaw

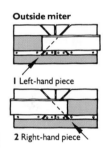

Outside miter

1 Left-hand piece

2 Right-hand piece

Inside miter

1 Left-hand piece

2 Right-hand piece

Crown molding can be used for an elegant treatment for the joint between wall and ceiling

EXTERIOR WALL FINISH

The exterior finish of a home serves two important functions: First, it weatherproofs the structure, and second, it provides a major decorative element that contributes to setting the style of the house.

Many different materials can be used to finish a house—among them various types of wood and composition shingles, wood and wood-product sidings such as plywood and hardboard, and aluminum, vinyl, brick and stucco. Each has its own advantages along with some characteristic disadvantages, and each has its own special procedures for installation, repair and maintenance. Some are easy; others are best left to professionals. The following pages will discuss various approaches to working with exterior finish materials.

Preparations for re-siding

In many cases you may simply be able to apply the new siding right over the old, but it is important to keep in mind that any moisture problems (◁) that led to the deterioration of existing siding must be corrected before new siding, whatever the type, is applied. Moisture problems are generally caused by seepage, inadequate ventilation or by a faulty vapor barrier. Any existing structural problems should also be corrected rather than merely covered over by a new application of siding.

This said, there are several basic approaches to preparing a house for new siding, and the one to choose will depend on the condition of the house, the existing siding and the type of siding that is to be applied. When there is evidence of moisture-induced rot or other structural problems, the best approach is to strip away the existing siding and possibly the sheathing as well, to expose the house frame, survey the extent of the damage, and replace any structural members affected. Other advantages of stripping off existing siding and sheathing include the opportunity to inspect existing insulation and improve it with batts or insulating sheathing, and to install new felt or a semipermeable house wrap over the sheathing to reduce air-infiltration levels. Stripping away existing siding is also the best approach if it is badly buckled.

If existing horizontal siding is sound, you may be able to prepare it for application of new horizontal board or aluminum or vinyl siding by attaching furring strips right over the existing siding to create a flat nailing plane for the new siding. Furring strips are also used to prepare masonry walls for siding. Still simpler, large plywood and hardboard siding panels can often be applied directly over existing siding without first installing furring.

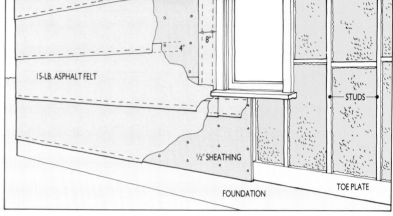

Restoring sheathing and felt
Sheathing and felt should be restored before siding is applied. Note that the perimeter of openings such as windows and doors is lined with 8-in. felt strips before horizontal courses are stapled to the entire wall surface, starting from the bottom and working up. All seams should overlap at least 4 in.

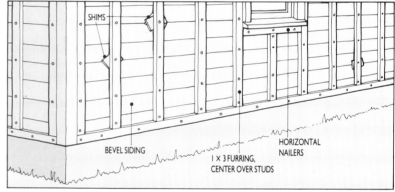

Applying new siding over existing siding
When applying new horizontal siding over existing horizontal siding, you need only install furring strips to provide a nailing base. If walls are slightly uneven, shim out the furring to create a smooth, flat plane for the new siding.

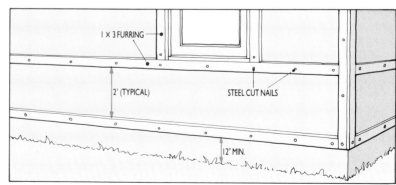

Preparing masonry
Prepare masonry walls for new siding by first nailing up furring strips. The pattern shown is appropriate for vertical board siding. For plywood or hardboard sheets, install vertical nailers on 4-ft. centers for securing the board edges, in addition to horizontal furring. To attach furring to brick or block, nail into the mortar joints.

Vertical siding

Tongue-and-groove boards fitted together and nailed to sheathing or furring make effective plain siding. Often this type is used on gables of masonry houses. Board-and-batten siding is nearly as easy to apply yet, because it is more decorative, can cover an entire house attractively.

Boards for board-and-batten siding are usually 1 × 12; battens 1 × 2. Attach the entire inner course of siding first, then fasten the outer course over the gaps. Overlap boards and battens at least ½ in. Follow the nailing patterns shown in the diagrams to allow for wood shrinkage and expansion.

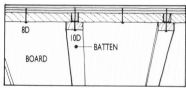
Board-and-batten siding

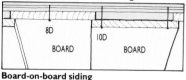
Reverse board-and-batten siding

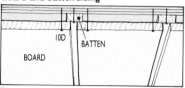
Board-on-board siding

Plywood panels

Sheets of plywood siding, available in a variety of surface textures, are economical, easy to install with a helper, and add strength to existing house frames. Panels come in 4-foot widths and 8-, 9-, and 10-foot lengths. Seal the edges with waterproof primer or caulk before joining. Panels may be nailed directly to studs, exterior sheathing or furring strips. Use noncorrosive 6d or 8d nails, spaced 6 inches on-center around the edges and 12 inches on-center within the panels, over studs or furring.

Plywood siding designs

Shingles

Wood shingles used as siding are the same as those used for roofs. They come in 16-, 18-, and 24-inch lengths, in four quality grades, and are sold in "bundles" covering 25 square feet at recommended exposure (half the shingle length minus ½ inch), and "squares" which cover 100 square feet. An advantage to shingles is that they can be applied by one person.

On walls, wood shingles may be applied either single-course (as on a roof) or double-course. Single-coursing covers walls with two thicknesses of shingles and three where rows overlap. With double-coursing, pairs of shingles are applied as one for greater weather protection and to produce strong shadow lines for attractive design. Utility-grade shingles may be used for the unexposed layer. Because double-coursed shingles have greater exposure, walls are also covered with two shingle thicknesses, but there are four where rows overlap. Calculate shingle layout as for bevel siding (see page 170).

Composition shingles

Shingles are also manufactured both from mineral fibers (containing asbestos) and asphalt. They are less expensive than wood and because more exposure is possible (even though they are laid single-course), less material and labor is needed. Asphalt "shingles" are even available in roll form, sometimes embossed to simulate masonry.

Shingle panels

Individual wood or composition shingles are available attached to fiberboard or other backing panels. These install quickly but because they overlap only 1 to 2 inches, they require careful layout.

SEE ALSO
Details for: ▷

House construction	120–121
Horizontal siding	170

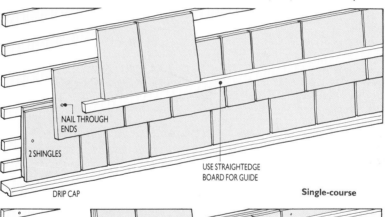

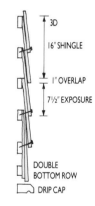

Single-course

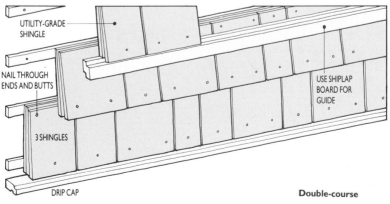

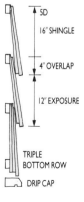

Double-course

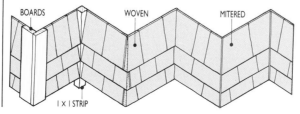
Corner styles

HORIZONTAL SIDING

ALUMINUM AND VINYL

Aluminum is one option for low-maintenance siding. It is available in a number of textures and finishes, and with insulated backing laminated to it. Layout and installation is similar to that for wood. However, framed openings, corners, eaves, and other areas require special trim pieces which often must be custom-formed using a bending brake. For this reason, most homeowners choose to have aluminum siding installed by professionals.

Vinyl siding is similar to aluminum expect that it doesn't bend. Preformed trim, cut to required lengths, is used at edges and openings. Although vinyl siding is usually applied by professionals, there's little reason for do-it-yourselfers to avoid the project.

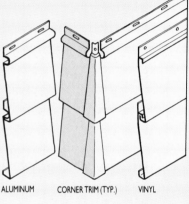

ALUMINUM   CORNER TRIM (TYP.)   VINYL

Wood

Bevel siding, which is wedge-shaped, is the most popular. Prime the ends with paint or sealer before you install it. Plan siding layout carefully to achieve a uniform exposure for all boards that is as close as possible to the recommended maximum: 6 inches for siding sold in nominal 8-inch widths; 8 inches for nominal 10-inch widths. For good looks and to minimize leaks, try to align the lower edges of siding boards with the tops and bottoms of window and door frames.

Use a straight length of lumber for a story pole (see diagram). Mark the heights of all windows and doors. (Average if necessary, or use only measurements from the front of the house.) Then set dividers to the recommended exposure and "walk off" intervals along the pole, starting at the window and door markings and working toward the ends. If necessary, decrease the exposure amount until correct spacing is achieved. Mark each interval onto the pole, then transfer marks to the sheathing and frame openings. Also make an exposure guide (see diagram) from a piece of scrap wood. Use it to align each board as you nail it into place.

Attaching siding

Snap a chalk line to connect the points marking the siding's lowest points. Check it with a level. Attach vertical strips of primed lumber at inside and outside corners for siding to butt against. Nail a primed lumber filler strip along the bottom of the sheathing ½ inch above the chalk line. Beginning at an inside corner, attach the bottom course of siding by aligning the bottom edge with the chalk line and nailing through the top edge into the sheathing or studs just above the filler strip. Continue all the way around the house, then snap another line to connect the next set of story-pole marks. Attach the second course of siding, checking the alignment of the boards by holding the exposure gauge against the siding below. Continue all the way up the house. Caulk corner and frame joints.

Windows and doors

At some window and other openings you may have to notch siding to fit. First, measure down from the sill to locate the butt line of the siding to be notched and snap a chalk line along the course of siding below. Then measure and cut the notch in the new siding, spread caulk around the opening, and fasten the siding into place. Follow the same procedure for notching at the top of openings.

SEE ALSO
◁ Details for:
Siding preparations   168
Shingles and panels   169

Wood siding types

CLAPBOARD   BEVEL   RABBETED

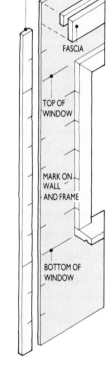

SHEATHING

STORY POLE

FASCIA

TOP OF WINDOW

MARK ON WALL AND FRAME

BOTTOM OF WINDOW

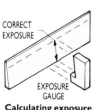

CORRECT EXPOSURE

EXPOSURE GAUGE

Calculating exposure

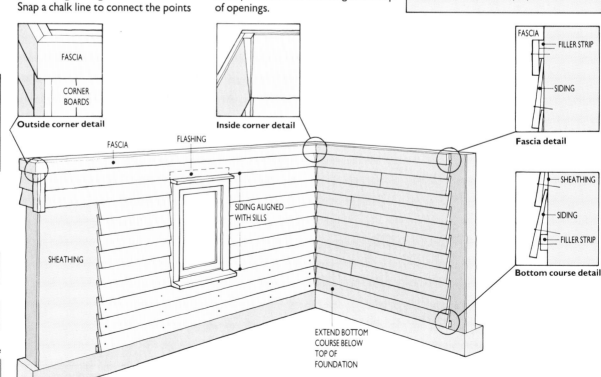

Outside corner detail

FASCIA

CORNER BOARDS

Inside corner detail

FASCIA   FLASHING

SIDING ALIGNED WITH SILLS

SHEATHING

EXTEND BOTTOM COURSE BELOW TOP OF FOUNDATION

Installing wood siding

Fascia detail

FASCIA   FILLER STRIP

SIDING

Bottom course detail

SHEATHING

SIDING

FILLER STRIP

MIXING STUCCO

Mix only as much stucco as you can use in an hour. Keep mixing tools and equipment thoroughly washed so that no mortar sets on them.

Measure level bucketfuls of sand onto a mortar board or smooth, level base such as a concrete driveway.

Using a second dry bucket and shovel, measure out the cement, tapping the bucket to settle the loose powder and topping it up as needed. Mix sand and cement together by shoveling them from one heap to another and back again (**1**) until it takes on a uniform gray color.

Form a well in the center of the heap and pour in some water (**2**).

Shovel the dry mix from the sides of the heap into the water until the water is absorbed (**3**). If you are left with dry material add more water as you go until you achieve firm, plastic consistency and even color. If after turning the mix it is still relatively dry, sprinkle it with water (**4**). But remember that too much water will weaken the mix.

Draw the back of your shovel across the stucco with a sawing action to test its consistency (**5**). The ribs formed by this action should not slump or crumble, which would indicate respectively that it is either too wet or too dry. The back of the shovel should leave a smooth texture on the surface of the stucco.

When you have finished, hose down and sweep the work area clean.

MASONRY

Veneer

Brick or stonework veneer used as siding is not load-bearing. It supports only its own weight. To apply it, the house foundation must have a ledge in front of the framing wide enough to build on. First install metal flashing atop the ledge, extending 6 inches up behind the sheathing. Then attach 15-pound building paper to the exterior of the sheathing (or old siding), and over that, metal masonry ties spaced 2 to 3 feet apart horizontally and 15 inches vertically. Erect the wall, leaving a 1/4-inch airspace between it and the sheathing, and anchor the masonry material to the ties as you go.

Stucco

Stucco is a mixture of portland cement and sand. It can be applied directly over brick, stone, or rough-surfaced concrete. Over wood or old siding, first attach building paper and furring strips, and across the furring nail sheets of metal lath. Self-furring lath is also available. It works best where shimming isn't necessary.

Apply the stucco in three layers. To mix the first, or scratch, coat, add 1 part cement to 3 parts sand (or up to 4 if it is coarse). Press generous amounts of scratch mix into the lath with a trowel. When a layer 1/8-inch-thick covers the lath, rake it with a leaf rake to groove the surface. Let stand two days. Spray frequently with water to prevent drying. To mix the second, or brown, coat, blend in 1–2 parts additional sand. Apply it as you did the first, in a 1/8-inch-thick layer. Roughen the surface only slightly. Keep moist for two days, then allow to dry for at least five days more. For the final, finish, coat, most DIY-ers purchase a dry premix colored to their specifications and containing lime to make the mix smooth and workable. Apply the finish coat in a thin layer, leveling it with a strip of lumber.

SEE ALSO

Details for: ▷	
Siding preparations	168
Shingles and panels	169
Horizontal siding	170

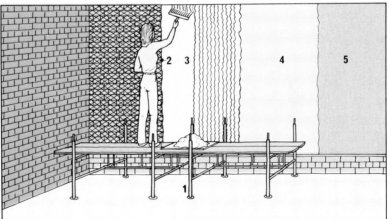

Applying stucco
1 Set up safe work platform.
2 Attach furring and lath.
3 Apply scratch coat; groove with rake.
4 Apply brown coat; roughen slightly.
5 Apply finish coat.

PATCH REPAIRS

Stucco should be applied with a metal plasterer's trowel and the top coat finished with a wooden float.

Take a trowelful of mortar and spread it on the wall with firm pressure, applying it with an upward stroke (**1**).

Build up the undercoat layer no more than two-thirds the thickness of the original or 1/8 inch, whichever is the thinner.

Level the mortar with a straight-edged strip of wood that fits within the cutout of the area being patched, then scratch grooves in the surface for the top coat (**2**). Leave the under-coat to set and strengthen for a few days.

Finish coat
Before applying, dampen the undercoat. When the coat is on, level it with a straightedge laid across the surfaces of the surrounding stucco and work it upward with a side-to-side motion.

1 Use firm pressure

2 Groove the surface

FLOORS: SUSPENDED FLOORS

Floor construction in most buildings is based on timber beams known as joists. These are rectangular in section, placed on edge for maximum strength, usually about 16 inches apart, and supported at the ends by the walls.

Such "suspended floors" contrast with the concrete "slab floors"—supported over their whole area by the ground— which are usually to be found in basements, and at ground level in modern houses.

Traditional suspended floors are usually finished with tongue-and-groove or plain-edged planks, though in modern houses flooring-grade chipboard is now being used on both types of floor.

Ground floors

The joists of a suspended ground floor are usually made from 2 × 8 to 2 × 12 lumber. Their ends are nailed to supporting lengths of 2 × 6s laid flat, called sills or plates, and these distribute the load from the joists to the walls, which, in turn, support them.

The ends of the joists are covered by lumber the same size as the joists, called headers. These are set on edge and fastened also to the sills or plates.

The relatively lightweight joists tend to sag in the middle and are therefore generally supported by girders running the length of the house, down the middle. Girders usually consist of three 2 × 10s or 2 × 12s nailed together, or a single steel I-beam. Both are supported by posts underneath. Their ends rest in notches cut into the foundation walls.

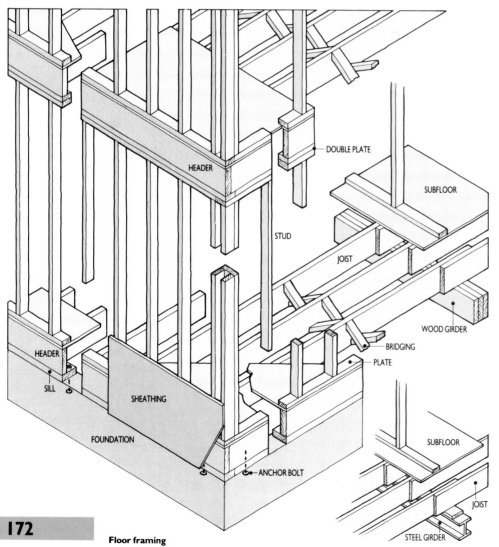

Floor framing

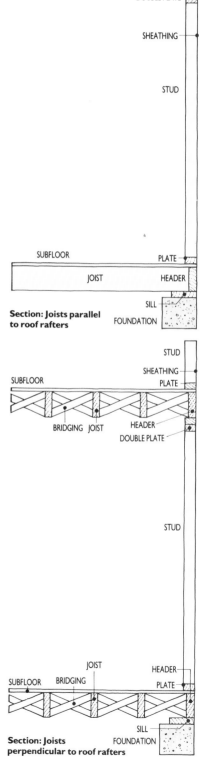

Section: Joists parallel to roof rafters

Section: Joists perpendicular to roof rafters

BRACING FLOORS

For extra stiffness, floor joists are braced with "blocking," solid sections of wood, nailed between them (1), or with "bridging," diagonal wooden braces (2).

Traditional bridging of 1 × 3 softwood, is preferable because it can compensate for timber shrinkage.

In modern floor construction, bridging is carried out with ready-made metal units (3), usually equipped with a drilled flange at each end for nailing between joists set on 16-, 18-, or 24-inch centers.

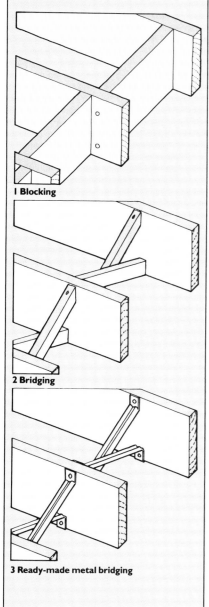

1 Blocking

2 Bridging

3 Ready-made metal bridging

SLAB FLOORS

Though slab floors are to be seen at all levels in large industrial buildings, in houses they are normally in basements.

A slab floor is essentially a concrete slab laid on a substratum of gravel. To lay such a floor the topsoil is first removed and the gravel then laid to consolidate the ground and level up the site. After tamping, the gravel is then covered with a layer of tough plastic (polyethylene) film which acts as a vapor barrier, and also prevents the cement from draining out of the concrete and into the gravel, which would cause the concrete to be weakened.

The concrete slab is usually about 4 to 6 inches thick and is laid over a layer of wire-mesh reinforcement. This is often supported off the vapor barrier on small stones during pouring so that the mesh becomes embedded in the concrete.

A slab floor can incorporate a foundation on which the walls are built, or the slab can be separate, laid within the confines of a perimeter foundation.

When resilient flooring such as linoleum or asphalt tile is to be applied directly to the floor, the concrete should be leveled by screeding and finished smooth with a trowel. For a nonslippery surface which is to be left bare, brush the leveled concrete with a stiff broom.

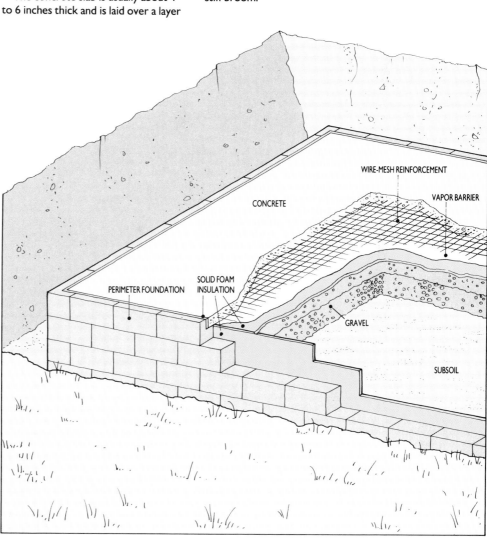

WIRE-MESH REINFORCEMENT

VAPOR BARRIER

CONCRETE

PERIMETER FOUNDATION

SOLID FOAM INSULATION

GRAVEL

SUBSOIL

Solid floors
A solid floor is often used in preference to a suspended floor as it can be cheaper to construct. A concrete floor can be laid after the foundations and first courses of brickwork are built above ground level or be an integral part of a reinforced concrete foundation (see above).

METAL FITTINGS FOR FLOORS

Floor construction is one of the many areas in which modern builders have been able to substitute the use of factory-made fittings for traditional methods of construction.

SEE ALSO

◁ Details for:
Suspended floors   172

FLANGE

STIRRUP

Joist hangers
Some joist hangers are made with a top flange.

The hanger must be a close fit to the wall

A poorly fitted hanger will distort

Framing anchors
Framing anchors reduce the risk of splitting the wood with toe-nailing as they are fixed with relatively short nails driven in squarely.

Lateral restraint straps
The straps are fastened to the joists to tie the floor and side joists

together. They may be set at right angles to or parallel with the line of the joists.

Joist hangers

Galvanized steel joist hangers are now in wide use. These are brackets which are fastened to walls to support the ends of the joists. There are various versions for securing to masonry walls and for constructing timber-to-timber joints.

The use of metal joist hangers allows brickwork or blockwork to be completely built up before the joists are fitted. It also saves the awkward notching of doubled headers, which was once common practice. The hangers must be fitted properly, with the top flange sitting squarely. Any shims that are used must cover the whole bearing surface. The rear face of the bracket must fully meet the face of the wood.

The ends of the joists are fastened into hangers with nails, one or two being driven through the holes in the side gussets.

Face-fixing hanger   **Straight-flange hanger**   **Hooked-flange hanger**   **Double hanger**

Framing anchors

Framing anchors are steel brackets which are used to make butt joints with other wood framing members. They are in growing use among builders to fasten trimmed joists instead of making time-consuming notched joints.

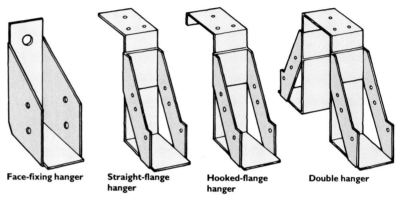

Framing anchors are made left- and right-handed

Lateral restraint straps

While the walls carry the weight of the floor, the floor adds to the lateral stiffness of the walls. In areas where the force of the wind can threaten the stability of modern lightweight walls, lateral restraint straps are used to provide ties between the walls and the floor. They are simply stiff strips of galvanized steel, perforated for nailing and bent in various ways to suit the direction of the joists.

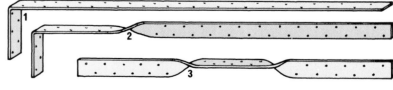

Lateral restraint straps
1 For tying joists parallel to an exterior wall
2 For tying joists at right angles to an exterior wall
3 For tying joists on either side of an interior wall

COVERED SLAB FLOORS

Most floor coverings, including wooden block flooring, can be bonded directly to a dry, smooth screeded floor, but floorboards cannot be directly bonded, and so must be fastened by other means.

The boards are nailed down to 2 × 2-inch furring strips, or sleepers. The sleepers are embedded in the concrete while it is wet or are later fastened to clips which have been embedded. In either case, the timber must be treated with a wood preservative. A vapor barrier must be incorporated, usually in the form of a sheet of polyethylene laid across the slab. A smooth, finished screed is unnecessary under a boarded floor.

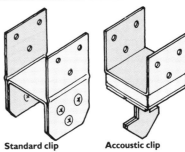

Standard clip   **Accoustic clip**

The clip method

This means of fastening requires the slab to be level and relatively smooth. The flanges of the clips are pressed into the surface of the concrete before it sets, while a marked guide strip is used to space the clips and align them in rows. The rows are normally set 16 inches apart on centers starting 2 inches from one wall. When the concrete is completely dry, the "ears" of the clips are raised from their folded position with a claw hammer. The sleepers, having been cut to length and their ends treated with a preservative, are nailed in place through the holes in the clips. The boards are nailed to the sleepers.

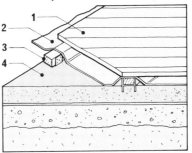

1 Clip method
Composition of floor
1 Floorboards
2 Vapor barrier
3 Clipped sleepers
4 Concrete slab

Embedded sleepers

These may be splayed in section so as to key into the concrete slab. Sometimes the slab is built up in two layers with a damp-proof asphalt membrane sandwiched between them. Before the top layer is laid, the treated sleepers are positioned on 16-inch centers and leveled on dabs of concrete. Strips of wood are nailed across them temporarily to hold them in position.

When the dabs of concrete are set and the sleepers firmly held, the wood strips are removed and the top layer of concrete is poured and compacted. It is leveled with a rule notched to fit over the sleepers, which is drawn along them and finishes the concrete ½ inch below their tops. When the concrete layer is fully dry, the boards are nailed on the sleepers in the conventional way.

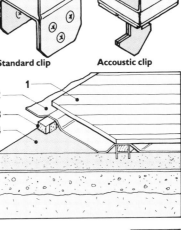

2 Embedded sleepers
Composition of floor
1 Floorboards
2 Embedded sleepers
3 Leveled concrete
4 Asphalt vapor barrier
5 Concrete slab

Particleboard floating floors

Flooring-grade particleboard is a relatively recent innovation as a material for installing over a slab floor. It is quicker and cheaper to lay a particleboard floor than one made of boards. It is also more stable and it can be laid without being fastened to the concrete slab.

It produces a floor of the type known as a "floating floor." The simplest floor of this kind is laid with ¾-inch high-density particleboard, either of the square-edged or tongue-and-groove variety.

First a sheet of insulating material such as rigid polystyrene or fiberboard is laid on the concrete slab; then, normally, a vapor barrier of polyethylene sheet is laid above the polystyrene. The vapor barrier must be a continuous sheet, with its edges turned up and trapped behind the baseboards. The particleboard, its edges glued, is then laid on the vapor barrier.

The particleboard flooring is held in place by its own weight, but is also trapped by the baseboards, which are nailed to the walls around its edges. The baseboards also cover a ⅛-inch gap between the particleboard and the walls, allowing for expansion across the floor.

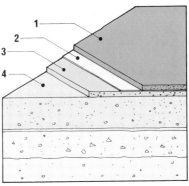

3 Chipboard floating floor
Composition of floor
1 Particleboard flooring
2 Vapor barrier
3 Polystyrene insulation
4 Leveled concrete

Sleeper-on-slab floor

This type of construction has become most common. The slab is swept clean and treated with sealer. Then 1 × 2 lumber strips treated with preservative are set in beads of waterproof construction adhesive and nailed to the slab with concrete nails. If strip flooring is to be laid directly (with no subfloor underneath), sleepers should lie on 16-inch centers perpendicular to the direction the strips will run.

Lay a sheet of polyethylene film over the treated sleepers to serve as a vapor barrier, then nail additional untreated 1 × 2 strips over the treated ones, sandwiching the film in between. Flooring or subflooring may then be nailed to the untreated sleepers.

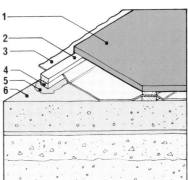

4 Sleeper-on-slab floor
Composition of floor
1 Particleboard flooring
2 Untreated sleepers
3 Vapor barrier
4 Treated sleepers
5 Adhesive
6 Concrete slab

175

FLOORING

Flooring is the general term used to describe the surface which is laid over the floor's structural elements—the floor joists or the concrete slab. This surface can *consist of hardwood planks or strips, or it can be constructed with manufactured boards of plywood or particleboard. Resilient vinyl flooring is another option.*

Floorboards

Hardwoods are generally used for making floorboards. The standard widths are from 1 to 3½ inches and thicknesses range from 5/16 to 2 inches. The standard thickness for tongue-and-groove flooring is 25/32 inch. The most popular width is 2¼ inches.

The narrow boards produce superior floors because they make any movement due to shrinkage less noticeable. But installing them is costly in labor, and they are used only in expensive houses. Softwood flooring of pine or hemlock is common in older homes, but seldom installed today.

The best floorboards are quarter-sawn (1) from the log, a method that diminishes distortion from shrinkage. But as this method is wasteful of timber, boards are more often cut tangentially (2) for reasons of economy. Boards cut in this way tend to bow, or "cup" across their width and they should be fastened

with the cupped side facing upwards, as there is a tendency for the grain of the other side to splinter. The cut of a board—tangential or quarter-cut—can be checked by looking at the annual growth rings on the end grain.

The joint of tongue-and-groove boards is not at the center of their edges but closer to one face, and these boards should be laid with the offset joint nearer to the joist. Though tongue-and-groove boards are nominally the same sizes as square-edged boards, the edge joint reduces their floor coverage by about ½ inch per board.

In some old buildings, you may find floorboards bearing the marks left by an adze on their undersides. Such old boards have usually been trimmed to a required thickness only where they sit over the joists, while their top faces and edges are planed smooth.

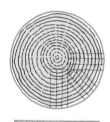

1 Quarter-sawn boards
Shrinkage does not distort these boards.

2 Tangentially sawn boards
Shrinkage can cause these boards to "cup"

SHEET FLOORING

Softwood and hardwood boards not only provide a tough flooring, but when sealed and polished they will also take on an attractive color. But sheet materials such as flooring-grade plywood or particleboard are purely functional, and are only as subfloor surfaces.

Plywood

Plywood is the most commonly used subfloor material. Standard thickness is 3/8 or 3/4 inch; sheets are normally 4 × 8 feet. Special 1⅛-inch plywood milled with tongue-and-groove edges is sometimes used to provide underlayment for carpeting. (Normally, underlayment is added as a separate layer.) Subfloor-grade plywood has one smooth side and one rough. Many grades are available. Most codes allow B-C, C-C, and C-D.

Particleboard

Particleboard for subflooring is allowed by some building codes. It is less expensive than plywood. Though particleboard does not warp, it does absorb moisture. Sheets come in 2 × 8- and 4 × 8-foot sizes, and for subfloor use, thicknesses of 3/8 to 3/4 inch. Both square-edged and tongue-and-groove panels are available. Particleboard is harder to nail into than plywood, and dulls sawblades faster. However, where the material is liable to become slightly damp only occasionally, some builders prefer it to plywood because it won't delaminate.

Types of flooring
1 Square-edged particleboard
2 T&G particleboard
3 T&G plywood
4 T&G softwood boards
5 Square-edged softwood board
6 T&G hardwood boards

TONGUE-AND-GROOVE FLOORING

You can detect whether your floorboards are tongue-and-groove by trying to push a knife blade into the gap between them.

To lift a tongue-and-groove board it is necessary first to cut through the tongues on each side of the board. Saw carefully along the line of the joint with a dovetail or tenon saw (1) held at a shallow angle. A straight strip temporarily nailed along the edge of the board may help you to keep the saw on a straight line.

With the tongue cut through, saw across the board and lift it as you would a square-edged one.

If the original flooring has been "blind nailed" (2), use finishing nails (3) to nail the boards back in place and conceal the recesses with a matching wood filler.

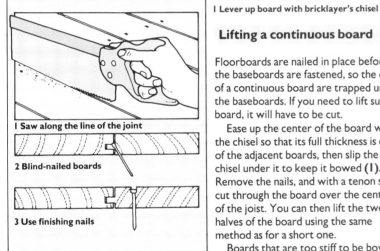

1 Saw along the line of the joint

2 Blind-nailed boards

3 Use finishing nails

REFITTING A CUT BOARD

The butted ends of floorboards normally meet and rest on a joist (1) and a board which has been cut flush with the side of a joist must be given a new means of support when replaced (2).

Cut a piece of 2 × 2-in. softwood and screw it to the side of the joists flush with the top. Screw the end of the floorboard to the support.

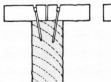

1 Boards share a joist   2 Support a cut board

LIFTING FLOORBOARDS

Floorboards are produced in random lengths which are an equal size per bundle—oak strips are often up to 16 feet long. When lifting floorboards, it is these shorter pieces that you should start with if possible. In many older homes, one or two boards will probably have been lifted already for access to services.

Square-edged boards

Tap the blade of a bricklayer's chisel (▷) into the gap between the boards close to the cut end (1). Lever up the edge of the board but try not to crush the edge of the one next to it. Fit the prybar into the gap at the other side of the board and repeat the procedure.

Ease the end of the board up in this way, then work the claw of a hammer under it until you can lift it enough to slip a cold chisel (▷) under it (2). Move along the board to the next set of nails and proceed in the same way, continuing until the board comes away.

1 Lever up board with bricklayer's chisel   2 Place cold chisel under board

Lifting a continuous board

Floorboards are nailed in place before the baseboards are fastened, so the ends of a continuous board are trapped under the baseboards. If you need to lift such a board, it will have to be cut.

Ease up the center of the board with the chisel so that its full thickness is clear of the adjacent boards, then slip the cold chisel under it to keep it bowed (1). Remove the nails, and with a tenon saw cut through the board over the center of the joist. You can then lift the two halves of the board using the same method as for a short one.

Boards that are too stiff to be bowed upwards, or are tongue-and-groove, will have to be cut across in place. This means cutting flush with the side of the joist instead of over its center.

Freeing the end of a board

The end of the board trapped under the baseboard can usually be freed by being lifted to a steep angle, when the gap between the joists and the wall should allow the board to clear the nails and be pulled free (1).

To raise a floorboard that runs beneath a partition wall, the board must also be cut close to the wall. Drill a starting hole and then cut the board as close to the wall as possible (2).

There is a special saw (3) that can be used for cutting floorboards. It has a curved cutting edge that allows you to cut a board without fully lifting it.

Locate the side of the joist by passing the blade of a padsaw (2) vertically into the gaps on both sides of the board (the joints of tongue-and-groove boards will also have to be cut (see left). Mark the edges of the board where the blade stops, and draw a line between these points representing the side of the joist. Make a starting hole for the saw blade by drilling three or four 1/8-inch holes close together at one end of the line marked across the surface.

Work the tip of the blade into the hole and start making the cut with short strokes. Gradually tip the blade to a shallow angle to avoid cutting into any cables or pipes that may be hidden below. Lever up the board with a chisel as described above.

1 Saw across the board

2 Find the joist's side

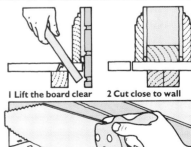

1 Lift the board clear   2 Cut close to wall

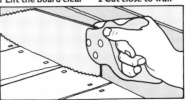

3 Use a floorboard saw if necessary

SEE ALSO

Details for: ▷
Bricklayer's chisel   480
Cold chisel   480

RE-LAYING A FLOOR

Though floors probably take more wear and tear than any other interior surface, this is not usually the reason why re-laying boards becomes necessary. Fire damage or wood decay—which would also affect the joists—or simply large gaps in the boards caused by shrinkage may require the floor to be relaid, or even entirely renewed.

If the floor is to be renewed, measure the room and buy your materials in advance. Leave floorboards or sheets of plywood to acclimatize—ideally in the room where they are to be laid—for at least a week before fastening them.

Removing the flooring

To lift the complete flooring you must first remove the baseboards from the walls (◁). If you intend to re-lay the boards, number them with chalk before starting to raise them. Lift the first few boards as described (◁), starting from one side of the room, then pry up the remainder by working a cold chisel or crowbar between the joists and the undersides of the boards. In the case of tongue-and-groove boards, two or three should be eased up simultaneously, to avoid breaking the joints, and progressively pulled away.

Pull all the nails out of the boards and joists, and scrape any accumulated dirt from the tops of the joists. Clean the edges of the boards similarly if they are to be reused. Check all boards for rot or insect infestation and treat or repair them as required (◁).

Laying new floorboards

Though the following deals with fixing tongue-and-groove floorboards, the basic method described applies equally to square-edged boards.

Lay a few loose boards together to form a work platform. Measure the width or length of the room —whichever is at right angles to the joists— and cut your boards to stop ⅜ inch short of the walls at each end. Where two shorter boards are to be butted end to end, cut them so that the joint will be centered on a joist and set the boards out so as to avoid such joints occurring on the same joist with adjacent boards. Any two butt joints must be separated by at least one whole board. Lay four to six boards at a time.

Fix the first board with its grooved edge no more than ⅜ inch from the wall and nail it in place with steel-cuts—or finishing nails that are at least twice as long as the thickness of the board.

Place the nails in pairs, one about 1 inch from each edge of the board and centered on the joists. Punch them in about 1/16 inch. Place one nail in the tongued edge if blind-nailing.

Lay the other cut boards in place and clamp them to the fixed one so as to close the edge joints. Special floorboard clamps can be rented for this, but wedges cut from 16-inch cut-offs of board will work just as well (1). To clamp the boards with wedges, temporarily nail another board just less than a board's width away from them. Insert the pairs of wedges in the gap, resting on every fourth or fifth joist, and with two hammers tap the wedges' wide ends toward each other. Nail the clamped-up boards in place as before, then remove the wedges and temporary board and repeat the operation with the next group of boards, continuing in this way across the room.

At the far wall, place the remaining boards, cutting the last one to width, its tongue on the "waste" side. It should be cut to leave a gap equal to the width of the tongue or ½ inch, whichever is less. If you cannot get the last board to slot in, cut away the bottom section of the grooved edge so that it will drop into place (2).

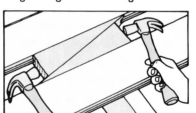

1 Make wedges to clamp boards

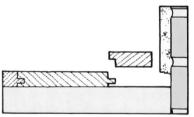

2 Cut away part of last board's grooved edge

FLOORBOARD CLAMP

This special tool automatically grips the joist over which it is placed by means of two toothed cams. A screw-operated ram applies pressure to the floorboards when the bar is turned.

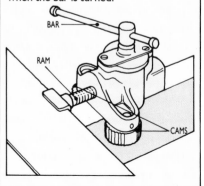

BAR

RAM

CAMS

• **Closing gaps**
You can re-lay floorboards without removing all the boards at once. Lift and renail about six boards at a time as you work across the floor. Finally, cut and fit a new board to fill the last gap.

Laying the boards
Working from a platform of loose boards, proceed in the following order:
1 Nail first board parallel to the wall.
2 Cut and lay up to six boards, clamp them together and nail.
3 Lay the next group of boards in the same way, continue across the floor and cut the last board to fit.

LAYING PARTICLEBOARD FLOORING

For a floor that is going to be invisible beneath some kind of covering— whether vinyl, cork, fitted carpet or whatever—particleboard is an excellent material. It is laid relatively quickly and is much cheaper than an equivalent amount of hardwood flooring. It comes in two types—square-edged or tongue-and-groove. Each has its own laying technique.

CUTTING TO FIT

Square-edge boards
The widths of the boards may have to be cut down (1) so that their long edges will butt on the joists' center lines.
Tongue-and-groove boards
Only the last boards need be cut in their width (2) to fit against the wall.

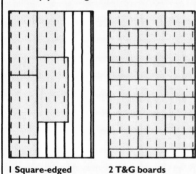

1 Square-edged boards   **2 T&G boards**

Square-edged boards

All the edges of a square-edged chipboard flooring must be supported. Lay the boards with their long edges along the joists and nail 2 × 4 blocking between the joists to support the boards' ends. The blocking against the wall can be placed in advance; those supporting joints must be nailed into place as the boards are laid.

Start with a full-length board in one corner and lay a row of boards the length of the room, cutting the last one to fit as required. Leave an expansion gap of about ⅜ inch between the outer edges of the boards and the walls. If the boards' inner edges do not fall on the center line of a joist, cut them down so that they do so on the nearest one, but cut the surplus off the outer edge, near the wall.

Nail the boards down close together, using 2- or 2¼-inch annular ring nails spaced about 1 foot apart along the joists and blocking. Place the nails about ¾ inch from the edges. Cut and lay the remainder of the boards with the end joints staggered on alternate rows.

Tongue-and-groove boards

Tongue-and-groove boards are laid with their long edges running across the joists. Blocking is needed only against the walls, to support the outer edges. The ends of the boards are supported by joists.

Working from one corner, lay the first board with its grooved edges about ⅜ inch from the walls and nail it into place.

Apply PVA wood adhesive to the joint along the end of the first board, then lay the next one in the row. Knock it up to the first board with a hammer for a good close joint, protecting the edge with a piece of scrap wood. Nail the board down as before, then wipe any surplus adhesive from the surface before it sets, using a damp rag. Continue in this way across the floor, gluing all of the joints as you go. Cut boards to fit at the ends of rows or to fall on the center of a joist, and stagger these end joints on alternate rows. Finally, fit the baseboard, which will cover the expansion gaps.

You can seal the surface of the particleboard with two coats of clear polyurethane if you wish, to protect it from dirt.

SEE ALSO

Details for: ▷

Floor covering	115
Baseboards	181

1 Arrangement for laying square-edged boards

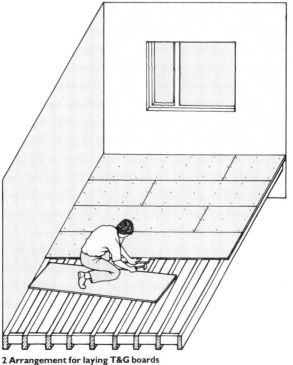

2 Arrangement for laying T&G boards

1 Square-edged boards
Lay the boards with their long edges on a joist and the ends supported with blocking.

2 Tongue-and-groove boards
Lay the boards across the joists with the ends falling on a joist.

FLOOR JOISTS

Floor joists are important structural elements of a house. Being loadbearing, their size and spacing in new structures are strictly specified by building code regulations and they must satisfy a building inspector. Spacing and lumber dimension are the most critical factors. In most cases, repairing and replacing joists may be done merely using the same size lumber as the originals. However, it is always recommended that you consult building regulations or a building inspector before beginning any task involving joists, especially in the case of older homes.

Fitting services

Service runs like heating pipes and electric cables can run in the void below a suspended first floor, but those running at right angles to the joists in upper floors must pass through the joists, which are covered by flooring above and a ceiling below.

So as not to weaken joists, the holes for cables and pipes should center on the joists depth, in any event at least 2 inches below the top surface to clear floor nails, and always within the middle two-thirds of the joist's length **(1)**.

Notches for pipe runs in the top edge should be no deeper than one-fourth the depth of the joist and within a quarter of the joist's length at each end. Otherwise, they will be weakened. Notched joists should be strengthened along their length with 2 × 4s **(2)**. Make notches by drilling through the joist, then sawing down to the hole.

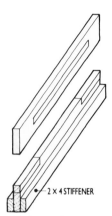

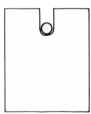

● ─ 2 × 4 STIFFENER

Fitting services
1 Make holes within the shaded line.
2 Place notches within shaded area.

Drill and saw notches to accommodate pipe

Repairing joists

Repairing joists is far simpler than replacing them. To fit new joists, long lengths must often be maneuvered where there is little headroom, and frequently fitting new joists causes uneven spots in an otherwise level floor.

If possible, repair joists by strengthening localized areas of damage, using either metal fittings such as joist hangers and angle iron, steel plates or ¾-inch plywood strips. Weak and sagging joists can be strengthened by attaching a long length of angle iron along their bottom edge, or by fastening them to new joists, running parallel.

Sometimes deteriorated wood can be treated with insecticide to prevent further damage, and new wood placed on either side, separated from the infected wood by a layer of 15-pound asphalt roofing felt placed in between. Check with an exterminator. However, in most cases of rot or insect damage, new wood is the only answer. Again, where code allows, you may be able merely to cut out the decayed wood and replace it with a new section properly strengthened. Where regulations require that new wood stretch from sill to sill or sill to girder, however, you will have to install full-length lumber.

Fitting a new joist

To replace joists resting atop sills, first notch the ends as shown. Position the joist on its side, next to the old joist, then tap it snugly into place on edge using a light sledgehammer. Stop and trim the upper edge of the joist if the floor shows signs of lifting. After the new joist is in place, jack both joists up slightly and insert thin shims against the notched surface. Lower the jacks, then nail the joists together using 16d common nails.

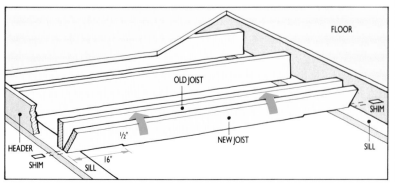

FLOOR

OLD JOIST

SHIM

NEW JOIST

SILL

HEADER

SHIM

SILL

½"

16"

STRENGTHENING A SAGGING FLOOR

When sections of flooring become uneven, usually a problem in older homes, the cause is seldom the joists but more often the weakening of a girder or supporting post. One remedy is to merely add another post, directly beneath the sagging section of girder. Rent a shoring jack and use it to raise the girder to level, plus a fraction of an inch more to allow for settling. Raise the jack very gradually, a partial turn or so per day over the course of a week or more. Adjust the height of the new post and make sure there is solid footing beneath (a 20-inch-square concrete slab 10 inches thick is standard). Then fit the post into position, check that it is exactly vertical, and lower the girder onto it as you remove the jack. Sometimes all that is necessary is to place shims between the girder and existing posts, using the same jacking method.

To determine the amount a girder must be raised to level it, stretch a string along one side of the beam, from the bottom corner at one end to the bottom corner at the other. The amount of wood showing below the string (where the sag is most extreme) is the distance the girder must be raised.

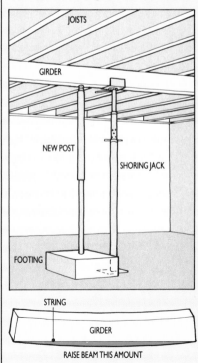

JOISTS

GIRDER

NEW POST

SHORING JACK

FOOTING

STRING

GIRDER

RAISE BEAM THIS AMOUNT

BASEBOARDS

Baseboards are protective "kick boards," but are usually also molded to form a decorative border between the floor and walls. Modern baseboards are relatively small and simply formed, with either a rounded or beveled top edge.

Baseboards found in older houses can be as much as 1 foot wide and quite elaborately molded, but those in newer homes are narrower and simpler. Many designs are available at lumberyards. Some will supply more elaborate designs to special order.

Baseboards can be nailed directly onto studs behind wallboard. Sometimes a strip of quarter-round molding is attached also, where the baseboard meets the floor.

Removing baseboard molding

Remove a baseboard by levering it away from the wall with a crowbar or bricklayer's chisel. Where a baseboard butts against door molding or an outside corner, it can be levered off, but a single length whose ends are mitered into inside corners will have to be cut before it can be removed.

Tap the blade of the chisel between the baseboard and the wall, and lever the top edge away sufficiently to insert the chisel end of the crowbar behind it. Place a thin strip of wood behind the crowbar to protect the wall, tap the chisel in again a little further, and work along the baseboard in this way as the nails loosen. With the board removed, pull the nails out through the back to avoid splitting the face. If you're careful, you can reuse the molding.

Cutting a long baseboard
A long stretch of baseboard will bend out sufficiently for you to cut it in place if you lever it away at its center and insert blocks of wood (1), one on each side of the proposed cut, to hold the board about 1 inch from the wall.

Make a vertical cut with a panel saw held at about 45 degrees to the face of the board (2) and work with short strokes, using the tip of the saw.

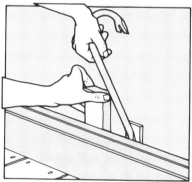

1 Pry board away from wall and shim it out

2 Cut through baseboard with tip of saw

Fitting new baseboard

A baseboard can be damaged by excessive moisture or dryness, or it can suffer in the process of being removed when a repair to a floor is being made. Restore the board if you can, especially if it is a special molding; otherwise try to make it up from various molded sections (see right). Standard moldings are easily available through lumberyards.

Measure the length of the wall. Most baseboards are mitered at the corners, so take this into account when you are measuring between inside and outside corners.

Mark the length on the plain bottom edge of the board, then mark a 45- degree angle on the edge and square it across the face of the board. Fix the board on edge in a vise and carefully cut down the line at that angle.

Sometimes molded baseboards are scribed and butt-jointed at inside corners. To achieve the profile, cut the end off one board at 45 degrees as you would for a miter joint (1), and with a coping saw cut along the contour line on the molded face so that it will "jig-saw" with its neighbor (2).

Fasten baseboards with cut nails when nailing to brickwork and with finishing nails when attaching them to wood wall framing.

BASEBOARD MOLDINGS

Most standard baseboard moldings are made in softwood ready for painting. Hardwood is not so common and is reserved for special decorative boards. Hardwoods are coated with a clear finish (▷). "Molded-reverse" baseboards have a different profile machined on each side of the board—providing two boards in one.

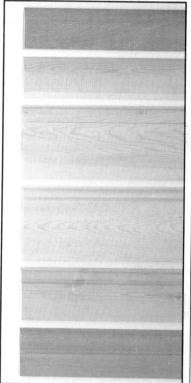

Selection of baseboard moldings
(From top to bottom) Beveled hardwoods. Beveled/rounded reverse. Ovolo/beveled reverse. Torus/beveled reverse. Ovolo/torus reverse. Hardwood baseboard.

SEE ALSO

Details for: ▷
Finishing wood	74–79
Coping saw	464

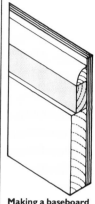

Making a baseboard
If you are unable to buy a length of baseboard to match your original, and the cost of having it specially machined is too high, make it up from various sections of molding.

1 Cut a 45-degree miter at the end

2 Cut the shape following the contour line

REPAIRING A CONCRETE FLOOR

Filling a crack

Clean all dirt and loose material out of the crack and, if necessary, open up narrow parts with a cold chisel to allow better penetration of the filler.

Prime the crack with a solution of 1 part bonding agent : 5 parts water and let it dry. Make a filler of 3 parts sand : 1 part cement mixed with equal parts of bonding agent and water; or use a ready-mixed quick-setting cement. Apply the filler with a trowel, pressing it well into the crack.

Foundation drainage

There are several techniques for draining perpetually wet basements. One is to dig a 1- to 2-foot-deep sump pit at one spot in the floor, near a corner if possible. Line the sides of the pit with a section of sewer tile and spread a 2- to 4-inch layer of gravel in the bottom. Install a sump pump to get rid of the water as it accumulates. Another method, to be installed before pouring a new floor, is to lay pipe in a slanting trench dug downward beneath the house footing. Digging under the footing is easier than drilling through a foundation wall; however, if the footings are located several feet below the level of the slab, it might make more sense to drill through the wall instead. Install a floor drain at the high end and connect the low end to the exterior foundation drain, or direct it into the gravel base around the footing. Fill in the trench, then pour the floor, sloping the surface toward the drain opening.

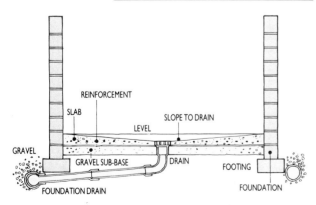

Sump pump details

SUMP PUMP
OUTLET LINE
SLAB
INTAKE GRAVEL FLOAT-SWITCH

REINFORCEMENT
SLAB
LEVEL
SLOPE TO DRAIN
GRAVEL
GRAVEL SUB-BASE
DRAIN
FOOTING
FOUNDATION
FOUNDATION DRAIN

Floor drain details

RESURFACING A CONCRETE FLOOR

Only in severe cases must a concrete slab floor be rebuilt. Have a concrete engineer or building inspector assess major cracking or other deterioration, but if the surface is spalled (flaked due to expanding moisture during freezing weather), chipped or even moderately cracked, and the floor is well supported, a new layer of concrete may be poured over the top and smoothed to a new finish relatively easily.

Preparing the surface

The first step is to clean and roughen the floor to provide good bonding for the new layer. Thoroughly sweep the surface and remove loose material from cracks. With a hammer and chisel, score shallow grooves in the floor, just deep enough to expose the coarse material below the finish surface. Consider renting a scarifying machine or a jack hammer if the floor is large. Scrub oil stains on the floor with a strong industrial detergent and rinse thoroughly with water to get rid of slick film.

Next, it is a good idea to etch the surface with hydrochloric or muriatic acid to ensure bonding. Commercial preparations containing these, especially for the purpose, are available at building supply centers. Make sure there is plenty of ventilation, and always wear a respirator, goggles, rubber boots and gloves. Spread the solution with a long-handled push broom. After the acid stops foaming, hose down the floor with plenty of water and scrub it with a clean broom. Remove all acid residue.

Setting forms

Most resurfacing doesn't require forms; the perimeter walls are usually adequate. However, in order to level the surface, you must install strips of wood whose top edges can serve as guides for screeding (see diagrams). Depending on the particular circumstances, you can either lay a double row of long strips running the entire length of the floor, or you can pour the concrete in 2-foot-wide bands, using only a single strip as a guide after the first pour has hardened. After each band is poured and screeded, relocate the board 2 feet further on and continue the process.

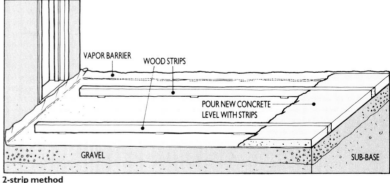

VAPOR BARRIER WOOD STRIPS
POUR NEW CONCRETE LEVEL WITH STRIPS
GRAVEL SUB-BASE

2-strip method

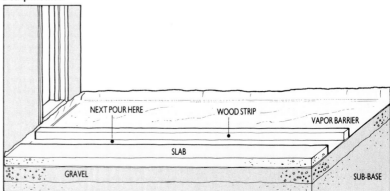

NEXT POUR HERE WOOD STRIP VAPOR BARRIER
SLAB
GRAVEL SUB-BASE

Single-strip method

CONCRETE FLOORS

Pouring

If the new floor will be more than 2 inches thick, cut and have ready squares of wire-mesh reinforcement to place between layers of concrete. Begin the actual pour by spreading a 1/8-inch layer of bonding grout (1 part cement/1 part sand/1/2 part water) over the prepared surface using a stiff push broom. Then, while the grout is still wet, immediately spread on the concrete, mixed 1 part cement/1 part sand/2 parts 3/8-inch-diameter crushed stone. Use a square-nose shovel to distribute the mix. When the layer is 1 inch thick, lay down the mesh if required, then spread the remaining concrete over it.

Spread grout with broom

Shovel on concrete

SEE ALSO

Details for: ▷	
Slab floors	173
Mixing concrete	439
Builder's tools	478–480

Screeding

Use a straight 2 × 4 laid across the embedded wood strips to level the poured concrete. Work the board back and forth with a sawing motion while simultaneously drawing it along the length of the strips. When you are finished, carefully remove the strips while kneeling on wide boards laid on the concrete to distribute your weight, fill in the troughs with concrete, and smooth with a wood float.

Level concrete with straightedge. Lift out and fill hollows left by strips

Floating and troweling

For a smooth-textured finish floor, work a wood float over the surface of the slab once the concrete is strong enough to bear your weight but is still soft enough to take an imprint. Concrete ready for floating has a frosted appearance. Small floats are available at hardware stores. Make or rent a long-handled one if space allows. For large floors, consider renting a gasoline-powered float. Lay two squares of plywood on the floor to kneel on. The boards should not sink more than 1/4 inch into the concrete.

Smooth the surface with a float

Later, when the concrete will bear no imprint, polish the surface with a steel trowel for a smooth, hard finish suitable as a base for carpet or other soft flooring. Do not trowel a floor that will be left bare. When wet it may become dangerously slick. Trowel the concrete only until it is smooth. Over-troweling causes the particulate matter in the concrete to sink, and the cement to rise, and later flake. Cover the finished concrete with plastic sheeting for a week or so to let it cure without drying out. Afterward, apply a masonry sealer.

Polish nearly cured concrete with steel trowels

DOORS: TYPES AND CONSTRUCTION

At first glance there appears to be a great variety of doors to choose from, but in fact most of the differences are simply stylistic. All doors are all based on a small number of construction methods.

The wide range of styles can sometimes tempt homeowners into buying doors that are inappropriate to the houses they live in. When replacing a front door you should be careful to choose one that is not incongruous with the architectural style of your house.

Buying a door

Doors in softwood and hardwood are available, the latter being the more expensive and normally used for a special interior or an entrance where the natural features of the wood can be exploited to the best effect.

Softwood doors are for more general use and are intended to be painted as opposed to clear-finished.

Glazed doors are becoming common features in the front and rear entrances of today's houses. They are traditionally of wooden frame construction, though modern aluminium-framed doors can be bought in the standard sizes, complete with double-glazing and accessories.

Wood-framed and panel doors are supplied in unfinished wood; these require trimming, glazing and fitting out with hinges, locks and letter plates.

Exterior flush door
A central rail is fitted to take a letter plate.

1 Planted molding

2 Bolection molding

DOOR SIZES

Doors are made in several standard sizes to meet most domestic needs.

The range of heights is usually 6 feet 6 inches, 6 feet 8 inches and occasionally 7 feet. The widths range from 2 feet to 3 feet in increments of 2 inches. Thicknesses vary from 1 3/8 to 1 3/4 inches.

In older houses it is common to find that larger doors have been used for the main room on the first floor than for others, but modern homes tend to have standard-size joinery and all interior doors the same size. The standard is usually 6 feet 8 inches × 2 feet 6 inches, though front entrance doors are always larger than interior ones to suit the proportions of the building.

When replacing doors in an old house, where the openings may well be nonstandard sizes, buy one of the nearest size and cut it down, removing an equal amount from each edge to preserve the frame's symmetry.

Panel doors

Panel doors are more attractive than flush doors but are also more expensive. They have hardwood or softwood frames, mortise-and-tenon joints, with grooves that house the panels, which can be of solid wood, plywood or glass.

1 Muntins
These are the central vertical members of the door. They are jointed into the three cross rails.

2 Panels
These may be of solid wood or of plywood. They are held loosely in grooves in the frame to allow for shrinkage without splitting. They stiffen the door.

3 Cross rails
Top, center and bottom rails are tenoned into the stiles. In cheaper doors the mortise-and-tenon joints are replaced with dowel joints.

4 Stiles
These are the upright members at the sides of the door. They carry the hinges and door locks.

Panel door moldings
The frame's inner edges may be plain or molded as a decorative border. Small moldings can be machined on the frame before assembly or pinned to the inside edge. Ordinary planted molding (**1**) can shrink from the frame, making cracks in the paintwork. Bolection molding (**2**) laps the frame to overcome this. It is decorative but more vulnerable.

Panel door

Flush doors

Flush doors are softwood frames with plywood or hardboard covering both sides and packed with a core material. Used mainly internally, they are lightweight, cheap, simple and rather lacking in character. Exterior flush doors have a central rail to take a letter plate. Firecheck doors are a special fire-retardant grade.

1 Top and bottom rails
These are tenoned into the stiles (side pieces).

2 Intermediate rails
These lighter rails, jointed to the stiles, are notched to allow passage of air and prevent the panels from sinking.

3 Lock blocks
A softwood block to take a mortise lock is glued to each stile.

4 Panels
The plywood or hardboard panels are left plain for painting or finished with a wood veneer. Metal-skinned doors may be had to special order.

Core material
Paper or cardboard honeycomb is sometimes sandwiched between the panels. In firecheck doors, a fire-retardant material is used.

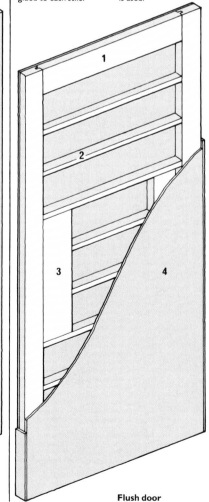

Flush door

Ledged and braced doors

These doors have a rustic, cottagey look and are often found in old houses, outbuildings and garden walls. They are weather-resistant, strong, secure and cheap, but a little crude. A superior framed version is tenon-jointed instead of being merely nailed.

1 Battens
Tongue-and-groove boards are nailed to the ledges.

2 Strap-hinges
Butt hinges will not hold in the end-grain of the ledges, so long strap-hinges take the weight.

3 Braces
These diagonals, notched into the ledges, transmit the weight to the hinges and stop the door from sagging.

4 Ledges
These are the cross rails to which the battens are nailed.

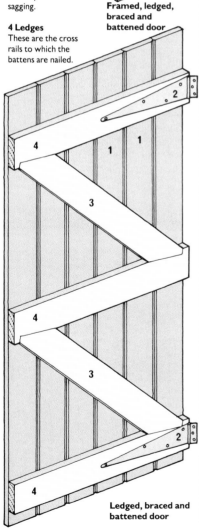

Framed, ledged, braced and battened door

Ledged, braced and battened door

DOOR FRAMES

Exterior doors

An exterior door is fitted into a heavy wooden frame consisting of the head jamb (1) at the top, the sill (2) below, fitted with a threshold and weatherstrip (inset), and the side jambs (3), which are usually joined to the other pieces by dado joints.

Normally, a section of the floor framing must be notched to accept the sill. However, some prehung exterior doors are made with adjustable sills which require no cutting. Thresholds come in several styles. They are designed to seal the door at the bottom, yet allow the door to swing freely.

Exterior door frame
1 Head jamb
2 Sill
3 Side jamb
4 Doorstop rabbet
5 Notched floor framing

DOOR
WEATHERSTRIP
THRESHOLD
SILL

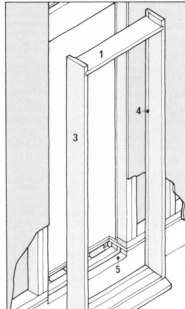

Interior doors

Interior doors are hung in frames similar to those for exterior doors, but less sturdy. No sill is present, although in some cases a threshold may be added. Usually, interior doors are trimmed during installation to leave a small amount of space above the top of the finish flooring.

The head jamb (1) and side jambs (2) are fastened to the framed rough opening with shims (3, 4) sandwiched between to level and plumb the frame, and to space it evenly within the opening. Wedge-shaped sections of cedar shingles make excellent shims. They are fastened in place with finishing nails driven through the jamb and into the pieces of the rough frame.

Most interior doors come prehung, already mounted in frames. When selecting interior doors, make sure the jamb width is sized to fit the thickness of the wall in which it will be installed, or else choose a doorframe with adjustable-width jambs, available from some manufacturers.

Interior door frame
1 Head jamb
2 Side jamb
3 Side shims
4 Head shims

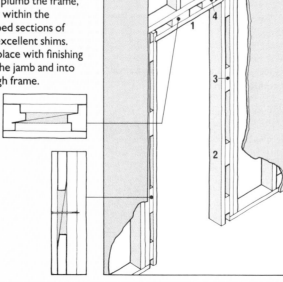

FITTING AND HANGING DOORS

Whatever the style of door you wish to fit, the procedure is the same, though minor differences between some exterior doors may show themselves. Two good-quality 4-inch butt hinges are enough to support a standard door, but if you are hanging a heavy hardwood door, you should add a third, central hinge.

All doors are fairly heavy, and as it is necessary to try a door in its frame several times to get the fit right, you will find that the job goes much more quickly and easily if you have a helper working with you.

Fitting a door

Before attaching the hinges to a new door, make sure that it fits nicely into its frame. It should have a clearance of $1/16$ inch at the top and sides and should clear the floor by at least $1/4$ inch. As much as $1/2$ inch may be required for a carpeted floor.

Measure the height and width of the door opening and the depth of the rabbet in the door frame into which the door must fit. Choose a door of the right thickness and, if you cannot get one that will fit the opening exactly, one which is large enough to be cut down.

Cutting to size

Transfer the measurements from the frame to the door, making necessary allowance for the clearances all around. To reduce the width of the door, stand it on edge with its latch stile upwards while it is steadied in a portable vise. Plane the stile down to the marked line, working only on the one side if a small amount is to be taken off. If a lot is to be removed, take some off each side. This is especially important with panel doors to preserve the symmetry.

If you need to take off more than $1/4$ inch to reduce the height of the door, remove it with a saw and finish off with a plane. Otherwise, plane the waste off (**1**). The plane must be sharp to deal with the end grain of the stiles. Work from each corner towards the center to avoid "chipping out" the corners. If you must trim a panel door by more than 4 inches, remove the waste entirely from the bottom. Then refit the spline in the exposed channel.

Try the door in the frame, supporting it on shallow wedges (**2**). If it still doesn't fit, take it down and remove more wood where appropriate.

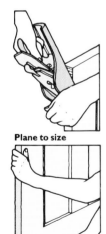

Plane to size

Wedge the door

Fitting hinges

The upper hinge is set about 7 inches from the door's top edge and the lower one about 10 inches from the bottom. They are cut equally into the stile and door frame. Wedge the door in its opening and, with the wedges tapped in to raise it to the right floor clearance, mark the positions of the hinges on both the door and frame.

Stand the door on edge, the hinge stile uppermost, open a hinge and, with its knuckle projecting from the edge of the door, align it with the marks and draw around the flap with a pencil (**1**). Set a marking gauge to the thickness of the mortise. Chisel out a series of shallow cuts across the grain (**2**) and pare out the waste to the scored line. Repeat the procedure with the second hinge, then, using the flaps as guides, drill pilot holes for the screws and fix both hinges into their mortises.

Wedge the door in the open position, aligning the free hinge flaps with the marks on the door frame. Make sure that the knuckles of the hinges are parallel with the frame, then trace the mortises on the frame (**3**) and cut them out as you did the others.

Adjusting and aligning

Hang the door with one screw holding each hinge and see if it closes smoothly. If the latch stile rubs on the frame, you may have to make one or both mortises slightly deeper. If the door strains against the hinges, it is what is called "hinge bound." In this case, insert thin cardboard strips beneath the hinge flaps to shim them out and retest door operation. When the door finally opens and closes properly, drive in the rest of the screws.

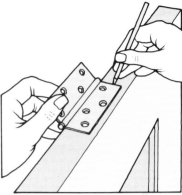

1 Mark around the flap with a pencil

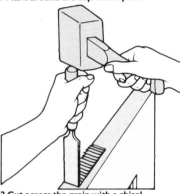

2 Cut across the grain with a chisel

3 Mark the size of the flap on the frame

MEASUREMENTS

A door that fits well will open and close freely and look symmetrical in the frame. Use the figures given as a guide for trimming the door and setting out the position of the hinges.

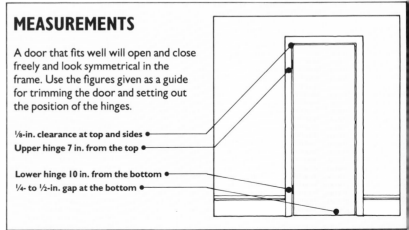

$1/8$-in. clearance at top and sides ●

Upper hinge 7 in. from the top ●

Lower hinge 10 in. from the bottom ●
$1/4$- to $1/2$-in. gap at the bottom ●

Rising butt hinges

Rising butt hinges lift a door as it is opened and are fitted to prevent it from dragging on thick pile carpet.

They are made in two parts: a flap, with a fixed pin, which is screwed to the door frame, and another, with a single knuckle, which is fixed to the door, the knuckle sliding over the pin.

Rising butt hinges can be fastened only one way up, and are therefore made specifically for left- or right-hand opening. The countersunk screwholes in the fixed-pin flap indicate the side to which it is made to be fitted.

Fitting

Trim the door and mark the hinge positions (see opposite), but before fitting the hinges, plane a shallow bevel at the top outer corner of the hinge stile so that it will clear the frame as it opens. As the stile ($\triangleright$) runs through to the top of the door, plane from the outer corner towards the center to avoid splitting the wood. The top strip of the door stop will mask the bevel when the door is closed.

Fit the hinges to the door and the frame, then lower the door onto the hinge pins, taking care not to damage the molding above the opening.

ADJUSTING BUTT HINGES

Perhaps you have a door catching on a bump in the floor as it opens. You can, of course, fit rising butt hinges, but the problem can be overcome by resetting the lower hinge so that its knuckle projects slightly more than the top one. The door will still hang vertically when closed, but as it opens the out-of-line pins will throw it upwards so that the bottom edge will clear the bump.

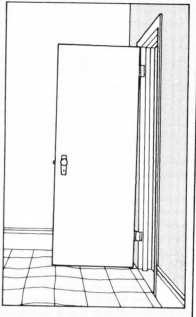

Resetting the hinge
You may have to reset both hinges to the new angle to prevent binding.

SEE ALSO

Details for: $\triangleright$
Door construction	184
Draftproofing	262–263

Weatherstripping a door

Weatherstripping is special molding fitted to the bottom of an exterior door to prevent moisture and the flow of air underneath. Many styles are available. Some require that the door be trimmed, some do not. Often, weatherstripping comes as an integral part of the threshold itself, and is easily installed merely by screwing the threshold to the sill.

When installing a new door, consider attaching a type of weatherstrip which mounts to the bottom of the door or to the threshold directly beneath it. When retrofitting weatherstripping, a style that attaches to the inside of the door at its lower edge is easier to apply, and adjustable as well.

Weatherstripping that flexes or is walked on will wear out in time. It is a good idea to check its condition each year and replace it if necessary. The best time to do this is *before* the onset of inclement weather.

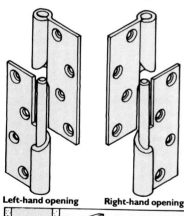

Left-hand opening   **Right-hand opening**

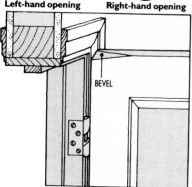

BEVEL

Plane a shallow bevel to clear the door frame

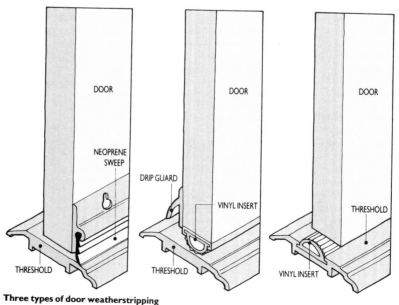

DOOR

NEOPRENE SWEEP

THRESHOLD

DOOR

DRIP GUARD

VINYL INSERT

THRESHOLD

DOOR

THRESHOLD

VINYL INSERT

Three types of door weatherstripping

REPAIRS AND IMPROVEMENTS

Repairing a battened door

The battens, or tongue-and-groove jointed boards, of a ledged and braced cottage or garage door can rot at the bottom because of the end grain absorbing moisture. The damage can be patch-repaired. Nailing a board across the bottom of the door is not the easy solution it may appear because moisture will be trapped behind the board and will increase the rot.

Remove the door and cut back the damaged boards to sound material. Where a batten falls on a rail, use the tip of a tenon saw, held at a shallow angle, to cut through most of it, then finish off the cut with a chisel. Use a padsaw or a saber saw where the blade can pass clear of the rail.

When replacing the end of a single batten, make the cut at right angles (1). When a group of battens is to be replaced, make 45 degree cuts across them (2). In this way the interlocking of the tongue-and-groove edges between old and new sections is better maintained.

When cutting new pieces of board to fit, leave them overlength. Apply an exterior woodworking adhesive to the butting ends of the battens but take care not to get any on the tongue-and-groove joints. Tap the pieces into place and nail each to the rail with two staggered finishing nails. Cut off the ends in line with the door's bottom edge and treat the wood with a good preservative (◁) to prevent any further rot damage.

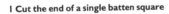

1 Cut the end of a single batten square

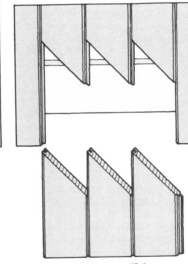

2 Cut a group of battens to 45 degrees

Easing a sticking door

If the bottom corner of a door is rubbing on the frame, it is probably swollen. Take it off its hinges and shave the corner down with a plane. If the top corner is rubbing, check the hinges before doing any planing. After years of use, hinges become worn so that the pins are slack and the door drops. In this case, fit new hinges, or, as a cheaper alternative, swap the old hinges, the top with the bottom, which will reverse the wear on the pins.

Swapping hinges ▶
Swap worn hinges, top with bottom, for a cheap and convenient repair.

An old framed-and-paneled door can be given a new lease on life by flush-paneling it with a sheet of hardboard or wood-veneered paneling on each side.

Using hardboard
The easiest way is to cut and fit a hardboard panel 1 inch smaller all around than the door. This can be done without removing the door.

Sandpaper the surface of the frame to roughen it, then apply contact adhesive to the frame members and to the corresponding areas on the back of the hardboard. Position the panels carefully and fix the edges with hardboard nails at 6-inch intervals. Tap all over the glued areas with a wood block and a hammer. Fill the nail recesses, prime the surfaces and paint as required.

Using a wood-veneered panel
This should extend to all four edges of the door, so the door must first be removed from the frame and the hinges and latch taken off.

Remove any paint from the long edges, scrape them back to bare wood and sandpaper them smooth.

Cut the panels slightly larger than the door, roughen the surface of the frame with abrasive paper and bond the panels to it with a contact adhesive.

When the adhesive is set, plane the panel edges flush with the door all around. With a chisel, trim away the edge of the panel where it overlaps the hinge mortise. Stain the stripped edges of the door and edges of the panel to match the color of the veneer.

Before rehanging the door, remove the doorstop strips. Fit the hinges and latch, rehang the door and replace the doorstops against the door while it is in the closed position.

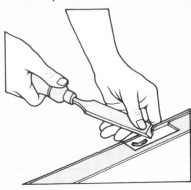

Trim the paneling at the hinge mortises

DOOR ACCESSORIES

Fitting a center pull

A period brass doorknob, kept well polished, or one of black iron, can be an attractive feature on a paneled door. Such knobs are now being reproduced in many traditional styles and patterns.

Decorative doorknobs are sometimes fitted on the center line of a paneled door. If a letter plate is occupying the middle rail, place the knob above it on the muntin, the central vertical member.

Drill a counterbore on the inside of the door to take the head of the screw that's used for fastening the knob, then a clearance hole for the thread that goes through the door (1).

The back plate of the knob usually has a locating peg on its back which stops the knob from turning when the screw is tightened. To mark its position, press the back plate onto the door so that the peg leaves an indentation, then drill a shallow recess there for the peg. Fit the assembly and tighten the screw.

For a neat finish, plug the counterbored hole on the inside to conceal the screw head.

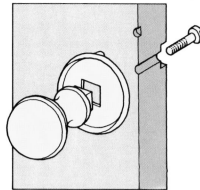

I Counterbore the hole for the attaching bolt

Fitting a letter plate

Letter plates, for fitting horizontally or vertically, are readily available in a variety of styles and materials—solid brass, stainless steel, plated, cast iron and aluminum. Horizontal plates are the more common and are usually fitted in the center rail of the door. Occasionally, in a fully glazed door, they are placed on the bottom rail, but this makes them awkward to reach. The problem can be overcome by fitting a plate vertically in one of the door's stiles (vertical side members), but this can weaken a door structurally.

Fitting a horizontal letter plate is dealt with at the right, but the method described applies to both types. Postal knockers, which incorporate a knocker with the letter plate, are fitted in a similar manner. Measure the width of the door and mark its center. From this mark out the opening, which must be only slightly larger than the hinged flap on the letter plate in the middle of the rail on the center line.

Drill a ½-inch clearance hole in each corner of the marked rectangle and cut the opening with a padsaw or saber saw. Or, working from the holes, trim the corners square with a chisel and clean up the cut edges.

Mark the centers for the attaching screw holes. These are usually close to the edge, so take care when drilling.

Drill counterbores on the outside of the door to take the threaded bosses on the back of the letter plate, and on the inside to take the heads of the machine screws. Then drill clearance holes for the screw threads through the centers of the counterbores (2).

Fasten the letter plate in place. You may have to shorten the screws to suit a thin door. Plug or fill the counterbores that house the screw heads.

Better still, fit an interior flap cover. These are made in metal or plastic and held with small wood screws. They will cut down drafts, look better and allow the letter plate to be removed easily if it is to be machine-polished from time to time.

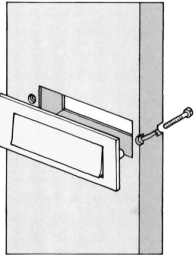

2 Counterbore the door for the plate and bolts

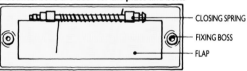

— CLOSING SPRING
— FIXING BOSS
— FLAP

Sizing the opening
Take dimensions from the flap and make the opening slightly larger.

Fitting a door knocker

A complete set of brass reproduction exterior-door accessories in the traditional manner comprises a letter plate, a doorknob and a knocker. Such sets are available in various patterns in Regency, Georgian, Victorian and other styles. Manufacturers all have their own interpretations of these styles, so if you plan to attach a set you should buy all of the items together.

You can, of course, fit items individually, and perhaps the one most widely used is the knocker, which can also be used as an alternative to a center pull. Being the most ornate item in a door set, a knocker is often used as a decorative feature rather than for its original function. Electric doorbells (▷) have made knockers obsolete.

On a paneled door, fit a feature knocker to the muntin at about shoulder height. Mark a vertical center line on the muntin at the required height and drill a counterbore and clearance hole for the attaching screw as described for installing a center pull. Plug the counterbored hole on the inside after attaching the backplate.

Reproduction brass fittings are finished with a clear lacquer to prevent tarnishing. When this wears through, regular polishing maintains the shine.

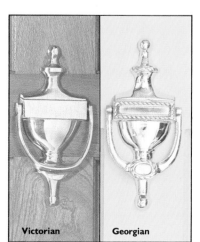

Victorian   **Georgian**

Knocker styles

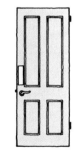

Fitting finger plates
Finger plates, used to protect the paintwork on interior doors, are screwed to each side of the lock stile just above the center rail.

INSTALLING A PRE-HUNG DOOR

Purchasing a door already attached to a matching frame saves a great deal of time and permits even novice DIYers to accomplish accurate work. Install the side of the door frame to which the door is attached first, by inserting it in the rough opening (**1**), wedged from below to allow clearance above finish flooring. Trim the lower ends of the jamb sides if necessary (**2**), then center the frame within the opening and align it horizontally and vertically using a level and plumb bob. Anchor the frame in place by shimming out the sides and head jamb with shims (**3**). Use finishing nails to fasten the shims securely to the frame and rough opening. Also drive finishing nails through the door casing into the edges of the rough opening members. If the door frame is the split-jamb type that adjusts to fit different wall thicknesses, complete the installation by attaching the other half of the frame into the rough opening from the other side (**4**).

SEE ALSO

◁ Details for:
Hanging doors	186
Masonry wall fasteners	498

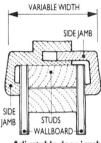

VARIABLE WIDTH

SIDE JAMB

SIDE JAMB · STUDS · WALLBOARD

Adjustable door jamb

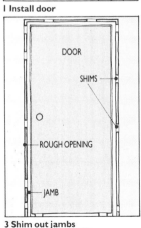

JAMB · CASING · ROUGH OPENING

I Install door

WEDGES

FINISH FLOOR

2 Trim with saw

DOOR · SHIMS · ROUGH OPENING · JAMB

3 Shim out jambs

CASING · JAMB

4 Attach remaining casing

REPAIRING EXTERIOR DOOR FRAMES

Exterior door frames are built into the brickwork as it is erected, so replacing an old one means some damage to the plaster or the outside stucco.

In older houses, the frames are recessed into the brickwork, the inside face of the frame is flush with the plaster work and the architrave covers the joint. Modern houses may have frames close to or flush with the outer face of the brickwork. Work from the side the frame is closest to.

Measure the door and buy a standard frame to fit, or make one from standard frame sections.

Removing the old frame

Chop back the plaster or stucco with a chisel to expose the back face of the door frame (**1**).

With a general-purpose saw (**2**) cut through the three metal brackets holding the frame in the brickwork on each side, two about 9 inches from the top and bottom and one halfway up.

Saw through the jambs halfway up (**3**), and if necessary cut the head member and the sill. Lever the frame members out with a crowbar.

Clear any loose material from the opening and repair a vertical vapor barrier in a cavity wall with gun-applied caulking to keep moisture out of the gap between inner and outer layers of brickwork.

Fitting the new frame

Fitting a frame is easier with its horns removed, but this weakens it. If possible, fit the frame with horns shaped like the old ones (see right).

Wedge the frame in position, checking that it is centered, square and plumb. Drill three counterbored clearance holes in each jamb for screws, positioned about 1 foot from the top and bottom with one halfway, but avoid drilling into mortar joints. Run a masonry drill through the clearance holes to mark their position on the brickwork.

Remove the frame, drill the holes in the brickwork and insert expandable metal wall plugs. Replace the frame and fix it with 4-inch steel screws. Plug the counterbores.

Pack any gap under the sill with mortar. Restore the brickwork, stucco or plasterwork and apply mastic sealant around the outer edge of the frame to seal any small gaps. Fit the door as described (◁).

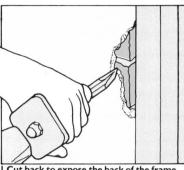

I Cut back to expose the back of the frame

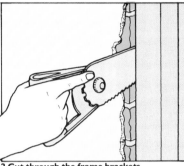

2 Cut through the frame brackets

3 Saw through the frame to remove it

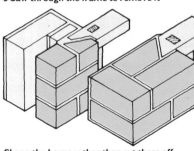

Shape the horns rather than cut them off

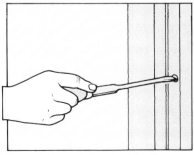

Screw the frame to the plugged wall

REPLACING A ROTTED FRAME

The great majority of exterior door frames are constructed of softwood, and this, if it is regularly maintained with good paint, will give years of excellent service. However, the ends of door sills and the frame posts are vulnerable to rot if they are subject to continual wetting. This can happen when the frame has moved because of shrinkage of the timber, or where old pointing has fallen out and left a gap where water can get in. Alternatively, old and porous brickwork or an ineffective moisture barrier can be the cause of moisture damage.

Prevention is always better than any cure, so check around the frame for any shrinkage gaps and apply a mastic sealant where necessary. Keep all pointing in good order. A slight outbreak of rot can be treated with the aid of a commercial repair kit and preservative.

Replacing a sill

You can buy 2 × 6 softwood or hardwood door sill sections that can be cut to the required length. If your sill is not of a standard-shaped section, the replacement can be made to order. It is more economical in the long run to specify a hardwood such as oak, as it will last much longer.

Taking out the old
First measure and note down the width of the door opening, then remove the door. Old jamb sides are usually tenoned into the sill, so to separate the sill from them, split it lengthwise with a wood chisel. A saw cut across the center of the sill can make the job of removing it easier.

The ends of the sills are set into the brickwork on either side, so cut away the bricks to make the removal of the old sill and insertion of the new one easier. Use a cold chisel to cut carefully through the mortar around the bricks, and try to preserve them for reuse after fitting the sill.

The new sill has to be inserted from the front so that it can be tucked under the jamb sides and into the brickwork. Cut the tenons off level with the shoulders of the jamb sides (**1**). Mark and cut shallow mortises for the ends of the jamb sides in the top of the new sill, spaced apart as previously noted. The mortises must be deep enough to take the full width of the jamb sides (**2**), which may mean the sill being slightly higher than the original one, so that you will have to trim a little off the bottom of the door.

Fitting the new
Try the new sill for fit and check that it is level. Before fastening it, apply a wood preservative to its underside and ends, and, as a moisture barrier, apply two or three coats of asphalt roofing sealer to the brickwork.

When both treatments are dry, glue the sill to the jamb sides, using an exterior woodworking adhesive. Wedge the underside of the sill with slate to push it up against the ends of the sides, toenail the sides to the sill and leave it for the adhesive to set.

Pack the gap between the underside of the sill and the masonry with a stiff mortar of 3 parts sand : 1 part cement, and rebond and point the bricks. Finish by treating the wood with preservative and applying a caulking sealant around the door frame.

1 Cut tenons off level with the joint's shoulder

2 Cut a mortise to receive the side

REPAIRING DOOR POSTS

Rot can attack the ends of door posts, particularly in exposed positions where they meet stone steps or are set into concrete, as is found in some garages. The posts may be located on metal dowels set into the step.

If the damage is not too extensive, the rotted end can be cut away and replaced with a new piece, either scarf-jointed or half-lap-jointed (▷) into place. If your situation involves a wooden sill, combine the following information with that given for replacing a sill.

First remove the door, then saw off the end of the affected post back to sound wood. For a scarf joint, make the cut at 45 degrees to the face of the post (**1**). For a lap joint, cut it square. Chip any metal dowel out of the step with a cold chisel.

Measure and cut a matching section of post to the required length, allowing for the overlap of the joint, then cut the end to 45 degrees or mark and cut a half lap joint in both parts of the post (**2**).

Drill a hole in the end of the new section for the metal dowel if it is still usable. If it is not, make a new one from a piece of galvanized steel pipe, priming the metal to prevent corrosion. Treat the new wood with a preservative and insert the dowel. Set the dowel in mortar, at the same time gluing and screwing the joint (**3**).

If a dowel is not used, fix the post to the wall with counterbored screws. Place hardboard or plywood shims behind it if necessary and plug the counterbores of the screw holes.

Apply a caulk sealant to the joints between the door post, wall and base.

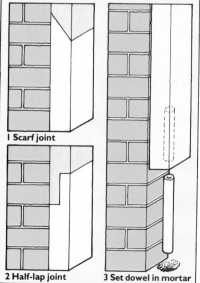

1 Scarf joint

2 Half-lap joint

3 Set dowel in mortar

SEE ALSO

Details for: ▷	
Woodworking	
joints	475–477
Treating rot	251
Moisture problems	253–255

FITTING ROOM-DIVIDING DOORS

SEE ALSO

◁ Details for:
Door frames   185

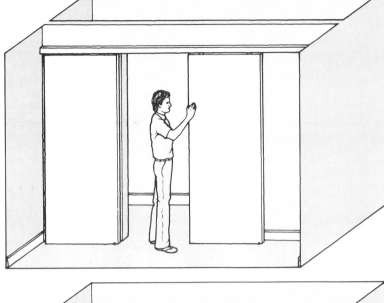

1 Sliding doors
Sliding doors are hung
from a track and are
most useful where
floor space is limited,
but they will require
clear wall space on one
or both sides of the
opening.

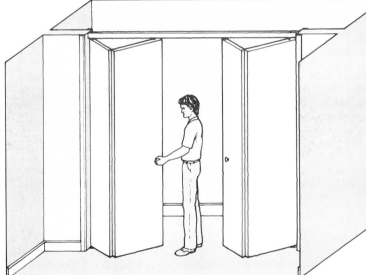

2 Bifold doors
Tracked systems are
easy to operate and
offer an attractive
means of diving a room
while not requiring as
much clear floor space
as conventional hinged
doors.

3 Multifold doors
Like bifold doors these
operate on a track
system but have
narrow door panels
which enable the door
to be stowed within
the thickness of the
wall.

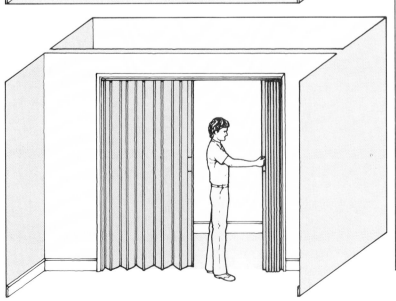

*It is now fashionable for houses to be built
with large through rooms in the "open
plan" style, and many owners of older
homes have adopted the style by
having two rooms converted to one.
But there are occasions when two rooms
would be preferable in the interests of
greater privacy within the family group.*

A reasonable compromise is to install a
door system which allows the living
space to be used either way. It is a
compromise because any door system
will in some way intrude into an
otherwise uncluttered room, and when
closed it is not as soundproof as a solid
wall. Sliding **(1)**, bifold **(2)** or multifold
(3) doors are the most suitable for this
kind of installation.
　　Complete door systems, ready for
installation, are available, or you can buy
the door mechanism only and fit doors
of your choice.

MEASURING THE OPENING

Before ordering a made-to-measure
door system, measure the opening
carefully. Then double-check, for your
money may not be refunded in case of
error. If you use a steel tape measure,
get a helper to keep it taut and avoid a
false reading. Measure the width at the
top *and* bottom of the opening and the
height at both ends. Take the smaller
dimension in each case.

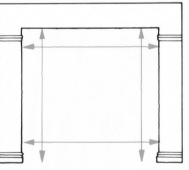

Checking the opening
If you are installing a system in an old house, check
that the opening is square—the house may have
settled unevenly—by measuring across both the
diagonals. If they are not the same you may have to
true up the frame or shim out the new system.

Sliding doors

A sliding-door system is a good space-saver. Whereas a hinged door needs clear floor space, an arc at least as wide as the door itself, a sliding door takes up no floor space, though it does require a clear stretch of wall at the side of the opening. Apart from such fixtures as radiators, this need not be a major problem. Furniture can be placed a little away from the wall, leaving a gap behind it to accommodate the thickness of the sliding door.

A range of standard door track sets is available for light, medium and heavy doors. The doors themselves can range in size from 1 foot 1 inch to 6 foot 6 inches in width and from $\frac{5}{8}$ inch to 2 inches in thickness, depending on the type chosen. For a double sliding door, two sets of rollers are necessary.

Though designs may vary, all track systems for sliding doors have adjustable hanger brackets which are fixed to the top edge of the door and attached to the rollers. A track screwed to the wall above the opening carries and guides the rollers. When the door is closed, it should overlap the opening by about 2 inches at each side.

Fitting the system

Following the manufacturer's instructions, set out the hangers and screw them to the top edge of the door. Plug and screw a furring strip for the track to the wall over the doorway. The strip must be as long as the track and equal in thickness to the baseboards and the casing. Sometimes it is possible to replace the top section of the casing with the furring strip. Screw the track to the furring strip, at the same time leveling it.

Assemble the hangers and rollers and suspend the door from the rack, then adjust the hangers to level if and as necessary. Fit the door guide to the floor, and then the stops to the track.

Cut cover molding twice as long as the door's width to cover the whole track. Fix it to the top edge of the furring strip or with metal brackets.

Bifold doors

Bifold doors offer a reasonable way of closing a door opening without intruding too much on the room space when open. The opening should be lined in the normal way and fitted with a casing. The top section of the casing can be lowered to cover shims on each side of the track.

The pivot hinge and track door rollers are available in standard sets for two or four doors of equal width, but up to six doors can be hung from one track; in this case a bottom guide track is also used. For extra-wide openings, more than one door set can be used. The doors range in thickness between $\frac{3}{4}$ and $1\frac{5}{8}$ inches, and in height up to 8 feet. Maximum width for bifolds is 2 feet per door.

Multifold doors

Multifold or concertina folding doors are designed to fold up and stack within the depth of the door opening. They are made up from narrow panels, hinged to each other and hung by sliders from a track in the top of the opening. No bottom track is necessary.

The panels are quite slim so that they will stack in the opening with a minimum of bulk. For this reason, they do not provide much in the way of sound insulation.

The doors are available for fitting in standard single-door openings or can be made to measure to fit larger openings, as, for example, where two rooms have been turned into one. They are supplied in kits, ready for fitting.

Fitting the system

Following the manufacturer's instructions, fit the pivot hinges into the top and bottom edges of the end door, also the pivoting hangers in the top edges of alternate doors, working away from the pivoted end door.

Hinge the doors together. They will swing to one side of the wall or the other, according to which way the knuckles of the hinges face. Set them out as you want them.

Locate the top pivot plate on the track, then fit the doors on the track and screw it to the underside of the opening. Fix the bottom pivot to the floor so that it is exactly plumb with the top one. Fit the door pivots in their plates and adjust them for level.

SEE ALSO

Details for: ▷

| Door frames | 185 |

Installing the system

Screw the lightweight track to the underside of the wall opening between two rooms or, where the opening is to full room height, fasten it to the ceiling. It is possible to inset the track in a plastered ceiling; however it is much easier to face-mount it and add a cover molding on each side.

Fit the track over the rollers of the stacked panels (**1**), then screw it into place. Screw the cover molding in place (**2**) to fill the gap between the soffit and the top of the door. Screw the end panel of the door to the jamb (**3**) and the latch-plate molding on the opposite side (**4**) to complete the installation of the system.

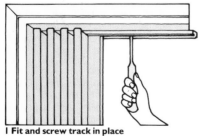
1 Fit and screw track in place

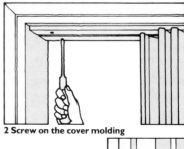
2 Screw on the cover molding

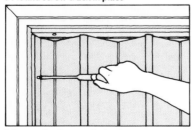
3 Screw the door to the jamb

4 Mount the door latch on opposite jamb

GARAGE DOORS

Garage doors, whether sectional or one-piece, should be maintained regularly for smooth operation.

SEE ALSO

◁ Details for:
Strap hinge   419

Styles of garage doors

Most garages today are fitted with sectional overhead doors. These are made up of horizontal sections, hinged together, which run on wheels on a continuous track from the vertical closed position to horizontal. The doors lift vertically and so are suitable for situations where the door must not swing out. Overhead doors utilize spring tension to make them easy to lift up and drop down. On most doors a large coil spring on each side stretches when the door is dropped. The accumulated tension assists when the door is raised, making it easier to lift. Large doors for two-car garages often are equipped with a single horizontal spring instead, which winds up as the door is lowered and unwinds when it is raised.

An older style of spring-assisted door is the one-piece variety which swings out from the bottom and slides

overhead, retracting either partially or completely into the garage. These are called "up-and-over doors". Those that retract only partially are called "canopy-type". Some up-and-over doors glide in tracks as do sectional overhead doors; some do not. The chief drawback of both types is that they require at least some clear space in front to open the door.

Requiring even more space, of course, are the traditional swinging garage doors still found on many old-fashioned properties. These are pairs of wide wooden doors fitted with heavy-weight strap hinges, usually with long arms that fasten a good part of the way across the width of each door. The doors are constructed on the ledged, braced and battened principle and may be plain or fitted with windows. These doors give long service if they are regularly painted, but they have a tendency to weaken after a time because of their weight, which makes the frame drop so that the doors begin to bind. If they touch the ground they can absorb moisture which will lead to rot.

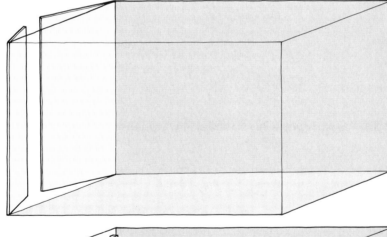

Traditional garage doors
Swinging doors, which are hinged to the side jambs, require more space and are more awkward to operate than modern garage doors.

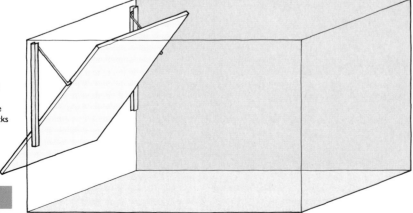

One-piece garage doors
These doors operate with a system of tracks and springs.

REPAIRING OVERHEAD DOORS

Because these are under spring tension and have so many mechanical parts, sectional overhead doors usually need frequent maintenance. If the door seems hard to lift or drops heavily, the spring tension may need tightening. Overhead doors are connected to their springs (whether coil or twist-up) by cables which run from the bottom corners of the door up through a system of pulleys to the springs, and then fasten either to large metal plates located above the curve of the door track (coil springs) or to the spring itself (twist-up). On doors with coil springs tighten the tension by hooking the end to one of the other holes in the attaching plates (**1**). On doors with twist-up springs, increase the tension by twisting the spring a few turns using a bar or long screwdriver, then tightening the locknut which holds the spring in place (**1A**). **WARNING:** Never loosen the locknut without at the same time applying force to the spring with the bar.

If overhead doors are hard to lower, or tend to "fly up" when raised, decrease the spring tension instead, by the same methods.

Binding may be caused by the track being out of alignment. To check, hold a level vertically alongside the track on each side of the door. Adjust the track by loosening the brackets slightly, tapping the track with a mallet until it is vertical, then retightening the brackets (**2**). You might also try oiling the rollers (**3**) and applying a thin coat of grease to the track.

If the door does not fit the contour of the floor when closed, you might want to recut the lower panel of the door to fit. Scribe the line by drawing a pencil compass simultaneously along the floor and bottom edge of the door (**4**). Set the compass to the widest gap between the floor and door before using. Cut the line with a saw or plane, after disassembling the door.

Lock problems can usually be solved by readjusting the lock-bar guide brackets on each side of the door so that the bars glide through them easily (**5**) or lubricating the lock mechanism itself (**6**). To do this, you must sometimes remove the lock and crank mechanism from the door.

PARTS OF A DOOR

Sectional overhead doors

These doors retract within their own space and can be used where a door may not swing out. Two types are common, one with large coil springs on both sides overhead, the other with a long horizontal spring centered above the door opening. Garage doors should be inspected and maintained often.

SEE ALSO

Details for: ▷	
Switches	310
Wiring	317–325

LOCKNUT

TWIST-UP (TORSION) SPRING

1 Adjust spring tension

TAP WITH MALLET

LEVEL

2 Tighten track flanges

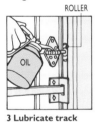

ROLLER

OIL

3 Lubricate track

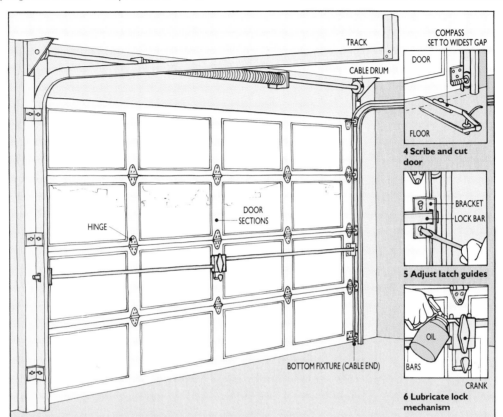

TRACK

COMPASS SET TO WIDEST GAP

DOOR

CABLE DRUM

FLOOR

4 Scribe and cut door

BRACKET

LOCK BAR

5 Adjust latch guides

OIL

BARS

CRANK

6 Lubricate lock mechanism

HINGE

DOOR SECTIONS

BOTTOM FIXTURE (CABLE END)

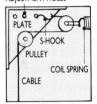

ADJUSTMENT HOLES

PLATE

S-HOOK

PULLEY

COIL SPRING

CABLE

Counterbalance system
Sectional garage doors operate with a system of springs, cables and pulleys that compensate for the weight of the door and make it easy to open and close.

AUTOMATIC GARAGE-DOOR OPENERS

Automatic garage-door openers are available for most types of garage doors. These systems allow you to open the door by remote control from inside your car and can also be equipped with switches for operating the door from inside the house. There are several proprietary systems designed for do-it-yourself installation, and these come with complete instructions.

Automatic garage-door openers shouldn't be regarded as a mere luxury—they can be absolutely essential for older and handicapped homeowners. These systems incorporate an electric motor mounted inside the garage with a track-and-pulley system that lifts the door. Most also have a light that goes on automatically and shuts off after a pre-set interval. Systems may operate either with an infra-red or radio-signal transmitter. The receiver will be mounted either outside the garage door or to the motor housing itself.

Transmitters and receivers have specially coded signals for security. Most systems also incorporate automatic safety devices that stop the door movement instantly if the door comes in contact with an obstruction.

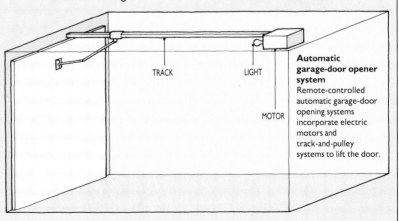

TRACK

LIGHT

MOTOR

Automatic garage-door opener system
Remote-controlled automatic garage-door opening systems incorporate electric motors and track-and-pulley systems to lift the door.

WINDOWS: TYPES AND CONSTRUCTION

The function of any window is to allow natural light into the house and to provide ventilation. Traditionally windows have been referred to as "lights", and the term "fixed light" is still used to describe a window or part of a window frame that doesn't open. A section that opens for ventilation, the "sash," is a separate frame that slides vertically or is hinged at its side, top or bottom edge. Windows of the hinged type are commonly referred to as casement windows.

A pane of glass can also be pivoted horizontally as a single sash, or several panes can be grouped together to make up a jalousie window.

Most window frames and sashes are made up from molded sections of solid wood. Clad-wood units offer the superior insulating properties and beauty of wood along with low maintenance. Steel and, more recently, aluminum or rigid vinyl frames are also used.

Casement windows

Window frames with hinged sashes—casement windows—are now produced in the widest range of materials and styles.

A traditional wooden window frame and its hinged sash are constructed in much the same way as a door and its frame. A jamb at each side is mortise-and-tenon jointed into the head member at the top and into a sill at the bottom (See below). The frame may be divided vertically by a "mullion", or horizontally by a "transom" **(1)**.

The sash, which is carried by the frame, has its top and bottom rails jointed into its side stiles. Glazing bars, relatively light molded sections, are used to sub-divide the glazed area for smaller panes **(2)**.

Side-hung sashes are fitted on butt hinges or sometimes, for better access to the outside of the glass, on "easy clean" extension hinges. A lever fastener, for securing the sash, is screwed to the middle of the stile on the opening side. A casement stay on the bottom rail holds the sash in various open positions and acts as a locking device when the sash is closed. Top-hung sashes, or vents, are secured with a stay only (◁).

Galvanized-steel casement windows **(3)** were once popular for domestic use. They are made in the same format as wooden hinged windows but have a slimmer framework. The joints of the metal sections are welded.

Steel windows are strong and long-lasting but vulnerable to rust unless protected by galvanized plating or a good paint. The rusting can be caused by weathering outside or by condensation on the inside.

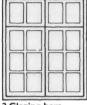

1 Casement window

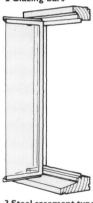

2 Glazing-bars

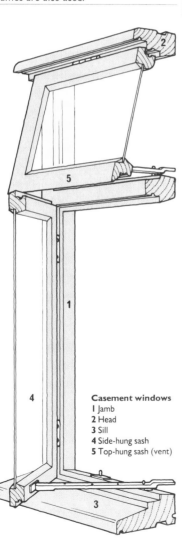

Casement windows
1 Jamb
2 Head
3 Sill
4 Side-hung sash
5 Top-hung sash (vent)

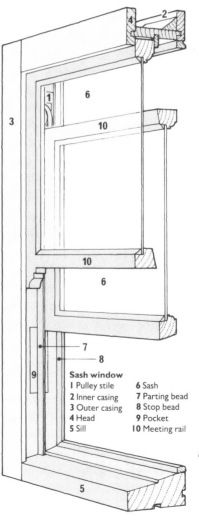

Sash window
1 Pulley stile	6 Sash
2 Inner casing	7 Parting bead
3 Outer casing	8 Stop bead
4 Head	9 Pocket
5 Sill	10 Meeting rail

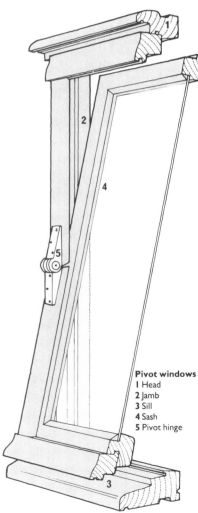

3 Steel casement type

Pivot windows
1 Head
2 Jamb
3 Sill
4 Sash
5 Pivot hinge

WINDOWS: TYPES AND CONSTRUCTION

Sash windows

Vertically sliding windows are commonly known as sash windows and when both top and bottom sashes can be opened they are referred to as "double-hung" sash windows.

The traditional wooden type (see opposite) is constructed with a "box frame" in which the jambs are made up from three boards: the pulley stile, the inner casing and the outer casing. A back completes the box that houses the sash counterweights. The head is made up in a similar way but without the back lining, and the sill is of solid wood. The pulley stiles are jointed into the sill and the linings are set in a rabbet.

The sashes of a double-hung window are held in tracks formed by the jamb, a parting bead and an inner stop bead. The beads can be removed for servicing the sash mechanism. Each sash is counter-balanced by two cast-iron weights—one at each side—which are attached by strong cords or chains that pass over pulleys in the stiles. Access to the weights is through "pockets"—removable pieces of wood—set in the lower part of the stiles.

The top sash slides in the outer track and overlaps the inner bottom sash at their horizontal "meeting rails." The closing faces of the meeting rails are bevelled, and their wedging action helps to prevent the sashes rattling. It also provides better clearance when the window is opened and improves security when it is locked. The sashes are secured by two-part fasteners of various types fitted on the meeting rails.

Spiral balances
Modern wooden or aluminum vertically sliding sashes have spring-assisted spiral balances which do not need a deep box construction. Rather than being concealed, the slim balances are fitted on the faces of the stiles.

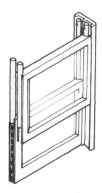

Spiral balances
The balances are usually fixed to the faces of the frame stiles and set in grooves in the sash stiles.

Pivot windows

Wooden-framed pivot windows (see opposite) are constructed in a similar way to casement windows, but the sash is held on a pair of strong pivot hinges which allow the window to be tilted right over for easy cleaning from inside. A safety roller arm can be fitted to the frame and set to prevent the window opening more than 4½ inches.

Pivoting roof windows are available for pitched roofs with slopes from 15- to 85-degrees. Like the standard pivoting windows, they can be fully reversed for cleaning. The windows are supplied double-glazed with sealed units, and ventilators are incorporated in the frame or sash. The wood is protected on the outside by a metal covering, and flashing kits are supplied for installing in roofs (▷).

Jalousie windows
A jalousie window is another form of pivot window. The jalousie are unframed "blades" of glass $5/32$ in. or $1/4$ in. thick, which have their long edges ground and polished. The panes are held at each end in light alloy carriers which pivot on an upright member, which is sometimes screwed to a wooden frame. One side is fitted with an opening and locking mechanism which links all of the panes so that they operate together as one.

Jalousie windows are effective as ventilators but they do not provide good security. They are also difficult to weatherseal.

Where an opening is more than 3 ft. 6 in. in width two sets of panes are best used, with the center pair of uprights set back-to-back in order to form a mullion.

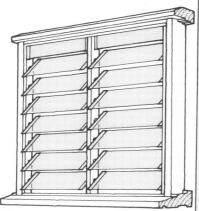

Use two sets of panes for a wide opening

ALUMINUM AND VINYL WINDOW FRAMES

Aluminum windows
These are now replacing old wooden and metal-framed windows. The aluminum is extruded into complex sections (1), to hold double-glazed sealed units and weather stripping and—ready finished in white, satin silver, black or bronze—is maintenance free. These windows are highly engineered and complete with concealed projection hinges and lockable fasteners. They need no stays to hold them open.

To combat condensation the latest designs incorporate a "thermal break" of insulating material in the hollow sections of the frame.

Most aluminum windows designed for replacement work are custom-made and fitted by contractors specializing in window installation.

Vinyl windows
Rigid vinyl windows (2) are similar to aluminum ones but are thicker through their sections. They are manufactured in white and brown, and once installed they require no maintenance.

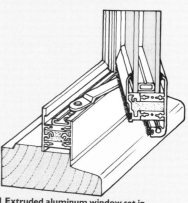

1 Extruded aluminum window set in wooden frame

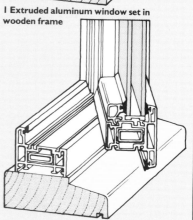

2 Metal tube-reinforced extruded-vinyl window

HOW WINDOWS ARE FITTED

Frame walls

Most new windows today are prefabricated and set into place as a single unit. Installing them is similar to installing doors.

First, measure the rough opening to be sure it is large enough to accept the window. Then, sheath all four sides of the opening with 15-pound building paper to prevent moisture damage (**1**). Set the window into the opening from outside. Center it, then raise it on shims from the inside to the specified height.

Set a level on top of the sill and adjust the shims until the frame is both plumb and horizontal. From outside, carefully drive one finishing nail into an upper corner of the casing, partway into a stud. Start a nail in the opposite corner, check that the window frame is level, and drive the nail through the casing into the stud.

Measure between diagonal corners of the frame to be sure it is square, then insert shims between the side jambs to hold it in position. Nail the lower corners in place carefully (**2**). After rechecking the frame for squareness, plumb and level, operate the sashes. If no further adjustment is necessary, finish nailing, trim shims flush, pack insulation between the window frame and rough opening from the inside, install a drip cap above the window, and caulk all seams to exclude moisture (**3**).

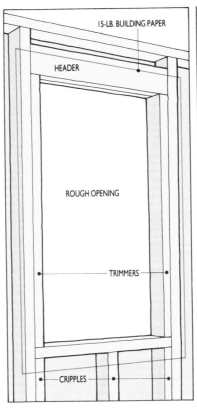

Labels: 15-LB. BUILDING PAPER · HEADER · ROUGH OPENING · TRIMMERS · CRIPPLES

1 Be sure opening matches window
To narrow an opening, install extra trimmers or strips of plywood. Widen an opening by adding a new stud next to the framed opening and removing a trimmer. Alter the height of an opening by rebuilding the sill and lower cripples, not the header.

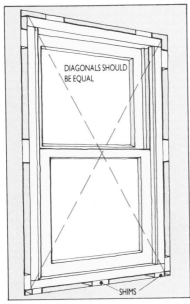

Labels: DIAGONALS SHOULD BE EQUAL · SHIMS

2 Tack window in place
Adjust with shims until all measurements are satisfactory and sash operates smoothly. Measurements taken between diagonals will be exactly equal if frame is square.

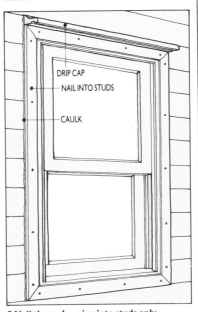

Labels: DRIP CAP · NAIL INTO STUDS · CAULK

3 Nail through casing into studs only
Do not nail into sheathing. If necessary, pre-drill holes to prevent splitting. Attach drip cap to top of casing. Fill all nail holes with putty. Apply caulk around all four sides.

Masonry walls

In older brick houses it is usual to find the window frame jambs set in recesses on the inside of the brickwork. The openings were formed before the windows were fitted and the frames were nailed or screwed into wooden plugs in the brickwork. No vertical damp-proof courses were fitted. Evaporation was relied on to keep the walls dry.

The frames in a 9-inch-thick wall were set flush with the inside. Thicker walls had inner reveals. All required sub-sills, usually stone ones, outside.

Brickwork above the opening in a traditional brick wall may be supported by a brick arch or a stone lintel. Flat or shallow curved arches were generally used, their thickness being the width of one brick. Wooden lintels were placed behind such arches to support the rest of the wall's thickness. Semi-circular arches were usually as thick as the wall.

Many stone lintels were carved to make decorative features. As with arches, an inner lintel shared the weight. Openings like this were never wide because of the relative weakness of the materials. The wide windows of main rooms had several openings divided by brick or stone columns.

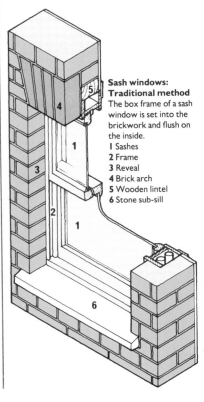

Sash windows: Traditional method
The box frame of a sash window is set into the brickwork and flush on the inside.
1 Sashes
2 Frame
3 Reveal
4 Brick arch
5 Wooden lintel
6 Stone sub-sill

TYPES OF GLASS

Glass is made from silica sand which, with such additives as soda, lime and magnesia, is heated until it is molten to produce the raw material. The type and quality of the glass produced for windows is determined by the method by which it is processed in the molten stage. Ordinary window glass is known as annealed glass. Special treatments during manufacturing give glass particular properties, such as heat-resistance or extra strength.

SHEET GLASS

Clear sheet glass is made for general glazing and was once the most common type used in windows. It is produced by a drawn process and can sometimes be recognized by its slight distorting effect, which is a result of the manufacturing process. Though the surfaces are given a smooth "fire-finish" they are not always quite flat or quite parallel.

Two qualities of clear glass are produced—the ordinary standard grade for general glazing and a "selected" one for better glazing work—in thicknesses from 1/16 to 5/32 inch.

Horticultural glass is a poorer category produced by the same method and made in 1/8- and 5/32-inch thicknesses for use in greenhouses only.

FLOAT GLASS

Float glass is now generally used for glazing windows. It is made by floating the molten glass on a bath of liquid tin to produce a sheet with flat, parallel and distortion-free surfaces. It has virtually replaced plate glass, which was a rolled glass ground and polished on both sides.

Clear float glass is made in thicknesses from 1/8 up to 1 inch, but it is generally stocked in only three: 1/8, 5/32 and 1/4 inch.

PATTERNED GLASS

Patterned glass is glass which has one surface embossed with a texture or a decorative design. It is available in clear or tinted sheets in thicknesses of 1/8, 5/32, 3/16 and 1/4 inch.

The transparency of the glass depends on the density of the patterning. Such "obscure" glass is used when maximum light is required while maintaining privacy, such as in bathroom windows.

Obscure glass, commonly known as rough-cast glass, is another form of patterned glass. It is made in a thicker range than patterned glass, 1/4 inch being the most common thickness. It is used mostly for commercial buildings.

TINTED GLASS

There is now special glass available which cuts down the heat received from the sun, and this is often used in roof lights. This tinted glass, which can be of the float, sheet, laminated or rough-cast type, also reduces glare, though at the expense of some illumination. It is available in thicknesses ranging from 1/8 to 1/2 inch, depending on the type.

NON-RELFECTIVE GLASS

Diffuse reflection glass is a 1/16-inch glass sheet with slightly textured surfaces, and is used for glazing picture frames. When placed within 1/2 inch of the picture surface the glass appears completely transparent, while eliminating the surface reflections associated with ordinary polished glass.

SAFETY GLASS

Glass which has been strengthened by means of reinforcement or a toughening process is known as safety glass. It should be used whenever the glazed area is relatively large or where its position makes it vulnerable to accidental breakage. Such hazardous areas common in domestic situations are glazed doors, low-level windows and shower screens.

WIRED GLASS

Wired glass is 1/4-inch-thick rough-cast or clear annealed glass with a fine steel wire mesh incorporated in it during manufacturing. Glass with a 1/2-inch-square mesh is known as Georgian wired glass. The mesh supports the glass and prevents it disintegrating in the event of breakage. The glass itself is not special and is no stronger than ordinary glass of the same thickness.

Wired glass is regarded as a fire-resistant material with a one-hour rating. Though the glass may break, its wire reinforcement helps to maintain its integrity and prevent the spread of fire.

TEMPERED GLASS

Tempered glass is ordinary glass that has been heat-treated to improve its strength. The process of treatment renders the glass about four to five times stronger than an untreated glass of similar thickness. In the event of breaking, it merely shatters into relatively harmless granules.

Tempered glass cannot be cut. Any work required, such as holes to be drilled for screws, must be done before the toughening process. Suppliers of doors and sindows usually stock standard sizes of tempered glass to fit standard frames.

LAMINATED GLASS

Laminated glass is made by bonding together two or more layers of glass with a clear tear-resistant plastic film sandwiched between. This safety glass will absorb the energy of an object hitting it, to prevent the object penetrating the pane. The plastic interlayer also binds broken glass fragments together and reduces the risk of injury from fragments of flying glass.

It is made in a range of thicknesses from 5/32 up to 9/16 inch, depending on the type of glass used. Clear, tinted and patterned versions are all available.

LOW-E GLASS

A microscopically thin coating on the surface of the glass is selectively permeable—it admits light but reflects heat. Depending on where the coated surface is positioned in an insulating glass unit, it can either help to reflect heat back into a room—thus offering energy savings during the heating season—or cut down on reflected heat during the air-conditioning season. Low-E glass is offered as an option by many window manufacturers.

BUYING GLASS

You can buy most types of glass from building supply and hardware stores. They will advise you on thickness, cut the glass to your measurements and also deliver larger sizes and amounts.

The thickness of glass, once expressed by weight, is now measured in inches. If you are replacing old glass, measure its thickness to the nearest 32nd, and, if it is slightly less than any available size, buy the next one up for the sake of safety.

Though there are no regulations about the thickness of glass, for safety reasons you should comply with the recommendations set out in the Uniform Building Code or your local code. The required thickness of glass depends on the area of the pane, its exposure to wind pressure and the vulnerability of its situation—e.g., in a window overlooking a play area. Tell your supplier what the glass is needed for—a door, a window, a shower screen, etc.—to ensure that you get the right type.

Measuring
Measure the height and width of the opening to the inside of the frame rabbet, taking the measurement from two points for each dimension. Also check that the diagonals are the same length. If they differ markedly and show that the frame is out of square, or if it is otherwise awkwardly shaped, make a cardboard template of it. In any case deduct 1/8 inch from the height and width to allow a fitting tolerance. When making a template allow for the thickness of the glass cutter.

When you order patterned glass, specify the height before the width. This will ensure that the glass is cut with the pattern running in the right direction. (Or take a piece of the old glass with you, which you may need to do in any case to match the pattern.)

For any asymmetrically shaped pane of patterned glass supply a template, and mark the surface that represents the outside face of the pane. This ensures that the glass will be cut with its smooth surface outside and will be easier to keep clean.

WORKING WITH GLASS

Always carry glass on its edge. You can hold it with pads of folded rag or paper to grip the top and bottom edge, though it is better to wear heavy working gloves.

Protect your hands with gloves and your eyes with goggles when removing broken glass from a frame. Wrap up the broken pieces in thick layers of newspaper if you have to dispose of them in your wastebasket, but before doing so check with your local glazier, who may be willing to take the pieces and add them to his cut-offs, to be sent back to the manufacturers for recycling.

Basic glass-cutting

It is usually unnecessary to cut your own glass as glass suppliers are willing to do it, but you may have surplus glass and want to cut it yourself. Diamond-tipped cutters are available, but the type with a steel wheel is cheaper and adequate for normal use.

Cutting glass successfully is largely a matter of practice and confidence. If you have not done it before, you should make a few practice cuts on waste pieces of glass and get used to the "feel" before doing a real job.

Lay the glass on a flat surface covered with a blanket. Patterned glass is placed patterned side down and cut on its smooth side. Clean the surface thoroughly.

Set a T-square the required distance from one edge, using a steel measuring tape (1). If you are working on a small piece of glass or do not have a T-square, mark the glass on opposite edges with a felt-tip pen or wax pencil. Use a straight edge to join up the marks and guide the cutter.

Lubricate the steel wheel of the glass cutter by dipping it in light machine oil or kerosene. Hold the cutter between middle finger and index finger (2) and draw it along the guide in one continuous stroke. Use even pressure throughout and run the cut off the end. Slide the glass forward over the edge of the table (3) and tap the underside of the scored line with the back of the cutter to initiate the cut. Grip the glass on each side of the score line with gloved hands (4), lift the glass and snap it in two. Alternatively, place a pencil under each end of the scored line and apply even pressure on both sides until the glass snaps.

1 Measure the glass with a tape and T-square

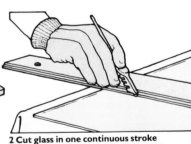
2 Cut glass in one continuous stroke

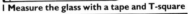

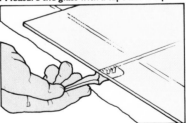
3 Tap the edge of glass to initiate the cut

4 Snap glass in two

Cutting a thin strip of glass

A pane of glass may be slightly oversize due to inaccurate measuring or cutting or if the frame is distorted.

Remove a very thin strip of glass with the aid of a pair of pliers. Nibble away the edge by gripping the waste with the tip of the jaws close to the scored line.

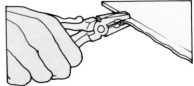
Nibble away a thin strip with pliers

CUTTING CIRCLES AND DRILLING HOLES

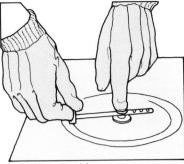

Fitting items such as an extractor fan may involve cutting a circular hole in a pane of glass. This can be done with a beam compass cutter.

Cutting a circle in glass

Locate the suction pad of the central pivot on the glass, set the cutting head at the required distance from it and score the circle around the pivot with even pressure (**1**). Now score another smaller circle inside the first one. Remove the cutter and score across the inner circle with straight cuts, then make radial cuts about 1 inch apart in the outer rim. Tap the center of the scored area from underneath to open up the cuts (**2**) and remove the inner area. Next tap the outer rim and nibble away the waste with pliers if necessary.

To cut a disc of glass, scribe a circle with the beam compass cutter, then score tangential lines from the circle to the edges of the glass (**3**). Tap the underside of each cut, starting close to the edge of the glass.

1 Score the circle with even pressure

SEE ALSO

Details for: ▷

| Repairing broken windows | 202 |
| Glass cutter | 480 |

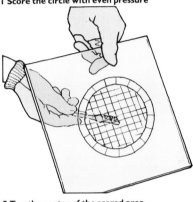

Smoothing the edges of cut glass

You can grind down the cut edges of glass to a smooth finish using wet-and-dry sandpaper wrapped around a wooden block. It is fairly slow work, although just how slow will depend on the degree of finish you require.

Start off with medium-grit paper wrapped tightly around the wood block. Dip the block complete with paper in water and begin by removing the "arris" or sharp angle of the edge with the block held at 45 degrees to the edge. Keep the abrasive paper wet.

Follow this by rubbing down the vertical edge to remove any nibs and go on to smooth it to a uniform finish. Repeat the process with progressively finer grit papers. A final polish can be given with a wet wooden block coated with pumice powder.

2 Tap the center of the scored area

3 Cutting a disc
Scribe the circle then make tangential cuts from it to the edge of the glass.

Using a glass-cutting template

Semi-circular windows and glazed openings in Georgian-style doors are formed with segments of glass set between radiating glazing-bars.

Windows with semi-circular openings and modern reproductions of period doors can be glazed with ready-shaped panes available from building suppliers, but for an old glazed door you will probably have to cut your own. The pieces are segments of a large circle, beyond the scope of the beam compass glass cutter (see above), so you will have to make a cardboard template.

Remove the broken glass, clean up the rabbet, then tape a sheet of paper over the opening and, using a wax crayon, take a rubbing of the shape (**1**). Remove the paper pattern and tape it to a sheet of thick cardboard. Following the lines on the paper pattern, cut the card to shape with a sharp knife, but make the template about 1/16 inch smaller all around, also allowing for the thickness of the glass cutter. The straight cuts can be aided by a straightedge, but you will have to make curved ones freehand. A slightly wavy line will be hidden by the frame.

Fix the template to the glass with double-sided tape, score around it with the glass cutter (**2**), running all cuts to the edge, and snap the glass in the normal way.

1 Take a rubbing of the shape with a crayon

• **Plastic glazing**
As an alternative to glass for awkward shapes you can use acrylic plastic, cutting it with a fret saw.

2 Cut around the template

Drilling a hole in glass

There are special spear-point drilling bits available for drilling holes in glass. As glass should not be drilled at high speed, use a hand-held wheel brace.

Mark the position for the hole, no closer than 1 inch to the edge of the glass, using a felt-tipped pen or a wax pencil. On mirror, glass work from the back or coated surface.

Place the tip of the bit on the marked center and, with light pressure, twist it back and forth so that it grinds a small pit and no longer slides off the center. Form a small ring with putty around the pit and fill the inner well with a lubricant such as kerosene or water.

Work the drill at a steady speed and with even pressure. Too much pressure can chip the glass.

When the tip of the drill just breaks through, turn the glass over and drill from the other side. If you drill straight through from one side, you risk breaking the surface around the hole.

Drilling glass
Always run the drill in a lubricant to reduce friction.

REPAIRING A BROKEN WINDOW

A cracked window pane, even when no glass is missing from it, is a safety hazard and a security risk. If the window is actually lacking some of its glass, it is no longer weatherproof and should be repaired promptly.

Temporary repairs

For temporary protection from the weather, a sheet of polyethylene can be taped or pinned with strips over the outside of the window frame, and a cracked window can be temporarily repaired with a special clear self-adhesive waterproof tape. Applied to the outside, the tape gives an almost invisible repair.

Safety with glass

The method you use to remove the glass from a broken window will to some extent depend on conditions. If the window is not at ground level, it may be safest to take out the complete sash to do the job. But a fixed window will have to be repaired on the spot, where it is.

Large pieces of glass should be handled by two people and the work done from a scaffold rather than ladders. Avoid working in windy weather and always wear protective gloves for handling glass.

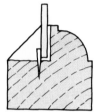

Weathered putty

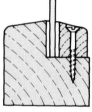

Wooden bead
Unscrew beading and scrape out mastic. Bed new glass in fresh astic and replace beading.

Repairing glass in wooden frames

In wooden window frames the glass is set into a rabbet cut in the frame's molding and bedded in linseed-oil putty. Small wedge-shaped nails called glazier's points are also used to hold the glass in place. In some wooden-framed windows a screwed-on beading is used to hold the pane instead of the "weathered" (outer) putty; this type of frame may have its rabbet cut on the inside instead of the outside.

Removing the glass

If the glass in a window pane has shattered, leaving jagged pieces set in the putty, grip each piece separately (wearing gloves) and try to work it loose (**1**). It is safest always to start working from the top of the frame.

Old dry putty will usually give way, but if it is strong it will have to be cut away with a glazier's hacking knife and a hammer (**2**). Alternatively, the job can be done with a blunt wood chisel. Work along the rabbet to remove the putty and glass. Pull out the points with pincers (**3**).

If the glass is cracked but not shattered, run a glass cutter around the perimeter of the pane about 1 inch from the frame, scoring the glass (**4**). Fasten strips of self-adhesive tape across the cracks and the scored lines (**5**) and tap each piece of glass so that it breaks free and is held only by the tape. Carefully peel the inner pieces away, then remove the pieces around the edges and the putty as described above.

Clean out the rabbet and seal it with a wood primer. Measure the height and width of the opening to the inside of the rabbets and have your new glass cut ⅛ inch smaller on each dimension to give a fitting tolerance.

Fitting new glass

Purchase new glazier's points and enough putty for the frame. Your glass supplier should be able to advise you on this but, as a guide, 1 pound of putty will fill about 13 linear feet.

Knead a palm-sized ball of putty to an even consistency. Very sticky putty is difficult to work with so wrap it briefly in newspaper to absorb some of the oil. You can soften putty that is too stiff by adding linseed oil to it.

Press a fairly thin, continuous band of putty into the rabbet all around with your thumb. This is the bedding putty. Lower the edge of the new pane on to the bottom rabbet, then press it into the putty. Press close to the edges only, squeezing the putty to leave a bed about ¹⁄₁₆ inch behind the glass, then secure the glass with points about 8 inches apart. Tap them into the frame with the edge of a firmer chisel so that they lie flat with the surface of the glass (**1**). Trim the surplus putty from the back of the glass with a putty knife.

Apply more putty to the rabbet all around, outside the glass. With a putty knife (**2**), work the putty to a smooth finish at an angle of 45 degrees. Wet the knife with water to prevent it dragging and make neat miters in the putty at the corners. Let the putty set and stiffen for about three weeks, then apply an oil-based undercoat paint. Before painting, clean any putty smears from the glass with paint remover. Let the paint lap the glass slightly to form a weather seal.

A self-adhesive plastic foam can be used instead of the bedding putty. Run it around the back of the rabbet in a continuous strip, starting from a top corner, press the glass into place on the foam and secure it with points. Then apply the weathered putty in the same way described above. Alternatively, apply a strip of foam around the outside of the glass and cover it with a wooden beading, then paint.

1 Work loose the broken glass

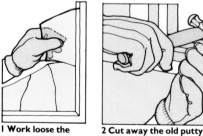

2 Cut away the old putty

3 Pull out the old points

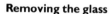

4 Score glass before removing a cracked pane

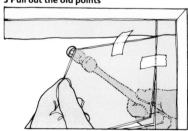

5 Tap the glass to break it free

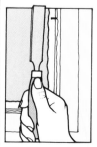

1 Tap in new points

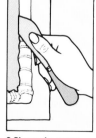

2 Shape the putty

Leaded lights are windows glazed with small pieces of glass joined together with strips of lead known as cames. The glass may be colored and cut to form a decorative design, as in churches, or it may be clear and set in a diamond-shaped or rectangular grid of cames.

SUPPORTING A LEADED LIGHT

Leaded lights are relatively weak and can sag with age. If you have such a window and it is bowing you can support it with the help of a ¼-inch mild steel rod.

Drill a ¼-inch hole on each side of the window frame. Place the holes about half-way up the sides and close to the lead strips. Drill one twice as deep as the other. Carefully flatten the window with the palm of a gloved hand or a board to spread the load.

To the back of the came(s) soft solder a few short lengths of tinned copper wire, stripped from household electrical cable, or some small tinplate strips cut from a food can. Set them in line with the line of the rod.

The length of the rod should equal the distance between the window frame sides plus the depth of the two holes, but *not* the extra depth of the one hole.

Locate the rod in the holes, inserting it in the deeper hole first. Twist the wires—or crimp the tinplate straps—around the rod so that the window is tied to it for support. Finish the rod with black enamel and wipe putty cement (see right) into the cames on the outside if necessary.

Support a sagging leaded light with a metal rod

Twisted wire tie

Tinplate strip tie

Replacing broken glass in leaded lights

It is always easier to replace a piece of glass with the window out of its frame, but leaded lights are rather fragile, so it is usually safer to carry out the repair with the window in place. If the complete unit must be removed, carefully hack out the putty and support the whole of the panel on a board as it is taken out.

Cut the cames around the broken pane at each joint, using a sharp knife **(1)**. Make the cuts on the outside if you are working with the window in place at ground floor level. The repair will then be less noticeable from inside. On the windows of an upper room the cames will have to be cut on the inside.

With a putty knife lift the edges of the cames holding the glass and pry the lead up until it is at right angles to the face of the glass **(2)**. Lift or tap out the broken pieces and scrape away the old putty cement. During this, if you are working with the leaded light in place, support it from behind with your hand

or with a board fixed across the window frame.

Take a paper rubbing of the open cames to give you the shape and size of the glass needed. Lay the new glass over the rubbing and follow the shape with a glass cutter and straightedge, keeping the cut a little inside the line **(3)**. Try the glass for fit and rub down corners and edges on wetted wet-and-dry sandpaper if necessary.

Mix a little gold size with linseed oil putty to make a putty cement, apply it to the open cames and bed the glass into it with even pressure.

Fold the edges of the cames over to secure the glass and burnish them flat with a piece of wood. Scrape away any surplus putty and gently wipe the glass and cames absolutely clean with paint remover.

Thoroughly clean the cut joints in the cames with fine steel wool and resolder them **(4)**, using an electric soldering iron and rosin-core solder.

SEE ALSO

Details for: ▷

Cutting glass	200
Soldering	488

Came styles

Round came

Flat came

Beaded came

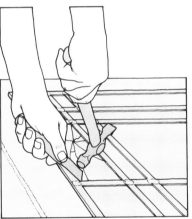
1 Cut the cames with a sharp knife

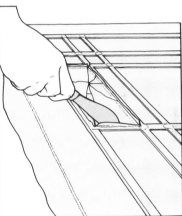
2 Pry the lead up with a putty knife

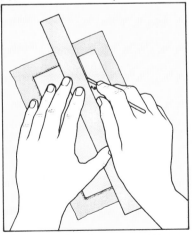
3 Cut the glass following a paper rubbing

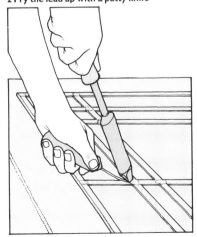
4 Resolder the joint after fitting the glass

DOUBLE-GLAZING UNITS

Using putty

SEE ALSO

◁ Details for:
Double-glazing   271-272

Using putty
Follow the sequence when fitting stepped double-glazing.
1 Set the packing in bedding putty.
2 Fit the glazing and secure with points.
3 Weatherproof the glass with putty.

Set stepped, sealed units in putty in the same way as for fitting new glass but place packing pieces of resilient material (supplied with the units) in the putty to support the greater weight of the double-glazing.

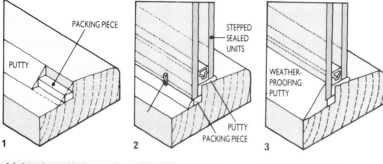

Using beading

Square-edged units are set in nonsetting glazing compound and held in place with wooden beading, a type of installation that is normally used for hardwood or metal window frames that are meant to be maintenance-free, i.e., not painted.

Apply two coats of sealer to the rabbet of a hardwood frame. When it is dry, lay a bed of the non-setting compound. Place the packing pieces on the bottom of the rabbet and the spacers, or distance pieces, against the back of it to prevent the glass from moving in the compound. Set the spacers about 2 inches from the corners and 1 foot apart opposite a screwhole in the bead.

Set the sealed unit into the rabbet and press it in firmly. Apply an outer layer of the nonsetting compound and another set of spacers against the glass positioned as before.

Cut the beading to length, making mitered ends, press it tight against the spacers and screw it into place with countersunk brass or plated screws. Countersunk screw cups are sometimes used instead of countersinking the holes in the beading. These give a neat finish.

Using beading
Set square-edged units in a nonsetting compound.
1 Set the packing and spacers in compound.
2 Fit the unit, apply more compound and place spacers at the bead fixing points.
3 Press the beads tight against the spacers and fix in place with screws.

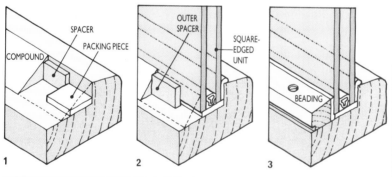

Metal-framed windows

Steel window frames are made with metal sections that form a rabbet for the glass. This type of window is glazed in much the same way as a wooden-framed window, but a special metal-quality putty is required. The putty is available from glass suppliers. The glass is secured in the frame with spring clips (**1**) which are set in putty and located in holes in frame. Replace glass in a metal frame following the sequence described for wooden frames but use clips instead of the springs mentioned. Treat any rust before fitting the glass and apply a metal primer.

Modern aluminum double-glazed frames use a dry-glazing system which involves synthetic rubber gaskets. These are factory-installed and should be free of the need for maintenance. If you break a pane in a window of this type, you should consult the manufacturers, as they usually have their own patented repair system.

RELIEVING STICKING WINDOWS

The sashes of wooden casement windows are liable to swell in wet weather, and this causes them to bind in the frame. If the windows have not been painted properly, it may be sufficient to wait for a period of dry weather, allowing the wood to shrink, and then apply a good paint.

The persistent sticking of a casement window in any weather may be due to a too-heavy buildup of paint. In this case, strip the old paint from the meeting edges of the sash and/or the frame rabbet and apply fresh paint. You may also have to plane the edge a little.

A window that was not opened when the frame was painted is likely to be glued shut by the paint. Free it by working a wallpaper scraper or thin knife between the sash and the frame.

The tolerances on wooden vertically sliding sashes are such that they do not stick unless they have been painted while shut, or the staff or parting beads have been badly positioned.

CURING RATTLING WINDOWS

The rattling of a casement window is usually caused by an ill-fitting lever fastener. If the fastener is worn you should either replace it with a new one or reset the plate on the frame into which the fastener locates.

Old wooden-sash windows are notorious for rattling. The cause is usually a sash, generally the bottom one, being a loose fit in its stile tracks. Remove and replace the inner stop bead with a new length so that it makes a close fit against the sash. Rub candle wax on both sliding surfaces.

A rattling top sash will have to be packed out, as there is no way of adjusting its track.

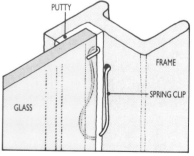

1 Use spring clips to hold the glass

REPAIRING ROTTED FRAMES

Softwood is the traditional material for making wooden window frames, and providing it is of sound quality and is well cared for, it will last the life of the building.

New frames or frames that have been stripped should always be treated with a clear wood preservative before being primed and painted (▷).

Regular maintenance

It is the bottom rail of a wooden window frame that is most vulnerable to rot if it is not protected. The water may be absorbed by the wood through a poor paint finish or by penetrating behind old shrunken putty. An annual check of all window frames should be carried out and any faults should be dealt with. Old putty that has shrunk away from the glass should be cut out and replaced.

Remove old, flaking paint, repair any cracks in the wood with a flexible filler and repaint, ensuring that the underside of the sash is well painted.

Replacing a sash rail

Where rot is well advanced and the rail is beyond repair, it should be cut out and replaced. This should be done before the rot spreads to the stiles of the frame. Otherwise you will eventually have to replace the whole sash frame.

Remove the sash either by unscrewing the hinges or—if it is a double-hung sash window—by removing the beading.

With a little care the repair can be carried out without the glass being removed from the sash frame, though if the window is large it would be safer to take out the glass. In any event, cut away the putty from the damaged rail.

The bottom rail is tenoned into the stiles (1), but it can be replaced by using bridle joints (▷). Saw down the shoulder lines of the tenon joints (2) from both faces of the frame and remove the rail.

Make a new rail, or buy a piece if it is a standard section, and mark and cut it to length with a full-width tenon at each end. Set the positions of the tenons to line up the mortises of the stiles. Cut the shoulders to match the rabbeted sections of the stiles (3) or, if it has a decorative molding, pare the molding away to leave a flat shoulder (4).

Cut slots in the ends of the stiles to receive the tenons.

Glue the new rail into place with a waterproof resin adhesive and reinforce the two joints with pairs of ¼-inch dowels. Drill the stopped holes from the inside of the frame and stagger them for greater rigidity.

When the adhesive is dry, plane the surface as required and treat the new wood with a clear preservative. Reputty the glass and paint the new rail within three weeks.

REPLACING A FIXED-LIGHT RAIL

The frames of some fixed lights are made like sashes but are screwed to the main frame jamb and mullion. Such a frame can be repaired in the same way as a sash (see left) after its glass is removed and it is unscrewed from the window frame. Where this proves too difficult, you will have to carry out the repair in place.

First remove the putty and the glass, then saw through the rail at each end. With a chisel, trim the rabbeted edge of the jamb(s) and/or mullion to a clean surface at the joint (1) and chop out the old tenons. Cut a new length of rail to fit between the prepared edges and cut mortises in its top edge at both ends to take loose tenons. Place the mortises so that they line up with the mortises in the stiles and make them twice as long as the depth of those mortises.

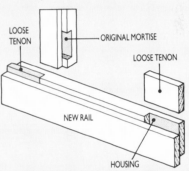

1 Cut the tenons and trim a new rail to fit

Cut two loose tenons to fit the rail mortises, and two packing pieces. The latter should have one sloping edge (2).

Apply waterproof woodworking adhesive to all of the joint surfaces, place the rail between the frame members, insert the loose tenons and push them sideways into the stile mortises. Drive the packing pieces behind the tenons to lock them in place. When the adhesive has set, trim the top edges, treat the new wood with clear preservative, replace the glass and reputty. Paint within three weeks.

SEE ALSO

Details for: ▷	
Painting windows	78
Wood joints	475–477
Removing glass	202

● **Removing glass**
Removing glass from a window frame in one piece is not easy, so be prepared for it to break. Apply adhesive tape across the glass to bind the pieces together if it should break. Chisel away the putty to leave a clean rabbet, then pull out the points. Work the blade of a putty knife into the bedding joint on the inside of the frame to break the grip of the putty. Steady the glass and lift it out when it becomes free.

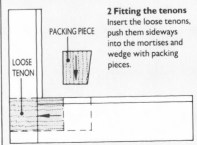

2 Fitting the tenons
Insert the loose tenons, push them sideways into the mortises and wedge with packing pieces.

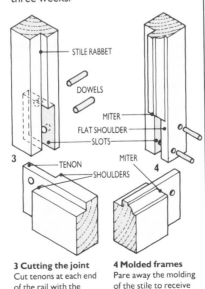

1 The original joint
The rail is tenoned into the stile and fitted with wedges.

2 Cutting out the rail
Saw down the shoulder lines of the joints from both faces of the frame.

3 Cutting the joint
Cut tenons at each end of the rail with the shoulders matching the sections of the stiles.

4 Molded frames
Pare away the molding of the stile to receive the square shoulder of the rail. Miter the molding.

REPAIRING ROTTED SILLS

The sill is a fundamental part of a window frame, and one attacked by rot can mean major repair work.

A window frame is constructed in the same way as a door frame and can be repaired in a similar way. All the glass should be removed first, preferably by removing the sashes. Be sure to check the condition of the subsill (part of the rough frame). Rot can extend into this region also if the opening was not covered with building paper. After repairs have been made, be careful to thoroughly weatherseal the window frame to prevent moisture from entering once again. Reapply fresh 15-pound asphalt-saturated building paper around exposed parts of the rough frame, then caulk all seams where the window frame itself contacts the exterior of the house. Repairing sills is difficult and time-consuming, so plan to do such work during warm weather when window openings can be covered with polyethylene while work progresses.

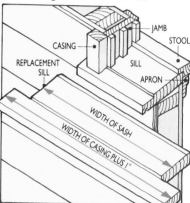

Double-hung window in frame wall

Replacing a wooden sill

Ideally, to replace a rotted window sill you should remove the entire window, carefully disassemble the old sill from the jamb sides, use it as a template, then cut and fit a new sill and replace the window. However, sills may be replaced with the window in place, provided you work patiently and have some skill at scribing and shaping wood with a chisel. Begin by carefully splitting out the old sill. Cut through it crosswise in two places with a saw to remove the middle portion, then gently pry the end sections away from the jambs. Hacksaw any nails holding the sill to the rest of the frame.

Use a piece of cardboard to make a template for a new sill, shaped to fit between the jambs but beneath the casing on the outside. Cut a 10-degree bevel along the upper outside edge of the sill, extending to the inside edge of the sash, then bevel the sash area so it is level when the sill is installed. Fill the area beneath the sill with insulation, install the sill with 16d finishing nails, then thoroughly caulk the seams.

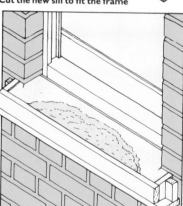

Cut the new sill to fit the frame

Repairing a stone subsill

The traditional stone sills featured in older houses may become eroded by the weather if they are not protected with paint. They may also suffer cracking due to subsidence in part of the wall.

Repair any cracks and eroded surfaces with a quick-setting waterproof cement. Rake the cracks out to clean and enlarge them, then dampen the stone with clean water and work the cement well into the cracks, finishing off flush with the top surface.

Depressions caused by erosion should be undercut to provide the cement with a good hold. A thin layer of cement simply applied to a shallow depression in the surface will not last. Use a cold chisel to cut away the surface of the sill at least 1 inch below the finished level and remove all traces of dust.

Make a wooden form to the shape of the sill and temporarily nail it to the brickwork. Dampen the stone, pour in the cement and tamp it level with the form, then smooth it with a trowel. Leave it to set for a couple of days before removing the form. Let it dry thoroughly before painting.

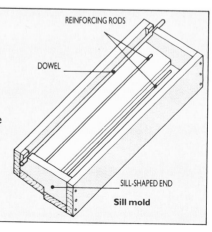

Make a wooden form to the shape of the sill

CASTING A NEW SUBSILL

Cut out the remains of the old stone sill with a hammer and cold chisel. Make a wooden mold with its end pieces shaped to the same section as the old sill. The mold must be made upside down, its open top representing the underside of the sill.

Fill two thirds of the mold with fine ballast concrete, tamped down well, and then add two lengths of mild steel reinforcing rod, judiciously spaced to share the volume of the sill, then fill the remainder of the mold. Set a narrow piece of wood such as a dowel into notches previously cut in the ends of the mold. This is to form a "throat" or drip groove in the underside of the sill.

Cover the concrete with polyethylene sheeting or dampen it regularly for two or three days to prevent rapid drying. When the concrete is set (allow about seven days), remove it from the mold and re-lay the sill in the wall on a bed of mortar to meet the wooden sill.

Sill mold

RE-CORDING A SASH WINDOW

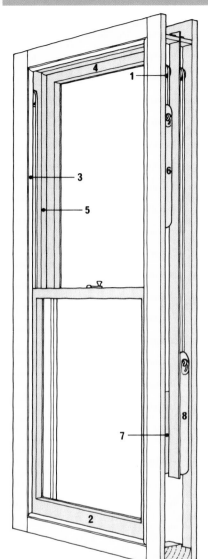

The workings of a double-hung sash window

1 Pulleys	**5** Parting bead
2 Bottom sash	**6** Bottom sash weight
3 Stop bead	**7** Pocket
4 Top sash	**8** Top sash weight

The sash cording from which the sashes are suspended will wear and in time will break. You should replace both cords even when only one has broken.

Waxed sash cording is normally sold in standard hanks, though some suppliers sell it by the foot. Each sash will require two lengths about three-quarters the height of the window. Sash chain is more durable than cord.

Removing the sashes

Lower the sashes and cut through the cords with a knife to release the weights. Hold on to the cords and lower the weights as far as possible before letting them drop. Pry off the side stop beads from inside the frame, starting in the middle and bowing them to make their mitered ends spring out and avoid breakage.

Lean the inner sash forward and mark the ends of the cord grooves on the face of the sash stiles. Reposition the sash and transfer the marks onto the pulley stiles (**1**). The sash can now be pulled clear of the frame.

Carefully pry out the two parting beads from their grooves in the stiles. The top sash can then be removed, after marking the ends of the grooves as before. Place sashes safely aside.

To gain access to the weights, take out the pocket pieces which were trapped by the parting bead and lift the weights out through the openings. Hanging pieces of thin wood known as parting strips may be fitted inside the box stiles to keep the pairs of weights apart. Push these aside to reach the outer weights.

Remove the old cord from the weights and sashes and clean them up ready for the new sash cords.

Fitting the sashes

The top sash is fitted first, but not before all of the sash cords and weights are in place. Clean away any buildup of paint from the pulleys. Tie a length of fine string to one end of the sash cord. Weight the other end of the string with small nuts or a piece of chain. Thread the weight—known as a mouse—over a pulley (**2**) and pull the string through the pocket opening until the cord is pulled through. Attach the end of the cord to a weight with a special knot (see below left).

Use the sash marks to measure the length of cord required. Pull on the cord to hoist the weight up to the pulley. Then let it drop back about 4 inches. Hold it temporarily in this position with a nail driven into the stile just below the pulley. Cut the cord level with the mark on the pulley stile (**3**).

Repeat this procedure for the cord on the other side, and then for the bottom sash.

Replace the top sash on the sill, removing the temporary nails in turn. Lean the sash forward, locate the cords into the grooves in the stiles and nail them in place using three or four 1-inch round wire nails. Nail only the bottom 6 inches, not all the way up (**4**). Lift the sash to check that the weights do not touch bottom.

Replace the pocket pieces and nail the parting beads in their grooves. Fit the bottom sash in the same way. Finally, replace the stop beads; take care to position them accurately.

SEE ALSO

Details for: ▷	
Spiral balances	197, 208
Replacement windows	209–210

HOW TO TIE A SASH WEIGHT KNOT

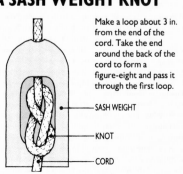

Make a loop about 3 in. from the end of the cord. Take the end around the back of the cord to form a figure-eight and pass it through the first loop.

— SASH WEIGHT

— KNOT

— CORD

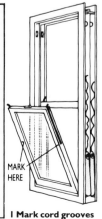

1 Mark cord grooves

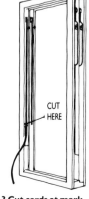

2 Pull cord through

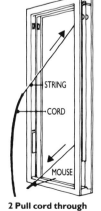

3 Cut cords at mark

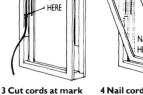

4 Nail cord to sash

SPIRAL BALANCES

Instead of cords and counterweights, modern sash windows use spiral balances which are mounted on the faces of the frame stiles, eliminating the need for traditional box sections. The balances are made to order to match the size and weight of individual glazed sashes and can be ordered through building supply stores or by mail.

Spiral balance components

Each balance consists of a torsion spring and a spiral rod housed in a tube. The top end is fixed to the stile and the inner spiral to the bottom of the sash. The complete unit can be housed in a groove in the sash stile or in the jamb of the frame.

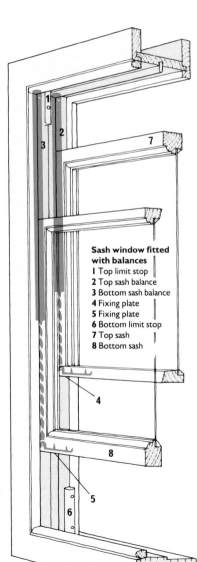

TUBE

SPIRAL

FIXING PLATE

A spiral balance unit

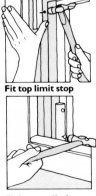

Fit top limit stop

Fit bottom limit stop

Sash window fitted with balances
1 Top limit stop
2 Top sash balance
3 Bottom sash balance
4 Fixing plate
5 Fixing plate
6 Bottom limit stop
7 Top sash
8 Bottom sash

Fitting the balances

You can fit spiral sash balances to replace the weights in a traditionally constructed sash window.

Remove the sashes and weigh them on your bathroom scales. Place your order, giving the weight of each sash and its height and width, also the height of the frame. Refit the sashes temporarily until the balances arrive, then take them out again and remove the pulleys.

Plug the holes and paint the stiles. Cut grooves, as specified by the manufacturers, in the stiles of each sash, to take the balances (1). Cut a mortise at each end of their bottom edges to receive the spiral rod mounting plates. Fit the plates with screws (2).

Sit the top sash in place, resting it on the sill, and fit the parting bead. Take the top pair of balances, which are shorter than those for the bottom sash, and locate each in its groove (3). Fix the top ends of the balance tubes to the frame stiles with the screw nails provided (4) and set the ends tight against the head.

Lift the sash to its full height and prop it with a length of wood. Hook the wire "key," provided by the makers, into the hole in the end of each spiral rod and pull each one down about 6 inches. Keeping the tension on the spring, add three to five turns counterclockwise (5). Locate the ends of the rods in the mounting plate and test the balance of the sash. If it drops, add another turn on the springs until it is just held in position. Take care not to overwind the balances.

Fit the bottom sash in the same way, refitting the staff bead to hold it in place. Fit the stops that limit the full travel of the sashes in their respective tracks (see left).

RENOVATING SPIRAL BALANCES

In time the springs of spiral balances may weaken. Retension them by unhooking the spiral rods from the mounting plates, then turning the rods counterclockwise once or twice.

The mechanisms can be serviced by releasing the tension and unwinding the rods from the tubes. Wipe them clean and apply a little thin oil, then rewind the rods back into the tubes and tension them as described above.

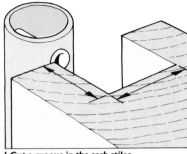

I Cut a groove in the sash stiles

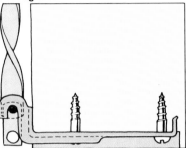

2 Fix the plates in their mortises with screws

3 Fit the sash and locate the tube in its groove

4 Nail the top end of the tube to the stile

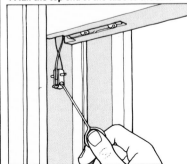

5 Tension the springs with the key provided

READY-MADE WINDOWS

Building suppliers offer a range of ready-made window frames in wood, vinyl and aluminum, and some typical examples are shown below.

Unfortunately, the range of sizes is rather limited, but where a ready-made frame is fairly close to one's requirements, it is possible to alter the size of the window's rough opening by cutting out or adding frame pieces, as described on page 198. In a wall of exposed brickwork, the window frame should be made to measure.

Casement windows

Vertical sliding sash windows

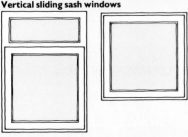

Pivot windows

REPLACEMENT WINDOWS

The style of the windows is an important element in the appearance of any house. Should you be thinking of replacing windows in an older dwelling you might find it better—and not necessarily more expensive—to have new wooden frames made rather than to change to modern windows of aluminum or vinyl.

Planning and building regulations

Window conversions do not normally need planning permission, as they come under the heading of home improvement or home maintenance. But if you plan to alter your windows significantly—for example, by bricking one up or making a new window opening, or both—you should consult your local building inspector.

All codes have certain minimum requirements, some pertaining to ventilation and some to the ratio of glass area to floor space.

You should also find out from your local authority if you live in a historic section, which could mean some limitation on your choice.

Buying replacement windows

Custom woodworking mills will make up wooden window frames to your size. Specify hardwood or, for a painted finish, softwood impregnated with a preservative.

Alternatively, you can approach one of the replacement window companies, though this is likely to limit your choice to aluminum or vinyl frames. The ready-glazed units can be fitted to your present framing or to new framing, should alteration be necessary. Most of the replacement window companies operate on the basis of supplying and also fitting the windows, and their service includes disposing of the old windows after removal.

This method saves time and labor, but you should carefully compare the various offerings of these companies and their compatibility with the style of your house before opting for one. Choose a frame that reproduces, as closely as possible, the proportions of the original window.

Replacing a casement window

Measure the width and height of the window opening. Windows in brick masonry will need a wood subframe. If the existing one is in good condition, take your measurements from inside the frame. Otherwise, take them from the brickwork. You may have to cut away some of the stucco first to get accurate measurements. Order the replacement window accordingly.

Remove the old window by first taking out the sashes and then the panes of glass in any fixed part. Unscrew the exposed hardware, such as may be found in a metal frame, or pry the parts of the frame out and cut through fasteners with a hacksaw. It should be possible to knock the frame out in one piece, but if not, saw through it in several places and lever the pieces out with a crowbar (**1**). Clean up the exposed masonry with a bricklayer's chisel to make a neat opening.

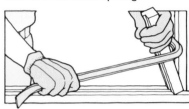

1 Lever out the pieces of the old frame

Cut the horns off the new frame if present, then plumb the frame in the window opening and wedge it (**2**). Drill screw holes through the stiles into the rough frame or masonry (**3**). Refit the frame, checking again that it is plumb before screwing it home.

Patch the wall on both sides if necessary. Gaps of ¼ inch or less can be filled with caulk. Glaze the new frame as required.

2 Fit the new frame   **3 Drill screw holes**

REPLACEMENT WINDOWS

Bay windows

A bay window is a combination of window frames which are built out from the face of the building. The side frames may be set at 90-, 60- or 45-degree angles to the front of the house. Curved bays are also made with equal-sized frames set at a very slight angle to each other to form a faceted curve.

The frames of a bay window are set on framing which is built to the shape of the bay, which may be at ground level only, with a flat or pitched roof, or may be continued up through all stories and finished with a gabled roof.

Bay windows in brick homes can break away from the main wall through subsidence caused by a poor foundation or differential ground movements. Damage from slight movements can be repaired once the ground has stabilized. Repoint the brickwork and apply mastic sealant to gaps around the woodwork. Damage from extensive or persistent movement should be dealt with by a builder. Consult your local building inspector and inform your homeowners insurance company.

Fitting the frame

Where the height of the original window permits it, standard window frames can be used to make up a replacement bay window. Using gasket seals, various combinations of frames can be arranged. Shaped hardwood corner posts are available to give a 90-, 60- or 45-degree angle to the side frames. The gasket is used for providing a weatherproof seal between the posts and the frames.

SEE ALSO
◁ Details for:
Removing sashes	207
Window types	197

Joining frames
A flexible gasket, which is sold by the foot, is available for joining standard frames. The frames are screwed together to fit the opening.

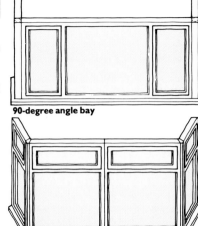
90-degree angle bay

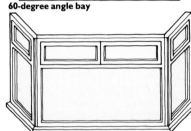
60-degree angle bay

45-degree angle bay

Hardwood bay window (detail)

Bow windows

These are windows constructed on a shallow curve, and they normally project from a flat wall. Complete bow window frames are available from window manufacturers, ready for installation. Bow windows can be substituted for conventional ones.

To install, build out the rough opening as necessary, cutting back the siding to receive the exterior trim if the window is precased. Center the window in the opening, shim it plumb and level, then nail it into place. Install purchased braces or ones you build yourself beneath the window to support it. Also, install a canopy to shed rain and snow from the top. Add flashing and new siding where necessary, then caulk all seams. Pack insulation between the window frame and rough opening from the inside, then install interior trim.

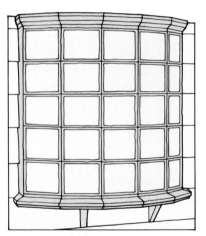
Bow window with braces

REPLACING A SASH WINDOW IN BRICK

An old vertically sliding sash window with cords and counterweights can be replaced with a new frame fitted with spiral balance sashes.

Remove the sashes (◁), then take out the old frame from inside the room. Pry off the casing, then the window jamb, and chop away the plaster as necessary. Most frames make a wedge fit, and you can loosen one by hitting the sill on the outside with a heavy hammer and a wood block. Lift the frame out of the opening when it is loose (**1**) and remove any debris from the opening once the window has been removed.

Set the new frame centrally in the opening so that its stiles are showing equal amounts on each side of the exterior brickwork reveals. Check the frame for plumb and wedge the corners at the head and the sill. Make up the space left by the old box stiles with mortared brickwork (**2**).

Metal brackets screwed to the frame's stiles can also be set in the mortar bed joints to secure the frame.

When the mortar is set, replaster the inner wall and replace the casing. In the meantime, glaze the sashes. Finally, apply a caulk sealant to the joints between the outside brickwork and the frame to keep the weather out.

1 Lift out old frame   **2 Fill gaps with brick**

Double-glazed roof windows are becoming increasingly popular for the modernizing of old-style skylights and as part of attic conversions. They are supplied ready-glazed and fully equipped with latches and ventilators. Flashing kits to fit the window frame and to suit high- or low-profile roofing materials are also available.

Center-pivoting sashes can be used on roofs with pitches between 15 and 85 degrees, and special emergency exit types may be installed. These can be converted to top-hung or side-hung sashes at the turn of a handle. The former are for roof pitches of 20 to 60 degrees and the latter are for those of 60 to 85 degrees.

Roof windows are relatively easy to install using only ordinary woodworking tools and often working only from the inside. Once they are fitted, the glass can be cleaned comfortably from the inside. Such accessories as blinds and remote opening devices are also available.

Roof windows reverse for easy maintenance

Blinds that fit the inside frame are available

Choosing the size

The manufacturers of roof windows offer a standard range of sizes and, apart from consideration of cost, the overall size should take account of the area of glass necessary to provide a suitable level of daylight in the room.

The height of the window is also quite important. It should be determined by the pitch of the roof in relation to how the window is going to be used. The manufacturers produce charts that give the recommended dimensions according to roof pitch. Ideally, if the window is to provide a good view, the bottom rails should not obstruct that view at normal seat height, nor should it cut across the line of sight of someone standing. Broadly speaking, this means that the shallower the pitch of the roof, the taller the window needs to be. The top of the window should remain within comfortable reach for accessibility.

Standard-size windows can be arranged side by side or one above the other to create a larger window. When deciding on the size of a window, bear in mind its proportions and its position in relation to the appearance of the building and its other features.

Though you will probably not need to get permission to install the window itself, code restrictions do apply when cutting through the roof, so check with a building inspector before you start your installation.

The manufacturers of roof windows supply comprehensive instructions to suit installation in all situations. Below is a summary of how to install a roof window in an ordinary pitched asphalt-shingle roof.

Fitting a window

Start by stripping off the roof-covering materials over the area to be occupied by the window. The final placing of the frame will be determined by the position of the rafters and the roofing. Start by setting the bottom of the window frame at the specified distance above the nearest full course of shingles and try to position it so as to have half or whole shingles at each side.

Brace the rafters from inside by inserting posts beneath them, then cut through the sheathing and rafters to make the opening, following the dimensions given by the manufacturer. Cut and nail headers and trimmers between the rafters to set the height of the opening, and a vertical trimmer or trimmers to set the width.

With the glazed sash removed, screw the window frame in place with the brackets provided. Mark a guide line clearly around the frame, level with the surface of the sheathing. Check that the frame is square by measuring across its diagonals; they should be equal.

Complete the outside work by fitting flashing and new shingles, working up from the bottom of the frame. Replace the glazed sash.

Cut and nail wallboard to the sides of the rafters on the inside and close the top and bottom of the opening with wallboard nailed in the groove provided in the frame and to the framing of the roof structure.

Finish off the joints with compound and tape to get ready for decoration.

SEE ALSO

Details for: ▷
Roofs   221–226, 232–233

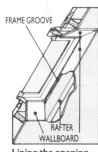
Height of window
The height should enable someone sitting or standing to see out of the window with ease.

FRAME GROOVE

RAFTER
WALLBOARD

Lining the opening with plasterboard
Section through window seen from the inside showing the lining on the side, top and bottom of the opening.

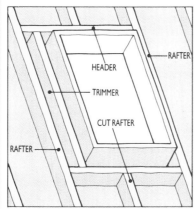
HEADER
TRIMMER
CUT RAFTER
RAFTER
RAFTER
Cut the opening and fit the trimmers

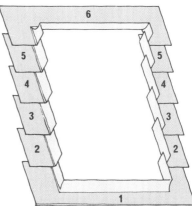
Flashing kit showing order of assembly

STAIRS

In simple functional terms, a stair is a series of steps that link one floor with another, but a staircase—traditionally the stair combined with that part of the building which surrounds it—can also be a powerful expression of the style of the house itself. By its location, invariably in the entrance hall, its sometimes impressive scale and its interesting shape or decorative features, the stair is an important element in the character of a home's interior.

In the staircases of some older houses, elaborate examples of the wood-joiner's art can be found. Unfortunately, joinery nowadays has lost much of the character of earlier periods. However, the spacious and airy quality of modern open-tread stairways, although simply constructed, makes them attractive in their own right.

An old, worn or creaking stair can be repaired, and though its decorative elements may be laborious to restore, the end result is worth the effort.

Types of stairs

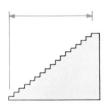

1 The run
The run of the stair is the horizontal measurement between the bottom and top riser.

The simplest stair is a straight flight of steps. This type of stair requires the greatest "run," that is, the horizontal distance between the face of the bottom step riser and the riser of the top step (**1**). In houses where space is limited, shorter flights may be used, an intermediate landing making a turn and linking one flight with another. Various elaborate arrangements—the dog-leg, open-well, quarter-turn and half-turn staircase—are also used (see right).

Most staircases use newel posts for their support and are known as newel stairs. The posts are a prominent feature, the newel at the foot of the stair often being larger and rather more decorative than those above. Stairs of this type usually have straight treads, though tapered treads known as winders are used at the top or bottom of a stair where the run is restricted.

Winders may be used exclusively, forming a sweeping curved or helical stair. This type, known as a geometric stair, does not include newel posts in its construction. A spiral staircase is a helical stair constructed around a central column. Unlike the sweeping curved stair, it can be used in small houses where space is limited. Reproductions of old spiral stairs and modern styles in wood, steel and concrete are made.

TYPES OF STAIRCASES

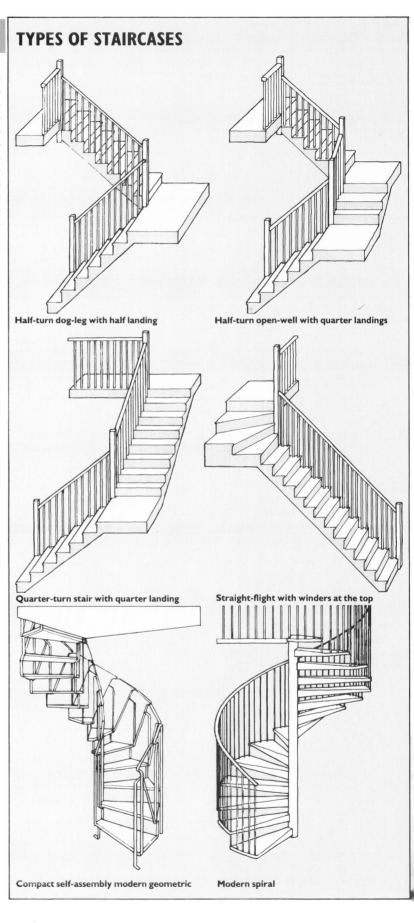

Half-turn dog-leg with half landing

Half-turn open-well with quarter landings

Quarter-turn stair with quarter landing

Straight-flight with winders at the top

Compact self-assembly modern geometric

Modern spiral

STAIR CONSTRUCTION

Softwood is most commonly used for the construction of traditional stairs, and expensive hardwoods such as oak, teak and mahogany are usually reserved for better-quality houses, though some hardwood is sometimes combined with softwood in stairs for such features as treads, newel posts and handrails.

Stone and metal are also used for stairs, though they are rarely found in ordinary domestic contexts other than in exterior staircases and spiral staircases.

Steps

Each step of an ordinary straight flight of stairs is made from two boards—the vertical riser that forms the front of the step and the horizontal tread, the board on which you walk. The riser is a stiffening member and is fixed between two treads, giving support to the front edge of one and the rear of the other.

Treads and risers may be joined in a number of ways (see below right), but always there are triangular blocks glued into the angles between risers and treads to give greater stiffness.

Open-tread stairs have thick treads and no risers. For increased strength, metal tie rods may be fitted across the stair in the gaps between the treads.

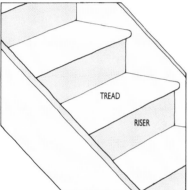

Each step of the common stair has a tread and riser

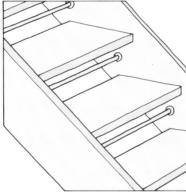

Open-tread stairs have no risers but sometimes use tie rods

Stringers

Steps are supported at their ends by wide boards set on edge, known as stringers, and these are the main structural members that run from one floor level to another. A wall stringer is an inner one that is fixed to the wall, while the stringer on the open side of the stair is called the outer stringer.

The appearance of the stair is affected by the style of the stringers, of which there are two types. The closed stringer has parallel long edges, while the cut or open stringer has its top edge cut away to the shape of the steps. The closed version is used for the wall stringer of a stair to pick up the line of the baseboard. The outer stringer can be either the simple closed type, preferred in modern houses, or the cut type that is generally found in older dwellings.

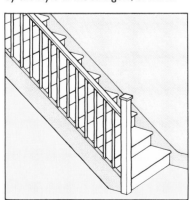

Closed stringers have parallel long edges

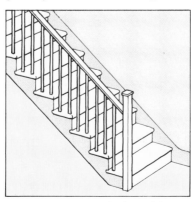

Open stringers are cut to the shape of the steps

Step/stringer joints

The treads and risers of stairs are set in mortises routed into the face of a closed stringer and secured with glued wedges. The wedges are driven in from the underside to make a tight joint.

In the case of an open stringer, the outer ends of the risers are mitered into the vertical cut edges and the treads are nailed down onto the horizontal edges. The nosing—the projecting rounded edge—of this type of tread, which usually has a scotia molding underneath it, is "returned" by a matching molding that covers the tread's end grain.

Additional decorative features of fretted wood may be pinned and glued to the side of the stringer underneath the tread moldings.

SEE ALSO	
Details for: ▷	
Removing a tread	216–217
Removing a riser	217

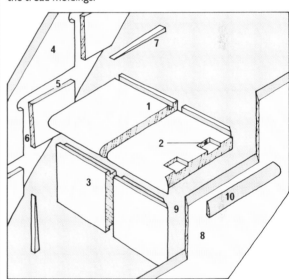

Step assembly showing typical stair joints
1 Grooved tread
2 Baluster housing
3 Tongued riser
4 Wall stringer
5 Tread housing
6 Riser housing
7 Wedge
8 Open stringer
9 Mitered butt joint
10 Molding

JOINTS BETWEEN TREAD AND RISER

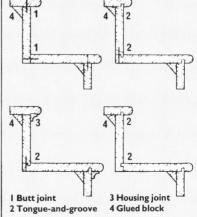

1 Butt joint
2 Tongue-and-groove
3 Housing joint
4 Glued block

213

STAIRS: CONSTRUCTION

Newels

The wall stringer is screwed to the wall at points underneath the treads and the outer stringer is tenoned into the newels at each end. Newel posts are at least 4 × 4 inches in section. They give support to the stair while securing it to the floor at the bottom and to the structural trimmer of the floor or landing above. The newel at the top of a stair, or the central newel on a stair with a landing, is usually continued down to the floor. The newels also carry the handrail, which is tenoned into them.

The balustrade

The space between the handrail and the outer stringer may be filled with traditional balusters, modern balustrade rails or framed paneling. The assembly is known as the balustrade, or banister.

Storage space

The space underneath a stair is often enclosed to make a cupboard and provide extra storage space. The triangular infilling between the outer stringer of the stair and the floor is known as the spandrel. It may be a wallboard

surface or one of wood paneling. It is not structural and can be removed if and when required. You might think twice before opening up this area, as the understair cupboard is a sensible use of a space that is otherwise of little value. Many families find it a good place for keeping such things as vacuum cleaners, folding chairs and TV trays.

The central bearer

Traditional stairs 3 feet in width should be supported on their underside by a central stringer. This is a length of "2-by" lumber as wide as the other stringers and is birdsmouth jointed onto the floorplate at the bottom and the floor header at the top. Short lengths of 1-inch-thick board known as rough brackets are sometimes nailed to alternate sides of the bearer to make a tight fit under each tread and riser.

If the finished underside of the stair is finished with wallboard, the central stringer also provides a nailing surface. The edges of the wallboard may be nailed to the edges of the stringers or to additional bearers that run down inside the assembly.

STAIRCASE DESIGN

Staircase dimensions and designs are strictly controlled by building codes which govern such measurements as tread size and shape, rise and run, minimum headroom, handrail position, and spacing of balusters. Consult a building inspector before building or modifying any staircase.

Calculating the rise and run of stairs is perhaps the most crucial consideration, for this determines the steepness of the staircase. Most codes allow 8 inches as the maximum vertical distance (rise) between treads, and 9 inches as the *minimum* horizontal distance (run). Minimum headroom between stairs and ceiling is usually 6 feet 8 inches. Properly designed, a finished staircase must fit the exact floor-to-floor height of the opening, and have level, uniformly sized and spaced treads and risers, all within code specifications. To check staircase calculations, building inspectors often employ one of these three formulas:

RISER HEIGHT + TREAD WIDTH
   = 17″ to 18″.
(2 × RISER HEIGHT) + TREAD WIDTH
   = 24″ to 27″.
RISER HEIGHT × TREAD WIDTH
   = 70″ to 75″.

Tread width does not include the nosing or lip that extends over the riser.

Manufactured staircases are available. To order, you must provide accurate measurements for the total rise of the staircase, the total run, and the width of tread you desire.

Storage space
The area below a stair is usually enclosed to provide storage space.

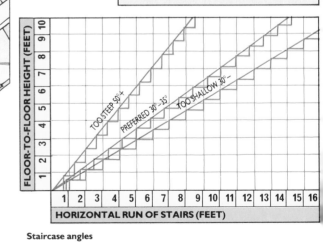

Stair components
1 Wall stringer
2 Outer stringer
3 Newel
4 Handrail
5 Balusters
6 Spandrel
7 Center stringer
8 Floor plate
9 Rough brackets
10 Tread
11 Riser

Staircase angles
Graph shows relationships of treads and risers for several angles of rise.

FLOOR-TO-FLOOR HEIGHT (FEET)

TOO STEEP 50°+
PREFERRED 30°–35°
TOO SHALLOW 30°–

HORIZONTAL RUN OF STAIRS (FEET)

CURING CREAKING STAIRS

Creaking in stairs begins when joints become loose and start rubbing. The slight gaps that allow this movement are often the result of the wood having shrunk, though general wear and tear will also contribute to the problem.

The method you choose for dealing with it will depend on whether you have access to the backs of the treads. A better repair can be carried out from underneath, but if that means cutting into the finish work, it will be more convenient to work on the stairway from above.

Working from underneath

If it is possible to get to the underside of the stairs, have someone walk slowly up the steps, counting them out loud, and from your position under the stairs, follow the counting, noting any loose steps and marking them with chalk. Have your helper work the loose treads while you inspect them to discover the source of the creaking.

Loose housing joint
If the tread or the riser is loose in its mortise in the string, it may be because the original wedge has become loose. Remove the wedge (**1**), clean it up, apply carpenter's wood glue and rewedge the joint (**2**). If the wedge has got damaged while being removed, make a new one out of hardwood.

Loose blocks
Check the triangular blocks that fit in the angle between the tread and the riser. If the glue has failed on one face, remove the blocks, clean off the old adhesive and reglue them in place. Before replacing the blocks, slightly pry open the shoulder of the tongue-and-groove joint with a chisel and apply new glue to it (**3**), then pull the joint up tight using 1½-inch countersunk screws set below the surface.

Rub the blocks into the angle (**4**). You can use panel pins to hold them while the glue sets. Try to avoid treading on the repaired steps before the glue dries.

If some of the blocks are missing, make new ones from lengths of 2 X 2-inch softwood. Set the wood upright in a vise and, sawing across the diagonal of the end, cut down the grain for about 7 inches. Remove the wood from the vise and, holding it on a bench hook or by repositioning it if you are using a Workmate bench, saw off 3-inch-long triangular blocks.

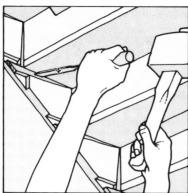

1 Pry out the old wedge with a chisel

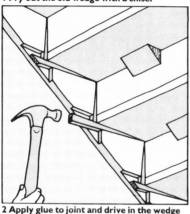

2 Apply glue to joint and drive in the wedge

3 Pry open the joint and inject glue

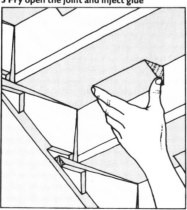

4 Rub the glued blocks into the angle

Working from the top

To identify the problem areas, walk slowly up the stairs—which should first be stripped of any covering—and stop at the creaking step, then shift your weight to and fro on the offending tread to discover which part is moving. It is best to do this late at night or early in the morning, when the house is quiet and small creaks will not be missed.

Nosing—loose joint
To cure looseness in a tongue-and-groove joint between the riser and the nosing of a tread, drill clearance holes for 1½-inch countersunk screws in the tread, centering on the thickness of the riser (**1**). Inject fresh woodworker's glue into the holes and work the joint a little so as to encourage the adhesive to spread into it, then pull the joint up tight with the screws. If the screws are not to be concealed by stair carpet you should counterbore the screw heads and plug the holes with matching wood.

Riser—loose joint
A loose joint at the back of the tread cannot be easily repaired from above. You can try working water-thinned glue into the joint but you cannot use screws to hold the joint fast until the glue sets.

One form of reinforcement which may be of help is made by gluing a section of ½ X ½-inch triangular molding into the angle between the tread and the riser (**2**), but this is possible only if it does not leave the remaining width of the tread narrower than the code specification for treads, 9 inches. Cut the molding slightly shorter than the width of the stair carpet, unless the carpet is of full stair width or a similar molding is fitted on all of the steps. Keep the details consistent.

1 Screw joint tight

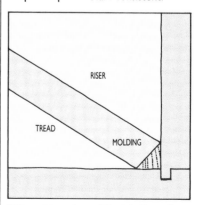

2 Glue a triangular molding into the angle

REPAIRING WORN STAIRS

REPLACING TREADS

Old wood stairs which have not had the protection of a floor covering will eventually become very worn. Worn treads and nosings are dangerous, and should be repaired promptly. If all the treads are badly worn, you should have the stairs replaced by a builder.

Treads fitted between closed stringers can be replaced only from below. If the stairs are enclosed underneath with plasterboard, you will have to cut an opening to reach the worn-out tread. Where a central stringer has been used in the construction of the stair the work involved in the repair can be extensive, and in such a case you should seek the advice of a professional builder since the job may be beyond your skills.*

Renewing a nosing

Wear on the nosing of a tread is usually concentrated in the center, and you can repair it without having to renew the whole tread.

Mark three cutting lines just outside the worn area, one set parallel with the edge of the nosing and the other two at right angles to it (**1**).

Adjust the blade depth of a portable circular saw to the thickness of the tread. Tack a strip the required distance from, and parallel to, the long cutting line to guide the edge of the saw's shoe, or baseplate.

Cutting out

Position the saw, switch it on, then make the cut by lowering the blade into the wood (**2**). Try not to overrun the short end lines. The cut made, remove the guide strip. Hand-saw the end lines, making cuts at 45 degrees to the face of the tread and taking care not to go beyond the first saw cut. Make these cuts with a tenon saw (**3**).

You will be left with uncut waste in the corners. Remove most of the cut waste with a chisel, working with the grain and taking care to avoid damaging the riser tongue and triangular reinforcing blocks. Pare away the waste from the uncut corners (**4**).

Replacement

In the underside of a new section of nosing, plane a groove to receive the tongue of the riser and cut its ends to 45 degrees. Check its fit in the opening, then apply wood glue to all of the meeting surfaces and attach it in place. Clamp it down with a strip screwed at each end of the tread (**5**). Place a packing strip of hardboard under the strip to concentrate the pressure, and a piece of polyethylene to prevent the hardboard from sticking. Drill and insert ¼-inch dowels into the edge of the nosing to reinforce the butt joint and, when the glue is set, plane and sand the repair flush. Reglue any blocks that may have fallen off.

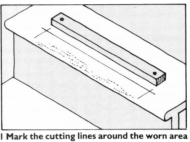
1 Mark the cutting lines around the worn area

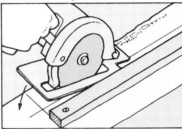
2 Make the cut with saw guided by strip

3 Make 45-degree cuts at each end

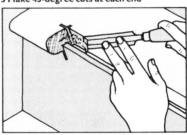
4 Pare away the waste from the corners

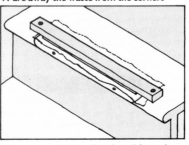
5 Clamp new section of nosing with a strip

Most stairs have tongue-and-groove joints between their risers and treads, though in some cases the tops of the risers are mortised into the undersides of the treads and in other stairs simple butt joints are used and secured with nails or screws.

You can determine which type of joint you are faced with by trying to pass a thin knife blade between the shoulders of the joint. It will help if you first remove any nails or screws. A butt joint will let the blade pass through, while a mortised or tongue-and-groove one will not do so.

As the joints effectively lock the treads and risers together, those in contact with the damaged tread must be freed before the tread can be removed. A butt joint is relatively easy to take apart; a mortise or tongue-and-groove joint will have to be cut.

Dismantling a butt joint

To take a butt joint apart, first take out the nails or screws and, if glue has been used, give the tread a sharp tap to break the hardened glue, or pry it up with a chisel. Remove the triangular glue-blocks in the same way.

Cutting a tongue

Where the tongue of a riser is joined to the underside of a tread, you cut it working from the front of the stair, and where the riser's tongue is joined to the top of the tread, it must be cut from the rear (**1**). If there is a scotia molding fitted under the nosing, try to pry it away first with a chisel.

Before cutting a tongue, remove any screws, nails and glued reinforcement blocks, then drill a line of ⅛-inch holes on the shoulders of the joint in which you can insert the blade of a padsaw (**2**). Make a saw cut; when it is long enough, continue with a panel saw.

The method you will now use to remove the tread will depend on whether it is fitted between closed strings or has an open string at one end (see opposite).

1 Cut the tongue from the front or rear

2 Start the cut with a hacksaw blade

Closed-stringer stair

Working from the underside of the stair, chisel out the tread-retaining wedges from the stringer mortises at the ends of the tread (**1**), then free the joints by giving the tread a sharp tap from above with a hammer and block.

Next, drive the tread backwards and out of its two mortises, alternately tapping one end and then the other (**2**).

Make a tread to fit, shaping its front edge to match the nosings of the other steps, and cut a new pair of wedges. Slide the new tread and wedges into place from underneath, measure the gaps left by the saw cuts at its front and back (**3**) and cut wooden packing strips or pieces of veneer to fill them.

Remove the tread, apply carpenter's wood glue and replace it, with the wedges and packing pieces. Secure the tread with 1½-inch countersunk wood screws into the risers.

1 Remove the wedges

2 Drive out the tread

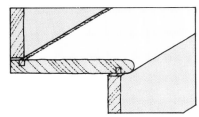

3 Pack out the saw cuts at front and back

Open-stringer stairs

Pry off the molding that covers the end grain of the tread, taking care not to split it (**1**). Remove the two balusters from the stair (▷).

Chisel the wedge out of the wall stringer mortise to free the inner end of the tread and drive the tread out from the rear of the stair with a hammer and a wood block on the outer end of its back edge (**2**). In this way the end of the tread fitted to the outer stringer is released while the inner end is still partly engaged in its mortise.

You will have to cut through or extract any nails that fasten the tread to the outer stringer before the tread can be pulled completely clear.

Use the original tread as a template and mark its shape out on a new board, then cut the board accurately to size. Take care to preserve the shape of the nosing which must follow that of the return molding.

Mark out and cut the mortises for the balusters (**3**) and make a new wedge for the inner tread mortise.

Fit the tread from the front, packing out and gluing and screwing it following the method described for a closed-stringer tread (see above).

Apply glue to the balusters and replace them. Finally, pin and glue the return molding to the end of the tread and replace any scotia molding.

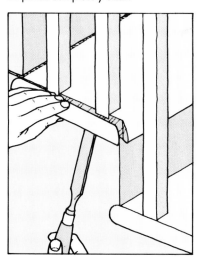

1 Pry off the return cover molding

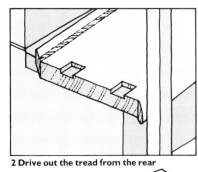

2 Drive out the tread from the rear

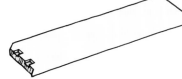

3 Cut the baluster housing in the new tread

REPAIRING A RISER

Risers take much less wear and tear than treads and will not ordinarily have to be replaced. Should a riser become weak through moisture damage, it can be reinforced from behind by having a piece of new board screwed and glued to it. Both the old and the new wood should be thoroughly treated to preserve them. A riser which is seriously weakened should be replaced.

Closed-stringer stair
In the case of a closed-stringer stair, remove the tread below the damaged riser using the method described (see left), but also saw through the tongue at the top of the riser. Knock the wedges out of the riser mortises, then knock or pry out the riser (**1**).

Measure the distance between the stringers and between the underside of one tread to the top of the other, then cut a new riser to fit. Though you could make tongue-and-groove joints on the new riser, it is easier simply to butt-join its top and bottom edges with the treads (**2**).

Glue and wedge the new riser into the mortises and to its top edge glue and screw the upper tread (**3**).

If yours is a "show-wood" staircase—one whose steps are not to be covered—counterbore the screw holes and use wood plugs to conceal the screws. Another way to secure a glued butt joint is by screwing and gluing blocks to both parts underneath.

Refit the tread as previously described (see left), but note that you need pack out only the front saw cut, as the new riser has been made to fit.

Open-stringer stair
First remove any scotia molding that is fitted under the nosing, then saw through the tongues at the top and bottom of the damaged riser and remove the wedge from its wall stringer mortise.

Knock apart the mitered joint between the end of the riser and the outer stringer by hammering it from behind. Once the mitered joint is free, pull the inner end of the riser out of its mortise, working from the front.

Make a new riser to fit between the treads, mitering its outer end to match the joint in the stringer. Apply glue and fit the riser from the front. Rewedge the inner mortise joint, screw the treads to the riser, nail the mitered end and replace the scotia molding.

SEE ALSO

Details for: ▷

Balusters	218
Stair joints	213–214

1 Pry out the riser

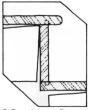

2 Cut riser to fit

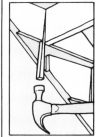

3 Wedge the riser

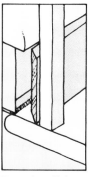

Free mitered joint

REPAIRING BALUSTERS

SPIRAL STAIRCASES

A broken baluster is potentially dangerous and it should be repaired or replaced promptly. If the baluster is a decorative one, it should be preserved, and if the damage is not too extensive, it can be repaired in place. Otherwise, if the damage is beyond repair, a new baluster can be made to replace it.

Buying balusters

Ready-turned balusters of various patterns are available from building suppliers and they can be used for replacing all the old and damaged ones where this would be more economical than having them made to order. They can also be used to replace old square balusters—perhaps originally fitted for economy reasons—and give added character to a staircase.

How balusters are fixed

Balusters are usually housed or stub-tenoned into the underside of the handrail and into the edge of a closed stringer or the treads of an open-stringer stair. Sometimes they are simply butt-joined and secured with nails, or are housed at the bottom but nailed at the top (see below). You can detect nails by examining or feeling the surface of the baluster at the back. You will find a slight bump or hollow. If the wood is stripped, the nail will be obvious. A light shone across the joint can also reveal a nail.

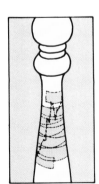

Typical examples of ready-made balusters/newels

Mending a baluster
Apply glue, and tape the split

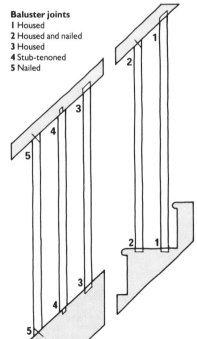

Baluster joints
1 Housed
2 Housed and nailed
3 Housed
4 Stub-tenoned
5 Nailed

Replacing a baluster

A damaged baluster that is butt-joined and nailed can be knocked out by driving its top end backward and its bottom end forward. If it is housed at the bottom, it can be pulled out of the housing once the top has been freed.

A baluster housed at both ends can be removed only by first cutting through the shoulder line of the joint on the underside of the handrail. It can then be pulled out of the lower housing.

When the baluster is fitted into an open stringer, remove the molding that covers the end of the tread and knock the bottom end of the baluster sideways out of its housing, then pull it down to disengage it from the handrail housing.

Fitting a baluster

Measure and mark out the required length on the new baluster, then mark out and cut the ends, using the old one as a pattern. If this cannot be done, take the angle of the handrail and stringer by setting an adjustable bevel on an adjacent baluster, then use the bevel to mark the new baluster for cutting. Fit and fasten the new baluster in the reverse order to the way in which the old one was taken out.

To replace a baluster which is mortised at both ends in a closed-stringer stair, first trim off the back corner of the top tenon (**I**), place the bottom tenon in its mortise and then swing the top end of the baluster into position (**2**).

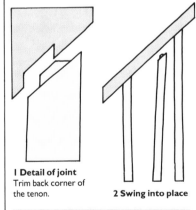

I Detail of joint
Trim back corner of the tenon.

2 Swing into place

Mending a baluster

A baluster that has split along the grain can be repaired in place. Work wood glue into the split and bind it with waxed string or masking tape until it dries (see far left). Before binding, squeeze the parts together and wipe any surplus glue with a damp rag.

Spiral staircases can be installed in small spaces or can be used to save space in a small room. However, their use is restricted by most building codes, so check with a building inspector before installing one. Most often, spiral staircases cannot be used as main staircases or fire exits. Consider also how you will move large objects between floors; spiral stairways can make maneuvering bulky furniture next to impossible.

Spiral stairway kits are popular and readily available. Usually they consist of a central pole which is fastened between floors and steps which spiral up around the pole. The inside ends of the steps are attached to the pole; the outer ends are fastened to balusters which are in turn fastened to a continuous handrail which spirals upward around the perimeter of the stair opening.

To install, first attach the central pole to the bottom floor, usually by lag-bolting it through the floor into the joists, and then slide on the treads. Fasten the top of the pole to the upper floor, usually by attaching the landing tread to the upper floor joists. Adjust the treads to spiral uniformly up the pole, then fasten them securely according to the manufacturer's directions. Attach the balusters to the ends of the steps, then connect their upper ends to the handrail.

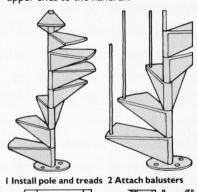

I Install pole and treads   2 Attach balusters

3 Attach handrail   4 Finished staircase

FITTING A HANDRAIL

Measuring and marking out

Mark a line on the wall to represent the top of the handrail, setting the height in accordance with building code regulations. Where there are tapered treads, some alterations of the rules may be necessary, but you should check with your local building inspector.

Set out the line by marking a series of points measured vertically from the nosing of each tread in a straight flight. Where tapered treads occur take the same measurement from the central winder tread and landing (1).

Marking tips and techniques

Marking the points can be greatly simplified by first cutting a straight wooden strip to the right height and then using it as a guide. Circle the points with your pencil as you make them so that you can find them easily later.

Marking out procedure

Using a straightedge, join up the marks to produce the line of the handrail, then draw a second line below and parallel to it at a distance equal to the thickness of the handrail. Where the rail changes direction, draw lines across the intersections (A) to find the angles at which the components must be cut (2).

Measure the run of the handrail and buy the required lengths, including such special sections as turns, ramps and the opening rise (see right). Also buy enough handrail brackets for spacing them at about 3-foot 3-inch intervals.

Assembling and fitting

Cut the components to the correct lengths and angles, then dowel and glue short sections together, or use special handrail screws. These require clearance holes in the ends of each part and mortises cut in the undersides for the nuts. When using handrail screws, you must also fit locating dowels (3) to keep the sections from rotating as they are pulled together. Assemble the rail in manageable sections.

Screw the brackets to the rail and hold it against the wall while a helper marks the mounting holes. Drill and plug the wall and screw the rail in place with No. 10 or No. 12 screws long enough to take a good hold in the studs and not just the wallboard (4).

Sand the handrail smooth and finish it with clear varnish or paint.

1 Laying out
Mark the wall above each tread and join the marks with a straightedge.

2 Changing angles
The junction of a sloping handrail with a horizontal one can be made with a ramp or left as a reflex angle.

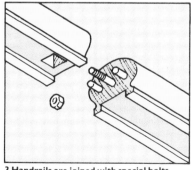

3 Handrails are joined with special bolts

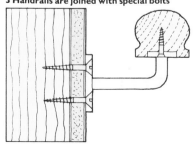

4 Securely fix handrail brackets to the wall

FIXING A LOOSE BALUSTRADE

When the whole balustrade, including the handrail and newel post, feels loose, it indicates a breakdown of the joints between the steps and the outer stringer. You should attend to it immediately, before the whole structure becomes dangerous and liable to collapse completely if someone were to fall against it.

Refasten to the steps a loose stringer and newel by first removing the wedges from the tread and riser mortises and then, working along the face of the stringer with a hammer and wood block, knocking it back into place to reseat the joints (1). If the stringer tends to spring away, hold it in place with lengths of timber braced between it and the opposite wall (2). Make new wedges, apply glue to the joints and drive the wedges in to make tight joints.

Reinforce the joint between the bottom step and the newel post with glued blocks rubbed into the angle on the underside of the stair. Alternatively, screw metal angle plates into the corners (3).

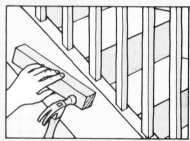

1 Reseat loose joints with a hammer and block

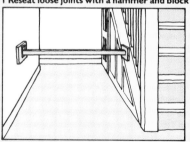

2 Brace the stringer against the opposite wall

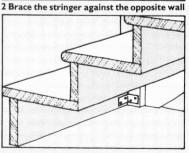

3 Reinforce the bottom joint

SEE ALSO

Details for: ▷	
Wood finishes	75
Stair construction	213–214
Replacing a balustrade	220
Dowel joints	476–477
Wall plugs	498

Handrail components
In addition to the normal handrail run, special matched components are available, such as turns, ramps and the open rise. These are joined with special handrail screws or dowels.

Horizontal cap turn

Horizontal turn

Opening rise

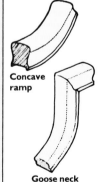

Concave ramp

Goose neck

REPLACING A BALUSTRADE

While the staircase of a house is a strong element in its interior character, the character of the staircase itself is very largely determined by the design of its balustrade and railing.

SEE ALSO

◁ Details for:
Stair
construction 213–214
Repairing balusters 218

Older houses, and even some tract houses in developments, were often fitted with attractive decorative features such as turned newel posts and balusters. But over the years, with changes in fashion, many of these old balustrades have been "modernized." Sometimes this has been done simply by paneling over the open balusters, sometimes by replacing turned ones with straight ones, and sometimes even by cutting away the whole assembly to achieve an "open plan" appearance (which, aesthetics apart, often does not comply with building code regulations; a new balustrade should be fitted for your own safety).

Balustrade components
1 Newel base
2 Newel center
3 Decorative knob
4 Turned balusters
5 Handrail
6 Base rail
7 Spacer fillets
8 Metal brackets
9 Cover buttons

Using a kit to replace a balustrade

A kit of parts is available which enables you to reinstate a traditionally designed balustrade. The kit consists of newel posts made up of three parts—a base section (1), a turned center section (2) and decorative knobs (3)—plus turned balusters in many styles (4) with a handrail (5) and machine-grooved base rail (6) in which to fit them. Spacer fillets (7) are also provided to make fitting and finishing of the balusters a straightforward job, and there are special metal brackets (8) for joining the ends of the handrails to the posts. You can use all or any of the parts to meet the demands of most types of wooden staircase; a straight-flight stair is taken as a typical example below.

Preparation

Remove all old hardboard or plywood paneling holding the balusters in place, and cut away, knock out or unscrew all old balusters, balustrade rails and handrails (◁).

Fitting the newels

The simplest way to start replacing the old or modified newels is to cut them off, leaving intact the joints between their bases and the string.

Cut the base of the bottom newel off square at a height of 8 inches above the pitch line—the stair nosing line—and cut the top newel 4⁷⁄₈ inches above the pitch line. Cut the base of an intermediate newel to a height of 7½ inches above the nosing.

Mark the diagonal lines across the cut ends to find their centers, then drill 2-inch-diameter holes to receive the center of the new newel posts. You can do this with a spade bit in a power drill or an expansion bit in a hand brace.

After drilling, finish the cut ends of the posts to a slightly convex contour and set the post centers in position, but do not glue them.

Fitting the rails

With an adjustable bevel, take the angle of the stair string where it meets the newel base. Hold the balustrade base rail against the stair, following the angle of the string exactly, and make a mark at each end where it meets the newels. Then mark the cutting lines at these points, using the bevel and a try square, and cut the rail to length.

Mark and cut the handrail in the same way, or use the base rail as a guide if it happens to be the same length. Screw the base rail to the string, then fix the special bolted handrail brackets into the posts and hand-tighten them with a wrench. Check that the posts are upright and that the rails fit properly, then glue the posts into place. Use a gap-filling powder-resin glue, or for a tight joint, woodworker's glue. Tighten the bolts fully, and when the glue has set, install the cover buttons (9) to conceal the nuts.

Fitting the balusters

Calculate the number of balusters you will need, allowing the equivalent of two per tread and one for the tread that is adjacent to the newel. In any event, they should not be spaced any more than 4 inches apart.

To find out how many spacer fillets will be needed, double the number of the balusters and add four.

Measure the vertical distance between the groove in the handrail and that in the base rail, then transfer this dimension to a baluster and mark it out, using the adjustable bevel to give the correct angle. Cut the baluster to size and check it for fit, then cut the others to suit. Space the balusters equally, using the precut fillets to even out the spacing over the total run.

Nail and glue the balusters and fillets in place, and when the adhesive has set, sand them down and finish the bare wood with clear varnish or paint as suits your tastes.

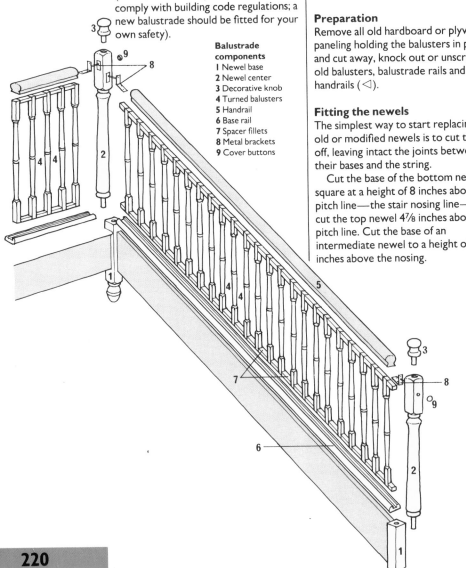

Most pitched roofs were once built on site from individual lengths of timber, but nowadays, for economy of time and materials, many builders use prefabricated from individual lengths of lumber, but specifically designed to meet the loading needs of a given house and, unlike traditional roofs, are usually not suitable for conversion because to remove any part of the structure can cause it to collapse.

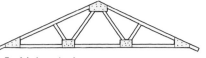

Prefabricated rafter truss

Basic construction

The framework of an ordinary pitched roof is based on a triangle, the most rigid and economical form for a load-bearing structure. The weight of the roof covering is carried by sloping members called rafters, which are set in opposing pairs whose heads meet against a central ridge board running the length of the roof, parallel to the long walls. The lower ends, or feet, of the rafters, are attached to the top plates of the walls.

To stop the roof's weight from pushing the walls out, horizontal members span between rafter ends. When these are level with the top of the walls they may serve as attic floor joists. In open-ceiling construction they are located nearer the ridge board and are called collar ties.

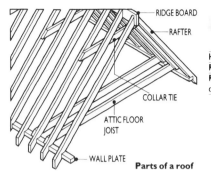

Parts of a roof

SEE ALSO

Details for: ▷	
House construction	120–121
Roof elements	222
Repairing roof coverings	225–227

PITCHED ROOF TYPES

There are a considerable number of roof styles. Nearly all, however, can be classified among these basic types:

FLAT ROOFS

Flat roofs may be supported on joists to which the ceiling material is also attached, or they may be constructed using trusses which have parallel top and bottom members supported by triangular bracing in between. Most flat roofs actually have a slight slope formed by the roofing material to provide drainage.

SHED OR LEAN-TO ROOFS

This is the simplest type of pitched roof. Sometimes it is called a lean-to roof. Inside the structure, the ceiling may be attached directly to the rafters, or supported by horizontal joists, forming a sloping loft above.

GABLE ROOFS

Two shed roofs joined together form the classic gable roof, the most commonly used in contemporary construction. Gable roofs are simple and economical to build, and have excellent loadbearing and drainage capabilities. The end (gable) walls are non-loadbearing.

GAMBREL ROOFS

By breaking the slope of a gable roof, more headroom becomes available in the attic area beneath the rafters, Gambrel and other styles of broken-gable roofs make construction of wide roofs easier also, because it is possible to use shorter lengths of lumber even for spanning large widths.

HIP ROOFS

By sloping the ends of a gable roof toward the center a hip roof is formed. An advantage of this type is the protective overhang formed on all four sides of a house.

INTERSECTING ROOFS

Many houses combine the same or different roof types at angles to each other, to form L- or U-shaped floor plans, as well as other shapes.

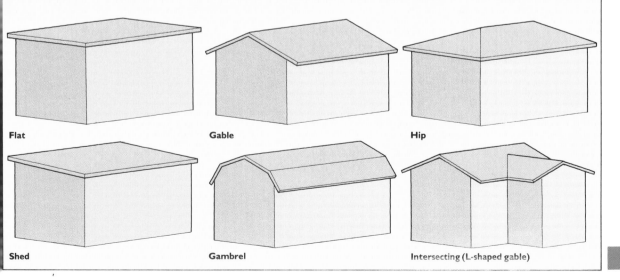

Flat

Gable

Hip

Shed

Gambrel

Intersecting (L-shaped gable)

ROOF ELEMENTS

Hips and valleys
Besides the components mentioned earlier, Gable roofs with intersecting dormers or secondary roofs have additional components. This illustration shows the parts and their names.

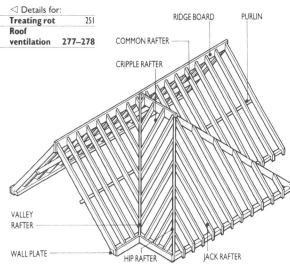

Hips and valleys

Eaves
The overhang of rafters past the outer walls is called the eaves, but sometimes rafters are cut flush with the walls and a fascia board along their ends protects them and supports the guttering (1). Projecting rafters can be left open, the ends exposed (2), and gutter brackets screwed to their sides or top edge.

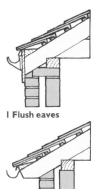

1 Flush eaves

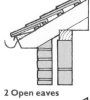

2 Open eaves

Closed eaves
The back of a fascia is usually grooved to take a soffit board, which closes the eaves (3). The board can be at 90 degrees to the wall or slope with the rafters, and it can be of various weather-proof materials. If attic insulation is laid, a roof with closed eaves must be ventilated by a small gap between soffit board and wall or by fitted vents (◁).

3 Closed eaves

The rake
The rake is the sloping edge of the roofing and can end flush with the wall or project past it. A flush rake means a roof structure that stops at the wall, with end rafters placed close to it and the roofing overlying it (4). An overhanging rake means framing extending beyond the wall to carry a fly rafter and fascia with a fascia fixed to it. Behind the fascia may be a soffit board to conceal the fly rafter (5).

ROOF STRUCTURE PROBLEMS

A roof structure can fail when members decay through inadequate weather-proofing, condensation or insect attack. It can also result from overloading caused by too-light original members, a new roof covering of heavier material or the cutting of a window opening that is not properly braced. You can detect any movement of a roof structure from outside. From ground level any sagging of the roof will be seen in the lines of the roof covering.

INSPECTION

The roof should also be inspected from inside. In any case, this should be done annually to check the weathering and for freedom from pest infestation. Work in a good light. If your attic has no lighting use a "trouble light" plugged into a down-stairs wall socket. In an unfloored attic place boards across the joists.

ROT AND INFESTATION

Rot in roof timbers is a serious problem which should be corrected by experts, but its cause should also be identified and promptly dealt with (◁).

Rot is caused by damp conditions that encourage wood-rotting fungi to grow. Inspect the roof covering closely for loose or damaged elements in the general area of the rot, although on a pitched roof water may be penetrating the covering at a higher level and so not be immediately obvious. If the rot is close to a gable wall you should suspect the flashing. Rot can also be caused by condensation, the remedy for which is usually better ventilation.

If you bring in contractors to treat the rot it is better to have them make all the repairs. Their work is covered by a guarantee which may be invalidated if you attempt to deal with the cause yourself to save money.

Insect infestation should also be dealt with by professionals if it is serious. Severely affected wood may have to be cut out and replaced, and the whole structure will have to be fumigated to ensure the problem is remedied.

STRENGTHENING THE ROOF

A roof that shows signs of sagging may have to be braced, though it may not be necessary if a sound structure has stabilized and the roof is weatherproof. In some old buildings a slightly sagging roof line is considered attractive.

Consult an engineer if you suspect a roof is weak. Apart from a sagging roof line, the walls under the eaves should be inspected for bulging and checked with a plumb line. Bulging may occur where window openings are close to the eaves, making a wall relatively weak. It may be due to the roof spreading because of inadequate fastening of the ties and rafters. If this is the case, call in a builder or roofing contractor to make the necessary alterations and improvements.

A lightly constructed roof can be made stronger by adding extra structural members. The method chosen will depend on the type of roof, its span, its loading and its condition. Where the lengths or section of new members are not too large the repair may be possible from inside. If not, at least some of the roof covering may have to be stripped off. Any given roof must be assessed and the most economical solution found for the particular circumstances.

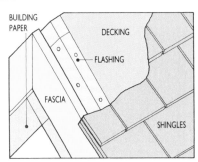

4 Flush rake

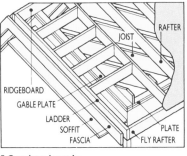

5 Overhanging rake

Generally speaking, the more durable the roof covering, the more expensive it will be, both in materials and labor costs. Try to afford a roof covering with an expected durability of at least 20 years. Besides cost, making a wise roof-covering decision must take into consideration structural factors (heavy roofs such as slate and tile often require more-than-ordinary roof framing), fire-resistance and appearance.

Types

Asphalt shingles: This is the most common roof covering used in the United States. Inexpensive, easy to install and repair, relatively durable, and providing tight protection from wind and rain, asphalt shingles come in many colors, textures and patterns. Different weights have different life-spans. Shingles weighing 235 pounds or more per "square" (the amount needed to cover 100 square feet) normally last 15 to 25 years. Though asphalt shingles are by far the most common type of roof covering, there are many other options.

Roll roofing: This is made from the same material as asphalt shingles, but is manufactured in long rolls. Roll roofing is applied in overlapping layers, giving it a varying lifespan of from 5 to 20 years depending upon the amount of overlap. Roll roofing is inexpensive, easy and quick to apply, but lacks good appearance. Do-it-yourself homebuilders often consider applying a roll roof initially, then reroofing with higher-quality material later when financing permits. Roll-roofing is only partially fire-resistant.

Wood shingles: These are normally sawn from cedar or redwood, come in uniform lengths and thicknesses, and when applied lie flat and smooth on the roof. Two grades are used: one for the starter course and the other for the rest of the roof. A separate grade is used for walls. Wood shingles add beauty and resale value to a home. However, though easy to install, the process is time-consuming, and the shingles themselves are expensive. Wood shingles offer no fire-resistance unless treated and are prohibited in some areas.

Wood shakes: Wood shakes are normally split from logs, rather than sawn, making them somewhat thicker and more irregularly-shaped than shingles. Resawn shakes—split shakes sawn in half through their thickness—have one smooth side and one rough, so they lie flatter when installed. Shakes may last 40 years or more, and because of their looks and durability add very high resale value to a home. Shakes frequently cost twice as much as asphalt shingles, and take much longer to apply. Like wood shingles, they are combustible.

Metal: Very expensive terne and copper roofing is available, but most homeowners choosing metal roof-covering select galvanized steel sheet or aluminum, which comes in 2-foot-wide strips up to 18 feet long. The panels overlap each other along raised crimps through which they are nailed with special nails. Sheet-metal roofing is very easy to apply, and has a life-span of 30 to 60 years. Sheet-metal roofing is also inexpensive, costing about the same as asphalt shingles yet requiring less labor to install. Metal roofs do not add appreciable resale value, however.

Slate: Because of its high expense and difficulty of application, slate is seldom used for new roofs, especially in areas where slate is not naturally-occurring. However, slate roofs frequently outlast their houses, and add high resale value. Slates are easily broken by falling tree branches, and their dark color retains heat in summer. Slate is, of course, fireproof.

Tile: There are several types on the market. Traditional clay tiles are time-consuming and difficult to apply; newer concrete tiles are easier and quicker, and some do not require extensive roof framing. Tile is beautiful, durable (30- to 60-year lifespan), and fireproof. But materials and labor expense is high and like slate, tile breaks easily under impact.

SEE ALSO

Details for: ▷	
House construction	120–121
Repairing roof coverings	225–227
Roll roofing	228

Asphalt shingles

Roll roofing

Wood shingles

Wood shakes

Slate

Tile

SLOPE AND PITCH

Slope and pitch are often incorrectly used as synonyms. While both terms do refer to the incline of a roof, slope identifies the incline as a ratio of the roof's vertical rise to the horizontal run of one side, but pitch identifies the incline as a ratio of the rise to *twice* the run, thus taking into account both sides of the roof.

Sometimes slope is expressed as a fraction, but, to use as an example a roof that rises 4 inches for each foot (12 inches) of run, usually such an incline is referred to as having a "4-in-12 slope." Pitch, on the other hand, is always expressed as a fraction. The pitch of a roof with a 4-in-12 slope is 1/6.

SLOPE = RISE / RUN   PITCH = RISE / 2 × RUN

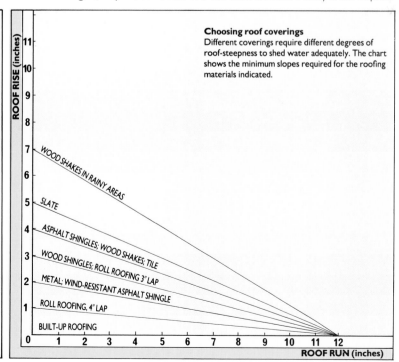

Choosing roof coverings
Different coverings require different degrees of roof-steepness to shed water adequately. The chart shows the minimum slopes required for the roofing materials indicated.

ROOF RISE (inches)

WOOD SHAKES IN RAINY AREAS
SLATE
ASPHALT SHINGLES; WOOD SHAKES; TILE
WOOD SHINGLES; ROLL ROOFING 3" LAP
METAL; WIND-RESISTANT ASPHALT SHINGLE
ROLL ROOFING, 4" LAP
BUILT-UP ROOFING

ROOF RUN (inches)

CHECKING FOR LEAKS

Most roof leaks become noticeable when they produce wet spots on ceilings.

Seldom, though, are the sources for leaks directly above the spots.

Analyzing the symptoms

Leaks near where chimneys pass close to walls or through roofs are relatively easy to pinpoint: generally they are the result of defective or damaged flashing. Leaks which appear elsewhere indicate the need for roof repair.

If the house has an unfinished attic, simply examine the underside of the decking near the wet spot during a rainstorm. Use a strong light, preferably a "trouble light" equipped with a 100-watt bulb. If the leak is not visible over the spot, search "uphill" of the leak until you find droplets of water entering through the decking at some point. You should then be able to trace their trail down to the spot. You can make a temporary repair by applying caulking compound over the area where the water is entering. Be sure to press the sealer in tightly. Or, you may opt for the traditional remedy of placing a large pan beneath a dripping area and emptying it as it becomes full. In either case, you should make permanent repairs as soon as possible. On the day of the repair, start by driving a small nail through the roof from the underside so that you can locate the leak from outside on the roof surface.

If the underside of the roof decking is covered, you may still be able to estimate the leak's source from below, and remove batts of insulation until you locate the trouble spot. However, if the attic is finished with wallboard, your only course of action is to locate the leak from the outside.

To do this, measure from the wet spot on the ceiling to some point of reference that is also visible outside, such as the chimney. Then, go up on the roof and duplicate the measurement. Search around the point and above it, bearing in mind that water can travel horizontally and diagonally in addition to straight down from its source to the point of entry, but it can never travel uphill. Look for curled, cracked or missing shingles, torn roofing paper, rotted decking, corroded flashing, any place that suggests it might admit moisture, especially if driven by wind.

Be especially cautious when climbing around on roofs. Wear sneakers and clothing that allows unrestricted movement, and stay off roofs in wet or very windy weather. Also, don't walk on roofing materials in near—or below—freezing temperatures, or in extremely hot weather. Cold makes asphalt brittle; heat can cause it to stretch and tear. In either situation you risk doing more damage to the roof than has already occurred. Under such conditions, or if the roof is steep-sloped or is covered with naturally-fragile materials (slate, tile, asbestos-cement shingles) use a lightweight roof ladder that hooks over the peak of the roof and affords safe access while distributing weight over a broad area.

When using a ladder, always be sure it is well-seated at the base, and that it extends at least 2 to 3 feet above the highest point you will be working on, so that you will have something to hold onto especially if you will be climbing on and off the ladder to reach the roof. Have a helper support the ladder from below while you are climbing up or down.

Carrying a ladder
Hold the ladder nearly vertical, braced with your body. Keep the base close to the ground.

Locating a ladder
Locate the foot of a ladder away from the wall ¼ the distance of its height; an angle of about 75°.

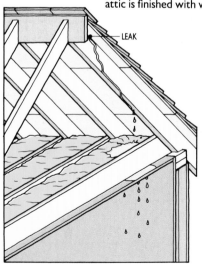

Locate leaks from inside

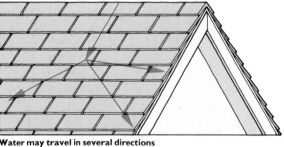

Water may travel in several directions

Drive nails to find leaks from outside

Working from a ladder
Do not reach sideways beyond the point where you must move your hips past the rails.

LEAK

ROOF SAFETY

Working on a roof can be hazardous, and if you are unsure of yourself on heights you should call in a contractor to do the work. If you do decide to do it yourself, do not use ladders alone for roof work. Rent a sectional scaffold tower and scaffold boards to provide a safe working platform.

Roof coverings are fairly fragile and should not be walked on. Rent crawl boards or special roof ladders to gain access. A roof ladder should reach from the scaffold tower to the roof's ridge and hook over it. On some models wheel the ladder up the slope and then turn it over to engage the hook (1).

Roof ladders are made with rails that keep the treads clear of the roof surface and spread the load (2), but if you think it's necessary you can place additional padding of paper-stuffed or sand-filled sacks to help spread the load further.

Never leave tools on the roof when they are not being used, and keep those that are needed safely contained inside the ladder framework.

1 Engage the hook of the ladder over the ridge

2 Roof ladders spread the load

REPAIRING ROOF COVERINGS

Repairing asphalt shingles

Curled shingles or those slightly torn or broken off can be repaired. Badly damaged shingles should be replaced. It is best to take the weather into account:

Work on a warm, sunny day if possible, so that shingle material will be pliable but not soft to the touch. Cold stiffens shingles, causing them to crack easily.

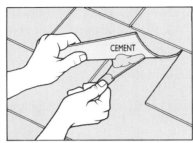

1 Fixing lifted or curled shingles
Apply a spot of roofing cement to the underside, then weight shingle with a brick. For torn shingles, apply cement liberally, press shingle down and nail both edges. Apply caulk, silicone sealer or roofing cement to nail holes before nailing heads down.

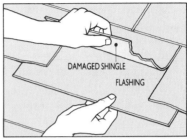

2 Repairing broken shingles
Cut a piece of metal flashing to size of original plus 3 in. on all sides. Apply roofing cement to underside of flashing, slide it in place beneath damaged shingle, then apply cement to top of flashing and press damaged shingle onto to it.

Replacing a shingle

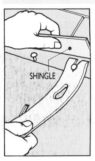
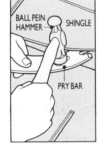

1 Replacing a shingle
Remove it from beneath those above. Carefully lift them and pry out the nails underneath using a putty knife and pry bar. If they won't come out, hammer them flat by laying the pry bar on the heads and striking it with hammer.

2 Sliding the new shingle into place
Align bottom edge of new shingle with the edges of the shingles on either side. Nail it in place, starting at one side and nailing across. Be sure overlapping shingles cover the nails by at least 1 in. Apply cement to the shingles lifted, and weight them flat.

Hips and ridges

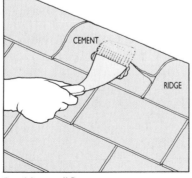
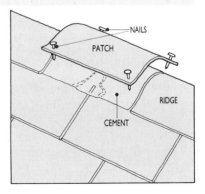

Repairing small flaws
Cover small damaged areas with roofing cement. If damage is more extensive, repair with flashing as shown above or with a patch made of shingle (shown here). Apply cement to the damaged shingle, press the patch over it and nail all four corners. Apply caulk, silicone sealer or roofing cement to nail holes before nailing heads down to discourage leaking.

SEE ALSO

Details for: ▷	
Reroofing	230–231
Flashing	232–233

REPAIRING ROOF COVERINGS

Repairing wood shingles

Thorough ventilation is the key to preserving wood shingles. Unless they can dry out after becoming wet they will rot. Shingle roofs often have wide spaces between decking boards to allow significant air flow underneath. However, even if solid decking such as plywood is used, underlayment—usually asphalt-saturated felt paper—is omitted between decking and shingles,

and between courses of shingles themselves. Under- and interlayment is recommended under and between wood shakes.

Work from a roof ladder when repairing wood shingles, to avoid damaging brittle shingles. The best time for shingle repair is the day after a soaking rain, when the shingles are still soft.

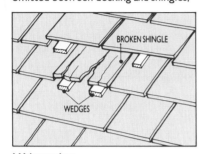

1 Using wedges
Drive wedges beneath damaged shingle and overlapping shingles in upper course.

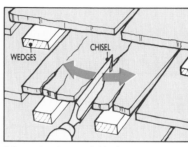

2 Removing damaged shingle
Remove damaged shingle by splitting it apart using a chisel.

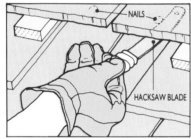

3 Sawing through nails
Saw through nails holding damaged shingle. Use a hacksaw blade wrapped with duct tape.

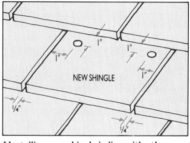

4 Installing new shingle in line with others
Leave ¼-in. gap on each side. Nail in place 1 in. from edges and top.

Replacing hips and ridges

Where shingles meet at hip and ridge seams, the most common treatment is the Boston ridge, which is formed by nailing together pairs of shingles or 1-inch-thick (nominal) boards along the seam. Nails holding each pair to the roof are covered by the overlapping pair next to it. Alternate the overlapping

ends of the boards making up each pair. As an alternative, several pairs of long boards can be butt-joined. To splice the boards, apply a layer of caulk to the ends and portions of the top and bottom surfaces, then nail metal flashing across the seam, pressing it down into the caulk.

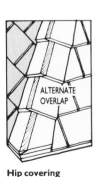

Hip covering

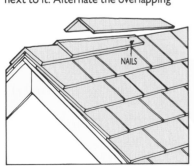

Boston ridge

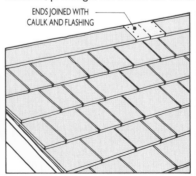

Single-board ridge

REPLACING A TILE

Individual tiles can be difficult to remove for two reasons: the retaining nibs on their back edges and their interlocking shape which holds them together.

You can remove a broken plain tile by simply lifting it so that the nibs clear the batten on which they rest, then drawing it out. This is made easier if the overlapping tiles are first lifted with wooden wedges inserted at both sides of the tile to be removed (**1**).

If the tile is also nailed try rocking it loose. If this fails you will have to break it out carefully. You may then have to use a slate hook or hacksaw blade to extract or cut any remaining nails.

Use a similar technique for single-lap interlocking tiles, but in this case you will also have to wedge up the tile to the left of the one being removed (**2**). If the tile is of a deep profile you will have to ease up a number of the surrounding tiles to get the required clearance.

If you are taking out a tile to put in a roof ventilator unit you can afford to smash it with a hammer. But take care not to damage any of the adjacent tiles. The remaining tiles should be easier to remove once the first is out.

1 Lift the overlapping tiles with wedges

2 Lift interlocking tiles above and to the left

CUTTING TILES

To cut tiles use an abrasive cutting disc in a power saw or rent an angle grinder for the purpose. Always wear protective goggles and a mask when cutting with a power tool.

For small work use a tungsten grit blade in a hacksaw frame or, if trimming only, use pincers but score the cutting line first with a tile cutter.

REBEDDING RIDGE TILES

Ridge tiles on old roofs often become loose because of a breakdown of the old lime mortar.

To rebed ridge tiles, first lift them off and clear all the old crumbling mortar from the roof, and from the undersides of the tiles.

Give the tiles a good soaking in water before starting to fasten them. Mix a new bedding mortar of 1 part cement to 3 parts sand. It should be a stiff mix and not at all runny. Load about half a bucketful and carry it on to the roof.

Dampen the top courses of the roof tiles and apply the mortar with the trowel to form a continuous edge bedding about 2 inches wide and 3 inches high, following the line left behind by the old mortar.

Where the ridge tiles butt together, or come against a wall, place a solid bedding of mortar, inserting pieces of tile in it to reduce shrinkage. Place the mortar for all the tiles in turn, setting each tile into place and pressing it firmly into the mortar. Strike off any squeezed-out mortar cleanly with the trowel, without smearing the tile. Ridge tiles should not be pointed.

Apply bands of bedding mortar on each side

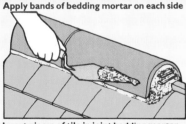
Insert pieces of tile in joint bedding mortar

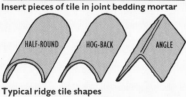
HALF-ROUND   HOG-BACK   ANGLE
Typical ridge tile shapes

REPAIRING ROOF COVERINGS

Mending metal roofing

Leaks due to broken nail heads, splits and small punctures can be patched with flashing cement or fiberglass asphalt-patching cement sold by building suppliers. If new roof sections are needed, try to match the old ones. Obtain sections long enough to reach from ridge to eaves if possible. Otherwise, overlap seams at least 6 inches and be sure top sections overlap those underneath. Lap vertical seams away from direction of prevailing winds. New galvanized roofing will not hold paint until weathered, usually one year. Wear sneakers when working on metal roofs; also gloves, especially if metal is hot.

SEE ALSO

Details for: ▷

Reroofing	230–231
Flashing	232–233

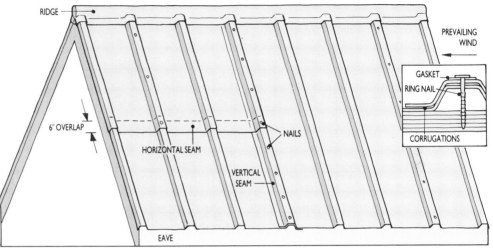

Installing new roof section
To install new roof section, overlap corrugations. Nail through ridges into decking. Use neoprene-gasketed ring-shank nails to prevent leaks and to hold fast despite fluctuations of metal due to temperature changes.

Removing and replacing a slate

A slate may slip out of place because its nails become corroded or because of a breakdown of the material of the slate itself. Whatever the cause, slipped or broken slates must be replaced as soon as possible.

Use a slate hook to remove the trapped part of a broken slate. Slip the tool under the slate and locate its hooked end over one of the nails (1), then pull down hard on the tool to extract or cut through the nail. Remove the second nail in the same way. Even where an aged slate has already slipped out completely you may have to remove the nails in the same way to allow the replacement slate to be slipped in.

You will not be able to nail the new slate in place. Instead cut a 1-inch-wide strip of copper to the length of the slate lap plus 1 inch and nail the strip to the sheathing, securing it between the slates of the lower course (2). Then slide the new slate into position and turn back the end of the lead strip to secure it (3).

1 Pull out nails

2 Nail strip to sheathing

3 Fold strip over edge

Cutting slate

With a sharp point mark out the right size on the back of the slate, either by measuring it out or scribing around another slate of that size. Place the slate, bevelled side down, on a bench, the cutting line level with the bench's edge, then chop the slate with the edge of a bricklayer's trowel. Work from both edges towards the middle, using the edge of the bench as a guide. Mark the nail holes and punch them out with a nail or drill them with a bit the size of the nails. Support the slate well while making the holes.

Asbestos cement slates
These can be cut by scribing the lines, then breaking the slates over a straight edge or sawing with a general-purpose saw. If you saw them, wear a mask, keep dust damped down well and sweep it into a plastic bag for disposal.

FLAT AND ROLL ROOFING

Flat (built-up) roofs

Flat roofs (most of which actually have a very slight pitch to promote drainage) depend on a seamless waterproof membrane to prevent leaks. Although some flat roofs are made of metal, the most common are made up of alternating layers of asphalt-saturated roofing felt and either liquid asphalt or melted coal tar. The first layer is nailed to the roof dry (with no liquid underneath) to prevent subsequent coatings from leaking through to the ceiling. Gravel, crushed stone or marble chips are spread over the top surface to reflect heat (which preserves the roofing) and provide coloring. Substitutes for the liquid coating—which must be applied hot—have recently come on the market and include synthetic rubber, mastic, fiberglass, and other compounds, all of which may be applied cold but with varying results. Unless only minor repairs are present, it is usually best to have flat roofs resurfaced professionally.

SEE ALSO

◁ Details for:
Roof types   221

Roll roofing

Roll roofing can be used on both flat and pitched roofs. It is sold in 36-foot rolls, 3 feet wide, and is applied using wide-head galvanized or aluminum shingle nails. On flat roofs and those with slopes to 1-in-12, each course is laid so that it overlaps the one underneath it by 19 inches. This method is called "double-coverage." Roll roofing designed to be applied in this way is made with only about half the width of the material coated with mineral granules. The smooth portion, which lies underneath each overlapping course, is called the selvage. On steeper roofs with slopes to 3-in-12, roll roofing with only 4-inch-wide, and even 3-inch-wide, selvage may be used. Because so little of each course overlaps the one beneath it this method of application is called "single-coverage." Roll roofing is easy to apply, repair and reapply. However, it must be unrolled in place the day before installation to allow it to expand, soften, and lie flat; otherwise it will buckle. When nailing roll roofing, always work from one end of a strip to the other, never from the ends toward the middle.

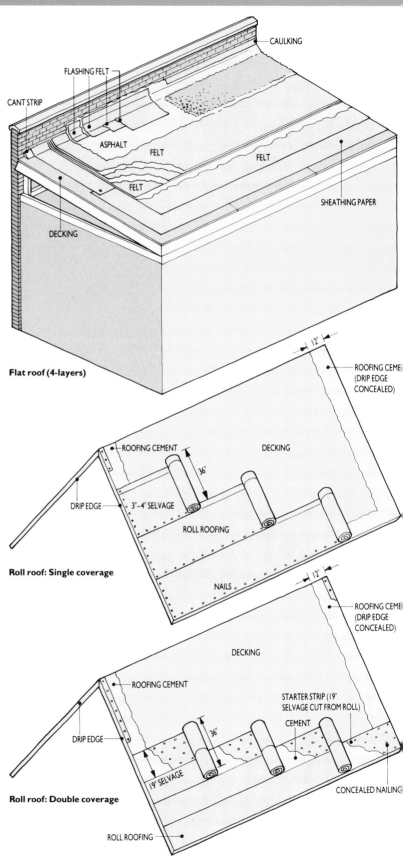

Flat roof (4-layers)

Roll roof: Single coverage

Roll roof: Double coverage

REPAIRING FLAT ROOFS

Mending blisters and splits

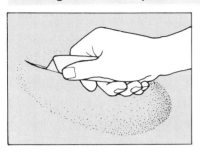

1 Slice through blistered layers
Use a sharp utility knife, and leave lower layers of roofing intact.

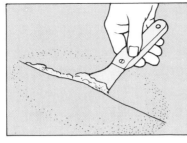

2 Work roofing cement under loose felt
Apply cement under both sides of slit, using a flexible-blade putty knife.

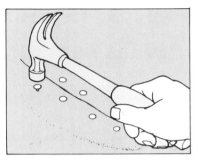

3 Nail both sides of split flat
Use wide-headed galvanized or aluminum shingle nails on both sides of the cut.

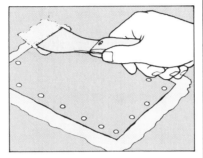

4 Cover repair with roof cement
Add patch of shingle. Nail patch around edges; seal with cement.

Patching damaged areas

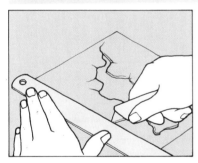

1 Cut out damaged area
Use sharp utility knife. Use straightedge to make square or rectangular cut.

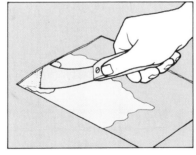

2 Apply roofing cement to exposed area
Using putty knife, lift edges carefully and force cement underneath as well.

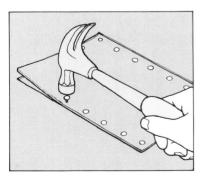

3 Nail down exact-size patch of shingle
Layer several together if necessary to bring patch level with the finished surface.

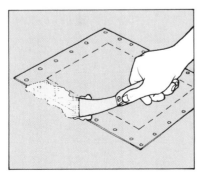

4 Apply cement, then nail down top patch
Top patch should be cut 2 in. oversize. Seal edges and nails with cement.

INSPECTION

Inspect flat roofs once a year. Do the job in two stages: once on a dry day, and again just after a rain so that you can observe standing pools of water. Wear soft-soled shoes and walk gently; one of the chief causes of leaks in a built-up roof is breakdown caused by careless walking on the roof in heavy work boots. If the roof is visited frequently install a wooden walkway supported on 2×4s laid horizontally to spread weight and distribute pressure over a large area. This prevents damage.

Leaks are generally located directly over their evidence on the ceiling below. Chief causes of leaks are moisture trapped between layers of roofing due to incorrect application, drying out or cracking of the layers due to deterioration caused by ultraviolet radiation, and inadequate flashing of roof edges and openings. Most leaks, in fact, appear where the roof meets the edges of the building.

Clean away debris—especially areas of damp slit or debris—from the roof and gutters. Look for blisters or ripples in the roof surface, as well as slits, cracks, areas of torn roofing and places where flashing has come loose or deteriorated. Do not tamper with untorn blisters or loose flashing until you are ready to make repairs. Blisters not located near ceiling damage and which do not expell water when pressure is applied should not be disturbed or repaired.

SEE ALSO

Details for: ▷
Flashing repairs   233

Treating the whole surface

A roof which has already been patched and is showing general signs of wear and tear can be given an extra lease on life by covering it with black asphalt roof coating—not roofing cement—especially designed for the purpose. Coating is available at many building supply and hardware stores.

First sweep the roof thoroughly to remove any loose debris, including pebbles which may have been part of the original roof covering. Then, apply the coating with a long-handled brush made for the job. Work only a small area at a time, resweeping as you go. Be sure to start at the highest point on the roof and work downward, also leaving yourself an escape route. Cover this path later, after the rest of the roof has dried. Spreading gravel or stone chips over modern flat-roof coatings is usually unnecessary. Consult the supplier or manufacturer to be sure.

REROOFING PITCHED ROOFS

When roofing has become so worn that massive or frequent repairs are needed, it is often more feasible to renew the entire roof. However, before you order the work, inspect the decking and rafters for signs of rot or damage. If the roof is quite old or you suspect it is unsound, perform the inspection first from in the attic underneath, to avoid risking an accident by walking on weakened roof members. Probe exposed wood with a penknife or awl. Remove insulation batts if necessary. Look for spongy or crumbly wood—indicating rot—and stained areas which mark present or past areas of leakage. Rotten areas must be replaced. If extensive, the entire roof should be resheathed and perhaps reframed.

New roofing over old

New asphalt or wood shingles can usually be laid directly over a single layer of old shingles, provided the roof deck and framing underneath is sound and the original shingles are not badly warped. New shingles, unless they are wood laid over an old layer of asphalt, will in time mold to the shape of those underneath, exaggerating any irregularities. Roofs with slopes greater than 6-in-12 may accept three layers of shingles provided the rafters are at least 2×8 and the combined weight of the additional shingles plus load factors meets code requirements. Check with your building inspector when planning the job.

To prepare an ordinary asphalt-shingled roof for reroofing, renail all loose or warped shingles and patch broken ones with asphalt scraps nailed in place to fill out their contours.

Remove any protruding nails. Break back shingles along the borders of the roof so they lie flush with the edges (or break them back further and attach lengths of 1×6 lumber as nailing surfaces) and install metal drip-edge flashing around the edge of the roof. Remove the ridge shingles.

Apply new shingles as you would to felt underlayment. Remove the nails from chimney and pipe flashing as you reach them and slide the new shingles underneath. When renailing flashing, apply roofing cement as well. At TV antennas, remove each guy wire as you reach it then refasten it in a new spot—and dab roofing cement over the fitting—after shingling the area. Around the mast plate, cut new shingles carefully and cover the seams with roofing cement.

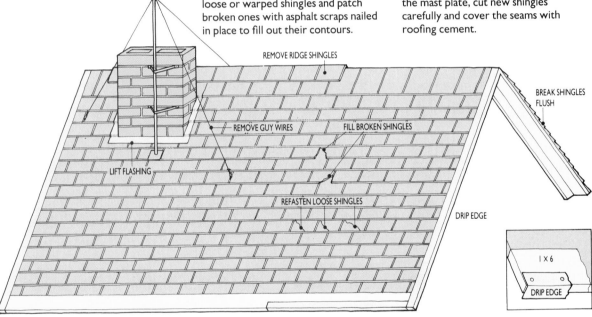

REMOVE RIDGE SHINGLES

BREAK SHINGLES FLUSH

REMOVE GUY WIRES

FILL BROKEN SHINGLES

LIFT FLASHING

REFASTEN LOOSE SHINGLES

DRIP EDGE

1 × 6

DRIP EDGE

Pry bar

Ice chopper

Stripping shingles

Badly warped roofs or those with several layers of shingles must be stripped before reroofing. Popular tools for this job are a long-handled ice chopper and a short, flat steel pry bar.

Choose a period of fair weather for working, and strip only as large an area as you can cover securely in case of rain. Work from a ladder or scaffold to remove the lower shingle courses then attach roofing jacks to the decking to remove shingles farther up. Spread plastic or a tarp on the ground below to make clean up easier. Bare roof decks can be slippery, so wear non-slip shoes and use extreme caution.

Roofing jacks

Roofing jacks, available at rent-it centers or easily made on the job, are wood or steel triangular brackets used for supporting horizontal planks along the length of pitched roofs. They're essential for safety when working on steeply pitched roofs. The brackets fasten with nails directly into the roof deck. The nail holes are filled with roof cement on removal. Commercial jacks adjust to match the slope of the roof.

Use 3 jacks to support a 16-foot length of 2×10 plank (or 2 brackets per 8-foot span). Install the end jacks first, using at least three 8d nails per bracket, then the middle one(s).

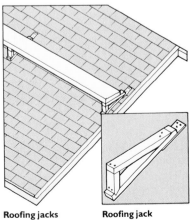

Roofing jacks   **Roofing jack**

REROOFING PITCHED ROOFS

Underlayment

Except with wood shingles, where optimum ventilation is essential, new decking and decking stripped of old roofing should be covered with 15-pound asphalt-saturated felt paper as underlayment. Felt paper prevents the passage of moisture but not vapor. Do not use plastic sheeting.

Professional roofers often cover the entire roof with underlayment before reshingling because of the extra protection it affords the deck in case of rain. However, because wind easily damages thin felt paper, you may wish to apply underlayment in stages.

To apply underlayment, first be sure the decking surface is dry, smooth, and free of protruding nails and splinters. Apply roofing cement to the upper surface of the drip edge and along the seam where it meets the decking, then set the roll of paper at one end of the roof and unroll it horizontally, allowing ¼ inch of the drip edge to extend beyond the paper. Staple the paper to the decking in as few places as possible, just enough to hold it in place until new shingles can be applied over top. Overlap subsequent courses of paper 2 inches over the course below; 4 inches at vertical seams. Always staple from one end of the course to the other to avoid producing a ripple in the center. At roof or hip ridges, fold the paper over the peak from each side to produce a double thickness. At valleys, overlap the flashing 4 inches on each side, also producing a double thickness of paper. Fasten the underlayment to the flashing using wide-head roofing nails made of metal compatible with the flashing material.

Bevel strips

When reroofing over wood or multi-layer asphalt shingles, the new layer of shingles will severely distort unless the tops of the new shingles are placed gainst the bottoms (butts) of the old. To level the old roof surface and permit greater freedom in laying the new shingles, nail strips of beveled wood siding against the butts of shingles before applying the new layer. Strips also form a solid nailing base for new shingles. Rip the siding so that its thickest edge equals the thickness of the shingle butts and attach it with that edge adjacent to the old shingles. Use 8d nails driven into rafters beneath decking.

Applying 3-tab asphalt shingles

Begin shingling at the eaves. First attach a single course of full-length shingles (trim 3 inches from their width at the tab ends) top-edge down along the length of the roof using wide-head shingle nails. Extend the shingles ¼-inch beyond the drip edge. Then nail a second layer of full-size shingles top-edge up over the first layer to complete the starter course.

So that the cutouts in each shingle will always center over the tabs in the course below, remove half a tab from the first shingle starting the second course. Attach the shingle so it exposes 6 inches of the one beneath. Lay the rest of the course, nailing 1 inch and 12 inches from each end, ⅝ inch above the cutouts. Space subsequent shingles to provide the same exposure. After completing the second course, start the third, removing an entire tab from the first shingle in the course.

Snap a horizontal chalk line measured from the eaves to mark the upper edge of the fourth course. Use a shingle with 1½ tabs removed to start, then lay the shingles to the line to compensate for errors in the previous 3 courses. Repeat the entire 4-stage process until you reach the ridge, then work up from the other side of the roof. Trim shingles to lie along the ridge. Cover their top edges with a strip of flashing folded lengthwise, then apply overlapping single shingle-tabs. Cover the nail heads of the last shingle with roofing cement to prevent leakage.

SEE ALSO

Details for: ▷
Roof coverings   223

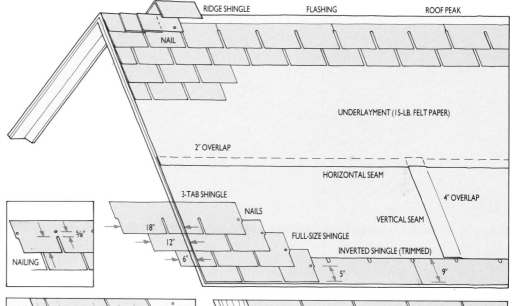

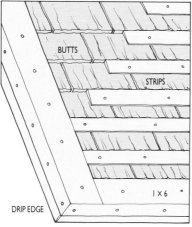

Details for reroofing over wood shingles

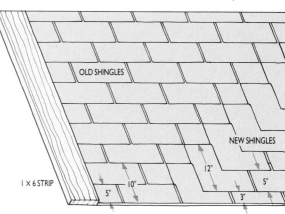

Covering old shingles
Trim and apply new shingles against butts of old layer.

231

FLASHING

Flashing is used to prevent moisture from entering under the roof covering wherever two or more planes of a roof meet or wherever the roof meets a vertical surface. It is also used along edges of roofs and other windows and doorways to direct moisture away from the house exterior and structural framing. Roll roofing material is widely used for flashing, particularly along ridges and hips, and at valleys. However, the most durable flashing materials are sheet aluminum, copper or galvanized steel. All are sold in rolls especially for the purpose.

SEE ALSO

◁ Details for:
Checking for leaks   224

Inspecting flashing

Inspect flashing at least once a year. It is a prime location for roof leaks. Look for cracks and separations where the flashing meets the chimney, vent stack, dormer and abutment walls, and where roof planes meet at valleys. Sometimes damaged flashing is discolored. Very old flashing sometimes develops pinholes which are hard to see so if possible, check the roof from below for leaks.

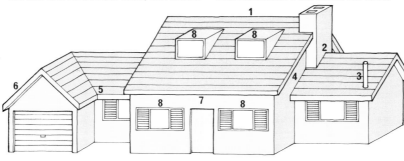

Flashing locations (typical)
1 Ridge
2 Chimney
3 Vent stack
4 Vertical wall
5 Valley
6 Rake
7 Eave
8 Drip edge

Maintenance and repair

It is not a bad idea to coat all flashing seams periodically with asphalt roofing cement, especially at chimney and vent-stack seams. Apply the cement using a small mason's trowel and smooth the contours of the cement so that it does not form hollows and ridges where water may collect and lead to leaks or damage. Where you find holes of 1-square-inch or more, cut a patch from the same material as the flashing, 1 inch larger all around than the hole. Apply cement to the damaged flashing, press the patch into place, then cover the entire area with cement and smooth the surface.

Repointing flashing

Rake out joint and repoint with fresh mortar

Where flashing meets brickwork it is usually embedded in mortar. Separations here require immediate repair since the loose flashing actually collects water and funnels it down beneath the roof where it may spread and do considerable damage. To repair, provided the flashing itself is sound, rake out the old mortar from the seam to a depth of about ¾ inch. Press the flashing back into place, wedging it if necessary with small stones, then fill the seam with fresh mortar, using a trowel. Smooth the seam carefully. Seal the flashing with asphalt roofing cement after the mortar has fully cured. If the flashing is corroded or damaged, you will have to replace it.

Galvanic action

Corrosion Table
1. Aluminum
2. Zinc
3. Steel
4. Tin
5. Lead
6. Brass
7. Copper
8. Bronze

Metals touching each other react when wet. As a result, metal flashing must be fastened with nails made of the same metal as the flashing, otherwise one or the other will corrode, often quickly. If it is impossible to match flashing and fasteners, use neoprene or asphalt washers with the fasteners to prevent direct contact between the two different metals. The chart shows commonly-used construction metals. When paired, metals farthest apart in the series corrode soonest and fastest. Metals in contact with certain acid-containing woods such as redwood and red cedar can also corrode. When purchasing flashing, exterior wood shingles or siding, and fasteners to match, ask your building-materials supplier for advice.

REPLACING CHIMNEY FLASHING

Chimney flashing is usually in two parts: the base (or step) flashing, which wraps completely around the base of the chimney and extends several inches under the roof covering, and the cap (or counter) flashing, which covers the top edges of the base flashing. Sometimes roofing felt extends up the sides of the chimney, taking the place of metal base flashing.

To replace, carefully chisel out the mortar joints securing the cap flashing and remove it. Then chisel the joints further, to a depth of 1½ inches. Remove any roof shingles or other covering overlapping the base flashing, and carefully pry it free. Use the old flashing as patterns to cut new pieces, preferably from copper sheet sold for the purpose. Bend the flashing to shape after cutting, then fasten it in place using asphalt roofing cement. Attach the front piece of base flashing first, then the sides. Fasten the back piece last.

Refasten or replace the shingles after attaching the base flashing. Then install the cap flashing (follow the same order—front, sides, back) and seal all the joints with fresh mortar where appropriate, and roofing cement.

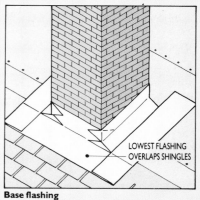

LOWEST FLASHING OVERLAPS SHINGLES

Base flashing

CAPS

SHINGLES OVERLAP FLASHING

Cap flashing

FLASHING REPAIRS

Flashing a vent stack

Sometimes you may be able to stop leaks by tightening the lead collar (if present) around the neck of the pipe where it passes through the roof. To do this, tap with a screwdriver or blunt mason's chisel and a hammer around the upper rim of the collar, sealing it against the stack. Also try coating the entire flashing area and lower portion of the vent stack with roofing cement.

To apply new flashing if repair is not possible, first remove the shingles covering the old flashing. In some cases you then may be able merely to slip a new piece of flashing over the old one and replace the roofing. Otherwise, pry up the old flashing as well, place a new piece of felt over the existing one, install the new flashing and then re-apply the roofing. The flashing must overlap the downhill shingles yet lie underneath those uphill.

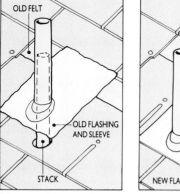

1 Remove shingles and old flashing

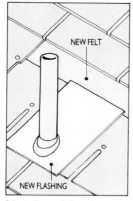

2 Install new felt and flashing

3 Reapply shingles

Renewing valley flashing

Where shingles are trimmed so that flashing is visible, the construction is termed "open valley." In a "closed valley," shingles overlap the flashing from view.

Small repairs to open valley flashing can be made with roofing cement. Larger holes can be patched as described on page 232, provided the upper edge of the patch can be slipped beneath an overlapping piece of flashing above. Leaks from no apparent source may sometimes be stopped by applying a bead of cement between the edges of the trimmed shingles and the flashing.

To repair closed valley flashing, first try slipping squares of copper or aluminum flashing material underneath the shingles in the damaged area. Loosen or remove the nails closest to the valley, then prebend and install the squares beginning at the bottom of the roof. Overlap them until they extend 2 inches beyond the damaged area. Renail the shingles and cover the nail heads with roofing cement. If leaks persist, remove the valley shingles and install new flashing. Then replace the shingles.

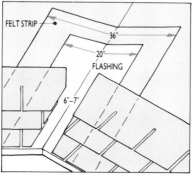

Open valley flashing

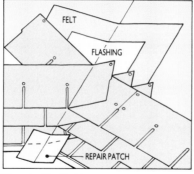

Closed valley flashing

Vertical wall flashing

A row of individual, overlapping flashing shingles are often installed where dormers join roofs and where roofs of different heights butt against each other. To locate and repair leaks in these areas, siding and roofing must be removed. Look for rotten or discolored sheathing, and evidence that settling has occurred which may have pulled house sections slightly apart. After remedying these problems, fill any gaps between building sections with strips of wood, apply new felt underlayment over the area, then reflash the area as you reshingle, by attaching a flashing shingle at the end of each course, fastened to the vertical surface with one nail at the upper corner. Each shingle should overlap the one underneath, and extend 4 inches up the vertical section and 2 inches under the roof covering. After the roofing is complete, attach new siding to cover the top edge of the flashing.

Drip flashing

During construction, strips of flashing are installed above doors and windows and along roof edges. These should extend several inches under the siding or roof covering and be nailed well away from the edges. On roofs, the drip edge goes on top of the underlayment along the rake and beneath it at the eaves. If minor repairs do not suffice, remove the siding or roof covering overlapping the flashing. Determine the cause of the leak, then refasten or (if necessary) replace the drip edge, cover the seams with roofing cement and reinstall the exterior material.

Repairing flat roof flashing

Felts comprising a built-up roof are generally left long at the edges and angled upward to create a raised flashing that directs water away from the edge. Cracks often develop where the angle begins. To repair, first cement down any loose flaps of roofing, then cover the area with a generous layer of roofing cement. Cut additional strips of felt, and build up the flashing by laying down alternate layers of felt and cement to obtain a smooth, even rise with no hollows that can retain water.

SEE ALSO

Details for: ▷

Checking for leaks	224
Repairing roofs	225–227

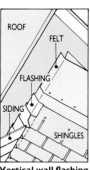

Vertical wall flashing

Drip edge

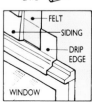

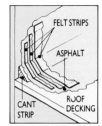

Flat roof

ROOF DRAINAGE

An adequate system of gutters and downspouts in good working condition is essential to maintaining the rest of the home. Gutters prevent water from running down the sides of the house, causing discoloration. Combined with downspouts, gutters also direct water away from the

foundation of the building, lessening the risk of basement flooding and foundation settling. Gutters also help to prevent the washing out of flowerbeds and other landscaping around the perimeter of the house. Keeping the system working requires regular inspection and maintenance.

Gutters and downspouts

Gutters are made of a number of materials. Wood was once traditional in America, along with cast iron or copper for masonry structures. Although new homes in some regions are still built with wood gutters, in most cases galvanized sheet metal (iron), stainless steel, aluminum, fiberglass and vinyl are most common.

The size and layout of a guttering system must enable it to discharge all the water from a given roof area. The flow load required depends mainly on the area of the roof. For roofs with areas less than 750 square feet, gutters with 4-inch-wide troughs usually suffice. Choose 5-inch gutters for roofs with

areas between 750 and 1400 square feet; 6-inch gutters are available for even larger roofs.

Downspouts also should be properly sized to carry away runoff adequately. For roof areas up to 1,000 square feet, 3-inch-diameter downspouts are ordinarily sufficient. Larger roofs require 4-inch-diameter spouts. The location of downspouts can affect the system's performance. A system with a central downspout can serve double the roof area of one with an end outlet. A right-angled bend in the guttering will reduce the flow capacity by about 20 percent if it is placed at a point near the outlet.

GUTTER HANGERS

Three styles of gutter-fastening hardware are popular. Although 30-inch spacing is standard, 24-inch spacing provides increased support necessary to withstand snow and ice loads.

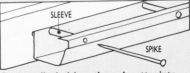

Gutter spike is driven through gutter into fascia board. Sleeve fits in trough

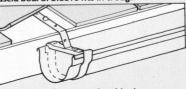

Strap hanger fastens under shingle

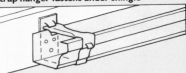

Bracket fastens to fascia board

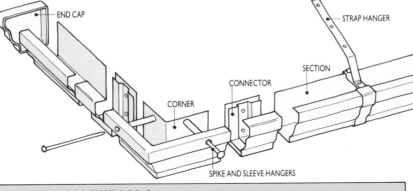

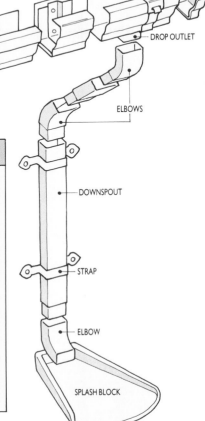

GUTTER MATERIALS

Wood gutters made of fir, redwood or red cedar (all decay-resistant) are used in some parts of the country, generally with wood-shingled roofs. Wood gutters are very sturdy and if maintained will last the life of the house.

Galvanized steel or iron gutters are often the lowest priced of all systems. Available unfinished or enameled, they have a short life compared to other materials unless frequently repainted. Paint will not adhere to galvanized metal until after one year. Use a special primer to prevent new paint from flaking.

Aluminum is very common as guttering material. Available in several enamel colors as well as unfinished it is lightweight and corrosion-resistant. However, aluminum guttering will not withstand ladder pressure. Sometimes aluminum guttering is cut and bent to shape on site. More often, systems are put together from components sold in standardized dimensions.

Plastic, especially vinyl, is becoming more popular than aluminum as gutter material. Sections and fittings are pre-colored and come in standard sizes.

Removing debris

Inspect and clean out the interiors of gutters at least twice a year (in autumn after the leaves have fallen, and again in early spring). Check more often if you live in a heavily wooded area. Use a ladder to reach the gutter. At least 12 inches should extend above the gutter to allow you to work safely.

First block the gutter outlet with a rag. Then, wearing heavy work gloves to avoid cuts, remove debris from the gutters. Scrape accumulated silt into a heap using a shaped piece of plastic or light sheet metal, then scoop it out with a garden trowel and deposit it in a bucket hung from the ladder. Sweep the gutter clean with a whisk broom, then remove the rag and flush the gutter using hard spray from a garden hose. Check whether the water drains completely or remains in standing pools, indicating a sagging gutter section.

Leaking seams where gutter sections are joined can be sealed using silicone caulk. For the best seal, disassemble the sections, apply caulk inside the seam, then reassemble the joint. Otherwise, spread caulk over the seam on the inside of the gutter, and smooth the surface to avoid producing ridges that might trap water.

If downspouts are clogged, free them using a plumber's snake or drain auger. Work from the bottom if possible, to avoid compacting debris further. If necessary, disassemble the downspout sections to get at the blockage. If downspout blockage is frequent, install leaf strainers in gutter outlets or, in severe situations, attach wire mesh leaf guards over the entire length of the gutters to slow the accumulation of debris.

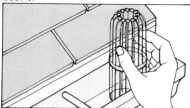
Leaf strainer

Wire mesh leaf guard

SEE ALSO

Details for: ▷	
Moisture problems	253–254

Repairing small holes

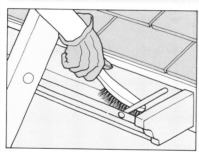

1 To repair pinholes and small rust spots
First clean the gutter and scrub the damaged area using wire brush or coarse sandpaper. Wipe away residue using a rag dipped in paint thinner.

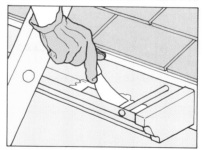

2 Apply coat of asphalt roofing cement
On holes larger than ¼ in., sandwich layers of heavy aluminum foil between coats of cement. Smooth top coat so water won't collect.

Patching large areas

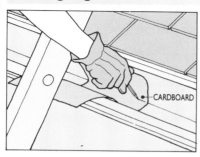
CARDBOARD

1 To repair a large hole
First use thin cardboard to make a pattern, then cut a patch of the same material as the gutter to fit over the damaged area, overlapping the hole at least 1 in.

2 Coat with asphalt roofing cement
Press the patch into place, then crimp over outer edge of gutter. Apply another layer of cement, smoothing it so water won't collect.

Maintaining wood gutters

Repaint wood gutters at least once every three years. Work during a period of warm, fair weather. First clear the gutter and allow a few days for the wood to dry thoroughly. Next, sand the interior of the gutter smooth and remove the residue with a whisk broom and hand-held vacuum. Wipe the sanded trough with paint thinner, then apply a thin coat of asphalt roofing cement mixed with paint thinner or turpentine to brushing consistency, so cement will enter wood pores. Apply a second thin coat two days later after the first has dried. Sand and repaint the gutter exterior with two coats of house paint.

Snow and ice

Plastic guttering can be badly distorted and even broken by snow and ice building up in it. Dislodge the build-up with a broom from an upstairs window if you can reach it safely. Otherwise climb a ladder to remove it.

If snow and ice become a regular seasonal problem you should screw a snow board made from 1 × 3 in. planed softwood treated with a wood preservative and painted. Fix it to stand about 1 in. above the eaves tiles, using 1 × ¼ in. steel straps bent as required.

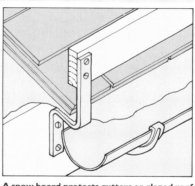
A snow board protects gutters or glazed roofs

FITTING NEW GUTTERS AND DOWNSPOUTS

When your old gutter system reaches the end of its useful life you should replace it. Try to do so with a system in the same style or, at least, one that goes with the character of your house. If you plan to install the guttering yourself a vinyl system is probably the best choice, being easy to handle.

SEE ALSO
◁ Details for:
Moisture problems   253–254

Installing gutters

An easy way to plan a new gutter system is to make a bird's-eye view sketch of the roof, as if you were looking straight down on it. Measure the distances between corners and note the locations of existing drains. Gutter sections are usually sold in 10-foot lengths, so you'll have to make up individual runs using combinations of section-lengths and couplings. Bring your plan with you when you purchase materials and ask your supplier to help determine the parts you will need.

After determining the high and low points of each run, and the slope (see "Positioning," this page), install a gutter bracket at the high point of a run and a downspout drop outlet at the low point. Stretch a string between the two fittings, then install the intermediate brackets needed to support the gutter, spacing them no more than 30 inches apart, 24 inches being best in areas where there is normally moderate to occasionally heavy snowfall.

Assemble the gutter runs on the ground. With help from an assistant hoist them into place, then seal the ends to the drop outlets using silicone caulk for metal gutters and manufacturer-recommended sealant for the vinyl guttering system you have chosen.

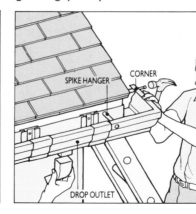

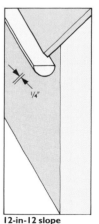

Installing downspouts

Assemble downspouts from elbow sections sold for the purpose and lengths of spouting. At the top, you will have to make up a "return" that joins the spout to the drop outlet yet allows the vertical section to lie along the side of the house. At the bottom, another elbow directs the flow of water away from the foundation, into a concrete splash block or underground drain.

To install downspouts after they are assembled, slip them into place at the top but do not fasten them with cement or permanent sealer; someday they may have to be removed. Do fasten the vertical pipe to the house trim, however. Use straps designed for the job, and predrill holes in the trim if necessary to prevent splitting. Install two straps for each 10-foot vertical length of downspout pipe.

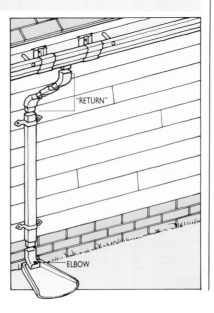

Positioning

Gutter runs should not exceed 35 feet per downspout. Longer runs normally slope from the middle to a downspout at each end, but may slope instead toward a central downspout. The slope should be constant, dropping approximately ¼ inch per foot from the highest point to the downspout drop outlet.

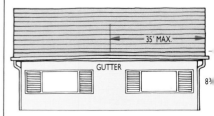

When mounting, center gutters so that roofing overlaps inner edge by half the gutter's width. The highest point of the gutter varies with the roof slope. Gutters should catch water falling vertically yet allow snow and ice to slide freely off the roof without touching the gutter to prevent damage.

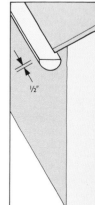

12-in-12 slope

7-in-12 slope

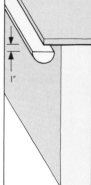

5-in-12 slope

No slope

4

HOME SECURITY

HOME SECURITY

All responsible homeowners will want to take reasonable precautions to protect themselves, their families and their property against the risks of fire and burglary. The cost and effort involved is *small by comparison with the possible expense of replacement or even rebuilding—not to mention the grief caused by personal injury and the loss of items of sentimental value.*

How a burglar gains entry

Many people innocently believe that they are unlikely to be burgled because they are not conspicuously wealthy. But statistics prove that most intruders are opportunists in search of one or two costly items, such as electrical hardware —typically the VCR, stereo and television set—jewelry or cash. And the average burglar takes only a few minutes to rob a house, and often in broad daylight, too.

Consequently, no house is immune to attack, especially those which afford an open invitation to thieves. It's virtually impossible to prevent a determined burglar from breaking in, but you can do a great deal to make it difficult for the inexperienced criminal. The illustration below indicates the vulnerable areas of an average house and the points listed in the box opposite suggest methods for safeguarding them. Check out each point and compare them with your own home to make sure your security is up to the minimum standard recommended.

Points of protection
1 The front door
An inadequately locked door invites a forced entry.
2 Darkened porch
Prevents identification of callers.
3 Back or side doors
Often fitted with minimal locks.
4 Burglar alarm
A useful deterrent.
5 Patio doors
Can be sprung with one well-placed blow.
6 Downstairs windows
A common means of entry when unlocked.

7 Upstairs windows
Vulnerable if they can be reached without effort.
8 Louvered windows
Their design permits silent entry.
9 Attic trap door
The only way to enter a house from the attic.
10 Skylight
A possible entrance if accessible from another building.
11 Garage
Possible access to main house as well as vehicle.
12 Shed
A source of housebreaking tools.
13 Ladders
An available ladder provides access to upper windows.

14 Downspouts
As good as a ladder to an agile thief.
15 Glass
Weak putty allows a thief to remove glass silently.

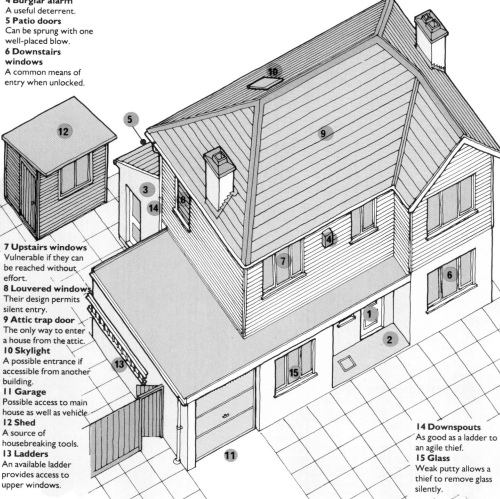

SEEKING EXPERT ADVICE

If, after reading the following information, you require further details, you can obtain free advice tailored to your needs.

Crime Prevention Officer
Local police usually have special officers responsible for advising commercial establishments and private individuals on ways to improve the security of their premises. Telephone your nearest police station to arrange for a confidential visit or meeting to discuss any aspect of home security that may concern you.

Fire Prevention Officer
Contact your local fire department for advice on how to balance your needs for security against the necessity to provide escape routes in case of fire. An officer will also explain the merits of simple firefighting equipment available to the homeowner.

Insurance companies
Check with your insurance company that your home and its contents are adequately covered against fire and theft. Most policies pay out only according to the value of objects at the time of their loss. This may or may not be adequate in replacing covered items with new ones.

However, they cannot allow for new items or improvements, and if you are underinsured you may receive only a percentage of the true value of lost or destroyed property. In some circumstances, an insurance company may insist on certain precautions, but they may also be willing to reduce your premium if you provide adequate security.

GUARDING AGAINST INTRUDERS

Simple precautions

Many burglaries can be prevented by adopting security-conscious habits. Most burglaries occur during daylight hours when the home is unoccupied. Discourage opportunistic burglars by closing and locking all windows and doors, even if you will be absent for a short time only.

Burglaries have occurred while the family is watching television in another room, so lock up before sitting down for the evening.

When you leave the house at night, close your curtains and leave a light on in a living room, not just in the hall. Alternatively, fit automatic time switches or random switches.

Make sure you open the curtains again in the daytime before you go out.

Bona fide officials from the gas or electric companies always carry identification. It's best to keep a security chain attached until you are satisfied that the identification is genuine.

When you go away on vacation, cancel all deliveries. If possible, ask a trusted neighbor to switch lights on and off for you, and open and close curtains. Have someone regularly collect your mail so that it won't pile up, or have it held by the post office. Don't advertise the fact that you will be absent, but tell the police and inform them that a neighbor has a key. Deposit valuables with the bank.

Mark your possessions by engraving or etching or with an invisible marker. Such measures help the police identify your belongings if they are recovered. Photograph jewelry or paintings which are difficult to mark, and keep a record at the bank in case of fire. Small floor or wall safes are available to store small valuables and important documents.

1 FRONT DOOR

An intruder will ring the doorbell and if there's no answer, he will force an entry. Fit a strong deadlock bolt that meets the recommendations of the police and your insurance company.

Fit a bolt top and bottom on the inside. If there is a glass panel in the door, the bolts must be lockable.

Attach a security chain or similar fitting to prevent an intruder from bursting in as you open the door a fraction. A door viewer allows you to identify a caller.

If you live in an apartment where the entrance door is the only vulnerable spot, consider having a multipoint lock fitted; it throws bolts into all four sides simultaneously.

2 DARKENED PORCH

Fit a porch light so that a door viewer is usable after dark. The light should make an intruder think twice before attempting to break in.

3 BACK OR SIDE DOORS

A burglar can often work unobserved at the rear or side of a house. Fit similar mortise locks and bolts to those described for the front door. If the door opens outward, fit hinge bolts, which will hold the door firmly in its frame, even if the hinge pins are driven out.

4 BURGLAR ALARM

An alarm is an additional deterrent but not a sufficient safeguard on its own.

5 PATIO DOORS

Sliding glass patio doors can easily be sprung. Fit rack bolts top and bottom.

6 DOWNSTAIRS WINDOWS

Always vulnerable, particularly at the back and side of the house. Fit locks and catches to suit the material and style of the window. They must have removable keys so that a thief can't break the glass and release them.

7 UPSTAIRS WINDOWS

If they can be reached only by ladder, it is probably safe enough to use a standard lock, but fit an inexpensive key-operated catch to be absolutely sure. Windows accessible by scaling drainpipes, flat roofs or walls must be secured as for those downstairs.

8 LOUVERED WINDOWS

Each individual pane can be removed silently simply by bending the aluminum holders. Use an epoxy adhesive to glue each one to its fitting, or attach bars.

9 ATTIC TRAP DOOR

Put a bolt on the trap door leading to your attic or roof space. Burglars have been known to break through the dividing walls of the adjoining house. Some terraced and semidetached houses have common attics.

10 SKYLIGHTS

Windows at roof level are at risk only if they can be reached easily by drainpipes, but fit a lock to deter thieves.

11 GARAGE

An unlocked garage door can provide burglars with entry to the home and vehicles. Keep door and vehicles locked.

12 SHEDS

Lock outbuildings to protect contents and to prevent an intruder from using your tools to break into your house. Fit a standard lock or padlock with a close-fitting or concealed shackle, so that it cannot be cut easily. Choose a design that covers the mounting screws. If possible, substitute bolts for screws to prevent the lock from being pried off.

13 LADDERS

Lock up ladders even if it means chaining them outside (to a garage wall, for instance). A loose ladder can be used to reach open windows upstairs.

14 DOWNSPOUTS

Paint downspouts with security paint to dissuade a burglar from climbing it. The substance remains slippery, preventing a good grip.

15 GLASS

Most people accept the risk that glass can be broken or cut. However, you can buy toughened or wired glass, or cover ordinary glass with a metal gate. A sliding gate on the inside can be concealed by curtains when it is not in use.

Double-glazing will deter a burglar to some extent, but don't rely on it alone as a security measure.

Keep window putty in good repair so that it cannot be picked out with a penknife to remove the pane.

Lead cames holding stained glass can be peeled silently and the glass removed, and the only way to prevent this is to fit the window with bars.

SECURING DOORS

Doors are vulnerable to forcing and often used by an intruder as a quick means of exit with his haul, even if he entered through a window. It makes good sense to fit strong locks and bolts. Don't rely on just the old nightlatch, which offers no security at all—it is only as strong as the screws holding it to the door, and a thief can easily break a pane of glass to operate it or simply slide back the bolt with a credit card. Front doors and back doors need different locking arrangements, and there are various mechanisms to choose for this purpose.

The choice of door locks

The door by which you leave the house—usually the front door—needs a particularly strong lock because it can't be bolted top and bottom, except at night, when you're at home and a break-in is less likely. Back and side doors need bolts top and bottom to prevent them from being smashed in from outside, plus a lock to stop thieves from making a getaway with their spoils. The basic choice of locks is between mortise and rim types.

How a mortise lock works

A mortise lock is fitted into a slot cut in the edge of the door, where it cannot easily be tampered with. There are various patterns to suit the width of the door stile and the location of the door. A two-bolt mortise is suitable for back and side doors. It has a handle or knob on each side to operate a springbolt, and a key-operated deadbolt which can't be pushed back once the door is closed. Mortise-and-cylinder rim locks are best for entrance doors.

Choose a lock that is advertised as 'pick-proof' and is strong enough to resist drilling or forcing, having a deadbolt of hardened steel. Some locks are intended for right-hand or left-hand opening doors.

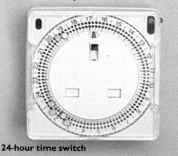

A mortise lock
1 Strike plate
2 Faceplate
3 Lock body

How a cylinder rim lock works

A cylinder rim lock is usually used on exit doors as an alternative to a mortise lock (or as an addition for extra security). It fits on the inner face of the door and shoots a bolt into a plate fixed to the face or into the edge of the frame. A rim lock automatically holds the door closed when it is pulled shut, can be opened from inside by a knob, but needs a key to be opened from outside.

Choose a rim lock which has a deadlockable bolt thrown by an extra turn of the latch key, or one that is automatically deadlocking. The best type has its staple fixed into the edge of the frame with screws or a metal stud. If it's only screwed to the face, a well-placed kick will rip out the screws.

A more secure type of rim latch incorporates a hook bolt, which is difficult to force open.

A cylinder rim lock
1 Cylinder
2 Mounting plate
3 Lock body
4 Staple

USING AUTOMATIC TIME SWITCHES

Give the impression that someone is home by using an automatic time switch plugged into an ordinary wall socket to control a table lamp or radio. By setting a dial you can have it switch the light on and off several times over a period of 24 hours, or buy a more sophisticated version that will control the lighting at different times for every day of the week.

A random switch can be fitted to a table lamp to control the lighting at undetermined periods.

24-hour time switch

INSTALLING A DOOR VIEWER

A door viewer enables you to identify callers before admitting them. Select a viewer with as wide an angle of vision as possible. You should be able to see someone standing to the side of the door or even crouching below the viewer. Choose one that is adjustable to fit any thickness of door.

Drill the recommended size hole right through the center of the door at a comfortable eye level, insert the barrel of the viewer into the hole from the outside then screw on the eyepiece from inside, using a coin to tighten it.

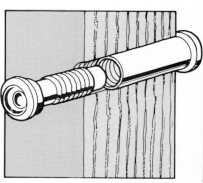

A telescopic viewer fits any size of door

FITTING LOCKS

Fitting a mortise lock

Scribe a vertical center line on the edge of the door with a marking gauge and use the lock body as a template to mark the top and bottom of the mortise (1). Choose a drill bit that matches the lock body thickness and drill out the majority of the waste.

Square up the edges of the mortise with a bevel-edged chisel (2) until the lock fits snugly in the slot. Mark around the edge of the faceplate with a knife (3), then chop a series of shallow cuts across the waste. Pare out the recess until the faceplate is flush with the edge of the door.

Hold the lock against the face of the door and mark the centers of the holes for the key and doorknob with an awl (4). Clamp a block of scrap wood to the other side of the door over the hole positions and drill right through on the center marks. The block of wood prevents the drill bit from splintering the face of the door as it bursts through on the other side.

1 Mark the mortise

2 Chop out the waste

3 Mark the faceplate

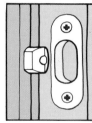
4 Mark the keyhole

Screw the lock into its recess and check its operation; screw on the faceplate and then the escutcheons over each side of the holes (5). With the door closed, operate the bolt; it may incorporate a marking device to gauge the position of the strike plate on the door frame. If it doesn't have a marking device, shoot the bolts fully open, close the door and draw around the bolts on the face of the frame (6).

Mark and cut the mortise and recess for the strike plate as described for the lock (7).

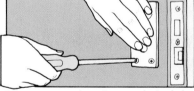
5 Screw on escutcheon to cover the keyhole

6 Mark bolt on frame

7 Fit strike plate

Fitting a cylinder rim lock

Tape the template provided with the lock to the door and mark; then drill holes to accept the cylinder (1). They vary in size among models. Pass the cylinder into the hole from the outside and connect it to the mounting plate on the inside with machine screws (2).

Drill and insert the wood screws to hold the plate to the door. Check the required length of the connecting bar, which projects through the plate. If necessary, cut it to the correct size with a hacksaw (3).

Mark and cut the recess for the lock in the door edge, and attach it to the door and mounting plate with screws (4). Mark the position of the lock on the frame and use the template to drill for staple mounting screws or studs. Hold the staple against the frame to mark its recess. Chop and pare out the recess, then screw on the staple.

1 Mark cylinder center

2 Fit mounting plate

3 Cut connecting bar

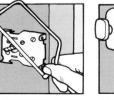
4 Screw lock to door

FITTING RACK BOLTS

There are many strong bolts for securing a door from the inside, but the rack bolt can be fitted into the door edge, secure and unobtrusive. Fit them to front, back and side doors in addition to mortise and rim locks.

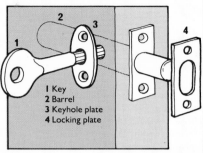

1 Key
2 Barrel
3 Keyhole plate
4 Locking plate

The components of a standard rack bolt

Drill a hole in the edge of the door—usually ⅜ inch in diameter—for the barrel of the bolt. Use a try square to transfer the center of the hole to the inside face of the door. Measure the keyhole and drill it with an ⅛-inch bit. Insert the bolt (1).

With the key in position, mark the recess for the faceplate (2), then cut it out with a chisel. Screw the bolt and keyhole plate to the door. Operate the bolt to mark the frame, then drill a ⅜-inch-diameter hole to a depth that matches the length of the bolt. Fit the locking plate over the hole.

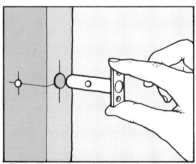
1 Drill holes for barrel and key then fit bolt

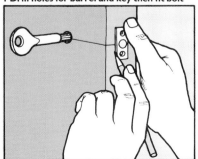
2 With the key holding bolt, mark faceplate

Fitting hinge bolts
Fix two bolts per door near the hinges. Drill hole in door edge for bolt and another in door frame. Recess the locking plate in frame.

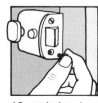

Attaching a security chain
No special skills are needed to fit a chain. Simply screw the fixing plates to the door and frame. Fit the chain just below the lock.

241

SECURING WINDOWS

Windows are a common means of entry for burglars, so take particular care to ensure they're secured, especially those in vulnerable locations. There are special locks for both wood and metal windows. The best type for wooden frames are set in mortises, whereas locks for metal frames are more limited due to the necessity of cutting threads in the material mounting hardware.

SEE ALSO

◁ Details for:

Windows	196–197
Repairing glass	202
Vulnerable windows	238
Rack bolts	241

How windows are locked

The way you lock a window depends on how it opens. Sliding sashes, for instance, should be secured by locking the two frames together; casements, which open like doors, should be fastened to the outer frame or locked by rendering the catches and stays immovable. But whichever type of lock you choose, it makes sense to buy the best you can afford for the most vulnerable windows and to spend less on those which are difficult to reach.

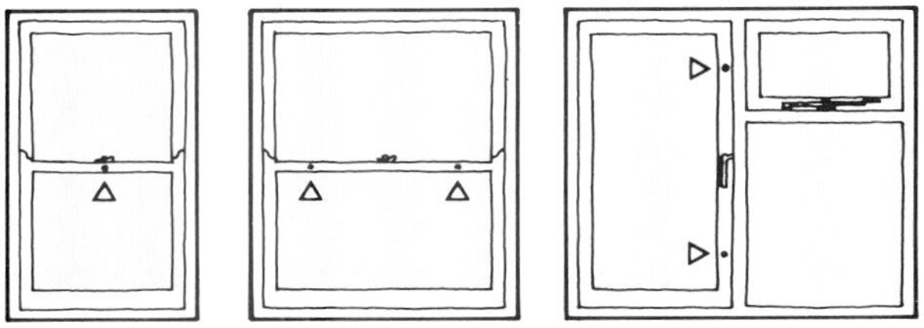

The best positions for window locks
The black dots in the illustrations above indicate where you should place bolts or locks.

Locks must be strong enough to resist forcing, and they must be situated correctly for optimum security. For small windows, fit one lock as close to the center as possible, but fit two locks spaced apart on large windows so that a thief cannot lever the opening edge and split the frame.

A window lock should be released by a removable key only. Some keys will open all locks of the same design (an advantage to some extent as you'll need to handle fewer keys—although a determined burglar may carry a range of standard keys). Other locks have several key variations.

Only fairly large windows can accommodate mortise-type locks, so many are surface-mounted. They're perfectly adequate, so long as the mechanism covers the screws, or where plugs are provided to seal them off once the lock is installed. If neither is the case, drill out the center of the screws once they are installed so that they cannot be withdrawn.

Fitting sash window locks

Installing dual screws

Cheap but effective, dual screws comprise a bolt which passes through both meeting rails so that the sashes are immobilized. There is little to see when the window is closed and they are simple to operate with a special key.

With the window closed and the standard catch engaged, drill through the inner meeting rail into the outer one. Tape the drill bit to gauge the depth. Slide the sashes apart and tap the two bolt-receiving devices into their respective holes. Close the window and insert the threaded bolt with the key until it is flush with the window frame. If necessary, saw the bolt to length.

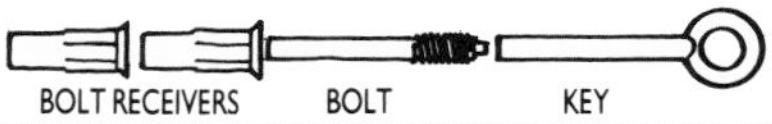

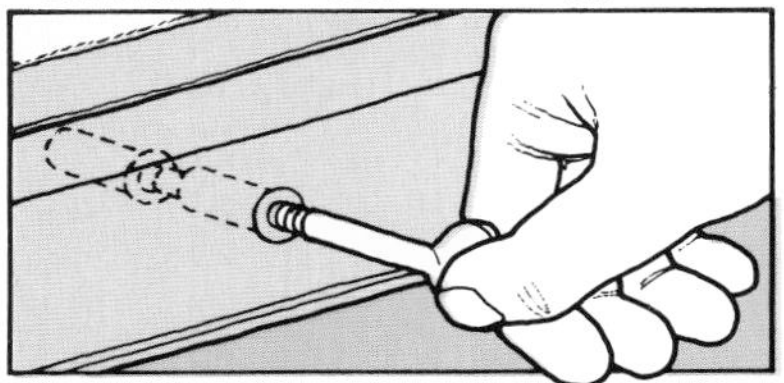

Turn a dual screw until it is flush with the frame

Using sash stops

When the bolt is withdrawn with a key, a sash stop fitted to each side of a window allows it to be opened slightly for ventilation. Apart from deterring a burglar, they will also prevent children from opening the window any further.

To fit the stop, drill a hole in the upper sash for the bolt and screw the faceplate over it. On close-fitting sashes, you will have to recess the faceplate. Screw the protective plate to the top edge of the lower sash.

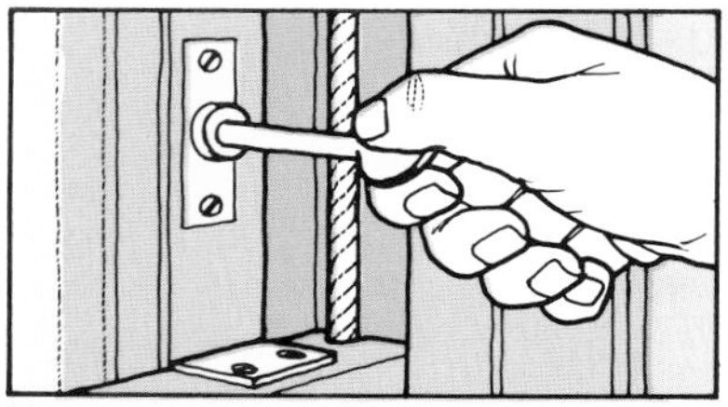

Extract sash stop with key to secure window

Lock for aluminum sash windows

Secure a metal sash window with the lock described for securing fanlights.

Fitting a key-operated sash lock

A key-operated cylinder sash lock can be screwed to the outer frame at top and bottom, and drives a small bolt into a reinforced bolt hole. It's more obtrusive than other sash locks.

Locking casement windows

Fitting rack bolts

On a large casement window, fit a rack bolt as described for doors.

Fitting a casement lock

A locking bolt can be attached to wooden window frames. The bolt is engaged by a simple catch but can only be released by a key.

With the lock body screwed to the opening part of the window, mark and cut a small mortise in the frame for the bolt. Screw on the cover plate.

For metal windows a similar device is a clamp which, fixed to the opening part of the casement, shoots a bolt that hooks onto the fixed frame.

Another metal casement lock fits within the metal section of the casement and a key-operated device expands the lock to secure the casement and frame together.

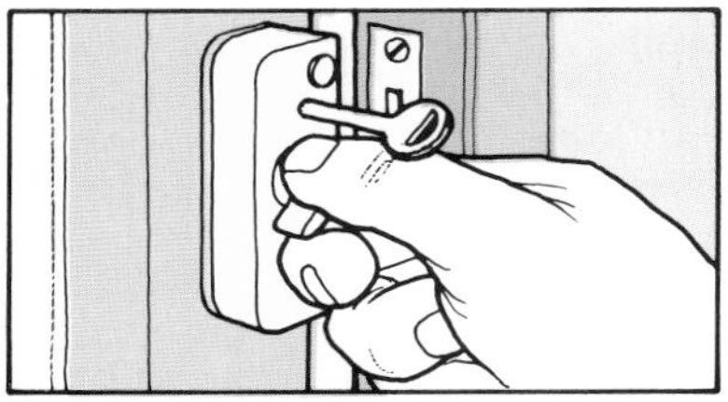

A good casement lock has a removable key

Locking the cockspur handle

The cockspur handle, which secures the opening edge of the casement to the fixed frame, can be locked using a device that you screw to the frame below the handle. When a key is turned, a bolt is extended to prevent the cockspur from moving. Lockable handles can be substituted for the standard handle; a key locks the handle, which can be fixed so the window is ajar for ventilation.

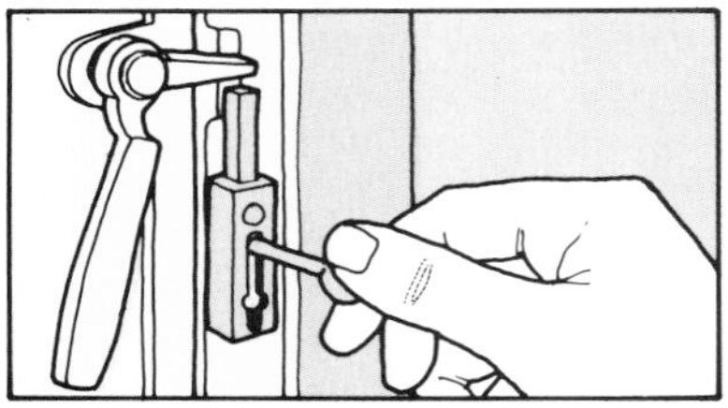

The extended bolt stops handle turning

Securing pivot windows

If a pivot window is not supplied with an integral lock, use the rack bolts or locks recommended for casement windows. Alternatively, fit the screw-mounted lock suggested for a fanlight window.

WINDOWS

Securing fanlight windows

Various types of casement and fanlight stay locks are available for securing the stay to the window frame. The simplest device is screwed below the stay arm and a key-operated bolt passes through one of the holes into it. Stays with built-in locks are also made.

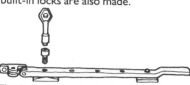

The device bolts a stay to the window frame

Fit a screw-mounted lock to wooden or metal fanlights. Attach the lock to the window then use it to position the staple on the fixed frame.

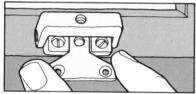

Position the staple to fit screw-mounted lock

Securing French windows

French windows or other glazed doors are vulnerable to forcing—a burglar only has to break a pane to reach the handle inside. Key-operated locks are essential to prevent a break-in.

Each side of a French window requires a rack bolt at the top and bottom, positioned so that the bolt shoots into the upper frame and the threshold below. Take each side off its hinges to fit the lower bolt.

Locking sliding doors

If you have aluminum sliding patio doors, fit additional locks at the top and bottom to prevent the sliding frame from being lifted off its track. These locks are costly, but offer good security.

Fit a lock top and bottom of a sliding door

BURGLAR ALARM SYSTEMS

Although they are no substitute for good locks and catches, an alarm system does provide an extra sense of security and may deter an intruder if there are other less well-protected premises nearby. An alarm must be reliable, but you and your family must be trained and disciplined in its use. If your neighbors are constantly subjected to false alarms, they're less likely to be vigilant and call the police in an emergency. Burglar alarm systems and installers vary in quality—the good ones are not always the most expensive.

A typical system

Alarm systems differ greatly but they fall into two basic categories: a passive system, which detects the presence of an intruder inside the house; or a perimeter system, which guards all likely means of entry. The best systems incorporate a combination of features for comprehensive security in case the perimeter detectors are bypassed.

Control unit
The control unit is the center of the system, to which all detectors are connected. From there, the signal is passed to a bell or siren. It should provide the necessary time for legitimate entry and exit from the premises. Units with separate zone monitoring allow you to set specific circuits while others are switched off. This facility provides freedom of movement upstairs, for instance, while the downstairs is fully guarded.

A control unit must be tamper-proof so that it will sound the alarm if disarming is attempted by any means other than with a key or digital code. Most systems are wired directly to the service panel but should be fitted with an additional battery in case of power failure.

Detectors
All entrances can be fitted with magnetic switches, which sound the alarm when broken by someone opening a door or window. Small detectors sense the vibration caused by an attempted entry, including breaking glass. They must be accurately placed and set to differentiate between an intrusion and other types of vibration from external sources.

A pressure mat activates the alarm when a person stands on it, closing two metallic strips. A mat can be placed under a carpet in the vicinity of a likely target or possible means of entry. Although efficient, pressure mats are not so popular nowadays, as experienced thieves are able to detect their presence.

Scanning devices
Sensors can be placed strategically to scan a wide area using infrared, ultrasonic or radio waves to detect movement or human presence. This type of detector is useful in a small apartment and can operate on house current or batteries.

The alarm
Most alarms are bells or sirens mounted on an outside wall. More sophisticated versions switch off after about twenty minutes but continue signaling with a flashing light. Some will automatically rearm themselves. A system can transmit a warning directly to the police or a monitoring center for swift response to a break-in.

Whatever alarm is incorporated, it must be capable of being triggered by an attempt to tamper with it by cutting wires or dismantling.

Personal attack button
Most systems provide the option of a button situated near the front door or in a bedroom, which you can operate in the event of an attack. It trips the alarm even when the rest of the system is switched off.

DIY systems

If you want to avoid the cost of professional installation, there are several DIY alarm systems on the market, which are quick and easy to install with minimal disruption to the house. Choose carefully, as many kits are inadequate for any but the smallest house.

A good system will enable you to select the type and number of detectors you require and should incorporate a reliable, tamper-proof control unit to avoid false alarms. Fitting and wiring instructions are provided with all kits but you'd be wise to discuss the procedure with the supplier so you know what the installation involves.

PROTECTING YOUR HOUSE AGAINST FIRE

No one needs to be reminded about the potential risk of fire, yet nearly all domestic fires are caused by careless *disregard of the dangers. Many could be prevented by simple awareness and sensible precautions.*

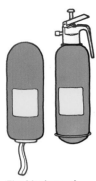

Fire blanket and extinguisher
Put one of each in the kitchen and garage.

Smoke detector
A detector will give you early warning of a fire when it can still be tackled easily.

Avoiding the risks

Make sure all your electrical installations and equipment are safe and in good order. Be sure all outlets in damp areas are equipped with ground-fault circuit interrupters. Don't overload power sockets with adapters—fit more sockets instead. Don't trail long extension coils under carpets or rugs. If they become damaged they could overheat and start a serious fire.

Never leave a fire unguarded, for safety's sake. And remember: You could be prosecuted if a young child is injured as a result of an unguarded fire or heater. Don't dry clothes in front of a fire—they could easily fall onto the elements or flames.

Take particular care with smoking materials. Empty ashtrays at night, but dampen the contents first, before discarding them in a trash can. Don't rest ashtrays on chair arms. A lit cigarette's center of gravity shifts as it burns and could topple off and ignite carpets and upholstery. Never smoke in bed. Many fires are caused by smokers falling asleep and setting light to the bedclothes.

Keep a workshop or garage clear of rubbish or shavings and dispose of oily rags—it's been known for them to ignite spontaneously. Store flammable chemicals and paints outside if possible, not under the stairs.

As a means of fighting a fire, install an all-purpose fire extinguisher and a fire blanket adjacent to the stove, and another set in the garage. Your local fire department will recommend reliable equipment for domestic use. Don't buy inferior items in preference.

Providing escape routes

Your first responsibility is to the occupants of a dwelling, so ensure that your family can escape safely from a burning building. Close interior doors before you go to bed to contain a fire, but don't lock them. A locked internal door rarely deters a burglar.

Although you should not leave a key in an exterior lock, keep it conveniently close by but out of reach of the door or window. Make sure everyone knows where the key is kept and make a habit of returning it to the same place after it has been used.

It is most important to keep stairs and hallways free from obstructions, as it may be difficult to see in dense smoke. In particular, avoid using a kerosene heater to warm these areas. It can be knocked over during an escape and spread the fire further.

Communal staircases to apartments are especially important, so talk to your neighbors about keeping them clear. Fire-check doors are a wise precaution and may be required by law in multistory dwellings. Never use an elevator to effect an escape.

Tackling a fire

Don't attempt to tackle a fire yourself unless you discover it early—and then only with the proper equipment. Throwing water onto an electrical fire, for instance, could be fatal.

Grease fire
When cooking fat or oil reaches a certain temperature, it ignites. Unattended frying pans are one of the most common causes of domestic fires. Don't attempt to move a burning pan:
● Turn off the source of heat.
● Smother the fire with a fiberglass blanket or soak a towel in water and drop it over the pan.

● Let the pan cool for half an hour before removing the towel or blanket.
● If the fire is not extinguished immediately, call the fire department.

Chimney fire
If a chimney catches fire, phone the fire department, then stand guard by the fireplace. Remove hearth rugs in case burning material drops to the grate.

Clothes on fire
If a person's clothes catch fire, throw him to the ground and roll him in a blanket or rug. Seek medical attention in the event of burns.

INSTALLING A SMOKE DETECTOR

You can't rely on your sense of smell to rouse you in the event of a fire—the toxic gases produced could render you unconscious before you have a chance to raise the alarm. A smoke detector will identify the presence of smoke even before flames start, and will sound a shrill warning. Although you can have detectors wired into an alarm system, self-contained, battery-operated units are easy to install.

There are two types of detectors. Photoelectric devices shine a beam of light into an open chamber, which just misses a photoelectric cell; if smoke fills the chamber, light is dispersed into the cell and the alarm sounds.

Ionization types have a minute radioactive source, which ionizes the air in an open chamber so it carries an electric current. Smoke entering the chamber spoils the conductivity and an alarm is sounded.

Photoelectric types can detect smoke from smoldering or slow-burning fires, while ionization types are more attuned to smoke from fast-flaming fires. Combination detectors are made. Choose a detector with a light that shines to guide you to an exit.

Siting a smoke detector
The best place to position a smoke detector is on the ceiling between potential sources of fire—the kitchen or garage, for instance—and a hall between the sleeping areas.

The detector should be kept out of drafts, away from shower areas (steam can trigger the alarm) and fixed either to the wall or ceiling no closer than 6 inches to a wall or ceiling angle, as the "dead air space" in the corner may prevent efficient working.

Fix the device's baseplate to the wall with screws driven into studs, or directly to the ceiling joists. Clip in the battery—and test the alarm. The detector cover simply clips on.

Linking detectors
To link several smoke detectors, first attach them to the wall or ceiling, then connect them with lengths of twin bell wire to the connector blocks within the devices. Run the wire by the most inconspicuous route around the house, clipping it at 1-foot intervals to the joists in the attic space or to the tops of picture rails, baseboards and around door frames.

5

INFESTATION/ROT & DAMP

INFESTATION: INSECTS

Our homes and surroundings are often invaded by various voracious insect pests. Some of them are quite harmless, although they cause a great deal of annoyance and even alarm, but certain insects can seriously weaken the structure of a building and it is these pests which often go unnoticed until the damage is done. At the first signs of infestation, try to identify and eradicate the cause as quickly as possible, before it escalates, causing even further damage.

Damp-wood termite

Termites

Termites are wood-eating insects, prevalent in nearly all parts of the country. Although if neglected they can cause severe damage, infestation is easily eradicable by professional pest-control experts and can be prevented in many cases by incorporating special, relatively inexpensive building techniques during construction.

Of the three significant species of termites in the U.S.—*subterranean*, *damp-wood*, and *dry-wood*—the subterranean variety do the most damage. These ¼-inch-long pests live underground—often at depths of up to 25 feet—and travel to the surface for food. They eat only cellulose, the material of wood fiber, and must avoid both light and the drying effects of open air. If they are shut off from moisture—which they receive by living in the ground—they die in only a few days.

Termites colonize as ants do, and their societies are formed of groups of specialized members. Within a colony there are winged termites, whose job it is to reproduce, and wingless termites, some of which act as soldiers and defend the colony, and others of which are workers, whose job it is to construct tunnels and forage for food. It is the workers which do the most damage.

Because termites avoid light, they feed entirely within the wood they find, so their presence is often hard to detect. As they travel upward from their nests, they feed on any wood in contact with the ground, and will sometimes build earth-covered tunnels several inches up the sides of impervious material such as masonry foundation walls or pipes to reach still higher. They can also burrow through weak mortar joints and poorly laid concrete.

Once a year, in spring or early summer, the winged, reproductive termites swarm, leaving their nest to fly to a new location to found another colony. Often the migration takes place only for a few hours. At the new site, the termites drop their wings and tunnel underground.

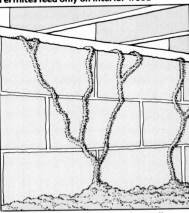

Termites feed only on interior wood

Termite tunnels along foundation wall

Damp-wood and dry-wood termites

Damp-wood termites do not require soil moisture. They may reach 1 inch in length and have a 2-inch wingspan. They inhabit only moisture-soaked wood and presently are a problem only along the Pacific coast.

Dry-wood termites resemble subterraneans, but require very little moisture to survive. Instead of dwelling underground, they bore directly into above-ground wood—even furniture—then plug their holes behind them as they begin to colonize. Currently, dry-wood termites are not a widespread problem in the U.S.—they threaten only a narrow zone along the Atlantic and Gulf coasts south from Virginia, the lower portions of Texas and the southwest, and the Pacific coast as far as northern California.

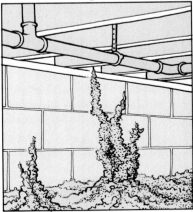

Freestanding termite tunnels

Termites
1 Winged adult
2 Soldier
3 Worker
4 Queen
5 King

Identifying termites

Winged subterranean termites are sometimes mistaken for flying ants, and vice versa, but the two can be distinguished by inspecting their wings and bodies. Termites have 4 equal-size wings. Flying ants also have 4 wings, but one pair is smaller than the other. Characteristic of ants' bodies is their distinctive pinched-in waist, separating their bodies into distinct sections—thorax and abdomen. Termites have thick waists and, compared to ants, their body sections are harder to distinguish.

Winged termites, like ants, are dark-colored (sometimes even black) and have completely formed, hard-walled bodies. Soldier termites are also dark. They have large, hard heads, strong jaws and strong legs, but their bodies are soft. They are blind. Workers are blind, too. Their bodies are pale yellow, grayish or white, and almost completely soft.

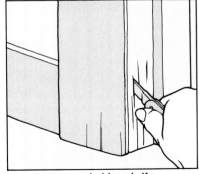

Probe suspect wood with penknife

INSECT INFESTATION

Locating termites

Termite inspections are required as part of most house sales, particularly when a mortgage is involved. In areas where infestation is common, once- or twice-yearly inspections should be made as well, although termites progress slowly and severe damage may take 2 or more years to develop. Here is where and how to look for termites:

Search for tunnels leading from moist earth towards a wood supply. Termite tunnels are half-round, approximately 1/4 to 1/2 inch in diameter, and appear as if made of cement. Normally tunnels are attached to some other surface, but in some instances they may be freestanding. Inspect foundation walls (inside and out), pipes rising from damp earth, and piers. Also check for evidence around foundation cracks, pipe openings, and especially sill joints—where the wood walls of a house rest on top of the foundation. Inspect the seams where concrete patio, garage, or basement slabs meet the house. Also check around basement windowsills and crawlspace ventilators.

Examine any wood that is in contact with the ground for direct entry of termites. Such sites include the bottoms of wooden stairs and railings, fence posts, trellises, firewood and lumber piles, even dead tree stumps.

In spring and early summer, watch for swarms of flying insects which may be termites. They normally enter wood at points near ground level, such as around house foundations, and leave piles of discarded wings at the entrance to the new colony.

Testing for damage

Because termite damage is seldom visible, probe suspect wood with a penknife, screwdriver, or ice pick. If the tool penetrates the wood easily to a depth of 1/2 inch or more, damage is present. Pry away a portion of the soft wood. If this procedure uncovers chambers or cavities, suspect termites or other wood-boring insects. If the wood seems intact but is uniformly spongy, most likely the problem is not termites, but rot.

Sources of termite infestation
1 Foundation too low
2 Sill and joists contact soil
3 Soil heaped against pier
4 Wood framing contacts soil
5 Porch and steps contact soil
6 Firewood, construction scraps left on dirt basement floor
7 Post extends through concrete
8 Exterior wood siding too near grade
9 Wood framing around vent contacts soil
10 Softened, cracked lime mortar in old brick wall
11 Improper roof drainage (runoff collects around foundation)
12 Loose stucco
13 Cracks in concrete slab floor
14 Unshielded girder end
15 Wood framing beneath chimney (heat attracts termites)
16 Insufficient crawlspace height
17 Rotting stumps and lumber scraps in yard
18 Untreated fence posts and clothesline posts contact soil

Control measures

Once termites are present, the only effective method of extermination is by treating the soil with chemicals to create a toxic envelope surrounding the house. Chlordane is the chemical used most often. Although the purchase of chlordane and other termite-controlling chemicals is still legal, their use may be banned in some regions of the country, or restricted to application only by licensed professionals. Pest-control poisons are hazardous and difficult both to handle safely and apply effectively. If you suspect or locate termite damage, contact a reputable extermination company for assistance.

TERMITE SHIELDS

Incorporating metal termite shields between foundation walls and wood sills, and around pipes entering the soil from the house structure above, is an effective way to prevent termite infestation. In addition, foundation walls should extend at least 6 inches above ground level, and the distance between joists and soil in crawlspaces should be a minimum of 18 inches.

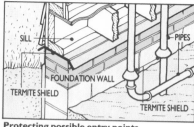

Protecting possible entry points

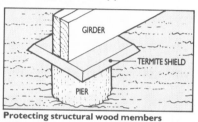

Protecting structural wood members

Dry-wood termites often invade attics
They can be controlled by fumigation with nontoxic silica gel dust which dehydrates (and thus kills) them.

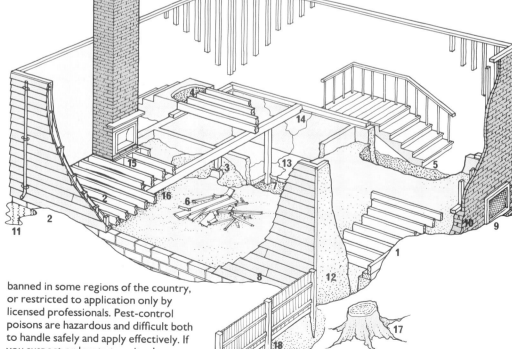

ERADICATING INSECT PESTS

Insecticides can be dangerous if allowed to contaminate food and they are also harmful to honey bees, so follow the manufacturer's instructions carefully when using them to eradicate insect pests of any kind.

SEE ALSO

◁ Details for:
Termites   246–247
Handling poisons
safely   250

Typical household pests
(Not to scale)
The insects shown below are more of a nuisance and a health hazard than a threat to the structure of your house.

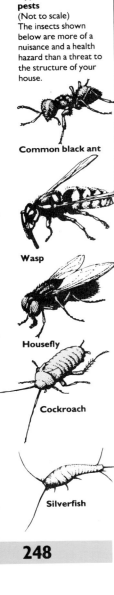

Common black ant

Wasp

Housefly

Cockroach

Silverfish

ANTS

The common black ant will enter a house foraging for food. Once established, the workers follow well-defined trails. In summer, great numbers of winged ants emerge from the nest to mate but the swarming is over in a matter of hours, and the ants themselves are harmless. If winged ants stray into the house, they can be overcome with an aerosol insecticidal spray.

To locate the nest, follow the trail of ants. It will be situated under a path, at the base of a wall, in the lawn or under a flat stone, perhaps 20 feet from the house. Destroy the nest by pouring boiling water into the entrances. If this will damage plants, use an insecticidal dust or spray.

WASPS

Wasps are beneficial in spring and early summer, as they feed on garden pests, but later in the year they destroy soft fruit. They will also kill bees and raid the hive for honey. Wasps sting when aroused or frightened.

Trap foraging wasps in open jam jars containing a mixture of jam, water and detergent. Flying wasps can be killed with an aerosol fly spray.

You can destroy wasps at the nest by depositing insecticidal powder near the entrances and areas where insects alight. Approaching a nest can be hazardous, so tie a spoon to a long stick to extend your reach. Alternatively, use a smoke generator where there is no risk of fire. Light a pellet, place it in the entrance and seal the opening.

Treat a wasp sting with a cold compress soaked in witch hazel or use an antihistamine cream or spray.

FLIES

Depending on the species, flies breed in rotting vegetables, manure, decaying meat and offal. They can carry the eggs of parasitic worms and spread disease by leaving small black spots of vomit and excreta on foodstuffs.

Cover food and keep refuse sealed in newspaper or plastic bin liners. Tight-fitting window screens and bead curtain hung in open doorways will prevent flies from entering the house.

An aerosol fly spray will deal with small numbers, but for swarming flies in a roof space, for instance, use an insecticidal smoke generator from a hardware store or agricultural supply store. Large numbers in a living room can be sucked into a vacuum cleaner: Suck up some insecticidal powder and wait a few hours before emptying the bag.

COCKROACHES

Cockroaches can appear anywhere there's a supply of food and water in warm conditions. Cockroaches are unhygienic, and smell unpleasant.

Being nocturnal feeders, cockroaches hide during the day in crevices in walls, behind cupboards and especially under cookers, fridges or near central heating pipes, where it is warmest. A serious outbreak should be dealt with by a professional, but you can lay a finely dusted barrier of insecticidal powder between suspected daytime haunts and supplies of food. Don't sprinkle insecticides near food itself. Use a paintbrush to stipple powder into crevices and under baseboards. When you have eradicated the pests, fill all cracks and gaps to prevent their return.

SILVERFISH

Silverfish are tapered, wingless insects about ½ inch long. They like moist conditions found in kitchens, bathrooms and cellars. You may find them behind wallpaper, where they feed on the paste, or in bookshelves because they also eat paper. Use an insecticidal spray or powder in these locations.

CARPENTER ANTS

Damage from carpenter ants is often mistaken for termite infestation. However, ants tunnel only to construct nesting places; they remove excavated wood to the outside of their nests and keep the passageways clear. Termite galleries, on the other hand, are packed with sawdustlike material which is actually woody feces. This difference in the appearance of infested areas is a positive means of identifying which pest is at work.

Carpenter ants may be seen entering and leaving wood. They vary widely in size but a common variety is approximately ½ inch long, and either all black or mixed with brown. All members of a colony are fully formed except the larvae, which are white and resemble grubs. Small, isolated colonies can be eradicated by injecting pesticide dust into the galleries or into holes drilled at intervals along infested timber. For best results, hire a licensed, professional exterminator.

Winged adult   **Worker**

CARPENTER BEES

Carpenter bees most often resemble large bumblebees. They have black bodies with patches of yellow, and may be 1 inch long. Bees bore an individual tunnel approximately ¾ inch in diameter directly into wood, then turn at right angles and excavate extensive galleries running in the same direction as the wood grain in which they lay eggs. Control is the same as for carpenter ants.

Carpenter bee

INSECTS

Powder-post beetles

Beetle damage occurs chiefly in dry wood, including furniture. Adult beetles enter the wood through small natural openings, then lay eggs. The larvae then feed on the wood as they develop, causing damage that looks a great deal like termite damage. Beetles breed in the same wood generation upon generation, often for hundreds of years. Eventually the wood becomes so honeycombed with burrows that, as with termite damage, the structure collapses of its own weight. Evidence of beetle infestation is only slightly more noticeable from the outside than infestation by termites: Tiny "shot holes" in the wood where adult beetles have chewed their way to the outside—particularly during spring or early summer—as part of their life cycle.

In the U.S., three types of wood-boring beetles are collectively termed powder-post beetles. The two most common are the death watch beetle and the true powder-post beetle. Both are tiny—approximately 1/8 inch long. Death watches in America attack primarily Douglas fir (European species are known for destroying hardwoods), whereas powder-posts are attracted especially to hickory, ash, and oak. The third type, commonly called the lead cable borer, reaches 1 inch in length. Presently it thrives only in the semiarid southwest and California. Named for its habit of chewing into lead-lined electrical cables and similar articles during hot weather, this beetle is also prevalent in much furniture and paneling made of oak and California laurel wood.

As with termites, extermination by professionals is the only reliable control. Infested furniture can be removed from the home and fumigated in a special chamber; on-site extermination in such woodwork as paneling and floors requires residents to vacate the building for up to a few days.

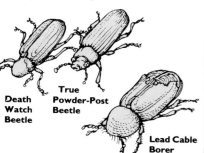

Death Watch Beetle **True Powder-Post Beetle** **Lead Cable Borer**

ERADICATING OTHER INSECT PESTS

CENTIPEDES AND MILLIPEDES

These multilegged pests inhabit damp, dark areas and decaying vegetable matter. Usually they remain out of doors; however, they may frequent unused basements and wander into the house from below or from outside. Some centipedes may bite if they are injured. If that happens, apply antiseptic to the swelling and call your physician if symptoms persist. To control centipedes and millipedes, apply insecticide on doorsills, windowsills, and other places where pests are entering the house. Pay particular attention to baseboard areas where pests may migrate from the basement.

EARWIGS

Easily recognized by their large rear pincers, these pests have become epidemic in many parts of the U.S. Earwigs inhabit moist, sheltered areas such as lawns and leafy garden vegetables, damp stored fabric or carpeting, the hollow tubing of lawn furniture, as well as foundation cracks, basements and behind baseboards. Control these pests with insecticide sprayed or applied to these areas. Major infestations are not a do-it-yourself proposition; seek professional pest-control advice.

CRICKETS

Crickets normally reside outdoors but may enter houses as autumn approaches or when populations increase during periodic cricket plagues. Whereas one or two of these insects are merely annoying because of their nocturnal chirping, an infestation can endanger many household items including woolens, silks and paper, not to mention fresh foodstuffs. To control crickets, spray insecticide around building entrances, baseboards and the edges of carpets. Also spray beneath furniture, in closets, and on floors behind drapery. Tight-fitting window screens and screen doors are effective along with other preventive measures to physically bar crickets from the house.

SPIDERS

Any area of undisturbed space within a house may be home to spiders; however, most prefer dark places. Though all spiders inject venom when they bite, only two species—the black widow and the brown recluse—are considered dangerous to humans. To be on the safe side, treat all spider bites with antiseptic and report them immediately to a physician. Regular and frequent sweeping and dusting can help keep spider populations down, but spraying insecticide is the best cure for infestations. To be sure of eradicating spiders, spray the webs with insecticide, then remove them after the spiders within them are dead. Black widows are especially fond of dry piles of lumber or firewood, and outdoor latrines. Use caution in these areas and spray often.

TICKS

Most ticks found in homes have been transported indoors by family pets, notably dogs. Filled with blood, the ticks drop off the animal and become lodged in bedding, upholstery, carpets and behind baseboards. Although many varieties of ticks carry diseases that affect humans, the common brown dog tick is considered harmless. To remove an individual tick, hold a lit cigarette close to its body, then pluck it away after it retracts its head from within the skin. You can also touch the tick with a red-hot needle, or swab it with kerosene or alcohol to remove it. Take an infested animal to a veterinarian for treatment. To effectively control ticks indoors, spray insecticide wherever an animal sleeps, and destroy old bedding by burning.

SEE ALSO

Details for: ▷

| Inspector | 17 |
| Termites | 246–247 |

House Centipede

Millipede

Earwig

Common Field Cricket

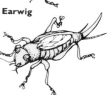

Black Widow Spider

Brown Recluse Spider

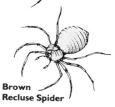

Tick (engorged) and normal tick

INFESTATION: ANIMALS

Domestic mouse
Not a serious threat to
health but they are
unhygienic.

Common rat
A serious health risk.
Seek expert advice.

Bat
Bats may cause rabies
and should be
considered a health
risk.

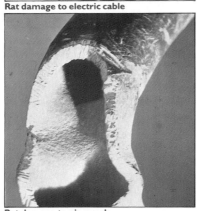

Insects aren't the only pests to set up home in your house: Mice and rats can be a menace, especially in houses that offer plenty of underfloor runs, where they can live and prosper uninterrupted and find a plentiful supply of food by invading your living quarters. Mice are a nuisance, but rats can be a definite health hazard and eradication is vital. Evan bats are known to shelter inside houses, usually occupying the roof space, and although they're beneficial—consuming large quantities of insects—they also harbor rabies, a potentially fatal disease.

Mice

Mice will be attracted by fallen food scraps, so the best remedy is to keep the floors spotlessly clean. However, mice will move readily from house to house through the roof spaces and wall cavities and under floors, so it is sometimes difficult to eradicate them completely. Contact your local Health Department if the mice persist.

Poisoned bait can be obtained, which you should sprinkle onto a piece of paper or card. In this way, uneaten bait can be removed easily. Keep pets and children away from the bait. If signs of mice are still evident after three weeks, you should resort to a trap. Humane traps capture mice alive in a cage, so that you can deposit them elsewhere, or you can use the spring-loaded snap-traps.

Most people set too few traps. Ideally, place them every 6 feet across mouse runs. The best place is against the baseboard, facing the wall. Bait traps with flour, oatmeal or chocolate molded onto the bait hook. Dispose of the mouse bodies by burying, burning or flushing down the toilet.

Rats

Serious rat infestations rarely occur in the average domestic situation but they can be a problem in rural areas or near rivers and docks. They can be killed with anticoagulant poisons, but as rats are a health hazard, always contact the Health Department for expert advice.

Bats

Bats prefer to roost in uninhabited structures—farm buildings, caves, mines and tunnels—but occasionally they will inhabit domestic housing. If possible, bats should be left undisturbed, since they eat large numbers of insects—particularly flies and mosquitoes. Only a few species of tropical bats suck blood or do direct damage, such as eating fruit crops. However, bats are known to harbor diseases, particularly rabies, and as such, constitute a health hazard. To rid an attic of a bat colony, seal all the openings except one, and install a bright light to shine directly on the roosting area. Wait a week, then approximately ½ hour after dark (while any bats that haven't already left the premises are out feeding), seal the remaining opening. Should an individual bat stray into a room, try to keep calm. They will avoid you if possible—and they don't become entangled in hair as the old wives' tale suggests. Open all windows and doors to the outside, turn off the lights, and allow the bat to escape.

Rat damage to plug

Rat damage to electric cable

Rat damage to pipework

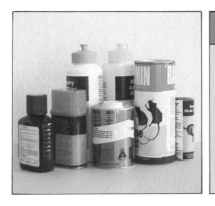

HANDLING POISONS SAFELY

Poisons designed to eradicate rodents are equally deadly to humans, so it is most important to follow the manufacturer's handling and storage instructions to the letter. Make sure poisons are always out of the reach of children, and where pets or other animals can get to them. Never store them under the kitchen sink where they might be mistaken for household products, or anywhere else where food could become contaminated. In the case of accidental consumption by animals or humans, keep the container so that the poison can be readily identified by a vet or doctor. Some containers are color-coded especially for the purpose. Wear protective gloves whenever you handle poisons and chemicals.

WET AND DRY ROT

Rot occurs in unprotected household timbers, fences and outbuildings, which are subjected to dampness. Fungal spores, which are always present, multiply and develop in these conditions until eventually the timber is destroyed. Fungal attack can be serious, requiring immediate attention to avoid very costly structural repairs to your home. There are two main scourges: wet and dry rot.

Recognizing rot

Signs of fungal attack are easy enough to detect but it is important to be able to identify certain strains which are much more damaging than others.

Mold growth

White, furry deposits or black spots on timber, plaster or wallpaper are mold growths; usually these are a result of condensation. When they are wiped or scraped from the surface, the structure shows no sign of physical deterioration apart from staining. Cure the source of the damp condition and treat the affected area with a solution of 16 parts warm water: 1 part bleach.

Wet rot

Wet rot occurs in timber with a high moisture content. As soon as the cause is eliminated, further deterioration is arrested. Wet rot frequently attacks the framework of doors and windows which have been neglected, enabling rainwater to penetrate joints or between brickwork and adjacent timbers. Peeling paintwork is often the first sign, which when removed reveals timber that is spongy when wet but dark brown and crumbly when dry. In advanced stages, the grain will have split and thin, dark brown fungal strands will be in evidence on the timber. Treat wet rot as soon as practicable.

Dry rot

Once it has taken hold, dry rot is a most serious form of decay. Urgent treatment is essential. It will attack timber with a much lower moisture content than wet rot, but—unlike wet rot, which thrives outdoors as well as indoors—only in poorly ventilated, confined spaces indoors.

Dry rot exhibits different characteristics depending on the extent of its development. It sends out fine, pale gray tubules in all directions, even through masonry, to seek out and infect other drier timber. It actually pumps water from damp timber and can progress at an alarming rate. The strands are accompanied by white cotton woollike growths, called mycelium, in very damp conditions. When established, dry rot develops wrinkled, pancake-shaped fruiting bodies, which produce rust-red spores that are expelled to rapidly cover surrounding timber and masonry. Infested timbers become brown and brittle, exhibiting cracks across and along the grain until it breaks up into little cubes. You may also detect a strong, musty, mushroomlike smell associated with the fungus.

Wet rot—treat it as early as possible

Dry rot—urgent treatment is essential

TREATING ROT

Dealing with wet rot

After eliminating the cause of the dampness, cut away and replace badly damaged wood, then paint the new and surrounding woodwork with three liberal applications of fungicidal wood preservative. Brush the liquid well into the joints and end grain.

Before decorating, you can apply a penetrating epoxy wood hardener to reinforce and rebuild damaged timbers, then repaint as normal.

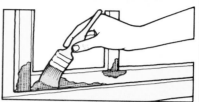

Fill rotted timbers with epoxy wood hardener

Dealing with dry rot

Dry rot requires more drastic action and should be treated by a specialist contractor, unless the outbreak is minor and self-contained. Remember that dry rot can penetrate masonry. Look under the floorboards in adjacent rooms before you are satisfied with the extent of the infection; check cavity walls for signs of rot.

Eliminate the source of water and ensure adequate ventilation in roof spaces or under the floors. Cut out all infected timber up to at least 1 foot 6 inches beyond the last visible sign of rot. Chop plaster from nearby walls, following the strands. Continue for another 1 foot 6 inches beyond the extent of the growth. Collect all debris in plastic bags and burn it or dispose of it away from the property.

Use a fungicidal preservative fluid to kill remaining spores. Wire-brush the masonry, then apply three liberal brush-coats to all timber, brickwork and plaster within 5 feet of the infected area. Alternatively, rent a sprayer and go over the same area three times.

If a wall was penetrated by strands of dry rot, drill regularly spaced but staggered holes into it from both sides. Angle the holes downwards so that fluid will collect in them to saturate the wall internally. Patch holes after treatment.

Treat replacement timbers and immerse the end grain in a bucket of fluid for five to ten minutes. If you are repairing a plaster eall, apply a zinc-oxychloride plaster.

ROT: PREVENTATIVE TREATMENT

Fungal attack can be so damaging that it is well worth taking precautions to prevent its occurrence. Regularly repaint and maintain window and door frames, where moisture can penetrate; seal around them with silicone caulk. Provide adequate ventilation between floors and ceilings; do the same in the attic. Check and eradicate any plumbing leaks and other sources of dampness, and you'll be less likely to experience the stranglehold rot can apply.

Looking after timberwork

Existing and new timbers can be treated with a preservative. Brush and spray three applications to standing timbers, paying particular attention to joints and end grain.

Immersing timbers

Timber in contact with the ground should be completely immersed in preservative. Stand fence posts on end in a bucket of fluid for 10 minutes. For other timbers, make a shallow bath from loose bricks and line it with thick polyethylene sheet. Pour preservative into the trough and immerse the timbers, weighing them down with bricks (**1**). To empty the bath, sink a bucket at one end of the trough, then remove the bricks adjacent to it so the fluid pours out (**2**), or use a bulb-type hand pump to suck up the liquid.

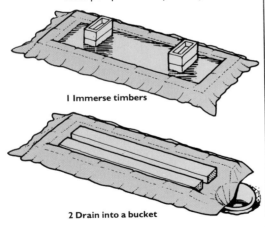

1 Immerse timbers

2 Drain into a bucket

WOOD PRESERVATIVES

Wood exposed to moisture should be treated with preservative to prevent rot. There are numerous types of wood preservatives, so be sure you choose the correct one for the timber you want to protect.

LIQUID PRESERVATIVES

For treatment of existing indoor and outdoor wood, choose a liquid preservative that you can apply by soaking or with a brush. Although all wood preservatives are toxic, the safest are copper and zinc napthenate, as well as copper-8-quinolinolate, tributyltin oxide (TBTO) and polyphase. Avoid using the traditional creosote or pentachlorophenol (penta). These chemicals are known carcinogens and highly toxic. If the wood must come into direct ground contact, use copper napthenate. Liquid preservatives, which are often sold as preservative stains, are readily available from paint stores, lumberyards and building supply stores.

PRESSURE-TREATED LUMBER

Consider using pressure-treated lumber for new outdoor construction and where wood will come in contact with ground or concrete. Use lumber stamped LP-22 for contact with soil; wood stamped LP-2 is only for above-ground use. Inhaling chemicals used to treat lumber can be harmful, so wear a mask when sawing and don't burn scraps.

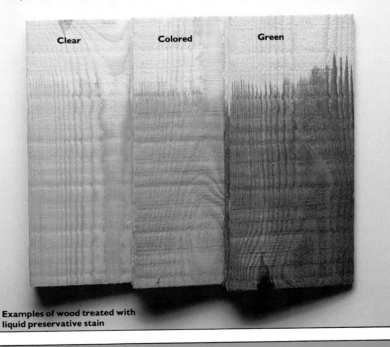

Clear   Colored   Green

Examples of wood treated with liquid preservative stain

SAFETY WITH PRESERVATIVES

All preservatives are flammable, so do not smoke while using them, and extinguish open flames.

Wear protective gloves at all times when applying preservatives and wear a face mask when using these liquids indoors.

Ensure good ventilation when the liquid is drying, and do not sleep in a freshly treated room for two nights to allow the fumes to dissipate fully.

MOISTURE PROBLEMS: PRINCIPAL CAUSES

Dampness, or rather the symptoms of it, can be most distressing both in terms of your health and the condition of your home. Try to locate the source of the problem as quickly as possible before it promotes its even more damaging side effects—wet and dry rot. Unfortunately, one form of moisture problem may obscure another, or may appear in an unfamiliar guise. Moisture may enter a house either by wicking through from the outside or rising by osmosis from below. By a third method—condensation—moisture may form entirely within the house itself.

Principal causes of penetrating moisture
1 Broken gutter
2 Leaking downspout
3 Missing shingle
4 Damaged flashing
5 Faulty pointing
6 Porous brick
7 Cracked masonry
8 Cracked stucco
9 Blocked drip groove
10 Defective seals around frames
11 Missing weatherstrip
12 Bridged cavity

Principal causes of rising moisture
Missing DPC or DPM
● Damaged DPC or DPM
● DPC too low
● Bridged DPC
● Earth piled above DPC

SEE ALSO

Details for: ▷	
Wet and dry rot	251
Damp-proof course	255

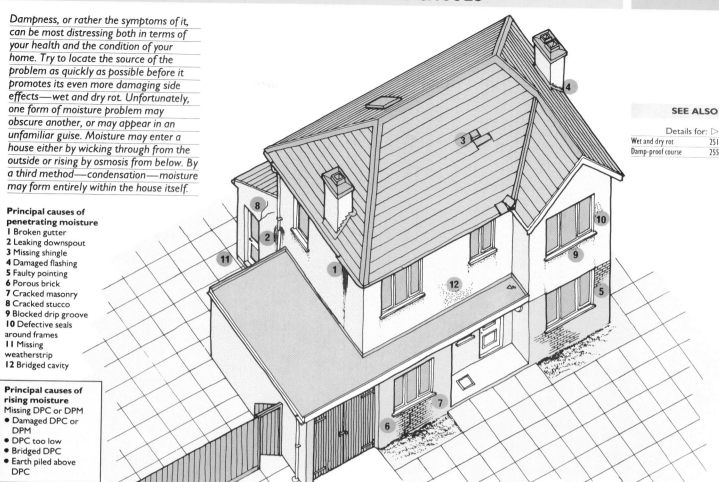

Penetrating dampness

Penetrating dampness is the result of water permeating the structure of the house from outside. The symptoms occur with wet weather only. After a few dry days, damp patches dry out but frequently leave stains.

Isolated patches are caused by a heavy deposit of water in one area and should pinpoint the source fairly accurately. General dampness usually indicates that the wall itself has become porous, but it could be caused by another problem.

Penetrating dampness occurs primarily in older homes with solid masonry walls. Relatively modern brick houses built with a cavity between two thinner brick skins are less likely to suffer from penetrating dampness, unless the cavity is bridged in one of several ways.

Rising dampness

Rising dampness is caused by water soaking up from the ground into the basement or slab floors, and walls of masonry houses. Most such houses are protected with an impervious barrier built into the walls and under concrete floors so that water cannot permeate above a certain level.

If the damp-proof course (DPC) in the walls or the damp-proof membrane (DPM) in a floor break down, water rises into the structure. Also, there may be something forming a bridge across the barrier so that water is able to flow around it.

Rising dampness is confined to solid floors and the lower sections of walls. It is a constant problem even in dry weather but becomes worse with prolonged wet weather.

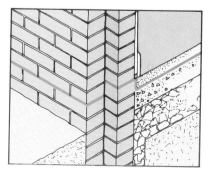

DPC in a solid wall
A layer of impervious material is built into a joint between brick courses, 6 in. above the ground.

DPC and DPM in a cavity wall structure
The damp-proof membrane in a concrete floor is linked to the DPC protecting the inner leaf of the wall. The outer leaf has its own damp-proof course.

253

PENETRATING DAMPNESS: PRINCIPAL CAUSES

CAUSE	SYMPTOMS	REMEDY
Broken or blocked gutter Rainwater overflows the gutter, typically at the joints of old metal types, and saturates the wall directly below, so that it is prevented from drying out normally.	Damp patches appearing near the ceiling in upstairs rooms. Mold forming immediately behind the leak.	Clear leaves and silt from the gutters. Repair the gutters, or replace a faulty system with a maintenance-free plastic setup.
Broken or blocked downspouts A downspout that has cracked or rusted douses the wall immediately behind the leak. Leaves lodged behind the pipe at the fixing brackets will produce a similar effect eventually.	An isolated damp patch, often appearing halfway up the wall. Mold growth behind the pipe.	Repair or replace the defective downspout, using a maintenance-free plastic type. Clear the blockage.
Loose or broken roof shingles Defective shingles allow rainwater to penetrate the roof.	Damp patches appearing on upstairs ceilings, usually during a heavy downpour.	Replace the faulty shingles. Renew damaged roof parts, if necessary.
Damaged flashing Ridges, joints and seams in a roof are sealed with flashing strips. When the flashing cracks, peels or corrodes, water trickles down the wall or down the chimney stack.	Damp patches on the ceiling extending from the wall or chimney breast; also on the chimney breast itself. Damp patch on the side wall near roof joints or lean-to extension; damp patch on the lean-to ceiling itself.	Repair the existing flashing by refitting if it appears undamaged, or replace it.
Faulty pointing Aging mortar between bricks will eventually dry and fall out; water then penetrates the remaining jointing mortar to the inside of the wall.	Isolated damp patches or sometimes widespread dampness, depending on the extent of the deterioration.	Repoint the joints between bricks, then treat the entire wall with water-repellent fluid or paint.
Porous bricks Bricks in good condition are weatherproof, but old, soft bricks become porous and often lose their faces so that the whole wall is eventually saturated, particularly on an elevation that faces prevailing winds, or where some other drainage fault occurs.	Widespread dampness on the inner face of exterior salls. A noticeable increase in dampness during a downpour. Mold growth appearing on internal plaster and trim.	Weatherproof the exterior with a clear silicone fluid or exterior paint, or cement-stucco the surface where the deterioration is extensive.
Cracked brickwork A crack in a brick wall allows rainwater (or water from a leak) to seep inside, then run to the inside face.	An isolated damp patch, which may appear on a chimney breast if the stack is cracked.	Fill the cracks and replace any damaged brickwork.
Defective stucco Cracked or ruined stucco encourages rainwater to seep between it and the brick wall behind. The water is prevented from evaporating and so becomes absorbed by the wall.	An isolated damp patch, which may become widespread. The trouble can persist for some time after rain ceases.	Fill and reinforce the crack. Chip off the damaged stucco, patch it with new sand-cement stucco, then weatherproof the wall by applying exterior paint.
Damaged coping If the coping stone on top of a roof parapet wall is missing, or the joints are open, water can penetrate the wall.	Damp patches on the ceiling against the wall just below the parapet.	Bed a new stone on fresh mortar and repair the joints.

PENETRATING DAMPNESS: PRINCIPAL CAUSES

CAUSE	SYMPTOMS	REMEDY
Blocked drip groove Exterior windowsills should have a groove running longitudinally on the underside. When rainwater runs under, it falls off at the groove before reaching the wall. If the groove becomes bridged with layers of paint or moss, water will soak the walls behind.	Damp patches along the underside of a window frame. Rotting wooden sill on the inside and outside. Mold growth appearing on the inside face of the wall below the window.	Rake out the drip groove. Nail a wood or aluminum strip to the underside of a wooden sill to form a deflection for drips.
Failed seals around windows and door frames Timber frames shrink, pulling weatherstripping from around the edge so that rainwater can penetrate the gap.	Damp surrounding frames and rotting woodwork. Sometimes the gap itself is obvious where caulking has fallen out.	Repair the frames. Seal around the edge with fresh caulk.
No weatherstrip A weatherstrip across the bottom of a door should shed water clear of the threshold and prevent water from running under the door.	Damp floorboards just inside the door. Rotting at the base of the door frame.	Fit a weatherstrip even if there are no obvious signs of damage. Repair the frame.
Bridged wall cavity In a brick building, mortar dropped onto a wall tie connecting the inner and outer leaves of a cavity wall allows water to bridge the gap.	An isolated damp patch appearing anywhere on the wall, particularly after a heavy downpour.	Open up the wall and remove the mortar droppings, then waterproof the wall externally with paint or silicone repellent.

RISING DAMPNESS: PRINCIPAL CAUSES

CAUSE	SYMPTOMS	REMEDY
No DPC or DPM If a house was built without either a damp-proof course or damp-proof membrane, water is able to soak up from the ground.	Widespread dampness at the baseboard level. Damp concrete floor surface.	Fit a new DPC or DPM.
Broken DPC or DPM If either the DPC or DPM has deteriorated, water will penetrate at that isolated point.	Possibly isolated but spreading dampness at the baseboard level.	Repair or replace the DPC or DPM.
DPC too low The DPC may not be the necessary 6 inches above ground level. Heavy rain is able to splash above the DPC and soak the wall surface.	Dampness at baseboard level but only where the ground is too high.	Lower the level of the ground outside. If it's a path or patio, cut a 6-inch-wide trench and fill with gravel, which drains rapidly.
Bridged DPC Exterior stucco taken below the DPC, or fallen mortar at the foot of a cavity wall (within the cavity), allows moisture to cross over to the inside.	Widespread dampness at, and just above, baseboard level.	Chip off stucco to expose DPC. Remove several bricks and rake out debris from the cavity.
Debris piled against wall A flower bed, rock garden or area of paving built against a wall bridges the DPC. Building material and garden refuse left there will do likewise.	Dampness at baseboard level in the area of the bridge only, or spreading from that point.	Remove the earth or debris and allow the wall to dry out naturally.

DPC too low

Render bridges DPC

Earth piled over DPC

1 Water drips to ground

2 A bridged groove

3 Drip molding

Apply caulk with an applicator gun

CURING DAMPNESS

Remedies for different moisture problems are suggested throughout the Principal Causes boxes on the previous pages, and you will find detailed instructions for carrying out many of them in other sections of the book, where they contribute to other factors such as heat loss, poor ventilation, and spoiled interior and exterior finish. The information below supplements those instructions, by providing advice on measures solely to eradicate dampness.

WATERPROOFING WALLS

Applying a water repellent to the outside of a wall not only prevents water infusion but also improves insulation, reducing the possibility of interstitial condensation. This occurs when water vapor from inside the house penetrates the wall until it reaches the damp, colder part of the structure within the wall, where it condenses and eventually migrates back to the inner surface, causing stains and mold growth.

There are several vapor-proof liquids, including interior house paint, for painting on the inside of a wall, but they should be considered a temporary measure only, as they do not cure the source of the problem. Apply two full brush coats over an area appreciably larger than the extent of the dampness. Once the wall is dry, you can decorate it as required with paint or a wallcovering.

Alternatively, apply a waterproof laminate or paper. It is hung using standard wallpapering techniques with the manufacturer's own primer and adhesive. However, seams must be lapped by ½ inch to prevent moisture penetration.

PROVIDING A DRIP MOLDING

Because water cannot flow uphill, a drip molding on the underside of an external windowsill forces water to drip to the ground before it reaches the wall behind (1). When painting, scrape the old paint or moss from the groove before it provides a bridge (2).

You can add a drip molding to a wooden windowsill that does not have a precut drip groove by pinning and gluing a ¼-inch-square hardwood strip 1½ inches back from the front edge (3). Paint or varnish the strip along with the windowsill.

SEALING AROUND WINDOW FRAMES

Scrape out old loose mortar or caulk from around the frame. Fill deep gaps with gap filler sold for the purpose, then seal all around with a flexible caulk. Caulk is available in cartridges to fit an applicator gun, or in tubes, which you squeeze just like toothpaste. Cut the end off the nozzle, then run it down the side of the frame to form a continuous, even bead. If the gap is very wide, fill it with a second bead when the first has set (follow directions). Most caulks form a skin and can be overpainted after a few hours, although they retain their waterproof characteristics even without being painted.

BRIDGED CAVITY

The simplest way to deal with a bridged wall cavity which allows water to flow to the inner leaf is to apply a water repellent to the outer surface.

However, this doesn't cure the cause, which may promote other moisture problems later. When it is convenient—when repointing perhaps—remove two or three bricks from the outside in the vicinity of the damp patch by chopping out the mortar around them. Use a small mirror and a flashlight to inspect the cavity. If you locate mortar lying on a wall tie, chip it off with a rod or opened metal coat hanger and replace the bricks.

Exposing a bridged wall tie
Remove a few bricks to chip mortar from a wall tie.

CONDENSATION

Air carries moisture as water vapor but its capacity depends on temperature. As it becomes warmer, air absorbs more water like a sponge. When water-laden air comes into contact with a surface that is colder than itself, it cools until it cannot any longer hold the water it has absorbed, and just like the sponge being squeezed, it condenses, depositing water in liquid form onto the surface.

Conditions for condensation

The air in a house is normally warm enough to hold water without reaching the saturation point, but a great deal of moisture is also produced by members of the household using baths and showers, cooking and even breathing. In cold weather when the low temperature outside cools the external walls and windows below the temperature of the heated air inside, all that extra water runs down window panes and soaks into the wallpaper and plaster. Matters are made worse in the winter by sealing off windows and doors so that fresh air cannot replace humid air before it condenses.

Dampness in a fairly new house which is in good condition is almost certainly due to condensation.

The root cause of condensation is rarely simple, as it is a result of a combination of air temperature, humidity, lack of ventilation and thermal insulation. Tackling one of them in isolation may transfer condensation elsewhere or even exaggerate the symptoms. However, the box opposite lists major contributing factors to the total problem.

Condensation appears first on cold glazing

CONDENSATION: PRINCIPAL CAUSES

CAUSE	SYMPTOMS	REMEDY
Insufficient heat The air in an unheated room may already be close to the point of saturation. (Raising the temperature increases the ability of the air to absorb moisture without condensing.)	General condensation.	Heat the room (but not with a kerosene heater, which produces moisture).
Kerosene A kerosene heater produces as much water vapor as the fuel it burns, and condensation will form on windows, walls and ceilings.	General condensation in the room where the heater is used.	Substitute another form of heating.
Uninsulated walls and ceilings Moist air readily condenses on cold exterior walls and ceilings.	Widespread dampness and mold. The line of ceiling joists is picked out as mold grows less well along these relatively "warm" spots.	Install attic insulation.
Cold bridge Even when a wall has cavity insulation, there can be a cold bridge across the window frames and studs in contact with both exterior and interior walls.	Damp patches or mold surrounding the window frames.	Try painting walls with vapor-barrier paint. If necessary, attach polyethylene vapor barrier over the inside wall, then cover with paneling.
Uninsulated pipes Cold water pipes attract condensation. It is often confused with a leak when water collects and drips from the lowest point of a pipe run.	Line of dampness on a ceiling or wall following the pipework. Isolated patch on a ceiling, where water drops from plumbing. Beads of moisture on the underside of a pipe.	Insulate the plumbing with fiberglass wrapping.
Cold windows Glass shows condensation usually before any other surface, due to the fact that it's very thin and constantly exposed to the elements.	Misted glass, or water collecting in pools at the bottom of the window pane.	Double-glaze the window. If condensation occurs inside a secondary glazing system, place some silica gel crystals (which absorb moisture) in the cavity between panes.
Sealed fireplace When a fireplace opening is blocked, the air trapped inside the flue cannot circulate and consequently condenses on the inside, eventually soaking through the brickwork.	Damp patches appearing anywhere on the chimney breast.	Ventilate the chimney by inserting a grille at a low level in the blocked-up part of the fireplace.
A___ ___tion blocking airways If ___ ___ blocks the spaces a___ ___ air cannot circulate in th___ ___ condensation is able to ___	Widespread mold affecting the timbers in the roof space.	Unblock the airways and, if possible, fit a ventilator grille in the soffit.
C___ ___cent building If ___ ___ork involving ne___ ___ especially pl___ ___ may be the result of ___ ___ing moisture as th___	General condensation affecting walls, ceilings, windows and solid floors.	Wait for the new work to dry out, then review the situation, before decorating or otherwise treating.

DAMP-PROOFING A CELLAR

Being at least partially below ground level, the walls and floors of a cellar or basement invariably suffer from dampness to some extent. If the problem cannot be tackled from the outside—usually most effective—you will have to seal out the moisture by treating the internal surfaces. Rising dampness in concrete floors, whatever the situation, can be treated as described below, but penetrating or rising dampness in walls other than in a cellar should be cured at the source. Merely sealing the internal surface encourages the dampness to penetrate elsewhere eventually. Also make sure a treated cellar is properly ventilated, and even heated to avoid condensation problems in the future.

Treating the floor

If you are laying a new concrete floor, incorporate a moisture barrier during its construction. If the barrier was omitted or has failed in an existing floor, seal the floor with a heavy-duty, moisture-curing polyurethane.

Preparing the surface
The floor must be clean and grease-free. Fill any cracks and small holes by priming with one coat of urethane, then one hour later apply a mortar made from 6 parts sand: 1 part cement plus enough urethane to produce a stiff paste. Although urethane can be applied to damp or dry surfaces, it will penetrate a dry floor better, so force-dry excessively damp basements with a fan heater before treatment. Remove all heaters from the room before you begin damp-proofing.

Applying urethane
Use a broom to apply the first coat of urethane using the coverage recommended by the manufacturer. If you are treating a room with a damp-proof barrier in the walls, take the urethane coating up behind the baseboard to meet it.

Two or three hours later, apply a second coat. Further delay may result in poor intercoat adhesion. Apply three or four coats in all.

After three days, you can lay any conventional floorcovering or use the floor as it is.

PATCHING ACTIVE LEAKS

Before you damp-proof a cellar, patch cracks which are active water leaks (running water) with a quick-drying hydraulic cement. Supplied as a powder for mixing with water, the cement expands as it hardens, sealing out the running water.

Undercut a crack or hole with a chisel and club hammer. Mix up cement and hold it in your hand until warm, then push it into the crack. Hold it in place with your hand or a trowel for three to five minutes until hard.

Treating a wall with bitumen latex emulsion
1 Skim coat of mortar
2 Coat of bitumen latex
3 Furring strips
4 Plasterboard

Moisture-curing polyurethane
Damp-proof a floor with three or four coats of urethane applied with a broom.

TREATING THE WALLS

If you want, you can continue with moisture-cured polyurethane to completely seal the walls and floor of a cellar. Decorate with latex or oil paints within 24 to 48 hours after treatment for maximum adhesion.

If you'd prefer to hang wallpaper, apply two coats of latex paint first and use a heavy-duty paste. Don't hang impervious wallcoverings such as vinyl, however, as it's important that the wall be able to "breathe."

Bitumen latex emulsion
Where you plan to sheetrock the basement walls, you can seal out dampness with a cheaper product, bitumen latex emulsion. It is not suitable as an unprotected covering to walls or floors, although it is often used as an integral damp-proof membrane (DPM) under the top layer of a concrete floor and as a waterproof adhesive for some tiles and wooden parquet flooring.

Chip off old plaster, if necessary, to expose the brickwork, then apply a skim coat of mortar to smooth the surface. Paint the wall with two coats of bitumen emulsion, joining with the DPM in the floor. Attach furring strips to the coated wall using construction adhesive, then install plasterboard.

Cement-based waterproof coating
In severe conditions, use a cement-based waterproof coating. Chip off old plaster or stucco to expose the wall. Then, to seal the junction between a concrete floor and the wall, cut a groove about ¾ inch wide by the same depth. Brush out the debris and fill the channel with hydraulic cement (see left), finishing it off neatly as an angled fillet.

Mix the powdered cement-based coating to a butterlike consistency, according to the manufacturer's instructions, then apply two coats to the wall with a bristle brush.

However, when brick walls are damp, they bring salts to the surface in the form of white crystals known as efflorescence, so before treating with waterproof coating, apply a salt-inhibiting stucco consisting of 1 part sulphate-resisting cement: 2 parts clean rendering sand. Add 1 part liquid bonding agent to 3 parts of the mixing water. Apply a thin troweled coat to a rough wall or brush it into a relatively smooth surface and allow it to set.

6

INSULATION & VENTILATION

INSULATION

No matter what fuel you use, the cost of heating a home has, over recent years, risen dramatically—and there's no reason to suppose it won't continue to rise, perhaps at an even faster rate. What makes matters worse for many homeowners is the heat escaping from their drafty, uninsulated homes. Even if the expense of heating wasn't an important factor, the improved comfort and health of the occupants would more than justify the effort of installing adequate insulation.

Specifications for insulation

Homes in nearly all parrts of the United States benefit from some amount of insulation. Even in the warmest parts of the country insulation is valuable in keeping excessive heat from infiltrating living spaces and in improving the efficiency of air conditioners by preventing cooled air from rapidly escaping. Reputable insulation contractors or your local building inspector can tell you the amount of insulation recommended for your region. When comparing thermal insulating materials, you'll encounter certain technical specifications:

U-values

The building materials that are already present in your house have been rated by the construction industry and government housing authorities according to the degree to which the materials conduct heat. For individual materials, these ratings are called K-values, and represent the total heat transmitted per square foot per hour between the surfaces of two materials when there is a temperature difference between the two of 1 degree F. When the passage of heat is measured through an entire structure—such as a wall, ceiling or floor, which is made up of several different materials plus air spaces—the rating is called the U-value. The higher the U-value, the more rapidly heat passes from one surface of the structure to another.

R-values

Adding insulation reduces U-values (but not K-values) by resisting the passage of heat through a structure. The degree of resistance is termed the R-value, and it is by this rating that insulation is compared and sold. Materials with superior insulating qualities have the highest R-values.

CHOOSING INSULATION PRIORITIES

To many people, the initial outlay for total house insulation is prohibitive, even though they will concede that it is cost-effective in the long term. Nevertheless, it's important to at least begin insulating as soon as possible —every measure contributes some saving.

Many authorities suggest that 35 percent of lost heat escapes through the walls of an average house, 25 percent through its roof, 25 percent through drafty doors and windows and 15 percent through the floor. At best, this can be taken as a rough guide only as it is difficult to define an "average" home and therefore to deduce the rate of heat loss. A town house, for instance, will lose less than a detached house of the same size, yet both may have a roof of the same area and a similar condition. Large, ill-fitting sash windows will permit far more drafts than small, well-fitting casements, and so on.

The figures identify the major routes for heat loss, but don't necessarily indicate where you should begin your program in order to achieve the quickest return on your investment or, for that matter, the most immediate improvement in comfort. Start with the relatively inexpensive measures.

1 HOT-WATER HEATER AND PIPES

Begin by insulating your hot-water storage heater and any exposed pipework running through unheated areas of the house. This treatment will constitute a considerable saving in a matter of only a few months.

2 RADIATORS

Apply metallic foil behind any radiators on an outside wall. It will reflect heat back into the room before the wall absorbs it.

3 DRAFTPROOFING

Seal off the major air leaks around windows and doors. For a modest outlay, draftproofing provides a substantial return both economically and in terms of your comfort. It is also easy to accomplish.

4 ROOF

Tackle the insulation of the roof next as, in addition to the eventual reduction in fuel bills, you may be eligible for assistance towards the cost of its insulation. Insulating the roof is usually the most cost-effective major insulating task.

5 WALLS

Depending on the construction of your house, insulating the walls may be a sound investment. However, it's likely to be relatively expensive, so it will take several years to recoup your initial expenditure.

6 FLOORS

Most of us insulate our floors to some extent by laying carpets or tiles. Taking extra measures will depend on the degree of comfort you wish to achieve and whether you can install more efficient insulation while carrying out some other improvement to the floor, such as laying new boards.

7 DOUBLE GLAZING (STORM WINDOWS)

Contrary to typical advertisements, double glazing will produce only a slow return on your investment, especially if you choose one of the more expensive systems. However, it may help to increase the value of your property— a double-glazed room is definitely cozier, and you will be less troubled by noise from outside, especially if you choose to install triple glazing.

INSULATING PIPES, WATER HEATERS AND RADIATORS

Insulating a hot-water heater

One of the least expensive, most effective energy-savers possible is to insulate your hot-water heater. Even so-called insulated heaters often have less than 1 inch of insulation surrounding the cylinder.

Many hardware, heating- and home-supply stores stock commercial kits containing precut fiberglass insulation for wrapping around hot-water tanks of the sizes shown on the package label. These are normally sufficient and so inexpensive that if you can obtain one to fit your hot-water heater, it makes economic sense to purchase a ready-made kit rather than make your own. However, making your own water-heater insulating jacket is simple. Merely cut strips of paper-backed fiberglass insulation material (the thicker the better), wrap them horizontally around the heater and fasten them in place with strips of duct tape. Be sure to leave the thermostat, pressure relief valve and control knobs exposed. On gas- or oil-fired heaters, cut the insulation to stop 2 inches from the vent stack (which usually connects to the furnace piping) and air intake (usually located at the base of the tank). Leave these areas exposed as well.

Insulating pipe runs

You should insulate hot-water pipes where their radiant heat is not contributing to the warmth of your home, and also cold-water pipe runs in unheated areas of the house, where they could freeze. You can wrap pipework in one of several types of tape, some of which are self-adhesive. However, it is more convenient to use foamed plastic tubes designed expressly for the purpose, especially along pipes running close to and clipped to a wall, which would be awkward and extremely difficult to wrap.

Plastic tubes are made to fit pipes of different diameters. More expensive tubing incorporates a metallic foil backing to reflect some of the heat back into hot-water pipes.

Most tubes are preslit along their length so that they can be sprung over the pipe (**1**). Butt successive lengths of tube end-to-end and seal the joints with PVC adhesive tape.

At a bend in the pipe, cut small segments out of the split edge so the plastic tube bends without crimping. Fit it around the pipe (**2**) and seal the closed joints with tape. If pipe is joined with an elbow fitting at the ends of the two lengths of tube, butt them together (**3**) and seal with tape.

Cut lengths of tube to fit completely around a tee-joint, linking them with a wedge-shaped butt joint (**4**) and seal with tape as before.

1 Spring onto pipe	**2 Cut to fit bend**
3 Miter over elbows	**4 Butt at tee-point**

Reflecting heat from a radiator

Up to 25 percent of the radiant heat from a radiator on an outside wall is lost to the wall behind. Reclaim perhaps half this wasted heat by installing a foil-faced, expanded polystyrene lining behind the radiator to reflect it back into the room.

The material is available as rolls, sheets or tiles to fit any size and shape of radiator. It is easier to stick the foil on the wall when the radiator is removed but it is not an essential requirement.

Turn off the radiator and measure it, including the position of the brackets. Use a sharp trimming knife or scissors to cut the foil to size so that it is slightly smaller than the radiator all around. Cut narrow slots to fit over the mounting brackets (**1**).

Apply heavy-duty fungicidal wallpaper paste to the back of the sheet and slide it behind the radiator (**2**). Rub it down with a radiator roller or smooth it against the wall with a wooden strip. Allow enough time for the adhesive to dry (follow manufacturer's instructions) before turning the radiator on again.

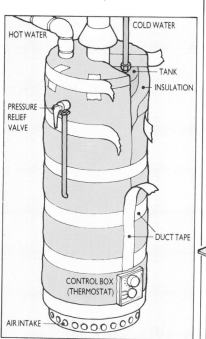

Insulating a hot-water heater
Fit insulation snugly around the tank and wrap insulating foam tubes (see above right) around the pipework, especially the hot-water outlet pipe.

1 Cut slots to align with wall brackets

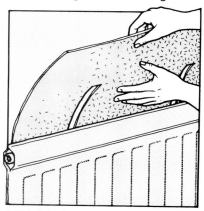

2 Slide lining behind radiator and press to wall

DRAFTPROOFING DOORS

A certain amount of ventilation is desirable for a healthy environment and to keep water vapor at an acceptable level; it's also essential to enable certain heating appliances to operate properly and safely. But using uncontrolled drafts to ventilate a house is not the most efficient way of dealing with the problem. Drafts account for a large proportion of the heat lost from the home and are also responsible for a good deal of discomfort. Draftproofing is easy to fit, requires no special tools, and there's a wide choice of threshold weatherstripping available to suit all locations.

Locating and curing drafts

Test exterior doors—and windows—first, and seal only those interior doors which are the worst offenders to provide "trickle" ventilation from room to room. Check out other possible sources of drafts, such as floorboards and baseboards, fireplaces, attic hatches, and overflow pipes from plumbing fixtures.

Locate drafts by running the flat of your hand along the likely gaps. Dampening your skin will enhance its sensitivity to cold, or wait for a very windy day to conduct your search.

There are so many manufacturers and variations of threshold weatherstripping excluders, it's quite impossible to describe them all, but the following examples illustrate the principles commonly employed to seal out drafts. Choose the best you can afford, but perhaps more importantly, try to decide which type of threshold system will suit your particular requirements best.

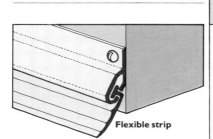
Flexible strip

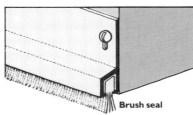
Brush seal

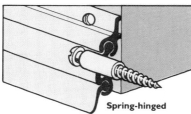
Spring-hinged

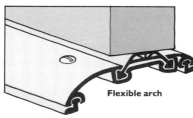
Flexible arch

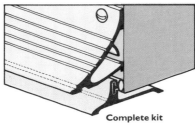
Complete kit

THRESHOLD WEATHERSTRIP SYSTEMS

The gap between the door and floor can be very large and will admit fierce drafts. Use a weatherstripped threshold to seal this gap. If it is to be used on an exterior door, make sure it is suitable for this purpose. Buy a device that fits the opening exactly, or cut it to fit from a larger size.

FLEXIBLE-STRIP WEATHERSTRIPPING

The simplest form of threshold weatherstrip is a flexible strip of plastic or rubber, that sweeps against the floorcovering to form a seal. The basic versions are self-adhesive strips that are simply pressed along the bottom of the door, but others have a rigid plastic or aluminum extrusion screwed to the door to hold the strip in contact with the floor. This type of weatherstrip is rarely suitable for exterior doors and quickly wears out. However, it is inexpensive and easy to fit. Most types work best over smooth flooring.

BRUSH SEAL

A nylon bristle brush set into a metal or plastic extrusion acts as a draft excluder. It is suitable for slightly uneven or textured floorcoverings; the same excluder works on both hinged and sliding doors.

SPRING-HINGED

A plastic strip and its extruded clip are spring-loaded to lift from the floor as the door is opened. On closing the door, the strip is pressed against the floor by a stop screwed to the door frame. This is a good-quality interior and exterior weatherstripping that reduces wear on the floorcovering.

FLEXIBLE ARCH

An aluminum extrusion with a vinyl arched insert presses against the bottom edge of the door. The extrusion has to be nailed or screwed to the floor, so it would be difficult to use on a solid concrete floor. If you fit one for an exterior door, make sure it is fitted with additional under-seals to prevent the rain from seeping beneath it. You may have to plane the bottom of the door.

DOOR KITS

The best solution for an outside door is a kit combining an aluminum weatherstrip, which sheds the rainwater, and a threshold with a built-in tubular rubber or plastic draft excluder. Components can be purchased individually or as a package.

WEATHERSTRIPPING THE DOOR EDGES

Any well-fitting door requires a gap of 1/16 inch at top and sides so that it can be operated smoothly. However, the combined area of a gap this large loses a great deal of heat. There are several ways to seal it, some of which are described here. The cheaper varieties have to be renewed regularly.

FOAM STRIPS

The most straightforward weatherstrip is a self-adhesive foam plastic strip, which you stick around the rabbet and is compressed by the door, forming a seal. The cheapest polyurethane foam will be good for one or two seasons (but it's useless if painted) and is suitable for interior use only. Better-quality vinyl-coated polyurethane, rubber or PVC foams are more durable and do not deteriorate on exposure to sunlight, as their cheaper counterparts do. Don't stretch foam weatherstripping when applying it, as it reduces its efficiency. The door may be difficult to close at first but the stripping soon adjusts.

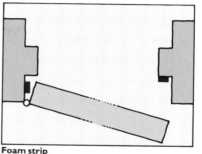

Foam strip

FLEXIBLE TUBE

A small vinyl tube held in a plastic or metal extrusion is compressed to fill the gap around the door. The cheapest versions have an integrally molded flange, which can be stapled to the door frame, but they are not as neat.

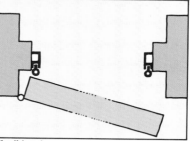

Flexible tube

SPRING STRIP

Thin metal or plastic strips with a sprung leaf are pinned or glued to the door frame. The top and closing edges of the door brush past the leaf, which seals the gap, while the hinged edge compresses it. It can't cope with uneven surfaces unless it incorporates a foam strip on the flexible leaf.

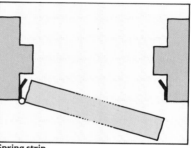

Spring strip

V-STRIP

A variation on the spring strip, the leaf is bent right back to form a V-shape. The strip can be mounted to fill the gap around the door or attached to the door stop so that the door closes against it. Most are cheap and unobtrusive.

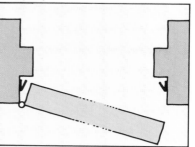

V-strip

SEAM SEALANT

With this method, a wad of rubberized sealant can be pressed into the door frame. Squeeze a wad of sealant onto the doorstop, then cover it with low-tack masking tape. Close the door, which will flatten the wad and force sealant against the door frame. Then remove the tape, leaving the sealant firmly attached.

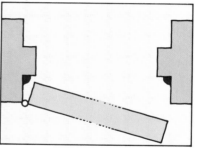
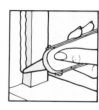

Sealant

SEALING KEYHOLES AND LETTERBOXES

Make sure the outer keyhole for a mortise lock is fitted with a pivoting coverplate to seal out drafts in the winter.

Special hinged flaps are made for screwing over the inside of a letterbox. Some types contain a brush seal behind the flap, forming an even better seal.

Keyhole coverplate
The coverplate is part of the escutcheon.

Letterbox flap
A hinged flap neatens and draftproofs a letterbox.

GENERAL DRAFTPROOFING

Hinged casement windows can be sealed with any of the draft excluders suggested for fitting around the edge of a door, but draftproofing a sliding sash window presents a more difficult problem.

Sealing a sash window

The top and bottom closing rails of a sash window can be sealed with any form of compressible weatherstripping; the sliding edges admit fewer drafts but they can be sealed with a brush seal fixed to the frame—inside for the lower sash, outside for the top one.

A spring or V-strip could be used to seal the gap between the central meeting rails, but you may not be able to reverse the sashes once it is fitted. Perhaps the simplest solution is to seal it with a reusable tubular plastic strip.

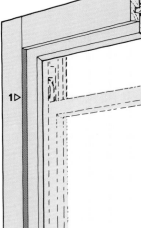

1 Brush seal

2 Spring or V-strip

3 Tubular strip

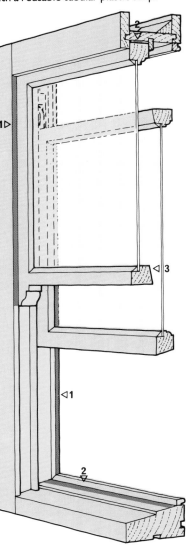

Clear liquid sealer

If you plan never to open a window during the winter, you could seal all gaps with a clear liquid draft seal, applied from a tube. It is virtually invisible when dry and can be peeled off, without damaging the paintwork, when you want to open the window again after the winter.

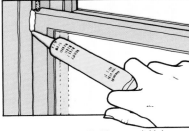

Liquid sealer is supplied in a special injector

Sealing a pivot window

As you close a pivot window, the moving frame comes to rest against fixed stops, but the stops for the top half of the window are on the outside of the house. These exterior stops, at least, must be sealed with draft excluders that are weatherproof, so use spring or V-strip compressible weatherstripping, or a good-quality flexible tube strip. Alternatively, use a draftproofing sealant.

DRAFTY FIREPLACES

A chimney can be an annoying source of drafts. If the fireplace is unused, you can seal it off completely, but be sure to fit a ventilator to provide ventilation for the flue.

If you want to retain the appearance of an open fireplace, cut a sheet of thick polystyrene to seal the throat but leave a hole about 2 inches across to provide some ventilation. Should you ever want to use the fireplace again, don't forget to remove the polystyrene, which is flammable.

DRAFTPROOFING FLOORS AND BASEBOARDS

The ventilated crawlspace below a wooden first floor is a prime source of drafts through gaps in the floorboards and between the wall and the baseboard. The best solution is to install fiberglass insulation beneath the floorboards. Seal the gap between the baseboard and the floor with caulk applied with an applicator gun or in the form of quarter-round strips. For a neat finish, pin molding to the baseboard to cover the sealed gap.

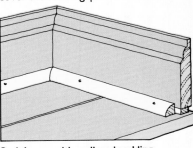

Seal the gap with caulk and molding

DRAFTPROOFING A DRYER VENT

An open dryer vent leading to the outside of the house can be a significant source of drafts both in winter and during windy weather. If yours is an electric dryer, check with a heating expert about the possibility of connecting the dryer vent to the furnace return duct, thus saving the heat generated by the dryer which is otherwise wasted by being expelled through the vent. Do not vent the dryer directly into the laundry area; dryer air is damp and you risk an indoor condensation problem. Gas dryers should remain vented to the outdoors.

To seal off the dryer vent permanently or for occasional use, merely disconnect the flexible dryer exhaust pipe from the wall opening and pack the opening with fiberglass insulation (enclose the insulation in a small muslin sack if it is to be removed often). Remove the insulation and reconnect the pipe each time you use the dryer.

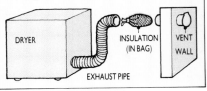

INSULATING ROOFS

About a quarter of the heat lost from an average house goes through the roof, so preventing this should be one of your priorities when it comes to insulating your home. Providing you're able to gain access to your attic floor, reducing substantial heat loss is just a matter of laying the insulation material between the joists: It's cheap, quick and effective. If you want to use the attic, insulating the sloping surface of the roof is a quite straightforward alternative.

Treating a flat roof

A flat roof—on an extension, for instance—may also need insulating, but since blowing in insulation between the rafters from outside may endanger overhead wiring and fixtures, the only really practical solution for most homeowners is to apply a layer of insulation to the ceiling surface, or remove the existing ceiling, insulate, then install a new ceiling. Installing ceiling tiles is an alternative, but their insulation value is minimal.

Preparing the attic

On inspection, you may find that the roof space has existing but inadequate insulation. It is worth installing extra insulation to bring it up to the recommended R-value rating for your climate region. Check roof timbers for pest damage or signs of rot so that they can be treated first. Make sure that the electrical wiring is sound; lift it clear so that you can lay insulation beneath it.

Plaster or plasterboard ceiling surfaces will not support your weight, so lay a plank or two, or a panel of chipboard, across the joists so that you can move about safely. Don't allow it to overlap the joists; if you step on the edge it will tip over.

If there is no permanent lighting in the attic, rig up a "trouble" light on an extension cord, so you can move it wherever it is needed, or hang it high up for best overall light.

Most attics are very dusty, so wear old clothes and a paper respirator. You may wish to wear protective gloves, particularly if you are handling fiberglass batts or blanket insulation, which can irritate sensitive skin.

TYPES OF INSULATION

There's a wide range of different insulation materials available. Assess your requirements and study the options before purchasing.

BLANKET INSULATION

Fiberglass and mineral- or rock-fiber blanket insulation is commonly sold as rolls made to fit snugly between the joists. The same material cut to shorter lengths is also sold as "batts." A minimum thickness of 3 1/2 inches is recommended for attic insulation. Blanket insulation may be unbacked, paper-backed to improve its tear-resistance, or have a foil backing as a vapor barrier (see below).

The unbacked type is normally used for laying on the attic floor. Blankets are 2 to 6 inches thick and typically 15 inches wide—suitable for the normal 16-inch joist spacing. For wider-than-usual joist spacing, choose the 23-inch width (cut in half with a panel saw before you unwrap it for narrow joist spaces). Rolls are sold by square-foot area. Blankets are usually sold in 4-foot lengths.

If you want to fit blanket insulation to the sloping part of the roof, make sure it has a lip of backing along each side for stapling to the rafters.

Both fiberglass and mineral fibers are nonflammable and proofed against moisture, rot and vermin.

LOOSE-FILL INSULATION

Loose-fill insulation in pellet or granular form is poured between the joists on the attic floor to a minimum depth of 3 1/2 inches, although a depth of 5 1/2 inches is recommended for the same value of insulation as 3 1/2-inch-thick blanket—but this could rise above some joists.

Exfoliated vermiculite, made from a mineral called mica, is the most common form of loose-fill insulation, but others such as mineral wool, polystyrene or cork granules may be available. Loose-fill is sold in bags containing enough material to cover a nominal 25 square feet to a depth of 4 inches.

It's inadvisable to use loose-fill in a drafty, exposed attic, because high winds can cause it to blow about. However, it's convenient to use if the joists are irregularly spaced.

BLOWN INSULATION

Professional contractors can provide interjoist attic insulation by blowing glass, mineral or cellulose fibers through a large hose. A minimum, even depth of 4 inches is required. Blown fiber insulation may be unsuitable for a house in a windy location, but seek the advice of a contractor.

RIGID INSULATION

Boards made of foamed plastic—polystyrene and polyurethane—are extremely efficient insulators. Most lumberyards and building supply stores stock them in 4 × 8-foot sheets, in thicknesses of 3/4 to 2 inches. Rigid insulation is easy to install where framing is level and uniform. Fire codes require that it has a minimum 1/2-inch-thick fireproof covering.

VAPOR BARRIERS

Installing insulation has the effect of making the areas of the house outside that layer of insulation colder than before, so increasing the risk of condensation either on or within the structure itself. In time this could result in decreased value of the insulation and may promote a serious outbreak of dry rot in the house framing.

To prevent this from happening, it's necessary to provide adequate ventilation for those areas outside the insulation or to install a vapor barrier on the inner, or warm, side of the insulation to prevent moisture-laden air from passing through. This is usually a plastic sheet or layer of metal foil. Foil vapor barrier sometimes makes up the backing of blanket or batt insulation. The vapor barrier must be continuous and undamaged or its effect is greatly reduced.

SEE ALSO

Details for: ▷

Ceiling tiles	112
Termites	246–247
Wet and dry rot	251
Condensation	256–257
Roof ventilation	277–278

R-VALUES FOR COMMON INSULATION MATERIALS

Material	Approx. R-Value (per inch)
Fiberglass	3.5
Mineral fiber	3.5
Cellulose	3.7
Polystyrene (beadboard)	4.0
Polystyrene (extruded)	5.0
Polyurethane	7.0
Isocyanurate	7.5

● **Ventilating the attic**
Laying insulation between the joists increases the risk of condensation in an unheated roof space above, but, provided there are vents at the eaves and/or ridge, there will be enough air circulating to keep the attic dry.

INSULATING THE ATTIC

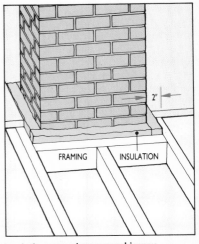

Insulating around ceiling light fixtures
Leave 3-in. space on all sides surrounding recessed ceiling light fixture to avoid fire hazard. Frame around fixture to prevent loose fill from creeping.

Laying blanket insulation

Seal gaps around pipes, vents or wiring entering the attic from outdoors with flexible caulk. Remove the blanket wrapping in the attic (it's compressed for storage and transportation but swells to its true thickness when released) and begin by placing one end of a roll into the eaves, vapor-barrier side down. Make sure you don't cover the ventilation gap—trim the end of the blanket to a wedge shape so it does not obstruct the airflow, or fit eaves vents.

Unroll the blanket between the joists, pressing it down to form a snug fit. If the roll is slightly wider than the joist spacing, allow it to turn up against the timbers on each side.

Continue at the opposite side of the attic with another roll. Cut it to butt up against the end of the first one, using a razor-knife or long-bladed pair of scissors. Continue across the attic until all the spaces are filled. Cut the insulation to fit odd spaces.

Do not cover the casings of any light fittings which protrude into the attic space. Avoid covering electrical cables, as there's a risk it may cause overheating. Instead, lay the cables on top of the blanket, or clip them to the sides of the joists above it.

If you have an attic cistern, do not insulate beneath it; heat rising from the room below will help to prevent freezing. Cut a piece of insulation to fit the hatch cover and attach it with glue. Fit foam weatherstripping around the edge of the hatch.

Laying loose-fill insulation

Take similar precautions against condensation to those described for blanket insulation. If the attic is poorly ventilated, install a polyethylene-sheet vapor barrier directly on top of the ceiling and joists. To prevent blocking the eaves, wedge strips of plywood or thick cardboard between the joists. Pour insulation between the joists and distribute it roughly with a broom. Level it with a spreader cut from hardboard to fit between the joists.

To insulate the entrance hatch, screw battens around the outer edge of the cover, fill with granules and nail on a hardboard lid to contain them.

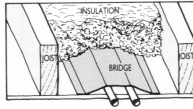

Insulating pipes between the joists

Double-thick blankets

You can install fiberglass insulation that is thicker than the height of the joists. First slash the vapor-barrier backing of the top layer of insulation every few inches, then lay it over the bottom layer at right angles to the existing layer. Take care not to block vents in the eaves.

INSULATING AROUND A CHIMNEY

Wood framing around a chimney should be 2 inches from masonry on all sides to avoid a fire hazard. To insulate, remove backing from fiberglass insulation and hand-pack area between framing and masonry.

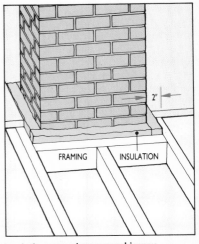

Insulating around masonry chimney

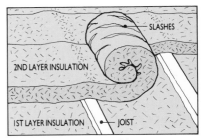

Installing new batts over old ones

Right
Seal gaps around pipes and vents (**1**). Place end of roll against eaves and trim ends (**2**) or fit eaves vents (**3**). Press rolls between joists (**4**).

Far right
Seal gaps to prevent condensation (**1**). Stop insulant from blocking ventilation with strips of plywood (**2**) or eaves vents (**3**). Cover cold water pipes with a cardboard bridge (**4**), then use a spreader to level the insulant (**5**). Insulate and draftproof the hatch cover (**6**).

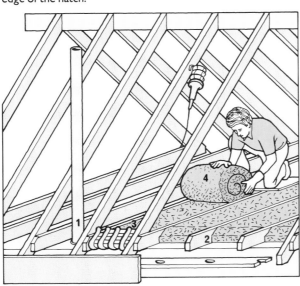

Laying blanket insulation in the attic

Spreading loose-fill insulation in the attic

INSULATING A SLOPING ROOF

Insulating between the rafters

If the attic is in use, you will need to insulate the sloping part of the roof in order to heat the living space. Repair the roof covering first, as not only will leaks soak the insulation, but also it will be difficult to spot them after insulating.

Condensation is a serious problem when you install insulation between the rafters, as the underside of the sheathing will become very cold. You must provide a 1 1/2-inch gap between the tiles and the insulation to promote sufficient ventilation to keep the space dry, which in turn determines the maximum thickness of insulation you can install. The ridge and eaves must be ventilated and you should include a vapor barrier

on the warm side of the insulation, either by fitting foil-backed blanket or by stapling sheets of polyethylene to the lower edges of the rafters to cover unbacked insulation.

Whatever insulation you decide on, you can cover the rafters with sheets of plasterboard as a final decorative layer. The sizes of the panels will be dictated by the largest boards you can pass through the hatchway. Use plasterboard nails or screws to hold the panels against the rafters, staggering the joints. Alternatively, fit solid insulation between the rafters, with a vapor barrier and plasterboard over that, to meet fire code requirements.

Attaching blanket insulation

Unfold the side flanges from a roll of foil-backed blanket and staple them to the underside of the rafters. When

fitting adjacent rolls, overlap the edge of the vapor barrier to provide a continuous layer.

Attaching solid insulation

The simplest method of attaching solid insulation is to cut the panels accurately so they wedge-fit between the rafters. If necessary, screw furring to the sides of the rafters to which you can fix the

insulating sheets. Allow a 1 1/2-inch air space. Staple a polyethylene sheet vapor barrier over the rafters. Double-fold the joints over a rafter and staple in place.

INSULATING AN ATTIC ROOM

If an attic room was built as part of the original dwelling, it will be virtually impossible to insulate the pitch of the roof unless you are prepared to remove the old plaster and proceed as left. It may be simpler to insulate from the inside as for a flat roof, but your headroom may be seriously hampered.

Insulate the short vertical wall of the attic from inside the crawlspace, making sure the vapor barrier faces the inner, warm side of the partition. Insulate between the joists of the crawlspace at the same time.

Fit blankets with vapor barrier facing the room

Insulating a room in the attic
Surround the room itself with insulation but leave the floor uninsulated so that the room benefits from rising heat generated by the space below.

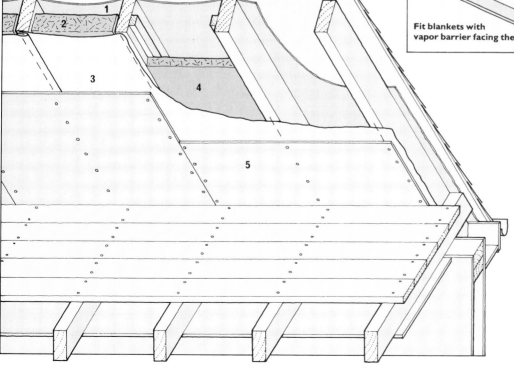

Insulating an attic from the inside
Fit blanket or sheet insulation between the rafters.
1 Minimum of 1 1/2 in. between insulation and roof for ventilation
2 Blanket or batts
3 Vapor barrier with double-folded joints stapled to rafters
4 Solid insulation fixed to battens
5 Plasterboard fastened over vapor barrier

267

INSULATING ABOVE RAFTERS

Installing insulation between the rafters and the roof covering results in a more complete thermal envelope because it avoids thermal bridging—the loss of heat from inside the house by conduction through the rafters (which are not covered by insulation). *Insulating this way is best done during new construction. Before retrofitting, carefully compare the costs of this method of insulating vs. results with an insulation contractor or home-energy analyst.*

Treatment over covered rafters

Where rafters are covered from view by ceiling material attached underneath, first lay down rigid foam insulation across the top surfaces of the rafters. Place strips of 1 × 2 lumber on top of the insulation, directly over the rafters, then, using nails which will penetrate at least 2 inches through the 1 × 2 strips into the rafters, fasten the insulation by nailing through the strips and insulation into the rafters. Attach roof decking over the insulation by nailing into the wood strips. Before installing the ceiling, staple sheets of polyethylene vapor barrier across the undersides of the rafters.

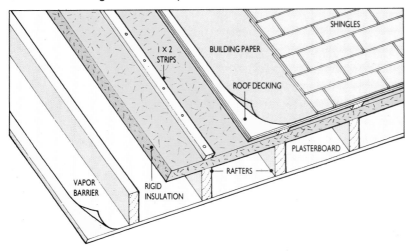

Treatment over exposed rafters

Where rafters are exposed, place insulation on top of the decking above. First lay down sheets of polyethylene vapor barrier. Then position rigid insulation on top, and nail through the insulation into the decking above the rafters. Cover the insulation with building paper before installing roof covering (no further decking is required).

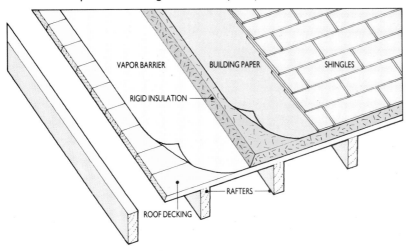

INSULATING WALLS

Although a great amount of heat escapes through the walls of a house, installing insulation in finished walls can be more expensive than the savings returned in decreased energy bills. If no insulation exists in the walls, plan on a payback period of from 5 to 10 years, the shorter time if you live in a cold climate, the longer time if you live where winters are moderate to mild. If the walls already contain some insulation, it is probable that the cost of adding more would not be offset by energy savings except over a very long period, perhaps as long as you own the home. Consult an insulation contractor and home-energy analyst for advice. If your home is completely uninsulated, check with local building authorities about the possibility of qualifying for municipal grants to help defray insulation expenses.

Options

In new construction or if you are considering major renovation, installing fiberglass-blanket insulation between the wall studs is the most common and generally the most practical method. The thickness of the insulation you'll be able to install depends upon the width of the lumber used for the studs, although by combining blanket insulation with additional insulation such as rigid foam or insulated vinyl siding applied to the exterior of the house, necessary R-values can be achieved. A typical stud-framed wall built with 2 × 4 lumber and finished on the inside with plasterboard and on the outside with wood siding already has an R-value of 5 to 7. Adding 3½-inch-thick fiberglass to that wall increases the R-value to approximately R-12.

With finished walls, common practice is to have a professional drill holes through the exterior sheathing and then blow loose-fill insulation into the cavities between the studs, using special pumping equipment.

If you are planning or prepared to re-side exterior walls, consider adding rigid insulation over the existing sheathing before re-siding. Nail the insulation to the bare sheathing, seal the seams between sheets with duct tape, apply caulk where the insulation meets any trim, then install the new siding. You'll have to increase the depth of door and window trim so it meets the siding properly. To do so, attach strips of molding around the edges, the same thickness as the insulation.

Installing fiberglass blankets

Choose insulation wide enough to fit tightly between wall studs. To cut, unroll insulation backing-side down, then use a framing square or straight-edged board to compress the insulation and act as a cutting guide. Cut the insulation 2 inches longer than the bay, using a utility knife. Afterward, pull the backing away from the fiberglass at each end to create 1-inch stapling tabs.

Press the insulation into each bay, with the backing facing toward the room. With foil-backed material, staple the tabs to the inside faces of the studs so the insulation is recessed at least ¾ inch. With paper-backed material, staple the tabs flat along the outer edges of the studs, leaving no recess. Fit insulation behind obstructions, such as pipes and electrical boxes, so it lies against the exterior sheathing. Pack unbacked insulation into gaps between window and door frames.

After installation is complete, staple polyethylene vapor barrier across the entire wall, allowing plastic to extend a few inches all around (to be covered later by finish floor, ceiling, and adjacent wall covering). Carefully cut out around windows, outlet boxes, and other openings before attaching interior wall covering.

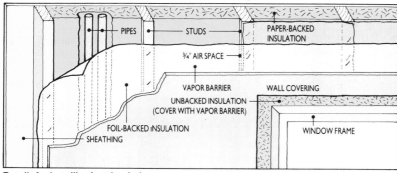

Details for installing batt insulation

Labels: PIPES, STUDS, PAPER-BACKED INSULATION, ¾" AIR SPACE, VAPOR BARRIER, WALL COVERING, UNBACKED INSULATION (COVER WITH VAPOR BARRIER), FOIL-BACKED INSULATION, SHEATHING, WINDOW FRAME

Insulating masonry walls

Above ground, masonry walls can be insulated with either blanket or rigid insulation. Below ground, because blanket insulation is susceptible to moisture damage, only rigid foam is recommended. (If you live in an extremely cold climate, insulating basement walls can cause foundation damage. Be sure to check with a local building inspector before proceeding.)

To apply blanket insulation, first cover the masonry surface with polyethylene vapor barrier, attaching it with dabs of construction adhesive. Then construct an ordinary stud wall against the masonry (nailing it to the floor and ceiling) and pack the bays with insulation as described on this page. Cover the insulation with a second vapor barrier before finishing with plasterboard or paneling.

To install rigid insulation, first attach a vapor barrier to the masonry as described, then power-nail vertical 1 × 2 furring strips to the wall, spaced 16 inches apart on center. Press insulation panels into the bays between strips—they should fit snugly—then cover the wall with vapor barrier and the finished wall covering, fastened to the furring strips.

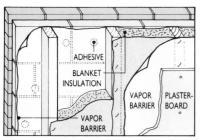

Above-ground masonry

Labels: ADHESIVE, BLANKET INSULATION, VAPOR BARRIER, PLASTER-BOARD, VAPOR BARRIER

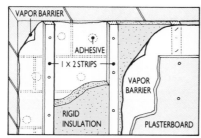

Below-ground masonry

Labels: VAPOR BARRIER, ADHESIVE, 1 × 2 STRIPS, VAPOR BARRIER, RIGID INSULATION, PLASTERBOARD

BLOWING-IN INSULATION

For most homeowners, this is a job best left to professional insulation contractors. However, equipment is available at rent-it centers if you wish to blow-in insulation yourself.

To perform the task, begin by locating all the wall studs, usually by noting the pattern of siding nails. Then shut off all power to the house. Remove a strip of siding 3 to 4 feet from the bottom of the walls and drill a pair of holes (the diameter recommended by the insulation or equipment supplier) side-by-side in each bay between studs. Check, using electrician's fish tape, for obstructions such as firestopping (horizontal boards fastened between studs) below the holes. If you find any, drill holes below them to gain access to the area beneath.

Insert the blower nozzle and blow insulation into each bay through one of the holes in each pair. Be sure the bays fill correctly, then plug the holes with corks. Drill another series of holes 4 feet above the first and repeat the procedure. Continue until you reach the top of the walls. When finished, reapply the siding.

Blowing in loose-fill insulation

Labels: HOLES, REMOVE SIDING, 4', STUDS, 4', FIRESTOPPING, LOOSE-FILL INSULATION

SAFETY

Fiberglass and mineral wool can severely irritate skin, lungs, eyes and mucous membranes. When handling, always wear long sleeves and trousers, gloves, goggles and a respirator.

INSULATING A FLOOR

Even with carpet or other covering above, heat can readily escape through the ground floor into an unheated basement or crawlspace below.

Floors are best insulated from underneath, by pressing fiberglass or mineral wool insulation between the floor joists, much the same way as in insulating a stud-frame wall. Foil-backed insulation is the best choice, since it reflects escaping heat back in the direction from where it came. Because joists are normally wider than wall studs, greater thicknesses of insulation may be used. Insulation may be pressed snugly against the subfloor (allow a ¾-inch gap if using foil-backed insulation), or be fastened level with the bottom edges of the joists. Be sure the insulation extends over the foundation sills at the ends of the joists. This is a primary heat-loss area.

No matter whether you use foil- or paper-backed insulation, the backing, which acts as a vapor barrier, must face the warm living space above. This makes fastening the insulation in place difficult, because the tabs on each side are no longer accessible. One solution is to staple wire mesh such as chicken wire across the joist edges as you install the insulation. The other—recommended especially if a basement ceiling must be installed—is to cut lengths of stiff wire each slightly longer than the distances between joists, and press them up at 18- to 20-inch intervals into each bay to hold the insulation in place above.

Insulating from below
To secure insulation between floor joists either staple wire mesh to lower edges of joists (right) or press lengths of heavy wire between joists (far right).

Crawlspaces

It is seldom necessary to fully insulate crawlspaces, provided insulation is installed beneath the house floor above. A polyethylene vapor barrier should be spread over the crawlspace floor and extended at least part way up the walls to prevent moisture buildup, and the space itself should be adequately vented to the outside. The vapor barrier may be left exposed if the space is unused.

Should insulation be required, proceed as for insulating a masonry wall or by merely draping fiberglass or mineral-wool blankets down from the foundation top. Anchor the insulation with bricks along the top, and with bricks or a length of lumber at the bottom.

BRICKS   JOIST

BLANKET INSULATION

FOUNDATION WALL

VAPOR BARRIER

2 × 4

Batt insulation for crawlspace

AIR DUCTS AND PIPES

Hot-air ducts running through unheated basements or crawlspaces should be insulated to prevent heat loss, unless such loss is desirable to warm the space. Also, ducts carrying air from central air-conditioning systems should be insulated to retain cool air if they pass through areas that are not air-conditioned. Fiberglass and mineral-wool blanket insulation, with and without a reflective vapor barrier, is sold for this purpose at heating and air-conditioning supply stores. Choose reflective-barrier insulation for air-conditioning ducts. Ordinarily, no barrier is needed for hot-air ducts.

To install the insulation, cut it into sections where necessary, wrap it around the duct, then secure the seams with duct tape.

Exposed steam and hot-water pipes should also be insulated. For these, purchase foam insulation sleeves sold especially for the purpose at plumbing and hardware stores. The sleeves are slit along one side. To install, slip the sleeve over the pipe, then seal the seam with duct tape. Insulated, adhesive pipe wrapping is also available. To attach this, merely remove the backing paper, then wrap the tape in a spiral, overlapping it slightly around the pipe along its entire exposed length.

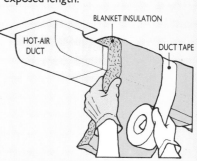

BLANKET INSULATION

HOT-AIR DUCT

DUCT TAPE

Blanket insulation for ducts

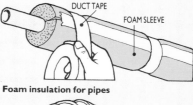

DUCT TAPE

FOAM SLEEVE

Foam insulation for pipes

ADHESIVE WRAPPING

Insulation tape for pipes

DOUBLE GLAZING

A double-glazed window consists of two sheets of glass separated by an air gap. The air gap provides an insulating layer, which reduces heat loss and sound transmission. Condensation is also reduced because the inner layer of glass remains relatively warmer than that on the outside. Factory-sealed units and secondary glazing are the two methods in common use for domestic double glazing. Both will provide good thermal insulation. Sealed units are unobtrusive, but secondary glazing can offer improved sound insulation. But which do you choose to suit your house and your lifestyle?

What size air gap?

For heat insulation, a ¾-inch gap provides the optimum level of efficiency. Below ½ inch, the air can conduct a proportion of the heat across the gap. Above ¾ inch, there is no appreciable extra gain in thermal insulation and air currents can occur, which transmit heat to the outside layer of glass. A larger gap of 4 to 8 inches is more effective for sound insulation. A combination of a sealed unit plus secondary glazing provides the ideal solution, and is known as triple glazing.

Double glazing will help to cut fuel bills, but its immediate benefit will be felt by the elimination of drafts. The cold spots associated with a larger window, particularly noticeable when sitting relatively still, will also be reduced. In terms of saving energy, the heat lost through windows is relatively small—around 10 to 12 percent—compared to the whole house. However, the installation of double glazing can halve this amount.

Double glazing will improve security against forced entry, particularly if sealed units, tempered or wired glass have been used. However, make sure that some accessible part of the window is openable to provide emergency escape in case of fire.

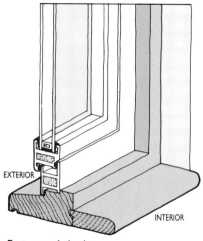

Factory-sealed unit
A complete frame system installed by a contractor.

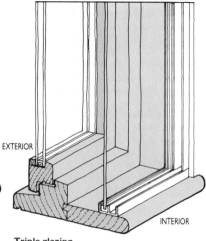

Secondary window system
Fitted in addition to the normal glazed window.

Triple glazing
A combination of secondary and sealed units.

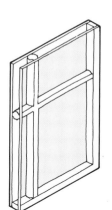

Georgian sealed unit

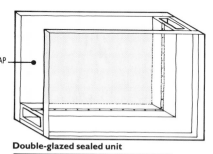

Double-glazed sealed unit

Double-glazed sealed units

Double-glazed sealed units are manufactured from two panes of glass separated by a spacer and hermetically sealed all around. The cavity between the glass may be ¼, ⅜, ½ or ¾ inch wide. The gap may contain dehydrated air to eliminate condensation between the glass, or inert gases which also improve thermal and acoustic insulation.

The thickness and type of glass is determined by the size of the unit. Clear float glass or tempered glass is common. When obscured glazing is required for privacy, patterned glass is used. Special heat-retentive sealed units are also supplied by some double glazing companies, incorporating special glass or a plastic film embodied within the unit.

For period-style windows, a leaded light and a Georgian version of the sealed unit are also produced. The former is made by bonding strips of lead to the outer pane of the glass, the latter by placing a molded framework of glazing bars in the cavity. The improved security, lack of maintenance and ease of cleaning in some way make up for their lack of character, compared with the original style of window.

Generally, these special sealed units are produced and installed by suppliers of ready-made double-glazed replacement windows. Sealed units are available for do-it-yourself installation or they can be installed by the window contractor to order by specialists. Square-edged units are made for frames with a deep rabbet, and stepped units for frames intended for single glazing.

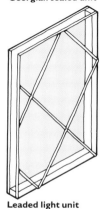

Leaded light unit

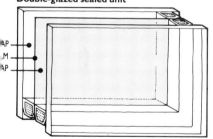

Heat-retentive sealed unit

271

SECONDARY DOUBLE GLAZING

Secondary double glazing comprises a separate pane of glass or plastic sheet which is normally fitted to the inside of existing single-glazed windows. It is a popular method for double glazing windows, being relatively easy for home installation—and usually at a fraction of the cost of other systems.

How the glazing is mounted

Glazing can be fastened to the sash frames (1), the window frames (2), or across the window reveal (3). The choice depends on the ease of installation, the type of glazing and personal requirements for ventilation.

Glazing fixed to the sash will cut down heat loss through the glass and provide accessible ventilation, but it will not stop drafts. That flxed to the window frame will reduce heat loss and stop drafts at the same time. Glazing fixed across the reveal will also offer improved sound insulation, as the air gap can be wider. Any system should be readily demountable or preferably openable to provide a change of air in a room without some other form of ventilation.

Rigid glazing of plastic or glass can be fitted to the exterior of the window opening if secondary glazing would spoil the appearance of the interior. In this case, windows which are set in a deep reveal, such as the vertically sliding sash type, are the most suitable (4).

Glazing with renewable film

Effective double glazing kits are available which consist of double-sided adhesive tape and thin plastic sheet to stretch across the window frame. Both can be removed at the end of the cold season without harming the paintwork.

Clean the window frame (1), then cut the plastic sheet roughly to size, allowing an overlap all around. Apply double-sided tape to the frame edges (2) and peel off its backing paper.

Attach the film to the top rail (3), then tension it onto the tape on the sides and bottom of the frame (4). Apply light pressure only until the film is positioned then rub it down onto the tape all around.

Use a hair dryer set to a high temperature to remove all creases and wrinkles in the film (5). Starting at an upper corner, move the dryer slowly across the film, holding it about ¼ inch from the surface. When the film is tensioned, cut off the excess plastic (6).

GLAZING POSITIONS

Secondary double glazing is particularly suitable for DIY installation, partly because it is so versatile. It is possible to fit a system to almost any style or shape of window.

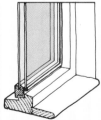

1 Sash-mounted
Glazing fixed to the opening window frame

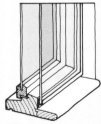

2 Frame-mounted
Glazing fixed to the structural frame

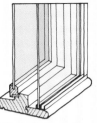

3 Reveal-mounted
Glazing fixed to the reveal and interior windowsill

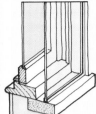

4 Exterior-fitted
Glazing fixed to the reveal and exterior windowsill

1 Wipe woodwork to remove dust and grease

2 Apply double-sided tape to the fixed frame

3 Stretch the film across the top of the frame

4 Pull the film tight and fix to sides and bottom

5 Use a hair dryer to shrink the film

6 Trim the waste with a sharp knife

PLASTIC GLAZING

Demountable systems

A simple method for interior secondary glazing uses clear plastic film or sheet. These lightweight materials are secured by self-adhesive strips or rigid molded sections, which form a seal. Most strip fastenings use plastic tracks or some form of rententive tape, which allows the secondary glazing to be removed for cleaning or ventilation. The strips and tapes usually have a flexible foam backing, which takes up slight irregularities in the woodwork. They are intended to remain in place throughout the winter and be removed for storage during the summer months.

Fitting a demountable system

Clean the windows and the surfaces of the window frame. Cut the plastic sheet to size. Place the glazing on the window frame and mark around it (1). Working with the plastic on a flat table, peel back the protective paper from one end of the self-adhesive strip. Tack it to the surface of the plastic, flush with one edge. Cut it to length and repeat on the other edges. Cut the mating parts of the strips and apply them to the window frame following the guidelines. Press the glazing into place (2).

When dealing with rigid molded sections, cut the pieces to length with mitered corners. Fit the sections around the glazing, peel off the protective backing and press the complete unit against the frame (3).

1 Mark around glazing

2 Position glazed unit

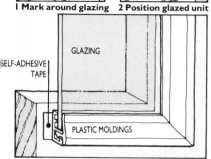

SELF-ADHESIVE TAPE

GLAZING

PLASTIC MOLDINGS

3 Rigid plastic moldings support the glazing

PLASTIC MATERIALS FOR DOUBLE GLAZING

For economy and safety, plastic sheet materials can be used in place of glass to provide lightweight double glazing. They are available in clear thin flexible films or clear, textured and colored rigid sheets.

Unlike glass, plastic glazing has a high impact-resistance and will not splinter when broken. Depending on thickness, plastic can be cut with scissors, drilled, sawn, planed and filed.

The clarity of new plastics is as good as glass but they will scratch. They are also liable to degrade with age and are prone to static. Plastic sheet should be washed with a liquid soap solution. Slight abrasions can be rubbed out with metal polish.

Film and semirigid plastics are sold by the square foot or in rolls. Rigid sheets are available in a range of standard sizes or can be cut to order. Rigid plastic is covered with a protective film of paper on both faces that is peeled off only after cutting and shaping to keep the surface scratch-free.

POLYESTER FILM

This is a plastic film used for inexpensive double glazing. Polyester film can be trimmed with scissors or a knife and fixed with self-adhesive tape or strip fasteners.

It is a tough, virtually tearproof film, which is very clear—ideal, in fact, for glazing living rooms. It is sold in rolls and is available in several widths and thicknesses.

POLYSTYRENE

This material is a relatively inexpensive clear or textured rigid plastic. Clear polystyrene does not have the clarity of glass and will degrade in strong sunlight. It should not be used for south-facing windows or where a distortion-free view is required. Depending on climatic conditions, the life of polystyrene is reckoned to be between three and five years. However, its working life can be extended if the glazing is removed for storage in summer. Polystyrene is available in several thicknesses and sheet sizes.

ACRYLIC

A good-quality rigid plastic with the clarity of glass. It costs about the same as glass and about half as much again as polystyrene. Its working life is considered to be at least 10 years. Acrylic is also available in a wide range of translucent and opaque colors. It is available in several thicknesses and sheet sizes.

POLYCARBONATE

A relatively new plastic glazing material, which is virtually unbreakable. It provides a lightweight vandal-proof glazing with a high level of clarity. The standard grade costs about twice the price of acrylic. It is made in clear, tinted, opal and opaque grades, some with textured surfaces. Thicknesses suitable for domestic glazing are $1/16$, $1/8$ and $5/32$ inch, although greater thicknesses are made, some in grades which are even bulletproof. Several sheet sizes are also available.

PVC GLAZING

PVC is available as a flexible film or as a semirigid sheet. The film provides inexpensive glazing where a high degree of clarity is not required, such as in a bedroom. PVC is ultraviolet-stabilized and is therefore suitable for outside or inside use. Consequently, it is very suitable for glazing sunspaces (and carport roofs). Several sheet sizes are available.

BRACKETS

Storm window mounting details

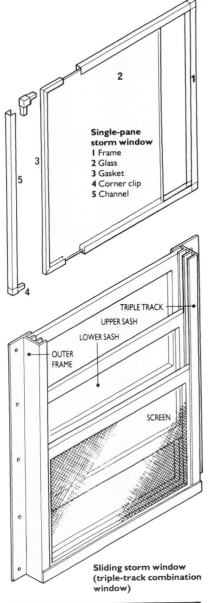

Single-pane storm window
1 Frame
2 Glass
3 Gasket
4 Corner clip
5 Channel

TRIPLE TRACK

UPPER SASH

LOWER SASH

OUTER FRAME

SCREEN

Sliding storm window (triple-track combination window)

Combination storm/ screen door
To fit, measure height (H) and width (W) of door opening in at least two places.

STORM GLAZING SYSTEMS

Secondary glazing applied to the exterior of windows usually takes the form of storm sashes, either one-piece, single-plate windows which are installed in the fall and taken down in spring, or permanently mounted sliding-sash panes which remain in place all-year-round. Single-plate storm windows can be homemade, often at considerable savings over purchased windows. However, sliding windows are best left to professional storm-window installers.

How to make a single-pane storm window

Measure the length and width of the window opening by holding the tape against the outside edges of the blind stop against which the storm window will seat. Single-pane storm window kits are often available at hardware and building supply stores and home centers. If you can't find a kit in the size you need, purchase lengths of aluminum storm-window channel (prefitted with U-section rubber glazing gasket), and friction-fit corner clips (usually sold with the channel) to make the frame. Don't attempt to make windows taller than 5 feet, because such large areas of glass are hard to handle.

Remove the gasket, then cut four pieces of channel so that when assembled, the outside dimension of the frame measures 1/8 inch less in both height and width than the window opening.

Assemble three sides of the frame using the corner clips to hold the pieces together. Drive the clips into the channel-ends using a small ball-peen hammer.

Purchase double-strength glass for the pane, cut so it will fit between the channels of the frame with the gasket installed. Fit the gasket around the edge of the pane, mitering the gasket sides at each corner with a utility knife (discard the triangular scraps of waste gasket), then slide the pane into the frame and install the final length of channel.

Attach two-piece storm-window hanging brackets from the top edge of the storm window, then mount the window to the outside of the opening. The storm window should seat firmly. However, you may wish to fasten it at the bottom and apply removable weatherstripping around the inside.

Sliding storm windows

Sliding storm windows, usually called double- or triple-track combination windows (because they incorporate a screen for use during summer), are available from home and building supply centers. Most often they are designed to fit the outside of double-hung window frames, and can be operated merely by raising the interior window to gain access to the latches controlling each sash. In triple-track units, the upper storm window sash is mounted—sometimes permanently—in the outermost track of the storm-window frame. The lower sash slides up and down in the middle track, and a screen slides up and down in the innermost track. In double-track units, the lower sash and screen are interchangeable, to be switched according to season.

It is important that sliding storm windows are well-made and tight-fitting. When purchasing, look for quality corner construction, gasketing on both sides of the glass, and deep tracks in the channel. Metal latches are more durable than plastic ones. At the bottom of each frame should be small (1/4-inch-diameter) holes to prevent condensation. When having storms installed, be sure caulk is applied to the existing frame before the storm frame is mounted. See that the windows operate smoothly before accepting the job.

Combination storm and screen doors

Combination storm doors are most often available made of aluminum. However, wood doors offer greater energy savings. Both are usually sold mounted in a frame, ready for installation. To measure the door opening, measure both the height and the width in at least two places. Use the smallest measurement in each case. For the height, measure between the door sill and the inside face of the top of the door frame or brick mold. For the width, measure between the two outermost offsets (rabbets) in the side pieces of the door frame. Usually, there must also be at least 1 inch of flat surface on the door frame boards or brick mold outside the door in order to mount the storm-door frame.

VENTILATION

Ventilation is essential for a fresh, comfortable atmosphere, but it has a more important function with regard to the structure of our homes. It wasn't a problem when houses were heated with open fires, drawing fresh air through all the natural openings in the structure. With the introduction of central heating, insulation and draftproofing, well-designed ventilation is vital. Without a constant change of air, centrally heated rooms quickly become stuffy, and before long the moisture content of the air becomes so high that water is deposited as condensation—often with serious consequences.

There are various ways to provide ventilation. Some are extremely simple, while others are much more sophisticated for total control.

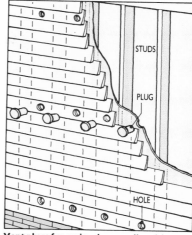
Vent plugs for curing damp wall cavities

Initial consideration

Whenever you undertake an improvement which involves insulation in one form or another, take into account how it is likely to affect the existing ventilation. It may change conditions sufficiently to create a problem in those areas outside the habitable rooms so that moisture and its side effects develop unnoticed under floorboards or in the attic. If there is a chance that damp conditions might occur, provide additional ventilation.

Ventilating wall cavities

Faulty vapor protection can lead to moisture accumulating within walls. The problem is common in renovated houses where insulation has been retrofitted into the original construction. Suspect the need for ventilation especially if you notice paint blisters on the exterior of the house.

To ventilate wall cavities, install vent plugs—small cylindrical louvers available in several diameters from hardware and building-supply stores. Drill holes from the exterior of the house into each cavity where moisture is suspected, at the bottom, top, and at 4-foot intervals in between, and insert the plugs.

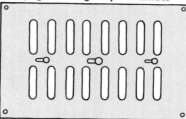
Hit-and-miss ventilator

Ventilating a fireplace

An open fire needs oxygen to burn brightly. If the supply is reduced by thorough draftproofing or double glazing, the fire smolders and the slightest downdraft blows smoke into the room. There may be other reasons why a fire burns poorly, such as a blocked chimney, for example, but if it picks up within minutes of partially opening the door to the room, you can be sure that inadequate ventilation is the problem.

One efficient and attractive solution is to cut holes in the floorboards on each side of the fire and cover them with a ventilator. Cheap plastic grilles work just as well, but you may prefer brass or aluminum for a living room. Choose a "hit-and-miss" ventilator, which you can open and close to seal off unwelcome drafts when the fire is not in use. If the room is carpeted, cut a hole in it and screw the ventilator on top into the floor.

Another solution is to install a sealed fireplace door unit, which comes with inlet pipes and a small blower. Cut holes in the exterior wall at each side of the fireplace, insert the pipes, and attach vents on the outside.

Ventilating an unused fireplace

An unused fireplace that has been blocked by brickwork, blockwork of plasterboard should be ventilated to allow air to flow up the chimney to dry out penetrating dampness or condensation. Some people believe a vent from a warm interior aggravates the problem by introducing moist air to condense on the cold surface of the brick flue. However, so long as the chimney is uncapped, the updraft should draw moisture-laden air to the outside. A brick vent installed in the flue from outside is a safer solution but it is more difficult to accomplish and, of course, impossible if the chimney is located within the house. Furthermore, the vent would have to be blocked should you want to reopen the fireplace later.

To ventilate from inside the room, leave out a single brick, form an aperture with blocks, or cut a hole in the plasterboard used to block off the fireplace. Screw a face-mounted ventilator over the hole or use one that is designed for plastering in. The thin flange for screw-fixing the ventilator to the wall is covered as you plaster up to the slightly protruding louver.

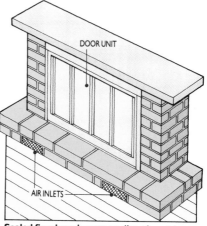
Sealed fireplace doors vent directly outdoors

Face-mounted ventilator for a fireplace

VENTILATING CRAWLSPACES

Because of their confined area, and because both cold and dampness are particularly likely to invade crawlspaces, ventilating them adequately is crucial. Whether the above-ground foundation walls are brick or block, louvered ventilators should be built into them on at least two opposite sides. If none are present, or if the number of ventilators seems inadequate, add additional ones or replace those existing with larger ones. Keep ventilators open except in inclement weather. Occasionally, vents become clogged with leaves or other debris.

Single ceramic brick vent

Double plastic brick vent

Assessing existing ventilation

Ideally, there should be a brick vent every 6 feet along an external crawlspace wall, but in many buildings there is less provision for ventilation with no ill-effects. Sufficient airflow is more important than the actual number of openings.

Pockets of noncirculating air in corners where drafts never reach are particularly prone to harboring the microorganisms which create dry rot. Frequently, these corners also are where the ends of floor joists rest on sills and against headers, which only increases the likelihood that moisture problems will eventually set in unless plenty of fresh air is kept flowing through the area.

If you suspect poor circulation in specific areas of a crawlspace, fit additional brick vents in the walls nearby, placing two vents at right angles, if possible, to create a cross-draft.

When checking the condition of existing vents, also be aware that even small holes can admit vermin unless screened over. Don't be tempted to block the opening. If you can't fix screen across it, or if the vent is damaged, replace it.

Installing or replacing a brick vent

Use a masonry drill to remove the mortar and a cold chisel to chop out the masonry you are replacing. You may have to cut some blocks to install a double-size vent. Having cut through the wall, spread mortar on the base of the hole and along the top and both sides of the new vent. Push it into the opening, keeping it flush with the face of the masonry. Repoint the mortar to match the profile used on the surrounding wall.

Installing brick vents
Brick vents or other louvered ventilators can be installed either by replacing foundation masonry or by cutting through the joist header that rests on the sill.

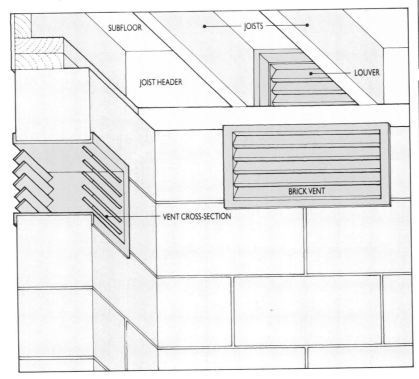

SUBFLOOR — JOISTS
JOIST HEADER
LOUVER
BRICK VENT
VENT CROSS-SECTION

VENTING A CAVITY WALL

If you build a vent into a brick cavity wall, bridge the gap with a plastic, telescopic unit, which in turn is mortared into the hole from both sides. If necessary, a louver can be screwed to the inner end of the telescopic unit. Where a vent is inserted above the damp-proof course, you must fit a cavity tray over the telescopic unit to stop water from running to the inner leaf of the cavity wall.

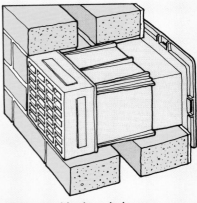

Brick vent with telescopic sleeve
Bridge a cavity wall with this type of unit.

Cavity tray
A galvanized cavity tray sheds any moisture which penetrates the cavity above the unit to the outer leaf of the wall. It is necessary only when the vent is fitted above the damp-proof course.

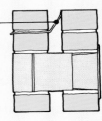

VENTING AN APPLIANCE

A flued, fuel-burning appliance must have an adequate supply of air to function efficiently and safely. If any alteration or improvement interferes with that supply, you must provide alternative ventilation. If you plan to block a vent, change the window or even install an exhaust fan in the same room as the appliance, consult a professional installer. He will tell you whether the alteration is advisable, what type and size of vent to install, and where it should be positioned for best effect. An appliance with a balanced flue draws air directly from outside the house, so will be unaffected by internal alterations.

VENTILATING THE ROOF SPACE

When insulating the attic first became popular as an energy-saving measure, homeowners were recommended to tuck insulation right into the eaves to keep out drafts. What people failed to recognize was the fact that the free flow of air is necessary in the colder roof space to prevent moisture-laden air from the dwelling below from condensing on the structure. Inadequate ventilation can lead to serious deterioration. Wet rot develops in the roof timbers and water drops onto the insulation, eventually saturating the material and rendering it ineffective as insulation. If water builds up into pools, the ceiling below becomes stained and there is a risk of short-circuiting the electrical wiring in the attic. Efficient ventilation of the roof space, therefore, is an absolute necessity for every home.

Ventilating the eaves

Building codes specify ventilation requirements, so check with a building inspector before installing vents yourself. One rule of thumb for estimating the amount of ventilation necessary is 1 square foot each of intake and outflow ventilation for every 300 square feet of roof.

The configuration of ventilators most suitable depends primarily on the amount of air that needs to circulate and the way in which the rafter ends are enclosed by the rest of the roof framing. Most sloping roofs incorporate vent plugs or strips installed in the soffit beneath the eaves for intake and gable-end louvers at each end of the house for outflow. In cases where gable-ends are not accessible, the peak of the roof can be opened and a ridge vent installed along its length. Other types of vents are designed for installation on some part of the sloping roof itself.

Installing eaves vents

In most houses where soffit vents do not already exist, installing vent plugs rather than strips is usually recommended. First, determine the locations of the rafter ends. Then, in the spaces between them, drill holes for the vents and apply caulk to their edges to prevent decay. Install the vents themselves by pressing them into place. Each plug should incorporate a screen to keep out pests. If necessary, install baffles between the rafters to prevent insulation from blocking airflow underneath the roof.

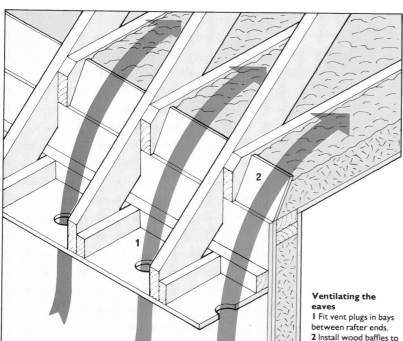

Ventilating the eaves
1 Fit vent plugs in bays between rafter ends.
2 Install wood baffles to contain insulation and maintain airflow.

COMMON VENT PATTERNS

Because warm air rises, air entering at eaves level is most effectively vented at the ridge. However, there are cases where vents must be located elsewhere on the roof.

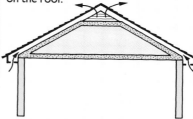

Eave vents and gable-end louver
This is the most common arrangement for pitched-roof buildings.

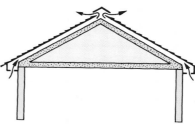

Ridge vent
Where gable ends are inaccessible or nonexistent—as on a hipped roof—a continuous ridge vent provides sufficient outflow ventilation.

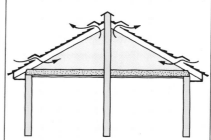

Pitched-roof vents
For venting special roof areas or when usual ventilation points are inaccessible, install pitched-roof vents. Place vents as high as possible to replace ridge vents, as low as possible to vent eaves.

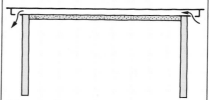

Flat roof
Install soffit vents beneath overhanging eaves to serve as both intake and outflow ventilators.

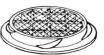

Soffit vent plug

Pitched-roof vent

Turbine vent

277

FITTING ROOF VENTS

Installing a ridge vent

A continuous ventilating strip running the length of the roof provides very effective outflow ventilation. Ridge venting may be installed on any pitched roof, during new construction or reroofing, or as a task by itself.

If a ridge vent is to be included in the new construction of a roof, the roof decking is laid to leave a gap on either side of the ridge board, creating an open slot along the roof peak approximately 2 inches wide. Determine the actual width from the size of the ridge vent. The gap allows exiting air to pass through. If felt roofing paper is laid, trim it even with the top edge of the decking. Fasten the ridge vent over the gap, nailing it into the decking and rafters on both sides. Lay the final

course of shingles on each side of the roof so that they cover the base of the vent.

To install a ridge vent to a finished roof, you will have to cut a gap along the roof peak to create a passage for exiting air. Use a chalk line to mark the cutting line on each side of the peak, then cut through the shingles and felt paper first, using a linoleum knife, to expose the decking. Set the blade of a circular saw to the thickness of the decking, then cut along each chalked line to open the roof. Be careful to avoid nails; also be sure not to cut into the rafters.

Caulk the underside of the ridge vent sides, then fasten it over the slot using gasketed roofing nails long enough to penetrate the rafters.

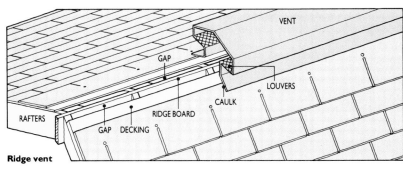

Ridge vent

Installing pitched-roof ventilators

Installing ventilators on the sloping portions of a roof requires careful cutting and sealing to prevent leaks. You may wish to hire a professional roofer to do the job.

First, determine the location of the vent. It must lie between rafters. Use the vent itself or a template made of cardboard (sometimes supplied with the vent) to mark the area of the roof to be cut out. It should be smaller than the overall dimensions of the vent base so that the vent can be slid beneath

adjacent shingles. Cut out the area by first removing the roof covering (use a linoleum knife to remove asphalt shingles), then sawing through the decking using a saber saw. Apply roofing cement to the underside of the vent. Then slide it into place and fasten it with galvanized roofing nails while, at the same time, holding neighboring shingles up and out of the way. Cover the nail heads with more cement, then smooth the shingles surrounding the vent so they lay flat.

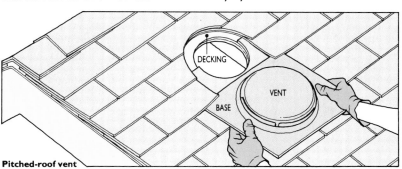

Pitched-roof vent

CALCULATING AIRFLOW CAPACITY

All vents positioned near the eaves should provide the equivalent of at least 1-inch continuous gap, depending on the pitch of the roof. The ones near the ridge should provide airflow to suit the construction of a particular roof.

Divide the specified airflow capacity of the vent you wish to use into the recommended continuous gap to calculate how many vents you will need. If in doubt, provide slightly more ventilation than is indicated.

Place eaves vents in the fourth or fifth course of shingles, slates or tiles. Position the higher vents a couple of courses below the ridge. Space all vents evenly along the roof to avoid any areas of "dead" air.

CLEARING THE OPENING

When replacing certain tiles or slates with a vent, it may be necessary to cut through a tile support strip to clear the opening. Nail a short length of wood above and below the opening to provide additional support.

Because roofing slates overlap each other by a considerable amount, you will have to cut away the top corners of the lower slates.

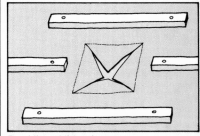

Providing additional support
Cut a strip that obstructs a hole, then place strips above and below to support the vent.

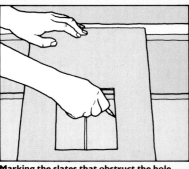

Marking the slates that obstruct the hole
When slates cover the opening for a vent, use a template to mark the corners, then remove them.

FITTING AN EXHAUST FAN

Kitchens and bathrooms are particularly susceptible to problems of condensation so it is especially important to have a means of efficiently expelling moisture-laden air along with unpleasant odors. An electrically driven exhaust fan will freshen a room faster than relying on natural ventilation and without creating uncomfortable drafts.

Positioning an exhaust fan

The best place to site a fan is either in a window or on an outside wall, but its exact position is more critical than that. Stale air extracted from the room must be replaced by fresh air, normally through the door leading to other areas of the house. If the fan is sited close to the source of replacement air it will promote local circulation but will have little effect on the rest of the room.

The ideal position would be directly opposite the source as high as practicable to extract the rising hot air (**1**). In a kitchen, try to locate the fan adjacent to the stove but not directly over it. In that way, steam and cooking smells will not be drawn across the room before being expelled (**2**). If the room contains a flued, fuel-burning appliance, you must ensure there is an adequate supply of fresh air at all times or the exhaust fan will draw fumes down the flue. The only exception is an appliance with a balanced flue, which takes its air directly from outside.

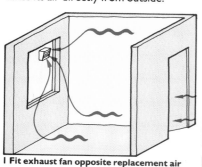

1 Fit exhaust fan opposite replacement air source

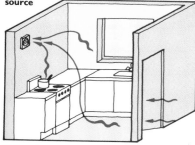

2 Place fan near a stove in a kitchen

Types of exhaust fans

Many fans have integral switches but, if not, a switched connection unit can be wired into the circuit when you install the fan. Some models incorporate built-in controllers to regulate the speed of extraction and timers to switch off the fan automatically after a certain time. Fans can be installed in a window and some, with the addition of a duct, will extract air through a framed or solid wall (see illustrations below). Choose a fan with external shutters that close when the fan is not in use, to prevent backdrafts.

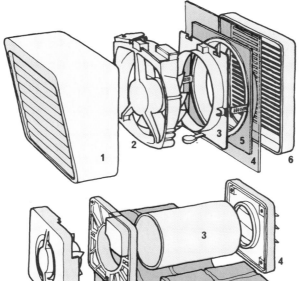

Window-mounted fan
1 Inner casing
2 Motor assembly
3 Interior clamping plate
4 Glass
5 Louver clamping plate
6 Exterior grille

Wall-mounted fan
1 Motor assembly
2 Interior backplate
3 Duct
4 Exterior louver

Choosing the size of a fan

The size of a fan, or to be accurate, its capacity, is determined by the type of room in which it is installed and the volume of air it must move.

A fan installed in a kitchen must be capable of changing the air completely ten to fifteen times per hour. A full bathroom requires fifteen to twenty air changes per hour and a powder room, ten to fifteen. A living room normally requires four to six changes per hour, but fit a fan with a slightly larger capacity in a smoky environment.

To calculate the capacity of the fan you require, find the volume of the room (length × width × height), then multiply that figure by the recommended number of air changes per hour. Choose a fan which is capable of the same or slightly higher capacity.

CALCULATING THE CAPACITY OF A FAN FOR A KITCHEN

SIZE

Length	Width	Height	Volume
11 ft.	10 ft.	8 ft.	880 cu. ft.

AIR CHANGES

Per hour	Volume	Fan capacity	
15	880 cu. ft.	13,200 cu. ft.	

Metal detector
Detect buried pipes or
cables by placing an
electronic sensor
against the wall.

1 Hold panel with plank

2 Seal plate fitting

3 Insert duct in hole

4 Attach louver

FITTING A WALL-MOUNTED UNIT

Satisfy yourself that there is no plumbing
or wiring buried in the wall by looking in
the attic or under the floorboards. Make
sure there are no drainpipes or other
obstructions.

Cutting the hole

Wall-mounted fans are supplied with a
length of plastic or metal ducting for
inserting in a hole which you must cut
through the wall to the outside. Plot the
center of the hole and draw its diameter
on the inside of the wall. Use a
long-reach masonry drill to bore a
central hole right through. Be sure to
hold the drill perpendicular to the wall.
To prevent the drill from breaking out
brickwork or stucco on the outside,
press a thick plywood panel against the
wall and wedge it with a scaffold board
supported by stakes in the ground (1).

Insert a keyhole saw or saber saw in
the center hole, then saw around the
inside of the planned opening to remove
most of the waste plasterboard. If
necessary, trim the hole larger using a
rasp. Saw through the exterior wall
from the outside, using the same
method. Keep the hole small enough so
that its edges will be hidden by the fan
mounting plate and exterior louver.

Fitting the fan

Most wall fans are fitted in a similar
manner, but check specific instructions.
Separate the components of the fan. If
necessary, attach a self-adhesive foam
sealing strip to the fitting on the
backplate to receive the duct (2).

Insert the duct in the hole so that the
backplate fits against the wall (3). Mark
the length of the duct on the outside,
allowing enough extra to fit the similar
fitting on the outer louver. Cut the duct
to length with a hacksaw. Reposition
the backplate and duct to mark the
mounting holes on the wall. Drill the
holes, then feed the electrical supply
cable into the backplate before
screwing it to the wall. Stick a foam
sealing strip inside the fitting on the
louver. Position it on the duct, then
mark and drill the wall mounting holes.
Use a screwdriver to stuff scraps of
fiberglass insulation between the duct
and the cut edge of the hole, then screw
on the exterior louver (4).

If the louver does not fit flush with
the wall, seal the gap with caulk. Wire
the fan and attach the motor assembly
to the backplate.

FITTING AN EXHAUST FAN

Installing a fan in a window

Some fans are designed to fit in fixed
windows. If you wish to fit one in a sash
window, it's necessary to secure the top
sash in which the fan is installed and fit a
sash stop on each side of the window to
prevent the lower sash from damaging
the casing of the fan should it be raised
too far.

To install an exhaust fan in an
hermetically sealed double glazing
system, ask the manufacturer to supply a
special unit with a hole cut and sealed
around its edges to receive the fan.
Some manufacturers supply a kit which
adapts a fan for installing in a window
with secondary double glazing. It allows
the inner window to be opened without
dismantling the fan.

Cutting the glass

A window-mounted fan requires a
round hole to be cut in the glass. The
size is specified by the manufacturer. It
is possible to cut a hole in an existing
window but stresses in the glass will
sometimes cause it to crack, and while
the glass is removed for cutting there is
always a security risk, especially if you
decide to take it to a glazier. All things
considered, it is advisable to fit a new
pane; it's easier to cut and can be
installed immediately once the old one
has been removed.

Cutting a hole in glass is not easy; it
may be more economical in the long run
to order it from a glazier. You'll need to
supply exact dimensions, including the
size and position of the hole. Use
strengthened glass in a thickness
recommended by the fan manufacturer
or glazier.

Installing the fan

The exact assembly may vary but the
following sequence is a typical example
of how a fan is installed in a window.
Take out the existing window pane and
clean up the frame, removing traces of
old putty and glazier's points. Fit the
new pane, with its hole precut, as for
fitting window glass.

From outside, fit the exterior louver
by locating its circular flange in the hole
(1). Attach the plate on the inside,
which clamps the louver to the glass.
Tighten the mounting screws in rotation
to achieve a good seal and an even
clamping force on the glass (2). Screw
the motor assembly to the clamping
plate (3). Wire up the fan following the
maker's instructions. Fit the inner casing
over the motor assembly (4).

WARNING
Never make electrical connections until the power is switched off at the service panel.

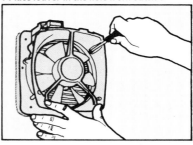

1 Place louver in the hole from outside

2 Clamp the inner and outer plates together

3 Screw the motor assembly to the plate

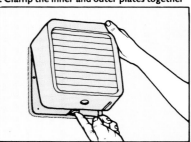

4 Attach the inner casing to cover the assembly

INSTALLING A RANGE HOOD

Window- and wall-mounted fans are designed for overall room extraction, but the ideal way to tackle steam and greasy cooking smells from a stove is to mount a specially designed exhaust hood directly over it.

Where to mount the range hood

Mount a range hood between 2 and 3 feet above the stovetop or about 1 foot 4 inches to 2 feet above an eye-level grill. Unless the manufacturer provides specific dimensions, mount a hood as low as possible within the recommended tolerances for best results.

Depending on the model, a range hood may be cantilevered from the wall or, alternatively, screwed between or beneath kitchen cupboards. Some kitchen manufacturers produce a stove hood housing unit, which matches the style of the cupboards. Opening the unit operates the fan automatically. Most range hoods have two or three speed settings and a built-in light fitting to conveniently illuminate the stovetop below.

Installing ductwork

When a range hood is mounted on an outside wall, air is extracted through the back of the unit into a straight duct passing through the rear wall. If the stove is situated against another wall, it is possible to connect the hood with the outside by means of fire-resistant ductwork. Straight and curved components plug into each other to form a continuous shaft running along the top of the wall cupboards, then through the wall.

Plug the female end of the first duct component over the outlet fitting on the top of the range hood. Cutting them to fit with a hacksaw or multisnips, run the rest of the ductwork, making the same female-to-male connections along the shaft. Some ducting is printed with airflow arrows to make sure each component is oriented correctly. If you were to reverse a component somewhere along the shaft, air turbulence might be created around the joint, reducing the effectiveness of the extractor. At the outside wall, cut a hole and fit an external louver to finish the job (see opposite).

Fitting a range hood

Recycling and extracting hoods are hung from wall brackets supplied with the machines. Screw mounting points are provided for attaching them to wall cupboards. Cut a ducting hole through a wall as for a wall-mounted fan (see opposite). Wire a range hood following the maker's instructions.

RECIRCULATION OR EXTRACTION?

The only real difference between one range hood and another is the way it deals with the stale air it captures. Some hoods filter out the moisture and grease before returning the freshened air to the room. Other machines dump stale air outside through a duct in the wall, just like a conventional wall-mounted exhaust fan.

Because the air is actually changed, extraction is the more efficient method, but it is necessary to cut a hole through the wall and, of course, the heated air is lost—excellent in hot weather but rather a waste in winter. Range hoods which recycle the air are much simpler to install but never filter out all the grease and odors, even when new. It is essential to clean and change the filters regularly to keep the hood working at peak efficiency.

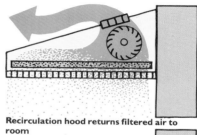

Recirculation hood returns filtered air to room

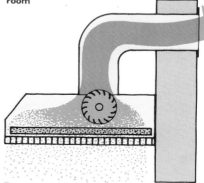

Extraction hoods suck air outside via ductwork

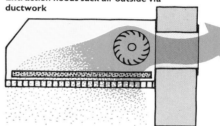

Alternatively, air is extracted directly to outside

◀ **Running ducts outside**
When a stove is placed against an inside wall, run ductwork from the extractor hood along the top of wall-hung cupboards.

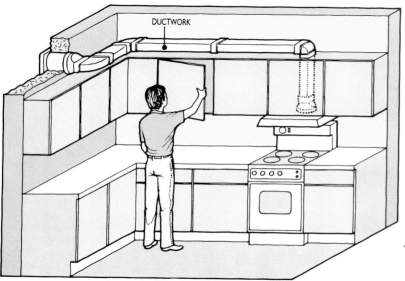

DUCTWORK

HEAT-EXCHANGING VENTILATORS

Most people naturally think of ventilating a room in hot weather when it is most likely to be unpleasantly stuffy. In all but the hottest of summers, it can be achieved simply by opening windows or using a mechanical fan. However, ventilation is equally important in the winter—but we keep our weatherstripped windows closed against drafts, promoting an unhealthy atmosphere and a rise in condensation.

Using a conventional exhaust fan solves the problem, but at the cost of throwing away heated air. A heat-exchanging ventilator is the answer. Two centrifugal fans operate simultaneously, one to suck in fresh air from the outside while the other extracts the same volume of foul air from inside. The system is perfectly balanced so the unit works efficiently.

The benefits of a heat exchanger

An important plus for heat-exchanging ventilators is that heat loss is cut to a minimum by passing the extracted air through a series of small vents sandwiched between similar vents containing cold outside air moving in the other direction. Most of the heat is transferred to the fresh air so it is blown into the room warmed.

If you want to install a heat exchanger in a kitchen or bathroom, check that the unit is suitable for steamy atmospheres and greasy air.

Heat exchangers are either wall-mounted much like a standard extractor fan, or flush-mounted so that the cabinet housing the unit is set into the wall. A slim, louvered casing is visible only from inside. The former version is relatively simple to fit but more obtrusive. To install a flush-mounted unit, it is necessary to cut a large rectangular hole through the wall and, in some cases, frame it with lumber.

How the ventilator functions
Hot, stale air is drawn into the unit (**1**), by a centrifugal fan (**2**). It is passed via the heat exchanger (**3**) to the outside (**4**). Fresh air is sucked from outside (**5**) by a fan (**6**) to be warmed in the heat exchanger and passed into the room (**7**).

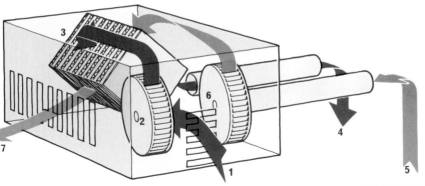

Fitting a wall-mounted ventilator

With the aid of a level, use the manufacturer's template to mark the position of the ventilator on the wall, including the centers of both ducts (**1**). Locate the unit high on the wall but with at least 2-inch clearance above and to the sides.

The ducting is likely to be narrower than that used for standard exhaust fans, so it may be possible to use a hole saw (**2**). Drill a pilot hole through both the interior wall covering and exterior sheathing and siding first. After cutting the hole in the interior wall, cut the hole in the exterior wall slightly lower so that the ducting will slope to drain condensation to the outside. If the ducting is too large to use a hole saw, use a keyhole or saber saw instead, and trim the holes using a rasp and file. Use a

hacksaw to cut the ducting to a length equaling the depth of the wall plus ⅜ inch. Use aluminum flashing tape to hold ducting to both fittings on the rear of the wall-mounting panel. Insert the ducting into the drilled holes (**3**), push the panel against the wall and mount it with screws.

Outside, plug the gaps around the ducting with fiberglass insulation (**4**) and screw the covers over the ends of the ducts. Seal around the edges of both covers with caulk (**5**). Fit the main unit to the mounting panel on the inside wall (**6**) and wire it to a fused connection box nearby.

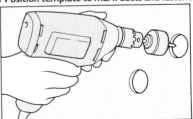

1 Position template to mark ducts and fasteners

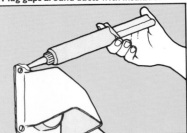

2 Bore holes for ducting with a hole saw

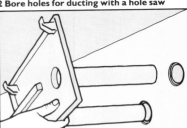

3 Pass both ducts through the wall

4 Plug gaps around ducts with insulation

5 Seal edge of duct covers with caulk

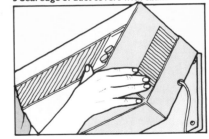

6 Fit the ventilator unit on the inside

VENTILATORS

Mounting a flush ventilator

Most flush-mounted ventilators require a wooden frame to line a hole cut through the wall. Make it to the dimensions supplied by the manufacturer of the ventilator. Construct the frame with lap joints or glued and screwed butt joints. Decide on the approximate position of the unit, then locate the wall studs to align one with the side of the unit. Mark the rectangle for the wooden lining onto the wall, then drill through the plasterboard at the corners of the outline. Cut out the rectangle with a keyhole saw or saber saw. Cut and remove the wall insulation. Working from outside, cut away the siding and sheathing along the same lines. Saw off any studs obstructing the hole flush with its edges. (Do not remove studs from a bearing wall without consulting a building inspector.)

Insert the lining. The ventilator must be angled downwards a few degrees towards the outside to drain away condensation. If this angle is built into the ventilator unit, the wooden lining can be set flush with the wall, otherwise tilt it a fraction by shimming it underneath before nailing. Measure the diagonals to make sure the lining is square in the hole.

Fit the main unit in the liner and screw it to the front edge of the lining. Fit the front panel onto the unit. Outside, seal the seams between the sheathing, lining and unit with caulk.

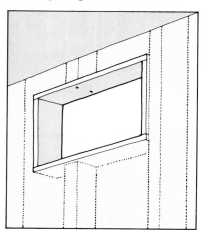

Mounting a flush ventilator
Fit a wooden liner in the wall close to the ceiling where it will be in the best position to extract hot, rising air. Screw the ventilator to the front edge of the liner.

FITTING A UNIT IN A MASONRY WALL

Decide on the approximate position of the unit, then mark its position on the wall by scribing around it with a pencil or awl. Use a masonry drill to bore a hole through the wall at each corner, then chop along the plaster between them with a bricklayer's chisel. Drill further holes around the perimeter of the hole and chop out the masonry with a cold chisel. Remove the whole bricks by drilling out the mortar joints. After cutting halfway through the wall, finish the hole from the outside.

Mounting a ventilator liner ▶
Cut a rectangular hole through the masonry. Construct a wood liner using butt joints at the corners. Insert the liner, tilting it slightly toward the outside if necessary.

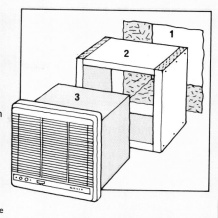

DEHUMIDIFIERS CONTROL CONDENSATION

To combat condensation you can remove the moisture-laden air by ventilation or warm it so that it can carry more water vapor before it becomes saturated. An alternative measure is to extract the water itself from the air using a dehumidifier. This is achieved by drawing air from the room into the unit and passing it over cold coils upon which water vapor condenses and drips into a reservoir. The cold but now dry air is drawn by a fan over heated coils before being returned to the room as additional convected heat.

The process is based on the refrigeration principle that gas under pressure heats up and when the pressure drops, so does the temperature of the gas. In a dehumidifier, a compressor delivers pressurized gas to the "hot" coils, in turn leading to the larger "cold" coils, which allow the gas to expand. The cooled gas returns to the compressor for recycling.

A dehumidifier for domestic use is built into a cabinet which resembles a large hi-fi speaker. It contains a humidistat, which automatically switches on the unit when the moisture content of the air reaches a predetermined level. When the reservoir is full, the machine shuts down

to prevent overflow and an indicator lights up to remind you to empty the water in the container.

When installed in a damp room, a dehumidifier will extract excess moisture from the furnishings and fabric of the building in a week or two. After that it will monitor the moisture content of the air to maintain a stabilized atmosphere. A portable version can be wheeled from room to room, where it is plugged into a standard wall stocket.

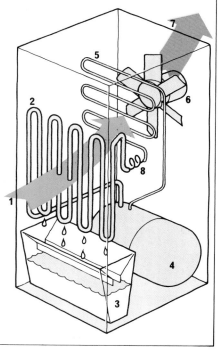

The working components of a dehumidifier ▶
The diagram illustrates the layout of a typical domestic dehumidifier.
1 Incoming damp air
2 Cold coils
3 Water reservoir
4 Compressor
5 Hot coils
6 Fan
7 Dry, warm air
8 Capillary tube where gas expands

AIR CONDITIONERS

Central air-conditioning systems should be checked once a year in early spring by a professional service technician. During the air-conditioning season, the homeowner should check and replace the filters once each month, or more frequently in dusty areas.

Even small window- or wall-mounted air conditioners are mostly factory-sealed and lubricated. However, it is important to keep the indoor and outdoor grillework dust-free to maintain optimum cooling efficiency and to prevent overstraining various components. Vacuum the front of the unit frequently. Once a year, remove the cover and vacuum behind it.

How air conditioning works

An air conditioner works on the same refrigeration principle described for a dehumidifier and incorporates similar gas-filled coils and a compressor. However, airflow within the unit is different. Individual units are divided into separate compartments within one cabinet. Room air is drawn into the cooling compartment and passed over the evaporation coils which absorb heat before a fan returns the air to the room at a lower temperature. As moisture vapor condenses on the coils, the unit also acts as a dehumidifier, a welcome bonus in hot, humid weather. Condensed water is normally drained to the outside of the house.

Gas in the evaporation coils moves on, carrying absorbed heat to the compartment facing the outside, where it is radiated from the condenser coils and blown outside by a fan.

A thermostat operates a valve, which reverses the flow of refrigerant when the temperature in the room drops below the setting. The system is automatic so that the unit can heat the room if it is cold in the early morning. As the sun rises and boosts the temperature, the air conditioner switches over to maintain a constant temperature indoors.

Choose a unit with variable fan speed and a method for directing the chilled air where it will be most effective in cooling the whole room. Usually this is at ceiling level, where the cold air falls slowly over the whole room area.

CHOOSING THE CAPACITY

To reduce the running costs of an air conditioner, try to match its capacity—the amount of heat it can absorb—to the size of the room it will be cooling. A unit which is too small will be running most of the time without complete success, while one that is much too large will chill the air so quickly that it won't be able to remove much moisture vapor, so the atmosphere may still feel uncomfortable when it is humid. Ideally, the unit should be working flat-out on only the hottest of days.

The capacity of a conditioner is measured in British Thermal Units (BTU). A unit with a capacity of 9000 BTU will remove the amount of heat every hour. As a rough guide to capacity, find the volume of the area you wish to cool (length × width × height), then allow 5 BTU per cubic foot. Ask the supplier to provide a more accurate calculation which will take into consideration other factors such as size and number of windows, insulation and heat-generating equipment in the room.

MOUNTING THE UNIT

Cut a hole through the wall and fit a wooden lining as for a heat-exchanging ventilator. Being a larger and heavier unit, an air conditioner will have some sort of supporting cage or metal brackets.

Units designed for installing in windows are supplied with adjustable frames and weatherstripping. After attaching the frame to the window opening, the conditioner is lifted into the window, then slid into place.

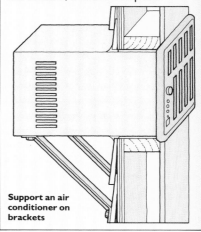

Support an air conditioner on brackets

How an air conditioner works
The diagram shows the mechanism of a small wall-mounted or window-mounted air conditioner but it illustrates the principle employed by all air conditioners.

Outside air (**1**) is drawn through the side vents (**2**) by fan (**3**) which blows it over the hot coils (**4**). The air extracts heat from the coils and takes it outside (**5**). Warm, humid air from the interior (**6**) is drawn over the cold coils (**7**) by a centrifugal fan (**8**) and returned to the room cooled and dry (**9**). The condensed

water drips into a reservoir (**10**) and drains to the outside (**11**). The motor (**12**) powers the fans and compressor (**13**), which pumps gas around the system.

7

ELECTRICITY

ELECTRICITY IN OUR HOMES

Electricity has been so much a part of our lives for so many years that now it is hard to imagine living without it. We instinctively reach for a switch in the dark and a light comes on. We give little thought to circuitry, to switches, to the flow of current. We expect it to be there, and most of the time it is. Only when our electrical systems fail do we give them much thought. And then we are likely to be more confused than curious. For many of us, it all seems an unapproachable mystery. Electricity sounds dangerous, and any discussion of it seems hopelessly and deliberately obscured by difficult technical jargon.

The truth of the matter is that electricity *is* complicated when used to do complicated things, as in advanced electronics. But you don't have to start at that level. No one does. You can start with the simplest repair and work up.

Electricity is learnable because it is logical, especially in practice. It is sequential, and therefore predictable. Electrical current runs along wires as simply as water passes through plumbing pipes. Switches interrupt current just as valves and faucets interrupt water. If this analogy seems too simple, it probably is, but learning to think in simple progressions is the key to understanding your home's electrical system. Don't try to understand the entire system. Instead, think in steps until the system becomes obvious.

Like so many other areas of home improvement, electrical projects are now made easier with improved materials. Electrical supply manufacturers are designing more and more items with the inexperienced do-it-yourselfer in mind. In many ways, electrical work has never been easier. Start by doing the little things. Small projects will give you the confidence to approach larger projects. Eventually, doing your own electrical work will offer real savings, in addition to the satisfaction of greater self-sufficiency.

Think safe to be safe

One of the most intimidating aspects of electricity is its ability to injure or even kill. With a few precautions, however, you can eliminate the danger factor and work without fear of being hurt. In fact, you are probably more likely to electrocute yourself through careless living habits than when attempting a do-it-yourself wiring project. The following list of do's and don'ts will protect you from electrical hazards, both in your daily living and when working on your home's electrical system.

- Always shut the power off at the main service panel to any circuit you intend to work on.
- Do not overload a receptacle with adapters and extension cords.
- Do not run extension cords under carpets or throw rugs. Constant traffic can fray a cord's insulation, creating a fire hazard.
- When holding electric razors, hair dryers or any bath or kitchen appliance, do not touch faucets or plumbing pipes, as most electrical systems are grounded through the plumbing system (◁).
- When bathing, keep radios, hair dryers and other small appliances beyond reach of the tub.
- When adapting a three-prong plug to a two-prong receptacle, make sure the adapter is grounded to the screw on the receptacle's coverplate and that the box is grounded (◁).
- When a fuse blows, never install a substitute fuse with a greater amperage rating (◁).

- Do not pull a plug from a receptacle by its cord. The cord will soon tear loose inside the plug, overheat and become a fire hazard.
- Always unplug an appliance or lamp before attempting a repair.
- Before starting any work, use a voltage tester to make sure the power is off. A lamp or small appliance will also work in testing outlets for power (◁).
- Do not use aluminum ladders when working near overhead service lines or when testing live circuits.
- If you must work on wet floors, wear rubber boots and stand on planks to provide a buffer between you and the moisture.
- Because most electrical systems are grounded through metal plumbing systems, never touch plumbing pipes while working on electrical projects.
- When making plumbing repairs, make sure that you do not splice a length of plastic pipe into a plumbing line that also serves as a grounding conductor.

ENERGY SAVINGS FOR PRACTICAL LIVING

Even if you understand nothing about the wiring in your home, you can still save on energy consumption by following these basic conservation measures.

Kitchen:
- Use flat-bottom pans roughly the same size as the burners when cooking on electric range tops.
- Cover foods when boiling to speed the heating process and reduce energy consumption.
- Use microwaves when possible, as they cook faster and use less wattage.
- When hand-washing dishes, use a sink stopper to hold water. A continually running hot rinse uses much more water.
- Clean dust and grease from refrigerator condensers at least three times a year. Dirty condensers are very inefficient to operate.

Heating and cooling:
- Set thermostats at 68 degrees F in winter and 78 degrees F in summer. Each degree under 68 degrees F and over 78 degrees F will save approximately 3 percent of your total heating or cooling costs.
- Open drapes facing the sun during the day in winter and close them during the day in summer. In wintertime, close all drapes at night to reduce heat loss.
- Apply caulk and weatherstripping to leaky windows and doors to further reduce heat loss.

Laundry and bath:
- Wash only full loads of clothing. When possible, wash with warm water and rinse with cold water.
- Because clogged filters interrupt efficient airflow, clean dryer lint filters after every load.
- Showers generally require less hot water than baths. To reduce further the amount of hot water needed, install a simple volume-reduction washer in the shower head.
- Repair all leaky faucets, as they can cost you hundreds of gallons of hot and cold water each year.

Waterbeds:
- The heater in an unmade waterbed can consume 30 percent more energy than when the bed is fully covered.

HOW MUCH SHOULD YOU DO?

If you own a single-family home, you can legally work on any of the electricity on your side of the meter. This does not mean that you can invent your own standards, however. The next person to live in your house has a right to be protected against dangerous or sub-standard workmanship and materials. It does mean that if you work to accepted standards, as defined by the National Electrical Code, you cannot be prohibited from doing your own wiring. All that is required is a work permit and a series of on-site inspections by code officials. Every major wiring project should begin with a visit to your local codes office for a consultation with officials.

When do you need a permit?

You need a permit anytime you alter or add to existing wiring or anytime new wiring is installed (▷). You will also need a permit when wiring major home appliances or when installing any outdoor or outbuilding wiring. When wiring will be covered up by finished walls or ceilings, a "rough-in" inspection is required, in addition to a "finish" inspection upon completion. Simple repairs, such as replacing switches and receptacles, generally do not require permits. When in doubt, call your municipal or county codes office.

Your local code authority will be happy to supply the forms you will need to apply for a permit. Inspectors are not hard to work with until you cross them. You will be charged a small fee to defray the costs of inspection and in some cases, you may be required to take a simple test to demonstrate your understanding of basic electrical principles. The test is not difficult. This chapter will give you more than enough information to pass it. Many authorities do not even require a test.

You may also be required to supply a rough drawing of the work you have in mind. Don't panic, this drawing need not be complicated, and besides, it offers the perfect opportunity for you to clarify any technical questions you might have.

UL listings

Just as you should maintain the highest standards of workmanship, you should use safe and tested materials. The best way to find quality materials is to look for a UL listing or the approval stamp of another major domestic testing laboratory. Electricity is only as safe as the materials used to bring it to you. A small savings on unapproved materials could cost you plenty in property damage or personal injury.

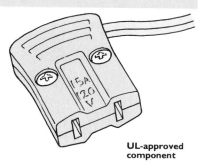

UL-approved component

Property insurance and your wiring

Home insurance policies are not likely to include exclusionary clauses concerning your electrical work. Even so, if a fire starts in your home and can be directly tied to your faulty electrical work, your insurance company may consider you a permanent bad risk and decide not to renew your policy.

Similar complications can result from work performed in your home by a licensed electrician who has not obtained a permit. Furthermore, you may be liable by a future owner of your home under the latent-defect laws of your state. If you knowingly hide an electrical defect when the contract is signed, the future owner can sue you for damages after the sale, or at least require you to correct the problem.

Conversely, acquiring a permit and setting up the proper inspections is the best insurance policy you can have. Once your code authority approves your work, you are in the clear. Any questions of liability will be directed elsewhere.

In short, acquire permits and follow code regulations. Codes protect you and the person who buys your home when you move on. In most cases, wiring to code does not make your work any more difficult or expensive, just safer. It only makes good sense to wire your home in the safest possible way. Prevention is still your best insurance.

CODES AND PERMITS

Codes and the grandfather clause

What if you are adding wiring to a home that does not meet current code requirements? When the inspector sees the existing wiring, will he make you upgrade it as well? The answer is almost always no. As codes change, you are not expected to change your home's wiring too. If your home was wired to code when it was built or remodeled, it falls under the grandfather clause. Only those sections you alter (and those sections affected by the alteration), must meet current code specifications.

Of course, there are exceptions. If existing wiring poses a serious threat to property and lives, you can be required to correct the problem.

About the NEC

The first electrical code in this country was proposed in 1881 by the National Association Of Fire Engineers. It was written in response to the many fires started by electricity then. It had only three rules. As we came to understand more about electricity, the code was expanded. The NEC guidebook is now a dense and highly technical book. Over 1,000 revisions were made in each of the last few updates. Today, it is considered a legal document, which makes it almost unreadable by amateurs. For the pertinent information it contains buy, instead, one of the simplified guidebooks available at bookstores.

Applying for an electrical permit

You may be required to take a simple test to demonstrate your electrical know-how. These tests are not difficult, and you will probably be tested only on those subjects listed in the permit application. Browse through this chapter before you go. You shouldn't have much trouble passing it.

You may also be required to sign an affidavit stating that you are the owner of the home listed in the permit application. If the home is not yours, don't expect to receive a permit. The house must be yours, and it must be a single-family dwelling. If it is a multi-family, you will not be issued a permit.

When a permit is issued to you, you must display it where it can be seen from the street. In most cases, you will have a year to complete the work, but expect inspectors to start looking in after a month or two.

● **Inspections**
You will be required to set up appointments with inspectors as you progress on a project. Usually two inspections are required, one before you cover up your work and one upon completion. When you call for an inspection, have the permit number handy and make sure you are there to open the house. Most codes departments will not allow their inspectors to enter a home alone.

HOW ELECTRICITY WORKS

Until you understand the basics of electricity, your electrical skills will be limited to simple repair projects. Luckily, once you get past the usual apprehensions, *electricity is quite easily understood. Electricity is logical and so can be learned in small steps. The basics are explained on this page.*

Volts × Amps = Watts

The electrons flowing through a circuit cause a current measured in *amperes*. The rate of flow can vary greatly, according to demand and power source. Current only flows when called for by an appliance. Amperes are moved along the circuit by pressure, called *voltage*. When we multiply voltage (pressure) times amperes (current) we get *wattage*, which is a measure of how much electricity is being used. If the current passes through a 75-watt bulb for example, the electricity consumed, or pulled out of the current, will be 75-watts.

Amperes

Amperes, often shortened to *amps*, are precise units of measurement. Approximately 6¼ billion billion electrons moving past a point in a circuit each second equals 1 amp.

Volts

Just as water pressure is measured in pounds, electrical pressure is measured in volts. The greater the voltage, the greater the pressure behind the amperes. Some voltage is lost when forced through a long conductor. This reduction is called *resistance*. Although a short and long conductor might have the same voltage input, the long conductor will deliver a lower output. The difference is lost to the resistance of the wire (also called a conductor) to the flow of current.

When voltage arrives at your service panel, it may fluctuate. This voltage ebb and flow may vary as much as ten or twelve units. You could be receiving from 114 to 126 volts at any given time. To establish some workable standard, the writers of the National Electrical Code have designed means of 120 and 240 volts. Today, all electrical materials are designed to these standards and rated accordingly.

Watts

Watts measure how much power is being used at a given time. To size a circuit and breaker, you must first determine the maximum wattage needed for a given room or group of rooms. We do this by adding up the watts as listed on light bulbs and appliances. A normal kitchen circuit might be quickly overloaded by a refrigerator, microwave, and a few small appliances.

We also need to know how many watts a 15- or 20-amp breaker will deliver, so we multiply 15 amps times 120 volts, to get 1,800 watts of potential power. If your maximum anticipated wattage is more than 1,800, extra circuits will be necessary (◁).

Watt-hours are also the measure used by power companies to keep track of the electricity we use. To make the billing more manageable, watt-hours are calculated in units of one thousand, known as kilowatt hours. Each kwh equals 1,000 watt hours, as measured by your service meter (◁).

Low-voltage circuits

Low-voltage wiring has long been used for doorbells and thermostats, because they require so little energy (◁). Recently, however, low-voltage systems have become popular in indoor track lighting and in landscape lighting as well. Low-voltage systems operate on approximately 12 volts. To reduce from 120 volts to 12 or less volts, small transformers are used (**1**). These transformers are usually supplied with low-voltage kits.

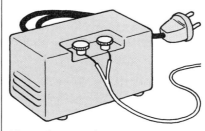

1 Low-voltage transformer

A SIMPLE CIRCUIT

For electricity to work, you must establish a circuit. A circuit is simply a wire loop that travels from an electrical source to an electrical outlet and back. Billions of electrons flow down one side of the loop, through the outlet and back along the other side. Only when a loop remains closed can electricity flow through it. If the loop is interrupted, as with a switch, the flow stops. The electrons must travel full circle to create a current. When a circuit is incomplete, it is said that a "short" exists. This can be the result of a broken wire or an improper connection (◁).

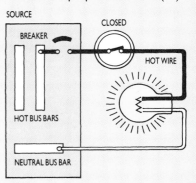

Closed loop
When a switch is closed, current flows.

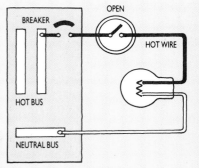

Open loop
When the switch is open, current cannot flow.

240-VOLT CIRCUITS

Many major appliances such as clothes dryers, water heaters and air conditioners require more voltage than can be handled by 120-volt conductors. To accommodate these greater voltage needs, two 120-circuits are joined in the service panel to create a single 240-volt circuit. Of course, 240-volt conductors, or cables, must sometimes be heavier to withstand the extra amperage (◁).

The rates listed below are for a specific area. Yours will be higher or lower. Information supplied by The Lincoln Electric System, Lincoln, Nebraska.

CONSUMPTION AND COSTS FOR COMMON ELECTRIC APPLIANCES

Appliance	Average Wattage	Avg Hrs Per Mo.	Avg Kwh Per Mo.	Avg Cost Per Mo.	Avg Cost Per Hour
FOOD PREPARATION					
Blender	386	3.2	1.24	$ .07	2.3¢
Coffee Maker (Drip)					
Brew	1440	3.0	4.32	$ .26	8.7¢
Warm	85	240.0	20.40	$ 1.23	.5¢
Deep Fryer	1448	4.7	6.80	$ .41	8.8¢
Electric Frying Pan	1196	13.0	15.50	$ .94	7.2¢
Electric Knife	92	1.0	.09	$ .01	.6¢
Garbage Disposal	445	6.0	2.70	$ .16	2.7¢
Microwave	1500	11.0	16.50	$ 1.00	9.1¢
Mixer (Hand)	127	1.0	.13	¢ .01	.8¢
Toaster	1146	3.0	3.40	$ .21	6.9¢
Toaster-Oven					
Toaster	1500	2.0	3.00	$ .18	9.1¢
Broiler	830	6.0	5.00	$ .30	5.0¢
Oven	1500	11.0	16.50	$ 1.00	9.1¢
Range					
Bake	2833	8.0	22.70	$ 1.37	17.1¢
Broil	2900	6.0	17.40	$ 1.05	17.5¢
Surface Units					
6" unit, high setting	1400	—	—	—	8.5¢
8" unit, high setting	2600	—	—	—	15.7¢
Sandwich Grill	1161	2.3	2.67	$ .16	7.0¢
Slow Cooker	200	57.0	11.40	$ .69	1.2¢
Waffle Iron	1161	1.6	1.90	$ .11	7.0¢
FOOD PRESERVATION					
Freezer					
15 cu. ft. upright	341	292.0	99.60	$ 6.02	2.1¢
15 cu. ft. upright frostless	440	334.0	147.00	$ 8.89	2.7¢
Refrigerator/Freezer					
15 cu. ft.	326	291.0	94.90	$ 5.74	2.0¢
15 cu. ft. frostless	615	248.0	152.50	$ 9.23	3.7¢
UTILITY					
Central Vacuum System	4300	8.0	34.40	$ 2.08	26.0¢
Clock	2	730.0	1.46	$ .09	—
Dishwasher	1200	25.0	30.00	$ 1.82	7.3¢
Dryer	4856	17.0	83.00	$ 4.99	29.4¢
Fluorescent Light (40 w)	40	92.0	3.68	$ .22	.2¢
Fluorescent Light (20 w)	20	92.0	1.84	$ .11	.1¢
Incandescent Light (100 w)	100	92.0	9.20	$ .56	.6¢
Iron	1100	12.0	13.00	$ .80	6.7¢
Sewing Machine	75	12.0	.90	$ .05	.5¢
Vacuum Cleaner	630	6.0	3.80	$ .23	3.8¢
Washing Machine (Automatic)	512	17.0	8.70	$ .53	3.1¢
Water Bed (King size— operating 50% of the time)	375	321.0	120.00	$ 7.28	2.3¢
Water Heater	4500	111.0	500.00	$30.22	27.0¢

*Summer Rate = 6.85¢/Kwh   **Winter Rate = 5.65¢/Kwh   Average = 6.05¢/Kwh

FROM THE SOURCE TO YOUR HOME

Electricity is created by generators that may be powered by water, oil, coal or nuclear reactor. From these generators electricity is pumped to distribution stations at very high pressure, or voltage. From the distribution stations, the voltage is reduced, split and distributed to major cities and rural areas.

From a local sub-station, electricity is pumped down your street, either through overhead wires or underground cables. Each home is then attached to the main distribution line by means of a residential service conductor. An older home might have a two-wire service capable of carrying only 30 amps of power at 120 volts of pressure. Homes built in the last 30 years are likely to have three-wire services capable of carrying from 60 to 200 amps at 120/240 volts.

SEE ALSO

◁ Details for:
Service entrance panel 291

UPGRADING YOUR SERVICE

With today's increased electrical needs, 30-amp services are seldom adequate. If you are willing to upgrade your service panel and possibly your home wiring, you can have your electrical supplier install an upgraded three-wire service (◁). Some municipalities will allow you to install your own service panel, but installing a new weather head, meter and service conductor should always be left to professionals. To determine if you will need upgraded wiring to accommodate a new service and panel, contact an electrician, your power company, or your local code authority. In any case, strict adherence to code specifications is a must.

One of the advantages of installing a new service is that you can usually convert from an overhead to an underground cable. Overhead services, called service drops, detract from the appearance of a home and are subject to storm damage. Overhead services can also kill you if you touch them with aluminum ladders or tree-pruning equipment. Even if you have an overhead three-wire service, you can have your power company convert it to an underground service, called a "service lateral," for a fee. Of course, your yard must be large enough to allow a trencher to maneuver. Patios and other large expanses of concrete also get in the way of trenchers and may prohibit going underground.

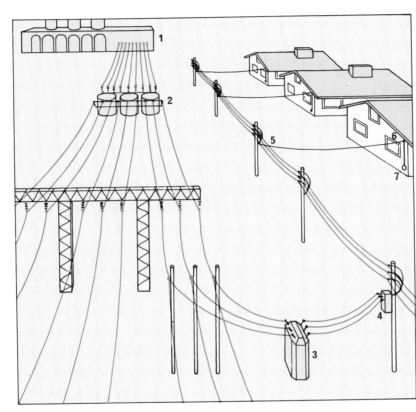

Electrical supply network
1 Generating station
2 Booster transformer
3 Distribution transformer
4 Residential transformer
5 Service drop
6 Weather head
7 Meter

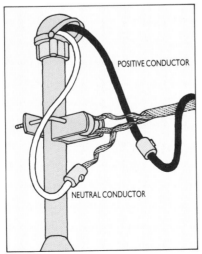

Two-wire service

POSITIVE CONDUCTOR

NEUTRAL CONDUCTOR

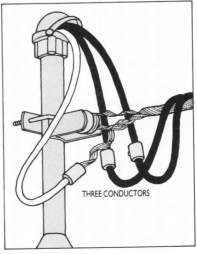

Three-wire service

THREE CONDUCTORS

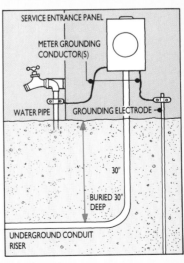

SERVICE ENTRANCE PANEL

METER GROUNDING CONDUCTOR(S)

WATER PIPE   GROUNDING ELECTRODE

30"

BURIED 30" DEEP

UNDERGROUND CONDUIT RISER

Service lateral

METERS AND SERVICE ENTRANCES

All the electricity you use is recorded in kwh by your meter. You can actually watch it count. A numbered disc spins when electricity is used and these revolutions are recorded by four or five small dials. The counter on your meter works much like the odometer in your car. Every watt consumed is recorded.

Your meter is banded in place and the band is sealed by your power company. It is actually part of the service entrance circuit. When a meter is removed, the circuit is interrupted. Only when it is plugged back in can you draw electricity from the power source.

If you wish to monitor your energy consumption, you can note the reading at the beginning of the month and again at the end of the month and subtract the former from the latter. Your meter will also give you an exact measure of energy saved when you experiment with energy-saving devices and practices. And of course, if you pay an estimated monthly bill, you can check for accuracy by comparing your actual use with the estimated billing (▷).

How to read a meter

If your meter is an older model, it will likely have only four dials. Newer models will have five dials. Each dial will be numbered from 0 to 9. As you look at these dials, you will see that they move in opposite directions. Starting from the left side, the first dial counts to the right, the second dial to the left and the third dial to the right again, and so on.

To record your meter reading, write down the numbers from each dial starting at the left. When a pointer reads between two numbers, record the lower number. When the pointer points directly to a number, look to the next dial. If the pointer to the right has reached 0, or has passed 0, write down the number indicated by the pointer at the left. If the pointer to the right has not reached 0, record the next lowest number from the dial on the left. Repeat this process until you have a number for each dial. That figure will give you the exact number of kilowatt hours consumed. To determine how much electricity you use in a month, read the meter at the beginning of the month and again at the end of the month.

Details for: ▷

Reading a meter
The reading indicated here would be 76579.

Service meter

THE SERVICE ENTRANCE PANEL

From the meter, your service wires enter your home, either through the roof or through a wall. (Thirty-amp services will have one black and one white wire, while 60- to 100-amp or greater services will have two black wires and one white wire.) Service wires are usually encased in metal or plastic conduit from the weather head to the service panel. Once inside the panel, the two hot (black) wires attach to a main switch, or disconnect. The neutral (white) wire is attached to the neutral bus bar. At this point, a ground wire, usually bare No. 6 copper, is connected to the bus bar as well and then fastened to a copper grounding rod or metal plumbing pipes or both. (Some panels have separate neutral and ground bus bars, which are bonded together in the panels.)

How your home's wiring connects to the service panel depends upon the age of the system and whether or not sub-panels are used. An older home may have a main panel with a disconnect switch, a bus bar and a ground conductor. In this case, the panel only serves as a distribution box and a main disconnect. From the main panel, one

black positive and one red positive wire, (the NEC no longer requires one hot conductor to be coded red), together with a white neutral wire and green ground, travel to one or more sub-panels where the positive wires are connected to "hot" bus bars and the neutral wire is connected to neutral bus bars. Older homes may also be wired directly to a main panel, without sub-panels. In this case, each circuit would have its own fuse in the main panel (▷).

A new home is likely to have a panel with built-in breakers. In this case, sub-panels are not generally used. All the circuits are connected to a bus bar through snap-in, or slide-in, breakers. In this configuration, the positive wire of every 120-volt circuit will be attached to the breaker and the neutral and ground wires will be connected to the neutral bus bar. Two-hundred forty-volt circuits will be similarly wired, except that two positive wires will be attached to each breaker. Once the panel is wired, connecting breakers and new circuits is relatively simple (▷).

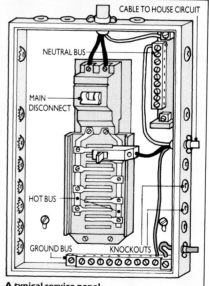

CABLE TO HOUSE CIRCUIT
NEUTRAL BUS
MAIN DISCONNECT
HOT BUS
GROUND BUS   KNOCKOUTS

A typical service panel

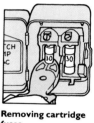

Removing cartridge fuses

MAIN FUSE BLOCK

Older service panels
These have pull-out fuse blocks.

BREAKERS AND FUSES

Fuses and breakers are safety buffers that keeps an electrical malfunction from starting a fire. A fuse can be blown or a breaker tripped when one of three things happens. The most frequent cause of trouble is an overloaded circuit. When too many lights or appliances are plugged into a circuit, they call for more amperage than the circuit can deliver. This amperage overload causes the conductors or wires to heat up, which causes the fuses to blow.

A short circuit will also cause a fuse to blow because of the greatly increased electrical charge it sends through the circuit. And finally, a fuse will blow when it is loose in its socket. This last cause is easy to fix, but the other two are not always so accommodating. It is crucial to determine exactly what may be causing a fuse to blow or a breaker to trip repeatedly.

Edison-base fuses
Used in older panels.

Time-delay fuses
Built to withstand brief amperage surges.

Type-S fuses
These keep homeowners from over-fusing a circuit.

Cartridge fuses
The knife-blade type protects heavier circuits.

Types of fuses

Edison-base fuses

A traditional Edison-base fuse contains a thin metal strip or wire that melts when a circuit heats up excessively. This metal strip is encased in ceramic and glass so that it can be screwed into its panel socket. When the strip melts, it separates and interrupts the flow of electrons. The glass and ceramic housing keeps the molten metal from escaping and becoming a fire hazard.

The glass window on the front of an Edison-base fuse allows you to see if the metal strip is intact. When an Edison-base fuse blows, the window also offers some clues in tracking down the source of the problem (◁). If the window is blackened by carbon, the cause of the overload is probably a short circuit (◁). A short circuit creates heat very quickly and burns the fuse at high temperature, which smokes the glass. If the glass is clear and you can see the melted strip, then the circuit probably heated up more slowly, as it would with an amperage overload.

If after replacing an Edison-base fuse, the new fuse blows as well, take notice of how long it took to blow. If it blows immediately, assume a short circuit. Often you will find the short in an appliance, most likely in its cord or plug. A lamp or appliance with a short will blow the fuse of any circuit you plug it into. Your only recourse is to repair the appliance and install a new fuse (◁).

If a single circuit blows frequently but with no apparent pattern, assume an overloaded circuit. You will have to unplug one or more lamps or appliances until a new circuit can be added (◁).

Time-delay fuses

Some heavy tools and electric motors require three times the amps to start as they do to run once started. If a fuse blows only when you start an electric shop tool or a window air conditioner, you can circumvent the start-up overload by installing a time-delay Edison-base fuse. If the time-delay fuse blows, however, unplug a few lamps or appliances or quit using the power tool until a new circuit can be installed.

Type S fuses

Through the years, many frustrated homeowners have installed 20-amp fuses in 15-amp sockets. This method does put an end to blown fuses, but it also cancels the only safety feature an electrical system has. If you are tempted to up-size a fuse, don't, under any circumstances. If an overloaded fuse in your panel can't overheat, the wiring in your home will. Overheated wires cause fires.

If you move into an older home, check to see that the previous owner has not made a dangerous substitution. To further protect yourself and all future owners, install non-tamperable Type S fuses. These fuses come with variously sized threaded adapters that screw into universal panel sockets. Once installed, they cannot be removed. From then on, only 15-amp fuses can be installed on 15-amp circuits because the thread sizes for 20-amp fuses are different.

Cartridge-type fuses

Cartridge fuses can be found in many older homes and are often used as main panel fuses. They may also be used to protect sub-panels, but the most common installation has two cartridge fuses at the main disconnect.

There are two types of cartridge fuse. The differences are in the end connections and in amp ratings. Ferrule-type cartridges can be rated between 10 and 60 amps and are frequently used in sub-panels and on branch circuits or appliance circuits. Knife-blade cartridges are the other type. The blade ends of these fuses snap into service panel clips. Because they are rated higher than 60 amps, they are often used as main panel protectors.

BREAKERS

Breakers have replaced fuses entirely in the last 25 years. Unlike a blown fuse, a tripped breaker does not have to be replaced. When a short or overload trips a breaker, all you will need to do is turn it back on. In addition to being a perpetually renewable circuit protector, a breaker can withstand the temporary amperage surges often created when electric motors first start up. So in a sense, a breaker has a built-in time-delay feature. You can also buy Edison-base replacement breakers that screw directly into older service panels. To reactivate these breakers, you simply push a small button in the center of the breaker.

Breakers differ slightly in appearance and operation from one manufacturer to another. The main difference is that some breaker switches do not return to the off position when tripped. You will have to shut them all the way off before flipping them on again. Breakers are also not universal in terms of how they snap into panels. You will have to buy breakers to match the brand name on your service panel.

Edison-base replacement breakers
By pushing the button, power is restored.

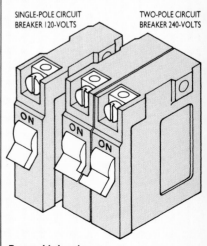

SINGLE-POLE CIRCUIT
BREAKER 120-VOLTS

TWO-POLE CIRCUIT
BREAKER 240-VOLTS

Renewable breakers
Modern panels use renewable breakers.

ASSESSING YOUR SYSTEM'S POTENTIAL

Two things determine the expansion capabilities of your home's electrical system. Most important is the amp rating of your service entrance. The other is the amount of circuit space left in your service panel.

To determine what rating your service panel has, open the panel cover and look for the amperage designation near the main disconnect. You should see the amp rating near the panel's brand name. If your service and panel are rated at 100 amps or more, you are in luck. If it is rated at 60 amps or less, expansion will be limited. If your needs require a substantial upgrade, you should consider having a larger service and panel installed. Contact a licensed electrician to determine whether the existing wiring will have to be replaced at the same time.

Your ability to install new circuits will depend on the number of breaker or fuse spaces left in the panel (▷). A home's wiring will seldom need all the breaker slots provided in a 100-amp, or greater, panel. If you see vacant breaker slots in your breaker panel, an expansion will be easy. Each slot will hold one new 15- or 20-amp circuit. If you have two vacant slots, your panel will accommodate a new 240-volt circuit.

If yours is one of the many older 60-amp panels, however, all available fuse spaces will likely be taken. A 60-amp service panel will also limit the number of 240-volt appliance outlets you can have. One 240-volt and four 120-volt circuits is the limit in 60-amp panels. If your 60-amp panel has the room and the available amperage, wiring a new circuit will be as easy as wiring from a new breaker. If the panel is full, but you still have some reserve amperage to work with, you can combine two underrated circuits in the panel and free one circuit for expansion.

Loose terminals

Loose terminal connections in older panels can cause a system to seem fully loaded when it is not. As connections expand and contract, they eventually loosen themselves. Loose connections blow fuses. Often you can solve the problem by shutting off power to the panel and tightening the screw terminals in the panel. With tight connections, fuses will not blow and you may even find that it will be possible for you to add an extra outlet or two (▷).

Mapping your home's wiring

Before you can know how much expansion your 60-amp system will safely handle, you will need to determine how much amperage is now being used by each circuit (▷). The best way to do this is to make a map of your home's circuitry. While tracing circuits sounds complicated, it need not be. All you will need is a floor plan drawing of your home, a voltage tester (▷) or lamp, and a little deductive reasoning.

Making the map

Start by drawing the perimeter of your home on graph paper. Use a simple 1/8-inch to 1-foot scale. In other words, each little square on the graph paper equals 1 square foot of living space. Then draw in the approximate location of all interior walls. If you have a lighted patio and a wired garage, draw them in too. Then indicate the location of each outlet box and each permanent light fixture in your home.

Start by removing the fuse or tripping the breaker on the first circuit in the panel. Mark that breaker or fuse No. 1. Then take your voltage tester or small lamp and plug it into all outlets near the circuit you've just interrupted. Next to each outlet on the map that doesn't work, place the number 1. Then go back to the service panel, restore power to the circuit you've just checked and shut off the power to the next circuit in the panel. Be sure to number each fuse or breaker in the panel as you go as well.

With power to the second circuit shut off, locate and number all fixtures and outlets on the map that do not work. Do this with each circuit until you have isolated each circuit and determined how many outlets and fixtures are served by each. When you are finished, every outlet and fixture should have a number. Tape the map to the inside of the panel cover for future reference.

SEE ALSO

Details for: ▷

How electricity works	288
Voltage testers	295
Circuits	306
Panels	307

Numbering the circuits

Each number represents a circuit.
⊕ Duplex outlet
⊕ Ceiling light
1 Kitchen appliance
2 Kitchen appliance
3 General lighting – dining/hall/bath/porch

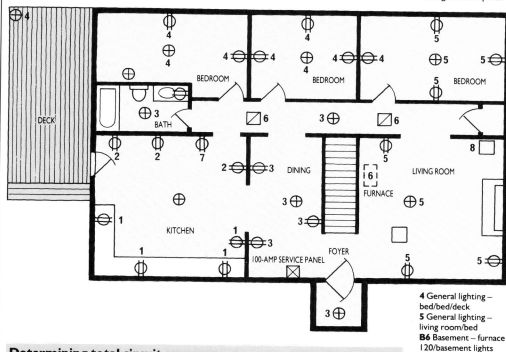

4 General lighting – bed/bed/deck
5 General lighting – living room/bed
B6 Basement – furnace 120/basement lights
7 240/120 range
B8 240 dryer – basement

Determining total circuit amperage

Each permanent light and outlet should be rated at 1.5 amps. This means that a 15-amp fuse or breaker (on No. 14 wire) will support 10 outlets. A 20-amp fuse or breaker (on No. 12 wire) will support 13 outlets. If your mapping identifies a circuit that can support additional outlets, you can tap into that circuit at any location to add new outlets.

If your map identifies two circuits with so few outlets that both circuits could be protected by a single fuse, you can combine those two circuits in the panel, thus freeing one whole circuit for expansion.

CONTINUITY TESTERS

Continuity testers allow you to test across conductors without having the power on, which makes them ideal for testing appliance switches and connections. Unlike voltage testers, continuity testers have their own battery-supplied power. The light in a continuity tester comes on when its circuit is completed by a switch, conductor or appliance. It is important to turn off power to any circuit or part before testing it with a continuity tester as house current will blow the tester bulb (◁).

Testing fuses

To see if a fuse is still working, touch the probe of the tester to the metal threads of the fuse and the alligator clip to the contact at the base of the fuse. If the fuse is good, the light in the tester's handle will glow.

To test a cartridge-type fuse, simply touch the probe to one end and the clip to the other. If the fuse completes the circuit and lights the tester bulb, it is good.

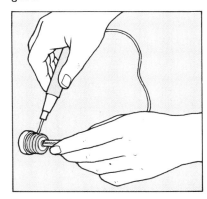

Testing an Edison-base fuse
Touch probe to base and clip to threads.

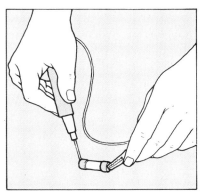

Testing a cartridge fuse
If the fuse is intact, the light will come on.

Testing lamp switches

To test a lamp switch, unplug the lamp and fasten the alligator clip to the brass-colored terminal screw and touch the probe to the contact tab inside the socket. When you turn the switch on, the light in the tester should glow. If it does not, replace the switch.

Testing three-way lamp switches

A three-way lamp switch has three opportunities to malfunction. If you have a lamp with a three-way switch that is giving you trouble, unplug the cord and remove the switch. Then attach the alligator clip to the brass screw terminal. (The other terminal will

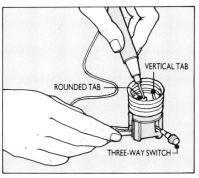

Testing a three-way lamp switch
Touch the probe to the vertical tab, the rounded tab, and finally, both tabs at once.

be bright silver colored.)

Then turn the switch to the first on position. When you touch the probe to the small vertical tab in the base, the tester light should come on. Then turn to the second on position. Touch the probe to the round center tab and the tester light should come on. Finally, turn the lamp to the third on position. If the tester light comes on when you touch both tabs simultaneously, the switch is not defective. You will probably find the problem in the cord or plug. If the tester fails to light in any one of the three on positions, replace the switch (◁).

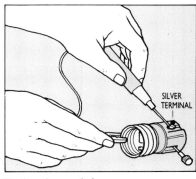

Testing a lamp switch
With the alligator clip clamped to the socket threads, touch the probe to the silver screw.

Testing toggle switches

When testing any switch with a continuity tester, shut off the power and remove the switch completely. To test a single-pole switch, place the alligator clip on one terminal and touch the probe to the other. When in the on position, the tester should light up.

To test three-way switches, determine which of the three terminal screws is the "common" terminal. Some manufacturers identify the common terminal by labeling it, while others color the common screw black or brass. The traveler screws will be bright silver. Place the alligator clip on the common screw and touch the probe to one of the other terminals. Flip the switch one way and the tester light should go on. Then touch the probe to the other terminal, the tester light should go on this time when the switch is in the opposite position.

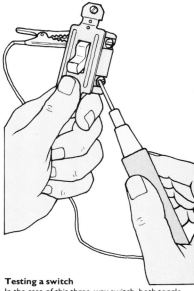

Testing a switch
In the case of this three-way switch, both toggle positions should be tested.

VOLTAGE TESTERS

A voltage tester is a simple, inexpensive device that tells you if there is electricity in a cable, outlet or switch. A voltage tester has no power of its own, but merely conducts voltage from one wire to another. As current passes through the wires, it lights a small neon bulb, which signals the presence of a current. Because a voltage tester can keep you from inadvertently touching a hot wire, you should buy one before you begin any wiring project. Voltage testers are also useful in testing your work for proper grounding and for determining which wire in a cable is hot.

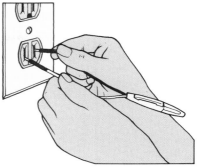

Testing a receptacle

To see if a receptacle is working, insert one wire of the tester into each plug slot. If the tester light comes on, the receptacle is energized. If not, the receptacle is defective or a fuse has blown. To determine if the problem is in one receptacle only, test the other receptacles on the circuit. If none works, the problem is in the circuit. If only one receptacle is defective, shut off the power to the entire circuit at the panel and test again to make sure the circuit is off, then replace the defective receptacle (▷).

Testing outlet
Testing for power at outlet with voltage tester.

Locating the hot wire in a cable

When working in a switch or receptacle box that contains two or more black wires, you will need to determine which black wire is hot. It is always possible that someone before you wired the white wire hot instead of the black wire, which can be confusing.

To find which wire is hot, separate the wires at the box so that they cannot make contact with one another. Then touch one tester probe to the metal box and the other to each of the black wires. The one that lights the tester bulb is the incoming hot wire. For future reference, you may wish to mark that wire with a piece of tape. If you are working inside a plastic outlet box, you will not be able to test the ground against the box. Instead, touch one probe to the bare ground wire in the box and the other to one of the black wires (▷).

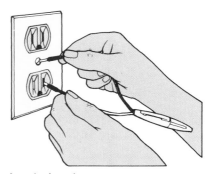

Testing fixture
Testing for power at fixture with voltage tester.

Checking for proper grounding

Properly grounded receptacles are very important to the safety of your electrical system (▷). Use your voltage tester to make sure every receptacle is grounded well. Insert one tester probe into the hot slot of the receptacle and touch the other probe to the coverplate screw. (The hot slot on newer receptacles is the smaller of the two. If the coverplate screw is painted, chip some paint from its head or turn the screw out far enough to reach the unpainted threads.) If the receptacle is a three-prong model, insert the ground probe into the U-shaped ground slot. The tester light should burn brightly. If the light seems weak, check for a poor ground connection.

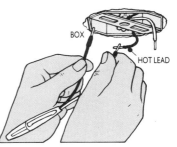

Locating hot wire
With the switch in the off position, only the incoming positive will be hot.

Testing a switch

To determine whether a switch is hot, remove the coverplate and touch one probe of your tester to the metal box or bare wire ground. Then touch the other probe to each of the wired terminals. If the light burns from each of these terminals, the switch is hot. If the switch is hot, shut the power off in the panel before working on the switch or the circuit (▷).

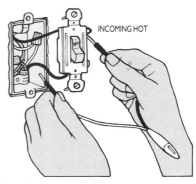

Checking grounding
If the box or the receptacle is grounded, the light will come on brightly. A dim light suggests a poor ground connection.

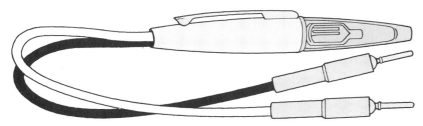

A typical voltage tester

DEALING WITH ELECTRIC SHOCK

Severe electric shock can arrest the heart and interrupt the breathing impulses controlled by the brain (◁). Often, when someone comes in contact with an electrical short, he or she will not be able to let go. If you see someone being electrocuted, use a towel or a broomstick or any poor conductor to pull him free of the current. If nothing else is available, try to knock them loose with a foot or a closed hand. Do not grab onto him or maintain contact for more than a split second. You too will become part of the short circuit, and will be unable to let go. The longer a person is in contact with a short, the more damage is done. You will have very little time to react, so move quickly.

SEE ALSO

◁ Details for:
Electrical safety 286, 302

Isolate the victim from the short circuit

Open the airway
Unless the victim's airway is opened, air cannot enter the lungs. If the victim is not breathing, the airway may be blocked. Clear the mouth of obstructions (food, gum, objects). Remove dentures only when they obstruct the airway. Lay the victim on his back and tilt his head back by placing your hand on his forehead and lifting the chin up with your other hand. The head-tilt helps keep the tongue from blocking the airway.

Clear away obstructions

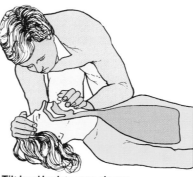

Tilt head back to open airway

Check for breathing
Once the airway is open, check for signs of breathing. Look to see if the victim's chest is rising and falling, listen for air being exhaled and feel with your cheek and ear for air escaping through the victim's nose and mouth. If the victim is not breathing, you should begin rescue breathing.

Check for breathing

Mouth-to-mouth
Keeping his head tilted back with one hand on his forehead, pinch the victim's nostrils shut with your thumb and forefinger. Take a deep breath and cover the victim's mouth with your own, making a seal. Blow deeply and slowly into the mouth, watching to see if the chest is rising and falling. Ventilate the victim's lungs two times with slow, full breaths. After the first two full breaths, continue giving one breath every 5 seconds for as long as you can. Check the victim often to see if he has begun breathing on his own.

Breathe into the victim's airway

Mouth-to-nose
If the victim's mouth is burned for any reason, you might breathe through his nose. Keeping the head tilted back, close the victim's mouth with your free hand by pushing the mouth shut. Place your mouth over the nose while sealing the mouth with your cheek, and proceed as with mouth-to-mouth.

Reviving a child
If the victim is a baby or small child, cover both the nose and the mouth at the same time with your mouth, then proceed as above, but use gentle puffs of air.

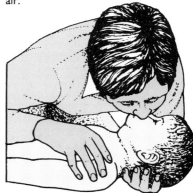

Breathe into a child's mouth and nose

Recovery
Once the victim starts breathing, place him in a semi-prone position. Observe him carefully to see that he continues to breathe regularly. Keep him warm with blankets or coats until medical help arrives.

A variety of cord types are used to supply lamps, power tools, portable heaters and small appliances. These cords usually consist of No. 16 or No. 18 stranded wire covered by two or three thin layers of paper insulation and plastic. The wire strands and the minimal insulation allow flex cords to be flexible. But these features also create problems. With years of flexing, the insulation breaks down and the protective covering wears thin. When bare wires are exposed, a short circuit can occur and can cause fires.

Years of use can threaten plugs as well. Plugs frequently tear loose, especially when pulled from receptacles by their cords. Rough handling can also break a plug's housing or cause a short between the prongs. And finally, plugs that are used a lot simply wear out.

To keep frayed flex cords and faulty plugs from threatening your home, inspect them regularly and replace them when they seem worn. If you find any cords that feel warm, change those immediately.

A FLEX CORD FOR EVERY PURPOSE

Flex cord manufacturers make cords for every use. Those shown here are designed for very specific purposes.

When replacing a cord, make sure you choose the correct replacement. Zip cord is the only type allowed for lamps.

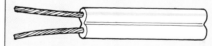
Fixture cord (zip cord)

Vacuum cleaner cord

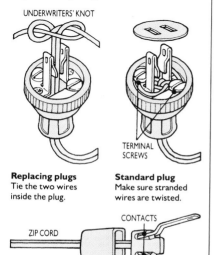
Heater cord

Power cord

SEE ALSO

Details for: ▷
Wiring 240-volt appliances 328

Replacing plugs

To replace a defective plug, cut the cord several inches away from the existing plug. Then separate the two wires for about 3 inches and strip ⅝ inch of insulation from each wire. Take the cover off the new plug prongs. Then feed the separated and stripped cord into the plug housing. Tie the two wires and fasten them to the terminals. Then replace the prong cover.

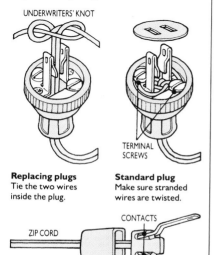

UNDERWRITERS' KNOT

TERMINAL SCREWS

Replacing plugs
Tie the two wires inside the plug.

Standard plug
Make sure stranded wires are twisted.

ZIP CORD

CONTACTS

PLUG HOUSING

Self-piercing plug
Each half pierces the cord, making contact.

Replacing cords

You can buy replacement flex cords by the foot or in pre-cut lengths that have plugs already on them. In the case of electric irons, replacement cords even have protective rubber sleeves on the appliance end to keep them from bending too sharply and breaking. The type you buy will depend mostly on the appliance and the appliance's proximity to a wall outlet.

Regardless of which cord you buy, the appliance end is a pretty simple hookup. In many cases, you will have to take the appliance apart, usually by loosening several screws in the housing. Some appliances have access panels that make connecting the cord easier. Many lamps have felt or cardboard base covers that can be pried loose. Others have a large enough cord opening to allow you to feed the new cord into the lamp stem. In any case, let the old cord be your guide to installing a new one. You can even tie the new cord to the old one

and pull it through.

Once you've brought the cord into the lamp or appliance, you will find two or three wire terminals, or in some cases, color-coded lead wires. If you find terminals, attach the wires to the terminals. Strip approximately ⅝ inch of insulation from the end of the wires. Twist the stranded wire and bend it into a clockwise hook. Lay the hook under the terminals and tighten them down. In most cases, two-wire cords cannot be cross-wired. If the cord wires are not color coded, don't worry about which terminal gets a given wire.

If you find two or three lead wires instead of terminals, you will have to join the new cord to the appliance leads with plastic solderless connectors. If your replacement cord has three wires, as is needed in a vacuum cleaner, fasten the green wire to the ground terminal (or green lead), and match the other two wires by color.

Replacing a lamp socket

Because lamp sockets get a lot of use, they wear out sooner than other components. Luckily, they are inexpensive and easy to replace. Start by unplugging the cord and removing the lamp shade and bulb. Then find the place on the socket marked "press." Press firmly against the socket and the components will separate. Once apart, remove all components and thread the new socket base onto the threaded nipple with the wires pulled through the new base. Then tie the two wires together and connect them to their respective terminals. Finally, replace the brass shell, bulb and shade.

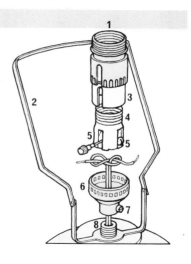

The components of a typical lamp
1 Socket shell
2 Harp
3 Insulating sleeve
4 Socket
5 Terminal screws
6 Socket cap
7 Set screw
8 Threaded center tube

REPLACING INCANDESCENT FIXTURES

Ceiling or wall-mounted light fixtures can be expected to last a long time. Even when they appear to be defective, often the problem can be traced to wall switches or defective wiring between the switch and fixture. Permanent light fixtures, therefore, are usually replaced for reasons of style or because not enough bulb sockets are available for adequate light. In bathrooms, wall lights might also be replaced so that new light/receptacle combinations can be installed. When shopping for a new light fixture, try to find one that has a cover, or canopy, as large as the one on your existing fixture. A smaller coverplate may require some touch-up painting or plaster repair. Whatever reason you have for replacing a light fixture, you will be glad to know that the project is a simple one.

Replacing light fixtures is easy because all fixtures, regardless of outward appearance, have similar internal parts. Likewise, nearly all fixtures are fastened to ceiling outlet boxes, which makes the fixture-to-box connection nearly universal.

If you are replacing an incandescent fixture because it no longer works, first check the switch, conductor and fixture leads to make sure that a new fixture will solve the problem (◁). When your diagnosis implicates the fixture, replace it.

Removing a light fixture

To remove an old ceiling or wall fixture, start by shutting the power off at the panel. Then loosen the set screws or center nut that holds the glass diffuser to the fixture body. With the diffuser off, undo the center nut or canopy screws from the decorative cover or canopy. Pull the canopy down to expose the wires and nipple strap. Then remove the nipple and strap from the box and pull the leads and wires out of the box. With the leads exposed, loosen each connection and remove the remaining components of the fixture.

Installing a new fixture

To install a new fixture, start by fastening the nipple strap to the box. Next, thread the nipple into the strap. Then, hold the fixture up to the box so that the fixture lead wires can be attached to the switch wires in the box. Hold each color-matched set of wires together and tighten a plastic solderless connector over them. No bare wire should be showing when the connectors are in place. With the switch wires connected to the lead wires, fasten the canopy to the nipple or nipple strap and connect the glass diffuser to the canopy.

One word of caution is in order when it comes to ceiling fixtures, especially those with closed diffusers: Never install a bulb with a higher wattage rating than the fixture is designed to hold. Bulbs of higher wattage can overheat the socket wiring. Hot fixtures start fires. You will find the recommended watt rating stamped somewhere on the fixture.

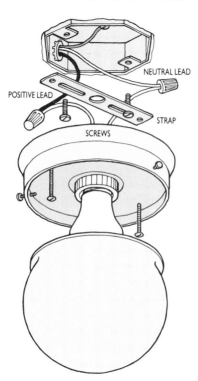

STRAP

Chandelier-type fixture connection

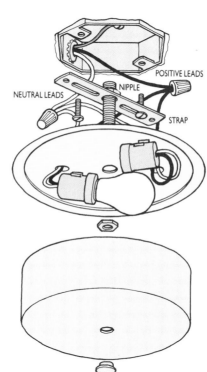

NEUTRAL LEAD

POSITIVE LEAD

STRAP

SCREWS

NEUTRAL LEADS

POSITIVE LEADS

NIPPLE

STRAP

Two common ceiling fixtures

HOT

SWITCH LOOP

NEUTRAL

Wall-mounted light with receptacle

INSTALLING AND REPAIRING FLUORESCENT FIXTURES

Fluorescent lights offer the best energy-buy around when it comes to lighting your home. You can receive five to six times more light from a fluorescent bulb than from an incandescent bulb of the same wattage. Fluorescent fixtures operate under a completely different principle from incandescent fixtures. When electricity is routed to a fluorescent fixture, a booster station, called a ballast, sends a surge of electricity into the fluorescent tube. Older models also include a starter to help the ballast reach maximum power in less time. This increased surge of electricity then charges gases in the bulb which in turn create a faint light. The light is then picked up and intensified by a chemical coating on the inner wall of the bulb. This three-step activation explains the familiar hesitation found in older models when first turned on. Newer models come on instantly.

Installing fluorescent fixtures

Installing fluorescent fixtures is no different than installing incandescent fixtures. In both cases, the body of the fixture is held to the ceiling by a threaded nipple or screws that go into a ceiling box (▷). Both have lead wires that are joined inside the ceiling box with approved connections. The rest is a matter of design variation.

When replacing an incandescent fixture, shut off the electricity, undo the center nut or screws that hold the canopy in place and remove the plastic connectors from the fixture leads. Then install the new threaded nipple and strap. Hold the lamp near the box and connect the fixture leads to the switch wires. With the wires connected, slide the fixture body, called the channel, over the threaded nipple and tighten the center nut. Larger channels may also need to be fastened to ceiling joists with wood screws. If you have trouble finding joists, use expansion inserts.

Diagnosing and repairing fluorescent fixtures

The most frequent problem you are likely to encounter with fluorescent lights is worn-out bulbs. Unlike incandescent bulbs, fluorescent tubes do not burn out abruptly. They flutter and flash on and off and act up in ways that lead homeowners to believe more serious problems exist. Don't assume the worst. Always start with the tube. If a tube will not come on at all, wiggle and twist it slightly in its sockets. Often the end pins are not seated properly.

To determine whether a troublesome tube needs to be replaced, look to the discoloration on each end. It is normal for a tube to show grey rings through the glass on each end, but when these rings turn black, the bulb needs to be replaced. Make sure that you replace it with a tube of the same wattage (▷).

Defective starters

When older, low-voltage fluorescent fixtures flutter but do not come on, the problem is likely to be the starter. A starter is a small cylinder located under one of the tubes near a socket. Twist the tube out so that you can reach the starter. Then, check to see if the starter is seated properly. Push it in and try to turn it to the right. If it moves or turns to the right, replace the bulb to see if re-seating it helped. If the light does not come on, you can assume a defective starter.

Remove the old starter by pushing in slightly and turning it a quarter-turn counterclockwise. Be sure to buy another starter with the same amp rating. Then push it into its socket and turn it to the right, until it seats. Finally, replace the tube and turn the power back on. The new starter should eliminate the flickering problem immediately.

Non-starter fixtures

Newer fluorescent fixtures come on instantly. Because of a few internal changes, starters are no longer needed and so maintenance problems have been greatly reduced. If you have a problem with one of these newer fixtures, first look to the tubes, then to the ballast for the problem.

REPLACING A BALLAST

The ballast is the heart of a fluorescent fixture and is therefore the most costly component to replace. In fact, if you watch for specials, you can often buy a completely new fixture for the same price as a new ballast.

A faulty ballast is characterized by a continuous buzzing sound, often accompanied by a sharp odor. To replace a ballast, shut the electricity off at the panel and remove the tubes and the channel lid. Inside, you will find the ballast screwed to the channel. Clip the wires near the ballast and loosen the retaining screws that hold the ballast in place inside the fixture.

Replacement ballasts come with lead wires. Simply fasten the new ballast to the channel and join the fixture wires to the ballast leads with plastic connectors. Follow the manufacturer's wiring diagram carefully to avoid cross-wiring.

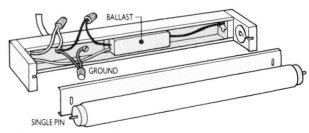

Instant-start fluorescent fixture

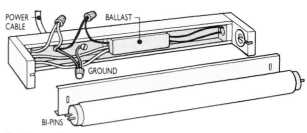

Rapid-start fixture

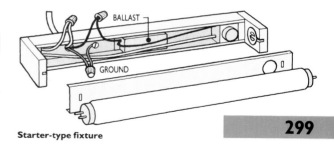

Starter-type fixture

LOW-VOLTAGE DOORBELLS AND THERMOSTATS

Repairing a broken door bell may require a little detective work, but is normally a simple enough task. The low-voltage current will do little more than tickle your fingers if you touch both wires (◁). Not until you reach the transformer will you need to shut the power off. All but the wiring will be surface-mounted.

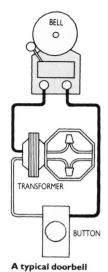

A typical doorbell loop

Testing the button

Start with the most likely culprit, the button. It gets the most use and abuse over the years. Undo the screws that hold the button to the house trim and locate the wires. Remove one of the two thin wires from its terminal and touch it to the other wire or terminal. If the bell rings, you probably need a new button. Simply attach the two existing wires to the terminals of the new button and fasten the new button to the door trim or house siding. Some buttons fasten directly, others have base plates. Low voltage requires no ground wire.

Repairing broken wires

As you work your way through the system, carefully check for loose connections, broken wires or frayed insulation. If you find broken wires, splice them with small wire connectors and tape (◁). If you find frayed insulation, tape each wire individually near the problem area. And of course, restore any loose connections you find.

Cleaning clapper and bell

If, when someone rings your doorbell, you hear a muffled buzz instead of the bell, suspect a dirty or gummed up clapper contact. Remove the cover and clean the clapper contact thoroughly. If it does not respond at all to an electrical charge, you probably need a new one. First, remove the old cover, bell and wall bracket. To keep the wires from falling into the wall space, pull them out as far as you can and guide them through the opening of the new wall bracket. Then screw the new bracket to the wall so that it is level. Connect the existing wires to the new terminals and snap the cover over the bell or chime mechanism.

Checking the transformer

If the bell does not ring when you test the button, look to the transformer. The transformer will be attached to the side of a 120-volt junction box, usually in the basement. To determine if the transformer is working, undo the two low-voltage wires and use a screwdriver to arc across the terminals. Lay the screwdriver on one terminal and lightly touch it to the other terminal. If you see a tiny spark, the transformer is sending current through the lines.

If no spark is produced, assume a faulty transformer. Before replacing it, shut the power off to the circuit that serves the transformer outlet. Then remove the screws that fasten the transformer to the outlet box. Attach the transformer leads to the 120-volt conductors in the box and replace the outlet cover. Finally, attach the low-voltage wires to the terminals and restore power to the circuit.

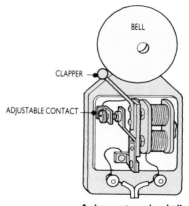

A clapper-type doorbell

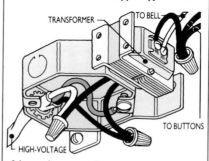

A low-voltage transformer

REPLACING A THERMOSTAT

Replacing a thermostat is an easy job when you buy the right replacement. Before shopping for a new one, pry the cover off of your current thermostat and check to see how many wires come through the wall. Furnaces without air conditioning will require only two wires, while furnaces with air conditioning require four and sometimes five wires. Make sure that the thermostat you choose is compatible with your existing system. Look for a brand name and model number and try for an exact replacement.

Start by removing the cover from the old thermostat. This will expose the wires and the heat-sensitive switch. Disconnect the wires, but make sure you note how they were hooked up. Then remove the screws holding the base plate to the wall. Be careful not to let the wires fall behind the wall finish back into the stud space.

Then slide the wires through the new base plate and fasten it to the wall. Make sure that the base plate is perfectly level, or the mercury switch may give you a false temperature reading. With the base installed, connect the wires to the terminal according to the manufacturer's instructions. (Wiring diagrams may vary with the manufacturer.) When you have the wires connected, snap the cover in place and test the thermostat with a setting greater than your current room temperature.

Set-back thermostats

Special set-back thermostats are available to help you save energy. They allow you to program a warmer or cooler setting for those hours when you are not home, or when you are asleep. A 6- to 10-degree setback can save a lot of energy in the course of a year.

Set-back thermostats are installed the same way as ordinary models. They too are available in two-wire and five-wire versions. The two-wire models have batteries that are continually charged by the available current. Four- or five-wire models operate directly off of the low-voltage circuit.

WORKING WITH WIRE

Most electrical wiring today is made of copper. Copper is a good conductor and is flexible enough to handle the twists and turns of a typical installation without breaking. Because the wires of a circuit, generally called conductors, will create a short circuit if they touch each other, they are usually encased in plastic insulation. Because all circuits require two or more conductors (▷), electrical supply manufacturers offer two or more conductors in a single plastic or nonmetallic sleeve. Wire in this form is called cable. Individual conductors that travel from one location to another without being part of a cable, must be encased in rigid or flexible conduit.

Electrical wire is sized by gauge number, starting with the smallest size, No. 18, and increasing to the largest residential size, No. 1. Wire size is a critical factor in a home's wiring system. Just as a small pipe size can carry only so many gallons of water, small conductors can carry only so many amperes. When a wire is forced to carry more amperes than its size can handle, resistance increases and the wire heats up. As a wire heats up, it either blows a fuse or becomes a fire hazard.

When you attempt any wiring project, make sure that you follow the NEC specifications (▷). The following sizing guide will help you choose the right wire size for each project. Other factors may dictate wire size, such as breaker capacity, so use this chart for general reference only (▷).

WIRE TYPES AND USES

The wire sizes used in a typical home range from No. 18 or No. 16 stranded wire for doorbells to No. 6 wire for grounding electrodes and service conductors.

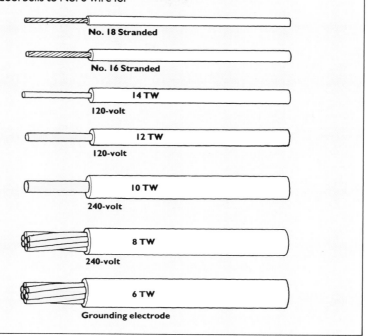

No. 18 Stranded

No. 16 Stranded

14 TW
120-volt

12 TW
120-volt

10 TW
240-volt

8 TW
240-volt

6 TW
Grounding electrode

RESIDENTIAL WIRE SIZING GUIDE

Wire Size	Common Use	Amps
#18	Low voltage (LV)	7
#16	LV/doorbells	10
#14	Lights, outlets	15
#12	Small appliances/120v	20
#10	Large appliance/120v	30
# 8	Larger appliance/120v	40
# 6	Single appliance/240	55
# 4	Single appliance/240	70

Identify wires by color

To give electrical wiring an instantly recognizable standard in the field, the NEC has designated an insulation color for each conductor function. A black wire, for example, is always the "hot," or positive side of a circuit. A red wire is also positive. If you see a black wire and a red wire in the same cable, you know that circuit has two hot wires and therefore must be a 240-volt circuit (▷). A white wire is always neutral, unless used as a traveler on a three-way switch (▷). In that case, the white insulation should be marked with black paint or black tape to distinguish it from the white neutral in the same box. Blue wires can also be hot when substituted for black in conduit. Green and yellow are always ground wires, as is bare copper wire.

While these designations are excellent indicators, don't trust your life to them. The home owner before you may have invented his own coding system. Protect yourself from nonconformists by testing each circuit you wish to work on with a voltage tester before starting work (▷).

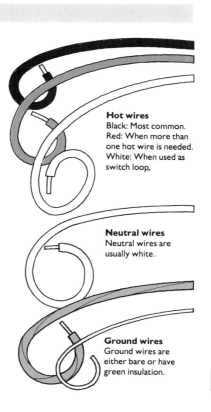

Hot wires
Black: Most common.
Red: When more than one hot wire is needed.
White: When used as switch loop,

Neutral wires
Neutral wires are usually white.

Ground wires
Ground wires are either bare or have green insulation.

CABLE TYPES AND USES

In the field, the terms wire and cable are often used interchangeably. To be exact, however, the term "wire" refers to a single conductor, insulated or uninsulated. The term "cable" is used to describe several wires encased in a single sleeve or sheath—12/2 cable with ground, for example, contains two insulated No. 12 wires and one paper-wrapped ground wire. This same arrangement of wires might also be run as single strands contained in conduit, but would not be called cable. And because the ground wire would not have the protection of a plastic sleeve as in insulated cable, it would need to be an insulated wire (◁).

Types of wire

Type T wire is most commonly used in residential installations. It has a tough insulation, called thermoplastic, that will accommodate both hot and cold weather extremes. Type TW is a designation for all-weather installations. Type TW can be used in above-ground outdoor installations. It has a slightly heavier plastic coating that provides more protection from temperature extremes and moisture. For extremely hot situations, type THW wire should be used.

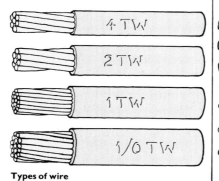

Types of wire

Types of cable

Because residential wiring is simpler than commercial wiring and requires fewer provisions for change, cable is used instead of conduit and wire. A variety of cable types have been developed to meet a variety of special needs. In most cases, the job will dictate the cable type you use (◁).

NM cable is the most commonly used in residential systems. It is made of two or more type T wires and a bare-wire ground, all encased in a plastic sleeve. The ground wire is wrapped in paper and is positioned between the two insulated wires. The paper wrap makes this type of cable unsuitable for damp situations.

NMC cable is specifically designed for damp situations. Instead of paper wrap,

all three wires are encased in a solid plastic strip. NMC is often used in basement installations.

UF cable is designed to be used in underground installations of outdoor lighting and as a lateral cable to outbuildings. It too is encased in plastic and is moistureproof (◁).

A last category, armored cable or BX, is rarely used today but must be reckoned with in older homes. It was designed to be used where ordinary cable might be punctured by nails. The distinguishing feature of armored cable is that the metal armor itself partially grounds the circuit it serves. To complete the ground, a thin metal strip runs next to the paper covered insulated wires.

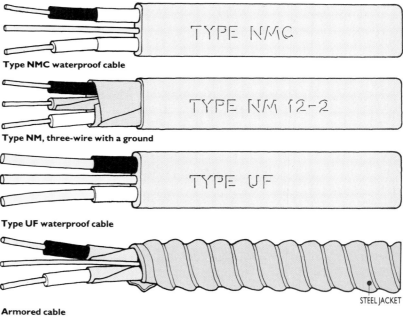

Type NMC waterproof cable

Type NM, three-wire with a ground

Type UF waterproof cable

Armored cable

STEEL JACKET

THE DANGER OF ALUMINUM WIRE

In the early fifties, manufacturers looking for a less expensive conductor introduced aluminum wire to the market. Because it was more economical, this wire was frequently used in homes built for speculation. The industry soon learned, however, that aluminum wire came with some very serious problems.

Aluminum is not as efficient a conductor as copper. As a result, it offers more resistance to current. As

the wire heats up, it expands. Repeated expansion and contraction eventually cause the wires to loosen under terminal screws. The short circuits that occur in the process regularly trip breakers and can cause fires.

A compromise wire was also manufactured. It too was made of aluminum, but was clad in copper. Copper-clad wire is allowed by some code authorities, but not by others.

To protect yourself against the

problems caused by aluminum wire, you can replace all switches and receptacles with those made to accommodate aluminum, or use a special pigtail connection with antioxidation paste in the plastic connector. If 15- or 20-amp switches and receptacles have no designation markings, don't use them. Use only those with "CO/ALR" designations. The NEC now forbids the use of aluminum No. 12 and No. 14 wire in new installations.

CUTTING, STRIPPING AND SPLICING WIRE

Working with wire does not require a large investment in tools. In fact, you can do a lot with needle-nose pliers and a sharp pocket knife. If you do more than replace an occasional receptacle, however, you should consider investing in a few wire-working tools. Your first purchase should be a multipurpose tool, pliers that cut and strip many different sizes of wire.

In residential wiring, every wire connection must be made within a box (▷). You should never splice two wires together outside of an outlet or junction box. Instead, bring a minimum of 6 inches of wire into each box and clamp it in place with the box clamps. Then strip the plastic sheathing from the wire.

Stripping wire

You can buy a sheathing stripper, but a sharp knife works just as well if you are careful (**1**). Because the uninsulated ground wire runs through the center of the sheathing, make your cut in the middle of one side. Make the cut shallow to avoid nicking the insulated wires. Then pull the split sheathing back from the wires and cut it off (**2**).

With the sheathing gone, strip approximately ½ inch of insulation from each insulated wire (**3**). You can use a knife, but a multipurpose tool works better. In any case, avoid cutting into the copper. Slide the end of the wire into the correct numbered slot in the handle of the tool (**4**), then squeeze, twist and pull. If you have the wire in the right hole, the insulation will strip right off. Work with 6 inches of wire outside the box.

Making connections

Wire connections, no matter where they are made, must be very tight. Loose connections create resistance, which in turn creates heat. Hot connections trip breakers and if they are allowed to spark, can cause fires.

To join two solid wires, strip ½ inch from each wire and twist them together with pliers in a clockwise direction. Then select a plastic connector large enough to slide over the twisted wires about half way. Insert the wires into the connector and turn it until the wire is drawn in and the connector no longer turns. The more wires you join, the larger the connector you will need. Make sure that no copper shows outside the connector. It is easier to join all corresponding wires out of the box where you can work unencumbered. Then carefully fold them into the box when finished.

Stranded wire connections

When connecting stranded wire, strip about ½ inch of insulation from each wire and twist the strands together in a clockwise direction until no loose ends can be seen. Then turn the connector on until it is tight.

When connecting stranded wire to solid wire, strip ½ inch of insulation from the solid wire and about ¾ inch from the stranded wire. Wrap the stranded wire tightly around the solid wire in a clockwise direction. Then tighten a connector over them (▷).

When connecting wires to switch or receptacle terminals, strip about ⅝ inch of insulation from each wire, then use needle-nose pliers to form a small loop or hook. Loosen the terminal screw until the loop fits under the screw clockwise. Then tighten the screw. Because receptacle terminals can hold only one wire, and because code now requires it, use a pigtail connection from the receptacle to the circuit wires (▷).

When connecting to a push-in switch or receptacle with self-locking slots, strip only ½ inch of insulation from the wires and push each into the back of the device until no copper can be seen. If any copper remains exposed, depress the locking clip next to the slot and pull the wire out. Then clip the end of the wire, and push it back in (▷).

Tighten a plastic connector over the wires

Wrap the longer stranded wire around the solid wire

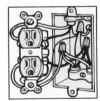

When joining a receptacle to a circuit, use pigtails

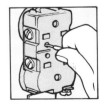

Most newer receptacles and switches have push-in wire slots

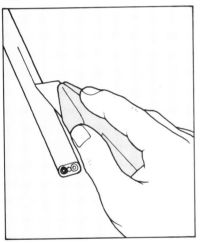

1 When cutting sheathing, cut in center only

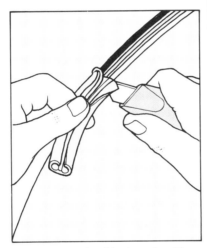

2 Cut the excess sheathing from the cable

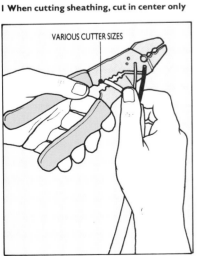
VARIOUS CUTTER SIZES

3 Select the correct wire size opening

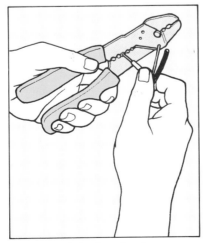

4 Pull the insulation from the wire

303

GROUNDING AN ELECTRICAL SYSTEM

You can always expect electricity to find the path of least resistance. Current will flow through a larger wire before it will a smaller wire. It will flow through copper more readily than it will through aluminum or iron. Given a choice, electricity would rather flow through copper than almost anything else, including a human body. This fact is the basis of the principle known as grounding. As long as we provide an easier grounding conductor, such as copper, we are kept from becoming conductors ourselves. Understanding grounding is critical to your understanding of a home's electrical system.

The electrical current in your home's system starts its circular flow at the main breaker, through the black wire (◁). It travels to its farthest destination, passes through a receptacle or appliance and travels back to the panel bus bar through the white wire. Both wires will carry the same amount of amperage in order to maintain a current, or circular flow.

Also tied to the bus bar is a ground wire and a grounding electrode. It is larger than the other wires in the panel so that it becomes the path of least resistance, should current become sidetracked. Connected to this heavy ground wire, is a smaller bare ground wire that travels next to the black and white wires of the circuit.

The heavy ground wire that fastens to the neutral and ground bus bars in your main panel carries any dangerous fault current into the ground around your home, where it dissipates. This is the origin of the term "grounding".

Short circuit

Occasionally, as when lamp cords fray or wear thin, a black hot wire comes in contact with a white neutral wire. When this happens, the current, or circular flow, takes a shortcut. For an instant, the flow increases dramatically. This "hot" surge usually creates a flash that burns away the contact surfaces. With the contact points burned off, the short no longer exists. What is left is a visible black char mark from the spark.

When a short circuit increases current flow beyond the breaker rating, the breaker opens and interrupts the flow. If a short circuit increases flow to a level just below the breaker rating, the breaker will not trip, but some part of the circuit may be destroyed.

Grounding a system

Grounding clamp

How your system is grounded will depend upon the age of your home and specific regulations of your local or municipal code (◁). Many homes are grounded through their water pipes to the city water main. In this case, the grounding wire travels from the panel bus bar to the house side of the water meter. It is then clamped to both sides of the meter. When a ground fault occurs, electricity is drained off through the water service and dissipates in the surrounding soil.

Other homes may be grounded directly through copper grounding rods. In this case, the grounding rod is driven into the ground at least 8 feet deep, usually near an outside basement wall. A simple grounding clamp ties the rod to the ground wire.

Many areas are now requiring that every electrical system be grounded both to the metallic plumbing system and to a grounding rod. Other codes require that the grounding electrode travel all the way to the water main on new construction installations. Ask your local code authority for grounding requirements in your area (◁).

GROUND FAULTS

A short, or ground fault, often happens when a black (positive) wire comes loose from its terminal and touches a metal outlet box or the metal housing of an electrical tool or appliance. Because a ground wire is attached to the metal surface, the current abandons the white neutral wire and travels back to the panel through the bare ground wire. While much of this misdirected electricity is dissipated in the soil, a great deal of resistance can be generated by the loose contact between the metal and the hot wire. If you touch the metal box or tool, you can become the ground conductor for this high-resistance circuit. This is essentially what happens when people are electrocuted in their workshops or bathrooms (◁).

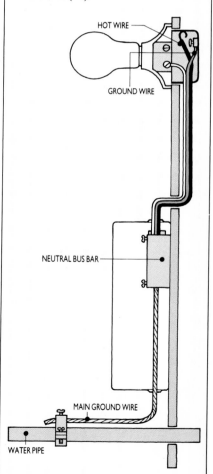

Grounding conductor
The plumbing pipe carries the misdirected current into the soil outside the house.

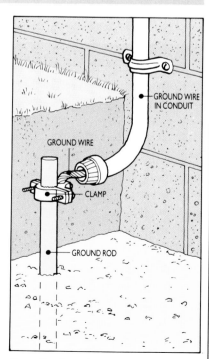

Grounding through copper grounding rods
When possible, the connection should be made below grade.

*Grounding the panel will be of little use if
every outlet is not tied to the grounding
electrode. The problem is that many older
homes have two-wire circuits and two-slot
outlets. If your home has three-wire
circuits, but two-slot receptacles, you can
upgrade to three-slot receptacles (▷).*

Checking for grounding

To determine whether you can make
such an upgrade, remove the coverplate
and pull the receptacle out of the box,
with the power off. If you see a bare
wire (**1**) fastened to the metal box, feel
free to install three-slot receptacles. If
you see no ground wire in the box (**2**),
definitely do not convert to three-slot
receptacles.

If the box is grounded, you can also
use three-prong adapters. Again, check
to see if the box is grounded. If not,
don't use them. If grounded, loosen the
coverplate screw and slide the
grounding wire under the screw. Then
tighten the screw and plug the adapter
into the receptacle. Every grounded
tool or appliance you plug into this
adapter will be grounded all the way to
soil outside your home.

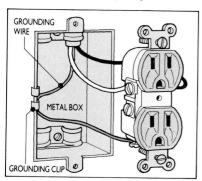

Copper compression ring
All ground wires can be crimped together.

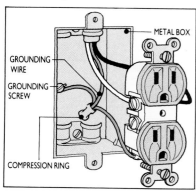

Grounding clip
If no grounding screw is present, use a grounding
clip.

GROUND FAULT CIRCUIT INTERRUPTERS

As already mentioned, a ground fault
can be dangerous. If you touch an
appliance or tool that has a loose
positive wire, the resistance created
there could send a shock through your
body. When you are on wet ground or
in a damp bathroom, your body
improves as a conductor. Water allows
you to conduct much more electricity.
In damp situations, a ground fault can be
fatal.

To protect yourself from a ground
fault shock, your bathroom, kitchen,
laundry room and workshop receptacles
should be equipped with ground
fault circuit interrupters, called GFCIs. GFCIs
are now mandatory in bathrooms and
garages and in all outdoor wiring. The
latest code now also requires GFCIs on
outlets near a kitchen sink.

GFCIs work by monitoring the
current in the black and white wires. As
long as current is equal in both wires,
the circuit remains closed. As soon as a

GFCI senses an imbalance, as typifies a
ground fault, it shuts off the power to
that circuit or receptacle within 1/40 of
a second.

You can acquire GFCI protection
with one of three devices. The most
expensive and most versatile GFCI is
contained in a breaker (**1**). When you
install a GFCI breaker, everything on
that circuit is protected (▷). The
second device is a GFCI receptacle that
is quite easy to install (**2**). When you
install this receptacle, all receptacles on
the circuit *after* the GFCI are also
protected (▷). A GFCI receptacle will
cost about 30 percent less than a GFCI
breaker. The last alternative is the
simplest. It is a GFCI receptacle adapter
(**3**). You simply plug this adapter into a
standard receptacle and then plug your
appliances into the adapter. An adapter
works well but only protects the
receptacle it is plugged into. Adapters
are a good choice in older bathrooms.

SEE ALSO

Details for: ▷
Breakers and fuses 292
**Installing
receptacles** 315–316

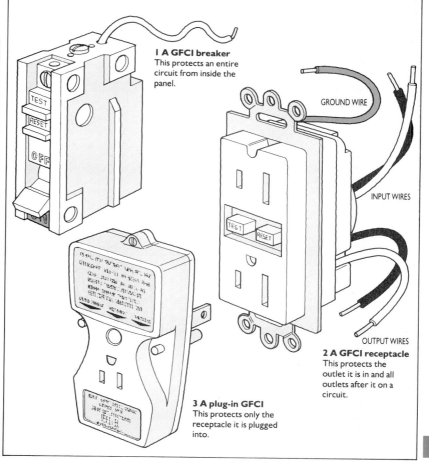

1 A GFCI breaker
This protects an entire
circuit from inside the
panel.

2 A GFCI receptacle
This protects the
outlet it is in and all
outlets after it on a
circuit.

3 A plug-in GFCI
This protects only the
receptacle it is plugged
into.

ELECTRICAL CIRCUITS

As mentioned earlier, a circuit is a flow of electricity that starts at the power source, or panel, continues through appliances and comes back to the source in a continuous pattern. But on a practical level, it helps to think of a circuit, not as a flow of electrons, but as the wires that carry that flow. It is easier to visualize wires threaded through our homes, carrying electricity to our lights and appliances. In any case, it is to these wires that we now turn our attention.

● **Do you need more
circuits?**
How do you know
when you need more
circuits? The most
obvious indicator will
be frequently blown
fuses or tripped
breakers. If you find
yourself plugging
adapters with several
extension cords into
certain outlets, that
should be another
clear signal. You
should also watch for
lights that flicker
when appliances,
such as refrigerators,
come on. And if the
image in your TV set
shrinks when some-
one turns on a major
appliance, it's probably
time to evaluate your
electrical needs.

Branch circuits

The circuits that serve the rooms of your home are called branch circuits. Indeed, if you could see through your home, these wires would look like branches, all reaching out from your service panel. In practice, there are three basic kinds of circuits. They are, lighting circuits, small-appliance circuits and individual circuits.

Lighting circuits serve the general purpose lights and outlets found in living rooms, bedrooms and bathrooms. They typically power ceiling lights, radios, televisions, lamps and all manner of low-wattage gadgets.

Small-appliance circuits are commonly found in kitchens and workshops. These circuits have larger wire and higher amp fuses or breakers. They run the usual gamut of small kitchen appliances, such as toasters, food processors and even refrigerators. The NEC now requires at least two circuits for kitchens, though many older homes get by with only one.

Individual circuits are dedicated to only one appliance. These include 240-volt circuits that serve clothes dryers and water heaters, but can include refrigerators, air conditioners, microwave ovens, computers and dishwashers. As a good rule of thumb, any appliance rated at 1,000 watts or greater should have its own circuit and breaker. Many individual circuits carry 240 volts to meet the greater demands of the appliances involved (◁). Others, like computer and microwave oven circuits, might be dedicated for other reasons. Computers are very sensitive to voltage dips and spikes, and so are sometimes given a circuit of their own and a switch with an isolated ground terminal. Microwave ovens, on the other hand, create voltage irregularities, and so are better kept on their own current.

When determining the best wiring scheme for your home, follow NEC regulations, but also use common sense. Remember that NEC rules pertain to minimum standards.

WORKING WITH DE-RATING

While your service panel may be rated at 125 amps, this does not mean you can commit that many amps to it. When a system is loaded to its maximum capacity, conductors and connectors will heat up and expand. When demand decreases, these conductors and connectors cool and contract. This continual movement will eventually loosen connections, which can heat trip breakers and cause fires.

For this reason, the NEC requires that you leave 20 percent of your panel's capacity in reserve. The method for calculating that reserve is called de-rating. You will have to use the de-rating method when determining your own expansion capabilities (◁).

Your system will be different, of course, but the following example will show you how to proceed. Assume a 1,000-square-foot home with a 125-amp service panel, two small appliance circuits, a laundry circuit and two heavy-duty circuits for a range and clothes dryer. (Heavy-duty circuits are not de-rated.) This example will approximate a typical middle-class home built in the early sixties.

The formula goes like this. Start by assigning 3 watts to each square foot of living space (3,000 watts.) Then assign 1,500 watts to each small appliance circuit and 1,500 watts to the laundry circuit. This would give you a subtotal of 7,500 watts for all 120-volt circuits.

Of this 7,500 watts, figure the first 3,000 watts at 100 percent and the remaining 4,500 watts at 35 percent. Add the de-rated figure (1,575 watts) to the original 3,000 watts for a subtotal of 4,575 watts. Finally, assign full load ratings to the two heavy-duty circuits (8,000 and 5,500 watts). Add these to the de-rated subtotal. Your de-rated total would then be 18,075 watts.

Because watts are the product of *volts times amps*, divide 18,075 watts by 240 volts, for a total of 75.3125, or 75 amps. Since a 125-amp service can be loaded to only 100 amps in the de-rated system, your expansion potential is limited to 25 amps.

Because the formula used to calculate heating and air-conditioning demands is complicated and varies from region-to-region, those factors were left out of this example. You can quickly find their load requirements in your home by checking the breaker ratings of the circuits that serve them.

The modern kitchen
A modern kitchen has at least two small-appliance circuits in addition to individual circuits for major appliances. Overhead lights can be part of a general lighting circuit.
1 120-volt, 20-amp circuit for refrigerator/small appliances
2 120-volt, 20-amp circuit for dishwasher
3 120/240-volt circuit to range
4 120-volt, 20-amp circuit for small appliances
5 Dishwasher
6 Range
7 Light switch
8 Overhead lights

PLANNING CIRCUITS

The number of circuits your home should have depends mostly on its size and also on your own special needs. The NEC requires one circuit for every 600 square feet of floor space, but many electricians prefer a 1/500 ratio to cover future needs. In the final analysis, your life-style, personal needs and your plans for the future have the most to do with how many circuits you install. For example, if you are converting a den into an entertainment center, your electrical needs in that room will be greater than before. If you plan to expand into the attic, you should keep that in mind when you plan your circuits (▷).

Adding outlets to a circuit

If you do not need a new circuit but would appreciate a few more outlets, you may be able to add outlets to existing circuits. If you determine that a 15-amp circuit has less than 10 outlets or a 20-amp circuit has less than 13, you can cut new boxes where you need them and run wire from one of the existing boxes to the first new box. From there on, you simply run wire from one box to another in sequence and install new receptacles (▷).

Making room in a full panel

In many cases, expansion will seem impossible because no fuse or breaker slots are left in the panel (▷). If this is the case in your home, don't panic. Expansion may still be possible by attaching a new sub-panel or by combining circuits in the existing service panel.

The easiest and sometimes only route is to combine circuits. The first step is to determine which two circuits serve so few outlets that together they could be protected by a single fuse or breaker (▷). For example, each outlet is given a rating of 1.5 amps, so a 15-amp breaker can protect 10 outlets. If you find one circuit that serves four outlets and another circuit that serves six, those two circuits can be combined. Kitchen circuits should not be combined.

To combine circuits, remove each wire from its breaker slot or fuse terminal and tie both wires and a short pigtail (a 4- to 6-inch piece of wire) together with a plastic connector. Then tie the pigtail wire to the fuse terminal or breaker. This will leave one circuit vacant for expansion.

ADDING A SUB-PANEL

Until recently, when 60-amp service panels were filled to capacity with fuses and wires, you could tie onto the tap screws between the four fuses and create a new sub-panel. The NEC has disallowed this practice because the tap screws, sometimes called water-heater taps, are not properly fused. The new ruling allows only six 120-volt circuits or one 240-volt circuit and four 120-volt circuits in a 60-amp panel (▷).

If you do have room in the panel, a sub-panel is still a good way to run several circuits to a remote location. If you need to run to an attic or an outbuilding, you can run one heavier wire to a sub-panel and then let the sub-panel serve several remote circuits.

Start by running the cable between panel locations. Attach the wires to the sub-panel first. Your sub-panel may have fuses or breakers. If yours has fuses, attach the positive wire(s) to the fuse terminals. If your sub-panel has breakers, attach the positive wire(s) to the breaker and snap the breaker in place on the positive bar.

The white neutral wire should attach to a neutral bus in the sub-panel, but the bus must not be bonded to the panel. (The neutral bus will be attached to the panel, but will be suspended on nonmetallic spacers. If you see a bonding screw in the bus that makes contact with the panel, remove it.) The ground wires should then be tied to a bonded grounding bus in the sub-panel and also to the main panel grounding bus.

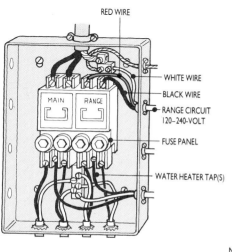

RED WIRE
WHITE WIRE
BLACK WIRE
RANGE CIRCUIT 120–240-VOLT
FUSE PANEL
WATER HEATER TAP(S)
MAIN   RANGE

This method is no longer allowed

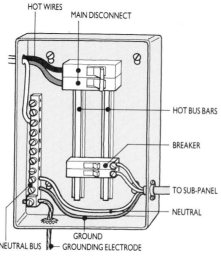

HOT WIRES
MAIN DISCONNECT
HOT BUS BARS
BREAKER
TO SUB-PANEL
NEUTRAL
GROUND
NEUTRAL BUS
GROUNDING ELECTRODE

The correct way to add a sub-panel

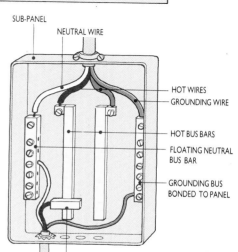

SUB-PANEL
NEUTRAL WIRE
HOT WIRES
GROUNDING WIRE
HOT BUS BARS
FLOATING NEUTRAL BUS BAR
GROUNDING BUS BONDED TO PANEL
CIRCUIT BREAKER

A properly wired sub-panel with breaker

EXTENDING CIRCUITS

There are several possible methods for extending circuits. The approach that will be best for you depends on available space *in the service panel and your existing wiring. Several options are discussed below.*

● **Drilling**
When drilling holes through studs and joists, drill only within the middle third of a joist or stud. Never, under any circumstances, notch the bottom of a joist. A notch on the bottom side of a joist seriously threatens its load capacity. When you drill near the edge of a stud, you are running the cable within reach of drywall fasteners. If you must drill near the edge of a stud or joist (less than 1¼ inch) cover its facing edge with a 1/16-inch protection plate.

A typical knob-and-tube extension
1 New circuit
2 Existing knob-and-tube wiring
3 Cable clamp
4 Grounding wire to neutral bus or to cold-water pipe
5 Soldered splice
6 Loom clamp
7 Junction box
8 Tube
9 Knob

Extending a knob-and-tube circuit

If you own one of the many thousand homes whose wiring is of the old knob-and-tube variety, your expansion capabilities are further limited. Knob-and-tube is a two-wire system. Each individual wire is encased in treated fabric. The wires run side by side through ceramic insulators that are knobs, either nailed to joists and rafters, or tubes inserted through drilled studs.

Knob-and-tube wiring can no longer be installed under current codes, but it can be extended providing you follow a fairly strict procedure. Start by shutting the power off to the circuit to be extended. Then, install a square junction box (◁) between or near the two knob-and-tube wires.

Next run the cable from the new outlets to the junction box. Clamp the cable in the box and cut the fabric sheath from the cable so that you have three 6-inch leads in the box. Then strip about 2 inches of insulation from both knob-and-tube wires near the junction box. Cut one black and one white TW wire (◁) long enough to reach the knob-and-tube wires. Slide these wires into a sheath made for this type of work called loom. Then clamp the loom-covered TW wires to the box with approved clamps.

To tie the TW wires to the knob-and-tube wires, first wrap each TW wire tightly around its knob-and-tube wire so that the wrap is at least ¾-inch long within the stripped area of the old wire. Then solder the connections with rosin-core solder. To heat the connection, hold a soldering iron to the wires until the solder melts and adheres to the wires. When the solder has cooled, wrap the exposed portions of the wire with electrical tape. For added protection, continue the tape at least 2 inches past the exposed area on each side.

With the soldered connections made, move back down to the junction box and join the cable leads to the loom-covered wires with plastic connectors. To ground the extension, connect the ground wire from the cable to a single insulated ground wire inside the box. Then replace the junction box coverplate. (Junction boxes must remain permanently accessible.)

The insulated ground wire you connected to the cable ground wire must then be run separately to a cold water plumbing pipe. Use a pipe clamp for a tight fit. If you are closer to the service panel than to a plumbing pipe, run the ground into the panel and fasten it to the neutral bus bar.

Using skinny breakers

If your service panel is a newer breaker model, but all the breaker slots are filled, you may be able to get one more circuit by substituting two extra narrow breakers (◁). Euphemistically called "skinnies," these narrow breakers allow you to attach one breaker to the existing circuit and another to a new circuit. Both breakers are then inserted in the space formerly occupied by the standard-size breaker.

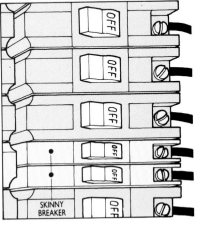

Skinny breakers
Two "skinny" breakers can be inserted into one regular breaker slot.

Common circuit routes

How you get from here to there with a circuit is largely a matter of choice (◁). However, it can be greatly influenced by the layout of the house and by whether you are wiring a new house or expanding the wiring in an older home. Circuits in new homes generally take a direct route, while new circuits in existing homes find the path of least resistance, both physically and financially.

As you plan your circuits, think first about how you will get from the service panel to the outlet area. Plan for the most economical use of cable. The cost of cable or conduit and wires makes long circuits more costly, of course, and long circuits also offer more resistance to the flow of current and, therefore, greater chance for overheating.

When possible, run several cables through the same holes until each must branch off to its own service area. This will result in fewer holes in load-bearing joists and less time spent drilling them. You will have to drill many holes; reduce that number when you can.

OUTLET AND FIXTURE BOXES

Outlet and fixture boxes now are made of metal, nonmetallic composition material or plastic. Plastic boxes cost substantially less than metal or nonmetallic boxes and in most situations work just as well as metal boxes. There is a notable practical difference, however. When wiring into metal boxes, you can attach the ground wires to the box. Plastic and nonmetallic are poor conductors, and so cannot be used in grounding a circuit (▷). In plastic or nonmetallic boxes, you tie all middle-of-run ground wires together and attach the end-of-run ground to the receptacle grounding terminal. Aside from this basic difference, wire is clamped to metal and nonmetallic boxes, whereas, in plastic boxes, wire is held in place by self-gripping plastic tabs.

MAXIMUM NUMBER OF WIRES PER BOX			
Size of Box	No. 14	No. 12	No. 10
Round or Octagonal			
4 × 1½	7	6	6
4 × 2⅛	10	9	8
Square			
4 × 1½	10	9	8
4 × 2⅛	15	13	12
Switch Boxes			
3 × 2 × 2¼	5	4	4
3 × 2 × 2½	6	5	5
3 × 2 × 2¾	7	6	5
3 × 2 × 3½	9	8	7
Junction Boxes			
4 × 2⅛ × 1⅞	6	5	5
4 × 2⅛ × 2⅛	7	6	5
All ground wires in a box can be counted as one wire.			

SEE ALSO

Details for: ▷

Grounding	304–305
Switches	311–313
Receptacles	314–316
Old-work boxes	321
Ceiling boxes	326

WHICH BOX SHOULD YOU USE?

The shape of a box is your best clue to its intended use (▷). Round boxes are most frequently used with ceiling fixtures, while square or rectangular boxes most often contain switches or receptacles. While wall fixtures and special adapter plates allow some crossover, shape is still a good indicator.

New-work boxes are designed to be attached directly to studs or rafters. A variety of fastening devices, including screws, nails, brackets and wire clips hold these boxes to framed walls or ceilings. Old-work boxes, on the other hand, attach to the wall finish between studs or joists. Take the time to familiarize yourself with the many kinds of boxes and their varied applications. When the time comes to start a project, you will know just which boxes to buy.

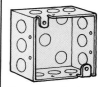

Square junction box

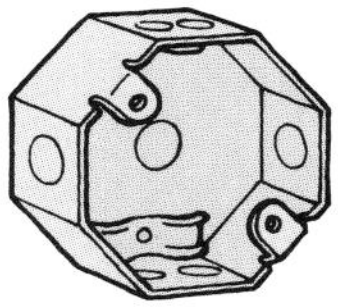

Octagonal junction box

Wall boxes

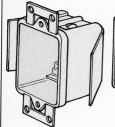

Old-work metal box

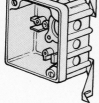

Old-work box nonmetallic

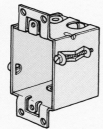

Nonmetallic new work box

Ceiling boxes

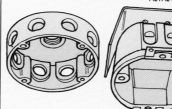

METAL CLAMP

Standard ceiling box

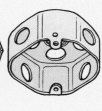

Cut-in box (old-work)

Weatherproof box

Methods of mounting

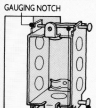

GAUGING NOTCH

DRIVE NAILS

Nail-in box

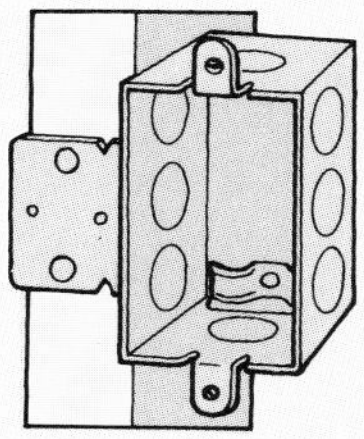

L-bracket box

CONNECTOR
CONDUIT

SCREW BOX TO WALL WITH ANCHORS

Utility (handy) box

Methods of mounting

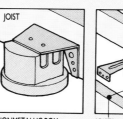

JOIST

NONMETALLIC BOX

Hanger bracket box

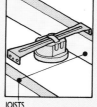

JOISTS

Bar hanger box

L-bracket box

SWITCHES

Switches are used to open and close circuits. When in the closed position, the circuit is completed and electrons flow according to demand. When in the open position, the circuit is interrupted and electrons cannot complete the circuit (◁).

Basic switches

There are four basic types of switches: The most basic and frequently used is the single-pole switch. Single-pole switches are used to open or close simple two-wire circuits. The next most frequently used is a three-way switch. Three-way switches are most often used to provide two switching locations for a single overhead light. The third most commonly used household switch is the four-way switch, which allows you control of an appliance from three or more locations. The fourth type is the double-pole switch. Double-pole switches can handle two hot wires and are therefore commonly used to switch 240-volt outlets and appliances. Like single-pole switches, double-poles have "on" and "off" toggle designations.

Toggle switches

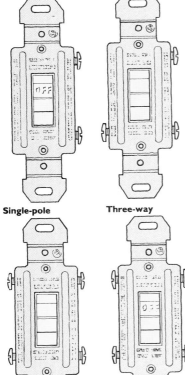

Single-pole   **Three-way**

Four-way   **Double-pole**

SWITCHES FOR SPECIAL NEEDS

In addition to the four basic wiring types, switches are also made for special needs and with special features. Some of these switches are just slightly more convenient, but others offer real advantages. You might consider installing one of these special switches to make some part of your life easier.

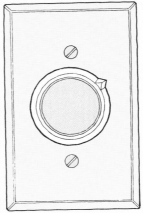
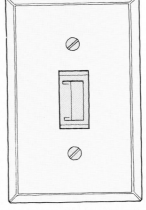

● **Dimmer switches**
Dimmer switches, or rheostats, are popular because they allow you to adjust standard lighting fixtures to create different lighting effects. Low light makes a room seem warmer and more inviting, while brighter light offers a better work environment. Dimmer switches give you both options and everything in between. If used properly, dimmer switches can also save energy by using less wattage.

● **Locking switches**
Locking switches do not have "on/off" toggles, but require a key to operate. These switches are ideal for protecting electrical tools, computers or stereo equipment from children. Simply switch an entire tool circuit with a locking switch.

● **Lighted toggle switches**
These switches are ideal for basement or garage use. The toggle lever contains a tiny light that remains on when the light is shut off. The light uses very little energy and will save you from having to feel your way to the switch in the dark.

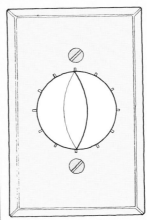

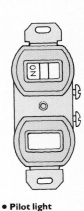

● **Time-delay switches**
Time-delay switches are perfect for those situations where you need to get from here to there before the light goes out. The most frequent use of a time-delay switch is on a flood light between a garage and house. You can turn the time-delay switch off in the garage and still have time to unlock the back door before the light goes out.

● **Timeclock switches**
Timeclock switches can be set to come on or go off at programmed intervals. They are commonly used to discourage burglars. They allow you to simulate your regular lighting habits when away.

● **Pilot light switches**
Pilot light switches tell you when they are on. If you have trouble remembering to shut the backyard light off, the glowing light will help you remember.

REPLACING A SWITCH

If you have never looked closely at a switch, now is a good time. A great deal of information is stamped into the metal yoke and the plastic body of a switch. You will see the amp rating, the volt rating, the approved wire type, the testing lab's approval, and the type of current it is approved to carry. Newer models will also give you a gauge to tell you how much wire to strip from the conductors. And if you make a mistake pushing the wires into the push-in terminals, the release slot is even marked so you can pull the wires back out without damaging the switch.

Read the switch you are about to buy carefully to make sure you get the one you need. Probably the most important designations on new switches are the UL approval stamp and the CO/ALR rating. The UL listing is your assurance of quality and the CO/ALR rating tells you that that particular switch can be safely used with aluminium, aluminum-clad or copper wires. Read your switches closely.

Connecting to terminals

Many switches come with push-in terminals and binding screw terminals. You can use either type. The gauges on the backs of push-in switches will show you exactly how much insulation you should strip from each conductor.

If you strip too much or too little insulation, you should redo the connection. To release the locking clip inside the switch, insert a piece of wire into the release slot next to the terminal and press in. At the same time, push the conductor in slightly and then pull it out.

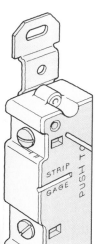

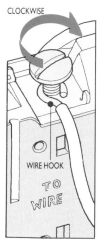

Push-in terminal connection

Screw-type terminal connection

Replacing a single-pole switch

Switches do eventually wear out. They may quit with one flick of the toggle, or they may work once in a while if you push on the toggle just right. In either case, there is no need to put up with a faulty switch. Single-pole switches are not expensive and are easy to replace (▷).

Start by shutting the power off to the circuit serving the bad switch. Then remove the coverplate and loosen the screws on the mounting yoke. Pull the switch out of the box so that you can work on it. You will notice that both wires fastened to the switch terminals are black. Because a switch needs only to control the hot side of the circuit, this makes perfect sense. You will also notice that the white wires are simply tied together and are not involved with the switch at all.

Check to make sure that your replacement looks like the faulty switch. It may have newer push-in terminals in addition to the screw terminals, but it should have only two. Because the existing conductors will be shaped to fit screw terminals, skip the push-in option and just use the screw terminals. Remove the old switch and attach the black wires to the new switch terminals. It will not matter which black wire you connect to which terminal. Slip the hook-shaped wires under the new screws so the open side of the hook is facing right, or clockwise. Then tighten the screws.

If the switch is in a metal box, fasten the ground wire to the hex-head ground screw on the switch or on the box. Use a pigtail from the ground wires to the switch. Finally, screw the mounting yoke onto the box and replace the cover plate. When you restore power to the circuit, you will have a switch that works. And if your old switch snapped off and on, you will be pleased to find that your new switch operates silently and smoothly.

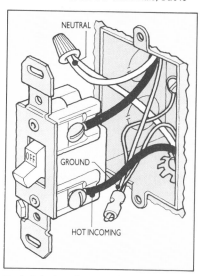

Typical single-pole connection

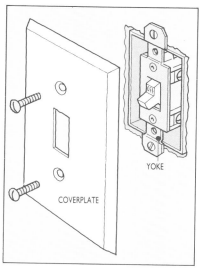

Coverplate screws mount to yoke

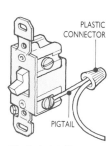

Typical pigtail connection
The term "pigtail" is the accepted vernacular for a short piece of TW wire. It is used as a lead to a receptacle, switch or fixture. A typical pigtail wire is about 6 inches long and is stripped on both ends. One end attaches to a terminal and the other is joined to the circuit wires in a plastic connector.

ALUMINUM WIRES AND SWITCHES

Because aluminum wire expands with current and contracts with no current, it eventually works loose under normal screw terminals (▷). Loose connections cause resistance and may cause sparks and a fire. Electrolysis also sets in to corrode, or oxidize, the connection. For this reason, CO/ALR rated switches should be used exclusively when connecting aluminum wire directly to switches. CU/AL switches can be used with aluminum wire if an indirect connection is made. In this case, a copper wire pigtail attaches to the switch and is then joined to the aluminum wire in a plastic connector filled with anti-oxidation compound. Of course, aluminum wires should never be used in push-in terminals. Their flexing will threaten the connection.

THREE-WAY AND FOUR-WAY SWITCHES

Three and four-way switches allow you to control a single overhead light from two or three locations. This is especially handy when that light is at the top of a stair or in the middle of a large room. Instead of making your way across a darkened room or up a dark stair, you can shut the light off when you leave the area, no matter which end you are on.

Installing three-way and four-way switches where only one switch has been before, requires cutting in new boxes and running new conductors through finished walls, ceilings and floors. If installing these switches in new construction or in an older home that has been gutted, the job is as simple as running an extra conductor or two.

Replacing a four-way switch

Four-way switches allow you to control a single fixture from three locations. Four-ways have four terminals and are used in conjunction with two three-way switches. To determine which of the three switches is defective, you will have to remove all three coverplates and test the two three-ways with the power off, using a continuity tester. If they are both working, hook them back up and buy a new four-way switch.

A four-way switch receives the two traveler wires from each of the two three-way switches. To replace a four-way switch, shut the power off and pull the switch from the box. Then disconnect the top two travelers and connect them to the top two terminals of the new switch. Do the same with the bottom two travelers. By transferring only two wires at a time, you will avoid making a wiring mistake.

A four-way switch

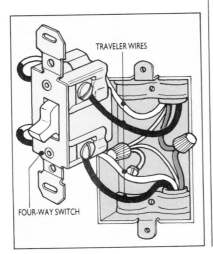

TRAVELER WIRES

FOUR-WAY SWITCH

Replacing a three-way switch

If you have one three-way switch, you must have another. If one of them fails, you will have to check both (with a continuity tester) in order to isolate the defective switch (◁). When you've determined which switch no longer works, shut the power off to that circuit. Then remove the coverplate and mounting yoke screws and pull the switch out of the box. To protect yourself further, test the circuit conductors with a voltage tester (◁).

The wiring to a three-way switch is more complicated than to a single-pole. With two three-way switches, three options are required: on/off, off/on and off/off. When you pull a three-way switch out of its box, you will see that it has three terminals and a grounding screw. Like single-pole switches, three-ways only control hot wires. You may see a red wire, a black wire and a white wire attached to the three terminals, but all are considered hot. Two of these hot wires are "travelers" and one is a common wire. The common wire will be attached to the third terminal, which will either be marked "COM" or will have a darker colored screw. The two travelers will be attached to matching screws of a lighter color.

When replacing a defective three-way switch, start by marking the common wire with a piece of tape. Then remove each wire from its terminal. Attach the two travelers to the two like-colored terminals of the new switch. It doesn't matter which terminal gets which traveler. Then fasten the common wire to the darker, or marked, screw. If the ground wire was connected to the defective switch only, use a pigtail to attach it to the new switch and to the metal box. If the box is nonmetallic, attach a pigtail from the switch to the other ground wires.

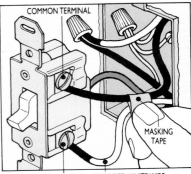

COMMON TERMINAL

MASKING TAPE

TRAVELER TERMINAL   RECODED WHITE WIRE

A typical three-way hook-up
Tape the common hot wire.

Creating a three-way circuit loop

If one of your ceiling lights is still an old-fashioned pull-chain model, you might consider installing a new fixture that can be controlled from either side of the room.

Start by shutting off the power to the circuit. Undo the old ceiling fixture so that you can see the wiring in the bracket box. Then check to see how best to run the new switch loop. When you have determined which is the easiest route to the new switch locations, cut old-work boxes into their respective walls. Then fish a two-wire (plus ground) cable across the ceiling and down one wall to the first switch box (◁).

From the first box, run a three-wire (plus ground) cable to the second box. Fasten the new cables to the new boxes and to the ceiling bracket box and strip all wires for the new connections. Then connect the new fixture and both new three-way switches to the cables and restore power to the circuit. With care you won't have to damage the wall.

A three-way circuit loop
1 Three-way
2 Four-way
3 Light fixture

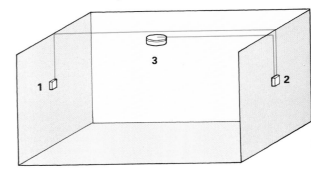

SPECIAL-USE SWITCHES

Special-use switches can make your existing lighting more effective and more useful (▷). They can also make your switches easier to see and easier to use. Dimmer switches, whether used on fluorescent or incandescent lights, can create softer moods and save money, too. The special switches examined earlier in this chapter are not overly expensive and are relatively easy to install. While each switch will come with wiring diagrams to suit a variety of situations, the following examples will help you through basic installations (▷).

Installing time-clock switches

Like pilot light switches, time-clock switches can only be installed in middle-of-the-run outlets. You will also need to use a voltage tester (▷) to locate the incoming black conductor. Time-clock switches sometimes come with wire leads instead of terminals, and so, must be connected with plastic connectors.

Start by shutting the power off and removing the old switch. Then fasten the special mounting bracket to the box. Tie the black lead to the incoming black wire and the red wire to the outgoing black wire. Connect the white neutral wire to the circuit neutral wires and the ground wire to the box. Then screw the switch to the mounting bracket and restore power to the circuit.

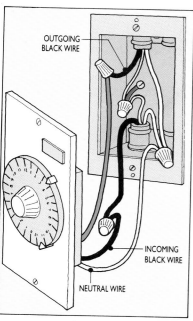

OUTGOING BLACK WIRE

INCOMING BLACK WIRE

NEUTRAL WIRE

A time-clock switch

Installing dimmer switches

To install a simple three-position dimmer switch on a two-wire circuit, shut the power off to the circuit and remove the single-pole switch. Shutting off the power here is doubly important because of the electronic circuits in the switch. A spark could easily ruin a diode rectifier. Then connect the black wire to the positive terminal and the white wire to the neutral terminal, just as you would a single-pole switch. Attach the ground to the box or switch and replace the switch and coverplate. These three-position switches can carry a maximum of 300 watts, so don't use them on circuits requiring more.

For circuits serving up to 600 watts, use a dimmer switch with a knob-controlled rheostat. These too are wired just like standard single-pole switches, unless you need a three-way version or a special fluorescent dimmer.

Installing a pilot light switch

Pilot light switches come in two varieties, but both must be installed in middle-of-the-run boxes. One has the light inside the toggle switch and the other has a larger light below a horizontal toggle. The lighted toggle version takes a switch coverplate and the separate light version requires a receptacle coverplate. They are wired a little differently, but the rest is a matter of preference. Before starting any switch replacement, be sure to shut the power off to that circuit.

If you choose the toggle-light version, you will find two brass terminals at the top of the switch and one silver-colored terminal at the bottom of the switch. Remove the single-pole switch and attach the incoming and outgoing black wires to the brass terminals on the new switch. Then join the incoming and outgoing white neutral wires to a pigtail inside the box and run the other end of the pigtail to the silver terminal on the new switch. Finish by attaching the ground wires to the metal box or to the ground screw on the switch. If after restoring power to the circuit, the pilot light stays on in the off position, reverse the black wires on the switch.

If you choose the separate light version, you will find three brass terminals and a silver terminal. Attach the outgoing black wire to the side with two brass terminals, either terminal will do. (Use a voltage tester to locate the

Three-way dimmer switches are wired the same as standard three-way switches, but will often come with wire leads instead of terminals. In this case, you will make all connections inside the box with plastic connectors.

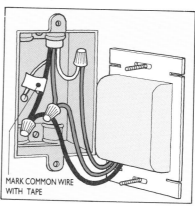

MARK COMMON WIRE WITH TAPE

Three-way dimmer switch

incoming hot conductor.) Then connect the incoming black wire to the brass screw on the other side of the switch. Finally, tie the white neutral to the silver screw terminal with a pigtail and connect the ground to the back of the metal box.

Fasten the yoke screws to the box and install the coverplate. Then test your work.

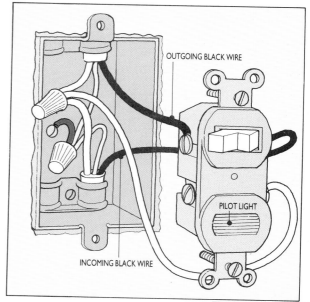

OUTGOING BLACK WIRE

PILOT LIGHT

INCOMING BLACK WIRE

A pilot light switch

RECEPTACLES

There are several reasons why you might want to replace a receptacle. You may wish to upgrade from two-socket to three-socket outlets to match your three-prong plugs. Of course, the circuit must be grounded if you intend to make this upgrade (◁). In most cases, you will install a new receptacle because the old one no longer works. If a fuse blows or a breaker trips only when you plug an appliance into a given receptacle, that receptacle is probably faulty. When receptacles fail, they often cause short circuits, which in turn trips a breaker.

In general terms, there are two basic types you can buy. One is side-wired, and features binding screw terminals on each side. The other is back-wired, and features the newer push-in terminals. If you are working with older wire that has already been shaped to fit under terminal screws, it is usually easier to use side-wired replacement receptacles. If you are working with new wire, or don't mind cutting and stripping existing wire, then go ahead and use back-wired receptacles (◁).

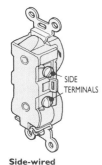

Side-wired
receptacle

SIDE
TERMINALS

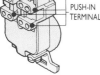

Back-wired push-in
terminals

RELEASE SLOT

PUSH-IN
TERMINALS

Switch-receptacle
combination

Receptacle/switches

A receptacle/switch combination offers greater versatility in a single box. These combinations are popular in simple remodeling projects where additional boxes are not feasible or practical.

This combination can be wired together or separately. For example, the switch might control a bathroom exhaust fan and light, while the receptacle half could be wired directly, so that it is always hot. In another situation, where an appliance needs to be controlled by a switch, the switch half of the combination would control the receptacle half. This combination is one way to add a receptacle to an older bathroom without a major rewiring project. Of course, every bathroom and appliance circuit must be protected by a ground fault interrupter to meet code. In this case, the GFCI could be installed in the panel. GFCI receptacles are also available for ungrounded circuits. Check with your local electrical outlet for your best alternative.

Receptacle/switch devices cannot be installed in end-of-the-run boxes (◁). Because every receptacle requires both a positive and a neutral terminal, and switches control only the positive sides of circuits, only middle-of-the-run configurations will do (◁).

READING RECEPTACLES

Like switches, receptacles are stamped with a variety of symbols that you should check before you buy. The ampacity and voltage rating will be stamped on the body, as will the testing lab's name and approval symbol. The mounting yoke may also tell you what type of wire each receptacle is approved to carry. If you are connecting solid copper wire, a CU CLAD rating is sufficient. If you are connecting aluminum wire, a CO/ALR rating is a must. If you connect aluminum wiring directly to an unapproved receptacle, you are risking a fire or at the very least, the regular annoyance of tripped breakers or blown fuses (◁).

The NEC does allow CU CLAD receptacles to be used with aluminum wire *if* the receptacle connection is made with a copper pigtail. The plastic connector joining the aluminum wire and the copper pigtail, however, must be filled with anti-oxidation compound to keep air from stimulating corrosion.

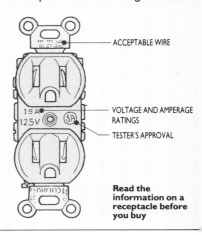

ACCEPTABLE WIRE

VOLTAGE AND AMPERAGE
RATINGS

TESTER'S APPROVAL

Read the
information on a
receptacle before
you buy

Receptacle/light combinations

In certain situations, such as above a bathroom vanity, a light with a receptacle is used. This combination is particularly useful in older bathrooms where outlets are limited or missing entirely. To meet code such a receptacle would have to be attached to a circuit that is ground-fault protected (◁).

These receptacle/light combination fixtures can be wired in one of two ways. The receptacle part can be wired to come on with the light from the switch, or it can be wired so that it is hot all the time. Most people prefer to wire the receptacle hot and switch only the light (◁).

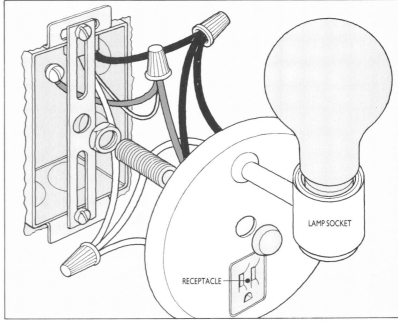

LAMP SOCKET

RECEPTACLE

Light/receptacle fixtures serve two functions

INSTALLING RECEPTACLES

There are two basic wiring methods for standard receptacles. The method you use will depend upon where the receptacle is located in the circuit (▷). If the receptacle you are about to install is in the middle of the circuit, you will follow the middle-of-the-run wiring method. If it is the last receptacle on a circuit, you will follow the end-of-run method (▷).

GROUND **INCOMING**

OUTGOING

A typical middle-of-the-run receptacle

Installing middle-of-the-run receptacles

Because a middle-of-the-run receptacle must pass electricity along to other receptacles on a circuit, it must be wired accordingly. A middle-of-the-run outlet box will contain two cables carrying six wires; two black, two white and two bare ground wires.

To wire a middle-of-the-run receptacle, tie the two black wires to the two brass colored terminals. Then

attach the two white wires to the two silver-colored terminals. To ground a receptacle in a metal box, make a pigtail connection between the two bare ground wires and the ground screw on the receptacle. Then attach another pigtail to the box with a machine screw or bonding clip. If installing a receptacle in a nonmetallic box (▷), simply tie the ground wires to the receptacle ground (▷).

HOT

NEUTRAL

GROUND

A typical end-of-the-run receptacle

Installing an end-of-the-run receptacle

An end-of-the-run receptacle only needs to be wired so that the circuit is completed across its own terminals. To wire an end-of-the-run receptacle, simply tie the single black wire to the brass terminal and the single white wire

to the silver terminal. Then pigtail from the incoming ground wire to the ground screw on the receptacle and to the metal box. If working with a nonmetallic box, tie the ground wire directly to the receptacle ground screw (▷).

INCOMING HOT

GROUND

ARMORED CABLE **OUTGOING HOT**

Armored cable uses its armor as ground

Armored cable and receptacles

Some older homes have armored cable, or BX (▷), instead of sheathed cable. Some armored cable uses the metal armor as a grounding conductor and has no separate ground wire. To ground

a receptacle with armored cable use a pigtail between the box and the receptacle ground screw. Because the metal box is fastened to the metal cable, a permanent ground connection is made.

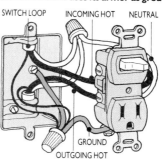

SWITCH LOOP **INCOMING HOT** **NEUTRAL**

GROUND

OUTGOING HOT

The switch controls a remote light

● **Pigtail connections**
Some municipal codes require that all standard receptacle connections be made with pigtail leads. In this case, the black pigtail is tied to one brass terminal and the white pigtail is tied to a silver terminal on the opposite side of the receptacle. In this way, one faulty terminal connection cannot disable an entire circuit. While this practice is not part of the NEC, local authorities may enforce its use. In any case, a pigtail should be used whenever more than one wire must be tied to a single terminal.

Installing a switch/receptacle combination

If you have a switch where you also need a receptacle, you can often have both in one unit. A switch/receptacle combination gives you both, while allowing you to use the wiring already in the switch box. But before buying a switch/receptacle unit, make sure you know which wiring method you will be able to use. The location of the unit on a circuit will dictate how the switch/receptacle will work.

The most popular use of a switch/receptacle combination has the receptacle wired hot and the switch controlling a remote light or small appliance. Because the receptacle must have both a hot and a neutral wire to complete the circuit, this switch/receptacle combination must be installed in a middle-of-the-run location. If you want the switch to control the

outlet and light, you will have to pull another cable to get a neutral for the receptacle.

To wire a switch/receptacle to a middle-of-the-run outlet, join the white neutral wires with a plastic connector and pigtail over to the silver-colored terminal screw. Attach the incoming black wire to one of the brass screws and the black outgoing switch wire to the copper screw. Then ground the receptacle and box with a pigtail to the receptacle ground screw.

To have the switch control the receptacle and the light at the same time, reverse the black wires. The incoming black wire should be connected to the copper screw and the outgoing black switch wire should be connected to the brass-colored screw.

SWITCH LOOP **OUTGOING HOT**

GROUND

The switch controls the receptacle

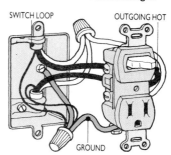

315

INSTALLING RECEPTACLES

Switching half of a receptacle

If most of the lights you use in your living room and bedrooms are lamps instead of permanent light fixtures, you may wish to wire half of some receptacles to switches. In this case, the bottom half of each outlet is wired directly and is always hot. TVs and other small appliances can be plugged into those. All lamps, on the other hand, could then be plugged into the switched half of the receptacles. The obvious advantage of this arrangement is that you can turn on lamps as you come through the door.

To split a receptacle so that half of it is hot full time and the other half is switch-controlled, start with the receptacle. As you hold a receptacle with the sockets facing you, you will see that the terminals on both sides are tied together with metal strips. You will also see that the strips have metal tabs that are scored part way through. These metal strips join both halves of the receptacle, which is what allows you to wire to only one terminal on each side and still have power to both sockets.

In the case of a split receptacle, you will no longer want the top and bottom sockets tied together on the hot side. To separate the top and bottom sockets, use pliers and break the tab off

of the metal strip on the hot side only. Do not break the tab on the neutral side.

Wiring split receptacles

To wire a split receptacle to a switch, use a 14/2 cable, with a ground wire. Bring this three-wire cable from the power source to the receptacle box and then continue it to the switch box. At the receptacle box, connect the incoming white wire to the silver terminal of the split receptacle. Then connect the outgoing white wire to a brass terminal. In this case, the white wire will be the hot wire of the switch loop. To keep it straight, code it with a piece of black tape.

Then tie all the black wires together and pigtail over to the remaining brass terminal. This will leave only the ground wires unattached in the receptacle box. Tie them together with a double pigtail. Tie one pigtail to the box and the other to the ground terminal on the receptacle.

To connect the switch, all you will have to do is tie the black wire to one terminal and the white, hot terminal to the other. Then tie the ground wire to the ground terminal on the switch and to the box.

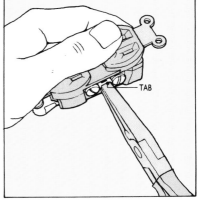

Split receptacles
To separate the top half of a receptacle from the bottom half, break the connecting tab.

INSTALLING A RECEPTACLE/LIGHT COMBINATION

Like a receptacle/switch combination, a receptacle/light combination is a good way to gain a receptacle without the work and expense of installing new boxes (◁). Receptacle/light combination units are most commonly used over bathroom lavatories, but can be installed elsewhere. They are usually rated at 15 amps, so only low-wattage appliances should be plugged into them. Electric razors and hair dryers will not overload receptacle/light combinations. Because the NEC requires every bathroom outlet to be protected from ground fault, a receptacle/light should always be protected by a GFCI (◁).

Receptacle/light combinations can also be wired in two ways. A switch can control both the light and receptacle, or the receptacle half of the fixture can be wired hot, leaving the switch to control only the light. How you wire your own receptacle/light combination will depend upon whether your existing light is in an end-of-the-run or middle-of-the-run outlet box (◁).

If only two wires enter your existing fixture box, you are dealing with an end-of-the-run connection, in which case, both the receptacle and the light must be operated by the switch.

If you find four wires (plus a ground) in your existing box, you will be able to wire the receptacle hot and switch the light independently.

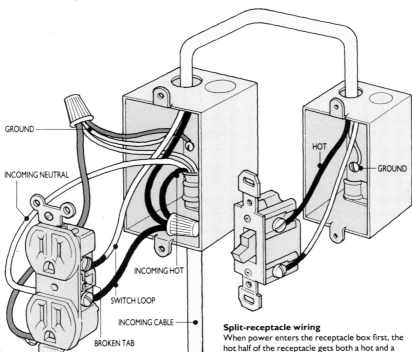

GROUND

INCOMING NEUTRAL

HOT

GROUND

INCOMING HOT

SWITCH LOOP

INCOMING CABLE

BROKEN TAB

Split-receptacle wiring
When power enters the receptacle box first, the hot half of the receptacle gets both a hot and a neutral wire. The other half of the receptacle is switched through the hot wire.

NEW WIRING FOR NEW ROOMS

If you will be wiring a new home, new addition or gutted older home, getting wiring from here to there seems an easy task. It is, in fact, much easier than fighting the structural barriers to remodeling work. Even so, there will be plenty of practical decisions to make and many considerations to weigh, not the least of which involves the most efficient use of costly materials.

This is where thinking through a wiring job is important. To do a professional job, amateurs always have to work harder than professionals, and that work starts with a well considered plan (▷). Do it on paper. Work it out so you know where your outlets and switches will be. Decide, in advance, how many circuits you will need (▷). And give some thought to your future needs while you are at it. Figure it out the best you can and then determine the most economical way to get it all done.

How many outlets?

Ultimately, the number of fixtures and outlets you install should be determined by your needs. Just remember, it will be far easier to install an extra outlet now than to cut one in later.

To make sure everyone installs enough outlets, however, the NEC has its own minimum standard that must be followed. In simple terms, you should have at least one outlet for every 12 feet of wall space. Any short wall 2 feet long or longer must have an outlet. In addition, you must place an outlet within 6 feet of the door.

Even with these rules, the layout of a home may be confusing. If for example, you measure 12 feet from one outlet to another, and the 12-foot location happens to fall in the middle of a closet door space, what then? You would have to place the outlet before the door, even if that would mean only 9 feet between the two outlets. If for some reason, you would rather have the outlet at 12 feet, in the middle of the door space, you would have to install an approved floor outlet. In either case, the next measurement should be figured from that outlet, be it 9 or 12 feet from the previous outlet.

Planning light locations

NEC lighting regulations are few, and in general, involve safety, not issues of practicality. The two areas of concern are fire protection and the prevention of personal injury due to insufficient lighting (▷).

Closet lighting

Lights in closets are not mandatory. Many builders prefer to let a ceiling fixture from an adjacent room spill light into a closet. In so doing, they avoid having to comply with some fairly stringent NEC codes concerning closet lighting.

The chief concern of code authorities and fire officials is that stored blankets and clothing would come in contact with exposed lights, thereby creating a fire hazard. In fact, many fires do start in closets every year. To guard against this possibility, exposed lights are prohibited in any closet less than 40 inches deep. In closets deeper than 40 inches, exposed lights must be at least 18 inches from combustible materials. The space between the bulb and the floor must also be unobstructed.

If your closets cannot be fitted with surface-mounted fixtures, you can circumvent the space requirements by installing recessed lights. Recessed lights have their own limitations, however. Those installed in closets must meet certain heat-resistance specifications and must also have solid lens covers. Recessed lights with solid lens covers and the correct heat rating can be used with a 6-inch clearance to combustibles.

Recessed lighting

Recessed lighting fixtures must be approved by your local code authority and fire department. Recessed lights are hidden in inverted canisters. These canisters can become quite hot and have caused quite a few fires in the past 10 years. Most started when homeowners blew cellulose insulation into their attics without protecting recessed fixtures.

To avoid this very real fire hazard, you must install fixtures that are insulated and rated to handle temperatures to 150 degrees F. Under-rated recessed lights must be surrounded by non-combustible shields that hold insulation and other flammable materials at least 3 inches away from the light canister or use type 1C rated fixtures with thermo-guards.

Front and back door lighting

The NEC stipulates that each entrance to a house must be lighted by an exterior fixture. The light does not have to be mounted near the door, but must be switched at the door and must illuminate the area around the entrance. For example, a light on a detached garage will qualify, if it is switched from the inside of the house and it illuminates the space between the garage and house. Time-delay switches are useful in these situations, but are not mandatory.

Other lighting considerations

As mentioned in the "Switches" section of this chapter, anytime a ceiling light is over a stair or in a large room with two entrances, a three-way switch should be used (▷). Dual switching locations are also handy in hallways, garages and in outbuildings with multiple entrances.

If you have a large yard and spend a lot of time in it, you might also consider installing landscape lighting (▷). Whether you are planning outlet locations or lighting locations, your decisions should be based on your needs. The minimum standards imposed by the NEC are just that: *minimum* standards. If you need more, install more. It will never be easier than before the walls are finished.

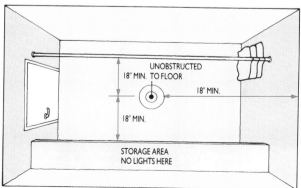

Closet light fixtures
These must be kept clear of combustible clothing or blankets.

UNOBSTRUCTED
18" MIN. TO FLOOR
18" MIN.
18" MIN.

STORAGE AREA
NO LIGHTS HERE

RUNNING NEW CABLES

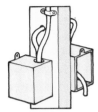

Wiring into boxes
Before bringing cable into metal boxes, you will have to pry one or more knockouts from each box. These knockouts have slots that allow you to twist them out with a screwdriver. Nonmetallic boxes have molded knockout areas that are very thin. To create an opening for a cable, force a screwdriver through the knockout area.

Stapling cables to studs and joists
Anytime you run cable along the side of a stud or joist, you must staple it, at least once every 4½ feet. The NEC also requires that any cable that enters a box must be stapled within 8 inches of the box. The exception to this rule is when fishing tape into old-work boxes on remodel projects, where studs and joists cannot be reached. In that case, boxes with connection clamps must be used.

When you know how you will run each circuit, start by installing boxes and drilling holes for the circuit cables (◁). With the boxes mounted and the holes drilled, start pulling cable through the holes, one circuit at a time.

Because you will have many cables of various sizes hanging near your panel when it comes time to install breakers, you should design some method of keeping them straight in your mind as you go. The best way is to write directly on the sheathing of each cable with a ballpoint pen. Each wire hanging near the panel will represent a circuit, serving a given area of the house. Write "#1 kitchen" on the first of two kitchen appliance circuits, for example. A professional electrician can walk up to a tangle of cables and somehow make sense of them. To most amateurs, however, a dozen unmarked cables is just one more can of worms.

Where to run circuit cables

As mentioned earlier, often the most efficient route for you to run cable is right down the center of the house. This will not be true of circuits near the panel, of course, but for those circuits serving the far end of the house, a trunk line approach is often the easiest. Start by drilling a slightly larger hole than usual, say ⅞ inch in diameter, in each joist near the center beam in the basement. If your home is built on a concrete slab, go through the attic. Then pull three cables through that single row of holes.

As you near each circuit's service location, route a cable to the first outlet box on that circuit. From there, thread a cable through drilled holes in the framed walls or ceiling until all outlets are connected. This trunk-line (with branch runs) approach will help you keep the layout clear in your mind and will also save a lot of unnecessary drilling and pulling (◁).

Mounting the boxes
Receptacle boxes should all be at a uniform height, usually 12 inches from the floor (◁). If a handicapped person will be using them, try a slightly higher level. Switch boxes should be mounted 48 inches from the floor and are usually on the lock side of the door (◁). Ceiling lights should be centered, or in the case of multiple fixtures, evenly spaced. Ceiling boxes should be installed with brackets to support heavier fixtures or ceiling fans (◁).

Where to drill
When threading wire through your home, you should always drill through the framed walls, ceiling joists and floor joists. Never staple a cable directly across a joist. The exception to this rule is in an attic, and then only near the eaves where there is less than 18 inches between ceiling joists and rafters. If you must lay a cable on top of ceiling joists, nail a furring strip on each side of the cable to protect it. The cable should not be in the open where it could be stepped on or caught by a foot.

When drilling holes in joists and studs, do everything you can to protect the wire and the structure. Always drill

through the center of a 2-by-4 stud. When you must drill closer to the edge of a stud than 1¼ inch, nail a ¹⁄₁₆-inch metal plate over the face of the stud to keep from nailing into the cable later. When drilling floor or ceiling joists, drill only in the center ⅓ of the board. If you drill near the bottom of a joist, you will weaken it.

Never, under any circumstances, notch the bottom of a joist. If you do, you seriously threaten its load-bearing capacity. Code officials may require that you replace those joists or laminate new joists to the damaged ones. In either case, you will have to tear the wiring out to get the job done. If your new home has floor trusses instead of joists, drill through the plywood center of the trusses and never through the bottom or top rails.

Once you branch off from the trunk, take the most direct route possible. Drill through toe plates and floor decking and pull the cable into the framed walls. From there, drill through each stud on your way to the outlet boxes. Drill these holes at a comfortable height, between 2 and 3 feet from the floor.

If you come to a door frame, drill above it, either through the short studs above the header or through the ceiling joists. Then travel back down and through the studs again. When you come to a framed corner with several thicknesses of 2-by-4s, drop down into the basement until you make it past the corner and then come back into the wall at a convenient location.

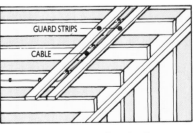

GUARD STRIPS

CABLE

Guard strips
When you must run cable across ceiling joists, protect it with guard strips.

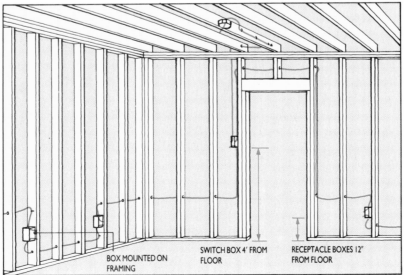

BOX MOUNTED ON FRAMING

SWITCH BOX 4' FROM FLOOR

RECEPTACLE BOXES 12" FROM FLOOR

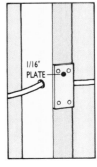

1/16" PLATE

Metal protection plates
Use when wires are within 1¼ in. of the face of a stud.

THE SERVICE PANEL

Connecting circuit breakers

Whether you are wiring a new home or a new addition, you are likely to start in the panel (▷). For the purposes of completeness, we will assume a new panel that is empty and de-energized. How you lay out your new panel, that is, in what order you install the new breakers, is really up to you. Electricians usually install the heavy-duty circuits at the top of the hot bus, just below the main disconnect. An average home might have three 240-amp breakers at the top, followed by six to ten 120-amp breakers below them for the kitchen appliance circuits and general lighting circuits (▷).

240-volt breakers

Practically speaking, a 240-volt circuit is two 120-volt circuits tied together in a panel and at a receptacle (▷). But technically, there is much more to it. A 240-volt circuit does draw power from two 120-volt circuits, but those circuits are from different phases of a transformer and are of opposite polarity. Transformers have three phases, but today, the third phase is reserved for commercial applications. Appliances requiring 240 volts are wired to draw from two phases through two hot wires.

Your 240-volt cables will each contain one red wire, one black wire, one white wire and one green or bare ground wire. As in 120-volt cables, the white wire (when required) will be neutral and the black and red wires hot.

Start by making sure that the main disconnect is shut off. (Even when you know the power is shut off, it is a good idea to avoid ever touching the positive

bus and the neutral bus at the same time.) Then insert the cable through one of the panel knockouts and fasten it with a clamp connector. Strip off all but ½ inch of the cable's sheathing inside the panel. Then fasten the white wire and the ground wire to the neutral bus bar. Fasten the black wire to one of the two terminals on the breaker. Follow by fastening the red wire to the other breaker terminal. With the hot wires connected, move the breaker into position on the positive bus. Tip one edge of the breaker under the small retainer on the bus and press the other end onto the two copper tabs projecting from the bus. The breaker should snap firmly in place. Different manufacturers will have slightly different breaker/bus connections.

120-volt breakers

Ordinary 120-volt breakers snap into place just like 240 breakers. The main difference is that a 120-volt breaker will only take up one breaker slot and cover only one copper tab (▷). Remember that each wire size must be matched to a compatible breaker ampacity.

Bring a 120-volt cable into another of the panel knockouts. If you have many circuits, you may wish to bring several cables into the panel through the same knockout opening. In that case, wait to fasten the clamp connector until all wires are installed. Strip the sheathing from the cable and connect the white neutral and bare ground wires to the neutral bus bar. (If a separate grounding bus is available, ground to it.) Then fasten the black wire to the single breaker terminal.

Grounding the panel

Just as every neutral and ground wire must be tied to the panel's bus bar, the bus must be connected to a grounding electrode (▷). The electrode (a heavy bare wire) must be fastened to a buried metal surface.

How you connect your system's grounding electrode will depend upon local code requirements. The most common connection is to a metal plumbing system. Other codes require a grounding electrode to be clamped to a ½-inch-by-8 foot grounding rod as well as to metal plumbing pipes.

If you fasten your grounding electrode to the plumbing system, make

sure that you use approved clamps. The NEC also requires that you bond a grounding electrode to both sides of the water meter, to circumvent the rubber washers or plastic components.

If you fasten your grounding electrode to a grounding rod, try to drive the rod into the ground at least 8 feet from a basement wall. While the NEC allows grounding rods next to basement walls, it is better to locate them farther away when you have a choice. The reason for this is that a grounded charge is dispersed in the soil in a V-shaped pattern. A wall reduces a rod's effectiveness.

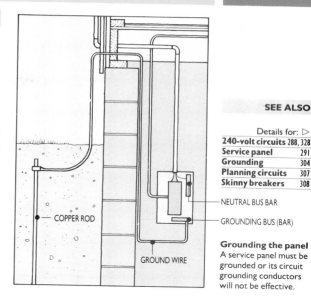

COPPER ROD — GROUND WIRE — NEUTRAL BUS BAR — GROUNDING BUS (BAR)

SEE ALSO

Details for: ▷

240-volt circuits	288, 328
Service panel	291
Grounding	304
Planning circuits	307
Skinny breakers	308

Grounding the panel
A service panel must be grounded or its circuit grounding conductors will not be effective.

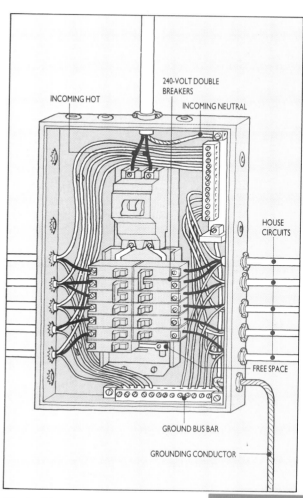

INCOMING HOT — 240-VOLT DOUBLE BREAKERS — INCOMING NEUTRAL — HOUSE CIRCUITS — FREE SPACE — GROUND BUS BAR — GROUNDING CONDUCTOR

Circuit cables exiting the sides of the panel
They could also exit the few knockouts at the top.

NEW WIRING FOR OLDER HOMES

The trick to electrical remodeling is in working past structural barriers in an inconspicuous way. A few specialized tools will be useful—fish tapes, saber saws and extension bits make reaching into blind spaces and blocked passage ways a lot easier, but a good understanding of how your home was built is your best help. Take some time to consider how your wall studs and floor and ceiling joists are laid out. Look for nail patterns that suggest the location of a stud or a joist. Check out your basement and attic to determine which way joists run and how far apart they are.

As a general rule, walls are laid out on 16-inch centers, that is, framing members are 16 inches apart when measured from the center of one joist or stud to the next. Ceiling joists may also be laid out on 24-inch centers.

These measurements are good standard references, especially for joists, but every home will have its exceptions. Joists, for example, will frequently be doubled for support under walls, while corners, doors, windows and intersecting walls all require extra studs. Be prepared to work with what you have.

Drilling top and bottom plates

The best places to run wiring are unfinished basement ceilings or unfinished attics. If you have either, make all of your long runs there and wire into the wall only to connect switches or receptacles.

In many cases, you will have to go from the basement to the attic at least once. If you have a two-story home, you may have to cut into walls at several levels. Two other options might be surface wiring or wiring through conduit (◁) on the outside of the house. You might also be able to use conduit in closets where it is not likely to show.

If you have a single-story home however, getting from the basement to the attic can be as simple as drilling through the top and toe plates of a center wall and fishing wire from one level to another. The secret to this and all remodeling work is accurate measuring. You will be able to see the top plate in the attic because the ceiling joists will be resting on it (**1**). In the basement, however, all you may see are the tips of nails showing through from the toe plate. You may not see even

that much. If not, you will have to measure for the exact location from an outside wall. Take the measurement from the upstairs center wall to an outside wall and transfer that measurement to the basement. Be sure to allow for the difference in wall thicknesses. If at all possible, check your measurement against some common reference, such as a plumbing pipe. Then drill into the wall from the basement and also from the attic.

If measuring is too difficult because of structural barriers, try driving a long thin nail right next to the wall from upstairs, then go into the basement and try to locate where the nail broke through the decking (**2**). Measure over 2 inches from the nail and drill straight up into the wall.

When both top and bottom plates are drilled, slide a fish tape into the wall cavity from each end and hook one with the other (**3**). Then pull the bottom tape out until the end of the tape from the attic is exposed. Attach a cable and pull it back through the wall and into the attic from above.

LOCATING STUDS AND FIRE BLOCKS

The easiest and most certain way to locate obstructions behind plaster or drywall is to buy an electronic density sensor (◁). These "stud finders" are not the usual magnetic sensors that react when near nails, but actually sense the extra density of a stud, joist or fire block. Furthermore, a density sensor will pinpoint the exact edges of a stud. They also work well through metal lath walls, where magnetic sensors are helpless. You can find a density sensor at most local hardware stores.

Density sensors are handy but certainly not necessary. You can locate most studs and fire blocks by visual inspection or by tapping on the wall and listening to its resonance. A rough estimate can be quickly made by rapping with your knuckles. A hollow sound suggests a hollow space between studs. A dull sound suggests the presence of a stud. To check for fire blocks (short 2-by-4s nailed crosswise between studs to stop the vertical spread of fire) rap every few inches between studs in a line between the floor and ceiling. A sudden dull sound between studs will indicate a blockage.

Another easy way to locate studs is by looking for nail holes in baseboards. Baseboard nail holes are usually covered with filler that is noticeable at close range. Always look to the nails at the top of the board for clues. The nails at the bottom may be driven into the toe plate of the wall, which is continuous and therefore deceiving. With a little close inspection, you will be able to predict where studs and joists are likely to be.

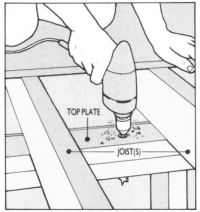
2 Drill a pilot hole guided by nail position

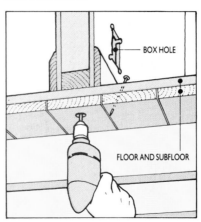
1 Ceiling joists rest on the top plate of a wall

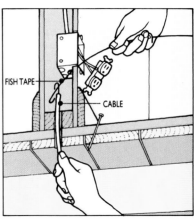
3 Use a fish tape and a cable

INSTALLING OLD-WORK BOXES

Old-work boxes are so-named because they are used exclusively in upgrading older electrical systems. Unlike standard boxes used in new construction, where walls are unfinished, old-work boxes are never fastened to studs or joists. They are, in fact, mounted directly to plaster or drywall, usually several inches away from studs and joists.

Old-work boxes come in several styles. The differences are in the clamping methods used on each. Some boxes have sheet-metal spring clamps, while others have wing nuts, expansion clamps or side brackets.

The kind you choose is less critical than how you mount it. In each case, you will have to custom fit the opening to the physical dimensions and characteristics of the box. And of course, what the wall is made of will have a lot to do with how you proceed (▷).

Cutting wood lath

Cutting into plaster and wood lath is really not much different than cutting into metal lath. The main difference is that wood is usually easier to cut than metal. You will find the cuts on one side of the opening relatively easy. This is because the lath is still supported from both directions. Once you cut through one side, however, the lath may vibrate too much when you cut it again. If it vibrates too much or tends to spring back when you cut, try a slightly different angle, speed or pressure. You can usually find a way by making minor adjustments in approach.

Cutting into drywall

Drywall is the easiest of any of the common wall finishes to cut. Again, the objective is to stay away from studs, joists or fire blocks. Drywall is thin and resonant, which makes finding studs easy. It will also reveal slight nail depressions, which are usually visible with bright side-light from a bare bulb. Use a drywall saw, keyhole saw or utility knife to make the cut.

When using a utility knife, always use sharp blades. Cut the paper all the way around first to establish the perimeter, then work the blade deeper with each cut thereafter. Cut in downward strokes with steady, even pressure.

Cutting into metal lath and plaster

Plaster-covered metal lath can be the most difficult kind of wall to cut. The problem is that the expanded metal base that holds the plaster will flex if you attempt to chisel or saw through it. Too much flexing will cause the wall to crack and can cause the plaster to let go.

Cutting old-work boxes into metal lath requires care, but it can be done, with very few special tools. Patience is the key here. Start by locating the studs in the area where you would like your new box. If you do not own a density sensing stud finder, rap on the wall to see if you can hear any variation in tone. Where the tone sounds most resonant, pick the spot for your new outlet. But before making a cut, drill a very small hole through the plaster and metal lath. Spend a little time reaming the back side of the plaster out with the drill bit. Then bend about 2 inches of a thin wire at a 90-degree angle. Slide the bent part of the wire into the drilled hole and spin it (1). If the wire hits a stud, move to the right or left accordingly. When the bent part of the wire spins all the way around without hitting anything, make your cut.

Before cutting into the plaster, cover the box area with masking tape (2). This will reinforce the plaster and keep it from chipping during the cut. Then hold the old-work box, or its paper template, up to the tape and trace around it (3). With the shape of the box established, use a sharp utility knife to cut into the plaster. Do not try to cut all the way through in one slice. Cut a little at a time until you reach the expanded metal. Then make several smaller cuts across the section to be removed so that it will come out easier.

With the plaster cut, use a sharp chisel to cut and pry the plaster square from the metal. Remember, you must not vibrate the lath too much. Just chip a little at a time, in a downward motion. Never tap the chisel straight back toward the lath.

With the plaster out, you will be ready to cut the lath. You can use a hacksaw or a saber saw (4). The hacksaw works well enough if you take your time. Be careful not to push too hard in case the blade binds against the wire. A quicker and safer way is to use a saber saw. Make sure that you use new blades for each cut and that you hold the base of the saw firmly against the wall. To reduce vibration further, you might hook a wire through the metal lath and pull toward you with roughly the same pressure you use against the saber saw. This will steady the saw and the lath. Then cut all sides slowly and consistently until the lath drops out.

SEE ALSO

Details for: ▷

Interior walls	123
House construction	120–121

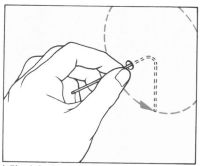

1 Check for blockage by inserting bent wire

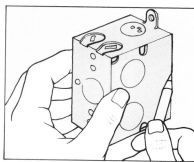

2 Trace around an old-work box

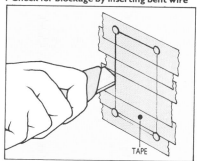

3 Tape the wall before cutting

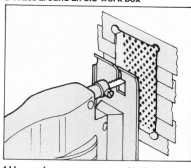

4 Use a saber saw to cut metal lath

PULLING WIRE WITH FISH TAPES

Fish tapes are the workhorse tools of remodeling. With them, you can reach into closed areas behind walls, ceilings and floors and pull new wire into otherwise inaccessible places (◁). They are simple to use. You simply drill into a wall or joist space and slide the tape along until you can reach it at another location. You can then tie cable to the end of the tape and pull it back through.

In really blind spots, you can slide two fish tapes into a space, one from each end. With a little maneuvering, you will be able to hook one tape with the other, giving you the choice of pulling wire from either direction. When working from above, where gravity is a factor in your favor, a fish tape and a small chain offer another option. Your home will dictate the method you use.

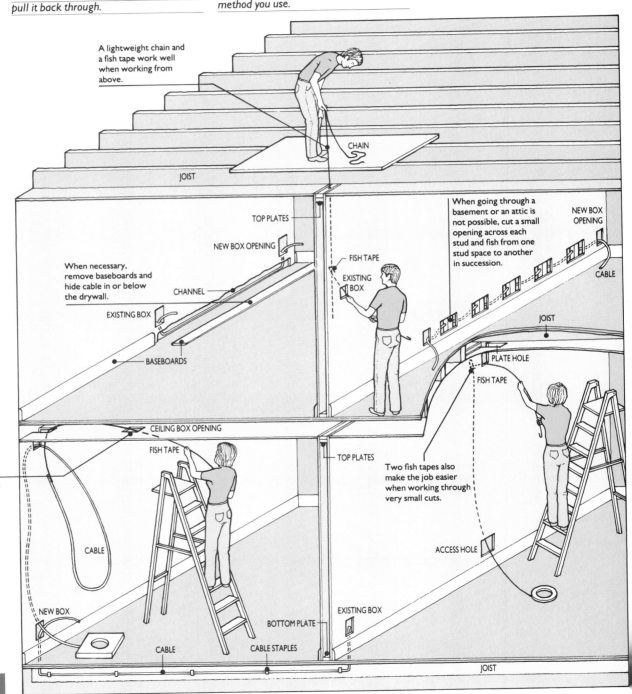

A lightweight chain and a fish tape work well when working from above.

CHAIN

JOIST

TOP PLATES

NEW BOX OPENING

FISH TAPE

EXISTING BOX

When going through a basement or an attic is not possible, cut a small opening across each stud and fish from one stud space to another in succession.

NEW BOX OPENING

CABLE

JOIST

When necessary, remove baseboards and hide cable in or below the drywall.

CHANNEL

EXISTING BOX

BASEBOARDS

PLATE HOLE

FISH TAPE

CEILING BOX OPENING

FISH TAPE

TOP PLATES

Two fish tapes also make the job easier when working through very small cuts.

Use a fish tape to reach deep into joist cavities and pull cable back.

CABLE

ACCESS HOLE

NEW BOX

CABLE

CABLE STAPLES

BOTTOM PLATE

EXISTING BOX

JOIST

RUNNING CABLE UNDER FLOORS

As you survey your home for possible electrical upgrades, you will see that many improvements could be made if you could only get cable from one wall to another. Fortunately, the problem is old enough to have a solution. All it will take is two fish tapes, a little planning and a lot of patience.

Start with particulars. Make sure that the circuit you wish to expand can handle more outlets (▷). Decide which existing outlet offers the easiest tie-in location. Then consider the best route to the new outlet location.

Start by shutting off the power to the circuit you will be tapping. Then remove the coverplate and receptacle from the tie-in box to make sure the circuit is grounded and the wiring is what you expected. For example, is it a middle-of-the-run or an end-of-the-run receptacle (▷)? While you are at it, remove a knockout from the bottom of the box for the new cable to come through.

When the existing box is ready, cut the box opening in the new location across the room. Then go into the basement and drill up into both walls below each box location. Use a ⅝-inch bit and stay near the center of the wall to avoid drilling into drywall or baseboard nails.

Slide one fish tape through the knockout in the existing box and another tape through the hole drilled from the basement **(1)**. You will need help at this point, but the object is to hook one tape with the other. When you hook them together inside the wall, pull the lower tape up and into the box. Fasten cable to the lower tape **(2)** and pull wire back into the basement and across the floor **(3)**. Then cut the cable so that it will reach well into the new box and push it up into the wall. Have someone reach into the new box opening and pull the wire into the room. Then staple the cable to the floor joists. Slide the cable into the new box and mount the box in the wall. Finally, wire the receptacles and install coverplates.

BEHIND WOODWORK

If you merely need to run wire down a wall or to the other side of a door but can't get there from an unfinished attic or basement, consider removing a little workwork and hiding the cable there. The most exacting part of this installation is removing baseboards or trim without damaging them. Use a flat pry bar and a small block of wood to pry against. Push the pry bar behind the trim and gently pry against the block, which you place against the wall. Pry a little at a time from several locations until the trim comes loose.

If the drywall is held up from the floor ½ inch, as it often is, tuck the cable under the drywall. If you do not find a gap under the drywall, use a chisel to cut a small channel for the cable so the trim will fit flat over it. When hiding cable behind door trim, tuck it between the frame and jamb. If the cable will not fit, you may have to chisel into the drywall or plaster. In either case, staple the cable in place as often as the situation allows. When you reach the box location, drill into the wall behind the trim and run the cable up to the opening from inside the wall.

SEE ALSO

Details for: ▷
Assessing your
system's potential 293
Receptacles 315

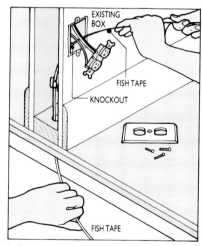

I Use two fish tapes to pull new wire into existing boxes

3 Pull the fish tape into the basement with cable attached

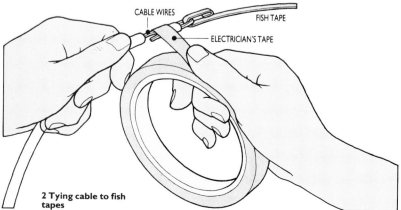

2 Tying cable to fish tapes

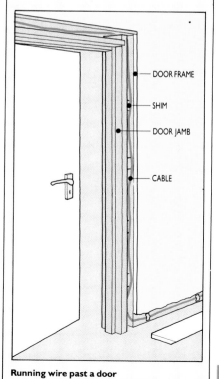

Running wire past a door

SURFACE WIRING

If cutting into finished walls, ceilings and floors is more than you feel like taking on, consider making your electrical improvements out in the open, through raceways. Surface-wiring kits have been popular for years and for just this reason. Because surface wiring adds to the cost of the job, plan carefully to avoid buying any unnecessary parts or making any wrong cuts. While wiring an entire house with surface-mounted raceway would be quite expensive, simpler projects will be affordable and convenient, especially when compared to wall repairs.

Working with raceways

Raceways come in pieces that you assemble to fit your needs. A raceway strip is actually a small rectangular tube that snaps into clips that screw directly to walls or baseboards. To cover in-line joints, small cover clips are provided. A variety of elbow and tee clips are used when turning corners, changing directions and branching off to switches, receptacles or fixtures.

When installing raceways, assemble all raceway strips and cover clips and then pull (or push) individual, color-coded wires from one box to another, just as you would in metal conduit. Leave elbow and tee clips off until you have routed all wires to their respective boxes. Then finish covering all exposed raceway joints and wire the boxes according to code.

Because raceway kits are now available in a variety of colors you should be able to choose an inconspicuous color that suits your decor (◁).

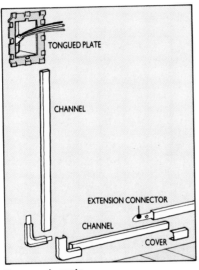

Raceway channels

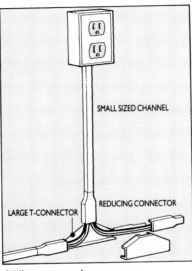

Adding a receptacle

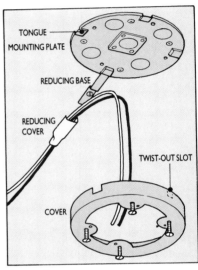

Fixture plates

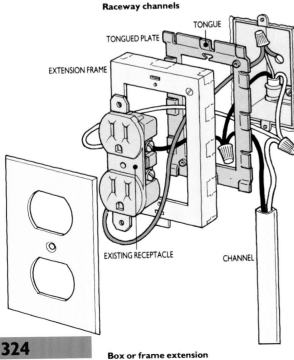

Box or frame extension

Tapping into existing receptacles

The advantage of surface wiring is that you can tap into an existing receptacle without cutting into the wall. This is accomplished by means of a receptacle extension adapter. The adapter fits over an existing box and the wires from the raceway are pigtailed to the receptacle wires to continue the circuit (◁).

To connect this adapter, start by shutting off the power to the circuit and removing the coverplate from the box. Then remove the receptacle and screw the adapter plate (also called "tongued plate") to the box. Follow by breaking out the slot you need in the frame for the raceway channel, place the extension frame over the channel and snap it onto the tongued adapter plate.

Wiring the tie-in receptacle

To connect the new raceway outlets to the tie-in receptacle, start by making four 5-inch pigtail wires; one black, one white and two green. Join the incoming black wire to the black raceway wire and the black pigtail wire inside a plastic connector. Then tie the other end of the black pigtail to the positive side of the receptacle. In like manner, join all white wires and pigtail over to the neutral side of the receptacle.

Because metal raceways can be used as grounding conductors, tie the green pigtail to the ground terminal of the receptacle and join it and the second green pigtail to the ground wire from the cable. Finally, tie the second green pigtail to the grounding screw in the box. If no screw exists, use a grounding clip and fasten it to the front edge of the box.

With the connection made, fasten the receptacle to the extension frame with screws and replace the coverplate. All other raceway receptacles should be wired in standard middle-of-the-run or end-of-the-run fashion, with metal fittings, and ground wire is needed.

EXTENDING EXISTING CIRCUITS

A junction box is simply an outlet box that is covered with a blank plate. Junction boxes are used to house and protect wire connections, or junctions. As discussed earlier, a wire connection must never be made outside of a box, even when hidden in an attic or crawl space. When you must splice wires together, do so inside a junction box. The NEC states that all junction boxes must remain permanently accessible. Never cover one or fasten one to the side of a joist.

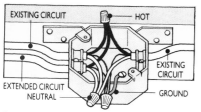

I Running a new circuit from an existing ceiling box

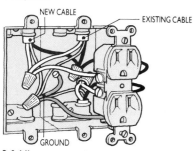

2 Running a new circuit from an existing receptacle

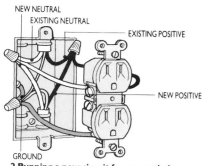

3 Adding an extension to an existing junction box

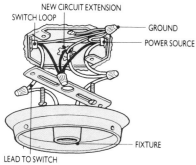

4 Extending circuit from an overhead fixture

Installing a new junction box

You will sometimes have the ampacity to add fixtures or outlets, but doing so will require cutting into the middle of a circuit (▷). A case in point would be when the easiest and most economical tie-in location is in the attic and not near receptacle or fixture boxes.

Start by shutting off power to the circuit. Then mount a round or octagonal box on an attic ceiling joist right next to the circuit cable (I). Cut the cable even with the box and pull as much slack out of the cable from each direction as you can. This will give you longer leads to work with in the box. Then bring both ends of the existing circuit and the new branch cable into the box. Secure each cable with a clamp connector or staple them within 8 inches of the box.

Assuming you already have the add-on boxes wired and covered, you will now be ready to tie the new branch line into the existing circuit. To make this connection, simply join each color-coded set of wires in the box with a plastic connector. To ground a metal junction box, you should also run a pigtail from the ground wires to the box screw. Finally, cover the box with a blank plate and restore power to the circuit. Remember, the plate of the box must remain accessible, so don't cover it up, even with insulation.

Converting an existing box

Often a receptacle box can serve as a junction box while continuing to serve its original purpose. (Ceiling boxes can also serve as junction boxes if they are not end-of-run outlets.) In strictest terms, these boxes are not junction boxes because they still hold receptacles or fixtures, but whenever possible, use them as junction boxes. Junction boxes are always in danger of being covered up by someone in the future. Ceiling and receptacle boxes generally are not.

End-of-the-run junctions

If you wish to add a circuit branch from a receptacle used as a junction box, try to find the last receptacle on the existing circuit. Because it will have only two existing wires, you will not be exceeding the NEC's allowable number of wires per box. You will also not have to worry about interrupting other receptacles down the line.

Just bring the new cable into the end-of-the-run box, remove the wires from the receptacle and tie each set of corresponding wires together with pigtails. Then connect the loose ends of the pigtails to opposing receptacle terminals (2). Of course, the power should be shut off during any of these procedures.

Middle-of-the-run junctions

Middle-of-the-run receptacles are more trouble, because by adding two more wires and a ground, you exceed the number of wires allowed by NEC for such a small box. You will either have to install a larger old-work box in place of the existing box or add a box extender (3). (Adding to the side of a box is possible only if the original box is the expandable type.)

Assuming that the position of the box or the box type allows you to provide a larger box, start by bringing the new branch cable into the box. Then join all corresponding wires with plastic connectors and pigtail the positive and neutral wires over to the original receptacle terminals. Pigtail out of the ground wire connection to the metal box. Finally, cover the receptacle and restore power to the circuit.

Ceiling box junctions

If a ceiling box is served by a fulltime hot cable, then it can be used as a junction box as well. Sometimes ceiling fixtures wired in this manner are switched by a pull chain, and at other times they are connected to a switch loop. When tapping into a fixture operated by a pull chain, just tie all corresponding wires together in the box with plastic connectors and pigtail over to the original fixture terminals (4).

When tapping into a box with a switch loop, start by cutting the white wire leading to the fixture. Then use a plastic connector to connect the white wire from the extension to the two wires produced by the cut. Next, find the connection joining the white wire from the switch (usually marked black with tape or paint) to the incoming black wire from the circuit. In like manner, use a plastic connector to join the black wire from the extension to these two wires.

SEE ALSO

Details for: ▷
Assessing your system's potential 293

INSTALLING A NEW CEILING BOX

If you would like a ceiling light or a ceiling fan added to a room but are put off by the prospect of cutting a new bracket box into your finished ceiling, don't despair. While ceiling installations can mean extensive ceiling and wall repair, in most cases, the damage will be minimal and easy to repair. The most difficult part of the job will be installing the bracket box. As usual, the design of your home will determine just how much trouble installing a ceiling fixture will be.

Working from above

If you live in a single-story home with an accessible attic, installing a ceiling box and running wire to it will be easy. Start by deciding exactly where you would like the fixture located. A central location is standard, but if the fixture would be better located over a table or work area, then put it there. When you determine your best location, drill a small pilot hole in the ceiling from below. Then insert a wire about a foot long through the pilot hole so that you can see it sticking above the insulation in the attic.

When you find the wire in the attic, clean all insulation away from the location and see if the bracket will fit between the two joists with the box centered over the pilot hole. Move the box position a little if necessary. Then, still using the pilot hole as a guide, hold the box up to the ceiling and trace around it with a pencil. Cut the opening carefully with a keyhole saw.

Working through floors

In many cases, working through a second-story floor is easier than cutting into a first-story ceiling (◁). Floors are sometimes easier to repair, especially when they will be covered with carpet. Of course, accurate measurements are a must.

Most homes have two layers of flooring: One is 1-inch subflooring and the other is tongue-and-groove flooring. To cut into the tongue-and-groove flooring, make two neat crosscuts, preferably on top of two joists. Then use a sharp chisel to cut through the tongue-and-groove joints. Finally, use a thin-bladed pry bar to ease the boards up.

When cutting through decking, make your cuts on top of the joists and on center. This will usually require pulling a few nails.

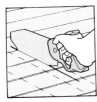

Working through floors

CHOOSING A CEILING BOX

The kind of ceiling box you buy will depend upon the access you have to the ceiling joists and the kind of fixture you wish to install. If you have access to joists from above or if you have no access and must cut an access hole in the drywall or plaster, then a bracket box is your best choice. Bracket boxes give the best support. If you are installing a lightweight ceiling fixture, an old-work box (also called a "cut-in box") or a pancake box will do the job. Of course, a pancake box should only be used in an end-of-the-run installation, because the box area is too small to contain more wires.

The 1987 NEC specifies that paddle-type ceiling fans must be installed in specially approved ceiling boxes. To give yourself even more protection, you should bolt these boxes to 2-by-4 cripples nailed between joists. If you install a ceiling fan, be sure to use a box that meets the new NEC specifications. It will be stamped accordingly.

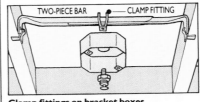

Clamp fittings on bracket boxes

TWO-PIECE BAR — CLAMP FITTING

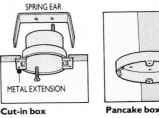

SPRING EAR

METAL EXTENSION

Cut-in box   **Pancake box**

Working from below

If fine hardwood floors or a flat roof prevent you from working from above, you may be constrained to cutting into the ceiling from below. While this will require some plaster or drywall repair, you should not let it get in the way of your lighting needs. Plaster and drywall repair can be learned in short order (◁). Even duplicating ceiling textures is not difficult if you practice first on a spare piece of drywall.

In any case, if you are going to cut into the ceiling from below, make a big enough access hole to fit a standard bracket box between joists or an NEC approved fan box and a 2-by-4 nailer. A larger hole will also make fishing cable to a power source or switch a lot easier. When it comes time to repair the ceiling, you will find that a large hole requires no more work than a small one.

The wiring method you use to bring power into the ceiling fixture will depend on the location of your most convenient power source. Another consideration is whether you wish to control the fixture from one or two locations.

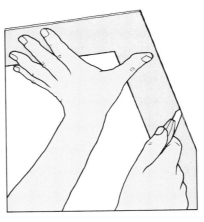

Making a square opening
Use a framing square to make a square opening. The opening will be easier to repair if it is uniform.

Replacing the drywall piece
You can often replace the same square of drywall you cut out, after you cut the box opening in it.

INSTALLING AN ATTIC FAN

Attics hold an incredible amount of heat in the summer. Temperatures that can easily exceed 150 degrees F are not much affected by simple louvers and vents. Very high attic temperatures put an extra load on your home's cooling system and in extreme cases, can damage plywood sheathing.

The solution is as simple as installing a power exhaust attic fan. A thermostatically controlled attic fan will make your home more comfortable in summer, and could save you up to 30 percent off your cooling bill.

Selecting a fan

There are two basic types of attic fans: One simply pulls cooler air through soffit and gable vents and exhausts the hot air trapped in the attic. This model is used in conjunction with your cooling system. The other is a whole house fan. This type works in conjunction with a large vent installed in an upstairs ceiling. When the exhaust fan is turned on, the ceiling vent opens and air is pulled through open windows throughout the house. A whole-house fan can replace the air in a home in a matter of minutes. They work especially well in climates with hot days and cool nights.

Except for the added task of cutting in a ceiling vent, the installation of these two fans is almost identical. When shopping for an attic fan, make sure you buy one with a large enough CFM (cubic feet per minute) rating. Your dealer should be able to help you select a size to fit your needs. If you prefer making your own estimates, multiply your attic's square footage by 0.7. The total will give you the CFM rating you need. If your shingles are black or very dark, add 10 to 15 percent to the CFM total.

Mounting the fan

Start by going into your attic and locating the best spot to install the fan. Choose a joist space near the center of your home and about 3 feet down from the peak of the roof, usually on the side opposite the street. Then measure for the center of the joist space and drill a small pilot hole **(1)** through the sheathing and shingles from the inside.

With the pilot hole made, take a saber saw, a utility knife and the fan up on the roof. Center the fan housing over the pilot hole and slide it to a position that requires the fewest number of shingles to be cut (▷).

Installed, the top two-thirds of the flashing will slide under the shingles and the bottom one-third will fit on top of the shingles. To do this, you may need to slide a hacksaw blade under some of the shingles and cut a few nails.

Mark the top and bottom positions of the flashing lightly with the knife and then set the fan aside. (If your fan comes with a template, use it to determine the best flashing position.) Then measure for the opening and use the knife to cut the shingles away. With the shingles and roofing felt removed, use a saber saw to cut through the sheathing **(2)**.

Then slide the upper part of the flashing under the shingles. Carefully lift the shingles and nail the flashing at each side so that the nails are under the shingles. While the bottom of the flashing is still loose, coat the underside with roofing compound and then nail the bottom over the shingles **(3)**.

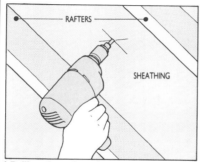

1 Drill up through roof at center of fan

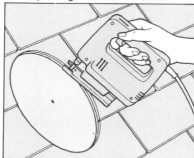

2 Cut through roof sheathing

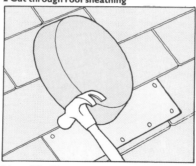

3 Install flashing around cowl

WIRING THE FAN

To get power to the fan, start by screwing the thermostat to a joist near the peak. Then run flexible conduit over to the fan motor and thread a black wire, a white wire and green ground wire between the motor and thermostat. Leads will be provided inside the fan and thermostat. Tie the corresponding color-coded wires together and fasten the ground wire to the ground terminals at each end.

The easiest way to get power to the thermostat is to tap into an existing circuit in the attic with a junction box. A good choice might be a ceiling light with incoming hot wires, or the cable that serves an attached garage (▷). Simply shut off the power to the circuit you wish to tap and mount a junction box on a joist next to that cable. Then bring a two-wire plus ground cable from the thermostat to the junction box. Either drill through the ceiling joists or staple the cable between two 1-inch furring strips. Once inside the box, tie the corresponding wires together with plastic connectors. Finally, install a blank coverplate on the junction box and restore power to the circuit.

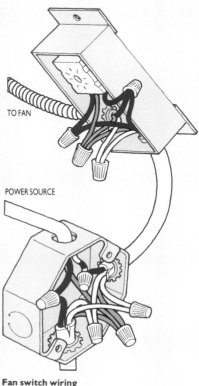

TO FAN

POWER SOURCE

Fan switch wiring

SEE ALSO

Details for: ▷
Roofs   221–233
Extending circuits   325

Temperature adjustments
Inside the thermostat box, you will see a set screw pointer on a dial. By turning this screw, you set the temperature at which the fan will come on. Try 90° F as a starting temperature. The fan will automatically shut off when the attic temperature drops 10°. If you find that the fan runs continuously, adjust the setting for a little higher start-up temperature.

WIRING 240-VOLT APPLIANCES

The major appliances that use 240-volt circuits make our lives a lot easier. Electric clothes dryers, water heaters and air-conditioners, for example, can make real differences in the way we live, or at least, how comfortably we live. If you need another 240-volt appliance and your service panel has the space and the ampacity to handle another 240-volt circuit, don't let working with 240 volts scare you, in some ways, 240-volt circuits are safer than 120-volt circuits because the amperage draw is split between two conductors.

If you can wire a 120-volt circuit, you already have the skills to wire a 240-volt circuit ($\triangleleft$). For all practical purposes, 240-volt circuits are just two 120-volt circuits tied together. In actuality, this is not so because each 120 volts comes from a separate phase of a transformer. But when you run wires and hook up breakers and receptacles, there isn't really much difference in the basic technique.

Two-wire and three-wire receptacles

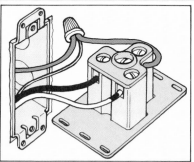

A dryer-type receptacle

HOT
NEUTRAL
HOT

A wall-mounted 120/240 receptacle

• **Running 240-volt cables**
Heavy-duty circuits require heavy wire, such as No. 10 or No. 8. When several of these thick wires are contained in a single cable, that cable is very stiff. In some situations, it is too stiff to be pulled through drilled joists and studs. To accommodate this problem, some code authorities allow No. 8 240 cable to be strapped or stapled directly to unfinished joists or to the sides of 2-by-4 inch running boards nailed to open joists. Others disallow any surface-mounted cable and require that any wire too stiff to pull through framing must be run inside conduit. Any drop from ceiling to appliance should also be encased in conduit.

RED WIRE

GROUND WIRE
NO. 6 CABLE

A range-type plug

Hooking up a range to a 120/240 circuit
The grounding strap must be turned around and screwed down to the neutral terminal.

It won't take you long to discover that the receptacle for your electric range does not look the same as the one for your electric dryer. For one thing, the socket holes are different. You can't plug a range into a dryer receptacle, or vice versa. These variations may seem superficial, but they are the electrical industry's gentle way of telling you there is a major difference in how 240-volt circuits are wired.

The main difference is that some 240-volt appliances, such as air conditioners, water heaters and dryers, need 240-volts only. Other appliances, like electric ranges, need both a 240-volt and a 120-volt circuit in a single receptacle. A range, for example, requires 240 volts for high heat, but might require only 120 volts for lower settings. Any built-in timers or lights would use only 120 volts, of course. As you can see, the needs of the appliance involved affect how many wires a circuit should have and therefore which receptacle you must use.

A 240-volt dryer type receptacle needs only two wires and a ground to complete its circuit. In this case, a black wire and a white wire (coded red) are brought into a three-terminal receptacle. The two hot wires are connected to the two hot terminals and the ground wire is connected by a pigtail to the ground wire (which travels uninterrupted to the neutral bus in the panel), and to the ground screw in the metal box. This is all there is to wiring a two-wire 240-volt receptacle.

Because a range-type receptacle must also supply a 120-volt circuit, one extra wire is needed. By bringing two hot wires and a neutral wire into the appliance, we are giving the appliance the option of pulling current from either circuit. When it needs 240 volts, it will pull from the two hot wires. When it needs only 120 volts, the

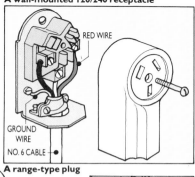

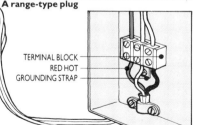

TERMINAL BLOCK
RED HOT
GROUNDING STRAP

WIRING AT THE SUB-PANEL

The sub-panel exception
The neutral bus bar in a sub-panel is never bonded directly to the panel when 240-volt circuits are involved ($\triangleleft$). It is attached to the panel, but only through non-conducting spacers. If the neutral wire were bonded to both panels, it would divide the circuit so that the breaker would read only half of a potential overload, thereby creating a fire hazard. Therefore, when running a 240-volt circuit through a sub-panel, four wires must be used. The neutral wire should travel uninterrupted to the main panel neutral bus bar. The ground wire, on the other hand, must be bonded to both the sub-panel and the grounding bus in the main panel, thus grounding the sub-panel and completing the short circuit path to the main grounding electrode.

Installing a 240-volt breaker
To install a 240-volt breaker, bring the heavy duty cable into the panel and fasten it with a clamp connector. Then strip the sheath from all but about 1/2 inch of the cable and bond the ground and/or neutral wires to the neutral bus bar. Then connect the black wire to one breaker terminal and the red wire to the other terminal and snap or slide the breaker onto the positive bus. With the receptacle connected and the breaker installed, replace the panel cover and turn the power on to the new circuit. Of course, any work in a panel should be done with the power off.

appliance can switch off one of the hot wires and create a lower voltage circuit out of the other hot wire and the neutral wire. Because a 120-volt circuit needs a separate grounding conductor, you will choose a three-wire plus ground cable whenever you wire into a 120/240-volt receptacle.

WIRING TO 120-VOLT APPLIANCES

While fixed appliances such as dishwashers, trash compacters and garbage disposers are sometimes found on kitchen appliance circuits, they should have their own circuits. Others that are not fixed but are considered major appliances should also be wired with individual circuits. Refrigerators are certainly large enough to warrant their own circuits. Microwaves should have their own circuits, simply because they create voltage irregularities in a home system. And, of course, computers should have their own circuits because they are so sensitive to voltage irregularities.

So much for the ideal. The truth of the matter is that many older homes simply do not have enough room in their service panels for that many circuits. If you are working against the limitations of an older home, follow the NEC's minimum standards and just do the best you can with the rest.

The NEC allows a fixed appliance to be plugged into an outlet only when the appliance has a factory-installed cord with a grounded plug. Other installations should be made with individual circuits. In some situations, a new dishwasher and a new disposer can share a circuit, but dedicated circuits are preferable.

Wiring a dishwasher

The method used to wire a dishwasher is similar to that used for a disposer, except that a dishwasher does not need an external switch. (Some local ordinances may require a disconnect switch in the cabinet.) Start by bringing 12/2 cable through the wall or floor of the dishwasher cabinet space. Because the cable will be hidden under the dishwasher and out of reach, you will not need to encase it in flexible conduit. Simply bring it into the cabinet space so that it is long enough to reach the front of the dishwasher. Slide the dishwasher into its space, level the legs and secure its brackets to the countertop. Then remove the access panel and complete the plumbing connections (▷).

With everything else connected, remove the plate from the box containing the lead wires. Bring the stripped cable into the box and fasten it with a clamp connector. Then join the dishwasher leads to the cable conductors and the ground wire to the ground screw in the box. Replace the box cover and the front access panel of the dishwasher and install a 20-amp breaker in the panel.

Wiring a disposer

If you are installing a garbage disposer in a sink that has not previously had one, you will have to bring power to a new switch nearby and then into the sink cabinet. A 12/2 cable with ground will give you the number of wires and the ampacity you need.

Start in the panel to make sure you have the expansion capabilities to support another appliance (▷). If you do, go ahead with the project. The first step will be to bring cable from the panel to the wall behind the sink. If the basement is open, simply run from the panel, directly to the sink wall and drill up into the toe plate of the wall. If much of the basement is finished, you may have to drill into a center wall and fish cable into the attic. Once in the attic, you can travel directly to the sink area and fish down into the wall through its top plate.

Next, cut an old-work box in the sink wall and pull the cable into the kitchen. Then fish a second cable from the sink cabinet to the box opening (▷). With both wires through the opening, bring them into the box and mount the box in the wall. While you are at it, tie the neutral wires together in the box and fasten a black wire to each terminal on a single-pole switch (▷). Then tie the ground wires together and run a pigtail to the ground screw on the switch. If the box is made of metal, ground it as well.

With the switch installed, go into the sink cabinet and slide flexible metal conduit (▷) over the cable from the disposer to the wall. The conduit should stick through the wall a little and be fastened to the disposer electrical access with a conduit connector. Inside the disposer housing, you will find a black stranded wire and a white stranded wire. You will also find a ground screw near the access plate just inside the disposer. Attach the ground conductor to the ground screw and pull the cable conductors and the stranded wires out through the access opening. Use plastic connectors to join the black cable conductor and the black disposer lead. Then join the white wires the same way. Finally, fold the wires and connectors into the disposer housing and fasten the plate over the opening. After you install the 20-amp breaker, your disposer should be safe and working.

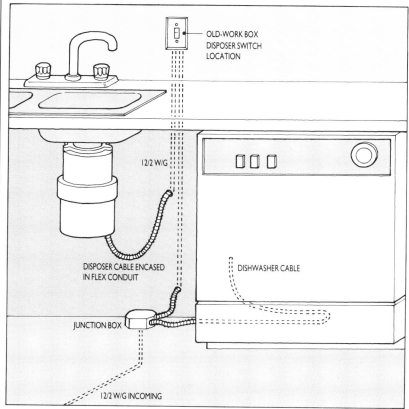

OLD-WORK BOX
DISPOSER SWITCH
LOCATION

12/2 W/G

DISPOSER CABLE ENCASED
IN FLEX CONDUIT

DISHWASHER CABLE

JUNCTION BOX

12/2 W/G INCOMING

Shared circuit, dishwasher/disposer
When possible, disposers and dishwashers should have their own circuits. When necessary, both can share a circuit as shown here.

CREATING INDIRECT LIGHTING

Architects are taught to think of lighting not only as a tool of daily living but as a part of a home's design. Today, lighting manufacturers are directing more and more of their energies to fixtures that can create dramatic effects (◁).

Even with all the technical advancements available to you, some of the most creative lighting techniques can still be created with inexpensive fixtures, common materials and a little imagination. You can change the entire mood of a room by hiding a few lights behind coves and valances and letting them spill soft light onto ceilings or down from cabinets. The object of indirect lighting is not to flood a room with light, but to direct attention toward or away from some feature of a room. If you would like your lighting to do more, you might consider the indirect approach.

SEE ALSO

◁ Details for:
Lighting   37–38

Choosing the right fixtures

Fluorescent fixtures are the most commonly used in indirect lighting. The reasons are that they produce soft white light that is without glare or hot spots. They also produce very little heat, and so, can be installed in tight spaces. Fluorescent lights come in a variety of sizes that can be easily adapted to any length of cove, soffit, valance or ceiling recess.

Wiring indirect lighting

Another advantage of fluorescent fixtures is that they can be easily ganged together and wired in sequence. Just mount the fixtures end-to-end and connect them with insulated jumper wires. Black ties to black and white ties to white, just as you would expect. Because the fixture channels are made of metal, all you have to do to ground each fixture is fasten a ground jumper wire to each channel. A continuous ground wire will not be needed. Then tie the last channel to the grounding conductor in the cable. With the fixtures tied together, switch the entire series with a single-pole switch from a two-wire circuit.

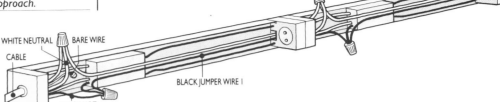

Wiring fluorescent lights in series
The channels can act as ground conductors and need only to be joined together by short jumper wires and then tied to the circuit ground.

WHITE NEUTRAL   BARE WIRE
CABLE
BLACK HOT
BLACK JUMPER WIRE

WHERE TO HIDE FIXTURES

Indirect lighting can be installed anywhere you feel like putting it provided NEC minimum clearances are observed. The three most common ways to hide indirect lights are behind a valance, cove or inside a soffit. In each case, you will build a trough to hide the fixture. You can be as creative as you wish, but remember to leave enough clearance so that the enclosure is not trapping too much heat and is accessible for maintenance.

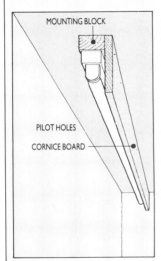

MOUNTING BLOCK

PILOT HOLES
CORNICE BOARD

Cornice boards
A cornice board hides the tube but spills light onto a nearby wall.

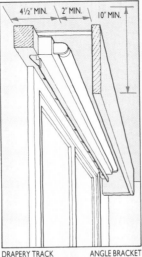

4½" MIN.   2" MIN.   10" MIN.

DRAPERY TRACK   ANGLE BRACKET
Valance boxes
Allow 10 in. between the fixture and ceiling.

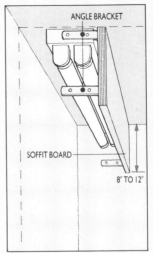

ANGLE BRACKET

SOFFIT BOARD

8" TO 12"

Soffit lights
Over a work space, use a two-tube light for added brightness.

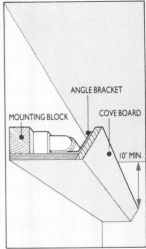

ANGLE BRACKET
MOUNTING BLOCK   COVE BOARD
10" MIN.

Cove lighting
Cove lighting bounces light onto the ceiling, into the room.

INSTALLING A BATHROOM FAN

The National Plumbing Code states that your bathroom must have either a window that opens or an exhaust fan. Even if you have a window offering cross-ventilation, a fan is a good idea. The reason is that building materials and high concentrations of moisture do not get along. Excess moisture causes paint to peel and can cause dry rot. Moisture tends to warp plywood or particleboard cabinet doors. It also fills a bathroom with mold spores, which are a common cause of allergic reaction.

Exhaust fans come in a variety of styles with a choice of extra features. A simple exhaust fan is easiest to install and supply with power, but fan/light combinations and fan/heater combinations offer greater utility in a single fixture. In many cases, you will be able to install a fan/light combination in place of an existing overhead light fixture, thereby saving a light and adding a fan. If your bathroom feels cold when you step out of the tub, a fan/heater combination can help take the chill out of the air. The kind of fan you choose should depend upon your needs, of course, but structural constraints will play a part, too. If you cannot run a three-wire cable from an existing switch to the fan location without breaking walls, you might have to settle for a simple fan or fan/light combination. Check your bathroom's wiring before buying.

Fan or fan/light installation

If you use the switch loop from an existing light to control a new fan/light combination, both the fan and the light will go on when you flip the switch. Start by shutting off the power to the circuit and removing the old fixture and ceiling box. Then measure carefully and cut the ceiling to accept the fan housing. Fasten the housing to the ceiling joists and bring the switch conductors into the housing. If the fan and light are not factory-installed in the housing, install these components and plug each into its receptacle. Then tie the switch conductors to the fixture leads and attach the grounding conductor to the grounding screw in the box. Finally, install the light diffuser and decorative cover and restore power to the circuit.

If separate switches for the fan and light are important to you, then you will have to run a three-wire cable between the switch box and fixture and install a double switch in the switch box. The connection you make will be similar to that of a three-way switch (▷). A common wire will serve both fixture components and two travelers will complete the circuit for each switch.

Fan/light/heater installations

A three-component fixture will require four wires, one for each traveler and one common wire. You can bring these four wires in as two two-wire cables, or you can run a single length of flexible conduit between the switch and fixture. In this case, you would pull four separate insulated wires and a ground wire through the conduit. Either way is legal, but conduit is a neater installation (▷). Four-wire fixtures usually come with combination switches so you do not have to install three separate switches in an expanded box.

Venting the fan

The way you vent your bathroom fan is important. When improperly vented, condensation will form and run back into the ceiling causing stains and ruining drywall. The best way to vent a fan is to connect a flexible plastic dryer vent between the fan and the soffit vent. A dryer vent is easy to cut and bend and slips easily into tight spaces. When in a horizontal position, condensation is not likely to run back into the ceiling.

Another method is to cut a vent flashing into the roof and vent the fan through a vertical exhaust pipe. This method is acceptable, but includes several pitfalls. One potential troublespot is the flashing. Cutting into an existing roof is tricky and anything less than a perfect seal will leak, perhaps not always, but whenever there is a driving rain. Secondly, with the vent pipe in a vertical position, condensation can run straight back into the fan and ceiling. When you have a choice, vent horizontally to a soffit, either by using a dryer vent or galvanized sheetmetal pipe and fittings.

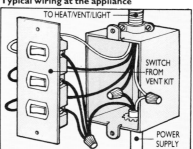

Anchor fan housing into ceiling from above

Typical wiring at the appliance

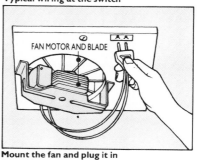

Typical wiring at the switch

Mount the fan and plug it in

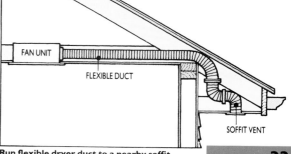

Run flexible dryer duct to a nearby soffit

INSTALLING OUTDOOR WIRING

If you can do your own wiring inside your home, you can certainly do it outside as well. The principles are the same. Because outdoor wiring is exposed to all kinds of weather, it must be impervious to water. It must also be resistant to the effects of extreme hot and cold temperatures. Knowing how to work with these materials is most of what you need to know to run electricity outdoors.

Connecting to the house circuits

You can bring indoor electricity outside with one of two exterior fittings:

90° fittings

If you are starting with a new circuit in the breaker panel or tapping into an existing circuit with a junction box, the fitting you will use to get through the house wall will be an LB, or conduit (◁). (An LB cannot be installed underground, however.) An LB allows you to come through an exterior wall and make a 90-degree turn along the wall. It is threaded on each end to accept conduit adapters or pipe nipples. Because it creates a 90-degree turn, its front can be removed so that you can help the wires make the turn. The coverplate for this opening fits over a rubber gasket, which makes the box water tight.

An LB is always installed between two pieces of conduit. In some cases, an LB might fit back-to-back with an outlet box, with the outlet box just inside the wall and the LB flush with the outside. Because no splices with plastic connectors are allowed inside smaller LB's, the conversion between cabled wire and individual wire should be made inside the junction box.

If you choose to run buriable cable inside the conduit instead of individual wires, a plastic connector conversion will not be necessary. In that case, a junction box inside the wall will not be necessary either. The LB could just be fastened to a short nipple through the wall. You could then run buriable cable uninterrupted from the panel to its first box. If you wish to exit a basement wall below ground level, do not use an LB. Use instead, a junction box mounted to the inside wall, then run conduit through the wall.

Extension boxes

If you are tapping into an outside outlet or light, you will not need an LB. Instead you can sandwich a weatherproof extension box between a receptacle, or fixture, and its outlet box.

To install an extension box, shut the power off, remove the coverplate and receptacle or fixture and pull the wires out of the box. Then screw the extension box to the outlet box mounted in the wall. Bring the conduit into the extension box and pull the conduit wires through the opening so that you can work on them comfortably. Connect all corresponding wires with plastic connectors and pigtail over to the receptacle or fixture. In this way, the existing circuit still serves the receptacle or fixture, but also serves the new wiring in the conduit. Then ground the outlet (◁) and replace the existing receptacle or fixture using the weathertight gaskets provided (◁).

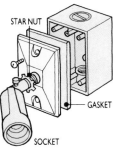

Features of an outdoor receptacle box

COVER GASKET SCREW-IN PLUG BOX GASKET

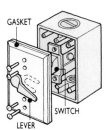

Features of an outdoor floodlight box

STAR NUT GASKET SOCKET

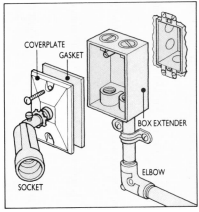

COVERPLATE GASKET BOX EXTENDER ELBOW SOCKET

Tapping an existing light or receptacle

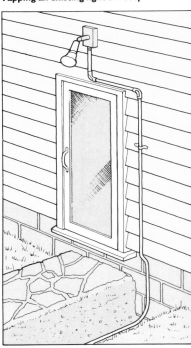

Connecting a new circuit
A box extender and metal conduit.

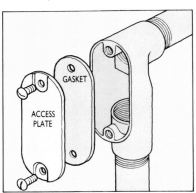

GASKET ACCESS PLATE

An LB allows you to wire at a 90° angle

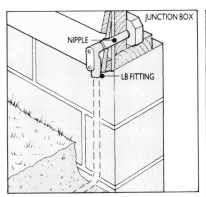

JUNCTION BOX NIPPLE LB FITTING

An LB and a junction box back-to-back

GASKET LEVER SWITCH

Uses a standard switch with an external lever

WORKING BEYOND THE HOUSE

All outdoor wiring must be encased in conduit unless it is buried 30 inches deep. All fixtures and boxes, including switch and receptacle boxes, must be weathertight and rated for exterior use. And all floodlights and their sockets must be rated for exterior use. As long as you satisfy these requirements, the improvements you make can be as varied as your outdoor needs.

OUTDOOR RECEPTACLES

Installing an outside receptacle

If an outside receptacle mounted to your house would make your outdoor cooking or lawn and garden work easier, you will be happy to know that the job is not that difficult. You may wish to create a new circuit for your outdoor receptacle, but in most cases, tapping an existing circuit will work just as well. Before you cut into any wall, however, shut the power off to the circuit inside that wall.

Start by finding a receptacle on the inside near where you would like one on the outside. Then take careful measurements and mark the box location on the outside of your home. Hold an old-work box or its template up to the siding and trace around it to mark the cut. To keep the corners neat, drill each with a 1/4-inch bit. Drill completely through the siding and the sheathing. Then, use a saber saw to cut the box opening.

With the opening made, probe through it to find the existing box. If insulation is in the way, push it up and away from your work area. Then go back inside and remove the receptacle from the existing box and open a new knockout hole at the bottom of it. Push a short length of cable through the knockout opening until you think you've pushed enough to reach the new box. Then go back outside and pull the cable out through the opening.

With the cable in place and the new box ready to install, pull the insulation back down. Insert the cable through a knockout opening and mount the box in the wall.

Installing isolated receptacles

If you cut your grass with an electric mower, or if you need an electric trimmer to reach under a backyard fence, you might consider installing receptacles nearer your work. All you will need is a few weathertight receptacle boxes, conduit, wire, concrete blocks and the will to dig a trench between your house and the new receptacle locations.

Once you have power ready at some point along your foundation, plan the most efficient route for your outdoor circuit. You might even want to drive several stakes and draw a string between them as a guide for your shovel. Use a tile spade and cut the sod twice about 4 inches deep and 12 inches across. Dig the sod up and pile it on one side of the ditch. Then dig the trench about 18 inches deep along its entire length. To protect your lawn further, pile the loose dirt on a row of newspapers on the other side of the ditch.

With the ditch ready, run plastic conduit (▷) between the house and the receptacle locations. At every receptacle location, sweep the conduit up out of the ground with pre-molded bends called "factory elbows". Then use another bend to re-enter the ditch in the direction of the next receptacle. Factory elbows are connected with glue.

When you have all conduit laid, fish the cable or individual wires through the conduit and leave a loop at each receptacle location. Then, to secure the conduit risers, or bends, slide a concrete block over each set of risers and cement them in. You will not need to wait for the concrete to set, so go ahead and cover the ditch, tamp the loose soil with your feet and replace the sod.

With the conduit and supports in place and the wires ready, install a weathertight junction box on each set of two risers. Use plastic fittings that screw into the box and glue to the conduit risers. Then install a short riser above the junction box and fasten a receptacle box to it. At the end of the run, you will only have one riser. You will not need a junction box there. Simply fasten the receptacle box directly to the riser. A single riser and outlet box should be fastened to a metal or redwood stake.

All that will remain is to install the receptacles and connect the conduit wires to the circuit at the house. Of course, all boxes between the house and the last box will require middle-of-the-run installations, while the last box will be wired as an end-of-the-run receptacle (▷).

Other outdoor options

Other electrical options might include a string of landscape lights or a front yard pole light. The installation of these fixtures does not differ substantially from that of the receptacles described here. Just remember that all wiring, except low-voltage systems (▷), must be encased in conduit, and all fixtures must be impervious to water.

Installing an outside GFCI

STUD — EXISTING CIRCUIT — NEW CABLE — SIDING — NEW GFCI RECEPTACLE — GASKET — COVER

Supporting the conduit
A concrete block gives the support it needs.

RECEPTACLE BOX — CINDER BLOCK — READY-MIX CONCRETE — BENT CONDUIT

SEE ALSO

Details for: ▷

Low-voltage	
systems	288, 335
Receptacles	314–316
Conduit	334

● **Installing a GFCI**
Every exterior receptacle or fixture must be protected from ground fault. When installing a new circuit, you might install a GFCI breaker, but when wiring only one box, use a GFCI receptacle. A GFCI receptacle senses any imbalance between the positive and neutral sides of the circuit. When an imbalance occurs, as it does with a short, the sensing mechanism immediately interrupts the flow of electricity.

The only real difference between installing a GFCI and a standard receptacle is that a GFCI often has leads.

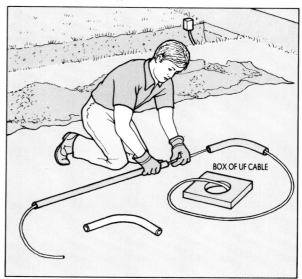

BOX OF UF CABLE

Inserting the cable
Slide cable through as you go.

333

WORKING WITH CONDUIT

Not many residential electrical improvements will require the use of conduit, but some will, and you should know what is available and how to use it. Conduit is required anytime individual wires are run in place of cabled wire. It is also required when a cable or wire is in danger of being cut, torn loose or stepped on, that is, when it is in harm's way. There are several different types.

SEE ALSO
◁ Details for:
Surface wiring   324

Types of conduit

There are three basic types of conduit: galvanized metal, galvanized flexible metal and plastic. All have at least two variations in wall thickness.

Metal conduit comes in 10-foot lengths and in three wall thicknesses. The heaviest is rigid metal. Rigid is usually hand-threaded and put together with threaded fittings. Because it is so heavy, you have to bury it only 6 inches deep in outdoor installations. The next heaviest metal conduit is known as "intermediate weight." It can be bent with a bending tool, so fewer fittings are needed. It can also be threaded for use with threaded fittings. The lightest weight metal conduit is called "thin-wall." It is put together with threadless fittings. It can be bent and shaped to follow the contours of any wall, ceiling or floor. Both intermediate and thin-wall conduit must be buried at least 18 inches deep when used outdoors. Thin-wall conduit is also prohibited for underground use in areas that have acidic soil compositions.

Flexible conduit, known in the trades as greenfield, resembles a hose more than a pipe. It is available in two thicknesses. It is very flexible and does a good job in protecting lead wires into appliances, such as disposers, water heaters and dishwashers. The NEC allows the heavier version to be buried, but many local ordinances disallow it for use underground. Flexible conduit is connected to appliances and outlet boxes with special clamp connectors.

As with plumbing pipes, plastic conduit is popular with homeowners. The reason is that plastic conduit does not have to be shaped and can be glued together. (Electricians do shape plastic conduit with special benders that heat the pipe until it is malleable.) When you want a bend in a plastic pipe, all you do is buy a bend fitting and glue it in place. These fittings, called factory elbows, are available in 45-degree and 90-degree angles. Plastic pipe is especially handy when running wire underground and along support beams in homes. Because it is not as rigid as metal conduit, however, it should not be used out in the open where it cannot be secured to walls or other rigid supports. It must be buried 18 inches deep for below-ground installations.

When cutting any kind of conduit, use a hacksaw or wheel cutter, then trim the sharp burrs inside the pipe with a reamer.

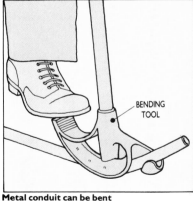

Metal conduit can be bent

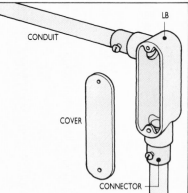

LBs make fishing at right angles easy

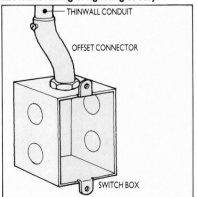

Offsets keep conduit tight against walls

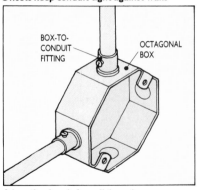

A junction box is for splicing wires

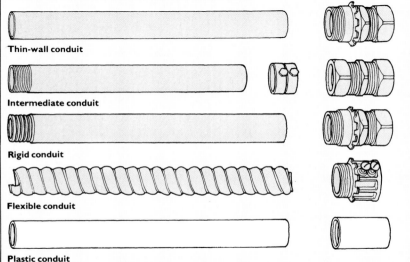

TYPES OF ELECTRICAL CONDUIT

Thin-wall conduit

Intermediate conduit

Rigid conduit

Flexible conduit

Plastic conduit

LOW-VOLTAGE ALTERNATIVES

Low-voltage wiring was once limited to doorbells and thermostats (▷). Today, however, low-voltage lighting is being used in places unheard of a generation ago. The reason, of course, is that low-voltage systems give you more light for less money, and rising electric rates have made efficiency an issue. Low-voltage wiring is also safe, if you short circuit a low-voltage system, the shock you get will feel more like a tickle than the life-threatening bite of a 120-volt system.

There are literally dozens of low-voltage lighting systems available today. You can run tiny low-voltage lights under the tread of each step in a stairway. You can run a string of mini-lights along a beam. You can highlight a favorite wall hanging or work of art with low-voltage track lighting. You can even frame the object with lights that have barn doors and focusing lenses. And finally, you can install low-voltage landscape lighting in your back yard that costs you only pennies a day to operate. If you've got something special in mind, you can do it with low-voltage systems already on the market.

Low-voltage kits

The best way to buy low-voltage components is in kit form. You won't necessarily save money that way, but you won't have to design your own system either. When you buy a kit, for example, the transformer size, the length and size of the wire and the number of allowable fixtures is all figured for you. If you install the kit according to instructions, you won't run the risk of over extending the system.

Contrary to popular opinion, low-voltage systems can start fires when over-extended. Too many fixtures or too long a run can cause low-voltage wires to overheat. If you hope to design your own system, make sure you use a transformer with a built-in breaker.

If you don't find exactly the combination of features you want in one brand, try another brand or another style. Track lighting offers a good illustration of this point. You can get a fixture that fastens to the ceiling and has a surface cord that runs to a transformer that you plug into a socket. You can find one the same size with a surface-mounted transformer that ties to a ceiling box. And you can find one that has a transformer hidden in a recessed fixture so that you can't see it at all. Kit lights need not limit your design options.

Installing a transformer

In order to reduce your house current from 120 volts to 12 volts, a transformer will be needed. There are several sizes of transformers to meet a variety of needs. Most transformers used in residential wiring are rated at 100 to 300 watts. The greater the rating, the more 100-foot branch circuits can be served. If a transformer is underrated, the lights it serves will not go on or the wire that serves them will overheat.

As mentioned earlier, transformers for indoor fixtures can be located in a number of places on or near their fixtures. In some fixtures, they can be part of an electronic circuit, similar to that of a stereo. But in many cases, you will fasten the transformer directly to a 120-volt metal outlet box. Just remove a knockout plug and fasten the transformer to the box with a clamp.

Then fasten the leads from the transformer to pigtail connections inside the box. The low-voltage UF wires can then be tied to the terminals of the transformer.

A transformer designed to be used outdoors, however, must be sealed in its own weathertight box. You can buy transformers with on/off switches built in, or you can use a conventional switch between the outlet and the transformer. The transformer box must be connected to the outlet box with weathertight conduit (▷). Then, from the transformer, low-voltage UF cable should be laid underground to each fixture. Low-voltage fixtures do not need to be grounded and because they pose no physical threat, do not have to be buried deep or encased in conduit when installed outdoors. Keep them out of harm's way, however.

Low-voltage fixture connections

Low-voltage connections are made inside protective boxes on indoor lighting fixtures. In some cases, the low-voltage side of the fixture is wired and sealed at the factory. When you install these fixtures, you will only have to wire the 120-volt connection. Terminals on the low-voltage side of a transformer can remain exposed provided the transformer is not covered by drywall or otherwise concealed.

All outdoor connectors must be made inside weathertight boxes (▷),

of course. They can be made the conventional way with binding screws or with special low-voltage connectors. These connectors use a screw-and-clamp device. The cable is placed in a slot and the clamp is screwed down over it. As the clamp tightens, it pierces the cable, making contact with the wires inside. In this case, you do not even have to cut the wire at the fixture. Both connections are legal in outdoor installations provided they take place in weathertight boxes.

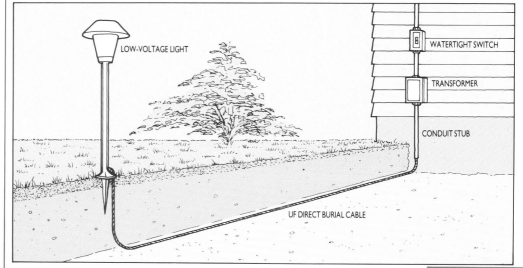

Burying low-voltage UF wire
Low-voltage UF wire can be buried without conduit after it reaches ground level.

PROTECTING AGAINST LIGHTNING

Lightning is a very real electrical threat to every home. When lightning strikes, the results are unpredictable. It can melt circuit cables, destroy the electrical components in appliances, and, of course, burn a home to the ground. A well grounded home has better protection against lightning than a poorly grounded home. Homes with lightning rods connected to heavy grounding conductors are even better protected. And those with lightning arresters installed in their service panels or at their meters are safest.

Ironically, the improvements we make to our homes may pose the greatest threats. Ungrounded steel or aluminum siding and ungrounded TV antennas and satellite dishes pose real hazards which many homeowners overlook. Replacing steel or copper water pipes with plastic can also remove the protection given our homes when they were first built. If you are contemplating improvements in these areas, be sure to keep the threat of lightning in mind and plan your work accordingly.

Antennas can be grounded with approved clamps, No. 6 wire and ground rods

1 Iron antenna
2 Approved clamp
3 No. 6 conductor
4 Finished grade
5 ½" × 8' ground stake
6 Undisturbed soil
7 Concrete pad

Grounding antennas

TV antennas and satellite dishes also attract lightning. A lightning charge can easily blow the circuitry of a television connected to an ungrounded antenna or dish. If you have either, make sure it is grounded properly.

Grounding an antenna is easy. Just fasten an approved clamp to the frame of the antenna, near the bottom. Then run a No. 6 ground wire to a second clamp fastened to a copper clad grounding rod just below grade.

Because some satellite dishes do not have grounding terminals, you may have to improvise a connection. The best method is to drill and tap a ¼-inch hole in the support post and fasten the ground wire to the frame with a brass bolt. Then run the No. 6 bare wire to an approved clamp and ground rod. Again, the rod connection should be made just below grade.

Grounding aluminum siding

Because aluminum and steel sidings are metal, they can attract and conduct electrical charges generated by lightning. For this reason, the NEC suggests that all metal sidings should be grounded. Most homeowners and many installers are not aware of this requirement and because siding installations do not always require building permits, thousands of American homes are without the lightning protection they need.

If your siding is not grounded, tuck a No. 10 bare wire under the lip of the bottom most layer of siding and secure it about every 10 feet with sheet metal screws. From the No. 10 wire, on two opposing corners of your home, run a No. 6 wire down to a copper clad grounding rod (◁). Use approved clamps and bury the connection just below grade.

When installing new siding (◁), run a grounding wire around the perimeter of your home under the first layer of siding. For added protection, run wires vertically from the perimeter wire to the soffit at 10-foot intervals. You can secure these wires by wrapping them around the siding fasteners as you go. Finally, attach the perimeter wire to grounding rods on two opposing corners of your house.

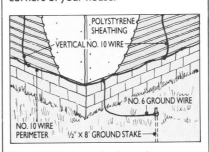

Ground siding by placing bare wire conductors next to siding

Installing a lightning arrester

A lightning arrester is a small rectifier that routes a high-voltage lightning charge away from an electrical system and into the earth. Lightning arresters are inexpensive and are not that difficult to install. Because they must be installed on the hot side of a home's main disconnect switch (◁), however, you will have to have the power to your home shut off by your local utility or a licensed electrician. Never attempt to install a lightning arrester with the power on.

With the power off, locate a knock-out plug on the top of your service panel the size of the threaded nipple on your arrester. Remove this plug and insert the nipple through the opening. Then tighten the arrester in place with the provided fastening nut.

Next, slide the white wire from the arrester under an unused terminal on the neutral bus bar and tighten the terminal screw. Then loosen one of the terminal screws on the incoming side of the main disconnect switch. Slide one of the black wires from the arrester under that terminal, next to the incoming service wire already in place, and retighten the screw. Finally, fasten the other black arrester wire under the remaining disconnect terminal.

Before calling for an inspection, make sure that the two main disconnect screws are very tight. You may wish to use a torque wrench or screwdriver. As manufacturer specifications vary, check with local suppliers for the proper torque rating for your panel.

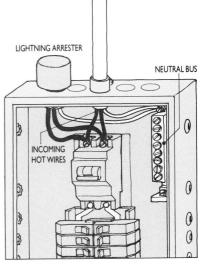

LIGHTNING ARRESTER

NEUTRAL BUS

INCOMING HOT WIRES

Lightning arrester installed in typical panel

8

PLUMBING

UNDERSTANDING THE SYSTEM

Today, more and more homeowners are willing to tackle their own plumbing repair and remodeling projects. As with most do-it-yourself endeavors, cost is a motivating factor. The lion's share of most plumbing bills is the cost of professional labor, so doing your own repairs and installations makes good economic sense, and offers as a bonus the satisfaction of greater self-sufficiency.

Fortunately for the do-it-yourselfer, the plumbing supply industry has wasted no time in recognizing the growing consumer market open to them. Instead of selling plumbing supplies in bulk quantities to wholesale houses and plumbers, manufacturers are now marketing for the consumer as well. They are also making their products easier to use. Repair and replacement parts are now likely to be attractively packaged with instructions and a "you-can-do-it" pep talk on the back of each blister pack.

To the further benefit of the homeowner, design and manufacturing trends have also steered the industry in the direction of lighter, less expensive and easier to install materials. City code authorities have recognized the need to make plumbing more affordable in new construction and have adjusted their material requirements accordingly.

The upshot of all of this is that basic plumbing has never been easier and has never required so few specialized tools. Still, the most important ingredient in any do-it-yourself project is confidence. Confidence starts with a basic understanding of how plumbing works and increases with every project you complete.

A typical plumbing system

A residential piping system can be divided according to function into five basic categories. These categories are: pressurized water and fuel pipes, gravity-flow soil pipes, vent pipes and fixtures and appliances. All pipes in a system serve specific fixtures (sinks, lavatories and tubs) and appliances (water heaters, disposers, dish washers and clothes washers).

Take time to familiarize yourself with this network of pipes in your home before beginning any repair or remodeling project. An understanding of how each component in your system works with other components will help you feel more confident about the project at hand. Think about each pipe, valve and fixture in your home as it fits within one of the five basic categories of function. Consider each item within the system separately. Until each element is examined according to its use, the system as a whole will likely remain a mystery. Plumbing is better learned one step at a time.

PLUMBING REGULATIONS

If you own a single-family dwelling, you can work on any of its plumbing. Your work will have to meet accepted plumbing standards as defined by local code regulations. Plumbing codes are written and enforced locally in the United States, but are based on specifications of the national *Uniform Plumbing Code*.

Before starting any major plumbing project, check with your local code office to see if the work you have planned meets specific code requirements. Any major project involving new piping or piping changes will require a permit and a series of inspections. Most plumbing appliance installations also require permits.

Plumbing standards are important because they protect us from health-threatening plumbing materials and practices. They benefit us all and should be supported by everyone.

A typical plumbing scheme

ROOF FLASHING

KITCHEN VENT TIED TO MAIN STACK

2" STOOL VENT

VENT

WATER HEATER COLD

1 1/2" VENT

STOOL SUPPLY

LAV

TUB

SINK/KITCHEN

SILLCOCK

SILLCOCK

GAS OR FUEL

3" STACK

WASHER HOT

WASHER COLD

HOT WATER SUPPLY

DRAIN

GAS

METER VALVES

GAS METER

CLEANOUT

DRYER

WASHER

GAS WATER HEATER

WATER SERVICE

FLOOR DRAIN

CLEANOUT

4" SOIL PIPE

SEWER SERVICE

A GENERAL OVERVIEW

*A brief look at the fundamental
components of a plumbing system will
help you think through any problems you
may be having.*

Supply lines

Cold water service
The water that flows from your tap
enters your home through a single
water service pipe (**1**). This pipe is
buried below frost level in your yard
and extends from the city water main to
a meter valve just inside your home. If
water is supplied from a well, it flows to
a pressure tank where it is stored until
needed. In some cases, the water meter
will be located in a meter pit just
outside the home.

Cold water lines
The water service is then connected to
a meter, which measures the amount of
water you use. From the meter, a single
trunk line usually travels up and along
the center girder of a home. At
convenient intervals along the way,
smaller branch lines extend from the
trunk line to service various fixtures
throughout the house.

Hot water lines
At some centrally located point, a cold
water trunk line branches off to enter a
water heater tank. Some of the
incoming water flows past the heater to
other cold water outlets, but some
enters the tank and fills it. The hot
water outlet pipe extends from the
other side of the tank and typically rises
to the floor joist next to the center
beam, becoming a hot water trunk line.
This hot water trunk usually travels
side-by-side with the cold water trunk
and branches off to serve the hot water
requirements of fixtures and appliances.

Drainage lines

Drainage lines are the pipes that carry
soiled water from your fixtures to the
public sewer system. They generally
consist of one or more vertical stacks
with horizontal drains attached. It is
important that drainage lines are
installed at just the right pitch. Too little
fall will cause water and solids to drain
sluggishly and may cause the line to clog.
Too much fall, particularly on long runs,
will cause the water to outrun the
solids, which may also cause the line to
clog. A fall of 1/8 inch per foot is ideal.
Use a level on each pipe.

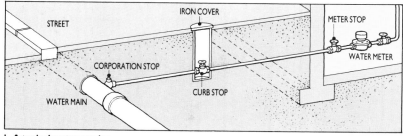

1 A typical water service

Fixture traps

As a public sewer system is vented
through the roofs (via plumbing stacks)
of the homes connected to it, sewer gas
is always present in large quantities in
drainage systems. Each fixture must
therefore have a seal to keep noxious
sewer gases from entering the home
through fixture drains. This seal is
created by a U-shaped pipe, called a
trap, beneath each fixture. Traps allow
water to pass through them when a
fixture is drained. After a fixture is
drained, however, the trap holds a
measured amount of water in its bend
so that sewer gas cannot pass through
the pipe and into your home. Every
fixture in your home must have a trap,
and every trap must be vented.

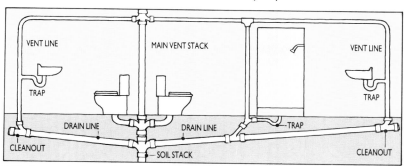

2 Stack-vented toilets with re-vented lavs and shower

Venting

Venting is one of the most critical
aspects of a drainage system. Without
properly vented drain lines, stools won't
flush properly, sink and lavatory drains
choke and high-volume appliance drains
may overflow. But most importantly,
unvented drain lines siphon water from
fixture traps. Once a trap seal is broken,
sewer gas quickly enters your living
quarters. Sewer gases can cause
respiratory problems and headaches
in quantities too small to detect by
smell.

A fixture trap may be vented in one
of two ways. The simplest way is to size
horizontal drains so that the top half of
the drain serves as the vent for that
fixture. This is called stack venting (**3**).

The second method is called
re-venting (**2**). A re-vent is a separate
vent that is installed on the highest part
of a drain pipe and within a few feet of
the trap. It then extends through the
roof independently or ties back into the
main vertical stack above the flood
plane of the highest fixture, often in the
attic. The type of vent used depends
upon the number of fixtures and floor
levels involved and the structural
constraints peculiar to each home.

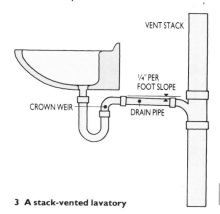

3 A stack-vented lavatory

SEE ALSO

Details for: ▷

Emergency repairs	341
General piping considerations	342

● **Gas and fuel lines**
Natural gas and fuel
oil piping will often
run next to the
plumbing pipes in
your home. Because
appliances such as
clothes dryers and
water heaters are
often gas-fired, you
will need to learn
enough about gas
piping to service and
replace these
appliances.

Gas is brought to
your meter through
an underground
service pipe made of
plastic or coated
black iron. Its
pressure is reduced
from around 25 psi
to about 6 ounces
before entering your
private system. Once
inside your home, it
is piped directly to
your gas appliances.

Fuel oil piping is
usually plumbed in
iron and makes its
way to the furnace
under low pressure
gravity flow.

DRAINING A WATER SYSTEM

Being able to locate and shut off your meter valve or, if you live in the country, your pump switch, is an important homeowner responsibility. You must be able to act quickly in an emergency.

Locating your meter

The main shutoff can be found at the water meter (◁). Water meters are made of brass and are usually not larger than 6 inches in diameter. At the top of the meter you will find a glass or plastic housing that contains a dial and a counter similar to the odometer on your car. Meters are often just inside the basement wall closest to the street. As previous owners may have covered your meter with cabinetry or a pipe chase, look for an access panel. Utility rooms and basement stairwells are also good places to look. If all else fails, follow the cold water inlet pipe from your water heater back to its source.

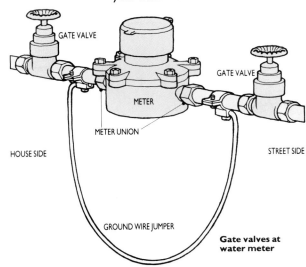

Gate valves at water meter

Shutting off your meter

Once you have located your meter, notice that there is a valve on each side of it. Many meter valves have handles, but some will have only a bar that must be turned with a wrench. Both of these valves will stop water from entering your home. The valve on the street side of the meter will stop the water before it enters your meter. Conversely, the valve on the house side of the meter will stop the water from entering your plumbing system.

If you merely wish to shut the water off, as when you leave on vacation, or in the event of an emergency, either valve will do the job. If, however, you need to drain your water system, then both valves will need to be closed.

Draining the system

To drain your water system, first shut the street side of the meter off. Then shut the house side of the meter off. When both valves are closed, place a bucket under the meter and loosen the meter union next to the house side valve. The small amount of water trapped in the meter will trickle through the opened union. Then go through your home and open all faucets to prevent air lock. When all faucets are open, return to the basement and open the house side valve and slowly drain the water into the bucket.

Draining your water heater

There can be several reasons why you might want to drain your water heater (◁). The most likely occasion will be when removing an old heater. Sediment, faulty electrical elements and stuck relief valves are three other common problems that require draining.

Start by shutting off the water supply to the heater. If your heater has a cold-water inlet valve, use it and leave the cold water side of the system on. If no inlet valve is present, you will have to shut the water supply to the entire house down at the meter.

Once water to the heater is shut off, open all hot water faucets in the house to prevent air lock. Then, open the spigot or drain valve at the base of the heater and drain off as much as you need for the repair. If yours is an electric heater, one added precaution is in order: Because energized electrical elements burn out in a matter of seconds when not immersed in water, you will need to shut off the power to the heater *before* draining it.

Partial drain downs

In many instances, such as toilet repairs, there will be no need to drain the entire system. A toilet usually has a shutoff valve between the riser and the supply line under the tank. Some homes have shutoff valves under sinks and lavatories as well. When these valves are present, use them. It is almost always easier to isolate a single fixture than to put the entire system out of order.

Recharging the system

Just as you opened all faucets to prevent an air lock when draining the system, you will need to open them to bleed air from the lines when recharging the system with water. Open the meter valves only part way. Then bleed the air from the newly charged lines. After all air in the system has escaped through the faucets, turn the faucets off and turn the meter valves all the way open. Small bursts of air may still escape through your faucets when you first use them after recharging, but all air should be dissipated after the first full pressure draw. If you do not bleed trapped air from supply lines, the shock of air released under full pressure could damage faucet and supply tube seals.

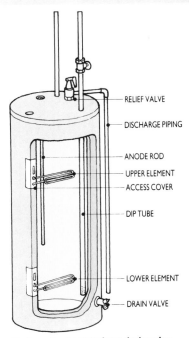

RELIEF VALVE

DISCHARGE PIPING

ANODE ROD
UPPER ELEMENT
ACCESS COVER

DIP TUBE

LOWER ELEMENT

DRAIN VALVE

Drain water heaters from drain valve

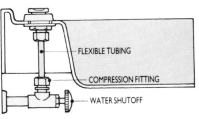

FLEXIBLE TUBING

COMPRESSION FITTING

WATER SHUTOFF

Independent shutoff under fixture

EMERGENCY REPAIRS

It seems that plumbing leaks occur when we are least prepared to deal with them. In such cases, a plumber may not be available, and you may not have the time or materials to make a permanent repair. There are, however, a number of stopgap measures that you can use to repair leaks temporarily.

A LAST-DITCH REPAIR

If conventional repair materials are not available, you can sometimes make do with materials found around the house or at your local all-night service station. To create a makeshift sleeve coupling, use a piece of bicycle or car tire inner tube and a few radiator hose clamps. Wrap the inner tube around the split pipe several times and clamp it in place with hose clamps. This is at best a stopgap measure, but it will slow the leak until you can make a more permanent repair.

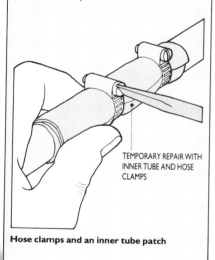

TEMPORARY REPAIR WITH INNER TUBE AND HOSE CLAMPS

Hose clamps and an inner tube patch

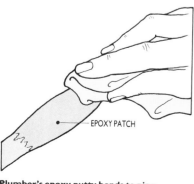

EPOXY PATCH

Plumber's epoxy putty bonds to pipe

Frozen and split pipes

In colder climates, pipes located in exterior walls, crawlspaces and attics are often subject to freezing. The best preventive measure is to insulate these pipes. Even insulated pipes, however, can freeze when exposed to cold drafts of air. When a pipe freezes, a plug of ice forms in a small section of the pipe and expands against the pipe walls. The expansion swells the pipe, and in most cases, ruptures the pipe wall.

Even a well protected pipe may crack after years of use. Factory defects and corrosion are often responsible for these leaks. Regardless of how a pipe cracks or splits, emergency repair methods are usually the same.

A sure sign that a pipe has frozen is when no water passes through the pipe to the faucets nearest the freeze. You will often be able to feel along the pipe and locate the frozen area. If the pipe has not yet ruptured, use a portable hair dryer to warm the frozen area until water again flows to the nearest faucet. Once thawed, you should wrap the pipe

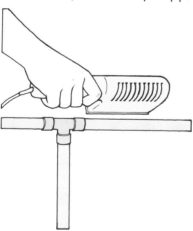

A hair dryer works well in thawing pipes

with insulation. If no insulation is available, use old rags and fasten them to the pipe with tape, string or wire.

If you can see that the pipe has already split, you will need to drain the system before thawing the frozen area. Once thawed, you will need to make some sort of emergency repair. If you are able to find a plumbing supply outlet, the best solution is to buy a sleeve-type repair coupling. These couplings can be purchased in a number of standard sizes. They consist of two metal halves that are hinged on one side and bolted together on the other. A rubber sleeve fits inside and wraps completely around the pipe.

To install a sleeve repair coupling, first clean the pipe with a wire brush or sandpaper. Then fit the rubber sleeve around the pipe so that the seam is opposite the leak. Fit the metal halves of the collar over the sleeve and tighten the two halves together. While this method is an emergency repair, it is also permanent.

SEE ALSO

Details for: ▷

Plastic pipe fittings	343–344
Steel pipe	345
Repair fittings	346

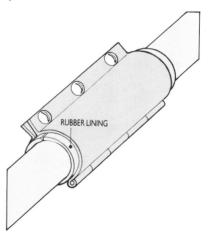

RUBBER LINING

A repair coupling for permanent repairs

Epoxy patch repair

If you do not have access to plumbing materials, you may still be able to buy a general-purpose epoxy kit. These kits consist of two sticks of putty that you knead together. Once the parts are completely mixed, you will have about fifteen minutes to work before the mixture begins to set. Start by cleaning and drying the area around the split with sandpaper and alcohol. Knead the two components until they are a single consistent color and begin to give off heat. Then press the epoxy putty

around the pipe. Smooth the ends with water until the epoxy forms a seamless bond around the pipe several inches on either side of the split.

Epoxy takes a full 24 hours to cure, but after a few hours, you should be able to turn the water on slightly. Do not put full pressure in the pipes for at least 24 hours after applying an epoxy patch. You will have to put up with slow-running faucets and toilets, but you will have the water you need to run a normal household until the epoxy cures.

WORKING WITH PIPE

Until you learn to work with pipe, your plumbing capabilities will be limited to simple maintenance. While Neoprene gaskets, no-hub couplings and plastic pipe and fittings have greatly reduced the need for special knowledge and specialized tools, most remodeling still requires that you understand how traditional plumbing materials are put together. In most cases, these newer, easier-to-use materials will still have to be tied into existing pipes. You may also need to dismantle some existing piping in order to repair or extend your

plumbing system. In short, knowing how to use plastic pipe is of little use if you do not also know how to tie it to other kinds of pipe in your existing system.

The good news is that the skill needed to work with cast-iron, steel and copper pipe has been seriously overrated. You can do it. You may need a few specialized tools, but you can rent those. What you need most is a basic understanding of how these materials are put together and what fittings and tools make the job easier. The rest is a matter of practice.

Making the connection

With the acceptance of plastic as a plumbing material, several new methods of joining plastic to conventional soil pipe have also been developed. These connectors have virtually eliminated the skill once needed to form mechanical joints. Where once molten lead and oakum (an oily, ropelike material) were packed into bell and spigot joints, now Neoprene gaskets make the seal. Now, instead of dismantling a run of pipe all the way back to its nearest hub, you can join two hubless pipes in minutes with no-hub couplings.

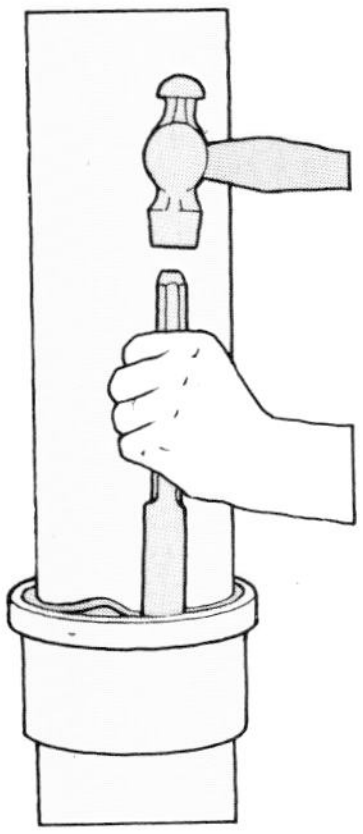

Bell and spigot gaskets
Neoprene gaskets are made for every standard size cast-iron soil pipe. They are fitted rubber collars that snap into the bell of a cast-iron pipe. The inside of the gasket is then lubricated with detergent (dish soap works well), and the male end of the adjoining pipe is forced into the gasket until it seats.

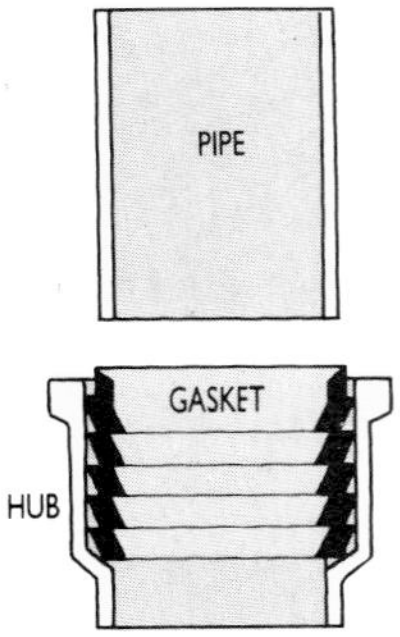

No-hub couplings
No-hub couplings are rot-resistant rubber sleeves with stainless-steel bands around them. They are designed for use on drainage pipes and are approved by most code authorities. To install no-hub

couplings, you simply slide one end of each pipe into the sleeve and tighten the bands. No-hubs come in many sizes, including increasing and decreasing couplings that allow you to join different pipe sizes to one another. They are particularly handy in joining dissimilar pipe materials, such as cast iron and plastic or plastic and copper.

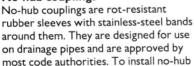

Lead-and-oakum joint
Made by packing a hub with ⅔ oakum and ⅓ lead.

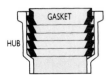

Neoprene gaskets
Neoprene gaskets are easy substitutes for lead-and-oakum joints.

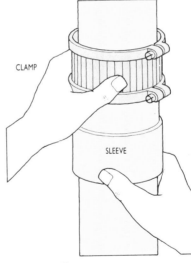

CLAMP

SLEEVE

No-hub coupling

DRAIN AND VENT SIZING CHART

FIXTURE	DRAIN SIZE	VENT SIZE	MAX. LENGTH STACK VENT
Toilet	4"	2"	10'
Toilet	3"	2"	6'
Sink	1½"	1½"	3.5'
Lavatory	1½"	1½"	3.5'
Tub	1½"	1½"	3.5'
Shower	2"	1½"	5'
Laundry	2"	1½"	5'
Floor drain*	2"	1½"	5'

* Vents waived by some codes.

GENERAL PIPING CONSIDERATIONS

When installing drainage pipe, there are a few rules you will need to follow in order to ensure mechanically sound joints and even flow patterns. They are as follows:

1. The grade, or elevation of a drainage pipe should not be less than 1/16 inch or not greater than 1/4 inch per running foot of pipe. In total, the fall of a given pipe run should not be greater than the diameter of the pipe involved. For example, a 2-inch pipe should not drop more than 2 inches along its entire length. If structural constraints require that a pipe drop more than its diameter, fittings should be used to "step" the pipe down to a lower plane. In this case, a re-vent will be required before stepping down.

2. When drainage pipes are wet, or carry water, fittings with gradual flow patterns should be used. For example, tees should be used only when they are the highest fittings on a vertical pipe. They should never be used in horizontal positions or when other fixtures are served above them. Because wyes offer much more gradual flow patterns, they should always be used instead of tees, except as the highest branch fitting on a vertical stack.

3. When drainage pipes are suspended from floor or ceiling joists, they should be supported by pipe hangers at a rate of at least one every 6 feet, or one for every pipe less than 6 feet long.

4. Every vertical stack must have a cleanout fitting at its base before entering a concrete floor.

5. All pipes installed underground or under concrete must be laid on even, solid soil. No voids or low spots are permitted under a pipe. If voids exist, or if the grade has been overexcavated, the ditch should be lined with fill sand. You should never fill voids or raise a pipe with soil. Soil is sure to settle with time, causing the pipe to sag and clog, or to shear off entirely.

When excavating a ditch for soil pipe, dig a small impression in the soil for each pipe hub. This will keep the entire length of the pipe from resting only on the hubs. Because soil pipe is buried permanently, either underground or under concrete, always work for a permanent installation.

PLASTIC DRAINAGE PIPE AND FITTINGS

Plastic pipe is the easiest pipe to handle because it is lightweight, can be cut with a hacksaw and is joined to its fittings with glue. Plastic drainage pipe comes in two forms. ABS pipe is black and PVC is white. Both are schedule #40 weight, which is the wall thickness required by code for drainage pipe. There is no appreciable difference between the two, except that ABS has become more expensive in recent years and the plumbing industry in general seems to be moving away from it. In the interest of consistency, you should match the type already in your home.

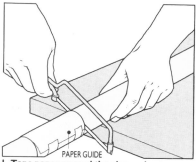

1   Tape paper around the pipe and cut

Cutting and assembling plastic pipe

To cut and fit plastic pipe, measure for the desired length and mark the pipe with a pencil. Then, using a hacksaw, cut carefully across the pipe (1). Take particular care in making straight cuts. A crooked cut will keep the end of the pipe from fitting properly into the bell of the fitting. Smooth the cut edge with a file (2).

It is always a good idea to assemble pipe and fittings before gluing to make sure that all measurements are accurate and all fitting angles correspond. Then, before dismantling, mark the fitting and pipe (3) at each joint so that you will have an easy reference point when gluing them together permanently (4).

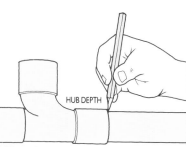

2   File away any burr left by the saw

Gluing plastic pipe

Gluing pipe and hubs is easy but requires accuracy and speed. Apply glue to the inside of the hub of the fitting. Then glue the outside of the pipe, covering a depth consistent with the depth of the hub (5). Press the fitting onto the pipe with the pencil marks about an inch apart. When the pipe is in all the way, turn the fitting so that the pencil marks line up. By turning the fitting on the pipe, the glue is spread out and the friction helps cement the joint.

Glued joints (technically, cemented joints) set in about 30 seconds, so if you make a mistake, you have to pull the joint apart very quickly. Plastic pipe cement does not really glue one surface to another; rather, it melts the two surfaces, causing them to fuse. Once a joint has set, it is permanent.

When buying materials, be sure to choose a cement made for the type of pipe you buy. ABS glue will not cement PVC pipe and fittings. PVC glue does work with ABS pipe, so it is always better to use compatible materials.

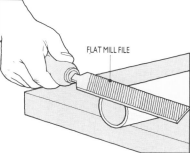

3   Mark the depth of the hub on the pipe

- **Supporting pipe runs**
  Plastic pipework should be supported with clips or saddles similar to those used for metal pipe, but because it is more flexible, you will have to space the clips closer together. Check with manufacturers' literature for exact dimensions. If you plan to surface-run flexible pipes, consider ducting or boxing-in because it's difficult to make a really neat installation.

Installing drainage pipe

Drainage pipe must often be installed in interior walls. Because plastic pipe expands and contracts with hot and cold water, make sure that holes drilled in the wall studs are large enough to allow for this expansion. Stud and joist holes should be at least 1/8 inch larger than the exterior diameter of the pipe. Plastic pipe should never be shimmed tightly against wood. Without room for expansion, plastic pipe will produce an annoying ticking sound in the wall after hot water has been drained through.

Plastic drainage pipe can be joined to pipes made of steel or copper in two ways. One way is to use a male or female adapter. One end of the adapter is glued to the plastic pipe and the other end threads into a female fitting. No-hub couplings make quick and easy connections and are also good fittings for drain cleanouts.

4   Mark pipe and hub as reference

Joining plastic to cast iron

When joining plastic to a cast-iron hub, use a Neoprene gasket. Fold the gasket into the hub and lubricate it. Then file down the sharp edge on the end of the plastic pipe and push the pipe into the gasket. To join plastic pipe to the hubless end of a pipe, use a no-hub (or banded) coupling.

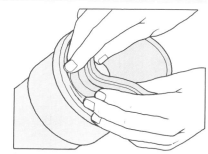

Neoprene gasket for cast-iron hub

5   Apply cement to both pipe and fitting

PLASTIC WATER PIPE AND FITTINGS

With one exception, CPVC plastic water pipe is put together the same way as plastic drainage pipe. Plastic pipe has a shiny residue on its surface that should be either sanded or treated with primer solvent before cement is applied. A fine-grit sandpaper works well when sanding the ends of each pipe and inside of a fitting, but solvent is faster and more thorough. Simply brush the surfaces to be glued, wait a few seconds and wipe them clean with a soft cloth. Then brush the glue on the pipe and fitting and push them together with a slight twist.

JOINING CPVC PIPE TO DISSIMILAR MATERIALS

Plastic water pipe can also be joined to steel and copper pipe by means of plastic threaded adapters. Both male and female plastic adapters are available. One end of the plastic adapter is glued to the plastic pipe and the other threaded into a fitting or onto a pipe. When joining plastic water pipe to existing metal piping, wrap the male threads with plastic pipe joint sealant tape. Because plastic female adapters can expand when threaded onto male threads, a better choice is to use a plastic male adapter threaded into an iron or copper female adapter or fitting.

STEEL ELBOW

PLASTIC MALE ADAPTER

Adapters connect plastic to existing steel

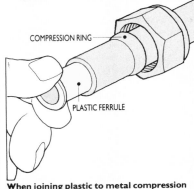

COMPRESSION RING

PLASTIC FERRULE

When joining plastic to metal compression fittings, use a plastic ferrule

Polybutylene pipe

PB pipe is a relative newcomer to the plumbing industry. It is not directly compatible with other plastics, but offers several real advantages. The first advantage is that it will take a freeze without splitting. The second is that PB fittings contain mechanical joints. They can be turned and adjusted in place and are therefore more forgiving of beginner error. And finally, PB pipe is bendable, which greatly reduces the need for elbow fittings. As PB piping is not universally accepted by code authorities, check to see if you can use it before starting a piping job.

The manufacturers of PB pipe have designed connector fittings to match nearly all water pipe materials and sizes. These fittings come in two styles. One is a simple compression fitting and the other has a push-fit O-ring combination. A good choice for supply pipe installations is the push-fit type. It goes together easily and almost never leaks. PB fittings adapt well to other materials, such as copper and CPVC. A threaded adapter is also available for threaded pipe hookups. PB valves come in many sizes for a variety of special-use situations.

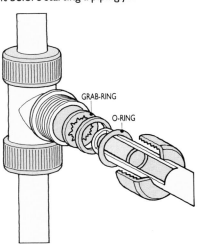

GRAB-RING

O-RING

Push-fit O-ring fitting
Just lubricate the pipe and push it in until it seats.

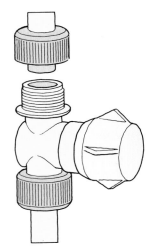

Compression valve
This valve is an ideal in-line toilet supply shutoff.

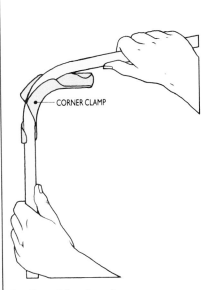

CORNER CLAMP

Bending polybutylene pipe
Polybutylene pipe saves fittings because it can be bent around corners.

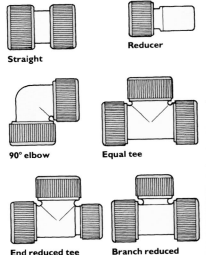

Straight

Reducer

90° elbow

Equal tee

End reduced tee

Branch reduced

Plastic pipe fittings
Some of the basic fittings for connections are shown.

WORKING WITH STEEL PIPE

Steel pipe is available in galvanized and black iron forms. Galvanized pipe is used for water supply lines and drainage and vent lines, while black iron is used primarily for gas piping. Though they are put together in exactly the same way, you should never mix the two. When galvanized iron is used on gas installations, the gas in the line will attack the zinc plating and cause it to flake off. These zinc flakes will be carried through the system and can easily clog the orifice and control valve of a water heater or furnace. On the other hand, if black iron pipe is used in water supply lines, it will rust shut in a matter of months.

Steel pipe is put together with threaded joints. Because steel was the predominant piping material of residential plumbing for the first 60 years of this century, you will find it in many older homes. You may never need to install steel piping, but chances are you will have to deal with it when making changes and repairs.

Steel pipe comes in 21-foot lengths and is threaded on each end at the factory. It also comes in short precut, prethreaded lengths called nipples that graduate in ½-inch increments from 1 foot to approximately 1 inch in length. When you need custom-cut lengths, you will have to cut and thread them yourself, using a die cutter.

Cutting and threading steel pipe

Steel pipe can be cut with a hacksaw. In fact, when cutting out a section of existing pipe, a hacksaw is your best choice. When you intend to thread the cut end, however, a wheel cutter will give you a much more uniform cut. Wheel cutters can be found at most rental stores along with the threading dies you may need.

To determine the exact length of pipe you need, measure between the two fittings and add the depth of the threads inside each fitting for your total length. Then mark the pipe with a soapstone or crayon. Place the pipe in a pipe vise and tighten the cutter on the pipe so that the wheel is directly on your mark. Then tighten the wheel one-half turn and rotate the cutter around the pipe. When the cutting wheel turns in its groove easily, tighten it another turn and rotate the cutter again. Repeat this process until the pipe is cut completely through.

When the cut is made, leave the pipe in the vice and get ready to cut new threads. Cover the first inch of the pipe

with cutting oil and slide the cylinder of the die onto the pipe. Set the lock on the die to the "cut" position. Then, while pressing the die onto the pipe with the palm of your hand, crank the die handle. When the die teeth begin to cut into the metal, you will feel some resistance. You will then be ready to crank the handle steadily around the pipe to cut the threads (**1**).

About every two rounds, stop and pour oil through the die head and onto the new threads. This is very important. Without oil, the pipe will heat-up and swell until you can no longer turn the handle. Dry pipe threads will also ruin the die cutters in short order.

Continue cranking and oiling until the first of the new threads shows through the front of the die. Then, reverse the direction lock on the handle and spin the die off the pipe. Thread the other end and you will be ready to install that length. All threaded steel joints should be put together with plastic pipe joint sealant tape or pipe joint compound, on the male side only.

SEE ALSO

Details for: ▷

Emergency repairs	341
General piping considerations	342
Plastic pipe	343–344
Repair fittings	346
Plumbing tools	486–491

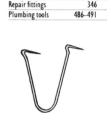

Wire pipe hook

Pipe strap

Two-hole strap

Hole strap

Pipe supports
Use standard pipe hooks and fasteners to support iron pipes.

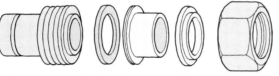

Plastic spacers
A dielectric union prevents corrosion by separating the metals with a plastic spacer.

Pipe adapter   Washer Pipe adapter Plastic spacer Fastening nut

IRON PIPE FITTINGS

You will find a fitting for nearly every possible piping configuration. Here are nine common fittings you will find at your local plumbing outlet.

Union   **Male/female adapter**   **Threaded nipple**

Coupling   **Reducer coupling**   **Reducing tee**

90° ell   **Reducing ell** **Combination tee**

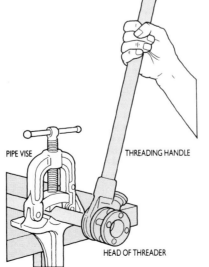

PIPE VISE   THREADING HANDLE

HEAD OF THREADER

1 Threading an iron pipe
Lock the pipe in a pipe vise and use a threading die.

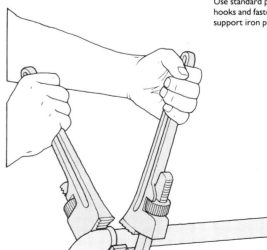

Removing a threaded fitting
Use a second pipe wrench to back-hold the pipe.

FITTINGS FOR REMODELING AND REPAIR

Repair and remodeling work often require that you cut a section of pipe from between two fittings. This is easily enough done with a hacksaw. Once the cut is made, you will need to back each section of remaining pipe from its fitting. Use two pipe wrenches, one to back the pipe out and one to hold the fitting so that no joints further down the line are disturbed. Otherwise, you might cause leaks.

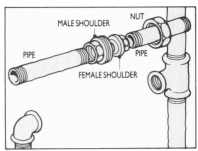
Fittings for reconnecting cast-iron pipe

Reconnecting with steel pipes, fittings and unions

To reconnect the removed portion of the line with steel, you will need a union. If a new tee or wye fitting is to be spliced into the new line, thread it onto a length of pipe and thread the pipe into one of the existing fittings. Thread another pipe into the other existing fitting. This pipe should come to within 6 inches of the new tee or wye. Finish with nipples and a union.

Reconnecting with copper or plastic pipe

Splicing in new pipe between two existing steel fittings is easier to do with copper or plastic. In each case, threaded adapters can be screwed into the steel fittings. In the case of copper, the remaining joints will be soldered. In the case of plastic drainage or water pipes, all other joints will be glued. PB pipe, of course, would be fitted with mechanical PB fittings and adapters. Because plastic water pipe is not universally accepted, you should check with your local code authorities before installing CPVC or PB piping materials.

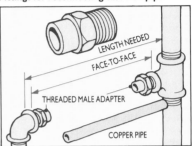
Fittings for splicing copper to iron pipe

Working with copper pipe

Copper pipe is available in four wall thicknesses. *Type K* is the thickest and is used primarily for underground water services and under concrete for supply lines. It comes in soft coils.

Type L offers the next thickest pipe wall. It is available in soft coils or rigid sticks. The soft version is typically used in gas pipe installations and is connected with flare fittings.

The thinnest allowable supply line pipe is *type M*. It is made only in 20-foot rigid lengths and is the most widely used in residential water systems.

The thinnest-walled copper pipe is *DWV*. As its initials imply, it is used as drain, waste and vent piping. Although seldom used now for drainage and vent piping, it was widely used in the '50s.

All copper pipe can be cut with a hacksaw, but if you intend to use flare fittings on soft copper, a wheel cutter (◁) will give a more uniform edge. All copper can be soldered, and all soft copper can be flared for use with flare fittings. Copper drainage pipe can be joined to steel, plastic or cast-iron pipe with no-hub couplings. Hard copper supply connections can also be joined with compression fittings.

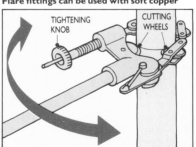
Flare fittings can be used with soft copper

Flare and compression fittings

As its name implies, a flare fitting requires that you flare the pipe to fit the fitting. Slide the flare nut onto soft copper pipe and clamp the flaring die within 1/8 inch of the end of the pipe. Thread the flaring tool against the pipe end until it expands evenly against the tapered die seat. Remove the tool and draw the fitting together with two wrenches.

A compression fitting operates in reverse fashion and so does not require a special tool. Simply slide the fitting nut and brass compression ring onto hard or soft copper pipe and thread the nut onto its fitting. Tighten hand tight, plus one to one and a half turns. Use pipe-joint compound on flare and compression fittings.

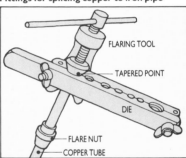
Cut cast-iron pipe with a snap cutter

Working with cast-iron pipe

You can cut cast-iron with a chisel by tapping lightly in a line around the pipe until it breaks. But the best way is to use a snap cutter. A snap cutter (◁) is a ratchetlike tool with a chain that wraps around pipe and cutting wheels that clamp onto the pipe. Snap cutters are available at most tool rental outlets.

Traditional hub and spigot joints are now made with Neoprene gaskets. Where hubs are not available or where hubless cast-iron is joined to plastic, steel or copper DWV pipe, no-hub couplings make the easiest connection.

Compression fittings for copper-to-copper joints

DRAIN-CLEANING TECHNIQUES

Soap, hair, food particles and cooking grease all help to clog drainage lines. Occasionally a fixture trap will accumulate a blockage that can be forced clear with a plunger, compressed air or a blow bag. Most blockages build up inside pipes over an extended period of time, however, and must be cabled, or "snaked," to be opened. The method you choose will depend upon the fixture involved and the size of the drainage line.

Forcing fixture traps

Plungers, blow bags and cans of compressed air can all be used to free simple trap clogs. When forcing a clog from a trap with any of these, be sure to plug any connecting airways. When plunging a lavatory, for example, use a wet rag to plug the overflow hole in the basin. When forcing the trap of a two-compartment sink, plug the opposite drain. After the clog has been forced through the trap and into the drain line, run very hot water through the line to move the clog into the main stack or soil pipe.

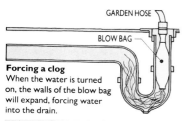

GARDEN HOSE

BLOW BAG

Forcing a clog
When the water is turned on, the walls of the blow bag will expand, forcing water into the drain.

Snaking a shower

If drain water backs up into a tub or shower from another fixture, it probably means that the main sewer line is clogged. If a tub or shower drains slowly or not at all, then you should snake the tub or shower trap and drain line. To snake a tub, remove the cover plate from the overflow valve and push the cable into the overflow pipe. Do not attempt to cable through the drain opening.

To clean a shower drain, start by removing the drain screen. If the screen is fastened to the drain with screws, remove them and pry the screen up with a knife. If the screen snaps in place, simply pry it up. Use a flashlight to look into the trap. If the trap is clogged by soap and hair, you can usually pick the clog out with a wire hook. If the trap is clear but the line is clogged, push the cable through the trap and cable the line to the main stack, or the nearest soil line.

Snaking fixture drains

When you wish to clean the drain line of any fixture with a snake, you will first have to remove the trap. Use a pipe wrench or adjustable pliers to loosen the nuts at the top of the trap and at the drain connection near the wall. With S-traps, loosen the nuts near the floor and at the trap weir. To avoid cracking or breaking a P-trap, hold it firmly and turn the nut with steady, even pressure.

With the trap removed, slide the snake cable into the drain line until you feel resistance. Then tighten the lock nut on the snake housing and slowly crank and push the cable deeper into the line. All bends in the line will offer some resistance, but slow, persistent pushing and cranking will force the cable around bends.

If the cable comes up against a blockage and begins to kink inside the line, back up a foot or so and try again. If you feel steady resistance, keep pushing and cranking. Every 3 feet or so, stop, pull the snake back a little and then crank forward again. Try to determine how many feet it is from the trap to the main stack and cable all the way to the stack, even if you break through the clog. When pulling the snake out for the final time, crank in a clockwise direction. If the clog was caused by a foreign object, like a piece of a sponge or dish cloth, the clockwise coil on the end of the cable will hang onto the object and pull it out as well.

After you have snaked the drain, replace the trap. If the trap washers seem hard and brittle, replace them with new washers. Because much of the debris from the clog will remain in the line, flush with plenty of hot water. If the fixture drain backs up, plunge it thoroughly and flush the line again.

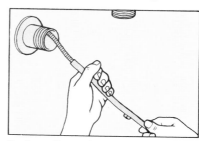

To clean a fixture drain, remove the trap

SEE ALSO

Details for: ▷

| Typical plumbing system | 338 |
| Plumbing tools | 486–491 |

SNAKING A SEWER LINE

Before you rent a sewer cleaning machine, get several bids from professional drain cleaners. Often drain cleaning companies can do the job for only a little more than the cost of machine rental.

If you decide to clean your own sewer line, start by removing the cleanout plug from the main line. If the cleanout plug is made of brass and is threaded into a cast-iron fitting, you may have to chisel it out. Use a sharp chisel and tap it into the brass threads in a counter clockwise direction. Continue to tap the chisel until the plug breaks loose. Because brass plugs are nearly always difficult to remove, you may wish to install a plastic plug when finishing the job. If the cast-iron threads are damaged, you can insert an expandable rubber plug in place of the conventional threaded type.

When using a heavy sewer cleaning

ROOT-CUTTING BLADES

machine, always wear leather gloves to avoid injuring your hands. Pay particular attention to the load on the motor. If the motor pulls down too far, stop, pull the cable out and start over.

Most sewer clogs fall into two categories: tree roots and collapsed pipes. Run the cable into the sewer until you feel and hear real resistance. Then pull the cable out and examine the blades. If you find hairlike tree roots, continue snaking until you pull the roots out or push them through. If you find dirt on the end of the pilot, stop. Dirt on the pilot suggests a collapsed line or fitting. You will have to dig the line up to make the repair.

Cleaning a sewer line
Monitor the action of the blades by the sound of the motor.

LEARNING HOW TO SOLDER

Soldered joints are often found in runs of copper water supply pipe. If one should need repair, all you will need is an inexpensive torch, the correct solder and flux, and a willingness to try.

Torches

Most hardware stores offer small, inexpensive torch kits. A typical kit will include a replaceable propane bottle, a regulator valve and a flame tip. The best of these kits offer a turbo tip that spins the flame as it exits the tip. Turbo tips are useful because they wrap flames around a pipe so that you do not have to heat both sides of a fitting. Any of these torch kits will work, however, and you should not have to invest more than $20.

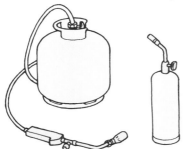

Bottle-type gas torches can be rented but inexpensive, hand-held torches also work well

Flux and solder

The next ingredient you will need is a good, self-cleaning flux. The right flux is critical to achieving a leakproof soldering job. Because you will sometimes need to reflux heated fittings, you will want to avoid soldering paste. Choose, instead, a can or jar of flux that has the consistency of butter. Then buy several acid brushes so that you can brush additional flux onto a hot fitting without burning yourself. Make sure that the flux you buy is self-cleaning. The cleaning agents in self-cleaning flux boil away any chemical residues and tarnish that build up on copper. With self-cleaning flux, you will have to clean only those fittings that are dirty or corroded.

Choosing the right solder is also important. Above-ground residential soldering should be done with 95/5 solder; 50/50 solder has been used for years, but the EPA has recently cited it as a source of potential lead poisoning. Resist any urging by sales people to buy acid-core solder for plumbing.

Preparing the joint

Start by making sure that both the end of the pipe and the inside of the fitting are free of dirt and corrosion. If needed, clean the surfaces to be soldered with emery cloth or a wire brush. Then apply flux to the end of the pipe. Flux as much of the pipe as will be covered by the fitting. Then push the pipe into the fitting. When the pipe is fitted and secured with pipe hooks every 4 to 6 feet, you will be ready to solder several joints.

Applying solder

Because comfort and dexterity are important when soldering at odd angles, you will not want to hold solder by the spool. Cut about 2 feet of solder from the spool and wrap all but about 10 inches around your hand. Then pull the loop from your hand and squeeze it into a handle. Finally, bend the last 2 inches of the 10-inch wire at a 90-degree angle. This will give you the greatest maneuverability. The 90-degree angle of the solder wire will allow you to reach all sides of a fitting simply by rotating your wrist. As you use the solder, unwind more from the loop and bend a new angle 2 inches from the end of the wire.

If you are right-handed, place the solder in your right hand and the torch in your left. Light the torch and open the valve all the way. Place the torch tip so that the flame hits the hub of the fitting straight on. The tip should be about ¾ inch away from the fitting. If yours is not a turbo tip, heat one side for a few seconds until the flux begins to liquefy, and then move around the fitting and heat the far side while touching the solder to the fitting.

Keep the solder opposite the torch flame and continue to touch the fitting until the solder liquefies and wraps around the fitting quickly. As soon as the fitting is hot enough to pull solder around it, take the heat away and push solder into the fitting.

If the fitting will not take solder easily, pull the solder away and heat the fitting for a few more seconds. Then push the solder in. A ¾-inch fitting should take about ¾ inch of solder. When the hub has taken enough solder, move onto the next hub on that fitting. Always start with the bottom joint on a fitting and work up. When all joints on that fittings are soldered, watch the rim of the last joint carefully. When the fitting starts to cool, it will draw solder into the joint. This cooling draw is your assurance that the joint is a good one. If the solder around the rim of a joint stays puddled and does not draw in when it cools, heat until the solder liquefies, and then wait again for it to draw in slightly. When you are satisfied that the last joint is a good one, wipe the fitting of excess solder and move on to the next fitting. When all fittings have cooled, turn the water on and check each joint periodically for leaks.

FIRE PRECAUTIONS

Of course, working with a torch requires a few precautionary measures. When soldering a fitting that is next to a floor joist or any combustible surface, you will have to protect that surface. The simplest protection method is to fold a piece of sheet metal over so that it has a double thickness. Then slide this double wall of metal between the fitting and the combustible surface. If you cannot sufficiently protect the area around the fitting, you may wish to solder that section elsewhere and install it already soldered.

To avoid scorching the rubber washers and diaphragms inside valves, always solder them with the handles turned open. This will defuse enough heat to keep the seals from being ruined. Remember, use only as much heat as is needed to draw the solder evenly around the joint. The most common beginner mistake is too much heat, not too little.

Using a heat shield
When soldering near a combustible surface, use a double-thickness of sheet metal as a shield.

SOLDER

TORCH

Bending solder
Always bend solder to achieve the greatest maneuverability.

FAUCET INSTALLATION AND REPAIR

Faucet installation has not changed much over the years. While plastic fasteners and flexible supply risers have made the job a little easier, the process remains much the same. These connections still need to be made carefully.

Replacing a faucet

The most troublesome part of replacing a faucet is getting the old faucet off. Start by shutting the faucet's water supply off, either at the meter or under the cabinet. Turn the faucet on to relieve the pressure. Then, loosen the nuts that connect the riser pipes to the supply lines and the faucet. A basin wrench will help you reach the coupling nuts high up under the cabinet. When these nuts are loose, bend the risers slightly so that they can be pulled out of the faucet and supply fittings.

Next, use a basin wrench to undo the nuts that hold the faucet to the sink. If the faucet is old and the nuts corroded, first spray penetrating oil on the threads. If this does not help loosen the nuts, use a small chisel and hammer and gently tap the nuts in a counter-clockwise direction to break them loose. Once broken loose, back the nuts off with a basin wrench.

In a few cases, even these methods will not free the fastening nuts. If this

happens to you, your only recourse is to saw through the nut with a hacksaw blade.

Some faucet styles mount from the bottom and are held to the sink or countertop by a locknut under the handle escutcheon. To remove a bottom-mounted faucet, first remove the handles, then the escutcheons. Escutcheons are usually screwed on and can be removed by threading them counterclockwise. Under the escutcheon, you will find the locknuts. Undo these nuts and the faucet should fall out.

Because years of soap and mineral buildup can leave a ridge around the edge of the faucet plate, you may have to clean the faucet area of the sink before installing a new faucet. A 50-50 mixture of white vinegar and warm water used in conjunction with a single-edged razor blade will help you remove this ridge. Just soak the buildup and scrape it away.

Installing a new faucet

After you've cleaned the sink, set the new faucet in place with the rubber or plastic spacer between the faucet and sink. Then reach under the sink and thread the new washers and nuts onto the faucet until the nuts are finger-tight. Before tightening the faucet nuts, however, go back and straighten the faucet so that the back of the coverplate is parallel with the back edge of the sink. When the faucet is straight, tighten the nuts with a basin wrench.

When the faucet is fastened in place, you will be ready to reconnect the supply risers. It is usually a good idea to start with new risers. Some municipal

codes allow PB riser pipes. If PB risers are permitted in your locale, use them. Because they are flexible and can be cut with a knife, you will find them much easier to use. PB risers, like copper or chrome risers, include a bulb-shaped head that fits into the ground joint surface of the faucet's hot and cold water inlets. The riser nuts slide onto the risers from the other end. When you tighten the riser nuts to the faucets, the fitted end of the riser is pressed into the ground joints and conforms to make a watertight seal. The supply line ends of the risers are connected with compression fittings.

Basic faucet repairs

Faucet repair is as simple or as complex as the design of the faucet involved. In general terms, there are four basic faucet mechanisms in use today. The oldest type, still used in many faucets and in most valves, uses the stem-and-seat principle. More recent faucet designs feature replaceable cores, rotating balls and ceramic disks. With each of these more recent faucet types,

the internal mechanism turns or rotates until holes in the mechanism align with holes in the faucet, allowing water to pass through. The degree of alignment determines the mixture of hot and cold water. In each case, repair is relatively simple and inexpensive. Only when a faucet body itself is defective is faucet replacement absolutely necessary. If your faucet falls apart, replace it.

SEE ALSO

Details for: ▷
Seat-and-spring faucets   351
Washerless faucets   352–353

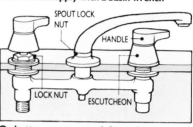

Disconnect supply with a basin wrench

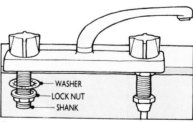

On bottom-mount, work from above

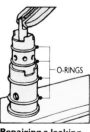

On top-mount, work from below

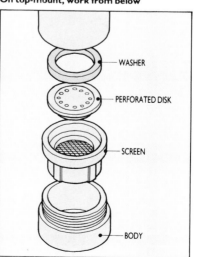

Uneven pressure
When one faucet has less pressure than others, clean its aerator.

Repairing a leaking spout collar
Cut the O-rings and replace them.

STEM-AND-SEAT FAUCETS

● **Heat-proof grease**
Before reassembling the faucet, cover all moving parts with heat-proof grease. As the name implies, heat-proof grease will not dissolve in hot water. It greatly increases the life of replacement parts and makes the faucet much easier to take apart the next time service is needed. Remember to grease the handle sockets as well. Heat-proof grease will separate dissimilar metals enough to prevent corrosion.

INDEX CAP

HANDLE SCREW

HANDLE

BONNET NUT

STEM

O-RING PACKING

STEM THREADS

SEAT WASHER

WASHER SCREW

BODY

Typical stem-and-seat faucet

Replacing stem packing

PACKING
STRING

Replacing stem packing
Wrap packing string around the stem and tighten the packing nut.

If a faucet leaks around the handle when you turn the water on, the packing washer is defective. Before replacing the stem, packing gland, packing nut and handle, check the packing washer. Packing washers are made of graphite, leather, rubber or nylon, depending on the age and make of the faucet. When a packing nut or packing gland is tightened, it compresses the packing washer which seals against the stem. If your faucet has a visible brand name, you can buy replacement packing washers. If you are unable to find a replacement washer, or if your faucet's original packing was made of packing string, then your best alternative is to repack the stem with graphite or plastic packing string. Simply wrap the stem below the nut several times and thread the nut in place. The string will compress and fill in any voids against the stem.

Repairing stem-and-seat faucets

To repair stem-and-seat faucets, start by removing the handles. Most handles have decorative coverplates under which you will find handle screws. These coverplates are also called "index caps" because they indicate hot and cold water. Pry the caps off and remove the screws. If a handle has not been removed recently, it may be stuck to the stem. Gently pry up under both sides of the handle with two screwdrivers to free the handle. If the handle will still not loosen, you may need to buy an inexpensive handle puller from your local hardware dealer.

On better faucets, all external parts are made of chromium-plated brass. Brass faucets usually come apart easily. Manufacturers of more competitive faucets, however, often substitute chrome-plated pot metal for brass on handles, coverplates and escutcheons. Pot metal will corrode, through electrolysis, when in contact with dissimilar metals. Pot metal handles, in particular, are often difficult to remove and are easily damaged when force is applied. If you must damage a handle to get it off, your best bet is to replace it with a universal-fit replacement handle.

When you have the handle off, undo the escutcheon so that you can get to the packing nut and locknut. When you

reach the locknut or packing gland, loosen it with a thin adjustable wrench. If the locknut backs out several rounds and then stops, turn the stem in or out, depending on the brand, to free the locknut. When the locknut is loose, back the stem out of the faucet. Most stems will turn out counterclockwise.

On the end of the stem you will find a rubber washer secured by a brass screw. Undo this screw and find a replacement washer that fits the rim of the stem. A tight fit is important here. The washer should not be too big or too small. Press the washer in place and replace the screw. Because brass screws can become brittle with age, you may wish to replace the washer screw as well. Washer screws often come with washer assortment packets.

The kind of seat your faucet has will determine the kind of replacement washer you will need. Recessed, beveled seats require beveled washers. Seats that have raised rims require flat washers to make a seal. When in doubt as to which type of washer you should use, check the shape of the seat. Because someone before you may have repaired your faucet with the wrong shape washer, using an old washer to determine the shape of the new is not a good idea.

DEALING WITH SEAT DAMAGE

When a defective washer is allowed to leak for an extended period of time, the pressure of the water will cut a channel in the faucet seat. For this reason, always repair a leaking faucet immediately. A defective seat will chew up new washers in short order. Always check the faucet seat when you replace a washer.

If you find a channel in the surface of a seat, replace the seat. A seat wrench will allow you to unscrew a removable seat from a faucet body.

Some seats are machined into the brass body of a faucet and therefore cannot be removed. If your faucet seats are pitted and cannot be replaced, your only alternative is to grind the entire seat rim to a level below the surface of the pit. While this may sound difficult, it is not. You can buy an inexpensive seat grinder from your local hardware dealer and once the faucet is apart, you can complete the job in a matter of minutes.

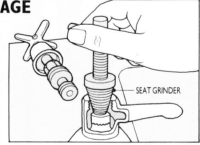

SEAT GRINDER

Damaged seats can be refurbished

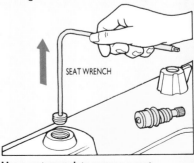

SEAT WRENCH

Use a seat wrench to remove a seat

SEAT-AND-SPRING FAUCETS

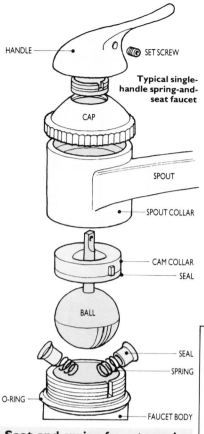

HANDLE

SET SCREW

Typical single-handle spring-and-seat faucet

CAP

SPOUT

SPOUT COLLAR

CAM COLLAR

SEAL

BALL

SEAL

SPRING

O-RING

FAUCET BODY

Repairing handle leaks

If your seat-and-spring faucet leaks around the handle but does not drip, all you have to do is tighten the body cap. The cap is the threaded dome that holds the mechanism in place. The repair kit comes with a small cap wrench, or if you prefer, you can use a slip-joint pliers to tighten a cap. You simply slip the wrench onto the cap and turn it clockwise until the leak stops. Do not overtighten. If you use a pliers on the knurled surface of the cap, wrap the jaws of the pliers with a soft cloth to avoid stripping chrome from the cap.

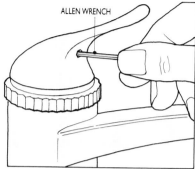

ALLEN WRENCH

Use an Allen wrench to remove handle

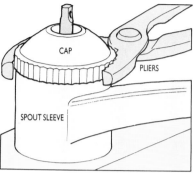

CAP

PLIERS

SPOUT SLEEVE

Use pliers to turn the cam cover

SEE ALSO

Details for: ▷
Faucet installation	349
Washerless faucets	352–353
Plumbing tools	486–491

Seat-and-spring faucet repairs

Seats-and-spring type faucets, one of a variety that have come to be known as 'washerless' faucets, have become quite popular in recent years, both because of their durability and because they are easy to repair. The operating mechanism of a seat-and-spring faucet consists of a stainless-steel or plastic ball that is turned and aligned with water openings in the faucet body as the single handle is manipulated. The openings in the faucet body contain spring-loaded rubber caps, or seats, which press against the globe and prevent leaking when in the off position. When this type of faucet drips, it is because these rubber cups and springs are worn.

Repair kits for seat-and-spring faucets are inexpensive and come with everything needed to completely rebuild a faucet. It is important to identify the faucet by brand name when asking for a repair kit in order to get the correct parts. The common brand names are Delta and Peerless. Kits come with complete instructions. The repairs you make will depend upon the location and nature of the leak.

REPLACING SEATS AND SPRINGS

If the faucet drips, you must take the faucet apart. This is easily enough done by using the proprietary cap wrench. Use the Allen wrench side of the tool to loosen the handle set screw. Pull the handle off. Then use the cap wrench to loosen and remove the cap. Under the cap you will find a nylon and rubber cam covering a stainless-steel ball. Remove the cam assembly and pull the ball up and out of the faucet body. Inside the faucet you will see two hollow rubber caps, or seats, mounted on two small springs.

Insert a needlenose pliers into the faucet body and pull the seats and springs out. Throw the worn seats and springs away. It is too easy to get the old confused with the new. Then slide the new springs and seats onto a screwdriver and slide them into the faucet holes. When the spring-loaded seats are in place, you will be ready to replace the ball-and-cam assembly.

The kit will come with a new cam seal as well. The cam assembly will have a tab on one side that corresponds with a slot in the faucet. Match the tab with the slot and press the cam assembly in place over the ball. You can then tighten the cap and replace the handle.

If your seat-and-spring faucet also leaks around the spout collar, you should replace the collar O-rings before putting the cap and handle back on. To replace collar O-rings, pull up evenly and firmly on the spout until it comes free. Use a knife to cut the old O-rings from the slots and slide the new rings over the body until they fit into the O-ring slots. Then grease the rings with liquid detergent or heatproof grease and press the spout collar back on, rotating it gently as you go.

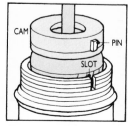

CAM

PIN

SLOT

Align the cam pin

SEAL

Retrieve seats and springs

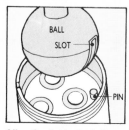

BALL

SLOT

PIN

Align the slot in the ball

WASHERLESS FAUCETS

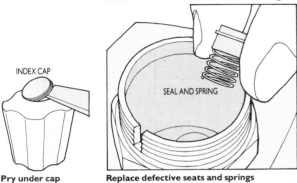

LOCK NUT

Remove the locknut to reach the cartridge

INDEX CAP

Pry under cap

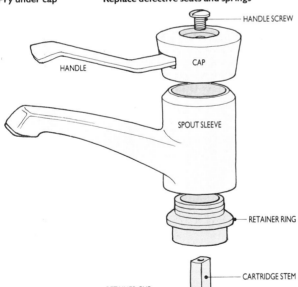

SEAL AND SPRING

Replace defective seats and springs

Repairing washerless two-handle faucets

Washerless faucets are also available in two-handle designs. These faucets are also easy to repair. The repair kit includes a cylinder, or cartridge, and seat assembly, which is similar to the seat-and-spring combination used in the single-handle washerless faucets. These cartridges come with new O-rings already installed.

To repair a two-handle washerless faucet, pry the index cap from the handle and remove the handle screw. Plastic two-handle washerless handles come off easily. When the handle is off, use a wrench to undo the locknut that holds the cartridge in place. Then pull the old cartridge assembly straight up and out of the faucet. Replace the seat and spring as you would with a single-handle faucet.

The new cartridges must first be properly aligned before they can be installed. On the side of each cartridge you will see a tab and a slot separated by an O-ring. The tab is called a key and its corresponding slot is called a keyway. You will also see a raised stop at the top of the cartridge next to the handle stem. Align the key so that it is directly over the keyway. Then insert the cartridge so the stop is facing the spout. If you are replacing hot and cold cartridges, both stops should be facing the spout. When the cartridge is properly positioned, press it into the faucet. Replace and tighten the locknut until it is snug. Press the handle onto the new stem and replace the handle screw and index cap.

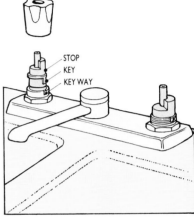

STOP
KEY
KEY WAY

Align keys and keyways

Repairing cartridge-type single-handle faucets

Cartridge-type washerless faucets have also enjoyed wide popular use because of their simplicity and durability. They are available in single-handle and two-handle versions. Unlike the single-handle seat-and-spring mechanism, the cartridge type has a core instead of a ball. This type of faucet is marketed widely under the Moen trade name.

All single-handle Moen faucets use the same core mechanism, but other aspects vary with price. The major differences are in exterior construction and style. In terms of repair, the only notable difference is in the way the spout/handle covers come off.

If your Moen single-handle faucet has a flat chrome coverplate with the trade name pressed into it, you must first pry the coverplate up with a knife to get to the handle screw. Other models have a plastic hood that covers the handle screw and top of the faucet. These hoods simply pull up and off. In the case of lavatory faucets, the handle screw is reached by prying off a plastic index cap at the top of the handle.

Below the handle you will find the core stem. If yours is a chrome coverplate model, you will also need to remove a retainer pivot nut. Just below the stem, or pivot nut, you will see a brass clip inserted into the side of the cartridge stem. This clip locks the cartridge in place. Assuming you have the water turned off, pull the clip out of the faucet with pliers. When the clip is removed, you will be able to pull the cartridge out of the faucet body.

Press the new core in place, making sure that the keys of the cartridge are aligned front to back. Seat the cartridge by pressing on the keys until the cartridge is in far enough to accept the clip. Then slide the clip back into the faucet body until it grips the far side of the faucet wall. Then replace the retainer pivot nut and handle. Make sure that the handle slips into the groove in the retainer pivot nut before replacing the screw. You will know that the handle is working properly when it lifts and lowers the stem of the cartridge smoothly. If the spout has been leaking when the faucet is in the on position, you should replace the spout collar O-rings before replacing the handle.

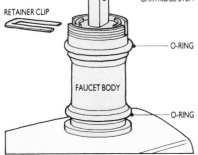

HANDLE SCREW
CAP
HANDLE
SPOUT SLEEVE
RETAINER RING
CARTRIDGE STEM
RETAINER CLIP
O-RING
FAUCET BODY
O-RING

Typical single-handle cartridge-type faucet

Repairing two-handle Moen faucets

Two-handle Moen kitchen and bath faucets also use cartridges for their internal mechanisms. The cartridges for two-handle faucets are smaller than single-handle cartridges of the same make. They are easy to install.

To remove a defective two-handle cartridge, start by removing the handle. The index cap will pry off with a thin-bladed knife so that you can get at the handle screw. Under the handle you will find a large nut that holds the cartridge in place. Undo this nut with pliers (**1**). Then lift the cartridge out by

the stem, pulling straight up.

To install a new cartridge, turn the cartridge stem in a counterclockwise direction (**2**) so that the holes of the cartridge are aligned (**3**). Then push the cartridge straight down into the faucet, making sure that the key at the top of the cartridge fits into the slot in the faucet. When you've seated the cartridge, screw the cartridge nut back on until it is hand-tight. Tighten with pliers until snug. Be careful not to strip the threads. Then replace the handle, handle screw and index cap.

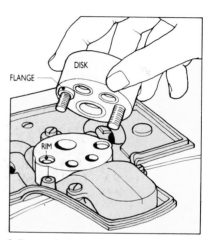

Moen assembly

1 Loosen lock nut

2 Turn cartridge stem

Repairing ceramic-disk faucets

When a ceramic-disk faucet leaks, it is likely to show up around the base of the faucet or on the floor below. Getting to the operational part of these faucets is a little different than with other models. Instead of prying off the index cap to remove the handle, you must tip the handle back to reveal a set screw under the front of the handle. Use an Allen wrench to loosen the screw. But having the handle removed still does not give you access to the internal mechanism. You must also remove the chrome faucet cover. With older models, you will need to loosen the pop-up drain lever and undo two brass screws from the underside of the faucet. Newer models have a slot screw in the handle

and a brass keeper ring that allows you to remove the cover from above.

When the faucet cover is off, you will find a ceramic disk secured by two brass bolts to the base of the faucet. Undo these bolts and the disk should lift off. Take this disk with you to your plumbing outlet and buy an identical replacement disk.

To install the new disk, align the ports of the disk with those of the faucet base and make sure that the flange under one of the cartridge bolt holes fits into the rim around one of the bolt holes in the body plate. When all is perfectly aligned, replace the disk bolts and refasten the faucet cover and handle. Then turn the water on and test for leaks.

3 Remove body to reach the disk

Sillcock repair

A sillcock is simply a stem-and-seat faucet with a long stem. Depending upon the length of the drain chamber, the stem can be from 6 to 30 inches long.

Start by shutting off the water at the meter. With the stem in the open position, loosen the locknut and pull the stem straight out. If the stem is particularly stubborn, twist and pull it out with a locking pliers. When you have the stem out, replace the washer, apply heat-proof grease and replace the stem.

Sillcocks often wear out faster than ordinary faucets because of a common error in judgment. As water continues to drain from the chamber after the flow has stopped, many homeowners continue to turn the handle. This extra, unnecessary pressure ruins stem washers in a hurry.

REPLACING FREEZELESS SILLCOCKS

Freezeless sillcocks differ from ordinary outside faucets in that they can be left on during freezing weather. Instead of stopping the water on the outside of the home, they stop water inside the home by means of a long faucet stem. The only way a freezeless sillcock can freeze is if a hose is left connected in cold weather or if it has been installed without sufficient pitch to drain. When either situation occurs, sillcocks will freeze and split just inside the home near the valve seat.

If a damaged sillcock is not buried in a basement ceiling, replacing it will be easy. First, shut the water off and undo the screws from the outside flange. Then, unthread the sillcock from the pipe in the basement. If it is soldered to a copper line, you will have to cut the line to pull the sillcock out. With the old sillcock out, buy a new one the same length and thread it onto the supply line. Copper connections, of course, will require soldering a splicing coupling between the cut pipe and sillcock.

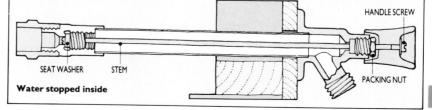

Water stopped inside

• **Replacing a concealed sillcock** Often sillcocks are buried in walls and ceilings. To avoid a troublesome wall or ceiling repair, measure carefully to determine the exact location of the connection and cut a 6-by-10-inch hole in the drywall or plaster. Make the change through this hole and then cover it with a furnace grill. The grill will successfully hide the opening and the louvers will allow warm air in around the sillcock, thus preventing a future freeze. Because a sillcock must drain any water left between its seat and hose connection, make sure that you install yours with enough pitch to drain the chamber completely.

LAVATORIES AND SINKS

INSTALLING A FAUCET AND POP-UP

Replacing a wall-hung lavatory with a vanity cabinet and countertop basin will greatly improve the appearance of your bathroom while adding valuable storage space. This is one project that will add real value to your home with less than a weekend's time invested. The amount you spend on materials will depend on the size and construction of the cabinet and the type of faucet and basin you choose.

How to replace a wall-hung lavatory with a vanity and basin

The first step is to measure the space around the existing lavatory to determine what size cabinet your bathroom will allow. Factory-made cabinets and countertops come in standard dimensions to fit many opening widths and depths. Buying one of these cabinets is generally the less expensive alternative to having one custom made. If the space you have will not accept a standard size cabinet, your next option is to have a cabinet built to fit the available space.

Countertops and lavatory basins are other major considerations. For standard-size cabinets, cultured-marble tops with basins molded into them are a good choice. Another option is to mount a china, cast-iron, plastic or enameled-steel basin in a particleboard deck that has been finished with a decorative plastic laminate. Countertop coverings are available in a variety of textures and colors to match nearly any home style or decor.

If your cabinet is custom made for a nonstandard dimension, a cultured-marble top is not likely to fit. Beyond this restriction, the combination you choose will be a matter of taste and adhering to your budget.

Removing a wall-hung lavatory

To remove a wall-hung lav, start by disconnecting the trap and water risers. If your lav does not have shutoff valves between its risers and supply lines, now might be a good time to install them. With stops on both supply lines, you will not have to shut the entire system down while you work.

When the piping has been disconnected, check to see if the back of the lavatory is secured to the wall by anchor screws. These screws will be located at the back of the lav just under the apron. If anchor screws are present, remove them. Then grab the lav by its sides and pull up. It should lift right off the mounting bracket. Remove the mounting bracket by undoing the screws that fasten it to the wall.

Before installing the new vanity, check to see if the wall above the vanity needs to be repaired or painted. Often the screw holes from the mounting bracket will show above the new vanity. Filling these holes and other cosmetic repairs may be necessary before the vanity can be set in place.

With the opening ready, slide the new vanity in place and secure it to the wall with long screws through the back of the cabinet. In some cases you may have to cut openings for the drainpipe and supply lines. With the cabinet in place, you are ready to set the countertop or premolded top and basin. In the case of a cultured-marble top, simply set it on the vanity and glue it to the cabinet top with construction adhesive. In the case of a factory or custom-made countertop, screw the top to the corner brackets of the cabinet from the underside.

Cutting a basin opening

The lav basin you buy will come with a paper template. Position this template where you want it on the countertop and tape it down. Then use a jigsaw (◁) to cut the opening for the basin along the dotted line of the template. To avoid chipping the plastic laminate, use a fine-tooth blade and advance the saw with steady, even pressure.

Because it is much easier to install a faucet and pop-up assembly sitting down than while on your back in a cramped space, you will want to fasten the faucet and pop-up to the basin before installing the basin in its countertop opening.

To install a lavatory faucet, insert the faucet supply shanks through the basin faucet holes. Then slide the large spacing washer onto the shanks from below and tighten the locknut on each shank. Make sure that the faucet is centered before tightening the locknuts.

To install a pop-up drain assembly, pack putty around the drain flange and thread the pop-up waste pipe into the basin gasket until the flange is seated in the drain opening. Follow by threading the tailpiece into the pop-up waste pipe.

To connect the pop-up mechanism, insert the lift rod into the opening at the back of the faucet. Then slide one end of the adjustment lever onto the lift rod and the other onto the pop-up lever. Finally, pull the pop-up lever all the way down and tighten the adjustment screw.

When the basin is in place and hooked up to its trap and water supplies, use water-soluble latex caulk to seal the basin to the counter. Wet the areas to be caulked first. Then apply a bead of caulk around the faucet base. Push caulk into the cracks. Then wipe all excess caulk away with a damp cloth.

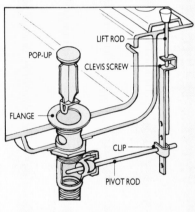

Typical pop-up drain assembly

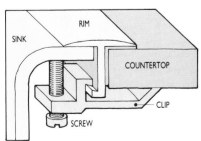

Removing a wall-hung lavatory Pull the lavatory off the wall bracket.

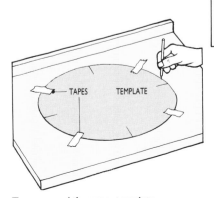

Trace around the paper template

Typical sink rim fastening details

REPLACING A KITCHEN SINK

Replacing a kitchen sink is not a difficult task. How you proceed, however, depends upon whether or not you replace the countertop as well.

Removing the old sink

If you plan to replace your old countertop, there is probably no need to pull the sink from the counter. Simply disconnect the trap, disposer and water supplies, remove the screws from the underside of the countertop and pull the sink and countertop up together. If you wish to save the basket strainers, disposer flange or faucet, these are much easier to remove when the countertop has been removed.

If you plan to save the countertop and replace only the sink, first remove the old sink without damaging the countertop. Start by disconnecting the water supplies, trap and disposal. Then loosen the clips around the underside of the sink rim. A special tool, called a Hudec wrench, will allow you to reach these clips with less strain, but a simple nut-driver socket will work.

When the clips have all been removed, lift the sink straight up by placing one hand around the faucet base and another through the disposer opening. With the sink out, you will likely need to clean a mineral, putty and soap buildup from the counter where the old sink rim rested. A putty knife and household cleanser work well in removing any buildup, but work carefully to avoid scratching the surface.

Replacement sinks

The replacement sink you choose will have one of three possible rims. If you select an enameled cast-iron sink, you will be able to choose between a "self-rimming" model and one that requires a sink rim to fasten it to the countertop. The "self-rimming" type has a rolled edge that rests on top of the counter and is caulked in place. The edge of the sink is raised and sets above the counter. The disadvantage of a self-rimming cast-iron sink is that when wiping the counter, you cannot simply push spills and food particles into the sink. As a result, some homeowners prefer a cast-iron sink that fits flush with the countertop. For a flush fit, choose a sink that uses a sink rim to suspend it in the counter opening. Sink rims are also required on porcelain steel sinks. A third rim seal is found on stainless-steel sinks. No separate rim is needed but rim clamps are used to fasten the sink to the countertop.

Cutting into a new countertop

Most new sinks will come with a paper template to help you make the right size cut in a new countertop. Position this template on the counter over the sink cabinet so that it is centered. Try to leave at least ½ inch between the sink rim and the backsplash. Then tape the template down and make the cut through the paper with a saber saw. It helps if you can have someone hold the section being cut from below so that it does not fall through and crack the countertop.

If you wish to install a used sink in a new countertop, you will have to do without a template. You can measure the dimensions to be cut, but it is easier and more exact to lay the sink rim on the counter and trace around it. Remember that your cut will need to be made from the center of the rim so that the outside of the rim can grip the countertop. If you are installing a self-rimming sink without a template, remove the faucet and lay the sink upside down on the counter. Trace around it lightly with a pencil. Remove the sink and draw a new line ½ inch inside the traced line. Then make the cut on the inside line.

SEE ALSO

Details for: ▷
Installing faucets	349
Plumbing tools	486–491

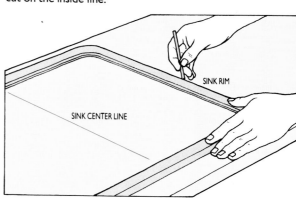

Set rim in place on counter and trace around it

Mounting a stainless-steel sink

Stainless-steel sinks are available in a wide range of prices. The more shiny the surface, the more expensive the sink. Stainless-steel sinks do not require sink rims to hold them in place. Instead, the rim of the sink rests on the top of the counter and is held against the countertop by fastening clips from the underside of the counter. Stainless-steel sinks will usually fit the same opening as a sink rim and therefore make good replacements. Measure before you buy.

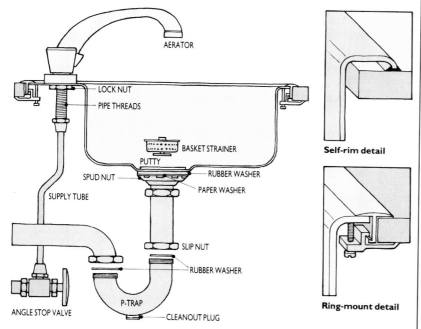

AERATOR

LOCK NUT

PIPE THREADS

BASKET STRAINER

PUTTY

SPUD NUT

RUBBER WASHER

PAPER WASHER

SUPPLY TUBE

SLIP NUT

RUBBER WASHER

ANGLE STOP VALVE

P-TRAP

CLEANOUT PLUG

Typical sink installation details

Self-rim detail

Ring-mount detail

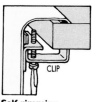

Self-rimming stainless-steel sink mounting detail

CLIP

355

STRAINERS AND DISPOSERS

The chrome trim you see in the drains of your sink are not part of the sink basin. They are merely the most visible parts of your disposer and drain spud. As such, they can be replaced when cosmetic or mechanical problems arise. The job is involved but not difficult and requires only a few tools.

SEE ALSO
◁ Details for:
Kitchen sinks   355

Replacing a basket strainer/drain spud

To remove a basket strainer, disconnect the drainpipe from the basket drain spud. Then use a spud wrench or a large adjustable pliers to loosen the locknut. To keep the strainer body from turning when you loosen the locknut, insert the handles of a small pliers into the drain crosspiece from the top. While you turn the nut from below, have someone hold the pliers with a wrench or screwdriver from above.

If the nut is corroded on the strainer body, you may need to use a small chisel and a hammer to break the threads loose. If the hammer and chisel do not loosen the threads, use a hacksaw blade to cut the locknut. Tape one end of a hacksaw blade to create a handle. Cut across the nut in an upward, diagonal motion.

When the locknut is loose, push the strainer body up through the drain opening. Clean the brittle, old putty from the recessed flange of the sink opening. Then roll new putty out between the palms of your hands so that the putty forms a soft rope about ½ inch in diameter. Press this putty around the flange of your new strainer and press the strainer in place.

Then slide the rubber washer onto the spud from below. Next, slide the fiber washer on, followed by the new locknut. Tighten the locknut until it no longer turns or until the strainer body also begins to turn. From above, clear the excess putty from the rim of the strainer and tighten the locknut again.

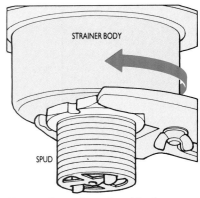

Use a spud wrench or adjustable pliers

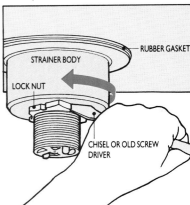

If the spud nut sticks, tap it loose

Installing a disposer in an existing sink

A disposer can be installed in any sink that has a full-size drain opening. All you will need is a disposer waste kit and access to electricity.

To install a disposer in an existing two-compartment sink, you must first remove the waste connector that joins the two drains to the P-trap. Then remove the strainer and clean any remaining putty from the recessed sink flange.

With the basket strainer removed, you are ready to install the disposer sink flange. Press putty around the sink flange and press the flange into the recessed sink opening. Then slide the rubber gasket, fiber gasket and mounting ring onto the spud from below. While holding the flange in place, snap the retaining ring over the ridge on

the mounting ring. Tighten the screws on the mounting ring until nearly all putty is forced from between the sink and flange, then trim the putty.

With the flange mounted in the sink opening, attach the disposer. Some disposers fasten to the flange by means of a stainless-steel band. Hold the disposer up so that the rubber collar on the disposer fits over the flange. Then tighten the stainless-steel band with a nut-driver or screwdriver.

Other models attach to their flanges by means of fastening rings. If the model you buy has this type of fastener, hold the disposer up to the flange and turn the fastening ring until its guides catch the tabs on the mounting ring. Then turn the fastening ring until it seats over the ridges on the upper mounting ring.

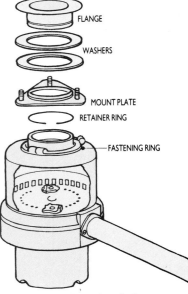

Typical disposer flange installation

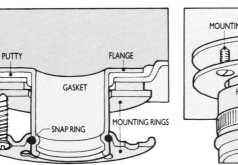

Fastening ring assembly

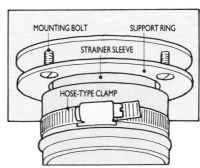

Hose clamp connection

CONNECTING TO WASTE LINES

Most disposers on the market today come with a discharge tube that connects directly to the P-trap under your sink. These discharge tubes, however, work only if you are installing a disposer in a single-compartment sink or if you are replacing a disposer that was previously hooked up to its own trap.

When connecting a disposer under a two-compartment sink, both compartments can be drained through a single trap. To make this connection, do not use the discharge tube that came with the disposer. Instead, buy a disposer waste kit. This kit consists of a baffled tee, a rubber gasket and a flanged tailpiece. Install the tee vertically between the P-trap and the tailpiece extension from the other compartment. The center of the tee branch opening should be only slightly lower than the discharge opening of the disposer.

With the tee installed at the proper height, slip the rubber gasket onto the flange of the tailpiece and hold it between the disposer opening and the tee opening. The tailpiece will be longer than needed, so you will have to cut to fit. Insert the flange in the disposer discharge opening and hold the other end of the tailpiece against the hub of the tee to determine the desired length. Remember to include the depth of the hub in your measurement.

Next, slide the metal flange onto the tailpiece followed by the compression nut and compression ring. Insert the compression end in the hub of the tee and the gasket end into the disposer. Bolt the flange to the disposer and tighten the compression nut to the tee.

To keep cooking grease from clinging to the sidewalls of the disposer and drain, always run cold water through your disposer when the motor is on. Cold water causes grease to coagulate and flow through the pipes. Hot water thins grease and allows it to build up in pipes.

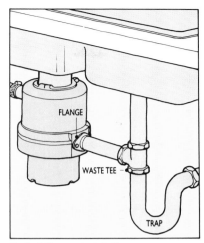
Typical disposer installation

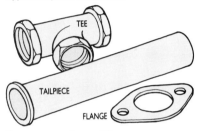
Components of waste kit

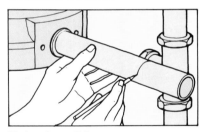
Mark and cut tailpiece

Waste flange tailpiece

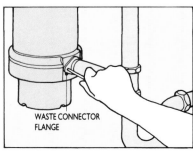
Fasten the flange screws

ELECTRIC HOOKUPS

If you are installing a disposer in a sink that has not had a disposer before, you will have to find some way to get electricity to the disposer and to a switch near the sink. If the basement ceiling beneath your sink is not finished, the easiest alternative might be to run a separate cable from your service panel (▷) into the wall behind your cabinet to a switch and then back down into the cabinet to your disposer. To meet code requirements, however, the leader wire in the cabinet must be encased in flexible conduit (▷).

If this option is not available to you, then you may wish to convert an existing outlet box above your counter into a switch box and fish a short length of wire down the wall and into the cabinet to the disposer.

Once inside the cabinet, the electrical hookup is simple. Remove the coverplate from the bottom of the disposer and pull out the white and black wires. Then, using plastic insulating connectors, connect the two insulated wires from the switch box to the insulated wires in the disposer. Connect black to black and white to white. Then fasten the uninsulated ground wire from the switch to the ground screw inside the disposer. Replace the coverplate and test the disposer.

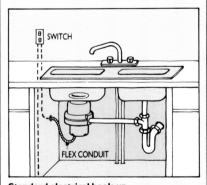
Standard electrical hook-up

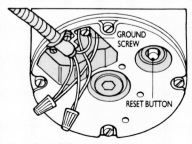
Bottom view of disposer

● **Servicing your disposer**
Disposers work very well on most foods but have real problems with anything hard or stringy. Chicken bones, fruit seeds, eggshells and celery can stop a disposer cold. When the motor pulls against too much resistance, a safety breaker built into the disposer will trip, cutting the power to the motor. To get a stopped disposer started again, first dislodge the motor blades from the blockage. To do this, use the wrenchette that came with the disposer to reverse the motor manually. The wrench should fit into a key slot on the bottom side of the disposer. Turn the motor back and forth until it spins easily in both directions. Next, find the reset button on the underside of the disposer and press it. Finally, run cold water through the disposer drain and turn the disposer on. This wrench and reset procedure will free most blockages. If the disposer stops again, repeat the procedure.

INSTALLING A BUILT-IN DISHWASHER

Like all things mechanical, dishwashers wear out. Hiring someone to replace your old dishwasher can easily add $100 to the price of a new one. Dishwashers are not terribly difficult to install, but one

precaution is in order. Because you must work with both electricity and water, make sure that you shut the electricity off at the main service panel before beginning dishwasher removal or installation.

Removing your old dishwasher

After shutting off the electrical current to your old dishwasher, look under the sink for the valve that shuts the water off (◁). In many cases this valve will be an in-line globe valve that is soldered or threaded in place. If you find no valve isolating your dishwasher, you will have to shut off the supply to the entire house at the meter.

With the water shut off, disconnect the discharge hose from the garbage disposer or the dishwasher tailpiece under the sink. In each case, the discharge hose will be held in place with a hose clamp. Simply undo the clamp and pull the hose out.

Next, remove the cover panel beneath the door of the dishwasher. This will give you access to the water and electrical connections. You may have to open the door to gain access to these screws. When the screws are removed, the panel should lift off.

Under the dishwasher, on the left-hand side near the front, you will find the water supply pipe and fitting attached to the solenoid valve. In most cases, the supply pipe will be ⅜-inch soft copper and the fitting will be a ½-inch threaded male iron pipe by ⅜-inch compression angle adapter. This fitting is used so universally on dishwashers that it is called a

"dishwasher ell." Loosen the compression nut and pull the copper tubing out. Keep a shallow cake pan handy to catch the water trapped in the line. Leave the copper tubing in place under the dishwasher, in most cases it can be connected directly to the new dishwasher unit.

Near the solenoid valve you will see the metal box that contains the electrical connection. Undo the screws from the coverplate and pull the wires out of the box. Undo the connections of the three wires and save the plastic connectors for the new installation.

Most dishwashers are fitted with brackets that fasten to the underside of the countertop. Remove the screws from these brackets, but before you pull the machine out, turn each of the four leveling legs in so that the top of the dishwasher will clear the edge of the countertop. Then tilt the dishwasher back and slide a large piece of cardboard under both front legs. This will keep you from tearing or gouging your floor covering. With everything disconnected and the cardboard in place, ease the old dishwasher out. Before hauling the old dishwasher away, however, tip it up, and remove the dishwasher ell from the water supply inlet. You may need it for your new supply connection.

Installing your new dishwasher

The dishwasher you buy will come in a cardboard box and will be bolted to a wooden skid. Cut the box around the bottom and lift it off. Then tilt the dishwasher up and undo the lag bolts from the skid. Remove the access panel and thread the dishwasher ell into place. Be sure to use pipe joint sealant tape or pipe joint compound on the male threads of the ell. Tighten the ell until nearly snug and then tighten one more round until the compression nut points in the direction of the existing water supply pipe.

Slide the dishwasher up to the cabinet and start the drain hose through the existing opening at the back of the cabinet. Slowly push the dishwasher into place. As the dishwasher goes in, have someone pull the discharge hose into the sink cabinet.

Align the sides of the dishwasher evenly in the cabinet. Make sure that the front of the dishwasher (not the front of the door) is flush with the cabinet. Then extend the leveling legs so that the fastening brackets meet the bottom of the countertop. Open and shut the door several times to test it. If the door rubs against the cabinet stiles, adjust the position of the dishwasher and then fasten the brackets to the countertop with short screws.

TESTING FOR LEAKS

Before replacing the access panel, run the dishwasher through an entire cycle so that you can check your work. If the frame of the dishwasher vibrates too much, you may need to adjust one of the leveling legs. If a small amount of water appears beneath the water connections, a quick tightening of compression nuts will usually correct the problem. Be careful not to overtighten. If the pump motor or electrical features fail to work, check the fuse or breaker.

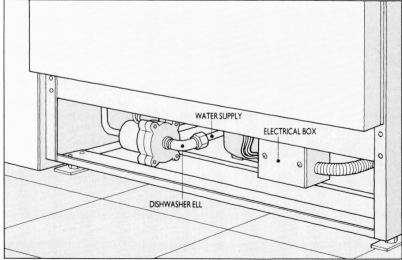

Typical dishwasher installation

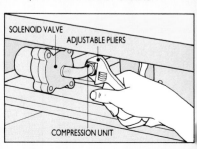

CONNECTING A DISHWASHER

Connecting the discharge hose

A discharge hose has an inside diameter of ⅝ inch, which is smaller than the fitting on a garbage disposer. You will need to compensate for this difference by installing a dishwasher adapter kit between disposer and discharge hose. This adapter is merely a rubber fitting that enlarges in ½-inch increments from ½ inch to 1⅛ inches. Each end is banded with hose clamps. Cut the adapter at the approximate size and insert the hose directly into it. Then band the adapter to the hose.

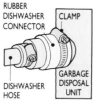

In-line dishwasher tailpiece

Dishwasher waste kit

The most important thing to remember when hooking up a discharge hose, however, is that the hose must arch high up in the cabinet before descending to the disposer or dishwasher tailpiece. If your kitchen sink ever backs up, bacterial-laden sewage will flow into your dishwasher if no loop is there to stop it.

Some codes may require that a vacuum breaker be installed in the discharge hose. A vacuum breaker provides an air gap that prevents siphoning, and because the hose connects to it just under the countertop, it creates its own loop. The most likely spot to install a vacuum breaker is in the fourth hole in your sink. If no extra sink hole exists, cut a hole in your countertop with a hole saw. The top half of the vacuum breaker will fit on the top and the hose attachments will fit under the counter.

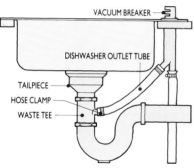

Some codes require a vacuum breaker

Making the water connection

If the previous water connection was made in ⅜-inch O.D. or I.D. soft copper pipe, the new connection will be easy. With the dishwasher ell transferred from the old dishwasher to the new, all you will have to do is apply pipe joint compound to the ferrule already on the pipe, insert the end of the copper into the ell and tighten the compression nut.

If your old dishwasher was piped in rigid copper with soldered joints, the process becomes a little more complicated. Rigid copper supply pipes enter the dishwasher compartment in one of two ways. The most common approach is directly through the floor. In this case a union is located under the dishwasher, and a valve is located just below the floor in the basement. If the water supply does not come through the floor, then it will take off from the hot water supply line in the sink cabinet, enter the dishwasher compartment and travel along the floor to the dishwasher water inlet. In either case, it is usually best to cut the supply line just after the valve and install a ⅝ × ⅜-inch compression adapter. You will then be able to run ⅜-inch soft copper pipe through the cabinet wall or kitchen floor to the compression end of the dishwasher ell. If manufacturer specifications insist on larger supply lines, use larger soft copper pipe.

Making the electrical connection

Most codes require that the non-metallic sheathed cable that extends from the wall to the dishwasher within the dishwasher compartment be encased in flexible conduit (▷). If your wire is not, now is a good time to do it. Just slide a length of conduit over the wire so that it enters the drywall. Then cut the other end so that it can be fastened to the electrical box on the dishwasher.

With the conduit in place, use plastic wire connectors to connect the respective wires inside the box. Attach black to black, white to white and fasten the ground wire to the ground screw inside the box.

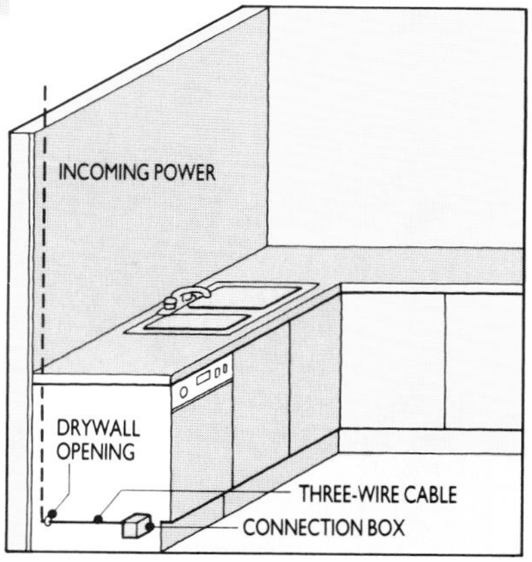

SEE ALSO

Details for: ▷

Flexible conduit	334
Wiring a dishwasher	329

A dishwasher ell adapts soft copper to a solenoid inlet

Run a new cable from service panel

KEEP YOUR DISHWASHER WORKING SMOOTHLY

If you are installing your home's first dishwasher, you should also have your kitchen drain line cleaned. Often a partially plugged drain line will accommodate the relatively low output of a kitchen sink, but when a dishwasher is added, the line will overflow. If you snake the line first, you will prevent the chance of water damage. Because a dishwasher forces a lot of water through a drain line and because that water is always very hot, a snaked kitchen line will remain clean almost indefinitely.

Dishwashers are designed to retain some water. Their pumps contain rubber O-rings and seals that must stay wet. Without this water, your dishwasher's seals will dry out, causing the pump to seize up or leak. If you are going to be away from your home for two weeks or longer, pour a thin layer of mineral oil into the base of your dishwasher. The oil will float on top of the water and seal it so that evaporation does not occur.

Contrary to popular belief, dishwashers do not sterilize dishes. The water temperature would have to be at least 180 degrees F to sterilize, and water at that temperature is a safety hazard at your faucets and in your shower. You should set your water heater between 135 and 140 degrees F. To see what your current hot water temperature reads, use a meat thermometer under one of your faucets. Make sure you hold it there long enough for the thermometer to give an accurate reading.

TOILET INSTALLATION AND REPAIR

There are several reasons why you might need to remove a toilet. If you wish to install a new one, of course, you will first have to remove the old. You might also need to repair part of the bathroom floor or replace a broken cast-iron stool flange. If you intend to install new vinyl floor covering, you may wish to remove the toilet and reset it after the new flooring is down. Installing or resetting a toilet is not a difficult job, but it is one that contains a number of pitfalls. Learning to avoid or work around these pitfalls is at least half the job.

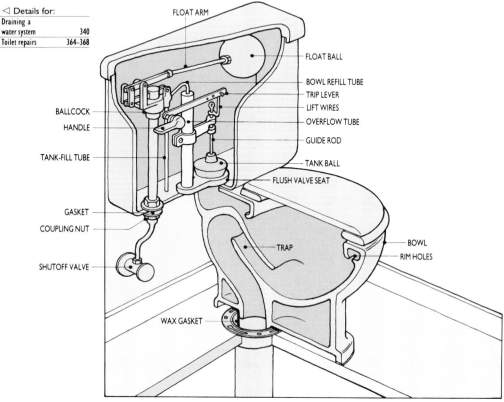

FLOAT ARM
FLOAT BALL
BOWL REFILL TUBE
TRIP LEVER
LIFT WIRES
OVERFLOW TUBE
GUIDE ROD
TANK BALL
FLUSH VALVE SEAT
BALLCOCK
HANDLE
TANK-FILL TUBE
GASKET
COUPLING NUT
SHUTOFF VALVE
TRAP
BOWL
RIM HOLES
WAX GASKET

The basic components of a toilet

Removing an existing toilet

While toilets are heavy and unwieldy, they are also fragile. To complicate the matter, old brass bolts and working parts become brittle with age and fall apart easily. If you wish only to remove a toilet in order to lay flooring, don't separate the tank from the bowl. While the unit will be heavier to move, you will avoid the possibility of damaging tank bolts and spud gasket seals.

Start by shutting off the water at the stool supply valve. Then flush the toilet and sponge the remaining water out of the tank. When the tank is dry, use a paper cup to dip the remaining water out of the bowl. Then, undo the water supply at the valve.

Next, pry the bolt caps from the base of the stool. Under these caps you will find the closet bolts. Older stools may have four bolts instead of the two bolts found on more modern stools. The front two bolts will be lag bolts with removable nuts and the back two will be standard closet bolts mounted through the stool flange. Use a small adjustable wrench to remove the nuts.

When you have the closet nuts loose and the supply tube disconnected, rock the bowl slightly in each direction to break it free from the floor and bowl gasket. Then grab the toilet by the bowl rim just in front of the tank and lift up. Because the bowl gasket will be sticky and dirty, have a newspaper ready to set the stool on. Then use a putty knife to scrape the remaining wax or putty from the stool horn and stool flange. Discard the old stool bolts. They are usually too damaged to be reused.

Resetting a stool

Before resetting a toilet, you will need to buy a new stool gasket and two new closet bolts. Stool gaskets come in two varieties. You can buy a traditional bowl wax or a rubber gasket. The advantages of a bowl wax are that one size fits all and that it costs much less than a rubber gasket. The disadvantage is that once used, a bowl wax cannot be used again. A rubber gasket can be used over and over again and tends to be more forgiving of beginner error.

Slide new closet bolts into the slots in the closet flange and center them so that each is the same distance away from the wall. Then press the stool gasket down on the flange. With these two items in place, you are ready to set the stool and fasten it down.

Lift the toilet as before, by the bowl rim near the tank, and carry it over to the flange. Carefully align the holes in the stool base with the closet bolts and slowly set the stool down. Press down evenly with all your weight. Then slide the cap retainers, closet washers and nuts onto the closet bolts and tighten each side a little at a time. When the base meets the floor and the nuts on the closet bolts seem snug, try rocking the bowl a little. If it moves, tighten the closet nuts another round. If the bowl does not move, stop. Both flanges and toilet bowls can break if you overtighten the bolts.

Use the stool a few days and then check the closet bolt nuts again. If the bowl has settled, tighten each nut another round or so until they feel snug. Then use a small hacksaw to saw the closet bolts off above the nuts. Finally, snap the bolt caps in place.

Clean away any wax

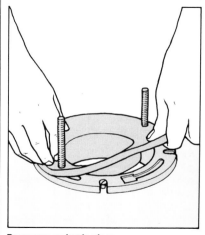

Press new gasket in place

Making the water connection

If you are resetting a toilet that you've just recently taken up, chances are you will be able to use the original stool supply tube. Apply a thin layer of pipe joint compound to the compression ferrule. Insert the compression end into the stool valve and then push down on the valve to gain the clearance needed to slide the cone washer end into the ballcock. If you cannot push the valve down, bend the supply tube slightly to gain the clearance you need. When both ends are in place, straighten the tube and tighten the compression nut.

If you add tile or another layer of flooring, you will not be able to use the original supply tube. The good news is that installing a new supply tube will probably be easier anyway, thanks to improved, more forgiving supply tube materials and designs.

While chromium-plated copper supply tubes are flexible and bendable, they kink very easily. And if the bend is too close to the end of the tube, the compression ferrule and the nuts will not slide over the pipe or seal properly. To avoid these installation problems, choose chromium-plated copper supplies that are ribbed. These more flexible supplies can almost be tied into knots without kinking. In tight situations, you can create a loop in the supply just to avoid cutting it to size.

Also on the market are plastic supply tubes encased in stainless-steel mesh. The plastic makes it flexible and the steel mesh makes it tough and durable. While this type of supply tube is more costly, it may be worth your while in time saved.

And finally, polybutylene plastic tubes are very flexible, inexpensive, corrosion-proof and easy to use. The problem with PB supply tubes, however, is that they are not universally accepted by code authorities. You will have to check with your local code administrators to see if they are allowable in your area.

No matter which type of supply tube you choose, you will find that the end that connects to the ballcock of your stool will be shaped to accept either a flat washer or a cone washer. The other end is designed to accept the compression nut and ferrule from the stool valve.

If the supply tube you intend to use must be cut to size, hold it against the ballcock threads and estimate how much

you will have to bend it to make it meet the stool valve. Then make the two bends as near the ballcock end of the tube as possible. To avoid kinking the tube without using a tubing bender, apply steady even pressure at several points along the tube.

Hold the supply in place again and mark where the cut should be made. Be sure to add the depth of the valve socket to the length of the supply. Use a wheel cutter to make the cut. Then slide the ballcock nut on the tube from the unshaped end, followed by the compression nut and ferrule. Fit the compression end into the stool valve socket and the shaped end against the tapered ballcock and tighten the nuts. Tighten the compression nut one full round after you feel resistance. When tightening the ballcock nut, reach into the tank and hold the ballcock to keep it from spinning.

The procedure with other types of supplies is the same, except that with flexible supplies, you may not have to cut them to fit. PB supply tubes can be cut with a knife and come with their own plastic ferrules. Plastic supplies and ferrules should not be tightened as much as copper or brass—snug plus a half turn is usually plenty.

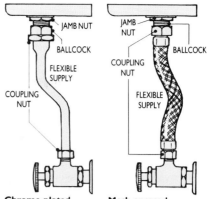

Chrome-plated tubing   **Mesh-encased polymer tubing**

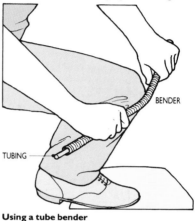

Using a tube bender

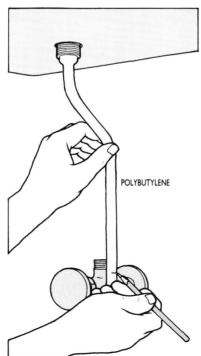

Mark and cut tubing

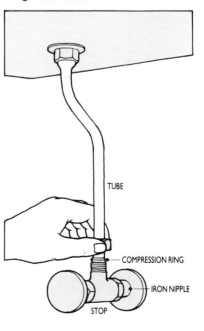

Connect to valve with compression fitting

SETTING A NEW STOOL

Your new toilet will come in two boxes. One will contain the bowl and the other the tank. You will have to install the bowl first, but open both boxes. Inside the tank box, you will find closet bolt caps and retainers needed to install the bowl.

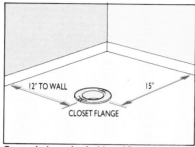

Center bolts on both sides of flange

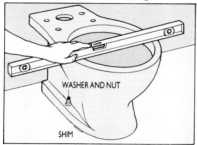

WASHER AND NUT

SHIM

Shim level when floor is uneven

Typical tank assembly
1 Tank bolt
2 Rubber washer
3 Tank washer
4 Tank cushion
5 Spud nut
6 Spud washer

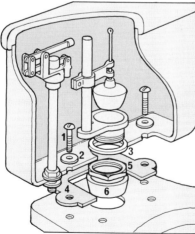

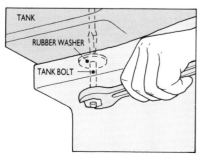

TANK

RUBBER WASHER

TANK BOLT

Tighten bolts until snug

Fitting a new toilet and tank

Insert new closet bolts into the slots of the stool flange so that both are the same distance from the wall. Then center the new bowl wax on the stool flange and press down to make even contact. With the bolts and wax in place, lift the bowl over the flange and guide the closet bolts through the holes in the stool base. If there is a slight angle in the position of the stool, straighten carefully before you press down on the stool. Then slide the bolt cap retainer rings and washers over the bolts and thread the nuts on. Tighten the nuts until you feel stronger resistance, push down on the bowl again and tighten the nuts another turn. Do not overtighten these nuts. It is always better to have to tighten them more after the stool has settled than to break the vitreous china bowl by overtightening the nuts.

Setting the tank

The same parts packet that contained the stool caps and retainer rings will contain a large rubber spud gasket and the tank bolts and washers. Press the spud gasket over the flush valve spud nut that protrudes through the bottom of the tank. Then sort the tank bolts and washers into sets. Start by sliding a rubber washer onto each bolt and installing the bolts in the tank holes. Set the tank on the bowl so that the bolts go through the holes in the bowl and the tank rests on the spud gasket. Then install a brass washer and a nut on each bolt and tighten each bolt a little at a time to equalize the pressure.

The stool you buy may have two bolts or it may have three. The thing to remember is that the bolts should be tightened in sequence so that the tank rests evenly on the bowl when you are finished. Tighten them only until you feel firm resistance. With some models, the tank may not meet the bowl, but will remain suspended by the thickness of the spud gasket. After the tank is installed, connect the flush valve chain to the flush handle so that very little slack is left in the chain.

Making the water connection

Given the choice now available in closet supply tubes (◁), you are likely to choose one of the flexible types and avoid cutting and shaping chromium-plated copper tubes altogether. Flexible supplies cost a little more, but are much easier to use. This is an important consideration to many homeowners.

REPLACING A TOILET SEAT

The item most likely to wear out and often the most difficult to remove is your toilet seat. The nuts on metal seat bolts almost always rust or corrode to the bolts. When you attempt to loosen these nuts, the bolts, which are molded into the seat hinge, break loose inside the hinge and turn in place. The only alternative left is to saw the bolts off at bowl level with a small hacksaw.

To avoid chipping or scarring the porcelain surface, apply duct tape to the bowl around the seat hinge. In this way, you will be able to lay the saw blade flat on the bowl and cut under the seat hinge. It is tedious work, but once done it should not need to be done again. Seats manufactured today use plastic bolts and nuts.

Once you are rid of your old-fashioned seat with its brass bolts, your next replacement will be much easier. When shopping for a seat and lid, choose a painted wooden one. The plastic models on the market do not hold up as well.

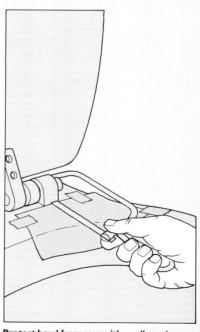

Protect bowl from saw with cardboard scrap

REPAIRING DAMAGED FLANGES

Toilet flanges do occasionally break. The method of repair depends mostly upon the material of the flange and soil pipe connected to it. Cast-iron flanges break most easily because of the nature of the metal. Brass flanges can also become brittle with age and break, while copper flanges will tear out at the slots. Plastic flanges can also tear or break at the slots. And, of course, any flange connected to a lead riser is easily threatened. When a toilet is tightened down too much, either the stool or the flange will break.

REPLACING A ROTTED FLOOR

When a stool is allowed to leak for months at a time, the water almost always damages the floor around it. If you have dry rot around your stool, you will have to take it up and replace a section of the floor. This is an involved task, but not a difficult one.

Take the stool up and cut the rotted layer of flooring out with a circular saw. Measure the area and cut a plywood replacement to fit the removed section. Then measure and cut the opening around the stool flange. Keep in mind that the flange rim must rest on top of the plywood.

Cut the plywood in two so that the center of the flange opening is the center of the cut. Slide each plywood half under the flange and nail down. Then screw the flange to the new floor.

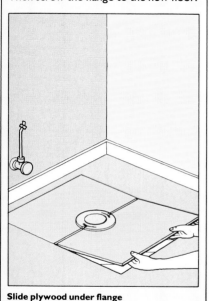

Slide plywood under flange

Replacing a defective toilet flange

If your cast-iron flange breaks at one of its side slots, you may be able to effect a quick-fix that is also permanent: You can buy a simple strap-metal repair item that works quite well in most situations. The strap is curved and shaped to slide under an existing flange. Just insert a closet bolt through the repair strap and slide the strap under the broken side of the flange. The strap is long enough to catch under the remaining edges of the flange. The pressure from the closet bolt keeps the repair piece tightly in place.

Replacing a cast-iron flange

If your cast-iron flange is badly broken, you will need to replace it. To remove a cast-iron stool flange, take up the stool and clean the excess putty or wax from the flange. If the flange is screwed to the floor, remove the screws. Then use an old screwdriver and hammer to pry the lead out of the joint between the flange and soil pipe. Hammer the screwdriver into the lead about ½ inch deep and pry up as you go.

Slide the new flange over the soil pipe and make sure that both closet bolt slots are the same distance from the wall. Then use heavy wood screws to fasten the flange to the floor.

To make a leakproof lead-and-oakum joint, push oakum into the joint and press it down so that it seats against the rim of the flange. Then use a hammer and packing iron to pack the oakum completely around the joint. Add more oakum until you have filled the joint two-thirds full with firmly packed oakum. Finally, fill the remainder of the joint with lead wool and pack it on top of the oakum until the hub is full.

Replacing a plastic stool flange

Usually one of the slots breaks or tears loose. If the ceiling below your stool is open, such as in a basement, the easiest way to remove a plastic stool flange is to cut the soil riser just below the flange. Then remove the flange screws and pull the damaged flange out.

Buy a new flange and a coupling. Then glue the new flange to a short stub of pipe and join the pipe to the riser with the coupling. Make sure the slots are the same distance from the wall before the glue sets (**2**). Then screw the flange to the floor and reset the stool.

If the soil riser is 4-inch plastic, cut the lip of the flange from above using a reciprocating saw. Saw around the joint where the top of the soil pipe meets the flange, then glue the flange inside the riser and screw the flange to the floor.

Removing a cast-iron flange and lead riser

Many older homes have cast-iron flanges connected to lead risers. Because lead is soft and becomes brittle with age, this combination should be replaced. Lead risers were used because lead is easier to work than cast-iron. One end of the riser would be bonded to a cast-iron insert that fits inside the nearest hub of cast-iron soil pipe. The other end comes through the bathroom floor and is flared out under a flat cast-iron flange. The best solution is to remove the flange and most of the lead riser and convert to plastic.

First remove the flange from the floor. Then cut the lead where it meets the cast-iron insert (**1**). Install a 4 × 3-inch no-hub coupling over the insert at the nearest cast-iron hub (**2**) and continue the rest of the way in plastic. The bolt slots should be 12 inches from the wall.

SEE ALSO	
Details for: ▷	
Flooring	178–179
Toilet repairs	364–368

REPAIR STRAP
Broken flange

Glue flange to riser

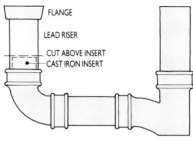

1 Connection details for installation with a lead riser

FLANGE
LEAD RISER
CUT ABOVE INSERT
CAST IRON INSERT

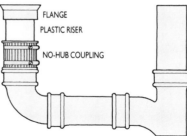

2 Connection details for installation with a plastic riser

FLANGE
PLASTIC RISER
NO-HUB COUPLING

TOILET REPAIRS

Toilets are a marvel of mechanical simplicity. With only a few moving parts, your toilet is responsible for half the water used in your home every day. It is easy to take toilets for granted, until they start to malfunction. Then we wonder how so few parts can cause so much trouble.

When you come to understand how a toilet really works, repair will no longer be a mystery. Mechanically, the components of a two-piece toilet haven't changed much since the turn of the century. The changes that have been made over the years have been modest. The changes you will see in the future will stem from the need to conserve water. You can expect toilets in the very near future to flush with under a gallon of water. Some European models work this way already. Even so, the age-old concept of gravity-flow flush valves and float-controlled ballcocks is likely to endure.

SEE ALSO

◁ Details for:
Toilet installation   360–363

How toilets work

Your bathroom stool has only three mechanical components: the trip lever, flush valve and ballcock. The physical design of the toilet allows it to work so simply.

A two-piece toilet consists of a bowl, which rests on the floor, and a tank, which mounts on the bowl. The bowl contains a built-in trap that holds a consistent amount of water. The amount of water held by each model is determined by the height of the trap weir. The water trapped in the bowl keeps the bowl clean and keeps sewer gases from escaping from soil pipes into living areas.

The rim of the bowl is hollow. Water from the tank rushes into the rim and sprays through holes on its underside (and through a tube exiting opposite the drain opening). These holes are drilled at an angle, which causes the water to stream down the sides of the bowl at an angle. This angled spray serves two very important purposes. It scours and cleans the sides of the bowl, and it starts the water in the bowl spiraling more efficiently over the trap weir. The spiraling water also starts the siphoning action that pulls the water out of the bowl, over the trap and into the soil stack. Once the water in the bowl

begins siphoning over the trap, the water draining out of the tank keeps the siphon going until all wastes have passed into the soil pipe below. When the tank is empty and the flow is stopped, the siphon breaks, which causes the water climbing the trap to fall back into the bowl.

If you want to see a stool flush without a tank, pour a gallon of water directly into the bowl. The added water will force the trap, which will start the siphon, which will flush the stool.

The tank is a matter less of design and more of mechanics. All the tank does is hold water. Water is brought into the tank through a ballcock and is released through a flush valve. When you press down on the flush lever of your stool, a chain pulls a ball or flapper off the flush valve opening. Water then rushes into the hollow stool rim and spirals into the bowl. The water level drops in the tank, which lowers the ballcock float, which opens the ballcock to incoming water. When most of the water passes through the flush valve, the ball or flapper settles back into place and the tank begins to fill again. When the water level reaches a certain point, the float shuts off the incoming flow of water through the ballcock.

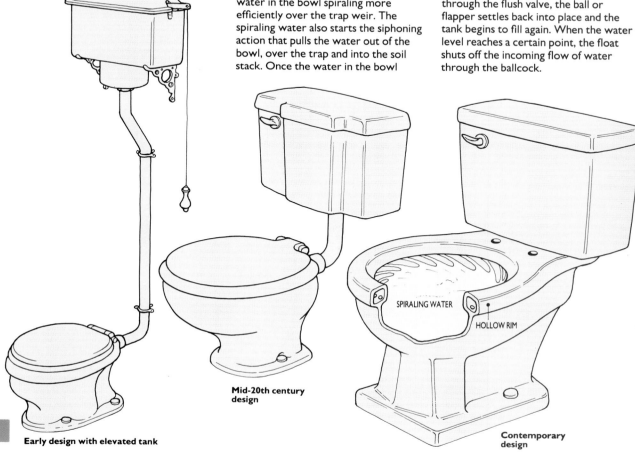

SPIRALING WATER

HOLLOW RIM

Mid-20th century design

Early design with elevated tank

Contemporary design

REPLACING A BALLCOCK SEAL

When a ballcock assembly wears out, some external component may break or the diaphragm gaskets may become too porous or brittle to make the seal. If an external part breaks, you will have to replace the entire ballcock assembly. If the internal seals wear out, you may wish to replace them without replacing the ballcock. The type of ballcock you have and its age will have a lot to do with the choice you make.

If the ballcock in your stool is made of brass and has been in service for many years, you should probably replace it. If your stool is not that old, or if the ballcock is made of plastic, you can probably get by with changing only the diaphragm seals (1). Start by shutting the water off below the stool or at the meter. Then flush the stool and undo the screws on the diaphragm cover. When all cover screws are removed, lift the float arm assembly and cover straight up and lay it aside. Remove all rubber or leather parts from the float arm assembly and diaphragm and examine the rim of the seat. If you can feel pits in the rim surface, you will have to replace the entire ballcock. If not, take the rubber washers and gaskets to your local plumbing outlet and buy replacement parts to match them.

Cover the new rubber washers and gaskets with heatproof grease and press them in place. On most models, you will have to replace the seat washer and the cover gasket.

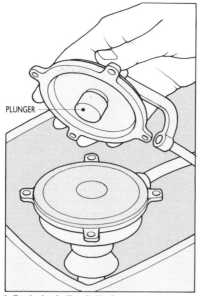

1 Replacing ballcock diaphragm seals

HEATPROOF GREASE

PLUNGER

Apply heatproof grease

CHOOSING A REPLACEMENT BALLCOCK

When replacing a ballcock, you will find that there are several designs on the market from which to choose. All work, but each has its advantages and disadvantages. Still widely used is the traditional brass ballcock with flush arm assembly. The term "ballcock" refers to this specific mechanism. The ball on the end of a float arm rises and falls with the water level, thus closing and opening a valve cock mechanism.

This design was universally used for so long that all mechanisms that fill a tank are often called ballcocks, even though their floats are not ball-shaped or their valves even float-operated. Brass ballcocks will last a long time, but they are considerably more expensive than some of their newer replacements.

The Fluidmaster design offers two real advantages. First, Fluidmasters are available with antisiphon valves, which prevent contamination of household water, and second, they can be easily twisted apart at valve level should you need to clean the diaphragm. This second feature is particularly important if you live in an older home, where mineral deposits from an aging piping system frequently lodge under diaphragm washers.

A third design, marketed under the trademark Fillmaster, uses no float at all. Instead, a built-in regulator allows a measured amount of water into the tank and then shuts off automatically. The advantage of this mechanism is that it is simple. You can adjust the intake volume to meet the needs of the type of stool you have.

Replacing a ballcock

To install a replacement ballcock, shut the water off at the toilet or at the meter. Then flush the stool and sponge all remaining water out of the tank. Loosen the coupling nut that holds the supply tube to the ballcock inlet. With the supply tube nut off, remove the fastening nut (or jamb nut) just above it. While loosening the jamb nut, however, reach into the tank with your other hand and hold the top of the ballcock so that it does not spin into the overflow tube on the flush valve.

With the fastening nut removed, pull the ballcock straight up and out of the tank. If putty was used on the old ballcock, scrape any remaining putty from the bottom of the tank and clean the area with a rag.

To insure a leakproof connection, apply pipe-joint compound to the new ballcock gasket. Then insert the shank of the ballcock through the hole in the tank. From underneath the tank, thread the jamb nut onto the ballcock and tighten it with your fingers. Before tightening the nut completely, make sure that the float will not rub against the tank wall or catch on the flush valve overflow. Then tighten the jamb nut with a wrench until the gasket is flattened out and the nut feels tight. Fasten the refill tube inside of the overflow tube of the flush valve.

Connecting water to the new ballcock will pose one obvious problem. Because of the compression nut, the coupling nut will not slide off the supply tube, nor will the new coupling nut slide on. Either you will have to install a new supply tube or fasten the old nut to your new ballcock. If the old nut is in good condition, there is really no reason why you shouldn't use it, but a new supply tube and coupling nut will look more professional. Whether you install a new supply tube or not, be sure to coat the cone washer with pipe-joint compound or petroleum jelly before tightening the coupling nut.

Ballcock adjustments

While minor adjustments can be made by turning the screw on the float arm near the diaphragm, gross adjustments should be made by carefully bending the brass float rod. For a high water level, bend the float rod up. For a lower water level, bend the float rod down. Set the water level so that it is about 1 inch below the top of the overflow.

SEE ALSO

Details for: ▷	
Adjusting ballcocks	366
Flush valves	366

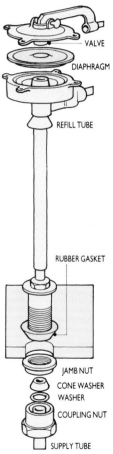

VALVE

DIAPHRAGM

REFILL TUBE

RUBBER GASKET

JAMB NUT

CONE WASHER

WASHER

COUPLING NUT

SUPPLY TUBE

Typical ballcock assembly
All components are replaceable.

ADJUSTING BALLCOCKS

Adjusting a Fluidmaster valve

The only adjustment you will make on a Fluidmaster valve will be in the level of the float. To adjust the float, pinch the stainless-steel clip on the adjustment rod and slide the float up or down.

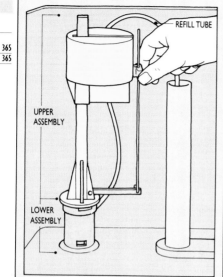

Fluidmaster fill valves

Adjusting a Fillmaster valve

The Fillmaster valve works without a float and relies on the hydraulic pressure of the water to open and shut the fill valve. An internal diaphragm measures the head pressure of the water to determine when to shut off. On top of the Fillmaster, you will see an adjustment screw marked "ADJ." Each complete turn of this screw will adjust the water level in the tank 1 inch. Fillmaster also offers an antisiphon model for cities that require them.

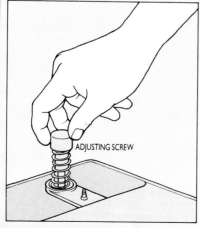

A Fillmaster uses no float mechanism

FLUSH VALVES

Flush valves can be very persistent sources of trouble. Luckily, most flush valve problems can be corrected with replacement tank balls.

Replacing a tank ball and assembly

Some toilets have a tank ball, trip wire and guide instead of a flapper and chain. If you need to replace just the tank ball, shut off the water to the toilet. Then reach into the tank, hold the ball still and thread the lift wire out of the top of the ball. If the ball is very old and brittle, the threaded inset may tear out of the rubber. If this happens, hold the inset with pliers and back the lift wire out.

With the tank ball removed, check the seat for calcium buildup and sand the valve seat if necessary. Then thread the lower lift wire into the new tank ball. You may also need to replace the top lift wires.

To replace a lift wire guide, use a thin-bladed screwdriver to loosen the guide from the overflow tube. Be very careful to avoid breaking the overflow tube off in the flush valve. If you do break the overflow tube, you will have to pry the remaining threads out of the flush valve with a pocket knife. Try to avoid damaging the threads inside the valve. Then coat the threads of the new tube with pipe-joint compound and carefully thread it in place.

Some flush valves have two lift wire guides clamped to the overflow tube, others require only one. In any case, fasten the guide clamps around the tube but do not screw them down tightly. Some adjustments will surely be necessary. Slide the lift wires through the guides so that they are centered over the flush valve. Then thread the lower lift wire into the new tank ball. Hold the upper lift wire next to the trip lever and move the wire and ball up and down to determine where the upper wire should fasten to the trip lever. Feed the upper wire through the nearest hole in the trip lever and bend it over on the other side.

Then, fill the tank with water and flush the toilet several times. The ball should drop straight down onto the flush valve. If it falls to one side, move the guides left or right to achieve the best alignment. When the ball drops straight on top the flush valve consistently, tighten the guide clamps and test several times more.

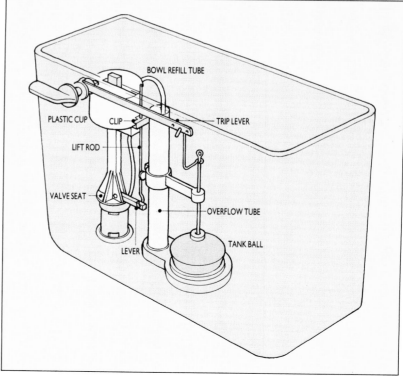

To install a tank ball, unscrew the ball from the lower lift wire

REPLACING A FLAPPER BALL

Flush valve problems occur when the flapper no longer holds water in the tank. In most cases, all that is needed is a new flapper.

To replace a flapper, first shut off the water to the tank. Then reach into the tank and carefully pull the rubber eyelets off the flush valve pegs. Disconnect the chain from the trip lever and discard the old flapper. Then run your finger around the flush valve to check for defects or pits in the rim of the seat. Even if no noticeable defects can be felt, it is a good idea to scour the seat rim with steel wool or emery cloth to remove any calcium buildup.

Some flush valves have no pegs through which the flapper eyelets hook. In this case, slide the collar of the flapper over the overflow tube until it seats against the bottom of the flush valve. Chances are that the flapper you buy will be designed for both applications and can be adapted to fit your needs. If your toilet's flush valve has no pegs, just slide the collar over the overflow tube without alteration. If the flush valve does have pegs, you will have to cut the collar from the flapper before hooking the eyelets to the pegs. Most universal replacement flappers are clearly marked so that you can make the cut in the right place.

After the flapper is in place, hook the chain to the trip lever so that there is not more than 1/2-inch slack in the chain.

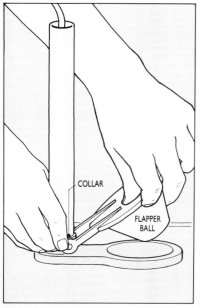

Unhook the collar eyelets

FAULTY FLUSH VALVES

Dealing with a faulty flush valve

If a flush valve seat is pitted or defective in any way, replacing the flapper or tank ball will do little good. The best solution is to separate the tank from the bowl and replace the entire flush valve. If this seems too intimidating, you might choose to install a replacement seat over the defective seat.

Installing a replacement seat

A seat replacement kit consists of a stainless-steel seat rim, flapper ball carriage, a flapper ball and epoxy putty. To install a seat replacement kit, you must first remove the flapper or tank ball and dry the defective flush valve completely. Press the new seat over the old so the epoxy is flattened evenly against both surfaces. Then allow the epoxy to dry for 12 hours.

Replacing a flush valve

A more permanent and much preferred solution is to replace the entire flush valve. To do this, you must first remove the tank from the bowl. Because tank bolts are likely to break in the process, you should buy new tank bolts when you buy the replacement flush valve.

Disconnect the water supply tube at the ballcock. Then remove the two or three tank bolts that hold the tank to the bowl. Lift the tank straight up and lay it on its side on the floor. Remove the large rubber spud washer from the flush valve shank. Then use a spud wrench or a large adjustable pliers to undo the spud nut from the old flush valve assembly.

If any putty or pipe-joint compound is stuck to the bottom of the tank, scrape it clean with a putty knife and sand the area around the opening. Then apply pipe-joint compound to the spud washer. Insert the spud through the tank opening and fasten it in place with the new spud nut. Make sure that the overflow tube is not in the way of the float arm inside the tank. Then press the large rubber spud washer over the spud nut and set the tank back on the bowl.

Apply pipe-joint compound to the rubber washers on the tank bolts and slide the bolts through the tank holes and bolt holes. (Some tanks require that you fasten the tank bolts to the tank with a second set of nuts and washers before setting the tank in place. Other models require rubber spacers between tank and bowl ($\triangleright$).) Then tighten the tank bolts a little at a time until the tank rests firmly on the bowl, and reconnect the water supply tube.

Finally, attach the flapper ball to the overflow tube and make minor adjustments as needed. After the toilet has been flushed several times satisfactorily, check for tank leaks by running your hand under it and under the tank bolts.

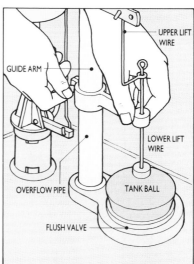

UPPER LIFT WIRE

GUIDE ARM

LOWER LIFT WIRE

OVERFLOW PIPE

TANK BALL

FLUSH VALVE

Adjusting a tank ball

Replacing a faulty trip lever

Replacing a handle/trip lever is not difficult, but the left-hand threads of the retaining nut have stumped a lot of beginner plumbers. The threads are machined on the shank counterclockwise so that the downward motion of the flush lever will not loosen the nut.

Take the lid off of the tank and use an adjustable wrench to loosen the retaining nut. When the nut is loose, slide it off of the trip lever. (Some models have set screws instead of retaining nuts.) Then pull the lever out through the tank opening.

To install a new trip lever, feed the lever into the opening until the handle seats. Then slide the nut over the lever until it makes a right-angle turn and rests against the left-hand threads of the shank. Tighten the nut and connect the flapper chain to the most convenient hole in the lever. Follow with several test flushes.

SEE ALSO

Details for: $\triangleright$
Setting a new tank   362

Replacement seat kit
Kits come with epoxy putty.

RETAINING NUT

TRIP LEVER

Replacing a tank trip lever
Loosen the set screw or undo the locknut.

MAINTAINING TOILETS

Dealing with sweating tanks

Condensation appears on the outside of a stool tank when cold water from the water system meets the warm humid air of a bathroom. The water that collects on the surface of the tank eventually falls to the floor, often causing water damage over time.

Air-conditioned homes do not have tank sweating problems. If your home is not air-conditioned, your best alternative is to insulate the tank from the inside. There are polystyrene insulating liners on the market, but you can just as easily make your own, using ½-inch polystyrene or foam rubber.

Drain and dry the stool tank. Cut a piece for each wall and several pieces for the bottom of the tank. Then glue them in place with silicone cement and allow the glue to dry for a full day.

You can also reduce the temperature extremes by mixing hot water with the cold before it enters the tank valve. This method wastes a lot of hot water, of course, and unless you install a check valve on the hot water side of the connection, the other fixtures in your home will back-siphon hot water through their cold water outlets.

A temperature, or check valve, is available for this purpose and is not difficult to install. In a typical installation, you will tap into the hot water supply of your lavatory and run a ⅜-inch soft copper line to the temperature valve. The temperature valve should be installed just before the toilet valve. The cold water inlet of the temperature valve threads into the toilet valve and onto the toilet supply line, while the hot water pipe is connected to the temperature valve by means of a ⅜-inch compression fitting. If your basement ceiling is not finished, you can also tap onto the hot water line below the floor. A through-the-floor installation offers a much neater appearance. It also saves cutting into vanity cabinets.

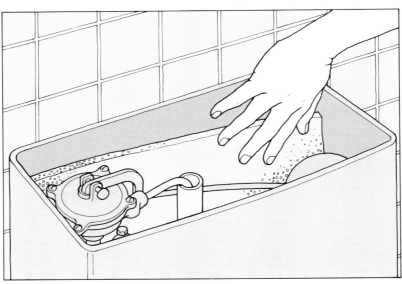

Glue foam rubber or polystyrene to the inside of the tank

Repairing wall-mounted stool tanks

Repairing a leaking flush ell
Loosen the nuts and wrap the threads with sealant tape.

Many older toilets have wall-mounted tanks that are joined to their bowls by means of a 90-degree pipe, called a "flush ell." While the working parts of these toilets are the same as in newer models, dealing with flush ells requires special care. When flush ells leak, carefully undo the nuts with a pipe wrench and wrap the threads with plastic pipe-joint sealant tape. When tightening the spud nut, hold on to the

ell firmly to avoid cracking it.

Because wall-mounted tank stools waste so much water, and because their flush ells make them harder to repair, you should think about replacing them when they need extensive work. For minor repairs, choose repair kits that do not require taking off the flush valve. Instead of replacing flush valves in wall-mounted tanks, use one of the stainless-steel seat replacement kits.

CLOGGED TOILETS

Occasionally, a toilet will clog and overflow. Often the water will seep away but the solids and paper will not. Most toilets clog at the top of the trap because that is where the trap is smallest. Clogs can be caused by too much paper or any of a number of bathroom items. Tooth paste caps, hair pins and combs are regular culprits.

Start by trying to plunge the toilet trap. A plunger with a collapsible funnel works best in toilets. If plunging does not do the job, dip the water out of the bowl and use a small pocket mirror and a flashlight to look up into the trap. If you can see the obstruction, chances are you can reach it with a wire hook.

If all else fails, rent a closet auger from your local tool rental outlet and crank the auger through the trap several times. A closet auger cable is just long enough to reach the toilet flange. When pulling the cable out of the trap, keep cranking in a clockwise direction to avoid losing the material causing the clog. Then test flush.

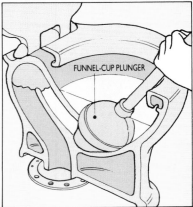

A funnel-cup plunger for a stool

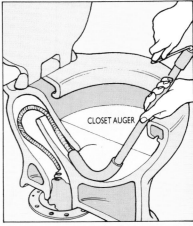

Feed the closet auger into the trap

BATHTUB INSTALLATION AND REPAIRS

For many years, bathtub designs consisted of various size free-standing leg tubs. Today, most tubs are of standard dimensions and are built into tub walls with an apron covering the side of the tub left exposed. Except for whirlpools, basic designs have changed very little in the last forty years, but some important material changes have taken place. Tubs today may be made of enameled cast-iron, porcelain-covered steel or molded fiberglass. The installation of tubs, however, remains much the same as it has always been.

Installing a built-in tub

To install a tub, you will need a framed opening that is 60 1/16 inches long by at least 31 inches deep. On the drain opening side, cut a hole in the floor that is 8 inches wide by 12 inches long. Center this hole 15 inches from the back wall. Then nail braces between the studs all around the tub centered 14 inches above the floor.

Walk the tub toward the opening in an upright position. Stay to one side wall or the other. When you have the tub standing upright in the opening, gradually tip it down. At some point, the tub will likely turn on one corner and wedge itself diagonally in the opening. If your tub is made of fiberglass or steel, just lift and pull it into position. If your tub is a 375-pound cast-iron model, however, keep your feet and fingers away. Instead, use a 2-by-4 to pry the tub into place.

If your tub is made of steel or fiberglass, screw the lip of the tub to the backing you've installed between the studs. Cast-iron tubs have no lip and are held in place by subflooring and wall finish alone.

Installing a waste and overflow drain

The waste and overflow you buy will come in several pieces. Start by locating the drain shoe, drain gasket and drain strainer. Wrap a small roll of plumber's putty around the flange of the strainer. Then reach below the tub and hold the drain shoe against the tub opening with its rubber gasket sandwiched between the drain shoe and tub. Thread the strainer into the drain shoe.

Next, assemble the overflow tube, tripwaste tee and tailpiece, and connect the tee to the drain shoe with the compression nuts provided. You may also attach the tailpiece to the soil P-trap and ground joint adapter at this step in the process.

When the waste and overflow components are assembled and connected to the drainage system, you will be ready to install and adjust the tripwaste mechanism. Feed the plunger into the overflow tube and fasten the coverplate screws. Pour water into the tub and open and close the trip lever to determine what adjustments are needed for the best flow.

Adjusting a tripwaste

There are two basic tripwaste designs. One has a plunger cylinder attached to the end of the trip wire. The cylinder slides up and down inside the tripwaste tee when you activate the trip lever. In the down position, the cylinder slides into the tee and closes it.

The other design features a pop-up lever and plug in the drain opening of the strainer. This model has a large spring attached to the lift wire that moves the pop-up lever up or down. When the spring is in the down position, the pop-up lever pushes the plug up and drains the tub. When the spring is in the up position, the pop-up seats itself in the drain opening and closes the drain.

SEE ALSO

Details for: ▷
Showers   371–372

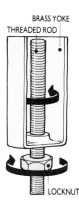

Adjusting a tripwaste
Loosen the locknut on the lift wire and thread the wire up or down.

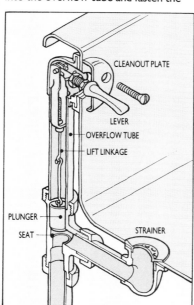

Typical plunger-type waste and overflow

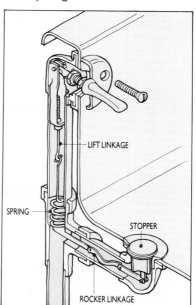

Typical pop-up waste and overflow

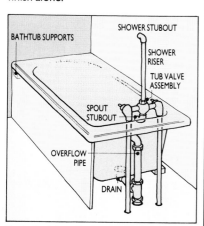

Typical tub installation

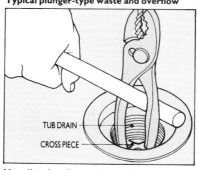

Use pliers handles to tighten the spud

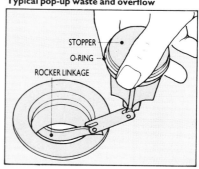

Pull the pop-up plug and lever out

369

MAINTAINING BATHTUBS

Tub valves and shower heads

Most tub/shower valves on the market come with a diverter spout and shower head. Start by installing the faucet body. Bring ½-inch copper water supplies up in the tub wall to a height of 28 inches. Then cut a 44-inch length of copper for the shower riser and a 4½-inch length for the tub spout rough-in. Thread or solder the valve in place, close enough to the wall so that the coverplate screws will reach through the tile and drywall and into the faucet. Then solder a sweat/FIP fitting, called a "drop eared ell," to the shower stem and to the spout leg. Plug the shower head fitting and the spout fitting and turn the water on to test the installation. Turn both the hot and cold sides of the valve on and watch for leaks.

After testing the piping for leaks, drywall and tile the walls and thread the shower head into its fitting with plastic pipe-joint sealant tape. To install the spout, measure from the surface of the tile to ⅜ inch inside the spout fitting and buy a ½-inch nipple that length. Wrap sealant tape around both ends of the nipple and thread the nipple into the spout fitting. Then turn the spout onto the nipple and caulk around the spout and faucet coverplate.

Installing a shower
Rough-in a tub valve 28 in. from the floor.

60" to 66"

6"

GROUT

Push grout into joints

Maintaining tiled tub walls

Eventually, every tiled tub/shower wall will need repair, but you can extend the life of your tile with a few simple maintenance procedures. The danger signs are loose or missing grout and excessive mildew in grout joints. To regrout a tiled wall, start by digging all soft or loose grout from between tiles with a grout removal tool, available from any tile outlet. All joints to be regrouted should be scraped to a depth of at least ¹⁄₁₆ inch. Then wipe away the loose grout and clean the entire wall with a good tile cleaner.

With the tile prepared, select a small container of premixed, ready-to-use grout and force a liberal amount into each prepared joint with your fingers. Use a damp sponge to smooth the grout. Wipe in large diagonal patterns until the grout is uniform. Then allow it to set for one-half hour and wipe the surface again to remove any residue. After the grout has cured for 24 hours, apply clear silicone sealer to the entire wall with a soft cloth. Reseal your tile at least every six months thereafter.

Replacing ceramic tiles

When water is allowed to seep behind tiles, it ruins the tile mastic and the wallboard. Eventually, tiles will loosen and fall out. To replace them, you may need to remove all tiles that have come in contact with moisture and replace a section of drywall.

Use a knife or screwdriver to pry under the tiles. If tiles come up easily, take them out. Then cut out the affected wallboard and nail a new piece of water-resistant wallboard in its place. If the edges fit together neatly, you will not have to tape the seams. Prime the new wallboard with clear sealer or oil-base paint and allow the primer to dry completely.

To strip the paper and mastic from the removed tile, soak each tile in very hot water and scrape it clean with a putty knife. Lay the tiles out on the floor in the order in which they will go back on. Apply wall-grade tile mastic to the wall or tile with a notched trowel. A ⅛-inch notch will provide enough gap in the cement to hold the tile to the wall.

With the cement on the wall, press the old tiles back in place. Clean away any tile cement from the tile surfaces

and allow the cement to cure for 48 hours. (If you grout the joints too soon, the gases escaping from the cement will cause pinholes to appear in the grout.) When the cement has cured, grout the new tile joints and seal the entire wall with clear silicone sealer.

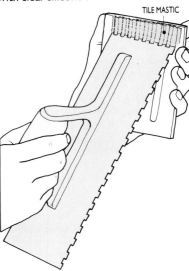

TILE MASTIC

Apply cement with a notched trowel

Adjusting and cleaning a tub drain

Often slow-draining tripwastes just need adjustment. Start by undoing the screws that hold the coverplate to the overflow opening. Pull the coverplate and lift wire up and out of the overflow tube. Part way down the wire, you will see adjustment slots, or a threaded adjustment wire. If your lift wire has a slot adjustment, pinch the two bottom wires together and move them up or down into the next slot level. If your tripwaste has a threaded wire adjustment, loosen the locknut and thread the wire up or down about ⅛ inch and retighten the locknut. Then slide the tripwaste back into the overflow and replace the coverplate screws.

If you do not find a clog at the tripwaste mechanism, you will have to snake the trap and drain line. Because tubs are snaked through the overflow and not through the drain, you will need to remove the coverplate and tripwaste components. Feed a small hand snake into the overflow until you feel resistance at the trap bend. When you feel the trap, start cranking the snake in a clockwise direction while pushing the cable slightly. After you

crank through the trap, pull the snake out to see if you've snagged the clog. If not, snake the entire tub line to where it enters the main stack. Then replace the tripwaste components and flush with plenty of hot water.

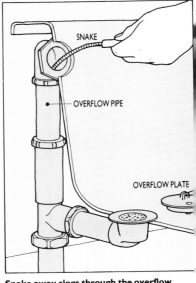

SNAKE

OVERFLOW PIPE

OVERFLOW PLATE

Snake away clogs through the overflow

SHOWERS

Shower stalls come in several varieties. All-metal or plastic freestanding showers can be installed anywhere near a floor drain. They are popular in unfinished basements and are often thought of as utility showers.

One-piece fiberglass stalls are built into framed walls and are popular in finished bathrooms, both upstairs and down. They drain into dedicated traps and are plumbed permanently.

A more traditional shower consists of a separate pan built into a framed wall and plumbed into a dedicated trap. The framed walls are covered with water-resistant drywall or concrete board and finished with ceramic tile, molded plastic or fiberglass shower walls.

Installing a freestanding shower

A freestanding shower consists of a raised pan, three wall panels, cornerbraces, a drain spud and a valve and shower head. All of these parts will come in a box and must be assembled on site. Start by setting up the pan and plumbing the drainpipe to the nearest floor drain. Then install the walls and cornerbraces and fasten the walls to the pan according to directions.

Next, assemble the valve and shower riser and mount the valve and shower head to the plumbing wall of the shower. Some freestanding shower stalls will have predrilled valve holes, but other models will have to be drilled. If you are plumbing the supply lines in steel, use a union on each side. If plumbing in plastic or copper, plumb into the valve with male adapters.

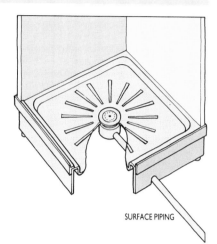

SURFACE PIPING

Plumbing the drain pipe
Run surface piping to the nearest floor drain.

A freestanding shower stall

FLANGE   SHIELD

Hardboard shield
Use hardboard to keep from hitting the shower wall.

Installing a one-piece fiberglass shower

To install a one-piece fiberglass shower, start by framing the walls. The width of the opening should not be more than $\frac{1}{16}$ inch wider than the width of the fiberglass stall. The depth of the opening should exceed the front drywall lip of the shower by 2 inches. With the framing completed, cut the drain hole in the floor. Take the measurements from the bottom of the shower stall to find the center of the drain, and make the opening at least 5 inches in diameter so you will have room to work.

Next, install the drain spud in the pan opening. Wrap the underside of the drain flange with plumber's putty and press it into the opening. Then slide the gasket over the spud from below and tighten the spud nut.

With the drain in place, you will be ready to set the shower in its frame. Because fiberglass shower floors tend to flex when you stand in them, it is a good idea to support the floor with a little perlited plaster. Mix enough wet plaster to cover the wooden floor 1 inch deep and about 1½ feet around the drain hole. Then set the shower in place on

top of the plaster. Level the shower walls and step into the shower to settle the base into the plaster. Nail the wall-board lip of the shower walls to the studs with galvanized roofing nails and connect the drain spud to the P-trap below the floor.

With the stall in place, measure for the shower valve cut. The valve should be 48 inches off the floor and the shower head should be 6 feet or more from the floor. Use a hole saw to cut the shower valve holes. Solder the shower valve, supply lines and shower head together and mount the shower valve through the stall wall. With the valve in place, install the shower head and nail 2-by-4 braces behind the valve and the shower head. Secure the valve and head firmly to the braces with pipe hooks. Then connect the water supply lines to the water system and test the solder joints under full pressure.

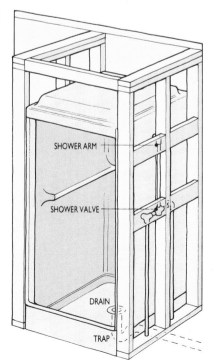

SHOWER ARM

SHOWER VALVE

DRAIN

TRAP

Framing the opening
Frame an opening the exact size of the shower.

INSTALLING SHOWERS

Installing a fiberglass shower

Like a one-piece shower, a shower pan is installed in a framed opening. Simply frame the stall as you would with a one-piece shower and cut the drain opening in the floor. Install the drain spud in the pan, using putty under the flange, and set the pan in place.

Shower pans often have metal drain spuds. The drainpipe from the P-trap then extends through the spud to just below the drain screen. You can use a rubber gasket to seal the joint or use a traditional lead wool and oakum seal.

With the pan installed and connected to the drain line, install the valve and shower head rough-in in the framed wall and secure both with pipe hooks and 2-by-4 bracing. Test the piping and cover the walls with water-resistant wallboard. You can then cover the wallboard with ceramic tile or a molded shower surround.

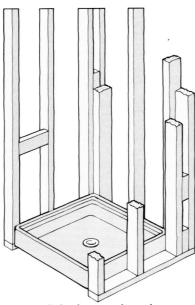

Frame walls for the pan and trap riser

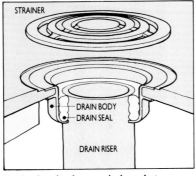

STRAINER

DRAIN BODY
DRAIN SEAL

DRAIN RISER

Use lead-and-oakum or drain gasket

Installing a tub or shower surround

Molded fiberglass or plastic tub and shower surrounds are easy to install and offer long-term durability. The appeal of these molded shower walls is that they have very few seams, and therefore few opportunities to leak. The only situation that prohibits the use of surrounds is crooked walls. Even with slightly out-of-plumb walls, a little bottom edge trimming will create an effective seal.

Most tub or shower surrounds come in three pieces. You will have to cut the valve and spout rough-in holes, but beyond that, they are ready to install. Before installing any of the panels, put a level on all walls and on the top of the tub to make sure they are reasonably plumb and level. If everything is straight and level, mark the exact center of the back wall of the tub. Then mark the center of the back wall shower panel.

Apply several beads of panel adhesive to the back of the center panel. Then peel the paper from the adhesive strips around the edges, if present. Lift the panel up to the back tub rim so that the bottom of the panel is an inch away from the wall. Rest the panel on several match sticks laid on the back rim of the tub. When the center of the panel is aligned with the center of the back wall, press the bottom of the panel against the wall. Work from bottom to top until the adhesive strip has sealed the entire panel. Then rub the panel firmly with the palm of your hand to flatten the panel adhesive to the wall.

Next, install the corner panel opposite the plumbing wall. Use the same method you used for the back panel, but press the corner in first. The corner panel will lap the back panel by several inches.

To cut the valve handles and tub spout in the plumbing wall panel, remove the spout and handles and measure from the tub rim and inside corner. Use a hole saw to cut the openings. Even a small cutting error will ruin the panel, so double-check all measurements before cutting. With the holes made, slide the panel over the handle stems and spout rough-in to make sure that everything fits. Then apply panel adhesive, peel the paper from the adhesive strip and press the corner in place.

When the adhesive dries, caulk the bottom seam and the valve flanges with white silicone sealant and both corners with latex tub and tile caulk.

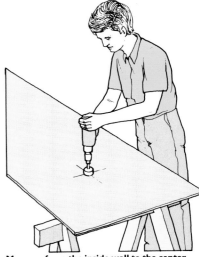

Measure from the inside wall to the center

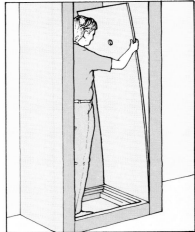

Set bottom of wall panel first

Apply panel adhesive liberally

It is hard to imagine living an active life without instant access to hot water. When your water heater fails, don't panic. A little troubleshooting, adjustment and repair may extend its life.

Water heaters are fairly simple appliances, but when problems arise, they can present an array of confusing symptoms. Because problems can occur in any part of your hot-water system, don't limit your investigation to the heater alone. The diagnostic charts on the next page will help you locate the source of your hot water trouble.

The piping system

In some cases, water heater problems turn out to be piping problems instead. For example, high operating costs can often be traced to dripping faucets or leaking pipes. Several dripping faucets in your home can waste hundreds of gallons of water a year. A simple, inexpensive faucet repair can pay for itself in energy saved.

Long, uninsulated piping runs also waste hot water. When you draw water from a faucet at the end of a run, hot water from the tank must first push the cooled water through the pipe. This not only wastes water, but energy as well. Uninsulated pipes dissipate heat much as a radiator does. To keep the energy you buy from escaping through the walls of hot water pipes, you should consider insulating all hot water lines.

Problems inside the tank

An aging water system can carry *sediment* into a tank, or sediment may collect in flakes of calcium and lime. In electric models, sediment-covered heating elements will burn out quickly. In gas water heaters, sediment accumulates in the bottom of the tank and forms a barrier between the heat source and the water. Not only does sediment make your heater very inefficient, but air bubbles created by the heat percolate through the sediment and cause a continuous rumbling sound. So, if your electric heater burns up lower elements frequently, or if your gas heater rumbles, sediment may be the culprit.

To remove sediment, drain as much water as possible from the tank. Then turn the water supply on and allow the new water to flush through the drain valve for a few minutes.

Dip tubes

A *dip tube* is a plastic pipe that delivers incoming cold water to the heat source near the tank bottom. Occasionally, a dip tube will slip through the cold-water inlet fitting and fall into the tank. When this happens, cold water entering the tank is drawn through the hot-water outlet without being heated. To replace a dip tube, disconnect the inlet pipe from the tank. Cut a length of ½-inch I.D. soft copper pipe long enough to reach within 12 inches of the tank bottom. Flare the pipe end so it is large enough to rest on the rim of the inlet fitting. Slide the tube into the fitting and reconnect the inlet pipe.

Anode rods

New water heaters are equipped with magnesium *anode rods* that coat any voids that develop in the porcelain tank lining. An anode rod acts as a sacrificial element. It has a slightly different electrical charge than the other metals in the tank and draws rust and corrosion to it. These rods are usually trouble free, but problems can occur when water contains an unusually high concentration of dissolved mineral salts. As a result, the water will have a gassy odor or taste. To correct this problem, unscrew the magnesium rod and replace it with an aluminum rod.

Relief valves

A *relief valve* keeps a heater from exploding in the event a thermostat becomes stuck. When pressure builds and the water gets too hot, the relief valve opens until the pressure is equalized. However, the spring mechanism in some valves weakens with age and valves release water with the slightest variation in pressure. To correct this, simply remove the old valve with a pipe wrench and thread in a new one.

SEE ALSO

Details for: ▷

| Water heater trouble-shooting | 374 |
| Common water heater problems | 375–376 |

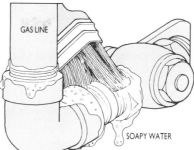
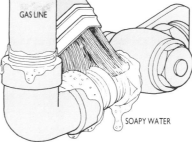

Test for gas leaks with soap and water

GAS LINE

SOAPY WATER

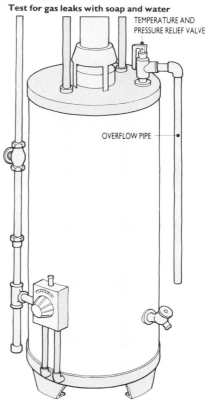

TEMPERATURE AND PRESSURE RELIEF VALVE

OVERFLOW PIPE

Testing valves Water should rush out if not stuck.

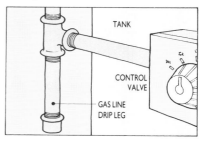

TANK

CONTROL VALVE

GAS LINE DRIP LEG

Drip legs
Install a drip leg near the control valve.

GAS WATER HEATER DIAGNOSTIC CHART

SEE ALSO
◁ Details for:
Common water
heater problems   375–376

CAUSES	Burner will not light	Burner flame floats—Lifts off	Burner flame yellow—Lazy	Burner flame noisy	Burner flame too high	Burner pops when turned off or on	Flame burns at orifice	Pilot will not stay lit	High operating costs	Insufficient hot water	Slow hot-water recovery	Pounding and steaming at faucet	Dripping relief valve	Thermostat fails to close	Condensation	Combustion odors	Smoking—carbon formation	Pilot flame too small	Pilot flame too large	SOLUTIONS
Insufficient secondary air		•		•						•						•	•			Provide ventilation
Dirt in main burner orifice	•	•		•	•		•	•	•							•	•			Clean—Install dirt trap
Dirt in pilot burner orifice			•	•				•								•	•		•	Clean—Install dirt trap
Flue clogged		•	•					•									•			Remove—Blow clean—Reinstall
Pilot line clogged	•							•												Clean—Install dirt trap
Burner line clogged	•							•												Clean—Check source and correct
Wrong pilot burner	•							•										•	•	Replace with correct pilot burner
Loose thermocouple								•												Finger-tight plus 1/4 turn
Defective thermocouple lead	•																			Replace thermocouple
Defective thermostat	•					•						•		•		•				Replace thermostat—(Call plumber)
Improper calibration									•	•	•	•	•							Replace—(Call plumber)
Heater in confined area	•	•	•												•	•	•			Install vent in wall or door
Heater not connected to flue		•	•		•										•	•	•			Provide and connect to proper flue
Sediment or lime in tank									•	•	•		•							Drain and flush—Repeat
Heater too small										•	•									Upgrade to larger heater
Gas leaks										•										Check with utility—Repair immediately
Excess draft		•		•							•									Check source, stop draft
Long runs of exposed piping										•	•									Insulate hot lines only
Surge from washer solenoid valve													•							Install air cushion pipe
Faulty relief valve													•							Install rated T & P valve—Soon
Dip tube broken										•	•	•								Replace dip tube

ELECTRIC WATER HEATER DIAGNOSTIC CHART

CAUSES	No hot water	Insufficient hot water	Slow hot-water recovery	Steaming and pounding at faucet	High operating costs	Dripping relief valve	Excessive relief valve operation	Condensation	Element failure	Blown fuse—Tripped circuit breaker	Service wires charred or hot	Continuous operation	Singing thermostat	Wet heater insulation	Gas odor or taste in water	Fluctuating temperatures	Rusty or discolored water	Rumbling-pounding in tank	SOLUTIONS
No power	•									•									Check fuses breakers–Reset
Undersize heater		•										•				•			Install larger heater
Undersize elements		•	•									•							Replace with rated element
Wrong wiring connections	•	•		•					•	•	•								See manufacturer's instructions
No relief valve				•															Install relief valve—Soon
Leaking faucets		•		•										•					Locate and repair
Leaks around heating elements	•			•				•						•					Tighten tank flange
Sediment or lime in tank		•		•													•	•	Drain and flush—Water treatment?
Lime formation on elements		•	•														•	•	Replace elements
Thermostat not flush with tank		•	•									•	•			•			Reposition
Faulty wiring connection	•	•								•	•	•							Locate, reconnect
Faulty ground		•	•									•							See maker's grounding instructions
Short	•		•						•	•	•								Locate short circuit—Correct
Gas from magnesium anode rod															•		•		Install aluminum anode rod
Damage from electrolysis																	•		Install dielectric unions
Excessive mineral deposits			•														•		Flush tank—Install water filter
Improper calibration	•	•	•	•	•	•						•							Replace thermostat—(Call plumber)
Eroded anode rod																•	•		Replace
Faulty thermostat	•	•	•									•				•		•	Replace—(Call plumber)
Faulty high limit (ECO)	•	•	•									•				•		•	Replace
Open high limit (ECO)	•	•																	Reset button or replace
Dip tube broken		•	•		•							•					•		Replace dip tube

COMMON PROBLEMS WITH GAS WATER HEATERS

A typical gas heater consists of a steel tank, a layer of insulation and a sheet-metal jacket.

The bottom of the tank is heated by a gas-fixed burner that is controlled by a thermocouple and a regulator valve.

To vent excess heat and noxious fumes, a gas heater tank is equipped with a hollow tube through its center, which connects to a home's flue.

A supply of secondary air

For a gas heater to burn evenly and efficiently, it must have an ample supply of *secondary air*. If your water heater shares space with a furnace and clothes dryer, then a continuous air supply is especially important, because they compete with the heater for air. When a heater is starved for air, the flame will burn orange, jump and pop. An orange flame means higher operating costs. Be sure that the heater has a sufficient supply of secondary air by opening doors in confined areas or by installing louvered vents in the doors.

A clogged flue

A *clogged flue* is caused by rust or debris that accumulates at tight bends in the flue piping. A clogged flue is a serious health hazard. Deadly carbon gases, unable to vent through the roof, are forced into living quarters. An easy way to check if the flue is working properly is to place a lit cigarette near the flue hat while the heater is on. The smoke should be drawn into the flue. To locate an obstruction, turn the heater to pilot, disassemble the tin vent pipes and inspect and clean each piece, then reassemble the flue.

Dirt in gas lines

Dirt in gas lines often makes its way into the heater's controls and burner systems. A dirty pilot line or burner line will cause the heater to burn unevenly or to stop burning entirely. To clean these lines, disconnect them from the regulator and slide a thin wire through each line. Then, blow air through the lines. If dirt is lodged in the gas control valve, call a plumber. Control valves are delicate mechanisms that can be dangerous if serviced improperly.

Thermocouple breakdown

A *thermocouple* is a thick copper wire that has a heat sensor on one end and a plug on the other. Heat from the pilot flame sends a tiny millivolt charge through the wire, which causes the plug to open the control valve. When a thermocouple's sensor burns out, the heater's magnetic safety valve remains closed and the pilot light won't burn.

To replace a thermocouple, turn off the gas and disconnect the entire burner assembly from the control valve. Remove the thermocouple from its retainer clip near the pilot and snap a new one in its place. Be sure to position the sensor directly in line with the pilot flame. Finally, reconnect the burner assembly to the control valve.

Gas leaks

If you smell a strong gas odor, it's likely there is a *gas leak*. Leave the house immediately and call your gas or utility company. If you smell only a slight trace of gas, it may be a leaky pipe joint. To find the leak, brush every joint with a mixture of dish detergent and warm water. Soap bubbles will appear around the leaky joint. Shut off the gas at the meter. Bleed the line at the union located above the heater and ventilate the area.

Cut the pipe a few inches away from the leaking fitting. Unscrew the bad fitting and thread a new fitting in its place. Then thread the cut pipe end. Connect the new fitting to the newly threaded pipe with a short nipple and union. Finally, turn the gas back on, bleed the air from the line and retest all pipe joints with soap and warm water.

SEE ALSO

Details for: ▷

Electric water
heater problems   376

**Typical gas water
heater**
1 Tin vent
2 Cold water inlet
3 Hot water outlet
4 Flue hat
5 Union
6 Relief valve
7 Discharge pipe
8 Anode rod
9 Water
10 Tank
11 Dip tube
12 Insulation
13 Flue baffle
14 Gas control
15 Gas pipe
16 Temperature control
17 Gas valve
18 Burner
19 Draincock
20 Thermocouple lead
21 Pilot line
22 Burner supply
23 Thermocouple

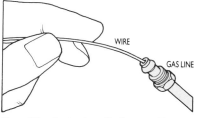

Use a thin wire to clear dirt from gas lines

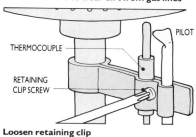

Loosen retaining clip

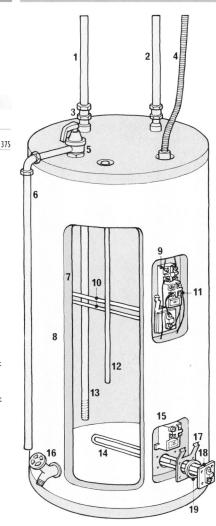

**Typical electric
water heater**
1 Inlet
2 Outlet
3 Union
4 Power cable
5 Relief valve
6 Discharge pipe
7 Insulation
8 Tank
9 High limit
10 Upper element
11 Upper thermostat
12 Anode rod
13 Dip tube
14 Lower element
15 Lower thermostat
16 Draincock
17 Bracket
18 Element flange
19 Gasket

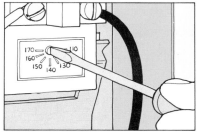

Test switch with ohmmeter

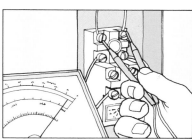

Adjust the new temperature setting

COMMON PROBLEMS WITH ELECTRIC HEATERS

If your electric water heater fails, first check for burned-out fuses or tripped circuit breakers at the main service panel. If the problem is not in the service panel, go to the heater. Remove the access panels and press the reset button on each thermostat and listen for a ticking noise caused by expansion as the elements begin to heat up. If this procedure doesn't produce hot water, the problem may be in the wiring, thermostats or elements.

Loose wires

Check to be sure that no wire has come loose from its terminal. If a wire is loose or disconnected, turn off the power to the heater before refastening the wire.

Defective thermostat element

To determine if the problem is in the element, thermostat or high-limit protector, test each part with a volt-ohmmeter (VOM). If you do not have a VOM, try simple logic. If the heater produces plenty of warm water but no hot water, then the top element or thermostat is probably defective. If you get a few gallons of very hot water followed by cool water, then the bottom element or thermostat probably needs replacing. Since elements fail much more often than thermostats, assume a faulty element or test with a VOM.

Replacing an element
To replace a defective element, first shut off the power and water supply to the heater. Next, drain the tank to a level below the element to be replaced. Disconnect the wires from the terminals and unscrew the element. Pull the element straight out of the tank. Then clean the gasket surface, coat it lightly with pipe-joint compound and seat a new gasket. Attach the new element to the heater and reconnect the wires to the terminals. (Some elements thread into a threaded tank opening, while others bolt to a gasket flange.) Before turning the power on, fill the tank with water and bleed all trapped air through the faucets. An element that is energized when dry will burn out in seconds.

Finally, replace the insulation, thermostat protection plates and access panel. Then, turn on the power. If after 45 minutes you still don't have sufficient hot water, then a replacement thermostat is in order.

Replacing a thermostat
Shut off the power and disconnect the wires from the thermostat's terminals. Pry out the old thermostat and snap the new one into the clip. Then, reconnect the wires, replace the insulation and turn the power back on. Allow both elements to complete their heating cycles and then test the water temperature at the faucets using a meat thermometer. Adjust the thermostat until the water temperature is between 130 and 140 degrees F.

New designs in electric water heaters

For years, electric water heaters have been made with metal storage tanks. All other components were replaceable, but when a tank developed a leak, the entire heater had to be replaced. The longevity of the tank, then, determined the longevity of the heater. While most manufacturers still prefer metal tanks, at least one offers a plastic tank. Because plastic cannot rust through, and because mineral salts will not adhere to it, this new design seems to have real potential.

Another recent design rejects the principle of storing hot water entirely. The makers of this design maintain that heating and reheating stored water is too wasteful. They offer, instead, a system that heats cold water as it passes through a heating element. In this way, only the water used is heated. With careful use and planning, these units should offer real savings. If you regularly take showers while your clothes washer or dishwasher are operating, then this system may have trouble keeping up. In any case, consider your needs before investing.

WATER SOFTENERS AND WATER FILTERS

The water we pump into our homes varies greatly in quality from region to region, and even from well to well. The degree of mineral content in groundwater accounts for these differences and can also account for a few health and plumbing problems as well. Most municipal water systems *provide water that falls within tolerable limits of hardness and dissolved mineral salts. Others, especially rural systems, do not. When mineral levels are too high, water must be treated or filtered to bring it within the acceptable tolerances for domestic use.*

Water softeners

The purpose of a water softener is to substitute sodium for calcium, magnesium or iron. These minerals, in high enough concentrations, can cause clogged pipes and appliances and can give drinking water a foul smell. Water softeners neutralize these minerals, which makes conditioned water feel softer. It helps eliminate soap scum on fixtures and reduces the amount of mineral sediment in water heaters.

Water softeners cause problems of their own, however. They naturally raise the salt content of drinking water. Too much salt presents certain health risks, especially for those on low sodium diets. There are two sides to this issue, of course, but softeners are probably installed more often than are needed. If soap does not dissolve well in your water or if mineral buildup occurs on your fixtures, then you may need a softener. If you are uncertain, you might have your water tested by a local lab or by your state health department.

If you do need a water softener, make sure you isolate your main cold water drinking faucets and your outdoor hydrants. Salt water will kill a lawn in short order. The easiest installation in a home with finished basement ceilings is to tie the intake of the softener to the inlet line of your water heater. With a hot-water-only installation, you get soft water where you need it most, in your clothes washer and dishwasher. You will also get some soft water in your tub/shower or wherever you mix hot and cold water. You will also prevent mineral buildup in your water heater.

For a more complete installation, you should tie the softener into the incoming water trunk line before it reaches any branch fittings. To isolate cold water drinking faucets and outdoor hydrants, cut and cap the branch fittings that serve these lines and tie all hard water lines in at a new location, somewhere between the meter and the soft water inlet fitting.

All water softeners must be equipped with a three-way bypass valve or a three-valve bypass configuration. You can buy one three-way valve and splice it into the inlet and outlet lines of the softener, or you can install a separate globe valve in the inlet line and another in the outlet line. Then install two tees in each pipe above these valves, joined by a third valve that will act as a bypass. When the softener is in service, the two line valves are open and the center valve is closed. When the softener is not in service, the two line valves are closed and the center valve is opened to allow water to pass from the inlet line to the outlet line without entering the water softener.

Water filters

Unlike softeners, which treat mineral salts, filters only screen unwanted sediment, minerals and chemicals. They strain water through fiber or charcoal cores designed for specific problem water conditions. While most filters are used to trap sediment, others are specially designed to filter mineral salts, like iron, calcium and sulfur. Other filter cores are designed to trap health-threatening nitrates, although the effectiveness of nitrate filters is debated by experts.

Many of these filters can be reused after they are back-flushed, but others must be discarded when they reach a saturation point. In any case, you should research filters thoroughly before investing in a filter system.

COMPRESSION FITTING

FILTER

Horizontal installation

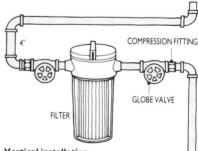

4"   COMPRESSION FITTING

GLOBE VALVE

FILTER

Vertical installation

How to install a filter

Filters are easy to install, but keep in mind that they must remain upright to work. Horizontal installations are easiest. Simply cut a section of pipe from the main trunk line and install gate valves on each new end. Then install the filter between the two valves with nipples and unions. With copper or plastic pipe, use male adapters.

For a vertical pipe installation, you will have to cut the pipe and create a horizontal loop for the filter. Use gate valves unions and nipples to make the necessary connections.

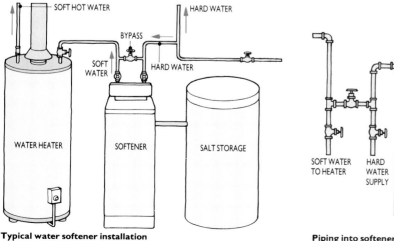

SOFT HOT WATER   HARD WATER

BYPASS

SOFT
WATER   HARD WATER

WATER HEATER   SOFTENER   SALT STORAGE

Typical water softener installation

SOFT WATER   HARD
TO HEATER   WATER
SUPPLY

Piping into softener

RURAL SEPTIC SYSTEM MAINTENANCE

Only two types of private waste disposal systems are allowed by most code authorities and health departments. They are underground (anaerobic) and above ground (aerobic) systems. Raw sewage seepage, as in cesspools, is no longer permitted, for obvious reasons.

An anaerobic system consists of a closed septic tank and a gray water leach field. When well maintained, this system will last the life of a home. When not properly maintained, a system can fail in five years. Once a system fails, it cannot be reclaimed. A new system will have to be installed at great cost.

Septic tanks

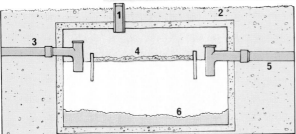

Typical septic tank system
1 Cleanout
2 Ground level
3 Inlet
4 Bacterial crust
5 Outlet
6 Sludge

To understand the need for routine maintenance, you must first understand how a septic system works. As raw sewage is drained into the septic tank, bacteria break the sewage down into gray water, bottom sludge and surface scum. As more sewage enters the tank, gray water rises through a baffle and floats out into the leach field. Once in the field, around 60 percent of the gray water is consumed by plants. The remaining 40 percent is lost through surface evaporation. The nitrate residue left behind is then consumed by another kind of bacteria found only in the top 4 feet of soil.

Because of the scum and sludge left in the tank, your septic tank must be pumped out every two or three years. If you do not have your tank pumped, the sludge at the bottom will rise, thus reducing the capacity of the tank. The scum will continue to build up at the top of the tank until it is deep enough to make its way through the baffle and into the leach field. Once inside the leach field, it will coat the walls of the trench and clog the gravel storage area. When the walls of the leach field are sealed, the leach field will fail.

To keep your septic tank and leach field in working order, have the tank pumped at least once every three years and avoid planting trees near the tank or on top of the leach field.

Repairing a collapsed leach field

Leach field water is transported through perforated pipe (**1**) or under concrete half culverts inverted on concrete blocks (**2**). While perforated pipe is packed in gravel and will not collapse when you drive on it, half culverts often do collapse with the weight of a vehicle. As a general rule, you should not drive over leach fields. If a section does collapse, you can dig it up and replace a broken section with a little shovel work.

Because leach fields work best near the surface, you will find the top of the half culvert only a foot or two down. Dig the dirt above the culvert away and keep it to one side of the ditch. When you hit gravel, dig it out of the trench and store it on the other side.

Each culvert will be 3 to 4 feet long. When you've removed the gravel from around the broken culvert, pull it out. Clean most of the gravel out of the ditch and set a new length of half culvert on the blocks. Shovel the gravel back into the ditch until the dome of the culvert is covered. Then lay several thicknesses of newspaper over the gravel and fill the remainder of the ditch with dirt. Because uncompacted dirt will settle in time, leave a 4-inch mound over the trench. Then soak the dirt and replace the sod.

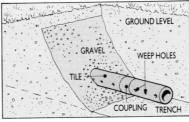

1 Gray water flows in and out of weep holes

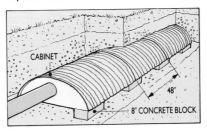

2 Inverted half-moon culverts

LAGOON DISPOSAL SYSTEMS

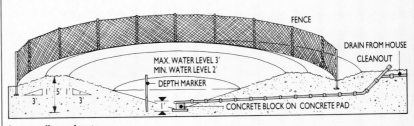

Lagoon disposal system

Aerobic systems are called lagoons. They rely on evaporation and aerobic bacteria to dispose of sewage. The secret to lagoon sewage disposal is in the shape and design of the lagoon. A lagoon is a 3-foot-deep hole with sloping sides and a flat bottom about 30 feet in diameter. The sewer line steps down just before it enters the lagoon and discharges about 3 feet below the water level. Bacteria breaks the solids down and evaporation keeps the lagoon

from overflowing. Naturally, lagoons are better suited to windy climates. And for safety reasons, every lagoon must be fenced.

To keep a lagoon working smoothly, keep tall weeds away from the berm so that wind can churn the water and sweep as much moisture away as possible. For the same reason, avoid planting trees in the path of prevailing winds. A lagoon is a self-regulating system that works well with little odor.

SPRINKLER SYSTEMS

With the introduction of polybutylene pipe and fittings to the plumbing market, simple do-it-yourself sprinkler systems are a lot easier to install, even in cold weather climates. Polybutylene pipe will take a *freeze, so drainage is not as critical as with other piping materials. Still, the most difficult aspect of any underground sprinkler job is the layout. Plan your work and work your plan.*

Installing a system

You will have to make a scale drawing of your lawn and include features such as driveways and sidewalks, which may present piping barriers. You should be able to cover your lawn evenly by matching sprinkler heads to specific areas. Use single-direction pop-up heads for terraces and flower gardens, 45- and 90-degree heads for corners and along drives and 360-degree heads for open spaces. No matter which combination you use, you will have some overlap. Overlapping patterns are not a real problem because coverage is lighter farther away from the heads. By researching the products on the market, you can get a good idea of how each head works and in which situation each should be used. You can do the layout yourself, or you may be able to get help from your local dealer.

Another important factor in planning your system is the water pressure in your home. With high pressure, you may be able to feed all heads from a single line and valve. With less pressure, you may need to divide the system up into two or three separately controlled lines so that one section can be charged at a time. Most sprinkler dealers will lend you a pressure gauge designed to be used on outside faucets. When testing for water pressure, make sure that none of the indoor fixtures is running at the same time.

Burying the lines

To bury the lines, start by marking each head location with a stake. Stretch a string from one stake to another and cut the sod along the string line. Make two cuts in rows about 6 inches apart and about 3 inches deep. Lift the sod up and lay it along the ditch. Then dig an additional 4 to 6 inches deep and level the bottom of the ditch as best you can.

With the ditches ready, roll the plastic pipe along the ditch and cut it at each head and at each intersecting fitting. Connect the tees, elbows and riser pipes at each head location. Then cover the pipe with loose dirt the length of each run. Hold each head level with the ground alongside the riser pipe to determine where to cut the riser. Cut the risers and install each head as you go. All joints will go together with O-ring compression fittings or push-fit fittings.

MAKING THE WATER CONNECTION

With all heads installed, replace the sod all the way up to the house connection. At the house, you will have a decision to make. You can connect directly to the sillcock, or bore through the rim joist or basement wall to connect the pipes inside. A sillcock connection is simpler, but a basement connection gives a cleaner appearance.

To connect to a sillcock, first install a hose-thread-adapted vacuum breaker. A vacuum breaker is necessary to keep your in-house plumbing from back-siphoning contaminated water. It will also allow your heads to drain properly. Then thread the sprinkler adapter to the vacuum breaker and turn on the water. If you need to use the sillcock separately, disconnect the sprinkler fitting temporarily. Of course, in colder climates, the sprinkler system should be disconnected in winter.

Permanent indoor connections

If more than one line must be connected, you are better off connecting inside the basement. Before each line goes into the house, install a backflow preventer. You can use the right angle of the backflow preventer as your elbow into the house. Once inside, run all lines to the nearest ¾-inch water pipe. About a foot before the supply line, install a valve on each line. Then tie the lines together and install a drain valve and another gate valve before tapping into the supply line. This will allow you to drain all lines each winter without shutting off the house water.

SEE ALSO

Details for: ▷

Plumbing outdoors	380
Garden planning	406–409

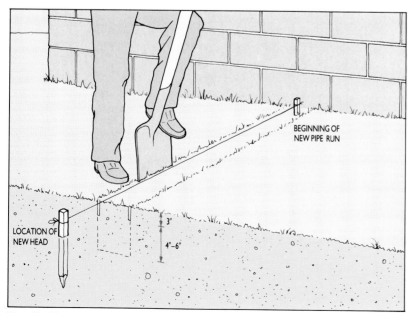

LOCATION OF NEW HEAD

BEGINNING OF NEW PIPE RUN

3"

4"–6"

Use a flat-bladed shovel to cut sod

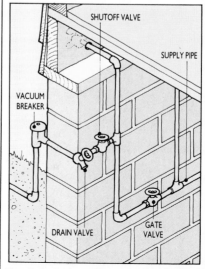

SHUTOFF VALVE

SUPPLY PIPE

VACUUM BREAKER

DRAIN VALVE

GATE VALVE

Details for linking sprinkler system to house

PLUMBING OUTDOORS

Outdoor plumbing can be a welcome alternative to stringing garden hoses across your yard. A freezeless spigot in your garden is convenient and a lot less messy than hoses. A seepage pit to serve a drain in your garage workshop can also make life easier. In the final analysis, outdoor plumbing is not much more difficult to install than indoor plumbing. The obvious difference is that in some locations, outdoor plumbing must be able to withstand subzero temperatures.

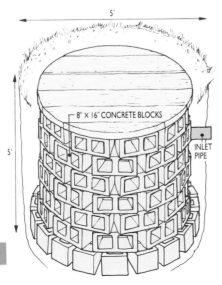

1 A freezeless yard hydrant provides water to remote locations year round

Freezeless yard hydrants

Yard hydrants (**1**) have their shutoff locations buried below frost level. When you lift the handle at the top of the hydrant, you pull a long stem inside the casing upward. The stopper at the lower end of the stem is lifted out of its seat and water travels up through the pipe casing to the spout. When you push the handle down, the stem pushes the stopper back into its seat and interrupts the flow of water. The water left standing in the pipe casing then drains back through an opening at the bottom of the hydrant, just below frost level.

2 Backflow preventers keep contamination from entering your piping

3 Seepage pits dispose of gray water only

Installing a hydrant

Whether you bring water from a basement wall or a buried rural line, you will have to rent a trenching machine. The depth of the trench you dig will be dictated by how deep the ground freezes in your area. Hydrants can be purchased in several lengths for a variety of conditions. A 5-foot depth is common in colder climates.

If you intend to bring water from a house system through a basement wall, simply start the trencher a few inches away from the wall and trench to the hydrant location. At the hydrant location, force the trencher to dig a foot or so deeper. Then, trench a few feet past where the hydrant will be located to avoid having loose soil fall back into the trench.

With the trench ready, measure carefully and drill directly into the open trench from inside the basement. Then slide one end of a coil of buriable plastic pipe through the wall from the outside and reel the coil out in the trench to the hydrant location. Leave the hydrant end of the coil out of the ditch so that you can attach the conversion fitting. The conversion fitting should be a male thread by male insert fitting, preferably made of brass. First, thread the fitting into the hydrant with pipe joint compound. Then, slide two stainless-steel hose clamps onto the plastic pipe and push the insert side of the fitting completely into the pipe. Finally, tighten the clamps around the pipe with a nut driver or small wrench.

Before setting the hydrant down into the trench, pour about 50 pounds of

gravel into the section of the ditch that you've made deeper. This will provide a small reservoir for the drain water when the hydrant is in use. Then set the hydrant in place and pour a few more pounds of gravel over the bottom of the hydrant. Before backfilling the trench, seal the wall opening with tar.

Finally, use another insert fitting inside the wall and make the water connection with copper pipe. Because plastic pipe cannot withstand heat, you may wish to use galvanized fittings to get a safe soldering distance away.

If you are splicing into an existing underground plastic line, installation is much the same. The only real difference is that instead of using a copper wye insert fitting, you will use an insert tee. The piping size you use will depend upon the hydrant's inlet size and your system's water pressure. A 1¼-inch line is commonly used.

Preventing backflow

Because both sillcocks and yard hydrants are frequently used to apply lawn and garden chemicals, water contamination becomes an issue. Contaminated hoses can easily backwash when fire hydrants are opened or when other high-volume draws are made on city piping near your home. This is especially true when a section of city main is shut down for repairs. To protect yourself and your neighbors, you should install backflow preventers (**2**) on all outdoor faucets. Backflow preventers allow water to pass in one direction only, thereby checking any system backwash.

Installing seepage pits

Seepage pits (**3**) are miniature leach fields designed to dispose of gray water discharged from appliances and floor drains. If your drainage system is served by a municipal sewer, seepage pits will not be needed, and in most cases, not allowed. If, however, yours is a home built in the country, a seepage pit can save you the trouble of tapping into your septic system when outbuildings are some distance from the house.

The size of the pit you build will depend upon anticipated volume. For a garage or workshop, a 3-by-4-foot inside diameter is often sufficient. Before starting the job, however, check with local code authorities for structural guidelines.

Start by digging a more or less round pit roughly 5 feet deep and 5 feet in diameter. Then lay a starter course of concrete blocks side-by-side around the outside walls of the pit. Follow with a series of courses until you are within 1½ feet of grade. At this point, you can trench the drainage pipe to the pit. If you slide the drainpipe through an opening in one of the top blocks, it will be held permanently in place. Finally, construct a cover from treated lumber.

For sandy soil, you may wish to tape layers of newspaper around the outside perimeter of the block to keep the soil from sifting in when you backfill. The newspaper will decompose after the soil settles.

9

HEATING

OPEN FIRES

For centuries open fires were our only domestic heating. Inefficient and wasteful, their only benefits were the radiant heat from the burning fuel and some milder *warmth from heated chimneys. They are nowadays used mainly as attractive focal points in homes heated by more modern means.*

How an open fire works

To burn well, any fire needs a good supply of oxygen (1) and a means for its smoke and gases to escape (2). If either of these is cut off the fire will be stifled and will eventually go out.

The domestic open fire is built on a barred grate (3) through which ash and debris fall into a removable tray and oxygen is sucked up into the base of the fire to maintain combustion.

As the fuel burns it gives off heated gases which expand and become lighter than the surrounding air so that they rise (4). To prevent the gases and smoke from drifting out and filling the room, a chimney above the fire gives them an escape route, taking them above the roof level of the house to be harmlessly discharged into the atmosphere beyond.

As the hot gases rise they cause the suction at the bottom of the fire which draws in the supply of oxygen that keeps it burning. For this reason, a good fire needs not only an effective chimney but also good ventilation in the room where it is burning so that the air consumed by the fire can be continually replenished. Sometimes efficient draftproofing at doors and windows can cause problems with a fire, and prevent its burning properly by denying it the constant supply of air that it needs. In such a case, the ventilation must be provided by means of a vent, or opening a window slightly; underfloor ventilation is another possibility.

The simple workings of a traditional open
1 Air is sucked in as gases rise
2 Gases escape up t narrow flue
3 The grate lets ash and air in
4 Gases vent to the outside

CHIMNEY FLUE

SMOKE SHELF

DAMPER

GRATE

FIREPLACE

CLEAN-OUT DOOR

ASH PIT

Sweeping chimneys

- **Vacuum sweeping**
You can rent a special vacuum cleaner for chimney sweeping. Its nozzle is inserted from above or below and sucks out the soot—a very clean method but no use for heavy soot deposits or other obstructions.

- **Chemical cleaning**
There are chemicals which remove light soot deposits and stop further sooting up. In liquid or powder form, sprinkled on the hot fire, they make a nontoxic gas which causes soot to crumble away from the chimney sides.

All solid fuels give off dust, ash, acids and tarry substances as they burn, and this material is carried up through the chimney, where a part of it collects as soot. If too much soot collects in a chimney, it effectively reduces the diameter, and therefore the gas flow, and prevents the fire from burning properly. It can even cause a blockage, particularly at a bend, or the more serious hazard of a chimney fire.

To prevent soot build up, sweep your chimneys at least twice a year, once during the heating season and once at the end to prevent acids in the soot from attacking the chimney's lining and mortar joints during the summer. If a chimney is left unswept for too long a period, the consumption may increase, smoke may start billowing into the room and soot may occasionally drop into the fire.

Though it's seemingly a dirty job, you can sweep a chimney without making a great deal of mess to be cleaned up afterwards, provided you take some care. You can rent the brushes. The modern ones have nylon bristles and "canes" made from polypropylene.

Remove all loose items from the fire surround and the hearth, then roll back the carpet and cover it with a dropcloth or newspapers for protection. Drape a large old sheet or blanket over the fire surround, weighting it down along the top and leaning something heavy against each side to form a seal with the edges of the fire surround.

Actual sweeping may be done by pushing a brush up from the fireplace, or by forcing it down from the chimney top. If the roof is dangerous or the chimney is covered by a nonremovable chimney cap, sweep from inside the house (you may have to remove the damper plate at the base of the flue to fit the brushes). If possible, sweep from the top down. To do this, first be sure the fireplace opening is tightly covered with dropcloths. From the roof, insert a correct size brush (it should fit tightly) into the chimney top and push it down toward the fireplace opening below. Screw on additional lengths of cane as necessary to reach the proper depth. Work the brushes up and down, being careful not to damage any mortar inside the chimney. When you reach the bottom, withdraw the brush. Wait one hour for the dust to settle, then vacuum the debris from the fireplace floor and smoke shelf using a heavy-duty industrial vacuum cleaner available from rent-it centers.

Though using a brush and canes is the most time-honored—and the most effective—way of sweeping a chimney, in recent years some other methods have been found for doing this dirty job (see left).

Cleaning from above
Insert brush and canes at chimney top. Brush up and down, being careful not to disturb mortar joints.

Cleaning from below
Seal off the fireplace with an old sheet and feed the canes up under it.

CURING A SMOKY FIREPLACE

A well-functioning fireplace is the product of many design elements working together in harmony. When fireplace smoke drifts outward into the room rather than escaping smoothly up the chimney, there may be several causes. If the fireplace has always been a smoky one, chances are that its construction includes one or more design flaws. If the condition is a recent development or is intermittent, solving the problem may mean only simple adjustment or cleaning.

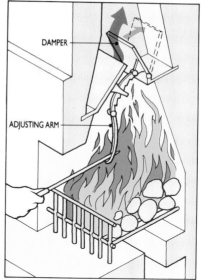

Remedying simple problems

If the fireplace smokes only occasionally, or has just begun to smoke, run through this checklist of minor adjustments. First, be certain that when the fire is burning, the damper is fully open. Most dampers can be adjusted when hot by pushing the protruding end of the handle with a poker. Check, too, that the chimney is free of obstructions, especially if a normally clean-burning fireplace suddenly starts smoking. Along with this, make sure that the chimney is kept regularly swept. Accumulated soot can eventually cause smoking and, worse, a chimney fire.

Check that the fire is built well back in the firebox so that no burning logs project beyond the fireplace opening. Try raising the height of the fire several inches by placing the logs on a grate elevated on firebricks. Inadequate inflow of air—too little to support combustion or feed the chimney's updraft—may also be the culprit, especially if you have altered the ventilation pattern in the room by adding insulation and weatherstripping. To alleviate this cause of a smoky fireplace, open a door or window to admit more air.

Regulating updraft
Regulate chimney updraft by adjusting damper. Operate adjusting arm using poker when fire is burning.

Correcting chimney faults

To produce an updraft, air must flow steadily across the opening at the top of a chimney, creating a partial vacuum within, which aids in drawing the heated air from the fireplace upward. In order for the air to be unobstructed as it flows, a chimney must be at least 3 feet higher than any object within a 10-foot radius, including roof peaks, trees, television antennas or other chimneys. If you cannot increase the height of a too-short chimney by adding to it, attaching a chimney cap or smoke puller (a fan mounted in the chimney opening) may help. Before undertaking such modifications, consult a professional chimney mason.

Uncapped chimneys should have a sloping cowl of mortar on all four sides to direct passing air upward and over the opening. Otherwise, air striking the chimney will eddy and swirl erratically.

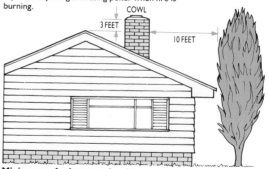

Minimum safe clearance for chimneys

Correcting fireplace proportions

To draw smoke upward properly, the dimensions of the chimney flue must bear a certain proportional relationship to those of the brick-lined or steel-lined area where the fire is actually built, called the firebox. Also, the firebox itself must be built to a certain shape, in order to both reflect heat outward yet direct smoke upward. Often, either the firebox is built too large for the flue rising inside the chimney, or the flue (usually a retrofit inserted into a chimney that was originally built without one) is too small.

One solution is to fit a metal fireplace hood, available from fireplace and woodstove supply stores and some home centers, across the top of the fireplace opening to decrease its overall size and also trap smoke that might otherwise seep out. To install the hood, first determine how large it must be by holding a piece of metal or dampened plywood across the top of the fireplace when a fire is burning. As the fireplace begins to smoke, gradually lower the sheet of material until the smoking is contained. Purchase a hood this size. Most hoods attach to the fireplace surround by means of special masonry hangers.

Another solution is to fit glass doors across the entire front opening of the fireplace. These, too, are available in many sizes from fireplace and woodstove stores, as well as home centers. Although some heat may be lost to the room when the doors are closed the fire is entirely enclosed and smoke completely contained. (There are, however, energy-efficient models which actually enhance the amount of heat produced by the fireplace.)

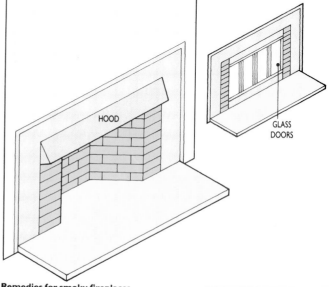

Remedies for smoky fireplaces
A hood or glass doors can prevent smoke from entering a room.

REMOVING AN ANTIQUE FIREPLACE

To take out an antique fire surround and hearth is easy enough, but it can create much dust and debris. Any hammering is likely to cause quantities of soot to fall down the chimney. Before you start, sweep the chimney, move all furniture as far from *the fireplace as possible, roll back the carpet and cover everything with drop-cloths. There is a good demand for Victorian fire surrounds and some are valuable. If you remove yours undamaged, you may be able to sell it.*

Removing the hearth

Most old-fashioned hearths were laid after the fire surround had been fitted and so must come out first, but check beforehand that your surround has not been installed on top of the hearth.

Wear safety goggles and heavy gloves against flying debris and use a 2-pound sledgehammer and bricklayer's chisel to break the mortar bond between the hearth and the subhearth below.

Knocking in wood wedges will help. Lever the hearth free with a crowbar or the blade of a strong garden spade and lift it clear. It will be heavy, so get someone to help.

Some older hearths are laid level with the surrounding floorboards and have a layer of tiles on top of them. Here all that's needed is to lift the tiles off carefully with a bricklayer's chisel.

Removing the surround

- **Saving a fireplace**
Fire surrounds can be very heavy, especially stone or marble ones. If you wish to keep yours intact for sale, lay an old mattress in front of it before you pull it from the wall so it will be less likely to break if it should fall.

Most fire surrounds are held to the wall by screws driven through metal lugs set around their edges. They will be concealed in the plaster on the chimney breast. To find the lugs, chip away a 1-inch strip of plaster around the surround, then expose the lugs completely and take out the screws. If they are rusted and immovable, soak them in penetrating oil, leave for a few hours and try again. If that fails, drill out their heads. The surround will be heavy, so have some help available when you lever it from the wall and lower it carefully onto the floor (see left).

Brick and stone surrounds
A brick or stone surround can be removed a piece at a time, using a bricklayer's chisel to break the mortar joints. There may also be metal ties holding it to the wall.

A wooden surround
A wooden surround will probably be held by screws driven through its sides and top into strips fixed to the chimney breast inside the surround. The screw heads will be hidden by wooden plugs or filler. Chisel these out, remove the screws and lift away the surround.

Taking out a fireplace
1 The hearth chipped free
2 The subhearth at floor level
3 The fireback, to be broken out
4 The fire surround; a brick or stone one can be taken out in bits
5 Metal lugs hold most surrounds in place

REPLACING CRACKED TILES

Cracked or broken tiles in a hearth or fire surround should be replaced with sound ones, but you may not be able to match those in an old fireplace. One solution here is to buy some new tiles that pleasantly complement or contrast with the originals and replace more than just the damaged one or two, making a random or symmetrical pattern.

Break out the damaged tile with a hammer and cold chisel, working from the center outwards. Wear thick gloves and safety goggles against flying bits of tile and protect nearby surfaces with dropcloths. When the tile is out, remove all traces of old adhesive or mortar and vacuum up the dust.

If necessary, cut the new tile to shape. Spread heat-resistant tile adhesive thickly on its back and on the surface where it is to go. Don't get adhesive on its edges or the edges of surrounding tiles. Set the tile in place, taking care that the clearance is equal all around, and wipe off any excess adhesive. Leave it to set and then apply grout.

If you are replacing only one tile, it's not worth buying a tub or packet of adhesive. Instead, mix a paste from coarse sawdust and wood glue, which will work just as well. If the tile is very close to the fire you can use some fire cement.

Chipping out a damaged tile
Start in the middle and work out to edges. Clean out all old mortar or adhesive.

Complete retiling
If a lot of the tiles are damaged or crazed, your best course may be to retile the surround and hearth entirely. This is much less trouble than it sounds, as you can simply stick the new tiles directly on top of the old ones. First make sure that the old tiles are clean and remove any loose pieces, then apply your tile adhesive and stick the tiles on in the ordinary way.

INSTALLING AN OLD-FASHIONED FIREPLACE

In the past 30 years or so traditional fireplaces have vanished from many older houses, swept away in the name of modernization. But now they are being appreciated again and even sought after. You can reinstate an old-fashioned fireplace as described here.

Most period fire surrounds are held in place by lugs screwed to the wall, but some can be attached with mortar. A plaster surround can be held with dabs of bonding plaster.

First, remove a strip of plaster from around the fire opening about 2 inches wider all around than the surround.

If the surround incorporates a cast-iron centerpiece, it must be fitted first. Most of them simply stand on the back hearth, but some have lugs for screwing to the wall. If yours has lugs, use metal wall plugs or expanding bolts. Fit lengths of asbestos-substitute packing as expansion joints where the grate or centerpiece touches the fireback.

Hold the surround in place, mark the wall for the screw holes and drill them. Use a level to check that the surround is upright and the mantel horizontal, and make any needed corrections by fitting wooden wedges behind the surround or bending the lugs backward or forward.

An alternative method for plaster surrounds is to apply mortar or plaster to the wall and prop the surround against it with boards until the mortar or plaster sets.

Replace the hearth or build a new one. Set the hearth on dabs of mortar and point around the edges with the same material.

Replaster the wall and fit new baseboard molding between the hearth and the corners of the chimney breast.

Hold a light surround in place with boards while the plaster sets

SEALING A FIREPLACE OPENING

If you have removed an old fireplace, you can close the opening by bricking it up or by covering it with plasterboard. The latter will make it easier to reinstate the fireplace if you want to at some time in the future. In either case, you must fit a ventilator in the center of the opening just above baseboard level. This will provide an airflow through the chimney and prevent condensation from forming and seeping through the old brickwork to damage wall decorations.

Restoring the floor

If the floor is solid, you need only bring the subhearth up level with it, using cement. You can also do this with a wood floor if it is to be carpeted. If you want exposed floorboards, the subhearth will have to be broken away with hammer and cold chisel to make room for a new joist and floorboards to be fitted.

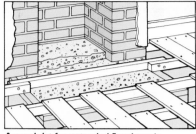

A new joist for extended floorboards

Sealing the opening with bricks

If you wish to brick up the firebox opening, remove bricks from alternate courses at the edges of the opening so that the new brickwork can be "toothed in." Provide ventilation for the chimney by fitting a brick vent centrally in the brickwork and just above baseboard level. Plaster the brickwork and allow it to dry out thoroughly before you redecorate the wall.

Finally, lever the old pieces of baseboard from the ends of the chimney breast and replace them with a full-length piece from corner to corner.

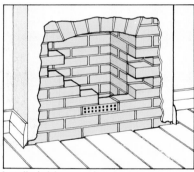

Install a brick vent at baseboard level

Sealing the opening with plasterboard

Cut a panel from ⅜-inch plasterboard and nail it onto a wood frame mounted inside the fire opening.

Use 2 × 2-inch sawn lumber for the frame. Nail it into the opening with masonry nails, setting it in so that when the plasterboard is nailed on, it will lie flush with the surrounding wall if it is to be papered. Place it ⅛ inch deeper if a plaster skim is to be added. For papering, fix the plasterboard with its ivory side out; for a plaster skim, the gray side should be showing. After decorating or plastering the panel, fit a ventilator.

Attach plasterboard panel to inset wood frame

Closing off the chimney top

When you close off a fireplace opening, you will have to cap the chimney in such a way as to keep rain out while allowing the air from the vent in the room to escape. Use a half-round ridge tile bedded in cement, or a metal cowl, either of which will do the job.

Half-round ridge tile   **Commercial cowl**

INSTALLING A COMBINATION INSERT

Easy-to-install fireplace inserts, consisting of an energy-efficient tubular fireplace grate and blower unit plus glass doors that fully cover the fireplace opening, are widely available and can significantly boost the amount of heat produced by an ordinary fireplace.

Although there are many different varieties, installation of most combination inserts involves first assembling the grate, usually by bolting the convection tubes in sequence to the grate supports which elevate the unit off the firebox floor, and then fitting the unit into the firebox, to be followed by the assembled doors. Many grates are free-standing, and may be merely slid in and out for periodic cleaning.

The tops of the convection tubes generally seat against a vented portion along the top of the door frame, so that the heated air rising through them as the fire burns is directed outward. A blower assembly attaches to the lower portion of the door to draw air needed for combustion into the lower ends of the tubes and assist in forcing it upward and out again, into the room.

The doors themselves fit around the perimeter of the fireplace surround and are held in place with masonry bolts. Installation is usually a matter of drilling into the masonry, installing bolt inserts, then attaching the door frame using the bolts supplied with the unit. In addition, most manufacturers recommend sealing the gap between the insert frame and fireplace surround with fiberglass insulation to prevent heat leaks.

Flue box
Connecting the flue of a log-burning stove to a flue box set into a bricked-up fireplace may be preferred to using a horizontal or vertical closure plate. A flue box is a cast-iron frame with a hole in the center for the flue outlet.

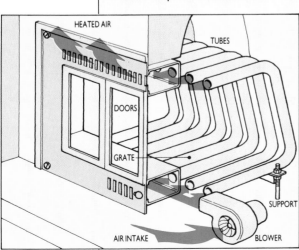

Combination tube and glass-door insert
This installs easily and increases fireplace efficiency.

WOOD HEATERS AND INSERTS

A modern enclosed fireplace, or room heater, can be freestanding or inset (built-in). Both are very efficient at heating individual rooms and, with the addition of back boilers, can provide domestic hot water and central heating, too. The toughened-glass doors of closed fireplaces and inserts, which allow the glow of the fire to be seen, open for extra fuel to be added.

A freestanding heater on the hearth

Freestanding room heaters are designed to stand on the hearth forward of the chimney breast. They radiate extra warmth from their casings but their size can make them obtrusive in small rooms. You may also have to extend the hearth to the required 18 inches in front of the heater.

A heater of this type has a flue outlet at its rear which must be connected to the chimney, and the easiest way of arranging this is to seal the outlet into a metal backplate that closes off the fire opening. The projecting end of the outlet must be at least 4 inches from the back wall of the firebox.

The closure plate should be of steelboard (metal-covered asbestos), which is sold at woodstove supply stores. Use metal wall plugs to hold the screws, and seal the joint between plate and opening with asbestos-substitute packing and fire cement. Alternatively, stovepipes can be fitted into the fireplace damper opening after removing the damper plate.

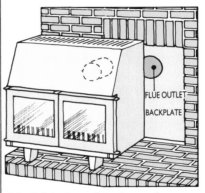

A backplate closes off the fire opening

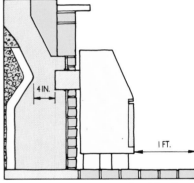

Key measurements for an enclosed fireplace

A freestanding heater in the fireplace

Some freestanding room heaters are designed to stand in the fire opening. This type of heater has a flue outlet in its top which must be connected to a closure plate set in the base of the chimney.

The plate can be of metal or precast concrete. For access to fit it, remove some bricks from the chimney breast just above the opening but below the load-bearing lintel. If the plate is of concrete, take out a course of bricks around the bottom of the chimney to support it properly. You can insert a metal plate into a chased-out mortar joint or fasten it with expansion bolts. Bed the plate on fire cement, sealing the edges above and below. Check that the heater's outlet enters the chimney flue, and seal the plate joint with asbestos-substitute packing and fire cement.

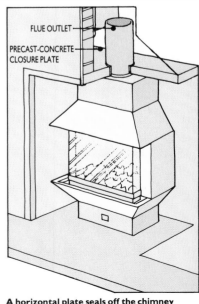

A horizontal plate seals off the chimney

An inset room heater

An inset room heater has its flue outlet mounted on top to be connected to a chimney closure plate or stovepipe rising through the chimney.

This type of appliance is designed to fill and seal the fire opening completely, so to install one you may have to modify your present fire surround or, if the opening is very large, even build a new one. The sides of the surround must be exactly at right angles to the hearth, as the front portion of the heater's casing has to be sealed to both. If the surround and the hearth form an odd angle, a good seal with the heater casing will be impossible. The seal is made with asbestos-substitute packing material.

More inset room heaters are screwed down to the firebox floor, and some may need a vermiculite-based infill around the back of the casing which must be in place before the chimney closure plate is fitted and the flue outlet connected.

Some come supplied with their own fire surrounds, complete with drop-in closure plates designed to make their installation easier.

Finish the job by restoring the brickwork of the chimney breast and replastering it if necessary.

One of the most economical ways to keep a room warm is by means of a modern slow-combustion log-burning stove—if you have access to cheap wood. Like fireplace inserts or inset room heaters, they can be stood on the hearth with rear flue outlets or installed in the fireplace with top-mounted outlets. A good log-burning stove can burn all day or night on one load of wood.

A log-burning stove is best installed forward of the chimney breast so that you get the full benefit of the heat that radiates from its casing. You can stand it on your present hearth provided that the hearth projects the required minimum of 18 inches in front of the stove and at least 12 inches on each side of it (36 inches from the nearest combustible surface). Otherwise you will have to make a new and bigger hearth. The hearth must be level and constructed of stone, brick or tiles.

A log-burning stove can be fitted with a stainless-steel, insulated flue pipe and this can be passed through a vertical back closure plate that seals off the whole fireplace opening or through a horizontal plate that closes off the base of the chimney. It may even be passed through a fitting—called a thimble—in the face of the chimney itself.

As an alternative to all this you can brick up the fireplace completely and install a flue box (see opposite).

If the flue pipe is connected to a stovepipe, the connection should include an extension of pipe below the joint, to serve as an ash pit. The installation must incorporate good access for efficient chimney sweeping, which will be needed often.

It's important to follow local fire codes and building regulations when installing a wood stove. These generally include setting the unit at a safe distance from combustibles, making a positive connection between the stovepipe and flue and being sure the flue extends at least 36 inches above the roof.

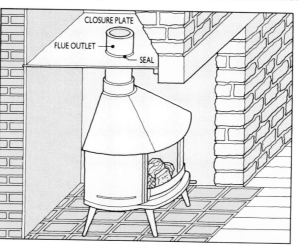

Vertical flue outlet
This type of stove has its flue sealed into the opening of a horizontal closure plate in the base of the chimney.

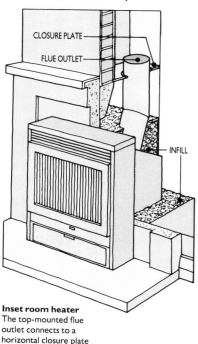

Inset room heater
The top-mounted flue outlet connects to a horizontal closure plate in the chimney base. Some versions need an infill around the rear casing.

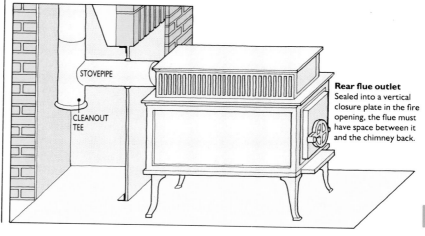

Rear flue outlet
Sealed into a vertical closure plate in the fire opening, the flue must have space between it and the chimney back.

INSTALLING A FLUE LINER

If your house was built before World War II, there's a good chance that its chimney is unlined and is simply a rectangular duct whose brickwork is either stuccoed with cement or quite exposed.

Over the years corrosive elements in the rising combustion gases eat into the chimney's mortar and brickwork and weaken it, allowing condensation to pass through and form damp patches on the chimney breast and, in extreme cases, letting smoke seep through. This is particularly true where coal or wood-burning appliances are in use.*

Choosing a flue liner

You can deal with these problems by installing a flue liner, which will prevent the corrosive elements from reaching the brickwork. It will also reduce the "bore" of the flue, and that will speed up the flow of gases and prevent their cooling and condensing. The draft of air through the flue will improve and the fire will burn more efficiently.

However, it is important to fit the type of liner that's appropriate to the kind of heating appliance being used and to be sure the size is large enough to prevent the fireplace from smoking. Ask the appliance supplier or building inspector. Linings are tubes, one-piece or in sections, of metal or other rigid, noncombustible material.

ROOF ACCESS

You can rent easy-to-use light alloy roof scaffolding. Two units will make a half platform for a central or side chimney; four will provide an all-around platform.

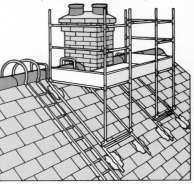

Scaffolding is essential for safe working

Installing a one-piece flue liner

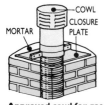

Approved cowl for gas

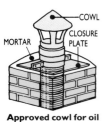

Approved cowl for oil

A popular type of liner is a one-piece flexible corrugated tube of stainless steel that is easily fed into a chimney that has bends in it. Unfortunately, this type of liner is not suitable for use with coal or wood-burning appliances. To install it you must get onto the roof and erect scaffolding around the chimney (see above right).

First sweep the chimney, then chop away the mortar around the base of the chimney pot with a hammer and cold chisel, remove the pot—it will be very heavy, so take care—and lower it to the ground on a rope. Clean up the top of the chimney to expose the brickwork.

The liner is fed into the chimney from the top. Drop a strong weighted line down the chimney (1) and attach its other end to the conical endpiece of the flue liner. Have an assistant pull gently on the line from below while you feed the liner down into the chimney (2). When the conical endpiece emerges below, remove it and connect the liner to a closure plate set across the base of the chimney or to the flue outlet of the heating appliance, and seal the joint with an asbestos-substitute packing and some fire cement.

Return to the roof, fit the top closure plate and bed it in mortar laid on the top of the chimney, adding extra mortar to match the original (3). Finally, fit a cowl to the top of the liner, having chosen one appropriate to the heating appliance being used (see left).

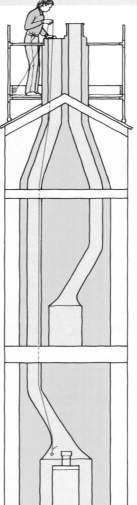

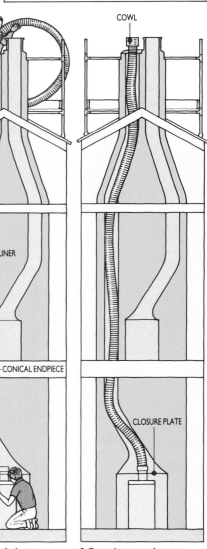

1 Lower attached line   **2 Feed liner to helper**   **3 Complete top closure**

Installing a sectional flue liner

A sectional flue liner has the space around it filled with a lightweight concrete that strengthens and insulates the chimney but needs good foundations for the added weight. Like the one-piece liner (see opposite), it is inserted from the top. First, cement a steel base plate across the bottom of the chimney.

Tie the first flue section to a rope and lower it into the chimney. Connect the next section to it by one of the steel collars supplied and lower the two farther down. Continue adding sections and lowering the liner until it reaches the base plate, then seal it in place.

If there are any bends in the chimney, you will have to break into it at those points to feed the sections in. This may be a job for a professional.

For filling in the chimney around the liner use concrete made with a lightweight aggregate such as expanded clay or vermiculite. Pour this into the chimney around the liner and finish off the mortar cap at the top.

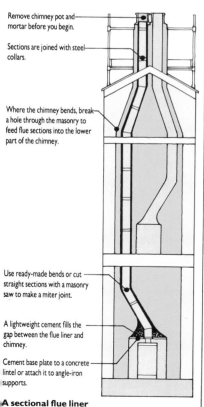

Remove chimney pot and mortar before you begin.

Sections are joined with steel collars.

Where the chimney bends, break a hole through the masonry to feed flue sections into the lower part of the chimney.

Use ready-made bends or cut straight sections with a masonry saw to make a miter joint.

A lightweight cement fills the gap between the flue liner and chimney.

Cement base plate to a concrete lintel or attach it to angle-iron supports.

A sectional flue liner
Installing a sectional flue liner can be such a complicated procedure that it is worth asking for professional quotes before you decide to tackle the job yourself.

MAINTAINING FIREPLACE SURROUNDS

Though fireplace surrounds and hearths get a great deal of wear and tear, they will keep their appearance if they're looked after and if certain elementary care is taken. For example, avoid standing cups, glasses and ashtrays on them and be especially careful with such drinks as coffee, tea, alcohol and fruit juices, which can be very damaging to some surfaces, particularly marble.

Always let the hearth and surround cool down before you clean them, and avoid standing on the hearth when you clean the surround.

The different materials respond to different cleaning methods.

STONE

This can be sponged off with warm water that has a little detergent mixed into it. You can remove the more stubborn stains with a stiff brush.

MARBLE AND GRANITE

It is easy to damage the fine finish on these stones, so they should be treated with some care. Wash them regularly with warm, soapy water and polish them with a chamois leather or a good-quality wax polish. Patch small chips with a putty made from kaolin powder (china clay) and epoxy glue. Rub down the hardened filler with silicon carbide paper and touch up with lacquer.

CERAMIC TILES

Wash these with warm water containing a little detergent. Never use any kind of abrasive cleaner on them.

BRICKS

Dust bricks off occasionally with a soft brush, but never use soapy water on them. If you have built your own brick surround, you should treat it with a commercial sealer to prevent "dusting." Broken bricks can be stuck together again with an epoxy adhesive, or you can cut them out and replace them with new ones, using fresh mortar.

SLATE

Wash this with warm water mixed with a little detergent, using a stiff brush. If the slate is unpolished, remove stubborn stains with an abrasive cleaner.

METALWORK

Wash this with warm, soapy water and take off stubborn tar and soot stains with commercial metal cleaner. Clean up cast-iron surrounds with wet-and-dry abrasive paper or emery cloth, then finish with stove blacking.

WOODWORK

If the grain is exposed, maintain the finish with a good wax polish. Fill any cracks or gouges with a commercial wood filler tinted to match with a little wood stain. The woodwork can also be painted in the ordinary way.

Stone surround

Marble surround

Wood surround

● **Casting a flue liner**
Professional installers can cast a flue liner in place. A deflated tube is lowered into the chimney. It is inflated, and a lightweight infill is poured into the gap between the tube and chimney. When the infill has set, the tube is deflated and removed, leaving a smooth-bore flue.

CENTRAL HEATING SYSTEMS

A central heating system supplies heat from a single source to selected rooms—or all the rooms—in the house. It is a much more efficient arrangement than having an individual heater in each room as it has only one appliance to be controlled, cleaned and maintained.

Categories of heating systems

Central heating systems are categorized by the medium used to deliver the heat from its source to the various outlets around the house. The three most common systems are forced-air, circulating hot water, and steam. Heat sources for these are normally a gas- or oil-fired furnace (though in some areas coal- and even wood-fueled systems are still in use), which in turn either heats water in a boiler or air passing directly past the flame. Electric heating systems, which derive heat through simple resistance wiring usually embedded in ceilings or floors, or which feed heated air through a blower, are a less popular system, due to expensive energy costs. Their advantages, however, are cleanliness and high efficiency.

Forced-air systems

Modern forced-air heating systems consist of a furnace which heats air, a large squirrel-cage blower which circulates that air, and a system of air ducts through which the heated air is directed throughout the house. A secondary system of ducts is also part of the system. Through it, cooled air returns to the furnace.

Because of the size and unwieldy nature of the air ducts, forced hot-air heating systems are almost always installed during new construction. Rarely are they feasible as retrofits. From the main duct leading away from the blower chamber the delivery ducts branch off, running between floor joists and wall studs to their openings at louvered registers normally located in outside walls, a short distance up from the floor. Cool air returns via larger-size ducts, which generally open directly into the floor, most often near inside walls or near the center of a room, but also in natural air traps such as stairwells. Since hot air rises and cold air descends, the warm air rising along the outside walls heats the rooms; then, as it cools, descends and enters the return ducts, creating a convection current which serves the entire enclosed area.

In large systems, the ductwork is usually designed to produce heating zones, groups of rooms or areas served by a single branch-duct system which can be isolated from the rest. By the use of dampers which physically close off key ducts (dampers are operated manually or by thermostats), the amount of heat directed throughout the house can be adjusted so that unused rooms receive less heat, while frequently inhabited rooms receive more.

Typical gas-fired forced-air system
1 Furnace (gas)
2 Motor
3 Blower
4 Cold-air return
5 Warm-air delivery
6 Warm-air registers
7 Cold-air registers
8 Exhaust (to chimney)

BALANCING A FORCED-AIR SYSTEM

Adjusting the air flowing through a forced-air heating system—a process called balancing—assures that each room receives the most comfortable amount of heat. Whereas the registers at the ends of each duct run are generally louvered and adjustable, it is best to use these merely as a means of directing air up or down within a room. To actually control the amount of air passing through the registers, most duct systems are fitted with metal plates called dampers inside strategically located sections. Dampers are controlled by means of a handle on the outside of the duct. Turning the handle so it is parallel with the run of the duct allows maximum airflow; turning it toward perpendicular, the less air flows through.

To balance the system, you must merely adjust the dampers until the appropriate settings are achieved. The process is simple but, because each room requires 6 to 8 hours to become properly heated, takes time. Balance the system during a cold spell, when the furnace is running at its peak. Begin by closing down the damper to the most uncomfortably hot room nearest the furnace. This will send correspondingly greater amounts of heat to more distant registers, so, after waiting the required heating-up time, move on to the next uncomfortably hot room and adjust the damper there. You may determine the desired temperature of a given room by "feel," or by holding a thermometer in the room a few feet above floor level.

After you have moved through the entire house and adjusted all the dampers once (a process that may have taken a week or more), go back and fine-tune your work by making minor adjustments to the dampers that seem to require it. Wait the necessary time between each. When you are finished, mark with white paint on the duct the positions of all the damper handles so that they are permanently recorded.

If, after balancing, there exist rooms at the far end of duct runs that receive insufficient heat, a common solution is to increase the speed of the squirrel-cage blower. This is done by adjusting or replacing one of the drive pulleys on the motor. However, since increasing blower speed places additional strain on the motor, consult a furnace repair person beforehand.

CENTRAL HEATING SYSTEMS

Circulating hot-water

The most popular form of central heating is a circulating hot-water system. Water is heated to between 120 and 180 degrees F in a furnace-fired boiler and then is forced by a circulator pump through a system of pipes leading to and from radiators or convectors located throughout the house. Some layouts pump water through a single loop of pipe, off which branch piping both feeds hot water and returns cooled water to each radiator in sequence. With these systems, careful balancing (as for forced-air systems) is necessary to assure that radiators at the far end of the pipe loop obtain sufficient heat. A better type of layout is one made up of two sets of pipe runs, one to carry only the hot water, and one to return only the cooled. These systems require far less adjustment, since water flowing to the farthest radiator does not become mixed with cooled water returning from radiators along the way.

Hot-water systems include an expansion tank—normally located near the boiler—which contains air. As water in the system becomes heated and expands, the air in the tank is compressed, in turn placing the water in the system also under pressure, and thus preventing it from becoming steam.

Steam heat

Few contemporary homes are built with steam heating systems. However, they are still to be found in many older homes, especially those built prior to World War II. Steam systems operate much like a single-pipe circulating hot-water system (see above). Water heated in a boiler until it becomes steam travels under its own pressure through a single pipe forming a loop around the house, off which branch plumbing services each radiator. As the steam cools by giving up its heat to the radiators, it changes back to water and returns to the boiler by gravity via the same pipe from which it was originally dispersed. Steam systems require neither a circulator nor an expansion tank. Piping must, however, slope downward from all points toward the boiler, and balancing is necessary to properly distribute steam to each room. In addition, steam radiators must be frequently drained of both air and water to remain in working order.

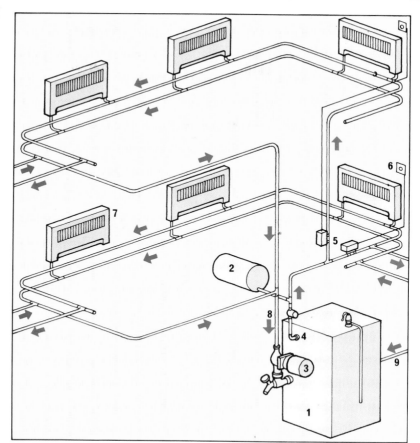

Typical circulating hot-water system
1 Boiler (oil-fired)
2 Expansion tank
3 Circulator pump
4 Hot-water supply
5 Control valves
6 Thermostats
7 Convectors
8 Cooled-water return
9 Main water supply

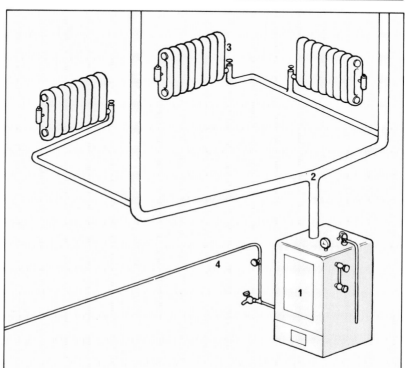

Typical steam/heat system
1 Boiler (oil-fired)
2 Steam supply/return pipe
3 Radiator
4 Main water supply

CENTRAL HEATING SYSTEMS

**Typical radiant
electric ceiling
(cable-embedded)**
1 Service panel
2 Heating-cable grids
3 Thermostats

Electric heat

Electric central heating systems have long been popular in Europe and have been available in the U.S. for approximately fifty years. Their popularity reached its peak during the 1960s, prior to the worldwide increase in energy costs, which has subsequently caused large-scale electric heating systems to be expensive to operate. Still, electric heat offers distinct advantages of comfort—quick, efficient, draft-free warmth—and, since no fuel is actually burned, the lack of need for such apparatus as a chimney, fuel storage tank, and in many systems even ductwork, piping, and vents.

Because most electric systems operate on the principles of radiant, rather than convective, heat, they provide the most uniform heat and achieve their greatest energy efficiency when installed over the greatest possible area. Installing radiant heating is similar to installing electric lighting: Many small, low-intensity units covering a broad area produce better results than only a few high-intensity units widely spaced.

Embedded tubes and cables

In new-floor and -ceiling construction, grids of electric resistance heating cable are often embedded between layers of whatever building material is used, with insulation placed below (in the case of floors) or above the wiring (in the case of ceilings) to direct all heat toward the living area. Each grid forms a separate heating zone and is wired as an individual circuit to a central service panel (generally not the same panel that controls the other household circuitry), and is controlled by an individual thermostat.

In place of cable, grids of copper tubing are sometimes embedded which circulate electrically heated hot water. Such systems are actually a form of circulating hot-water heat, and are easily as capable of being oil- or gas-fired.

INSTALLING RADIANT CEILING PANELS

Flexible and rigid panels containing electric heating grids are available for retrofitting or new construction. Some types fasten to standard framing prior to installing the finished ceiling; others are embedded in gypsum and may be installed using drywall screws or nails.

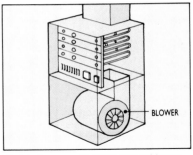

Baseboard heaters

Electric baseboard heaters are the most popular form of electric heat in the U.S. Each unit contains one or more horizontal heating elements, the entire unit being thermostatically controlled. Often, units are ganged around the perimeter of the area to be heated.

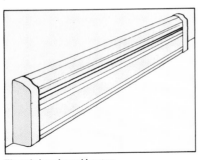

Electric baseboard heater

Wall heaters

Individual electric wall heaters are often installed in special-use areas such as bathrooms and laundry rooms to provide supplementary or occasional heat. Most of these units include a small fans which aids in circulating heated air throughout the room.

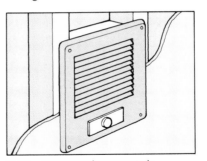

Wall heater mounts between studs

Electric furnace

Electric furnaces are small and require no chimney or vents. They usually consist of several cooking-oven type heating elements plus a squirrel-cage blower. The furnace is linked to a duct system and operates as a form of forced hot-air heating.

Electric furnace with squirrel-cage blower

FUEL-BURNING FURNACES

The furnace is the heart of any heating system, whether forced-air, circulating hot-water, or steam. By far the most common furnaces in use today are fuel-burners—gas- or oil-fired. Either may in turn be used to heat air or water for circulation throughout the house. Fuel-burning furnaces require regular adjustment and periodic care. If they are properly looked after, however, modern furnaces can be economical and efficient heat producers and will provide years of dependable service, often equal to the life of the house.

SEE ALSO

Details for: ▷

Furnace maintenance	397
Trouble-shooting	404

Oil burners

Oil burners spray fuel oil into a combustion chamber which is then ignited to produce heat. The two most popular burner designs are the pressure (gun) type and the vaporizing (pot) type. Pressure burners are by far the most popular furnaces in the U.S. today. Of the various designs, both high- and low-pressure types are available. The most common variety is high-pressure.

In a high-pressure oil burner, a fine spray of oil is jetted under pump pressure through a nozzle, mixed with air and then ignited by an electric spark derived from household current. Low-pressure burners are somewhat similar, the difference being that the oil and air are mixed before exiting the nozzle and pumped into the combustion chamber under far less pressure and through a much larger opening.

Vaporizing burners do not operate under pressure of any sort. The combustion area consists of an enclosed shallow pan into which oil is admitted by regulating a manually operated valve. The oil is ignited by hand or by a simple electric igniter, which causes it to vaporize, then is kept burning by a small pilot flame. Some units feature a small blower to increase the amount of air drawn into the furnace for combustion. Because vaporizing oil burners are compact and make very little noise, they are sometimes installed in kitchens or utility rooms. Pressure-type oil burners, on the other hand, are nearly always installed in basements.

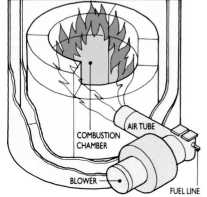

Pressure burner

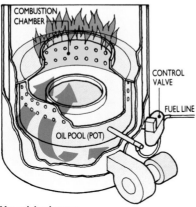

Vaporizing burner

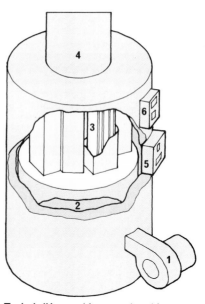

Typical oil burner (shown equipped for circulating hot water)

Parts of an oil furnace
1 Motor/blower
2 Combustion chamber
3 Heat exchanger
4 Chimney vent
5 On/off switch
6 Combination gauge

Gas burners

Gas burners are far simpler than oil burners and, since gas itself burns much more cleanly than fuel oil, require less regular maintenance. Still, they should be cleaned and services at least every 2 or 3 years.

Whether supplied by natural gas or liquefied petroleum (LP gas), furnaces of this type consist merely of a burner layout and gas-regulating valve. No pressurizing system is employed. The burners may be of a type that spread their flame over a large area or they may merely have multiple openings (or jets), as on a gas kitchen range.

For safety, gas burners incorporate a thermocouple device which automatically shuts off the gas-supply valve when no heat is detected in the combustion area. Should the odor of gas ever be detected near a gas burner, immediately open windows, extinguish any open flame or cigarettes, then leave the premises and telephone your gas or utility company from a phone outside the house. Do not touch any electrical switches—doing so many produce a static charge sufficient to ignite escaping gas.

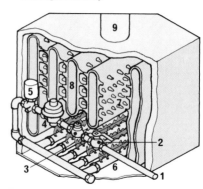

Typical gas burner (equipped for circulating hot water)

Parts of a gas furnace
1 Gas supply
2 Manual shutoff valve
3 Thermocouple
4 Pressure regulator
5 Automatic supply valve
6 Burners
7 Combustion chamber
8 Heat exchanger
9 Chimney vent

RADIATORS AND CONVECTORS

The hot water from a central heating boiler is pumped through the house along narrow pipes which may be connected to radiators or to special convector heaters that extract heat from the water and pass it out into their respective rooms.

You can feel radiant heat being emitted directly from the hot surface of an appliance, but convected heat warms the air that comes into contact with the hot surface. As the warmed air rises toward the ceiling, it allows cooler air to flow in around the appliance, and this air in turn is warmed and moves upwards. Eventually a steady but very gentle circulation of air takes place in the room, and the temperature gradually rises to the optimum set on the room thermostat.

Radiators

Ordinary radiators are made of heavy cast iron which absorbs and then radiates heat for a long time. For hot-water use only, lightweight radiators made of pressed sheet metal are sometimes available as imports. In either type, water flows in through a manually adjustable valve at one corner and then out through a return valve at the other (except in the case of most steam radiators—see box at right). A bleed valve is placed near the top of the radiator on the end opposite the inflow valve to let air out and prevent airlocks which stop the radiator from heating up properly. Cast-iron radiators are normally freestanding. However, special brackets are available to hang them from sturdy wall studs. Sheet-metal radiators are usually wall-hung.

Despite their name, radiators deliver only about half their output as radiant heat; the rest is emitted through natural convection as the surrounding air comes into contact with the hot surfaces of the radiators.

Radiators come in a wide range of sizes, and the larger they are, the greater their heat output. Maximum efficiency dictates that radiators be fully exposed in a room, however, not recessed or covered by a vented housing. Nor should they be painted or hidden behind furniture or drapes. A better way to deal with unsightly radiators in an interior decor is to replace them with less obtrusive convectors.

Cast-iron radiator
1 The manual valve controls inflow.
2 The return valve controls outflow to keep the radiator hot.
3 The bleed valve is to disperse airlocks.

Heat emission
The large arrow shows the flow of air during convection. The small arrows indicate how heat radiates from the radiator's surface.

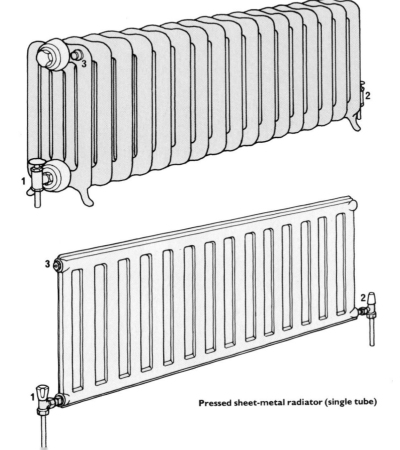

Pressed sheet-metal radiator (single tube)

STEAM UNITS

Cast-iron radiators designed for steam heat look similar to those used for hot water and, with minor modifications, are interchangeable. In most cases steam radiators have only one pipe connecting them with the main supply line; water that has condensed as the steam gives up its heat makes its way back to the boiler the way it came. The other difference is that in place of a bleed valve, steam radiators have an automatic vent built into the end of the radiator opposite the inlet pipe. The vent permits air to bleed out automatically as the radiator fills with steam. However, the steam itself does not escape.

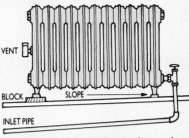

To cure noisy radiator, slope end toward inlet. Pipe should slope toward furnace.

If radiator heats unevenly, remove vent and listen for escaping air. Replace with new vent.

Maintenance

Many steam radiators produce knocking and banging noises as they heat up. The sound is actually made by water which has become trapped striking the walls of the radiator or piping as the steam seeks to get past. To cure the condition, make sure that the radiator slopes slightly downward toward the inlet pipe and the pipe itself slopes downward toward the furnace.

If the radiator will not heat properly all the way across, suspect a blocked vent. Air that cannot escape prevents steam from diffusing throughout the radiator. Shortly after turning on the heat, unscrew the vent and remove it. As the steam rises, air should escape from the hole, followed by steam, indicating that the radiator itself is functioning properly. Purchase a new vent and install it in place of the old one.

CONVECTORS

You can install convector heaters in your circulating hot-water heating system to replace conventional cast-iron radiators.

Unlike radiators, convector heaters emit none of their heat in the form of direct radiation. The hot water from the boiler passes through a finned pipe inside the heater, the fins absorbing the heat and transferring it to the air surrounding them. The warmed air escapes through an opening at the top of the appliance and at the same time cool air is drawn in through the open bottom, to be warmed in turn.

Most convector heaters have a damper that can be set to control the airflow. Some are designed for inconspicuous mounting at baseboard level. An advance is a fan-assisted type in which the airflow over the heating fins is forced, making for fast room heating.

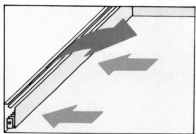
Rising warm air draws cool air in below

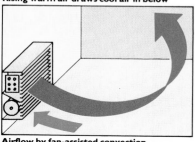
Airflow by fan-assisted convection

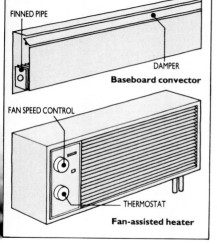
FINNED PIPE

DAMPER
Baseboard convector

FAN SPEED CONTROL

THERMOSTAT
Fan-assisted heater

PLACING YOUR HEATERS

At one time central heating radiators or convectors were nearly always placed under windows to balance the chill of the panes and cut the drafts caused by warmed air cooling against them. If double glazing deals with both of these problems you can place radiators or convectors with an eye to maximum comfort—but keep the other on the length and consequent cost of pipe runs.

Convenience and cost

Your radiators and convector heaters can be positioned anywhere that's convenient, that suits the shape of the rooms and that keeps costly pipe runs to a reasonable minimum. Probably you'll want to take all of these considerations into account.

While double glazing means that the appliances can be sited elsewhere than under windows, there is a slight drawback to placing them against walls. The warm air rising from them will tend to discolor the paint or wallpaper above. You can guard against this by fitting radiator shelves immediately above them to direct the warm air clear of the walls.

Never hang curtains or stand furniture in front of radiators or convectors. They will absorb radiated heat, and curtains will trap convected heat between themselves and the walls. While convectors radiate almost no heat, you should never obstruct warm air leaving the appliance nor cool air being drawn into it.

A room's shape can affect the siting of appliances and perhaps their number. For example, you cannot heat a large L-shaped room from a radiator in its short end. A heating installer can work out a combination of appliances—and their positions—to heat a room properly.

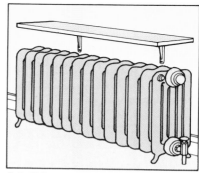
A shelf directs warm air clear of the wall

Selecting the size of heaters

A house loses heat constantly—whenever a door or window is opened; because of cold drafts; through the fabric of the doors, windows, walls, floors, ceilings and roof. To work out the heating needs of the rooms in a house, the designer has to take into account the rate at which they lose heat. This varies with the materials and construction of the walls, floors and ceilings. For example, heat is lost more quickly through a solid brick wall than through an insulated wood-frame wall. Also, the temperature on the other side of walls, floors and ceilings will come into the equation.

The designer also needs to know the temperature to which each room must be heated, and there are standard levels for particular rooms. The designer's calculations will produce a heating requirement for each room, expressed in kilowatts; the next step is to select radiators or convectors of appropriate outputs. Then all the heat output figures are totaled to give the output required from the boiler.

When you install your central heating, be sure to choose radiators and convector heaters that meet the standards approved by your local building inspector.

SEE ALSO

Details for: ▷	
Reflective foil	261
Double-glazing	271–274
Radiators	394

IDEAL ROOM TEMPERATURES

A central heating designer/installer aims at a system that will heat rooms to standard or customer-specified temperatures. Such a design might look like this:

ROOM	TEMPERATURE
Living room	70°F
Dining room	70°F
Kitchen	60°F
Hall/landing	65°F
Bedroom	60°F
Bathroom	72°F

CENTRAL HEATING CONTROLS

A range of automatic control systems and devices for circulating central heating can, if used sensibly, enable you to make useful savings in running costs. They can ensure that your system never "burns up money" by producing unwanted heat.

Timer

Room thermostat

Programmable

Thermostatic radiator valve

Heating controls
There are several ways to control the temperature:
1 Programmable type controls boiler and pump.
2 A timer is used to control a zone valve. It can be used to regulate boiler and pump.
3 Room thermometer controls pump or a zone valve.
4 A nonelectrical radiator valve controls an individual heater.

Three basic devices

While considerable sophistication is now available in automatic control, the systems can be divided into three main types: temperature controllers (thermostats), automatic on-off switches (timers and programmers) and heating circuit controllers (zone valves).

These devices can be used individually or in combination to provide a very high level of control.

It must be added that automatic controls are really effective only with gas- or oil-fired boilers, which can be switched on and off at will. Linked to coal or wood systems, which take time to react to controls, the systems will be less effective and can be dangerous.

ZONE CONTROL VALVES

It is not often that all the rooms in a house are in use at once. During the day it is normal for the upstairs rooms to be unused for long periods, and to heat them permanently would be very wasteful. To avoid such waste you can divide your central heating system into circuits, or zones—the usual ones being upstairs and downstairs—and heat those areas only when it's necessary.

Control is provided by motorized valves linked to a timer or programmer that directs the flow of heating water through preselected pipes at preselected times. Alternatively, zone valves can be used to provide zone temperature control by being linked to individual zone thermostats.

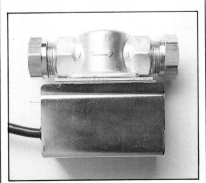

A motorized zone control valve

Thermostats

All steam and hot-water systems incorporate thermostats to prevent overheating. A gas- or oil-fired tank will have one that can be set to alter heat output by switching the unit on and off. Another, called an aquastat, can be set to monitor the temperature of the water circulating through the pipes.

Room thermostats are common forms of central heating control, often the only ones fitted. They are placed in rooms where temperatures usually remain fairly stable, and work on the assumption that any rise or drop in room temperature will be matched by similar ones throughout the house. Room thermostats control temperatures through simple on-off switching of the heating unit—or its pump if a boiler must run constantly to provide a constant supply of domestic hot water.

The room thermostat's drawback is that it can make no allowance for local temperature changes in other rooms caused, for example, by the sun shining through a window or a separate heater being switched on. Much more sophisticated temperature control is provided by thermostatic radiator valves, which can be fitted to radiators instead of the standard manually operated inlet valves. Temperature sensors open and close them, varying heat output to maintain the desired temperatures in individual rooms.

Thermostatic radiator valves need not be fitted in every room. You can use one to reduce the heat in a kitchen or reduce the temperature in a bathroom while using a room thermostat to regulate the temperature in the rest of the house or separate zones.

Other available thermostatic controls include devices for regulating the temperature of domestic hot water and for giving frost protection to a unit switched off during winter holidays.

Timers and programmers

You can save a lot in running costs by ensuring that your heating system is not working when you don't need it—while you're out, for instance, or while you sleep. A timer can be set to switch the system on and off to suit the regular comings and goings of the family. It can switch on and warm the house just before you get up, then off again just before you leave for work, on again when you come home, and so on.

The simpler timers offer two "on" and two "off" settings which are repeated daily, though a manual override allows variations for weekends and such. More sophisticated programmable versions offer a number of on-off options—even a different one for each day of the week—as well as control of hot water.

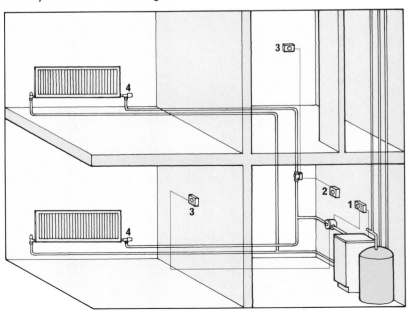

REGULAR FURNACE MAINTENANCE

Routine cleaning, maintenance and adjustment will give your central heating furnace a longer life and prolong its efficiency.

Both gas and oil-fired furnaces should be serviced once a year by qualified service persons, but you can do a certain amount of cleaning and tuning up yourself.

Servicing oil burners

Here are several maintenance chores you can perform which do not involve making adjustments to the combustion components of the furnace. Unless you are skilled and have the proper testing instruments, leave those to a service professional. Before starting any maintenance task, turn the furnace completely off.

Maintaining gas burners

Because gas furnaces involve less complicated equipment and technology than oil burners (combining gas and air for combustion is much easier than combining fuel oil and air), frequent maintenance of gas furnaces is less necessary than with oil-fired units. Inspection of the flame and pilot mechanisms should be carried out yearly by a professional service technician, of course. Cleaning—a task suitable to do-it-yourselfers—normally need take place only every 2 or 3 years. Before beginning any maintenance task, be certain to turn off the main gas supply line, pilot light, and burners.

Cleaning a pressure-type oil burner

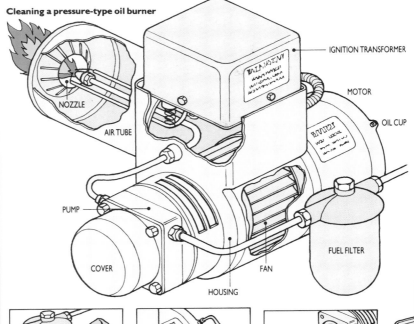

IGNITION TRANSFORMER

MOTOR

OIL CUP

AIR TUBE

NOZZLE

PUMP

COVER

FAN

HOUSING

FUEL FILTER

SEE ALSO

Details for: ▷

| Heating contractors | 21 |
| Gas/oil burners | 393 |

Change fuel filter
Place pan beneath filter area. Unscrew cup. Remove and replace cartridge and gasket.

Lubricate motor
Locate oil cups at each end of motor (if none are present, motor is self-lubricating and requires no treatment). Squirt 3 to 6 drops SAE 10W nondetergent electric motor oil in each cup. Do not overlubricate.

Clean pump strainer
Remove pump cover and gasket. Soak strainer in solvent, then brush clean with toothbrush. Replace, using new gasket. (Note: Some pumps do not have strainers.)

Clean fan
Unbolt transformer and swing aside to access fan. Clean blades with bottle brush or lint-free cloth attached to popsicle stick; wipe interior of housing with rag.

PROFESSIONAL SERVICE PLANS

The very high efficiency of modern gas and oil furnaces largely depends on their being regularly checked and serviced. It should be done annually, and because the mechanisms involved are so complex, the work should be done by qualified service persons.

For either type of furnace you can enter into a contract—with either the original installer or the fuel supplier—for regular maintenance.

Gas-fired installations
Many gas utilities offer a choice of several service arrangements for gas furnaces. These cover their own installations, but they can often be arranged for systems put in by other installers on condition that the utility inspect the installation before writing the contract.

The simplest maintenance contract plan provides for an annual check and adjustment of the furnace. If any repairs are found to be necessary, either at the time of the regular check or at other times during the year, the labor and the required parts will be charged separately. But for an extra fee it is possible to have both free labor and free parts for furnace repairs at any time of the year. Most utilities will also extend the arrangement to include a check of the whole heating system at the same time as the furnace is being checked.

It may be that your own installer can offer you a similar choice of service plans. The best course is to compare the charges and decide which gives the best value for your money.

Oil-fired installations
The installers of oil-fired central heating systems and the suppliers of fuel oil offer service plans similar to those outlined above for gas-fired systems. The choice of plans ranges from the simple checkup each year to complete coverage for new parts and labor if and when any repairs should become necessary.

Again, as with the plans for gas, it is wisest to shop around and make a comparison of the various services offered and the changes for them.

DRAINING A HOT-WATER SYSTEM

Circulating hot-water systems rarely need complete draining. However, if the water has become overly contaminated, or if a component fails and must be removed for replacement, by following the procedures outlined here, the task of removing the water from the boiler and piping can be done fairly easily.

Steps in draining hot-water system
1 Extinguish furnace
2 Shut off water supply line
3 Open draincock
4 Open radiator bleed valves
5 Drain expansion tank

Draining the system

The most frequent reason for draining a hot-water system is excessive rust in the circulating water. Each year, a small amount of water should be drained from the boiler into a clear glass via the draincock usually located near the base of the unit. Should the water appear unusually cloudy, draining the system, flushing it clean, and then refilling it is in order.

Begin by turning off the furnace. Remember that with a gas furnace this means also turning off the pilot flame and main gas inlet. Next, turn off the water supply line to the boiler. Connect a garden hose to the draincock and lead the other end of the hose to a floor drain. If no drain is present, position a bucket beneath the draincock. After waiting until you are certain the water has cooled sufficiently, open the draincock and let the water drain out. While it is draining, open the bleed valves on the radiators in the house to avoid creating a partial vacuum which will prevent complete drainage. At the same time, drain the expansion tank (see below).

Flushing

To rid the boiler of accumulated rust and sediment, leave the draincock open after the water stops flowing, then reopen the water supply line to admit fresh water into the system. When the water runs clear, close the draincock and let the boiler fill.

REFILLING THE SYSTEM

When you are ready to refill the boiler, close the draincock used for flushing the system. If you wish to add a commercial rust inhibitor to forestall further corrosion in the pipes, do so by closing off the water supply line, removing the pressure relief valve from the boiler tank and pouring the recommended amount of inhibitor (see manufacturer's instructions) into the hole, then replacing the valve. Reopen the water supply line. Wait until the boiler fills, then turn on the furnace. Reclose the radiator bleed valves when you hear water rising in the radiators. Wait several hours with the system running, then bleed all the radiators.

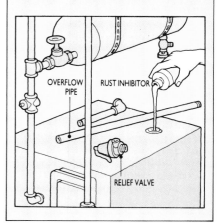

Draining the expansion tank

Conventional expansion tanks are merely cylinders partially filled with water. As the water in the circulating system heats and expands, air present in the tank is compressed, relieving the excess system pressure created and also preventing the hot water from turning to steam. Over a period of time, however, most tanks gradually accumulate too much water, which forces the air out and thus prevents the tank from functioning properly. The solution is to drain the tank, an operation that must be done also if the entire system is to be drained.

To drain a conventional expansion tank, attach a garden hose or a bucket to the draincock, usually located on the underside of the tank. Close off the inlet pipe leading to the tank, then open the draincock. If no inlet valve is present, you must drain the entire system in order to drain the tank as well.

Diaphragm expansion tanks

Some expansion tanks physically separate air and water by means of a rubber partition (diaphragm) which divides the tank into two chambers. Instead of draining the water from such tanks, they are periodically recharged with air. To do so, check the air pressure in the chamber using an ordinary tire-pressure gauge attached to the recharge valve, usually located on the underside of the tank. Then use a bicycle pump to add air until gauge readings match the tank's recommended pressure. NOTE: A diaphragm tank which requires even moderately frequent recharging may be leaking and should be replaced.

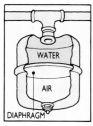

Diaphragm expansion tanks never need draining
To recharge air chamber, use a bicycle pump.

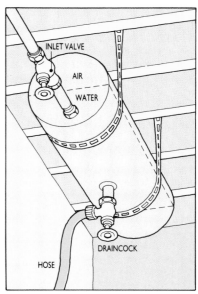

Conventional expansion tank

If a radiator feels cooler at the top than at the bottom, it's likely that a pocket of air has formed in it and is stopping full circulation of the water. Getting the air out—"bleeding"—is a simple matter.

Opening a bleed valve

Bleed radiators with the circulator running. Each radiator has a bleed valve at one of its top corners, near the end opposite the water inlet. Usually the valve is slotted for a screwdriver, but on many new models the valve is a square-section shank in the center of the round blanking plug. You should have been given a key to fit these shanks by the installer, but if you weren't, you can buy one at a plumbing supply store.

Use the key to turn the shank of the valve counterclockwise about a quarter of a turn. It shouldn't be necessary turn it further, but have a small container handy to catch any spurting water if you do open the valve too far.

You will hear a hissing sound as the air escapes. Keep the key on the shank of the valve and when the hissing stops and the first dribble of water appears, close the valve tightly.

In no circumstances must you be tempted to open the valve any more than is needed to let the air out, or to remove it completely, as this will produce a deluge of water.

Dispensing the air pocket in a radiator

Radiator key
Keep your radiator key in a handy place where you can find it on short notice. There is no substitute for it.

Fitting an automatic bleed valve

If you find yourself having to bleed one particular radiator regularly it will save you trouble if you replace its bleed valve with an automatic one that will allow air to escape but not water.

First drain the water from the system, then use your bleed-valve key to unscrew the old valve completely out of the blanking plug (**1**). Wind some Teflon tape around the threads of the automatic valve (**2**) and screw it finger-tight into the blanking plug (**3**).

Refill the system; if any water appears around the threads of the new valve, tighten it further with a wrench (**4**).

If, when the system is going again, the radiator still feels cool on top, it may be that a larger amount of air has collected than the bleed valve can cope with. In this case, unscrew the valve until you hear air hissing out. Tighten it again when the hissing stops and the first trickle of water appears.

 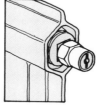 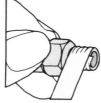 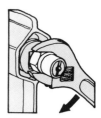

1 Unscrew old valve **2 Tape the new one** **3 Screw it finger-tight** **4 Stop any leak in use**

HOW TO REMOVE A RADIATOR

You can remove an individual radiator while the wall behind it is decorated without having to drain the whole system. You simply close the valves at the ends of the radiator, drain it and then remove it.

Shut off both valves, turning the shank of the return valve clockwise with a key or an adjustable wrench (**1**). Note the number of turns needed to close it so you can reopen it by the same number of turns later.

Make sure that you have plenty of rags for mopping up spillage, also a jug and a large bowl. As the water in the radiator will be very dirty, you should also roll back the floorcovering before you start, if possible.

Unscrew the capnut that holds one of the valves to the adapter in the end

of the radiator (**2**). Hold the jug under the joint and open the bleed valve slowly (**3**) to let the water drain out. Transfer the water from jug to bowl and keep going until no more can be drained.

Unscrew the capnut that holds the other valve on the radiator. If the radiator is not freestanding, lift it free from its wall brackets (**4**) and drain any remaining water into the bowl. Unscrew the wall brackets to decorate.

To replace the radiator after decorating, screw the brackets back in place, hang the radiator on them and tighten the capnuts on both valves. Close the bleed valve and open both radiator valves. Adjust the return valve by the same number of turns as you used to close it. Finally, use the bleed valve to release any trapped air.

1 Close the valve **2 Unscrew capnut**

3 Open bleed valve

4 Final draining
Lift radiator from brackets and drain off any remaining water.

RADIATOR VALVES

VALVE HEAD

GLAND NUT

Tightening gland nut
Tighten the gland nut with a wrench to stop a leak from a radiator valve spindle. If the leak persists, replace the valve (see right).

Curing a leaking radiator valve

If an inlet valve or return valve on a radiator seems to be leaking, its most likely that one of the capnuts that secures it to the water pipe and to the radiator's valve adapter needs some tightening up.

Tighten the suspect capnut with an adjustable wrench while you hold the body of the valve with a pipe wrench to prevent it from moving. If this doesn't work, the valve will have to be replaced.

If the leak seems to be from the valve adapter in the radiator, the joint will have to be repaired in the same way as when a new valve is fitted (see below). If the leak seems to be from the valve spindle, tighten the gland nut (see left) or replace the valve.

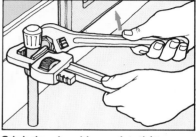
Grip leaky valve with wrench to tighten capnut

Replacing a worn or damaged valve

Be sure that the new valve is exactly like the old one, or it may not align with the water pipe. Drain the heating system and lay rags under the valve to catch any remaining dregs that may come out.

Hold the body of the valve with a pipe wrench and use an adjustable wrench to unscrew the capnuts that hold the valve to the water pipe and to the adapter in the end of the radiator (**1**). Lift the valve from the end of the pipe (**2**). If the valve being replaced is a return valve, don't remove it before you have closed it, counting the number of turns needed so that you can open the new valve by the same number to balance the radiator.

Unscrew the adapter from the radiator (**3**). You may manage this with an adjustable wrench or you may need an Allen wrench, depending on the type of adapter.

Fitting the new one
Ensure that the threads in the end of the radiator are clean and wind Teflon tape four or five times around the thread of the new valve's adapter, then screw it into the end of the radiator by hand and tighten it a further 1½ turns with an adjustable or Allen wrench.

Slide the valve capnut and a new ferrule over the end of the water pipe and fit the valve to the end of the pipe (**4**), but don't tighten the capnuts at this stage. First align the valve body with the adapter and tighten the capnut that holds them together (**5**). Hold the valve body firm with a wrench while you do this. Now tighten the capnut that holds the valve to the water pipe (**6**).

Finally, refill the system, check for leaks at the joints of the new valves and tighten the capnuts some more if that seems necessary.

DEALING WITH A JAMMED FERRULE

If the ferrule is jammed onto the pipe, cut the pipe off below floorboard level and make up a new section. Join it to the old pipe by means of either a soldered joint or a compression joint.

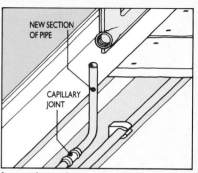

NEW SECTION OF PIPE

CAPILLARY JOINT

New section replaces pipe with jammed ferrule

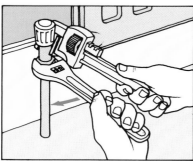
1 Hold the valve firm and loosen both capnuts

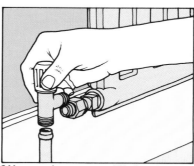
2 Unscrew the capnuts and lift the valve out

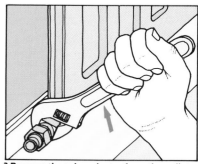
3 Remove the valve adapter from the radiator

4 Fit new adapter, then fit new valve to pipe

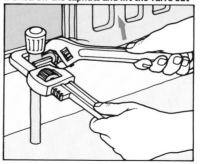
5 Connect valve to adapter and tighten capnut

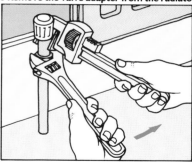
6 Tighten capnut holding valve to water pipe

REPLACING A CORRODED OR DAMAGED RADIATOR

Try to obtain a new radiator of exactly the same model as the one you wish to replace. This will make the job easier.

Simple replacement

Drain and remove the old radiator. With it clear of the wall, unscrew the valve adapters from the bottom with an adjustable wrench or, if necessary, an Allen wrench. Unscrew the bleed valve with its key, and then the two blanking plugs from the top of the radiator, using a square or hexagonal Allen wrench (**1**).

With steel wool, clean up the threads of both adapters and both blanking plugs (**2**), then wind four or five turns of Teflon tape around the threads (**3**). Screw them into the new radiator and the bleed valve into the blanking plug.

Position the new radiator and connect the valves to their adapters. Open the valves and fill and bleed the radiators.

Replacement with a different pattern radiator

Rather more work is involved in the replacement if you can't get a radiator of the same pattern as the old one. If it is not freestanding, you'll have to fit new wall brackets. Possibly you'll also have to alter the water pipes.

Drain the system. Then for a wall-hung unit, take the old brackets off the wall. Lay the new radiator face down on the floor and slide one of its brackets onto the hangers welded to the back of the radiator. Measure from the top of the bracket to the bottom of the radiator, add 4 or 5 inches for clearance under the radiator, then mark a horizontal line on the wall that distance from the floor. Now measure the distance between the centers of the radiator hangers and make two marks on the horizontal line that distance apart and at equal distances from the two water pipes (**1**).

Line up the brackets with the pencil marks, mark their mounting screw holes, drill and plug the holes and install the brackets in place (**2**).

Lift up the floorboards below the radiator and cut off the vertical portions of the inlet and return pipes. Connect the valves to the radiator and hang it on its brackets. Slip a short length of pipe into each valve as a guide for any further trimming of the pipes. Connect these lengths to the original pipes (**3**) with soldered or compression fittings, then connect the new pipes to the valves. Refill the system and check for leaks.

1 Removing the plug
Use an Allen wrench to unscrew the blanking plug at each end of the radiator.

2 Cleaning the threads
Use steel wool to clean any corrosion from the threads of both blanking plugs and valve adapters.

3 Taping the threads
Make the threaded joints watertight by wrapping Teflon tape several times around each component before screwing them into the new radiator.

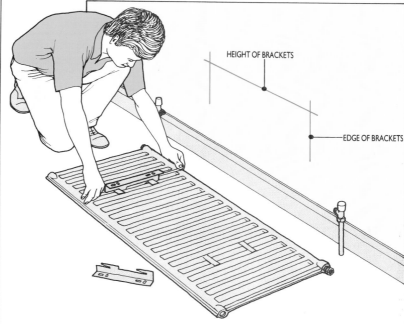

HEIGHT OF BRACKETS

EDGE OF BRACKETS

1 Taking the measurements
Measure the positions of the radiator brackets and transfer the measurements to the wall. Double-check the results to make sure the radiator is equidistant between the two pipes projecting from the floor.

2 Securing the brackets
Screw the mounting brackets to the wall. Make sure they are on the right side of the line.

3 Connecting up
Connect the new section of pipework. The vertical pipe aligns with the radiator valve.

CIRCULATING PUMPS

Forced hot-water heating depends on a steady cycle of hot water from boiler to radiators and back to the boiler for *reheating. This is the pump's job. A faulty pump means poor circulation. A failed pump means no circulation.*

Bleeding the pump

If your radiators don't seem to be warming up, though you can hear or feel the pump running, it's likely that an airlock has formed in the pump and its impeller is spinning in air. The air must be bled from the pump, a job that's done in the same way as bleeding a radiator. You'll find a screw-in valve for the purpose in the pump's outer casing.

The valve's position varies with the different makes, but it is usually marked.

Switch off the pump, have a jug or jam jar handy to catch any water spillage and open the valve with a screwdriver or vent key. Open it only slightly, until you hear air hissing out. When the hissing stops and a drop of water appears, close the valve fully.

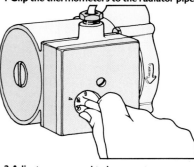

Open the bleed valve with a screwdriver

Adjusting the pump

Central heating pumps are of two kinds: fixed-head and variable-head. Fixed-head units run at a single speed, forcing the water round the system at a fixed rate. Variable-head pumps can be adjusted to run at different speeds, circulating the water at different rates.

When a variable-head pump is fitted as part of a central heating system, the installer adjusts its speed after balancing all the radiators so that each room reaches its "design temperature." If you find that your rooms are not as warm as you would like, though you have opened the inlet radiator valves fully, you can adjust the pump speed. But first check that all radiators show the same temperature drop between their inlets and outlets. You can get clip-on thermometers for the job from a

plumber's supply store. You will need a pair of them.

Clip one thermometer to the feed pipe just below the radiator valve and the other to the return pipe below its valve (**1**). The difference between the temperatures registered by the two should be about 20 degrees F. If it is not, uncover the return valve and close it further (to increase the difference) or open it more (to reduce the difference).

Having balanced the radiators you can now adjust the pump. Switch it off and then turn the speed adjustment up (**2**), one step at a time, until you are getting the overall temperatures you want. You may be able to work the adjustment by hand or you may need some special tool, such as an Allen wrench, depending on the make and model of your pump.

RETURN PIPE   FEED PIPE

I Clip the thermometers to the radiator pipes

2 Adjust pump speed to increase temperature

Replacing a worn pump

If you have to replace your circulating pump, be quite sure that the one you buy is of exactly the same make and model as the old one, or seek the advice of a professional installer.

Turn off the boiler and close the isolating valves, on each side of the pump. If there are no isolating valves you will have to drain down the whole system.

Identify the electrical circuit that controls the circulating pump and trip the circuit breaker for that circuit at the service panel, then take the cover plate off the pump and disconnect its wiring (**1**).

Have a bowl or bucket at hand to catch any water left in the pump, also some old rags for any mopping up that you may have to do. Undo the retaining nuts that hold the pump to the valves or the pipework with an adjustable wrench

(**2**) and catch the water as it flows out.

Remove the pump and fit the new one in its place, taking care to fit correctly any sealing washers that are provided (**3**), then tighten up the retaining nuts.

Take the cover plate off the new pump, feed in the electrical cable, connect the wires to the pump's terminals (**4**) and replace the cover plate. If the pump is of the variable-head type (see above), set the speed control to the speed indicated on the old pump.

Open both isolating valves—or if the system has been drained, refill it—check the pump connections for leaks and tighten them if necessary. Then open the pump's bleed valve to release any air that may have become trapped in it. Finally, restore power to the circuit and test the pump.

I Remove cover plate

2 Undo connecting nuts

3 Attach new pump

4 Connect power cable

CONTROL VALVES

The control valves are vital to the effective working of a modern central heating system, for it is through them that the various timers and thermostats are able to adjust the levels of heating precisely to the programmed requirements you set for comfort.

Worn or faulty control valves can seriously affect the reliability of the system and should be replaced promptly.

Replacing a faulty valve

First ensure that the replacement valve that you buy is of exactly the same pattern as the faulty one, or seek professional advice.

Drain down the system, then identify the electrical circuit that services the central heating controls and turn off its power at the service panel.

The electrical cable from the valve will be connected to the terminals of a nearby junction box, which will also be linked to the heating system's other controls. Take the cover off the junction box and disconnect the wiring for the valve. As you do this you should carefully note the connections so as to make reconnection easier.

You will probably not be able to take the old valve out of the pipe run by simply unscrewing its capnuts, as you won't be able to pull the ends of the pipe free of their sockets in the valve. Instead, cut through the pipe on each side of the valve (**1**) and take out the section, complete with valve, then make up two pieces of pipe to fit on either side of the new control valve.

Assemble the valve with its ferrules and capnuts, pipes and joints, but only loosely at first, and fit the assembly into the pipe run (**2**).

There should be enough play in the joints to allow the assembly to be sprung into place, and this may be helped if the original pipes on each side of the valve position are first freed from their clips.

When the pipes and valve are in place, connect them to the original pipework with compression or soldered joints, then tighten the valve capnuts. Hold the body of the valve with a second wrench to prevent it from turning (**3**).

Reconnect the cable to the terminals of the junction box and replace its cover plate, then restore power to the circuit.

Refill the heating system and check the working of the valve by adjusting the timer or thermostat that controls it.

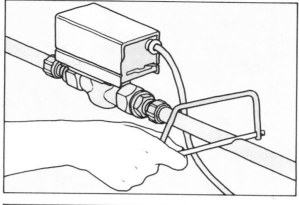

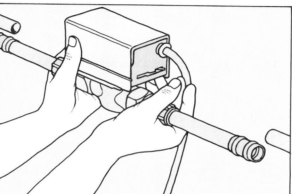

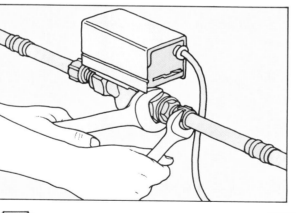

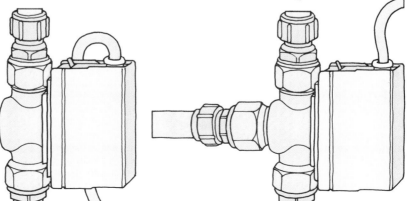

1 Removing the valve
If you cannot disconnect the valve, cut through the pipe on each side of it with a hacksaw.

SEE ALSO	
Details for: ▷	
Service panel	291, 319
Junction box	309
Pipe joints	342–346
Heating controls	396
Draining system	398
Refilling system	398

2 Fitting new valve
With the new valve connected to short sections of pipe, spring the assembly into the pipe run.

3 Closing the joints
Having connected the pipework, tighten the valve capnuts on each side with a pair of wrenches.

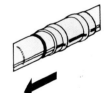

Slip coupling
If you cannot spring pipework to locate a conventional soldered joint, use a slip coupling which is free to slide along the pipe to cover the junction.

Far left
Two-port control valve
A two-port valve seals off a section of pipework when water within that section has reached the required temperature.

Left
Three-port control valve
This type of valve can independently isolate central heating or hot-water circuits.

HEATING SYSTEM TROUBLE-SHOOTING

SYMPTOM

Hissing or banging sounds from boiler or pipework.

Overheating caused by:

- **Blocked chimney (with coal furnace).**
  Check flueway for substantial soot fall. Sweep chimney.

- **Heavy scale deposits in system due to hard water.**
  Shut down boiler and pump. Have a specialist treat system with a descaler, then drain, flush and refill system.

- **Faulty boiler thermostat.**
  Shut down boiler.
  Leave pump working to circulate water around system and cool it quickly. With system cool, operate boiler thermostat control. If you do not hear a clicking sound, call in a repair person.

- **Incorrectly sloping pipework (with steam systems).**
  Check to see that radiators and pipe runs carrying steam slope downward at all points, so that water can travel freely back to boiler. Insert wooden wedges under improperly sloping radiators. Rehang improperly pitched pipe. Check results using carpenter's level.

- **Circulating pump not working (with coal furnace).**
  Shut down boiler, then check that the pump is switched on.
  If pump won't work, turn off power and check wired connections to it. If pump seems to be running but outlet pipe is cool, check for airlock by using bleed screw. If pump is still not working, shut it down, drain system, remove pump and check it for blockage. Clean pump or replace it if necessary.

SYMPTOM

Pressure-relief valve on circulating hot-water boiler opens, sending water through overflow pipe.

- **Excess pressure in piping caused by malfunctioning expansion tank.**
  Drain conventional tank by first closing inlet valve leading to tank, then opening draincock on underside of tank. For tanks with diaphragm-design, recharge air chamber using bicycle pump, or replace tank.

SYMPTOM

All radiators remain cool though boiler is operating normally.

- **Pump not pumping.**
  Check that pump is working by feeling for motor vibration or by listening. If pump is running, check for airlock by operating bleed valve. If this has no effect, the pump outlet may be blocked. Switch off boiler and pump; remove pump and clean or replace as necessary.

- **Pump's thermostat or timer is set incorrectly or is faulty.**
  Check thermostat or timer setting and reset if necessary. If this makes no difference, switch off power and check wiring connections. If connections are in good order, call in repair person.

SYMPTOM

Radiators in one part of the house do not warm up.

- **Timer or thermostat which controls zone valve not set properly or faulty.**
  Check timer or thermostat setting and reset if necessary. If this has no effect, switch off the power supply and check wired connections. If this makes no difference, call in repair person.

- **Zone valve itself faulty.**
  Drain system and replace valve.

SYMPTOM

Single radiator does not warm up.

- **Manual inlet valve closed.**
  Check setting of valve and open it if that is necessary.

- **Thermostatic radiator valve not set properly or faulty.**
  Check setting of valve and reset it if necessary. If this has no effect, drain radiator and replace valve.

- **Return valve not set properly.**
  Remove return valve cover and adjust valve setting until radiator seems as warm as those in adjacent rooms. Have valve properly balanced next service.

- **Inlet/outlet blocked by corrosion.**
  Close inlet and return valves, remove radiator and flush out and refit or replace as necessary.

SYMPTOM

Area at top of radiator stays cool while the bottom is warm.

- **Airlock at top of radiator preventing water from circulating fully.**
  Operate bleed valve to release the trapped air.

SYMPTOM

Cool patch in center of radiator while top and ends are warm.

- **Heavy deposits of corrosion at bottom of radiator are restricting circulation of water.**
  Close inlet and return valves, remove radiator, flush out, then refit or replace as necessary.

SYMPTOM

Water leaking from system.

- **Loose pipe unions at joints, pump connections, boiler connections, etc.**
  Switch off boiler and turn furnace off completely—switch off pump and tighten leaking joints. If this has no effect, drain the system and remake joints completely.

- **Split or punctured pipes.**
  Wrap damage in rags temporarily, switch off boiler and pump and make a temporary repair with hose or commercial leak sealant. Drain system and fit new pipe.

SYMPTOM

Boiler not working.

- **Thermostat set too low.**
  Check that room or boiler thermostat is set correctly.
- **Timer or programmer not working.**
  Check that unit is switched on and set correctly. Have it replaced if the fault persists.
- **Pilot light goes out.**
  Relight a gas boiler pilot light following the manufacturer's instructions, which are usually found on the back of the boiler's front panel. If the pilot fails to ignite after second try, have the unit replaced.

10

WORKING OUTDOORS

PLANNING A GARDEN

SEE ALSO

◁ Details for:
Building regulations   18

Designing plantings and structures for a yard is not an exact science. Plants may not thrive even though you select the right soil conditions and check the amount of daylight, and shrubs and trees may never reach the maximum size specified for them in a catalogue. Nevertheless, advance planning will produce a more satisfactory result than a haphazard approach, which could involve expensive mistakes like laying a patio where it will be in shade for most of the day, building a boundary wall that is too high to meet with zoning board approval, or putting in a patio that drains poorly. It is these permanent features of a garden which you should concentrate on planning first, always, of course, considering how they will fit and function. No one wants to live in a concrete jungle.

Deciding on the approach

Before you even put pencil to paper, get a feel for the style of yard you would prefer and consider whether it will sit happily with the house and its immediate surroundings. Is it to be formal, laid out in straight lines or geometric patterns—a style which often marries successfully with modern architecture? Do you prefer the more relaxed style of a rambling cottage garden? Natural informality may not be as easy to achieve as you think, and it will certainly take several years to mature into the established garden you have in mind. Or, consider a blend of both, where every plant, stone and pool of water is carefully positioned. A Japanese-style garden bears all the hallmarks of a man-made landscape yet conveys a sense of natural harmony.

There is no shortage of material from which to draw inspiration—countless books and magazines are devoted to the design of gardens. Don't expect to find a total solution which fits your plot exactly—no two gardens are alike—but you may be able to adapt a particular approach or develop a small detail into a design for your own garden. Visiting other gardens is even better. Large country estates and city parks will have been designed on a much grander scale, but at least you will be able to see how a mature shrub should look, or gain a fresh idea on combining plants, stone and water in a rockery or water garden. Don't forget that your neighbors and friends may also have had to tackle problems identical to yours. If nothing else, you might learn by their mistakes!

1 Cottage-style garden
The informal character of abundant flowers planted between areas of natural-stone paving ideally complements traditional architecture.

2 Consider the details
Good design does not rely on having a large garden. A successful combination of natural forms can be just as rewarding on a small scale.

3 A natural-looking rock garden
Once plants become established, a rock garden should blend into a landscape without a hint of artificiality. The effect relies on the careful positioning of stones during construction.

4 A simple layout
Simplicity is often the best approach, but the proportions of the various elements must be carefully considered to avoid a boring result.

SURVEYING THE PLOT

Measuring the plot
Measure your plot of land accurately, including the diagonals, because what might appear to be square or rectangular may taper towards one end or do something equally unexpected.

Slopes and gradients
Make a note of how the ground slopes. An accurate survey is not necessary, but at least jot down the direction of the slope and plot the points where it begins and ends. You can get some idea of the difference in levels by using a long straightedge and a level. Place one end of the straightedge on the top of a bank, for instance, and measure the vertical distance from the other end to the foot of the slope.

Climatic conditions
Check the path of the sun and the direction of prevailing winds. Don't forget that the angle of the sun will be higher in summer and a screen of deciduous trees will be less of a windbreak when they drop their leaves.

Soil conditions
Make a note of soil conditions. You can easily adjust soil content by adding peat or fertilizers. A peat or clay soil is not very stable, however, and will affect the type of footings and foundation you may want to lay.

Existing features
Plot the position of features you want to retain in your plan, such as existing pathways, areas of lawn, established trees and so on.

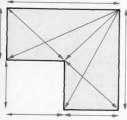

Measuring a plot
Note the overall dimensions, including the diagonals, to draw an accurate plan.

Gauging a slope
Use a straightedge and level to measure the height of a bank.

1△

SEE ALSO

Details for: ▷	
Footings/foundations	427
Retaining walls	437
Paving	448
Water gardens	455–459
Building a rock garden	459

1 Japanese-style garden
The overall effect should be one of tranquillity.

◁2

3▷

4▽

2 Using textures
Still water punctuated with rugged stones makes for a pleasing contrast of textures.

3 A sloping site
Some of the most dramatic gardens are a result of having to contend with a sloping site. Here, retaining walls are used to terrace a steep bank of colorful shrubs.

4 A formal garden
Use public parks or country estates as inspiration for planning a formal garden. These miniature hedges with selected plantings outline a geometric layout of pathways.

YARD PLANNING: BASIC CONSIDERATIONS

Having surveyed your plot, it is worth taking the time to plan all aspects of the design of your garden. Practical problems will need careful thought.

DRAWING A PLAN

Draw a plan of your garden on paper. It must be a properly scaled plan or you are sure to make some gross errors, but it need not be professionally perfect. Use graph paper to plot the dimensions, but do the actual drawing on tracing paper laid over the graph paper. This allows you to try out several different ideas and adapt your plan without having to redraw it every time.

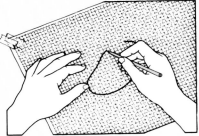
Make a garden plan on tracing paper

PLOTTING YOUR DESIGN

Planning on paper is only the first stage. Gardens are rarely seen from above, so it is essential to plot the design on the ground to check your dimensions and view the features from different angles. A pond or patio which looks enormous on paper can be pathetically small in reality. Other shortcomings, such as the way a tree will block the view from your proposed patio, become obvious once you lay out the plan full-size.

Plot individual features by driving pegs into the ground and stretching string lines between them. Scribe arcs on the ground with a rope tied to a peg, and mark the curved lines with stakes or a row of bricks. Use a garden hose to mark out less regular curves and ponds. If you can scrape areas clear of weeds, it will define the shapes still further.

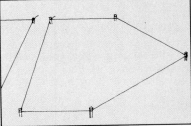
Mark out lines with stakes and string

PRACTICAL EXPERIMENTS

When you have marked out your design, check that it works with a few practical experiments. Will it be possible, for instance, for two people to pass each other on a footpath without stepping onto flowerbeds? Can you set down a wheelbarrow onto the path without one of its legs slipping into the pond?

Try placing some furniture on the area marked out for a patio to make sure you can sit comfortably and even serve a meal when visitors arrive. Most people build a patio alongside the house, but if you have to put it elsewhere to find a sunny spot, will it become a chore to walk back and forth for food?

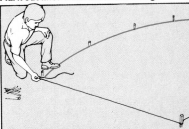
Use rope tied to a peg to scribe an arc

SITING PONDS

Site a pond to avoid overhanging trees and where it will catch at least a half-day's sunlight. Check that you can reach it with a hose for filling and that you can run electrical cables to power a pump or decorative lighting.

COMMON-SENSE SAFETY

Don't make your garden an obstacle course. A narrow path alongside a pond, for instance, could be intimidating to an elderly relative. Low walls or planters near the edge of a raised patio could cause someone to trip.

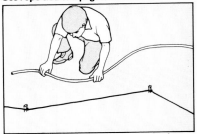
Try out irregular curves with a garden hose

DRIVEWAYS AND PARKING SPACES

Allow a minimum width of 10 feet for a driveway, making sure there is enough room to open the car doors if you park alongside a wall. Remember that vehicles larger than your own might need to use the drive or parking space—delivery trucks, for instance. When you drive in or out, will you be able to see? Try out the turning circle of your car in an empty parking lot.

CONSIDER THE NEIGHBORS

There may be legal restrictions on what you can erect in your garden (◁), but even if you have a free hand it is only wise to consult your neighbors if anything you plan might cause discomfort or inconvenience. A wall or even trees which are high enough to shade their favorite sun spot or block out the light to a window could be the source of argument for years to come.

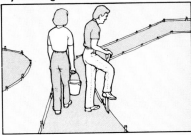
Make sure two people can pass on a path

TREE ROOTS AND FOUNDATIONS

As a permanent feature of your yard, you will probably want to plant at least one tree. You will need to think carefully about your choice of trees and their position—they could be potentially damaging to the structure of the house if planted too near.

GROWING IVY ON WALLS

There is a widely held misconception that a climbing ivy will damage any masonry wall. If stucco or the mortar between bricks or stonework is in a poor condition, then an exuberant ivy plant will undoubtedly weaken the structure as its aerial roots attempt to extract moisture from the masonry. The roots invade broken joints or cracks and on finding a source of nourishment for the main plant, they expand and burst the weak material, which accelerates deterioration by encouraging moisture penetration. If the ivy is allowed to grow unchecked, the weight of the plant can eventually topple a weakened wall.

However, with modern hard bricks and mortar, ivy can do no more than climb by the aid of training wires and its own suckerlike roots. So long as the structure is sound and moistureproof, there is some benefit from ivy clothing a wall in that its close-growing mat of leaves, mostly with their drip tips pointing downwards, acts as insulation and a watershed against the elements. Where ivy is permitted to flourish as a climber, it must be hard-pruned to prevent it from penetrating between roofing joints and vents and clogging gutters and downspouts.

Don't allow ivy to grow out of control

Cracks: subsidence and heaving

Minor cracks in siding, stucco and even brickwork are often the result of shrinkage as the structure dries out. These sorts of cracks are not serious and can be repaired during normal maintenance, but more serious structural cracks are due to movement of foundations. Trees planted too close to a building can add to the problem by removing moisture from the site, causing subsidence of the foundations as the supporting earth collapses. The felling of trees can be just as damaging. The surrounding soil, which had become stabilized over the years, swells as it takes up the moisture which had been removed previously by the tree root system. Upward movement of the ground, known as heave, distorts the foundations until cracks appear.

Siting trees

Growing tree roots search out moisture, and this can result in an expensive repair or replacement of the house drainage system. Large roots can fracture rigid pipework or penetrate joints until the drain becomes blocked.

Before you plant a tree close to a building, find out the likely spread of the mature root system. As a rough guide, make sure there is a distance of at least two-thirds the mature height of a tree between it and nearby buildings. If an existing tree is likely to cause a problem, ask your local building department for advice—the tree may be protected by a preservation order and you could be fined if you cut it down without permission. It may be possible to prune the branches and roots to lessen the likelihood of future damage.

SEE ALSO	
Details for: ▷	
Repairing cracks	48–49
Penetrating damp	254

Subsidence
A mature tree planted close to a house can drain so much water from the ground that the earth collapses, causing the foundation to subside.

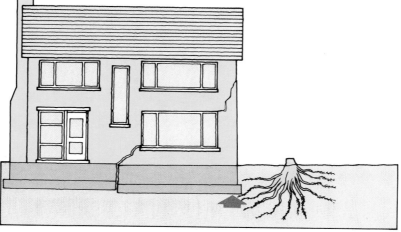

Heave
When a mature tree is felled, the earth can absorb more water, causing it to swell until it displaces the foundation of a building.

FENCES: CHOOSING

A fence is the most popular form of boundary marker or garden screen because of its advantages over other methods of dividing plots of land. A fence takes very little time to erect when compared with a wall or especially a hedge, which takes years to establish. Most fencing components are relatively lightweight and are therefore easy to transport and handle on site.

Economics and maintenance

In the short term a fence is cheaper than a wall built of masonry, although one can argue that the cost of maintenance and replacement over a very long period eventually cancels out the saving in cost. Wood does have a comparatively short life because it is susceptible to insect infestation and rot (◁) when exposed to the elements, but a fence will last for many years if it is treated regularly with a chemical preservative. In any case, if you are prepared to spend a little more money on plastic or concrete components, you can erect a virtually maintenance-free fence.

Choosing your fencing

When you measure even a small garden, you will be surprised by the overall length of fencing required to surround your property, so it is worth considering the available options carefully to make sure that you invest your money in the kind of fence that will be most suitable. Unless your priority is to keep neighborhood children or animals out of your garden, the amount of privacy afforded by a fence is likely to be your most important consideration. There are a number of privacy options, but you may have to compromise to some extent if you plan to erect a fence on a site exposed to strong prevailing winds. In that case you will need a fence which will provide a decent windbreak without offering such resistance that the posts will work loose within a couple of seasons due to constant buffeting by the wind.

Planning and planning permission

You can build any fence up to about 6 feet high without a zoning variance (◁) unless your boundary adjoins a highway, in which case permissible fence height may be limited. In addition, there may be local restrictions on fencing if the land surrounding your house has been designed as an open-plan area. Even so, many authorities will permit low boundary markers such as a ranch-style or post-and-chain fence.

At least discuss your plans with your neighbors, especially as you will require their permission to enter onto their properties, and it is always an advantage to be able to work from both sides when erecting a fence. Check the line of the boundaries to make certain that you do not encroach on neighbors' land. The fence posts should run along the boundary or on your side of the line. Before you dismantle an old fence, make sure it is yours to demolish. If a neighbor is unwilling to replace an unsightly fence, or even to allow you to replace it at your expense, there is nothing to stop you from erecting another fence alongside as long as it is on your property. It is an unwritten law that a good neighbor erects a fence with the post and rails facing his or her own property, but there are no legal restrictions which force you to do so.

TYPES OF FENCING

CHAIN-LINK FENCING

Chain-link fencing is a utilitarian form of barrier constructed from wire netting stretched between fence posts. A true chain-link fence is made from strong galvanized or plastic-coated wire woven into a diamond-shape mesh, suspended from a heavy-gauge wire tensioned between the posts. A cheap fence can be made from soft wire netting or chicken wire. However, it is not very durable and will stretch out of shape if a large animal leans against it. Decorative wire fencing is available at many garden centers; it is designed primarily for low boundary markers or to support lightweight climbing plants. In fact, any chain-link fence will benefit from a screen of climbers or hedging plants.

TRELLIS FENCING

A concertina-fold trellis formed from thin softwood or cedar laths joined together is virtually useless as a fence in the true sense, relying exclusively on the posts and rails for its strength. But a similar fence made from split rustic poles nailed to heavy rails and posts forms a strong and attractive barrier. Both types of trellises are ideally suited as plant supports for climbers.

POST-AND-CHAIN FENCING

A post-and-chain fence is simply a decorative feature to keep people from wandering off a path or pavement onto a lawn or flowerbed. Lengths of painted metal or plastic chain are strung between short posts sunk into the ground.

Chain-link fencing

Trellis fencing

Post-and-chain fence

TYPES OF FENCING

CLOSEBOARD FENCING

A closeboard fence is made by nailing overlapping bevel siding or "featherboard" strips to the horizontal rails. Featherboards are sawn planks which taper across their width from 5/8 inch at the thicker side down to about 1/8 inch. The boards are 4 to 6 inches wide, and the best quality are made from cedar. However, treated pine may also be used. Although it is expensive, closeboard fencing forms a strong and attractive screen. Being fixed vertically, the boards are difficult to climb from the outside—ideal for keeping children out!

Closeboard fencing

PREFABRICATED PANEL FENCING

Fences made from prefabricated panels nailed between wood posts are very common, perhaps because they are particularly easy to erect. Standard panels are 6 feet wide, and rise in 1-foot steps from approximately 2 feet to 6 feet in height. Most panels are made from interwoven or overlapping strips of pine or cedar sandwiched between a frame of 2 × 4s. The overlapping strip panels may be either sanded or rough-sawn. Some panels are pressure-treated to resist decay. Cedar may be left untreated to weather naturally.

A panel fence offers good value as a reasonably durable screen. But choose the lapped type for privacy. In the summer, interwoven strips will shrink to some extent, leaving gaps.

Panel fence

INTERLAP FENCING

An interlap fence is made by nailing square-edged boards to the horizontal rails, fixing them alternately on one side, then the other. Spacing is a matter of choice. For privacy, overlap the edges of the boards, or space them apart for a decorative effect.

This is the type of fence to choose for a windy site as it is substantial, yet the gaps between the boards allow the wind to pass through without exerting too much pressure. Because of its construction, an interlap fence is equally attractive from either side.

Interlap fencing

PICKET FENCING

The traditional, low picket fence is still popular as a barrier at the front of the house where a high fence is unnecessary. Narrow, vertical poles, with rounded or pointed tops, are spaced about 2 inches apart. As they are laborious to build by hand, most picket fences are sold as ready-made panels constructed from softwood or plastic to keep down the cost.

Picket fencing

RANCH-STYLE FENCING

Low-level fences made from simple, horizontal rails fixed to short, stout posts are the modern counterpart of picket fencing. Used extensively in today's housing developments, this ranch-style fencing is often painted, although clear-finished or stained wood is just as attractive and far more durable. Softwoods and some hardwoods are used for fencing, but plastic ranch-style fences are becoming increasingly popular for their clean, crisp appearance, since they do away with the chore of repainting for maintenance.

Ranch-style fence

CONCRETE FENCING

A cast concrete fence offers the security and permanence of a masonry wall and needs minimal maintenance. Interlocking, horizontal sections are built one upon the other up to the required height. Each screen is supported by grooves cast into the sides of specially designed concrete fence posts.

Concrete fencing

FENCE POSTS

Whatever type of fence you plan to erect on your property, its strength and durability rely on good-quality posts set solidly in the ground. Buy the best posts you can afford, and erect them carefully. It is worth taking longer over its construction to avoid having to dismantle and repair a poorly built fence in the future.

TYPES OF POSTS

In some cases, the nature of the fencing will determine the choice of post. Concrete fencing, for instance, must be supported by compatible concrete posts, but usually, you can choose the material and style of post which suits the appearance of the fence.

TIMBER POSTS

Most fences are supported by square-section wooden posts. Standard nominal sizes are 4 × 4 and 6 × 6 inches; 8 × 8 posts are also available. Most lumberyards supply pretreated softwood posts unless you ask specifically for hardwood.

CONCRETE POSTS

A variety of 4 × 4-inch reinforced-concrete posts exists to suit different styles of fence: drilled for chain-link, mortised for rails and recessed or grooved for panels. Special corner and end posts are notched to accommodate bracing struts for chain-link fencing.

METAL POSTS

Angle iron or plastic-coated steel posts are made to support chain link or plastic fences. Although angle iron posts are very sturdy, they do not make for a very attractive garden fence.

PLASTIC POSTS

PVC posts are supplied with plastic fencing, but most have to be reinforced internally by a wooden insert for fences over 2 feet 6 inches in height.

Preserving fence posts

Even when a wood post is pretreated to prevent rot, provide additional protection by soaking the base of each post in a bucket of chemical preservative for at least ten minutes, and longer if possible (◁).

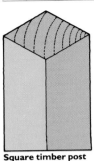

Capping fence posts
If you simply cut the end of a timber post square, the top of the post will rot relatively quickly. The solution is to cut a single or double bevel to shed the rainwater, or nail a wooden or galvanized metal cap over the end of the fence post.

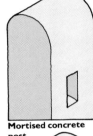

Square timber post

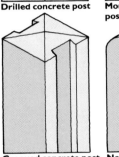

Drilled concrete post

Mortised concrete post

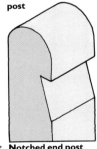

Grooved concrete post

Notched end post

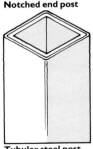

Angle iron post

Tubular steel post

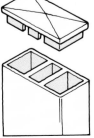

Capped plastic post

REMOVING OLD FENCE POSTS

Fixing posts in virgin soil is straightforward, but if you are replacing a fence you may want to put the new posts in the same positions as the old ones. Remove the topsoil from around each post to loosen the grip of the soil. If one is bedded firmly, or sunk into concrete, lever it out as shown below. Drive large nails in two opposite faces of the post, about 1 foot from the ground. Bind a length of rope around the post just below the nails, and tie the ends to the tip of a length of heavy lumber. Build a pile of bricks close to the post and use it as a fulcrum to lever the post out of the ground.

Levering a rotted fence post
Use a pile of bricks as a fulcrum to lift the post.

FIXING TO A WALL

If a fence runs up to the house, fix the first post to the wall with three expanding masonry bolts (◁). Place a washer under each bolt head to stop the wood from being crushed. Check with a level that the post is vertical, driving shims between the post and wall to make slight adjustments.

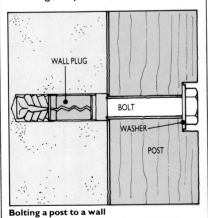

WALL PLUG

BOLT

WASHER

POST

Bolting a post to a wall
If you are fitting a prefabricated panel against a wall-fixed post, counterbore the bolts so that the heads lie flush with the surface of the wood.

USING METAL SPIKES

Instead of anchoring fence posts in concrete, you can plug the base of each post into the square socket of a metal spike driven into firm ground. Use a 2-foot spike for fences up to 4 feet high, but use a 2-foot 6-inch spike for a 6-foot-high fence.

Place a scrap of hardwood post into the socket to protect the metal, then drive the spike partly into the ground with a sledgehammer. Hold a level against the socket to make certain the spike is plumb (1). Continue to hammer the spike into the ground until only the socket is visible. Insert the post and secure it by screwing through the side of the socket or by tightening clamping bolts (2), depending on the design of the spike you are using.

If you are erecting a panel fence, use the edge of a fixed panel to position the next spike (3).

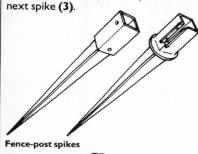

Fence-post spikes

1 Check with a level that spike is vertical

2 Fix the post   **3 Locate next spike**

ERECTING FENCE POSTS

The type of fence you choose to erect often dictates whether you erect all the posts first or one at a time along with the other components. When building a prefabricated panel fence, for instance, fix the posts in the ground as you erect the fence, but complete the run of posts before you install chain-link fencing.

Marking out

Drive a stake into the ground at each end of the fence run and stretch a line between. If possible, adjust the spacing of the posts to avoid obstructions such as large tree roots. If one or more posts have to be inserted across a paved patio, lift enough slabs to dig the necessary holes. You may have to break up a section of concrete beneath the slabs using a cold chisel and hammer.

Erecting the posts

Digging the hole
Bury one-quarter of each post to provide a firm foundation. For a 6-foot-high fence, dig a 2-foot hole to take an 8-foot post. You can rent a post hole auger to remove the central core of earth. Twist the tool to drive it into the ground (1) and pull it out after every 6 inches to remove the soil. When you have reached a sufficient depth, taper the sides of the hole slightly so that you can pack gravel and concrete around the post.

Anchoring the post
Ram a layer of gravel, broken bricks or small stones into the bottom of the hole to support the base of the post and provide drainage. Get someone to hold the post upright while you brace it with supports nailed to the post and to stakes driven into the ground (2). Use a level to check that it is vertical. (Use guy ropes to support a concrete post.)

Pack more coarse fill around the post, leaving a hole about 2 feet deep for filling with concrete. Mix some concrete to a firm consistency using the proportions 1 part cement: 2 parts sand: 3 parts aggregate (▷). Use a trowel to drop concrete into the hole all around the post and tamp it down with the end of a 4 × 4 (3). Build the concrete just above the level of the soil and smooth it to slope away from the post (4). This will help shed water and prevent rot. Let the concrete harden for about a week before removing the struts. To support a panel fence temporarily, wedge struts against the posts.

Post hole auger

1 Notch post

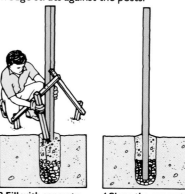

1 Dig the post hole **2 Brace the post** **3 Fill with concrete** **4 Slope the concrete**

2 Concreting end post

Supporting end posts

Chain-link fence posts must resist the tension of the straining wires (▷). Brace each end post (and some intermediate posts (▷) over a long run) with a strut made from a length of fence post. Shape the end of the strut to fit a notch cut into the post (1) and nail it in place. Order special posts and precast struts for concrete components.

Anchor the post in the ground in the normal way, but dig a 1½-foot-deep trench alongside for the strut. Wedge a brick under the end of the strut before tamping gravel around the post and strut. Fill the trench up to ground level with concrete (2).

Support a corner post with two struts set at right angles. Where a fence adjoins a masonry wall, fix as described in the box on the opposite page.

413

ERECTING A CHAIN-LINK FENCE

Set out a complete row of wood, steel, concrete or angle iron posts to support chain-link fencing, spacing them no more than 10 feet apart. Brace the end posts with struts (◁) to resist the pull of the straining wires. A long run of fencing will need a braced intermediate post every 225 feet or so.

Using wooden posts

Support the chain-link fencing on straining wires (see right). As it is impossible to tension this heavy-gauge wire by hand, use large straining bolts to stretch it between the posts. Mark the height of each wire on the posts—one to coincide with the top of the fencing, one about 6 inches from the ground, and the third midway between. Drill ⅛-inch-diameter holes right through the posts, insert a bolt into each hole and fit a washer and nut, leaving enough thread to provide about 2 inches of movement once you begin to apply tension to the wire (**1**).

Pass the end of the wire through the eye of a bolt and twist it around itself with pliers (**2**). Stretch the wire along the run of fencing, stapling it to each post and strut, but leaving enough slack for the wire to move when tensioned (**3**). Cut the wire to length and twist it through the bolt at the other end of the fence. Tension the wire from both ends by turning the nuts with a wrench (**4**).

Standard straining bolts provide enough tension for the average garden fence, but over a long run (200 feet or more), use a turnbuckle for each wire, applying tension with a metal bar (see left).

Using concrete posts

Fix straining wires to concrete posts using a special bolt and cleat (see right). Bolt a stretcher bar to the cleats when putting on the wire netting.

Tie the straining wire to intermediate posts with a length of galvanized wire passed through the predrilled hole.

Using angle iron posts

Winding brackets are supplied with angle iron fence posts to attach stretcher bars and to apply tension to the straining wires (see right). As you pass the straining wire from end to end, pass it through the predrilled hole in every intermediate post.

Using a turnbuckle
Apply tension by turning the turnbuckle with a metal bar.

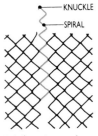
KNUCKLE
SPIRAL

Joining wire mesh
Chain-link fencing is supplied in standard lengths. To join one roll to another, unfold the knuckles at each end of the first wire spiral, then turn the spiral counterclockwise to withdraw it from the mesh. Connect the two rolls by rethreading the loose spiral in a clockwise direction through each link of the mesh. Bend over the knuckle at the top and bottom.

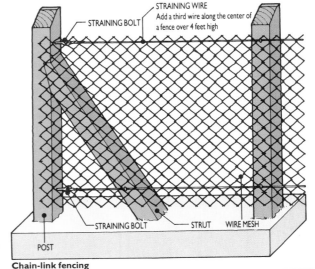
STRAINING WIRE
Add a third wire along the center of a fence over 4 feet high
STRAINING BOLT
STRAINING BOLT — STRUT WIRE MESH
POST
Chain-link fencing

Attaching the mesh
Staple each end link to the post. Unroll the mesh and pull it taut. Tie it to straining wires every foot or so with galvanized wire. Fix to post at other end.

Staple mesh to post

Tie with wire loops

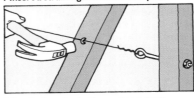
1 Insert a straining bolt in the end post

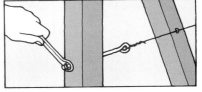
2 Attach a straining wire to the bolt

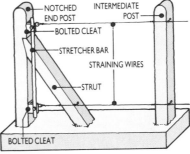
3 Staple the wire to the post and strut

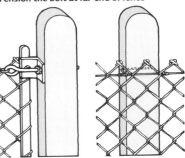
4 Tension the bolt at far end of fence

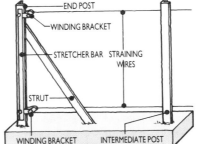
NOTCHED END POST
INTERMEDIATE POST
BOLTED CLEAT
STRETCHER BAR
STRAINING WIRES
STRUT
BOLTED CLEAT
Concrete fence posts

Cleat and stretcher bar **Tie wire to post**

END POST
WINDING BRACKET
STRETCHER BAR STRAINING WIRES
STRUT
WINDING BRACKET INTERMEDIATE POST
Angle iron posts

Winding bracket **Pass wire through post**

ERECTING A CLOSEBOARD FENCE

The bevel siding panels used for this type of fence are nailed to triangular-section rails known as arris rails. The arris rails are mortised into the fence posts. Concrete posts—and some that are made of wood—are supplied ready-mortised, but if you buy standard timber posts you will have to cut the mortises, a job you may not want to do. The unprotected end grain of the panels is liable to rot, especially if they are in contact with the ground. So fix horizontal 1 × 6 gravel boards at the foot of the fence, and nail wooden capping strips across the tops of the bevel siding. Space the fence posts no more than 10 feet apart.

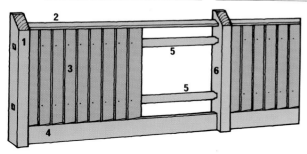

Closeboard fencing
1 End post
2 Capping strip
3 Featherboards
4 Gravel board
5 Arris rail
6 Intermediate post

REPAIRING A DAMAGED ARRIS RAIL

The arris rails take most of the strain when a closeboard fence is buffeted by high winds. Not surprisingly, they eventually crack across the middle or break where the tenon enters the mortise. You can buy galvanized metal brackets for repairing broken arris rails.

If you wish, you can use end brackets to construct a new fence instead of cutting mortises for the rails. However, it will not be as strong as a fence built with mortise-and-tenon joints.

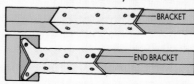
←BRACKET

←END BRACKET

Erecting the framework

If you are using plain wooden posts, mark and cut mortises for the arris rails about 6 inches above and below the ends of the fixed paneling. For fencing over 4 feet high, cut mortises for a third rail midway between the others. Position the mortises about 1 inch from the front face of each post (the paneled side of the fence).

As you erect the fence, cut the rails to length and shape a tenon on each end with a coarse rasp or Surform file (1). Paint preservative onto the shaped ends and into the mortises before you assemble the rails.

Erect the first fence post and pack gravel around its base (▷). Get someone to hold the post steady while you fit the arris rails and erect the next post, tapping it onto the ends of the rails with a mallet (2). Check that the rails are horizontal and the posts are vertical before packing fill around the second post. Construct the entire run of posts and rails in the same way. If you cannot maneuver the last post onto tenoned rails, cut the rails square and fix them to the post with metal brackets (see box right).

Check the whole fencing run once more to ensure that the arris rails are bedded firmly in their mortises and that the framework is true. Then secure each rail by driving a nail through the post into the tenon (3). Or drill a hole through the post and tenon and insert a wooden dowel. Pack concrete around each post (▷). Allow it to cure.

Fitting the boards

Gravel boards
Some concrete posts are mortised to take gravel boards. In this case they must be fitted with the arris rails. To fit gravel boards to wooden posts, toenail treated wooden cleats at the foot of each post, then nail the gravel boards to the cleats (4).

If a concrete post is not mortised for gravel boards, set wooden cleats into the concrete filling at the base of the post, and screw the board to the cleat when the concrete is set.

Featherboards
Cut the featherboards to length and treat the end grain. Stand the first board on the gravel board with its thick edge against the post. Nail the board to the arris rails with galvanized nails positioned ¾ inch from the thick edge. Place the next board in position, overlapping the thin edge of the fixed board by ½ inch. Check that it is vertical, then nail it in the same way. Don't drive a nail through both boards or they will not be able to move when they shrink. To space the other boards equally, make a spacer block from a scrap of wood (5). Place the last board to fit against the next post and fix it, this time with two nails per rail (6).

When the fence is completed, nail capping strips across the tops of the featherboards, cut the posts to length and cap them (▷).

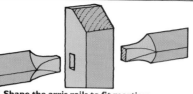
1 Shape the arris rails to fit mortises

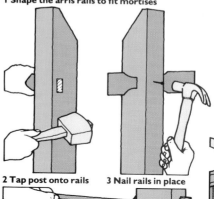
2 Tap post onto rails   **3 Nail rails in place**

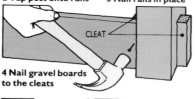
CLEAT→

4 Nail gravel boards to the cleats

5 Position panels with a spacer block

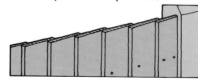
6 Fix last board with two nails

Capping the fence
Nail a wooden capping strip to the ends of the featherboards to shed rainwater.

ERECTING A PANEL FENCE

To prevent a prefabricated panel from rotting, either fit gravel boards as for a closeboard fence or leave a gap at the bottom by supporting a panel temporarily on two bricks while you nail it to the fence posts.

Using timber posts

Pack the first post into its hole with gravel (◁), then get someone to hold a panel against the post while you toenail through its framework into the post (**1**). If you can work from both sides, drive three nails from each side of the fence. If the frame starts to split, blunt the nails by tapping their points with a hammer. Alternatively, use metal angle brackets to secure the panels (**2**). Construct the entire fence erecting panels and posts alternately.

Nail capping strips across the panels if they have not been fitted by the manufacturer. Finally, cut each post to length and cap it (◁).

Wedge struts made from scrap lumber against each post to keep it vertical, then top up the holes with concrete (◁). If you are unable to work from both sides, you will have to fill each hole as you build the fence.

Using concrete posts

Panels are supported by grooved concrete posts without additional fasteners (**3**). Recessed posts are supplied with metal brackets for fastening the panels with screws (**4**).

Building a panel fence
Posts and panels are erected alternately. Dig a hole for the post (**1**) and hold it upright with gravel fill (◁). Support a panel on bricks (**2**) and have a helper push it against the post (**3**) while you nail it (**4**). Fit gravel boards (**5**), capping strips (**6**) and cap the posts (**7**). Fill the holes with concrete (**8**) and allow it to set.

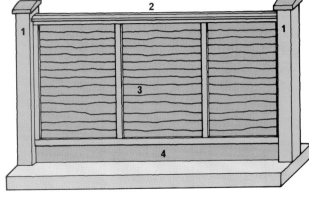

Panel fence
1 Fence posts
2 Capping strip
3 Prefabricated panel
4 Gravel board

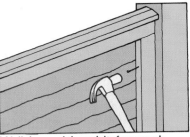

1 Nail the panel through its framework

2 Or use angle brackets to fix panel to posts

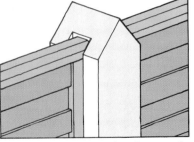

3 A grooved concrete post for a fence panel

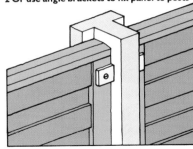

4 A recessed concrete post with bracket

ERECTING A POST-AND-RAIL FENCE

A simple ranch-style fence is no more than a series of horizontal rails fixed to short posts set into concrete in the normal way (▷). A picket fence is made in a similar way, but with vertical poles fixed to the rails.

Fixed horizontal rails

You can simply screw the rails directly to the posts (1), but the fence will last longer if you cut a shallow notch in the posts to locate each rail before you join it permanently (2).

Join two rails by butting them over a post (3). Arrange to stagger these joints so that you don't end up with all the rails butted on the same post (4).

Fastening picket panels

When you construct a picket fence from ready-made panels, buy or make metal brackets for fixing two panels to a single post.

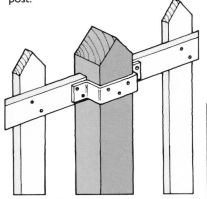

Use a metal bracket to fix picket-fence panels

Supporting a rotted post

A buried timber post will quite often rot below ground level, leaving a perfectly sound section above. To save buying a whole new post, brace the upper section with a concrete spur.

Erecting a spur
Dig the soil from around the post and remove the rotted stump. Insert the spur and pack gravel around it (1), then fill with concrete (2). Drill pilot holes for coach screws—wood screws with hexagonal heads (3). Insert the screws with a wrench to draw the post tightly against the spur.

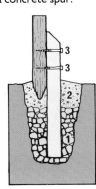

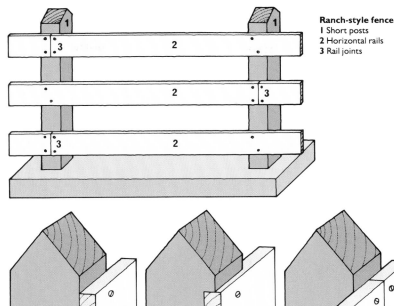

Ranch-style fence
1 Short posts
2 Horizontal rails
3 Rail joints

SEE ALSO

Details for: ▷
| Erecting posts | 413 |
| Retaining walls | 420 |

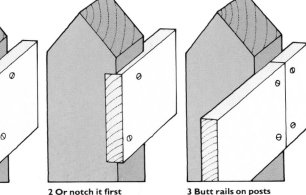

1 Screw rail to post   2 Or notch it first   3 Butt rails on posts   4 Stagger rail joints

ERECTING FENCES ON SLOPING GROUND

Crossways slope
If a slope runs across the garden, so that your neighbor's garden is higher than yours, build brick retaining walls between the posts or set paving stones in concrete to hold back the soil.

Downhill slope
The posts must be set vertically even when you erect a fence on a sloping site. Chain-link fencing or ranch-style rails can follow the slope of the land if you wish, but fence panels should be stepped and the triangular gaps beneath filled with gravel boards or retaining walls.

A retaining wall for a crossways slope

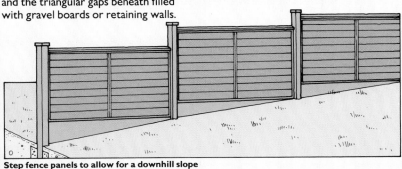

Step fence panels to allow for a downhill slope

• **Building plastic fences**
The basic construction of a plastic ranch-style fence is similar to one built from wood. But follow the manufacturer's instructions concerning the method for joining rails to posts.

417

GATES: CHOOSING

There are several points to consider when choosing a gate, not the least being the cost. All gates are relatively expensive, but don't buy one merely because it is cheaper than another. A garden gate must be constructed sturdily if it is to be reasonably durable, and, perhaps even more important, it must be mounted on strong posts.

Choose a style of gate which matches the fence or complements the wall from which it is hung, with due consideration for the character of the house and its surroundings. As a guide, aim for simplicity rather than the elaborate.

Side gates

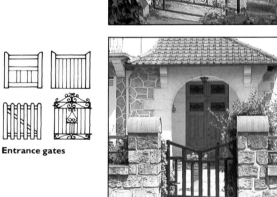

Entrance gates

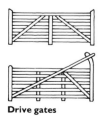

Drive gates

GATES FOR DIFFERENT LOCATIONS

When you browse through suppliers' catalogues, you will find gates grouped according to their intended location, because it is where it is to be sited that has most influence on the design of a gate and dictates its function.

SIDE GATES

A side gate is designed to protect a pathway next to a house from intruders. Side gates are invariably 6 feet 6 inches high and usually made from heavy lumber or metal. As a result, these gates are heavy and therefore braced with strong diagonal members to keep them rigid. With security in mind, choose a closeboard or tongue-and-groove gate—vertical boards are difficult to climb. When you hang a side gate, fit strong bolts top and bottom.

ENTRANCE GATES

An entrance gate is designed as much for its appearance as its function, but because it is in constant use, make sure it is properly braced with a diagonal strut running from the top of the latch stile down to the bottom of the hanging or hinge stile. If you hang a gate with the strut running the other way, the bracing will have no effect whatsoever.

Common fence structures are reflected in the style of entrance gates. Picket, closeboard and ranch-style gates are available, as is a simple and attractive frame and panel gate. With the latter style of gate, the solid wood or exterior-grade plywood panels keep the frame rigid. If the tops of both stiles are cut at an angle they will shed rainwater, reducing the likelihood of rot—a small but important feature to note when buying or designing a wooden gate.

Decorative iron gates are often used for entrances, but make sure the style is not too ostentatious for the building or its location. A very elaborate gate might look ridiculous in the entrance of a simple modern house or a traditional country cottage.

DRIVE GATES

First decide whether hanging a gate across a drive to a garage is such a good idea. Parking the car in a busy road in order to open the gate can be a difficult maneuver unless you have enough room to set the gate back from the entrance to leave enough space to pull the car off the road even when the gate is closed. Gates invariably open into the property, so make certain there is enough ground clearance for a wide gate if the drive slopes up towards a garage. Or hang two smaller gates to meet in the center. If you decide on a wide gate, choose a traditional five-bar gate for both strength and appearance.

GATE POSTS AND PIERS

Gate posts and masonry piers have to take a great deal of strain, so they must be strong in themselves and anchored securely in the ground.

Choose hardwood posts whenever possible, and select the section according to the weight of the gate. 4 × 4 posts are adequate for entrance gates but use larger posts for higher gates. For a wide gate across a drive, choose 6 × 6 or 8 × 8 posts.

Concrete posts are a possibility but unless you find a post predrilled to accept hinges and catch, you will have to screw them to a strip of lumber bolted to the post, so the fittings will not be securely fastened.

Square or tubular metal posts are available with hinge pins, gate-stop and catch welded in place. Like metal gates they must be protected from rust with paint, unless they have been coated with plastic at the factory.

A pair of masonry piers is another possibility. Each pier should be a minimum of 14 inches square and built on a firm concrete footing (◁). For large, heavy gates, the hinge pier at least must be very sturdy. It should be reinforced with a metal rod buried in the footing and running centrally through the pier.

HARDWARE FOR GATES

Rather specialized hardware has been developed to allow for the considerable strain on its hinges and catch imposed by a garden gate.

HINGES

Strap hinges
Side gates and most wooden entrance gates are hung on strap hinges, or T-hinges. Screw the long flap horizontally to the gate rails and the vertical flap to the face of the post. Heavier gates need a stronger version which is bolted through the top rail.
Wide drive gates need a double strap hinge with a long flap bolted on each side of the top rail. These heavy-duty hinges are supported by bolts which pass through the gate post.

Hinge pins
Metal collars, welded to the hinge side of metal gates, drop over hinge pins attached to gate posts in a variety of ways: screwed to wooden posts; bolted through concrete; built into the mortar joints of masonry piers; welded to metal posts. The gate can be lifted off its hinges at any time, unless you reverse the top pin or drill a hole and fit a split pin and washer.

LATCHES

Automatic latches
Simple wooden gates are fitted with a latch that operates automatically as the gate is closed. Screw the latch bar to the latch stile of the gate and use it to position the latch on the post.

Thumb latches
Cut a slot through a closeboard side gate for the latch lifter of a thumb or Suffolk latch. Pass the lifter bar through the slot and screw the handle to the front of the gate. Screw the latch bar to the inner face so that the lifter releases the bar from the catch plate.

Ring latches
A ring latch works in a similar way to a thumb latch but is operated from inside only, by twisting the ring handle to lift the latch bar.

Chelsea catches
Bolt a Chelsea catch through a drive gate. The latch pivots on the bolt to drop into a slot in the catch plate screwed to the post.

Loop-over catches
When two wide gates are used in a drive entrance, one gate is fastened with a drop bolt located in a socket set in concrete. A simple U-shaped metal bar, bolted through the latch stile of the other gate, drops over the stile of the fixed gate.

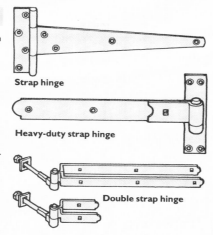
Strap hinge

Heavy-duty strap hinge

Double strap hinge

Hinge pin

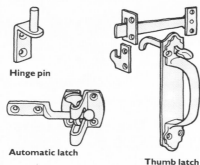
Automatic latch

Thumb latch

Ring latch

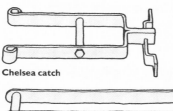

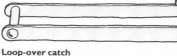
Chelsea catch

Loop-over catch

Materials for gates

Many wooden gates are made from softwood simply for economy, but a wood such as cedar or oak is a better investment. Most so-called wrought-iron gates are made from mild steel bar which must be primed and painted ($\triangleright$) if they are to last.

Hang a heavy drive gate on a stout post

GATE POSTS

Gate posts are set in concrete like ordinary fence posts but the post holes are linked by a concrete bridge to provide extra support.

Side and entrance gate posts

Lay the gate on the ground with a post on each side. Check that the posts are parallel and the required distance apart to accommodate hinges and catch. Nail two horizontal braces from post to post and another diagonally to keep the posts in line while you erect them (**1**).

Dig a 1-foot-wide trench across the entrance and long enough to accept both posts. It need be no deeper than 2 feet at the center, but dig an adequate post hole at each end—about 2 feet deep for a low entrance gate, 3 feet deep for a taller gate. Set the braced gate posts in the holes with gravel and concrete as for fence posts ($\triangleright$), using temporary braces to hold them upright until the concrete sets (**2**). Fill the trench with concrete at the same time and either level it flush with the pathway or allow for the thickness of paving slabs or blocks ($\triangleright$).

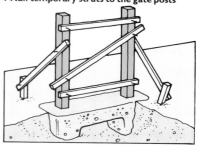
1 Nail temporary struts to the gate posts

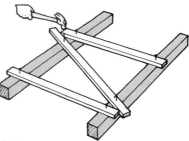
2 Support the posts until the concrete sets

Drive gate posts

Hang wide farm-style gates on posts set in 3-foot-deep holes (**3**). Erect the latch post in concrete like any fence post, but bolt a heavy piece of lumber across the base of the hinge post before anchoring it in concrete.

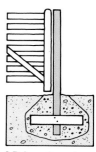
3 Drive gate post
Bolt a wood "deadman" to the post to help support the weight of the gate.

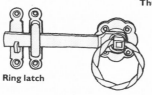

MASONRY: BUILDING WALLS

Whatever structure you build with masonry, the basic techniques for laying brick, stone or concrete block remain the same. On the other hand, it must be recognized that it is wise to hire a professional builder when the structure is complicated, extensive or must withstand considerable loads or stress.

A stone-built retaining wall

A boundary wall of yellow brick

Facing blocks make attractive dividing walls

A decorative pierced-block screen

Amateur bricklaying

It is difficult to suggest when a particular job is beyond the level of skill or confidence of an amateur bricklayer, clearly differing from individual to individual. It would be foolhardy for anyone to attempt to build a two-story house, for instance, unless they had had a lot of experience and, possibly, professional training, but building even a high boundary wall, which in terms of pure technique is simple, would be an arduous task if it were very long or had to allow for changes in gradient. The simple answer is to begin with low retaining or dividing walls and screens until you have mastered the skills of laying bricks and blocks solidly upon one another, and the ability to build a wall both straight and vertical without danger of possible collapse.

WALLS FOR DIFFERENT LOCATIONS

RETAINING WALLS

Raised planting beds are made with low retaining walls, but a true retaining wall is designed to hold back a bank of earth, usually to terrace a sloping site. As long as it is not too high, a retaining wall is easy to build, although, strictly speaking, it should slope back into the bank to resist the weight of the earth. Also, you must allow for drainage, to reduce the water pressure behind the wall. Retaining walls are built with bricks, concrete blocks or stone, sometimes dry-laid with earth packed into the crevices for planting—it is a matter of personal choice.

BOUNDARY WALLS

A brick or stone wall surrounding your property provides security and privacy while forming an attractive background to trees and shrubs. New, crisp brickwork complements a formal garden or modern setting, while second-hand materials or undressed stone blend with an old, established garden. If you cannot match exactly the color of existing masonry, encourage the growth of lichen with a wash of liquid fertilizer, or disguise the junction with a well-chosen climber. You may need local authority approval if you want to build a wall higher than 3 feet that will adjoin a road or public sidewalk (◁).

DIVIDING WALLS

Many gardeners divide a plot of land with walls to form a visual break between patio and lawn, to define the edges of pathways, or simply to add interest to an otherwise featureless site. Dividing walls are often merely low walls, perhaps only a foot or two in height. They make perfect structures upon which to practice basic techniques.

Use simple concrete block or brick walls to divide interior spaces—for a workshop or hobbies room.

SCREEN WALLS

Screens are also dividing walls, but they provide a degree of privacy without completely masking the garden beyond. Screens are built with decorative pierced blocks, often with solid block or brick bases and concrete piers.

STRUCTURAL WALLS

Walls of even a small building have to support the weight of a roof and, depending on the complexity of the structure, will have to incorporate door and window frames. In most cases, a moisture resistance will have to be built into the walls to control dampness, and some walls are constructed with a cavity between two leaves of masonry to provide insulation and weatherproofing. A brick foundation for a sun space is no more difficult to build than a simple garden wall, but make certain you are familiar with building methods before you attempt to build a garage or similar outbuilding.

CHOOSING BRICKS

More than 10,000 different types of bricks are produced in this country and throughout the world. Generally, your choice will be limited to bricks manufactured in your local area, since long-distance hauling of these heavy materials is prohibitively expensive. When creating brick designs and purchasing brick, it's important to understand the basic classifications as they relate to size, appearance and weathering characteristics.

The variety of brick

Face brick
Face bricks are suitable for any type of exposed brickwork. They are water- and frost-resistant. Being visible, face bricks are made as much for their appearance as their structural qualities and, as such, are available in the widest range of colors and textures. Face bricks are graded carefully to meet standards of strength, water absorption and uniformity of shape.

Building brick
Building bricks are cheap general-purpose bricks used primarily for interior brickwork which is to be plastered, or stuccoed if used externally. They are not color-matched carefully but the mottled effect of a wall built with building bricks is attractive.

Although they could become damaged or cracked by frost if used on an exposed site, building bricks can be used for garden walls.

Fire brick
Fire bricks are pale yellow in color and made from specially chosen clays and carefully fired. They're designed and used to line fireplaces, kilns and barbecues and must be laid with heat-resistant mortar.

Weathering classifications of brick

Building brick is manufactured in three grades that differentiate weathering characteristics and indicate the conditions a particuular kind of brick is best suited for. For any particular project, check which kind of brick is required by the building department regulations in your area.

Type SW (severe weathering) bricks are best suited for outdoor projects in areas prone to prolonged periods of freezing. Always choose Type SW brick for patios and driveways. While there is a separate classification of bricks known as "paving bricks," these are meant for public, high-traffic areas and are not required for residential projects.

Type MW (moderate weathering) bricks can be used outdoors in areas where there is little or no frost. In most cases, Type MW bricks can be used for constructing garden walls, even in cold regions.

Type NW (no weathering) bricks are meant only for indoor use, but they can be used for outdoor structures where they'll be protected from the ravages of rain and snow.

Types of brick

Solid bricks
The majority of bricks are solid throughout, either flat on all surfaces or with a depression known as a "frog" on one face. When filled with mortar, the frog keys the bricks.

Cored or perforated bricks
Cored bricks are made with holes running through them, providing the same function as the frog. A wall made with cored bricks must be finished with a coping of solid bricks.

Special shapes
Specially shaped bricks are made for decorative brickwork. Master bricklayers use the full range to build arches, chamfered or rounded corners and curvilinear walls. A number of shaped bricks are made for coping garden walls.

BUYING BRICKS

Ordering bricks
Bricks are normally sold by the thousand, but builders' supply yards are usually willing to sell them in smaller quantities. It is cheaper to order them direct from the manufacturer, but only if you buy a sufficient load to make the delivery charge economical.

Estimating quantities
The size of a standard brick is $2\frac{1}{4} \times 3\frac{3}{4} \times 8$ inches, but because dimensions may vary by a fraction of an inch, even within the same batch of bricks, manufacturers normally specify a nominal size which includes an additional $\frac{1}{4}$ to $\frac{1}{2}$ inch to each dimension to allow for the mortar joint. To calculate how many bricks you need, allow about 48 bricks for every square yard of single-skin wall. Add a 5 percent allowance for cutting and breakage.

Storing bricks
When bricks are delivered, have them unloaded as near as possible to the building site, and stack them carefully on a flat, dry base. Cover the stack with polyethylene sheet or a tarpaulin until you are ready to use them, to prevent their becoming saturated with rain. This could cause staining and an increased risk of frost damage to the mortar and the bricks themselves.

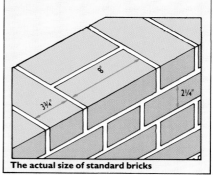

The actual size of standard bricks

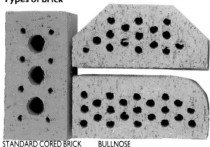

Types of brick

STANDARD CORED BRICK   BULLNOSE   DOUBLE-CANT COPING

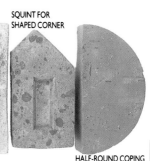

STANDARD BRICK WITH FROG   SQUINT FOR SHAPED CORNER   HALF-ROUND COPING

THE COLOR AND TEXTURE OF BRICKS

The popularity of brick as a building material stems largely from its range of subtle colors and textures, which actually improve with weathering. Unfortunately, weathered brick can be difficult to match by using a manufacturer's catalogue. If you have spare bricks, take one to the supplier to compare with new bricks, or borrow samples from the supplier's stock to match when you get home.

Color

The color of bricks is determined by the type of clay used in their manufacture, although it is modified by the addition of certain minerals and the temperature of the firing. Large manufacturers supply a complete range of colors from black or purple to white, plus reds, browns and yellows. There are also brindled bricks—multicolored or mottled—especially useful for blending with existing masonry.

Texture

Texture is as important to the appearance of a brick wall as color. Simple rough or smooth textures are created by the choice of materials. Others are imposed upon the clay by scratching, rolling, brushing and so on. A brick may be textured all over or on the sides and ends only.

Brick colors and textures
A small selection from the extremely wide range of colors and textures.
1 Smooth blended
2 Handmade
3 Sand-faced yellow
4 Smooth blue engineering
5 Sand-faced gray
6 Smooth red stock
7 Wire-cut brindle
8 Textured multibuff
9 Second London stock
10 Wire-cut blue
11 Red common
12 Coarse fletton
13 Molded fletton
14 Dragwire multired

Pattern formed by projecting headers

Decorative combination of colored bricks

Look out for second-hand molded bricks

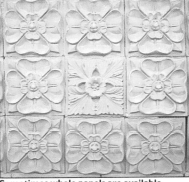

Sometimes whole panels are available

Weathered antique bricks are attractive

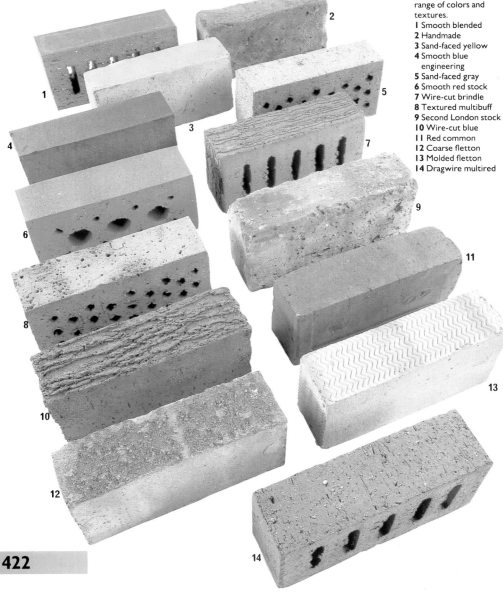

CHOOSING CONCRETE BLOCKS

Cast concrete building blocks are not as standardized as clay bricks, but to describe them using the same specifications—variety, quality and type—makes for a useful comparison when choosing which to use.

Variety of block

Structural blocks
Simple rectangular blocks, cement gray or white in color, are used as the structural core of a wall which will be stuccoed or plastered. Consequently, they are often made with a zigzag key on the surface to encourage the finish to adhere. Since they are not intended as visible masonry, they have no aesthetic qualities whatsoever. A wall can be constructed quickly with blocks because they are considerably larger than standard bricks, and the wall will be relatively cheap.

Facing blocks
These are blocks with one decorative face and end for walls which are to be left exposed. They are often made to resemble natural stone by including crushed stone aggregate. There is a sufficient range of colors to blend with the local stone in most areas of the country. Facing blocks are used for the external skin of cavity walls, backed by the cheaper structural blocks. They are also used for ornamental garden walls for which matching coping slabs are available as a finishing touch.

Screen blocks
Screen blocks are pierced decorative building units for constructing a lightweight masonry trellis or screen. They are not bonded like brickwork or structural blocks and therefore require supporting piers made from matching pilaster blocks with locating channels to take the pierced blocks. Coping slabs finish the top of the screen and piers.

Quality of block

Load-bearing blocks
Structural blocks are used to construct the load-bearing walls of a building. Those made with lightweight aggregate are easier to handle, but when the loads are excessive, use stronger blocks made from dense concrete.

Nonload-bearing blocks
Nonload-bearing blocks are used to build internal, dividing partitions. They are either lightweight-aggregate blocks or low-density foamed-concrete blocks which are easy to cut to shape or chase for electrical wiring. Foamed blocks are also made in a load-bearing quality.

Decorative blocks
Pierced screen blocks should not be used in the construction of load-bearing walls. However, they are capable of supporting a lightweight structure such as a wood and plastic carport roof.

Insulating blocks
Foamed blocks are often used for constructing the inner leaf of a cavity wall. They have good insulating properties and meet minimum building code standards without the need for secondary insulation. Use ultralight foamed blocks when improved insulation is required.

Type of block

Solid blocks
Solid blocks are constructed two ways—with lightweight aggregate or foamed concrete.

Cored blocks
To reduce their weight, large dense-concrete blocks are virtually hollow with supporting ribs between the outer skins. Stretcher blocks are used for the main part of the wall, while corner blocks are used when the end of a wall is exposed. Solid-top blocks, partly hollowed out on the underside, are used to support joists.

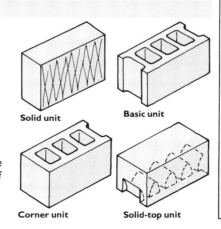

Solid unit

Basic unit

Corner unit

Solid-top unit

BUYING CONCRETE BLOCKS

Estimating quantities
Blocks are available in such a variety of sizes that in order to calculate the number required you must divide a given area of wall by the dimensions of a specific type of block. Blocks are sometimes specified in nominal sizes (larger than actual size) but with the 2⅜-inch allowance for mortar on the length and height only. Block walls are normally constructed with one skin of masonry, so the thickness of a block remains as the actual size.

Available sizes and designs
Standard blocks are nominally 16 inches long, 8 inches high and 8 inches thick. Many other sizes are available, as well, including half and three-quarter units. Available shapes vary widely: Units with keyed ends are used in ordinary wall construction, square-end blocks for corners. Single- and double-bullnose units can be used for decorative designs, and other blocks are designed for door jamb surrounds and lintels. There are also many decorative blocks, including pierced ornamental blocks and "tile" units.

Storing blocks
When blocks are delivered, have them unloaded as near as possible to the construction site to reduce the possibility of damage—they are brittle and chip easily. Stack them on a flat, dry base and protect them from rain and frost with a polyethylene tarpaulin.

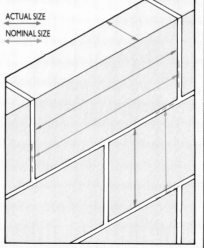

ACTUAL SIZE

NOMINAL SIZE

Sizes of structural blocks
The nominal size of a block refers to the length and height only. Thicknesses are always specified as an actual size.

SEE ALSO

Details for: ▷	
Loadbearing walls	122
Blocks	424
Laying blocks	434–435

BLOCKS AND STONES

Precast blocks made from poured concrete are available in a variety of colors, shapes and sizes. Aesthetically, however, nothing can surpass quarried *stone such as granite or sandstone. Hewn roughly in natural shapes and textures, or as dressed blocks, natural stone is durable and weathers well.*

Semidressed natural stone blocks

Dry-stone retaining wall

Man-made concrete blocks
1 Solid, dense concrete
2 Lightweight
3 Lightweight aggregate
4 Pierced decorative
5 Solid decorative
6 Pitched-face reconstituted stone
7 Pilaster block
8 Pilaster coping
9 Multistone block
10 Screen coping
11 Split-face facing
12 Hewn-stone facing

Split-stone walling

Knapped-flint boundary wall

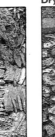
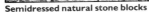

CHOOSING NATURAL STONE

Practical considerations
In practical terms, the type of natural stone you choose for walls depends almost entirely on where you happen to live. In some parts of the country there are local restrictions governing the choice of building materials, and, in any case, a structure built from stone that is indigenous to a locality is more likely to blend sympathetically into its surroundings. Furthermore, buying stone from a local quarry makes economic sense—transporting stone over long distances can be very costly.

Where to obtain stone
If you live in a large town or city, obtaining natural stone can be a real problem. You might be prepared to buy a few small boulders for a rock garden from a local garden center, but the cost of buying enough stone for even a short run of walling is likely to be prohibitive. Masonry supply yards may carry some varieties of natural stone and can order others on your behalf, but transportation costs tend to inflate the price of the material.

Another source of materials, and possibly the cheapest way to obtain dressed stone, is to visit a demolition site. Prices vary considerably, but the cost of transport may be less than a supplier might offer.

Estimating quantities
As most quarries sell stone by the ton, it is difficult to estimate the quantity you need. Having worked out the approximate dimensions of the wall in question, telephone the nearest quarry for advice. Not only can you get an estimate of the cost of the stone, but you will be in a position to arrange for transport on your own.

Types of stone
Limestone, sandstone and granite are all suitable for building walls. Flint and slate require specialized building methods and are often used in combination with other materials. Stone bought in its natural state is classed as undressed; it is perfect for dry-stone walls in an informal garden. A more regular form of masonry is semidressed stone, which is cut into reasonably uniform blocks but with uneven surfaces, or fully dressed stone with machine-cut faces. The cost of stone increases in proportion to its preparation.

When building a wall, mortar is used to bind together the bricks, concrete blocks or stones. The durability of a masonry structure depends on the quality of the mortar used in its construction. If it is mixed correctly to the right consistency, the mortar will become as hard and strong as the masonry itself, but if the ingredients are added in the wrong proportions, the mortar will be weak and prone to cracking. If too much water is used, the mortar will be squeezed out of the joints by the weight of the masonry, and if the mortar is too dry, adhesion will be poor.

BRICKLAYERS' TERMS

Bricklayers use a number of specialized words and phrases to describe their craft and materials. Terms used frequently are listed below while others are described as they occur.

BRICK FACES The surfaces of a brick.
Stretcher faces The long sides of a brick.
Header faces The short ends of a brick.
Bedding faces The top and bottom surfaces.
Frog The depression in one bedding face.

COURSES The individual, horizontal rows of bricks.
Stretcher course A single course with stretcher faces visible.
Header course A single course with header faces visible.
Coping The top course designed to protect the wall from rainwater.
Bond Pattern produced by staggering alternate courses so that vertical joints are not aligned one above the other.
Stretcher A single brick from a stretcher course.
Header A single brick from a header course.
Closure brick The last brick laid in a course.

CUT BRICKS Bricks cut with a bolster chisel to even up the bond.
Bat A brick cut across its width, e.g. half-bat, three-quarter bat.
Queen closer A brick cut along its length.

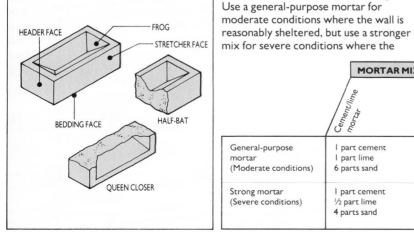

HEADER FACE — FROG — STRETCHER FACE — BEDDING FACE — HALF-BAT — QUEEN CLOSER

The ingredients of mortar

The ingredients of general-purpose mortar are portland cement, hydrated lime and sand, mixed with enough water to make a workable paste.

Cement is the hardening agent which binds the other ingredients together. The lime slows down the drying process and prevents the mortar setting too quickly. It also makes the mix flow well so that it fills gaps in the masonry and adheres to the texture of blocks or bricks. The sand acts as fine aggregate, adding body to the mortar, and reduces the possibility of shrinkage.

Use fine builders' sand for general-purpose mortar. However, use silver sand if you want a paler mortar to bond white screen blocks.

Mixing mortar

Mortar must be used within two hours of mixing or be discarded, so make only as much as you can use within that time. An average of about two minutes to lay one brick is a reasonable estimate.

Choose a flat site upon which to mix the materials—a sheet of plywood will do—and dampen it slightly to prevent its absorbing water from the mortar. Make a pile of half the amount of sand to be used, then add the other ingredients. Put the rest of the sand on top, and mix the dry materials thoroughly.

Scoop a depression in the pile and add clean tap water. Never use contaminated or salty water. Push the dry mix from around the edge of the

Plasticizers

If you are laying masonry in cold weather, substitute a proprietary plasticizer for the lime. Plasticizer produces aerated mortar—the tiny air bubbles in the mix allow the water to expand in freezing conditions and reduce the risk of cracking. Premixed masonry cement, with an aerating agent, is ready for mixing with sand.

Ready-mix mortar

Ready-mix mortar contains all the essential ingredients mixed to the correct proportions. You simply add water. It is a more expensive way of buying mortar but convenient to use and is available in small quantities.

pile into the water until it has absorbed enough for you to blend the mix with a shovel, using a chopping action. Add more water, little by little, until the mortar has a butterlike consistency, slipping easily from the shovel but firm enough to hold its shape if you make a hollow in the mix. If the sides of the hollow collapse, add more dry ingredients until the mortar firms up. Make sure the mortar is not too dry or it won't form a strong bond with the masonry.

If mortar stiffens up while you are working, add just enough water to restore the consistency. Dampen the mixing board again.

Proportions for masonry mixes

Mix the ingredients according to the prevailing conditions at the building site. Use a general-purpose mortar for moderate conditions where the wall is reasonably sheltered, but use a stronger mix for severe conditions where the

wall will be exposed to wind and driving rain, or if the site is elevated or near the coast. If you are using plasticizer instead of lime, follow the manufacturer's instructions regarding the quantity you should add to the sand.

SEE ALSO

Details for: ▷	
Cutting bricks	428
Floats and trowels	478

Correct consistency
The mortar mix should be firm enough to hold its shape when you make a depression in the mix.

● **Estimating quantity**
As a rough guide to estimating how much mortar you will need, allow approximately 1 cu. yd. of sand (other ingredients in proportion) to lay: 1600 to 1650 bricks; 69 to 70 sq. yds. average facing blocks; 100 to 105 sq. yds. screen or structural blocks.

MORTAR MIXING PROPORTIONS

	Cement/lime mortar	Plasticized mortar	Masonry cement mortar
General-purpose mortar (Moderate conditions)	1 part cement 1 part lime 6 parts sand	1 part cement 6 parts sand/ plasticizer	1 part cement 5 parts sand
Strong mortar (Severe conditions)	1 part cement ½ part lime 4 parts sand	1 part cement 4 parts sand/ 3 parts sand plasticizer	1 part cement 3 parts sand

DESIGNING A WALL FOR STABILITY

It is easy enough to appreciate the loads and stresses imposed upon the walls of a house or outbuilding, and therefore the necessity for solid foundations and adequate methods of reinforcement and protection to prevent their collapsing. It is not so obvious, but even a simple garden wall requires similar measures to ensure its stability. It is merely irritating if a low dividing wall or planter falls apart, but a serious injury could result from the collapse of a heavy boundary wall.

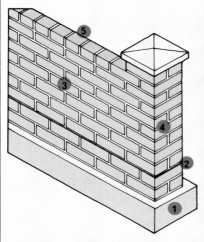

The basic structure of a wall
Unless you design and build a wall in the correct manner, it will not be strong and stable.

1 Footings
A wall must be built upon a solid concrete platform known as a strip footing. The dimensions of the footing vary according to the height and weight of the wall.

2 Damp-proof course
A layer of waterproof material 6 inches above ground level stops water from rising from the soil. It is not needed for most garden walling unless it abuts a building with a similar DPC. Not only does it protect the house from dampness, but it reduces the likelihood of freezing water expanding and cracking the joints.

3 Bonding
The staggered pattern of bricks is not merely decorative. It is designed to spread the static load along the wall and to tie the individual units together.

4 Piers
Straight walls over a certain height and length must be buttressed at regular intervals with thick columns of brickwork known as piers. They resist the sideways pressure caused by high winds.

5 Coping
The coping prevents frost damage by shedding rainwater from the top of the wall where it could seep into the upper brick joints.

BONDING BRICKWORK

Mortar is extremely strong under compression, but its tensile strength is relatively weak. If bricks were stacked one upon the other so that the vertical joints were continuous, any movement within the wall would pull them apart and the structure would be seriously weakened. Bonding brickwork staggers the vertical joints, transmitting the load along the entire length of the wall. Try out the bond of your choice by dry-laying a few bricks before you embark on the actual building work.

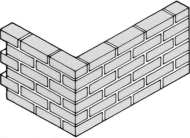

Stretcher bond
The stretcher bond is the simplest form of bonding, used for single-thickness walls, including the two individual leaves of a cavity wall found in the construction of modern buildings. Half-bats are used to make the bond at the end of a straight wall, while a corner is formed by alternating headers and stretchers.

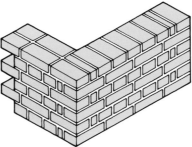

English bond
If you build an 8-inch-thick wall by laying courses of stretcher-bonded bricks side by side, there would be a weak vertical joint running centrally down the wall. An English bond strengthens the wall by using alternate courses of headers. Staggered joints are maintained at the end of a wall and at a corner by inserting a queen closer before the last header.

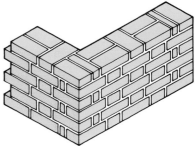

Flemish bond
The Flemish bond is an alternative method to English bond for building a solid, 8-inch-thick wall. Every course is laid with alternate headers and stretchers. Stagger the joint at the end of a course and at a corner by laying a queen closer before the header.

Decorative bonds
Stretcher, English and Flemish bonds are designed to construct strong walls—decorative qualities are incidental. Other bonds, used primarily for their visual effect, are suitable for low, nonload-bearing walls only, supported by a conventionally bonded base and piers.

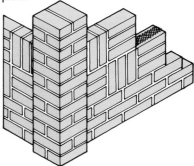

Stack bonding
A basketweave effect is achieved by stack bonding bricks in groups of three. Strengthen the continuous vertical joints with wall ties (◁).

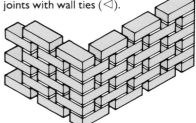

Honeycomb bond
Build an open, decorative screen using a stretcherlike bond with a quarter-bat-size space between each brick. Build the screen carefully to keep the bond regular, and cut quarter-bats to fill the gaps in the top course.

CONSTRUCTING STRIP FOOTINGS

Stringent code regulations govern the size and reinforcement required for the footings to support high and especially *structural walls, but most garden walls can be built upon concrete footings laid in a straight-sided trench.*

Size of footings

The footings must be sufficiently substantial to support the weight of the wall, and the soil must be firm and well drained to avoid possible subsidence. It is unwise to set footings in ground which has been filled recently, such as a new building site. Also, take care to avoid tree roots and drainpipes. If the trench begins to fill with water as you are digging, seek professional advice before proceeding.

Dig the trench deeper than the footing itself so that the first one or two courses of brick are below ground level. This will allow for an adequate depth of soil for planting right up to the wall.

If the soil is not firmly packed when you reach the required depth, dig deeper until you reach a firm level, then fill the bottom of the trench with compacted hardcore up to the lowest level of the proposed footing.

RECOMMENDED DIMENSIONS FOR FOOTINGS

Type of wall	Height of wall	Depth of footing	Width of footing
One brick thick	3 ft.	4 to 6 in.	12 in.
Two bricks thick	3 ft.	9 to 12 in.	18 in.
Two bricks thick	3 to 6 ft.	16 to 18 in.	18 to 24 in.
Retaining wall	3 ft.	6 to 12 in.	16 to 18 in.

Setting out the footings

For a straight footing, set up two form boards made from 2-inch-thick (nominal) lumber nailed to stakes driven into the ground at each end of the proposed trench but well outside the work area.

Drive nails into the top edge of each board and strentch lines between them to mark the front and back edges of the wall. Then drive nails into the form boards on each side of the wall line to indicate the width of the footings, and stretch more lines between them (1).

When you are satisfied that the setting out is accurate, remove the lines marking the wall but leave the nails in place so that you can replace the lines when you come to lay the bricks.

Place a level against the remaining lines to mark the edge of the footing on the ground (2). Mark the ends of the footing extending beyond the line of the wall by half the wall's thickness. Mark the edge of the trench on the ground with a spade and remove the lines. Leave the boards in place.

Turning corners

If your wall will have a right-angled corner, set up two sets of form boards as before, checking carefully that the lines form a true right angle using the 3:4:5 right triangle method (3).

Digging the trench

Excavate the trench, keeping the sides vertical, and check that the bottom is level, using a long, straight piece of wood and a level.

Drive a stake into the bottom of the trench near one end until the top of the stake represents the depth of the footing. Drive in more stakes at 3-foot intervals, checking that the tops are level (4).

Filling the trench

Pour a foundation mix of concrete (▷) into the trench, then tamp it down firmly with a heavy piece of lumber until it is exactly level with the top of the stakes. Leave the stakes in place and allow the footing to harden thoroughly before building the wall.

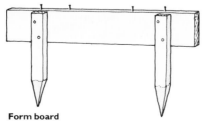

Form board

FOOTING FOR A SLOPING SITE

When the ground slopes gently, simply ignore the gradient and make the footing perfectly level. If the site slopes noticeably, make a stepped footing by placing plywood form stops across the trench at regular intervals. Calculate the height and length of the steps using multiples of normal brick size.

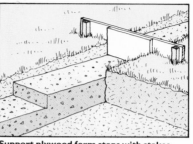

Support plywood form stops with stakes

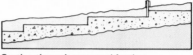

Section through a stepped footing
A typical stepped concrete footing with one of the plywood form stops in place.

SEE ALSO

Details for: ▷	
Concrete mixes	441
Level	428, 478

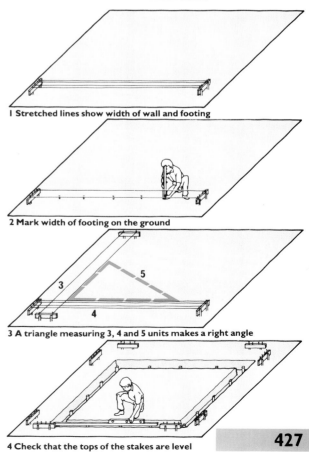

1 Stretched lines show width of wall and footing

2 Mark width of footing on the ground

3 A triangle measuring 3, 4 and 5 units makes a right angle

4 Check that the tops of the stakes are level

BRICKLAYING TOOLS

You can make or improvise some builder's tools (◁) but you will have to buy some of the more-specialized bricklayer's tools.

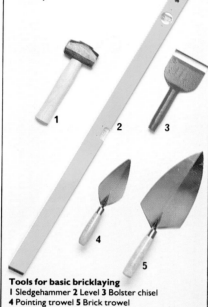

Tools for basic bricklaying
1 Sledgehammer 2 Level 3 Bolster chisel
4 Pointing trowel 5 Brick trowel

LAYING BRICKS

Spreading a bed of mortar—throwing a line—requires practice before you can develop speed, so concentrate at first on laying bricks neatly and accurately. Mortar mixed to the right consistency (◁) helps to keep the visible faces of the bricks clean. In hot, dry weather, dampen the footings and bricks, but let any surface water evaporate before you begin to lay bricks.

Bricklaying techniques

Hold the brick trowel with your thumb in line with the handle, pointing towards the tip of the blade (1).

Scoop a measure of mortar out of the pile and shape it roughly to match the shape of the trowel blade. Pick up the mortar by sliding the blade under the pile, setting it onto the trowel with a slight jerk of the wrist (2).

Spread the mortar along the top course by aligning the edge of the trowel with the center line of the bricks. As you tip the blade to deposit the mortar, draw the trowel back towards you to stretch the bed over at least two to three bricks (3).

Furrow the mortar by pressing the point of the trowel along the center (4).

Pick up a brick with your other hand, but don't extend your thumb too far onto the stretcher face or it will disturb the builders' line every time you place a brick in position. Press the brick into the bed, picking up excess mortar squeezed from the joint by sliding the edge of the trowel along the wall (5).

With the mortar picked up on the trowel, butter the header of the next brick, making a neat 1/8-inch bed for the header joint (6). Press the brick against its neighbor, scooping off excess mortar with the trowel.

Having laid three bricks, use the level to make sure they are horizontal. Make any adjustments by tapping them down with the trowel handle (7).

Hold the level along the outer edge of the bricks to check that they are in line. To move a brick sideways without knocking it off its mortar bed, tap the upper edge with the trowel at about 45 degrees (8).

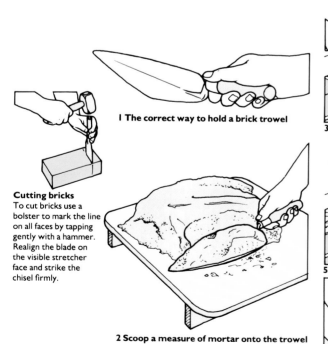

Cutting bricks
To cut bricks use a bolster to mark the line on all faces by tapping gently with a hammer. Realign the blade on the visible stretcher face and strike the chisel firmly.

1 The correct way to hold a brick trowel

2 Scoop a measure of mortar onto the trowel

3 Stretch a bed of mortar along the course

5 Push down brick and remove excess mortar

7 Level the course of bricks with the trowel

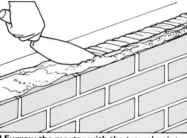

4 Furrow the mortar with the trowel point

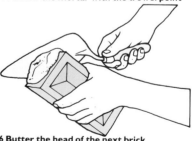

6 Butter the head of the next brick

8 Tap the bricks sideways to align them

BUILDING A STRETCHER-BONDED WALL

A single-width brick wall looks unsubstantial and, over a certain height, is structurally weak unless it is supported with piers or changes direction by forming right-angle corners. In any case, the ability to construct strong, accurate corners is a requirement for building most structures, including simple garden planters. Building a wall with another type of bond is a little more complicated in detail ($\triangleright$), but the basic construction principles remain the same.

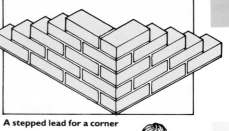

A stepped lead for a corner

Setting out the corners

Mark out the footings and face of the wall by stretching string lines between profile boards ($\triangleright$). When the footings have been filled and the concrete has set, use a plumb line or hold a level lightly against the line to mark the corners and the face of the wall on the footing (**1**). Join the marks with a pencil and straightedge, and check the accuracy of the corners with a builder's square. Stretch a line between the corner marks to check the alignment.

1 Mark the face of the wall on the footing

Building the corners

Build the corners first as a series of steps or "leads" before filling between. It is essential that they form true right angles, so take your time.

Throw a bed of mortar, then lay three bricks in both directions against the marked line. Check that they are level in all directions, including across the diagonal, by laying a level between the end bricks (**2**).

Build the leads to a height of five stepped courses, using a gauge stick to measure the height of each course as you proceed (**3**). Use alternate headers and stretchers to form the actual point of the corner.

Use a level to plumb the corner, and check the alignment of the stepped bricks by holding the level against the side of the wall (**4**).

• **Covering the wall**
Cover finished or partly built walls overnight with sheets of polyethylene or tarpaulin to protect the brickwork from rain or frost. Weight the edges of the covers with bricks.

2 Level the first course of bricks

3 Check the height with a gauge stick

4 Check that the steps are in line

Building the straight sections

Stretch a builder's line between the corners so that it aligns perfectly with the top edge of the first course (**5**).

Lay the first straight course of bricks from both ends toward the middle. As you near the middle point, lay the last few bricks dry to make certain they will fit. Then mortar them in, finishing with the central or "closure" brick. Spread mortar onto both ends of the closure brick and onto the header faces of the bricks on each side. Lay the closure brick very carefully (**6**), and scoop off excess mortar with the trowel.

Lay subsequent courses between the leaders in the same way, raising the builder's line each time. To build the wall higher, raise the corners first by constructing leads to the required height, then fill the spaces between.

5 Stretch a builder's line for the first course

6 Carefully lay the last or closure brick

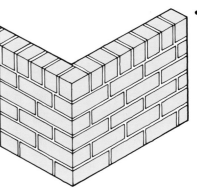

• **Building a straight wall**
To build a straight wall without a corner, follow the procedure described left, building end leads—straight stepped sections—at each end of the wall, then fill between with bricks.

Coping the wall
You could finish the wall by laying the last course frog downwards, but a coping of half-bats laid on end looks more professional. Alternatively, use proprietary coping bricks or blocks ($\triangleright$).

POINTING BRICKWORK

Finishing the mortar joints—pointing—compresses the materials to make a packed, watertight joint and enhances the appearance of the wall. Well-struck joints and clean brickwork are essential if the wall is to look professionally built, but the mortar must be shaped at the right time for best results.

Flush joint

Concave joint

"V" joint

Raked joint

Weather joint

Colored mortar
You can add colored powders to your mortar mix. Make a trial batch to test the color when dry. Rake out the joint and apply with a tray to avoid staining the bricks.

Mortar for pointing work

If the mortar is still too wet, the joint will not be crisp and you may drag mortar out from between the bricks. On the other hand, if it is left to harden too long, pointing will be hard work and you may leave dark marks on the joint.

Test the consistency of the mortar by pressing your thumb into a joint. If it holds a clear impression without sticking to your thumb the mortar is just right for pointing. Because it is so important that you shape the joint at exactly the right moment, you may have to point the work in stages before you can complete the wall.

Shape the joints to match existing brickwork or choose one that is suitable for the prevailing weather conditions.

How to make pointing joints

Flush joint
Rub a piece of sacking along each joint to finish the mortar flush with the bricks. This is a utilitarian joint for a wall built with second-hand bricks which are not of a sufficiently good quality to take a crisp joint.

Concave joint
Buy a shaped jointing tool to make a concave joint, or improvise with a length of bent tubing. Flush the mortar first, then drag the tool along the joints. Finish the vertical joints, then do the long, continuous horizontal ones.

Shape the mortar with a jointing tool

"V" joint
Produced in a similar way to the concave joint, the "V" joint gives a very smart finish to new brickwork and sheds rainwater well.

Raked joint
Use a piece of wood or metal to rake out the joints to a depth of about 1/4 inch, then compress them again by smoothing the mortar lightly with a piece of rounded dowel rod. Raked joints do not shed water so don't use them on an exposed site.

Weather joint
The angled weather joint is ideal, even in harsh conditions. Use a small pointing trowel to shape the vertical joints (**1**). They can slope to the left or right, but be consistent throughout the same section of brickwork. Shape the horizontal joints allowing the mortar to spill out slightly at the base of each joint. Professionals finish the joint by cutting off excess mortar with a tool called a Frenchman, similar to a table knife with the tip at 90 degrees. Improvise a similar tool with a strip of bent metal. Align a straightedge with the bottom of the joint to guide the tool and produce a neat, straight edge to the mortar. Nail two scraps of plywood to the guide to hold it away from the wall (**2**).

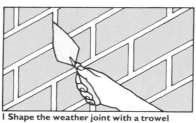

I Shape the weather joint with a trowel

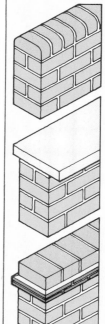

2 Remove excess mortar with a Frenchman

Brushing the brickwork
Let the shaped joints harden a little before you clean scraps of mortar from the face of the wall. Use a medium-soft brush, sweeping lightly across the joints so as not to damage them.

COPINGS FOR BRICK WALLS

The coping, which forms the top course of the wall, protects the brickwork from weathering and gives a finished appearance to the wall. Strictly speaking, if the coping is flush with both faces of the wall, it is a capping. A true coping projects from the face so that water drips clear and does not stain the brickwork.

You can lay a coping of bricks with their stretcher faces across the width of the wall. Use the same type of brick employed in the construction of the wall or specially shaped coping bricks designed to shed rainwater. Engineering bricks are sometimes used for copings. The dense water-resistant quality of the brick makes an advantage and the color makes a pleasing contrast with regular brickwork.

Stone or cast concrete slabs are popular for garden walls. They are quick to lay and are wide enough to form low, bench-type seating.

On an exposed site, consider installing a damp-proof course (◁) under the coping to reduce the risk of frost attack. Use a standard bituminous felt DPC or lay two courses of plain roof tiles with staggered joints and a brick coping above. Let the tiles project from the face of the wall but run a sloping mortar joint along the top of the projection to shed water.

Brick coping
Specially shaped bricks are made to cope a wall.

Slab coping
Choose a concrete or stone slab that is wider than the wall itself.

Tile and brick coping
Lay flat roof tiles or specially made creasing tiles beneath a brick coping to form a weatherproof layer which allows water to drip clear of the wall.

BUILDING INTERSECTING WALLS

When building new garden walls which intersect at right angles, either anchor them by bonding the brickwork (see below), or take the easier option to link them with wall ties at every third course (▷). If the intersecting wall is over 6 feet in length, make the junction a control joint by using straight metal strips as wall ties (▷).

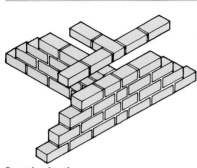

Stretcher bond

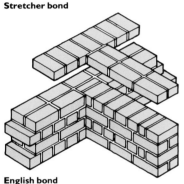

English bond

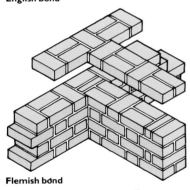

Flemish bond

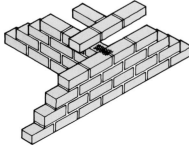

Using a wall tie

Building up to an existing wall

When you build a new wall to intersect the existing wall of a house, you must include a damp-proof course to prevent water from bridging the house DPC via the new masonry (▷) and you must make a positive joint between the two walls.

Inserting a DPC
Good building practice requires a damp-proof course in all masonry construction to prevent rising dampness. This consists of a layer of impervious material built into the mortar bed about 6 inches above ground level. When you build a new wall, its DPC must coincide with the DPC in the existing structure. Use a roll of bituminous felt chosen to match the thickness of the new wall.

Locate the house DPC and build the first few courses of the new wall up to that level. Spread a thin bed of mortar on the bricks and lay the DPC upon it with the end of the roll turned up against the existing wall (**1**). The next course of bricks will trap the DPC between the header joint and the wall. Lay more mortar on top of the DPC to produce the standard ⅜-inch joint ready for laying the next course in the normal way. If you have to join rolls of DPC, overlap the ends by 6 inches.

Tying in the new wall
The traditional method for linking a new wall with an existing structure involves chopping recesses in the brickwork at every fourth course. End bricks of the new wall are set into the recesses, bonding the two structures together (**2**). An alternative and much simpler method, however, is to screw a special stainless metal channel to the wall, designed to accept bricks or concrete blocks and provide anchoring points for standard wire wall ties (▷). Channels are available for masonry units in standard sizes.

Screw the channel to the old wall above the DPC with stainless-steel lag screws and wall plugs or use expanding bolts (**3**). Though not essential, trap 3 feet of DPC felt behind the channel.

Mortar the end of a brick before feeding it into the channel (**4**). As the brick is pushed home, the mortar squeezes through the perforated channel to make a firm bond.

At every third course, hook a wall tie over the pressed lugs in the channel and bed it firmly into the mortar joint (**5**).

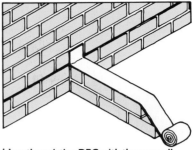

1 Lap the existing DPC with the new roll

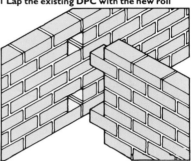

2 You can tooth the wall into the brickwork

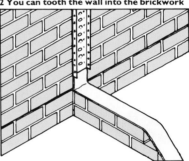

3 But it is easier to use a special channel

4 Locate the brick ends in the channel

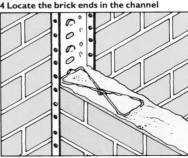

5 Hook wire wall ties over the pressed lugs

DPC on a sloping site
When the site slopes noticeably, the wall footing is stepped to keep the top of the wall level (▷). If you include a DPC in the wall, that, too, must follow the line of the steps to keep it the required height above ground level.

BRICKWORK PIERS

A pier is a free-standing column of masonry used to support a porch. It can be used as an individual gatepost as well. When it is built as part of a wall, it is more accurately termed a pilaster. In practice, however, the word "column" often covers either description. Columns bonded into a masonry base but extending up each side of a wooden trellis to support a pergola is a typical example. To avoid confusion, any supporting brick column will be described here as a pier. Thorough planning is essential when building piers.

Structural considerations

Any free-standing straight wall over a certain length and height must be buttressed at regular intervals by piers. Wall sections and piers must be tied together, either by a brick bond or by inserting metal wall ties in every third course of bricks. Any single-width brick wall, whatever its height, would benefit from supporting piers at open ends and gateways where it is most vulnerable; these will also improve the appearance of the wall. Piers over 3 feet, and especially those supporting gates, should be built around steel reinforcing rods set in the concrete footings. Whether reinforcing is included or not, allow for the size of piers when designing the footings (◁).

Designing the piers

Piers should be placed no more than 10 feet apart in walls over a certain height (see chart). The wall itself can be flush with one face of a pier, but the entire structure is stronger if it is centered on the column.

Piers should be a minimum of twice the thickness of a 3¾-inch-thick wall, but build 1-foot-square piers when reinforcement is required, including gateways, and to buttress 8-inch-thick walls.

INCORPORATING PIERS IN A BRICK WALL		
Thickness of wall	Maximum height without piers	Maximum pier spacing
3¾ in.	2 ft. 6 in.	10 ft.
8 in.	4 ft. 6 in.	10 ft.

BONDING PIERS

If you prefer the appearance of bonded brick piers, construct them as shown below, but it is easier, especially when building walls centered on piers, to use wall ties to reinforce continuous vertical joints in the brickwork.

Various types of galvanized metal wall ties are available. Wire is bent into a butterfly shape (**1**). Stamped metal steel strips have forked ends and are known as "fish tails" (**2**). Expanded metal mesh is cut in straight strips (**3**).

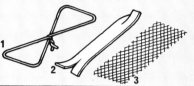

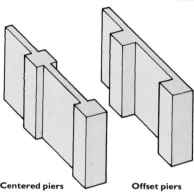

Centered piers   Offset piers

- **Bonding piers**
  It is simpler to tie any wall to a pier with wall ties (see above right) but it is relatively easy to bond a pier into a single-brick width wall.

Color key
You will have to cut certain bricks to bond a pier into a straight wall. Whole bricks are colored with a light tone, three-quarter bats with a medium tone, and half-bats with a dark tone.

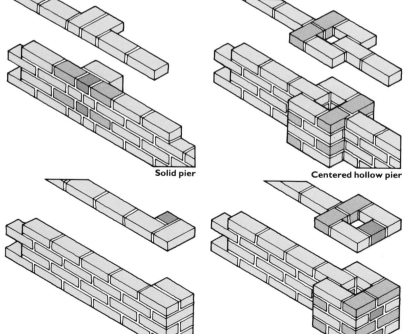

Solid pier   Centered hollow pier   Offset hollow pier

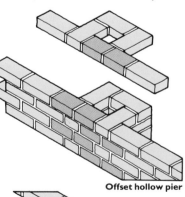

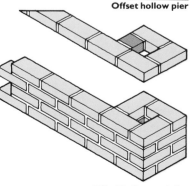

Solid end pier   Centered hollow end pier   Offset hollow end pier

BUILDING PIERS

Mark out accurately the positions of piers and the face of the wall on the concrete footing (▷). Lay the first course for the piers using a builder's line stretched between two stakes to align them (**1**). Adjust the position of the line if necessary, and fill in between with the first straight course working from both ends toward the middle (**2**). Build alternate pier and wall courses, checking the level and the vertical faces and corners of the piers. At the third course, push metal wall ties into the mortar bed to span the joint between wall and pier (**3**). Continue in the same way to the required height of the wall, then raise the piers to their required height (**4**). Lay a coping along the wall and cap the piers with concrete or stone slabs (**5**).

Incorporating control joints

Although you would never notice, a brick wall is constantly moving due to ground settlement as well as expansion and contraction of the materials. Over short distances, the movement is so slight that it hardly affects the brickwork, but the combined movement of masonry in a long wall can crack the structure. To compensate for this movement, build unmortared, continuous vertical joints into a wall at intervals of about 20 feet. These control joints can be placed in a straight section of wall, but it is neater and more convenient to place them where the wall meets a pier. Build the pier and wall as normal, but omit the mortar from the header joints of the wall. Instead of inserting standard wall ties, embed a flat, 1/8-inch-thick galvanized strip in the mortar bed. Lightly grease one half of the strip so that it can slide lengthwise to allow for movement yet still key the wall and pier together. When the wall is complete, fill the joint from both sides with mastic.

Incorporating reinforcement

Use 5/8-inch steel reinforcing bars to strengthen brick piers. If the pier is under 3 feet in height, use one continuous length of bar (**1**), but for taller piers, embed a bent starter bar in the footing, projecting a minimum of 24 inches above the level of the concrete (**2**). As the work proceeds, bind extension bars to the projection with galvanized wire up to within 2 inches of the top of the pier. Fill in around the reinforcement with concrete as you build the pier, but pack it carefully, trying not to disturb the brickwork.

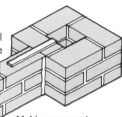

Making a control joint
Tie the pier to the wall with galvanized-metal strips when making a control joint (shown here before it's set in mortar). The mastic is squeezed into the joint between the wall and the pier.

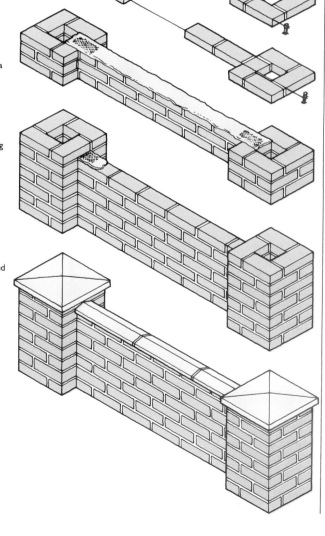

1 Lay pier bases
Stretch a builder's line to position the bases of the piers.

2 Lay first wall course
Move the line to keep the first course straight.

3 Lay pier ties
Tie the piers to the wall by inserting wall ties into every third course. Put a tile into alternate courses for a gate-supporting pier.

4 Raise the piers
Build the piers higher than the wall to allow for a decorative coping along the top course.

5 Lay the coping
Lay the coping slabs and cap the piers.

BRICK PIER

REINFORCEMENT BAR

CONCRETE INFILL

FOUNDATION

1 A reinforced pier   2 Starter bar

433

BUILDING WITH CONCRETE BLOCKS

The methods for laying concrete blocks are much the same as for building with bricks. Block walls need similar concrete footings, and the same type of mortar, although heavy blocks should be laid with a strong, firm mix (◁) to resist the additional weight of the freshly constructed wall. As blocks are made in a greater variety of sizes, you can build a wall of any thickness with a simple stretcher bond (◁). However, don't dampen concrete blocks before laying them—wet blocks can shrink and crack the mortar joints as the wall dries out. When you are building decorative walls with facing blocks, use any of the pointing styles described for bricks (◁), but flush-joint a wall built with structural blocks which is to be stuccoed.

● **Building piers**
High, free-standing garden walls constructed from blocks must be supported by piers at 10-foot intervals (◁).

CONTROL JOINTS

Walls over 20 feet in length should be built with a continuous, vertical control joint to allow for expansion (◁). Place an unmortared joint in a straight section of wall or against a pier, and bridge the gap with galvanized-metal dowels as for brickwork (◁). Fill the gap with mastic.

It is unlikely, but if you need to insert a control joint in a dividing wall, form the joint between the door frame and wall. In this case, fill the joints with mortar in the normal way but rake them out to a depth of ¾ inch around one end of the lintel and vertically to the ceiling on both sides of the wall. Fill the control joint flush with mastic.

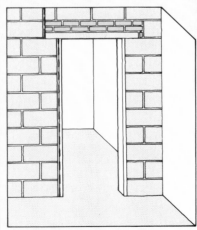

A control joint next to a door opening
Take the joint around the lintel and up to the ceiling on both sides of the wall.

Building a dividing wall

Building a nonload-bearing stud partition (◁) is the usual method for dividing up a large internal space into smaller rooms, but if your house is built on a concrete pad, a practical alternative is to use concrete blocks. If you install a doorway in the dividing wall, plan its position to avoid cutting too many blocks. Allow for the wooden door frame and lining (◁) as well as a precast lintel to support the masonry above the opening (◁). Fill the space above the lintel with cut blocks or bricks to level the courses.

Screw galvanized pressed-metal channels (◁) to the existing structure to support each end of the dividing wall. Plumb them accurately or the new wall will be out of true. Lay the first course of blocks without mortar across the room to check their spacing and the position of a doorway if one is to be included. Mark the positions of the blocks before building stepped leads at each end as for brickwork (◁). Check for accuracy with a level. Fill between the leads with blocks.

Build another three courses, anchoring the end blocks to the channels with wall ties in every joint. Leave the mortar to harden overnight before you continue with the wall.

Building a dividing wall

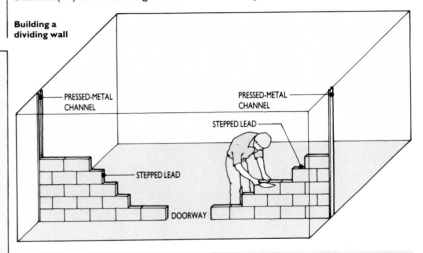

PRESSED-METAL CHANNEL

PRESSED-METAL CHANNEL

STEPPED LEAD

STEPPED LEAD

DOORWAY

Building intersecting walls

Butt intersecting garden walls together with a continuous vertical joint between them, but anchor the structure as for brickwork (◁) with wire-mesh wall ties **(1)**. If you build a wall with heavy, but hollow, blocks, use stout metal tie bars with a bend at each end. Fill the block cores with mortar to embed the ends of the bars **(2)**. Install a tie in every course.

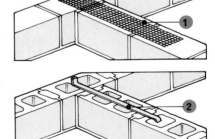

1 Wire-mesh wall tie for solid blocks ▶
2 Metal tie bar for hollow blocks

Cutting blocks

Use a bolster chisel and straightedge to score or cut a line around a block. Deepen the groove by tapping the chisel with a hammer. The chisel will ring with each blow until a crack makes its way through the block with a dull thud. One more sharp blow should split the block.

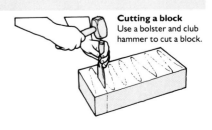

Cutting a block
Use a bolster and club hammer to cut a block.

BUILDING A DECORATIVE BLOCK SCREEN

Basic bricklaying techniques and tools (▷) are used to build a pierced concrete screen, but because the blocks are stack-bonded—with continuous vertical joints—the wall must be reinforced vertically with ⅝-inch steel bars, and horizontally with galvanized mesh if it is built higher than 2 feet. Build the screen with supporting piers located no more than 10 feet apart using matching pilaster blocks. Or you might prefer the appearance of contrasting masonry; in that case, construct a base and piers from bricks or facing blocks.

Constructing the screen

Set out and fill the footings (▷) twice the width of the pilaster blocks. Embed pier reinforcing bars in the concrete (◁) and support them with guy ropes until the concrete sets.

Lower a pilaster block over the first bar, setting it onto a bed of mortar laid around the base of the bar. Check that the block is perfectly vertical and level, and that its locating channel faces the next pier. Pack mortar or concrete into its core, then proceed with two more blocks so that the pier corresponds to the height of two mortared screen blocks (1). Construct each pier in the same way. Intermediate piers will have a locating channel on each side.

Allow the mortar to harden overnight, then lay a mortar bed for two screen blocks next to the first pair. Butter the vertical edge of a screen block and press it into the pier locating channel (2). Tap it into the mortar bed and check it is level. Mortar the next block and place it alongside the first.

When buttering screen blocks, take special care to keep the faces clean by making a neat, chamfered bed of mortar on each block (3).

Lay two more blocks against the next pier, stretch a builder's line to gauge the top edge of the first course, and then lay the rest of the blocks toward the center. Lay the second course in the same way, making sure the vertical joints are aligned perfectly.

Before building any higher, embed a wire reinforcing strip running from pier to pier in the next mortar bed (3). Continue to build the piers and screen up to a maximum height of 6 feet, inserting a wire strip into alternate courses. Finally, lay coping slabs at the top of each pier and along the top of the screen (5).

If you don't like the appearance of ordinary mortar joints, take out some of the mortar and repoint with mortar made with silver sand. A concave joint suits decorative screening (▷).

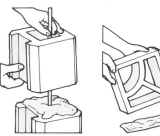

1 Build the piers

2 Fit block to pier

3 Butter edge of block

4 Lay a wire reinforcing strip into the mortar

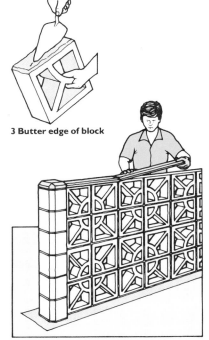

5 Lay coping slabs along the wall

CAVITY WALLS

Cavity walls are used in the construction of buildings to prevent the passage of moisture through the wall to the interior. This is achieved by building two independent leaves of masonry with a clear gap between them. The gap provides a degree of thermal insulation but the insulation value increases appreciably if an efficient insulant is introduced to the cavity (▷). The exterior leaf of most cavity walls is constructed with facing bricks. The inner leaf is sometimes built with interior-grade bricks but more often with concrete blocks. Whatever type of masonry is used, both leaves must be tied together with wall ties spanning the gap. Cavity walls are likely to be load-bearing, and so have to be built very accurately—hire a professional to construct them. Make sure the bricklayer includes a DPC in both leaves and avoids dropping mortar into the gap. If mortar collects at the base of the cavity, or even on one of the wall ties, moisture can bridge the gap leading to dampness on the inside.

Cavity wall construction
A section through a typical cavity wall built with an exterior leaf of bricks tied to an inner leaf of plastered concrete blocks.

Building a brick base and piers
Build piers and a low base of bricks or facing blocks (▷), including reinforcing bars in the center of each pier. Lay coping slabs along the wall and continue to build the piers along with the screen. Tie the screen and piers together with reinforcing strips as described at left, but insert standard wall ties in alternate courses to provide additional location and support.

BUILDING WITH STONE

Constructing garden walls with natural stone requires a different approach than that needed for bricklaying or building with concrete blocks. A stone wall must be as stable as one built with any other masonry material, but its visual appeal relies on less regular coursing. In fact, there is no real coursing at all in the usual sense when the wall is built with undressed stone or rubble.

Structural considerations

Stone walls don't necessarily require mortar to hold the stones together, although it is often used, especially with dressed or semidressed stone, to provide additional stability. As a result, many stone walls taper, having a wide base of heavy, flat stones and gradually decreasing in width as the wall rises.

This traditional form of construction developed to prevent a wall of unmortared stones from toppling sideways under the pressure of high winds or animals. Far from detracting from its appearance, the inherent informality of natural stone walling suits a country-style garden perfectly.

Building a dry-stone wall

A true dry-stone wall is built without mortar, relying instead on a selective choice of stones and careful placement to provide stability. Experience is needed for perfect results, but there is no reason why you cannot introduce mortar, particularly within the core of the wall, and still maintain the appearance of dry-stone construction. You can also bed the stones in soil, packing it firmly into the crevices as you lay each course. This enables you to plant ferns or other suitable plants in the wall, even during construction.

When you select the masonry, look out for flat stones in a variety of sizes, and make sure you have some large enough to run the full width of the wall, especially at the base of the structure. These bonding stones, placed at regular intervals, are important components which tie the loose rubble into a cohesive structure. Even a low wall will inevitably include some heavy stones. When you lift them, keep your back straight and your feet together, using the strong muscles of your legs to take the strain.

Constructing the wall

Assuming you are using soil as a jointing material, spread a 1-inch layer over the footing and place a substantial bonding stone across the width to form the bed of the first course (1). Lay other stones about the same height as the bonding stone along each side of the wall, pressing them down into the soil to make a firm base. It is worth stretching a builder's line (◁) along each side of the wall to help you make a reasonably straight base.

Lay smaller stones between to fill out the base of the wall (2), then pack more soil into all the crevices.

Spread another layer of soil on top of the base and lay a second course of stones, bridging the joints between the stones below (3). Press them down so that they angle inwards towards the center of the wall. Check by eye that the coursing is about level as you build

the wall and remember to include bonding stones at regular intervals.

Introduce plants into the larger crevices or hammer smaller stones into the chinks to lock the large stones in place (4).

At the top of the wall, either fill the core with soil for plants or lay large, flat coping stones, firming them with packed soil. Finally, brush loose soil from the faces of the wall.

DESIGNING THE WALL

Every dry-stone wall must be "battered." In other words, it must have a wide base and sides that slope inward. For a wall about 3 feet in height (and it is risky to build a dry-stone wall any higher) the base should be no less than 18 inches wide. You should aim to provide a minimum slope of 1 inch for every 2 feet of height.

Traditionally, the base of this type of wall rests on a 4-inch bed of sand laid on a compacted soil at the bottom of a shallow trench. For a more reliable foundation, lay a 4-inch concrete footing (◁), making it about 4 inches wider than the wall on each side.

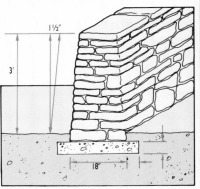

Proportions of a stone-built wall

1 Lay a bonding stone at the end of the wall

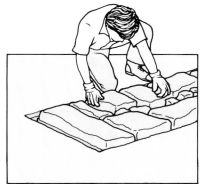

2 Fill out the base with small stones

3 Lay a second course of stones

4 Fill the chinks

BUILDING RETAINING WALLS

Retaining walls hold back a bank of earth. But don't attempt to cut into a steep bank and restrain it with a single high wall. Apart from the obvious danger of the wall collapsing, terracing the slope with a series of low walls is a more attractive solution which offers opportunities for imaginative planting.

Choosing your materials

Bricks and concrete blocks are perfectly suitable materials to choose for constructing a retaining wall, providing they are built sturdily. It is best to support these walls with reinforcing bars buried in the concrete footing (▷). Run the bars through hollow-core blocks (**1**) or build a double skin of brickwork, rather like a miniature cavity wall, using wall ties to bind each skin together (**2**).

The mass and weight of natural stone make it ideal for retaining walls. The wall should be battered to an angle of 2 inches to every foot of height so that it virtually leans into the bank (**3**). Keep the height below 3 feet for safety.

A skillful builder could construct a dry-stone retaining wall perfectly safely, but use mortar for additional ridigity and support if you are an amateur.

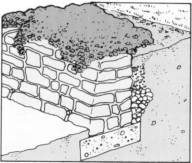

Terracing with retaining walls

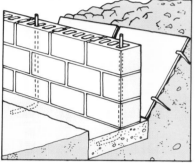

1 A retaining wall of hollow concrete blocks

2 Use two skins of brick tied together

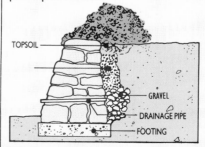

3 Lean a stone wall against the bank of earth

Constructing a stone wall

Excavate the soil to provide enough room to dig the footing (▷) and construct the wall. If the soil is loosely packed, restrain it temporarily with sheets of scrap plywood, corrugated iron or similar sheeting. Drive long metal pegs into the bank to hold the sheets in place (**1**). Lay the footing at the base of the bank and allow it to set before building the wall.

Lay uncut stones as if you were building a dry-stone wall (▷), but set each course on mortar. If you use regular stone blocks, select stones of different proportions to add interest to the wall, and stagger the joints. Use standard bricklaying methods (▷) to bed the stones in mortar.

It is essential to allow for drainage behind the wall to prevent the soil's becoming waterlogged. When you lay the second course of stones, embed ¾-inch plastic pipes in the mortar bed, allowing them to slope slightly toward the front of the wall. The pipes should be placed at about 3-foot intervals and pass right through the wall, projecting a little from the face (**2**).

FINISHING STONE WALLS

When the wall is complete, rake out the joints to give a dry-wall appearance. An old paintbrush is a useful tool for smoothing the mortar in deep crevices to make firm, watertight joints. Alternatively, point regular stones as for brickwork (▷).

Allow the mortar to set for a day or two before filling behind the wall. Lay gravel at the base to cover the drainage pipes to help reduce the force of groundwater pressure. Provide a generous layer of topsoil so that you can plant up to the wall.

1 Hold back the earth with scrap boards

2 Set plastic pipes in the wall for drainage

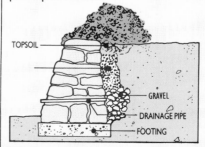

TOPSOIL —

GRAVEL

DRAINAGE PIPE

FOOTING

Filling behind a stone wall

PATHS, DRIVES AND PATIOS

For many people, paving of any kind is associated with an unpleasant urban environment, conjuring up an image of a concrete patch devoid of plants, trees and grass—inhuman and unattractive. In reality, introducing paving to a garden provides an opportunity to create surprising contrasts of color and texture intensified by sunlight and deep shadows. The harshness of a hard, unyielding surface is softened by the addition of foliage, while certain sculptural plants which recede into a background of soil and grass are seen to advantage against stone and gravel.

A paved patio
A paved area surrounded by stone or brick walls makes a perfect suntrap for swimming and relaxing.

Designing paved areas

The marriage of different materials offers numerous possibilities. It may be convenient to define areas of paving as paths, drives and patios, but they are only names to describe the function of those particular spaces in the garden. There is no reason why you cannot blend one area into another using the same material throughout, or use similar colors to link one type of paving with another. On the other hand, you could take a completely different approach and deliberately juxtapose coarse and smooth textures, or use pale and dark tones to make one space stand out from the next.

Having so many choices at your disposal does have its drawbacks. There is a strong temptation to experiment with any and every combination until the end result is a distracting mishmash. A few well-chosen materials which complement the house and its surroundings produce an environment which is not only more appealing in the short term, but actually improves as the garden matures.

Working with concrete

Concrete might not be everybody's first choice for paving a garden, but it is such a versatile material that you may not even be aware of its use. When it is cast into paving slabs (◁), for instance, it can be mistaken for natural stone, or you might be more aware of the geometric pattern created by the combination of individual units rather than the material itself. Even ordinary concrete can be finished with a surprising variety of textures, and is incomparable as a material for the foundations of outbuildings or extensions.

THE INGREDIENTS OF CONCRETE

Concrete in its simplest form consists of cement and fine particles of stone—sand and pebbles—known as aggregate. The dry ingredients are mixed with water to create a chemical reaction with the cement which binds the aggregate into a hard, dense material. The initial hardening process takes place quite quickly. The mix becomes unworkable after a couple of hours, depending on the temperature and humidity, but the concrete has no real strength for three to seven days. The process continues for up to a month, or as long as there is moisture present within the concrete. Moisture is essential to the reaction and the concrete must not dry out too quickly in the first few days.

CEMENT

Standard portland cement, sold in 94-pound bags from builders' supplies or DIY outlets, is used in the manufacture of concrete. In its dry condition, it is a fine, gray powder.

SAND

Sharp sand, a rather coarse and gritty material, constitutes part of the aggregate of a concrete mix. Don't buy fine builders' sand used for mortar, and avoid unwashed or beach sand, both of which contain impurities that could affect the quality of the concrete. Sharp sand is sold by the cubic yard from a builders' supply, although it is perhaps more convenient to buy it in large plastic bags if you have to transport it by car or van.

COARSE AGGREGATE

Coarse aggregate is gravel or crushed stone composed of particles large enough to be retained by a 1/4-inch sieve up to a maximum size of 3/4 inch for normal use. Once again, it can be bought loose by the cubic yard or in smaller quantities packed in plastic sacks.

PIGMENTS

Special pigments can be added to concrete, but it is difficult to guarantee an even color from one batch of concrete to another.

COMBINED AGGREGATE

Naturally occurring sand and gravel mix, known as ballast, is sold as a combined aggregate for concrete. The proportion of sand to gravel is not guaranteed unless the ballast has been reconstituted to adjust the mix, and you may have to do it yourself. In any case, make sure it has been washed to remove impurities.

DRY-MIXED CONCRETE

You can buy dry cement, sand and aggregate mixed to the required proportions for making concrete. Choose the proportion that best suits the job you have in mind (◁). Concrete mix is sold in various size bags up to 100 pounds. Available from the usual outlets, it is a more expensive way of buying the ingredients, but is a simple and convenient method of ordering exactly the amount you will need. Before you add water to the mix, make sure the ingredients are mixed thoroughly.

WATER

Use ordinary tap water to mix concrete, never river or sea water.

PVA ADDITIVES

You can buy PVA additives from builders' suppliers to make a smoother concrete mix which is less susceptible to frost damage.

MIXING CONCRETE

You can rent small mixing machines if you have to prepare a large volume of concrete, but for the average job it is just as convenient to mix concrete by hand. It isn't necessary to weigh out the ingredients when mixing concrete. Simply mix them by volume, choosing the proportions that suit the job at hand.

Mixing by hand

Use large buckets to measure the ingredients, one for the cement and an identical one for the aggregate, in order to keep the cement perfectly dry. Different shovels are also a good idea. Measure the materials accurately, leveling them with the rim of the bucket. Tap the side of the bucket with the shovel as you load it with sand or cement to shake down the loose particles.

Mix the sand and aggregate first on a hard, flat surface. Scoop a depression in the pile for the measure of cement, and mix all the ingredients until they form an even color.

Form another depression and add some water from a watering can. Push the dry ingredients into the water from around the edge until surface water is absorbed, then mix the batch by chopping the concrete with the shovel (1). Add more water, turning concrete from the bottom of the pile, and chop it as before until the whole batch has an even consistency. To test the workability of the mix, form a series of ridges by dragging the back of the shovel across the pile (2). The surface of the concrete should be flat and even in texture, and the ridges should hold their shape without slumping.

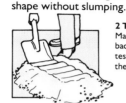

1 Mixing ingredients
Mix the ingredients by chopping the concrete mix with the shovel. Turn the mix over and chop again.

2 Testing the mix
Make ridges with the back of the shovel to test the workability of the mix.

Mixing by machine

Make sure you set up the concrete mixer on a hard, level surface and that the drum is upright before you start the motor. Use a bucket to pour half the measure of coarse aggregate into the drum and add water. This will clean the drum after each batch has been mixed. Add the sand and cement alternately in small batches, plus the rest of the aggregate. Add water little by little along with the other ingredients.

Let the batch mix for a few minutes. Then, with the drum of the mixer still rotating, turn out a little concrete into a wheelbarrow to test its consistency (see above). If necessary, return the concrete to the mixer to adjust it.

Storing materials

If you buy sand and coarse aggregate in sacks, simply use whatever you need at a time, keeping the rest bagged up until required. If you buy the materials loose, store them in piles, separated by a wooden plank if necessary, on a hard surface or thick polyethylene sheets. Protect the materials from prolonged rain with weighted sheets of plastic.

Storing cement is more critical. It is sold in paper sacks which will absorb moisture from the ground, so pile them on a board propped up on spacers. Keep cement in a dry shed or garage if possible, but if you have to store it outdoors, cover the bags with sheets of plastic weighted down with bricks. Once open, cement can absorb moisture from the air. Keep a partly used bag in a sealed plastic sack.

READY-MIXED CONCRETE

If you need a lot of concrete for a driveway or large patio it may be worth ordering a supply of ready-mixed concrete from a local supplier. Always speak to the supplier well before you need the concrete to discuss your particular requirements. Specify the proportions of the ingredients and say whether you will require the addition of a retarding agent to slow down the setting time. Once a normal mix of concrete is delivered, you will have no more than two hours to finish the job. A retarding agent can add up to two hours to the setting time. Tell the supplier what you need the concrete for and accept his advice.

For quantities of less than 6 cubic yards you might have to shop around for a supplier who is willing to deliver without an additional charge. Discuss any problems of discharging the concrete on site. To avoid transporting the concrete too far by wheelbarrow, have it discharged as close to the site as possible, if not directly into place. The chute on a delivery truck can reach only so far, and if the truck is too large or heavy to drive onto your property you will need several helpers to move the quantity of concrete while it is still workable. A single cubic yard of concrete will fill 25 to 30 large wheelbarrows. If it takes longer than 30 to 40 minutes to discharge the load, you may have to pay extra.

Storing sand and aggregate
Separate the piles of sand and aggregate with a wooden plank.

Storing cement
Raise bags of cement off the ground and cover them with plastic sheeting.

● **Professional mixing**
There are companies who will deliver concrete ingredients and mix them to your specification on the spot. All you have to do is transport the concrete and pour it into place. There is no waste as you only pay for the concrete you use. Telephone a local company for details on price and minimum quantity.

DESIGNING CONCRETE PAVING

The idea of having to design simple concrete pads and pathways might seem odd, but there are important factors to consider if the concrete is to be durable. At the least, you will have to decide on the thickness of the concrete to support the weight of traffic, and determine the angle of slope required to drain off surface water. When the area of concrete is large or a complicated shape, you must incorporate control joints to allow the material to expand and contract without cracking. If a pad is for a habitable building, it must include a damp-proof membrane to prevent moisture from rising from the ground (◁). Even the proportions of sand, cement and aggregate used must be considered carefully to suit the function of the paving.

Deciding on the slope

In theory, a free-standing pad can be laid perfectly level, especially when it is supporting a small outbuilding, but, in fact, a very slight slope or fall prevents water from collecting in puddles if you have failed to get the concrete absolutely flat. When a pad is laid directly against a house, it must have a definite fall away from the building, and any parking area or drive must shed water to provide adequate traction for vehicles and to minimize the formation of ice. When concrete is laid against a building, it must be at least 6 inches below the existing damp-proof course.

USE OF PAVING	ANGLE OF FALL
Pathways	Not required
Drive	1 in 40 1 in. per yard
Patio Parking area	1 in 60 away from building 1 in. per yard
Outbuildings	1 in 80 toward the door ½ in. per yard

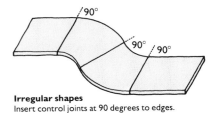

Irregular shapes
Insert control joints at 90 degrees to edges.

RECOMMENDED THICKNESSES FOR CONCRETE

The natural thicknesses recommended for concrete paving assumes it will be laid on a firm subsoil, but if the soil is clay or peat, increase the thickness by about 50 percent. The same applies to a new site where the soil might not be compacted. Unless the concrete is for pedestrian traffic only, lay a subbase of compacted gravel below the paving. This will absorb ground movement without affecting the concrete itself. A subbase is not essential for a very lightweight structure like a small wooden shed, but since you might want to increase the weight at some time, it is wise to install a subbase at the outset.

PATHWAYS

For pedestrian traffic only
Concrete: 4 in.
Subbase: Not needed

PATIOS

Any extensive area of concrete for pedestrian traffic
Concrete: 4 to 6 in.
Subbase: 4 in.

DRIVEWAYS

A drive which is used for an average family car only
Concrete: 4 in.
Subbase: 4 in.
For heavier vehicles like delivery trucks
Concrete: 6 in.
Subbase: 4 in.

LIGHT STRUCTURES

A support pad for a wooden shed, green-house, and the like
Concrete: 4 in.
Subbase: 3 in.

PARKING SPACES

Exposed paving for parking the family car
Concrete: 4 in.
Subbase: 4 in.

GARAGES

Thicken up the edges of a garage pad to support the weight of the walls
Concrete:
Floor: 4 in.
Edges: 8 in.
Subbase:
Minimum 4 in.

Allowing for expansion

Changes in temperature cause concrete to expand and contract. If this movement is allowed to happen at random, a pad or pathway will crack at the weakest or most vulnerable point. A control joint, composed of a compressible material (◁), will absorb the movement or concentrate the force in predetermined areas where it does little harm. Joints should meet the sides of a concrete area at more or less 90 degrees. Always place a control joint between concrete and a wall, and around inspection chambers.

Positioning control joints
The position of control joints depends on the area and shape of the concrete.

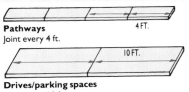

Pathways
Joint every 4 ft.   4 FT.

Drives/parking spaces
Joint every 10 ft.   10 FT.

Concrete slabs
Joints no more than 10 ft. apart and around drains   10 FT.

Divide a pad into equal bays if:
● Length is more than twice the width.
● Longest dimension is more than 40 × thickness.
● Longest dimension exceeds 10 ft.

CALCULATING QUANTITIES OF CONCRETE

Estimate the amount of materials you require by calculating the volume of concrete in the finished pad, path or drive.

Measure the surface area of the site and multiply that figure by the thickness of the concrete.

Estimating quantities of concrete

Use the gridded diagram to estimate the volume of concrete by reading off the area of the site in square yards and tracing it across horizontally to meet

the angled line indicating the thickness of the concrete. Trace the line up to find the volume of concrete needed for your job in cubic yards.

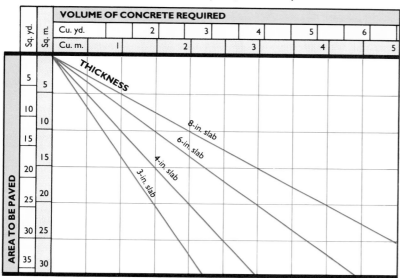

Estimating quantities of ingredients

Use the bar charts to estimate how much cement, sand and aggregate is needed to mix up the volume of concrete worked out by using the chart above.

The figures are based on the amount of ingredients used to mix one cubic yard of concrete using a particular type of mix (see below) plus about 10 percent for waste.

CUBIC YARDS OF CONCRETE	1.00	1.50	2.00	2.50	3.00	3.50	4.00	4.50	5.00
GENERAL-PURPOSE MIX									
Cement (94-lb. bags)	3.50	5.25	7.00	8.25	10.50	12.25	14.00	15.75	17.50
Sand (Cu. yds.)	0.50	0.75	1.00	1.25	1.50	1.75	2.00	2.25	2.50
Aggregate (Cu. yds.)	0.75	1.15	1.50	1.90	2.25	2.65	3.00	3.40	3.75
Ballast (Cu. yds.)	0.90	1.35	1.80	2.25	2.70	3.15	3.60	4.05	4.50
FOUNDATION MIX									
Cement (94-lb. bags)	3.00	4.50	6.00	7.50	9.00	10.50	12.00	13.50	15.00
Sand (Cu. yds.)	0.55	0.80	1.10	1.40	1.65	1.95	2.20	2.50	2.75
Aggregate (Cu. yds.)	0.75	1.15	1.50	1.90	2.25	2.65	3.00	3.40	3.75
Ballast (Cu. yds.)	1.00	1.50	2.00	2.50	3.00	3.50	4.00	4.50	5.00
PAVING MIX									
Cement (94-lb. bags)	9.00	13.50	18.00	22.50	27.00	31.50	36.00	40.50	45.00
Sand (Cu. yds.)	0.45	0.70	0.90	1.15	1.35	1.60	1.80	2.00	2.25
Aggregate (Cu. yds.)	0.75	1.15	1.50	1.90	2.25	2.65	3.00	3.40	3.75
Ballast (Cu. yds.)	1.00	1.50	2.00	2.50	3.00	3.50	4.00	4.50	5.00

CALCULATING AREA

Squares and rectangles
Calculate the area of rectangular paving by multiplying width by length:

Example:
2 ft. × 3 ft. = 6 sq. ft.
78 in. × 117 in. = 9126 sq. in. or 7 sq. yds.

Circles
Use the formula πr^2 to calculate the area of a circle. $\pi = 3.14$. r = radius of circle.

Example:
3.14×2 ft.$^2 = 3.14 \times 4 = 12.56$ sq. ft.
3.14×78 in.$^2 = 3.14 \times 6084 = 19,104$ sq. in. or 14.75 sq. yds.

Irregular shapes
Draw an irregular area of paving on graph paper. Count the whole squares and average out the portions to find the approximate area.

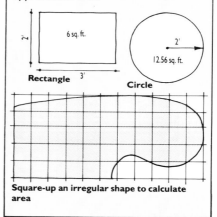

Square-up an irregular shape to calculate area

CLEANING TOOLS AND MACHINERY

Keep the shovel as clean as possible between mixing batches of concrete, and at the end of a working day wash all traces of concrete from your tools and wheelbarrow.

When you have finished using a concrete mixer, add a few shovels of coarse aggregate and a little water, then run the machine for a couple of minutes to scour the inside of the drum. Dump the aggregate, then hose out the drum with clean water.

Shovel unused concrete into sacks ready for disposal at a refuse dump and wash the mixing area with a stiff broom. Never hose concrete or any of the separate ingredients into a drain.

POURING A CONCRETE SLAB

Laying a simple slab as a base for a small shed or similar structure involves all the basic principles of concrete work: building a retaining formwork, as well as the pouring, leveling and finishing of concrete. As long as the base is less than 6 square feet, there is no need to include control joints.

Mixing concrete by volume

Mixing the ingredients by volume is the easiest and most accurate way to guarantee the required proportions. Whatever container you use to measure the ingredients of concrete—shovel, bucket or wheelbarrow—the proportions remain the same.

MIXING CONCRETE BY VOLUME		
Type of mix	Proportions	For I cu. yd. concrete
GENERAL PURPOSE		
Use in most situations including covered pads other than garage floors	1 part cement	3 bags (94-lb.)
	2 parts sand	0.5 cu. yd.
	3 parts aggregate	0.7 cu. yd.
	4 parts ballast	0.9 cu. yd.
FOUNDATION		
Use for footings at the base of masonry walls	1 part cement	2.5 bags (94-lb.)
	2½ parts sand	0.5 cu. yd.
	3½ parts aggregate	0.7 cu. yd.
	5 parts ballast	1.0 cu. yd.
PAVING		
Use for exposed pads such as drives, parking areas or footpaths, but also for garage floors	1 part cement	4 bags (94-lb.)
	1½ parts sand	0.5 cu. yd.
	2½ parts aggregate	0.7 cu. yd.
	3½ parts ballast	1.0 cu. yd.

Excavating the site

Mark out the area of the pad with string lines attached to pegs driven into the ground outside the work area (**1**). Remove them to excavate the site but replace them later to help position the formwork which will hold the concrete in place.

Remove the topsoil and all vegetation within the excavation site down to a level which allows for the combined thickness of concrete and subbase (◁). Extend the area of excavation about 6 inches outside the space marked out for the pad. Cut back any roots you encounter. Put the turf aside to cover the infill surrounding the completed pad. Level the bottom of the excavation by dragging a board across it (**2**), and compact the soil with a garden roller.

Erecting the formwork

Until the concrete sets hard, it must be supported all around by formwork. For a straightforward rectangular slab, construct the formwork from 1-inch-thick wood planks set on edge. The planks, which must be as wide as the finished depth of concrete, are held in place temporarily with stout 2 × 2-inch wooden stakes. Secondhand or form-grade lumber is quite adequate. If it is slightly thinner than an inch, just use more stakes to brace it. If you have to join planks, butt them end to end, nailing a cleat on the outside (**3**).

Using the string lines as a guide, erect one board at the higher end of the pad, and drive stakes behind it at about 3-foot intervals or less, with one for each corner. The tops of the stakes and board must be level and correspond exactly to the proposed surface of the pad. Nail the board to the stakes (**4**).

Set up another board opposite, but before you nail it to the stakes, establish the crossfall (◁) with a straightedge and level. Work out the difference in level from one end of the pad to the other. For example, a pad which is 6 feet long should drop an inch over that distance. Tape a shim to one end of the straightedge, and with the shim resting on the low stakes, place the other end on the opposite board (**5**). Drive home each low stake until the level reads horizontal. Then nail the board flush with the tops of the stakes.

Erect the sides of the formwork, allowing the ends of the boards to overshoot the corners to make it easier to dismantle them when the concrete has set (**6**). Use the straightedge, this time without the shim, to level the boards across the formwork.

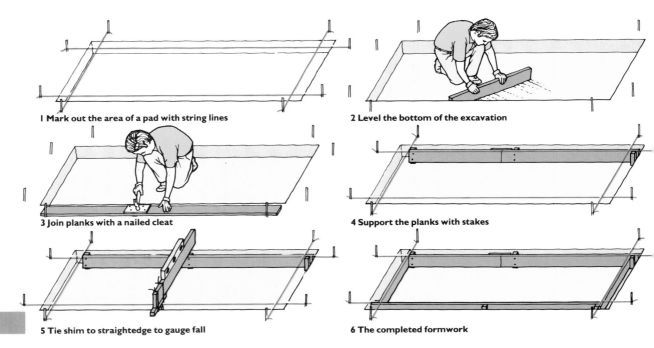

I Mark out the area of a pad with string lines

2 Level the bottom of the excavation

3 Join planks with a nailed cleat

4 Support the planks with stakes

5 Tie shim to straightedge to gauge fall

6 The completed formwork

POURING A CONCRETE SLAB

Laying the subbase

A mixture of gravel and sand is an ideal material for a subbase, but you can use crushed stone or brick as long as you throw out any plaster, scrap metal or similar rubbish. Also remove large lumps of masonry as they will not compact well. Pour gravel into the formwork and rake it fairly level before tamping it down with a heavy length of wood (**7**). Break up any stubborn lumps with a heavy hammer. Fill in low spots with more gravel or sharp sand until the subbase comes up to the underside of the formwork boards.

Filling with concrete

Mix the concrete as near to the site as is practicable and transport the fresh mix to the formwork in a wheelbarrow. Set up firm runways of scaffold boards if the ground is soft, especially around the perimeter of the formwork. Dampen the subbase and formwork with a fine spray and let surface water evaporate before tipping the concrete in place. Start filling from one end of the site and push the concrete firmly into the corners (**8**). Rake it level until the concrete stands about ¾ inch above the level of the boards.

Tamp down the concrete with the edge of a 2-inch-thick plank long enough to span across the formwork. Starting at one end of the site, compact the concrete with steady blows of the plank, moving it along by about half its thickness each time (**9**). Cover the whole area twice, then remove excess concrete using the plank with a sawing action (**10**). Fill any low spots, then compact and level once more.

Cover the pad with sheets of polyethylene, taped at the joints to retain the moisture and weighted down with bricks around the edge (**11**). Alternatively, use wet burlap which you must keep damp for three days using a fine spray. Try to avoid pouring concrete in very cold weather, but if it is unavoidable, spread a layer of earth or sand on top of the sheeting to insulate the concrete from frost. You can walk on the concrete after three days, but leave it for about a week before removing the formwork and erecting a shed or similar outbuilding on it.

Extending a slab
If you want to enlarge a patio, simply butt a new section of concrete against the existing slab. The butt joint will form a control joint. To add a narrow strip, for a larger shed for instance, drill holes in the edge of the pad and use epoxy adhesive to glue in short reinforcing rods before pouring the fresh concrete.

Finishing the edges
If any of the edges are exposed, the sharp corners might cause a painful injury. Round the corners with a homemade edging float. Bend a piece of sheet metal over a ¾-in.-diameter rod or tube and screw a handle in the center. Run the float along the formwork as you finish the surface of the concrete.

SEE ALSO

Details for: ▷	
Mixing concrete	439
Control joints	444
Floats and trowels	478
Adhesives	495–496

7 Level gravel base with a heavy tool made of heavy lumber

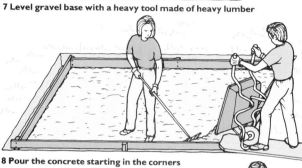

8 Pour the concrete starting in the corners

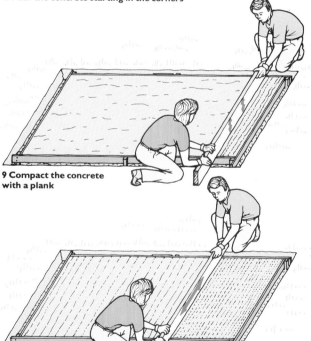

9 Compact the concrete with a plank

10 Use a sawing action to remove excess concrete

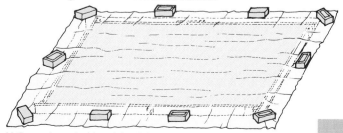

11 Cover the pad with weighted sheets of plastic

443

POURING PATHS AND DRIVES

Paths and drives are poured and compacted in the same way as simple rectangular slabs, using similar framework to contain the fresh concrete. But the proportions of most paths and drives necessitate the inclusion of control joints to allow for expansion and contraction (◁). You must install a subbase beneath a drive, but a footpath can be poured on compacted soil leveled with sharp sand. Establish a slight fall across the site to shed rainwater (◁). Don't use a vehicle on concrete for 10 days after laying.

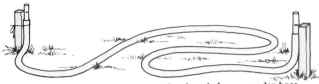

1 A water level made from a garden hose

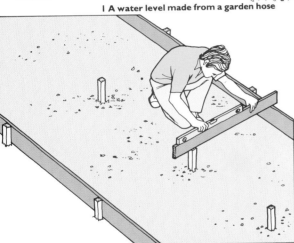

2 Level formwork using a reference stake

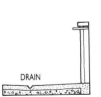

A sloping drive
If you build a drive on a sloping site, make the transition from level ground as gentle as possible. If it runs toward a garage, let the last 6 ft. slope up toward the door. Use a pole to impress a drain across the wet concrete at the lowest point.

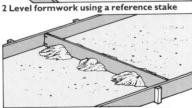

5 Support board with concrete and nails

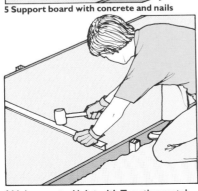

6 Make a control joint with T-section metal

Setting out paths and drives

Excavate the site, allowing for the thickness of subbase and concrete. Level the bottom of the excavation as accurately as you can, using a board to scrape the surface flat.

Drive accurately leveled pegs into the ground along the site to act as datum points for the formwork. Space them about 6 feet apart down the center of the pathway. Drive in the first peg until its top corresponds exactly to the proposed surface of the concrete. Use a long straightedge and level to position every other peg or, better still, use a homemade water level. Push a short length of transparent plastic tubing into each end of an ordinary garden hose. Fill the hose with water until it appears in the tube at both ends. As long as the ends remain open, the water level at each end is constant so that you can establish a level over any distance, even around obstacles or corners. Tie one end of the hose to the first reference stake so that the water level aligns with the top of the peg. Use the other to establish the level of every other peg along the pathway (**1**). Cork each end of the hose to retain the water as you move it.

To set a fall with a water level, make a mark on one tube below the surface of the water and use that as a gauge for the top of the peg.

Erecting formwork

Construct formwork from 1-inch-thick planks as for a concrete slab (◁). To check that it is level, rest a straightedge on the nearest reference stake (**2**).

If the drive or path is very long, wood formwork can be expensive. It might be cheaper to rent metal road forms (**3**). Straight-sided formwork is made from rigid units, but flexible sections are available to form curves.

If you want to bend wooden formwork, make a series of parallel saw cuts across the width of the plank in the area of the curve (**4**). The wood is less likely to snap if you place the saw cuts on the inside of the bend.

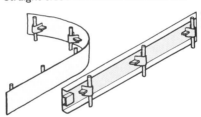

3 Curved and straight road forms

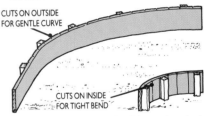

CUTS ON OUTSIDE FOR GENTLE CURVE

CUTS ON INSIDE FOR TIGHT BEND

4 Curved formwork made with wooden planks

Installing control joints

Install a permanent expansion joint every 4 feet for a footpath and every 10 feet along a drive. Cut strips of treated hardboard or ¾-inch-thick softwood to fit exactly between the formwork and to match the depth of the concrete. Before pouring, hold the control joints in place with mounds of concrete and nails on each side of the board driven into the formwork (**5**). Pack more concrete carefully on each side of the joints as you fill the formwork and tamp toward them from both sides so that they are not dislodged.

As the joints are permanent fixtures, make sure they are level with the surface of the concrete. Install similar joints in a patio or use an alternate-bay construction (see opposite page).

To prevent concrete from cracking between joints on a narrow path, cut ¾-inch-deep grooves across the compacted concrete to form dummy joints alternating with the actual ones. The simplest method is to cut a length of T-section metal to fit between the formwork boards. Place it on the surface of the wet concrete and tap it down with a mallet (**6**). Carefully lift the strip out of the concrete to leave a neat impression. If the concrete should move, a crack will develop unnoticed at the bottom of the groove.

Place strips of thick bituminous felt between concrete and an adjoining wall to absorb expansion. Hold the felt in place with mounds of concrete, as described at left, before pouring the full amount of concrete.

ALTERNATE-BAY METHOD OF CONSTRUCTION

It is not always possible to pour all the concrete in one operation. In such cases it is easier to divide the formwork crosswise with additional planks known as stop ends to form equal-size bays. By filling alternate bays with concrete, you have plenty of time to compact and level each section and more room in which to maneuver. It is a convenient way to pour a large patio which would be practically impossible to compact and level all at once, and it is the only method to use for drives or paths butting against a wall which makes it impossible to work across the width. Alternate-bay construction is often used for drives on a steep slope to prevent concrete from slumping downhill.

There is no need to install physical control joints as the simple butt joint between the bays is sufficient allowance for movement within the concrete.

Pouring concrete in alternate bays
Stand in the empty bays to compact concrete laid against a wall. When the first bays are set hard, remove the stop ends and fill the gaps, using the surface of the firm concrete as a level.

INSPECTION CHAMBERS

Prevent expansion from damaging grating by surrounding it with control joints. Place formwork around the chamber and fill with concrete. When set, remove the boards and place felt strips or treated wood boards on all sides.

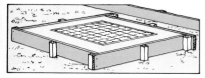

Surround grating with formwork

SURFACE FINISHES FOR CONCRETE

The surface finishes produced by tamping or striking off with a sawing action are perfectly adequate for a skid-proof, workmanlike surface for a slab, drive or pathway, but you can produce a range of other finishes using simple hand tools once you have compacted and leveled the concrete.

Float finishes
Smooth the tamped concrete by sweeping the wooden float across the surface, or make an even finer texture by finishing with a trowel (steel float). Let the concrete dry out a little before using a float or you will bring water to the top and weaken it, eventually resulting in a dusty residue on the hardened concrete. Bridge the formwork with a stout plank so that you can reach the center, or rent a skip float with a long handle for large pads.

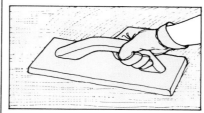

Make a smooth finish with a wooden float

Brush finishes
Make a finely textured surface by drawing a yard broom across the setting concrete. Flatten the concrete initially with a wooden float, them make parallel passes with the broom held at a low angle to avoid tearing the surface.

Texture the surface with a broom

Brush-finishing concrete

Exposed-aggregate finish
Embedding small stones or pebbles in the surface makes a very attractive and practical finish, but it takes a little practice to be successful.

Scatter dampened pebbles onto the freshly laid concrete and tamp them firmly with a length of timber until they are flush with the surface (**1**). Place a plank across the formwork and apply your full weight to make sure the surface is even. Let the concrete harden for a while until all surface water has evaporated, then use a very fine spray and a brush to wash away the cement from around the pebbles until they protrude (**2**). Cover the concrete for about 24 hours, then lightly wash the surface again to clean any sediment off the pebbles. Cover the concrete again and leave it to harden thoroughly.

1 Tamp pebbles into the fresh concrete

2 Wash the cement from around the pebbles

Exposed-aggregate finish

SEE ALSO

◁ Details for:
Brick paving   449

PRECAST PAVING UNITS

If your only experience with paving slabs is the rather bland variety used for public footpaths, then cast concrete paving may not seem a very attractive proposition for
a garden. However, manufacturers can supply products in a wide range of shapes, colors and finishes that are sure to please.

Colors and textures

Paving units are made by hydraulic pressing or casting in molds to create the desired surface finish. Pigments and selected aggregates added to the concrete mix create the illusion of
natural stone or a range of muted colors. Combining two or more colors within the same area of paving can be very striking.

1 Cobbles or sets
Large units resemble an area of smaller cobbles or sets. Careful laying and filling are essential. Sets are patterned in straight rows or as curves.

2 Planter
Four planter stones laid in a square leave a circle for a tree or shrub.

3 Exposed aggregate
Crushed-stone aggregate has a very pleasing mottled appearance, either exposed to make a coarse gritstone texture or polished flat to resemble terrazzo.

4 Brushed finishes
A brush-filling unit, textured with parallel grooves as if a stiff broom had been dragged across the wet concrete, is practical and nonslip. Straight or swirling patterns are available.

5 Riven stone
The finish resembles that of natural stone. The best-quality units are cast from real stone originals in a wide variety of subtle textures. If the texture continues over the edge of the slabs, they can be used for steps and coping.

SHAPES AND SIZES

Although some manufacturers offer a wider choice than others, there is a fairly standard range of shapes and modular sizes. You can carry the largest slabs by yourself, but it is a good idea to have an assistant when maneuvering them carefully into place.

Square and rectangular
One size and shape make gridlike patterns or, staggered, create a bonded brickwork effect. Rectangular slabs can form a basketweave or herringbone pattern. Or, combine different sizes to create the impression of random paving.

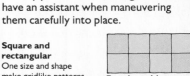

Regular grid

Staggered slabs

Basketweave pattern

Herringbone pattern

Random paving

Hexagonal
Hexagonal slabs form honeycomb patterns. Use half slabs, running across flats or from point to point, to edge areas paved in straight lines.

Hexagonal slab

Half-hexagonal slabs

Honeycomb pattern

Tapered slabs
Use tapered slabs to edge ponds, or around trees, and for curved paths or steps. Lay them head to toe to make straight sections of paving. Use right- or left-hand half slabs at the ends.

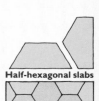

Full and half-tapered slabs

Straight section

Circular
Circular slabs make perfect individual stepping stones across a lawn or flower bed, but for a wide area, fill the spaces between with cobbles or gravel.

Butted circular slabs

LAYING PAVING UNITS

Laying heavy paving units involves a fair amount of physical labor, but in terms of technique it is no more complicated than tiling a wall. Accurate setting out and careful laying, especially during the early stages, will produce perfect results. Take extra care when laying hexagonal units to ensure that the last of them fit properly.

CUTTING CONCRETE PAVING UNITS

Mark a line across a unit with a soft pencil or chalk. Then, using a bolster and hammer, chisel a groove about ⅛ inch deep following the line (**1**). Continue the groove down both edges and across the underside of the unit. Place the unit on a bed of sand and put a block of wood at one end of the groove. Strike the block with a hammer while moving it along the groove until a split develops through the slab (**2**). Clean up the rough edge with a bolster.

For a perfectly clean cut each time, hire an angle grinder fitted with a stone-cutting disc. Score a deep groove on both sides of the slab and across the edges. Tap along the groove with a bolster to propagate a crack.

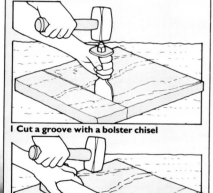

1 Cut a groove with a bolster chisel

2 Strike block over groove with a hammer

Setting out the area of paving

Wherever possible, to eliminate the arduous task of cutting units to fit, plan an area of paving to be laid with whole slabs only. Use a straight wall as a reference line and measure away from it, or allow for a 4- to 6-inch margin of gravel between the paving and wall if the location dictates that you have to lay slabs toward the house. A gravel margin not only saves time and money by using fewer slabs, but also provides an area for planting climbers and adequate drainage to keep the wall dry. Even so, establish a ⅝-inch-per-yard slope across the paving so that most surface water will drain

Preparing a base for paving

Paving units must be laid upon a firm, level base, but the depth and substance of that base depends on the type of soil and the proposed use of the paving.

For straightforward patios and paths, remove vegetation and topsoil to allow for the thickness of the paving and a 1-inch layer of sharp sand. Set the paving about ¾ inch below the level of surrounding turf to avoid damaging the lawn mower when you cut the grass. Having compacted the soil using a

into the garden. Any paving must be 6 inches below a damp-proof course to protect the building.

Since paving units are made to reasonably precise dimensions, marking out an area simply involves accurate measurement, allowing for a ¼-inch gap between slabs. Some units are cast with sloping edges to provide a tapered joint (**1**) and should be butted edge to edge. Use stakes and string to mark out the perimeter of the paved area, and check your measurements before you excavate.

garden roller, spread the sand with a rake and level it by scraping and tamping with a length of wood (**2**).

To support heavier loads, or if the soil is composed of clay or peat, lay a subbase (▷) of firmly compacted gravel—broken bricks or crushed stone—to a depth of 3 to 4 inches before spreading the sand to level the surface. If you plan to park vehicles on the paving, then increase the depth to 6 inches.

Laying the paving slabs

Set up string lines again as a guide and lay the edging slabs on the sand, working in both directions from a corner. When you are satisfied with their positions, lift them one at a time and set them on a bed of mortar (1 part cement: 4 parts sand). Add just enough water to make a firm mortar. Lay a fist-size blob under each corner and one more to support the center of the slab (**3**). If you intend to drive vehicles across the paving, lay a continuous bed of mortar about 2 inches thick.

Lay three units at a time with ¼-inch wooden spacers between them. Level each unit by tapping with a heavy hammer, using a block of wood (**4**).

Gauge the slope across the paving by setting up reference stakes along the high side (▷). Drive them into the ground until the top of each corresponds to the finished surface of the paving, then use the straightedge to check the fall on the slabs (**5**). Lay the remainder of the units, working out from the corner each time to keep the joints square. Remove the spacers before the mortar sets.

SEE ALSO

1 Tapered joint

2 Level the sand base

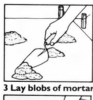

3 Lay blobs of mortar

4 Level the units

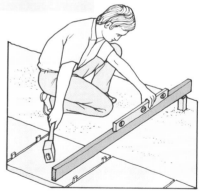

5 Check the fall with a level

Filling the joints

Don't walk on the paving for two to three days until the mortar has set. If you have to cross the area, lay planks across the slabs to spread the load.

To fill the gaps between the units, brush a dry mortar mix of 1 part cement: 3 parts sand into the open joints (**6**). Remove any surplus material from the surface of the paving, then sprinkle the area with a very fine spray of water to consolidate the mortar. Avoid dry mortaring if heavy rain is imminent; it may wash the mortar out.

6 Fill the joints

447

LAYING CRAZY PAVING

The informal nature of paths or patios laid with irregular-shaped paving stones has always been popular. The random jigsaw effect, which many people find more appealing than the geometric accuracy of neatly laid slabs, is also very easy to achieve. A good eye for shape and proportion is more important than a practiced technique.

Materials for crazy paving

You can use broken concrete slabs if you can find enough but, in terms of appearance, nothing compares with natural stone. Stratified rock which splits into thin layers of its own accord as it is quarried is ideal for crazy paving, and can be obtained at a very reasonable price if you can collect it yourself. Select stones which are approximately 1½ to 2 inches thick in a variety of shapes and sizes.

Crazy paving from broken concrete slabs

SETTING OUT AND LAYING A BASE

You can, if you wish, set out string lines to define straight edges to crazy paving, although they will never be as precisely defined as those formed with cast concrete slabs. Or, allow the stones to form a broken irregular junction with grass or shingle, perhaps setting one or two individual stones out from the edge of the paving to blend one area into the other.

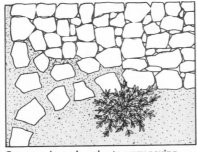

Create an irregular edge to crazy paving

Laying the stones

Arrange an area of stones, selecting them for a close fit but avoiding too many straight, continuous joints. Trim those that don't quite fit with a bolster and hammer. Reserve fairly large stones for the perimeter of the paved area, as small stones tend to break away.

Use a mallet or block of wood and a hammer to bed each stone into the sand (**1**) until they are all perfectly stable and reasonably level. Having bedded an area of about a square yard, use a straightedge and level to true up the stones (**2**). If necessary, add or remove

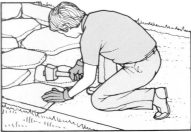

1 Bed the stones in the sand base

3 Fill the gaps with small stones

sand beneath individual stones until the whole area is level. When the main area is complete, fill in the larger gaps with small stones, tapping them into place with a mallet (**3**).

Fill the joints by spreading more sand across the paving and sweeping it into the joints from all directions (**4**). Alternatively, mix up a stiff, almost dry, mortar and press it into the joints with a trowel, leaving no gaps.

Use an old paintbrush to smooth the mortared joints and wipe the stones clean with a damp sponge.

2 Check the level across several stones

4 Sweep dry sand into the joints

Laying stepping stones

Place individual stones or slabs across a lawn to form a row of stepping stones. Cut around the edge of each stone with a spade or trowel and remove the area of turf directly beneath. Scoop out the earth to allow for a one-inch bed of sharp sand plus the stone, which must be about ¾ inch below the level of the surrounding turf. Tap the stone into the sand until it no longer rocks when you step on it.

Cut around a stepping stone with a trowel

Stepping stones preserve a lawn

BRICK PATTERNS

Concrete bricks have one surface with chamfered edges all around, and spacers molded into the sides to form accurate joints. Common bricks can be laid on edge or face down showing the wide face normally unseen in a wall.

Unlike brick walls, which must be bonded in a certain way for stability (▷), brick paths can be laid in any pattern that appeals to you.

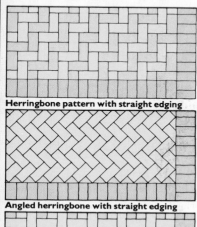

Herringbone pattern with straight edging

Angled herringbone with straight edging

Whole bricks surrounding colored half-bats

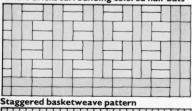

Staggered basketweave pattern

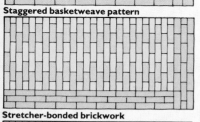

Stretcher-bonded brickwork

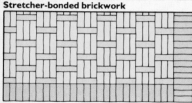

Cane-weave pattern

PAVING WITH BRICKS

Bricks make charming and attractive paths in a garden or lawn setting. The wide variety of textures and colors available gives endless possibilities of pattern, bearing in mind the sort of use your paving can expect.

Materials for brick paving

Common bricks are often selected for paths, and also small patios, even though there is the risk of spalling in freezing conditions unless they happen to be engineering bricks (▷). The slightly uneven texture and color are the very reasons why secondhand bricks in particular are so much in demand for garden paving, so a little frost damage is usually acceptable.

Common bricks are not really suitable if the paved area is to be a parking space or drive, especially if it is to be used by heavy vehicles. For a durable surface, even under severe conditions, use modular bricks. They are slightly smaller than standard bricks, being $2\frac{1}{4} \times 3\frac{5}{8} \times 7\frac{5}{8}$ inches. Red or yellow are widely available and you can obtain other colors by special order.

Brick pavers
Clay brick pavers (top row) are made in a wide variety of colors and textures. *Concrete pavers* (bottom row) are less colorful but are available in more shapes.

Providing a base for brick paving

Lay brick footpaths and patios on a 3-inch gravel base (▷) covered with a 2-inch layer of sharp sand. To lay concrete bricks for a drive, increase the depth of gravel to 4 inches.

Fully compact the gravel and fill all voids that may have occurred so that sand from the bedding course is not lost to the subbase.

Provide a cross-fall on patios and drives as for concrete (▷), and ensure that the surface of the paving is at least 6 inches below a damp-proof course to protect the building.

Retaining edges

Unless the brick path is laid against a wall or some similar structure, the edges of the paving must be contained by a permanent restraint. Lumber, treated with a chemical preservative, is one solution, constructed like the formwork for concrete (▷). The edging boards should be flush with the surface of the path, but drive the stakes below ground so that they can be covered by soil or turf (**1**).

As an alternative, set an edging of bricks in concrete (**2**). Dig a trench deep and wide enough to accommodate a row of bricks on end plus a 4-inch concrete foundation. Lay the bricks while the concrete is still wet, holding them in place temporarily with a staked board while you pack more concrete behind the edging. When the concrete has set, remove the board and lay gravel and sand in the excavation.

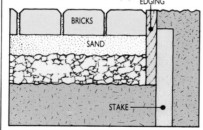

1 Wooden retaining edge

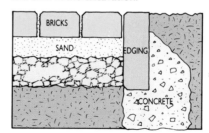

2 Brick retaining edge

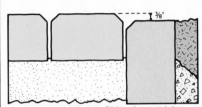

Cutting bricks
Rent an hydraulic
brick-cutting guillotine
to cut pavers.

LAYING THE BRICKS

Having chosen your bricks, prepared the ground and set retaining edges (▷), you can start laying your paving. When bricks are first laid upon the sand they should project ⅜ inch above the edging restraints to allow for bedding them in at a later stage (**1**). To level the sand for a path, cut a notched spreader to span the edging (**2**). If the paving is too wide for a spreader, lay leveling strips on the gravel base and scrape the sand to the required depth using a straightedge (**3**). Remove the strips and fill the voids carefully with sand. Keep the sand bed dry at all times. If it rains before you can lay the bricks, either let the sand dry out thoroughly or replace it with dry sand.

Lay an area of bricks on the sand to your chosen pattern. Work from one end of the site, kneeling on a board placed across the bricks (**4**). Never stand on the bed of sand. Lay whole bricks only, leaving any gaps at the edges to be filled with cut bricks after you

have laid an area of about a square yard. Concrete bricks have fixed spacers, so butt them together tightly.

Fill any remaining spaces with bricks cut with a bolster (◁). If you are paving a large area, you can rent an hydraulic guillotine (see left).

When the area of paving is complete, tamp the bricks into the sand bed by striking a 2 × 4 with a heavy sledgehammer. The 2 × 4 must be large enough to cover several bricks to maintain the level (**5**). For a really professional finish, rent a powered plate vibrator. Pass the vibrator over the paved area two or three times until it has worked the bricks down into the sand and flush with the outer edging (**6**). The act of vibrating bricks works sand up between them, but complete the job by brushing more sand across the finished paving and vibrate the sand into the open joints.

Plain concrete-brick drive and parking space

Mottled-brick garden path

Interlocking concrete pavers

Bricks laid to a herringbone pattern

1 Start by laying bricks ⅜ in. above edging

2 Level the sand with a notched spreader

3 Or lay level battens on the gravel

4 Lay the bricks to your chosen pattern

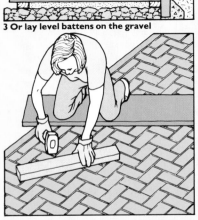

5 Tamp the bricks with a hammer and 2 × 4

6 A vibrator levels brick paving perfectly

COBBLESTONES AND GRAVEL

Areas of cobblestones and gravel are used more for their decorative quality than as functional paving for drives or pathways. Cobbles, in particular, are most uncomfortable to walk on and, although a firmly consolidated area of gravel is fine for vehicles, walking on a gravel footpath can be rather like treading water. Both materials come into their own, however, when used as a foil for areas of flat paving slabs or bricks, and to set off plants such as dwarf conifers while keeping weed growth to a minimum.

Laying cobbles

Cobbles, large flint pebbles found on many a beach, can be laid loose, perhaps with larger rocks and plants. However, they are often set in mortar or concrete to create formal areas of texture.

Consolidate a layer of gravel (▷) and cover it with a leveled layer of dry concrete mix about 2 inches deep (▷).

Press the cobbles into the dry mix, packing them tightly together and projecting well above the surface. Use a 2 × 4 to tamp the area level (1). Then lightly sprinkle the whole area with water, both to set off the concrete hardening process and to clean the surfaces of the cobbles.

Large cobbles as a background to plants

Tamp the cobbles into a dry concrete mix

Laying gravel

If an area of gravel is to be used as a pathway or for motor vehicles, construct retaining edges of brick, concrete curbs or wooden boards as for brick paths (▷). This will stop gravel being spread outside its allotted area.

To construct a gravel drive, the subbase and the gravel itself must be compacted and leveled to prevent cars from skidding and churning up the material. Lay a 4-inch bed of firmed fill (▷) topped with 2 inches of very coarse gravel mixed with sand. Roll it flat. Rake a ¾- to 1-inch layer of fine pea gravel across the subbase and roll it down to make firm.

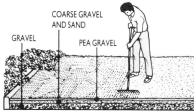

GRAVEL
COARSE GRAVEL AND SAND
PEA GRAVEL

Rake pea gravel across the surface of a drive

Making a gravel garden

To lay an area of gravel for planting, simply excavate the soil to accept a 1-inch-deep bed of fine gravel. Either set the gravel ¾ inch below the level of the lawn or edge the gravel garden with bricks or flat stones. Scrape away a small area of gravel for planting, then sprinkle it back again to cover the soil surrounding and right up to the plant itself.

Gravel and conifer garden ▶

WOODEN PATHWAYS

If you live in a rural district where large logs are plentiful or perhaps a mature tree has been felled in your garden, you can use 6-inch lengths of sawn logs set on end to make a practical and charming footpath. Either lay the logs together like crazy paving or use large individual pieces of wood as stepping stones. Hold wood rot at bay by soaking the sawn sections in buckets of chemical preservative.

Laying a log pathway

Excavate the area of the pathway to a depth of 8 inches and spread a 2-inch-deep layer of gravel and sand mix across the bottom. Use concreting ballast—combined aggregate—or make up the mix yourself (▷). Level the bed by scraping and tamping with a straightedge.

Place the logs on end on the bed, arranging them to create a pleasing combination of shapes and sizes (1). Work them into the sand until they stand firmly and evenly, then pour more sand and gravel between them (2). Brush the material across the pathway in all directions until the gaps between the logs are filled flush with the surface (3). If any logs stand proud so that they could cause someone to trip, tap them down with a heavy hammer.

If you want to plant between the logs, scrape out some sand and gravel and replace it with the appropriate soil.

1 Arrange the logs on end

2 Shovel sand and gravel mix between the logs

3 Brush more mix into the joints

PAVING
STONES/WOOD

SEE ALSO

Details for: ▷

Combined aggregate	438
Concrete mixes	441
Laying subbase	443
Retaining edges	449
Preservatives	252

● **Use a heavy roller**
A lightweight garden roller is fine for compacting earth or sand, but use one weighing about 300 lbs. when leveling gravel.

451

- **Laying a new path**
  Although cold cure tarmac is primarily a resurfacing material, it can be applied to a new gravel base as long as it is firmly compacted, leveled and sealed with a slightly more generous coat of bitumen emulsion.

- **Treating for heavy wear**
  At entrance to drives and on bends, vehicle tires cause more wear than normal. Treat these areas with ¾-inch rolled layer of cold cure tarmac (see far right) before applying a dressing of stone chippings.

- **Double dressing**
  If the surface you are dressing is in very poor condition or exceptionally loose, apply a first coat of bitumen emulsion at 7.25 lbs. per sq. yd. Cover with chippings and roll thoroughly. Two days later, sweep away loose chippings and apply a second coat of emulsion at 3.5 lbs. per sq. yd. and finish with chippings as described at right.

DRESSING WITH STONE CHIPPINGS

As an alternative to asphalt, completely resurface a path or drive with natural stone chippings embedded in fresh bitumen emulsion. Chippings in various colors are available in sacks which cover varied areas depending on weight. Apply weedkiller and fill potholes as for tarmac (see right).

Bitumen emulsion sets by evaporation in about 12 hours, but until that time it is not completely waterproof. So check the weather forecast to avoid wet conditions. You can lay emulsion on a damp surface but not on one that is icy.

Apply emulsion according to the manufacturer's instructions for the type of base you are surfacing.

SURFACE	BITUMEN EMULSION
Concrete and smooth surfaces	2.6 lbs. per sq. yd.
Other firm, dense surfaces	3.4 lbs. per sq. yd.
Open textured, loose surfaces	7.25 lbs. per sq. yd.

Decant the emulsion into a bucket to make it easier to pour onto the surface, brushing it out, not too thinly, with a stiff broom as for laying tarmac (see right). Having brushed out one bucket of emulsion, spread the stone chippings evenly with a spade. Hold the spade horizontally just above the surface and gently shake the chippings off the edge of the blade (**1**). Don't pile them too thickly, but make sure the emulsion is covered completely. Cover an area of about 5 square yards, then roll the chippings down. When the entire area is covered, roll it once more. If traces of bitumen show between the chippings, mask them with sharp sand and roll again. (See margin notes left for applying dressing to heavy-wear areas.)

You can walk or drive on the dressed surface immediately. One week later, gently sweep away any surplus chippings. Patch any bare areas by re-treating them with emulsion and chippings.

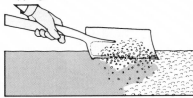
Sprinkle a layer of chippings with a spade

RESURFACING WITH TARMAC

Smarten up an old tarmac path or drive, or any basically sound but unsightly paved area, by resurfacing with cold cure tarmac. It makes a serviceable surface and is ready to lay from the sack. Roll the tarmac flat with a heavy garden roller—a light roller will do, but you will have to make extra passes.

Choosing the materials

Choose between red or black tarmac. It is available in sacks that will cover up to about 10 square feet at a thickness of about ½ inch. Each sack contains a separate bag of decorative stone chippings for embedding in the soft tarmac as an alternative finish. Cold cure tarmac can be laid in any weather, but it is much easier to level and roll flat on a warm, dry day. If you have to work in cold weather, store the materials in a warm place the night before laying. While not essential, edging the tarmac with bricks, concrete curbs or wooden boards (◁) will improve the appearance of the finished surface.

Preparing the surface

Pull up all weeds and grass growing between the old paving, then apply a strong weedkiller to the surface two days before you lay the tarmac. Sweep the area clean, and level any potholes by first cutting the sides vertical, then remove dust and debris from the hole. Paint with bitumen emulsion, supplied by the tarmac manufacturer. Wait for it to turn black before filling the hole with ¾-inch-thick layers of tarmac, compacting each layer until the surface is level.

Apply a tack coat of bitumen emulsion to the entire surface to make a firm bond between the new tarmac and the old paving. Mask surrounding walls, curb stones and drain gratings. Stir the emulsion with a stick before pouring it from its container, then spread it thinly with a stiff-bristled broom. Try not to splash, and avoid leaving puddles, especially at the foot of a slope. Let the tack coat set for about 20 minutes and, in the meantime, wash the broom in hot, soapy water. Don't apply the tack coat when it is likely to rain.

Apply a tack coat of bitumen emulsion

Applying the tarmac

Rake the tarmac to make a layer about ¾ inch thick (**1**), using a straightedge to scrape the surface flat. Press down any stubborn lumps with your foot. Spread the contents of no more than three sacks before the initial rolling. Keep the roller set (**2**) to avoid picking up specks of tarmac. Don't run the roller onto grass or gravel or you may roll particles into the tarmac.

Spread and roll tarmac over the whole area, then achieve the final compaction by rolling it thoroughly in several directions. Lightly scatter the chippings (**3**) prior to the final pass.

You can walk on the tarmac immediately, but avoid wearing high-heeled shoes. Don't drive on it for a day or two, and leave a note on the gate to warn others that the paving is not completely cured. You should always protect tarmac from oil and gasoline spillage, but take special care while the surface is fresh.

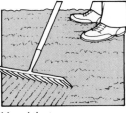
1 Level the tarmac

2 Keep the roller wet

3 Scatter chippings

BUILDING GARDEN STEPS

Designing a garden for a sloping site is an exciting challenge. It offers many possibilities for interesting changes of level by terracing areas of paving or with planting beds held in place with retaining walls (▷). But to move safely from one level to another requires at least one flight of steps.

Designing steps

If you are fortunate enough to own a large garden, and the slope is very gradual, a series of steps with wide treads and low risers can make an impressive feature. If the slope is steep, you can avoid a staircase appearance by constructing a flight of steps composed of a few treads interposed with wide, flat landings, at which points the flight can change direction to add further interest and offer a different viewpoint of the garden. In fact, a shallow flight can be virtually a series of landings, perhaps circular in plan, gradually sweeping up the slope in a curve.

The proportion of tread (the part you stand on) to riser (the vertical part of the step) is an important factor if using the steps is to be both safe and comfortable. As a rough guide, construct steps so that the depth of the tread (from front to back) plus twice the height of the riser equals 26 inches. For example, 12-inch treads should be matched with 7-inch risers, 14-inch treads with 6-inch risers and so on. Never make treads less than 12 inches deep or risers higher than 7 inches.

Garden steps built with natural stone

Using concrete slabs

Concrete paving units in their various forms (▷) are ideal for making firm, flat treads for garden steps. Construct the risers from concrete facing blocks or bricks, allowing the treads to overhang by an inch or two to cast an attractive shadow line which also defines the edge of the step.

Measure the difference in height from the top of the slope to the bottom to gauge the number of steps required. Mark the positions of the risers with pegs and roughly shape the steps in the soil as confirmation (**1**).

Either lay concrete slabs, bedded in sand (▷), flush with the ground at the foot of the slope or dig a trench to contain gravel and a 4- to 6-inch concrete base to support the first riser (**2**). When the concrete has set, construct the riser using normal bricklaying methods (▷). Check its alignment with a level (**3**). Fill behind the riser with compacted gravel until it is level, then lay the tread on a bed of mortar (**4**). Using a level as a guide, tap down the tread until it slopes very slightly towards its front edge to shed rainwater and so prevent ice from forming in cold weather.

Measure from the front edge of the tread to mark the position of the next riser on the slabs (**5**), and construct the step in the same way. Set the final tread flush with the area of paving, pathway or lawn at the top of the flight of steps.

Dealing with the sides

It is usually possible to landscape the slope at each side of the flight of steps, and turf or plant it to prevent the soil from washing down onto the steps. Alternatively, extend the riser to edge each tread or build a wall or planter on each side of the steps. Another solution is to retain the soil from with large stones, perhaps extending into a rock garden on one or both sides.

1 Cut the shape of the steps in the soil

2 Dig the footing for the first riser

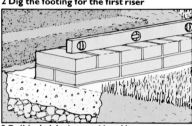

3 Build a brick riser and level it

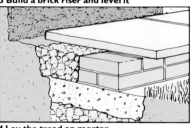

4 Lay the tread on mortar

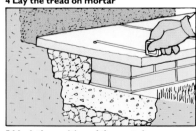

5 Mark the position of the next riser

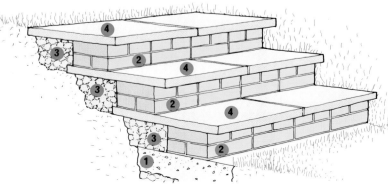

Concrete-slab steps
A section through a simple flight of garden steps built with bricks and concrete paving slabs.
1 Concrete footing
2 Brick-built riser
3 Gravel fill
4 Concrete-slab tread

• **Dealing with slippery steps**
Algae will grow in damp conditions, especially under trees, and steps can become dangerously slippery if it is allowed to build up on the surfaces. Brush with a solution of 1 part household bleach: 4 parts water. After 48 hours, wash with clean water and repeat if the fungal growth is heavy. You can also use a proprietary fungicidal solution, but follow manufacturers' instructions carefully.

REPAIRING CONCRETE STEPS

Casting new steps in concrete needs such complicated formwork that the end result hardly justifies the amount of effort required, especially when better-looking steps can be constructed from cast concrete slabs and blocks. Nevertheless, if you have a flight of concrete steps in your garden you will want to keep them in good condition. Like other forms of masonry, concrete suffers from spalling, where frost breaks down the surface and flakes off fragments of material. It occurs a great deal along the front edges of steps where foot traffic adds to the problem. Repair broken edges as soon as you can. Not only are they ugly, but the steps are not as safe as they might be.

Building up broken edges

Wearing safety goggles, chip away concrete around the damaged area and provide a good grip for fresh concrete. Cut a board to match the height of the riser and prop it against the step with bricks (**1**). Mix up a small batch of general-purpose concrete but add a little PVA bonding agent to help it stick to the damaged steps. Dilute some bonding agent with water, say 3 parts water: 1 part bonding agent, and brush it onto the damaged area, stippling it into all the crevices. When the painted surface becomes tacky, fill the hole with concrete mix flush with the edge of the board (**2**). Round the front edge slightly with a homemade edging float (◁), running it against the board (**3**).

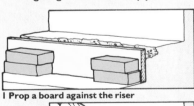
1 Prop a board against the riser

2 Fill the front edge with concrete

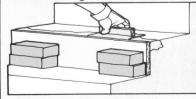
3 Run an edging float against the board

CURVED STEPS/LOG STEPS

Building curved steps

To build a series of curved steps, choose materials which will make the job as easy as possible. You can use tapered concrete slabs (◁) for the treads, designing the circumference of the steps to suit the proportions of the slabs. Or, you can construct the treads from crazy paving (◁), selecting fairly large stones for the front edge. Use bricks laid flat or on edge to build the risers. Set the bricks to radiate from the center of the curve, and fill the slightly tapered joints with mortar.

Use a length of string attached to a peg driven into the ground as an improvised compass to mark out the curve of each step. Tie a stake to the string to help you gauge the front edge of the lower steps (**1**). Roughly shape the soil and lay a concrete foundation for the bottom riser (◁). Build risers and treads as for regular concrete slab steps, using the improvised string compass as a guide.

Building circular landings

To construct a circular landing, build the front edge with bricks and paving as for a curved step. When the mortar has set, fill the landing area with compacted coarse gravel (◁) and lay pea gravel up to the level of the tread (**2**).

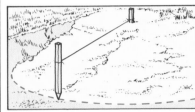
1 Mark the edge with an improvised compass

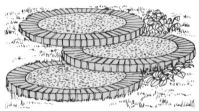
2 Circular landings made with bricks and gravel

Making log steps

For an informal garden, build steps from lengths of logs soaked in a chemical preservative. Try to construct risers of a fairly regular height, otherwise someone might stumble if they are forced to break step. As it is not always possible to obtain uniform logs, you may have to make up the height of the riser with two or more slimmer logs.

Cut a regular slope in the earth bank and compact the soil by treading it down. Drive stakes cut from 3-inch-diameter logs into the ground, one at each end of a step (**1**). Place one heavy log behind the stakes, bedding it down in the soil (**2**), and pack coarse gravel behind it to construct the tread of the step (**3**). Shovel a layer of pea gravel on top of the coarse to finish the step.

If large logs are in short supply, build a step from two or three slim logs, holding them against the stakes with gravel as you construct the riser (**4**).

Log-built garden steps

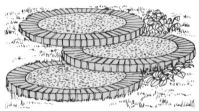
1 Drive a stake at each end of a step

2 Place a log behind the stakes

3 Fill behind the log with gravel

4 Make up a riser with two slim logs

CREATING WATER GARDENS

There is nothing like still or running water to enliven a garden. Cascades and fountains have an almost mesmeric fascination—it is practically impossible to take your eyes off them—and the sound of trickling water has a charming, soothing effect. Even a small area of still water will support all manner of interesting pond life and plants, with the additional bonus of the mirrored images of trees, rocks and sky reflected in its placid surface.

Pond liners

It is not by chance that the number of garden ponds has increased over recent years. There is no doubt that their popularity is due largely to the emergence of simply installed rigid and flexible pond liners, making it possible to create a complete water garden in return for a few days' work.

In the past it was necessary to line a pond with concrete. While it is true that concrete is a very versatile material, there is always the possibility of a leak developing through cracks caused by ground movement or the force of expanding ice. There are no such worries with flexible liners. In addition to the labor and expense involved in building forms for a concrete pond, it must be left to season for about a month, during which time it must be emptied and refilled a number of times to ensure that the water will be safe for fish and plant life. But you can introduce plants to a plastic- or rubber-lined pool as soon as the water itself has matured, which takes no more than a few days.

Ordering a flexible liner

Use a simple formula to calculate the size of liner you will need. Disregard the actual plan and ignore the size and shape of planting shelves. Simply take the overall length and width of the pond and add twice the maximum depth to each dimension to arrive at the size of the liner. If possible, adapt your design to fall within the nearest stock liner size.

SEE ALSO

Details for: ▷	
Installing liners	456
Building a waterfall	459

Garden pond
A well-planted water garden surrounded by flowering shrubs looks like a natural pond.

CHOOSING A POND LINER

The advantages of proprietary pond liners over concrete are fairly clear, but there are still a number of options to choose from, depending on the size and shape of the pond you wish to create and how much you propose to spend.

RIGID LINERS

Regular garden-center visitors will be familiar with the range of preformed plastic pond liners. The best liners are made from rigid glass-reinforced plastic which is very strong and resistant to the effects of frost or ice. As long as they are handled with reasonable care and installed correctly, rigid plastic pools are practically puncture- and leak-proof.

Rigid pond liner
Rigid liners are molded using glass-reinforced plastic.

SEMIRIGID LINERS

Semirigid liners, made from vacuum-formed plastic, are cheaper than those made from fiberglass, but the range of sizes is very limited. However, they make ideal reservoirs or header pools for a cascade or waterfall.

Rectangular or irregular-shaped liners are available in rigid or semirigid plastic, and a very acceptable water garden can be created with a carefully selected series of pond liners linked by watercourses.

FLEXIBLE LINERS

For complete freedom of design, choose a flexible-sheet liner designed to stretch and hug the contours of a pond of virtually any shape and size. In addition, a pond made with even the most expensive sheet liner is cheaper to construct and guaranteed to last longer than an equivalent rigid plastic liner.

Polyethylene liners, once the only type of flexible liner on the market, are still available but they are relatively fragile, and should be considered only for temporary pools. And even then, they should be lined with a double thickness of material. PVC liners, especially those reinforced with nylon, are guaranteed for up to 10 years of normal use, but if you want your pond to last for 50 years or more, choose a synthetic rubber membrane based on butyl. Not all butyl liners are of the same quality, so buy one from a reputable manufacturer offering a 20-year written guarantee if you want the very best product. Black and stone-colored butyl liners are made in a wide range of stock sizes, but if you can't find one to suit your needs, you can have one made to order.

Flexible liners
Best-quality flexible liners are made from butyl.

DESIGNING A POND

A pond must be sited correctly if it is to have any chance of maturing into an attractive, clear stretch of water. Never place a pond under deciduous trees. Falling leaves will pollute the water as they decay, causing fish to become ill and even die. Some trees are especially poisonous.

Positioning for sunlight

A pond must receive plenty of daylight. Although sunlight promotes the growth of algae, which causes ponds to turn a pea-green color, it is also necessary to encourage the growth of other water plant life. An abundant growth of oxygenating plants will compete with the algae for the mineral salts and, with shade provided by floating and marginal plants, will keep the pond clear.

Size and shape

The proportion of the pond is important in creating harmony between plants and fish. It is difficult to maintain the right conditions for clear water in a pond less than 40 square feet in surface area, but the volume of water is even more vital. A pond up to about 100 square feet in area should be 18 inches deep. As the area increases, you will have to dig deeper to about 24 inches or more, but it is rarely necessary to go below 30 inches.

A flexible liner will conform better to simple curves, but the section or profile must be designed to fulfill certain requirements. To grow marginal plants, you will need a 9-inch-wide shelf around the edge of the pond, 9 inches below the surface of the water. This will take a standard 6-inch planting flat with ample water above, and you can always raise the flat on pieces of paving or bricks. The sides of the pond should slope at about 20 degrees to prevent soil collapse during construction and to allow the liner to stretch without promoting too many creases. It will also allow a sheet of ice to float upwards without damaging the liner. Judge the angle by measuring 3 inches inwards for every 9 inches of depth. If the soil is very sandy, increase the angle of slope slightly for extra stability.

Accommodating a sloping site

On a sloping site, build up the low side with earth, turfing up to the paving surround. Cut back the higher side and build a low retaining wall, or bed stones against the earth to create a rock garden.

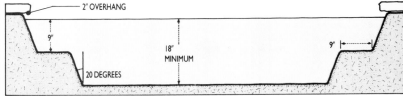

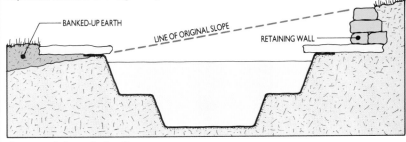

Important dimensions for a garden pond

Accommodating a sloping site

Installing a rigid liner

Stand up a rigid liner in position and prop it up with cardboard boxes, both to check its orientation and to mark its perimeter on the ground. Use a level to plot key points on the ground (**1**) and mark them with small stakes. You will need to dig outside this line, so absolute accuracy is not required.

As you move the topsoil, either take it away in a wheelbarrow or pile it close by ready to incorporate into a rock garden. Lay a straightedge across the top and measure the depth of the excavation (**2**), including marginal shelves. Keep the excavation as close as possible to the shape of the liner, but extend it by 6 inches on all sides. Compact the base and cover it with a

1-inch-deep level of sharp sand. Lower the liner down and bed it firmly into the sand. Check that the pool stands level (**3**) and wedge it temporarily with wooden stakes until the back-fill of soil or sand can hold it.

Start to fill the liner with water from a hose and, at the same time, pour sifted soil or sand behind the liner (**4**). There is no need to hurry as it will take some time to fill, but keep pace with the level of the water. Reach into the excavation and pack soil under the marginal shelves with your hands.

When the liner is firmly bedded in the soil, either finish the edge with stones as for a flexible liner (see opposite) or re-lay turf to cover the rim of the liner.

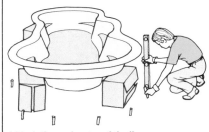

1 Mark the perimeter of the liner

2 Measure the depth of the excavation

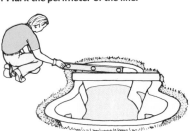

3 Make sure the liner stands level

4 Backfill with sifted soil or sand

CONSTRUCTING A POND: FLEXIBLE LINER

Excavating the pond

Mark out the shape of the pond on the ground. A garden hose is useful for trying out curvilinear shapes. Excavate the pond to the level of the planting shelf, then mark and dig out the deeper sections (1). Remove sharp stones and roots from the sides and base to make sure they won't puncture the liner.

The top of the pond must be level, and the surrounding stone or concrete slabs must be ¾ inch below the turf. For those reasons, cut back the turf to accommodate the stones and then drive wooden reference stakes into the exposed surround every 3 to 4 feet. Level the tops of all the stakes using a straightedge (2) and check the level across the pond as well. Remove or pack earth around the stakes until the compacted soil is level below them.

When the surround is level, remove the stakes and spread ½ inch of slightly damp sand over the base and sides of the excavation (3).

Installing a flexible liner

Drape the liner across the excavation with an even overlap all round, and hold it in place with bricks while you fill the pond with water from a hose (4). It will take several hours to fill a large pond, but check it regularly, moving the bricks as the liner stretches. A few creases are inevitable around sharp curves but you will lose most of them by keeping the liner fairly taut and easing it into shape as the water rises. Turn off the water when the level reaches about 2 inches below the edge of the pond. Cut off surplus liner with scissors, leaving a 6-inch overlap all round (5). Push 4-inch nails through the overlap into the soil so that the liner cannot slip while you place the edging stones.

Building the surround

Lay flat stones dry at first, selecting those which follow the shape of the pond with a reasonably close fit between them. Let the stones project over the water by about 2 inches to cast a deep shadow line and reflection. Cut stones with a bolster to fit the gaps behind the larger edging stones (▷). Lift the stones one or two at a time and bed them on two or three strategically placed mounds of mortar mixed with 1 part cement: 3 parts soft sand (6). Tap the stones level with a mallet and fill the joints with a trowel. Smooth the joints flush with an old paintbrush. Do not drop mortar in the water or you will have to empty and refill the pond before you introduce fish or plants.

INCORPORATING A DRAIN

The recommended water level for a pond is about 2 inches below the edging stones, but in exceptional circumstances such as a heavy storm, or if you forget to turn off the water when topping up, the water can rise fast enough to spill over and flood the garden. As a precaution, build a drain beneath the edging stones to allow excess water to escape. Not only does a drain prevent a flood, it provides a means of running electric cable into the pond to power a pump or lighting. Cut corrugated plastic sheet into two strips 6 inches wide and long enough to run under the edging stones. Pop-rivet the strips together to make a channel about an inch deep (1). Scrape earth and sand from beneath the liner to accommodate the channel (2), then lay edging stones on top to hold it in place. Dig a small soakaway behind the channel and fill it with rubble topped with fine gravel or turf up to the level of the stones.

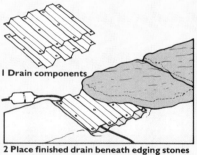

1 Drain components

2 Place finished drain beneath edging stones

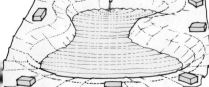

1 Dig the excavation as accurately as possible

2 Level the edge using reference stakes

3 Line the excavation with damp sand

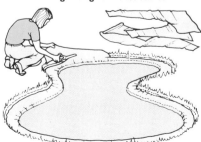

4 Stretch the liner by filling the pond

5 Cut the flexible liner to fit

6 Lay edging stones to complete the pond

MAKING A RAISED-EDGE POND

You can build a formal pond with a raised edge using bricks or concrete facing blocks. An edging about 18 inches high is safer for small children while also providing seating for adults. If you prefer a low wall—say, 9 inches high—create planting shelves at ground level, digging the pond deeper in the center. Place planting crates on blocks around the edge of a deep raised pond.

Building the pond

Lay 4- to 6-inch concrete footings (◁) to support the walls, which are constructed from two skins of masonry set apart to match the width of flat coping stones. Allow for an overhang of 2 inches over the water's edge and lap the outer wall by ½ to ¾ inch. To save money, build the inner wall from plain concrete blocks or cheap common bricks, reserving more expensive and decorative bricks or facing blocks for the outer skin of the wall. Raised ponds can be lined with a standard flexible liner or you can order a prefabricated fitted liner to reduce the amount of creasing at the corners. Trap the edge of whichever liner you select under the coping stones.

Raised-edge pond
A well-designed and constructed pond which is nicely integrated in a sloping site.

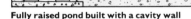

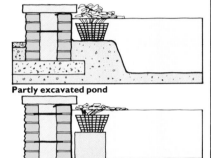

Partly excavated pond

Fully raised pond built with a cavity wall

ALTERNATIVE POND EDGING

Edging a pond with flat stones provides a safe and attractive footpath for tending to water plants and fish, but a more natural setting is often required, particularly for small header pools in a rock garden. Incorporate a shelf around the pond as for marginal plants, but this time for an edging of rocks. If you place them carefully there is no need to mortar them. Arrange rocks behind the edging to cover the liner **(1)**.

To create a shallow, beachlike edging, slope the soil at a very shallow angle and lay large pebbles or flat rocks upon the liner. You can merge them with a rock garden or let them form a natural water line **(2)**.

To discourage neighborhood cats from poaching fish from a pond, create an edging of trailing plants. Without a firm foothold, no cat will attempt to reach into the water. Bed a strip of soft wire netting in the mortar below flat edging stones. Cut the strip to overhang the water by about 6 inches as a support for the plants **(3)**. Once the plants are established, they will disguise the nature of the pool liner.

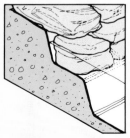

1 Rock-edged pond

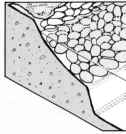

2 Pebble-strewn shelf

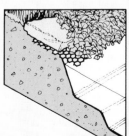

3 Wire edge holds plants

Pumps and fountains

Small submersible pumps for fountains and waterfalls are operated either directly from the house electrical supply or through a transformer which reduces the voltage to 12 volts. The combination of house electricity and water can be fatal, so consult an electrician if you plan to use a 12-volt pump. A low-voltage pump is safe and can be installed and wired simply (◁).

Place the pump in the water and run its electric cable beneath the edging stones, preferably via a drain (◁), to a waterproof connector attached to the extension lead of a transformer installed inside the house. This permits removal of the pump for servicing without disturbing the extension cable or transformer. Run pumps regularly, even in the winter months, to keep them in good working order, and clean both the pump and its filter according to the manufacturer's instructions.

There are so many waterfall pumps and fountain kits available that you should consult manufacturers' catalogues to find one that best suits your purpose. Place a submersible waterfall pump close to the edge of the pond so that you can reach it to disconnect the hose running to the waterfall when you need to service the pump. Stand fountain units on a flat stone or propped up on bricks so that the jet is vertical. Plant water lilies some distance away from a fountain as falling water will encourage the flowers to close up.

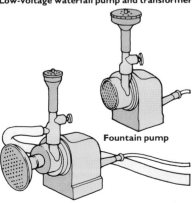

Low-voltage waterfall pump and transformer

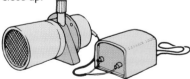

Fountain pump

Combination pump

BUILDING A ROCK GARDEN AND WATERFALL

A waterfall, complemented by a rock garden displaying clumps of ferns or graceful shrubs and trees such as Japanese maple or dwarf conifers, adds a further dimension to a water garden. The technique for building a series of watercourses is not as complicated as it may appear and, in doing so, you can also cover much of the groundwork needed for your rock garden.

Materials

You will be surprised by the amount of soil produced by excavating a pond. To avoid the waste and trouble of transporting it to a local dump, use it to create your poolside rock garden. If you include a small reservoir on the higher ground you can pump water into it from the main pond to be returned via a trickling cascade or waterfall.

You'll have plenty of soil, but obtaining enough stones to give the impression of a real rocky outcrop can be very expensive, that is, if you buy them from a local garden center. A cheaper way is to use hollow, cast reproduction rocks, which surprisingly will eventually weather-in quite well. However, your best option is to buy natural stone direct from a quarry.

Real rocks can be extremely heavy, so have them delivered as close to the site as possible, and have a sturdy cart on hand to move individual stones about the garden. A rock garden and waterfall are actually built as one operation but for the sake of clarity, they are described separately here.

AVOIDING STRAIN

Lifting stones
Keep your back straight when lifting heavy stones (right). Use a rope to lift and place large rocks (below).

Creating a waterfall

So that the waterfall can discharge directly into the main pond, form a small inlet at the side of the pond by leaving a large flap of flexible liner. Build shallow banks at each side of the inlet and line them with stones (**1**). Create a stepped watercourse ascending in stages to the reservoir. Line the watercourse with cutoffs of flexible liner which must be overlapped on the face of each waterfall. Tuck the edge of each lower piece of liner under the edge of the piece above, and hold them in place with stones. To retain water in small pools along the watercourse, cut each step with a slope toward the rear (**2**), placing stones along the lip for the desired effect (**3**). A flat stone gives a sheet of water whereas a layer of pebbles produces a rippling cascade.

Test the watercourse as the construction work progresses by running water from a hose—it is difficult to adjust the angle of stones once the watercourse has been completed.

Bury the flexible hose from the waterfall pump in the rockery, making sure there are no sharp bends which would restrict the flow of water. Cut the hose so that it emerges at the edge of the reservoir and cover it with a flat stone (**4**) to hold and hide it.

A rigid plastic reservoir will have a lip molded in an edge which will allow water to escape down the watercourse. If you construct a reservoir with flexible liner, however, shape the edge to form a low point and support a flat stone over the opening to hide the liner (**5**).

SEE ALSO

Details for: ▷	
Obtaining stone	424
Flexible liners	455

Cascade or waterfall
This section shows a cascade or waterfall running from a reservoir to a pond.
1 Pond inlet
2 Watercourse step
3 Overhanging stone creates a sheet of water
4 Hose from pump
5 Reservoir outlet
6 Reservoir

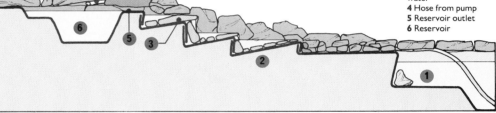

Constructing a rock garden

Select and place each stone in a rockery to create an illusion of strata, or layers, of rock. Stones placed haphazardly at odd angles tend to resemble a spoil heap rather than a natural outcrop. Take care not to strain yourself when lifting rocks. Keep your feet together and use your leg muscles to do the work, keeping your back as straight as possible. To move a particularly heavy rock, slip a rope around it (see left).

Lay large flat rocks to form the front edge of the rockery, placing soil behind and between them to form a flat, level platform. Compact the soil to make sure there are no air pockets which will damage the roots of plants. Lay subsequent layers of rock set back from the first, but not in a regular pattern. Place some to create steep embankments, others to form a gradual slope of wide steps. Pockets of soil for planting alpines or other small plants will form naturally as you lay the stones, but plan larger areas of soil for specimen shrubs or dwarf trees.

Building a rock garden
A rockery should have irregular rock steps along its front edge.

Incorporating a bog garden

An area of wet, boggy soil where specialized waterside plants will flourish complements a pond perfectly. When you excavate the pond, make a wide planting shelf covered with the flexible liner. Place a row of stones to form the edge of the pond, dividing the bog area from the deep water. Bed the stones in 2 inches of mortar. When the mortar has set, its lime content must be neutralized by painting on a solution of

waterproof powder available from pond specialists. Follow manufacturers' instructions for its use.

Incorporate the bog garden into a rockery by lining the perimeter with stones, then fill the area with soil. The liner beneath the soil will retain enough moisture to keep the garden permanently damp, but make sure the planting bed is deep enough to ensure plants are not waterlogged.

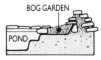

Bog garden
Construct a bog garden next to a pond for waterside plants.

CHOOSING A SWIMMING POOL

Owning a private swimming pool is no longer the exclusive privilege of the rich and famous. Many specialist companies offer reasonably priced pool kits which you can install yourself following the manufacturer's detailed instructions. It is worth hiring professional help for deep excavations and to remove soil from the site, and anything but the most basic heating equipment should be installed by a *qualified tradesperson. Local building departments and zoning boards have strict rules concerning in-ground pools. You must seek their permission. Pools generally need filling only once a year, and in areas with a cold winter climate, it's important to leave at least some water in the pool during the winter to resist ground heaving caused by freezing.*

Sunken-pool kits
Vinyl liners are used with block-built walls or a frame-and-panel construction.

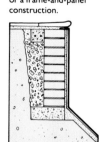

Block-wall construction

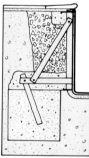

Frame-and-panel walling

● **Tiled concrete pools**
For a top-quality permanent pool, hire a professional contractor to install a reinforced-concrete structure. Hollow pool walls, constructed with cast-concrete sections, are filled with vibrated concrete, finished and lined with polished marble or mosaic tiles.

A self-assembly pool
Swimming pools made from self-assembly kits are just as attractive as professionally installed pools, but a fraction of the cost.

Siting a swimming pool

The size and shape of a swimming pool are largely dictated by the area of your garden, but it should be positioned away from trees so that it benefits from the sun and avoids falling leaves. Most people prefer to install a pool reasonably close to the house so that its facilities can be used to supply water, electricity and heating. As the pool filtration plant must be housed, an existing building such as a garage can be utilized. It is normally easier to install a pool on a level site, but you can partially bury one in a sloping bank and fill in the lower area below the pool with the excavated soil.

Above-ground pool kits

Above-ground pools are cheap and easy to erect. Most are circular or oval in plan, and are constructed by bolting together galvanized-steel panels and frame members. A heavy-duty vinyl liner and wide coping strips complete the basic pool. Above-ground pools are the least likely to be contaminated by wind-blown leaves and other debris, and they can be dismantled and moved when you buy another house. Young children cannot fall into the water once you have removed the steps. With some modification you can partially bury an above-ground pool and bank the excavated soil around the sides.

Sunken-pool kits

Sunken pools, in a wide range of shapes and sizes, can be built using prefabricated panels similar to those used for above-ground pools. The wall panels, which are anchored in concrete, line the perimeter of the pool to a depth of about 3 feet. A deeper hopper-shaped excavation at one end of the pool is finished with a sand and cement mix before a fitted vinyl liner is installed. The pool walls are backfilled with gravel to balance the water pressure. Finally, an edging of shaped coping stones is embedded in mortar.

Similar pools are built using standard concrete blocks laid on a concrete footing to construct the walls. The walls and floor of the pool are rendered to present a smooth face to the vinyl liner. You could hire a local builder to excavate and construct the pool, then backfill and line it yourself.

A swimming-pool liner will last for years but, should one become damaged accidentally, it can be patched without your having to empty the pool.

SWIMMING POOL ACCESSORIES

Some accessories like diving boards, water chutes and underwater lights merely add to the enjoyment of your pool. Others are absolutely essential to keep the water pure.

Skimmer and filter
A pump-operated skimmer built into the side of a swimming pool sucks lightweight floating debris into a filter housed outside the pool. The filtered water is returned to the pool via a separate inlet. The entire unit is supplied with most pool kits.

Pool vacuum cleaner
You will need a special vacuum cleaner to remove the heavier debris that sinks to the bottom of the pool. Its hose connects to the poolside skimmer.

Leaf net
Buy a net attached to a long pole to periodically remove floating leaves which might clog the filter.

Pool cover
Lightweight plastic covers are available for above-ground and sunken pools to keep leaves, twigs and other wind-blown debris out of the water during the winter months.

Test equipment
Chlorine or other chemicals must be added to the water at regular intervals to kill harmful bacteria and algae, but the water must be analyzed to maintain an effective chemical balance. Pool kits are supplied with simple test equipment which allows you to analyze water samples yourself.

Heating the water
Floating thermal blankets, which are removed prior to swimming, provide the cheapest method of raising the temperature of the water. They are essential to reduce the cost of heating the water by more sophisticated equipment. You can install a heat exchanger, which uses heat produced by the house central-heating boiler, or a separate boiler used exclusively for the pool. Both methods are expensive. Solar panels or mats provide free heat but installation costs are high. A heat pump, which extracts heat from the surrounding air, even during a cloudy day, is probably the most effective way to heat a swimming pool.

11

TOOLS & SKILLS

A TOOL KIT IS PERSONAL

If you talk to people who make a living using tools you'll find that they guard them jealously, are loath to lend them and even less likely to borrow them. Tools are very personal. The way a person uses or sharpens a tool, even his or her working stance, will shape and modify it until it works better for its owner than in other hands. This is particularly noticeable with old wooden tools. If you examine the sole of a well-used wooden jack plane, for example, you will see that it has worn unevenly to suit the style of one craftsman. Even the handle of a new plane feels unfamiliar after the feel of a plane you've used for years.

The choice of tools is equally personal. No two professionals' tool kits are identical and each might select different tools to do the same job. The tools shown and described in these pages will enable you to tackle all but the more specialized tasks involved in maintaining, repairing, extending and decorating your home and garden, but the final choice is yours.

No one buys a complete kit of tools all at once. Apart from the considerable cost, it makes more sense to buy tools as you need them. You may prefer to do your own decorating but hire a professional for electrical work, in which case you are better off spending your money on good-quality brushes, rollers or scrapers than spreading it thinly on a wider range of cheaper tools. Consequently, we have listed the essential tools for each "trade" under specific headings — plumber's tool kit, decorator's tool kit and so on. But a great many tools are common to all trades, and you'll find it necessary to buy only a few extra tools as you tackle a growing range of activities.

Even hand tools are expensive, but buy the best you can afford, for top-quality tools are always a wise investment. Not only will they perform well but if they are used, stored and maintained properly they will last a lifetime. Power tools are especially expensive, so unless you plan to use them regularly, it may be more economical to rent them. Make sure that rented tools are in good condition and ask for a set of written instructions or a demonstration before you leave the shop.

It is impossible to produce first-class work with blunt cutting tools, and they are more dangerous than sharp ones. Keep the blades in good condition and discard disposable ones when they no longer cut smoothly and easily. You'll find instructions for sharpening and maintaining hand tools, but have your power tools serviced professionally.

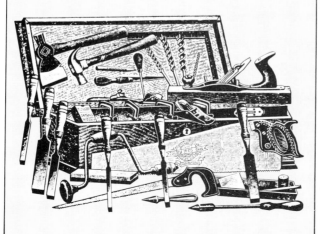

WOODWORKER'S TOOL KIT

A full tool kit for woodworking is enormous, but for general home maintenance you can make do with a fairly limited one. The most essential tools are listed in the page margin as a guide to building up a basic kit.

TOOLS FOR MEASURING AND MARKING

Take care of your measuring and marking tools. Thrown carelessly into a toolbox, squares can be knocked out of true and gauges can become blunt and inaccurate.

Tape measure and folding rule

A folding boxwood rule is the traditional cabinetmaker's tool for measuring, but a modern retractable steel tape measure is more versatile. Some can take measurements up to about 16 ft., including internal ones using the tip of the tape and the back of the case. The tape can be locked open at any point. Avoid letting the spring-loaded tape snap back into its case or the riveted hook on its end will become loose.

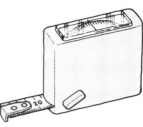

Try square

A try square is used to check the accuracy of square joints and planed timber, also for marking out timber which is to be sawn or cut square to its edge. Look for a try square with its blade and stock (handle) cut from one L-shaped piece of metal. One with a straight blade riveted to the stock may lose its accuracy. Some try squares have the top of the stock cut at 45 degrees for marking out miter joints. Buy the largest square you can afford. They come with blades up to 1 foot long.

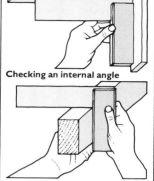

Checking an internal angle

Checking planed timber
View the work against the light to check that you are planing square.

Combination square

A combination square is a very versatile tool. It's essentially a try square, but instead of a fixed blade it has a calibrated rule that slides in the stock to make a blade of any length up to 10 inches. This works as a useful depth and marking gauge. The head has an angled face for marking miters and incorporates a small level for checking vertical and horizontal surfaces.

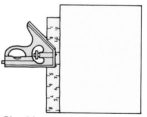

Checking horizontals
Remove the blade and place the stock face on the horizontal surface.

Checking verticals
Place the blade against a vertical face and read the level to check its accuracy.

Sliding or adjusting bevel

A sliding bevel is used like a standard try square, but its blade can be adjusted to "take" and mark any angle.

Marking knife

Before sawing timber, mark the cutting lines with a knife. It is more accurate than a pencil and prevents the grain from breaking out when you saw. The blade of a marking knife is ground on only one side, and its flat face is run against the square or bevel.

Marking gauge

With a marking gauge you can score a line parallel to an edge. Set the movable stock the required distance from the pin in the beam. Press the face of the stock against the edge of the board, tilt the gauge to an angle, the pin touching the wood's surface, then push the tool away from you to scribe the line.

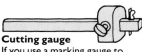

Cutting gauge

If you use a marking gauge to score a line across the grain of the wood, the pin will tear the surface. A cutting gauge is designed for the purpose, and has a sharp blade in place of the pin. The blade is held in the beam with a removable wedge.

Mortise gauge

A mortise gauge has two pins, one fixed and the other movable, for marking the parallel sides of mortise-and-tenon joints. First set the points apart the width of the mortise chisel, then adjust the stock to place the mortise the required distance from the edge of the wood. Having marked the limits of the mortise with a try square (1), score the two lines with the gauge (2). With the same setting mark the tenon rail.

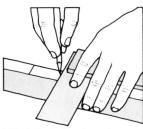

1 Mark the limits of mortise

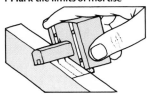

2 Score the lines

SAWS

Don't try to make do with just one or two saws in your kit. The right tool for the job will make for fast and accurate cutting.

HANDSAWS

Handsaws are a family of saws with flexible, unsupported blades. They are for sawing solid timber and man-made boards. They differ mainly in the ways that their teeth are shaped and sharpened.

Ripsaw

The ripsaw is made specifically for cutting solid timber along its length (ripping). Each of its teeth is like a tiny chisel that slices the timber along its grain. Alternate teeth are bent outward in opposite directions (set) so that the groove (kerf) cut in the timber is slightly wider than the thickness of the blade. Most saws are set in this way, or they would jam in the kerf.

Crosscut saw

Unlike ripsaw teeth, which are filed square with the face of the blade, those of a crosscut saw are filed at an angle to form points that score lines along both edges of the kerf before removing the wood between them. This allows the saw to cut across the grain of solid timber without tearing the fibers.

Panel saw

The teeth of a panel saw are set and shaped like those of a crosscut but are smaller and closer together and cut a finer kerf. The saw is used for cutting thin man-made boards like plywood and hardboard.

STORING SAWS

Glue dowel pegs into a stout strip and screw it to the wall. Hang your saws from the pegs and protect their teeth with some plastic weather-strip.

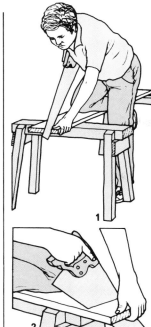

1

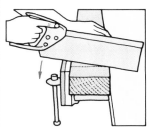

2

Using handsaws

Hold the saw with your forefinger extended towards the tip of the blade. This helps to keep the blade in line with your forearm and produces a straight cut.

To saw down the length of a board, support it on wooden sawhorses and start the cut at one end with short, light backward strokes only at first, to establish the kerf, while steadying the blade with the tip of your thumb against its flat face (1).

Continue cutting with slow, regular strokes, using the full length of the blade. Move the sawhorses as needed to allow the blade a clear path.

As you approach the end of the board, turn it around. Start a fresh cut at that end and saw back to meet the original kerf.

When crosscutting, support the work with your free hand (2) and finish the cut with slow, gentle strokes to avoid breaking off the last uncut layer of wood.

BACKSAWS

The blade of a backsaw is stiffened with a heavy metal strip folded over its top edge. Backsaws are for cutting narrow boards to length and for cutting joints.

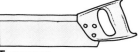

Tenon saw

A tenon saw has fine teeth shaped and set like those of a crosscut saw. It is the perfect saw for general-purpose woodworking and is especially useful for cutting molding joints.

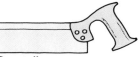

Dovetail saw

Because the tails and pins of a dovetail joint run with the grain, the teeth of a dovetail saw are like miniature ripsaw teeth. Use this saw for fine cabinetwork.

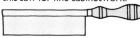

Gents saw

This cheap alternative to a dovetail saw has a straight wooden handle.

Using backsaws

Support the work in a vise or on a bench hook and hold the saw at a shallow angle to establish the kerf, gradually leveling the blade until you are sawing parallel to the face of the wood.

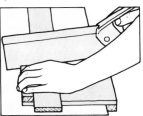

Using a bench hook

A bench hook, used in cross-cutting narrow boards, hooks against the front edge of the workbench while the wood is held firmly against its top block.

Using a miter box

When you cut 45-degree miter joints, use a miter box to guide your saw blade in slots set at that angle. Other slots, set at 90 degrees, can help you to cut square butt joints.

● **Essential tools**
Tape measure
Combination square
Marking knife
Marking gauge
Crosscut saw
Tenon saw

FRAME SAWS

A frame saw is fitted with a very slim blade for cutting curves. A strong metal frame holds the blade taut to keep it from bending.

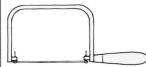

Coping saw

A coping saw is the most useful frame saw. Its teeth are coarse enough to cut fairly thick timber, yet it will cope with thin boards.

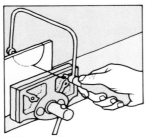

Using a coping saw

The blade is held between two pins that swivel so that you can turn it in the direction of the cut while keeping the frame out of the way.

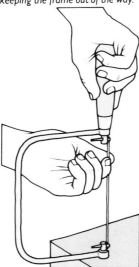

Fitting a coping saw blade

A coping saw's blade is replaced when it gets blunt or breaks. Unscrew the handle a few turns counterclockwise, hook the new blade into the pin farthest from the handle, press the frame down on the bench and locate the other end of the blade. Tension the blade by turning the handle clockwise. Make sure the teeth point away from the handle and that the two pins are aligned so that the blade isn't twisted.

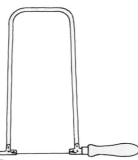

Fret saw

The blade of a fret saw is so fine that the spring of the frame alone keeps it under tension. The blade, its teeth pointing to the handle, is held at each end by a thumbscrew and plate.

Using a fret saw

Hold the work over the edge of the bench and saw with the blade upright, pulling on it from below.

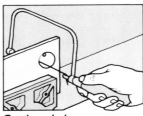

Cutting a hole

You can use a frame saw to cut a large hole in a piece of wood. Mark out the hole, drill a small hole inside the outline, pass the blade through it and connect it to the saw frame. Cut out the hole, adjusting the angle of the blade to the frame as needed, then dismantle the saw to free the blade.

Keyhole saw

A keyhole saw is for cutting holes in panels, but because of its relatively wide blade, it is easier to use on straight cuts, particularly on thick boards. With no frame restricting its movement, the saw can be used, for example, to cut the hole for a letterbox in a door. Take care not to bend the blade.

SHARPENING SAWS

A saw must be sharpened carefully with special tools if it is to cut properly, so you may prefer to have your saws sharpened by a professional, especially any that are finer than a tenon saw. If you want to keep the tools in tip-top condition yourself, buy a saw file for sharpening the teeth and a saw set for bending them back to their correct angle.

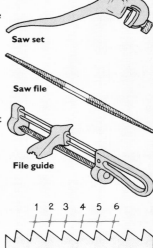

Saw set

Saw file

File guide

I Count the points in I in.

Saw-sharpening tools

A saw file is double-ended and triangular in section. Its length should relate to the spacing of the saw's teeth, strictly speaking, but in practice you can use one file about 6 inches long for handsaws and another 4 inches long for a tenon saw. You can also buy a file guide, which locates over the saw's teeth and keeps the file at a constant angle while in use.

Closing the handles of a saw set squeezes the saw tooth between a plunger and an angled anvil, which is first set to correspond with the number of tooth points per I inch on the saw blade (**1**). To set the anvil, close the handle, release the locking screw at the end of the tool, turn the anvil until the required setting number on its edge aligns with the plunger, then tighten the locking screw.

Jointing a saw

*Jointing restores all of a saw's teeth to the same height. It is not absolutely essential every time a saw is sharpened, but a light jointing will produce a spot of bright metal on each point that will help you to sharpen the teeth evenly. Near the top edge of a block of hardwood, plane a groove that will grip a smooth flat file (**2**). Clamp the saw, teeth up, between two strips in a vise, and with the wood block held against the flat of the blade, pass the file two or three times along the tops of the teeth (**3**) so that every one shows a tiny spot of bright metal.*

2 Mount a file in hardwood

3 Joint the saw with a file

Setting the teeth

*Adjust the saw set to the right number of points (see above) and, starting at one end of the saw, place the set over the first tooth facing away from you, aligning the plunger with the center of the tooth. Hold the set steady and squeeze the handles (**4**). Set every other tooth—those facing away—then turn the saw around and set those in between.*

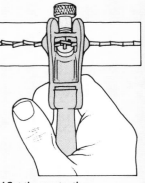

4 Set the saw teeth

● **Essential tools**
Coping saw

SHARPENING SAWS

Sharpening the teeth

To sharpen a ripsaw, clamp the blade between the strips with its teeth projecting just above the edges of the wood. Starting next to the handle, place the saw file against the front edge of the first tooth facing away from you and settle it snugly into the space between the teeth (the gullet). With the file square to the flat of the blade (5), make two or three strokes until the edge of the tooth is shiny right up to its point and half of the bright jointing spot has disappeared. File alternate teeth in this way, then turn the saw around and sharpen those in between until the bright spots are completely removed.

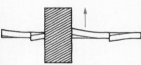

5 Filing ripsaw teeth

Sharpening a crosscut saw

To sharpen a crosscut saw, use the same procedure but hold the file at an angle of 60 to 70 degrees to the flat of the blade (6), with its handle slightly low.

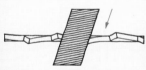

6 Filing crosscut saw teeth

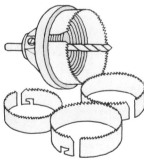

Hole saw

You can buy a set of hole saw blades for cutting perfectly round holes of different diameters. They clip into a backing plate clamped to a drill bit which fits in the chuck of a power drill. Place the tip of the drill bit at the center of the required hole and with the power tool at slow speed, slowly push the revolving saw against the wood. Always place a piece of scrap wood behind the work to keep the saw from breaking out the back.

POWER SAWS

Power saws are invaluable for cutting heavy framing lumber and large man-made boards. There are circular saw and jigsaw attachments for electric drills, but they are too small and low-powered for heavy work.

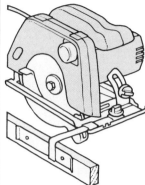

Portable circular saw

When you buy or rent a circular saw, choose one with a 7 1/2-inch blade. Its motor will be powerful enough to give a blade speed that can cut thick lumber and man-made boards without straining the saw or scorching the work. There are blades designed just for ripping and others for crosscutting, but for general use, choose a combination blade. This will cut efficiently both along and across the wood grain and is suitable for sawing man-made boards. There are also special blades and abrasive discs for cutting metal and stone.

On a good saw you can adjust the angle of the blade for cutting bevels.

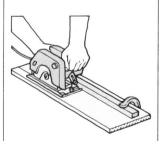

Making straight cuts

Circular saws have removable fences to guide the blades parallel to the edge of the work, but these are often too small to be of much use. You can extend the fence by screwing a length of wood to it or clamp a strip onto the work itself to guide the edge of the soleplate. By clamping the strip at various angles across the wood, you can crosscut boards or planks at these angles.

Sawing by eye

When accuracy of cut is not too important, you can use the saw freehand, guiding a notch in the soleplate along a line marked on the work. Place the tip of the soleplate on the work and align the notch with the line. Switch on, let the blade get up to speed, then advance the saw steadily.

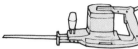

Reciprocating saw

Reciprocating saws, with powerful motors and blades up to I foot long, are especially useful for such jobs as cutting openings in stud partitions.

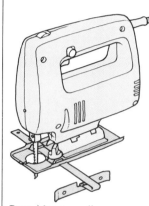

Portable power jigsaw

A portable jigsaw is primarily for making curved cuts in lumber and man-made boards. Most such saws have guide fences for straight cutting, but they are rarely sturdy enough to stop the blade from wandering. Discard jigsaw blades when they get blunt and keep some spares handy. As blades are fairly cheap, it's worth buying some of the special ones for cutting plastics, metal, plasterboard and even ceramics.

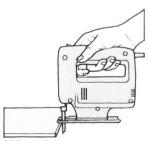

Using a jigsaw

Rest the front of the soleplate on the edge of the work, squeeze the saw's trigger and advance the moving blade into the work along the marked cutting line. Don't force or twist a blade or it will break, and let the blade come to rest before you put the saw down.

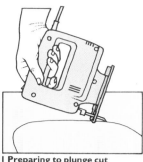

I Preparing to plunge cut

Cutting holes with a jigsaw

The simplest way to cut a large hole in a panel is first to drill a starter hole into which you then insert the jigsaw blade, but you can start the cut by "plunge cutting". Tilt the saw onto the front edge of its soleplate with the tip of the blade just above the surface of the work (1). Switch on the saw and gradually lower the blade into the wood until it is upright and the soleplate is flat on the surface.

POWER SAW SAFETY

A circular saw is perfectly safe to use as long as you follow the manufacturer's handling and fitting instructions carefully and observe the following safety guidelines:

- Always unplug the saw before you adjust or change the blade.
- Don't use a blunt blade. Have it sharpened professionally.
- Fit new blades according to manufacturer's instructions. The teeth at the bottom of the blade must face in the direction of the cut.
- All circular saws must have a fixed blade guard and a lower guard that swings back as the cut proceeds. Never use the saw without the guards in place, and make sure that the lower one will return to its position when the blade clears the work.
- The work must be held securely on a sawhorse or bench.
- Keep the electrical cable well behind the saw.
- Don't force the saw into a cut. If it jams, back off a little until the blade returns to full speed.
- Don't put the saw down before the blade stops moving.
- Don't wear loose clothing, a necktie or a necklace, any of which could become entangled in the machine.

Saw bench

You can clamp a circular saw upside down under a saw bench attachment and cut wood by passing it across the blade which projects up through the flat bed.

PLANES AND SPOKESHAVES

Unless lumber is to be used for crude framing, as in a stud partition or a bath panel, it must be planed to remove the marks of saw teeth. Planes are also used for reducing wood to size and shape. Wooden planes are still made, and many antique ones are for sale at reasonable prices, but most people find modern metal planes easier to adjust for the exact thickness of shaving they require.

BENCH PLANES

Bench planes are general-purpose tools for smoothing wood to make joints between boards or to level the surface of several boards glued together. Bench planes are all similar in design, differing only in the length of the sole.

Jointer plane

The jointer is the longest bench plane, with a sole up to 2 feet long. It is designed for truing up the long edges of boards that are to be butted and glued together, and for leveling large flat panels. Its long sole bridges minor irregularities until the blade shaves them down. A shorter plane would simply follow the uneven surface.

Jack plane

A jack plane 12 to 15 inches long is a good all-purpose tool. If you can afford only one bench plane choose a jack plane, which is light enough to cope with most planing without tiring you.

Smoothing plane

A finely set smoothing plane is used for putting the final surface on a piece of lumber after it has been reduced to size with a jack plane or jointer plane.

1 Checking the blade angle

Adjusting a bench plane

Before you use a bench plane adjust the angle and depth of the blade. Check the angle by sighting down the sole of the plane from the toe (1) and use the lateral adjustment lever behind the blade to set the cutting edge so that it projects an equal amount across the width of the sole. Use the knurled adjusting nut in front of the handle to set the depth to take off a fine shaving.

STORING PLANES

Never put a plane sole-down on the bench during work. Lay it on its side. Similarly, the plane should be stored on its side, even though the blade is withdrawn. For long-term storage, dismantle and clean the plane and grease bare metal parts lightly to protect them from rust.

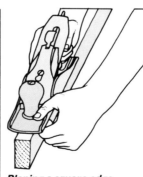

Planing a square edge

Keep the plane flat on the edge of the work by holding the toe down with the thumb of your free hand and pressing the fingers against the side of the wood to guide the tool along.

Planing a flat surface

To plane a wide surface as flat as possible, work the plane diagonally across the wood but following the general direction of the grain. Finish by working parallel to the grain, taking off very fine shavings.

Block plane

The blade of a block plane is mounted at a shallow angle so that its edge can slice smoothly through the end grain of lumber. Small and lightweight—it can be used in the palm of one hand—the plane is also ideal for all kinds of fine trimming and shaping.

Trimming end grain

Cut a line all around the work with a marking knife, then set it vertically in a vise. To prevent the wood from splitting, form a chamfer down to the line on one side by planing towards the center. Plane the end square, working from the other side down to the marked line so that the chamfer is removed.

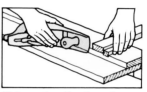

Using a shooting board

You can trim end grain with a bench plane on its side, running on a shooting board. The blade must be sharp and finely set. The work is held against the stop.

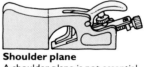

Shoulder plane

A shoulder plane is not essential for everyday use but, as its blade spans the whole width of its squarely machined body, it is ideal for trimming the square shoulders of large joints or rabbets. With the body removed the exposed blade can trim a rabbet right up to a stopped end.

Power plane

A power plane is useful for smoothing and shaping large structural timbers. Its revolving two- or three-cutter block can be used for planing rabbets if guided by a side fence.

Spokeshaves

A spokeshave is a miniature plane for shaping curved edges in wood. Use one with a flat base to shape a convex curve, one with a bellied base for a concave curve. When you use either tool, shape the curve from two directions so as to work with the grain all the time. Sharpen a spokeshave cutter as you would a plane blade.

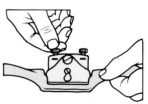

Adjusting the blade

Use the two adjusting screws to produce a fine setting, then fix the setting with the central locking screw.

Using a spokeshave

With a handle in each hand, your thumbs on their back edges, push the tool away from you. Rock it backward or forward as you work to produce a continuous shaving.

MOLDING PLANES AND ROUTERS

There are many times when it's necessary to cut grooves in wood, both with and across the grain, or to plane rabbets or moldings on the edges. A multi-plane or a power router—though neither can be called an essential tool—will produce any type of groove or molding and is extremely useful to the woodworker.

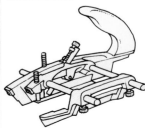

Combination plane

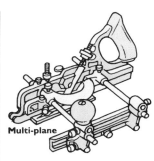
Multi-plane

Combination and multi-planes

Combination and multi-planes with variously shaped cutters can be used to plane grooves, rabbets and a number of molding profiles. Both tools have spurs—pairs of vertically adjusting blades—that cut parallel lines ahead of the cutter to prevent tearing of the wood fibers when a groove or housing is planed across the grain. Both tools can be used to cut tongue-and-groove joints along the edges of boards. The multi-plane has a larger selection of cutters than the combination plane.

Rabbet plane

A rabbet plane is similar to a bench plane, but its blade spans the whole width of its sole. With its depth gauge and guide fence set to the required dimensions, the plane will cut any number of identical rabbets.

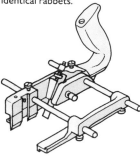

Plough plane

A plough plane has narrow blades for cutting grooves. It can be used only in the direction of the grain.

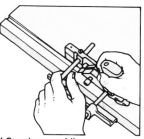
I Starting a molding

Using molding planes
Rabbet, plough, combination and multi-planes are all used in much the same way. Follow the maker's instructions for setting the depth gauge and guide fence, which control the position of the cutter relative to the surface and edge of the wood.

Hold the guide fence against the edge of the work at the far end and make short strokes to begin the molding (1), then move backwards, making longer and longer strokes until the depth gauge rests on the surface. Finish with one continuous pass along the length of the timber.

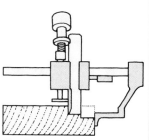

Cutting an extra-wide rabbet
To cut a rabbet wider than a standard cutter, first plane a rabbet on the outer edge, then adjust the guide fence to make a second cut that will make up the required width.

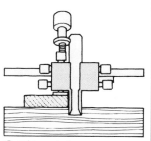

Cutting a dado
When you cut a dado—a groove across the grain—take off the guide fence and instead clamp a wooden strip across the work to guide the body of the plane.

SHARPENING PLANES

To keep its sharp cutting edge, a plane blade must be honed on a flat oilstone. Choose one with a medium grit on one side to remove metal quickly and a fine grit on the other for the final sharpening of the edge.

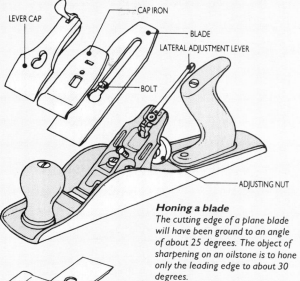

LEVER CAP — CAP IRON — BLADE — LATERAL ADJUSTMENT LEVER — BOLT — ADJUSTING NUT

Honing a blade
The cutting edge of a plane blade will have been ground to an angle of about 25 degrees. The object of sharpening on an oilstone is to hone only the leading edge to about 30 degrees.

Hold the blade against the stone at the correct angle and rub it to and fro to produce a sharp edge. A wide blade must be held at an angle across the stone so that the whole edge is in contact (1). Keep the stone lubricated with a little oil while you work.

Honing creates a burr along the cutting edge. Remove it by laying the back of the blade flat on the stone (2) and making several passes along the surface.

Removing and replacing a blade
The blade of a bench or block plane is clamped in place by a metal lever cap. Slacken the lever to remove the cap and lift the blade out of the plane. The blade of a bench plane has a cap iron bolted to it to break and curl the shavings as they are trimmed from the wood. Undo the bolt with a screwdriver and remove the cap iron before you sharpen the blade.

When you replace the cap iron, place it across the blade (1), then swivel it until the two are aligned (2). Don't drag the iron across the cutting edge but slide it to within 1/16 inch of it (1).

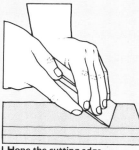
I Hone the cutting edge

2 Remove the burr

SEE ALSO
Details for: ▷
Bench planes   466

Using a honing guide
If you want to be certain that you are honing a blade to the correct angle, clamp it in a honing guide and roll the guide to and fro on the surface of the stone to sharpen the blade.

Repairing a chipped cutting edge
If you chip the cutting edge of a blade—against a nail, for example—regrind it on a bench grinder. Hold the blade against the tool rest and move the cutting edge from side to side against the revolving wheel until it is straight and clean. Use only light pressure and dip the blade in water regularly to cool it. Finally, hone the ground edge on an oilstone.

• **Essential tools**
Combination oilstone

467

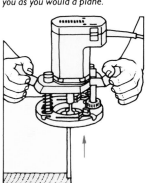

Hand router

Power router

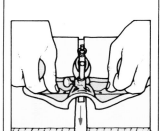

Power-router bits
1 Grooving bit
2 Edge-molding bit

● **Essential tools**
Wood chisels
$1/8$ to 1 in.
Bevel-edge chisels
$1/2$ to 1 in.
Gouges
Select sizes as required
Mortise chisels
Select sizes as required

ROUTERS

A hand router is used for finishing the bottom of a sawn housing after most of the waste has been cut out with a chisel. A power router is a sophisticated tool that performs all the tasks of combination and multi-planes and will follow a curved edge as easily as a straight one. The cutter revolves so fast that it produces as clean a cut across the grain as with it.

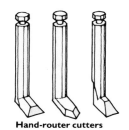

Using a hand router
To pare the bottom of a dado, hold one handle of the router in each hand and push the tool away from you as you would a plane.

Using a power router
Always let the bit run up to full speed before you allow it to come into contact with the work, and always lift it clear of the groove or molding before you switch off. The bit revolves clockwise; feed the machine against the rotation when molding an edge so that the cutter pulls itself into the wood.

Router cutters and bits
Hand-router cutters have square shafts that clamp into the tool and are adjusted vertically to set the chisel-like cutting edges at the required depth.

Power-router bits fit into a chuck at the base of the tool and are adjusted until they project through the baseplate. A grooving bit has two symmetrical cutting edges that run to its bottom end. An edge-molding bit has a cylindrical pilot tip below

the cutting edges that runs against the edge of the work to stop the cutter from biting too deeply.

Follow the manufacturer's instructions for fitting and adjusting bits or cutters.

Hand-router cutters

Honing a router cutter
Hone blunt hand-router cutters on an oilstone. Position the stone so that the cutter's shaft will clear the bench, then rub the cutter from side to side on the stone.

Cutting grooves and housings
*To cut a groove parallel to an edge, fit and set the adjustable guide fence (**1**) or run the edge of the baseplate against a wood strip clamped to the surface (**2**). To cut a wide dado, use two parallel strips to guide the bit along both outer edges (**3**), then rout out the center.*

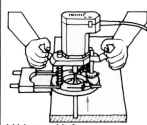

1 Using a guide fence

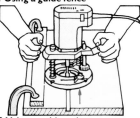

2 Using a guide strip

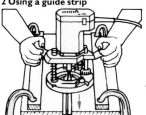

3 Cutting a wide dado

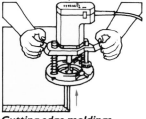

Cutting edge moldings
Rest the baseplate on the upper surface of the work and when the bit has run up to full speed, feed it against and along the edge.

When you mold all four edges of a rectangular piece of wood, do the end grain first, then run the router along each side.

SHARPENING A POWER-ROUTER BIT

You can grind and hone power-router bits yourself, though as they must be symmetrical it's better to have them done by a professional.

CHISELS AND GOUGES

Chisels are general-purpose woodcutting tools but are used mostly to remove the waste from joints or to pare and trim them to size. The size of a chisel refers to the width of its cutting edge. Though chisels range from $1/8$ inch in width up to 2 inches, a selection of sizes up to 1 inch is sufficient for most woodworking purposes.

Gouges are similar to wood chisels, but their blades are curved in cross section for such work as cutting the shoulders of a joint to fit against a turned leg or scooping out the waste from a finger pull on a drawer front or sliding door.

Most wood chisels and gouges have handles of boxwood or of impact-resistant plastic.

Wood chisel
A wood chisel has a strong, flat, rectangular-section blade for chopping out waste wood. It is strong enough to be driven with a mallet or hammer—though hammers must not be used on wooden handles.

Bevel-edge chisel
A bevel-edge chisel is used for paring, especially in trimming undercuts like dovetail joints or housings. Its bevels enable the blade to work in tight spaces that would be inaccessible to a thick wood chisel. It is not as strong as an unbeveled and may break if it is used for heavy work. If a little extra force is needed to drive the chisel forward, use your shoulder or the ball of your hand.

Mortise chisel
A mortise chisel has a thick blade, rectangular in section, for chopping and levering the waste out of mortise joints. Mallets are always needed to drive mortise chisels, so many of them have a shock-absorbent leather washer between the blade and the ferrule.

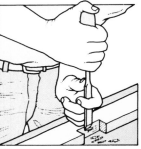

Chopping out waste wood
Don't try to chop out too much waste all at once. The wood will split or the chisel will be driven over the line of the joint, resulting in a poor fit. Remove the waste a little at a time, working back to the marked line. You can use a mallet at first, but finish off by hand.

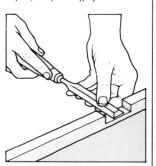

Paring with a chisel
Finish a joint by paring away very thin shavings with a bevel-edge chisel. Control the blade with finger and thumb, steadying your hand against the work while you apply pressure to the tip of the handle with the other hand.

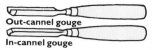

Out-cannel gouge

In-cannel gouge

Gouges

An in-cannel gouge is one whose cutting edge is formed by grinding the inside of the curved blade. It is used for trimming rounded shoulders. An out-cannel gouge is ground on the outside so that the blade will not be driven into the wood when it is scooping out shallow depressions.

STORING CHISELS

Make a wall-mounted rack for chisels and gouges by gluing two strips of plywood to leave slots for the blades. Screw the rack to the wall behind your workbench so that the chisels are in easy reach.

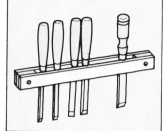

RASPS AND SURFORMS

Rasps are coarse files for shaping free curves in wood. Traditional ones have teeth formed in the solid metal to wear away the wood; modern Surform files have hollow blades pressed out to form a great many cutting edges. Surform files stay sharp for a long time, remove wood very quickly and do not get clogged up like rasps because the shavings fall through their hollow blades.

Cabinet rasp

Flat rasp

Round rasp

Rasps

Rasps are made in degrees of coarseness, designated as bastard, second-cut and smooth. Their names refer to their shapes: A cabinet rasp is half-round, with one flat and one curved face; a flat rasp has two flat faces and one cutting edge; a round rasp is circular in section, tapering towards the tip.

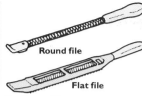

Round file

Flat file

Surform files

A round Surform file has a detachable handle and thumb-grip at the tip. A flat Surform has a disposable blade that fits into a hollow metal frame.

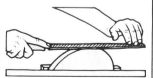

Using a rasp

A rasp cuts only on the forward stroke. Control its tip with your fingertips as you work, and never use one without first fitting a handle. Holding the bare pointed tang is very dangerous.

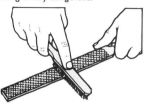

Cleaning a rasp

When a rasp gets clogged up with wood fibers, clear them with a file card—a fine wire brush made for the purpose.

SANDERS AND ABRASIVES

Abrasive papers are used for smoothing wood after it has been shaped with rasps or Surform files. Always sand in the direction of the grain. Tiny scratches made by cross-grain sanding may not appear until the work has been clear-varnished or polished. Though flat surfaces are often sanded smooth, you can get a better finish with a cabinet scraper.

Sanding by hand

Abrasive papers—sometimes called sandpapers—are graded by size and the spacing of the grit. There are coarse, medium and fine grits, but they are also designated by number—the higher the number, the finer the grit. Particles are spaced apart on open-coat papers to reduce clogging. Tightly packed close-coat papers produce a finer finish.

TYPES OF ABRASIVES

Flint or flint-coat paper is cheap and relatively soft. Use it for the first stages of sanding, especially on softwoods.

Garnet paper is reddish, comes in very fine grades and, being harder than flint-coat, wears more slowly. Use it on hardwoods.

Silicon-carbide paper, usually called wet-and-dry, is used mainly for smoothing paintwork, but it can be used dry for an extra-smooth finish on hardwoods.

Using abrasive papers

Tear a sheet of the paper into manageable strips over the edge of a bench. To smooth flat surfaces or square edges, wrap a strip around a sanding block (1); on curves, use your fingertips to apply the paper. To sand moldings, use a dowel (2) or a shaped block wrapped in the abrasive paper.

Use progressively finer grades of paper as you work. Before the final sanding, dampen the wood with water to raise the grain. When it dries, sand it with a very fine abrasive for a perfect finish.

To sand end grain, first rub the grain with your fingers. When rubbing in one direction feels less rough than in others, sand the grain in that direction only, not to and fro.

When the grit becomes clogged with wood dust, tap the paper against the bench to clear it, or use a file card.

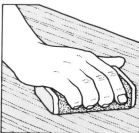

1 Sanding a flat surface

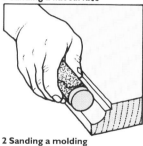

2 Sanding a molding

SHARPENING CHISELS AND GOUGES

Sharpen a chisel as you would a plane blade, but hone it across the whole surface of the oilstone in a figure 8 pattern to avoid uneven wear of the stone.

Honing an out-cannel gouge
Stand to the side of the oilstone and rub the bevel of the gouge from end to end of the stone in a figure 8 pattern (1) while you rock the blade to hone the edge evenly. Remove the burr from the inside with a slipstone (2)—a small oilstone shaped to fit different gouge sizes.

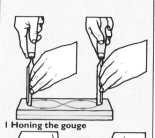

1 Honing the gouge

2 Removing the burr

Honing an in-cannel gouge
Hone the bevel on the inside of an in-cannel gouge with a slipstone (1), then remove the burr by holding the back of the blade flat on an oilstone and rocking it from side to side while you slide it up and down the stone (2).

1 Sharpening the edge

2 Removing the burr

● **Essential tools**
Combination oilstone
Slipstone
Sanding block
Range of abrasives
Choose a Surform in preference to a solid rasp, but buy as required.

POWER SANDERS

Sanding machines remove wood quickly and reduce the tedium of sanding large flat surfaces. But no power sander produces a surface good enough for a clear wood finish. Always complete the work by hand.

Belt sander

A belt sander has a continuous loop of abrasive paper passing around a drum at each end. The flat plate between the revolving drums presses the moving abrasive against the wood.

Using a belt sander

Switch on the machine and lower it gently onto the work, then make forward and backward passes with it, holding it parallel to the grain. The machine's weight is enough pressure to do the work, especially when the abrasive band is fresh. Cover the surface in overlapping bands, but don't let the sander ride over the edges or it will round them off. Lift the sander from the surface before you switch it off and do not put it aside before the belt comes to a stop.

Change to a finer-grade belt and remove the marks of the previous sanding. Always follow the manufacturer's instructions when fitting a belt.

Finishing sander

The finishing sander produces a surface that needs only a light further hand finishing. On the machine, a strip of abrasive paper is stretched across a flat rubber pad, which is moved by the motor in a a tight, rapid orbital pattern. Use only light pressure or the paper will leave tiny swirling marks on the wood.

- **Essential tools**
Flat cabinet scraper

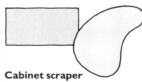

Rubber disc sander

Disc sander

Disc sanding is not suitable for fine woodwork. It inevitably leaves swirling scratches that have to be removed with a finishing sander or cabinet scraper before a clear finish can be applied. The sander removes old paint very successfully and is handy for cleaning up old floorboards that are inaccessible to a large floor-sanding machine.

The simplest disc sander has a flexible rubber pad with a central shaft that is gripped in the chuck of an electric drill. An abrasive-paper disc is bolted to the face of the pad.

Metal disc sander

A superior type has a rigid metal plate on a ball-and-socket joint that lets the disc stay flat on the work while in use.

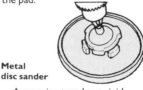

Using a rubber disc sander

With the drill running, flex the edge of the rubber disc against the wood. Keep the sander moving along the work to avoid deep scratching.

Foam drum sander

This is a flexible plastic-foam drum covered by an abrasive-paper band and attached to a power drill by a central shaft. The foam drum will deform against irregularly curved workpieces.

The abrasive bands are easy to take off and replace.

WOODSCRAPERS

Scrapers give wood the smoothest finish. They take off fine shavings, whereas abrasive paper always leaves minute scratches.

Cabinet scraper

This is a simple rectangle of thin steel used for scraping flat surfaces. Curved-edge versions are used for working moldings and carved wood.

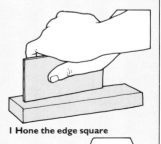

Using a cabinet scraper

Hold the scraper in both hands, pressing it into a slight forward curve with your thumbs, tip it away from you and scrape diagonally across the wood in two directions to keep the surface flat. Finally, scrape lightly in the direction of the grain.

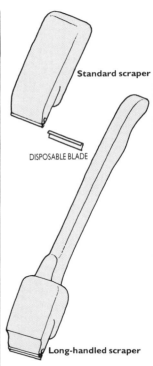

Standard scraper

DISPOSABLE BLADE

Long-handled scraper

Hook scraper

A hook scraper's disposable blade slides into a clip at the end of a wooden handle. Use the scraper by pulling it towards you along the grain of the wood, applying light pressure.

SHARPENING A CABINET SCRAPER

The scraper is sharpened by raising a butt along its edge and turning it over. Both types of scrapers are sharpened in the same way, though it is harder to turn an even burr along a curved edge. Draw-file the edge of the scraper and hone it perfectly square on an oilstone (1). Raise the burr with the curved back of a gouge. Lay the scraper flat on the bench, aligned with one edge, and stroke the edge of the scraper firmly several times with the gouge, holding its blade flat on the scraper (2). This stretches the metal along the edge of the scraper and forms the burr.

Turn the burr to project from the face of the scraper by holding the scraper upright against the bench and stroking the burred corner with the gouge held at an angle to the face (3).

1 Hone the edge square

2 Raise the burr

3 Turn the burr over

DRILLS AND BRACES

The versatile electric drill is the only essential power tool for a tool kit. However, it has not yet completely replaced the brace and the hand drill. These are still very useful, especially in places where it is inconvenient or impossible to run an extension lead for a power drill.

Brace
Use a brace for drilling the larger diameter holes. The bit is driven into the wood by the turning force on the handle plus pressure on the head of the tool.

A good brace will have a ratchet for turning the bit in only one direction when working in confined spaces where a full turn of the handle isn't possible.

I Tightening the chuck

Brace bits
Brace bits have square-section tangs that fit into the jaws of the tool's chuck. To fit a bit, grip the chuck in one hand and turn the handle clockwise to open the jaws. Drop the bit into the chuck and tighten it on the bit by turning the handle in the counterclockwise direction (I).

Auger bit
An auger bit has helical twists along its shank which removes the waste as the bit bores into the wood. The twisted shank, being the same diameter as the cutting tip, keeps the bit straight when you bore deep holes. A tapered lead screw helps to draw the bit into the work and knife-edge spurs cut the perimeter of the hole before the bit enters the wood.

Expansive bit
This bit has an adjustable spurred cutter for making holes of up to 3 inches in diameter.

Center bit
A center bit is fast-cutting because it has no helical twists to create friction, but it tends to wander off line. It's best for drilling man-made boards in which the holes are never very deep. Its relatively short shank makes it useful for working in confined spaces.

Using a brace
When you use a brace, don't let the bit burst through and split the wood. As soon as the lead screw emerges, turn the work over and complete the hole from the other side.

Hand drill
For small-diameter holes use a hand drill, also called a wheelbrace. Some have cast bodies enclosing their drive mechanisms to keep gear wheels and pinions dust-free.

Using a hand drill
Center the drill bit on the work. This is easier if the center for the hole has been marked with a bradawl puncture. Give the bit a start by moving the handle to and fro until the bit bites into the wood, then crank the handle to drive the bit.

Twist drills
Use standard twist drills with a hand drill. Fit a drill bit by turning the chuck counterclockwise, inserting the drill bit, then turning the chuck clockwise to tighten it. Check that a very thin bit is centered accurately between the chuck's three jaws.

SHARPENING TWIST DRILLS

You can sharpen a blunt drill on a bench grinder but it takes practice to center the point. An electric sharpener centers the point automatically. Drop the drill tip-down into the appropriate hole in the top of the machine and switch on for a few seconds to grind one cutting edge. Rotate the drill one-half turn to position the other edge and repeat the process.

SHARPENING BRACE BITS

Brace bits are sharpened with fine needle files. Put an edge on a spur by stroking its inside face with a flat file (I), then support the point of the bit on a bench and sharpen the cutting edge with a triangular file (2).

I Sharpening the spur

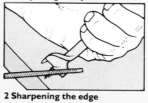

2 Sharpening the edge

Power drill
Buy a well-made drill that can cope with all the tasks you may have to tackle now and later. Choose one with a powerful motor especially if you plan to use it with power-tool attachments. Continuously using sanding attachments for a long time will burn out an underpowered drill. Most drills now have plastic bodies that are lighter than metal ones and will protect you from electric shock. A few drills are battery-powered and have plug-in rechargers.

SELECTING USEFUL FEATURES

Before you choose an electric drill, jot down the features that would be of most use to you and list them in order of priority, in case you can't find a tool that has them all.

● Drill speed
A power drill with one fixed speed is too limiting for general use. Some drills have from two to four fixed speeds and a switch for selecting the one appropriate to a

---

given job. A slow speed uses the drill's power to produce more torque (turning force) for drilling such materials as masonry and metal; a high speed gives a clean cut when drilling wood.

Run power-tool attachments at the speeds recommended by the manufacturer.

A variable-speed drill can be operated at any speed throughout its range by varying pressure on the trigger or setting a control dial. This lets you select the ideal speeds for drilling various materials, and is essential also if you want to use a screwdriver bit in a power drill.

● Trigger lock
A trigger lock button sets the drill for continuous running when it is used to drive attachments.

● Chuck size
Chuck size refers to the maximum diameter of drill shank or attachment spindle the chuck can accommodate. A ⅜-inch chuck is adequate for most purposes, though there are drills with a chuck size of ½ inch. You can drill holes of greater diameter than the chuck size by using special drilling bits with shanks attached to oversize cutters.

● Percussion or hammer action
By operating a lever you can convert some drills from smooth rotation to a hammer action that delivers several hundred blows per second to the revolving chuck. This is required only for drilling masonry, when the hammer vibration breaks up hard particles ahead of the special toughened bit before the debris is cleared by the helical flutes on the bit.

● Reverse rotation
If you want to use a screwdriver bit with your electric drill, make sure that its rotation can be reversed so that you can take screws out as well as insert them.

● Handgrips
Most power drills have a pistol-grip handle and a second handgrip for steadying the drill. Some manufacturers provide a handle that bolts onto the rear of the drill so that it can be controlled with both hands when pressure is needed directly behind the chuck.

● **Essential tools**
Brace
Set of auger bits
Hand drill
Set of drill bits
Power drill

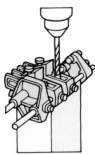

Doweling jig
A doweling jig clamped to the work ensures alignment of the holes and keeps the drill bit perpendicular to the work.

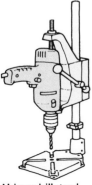

Using a drill stand
To bore holes absolutely square to the face of the work, mount your electric drill in a vertical drill stand.

● **Essential tools**
Set of spade or power-bore bits
Countersink bit
Claw hammer
Cross-peen hammer
Pin hammer
Carpenter's mallet
Nail set

POWER DRILL BITS

A variety of bits can be used in a power drill, depending on the kind of hole you want to bore.

Twist drill
You can use standard twist drill bits of any size to the maximum opening of the chuck. To bore larger holes, use reduced-shank drill bits.

Power-bore bit

Spade bit

Power-bore and spade bits
With a power-bore bit or a spade bit you can drill holes of up to 1½ inches in diameter. Either bit produces minimal friction. Place the sharp lead point of the bit on the center of the hole before pressing the trigger of the drill.

Countersink bit
To sink the head of a woodscrew flush with the surface of the work, make a tapered recess in the top of the clearance hole with a 'rose' or countersink bit. These bits can be used in hand drills and braces, but a high-speed electric drill forms a neater recess.

Except with a vertical drill stand, the countersink bit chatters if the hole has already been drilled, producing a rough recess. When you have to use the drill freehand, it's best to make the recess first, then drill the hole itself.

Screwdriver bit
With slotted-head or cross-head screwdriver bits you can use your electric drill as a power screwdriver. The drill must be capable of slow speeds.

Plug cutter
This special bit cuts cylindrical plugs of wood for concealing the heads of screws sunk below the surface of the work.

Dowel bit
This is a twist drill with a sharp lead point and cutting spurs that help to keep it on line when holes are bored for dowel joints.

Drill and countersink bit
This bit makes the pilot hole, clearance hole and countersink recess for a woodscrew in one operation. As it is matched to one specific screw size, it is worth purchasing only when you plan to use a fair number of identical screws.

Fitting a power drill bit
Turn the chuck counterclockwise to open its jaws and insert the bit. Close the jaws on the bit and tighten the chuck with the key supplied with the drill. Remove the key before starting.

USING A POWER DRILL SAFELY

● **Choose a drill with a plastic nonconducting body.**
● **Remove the chuck key before using the drill.**
● **Don't wear loose clothing, a necktie or a necklace while using the drill.**
● **Unplug the drill before fitting bits, accessories or attachments.**
● **Don't lift the drill by its power cord.**
● **Use a proper heavy-duty extension lead when you want to extend the drill's power cord.**
● **Always fit and use attachments according to the manufacturer's safety recommendations.**

SELECTING POWER DRILL ATTACHMENTS

Most manufacturers produce a range of attachments for turning an electric drill into a circular saw, jigsaw, sander, bench grinder—even a hedge trimmer. Most attachments fit only one make of drill, so check the quality of various attachments before you choose your drill.

HAMMERS AND MALLETS

Driving in a nail is so simple that one hammer would seem to be as effective for it as another, but having one of the right shape and weight for a given job makes for easier, trouble-free work.

Mallets have their own specific uses, and should never be used for hammering nails.

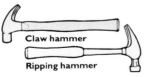

Claw hammer

Ripping hammer

Claw hammer
A claw hammer is a heavy-weight general-purpose tool, probably the most useful hammer to have in a tool kit. The split claw at the back of the head is for levering out nails, and to withstand the strain of this, the head must be fixed firmly to a strong shaft. The head has a deep square socket driven and wedged onto a tough but flexible hickory shaft. Standard weight is 16 ounces. The ripping hammer is an even heavier tool. Its tubular steel shaft won't bend or break, and the head can't work loose. The rubber grip is comfortable and shock-absorbing.

Cross-peen hammer
For those jobs too delicate for a heavy claw hammer, use a medium-weight cross-peen one. Its wedge-shaped peen is for setting (starting) a nail held between finger and thumb.

Pin hammer
A small lightweight tack hammer is perfect for tapping in fine panel pins and tacks.

Using a hammer
Set a nail in wood with one or two taps of the hammer to make it stand upright without support, then drive it home with firm steady blows, keeping your wrist straight and the hammer face square to the nail head.

Using a nail set
A nail set is a punch with a hollow-ground tip used for sinking nails below the surface of the wood. Nail sets are made in several sizes for use with large and small nails. Hold the tool upright between thumb and fingertips and place its tip on the nailhead while it still protrudes just above the surface. Tap the head of the nail set with your hammer. With a heavy hammer, very little force is needed to sink the nail.

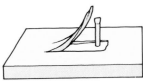

Blind nailing
To hide a nail. lift a flap of wood with a gouge, sink the nail with a nail set, then glue the flap and clamp it flat.

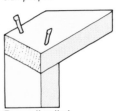

Dovetail-nailed

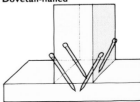

Toenailed

Making a strong nailed joint
The grip between the nails and the wood is usually enough to hold the joint together, but for stronger fixings, drive the nails in at an angle. When angled nails fix wood onto the end grain of another member, the technique is called dovetail-nailing. When they pass through the side of a section it's called toenailing.

Hammering small nails
◀ *If the nail is very small, set it with the hammer peen or push it through a piece of thin cardboard to steady it. Just before you tap the nail flush with the wood, tear the cardboard away.*

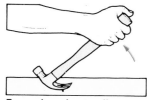

Removing a bent nail
If you bend a nail while driving it in with a claw hammer, you can lever it out by sliding the claw under the nailhead and pulling back on the end of the shaft. The curved head will roll on the wood without doing too much damage, but you can protect the work by placing a piece of thick cardboard or hardboard under the hammer head. A thick packing of this kind will give you extra leverage in removing a long nail.

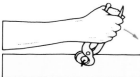

If a nailhead is too small to catch in a claw hammer, lever it out with carpenter's pliers. Grip the nail with the jaws resting on the wood, squeeze the handles together and roll the pliers away from you. Here again, cardboard or hardboard packing will protect the wood.

Sanding a hammer head
You're more likely to bend nails if your hammer head gets greasy and slippery. Rub the face on fine abrasive paper for a better grip.

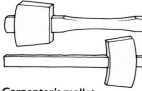

Carpenter's mallet
A carpenter's mallet is for driving a chisel or gouge into wood. Its striking faces are angled so as to deliver square blows to the end of the chisel. A loose mallet head is tightened by tapping the top of the tapered shaft on a bench.

Soft-faced mallet
Though you can use a hardwood carpenter's mallet to knock joints together or apart, a soft-faced one of rubber, plastic or leather is less likely to mar the surface of the wood.

SCREWDRIVERS
You need a number of screwdrivers of various sizes, both flat-tipped and Phillips-head-tipped, because it's important to match the size of the driver to the screw. If the tip is a little too big or too small, it can slip out of the slot while you work, damaging the screw or the surrounding woodwork, or both.

For the best grip, choose screwdrivers that have large, smooth handles.

Pump-action screwdriver
The tip of a pump-action screwdriver is turned by a thrusting action on the handle. The spring-loaded shaft moves in and out of a hollow handle containing a ratchet mechanism that controls the direction of rotation. Interchangeable Phillips-head and flat-tipped bits fit into a chuck on the end of the shaft.

Cabinet screwdriver
A cabinet screwdriver has a shaft ground on two sides to produce a flat, square tip. It may have a hardwood handle, strengthened with a metal ferrule, or a plastic one molded onto the shaft.

Phillips-head screwdriver
Always use a matching Phillips-head screwdriver to drive screws with cruciform slots. Using a flat-tip one instead invariably damages the screw.

Ratchet screwdriver
By using a ratchet screwdriver you can insert and remove screws without having to replace the tip in the slot after each turn or shifting your grip on the handle. You can select clockwise or counterclockwise rotation or lock the ratchet and use the tool like an ordinary fixed screwdriver.

HONING A FLAT TIP
If the tip of a screwdriver gets rounded through wear, it will no longer grip screws as it should. Reshape it by honing on an oilstone, then filing the end to a good, square shape.

Inserting a woodscrew
You may split wood if you drive in a screw without making a hole first. To make a starter hole for a small screw place the flat tip of a bradawl (1) across the grain of the wood and press it in and twist it. To guide a large screw, drill a pilot hole followed by a clearance hole for the shank (2). For the pilot hole, use a drill bit slightly narrower than the screw's thread, but drill the hole fractionally larger than the screw's shank.

Use a countersink bit to make recesses for the screw heads.

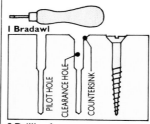

I Bradawl

PILOT HOLE | CLEARANCE HOLE | COUNTERSINK

2 Drilling for screws

Lubricating a screw
If a screw is too tight to fit in its clearance hole, withdraw it slightly and put a little grease on its shank.

Getting old screws out
Don't try to extract an old painted-over screw until you have cleared the slot. Scrape the paint out with the end of a hacksaw blade or by tapping the tip of a screwdriver through the slot with a hammer. For the best results, place a corner of the screwdriver tip in the slot (1) and tap it sideways into the slot until it is gripped snugly, then extract the screw.

Where a screw's slot has been completely stripped, remove the head by drilling it out. Mark the middle of the head with a center punch, then use progressively larger drill bits to remove the metal in stages.

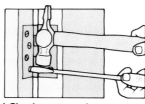

I Clearing a screw slot

CLAMPS
Clamps are for holding glued joints together while the glue sets, for assembling structures temporarily to see if they work or fit, and for holding small workpieces on a bench while they are worked on.

Bar clamp
A bar clamp is a long metal bar with a screw-adjustable jaw at one end and another jaw, the tail slide, that can be fixed at convenient points along the bar by a metal peg inserted in any of a series of holes. Bar clamps are for clamping large glued frames, and it's worth having a couple of medium-size ones in your tool kit. Rent additional ones as you need them.

Clamp heads
If you need a very long bar clamp, rent a pair of clamp heads. Use a 1 × 3-inch rail as a bar, locating the heads on it by plugging their pegs into holes drilled through it.

C-clamp
A C-clamp has a screw that grips the work between a shoe attached to its end and the cast metal frame. You will need at least one 6-inch and one 12-inch C-clamp.

Frame and miter clamps
The four plastic corner blocks of a simple frame clamp contain the glued corners of a mitered frame, while a cord pulled taut around the blocks applies equal pressure to all four joints, holding the frame square while the glue sets.

A cast metal miter clamp holds one joint at a time, holding the two mitered members against a right-angled fence.

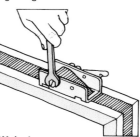

Web clamp
A web clamp acts like a frame clamp, forming a tourniquet clamp for large frames. Its nylon webbing is tensioned by adjusting a ratchet mechanism with a wrench or screwdriver.

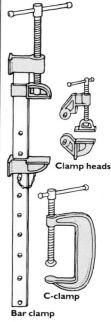

Clamp heads

C-clamp

Bar clamp

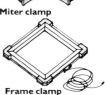

Miter clamp

Frame clamp

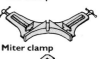

● **Essential tools**
Cabinet screwdriver
Phillips-head
screwdriver
Bradawl

473

Clamping a jointed frame

Prepare and adjust your bar clamps before you glue and assemble a jointed frame. If you waste time with them after the joints are glued, the adhesive may begin stiffening before you can close the joints properly. Set the tail slides to accommodate the frame and make sure that the adjustable jaws will have enough movement to tighten the joints. Use wood scraps to protect the work from the metal jaws. Place the clamps in line with the joints, then apply the pressure gradually, first with one clamp, then the other, until the joints are tightly closed (**1**).

Check that the frame is square by measuring both diagonals. If they are not equal, set the clamps at a slight angle to the frame so as to pull it square by squeezing the long diagonal (**2**).

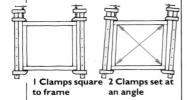

**1 Clamps square   2 Clamps set at
to frame   an angle**

Clamping boards together

To clamp several glued boards together edge to edge, use at least three bar clamps, one on top of the assembly (**1**) to prevent the boards from bowing under pressure from the other two. A long bar clamp will bend as it is tightened, so protect the wood with hardboard scraps between the bars and the work.

Lay a straightedge across the clamped boards to check that the panel is flat, and correct any distortion by adjusting the pressure of the clamps. To tap a misaligned board back into place, put a scrap across the joint and strike it firmly with a heavy hammer.

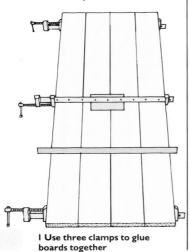

**1 Use three clamps to glue
boards together**

BENCHES AND VISES

A woodworking bench must be strong and rigid. Heavy timbers and man-made boards put a considerable strain on a bench, and the stress imposed by sawing and hammering will eventually weaken a poorly constructed one.

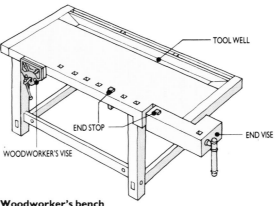

TOOL WELL

END STOP

WOODWORKER'S VISE

END VISE

Woodworker's bench

The hardwood underframe of a traditional woodworker's bench is constructed with large double-wedged mortise-and-tenon joints. The longer rails are usually bolted to the rigid endframes so that the bench can be dismantled for removal. The thick worktop is normally of short-grain beech. A storage recess, or tool well, keeps the worktop free of tools for laying large boards across it. Better-quality benches have a vise built onto one end of the top for clamping long timber sections between metal pegs called bench stops or "dogs."

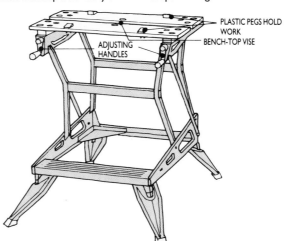

ADJUSTING
HANDLES

PLASTIC PEGS HOLD
WORK
BENCH-TOP VISE

Workmate bench

A Workmate is a portable bench that can be folded away between jobs. The two halves of the thick plywood worktop are, in effect, vise jaws operated by adjusting handles at the ends of the bench.

As the handles work independently, the jaws can hold tapered workpieces. Plastic pegs fit into holes in the worktop and hold work laid flat on it; they can be arranged to hold very irregular shapes.

Clamp-on vise ▶

This lightweight vise can be clamped temporarily to the edge of any worktop. Though not so rigidly fixed as a proper woodworker's vise, it is a lot cheaper to buy.

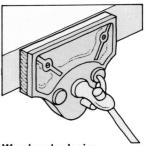

Woodworker's vise

A feature of most benches is a large woodworker's vise, screwed to the underside of the worktop, close to one leg, so that the top will not flex when you work on wood held in it. Wooden linings (pads) must be fixed inside the jaws to protect the work from the metal edges. A quick-release lever on the front of the vise lets you open and shut the jaws quickly, turning the handle only for final adjustments.

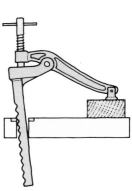

Holdfast

A holdfast is a bench-mounted clamp for holding a workpiece firmly against the worktop. The notched shaft of the tool is slipped into a metal collar which is let into the bench. When pressure is applied with the bar, the shaft rocks over to lock in the collar so that the shoe at the end of the pivoting arm bears down on the workpiece. One holdfast at each end of a bench is ideal for clamping long boards.

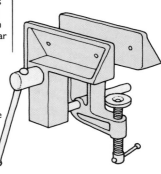

BASIC WOODWORKING JOINTS

Craftsmen have invented many ingenious ways of joining pieces of timber, some as decorative as they are practical, but general home maintenance and joinery require only a few basic woodworking joints.

BUTT JOINTS

When you cut a piece of wood square and simply butt it against its neighbor, you need some kind of mechanical attachment to hold the joint together. The end grain of wood doesn't glue well enough for glue alone to be used.

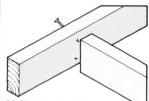

Nailed butt joints
When you nail a butt joint, drive the nails in at an angle to clamp the two pieces together.

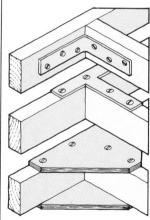

Brackets and plates
Screwed-on right-angle and T-shape metal brackets make strong, though not very neat-looking, butt joints. You can give similar reinforcement to a joint with a plywood plate nailed or screwed across it.

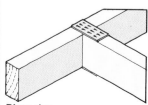

Plate ties
The sharp-pointed teeth of metal plate ties hammered onto a butt joint will grip the wood like a bed of nails.

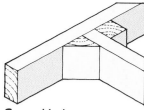

Corner blocks
Nail and glue, or screw, a square- or triangular-section block of wood into the angle between the two components.

LAP JOINTS

A lap joint can be simply one square-cut board laid across another and fixed with nails or screws, but the components of a true lap joint are cut to lie flush with each other.

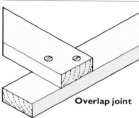

Overlap joint

Making an overlap joint
Clamp the components accutately together with a C-clamp and drill pilot holes for the screws through the top one and into the other. Make clearance holes of the necessary depth with a larger drill, and countersink if needed. Remove the clamp, apply glue, and screw the two components together.

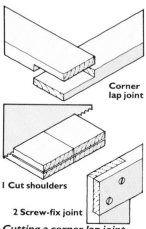

Corner lap joint

1 Cut shoulders

2 Screw-fix joint

Cutting a corner lap joint
To join two pieces of wood at a right-angled corner, cut identical tongues in their ends. Make each tongue as for a lap joint, but clamp the components together, side by side, and cut their shoulders simultaneously (**1**). Glue the joint and reinforce it with screws or with glued dowels (**2**).

Cutting a lap joint
Lay the crossrail on the side rail (**1**) and mark the width of the housing on it with a marking knife, extending the lines halfway down each edge of the rail. With a marking gauge set to exactly half the thickness of the rails, score the centerlines on both rails (**2**). Mark the shoulder of the tongue on the crossrail (**3**), allowing for a tongue slightly longer than the width of the side rail. Hold the crossrail at an angle in a vise (**4**) and saw down to the shoulder on one edge, keeping to the waste side of the line, then turn the rail around and saw down to the shoulder on the opposite edge. Finally, saw down square to the shoulder line (**5**). Remove the waste by sawing across the shoulder line (**6**).

To cut the dado in the side rail, saw down both shoulder lines to the halfway mark, then make several more saw cuts across the waste (**7**). With a chisel, pare out the waste down to the marked lines (**8**), working from both sides of the rail. Glue and assemble the joint, and when the glue is set, plane the end of the slightly overlong tongue flush with the side rail.

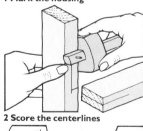

CROSSRAIL

SIDE RAIL

1 Mark the housing

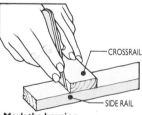

2 Score the centerlines

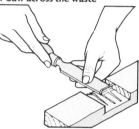

3 Mark the shoulder

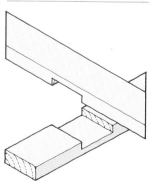

4 Saw with the rail at an angle

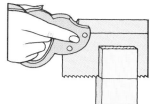

5 Saw square to the shoulder

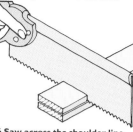

6 Saw across the shoulder line

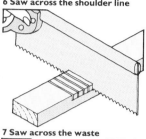

7 Saw across the waste

8 Remove the waste

HALVING JOINT

When one rail must cross another, cut equal dados to make a halving joint.

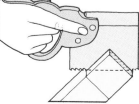

Cutting a halving joint
Cut it as described for a lap joint, but clamp the components together side by side and saw both sets of shoulders at the same time. Then separate them and remove the waste with a chisel.

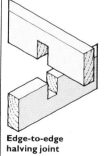

Edge-to-edge halving joint

RABBETED JOINT

A rabbeted joint is for joining two wide boards at a corner.

Rabbeted joint

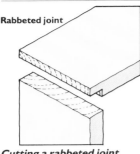

Cutting a rabbeted joint

Cut the square-ended board first and use it to mark out the width of the rabbet on the other (**1**). Set a marking gauge to about half of the board's thickness and mark out the tongue (**2**). Cut out the rabbet with a tenon saw, then glue and dovetail-nail the joint.

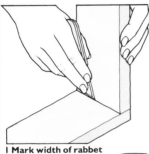

1 Mark width of rabbet

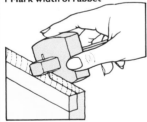

2 Mark out the tongue

BRIDLE JOINT

A bridle joint is used for making a strong joint in a frame.

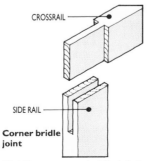

CROSSRAIL

SIDE RAIL

Corner bridle joint

Cutting a corner bridle joint

To make a corner bridle joint, cut equal-size tongues, two on the side rail and one center on the crossrail. Mark the tongues out with a mortise gauge, making them slightly longer than the width of the rails. Cut the waste away from both sides of the crossrail tongue with a tenon saw, as for a lap joint. To form the side rail tongues, saw down to the shoulder on both sides, keeping to the waste side of the two marked lines (**1**), then chop out the waste with a narrow wood chisel or mortise chisel. Glue and assemble the joint and, when the glue has set, plane the ends of the overlong tongues flush with the rails.

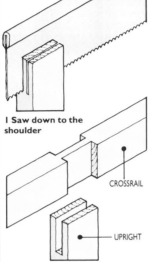

1 Saw down to the shoulder

CROSSRAIL

UPRIGHT

Through bridle joint

When a crossrail must join an upright rail to form a T, cut two tongues on the upright, as for a corner bridle joint, and a dado on each side of the crossrail, as for a lap joint. The depth of the dado must, of course, equal the thickness of the tongues.

DADO JOINTS

Dado joints are often used in shelving and similar constructions. A through dado can be seen from both sides of the structure while a stopped dado is not visible from the front.

Through dado   **Stopped dado**

Cutting a through-dado

Square the end of one board and use it to mark out the width of the dado on the other (**1**). Then with a marking gauge set at about a third of the board's thickness mark the depth of the dado on both edges (**2**). Saw along both sides of the dado (**3**), keeping just on the waste side of the two lines, then chisel out the waste, working from both edges of the board (**4**). A router is the ideal tool for leveling the bottom of the dado; failing this, pare it flat with the chisel.

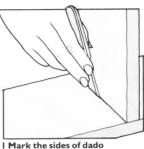

1 Mark the sides of dado

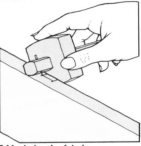

2 Mark depth of dado

3 Saw on each side

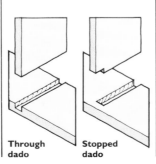

4 Chisel out waste

Cutting a stopped dado

Mark out the housing as described before but stop about ¼ inch short of the front edge. To give the saw clearance, cut about 1½ inches of the housing at the stopped end, first with a drill and then with a chisel (**1**). Saw down both sides of the housing and pare out the waste to leave a level bottom. In the front corner of the other board cut a notch (**2**) to fit the stopped dado so that the two edges lie flush when assembled.

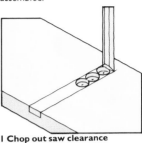

1 Chop out saw clearance

2 Cut a notch

DOWEL JOINTS

Dowel joints are strong and versatile. They can secure butt-joined rails, mitered frames and long boards butted edge to edge. Use wooden dowels about one-third the thickness of the wood to be dowel-joined.

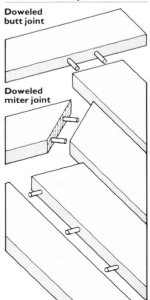

Doweled butt joint

Doweled miter joint

Doweled edge-to-edge joint

Cutting a dowel joint

Cut the dowels to a length equaling about two-thirds the width of the rails, but when joining boards edge to edge cut them about 1½ inches long. File chamfers on both ends of each dowel and saw a groove along each (**1**) to allow air and surplus glue to escape as the joint is assembled. For the smaller doweling jobs you can get ready-cut and chamfered hardwood dowels, grooved all around, in a limited range of sizes.

If you are using a doweling jig there's no need to mark the centers of the dowel holes. Otherwise, set a marking gauge to the centerline on both rails (**2**), drive panel pins into the edge of the side rail to mark dowel hole centers, then cut them to short sharp points with pliers (**3**). Line up the rails and push them together for the metal points to mark the end grain of the crossrail (**4**). Pull out the cut panel pins.

With the appropriate bit in a power drill, bore the holes to a depth just over half the length of the dowels, then glue and assemble the joint.

Drilling accurate dowel holes is much easier with the drill mounted in a vertical drill stand.

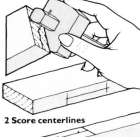
1 Saw glue escape slot

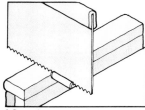
2 Score centerlines

3 Cut pins to sharp points

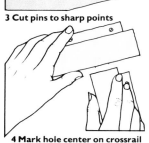
4 Mark hole center on crossrail

MORTISE-&-TENON JOINTS

Mortise-and-tenon joints make a strong joint in narrow sections of wood—an essential joint for chair and table frames. A through-tenon can be further strengthened with wedges but a stopped-tenon is neater.

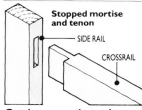
Stopped mortise and tenon
— SIDE RAIL
— CROSSRAIL

Cutting a mortise and tenon

Mark the width of the mortise, using the crossrail as a guide (**1**), and mark the shoulder of the tenon all around the crossrail (**2**) so that the tenon's length will be two-thirds of the side rail's width. Set a mortise gauge to one third of the crossrail's thickness and mark both mortise and tenon (**3**).

Cut the tenon as for the tongue of a lap joint. Remove the waste from the mortise with an electric drill—preferably mounted in a vertical stand—and square up the ends and sides with a chisel (**4**). Glue and assemble the joint.

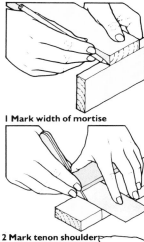
1 Mark width of mortise

2 Mark tenon shoulder

3 Mark thickness of joint

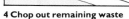
4 Chop out remaining waste

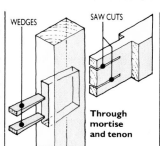
WEDGES   SAW CUTS

Through mortise and tenon

Cutting a through tenon

When a tenon is to pass right through a side rail, cut it slightly longer than the width of the rail and make two saw cuts through it. Glue and assemble the joint, then drive two glued hardwood wedges into the saw cuts to expand the tenon in the mortise. When the glue has set plane the wedges and tenon flush with the rail.

MITER JOINT

A miter joint is for joining corners of frames. Especially useful for decorative molded sections and baseboards.

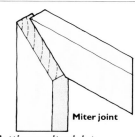
Miter joint

Cutting a miter joint

A right-angled miter joint is made by sawing the ends of two rails to 45-degree angles in a miter box and butting them together. Trim the joints with a finely set block plane and a shooting board and assemble the glued joint in a miter clamp. If the meeting faces of the rails are fairly large, glue alone will hold them together, but you can reinforce a miter joint by sawing two slots across the corner and gluing strips of veneer into them (**1**), planing the veneers flush with the rails after the glue has set.

1 Inserting veneer strips

SCARF JOINT

A scarf joint is for joining two lengths of lumber end to end.

Scarf joint

Making a scarf joint

Clamp the two lengths side by side, their ends flush, and mark out the angled cut. The span of a scarf joint should be four times the width of the board (**1**). Saw and plane both lengths down to the marked line simultaneously, then unclamp them. Glue the two angled faces together, securing them with wood strips and C-clamps while the glue sets (**2**).

A scarf joint that will be subject to a lot of stress can be reinforced with plywood plates screwed to both sides of the rails (**3**).

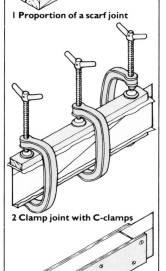
1 Proportion of a scarf joint

2 Clamp joint with C-clamps

3 A reinforced scarf joint

Using a pointing tray
A pointing tray makes the filling of mortar joints very easy. Place the flat lip of the tray just under a horizontal joint and scrape the mortar into place with a jointer. Turn the tray around and push mortar into vertical joints through the gap between the raised sides.

Continental-pattern trowels

● **Essential tools**
Brick trowel
Pointing trowel
Plasterer's trowel
Mortar board
Hawk
Level
Try square
Plumb line

BUILDER'S TOOL KIT

Bricklayers, carpenters and plasterers are all specialist builders, each requiring a set of specific tools, but the amateur is more like one of the self-employed builders who must be able to tackle several areas of building work, and so need a much wider range of tools than the specialist. The builder's tool kit suggested here is for renovating and improving the structure of a house and for erecting and restoring garden structures or paving. Electrical work, decorating and plumbing call for other sets of tools.

FLOATS AND TROWELS

For professional builders, floats and trowels have specific uses, but in home maintenance, the small towel for repointing brickwork is often found ideal for patching small areas of plaster, while the plasterer's trowel is as likely to be used for smoothing concrete.

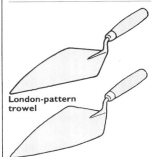

London-pattern trowel

Brick trowel

A brick trowel is for handling and placing mortar when laying bricks or concrete blocks. A professional might use one with a blade as long as 1 foot, but such a trowel is too heavy and unwieldy for the amateur, so buy a good-quality brick trowel with a fairly short blade.

The blade of a *London-pattern trowel* has one curved edge for cutting bricks, a skill that needs much practice to perfect. The blade's other edge is straight, for picking up mortar. This type of trowel is made in right- and left-handed versions, so buy the right one. A right-handed trowel has its curved edge on the right when you point it away from you.

A *Canadian-pattern trowel* is symmetrical, so it's convenient when people with different left- and right-hand preferences have to share one trowel.

Pointing trowel

The blade of a pointing trowel is no more than 3 to 4 inches long, designed for repairing or shaping mortar joints between bricks.

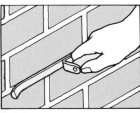

Pointer

A pointer is shaped for making 'V' or concave joints between bricks. The narrow blade is dragged along the mortar joint and the curved front end is used to shape the verticals.

Frenchman

A Frenchman is a specialized tool for cutting excess mortar away from brickwork jointing. You can make one by heating and bending an old table knife.

Wooden float

A wooden float is for applying and smoothing stucco and concrete to a fine, attractive texture. The more expensive ones have detachable handles so that their wooden blades can be replaced when they wear. But the amateur is unlikely to use a float often enough to justify the cost of buying one.

Plasterer's trowel

A plasterer's trowel is a steel float for applying plaster and stucco to walls. It is also dampened and used for "polishing," stroking the surface of the material when it has firmed up. Some builders prefer to apply stucco with a heavy trowel and finish it with a more flexible blade, but one has to be quite skilled to exploit such subtle differences.

BOARDS FOR CARRYING MORTAR OR PLASTER

Any convenient-sized sheet of ½- or ¾-inch exterior-grade plywood can be used as a mixing board for plaster or mortar. A panel about 3 feet square is ideal, and a smaller spotboard, about 2 feet square, is convenient for carrying the material to the actual work site. In either case, screw some wood strips to the undersides of the boards to make them easier to lift and carry. Make a small, lightweight hawk to carry pointing mortar or plaster by nailing a single strip underneath a plywood board so that you can plug a handle into it.

A homemade hawk

LEVELING AND MEASURING TOOLS

You can make several specialized tools for measuring and leveling, but don't skimp on essentials like a good level and a strong tape measure.

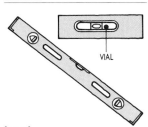

VIAL

Level

A level is a machine-made straightedge incorporating special glass tubes or vials that contain a liquid. In each vial an air bubble floats. When a bubble rests exactly between two lines marked on the glass, the structure on which the level is held is known to be exactly horizontal or vertical, depending on the vial's orientation. Buy a wooden or lightweight aluminum level 2 to 3 feet long. A well-made one is very strong, but treat it with care and always clean mortar or plaster from it before the material sets.

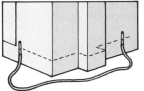

Water level

You can make a water level from a garden hose with short lengths of transparent plastic tube plugged into its ends. Fill the hose with water until it appears in both tubes. As water level is constant, the levels in the tubes are always identical and so can be used for marking identical heights even over long distances and around obstacles and bends.

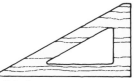

Builder's square

A large set square is useful when you set out brick or concrete-block corners. The best ones are stamped out of sheet metal, but you can make a serviceable one by cutting out a thick plywood right-angled triangle with a hypotenuse of about 2 feet 6 inches. Cut out the center of the triangle to reduce the weight.

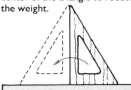

Checking a square
Accuracy is important, so check the square by placing it against a straight strip of wood on the floor, drawing a line against the square to make a right angle with the strip, then turning the square to see if it forms the same angle from the other side.

Try square

Use a try square for marking out square cuts or joints on timber.

Making a plumb line
Any small but heavy weight hung on a length of line or string will make a suitable plumb line for judging the verticality of structures or surfaces.

Bricklayer's line
Use a bricklayer's line as a guide for laying bricks or blocks level. It is a length of nylon string stretched between two flat-bladed pins that are driven into vertical joints at the ends of a wall. There are also special line blocks that hook over the bricks at the ends of a course. As an improvisation, you can stretch a string between two stakes driven into the ground outside the line of the wall.

Steel pins and line
Buy the special pins or make your own by hammering flats on 4-inch nails.

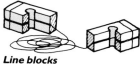

Line blocks
Blocks grip the brickwork corners; the line passes through their slots.

Plasterer's rule
A plasterer's rule is simply a straight wooden strip used for scraping plaster and rendering undercoats level.

Straightedge
Any length of straight, fairly stout lumber can be used to tell whether a surface is flat or, used with a level, to test whether two points are at the same height.

Gauge stick
For gauging the height of brick courses, calibrate a wooden strip by making saw cuts across it at 3-inch intervals—the thickness of a brick plus its mortar joint.

Tape measure
An ordinary retractable steel tape measure is adequate for most purposes, but if you need to mark out or measure a large plot, rent a wind-up tape up to 100 feet in length.

Marking gauge
This tool has a sharp steel point for scoring a line on lumber parallel to its edge. Its adjustable stock acts as a fence and keeps the point a constant distance from the edge.

HAMMERS
Very few hammers are needed on a building site.

Claw hammer
Choose a strong claw hammer for building wooden stud partitions, nailing floorboards, making door and window frames and putting up fencing.

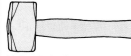

Light sledgehammer
A light sledgehammer is used for driving cold chisels and for various demolition jobs. It is also useful for driving large masonry nails into walls.

Sledgehammer
Rent a big sledgehammer if you have to break up concrete or paving. It's also the best tool for driving stakes or fence posts into the ground, though you can make do with a light sledge if the ground is not too hard.

Mallet
A carpenter's wooden mallet is the proper tool for driving wood chisels, but you can use a hammer if the chisels have impact-resistant plastic handles.

SAWS
Every builder needs a range of handsaws, but consider renting a power saw when you have to cut a lot of heavy structural timbers, and especially if you plan to rip floorboards down to width, a very tiring job when done by hand.

There are special power saws for cutting metal, and even for sawing through masonry.

Panel saw
All kinds of man-made building boards are used in house construction, so buy a good panel saw—useful also for cutting large structural timbers to the required lengths.

Tenon saw
A tenon saw accurately cuts wall studs, floorboards, panelling and joints. The metal stiffening along the top of the blade keeps it rigid and less likely to wander off line.

Padsaw
Also called a keyhole saw, this small saw has a narrow tapered blade for cutting holes in wood.

Coping saw
A coping saw has a frame that holds a fairly coarse but very narrow blade under tension for cutting curves in wood.

Floorboard saw
If you pry a floorboard above its neighbors you can cut across it with an ordinary tenon saw. But a floorboard saw's curved cutting edge makes it easier to avoid damaging the boards on either side.

Hacksaw
The hardened-steel blades of a hacksaw have fine teeth for cutting metal. Use one to cut steel concrete-reinforcing rods or small pieces of sheet metal.

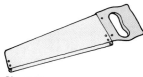

Sheet saw
A hacksaw's frame prevents its use for cutting large sheets of metal. For that job, bolt a hacksaw blade to the edge of the flat blade of a sheet saw, which will also cut corrugated plastic sheeting and roofing slates.

Universal saw
A universal or general-purpose saw is designed to cut wood, metal, plastics and building boards. Its short frameless blade has a low-friction coating and is stiff enough to make straight cuts without wandering. The handle can be set at various angles. The saw is particularly useful for cutting secondhand lumber, which may contain nails or screws that would blunt an ordinary saw.

POWER SAWS
A *circular saw* will accurately rip lumber or man-made boards down to size. As well as doing away with the effort of hand-sawing large timbers, a sharp power saw produces such a clean cut that there is often no need for planing afterwards.

A *power jigsaw* cuts curves in lumber and sheet materials but is also useful for cutting holes in fixed wall panels and sawing through floorboards so as to lift them.

A *reciprocating saw* is a two-handed power saw with a long pointed blade, powerful enough to cut heavy timber sections and even through a complete stud partition, panels and all.

Masonry saw
A masonry saw looks much like a wood handsaw but its tungsten-carbide teeth cut brick, concrete blocks and stone.

DRILLS
A powerful electric drill is invaluable to a builder, but a hand brace is useful when you have to bore holes outdoors or in attics and cellars that lack convenient electric sockets.

Power drill
Buy a power drill, a range of twist drills and some spade or power-bore bits for drilling lumber. Make sure that the tool has a percussion or hammer action for drilling masonry. For masonry you need special drill bits tipped with tungsten carbide. The smaller ones are matched to the size of standard wall plugs, though there are much larger ones with reduced shanks that can be used in a standard power-drill chuck. The larger bits are expensive, so rent them when you need them. Percussion bits are even tougher than masonry bits, with shatterproof tips.

Brace and bit
A brace and bit is the ideal hand tool for drilling large holes in lumber, and when fitted with a screwdriver bit, it gives good leverage for driving or extracting large woodscrews.

Drilling masonry for wall plugs
Set the drill for low speed and hammer action, and wrap tape around the bit to mark the depth to be drilled. Allow for slightly more depth than the length of the plug, as dust will pack down into the hole when you insert it. Drill the hole in stages.

Protect floor coverings and paintwork from falling dust by taping a paper bag under the position of the hole before you start drilling.

● **Essential tools**
Straightedge
Tape measure
Claw hammer
Light sledgehammer
Panel saw
Tenon saw
Hacksaw
Padsaw
Power-drill
Masonry bits
Brace and bit

ADDITIONAL BUILDER'S TOOLS

The following tools would be a useful addition to a builder's tool kit, especially when carrying out major repairs and improvements.

Crowbar

A crowbar, or wrecking bar, is for demolishing timber framework. Force the flat tip between components and use the leverage of the long shaft to pry them apart. Choose a bar that has a claw at one end for removing large nails.

● **Essential tools**
Glass cutter
Putty knife
Cold chisel
Bricklayer's chisel
Spade
Shovel
Rake
Wheelbarrow
Cabinet screwdriver
Phillips-head screwdriver
Jack plane

480

GLAZIER'S TOOLS

Glass is such a hard and brittle material that it can be worked only with specialized tools.

Glass cutter

A glass cutter doesn't really cut glass but scores a line in it. The scoring is done by a tiny hardened-steel wheel or a chip of industrial diamond mounted in the penlike holder. The glass will break along the scored line when pressure is applied to it.

Beam compass cutter

A beam compass cutter is for scoring circles on glass—when, for example, you need a round hole in a window pane to fit a ventilator. The cutting wheel is mounted at the end of an adjustable beam that turns on a center pivot which is fixed to the glass by suction.

Spear-point glass drill

A glass drill has a flat spearhead-shaped tip of tungsten-steel shaft. The shape of the tip reduces friction that would otherwise crack the glass, but it needs lubricating with oil, paraffin or water during drilling.

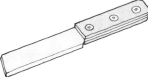

Hacking knife

A hacking knife has a heavy steel blade for chipping old putty out of window rabbets so as to remove the glass. Place its point between the putty and the frame and tap its thickened back with a hammer.

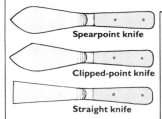

Spearpoint knife

Clipped-point knife

Straight knife

Putty knife

The blunt blade of a putty knife is for shaping and smoothing fresh putty. You can choose between spearpoint, clipped-point and straight blades according to your personal preference.

CHISELS

As well as chisels for cutting and paring wood joints, you will need some special ones for masonry work.

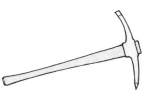

Cold chisel

Cold chisels are made from solid steel hexagonal-section rod. They are primarily for cutting metal bars and chopping the heads off rivets, but a builder will use one for cutting a chase in plaster and brickwork or chopping out old brick pointing.

Slip a plastic safety sleeve over the chisel to protect your hand from a misplaced blow with the sledgehammer.

Plugging chisel

A plugging chisel has a flat narrow bit (tip) for cutting out old pointing. It's worth renting one if you have a large area of brickwork to repoint.

Bricklayer's chisel

The wide bit of a bricklayer's chisel is for cutting bricks and concrete blocks. It's also useful for levering up floorboards.

WORK GLOVES

Wear strong work gloves whenever you carry paving stones, concrete blocks or rough lumber. Ordinary gardening gloves are better than none but won't last long on a building site. The best work gloves have leather palms and fingers, though you may prefer a pair with ventilated backs for comfort in hot weather.

DIGGING TOOLS

Much building work requires some kind of digging—for laying strip foundations and concrete pads, sinking rows of postholes and so on. You may already have the essential tools in your garden shed; others you can rent.

Pickaxe

Use a medium-weight pickaxe to break up heavily compacted soil, especially if it contains a lot of buried rubble.

 (see Pickaxe region)

Mattlock

The wide blade of a mattock is ideal for breaking up heavy clay soil, and it's better than an ordinary pickaxe for ground that's riddled with tree roots.

Spade

Buy a good-quality spade for excavating soil and mixing concrete. One with a stainless-steel blade is best, but alloy steel will last fairly well if it is looked after. For strength choose a D-shaped handle whose hardwood shaft has been split and riveted with metal plates to the crosspiece, and make sure that the shaft socket and blade are forged in one piece.

Square blades seem to be the most popular, though some builders prefer a round-mouth spade with a long pole handle for digging deep trenches and holes.

Shovel

You can use a spade for mixing and placing concrete or mortar, but the raised edges of a shovel retain it better.

Garden rake

Use an ordinary garden rake to spread gravel or level wet concrete, but be sure to wash it before any concrete sets on it.

Posthole auger

Rent a posthole auger to sink narrow holes for fence and gate posts by driving it into the ground like a corkscrew and pulling out plugs of earth.

Wheelbarrow

The average garden wheelbarrow is not really strong enough for work on building sites, which entails carrying heavy loads of wet concrete and rubble. Unless the tubular underframe is rigidly strutted, the barrow's thin metal body will distort and perhaps spill its load as you cross rough ground. Check, too, that the axle is fixed securely. Cheap wheelbarrows often lose their wheels when their loads are being tipped into excavations.

SCREWDRIVERS

One's choice of screwdrivers is a personal matter, and most people accumulate a collection of types and sizes over the years.

Cabinet screwdriver

Buy at least one large flat-tip screwdriver. The fixed variety is quite adequate but a pump-action one, which drives large screws very quickly, is useful when you assemble big wooden building structures.

Phillips-head screwdriver

Choose the size and type of Phillips-head screwdriver to suit the work at hand. There is no most useful size as the driver must fit the screw slots exactly.

PLANES

Your choice of planes depends on the kind of joinery you plan to do. Sophisticated framing may call for molding or grooving planes, but most woodwork needs only skimming to leave a fairly smooth finish.

Jack plane

A medium-size bench plane, the jack plane, is the best general-purpose tool.

DECORATOR'S TOOL KIT

Most of us decorate our own houses to some extent, and decorator's tools are fairly common. Though traditionalists will stick to tried and tested tools and materials of proven reliability, others will prefer recent innovations aimed at making the work easier and faster for the home decorator.

TOOLS FOR PREPARATION

Whether you are painting, papering or tiling, the surface to which the materials will be applied must be sound and clean.

Straight scraper

Serrated scraper

Wallpaper or paint scraper
The wide, stiff blade of a scraper is for removing softened paint or soaked wallpaper. The best scrapers have high-quality steel blades and riveted rosewood handles. One with a 4- to 5-inch-wide blade is best for stripping wallpaper, but a narrow one, no more than 1 inch wide, is useful for removing paint from window or door frames. A serrated scraper will score impervious wallcovering so that water or stripping solution can penetrate it faster. If you use one, try not to damage the wall behind the covering.

Vinyl gloves
Most people wear ordinary "rubber" gloves to protect their hands when washing down or preparing paintwork, but tough PVC work gloves are more hard-wearing and will protect you from a great many harmful chemicals.

WOODWORKING TOOLS

In addition to specialized decorating tools, you will need a basic woodworking tool kit for repairing damaged framing or floorboards and for installing wall paneling or laying parquet flooring.

RESERVOIR

SOLE PLATE

Steam wallpaper stripper
To remove wallpaper quickly, especially thick wallcovering, rent an electric steam stripper. All such strippers work on the same principle, but follow any specific safety instructions that come with the machine.

Using a steam stripper
Fill its reservoir and plug it into an outlet 15 minutes before starting work so as to generate a good head of steam. Hold the steaming plate against the wallpaper until the paper is soft enough to be removed with a scraper. The time for this will depend on the type of wallcovering.

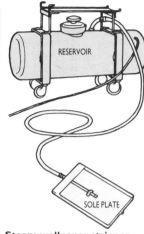

Straight-sided shavehook

Combination shavehook

Shavehook
This is a special scraper for removing old paint and varnish. A straight-sided triangular one is fine for flat surfaces, but one with a combination blade can also be used on concave and convex moldings. You pull a shavehook towards you to remove the softened paint.

Heat gun
The gas blowtorch was once the professional's tool for softening old paint so as to strip it, but the modern electric hot-air stripper is much easier to use. It is as efficient as a blowtorch but involves little risk of scorching woodwork. Early models were heavy and tiring to use, but today's are light enough to be used for long periods without fatigue. On some guns, the air temperature can be adjusted. Others have interchangeable nozzles shaped to concentrate the heated air or direct it away from glass panes.

Filling knife
A filling knife looks like a paint scraper but has a flexible blade for forcing filler into cracks in wood or plaster. Patch large areas of damaged wall with a plasterer's trowel, however.

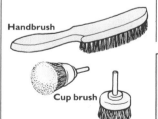

Handbrush

Cup brush

Wire brushes
A handbrush with steel wire bristles will remove flaking paint and rust particles from metalwork before repainting. The job is easier with a rotary wire cup brush in a power drill, but wear goggles or safety glasses if you use one.

Mastic guns
Nonsetting (permanently flexible) mastic is for sealing gaps between masonry and wooden frames and other joints between materials whose different rates of expansion will eventually crack and eject a rigid filler. You can buy mastic that is squeezed directly from its plastic tube like toothpaste, but it is easier to apply from a cartridge in a spring-loaded gun or an aerosol can with a special nozzle.

Tack cloth
A resin-impregnated cloth, called a tack cloth, is ideal for picking up particles of dust and hard paint from a surface prepared for painting. If you can't get a tack cloth, use a lint-free cloth dampened with denatured alcohol.

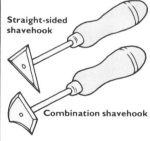

Dusting brush
A dusting brush has long, soft bristles for clearing dust out of moldings and crevices just before painting woodwork. You can use an ordinary paintbrush if you keep it clean and reserve it for the job.

WET-AND-DRY PAPER

Wet-and-dry abrasive paper is for smoothing new paintwork or varnish before applying the final coat. It is a waterproof backing paper with silicon carbide particles glued to it. Dip a piece in water and rub the paintwork until a slurry of paint and water forms. Wipe it off with a cloth before it dries, then rinse the paper clean and continue.

● **Essential tools**
Wallpaper scraper
Combination spokeshave
Filling knife
Heat gun
Wire brush

481

PAINTBRUSHES

Some paintbrushes are made from natural animal hair. Hog bristle is the best, but it is often mixed with inferior horsehair or oxhair to reduce cost. Synthetic-bristle brushes are usually the least expensive, and are quite adequate for the home decorator.

Bristle types

Bristle is ideal for paintbrushes because each hair tapers naturally and splits at the tip into even finer filaments that hold paint well. Bristle is also tough and resilient. Synthetic bristle, usually of nylon, is made to resemble the characteristics of real bristle, and a good-quality nylon brush will serve the average painter as well as a bristle one.

Paint bucket
To carry paint to a worksite, pour a little into a cheap, lightweight plastic paint bucket.

Choosing a brush

The bristles of a good brush—the "filling"—are densely packed. When you fan them with your fingers they should spring back into shape immediately. Flex the tip of the brush against your hand to see if any bristles work loose. Even a good brush will shed a few individual bristles at first, but never clumps. The ferrule should be fixed firmly to the handle.

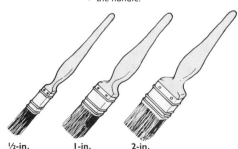

½-in.	1-in.	2-in.

● **Essential tools**
Flat brushes
1-, 1½- and 2-in.
Wallbrush
6-in.

Flat paintbrush

The filling is set in rubber—or occasionally in pitch or resin—and bound to the wooden or plastic handle by a pressed-metal ferrule. You will need several sizes up to 2 inches for painting, varnishing and staining woodwork.

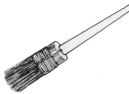

One-knot paintbrush

The bristles on a one-knot paintbrush are bound to a cylindrical handle with string, wire or a metal ferrule. Their grouping makes them very resilient, but when flexed against a surface, they will fan out like those of the more common flat paintbrush.

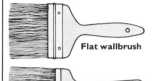

Flat wallbrush

Two-knot brush

Wallbrush

To apply latex paint by brush, use a 6-inch flat wallbrush or a two-knot brush of the kind favored by European painters and decorators.

Trim brush

The filling or cutting-in of a trim brush is cut at an angle for painting molded glazing bars right up into the corners and against the glass, though most painters make do with a ½-inch flat brush.

STENCIL AND GRAIN-EFFECT TOOLS

Stencil brush

A stencil brush has short stiff bristles. The paint is stippled on with their tips and a cutout template defines the painted shape.

Grainers

These are special brushes for reproducing the effects of natural woodgrain on paint or varnish. A "mottler" has a dense, soft filling of squirrel hair for lifting bands or streaks of color to simulate figured hardwoods. A "pencil grainer" has a row of fine brushes mounted in one handle for drawing patterns of parallel lines.

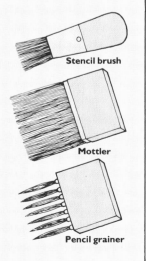

Stencil brush

Mottler

Pencil grainer

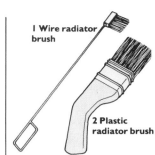

1 Wire radiator brush

2 Plastic radiator brush

Radiator brush

Unless you take a radiator off the wall for decorating, you need a special brush to paint the back of it and the wall behind it. There are two kinds: one with a standard flat paintbrush head at right angles to its long wire handle (**1**), the other like a conventional paintbrush but with a cranked plastic handle (**2**).

Banister brush

Use a household banister brush for painting rough or stuccoed walls.

Paint shield

Glass scraper

Paint shield and scraper

There are various plastic and metal shields for protecting glass when window frames and glazing bars are being painted, and glass that does get spattered can be cleaned with a razor blade clipped in a special holder.

CLEANING BRUSHES

● **Latex paint**
As soon as you finish working with latex paint, wash it from the brush with warm, soapy water, flexing the bristles between your fingers to work all paint out of the roots. Then rinse and brush in clean water and shake out the excess. Smooth the bristles and slip an elastic band around their tips to hold the shape of the filling while it dries.

Holding the shape of a brush

● **Oil paint**
If you are using oil paint, you can suspend the brush overnight in enough water to cover the bristles, blot it with paper towels the next day and continue painting.
When you have finished, brush excess paint out on newspaper, then flex the bristles in a bowl of thinner. Some finishes need special thinner, so check for this on the container; otherwise use turpentine or a chemical brush cleaner. Wash the dirty thinner from the brush with hot, soapy water, then rinse it.

Soaking a brush

● **Hardened paint**
If paint has hardened on a brush, soak its bristles in brush cleaner to soften the paint, which will become water-soluble and will wash out easily with hot water. If the old paint is unusually stubborn, dip the bristles in some paint stripper.

STORING PAINTBRUSHES

For long-term storage, fold soft paper over the bristles and secure it with a rubber band around paper and ferrule.

PAINT PADS

Paint pads are a fairly recent development aimed at helping inexperienced painters to apply oil and latex paint quickly and evenly. They are not universally popular, but no one disputes their value in painting large, flat areas. They cover quickly and are unlikely to drip paint if they are loaded properly.

Standard pads
There is a range of rectangular pads for painting walls, ceilings and flat woodwork. They have short mohair pile on their painting surfaces and handles on their backs.

Edging pad
To paint a straight edge—between a wall and a ceiling, for instance—use an edging pad with small wheels or rollers that guide it parallel to the adjacent surface.

Sash pad
A sash pad has a small mohair sole for painting glazing bars. Most sash pads have plastic guides on their backs to prevent them from straying onto the glass.

PRESSURIZED PAINTING SYSTEM

With a pressurized painting system, you can work continuously for as long as its reservoir contains paint. An ordinary siphon bulb delivers the paint at a slow but steady pace, and a control button on the handle releases it to the painting head, which is detachable and can be a roller, a brush or a pad as required. You can carry the reservoir or clip it to your belt for greater freedom of movement.

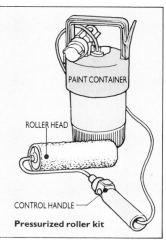

PAINT CONTAINER

ROLLER HEAD

CONTROL HANDLE

Pressurized roller kit

CLEANING PAINT PADS

Before dipping a new pad into paint, brush it with a clothes brush to remove any loose nylon filaments.

● When you finish painting, blot the pad on old newspaper, then wash it in the appropriate solvent—water for latex, turpentine or brush cleaner for oil paints, or any special thinners recommended by the paint manufacturer. Squeeze the foam and rub the pile with gloved fingertips, then wash the pad in hot, soapy water and rinse it.

● Even after washing, a new pad may be stained by paint, but the color will not contaminate the next batch of fresh paint.

Pad tray
Pads and trays are normally sold as sets, but if you buy a separate tray, get one with a loading roller that distributes paint evenly onto the sole of a pad drawn across it.

PAINT ROLLERS

A paint roller is efficient for painting large areas quickly. On the better type, the cylindrical sleeve that applies the paint slides onto a revolving sprung-wire cage on a cranked handle. The sleeves on this type of roller are easily changed. Don't buy one whose sleeve is held in place by a small nut and washer. Even if the nut doesn't get lost, corroded or paint-clogged it's much too tricky.

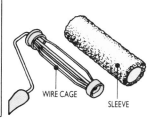

WIRE CAGE   SLEEVE

Sizes of roller sleeves
Sleeves for standard rollers range from 7 inches to about 12 inches in length, but there are smaller rollers for painting narrow strips of wall or woodwork.

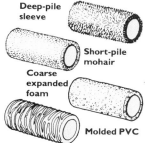

Deep-pile sleeve

Short-pile mohair

Coarse expanded foam

Molded PVC

Types of roller sleeves
There are roller sleeves of various materials to suit different paints and surface textures. Most are of *sheepskin* or *synthetic fiber*, both of which suit latex paint and leave an even, finely textured finish. Use a *deep-pile* sleeve to paint a heavily textured surface, a *medium-pile* one for smooth walls and ceilings.

Short-pile roller sleeves, usually of mohair, are made for use with oil paints.

The cheap *plastic-foam* sleeves are unsatisfactory with both oil and latex paints. They leave tiny air bubbles in the painted surface and the foam often distorts as it dries after washing. But they are cheap enough to be thrown away after use with finishes which would be hard to remove even from a short-pile roller sleeve.

Use a *coarse expanded foam* sleeve for applying textured coatings. There are also *molded PVC* rollers with embossed surfaces to pattern all kinds of textured paints and coatings.

Extending a roller
If your roller has a hollow handle, you can plug it onto a telescopic extension handle to be able to reach a ceiling from the floor. Loading an extended roller can be tricky, but you can buy one with a built-in reservoir that keeps the roller charged and holds enough paint for a large area.

CLEANING A ROLLER

Remove most of the excess paint by running the roller back and forth across old newspaper. If you plan to use the roller the next day, apply a few drops of the appropriate thinner to the sleeve and wrap it in plastic. Otherwise clean, wash and rinse the sleeve before the paint can set.

● Latex paint
If you've been using latex paint, flush most of it out under running water, then work a little liquid detergent into the pile and flush it again.

● Roller washer
You can mechanize the job with a roller washer that stands in the sink, its hose attached to a tap. Lower the roller, complete with sleeve, into the washer and turn on the tap. The force of the water spins the roller head and flushes the paint from it out of the base of the washer into the drain. The roller is cleaned in about one or two minutes.

● Oil paint
To remove oil paint, pour some thinner into the roller tray and slowly roll the sleeve back and forth in it. Squeeze the roller and agitate the pile with your fingertips. When the paint has all dissolved, wash the sleeve in hot, soapy water.

1   2   3

1 Corner roller
You cannot paint into a corner with a standard roller, so unless there are to be different adjacent colors, paint the corner first with a shaped corner roller.

2 Pipe roller
A pipe roller has two narrow sleeves, mounted side by side, which locate over the cylindrical pipework to paint it.

3 Radiator roller
This is a thin roller on a long wire handle for painting behind radiators and pipes.

Roller tray
A paint roller is loaded from a sloping plastic or metal tray whose deep end acts as a paint reservoir. Load the roller by rolling paint from the deep end up and down the tray's ribbed slope once or twice so as to get even distribution on the sleeve.

● **Essential tools**
Standard pads
2- and 8-in.
Sash pad
Large roller and selection of sleeves
Roller tray

PAINTSPRAYING EQUIPMENT

Spraying is so fast and efficient that it's worth considering if you plan to paint the outside walls of a building. The equipment is expensive to buy but it can be rented from most tool-rental outlets. You can spray most exterior paints and finishes if they are thinned properly but tell the rental company which one you wish to use so that they can supply the right spray gun with the correct nozzle. Rent goggles and a face mask at the same time.

Preparation
As far as possible, plan to work on a dry and windless day, and allow time to mask off windows, doors and pipework. Follow the setting-up and handling instructions supplied with the equipment, and if you are new to the work, practise a little beforehand on an inconspicuous section of wall.

Compressor-operated spray
With this equipment, the paint is mixed with pressurized air to emerge as a fine spray. Some compressors deliver compressed air to an intermediate tank and top it up as air is drawn off by the spray gun, but most rented ones supply air directly to the gun. The trigger opens a valve to admit air, at the same time opening the paint outlet at the nozzle. The paint is drawn from a container, usually mounted below the gun, and mixes with compressed air at the tip. Most guns have air-delivery horns at the sides of the nozzle to produce a fan-shaped pattern.

Spraying textured paint
Rent a special gravity-fed spray gun to apply textured finishes. The material is loaded into a hopper on top of the gun.

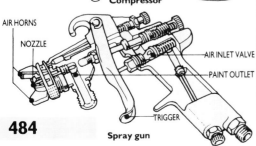

Compressor

AIR HORNS

NOZZLE

AIR INLET VALVE

PAINT OUTLET

TRIGGER

484

Spray gun

Airless sprayer
In an airless sprayer, an electric pump delivers the paint at high pressure to the spray gun. The paint is picked up through a tube inserted in the paint container and the pump forces it through a high-pressure hose to a filter and pressure regulator which is adjustable to produce the required spray patterns. The paint leaves the nozzle at such high pressure that it can penetrate skin, so most such spray guns have safety shields on their nozzles.

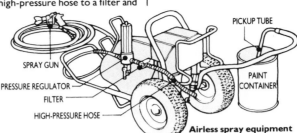

SPRAY GUN

PRESSURE REGULATOR

FILTER

HIGH-PRESSURE HOSE

PICKUP TUBE

PAINT CONTAINER

Airless spray equipment

CLEANING A SPRAY GUN

Empty out any paint left in the container and add some thinner. Spray the thinner until it emerges clear, then release the pressure and dismantle the spray nozzle. Clean the parts with a solvent-dampened rag and wipe out the container.

COMMON SPRAYING FAULTS

Streaked paintwork
An uneven, streaked finish results if you don't overlap the passes of the gun.

Patchy paintwork
Coverage won't be consistent if you move the gun in an arc. Keep it pointing directly at the wall and moving parallel to it.

Orange-peel texture
A wrinkle paint film resembling the texture of orange peel is usually caused by spraying paint that is too thick, but if the paint seems to be of the right consistency, you may be moving the spray gun too slowly.

Runs
Runs will occur if you apply too much paint, probably through holding the gun too close to the surface you're spraying.

Powdery finish
This is caused by paint drying before it reaches the wall. Hold the gun a little closer to the wall surface.

Spattering
Pressure that's too high will produce a speckled finish. Lower the pressure until the finish becomes satisfactory.

Spitting
A partly clogged nozzle will make the gun sputter. Clear the nozzle with a stiff bristle from a brush—never use wire—then wipe it with a rag dampened in thinner.

PAPERHANGERS' TOOLS

You can improvise some of the tools needed for paperhanging, but even specialized equipment is inexpensive so it's worth having a proper kit.

Tape measure
A retractable steel tape is best for measuring walls and ceilings to estimate the amount of wallcovering you'll need.

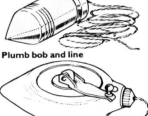

Plumb bob and line

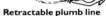

Retractable plumb line

Plumb line
Any small weight suspended on fine string can be used to mark the position of one edge of a strip of wallpaper. Hold the end of the line near the ceiling, allow the weight to come to rest, then mark the wall at points down the length of the line.

A true plumb line has a pointed metal weight called a plumb bob. In some versions the line retracts into a hollow plumb bob containing colored chalk and is coated with chalk as it is withdrawn. When the line hangs vertically stretched taut, then snap it against the wall like a bowstring to leave a chalked line.

Paste brush
Apply paste to the back of wallcovering with a wide wallbrush. Alternatively, use a short-pile mohair roller. Clean either tool by washing it in warm water.

PASTING TABLE

Though you can paste wallcoverings on any convenient flat surface, a proper pasting table is ideal. It stands higher than the average dining table and is only 1 inch wider than a standard roll of wallpaper, making it easier to apply paste without spreading it onto the work surface. The under frame folds flat and the top is hinged, so the table can be carried from room to room and stowed in a small space.

Paperhanger's brush
This is a brush used for smoothing wallcovering onto a surface. Its bristles should be soft, so as not to damage delicate paper, but springy enough to provide the pressure to squeeze excess paste and air bubbles from beneath the wallcovering. Wash the brush in warm water when you finish work to prevent paste hardening on the tips of the bristles.

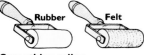

Seam roller
Use a hardwood or plastic seam roller to press down butted joints between adjacent strips of wallpaper, but not on embossed or delicate wallcoverings.

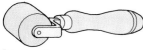

Rubber   Felt

Smoothing roller
There are rubber rollers for squeezing trapped air from under wallcoverings, but use a felt roller on delicate and flocked wallpapers.

Paperhanger's scissors
Any fairly large scissors can be used for trimming wallpaper to length, but proper paperhanger's scissors have extra-long blades to achieve a straight cut.

Craft knife
Use a knife to trim paper around light fixtures and switches and to achieve perfect butt joints by cutting through overlapping edges of paper. The knife must be extremely sharp to avoid tearing the paper, so use one with disposable blades that you can change easily when one gets dull. Some craft knives have short double-ended blades clamped in a metal or plastic handle. Others have long retractable blades that can be snapped off in short sections to leave a new sharp point.

TILING TOOLS

Most of the tools in a tiler's kit are for applying ceramic wall and floor tiles, but others are needed for laying soft tiles and vinyl sheeting.

Level
You will need a level for setting up temporary battens to align a field of tiles both horizontally and vertically.

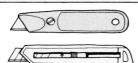

Profile gauge
A profile gauge is for copying the shapes of pipework or door moldings to provide a pattern for fitting soft floorcoverings. As you press the steel pins of the gauge against the object you wish to copy, they slide back, mirroring

the shape. When you want to copy another shape, press the needles against a flat surface to reposition them in a straight line.

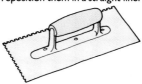

Serrated trowel
Make a ridged bed of adhesive for ceramic tiles by drawing the toothed edge of a plastic or steel tiler's trowel through the material.

Tile cutter
A tile cutter is a square-section rod of steel with a pointed tungsten-carbide tip. The tip is for scoring the glazed surface of a ceramic tile so that it will snap cleanly along the scored line. Other cutters have steel wheels like glass cutters.

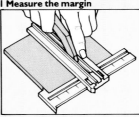

Saw file
A saw file has a bent metal frame that holds the thin wire rod under tension. The rod is coated with particles of tungsten-carbide hard enough to cut through ceramic tiles. Circular in section, the file will cut in any direction, so it can cut curved and straight lines with equal ease.

Squeegee
A squeegee has a blade of hard rubber mounted in a wooden handle. Use one for spreading grout into the gaps between ceramic tiles.

Nibblers
It is impossible to snap a very narrow strip off a ceramic tile. Instead, score the line with a tile cutter, then break off the waste little by little with tile nibblers. They resemble pliers but have sharper jaws of tungsten-carbide that open automatically when you relax your grip on the spring-loaded handles.

TILE-CUTTING JIGS

A tile-cutting jig greatly simplifies the cutting and fitting of border tiles to fill the edges of a field of tiles. With the one tool you can measure the gap, score the tile and snap it along the scored line.

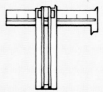

Using the jig
To measure the size of the tile to be cut, slide the jig open until one pointer is against the adjacent wall and the other is against the edge of the last full tile (1). The jig automatically allows for grouting.

Fit the jig over the tile to be cut and with the tile cutter, score the tile through the slot in the jig (2).

The cutter includes a pair of clippers with angled jaws for snapping the tile in two. Align the scored line with the pointer on the jaws and squeeze the handles until the tile breaks cleanly (3).

1 Measure the margin

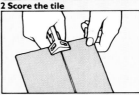

2 Score the tile

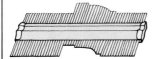

3 Snap the tile

Floor tile jig
Large cutting jigs for floor tiles can be rented or bought from good DIY suppliers.

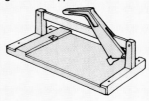

Staple gun
A staple gun is used for fixing mineral-fiber tiles to furring attached to a ceiling. The hand-operated type has a trigger that works a spring-loaded striker, which drives two-pronged staples into the work. It can be tiring to use with an outstretched arm. An electric stapler makes light work of the largest ceilings and is much more powerful than the hand-operated tool, though its force is adjustable to suit various materials.

Hand-operated gun

Electric stapler

● **Essential tools**
Steel tape measure
Plumb line
Paste brush
Paperhanger's brush
Seam roller
Scissors
Craft knife
Pasting table
Level
Serrated trowel
Tile cutter and jig
Nibblers
Saw file
Squeegee

485

● **Essential tools**
Sink plunger
Scriber
Center punch
Steel rule
Try square
General-purpose
hacksaw

PLUMBER'S AND METALWORKER'S TOOL KIT

The growing use of plastics in plumbing is likely to affect the trade considerably, and while plastics have been used for drainage for some years, the advent of plastics suitable for mains, pressure and hot water lines will have the greatest impact. But brass fittings and pipework of copper and other metals are still the most commonly used for domestic plumbing, so the plumber's tool kit is still basically a metalworker's kit.

SINK- AND DRAIN-CLEANING EQUIPMENT

There's no need to hire a plumber to clear blocked appliances, pipes or even main drains. The necessary equipment can be bought or rented.

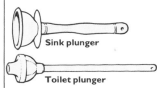

Sink plunger

Toilet plunger

Plunger

This is a simple but effective tool for clearing a blockage from the trap or toilet bowl. A pumping action on the rubber cap forces air and water along the pipe to disperse the blockage.

When you buy a plunger, make sure that the cup is big enough to surround the waste outlet completely. The cup of a toilet plunger may have a cone that makes a tight fit in the trap.

Compressed-air gun

A blocked wastepipe can be cleared with a compressed-air gun, if allowed by code. A hand-operated pump compresses air in the gun's reservoir, to be released into the pipe by a trigger. The gun has three interchangeable nozzles to suit different outlets.

Toilet auger

The short coiled-wire toilet auger, designed for clearing toilet traps, is rotated by a handle in a hollow rigid shaft. A vinyl guard prevents scratching of the toilet bowl.

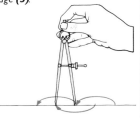

Drain auger

Toilet auger

Drain auger

A flexible drain auger of coiled wire will pass through small-diameter wastepipes to clear blockages. Pass the corkscrewlike head into the pipe until it reaches the blockage, clamp on the cranked handle and turn it to rotate the head and engage the blockage. Push and pull the auger until the pipe is clear.

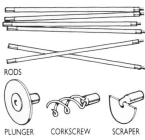

RODS

PLUNGER   CORKSCREW   SCRAPER

Drain rods

You can rent a complete set of rods and fittings for clearing main drains and inspection chambers. Traditionally, the rods are of flexible cane and wire, but modern ones come in lengths of polypropylene with threaded brass connectors. The clearing heads comprise a double-worm corkscrew fitting, small diameter rubber plunger and a hinged scraper for clearing the open channels in inspection chambers.

MEASURING AND MARKING TOOLS

Tools for measuring and marking metal are much like those used for wood but are made and calibrated for greater accuracy because metal parts must fit with great precision.

Scriber

For precise work, mark lines and hole centers on metal with a pointed hardened-steel scriber—but use a pencil to mark the center of a bend, as a scored line made with a scriber may open up on the outside of the bend when the metal is stretched.

Spring dividers

Spring dividers are like a pencil compass, but both legs have steel points. These are adjusted to the required spacing by a knurled nut on a threaded rod that links the legs.

Using spring dividers

Use dividers to step off divisions along a line (1) or to scribe circles (2). By running one point against the edge of a workpiece you can also scribe a line parallel with the edge (3).

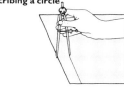

1 Stepping off

2 Scribing a circle

3 Parallel scribing

Center punch

A center punch is for marking the center of holes to be drilled.

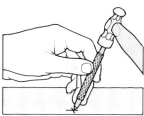

Correcting a center mark

Using a center punch

Place the punch's point on dead center and strike it with a hammer. If the mark is not accurate, angle the punch toward the true center, tap it to extend the mark in that direction, then mark the center again.

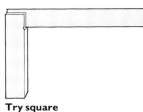

Steel rule

You'll need a long tape measure for estimating pipe runs and positioning appliances, but use a 1- or 2-foot steel rule for marking out components when absolute accuracy is important.

Try square

You can use a woodworker's try square to mark out or check right angles, but an all-metal engineer's try square is precision-made for metalwork. The small notch between blade and stock allows the tool to fit properly against a right-angled workpiece even when the corner is burred by filing. For general-purpose work, choose a 6-inch try square.

METAL-CUTTING TOOLS

You can cut solid bar, sheet and tubular metal with a hacksaw, but special tools for cutting sheet metal and pipes will give you more accuracy and speed the work.

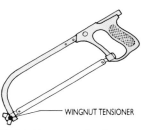

WINGNUT TENSIONER

General-purpose hacksaw

A modern hacksaw has a tubular steel frame with a light cast-metal handle. The frame is adjustable to blades of different lengths, which are tensioned by tightening a wingnut.

CHOOSING A HACKSAW BLADE

There are 8-, 10- and 12-inch hacksaw blades. Try the different lengths until you find which suits you best. Choose the hardness and size of teeth according to the metal to be cut.

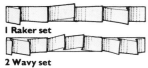

1 Raker set

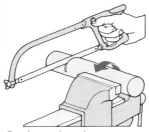

2 Wavy set

Size and set of teeth
There are fine and coarse hacksaw blades, graded by the number of teeth per inch. A coarse blade has 14 to 18 teeth per inch and a fine one has 24 to 32. The teeth are set—bent sideways—to make a cut wider than the blade's thickness and prevent it from jamming in the work. Coarse teeth are "raker set" (1), with pairs of teeth bent in opposite directions and every third or fifth one left in line with the blade to clear the cut of metal waste. Fine teeth are too small to be raker set and the whole row is "wavy set" (2).

Use a corase blade for cutting soft metals like brass and aluminum, which would clog fine teeth, and a fine blade for thin sheet and the harder metals.

Hardness
A hacksaw blade must be harder than the metal it is cutting or its teeth will quickly blunt. A flexible blade with hardened teeth will cut most metals, but there are fully hardened blades that stay sharp longer and are less prone to losing teeth. Being rigid and brittle, they break easily. High-speed steel blades for sawing very hard alloys are expensive and even more brittle than the fully hardened type.

Fitting a hacksaw blade
Adjust the length of the saw frame and slip the blade onto the pins at its ends, teeth pointing away from the handle. Then apply tension with the wingnut. If the new blade wanders off line when you work, tighten the wingnut.

If you have to fit a new blade after starting to cut a piece of metal it may jam in the cut because its set is wider than that of the old worn blade. Start a fresh cut on the other side of the workpiece and work back to the cut you began with.

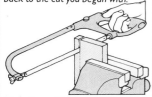

Turning a blade
Sometimes it's easier to work with the blade at right angles to the frame. Rotate the blade-attachment bars a quarter turn before fitting the blade on the pins.

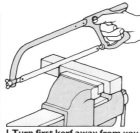

1 Turn first kerf away from you

Sawing metal bar
Hold the work in a machinist's vise, the marked cutting line as close to the jaws as possible. Start the cut on the waste side of the line with short strokes until it is about 1/16 inch deep, then turn the bar 90 degrees in the vise, so that the cut faces away from you, and make a similar one in the new face (1). Continue in this way until the kerf (cut) runs right around the bar, then cut through the remainder with long steady strokes. Steady the end of the saw with your free hand and put a little light oil on the blade if necessary.

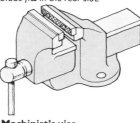

Sawing rod or pipe
As you cut a cylindrical rod or tube with a hacksaw, rotate the work away from you until the kerf goes right around it, then cut through it.

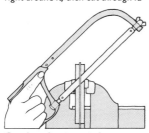

Sawing sheet metal
To saw a small piece of sheet metal, sandwich it between two strips of wood clamped in a vise. Adjust the metal to place the cutting line close to the strips, then saw down the waste side with steady strokes and the blade angled to the work.

Clamp thin sheet metal between two pieces of plywood and cut through all three layers at once.

Sawing a groove
To cut a slot or groove wider than a standard hacksaw blade, fit two or more identical blades in the frame at the same time.

Junior hacksaw
Use a junior hacksaw for cutting small-bore tubing and thin metal rod. In most types the blade is held under tension by the spring steel frame.

Fitting a new blade
To fit a blade, locate it in the slot at the front of the frame, then bow the frame against a workbench until the blade fits in the rear slot.

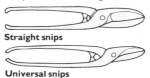

Machinist's vise
A large machinist's or metalworker's vise is bolted to the workbench, but small clamp-on ones are also available. Slip soft fiber liners over the jaws of a vise to protect workpieces held in it.

Cold chisel
Though plumbers use cold chisels to hack old pipework out of masonry, they are also for cutting metal rod and slicing the heads off rivets. Keep the tip of yours sharpened on a bench grinder.

Straight snips

Universal snips

Tinsnips
Tinsnips are heavy-duty scissors for cutting sheet metal. Straight snips have wide blades for cutting straight edges, and if you try to cut curves with them the waste gets caught against the blades. But it is possible to cut a convex curve by removing small straight pieces of waste and working down to the marked line. Universal snips have thick, narrow blades that will cut a curve in one pass and will also make straight cuts.

Using tinsnips
As you cut along the marked line, let the waste curl away below the sheet. If the metal is too thick to be cut with one hand, clamp one handle of the snips in a vise so that you can put your full weight on the other.

Try not to close the jaws completely each time, as it can cause a jagged edge on the metal. Wear thick work gloves when you are cutting sheet metal.

SHARPENING SNIPS

Clamp one handle in a vise and sharpen the edge with a smooth file; repeat with the other and finish by removing the burrs from the backs of the blades on an oiled slipstone.

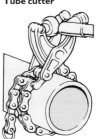

Sheet-metal cutter
Unlike tinsnips, which will distort a narrow waste strip on one side of the cutting line, a sheet-metal cutter removes a narrow strip as perfectly flat as the larger sheet. It is also suited to cutting rigid plastic sheet, which can crack if it is distorted by tinsnips.

Tube cutter
A tube cutter will cut the ends of pipes at exactly 90 degrees to their length. The pipe is clamped between the cutting wheel and an adjustable slide with two rollers, and is cut as the tool is revolved around it and the adjusting screw tightened before each turn. Keep the cutter lightly oiled when you use it.

Chain-link cutter
Cut large-diameter pipes with a chain-link cutter. Wrap the chain round the pipe, locate the end link in the clamp and tighten the adjuster until the cutter on each link bites into the metal. Work the handle back and forth to score the pipe and continue tightening the adjuster intermittently to cut deeper, until the pipe is severed.

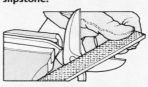

Sheet-metal cutter

Tube cutter

Chain-link cutter

● **Essential tools**
Junior hacksaw
Cold chisel
Tinsnips
Pipe cutter

● **Essential tools**
High-speed twist
drills
Variable or
two-speed power
drill
Bending spring
Soft mallet
Soldering iron
Gas torch

DRILLS AND PUNCHES

Special-quality steel bits are made for drilling holes in metal. Cut ½- to 1-inch holes in sheet metal with a punch.

Twist drills

Metal-cutting twist drills are much like those used for wood but are made from high-speed steel and with tips ground to a shallower angle. Use them in a power drill at slow speeds.

Mark the hole's center with a center punch to locate the drill point and clamp the work in a vise or to the bed of a drill stand. Drill slowly and steadily and keep the bit oiled.

To drill a large hole, make a pilot hole first with a small drill to guide the larger one.

When drilling sheet metal, the bit may jam and produce a ragged hole as it exits on the far side of the work. To prevent this, clamp the work between pieces of plywood and drill through the three layers.

Hole punch

Use a hole punch to make large holes in sheet metal. Mark the circumference of the hole with spring dividers, lay the metal on a piece of scrap softwood or plywood, place the punch's tip over the marked circle, tap it with a hammer, then check the alignment of the punched ring with the scribed circle. Reposition the punch and, with one sharp hammer blow, cut through the metal. If the wood gives and the metal is slightly distorted, tap it flat again with the hammer.

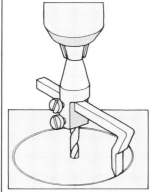

Tank cutter

Use a tank cutter to make holes for pipework in plastic or metal storage cisterns.

METAL BENDERS

Thick or hard metal must be heated before it can be bent successfully, but soft copper piping and sheet metal can be bent while cold.

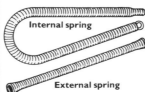

Internal spring

External spring

Bending springs

You can bend small-diameter pipes over your knee, but their walls must be supported with a coiled spring to prevent them from buckling.

Push an internal-type spring inside the pipe or an external-type one over it. Either type of spring must fit the pipe exactly.

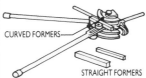

CURVED FORMERS

STRAIGHT FORMERS

Tube bender

In a tube bender, pipe is bent over one of two fixed curved formers that give the optimum radii for plumbing. Each has a matching straight former which is placed between the pipe and a steel roller on a movable lever. When this lever is moved towards the fixed one, the pipe is bent over the curved former. The formers support the pipe walls during bending.

You can get extra leverage by clamping the fixed lever in a vise and using both hands on the movable one.

Soft mallet

Soft mallets have heads of coiled rawhide, hard rubber or plastic. They are used in bending strip or sheet metal, which would be damaged by a metal hammer.

To bend sheet metal at a right angle, clamp it between stout wood strips along the bending line. Start at one end and bend the metal over one of the strips by tapping it with the mallet. Don't attempt the full bend at once but work along the sheet, increasing the angle and keeping it constant along the length until the metal lies flat on the strip. Then knock out any kinks.

TOOLS FOR JOINING METAL

You can make permanent watertight joints between metal components by using a molten alloy that acts like a glue when it cools and solidifies. Mechanical fasteners like compression joints, rivets and nuts and bolts are also used for joining metal.

SOLDERS

Solders are special alloys for joining metals and are designed to melt at temperatures lower than the melting points of the metals to be joined. Soft solder, a tin-and-lead alloy, melts at 183° to 250°C. Brazing, a method of hard soldering involving a copper-and-zinc alloy, requires the even higher temperature of some 850° to 1000°C.

Solder is available as a coiled wire or a thick rod. Use soft solder for copper plumbing fittings.

FLUX

To be soldered, a joint must be perfectly clean and free of oxides. Even after cleaning with steel wool or emery cloth, oxides will form immediately, preventing a positive bond between solder and metal. Flux forms a chemical barrier against oxidation. Corrosive, or "active" flux, applied with a brush, actually dissolves oxides but must be washed from the surface with water as soon as the solder solidifies or it will go on corroding the metal. A "passive" flux, in paste form, is used where it will be impossible to wash the work thoroughly. Though a passive flux will not dissolve oxide, it will exclude it adequately for soldering copper plumbing joints and electrical connections.

Some wire solder contains flux in its hollow core. The flux flows before the solder melts.

Soldering irons

Successful soldering needs the work to be made hot enough to melt the solder and cause it to flow; otherwise the solder will solidify before it can completely penetrate the joint. The necessary heat is applied with a soldering iron.

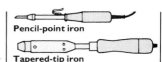

Tapered-tip iron

There are simple irons that are heated in a fire, but an electric iron is much handier to use and its temperature is both controllable and constant. Use a low-powered pencil-point iron for soldering electrical connections and a larger one with a tapered tip to bring sheet metal up to working temperature.

Tinning a soldering iron

The tip of a soldering iron must be coated with solder to keep it oxide-free and maintain its performance. Clean the cool tip with a file, then heat it to working temperature, dip it in flux and apply a stick of solder to coat it evenly.

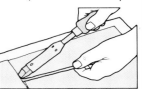

Using a soldering iron

Clean the mating surfaces of the joint to a bright finish and coat them with flux, then clamp the joint tightly between two wooden strips. Apply the hot iron along the joint to heat the metal thoroughly, then run its tip along the edge of the joint, following it with solder. Solder will flow immediately into a properly heated joint.

Gas torch

Even a large soldering iron cannot heat thick metal fast enough to compensate for heat loss away from the joint, and this is very much the situation when you solder pipework. Though the copper unions have very thin walls, the pipe on each side dissipates so much heat that an iron cannot get the joint itself hot enough to form a watertight soldered seal. Use a gas torch with an intensely hot flame that will heat the work quickly.

The torch runs on propane or Mapp contained under pressure in a disposable metal canister that screws onto the gas inlet. Open the control valve and light the gas released from the nozzle, then adjust the valve until the flame roars and is bright blue. Use the hottest part of the flame—about the middle of its length—to heat the joint.

Fiberglass mat
Buy a fireproof mat of fiberglass from a plumbers' supply to protect flammable surfaces from the heat of a gas torch.

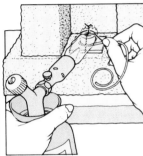

Hard-soldering and brazing
Use a gas torch to hard-solder or braze. Clean and flux the work—if possible with an active flux—then wire or clamp the parts together. Place the assembly on a fireproof mat or surround it with firebricks. Bring the joint to red heat with the torch, then dip a stick of the appropriate alloy in flux and apply it to the joint. When the joint is cool, chip off hardened flux, wash the metal thoroughly in hot water and finish the joint with a file.

Hot-air gun
Some hot-air guns, designed for stripping old paintwork, can also be used for soft soldering. You can vary the temperature of an electronic gun from 100° to 600°C. A heat shield on the nozzle reflects the heat back onto the work.

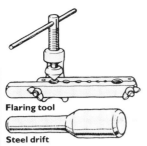

Flaring tool

Steel drift

Flaring tools
To make a nonmanipulative joint in plumbing pipework, the ends of the copper pipes are simply cut square and cleaned up to remove sharp edges. For a manipulative joint, the pipe ends must be flared to lock into the joint.

The simplest way to flare a copper pipe is with a steel drift. First slip one joint capnut onto the pipe, then push the narrow shank of the drift into the pipe. Strike the tool with a heavy hammer to drive its conical part into the pipe, stretching the walls to the required shape.

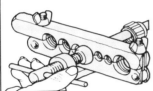

Using a flaring tool
A flaring tool will shape pipework more accurately. Again with the capnut in place, clamp the pipe in the matching hole in the die block, its end flush with the side of the block, then turn the screw of the flaring tool to drive its cone into the pipe.

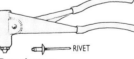

RIVET

Pop riveter
Join thin sheet metal with a pop riveter, a hand-operated tool with pliers-like handles. The special rivets have long shanks that break off and leave slightly raised heads on both sides of the work.

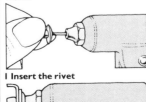

1 Insert the rivet

2 Squeeze the handles

Using a riveter
Clamp the two sheets together and drill holes right through the metal, matching the diameter of the rivets and spacing them regularly along the joint. Open the handles of the riveter and insert the rivet shank in the head (1). Push the rivet through a hole in the work and, while pressing the tool hard against the metal, squeeze the handles to compress the rivet head on the far side (2). When the rivet is fully expanded, the shank will snap off in the tool.

WRENCHES

A plumber uses a great variety of wrenches on a wide range of fittings and fixings, but you can rent the ones that you need only occasionally.

Open-end wrench
A set of the familiar open-end wrenches is essential to a plumber or metalworker. In most situations, pipework runs into a fitting or accessory and it is not possible to use anything but a wrench with open jaws. Most wrenches are double-ended, perhaps in a combination of sizes, and sizes are duplicated within a set for when two identical nuts have to be turned simultaneously, as on a compression joint, for instance.

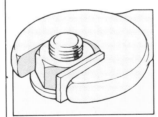

Achieving a tight fit
A wrench must be a good fit or it will round over the corners of the nut. You can pack out the jaws with a thin "shim" of metal if a snug fit is otherwise not possible.

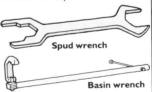

Box wrench
Being a closed circle, the head of a box wrench is stronger and fits better than that of an open-ended one. It is especially handy for loosening corroded nuts if it can be slipped onto them from above.

Square nut   **Hexagonal nut**

Choosing a box wrench
Choose a 12-point wrench. It is fast to use and will fit both square and hexagonal nuts. You can buy combination wrenches with rings at one end and open jaws at the other.

Socket tube
A socket tube is a steel tube with its ends shaped into hexagons—an excellent tool for reaching a nut in a confined space. Turning force is applied with a bar slipped into a hole drilled through the tube. Don't use a very long bar. Too much leverage may strip the thread of the fitting or distort the thin walls of the tube.

Adjustable wrench
Having a movable jaw, an adjustable wrench is not as strong as an open-end or box wrench but is often the only tool that will fit a large or painted-over nut. Make sure the wrench fits the nut snugly by rocking it slightly as you tighten the jaws. Grip the nut with the roots of the jaws. If you use just the tips, they can spring apart slightly under force and the wrench will slip.

Spud wrench

Basin wrench

Spud wrench and basin wrench
A spud wrench is a special double-ended wrench for use on large toilet and sink nuts.

A basin wrench has a pivoting jaw that can be set for either tightening or loosening hard-to-reach fittings.

Radiator wrench
Use a simple Allen wrench of hexagonal-section steel rod to remove radiator drain plugs. One end is ground to fit plugs with square sockets.

● **Essential tools**
Blind riveter
Set of open-ended wrenches
Small and large adjustable wrenches

489

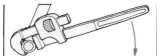

Pipe wrench

The adjustable toothed jaws of a pipe wrench are for gripping pipework. As force is applied, the jaws tighten on the work.

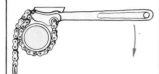

Chain wrench

A chain wrench does the same job as a pipe wrench but it can be used on very large-diameter pipes and fittings. Wrap the chain tightly around the work and engage it with the hook at the end of the wrench, then lever the handle towards the toothed jaw to apply turning force.

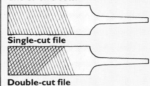

Strap wrench

With a strap wrench you can disconnect chrome pipework without damaging its surface. Wrap the smooth leather or canvas strap around the pipe, pass its end through the slot in the head of the tool and pull it tight. Leverage on the handle will rotate the pipe.

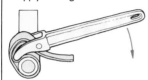

Locking pliers

These special pliers lock onto the work. They will grip round stock or damaged nuts and are often used as a small clamp.

Using locking pliers

Squeeze the handles to close the jaws while slowly turning the adjusting screw clockwise until they snap together (1). Release the tool's grip on the work by pulling the release lever (2).

I Adjusting the wrench

2 Releasing the wrench

- **Essential tools**
  Locking pliers
  Second-cut and
  smooth flat files
  Second-cut and
  smooth half-round
  files

FILES

Files are used for shaping and smoothing metal components and removing sharp edges.

CLASSIFYING FILES

The working faces of a file are composed of parallel ridges, or teeth, set at about 70 degrees to its edges. A file is classified according to the size and spacing of its teeth and whether it has one or two sets.

Single-cut file

Double-cut file

A *single-cut file* has one set of teeth virtually covering each face. A *double-cut file* has a second set of identical teeth crossing the first at a 45-degree angle. Some files are single-cut on one side and double-cut on the other.

The spacing of the teeth relates directly to their size: The finer the teeth, the more closely packed they are. Degrees of coarseness are expressed in numbers of teeth per inch. Use progressively finer files to shape a component and to gradually remove marks left by coarser ones.

File classification

Bastard file—Coarse grade (26 teeth per inch)—For initial shaping. *Second-cut file*—Medium grade (36 teeth per inch)—For preliminary smoothing. *Smooth file*—Fine grade (47 teeth per inch)—For final smoothing.

CLEANING A FILE

Soft metal clogs the teeth of files but can be removed by brushing along the teeth with a file card—a fine wire brush. Chalk rubbed on a clean file will reduce clogging.

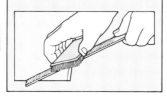

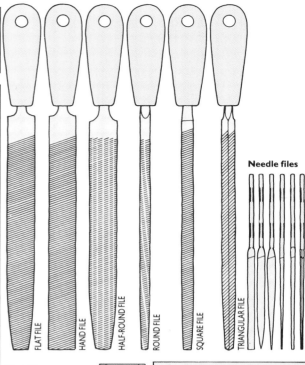

FLAT FILE

HAND FILE

HALF-ROUND FILE

ROUND FILE

SQUARE FILE

TRIANGULAR FILE

Needle files

Flat file

A flat file tapers from its pointed tang to its tip, both in width and thickness. Both faces and both edges are toothed.

Hand file

Hand files are parallel-sided but tapered in their thickness. Most of them have one smooth edge for filing up to a corner without damaging it.

Half-round file

This tool has one rounded face for shaping inside curves.

Round file

A round file is for shaping tight curves and enlarging holes.

Square file

This file is for cutting narrow slots and smoothing the edges of small rectangular holes.

Triangular file

The triangular file is for accurately shaping and smoothing undercut apertures of less than 90 degrees.

Needle files

Needle files are miniature versions of standard files and are all made in extra-fine grades. They are used for precise work and to sharpen brace bits.

FILE SAFETY

Always fit a wooden or plastic handle on the tang of a file before using it.

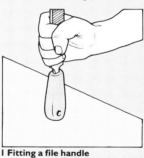

I Fitting a file handle

2 Knock a handle from the tang

If an unprotected file catches on the work, the tang could be driven into the palm of your hand. Having fitted a handle, tap its end on a bench to tighten its grip (1).

To remove a handle, hold the file in one hand and strike the ferrule away from you with a piece of wood (2).

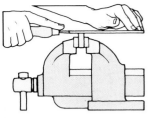

Using a file
When you use any file, keep it flat on the work and avoid rocking it on the forward strokes. Hold it steady with the fingertips of one hand on its tip and make slow, firm strokes with the full length of the tool.

To avoid vibration, hold the work low in a vice or clamp it between two strips of wood.

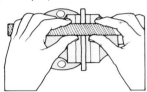

Draw filing
You can give metal a smooth finish by draw filing. With both hands, hold a smooth file at right angles to the work and slide it back and forth along the surface, then polish the work with emery cloth wrapped around the file.

PLIERS

Pliers are for improving your grip on small components and for bending and shaping metal rod and wire.

Machinist's pliers
For general-purpose work, buy a sturdy pair of machinist's pliers. The toothed jaws have a curved section for gripping round stock and side cutters for cropping wire.

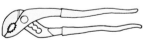

Slip-joint or waterpump pliers
The special feature of slip-joint pliers is a movable pivot for enlarging the jaw spacing. The extra-long handles give a good grip on pipes and other fittings.

FINISHING METAL

Apart from its appearance, metal must be clean and rust-free if it is to be painted or soldered.

Wire brush
Use a steel wire hand brush to clean rusty or corroded metal.

Steel wool
Steel wool is a mass of very thin steel filaments. It is used to remove file marks and to clean oxides and dirt from metals.

Emery cloth and paper
Emery is a natural black grit. Backed with paper or cloth for polishing metals, it is available in a range of grades from coarse to fine. For the best finish, work through the grades, using progressively finer abrasives as the work proceeds.

1 Glue paper to a board

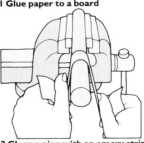

2 Clean a pipe with an emery strip

Using emery cloth and paper
To avoid rounding the crisp edges of a flat component, glue a sheet of emery paper to a board and rub the metal on it *(1)*.

To finish round stock or pipes, loop a strip of emery cloth over the work and pull alternately on each end *(2)*.

Buffing wheel
Metals can be brought to a shine by hand using liquid polish and a soft cloth, but for a really high gloss, use a buffing wheel in a bench-mounted power drill or grinder.

Using a buffing wheel
Apply a stick of buffing compound—a fine abrasive with wax—to the revolving wheel, then move the work from side to side against its lower half, keeping any edges facing down.

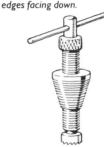

Reseating tool
When the seat of a faucet is so worn that even a new washer will not make a perfect seal, you can grind a new seat with a reseating tool. Remove the valve parts and screw the cone into the body of the faucet. Lower the threaded section with the knurled adjuster, then turn the bar to operate the cutter.

WOODWORKING TOOLS

A plumber needs basic woodworking tools to lift floorboards, notch joists for pipe runs and attach pipe clips.

● **Essential tools and materials**
Machinist's pliers
Wire brush
Steel wool
Emery cloth and paper

Flashlight
Keep a flashlight handy for checking your service box when a fuse blows on a lighting circuit. You may also need artificial light when working on connections below floorboards or in a loft, and a flashlight that stands unsupported is very helpful.

Diagonal cutters

● **Essential tools**
Terminal screwdrivers
Wire cutters
Wire strippers
Power drill and bits
Circuit tester
Flashlight
General-purpose tools

ELECTRICIAN'S TOOL KIT
You need only a fairly limited range of tools to make electrical connections. The largest number is needed for making cable runs and fixing accessories and appliances to the house structure.

SCREWDRIVERS

Buy good screwdrivers for tightening electrical terminals. The cheap ones are practically useless, being made from such soft metal that the tips soon twist out of shape.

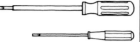

Terminal screwdriver
A terminal screwdriver has a long, slim cylindrical shaft ground to a flat tip. For work on the terminals in sockets and larger appliances, buy one with a plastic handle and a plastic insulating sleeve on its shaft. Use a smaller driver with a very slim shaft to work on ceiling roses or to tighten plastic terminal blocks on small fittings.

Cabinet screwdriver
You will need a woodworking screwdriver to fix mounting boxes to walls.

WRENCH

A small wrench is needed for making the ground connections in some appliances and for supplementary grounding.

WIRE CUTTERS

Use wire cutters for cutting cable and cord to length.

Electrician's pliers
These are machinist's pliers with insulating sleeves shrunk onto their handles. You'll need them to cut circuit conductors and to twist their ends together.

Diagonal cutters
Diagonal cutters will cut thick wires more effectively than electrician's pliers. To cut cable leads, you may need a junior hacksaw.

WIRE STRIPPERS

There are various tools for removing parts of the plastic insulation that covers cables and flexible cords.

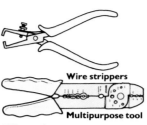

Wire strippers

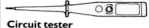

Multipurpose tool

Wire strippers
To remove the color-coded insulation from cable and cord, use a pair of wire strippers with jaws shaped to cut through the plastic without damaging the wire core. There is a multipurpose version that can both strip the insulation and cut the wires to length.

Sharp knife
Use a knife with sharp disposable blades for slitting and peeling the outer sheathing on conductors.

DRILLS

When you run circuit wiring, you need a drill and several special-purpose bits for boring through wood and masonry.

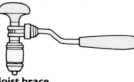

Joist brace
A joist brace has a chuck that takes standard brace bits, but its side-mounted handle and ratchet mechanism allow drilling in the restricted space between floor and ceiling joists.

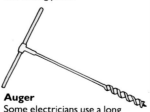

Auger
Some electricians use a long wood-boring auger to drill through the wall top plate and when running a cable from an attic down to its junction box. But it's hard to use such a long tool in the restricted roof space of a small modern house or apartment.

Power drill
A power drill is best for boring cable holes through timbers. As well as a standard masonry bit, you will need a much longer version for boring through walls and clearing access channels behind baseboards.

If you shorten the shaft of a wide-tipped spade bit, you can use it in a power drill between floor joists instead of renting a special joist brace.

TESTERS

Even when you have turned off the power at the service box, use a tester to check that the circuit is dead.

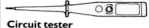

Circuit tester
A circuit tester has a light in its handle that glows when its screwdriverlike tip touches a live wire or terminal. You have to place a fingertip on the tool's metal gap for the light to work but there is no danger of a shock. A small test button on the handle tells if the tool is in working order.

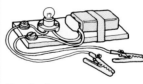

Continuity tester
A continuity tester will test whether a circuit is complete or an appliance is properly grounded. You can buy a tester or make one by connecting a battery and a bulb via short lengths of wire and alligator clips.

Using a continuity tester
Switch off the power at the service box before making the test. To discover, for example, which are the two ends of a buried disconnected cable, twist the black and white conductors together at one end, then attach the alligator clips to the same conductors at the other end (1). If the bulb lights up, the two ends belong to the same length of cable.

To check that a plug-in appliance is safely grounded, attach one clip to the ground pin of the plug—the longest of the three—and touch the metal casing of the appliance with the other clip (2). If the ground connection is good, the bulb will glow brightly; a

dimly glowing bulb indicates poor grounding, which should be checked professionally.

Don't use the appliance if the bulb lights up when you attach the clip to either of the other pins (3). It is dangerous and should be overhauled professionally. Make sure the plug fuse is working.

You cannot test a double-insulated appliance, as it has no ground connection in the plug.

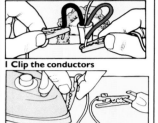

1 Clip the conductors

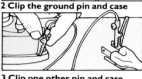

2 Clip the ground pin and case

3 Clip one other pin and case

GENERAL-PURPOSE TOOLS

Every electrician needs tools for lifting and cutting floorboards, for fixing mounting boxes and for cutting cable runs through a building.

Claw hammer
For nailing cable clips to walls and beams.
Light sledgehammer
For use with a cold chisel.
Cold chisel
For cutting channels in plaster and brickwork so as to bury cable or junction boxes.
Bricklayer's chisel
For levering up floorboards.
Wood chisels
For notching floor joists.
Padsaw or power jigsaw
For cutting through floorboards close to baseboards.
Floorboard saw
A floorboard saw is best for cutting across a pried-up board, though a tenon saw is a reasonable substitute.
Level
For checking that outlet boxes are being fixed horizontally.
Plasterer's trowel or filling knife
Use either tool for covering concealed cable with plaster or other filler.

12

REFERENCE & INDEX

LUMBER AND MAN-MADE BOARDS

Lumber is classified in two main groups, softwood and hardwood, according to the type of tree it comes from. Softwoods are from the evergreen coniferous trees like firs and pines, hardwoods from the deciduous broad-leaved ones. Most softwoods are in fact softer than most hardwoods, but that is not invariably so.

SOFTWOODS

Softwood used for construction is usually pine, spruce, fir, or hemlock. Most of the wood you see in a lumberyard is softwood, as it is by far cheaper and more widely used for structural house timbers, floorboards, stairs and simpler kinds of furniture.

Buying softwood
Most softwood is available in rough and smooth versions called, respectively, rough and surfaced. The rough unplaned surface of sawn timber means that it is suitable only for jobs where it will be out of sight. Where appearance is important you need planed wood—that is, of course, sawn and planed—which has been through a planing machine and is relatively smooth. But here a confusion can arise. Planed timber, or "S4S" (surfaced 4 sides), is always slightly thinner and narrower than its nominal dimensions. Machine planing takes about 1/2 to 3/4 inch off the width and 1/4 to 1/2 inch off the thickness, but the loss is not uniform and so the wood is always referred to in terms of its nominal size, the size before planing. You have to take this into account when you plan jobs involving softwood. Planed hardwoods are actually the size they are said to be.

Lumberyards use the board-foot system, but if you think and work in linear inches and feet, the men in the yards are experts at instant conversion.

Choosing softwood
A number of defects that can be found in softwood should be avoided, especially when a job's appearance is important. For this reason it is always best to go and pick out the wood yourself. Never simply order by phone.

Knots
Knots can look attractive in pine, but they must be "live" knots, the glossy brown ones. "Dead" knots, the black ones, will shrink and eventually drop out, leaving holes.

Warping
Is another common problem. Sight along the edges of each board to check that it is not bowed or twisted.

Shakes
Are cracks or splits in timber.

End shakes
These are splits in the ends of boards, and can be cut off, but the split section should not count in what you pay for.

Heart shakes
These are irregular cracks, usually accompanied by warping through the board's width.

Cup shakes
These can occur when a board comes from the center of a tree. The small center ring splits away along the board's length.

Surface checking
This is when many fine cracks appear on the timber's surface. Very fine ones may be removed by planing, or filled if the work is to be painted; wood with wider cracks should be rejected.

Other defects
Watch out for rough patches that have escaped the planer, damage from workmen's boots and calculations in ballpoint pen left on boards by other customers.

Cutting to size
At extra cost, a lumberyard with modern woodworking machinery can cut wood to size for you, but a busy yard worker with a handsaw won't produce an accurate result. It's best to buy a little over length and cut your own wood to size.

Most yards will cut a board to the length you want unless it leaves too small an offcut to be sold, in which case you have to buy the whole board.

Seasoning softwood
Softwood is not usually well seasoned and is often exposed to moisture in the yard, so it's best to let it dry out indoors for a week or so before use, preferably in the room where it is to be used, and lying flat.

Standard sizes and sections
Surfaced construction softwood comes in a range of standard thicknesses and widths, from nominal 1-inch to 6-inch thicknesses and in widths of nominal 2-inch intervals from 1 inch to 12 inches. Standard lengths are from 4 to 16 feet, in 2-foot intervals. It can also be bought tongue-and-groove and machined into a variety of sectional shapes known as moldings for such uses as architraves, baseboards and picture rails.

HARDWOODS

Hardwoods are much more expensive than softwoods and must usually be bought from specialty lumber suppliers. They are mainly used nowadays only to achieve a particular appearance or for special structural purposes.

Ordering hardwoods
Hardwoods—walnut, cherry, oak and many others—have to be ordered by their specific names.

Philippine mahogany
There is one relatively cheap hardwood called Philippine mahogany, now used widely for interior trim, cabinetry, paneling and some kinds of molding, and is also available in small-section strips and battens. Philippine mahogany is pale brown and seems almost grainless. It splits rather easily when nailed.

Simulated hardwoods
The expensive hardwoods have been supplanted in many of their traditional applications by man-made boards veneered with hardwood.

MAN-MADE BOARDS

Three man-made boards are used widely by woodworkers—plywood, particleboard and hardboard.

Plywood
Plywood is a sheet material made by bonding a number of thin wood veneers together under high pressure. It is exceptionally strong and much used in both construction and furniture-making.

The veneers, or plies, in plywood always lie with their grain directions alternating and always come to an odd number so that the grains of the two outer plies run in the same direction.

Plywood surfaces
The outer veneers of plywood are usually of softwood, but the material can also be obtained surfaced with quality hardwoods and with solid lumber instead of veneer plies making up the core.

Plywood sizes
The normally available thicknesses are from 1/8 to 3/4 inch and there are several sheet sizes. Standard sheets measure 4 × 8 feet.

Particleboard
Particleboard is made from small softwood chips bonded together under pressure. There are several grades, including a tough one for flooring and others for use in cabinetmaking.

Particleboard surfaces
Standard particleboard is sanded smooth on both sides and can be simply filled and primed for painting. There are also several brand-name products with plastic laminate surfaces especially for countertops.

Particleboard sizes
Standard particleboard sheets measure 4 feet by 8 feet and are available in 3/8-, 1/2-, 5/8- and 3/4-inch thicknesses. The thickest one is by far the most commonly stocked.

Hardboard
Is compressed softwood pulp in sheets. It has less structural strength than other man-made boards but is very cheap and effective for many uses.

Types of hardboard
Tempered hardboard is brown and 1/8 to 3/8 inch thick, with one shiny side and one matt side. Other types are: *pegboard*—perforated hardboard; *embossed hardboard*—with simulated wood-grain, basketweave or other patterns; *acoustic hardboard*—with perforations to absorb sound (particularly used for ceiling tiles); *standard hardboard*—a softer type; and *service grade*—not quite as smooth as standard.

Uses and sizes
Standard and tempered hardboard is light, easy to cut and ideal for small sliding doors, cabinet backs, drawer bottoms and underlay for floorcovering. The standard sheet is 4 × 8 feet, with up to 6 × 16 available.

ADHESIVES

Modern adhesives are greatly superior to the old glues they have supplanted and have very powerful bonding properties. Though there is no "universal adhesive" that will stick anything to anything, you can bond most materials to most others if you choose the right adhesive.

There is now an impressive range of adhesives for specific purposes; those discussed here relate to the procedures dealt with in this book.

Woodworking

To glue wood and man-made boards for use indoors, apply a polyvinyl acetate (PVA) woodworker's glue to one or both of the mating surfaces, clamp or weight the work and wipe off any excess glue squeezed from the joint with a damp cloth. The joint can be handled within 30 minutes and the bond is complete in 24 hours.

For outdoor work, use a waterproof powdered synthetic-resin glue that you mix with water for use, or a two-part (resorcinal and urea) adhesive whose parts are applied separately to the faces being glued. The latter sets when the faces come together. Both these glues require the work to be clamped or weighted during the setting period.

For indoor work where clamping or weighting is not possible—attaching wall panels to furring strips, for example—use a synthetic rubber-based contact adhesive. Apply it to both mating surfaces, allow it to become touch-dry, then press the surfaces together by hand. The bond is almost instantaneous.

An alternative for small nonclamping jobs is a two-part acrylic adhesive. The parts are not mixed for use; one is applied to each mating surface of the joint and bonding begins when they meet.

Fixing synthetic laminates

Contact adhesives were developed for attaching synthetic laminates to wood and other surfaces. No clamps or weights are needed, though some pressure improves the bond. The newer contact adhesives allow some repositioning of the mating surfaces; with the older ones the instant bond meant that laminates placed wrongly could not then be moved. So it's best to ensure that you choose a contact adhesive with what's called "slideability." Apply the adhesive to both surfaces, let it become touch-dry, then press them firmly together.

Attaching floorcoverings

Flooring adhesives must be versatile enough to fix a wide range of coverings—cork, vinyl, linoleum and many others—to such surfaces as floorboards, concrete, cement screed and hardboard underlays, to name only some. They must also be able to withstand regular floor washing and the spillage of various liquids. Such multipurpose flooring adhesives are of two types: rubber-resin and latex. Either will stick virtually any covering to any floor surface. They are semiflexible and will not crack or fail due to slight movement of the covering.

Attaching ceiling tiles

Expanded or foam-polystyrene ceiling tiles, and larger panels of that material, are fixed with a synthetic latex-based adhesive to plaster, cement, hardboard and lumber surfaces. The thick adhesive has gap-filling properties that allow the material to be fixed effectively to quite uneven surfaces, and the tiles or panels to be adjusted after they are in place.

Fixing ceramic tiles

Ceramic tiles are fixed with a white adhesive that may be had ready-mixed or in powder form. Ordinary "thin-bed" adhesives are for tiling on fairly flat surfaces, and there are "thick-bed" types for use on rough and uneven surfaces. There are water-resistant versions for use in kitchens and bathrooms and heat-resistant types for tiling around stoves and fireplaces.

Ceramic floor tiles are now often laid with a sand-and-cement mortar to which a special builder's adhesive—PVA bonding agent—is added to improve adhesion, a method also used for sand-and-cement stucco and concrete repairs.

Gluing metals

Metals can be glued with epoxy-resin adhesives, which produce such a powerful bond as to have replaced welding and riveting in some industries. The adhesives are in two parts, a resin and a hardener, and most require their parts be mixed together, then used within a certain time after mixing. Another type, acrylic-based, has two parts that are applied separately to the mating faces. These impose no time limit as they are dormant until the faces meet, when a chemical bonding reaction begins.

Epoxy-resin adhesives are also generally suitable for joining glass, ceramics, fiberglass and rigid plastic, though some products will not join all of these, so be sure that you get the right adhesive for the job.

Gluing stainless steel

Stainless-steel plumbing can be glued with a special adhesive and activator. Roughen the end of the tube and the inside of the fitting. Spray the activator onto both surfaces. After 30 seconds apply a ring of adhesive to the leading inside edge of the fitting and another to the end of the tube. Assemble the joint and leave it to harden for at least two minutes.

Cyanoacrylates

The cyanoacrylates, or "super glues," come close to being the universal adhesives that will stick anything. They rapidly bond a great many materials—including human skin, which led to cases of fingers, even eyelids, being glued together inadvertently when they were introduced (see Adhesive Solvents).

Usually supplied in tubes with fine nozzles, super glues must be used sparingly. They are commonly employed in joining small objects of metal, glass, ceramic, fiberglass and rigid plastic.

Glue guns

An electric "hot-melt" glue gun is loaded with a rod of solid glue that melts under heat when the gun is activated and discharged as a liquid onto the work. The components are pressed or clamped together and the glue bonds as it cools. Glue guns are useful for accurate spot-gluing, and there is a choice of glue rods for use with various materials. The glues normally cool and set within 20 to 90 seconds.

Cold gun-applied adhesive for attaching wallboards and ceiling tiles is supplied in cartridges fitted with nozzles. When the gun's trigger is pressed, a plunger pushes on the base of the cartridge and forces out the glue.

ADHESIVE SOLVENTS

When using an adhesive, you will inevitably get some where you don't want it, usually on your hands. So have the right solvent handy for the glue in question and use it promptly, as the more the glue has set, the harder it is to remove. Once a glue has set hard it might be impossible to dissolve it.

ADHESIVE	SOLVENT
PVA woodworking glue	Clean water
Synthetic-resin	Clean water
Resorcinal and urea	Clean water
Two-part acrylic	Paint thinner
Rubber-based contact glue	Acetone
Rubber-resin	Rubber cement thinner
Synthetic-latex	Clean water
Epoxy-resin	Acetone or paint thinner; liquid paint stripper if hard (not on skin)
Cyanoacrylates (super glues)	Special manufacturer's solvent
PVA tile adhesive	Clean water

NAILS

Nails, used with or without glue, provide an inexpensive, quick and simple fastening method for woodworkers, and there are also many special types of nails for other purposes.

Common wire nails
Rough general carpentry. Bright steel or galvanized finish. Size: 1 to 6 inches.

Finishing wire nails
Finish carpentry and cabinetmaking. Head can be punched into wood and concealed. Bright steel finish. Size: 1 to 4 inches.

Cement-coated common nails
General carpentry. Thinner and lighter than common nails, with greater holding power. Are 1/8 to 1/4 inch shorter than common nails, yet sold by same penny sizes. Size: 7/8 to 5 3/4 inches.

Annular-ring nails
For attaching man-made panels. Bright or blued steel. Size: 3/4 to 4 inches.

Spiral-shank nails
General-purpose. Twisted shank gives extra grip. Bright or blued steel. Size: 3/4 to 4 inches.

FASTENERS

An important part of any assembly or construction work is choosing the right fastening method. As well as the time-tested variety of nails and screws for woodwork, and the nuts, bolts and rivets for metal work, there are nowadays a number of patented devices that speed and simplify many jobs.

COMMON NAIL SIZES

PENNY SIZE	LENGTH (IN.) Length from underside of head to end of point	APPROX. NO. PER LB.
2d	1	847
3d	1 1/4	543
4d	1 1/2	296
5d	1 3/4	254
6d	2	167
7d	2 1/4	150
8d	2 1/2	101
9d	2 3/4	92
10d	3	66
12d	3 1/4	66
16d	3 1/2	47
20d	4	30
30d	4 1/2	23
40d	5	17
50d	5 1/2	13
60d	6	11

Key to types of adhesives
1 PVA woodworking glue
2 Synthetic-resin/ Resorcinal and urea
3 Rubber-based contact
4 Epoxy-resin
5 Rubber-resin
6 Synthetic-latex
7 Cyanoacrylates
8 Acrylic
9 PVA tile adhesive

Use this chart as a guide for gluing the materials on the left to those across the top.	WOOD AND MAN-MADE BOARDS	MASONRY	PLASTER	METAL	STONE	GLASS	CERAMIC	RIGID PLASTIC/ FIBERGLASS
WOOD/MAN-MADE BOARDS	1,2,3,7,8			8	8	8	8	
METAL	8			4, 7, 8	4, 7	4, 7, 8	4, 7, 8	7, 8
SYNTHETIC LAMINATES	3	3	3		3			
FLOORCOVERINGS	5, 6	5, 6			5, 6			
CEILING TILES/PANELS	6	6	6		6			
CERAMIC	8, 9	9	9	8	9	8	4, 7, 8	8
STONE		4			4	4		
GLASS	3, 4, 8	4	4	4, 7, 8		4, 7, 8	4, 7, 8	8
RIGID PLASTIC/FIBERGLASS	8			8		8	8	4, 7, 8

MEASURING NAILS

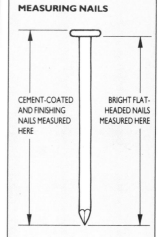

CEMENT-COATED AND FINISHING NAILS MEASURED HERE

BRIGHT FLAT-HEADED NAILS MEASURED HERE

Cut nails
General carpentry, though primarily used to attach wood to masonry. Steel or iron. Size: 1 to 6 inches.

Cut flooring nails
Nailing floorboards to joists. Steel or iron. Size: 1½ to 4 inches.

Powder-set nails
Joining wood to concrete. Nails are set by means of a special tool employing gunpowder charge. Hardened steel. Size: 1⅛ to 3⁷⁄₁₆ inches.

Barbed-shank nails
General fastening of soft materials, including plasterboard and asphalt shingles. Bright, galvanized, or cement-coated. Size: ¾ to 2 inches.

Panel pin
Attaching hardboard and light plywood. Blued or enameled steel. Size: ½ to 3½ inches.

Veneer pin
Applying veneers and small moldings. Bright steel. Size: ⅝ to 2 inches.

Fluted masonry nail
For fastening wood to concrete or brick masonry. Hardened steel. Size: ½ to 4 inches.

Roofing nail
Applying shingles to sloped roofs. Galvanized. Size: ¾ to 4 inches.

Casing nail
General carpentry. Conical head as opposed to round head of finishing nail. Often has depression in head to accept nail set. Size: 1 to 5 inches.

Roofing nail with neoprene washer
For use in flat roofing, skylights, or solar panels where potential for leakage is high. Galvanized. Size: 1½ to 2½ inches.

Wood shingle face-nail
Face-nailing wall shingles. Galvanized or enamel-coated. Size: 1½ to 3½ inches.

Duplex-head nail
Temporary construction bracing. Head extension used for removing nail. Bright steel or galvanized. Size: 1¾ to 4½ inches.

Glazier's point
Installing glass panes in windows and picture frames. Bright steel, aluminum. Size: ⅛ inch.

Escutcheon pin
Attaching keyhole plates, etc. Brass. Size: ⅝ or ¾ inch.

Upholstery nail
Upholstering furniture. Domed decorative head. Brass, bronze, chromed or antique. Size: ⅛ to ½ inch.

Carpet tack
Attaching carpeting to wood. Blued, galvanized or copper-clad steel. Size: ¼ to 1¼ inches.

Insulated masonry nail
Securing electric cable to masonry. Nail is driven through a plastic cable grip. Made in various shapes and sizes.

Timber connector
Making rough miter and butt joints in wood.

Corrugated fastener
Making rough miter and butt joints in wood.

Staple
Rough carpentry and attaching fencing wire. Bright steel or galvanized. Size: ⅜ to 1½ inches.

Wire dowel
Hidden fastener in woodwork, one point entering each component. Bright steel. Size: 1½ to 2 inches.

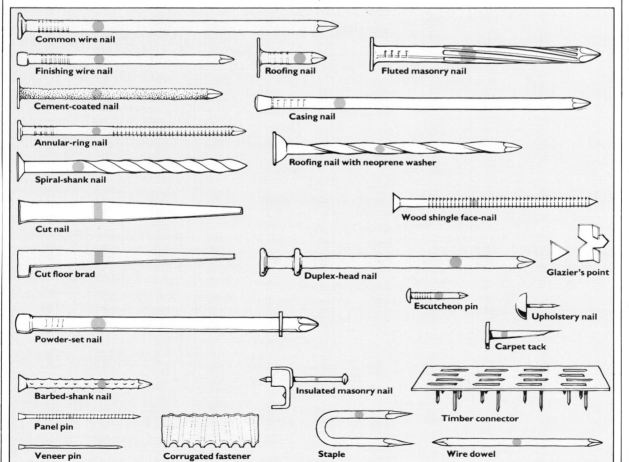

Key to diagram
Gray symbols superimposed on the nails and pins represent their cross section.

- **Preventing split wood**
  A blunt nail punches its way through timber instead of forcing the fibers apart. To avoid splitting, if that seems likely, blunt the point of a nail with a light hammer blow.

- **Removing a dent in wood**
  If you dent wood with a misplaced hammer blow, put a few drops of hot water on the dent and let the wood swell. When it is dry, smooth it with abrasive paper.

497

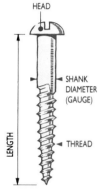

HEAD

SHANK
DIAMETER
(GAUGE)

LENGTH

THREAD

Parts of a screw
You will avoid confusion if you use the correct terminology when ordering screws.

SCREWS

Screws for woodworking and work partly involving wood come in a small range of head shapes suited to various purposes and in a choice of materials and finishes. Screws are ordinarily made of mild steel, but for corrosion-resistance and other special purposes, you can get brass, aluminum and stainless-steel screws as well as chromium-, zinc- and cadmium-plated and sherardized, bronzed and japanned ones.

Screwheads
There are three basic head shapes:

Flathead, for work where the screw must be recessed flush with the work surface or below it.

Roundhead, usually used with sheet material that is too thin for countersinking.

Oval-head, a combination of round- and flathead, often used for attaching metal items like door furniture to wood.

A further subdivision of all these screws is between those with traditional **slotted heads** and those with **cross-slotted heads**, which need special cross-section screwdrivers.

Drywall screws belong to a "new generation" of wood screws that are case-hardened to give them torsional strength and "abuse-proof" heads. They have narrow shanks and deep, sharp, widely spaced threads that make them easier and quicker to use while giving better holding strength. These, too, have cross-slotted heads.

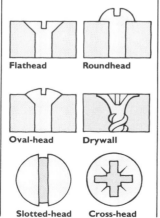

Flathead   Roundhead

Oval-head   Drywall

Slotted-head   Cross-head

Sizes and gauges
All screws, whatever their type, are described in terms of their length, given in inches, and their shank thickness, or gauge, expressed as a simple gauge number from 1 to 20. The length of a screw is the distance between its tip and the part of the head that will lie flush with the work surface. The thicker the screw, the higher its gauge number. Gauges in most general use are 4, 6, 8 and 10.

Woodscrews are available in lengths from 1/4 inch to 6 inches, but not every length, head shape and material is made, let alone stocked, in every gauge. Generally speaking, the largest range of lengths, head shapes and head slot screws is to be found in gauges 6 to 12.

Cups, sockets and caps
Flathead and oval-head screws may be used with metal screw cups or sockets, which increase their grip. Sockets also make for a neat appearance. Flathead screws can be concealed beneath brown or white plastic caps or wood plugs.

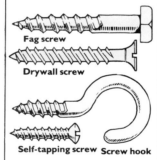

Fag screw

Drywall screw

Self-tapping screw   Screw hook

Special screws
Fag screws, for heavy-duty applications like building a workbench, have hexagonal or square heads which are turned into the work with a wrench. Large washers prevent the heads from cutting into the timber.

Drywall screws have a double spiral thread running throughout their length and taper only at the very end. These features enable them to get a strong grip in this relatively weak material.

Screw hooks and eyes in various styles and sizes are available for both light- and heavy-duty applications.

Self-tapping screws with slotted heads in all three styles are produced for attaching thin materials such as sheet metal or rigid plastic. They are so named because they cut their own threads as they are driven home.

WALL MOUNTINGS

To make secure mountings to any but solid wooden surfaces involves the use of various aids. These range from the simple plug to take a woodscrew in a hole drilled in brick or masonry up to fairly elaborate heavy-duty devices complete with bolts. There are also special products for making attachments to hollow walls.

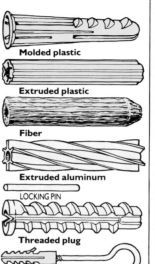

Molded plastic

Extruded plastic

Fiber

Extruded aluminum

LOCKING PIN

Threaded plug

Clothesline mounting

Wall plugs
There are light- to medium-duty **molded plastic wall plugs** to take a range of wood screws, generally from No. 4 gauge to No. 14. Some are color-coded for easy recognition. A wall plug is pushed into a drilled hole and the screw then driven into the plug, which expands to grip the sides of the hole tightly.

There are also **extruded plastic plugs,** simply straight tubes, which take only the thread of the screw and so must be shorter than the hole. These are cheaper than molded plugs but less convenient, as are the traditional **fiber** ones which serve the same purpose.

Aluminum wall plugs, both the molded and the extruded type, are used where heat might affect plastic ones, and there are **threaded plugs** for use in walls of crumbly material like aerated concrete. These plugs themselves are threaded outside and are screwed into the soft material to provide a socket for the screws.

A hole in masonry or brick too irregular to take a plug can be filled with **asbestos-substitute plugging compound,** which

molds itself to the shape of the hole. Wet the material, ram it into the hole, then pierce a hole in it for the screw. Let it dry out a little before inserting the screw.

Heavy-duty nylon wall plugs are supplied with lag screws or with screw hooks for use as clothesline and similar attachments.

Expansion bolt

Expansion bolts
These are for making very rugged mountings. There are various designs, but all work on one basic principle: A bolt is screwed into a segmented metal shell and engages the thread of an expander. As the bolt is tightened, the expander forces the segments apart to grip the sides of the hole. Some expansion bolts have built-in hooks and eyes.

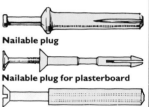

Nailable plug

Nailable plug for plasterboard

Hammer screw

Nailable plugs
These can be used to speed up jobs in which a great many attachments have to be made. There are two types: One is simply a flanged expansion sleeve with a masonry nail. The other consists of a ready-assembled wall plug and "hammer screw." Both are simply hammered in but the hammer screw of the second type has a thread and a slotted head, and can be removed with a screwdriver. Nailable plugs are often used for attaching furring strips and frames, wall linings, ducting and baseboards.

Frame mounting

Frame mountings
These are designed to speed up screw mounting by eliminating the need to mark out and predrill the pilot holes. Position the item to be attached and drill right through it into the wall, then insert the frame mounting, a long nylon plug with a plated screw, and tighten the screw. Typical uses for the device are attaching furring strips, wallplates, doors, window frames and fitted furniture to walls.

Mountings for hollow walls

There are many variations of each of several devices for making attachments to hollow walls of plasterboard on studs, lath and plaster and so on. All of them work on the principle of opening out behind the panel and gripping it in some way.

Special wall plugs, plastic toggles and *collapsible anchors* all have segments that open out or fold up against the inside of the panel. A rubber anchor comes complete with its own steel bolt which, when tightened, draws up an internal nut to make the rubber bulge out behind the panel.

Metal gravity toggles and *spring toggles* have arms that open out inside the cavity. A gravity toggle has a single arm, pivoted near one end so that its own weight causes it to drop. A spring toggle has two spring-loaded arms that fly open when they are clear of the hole and a bolt that draws them tight up against the panel.

A *nylon strap toggle* has an arm that is held firmly behind the panel while the screw is driven into its pilot hole.

The cheap special wall plugs and collapsible anchors remain in their holes if their screws have to be removed. Plastic toggles, nylon strap toggles and the more expensive gravity toggles and spring toggles are all lost in the cavity if their screws are taken out. The rubber anchor can be removed and used elsewhere.

None of these devices should be used for attaching a heavy load. Instead, locate the studs and mount directly into these. Even for moderate loads, the larger spring and gravity toggles should be used on lath and plaster walls rather than plug-type devices.

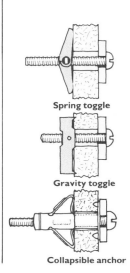

Spring toggle

Gravity toggle

Collapsible anchor

FITTING A ROLLER BLIND

Fitting a roller blind is fairly straightforward; many kits include manufacturer's instructions. A kit consists of a wooden roller with two plastic or metal end cups, one of them spring-loaded to work the blind; two support brackets; a narrow lath; and a pull-cord with a knob. You buy the fabric separately and cut it to width and length.

Rollers come in several standard lengths. Unless you find that one of these fits your window exactly, get the next largest and cut it down to size.

Measuring up

The blind can hang within the window aperture or down the front of it. The former leaves the sill accessible when the blind is down; the latter gives better draft protection but means fitting the supports to the wall, not the window frame.

Inside hanging

Fit the supports to the top of the window frame as close to the sides as possible. Remove the right-hand end cap, the one with a round pin, from the roller, cut the roller to fit neatly between the supports and replace the cap.

Front hanging

Measure the width of the frame and fit the supports that distance apart above and on either side of the window. If the frame is the old-fashioned type that projects from the wall, fix wood blocks of that thickness to the wall, then fix the supports to them. Cut the roller to fit between the supports as above.

The fabric

This must be cut exactly rectangular or it will not run evenly on the roller. Cut the width to fit between the two end caps, and the length to cover the window plus an extra 8 to 12 inches. Make a bottom hem 1/4 inch wide, then turn it up to form a sleeve for the lath. Glue and tack the other end of the fabric to the roller, taking care to align the top edge with the roller's axis. Fix the pull-cord to the lath.

Holding the roller with its flat spring-loaded peg on the left, roll the fabric up so that it hangs from the roller's far side. Place the roller in the supports and pull down the blind. Now make it return. If it returns sluggishly, it needs more tension. Pull it halfway down, carefully lift it off the supports, roll it up fully by hand and replace it. If it now flies back too violently take the rolled up blind off the supports, unwind it a little by hand and replace it.

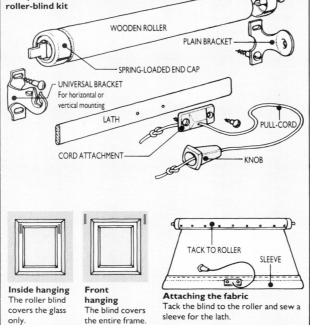

Components of a roller-blind kit

PLAIN END CAP
PIN
WOODEN ROLLER
PLAIN BRACKET
SPRING-LOADED END CAP
UNIVERSAL BRACKET
For horizontal or vertical mounting
LATH
PULL-CORD
CORD ATTACHMENT
KNOB

Inside hanging
The roller blind covers the glass only.

Front hanging
The blind covers the entire frame.

Attaching the fabric
Tack the blind to the roller and sew a sleeve for the lath.

TACK TO ROLLER
SLEEVE

FITTING CURTAIN RAILS

Modern plastic or aluminum curtain rails are easy to fit where there is a wooden window frame and only a little less so where there is not. In the latter case, use a wall mounting or screw a wooden strip to the wall above the window, paint it to match the wall and fix the rail supports to it. A similar mounting is often preferred for a small alcove window so that the rail can be extra long and the curtains can be drawn clear of the aperture for maximum daylight.

Measure the length of rail you need, allowing a little for cutting, and be sure to get the right number of gliders, hooks and support brackets.

The curtain rail can be bent to follow the curves of a bow window, but any curve should have a rail support on either side of it, which may mean buying extra ones. In a rectangular bay window, keep the curves gentle; curves that are too tight will obstruct the gliders.

Simply screw the rail supports to the window frame with the screws supplied, using a level to keep them properly aligned. Start with the two end supports, placing them so that they will be about 1 inch from the ends of the rail, then distribute the rest evenly between them. Some support brackets are designed for both window and ceiling attachment, so be sure that yours are the right way up.

Fit an end stop to the rail, slide the gliders onto it, fit the other end stop and mount the rail on the brackets. Some rails slide onto the supports, some clip into them and some have to be screwed to them.

Where a curtain rail must be fitted to the ceiling, the rail supports must be fixed to joists—though some builders install a special ceiling strip for the purpose—and longer screws may be needed. Check, of course, that the rail you buy is suitable for ceiling mounting.

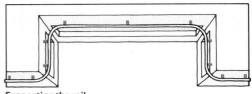

Supporting the rail
Mount rail support on each side of any curve.

Fixing to strip
Screw a straight curtain rail to a wall-mounted strip.

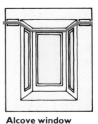

Alcove window
An extended rail allows curtain to be drawn clear.

Wall-mounted support bracket

Ceiling-mounted support bracket

SHELVING
Depending on where it is and what it is to be used for, shelving can be anything from a set of planks on functional-looking brackets in a garage to elegant spans of teak or plate glass on apparently delicate supports of colored light alloy.

Whatever its form or context, shelving is the cheapest, simplest and most economical kind of storage.

Mounting shelves
Shelves must not only stay up, they must not sag under their load. A load cantilevered on brackets from a back wall will impose great stress on the mounting screws, especially the top ones. If they are too short or of too small a gauge, or if the wall plugs are inadequate, the mountings may be torn out. The wider the shelf, the greater the danger of this. A shelf with its ends supported on strips within a brick or masonry alcove will not tear the screws out unless they are a great deal too small.

Shelf span
Sagging occurs when the span of a shelf between supports is too long in relation to its thickness or its load, or both. On this score, solid lumber and lumber-core plywood with its core running lengthways are best for sturdy shelving. Veneered particleboard, though popular because of its appearance, will eventually sag under relatively light loads, so it needs support at closer intervals than lumber does. But any of these materials can be stiffened with a hardwood strip glued along the underside.

A 1-inch-thick lumber shelf for a substantial load would need support about every 3 feet along its length, as would a plywood shelf of approximately the same thickness, whereas veneered chipboard of that gauge would have to be supported about every 2 feet 6 inches.

Even a short shelf on two brackets should have them placed well in from its ends to avoid central sagging. For this reason, alcove shelves resting on end strips must be quite thick in relation to their length.

Wall mounting
The type of wall involved has a bearing on all this. On solid brick or masonry, supports for a shelf may be attached almost anywhere; on a stud partition they must be fixed to the studs, unless you put up special cross braces for them between the studs.

For most ordinary shelving, brackets fixed to a back wall of brick or masonry with 2-inch screws and proper wall plugs should be adequate. Wide shelves intended for heavy loads such as a television set and/or stacks of LP records may need more robust mounts, though enough brackets to prevent sagging will also share the weight more effectively. Drill into the wall with a masonry bit, insert plastic wall plugs and screw the brackets to the wall. Brackets must be big enough to support almost the whole width of the shelf.

To fix end braces into the sides of an alcove, follow the same procedure, but remember to allow for the thickness of the braces when choosing screw lengths.

Fixing brackets to a stud partition involves simply making pilot holes for the screws in the studs, as does attaching them to cross braces, which are themselves fixed to the studs.

To install several shelves in an alcove, a good idea is to attach a wooden "ladder" on each of the alcove sides and rest the shelf ends on the "rungs." The ladder stands on the floor, and can be mounted to the brick or masonry with very few fastenings.

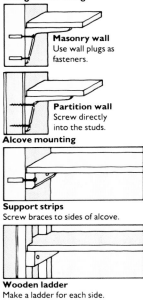

Straight-wall fixing

Masonry wall
Use wall plugs as fasteners.

Partition wall
Screw directly into the studs.

Alcove mounting

Support strips
Screw braces to sides of alcove.

Wooden ladder
Make a ladder for each side.

Patent shelving systems
There are many patent shelving systems on the market with brackets that slot or clip into metal upright supports which are screwed to the wall. In most of them, the upright has holes or slots that take lugs on the rear of the bracket, and these are at close enough intervals to allow considerable choice in the level at which the shelves can be placed. In one system, the upright has continuous slots over its whole length so that the brackets may be placed virtually at any level.

One advantage of such systems is that the weight and stress of loaded shelves are distributed down the supporting uprights. Another is that once the uprights are in place, more shelves may be added as the need arises with no need for more mounts. Yet another is that they allow shelving arrangements to be changed easily. Early versions of such systems were a little too "industrial" for some tastes, but today's have colors and finishes quite in keeping with good modern decor and furnishings.

Patent shelving systems

CLIP-IN BRACKET

Continuous-slot system

UPRIGHT SUPPORT

HOOKED BRACKET

Slotted-upright system

UPRIGHT SUPPORT

Alternative brackets

Glass-support bracket

Bookend brackets

Fitting shelving systems
The support must be properly vertical, and the best way of ensuring this is to mount it at first lightly, but not too loosely, to the wall by its top screw, then hold it vertical with the aid of a level and mark for the bottom screws (1). With the bottom screw in place you can check that the upright is vertical in its other plane, and not sloping outward because of a sloping wall. If it does slope you will have to place discreet packing behind it to correct it (2). Also put packing wherever the upright is away from the wall due to random hollows. Where there are very marked hollows, it may be necessary to use extra-long screws.

Put a bracket on the upright, then one on the second upright while it is held against the wall. Get a helper to lay a shelf across the brackets, then use a level to check that the shelf is horizontal. Mark the top hole of the second upright, then fix that upright as you did the first one.

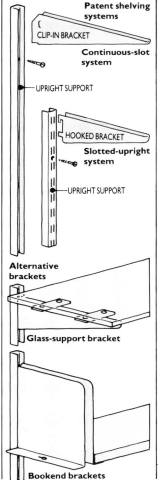

1 Plumb the upright support
Use a level to plumb the upright, then mark the bottom mounting hole on the wall.

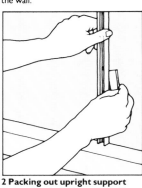

2 Packing out upright support
Push packing behind the upright if the wall is not vertical.

GLOSSARY OF TERMS

A

Accessory
An electrical component permanently connected to a circuit—a switch, socket outlet, connection unit, etc.

Aggregate
Particles of sand or stone mixed with cement and water to make concrete, or added to paint to make a textured finish.

Airlock
A blockage in a pipe caused by a trapped bubble of air.

Appliance
A machine or device powered by electricity. or A functional piece of equipment connected to the plumbing—a basin, sink, bath, etc.

Architrave
The molding around a door or window.

Arris
The sharp edge at the meeting of two surfaces.

B

Back-siphonage
The siphoning of part of a plumbing system caused by the failure of main water pressure.

Balanced flue
A ducting system which allows a heating appliance, such as a boiler, to draw fresh air from, and discharge gases to, the outside of a building.

Ballast
Naturally occurring sand and gravel mix used as aggregate for making concrete.

Baluster
One of a set of posts supporting a stair handrail.

Balustrade
The protective barrier alongside a staircase or landing.

Banister
See *balustrade*.

Batt
A short, cut length of fiberglass or mineral-fiber insulant.

Batten
A narrow strip of wood.

Batter
The slope of the face of a wall that leans backwards or tapers from bottom to top.

Blind
To cover with sand.

Blocking
A short horizontal wooden member between studs.

Blown
To have broken away, as when a layer of cement stucco has parted from a wall.

Bore
The hollow part of a pipe or tube. or To drill a hole.

Burr
The rough, raised edge left on a workpiece after cutting or filing.

Buttercoat
The top layer of cement render.

C

Came
The grooved strip of lead which holds the glass in a leaded light or a stained-glass window.

Cap-nut
The nut used to tighten a fitting onto pipework.

Casing
The wooden molding around a door opening.

Catenary wire
A length of wire cable suspended horizontally between two points.

Cavity wall
A wall of two separate masonry skins with an air space between them.

Chamfer
A narrow, flat surface on the edge of a piece of wood—it is normally at an angle of 45 degrees to adjacent surfaces. or To plane the angled surface.

Chase
A groove cut in masonry or plaster to accept pipework or an electrical cable. or To cut such grooves.

Circuit
A complete path through which an electric current can flow.

Concave
Curving inwards.

Conductor
A component, usually a length of wire, along which an electric current will pass.

Convex
Curving outwards.

Cornice
The continuous horizontal molding between walls and ceiling.

Counterbore
To cut a hole which allows the head of a bolt or screw to lie below a surface. or The hole itself.

Countersink
To cut a tapered recess which allows the head of a screw to lie flush with a surface. or The tapered recess itself.

Coving
A prefabricated molding used to make a cornice.

Cup
To bend as a result of shrinkage—specifically across the width of a piece of wood.

D

Dado
A groove cut into a piece of wood, running across the grain; a housing.

Damp-proof course
A layer of impervious material which prevents moisture from rising from the ground into the walls of a building.

Damp-proof membrane
A layer of impervious material which prevents moisture from rising through a concrete floor; vapor barrier.

Datum point
The point from which measurements are taken.

DPC
See *damp-proof course*.

DPM
See *damp-proof membrane*.

Drip groove
A groove cut or molded in the underside of a door or windowsill to prevent rainwater from running back to the wall.

Drop
A strip of wallpaper cut to length ready for pasting to a wall.

E

Eaves
The edges of a roof that project beyond the walls.

Efflorescence
A white powdery deposit caused by soluble salts migrating to the surface of masonry.

End grain
The surface of wood exposed after cutting across the fibers.

Ergonomics
The study of the physical relationship between the human body and its surroundings.

Extension
A length of electrical cable for temporarily connecting the short permanent cable of an appliance to a wall socket. or A room or rooms added to an existing building.

F

Face edge
In woodworking, the surface planed square to the face side.

Face side
In woodworking, the flat, planed surface from which other dimensions and angles are measured.

Fall
A downward slope.

Fascia board
Strip of wood which covers the ends of rafters and to which external guttering is fixed.

Feather
To wear away or smooth an edge until it is undetectable.

Fence
An adjustable guide to keep the cutting edge of a tool a set distance from the edge of a workpiece.

Flashing
A weatherproof junction between a roof and a wall or chimney, or between one roof and another.

Flaunching
A mortared slope around a chimney pot or at the top of a fireback.

Flute
A rounded concave groove.

Footing
A narrow concrete foundation for a wall.

Frass
Powdered wood produced by the activity of woodworm.

Frog
The angled depression in one face of some housebricks.

Furring battens
See *furring strips*.

Furring strips
Parallel strips of wood fixed to a wall or ceiling to provide a framework for attaching panels.

Fuse box
Where the main electrical service cable is connected to the house circuitry. or The service box.

G

Galvanized
Covered with a protective coating of zinc.

Gel
A substance with a thick, jellylike consistency.

Grain
The general direction of wood fibers. *or* The pattern produced on the surface of lumber by cutting through the fibers. See also *end grain* and *short grain*.

Grommet
A ring of rubber or plastic lining a hole to protect electrical cable from chafing.

Groove
A long, narrow channel cut in wood in the general direction of the grain. *or* To cut such channels.

Grounds
Strips of wood fixed to a wall to provide nail-fixing points for baseboards and door casings. See also *pallets*.

Gullet
The notch formed between two saw teeth.

H

Hardcore
Broken bricks or stones used to form a subbase below foundations, paving, etc.

Hardwood
Timber cut from deciduous trees.

Head
The height of the surface of water above a specific point—used as a measurement of pressure; for example, a head of 2 ft. *or* The top horizontal member of a wooden frame.

Heave
An upward swelling of the ground caused by excess moisture.

Helical
Spiral-shaped.

Hoggin
A fine ballast, usually with a clay content, used to form a subbase for concrete pads or paving.

Hone
To finely sharpen a cutting edge.

Horns
Extended door or window stiles designed to protect the corners from damage while in storage.

Housing
A long, narrow channel cut across the general direction of wood grain to form part of a joint.

I

Insulation
Materials used to reduce the transmission of heat or sound. *or* Nonconductive material surrounding electrical wires or connections to prevent the passage of electricity.

J

Jamb
The vertical side member of a door or window frame; sometimes the frame as a whole.

Joist
A horizontal wooden or metal beam used to support a structure like a floor, ceiling or wall.

K

Kerf
The groove cut by a saw.

Key
To abrade or incise a surface to provide a better grip when gluing something to it.

Knurled
Impressed with a series of fine grooves designed to improve the grip.

L

Lath and plaster
A method of finishing a stud-framed wall or ceiling. Narrow strips of wood are nailed to the studs or joists to provide a supporting framework for plaster.

Lead
A stepped section of brick- or blockwork built at each end of a wall to act as a guide to the height of the intermediate coursing.

Lintel
A horizontal beam used to support the wall over a door or window opening.

M

Marine plywood
Plywood meeting specific APA requirements governing continuing immersion in fresh and salt water.

Mastic
A nonsetting compound used to seal joints.

Microporous
Used to describe a finish which allows timber to dry out while protecting it from rainwater.

Miter
A joint formed between two pieces of wood by cutting bevels of equal angles at the ends of each piece. *or* To cut such a joint.

Mole
A tallow-soaked felt pad used to smooth a soldered lead joint.

Mono-pitch roof
A roof which slopes in one direction only.

Mortise
A rectangular recess cut in timber to receive a matching tongue or tenon.

Mouse
A small weight used to pass a line through a narrow vertical gap.

Mullion
A vertical dividing member of a window frame.

Muntin
A central vertical member of a panel door.

N

Needle
A stout wooden beam used with props to support the section of a wall above an opening prior to the installation of an RSJ or lintel.

Neutral
The section of an electrical circuit which carries the flow of current back to source. *or* A terminal to which the connection is made. *or* A color composed mainly of black and white.

Newel
The post at the top or bottom of a staircase that supports the handrail.

Nosing
The front edge of a stair tread.

O

Outer string
See *string*.

Oxidize
To form a layer of metal oxide, as in rusting.

P

Pallet
A wooden plug built into masonry to provide a fixing point for a door casing.

Pare
To remove fine shavings from wood with a chisel.

Parging
The internal stucco of a chimney.

Party wall
The wall between two houses and over which each of the adjoining owners has equal rights.

Penetrating oil
A thin lubricant which will seep between corroded components.

Pile
Raised fibers which stand out from a backing material, as with a carpet.

Pilot hole
A small-diameter hole drilled prior to the insertion of a woodscrew to act as a guide for the screw's thread.

Pinch rod
A wooden batten used to gauge the width of a door casing.

Plate
The top horizontal member of a stud partition.

PME
See *protective multiple earth*.

Point load
The concentration of forces on a very small area.

Positive
The part of an electrical circuit which carries the flow of current to an appliance or accessory. Also known as *live*.

Primer
The first coat of a paint system to protect the workpiece and reduce absorption of subsequent coats.

Profile
The outline or contour of an object.

Protective multiple earth
A system of electrical wiring in which the neutral part of the circuit is used to take earth-leakage current to earth.

PTFE
Polytetrafluorethylene—used to make tape for sealing threaded plumbing fittings.

Purlin
A horizontal beam that provides intermediate support for rafters or sheet roofing.

R

Rabbet
A stepped recess along the edge of a workpiece, usually as part of a joint. *or* To cut such recesses.

Rafter
One of a set of parallel sloping beams that form the main structural element of a roof.

Ratchet
A device that permits movement in one direction only by restricting the reversal of a toothed wheel or rack.

RCCB
See *residual-current circuit breaker*.

Residual-current circuit breaker
A device which monitors the flow of electrical current through the live and neutral wires of a circuit. When it detects an imbalance caused by ground leakage, it cuts off the supply of electricity as a safety precaution.

Reveal
The vertical side of an opening in a wall.

Riser
The vertical part of a step.

Rising main
The pipe which supplies water under mains pressure, usually to a storage cistern in the roof.

Rolled steel joist
A steel beam usually with a cross section in the form of a letter I.

RSJ
See *rolled steel joist*.

Rubber
A pad of cotton wool wrapped in soft cloth used to apply stain, shellac, polish, etc.

Rub joint
Glued wood rubbed together and held by its own suction until set.

Run
The horizontal measurement between the top and bottom risers of a stair or the depth of one tread.

S

Sash
The openable part of a window.

Score
To scratch a line with a pointed tool. See also *scribe*.

Scratchcoat
The bottom layer of cement stucco.

Screed
A thin layer of mortar applied to give a smooth surface to concrete, etc. *or* A shortened version of screed batten. Also, to smooth a concrete surface until level, using a sound batten.

Screed batten
A thin strip of wood fixed to a surface to act as a guide to the thickness of an application of plaster or render.

Scribe
To copy the profile of a surface on the edge of sheet material which is to be butted against it; to mark a line with a pointed tool. See also *score*.

Set
A small rectangular paving block.

Sheathing
The outer layer of insulation surrounding an electrical cable. *or* The outer covering of a stud-framed wall that is applied beneath the wall siding.

Short circuit
The accidental rerouting of electricity to ground which increases the flow of current and blows a fuse.

Short grain
When the general direction of wood fibers lies across a narrow section of timber.

Sill
The lowest horizontal member of a stud partition. *or* The lowest horizontal member of a door or window frame.

Sleeper wall
A low masonry wall used as an intermediate support for ground-floor joists.

Soakaway
A pit filled with rubble or gravel into which water is drained.

Soffit
The underside of a part of a building such as the eaves, archway, etc.

Softwood
Timber cut from coniferous trees.

Sole
Another term for a stud partition sill. *or* A wooden member used as a base to level a stud-framed load-bearing wall.

Spalling
Flaking of the outer face of masonry caused by expanding moisture in icy conditions.

Spandrel
The triangular infill below the outer string of a staircase.

Staff bead
The innermost strip of timber holding a sliding sash in a window frame.

Stile
A vertical side member of a door or window sash.

Stopper
A wood filler which matches the color of the timber.

Stringer
A board, which runs from one floor level to another, into which staircase treads and risers are jointed. The one on the open side of a staircase is an outer string, the one against the wall is a wall string.

Stucco
A thin layer of cement-based mortar applied to exterior walls to provide a protective finish. Sometimes fine stone aggregate is embedded in the mortar. *or* To apply the mortar.

Stud partition
An interior stud-framed dividing wall.

Studs
The vertical members of a stud-framed wall.

Subsidence
A sinking of the ground caused by the shrinkage of excessively dry soil.

Supplementary grounding
The connecting to earth of exposed metal appliances and pipework in a bathroom or kitchen.

T

Tamp
To pack down firmly with repeated blows.

Template
A cut-out pattern to help shape something accurately

Tenon
A projecting tongue on the end of a piece of wood which fits in a corresponding mortise.

Terminal
A connection for an electrical conductor.

Thinner
A solvent used to dilute paint or varnish.

Thixotropic
A property of some paints which have a jellylike consistency until stirred or applied, at which point they become liquefied.

Top coat
The outer layer of a paint system.

Torque
A rotational force.

Transom
A horizontal dividing member of a window frame.

Trap
A bent section of pipe below a bath, sink, etc. It contains standing water to prevent the passage of gases.

Tread
The horizontal part of a step.

U

Undercoat
A layer of paint used to obliterate the color of a primer and to build a protective body of paint prior to the application of a top coat.

V

Vapor barrier
A layer of impervious material which prevents the passage of moisture-laden air.

Vapor check
See *vapor barrier*.

W

Wall plate
A horizontal timber member placed along the top of a wall to support joists and to spread their load.

Wall string
See *string*.

Wall tie
A strip of metal or bent wire used to bind sections of masonry together.

Waney edge
A natural wavy edge on a plank. It might still be covered by tree bark.

Warp
To bend or twist as a result of damp or heat.

Water closet
A lavatory flushed by water.

Water hammer
A vibration in plumbing pipework produced by fluctuating water pressure

WC
See water closet.

Weathered
Showing signs of exposure to the weather. *or* Sloped so as to shed rainwater.

Weep hole
A small hole at the base of a cavity wall to allow absorbed water to drain to the outside.

Workpiece
An object being shaped, produced or otherwise worked upon. Sometimes shortened to "work."

INDEX

Picture sources

Key to photographic credits
L = Left, R = Right, T = Top, TL = Top left, TR = Top right, C = Centre, UC = Upper centre, LC = Lower centre, CL = Centre left, CR = Centre right, B = Bottom, BL = Bottom left, BR = Bottom right

Acquisitions Fireplaces Ltd. Page 389B
Albert Jackson. Pages 25BR; 406TR, BL, BR; 420T; 424TR, CL, CR; 450UC, B; 453
allmilmö Ltd. Page 34TR
Arthur Sanderson and Sons Ltd. Pages 29BL; 32TR; 33BL; BR
B. C. Sanitan. Page 35BR
Behr Furniture. Page 36C
Berger Decorative Paints. Page 32TL; 33TR; 72B
Blue Circle Industries PLC. Pages 49; 50T, B; 73
Cement & Concrete Association. Page 445
Clive Helm/EWA. Pages 31C; 32BL; 34BR; 35TR
Crown Decorative Products Ltd. Pages 27BL; 38BR; 72UC, C, LC
Faber Blinds (GB) Ltd. Pages 25CR; 34BL; 36T
Frank Herholdt/EWA. Page 31T
Harry Smith Collection. Pages 407T, CR; 448B; 451B; 455; 458
Howard Ceilings. Page 146
Jerry Tubby/EWA. Page 34TR
Magnet & Southerns. Pages 189; 210; 211
Michael Dunne/EWA. Pages 25BL; 35TL; 36B; 37; 38TR
Michael Nicholson/EWA. Page 38BL
Minsterstone (Wharf Lane) Ltd. Page 389T
Neil Lorimer/EWA. Pages 28BR; 38TL
Pat Brindley. Pages 406TL; 407T, B; 451T
Patrick Fireplaces. Page 389C
Paul Chave. Pages 26; 28T; 30; 63; 67; 74; 80; 82; 90; 91; 99; 100; 101; 113; 115; 252; 396; 421; 422L; 424B; 428; 446; 449
Peter Higgins. Pages 57R; 70; 71; 72T; 159; 176; 181
Rentokil Ltd. Pages 250T, UC, LC; 251R
Rodney Hyett/EWA. Pages 32BR; 35BL
Sheppard Day Designs. Page 31BR
Simon Jennings. Pages 44; 46; 48; 50C; 51; 55; 56; 57L; 59; 65; 240; 248B; 251L; 256; 263; 409; 410; 411; 418; 419; 420UC, LC, B; 422R; 424TL; 435; 438; 448; 450T, LC
Smallbone. Pages 29BR; 31BL; 33TL
Spike Powell/EWA. Pages 25TL; 27T
The Bisque Radiator Shop. Page 25TR
Tim Street-Porter/EWA. Page 27BR
Waterways Ltd./Dr. D. W. Davison. Page 460
Wrighton International Ltd. Page 28BL

SHOP GUIDE

CUSTOMARY TO METRIC (CONVERSION) Conversion factors can be carried so far they become impractical. In cases below where an entry is exact it is followed by an asterisk (*). Where considerable rounding off has taken place, the entry is followed by a + or a − sign.

Linear Measure

inches	millimeters
1/16	1.5875*
1/8	3.2
3/16	4.8
1/4	6.35*
5/16	7.9
3/8	9.5
7/16	11.1
1/2	12.7*
9/16	14.3
5/8	15.9
11/16	17.5
3/4	19.05*
13/16	20.6
7/8	22.2
15/16	23.8
1	25.4*

inches	centimeters
1	2.54*
2	5.1
3	7.6
4	10.2
5	12.7*
6	15.2
7	17.8
8	20.3
9	22.9
10	25.4*
11	27.9
12	30.5

feet	centimeters	meters
1	30.48*	.3048*
2	61	.61
3	91	.91
4	122	1.22
5	152	1.52
6	183	1.83
7	213	2.13
8	244	2.44
9	274	2.74
10	305	3.05
50	1524*	15.24*
100	3048*	30.48*

1 yard = .9144* meters
1 rod = 5.0292* meters
1 mile = 1.6 kilometers
1 nautical mile = 1.852* kilometers

Weights

ounces	grams
1	28.3
2	56.7
3	85
4	113
5	142
6	170
7	198
8	227
9	255
10	283
11	312
12	340
13	369
14	397
15	425
16	454

Formula (exact):
ounces × 28.349 523 125* = grams

pounds	kilograms
1	.45
2	.9
3	1.4
4	1.8
5	2.3
6	2.7
7	3.2
8	3.6
9	4.1
10	4.5

1 short ton (2000 lbs) = 907 kilograms (kg)
Formula (exact):
pounds × .453 592 37* = kilograms

Fluid Measure

(Milliliters [ml] and cubic centimeters [cc] are equivalent, but it is customary to use milliliters for liquids.)

1 cu in	= 16.39 ml
1 fl oz	= 29.6 ml
1 cup	= 237 ml
1 pint	= 473 ml
1 quart	= 946 ml
	= .946 liters
1 gallon	= 3785 ml
	= 3.785 liters

Formula (exact):
fluid ounces × 29.573 529 562 5* = milliliters

Volume

1 cu in	= 16.39 cubic centimeters (cc)
1 cu ft	= 28 316.7 cc
1 bushel	= 35 239.1 cc
1 peck	= 8 809.8 cc

Area

1 sq in	= 6.45 sq cm
1 sq ft	= 929 sq cm
	= .093 sq meters
1 sq yd	= .84 sq meters
1 acre	= 4 046.9 sq meters
	= .404 7 hectares
1 sq mile	= 2 589 988 sq meters
	= 259 hectares
	= 2.589 9 sq kilometers

Miscellaneous

1 British thermal unit (Btu) (mean)
    = 1 055.9 joules
1 horsepower = 745.7 watts
    = .75 kilowatts
caliber (diameter of a firearm's bore in hundredths of an inch)
    = .254 millimeters (mm)

1 atmosphere pressure = 101 325* pascals (newtons per sq meter)
1 pound per square inch (psi) = 6 895 pascals
1 pound per square foot = 47.9 pascals
1 knot = 1.85 kilometers per hour
1 mile per hour = 1.6093 kilometers per hour